Official Bulletin Of The National Society Of The Sons Of The American Revolution, Volumes 16-17...

Sons of the American Revolution

WALLACE McCAMANT

President General

FOREWORD TO OUR COMPATRIOTS

The Officers of the National Society and the Editors of the BULLETIN, following the direction of the National Congress and the Executive Committee, have discontinued the Year Book and instead have enlarged the BULLETIN to cover, to a certain extent at least, the information that was contained in the Year Book, which reached but a small proportion of our members. On account of the shortness of the time between the National Congress, held in Buffalo May 16 and 17, and the issuance of this BULLETIN, which, under the postal regulations, must be mailed before the end of June, this issue must necessarily be somewhat hastily compiled, and no doubt many errors have been made. However, it will be the endeavor of the Officers and Editors in the remaining issues of this year to make the BULLETIN a complete, interesting, and live record of all the matters pertaining to the best that is in this Society. The co-operation of the compatriots is cordially invited to assist the Editors in this work, and our members are assured that it will be the endeavor of those in charge to give space and prominence to all matters that affect the best interests of the Society of the Sons of the American Revolution.

MESSAGE OF THE PRESIDENT GENERAL

DEAR COMPATRIOTS:

There are two administrative matters to which the attention of the Society should be directed. One of them relates to the troublesome question of finances. The expenses of the National Society have increased out of all proportion to its income. Additional revenues are required if the balance is to be maintained on the right side of the ledger. The showing to this effect was so clear that there was no substantial difference of opinion on the subject at the Buffalo Congress. After canvassing the ways and means of increasing the revenues, the Congress voted by a large majority to increase the per capita tax from fifty cents to one dollar. The State Societies are earnestly requested to accept this increase in a proper spirit and to render the financial support which is essential to the important work the National Society is doing.

It is important that correct lists of the names and addresses of members be maintained by the State Societies and lodged with the Secretary General. I should be gratified if all the State Societies would immediately revise their membership rolls and forward correct records for the use of the National Society. The lists now in use urgently require revision.

I hope that during the coming year the Society may make its influence felt in the matter of patriotic education. The public schools are by far the most effective force making for Americanization. It is essential that their teaching be sound on the fundamentals of Americanism. There should be a nation-wide censorship of the text-books on history and constitutional government. Some of the text-books now in use are full of errors; others are inadequate in the emphasis they lay on the American Revolution and the sacrifices it involved; a few of them are sympathetic with radical propaganda. Students should be correctly taught the facts leading up to the creation of the American Commonwealth; they should be impressed, while still children, with the value of our political heritage.

The faculties of our institutions of higher learning should be purged of destructive radicals. Men out of harmony with the principles of the Constitution should not be given the floor at the students' assemblies in our universities. We are particularly within our rights when we ask that institutions supported by taxation be sound in their teaching and in the atmosphere they throw about their student bodies.

Residing as I do in a section of the Union remote from the great centers of population, it will not be possible for me to visit the State Societies so freely as some of my predecessors have done. I do hope to make one eastern trip in the course of the year, probably in February, 1922. I also hope to bring the Far Western Societies into closer touch with the National Organization than in times past.

WALLACE McCAMANT,
President General.

GENERAL OFFICERS ELECTED AT THE BUFFALO CONGRESS, MAY 17, 1921

President General:

WALLACE McCAMANT, Northwestern Bank Building, Portland, Oregon.

Vice-Presidents General:

GEORGE HALE NUTTING, 53 State Street, Boston, Massachusetts.

New England (Maine, New Hampshire, Vermont, Massachusetts, Rhode Island, and Connecticut).

PHILIP F. LARNER, 918 F Street N. W., Washington, District of Columbia

Middle and Coast District (New York, New Jersey, Pennsylvania, Delaware, Maryland, District of Columbia, Virginia, North Carolina, South Carolina, Georgia, and Florida).

MARVIN H. LEWIS, 201 Keller Building, Louisville, Kentucky.

Mississippi Valley, East District (Michigan, Wisconsin, Illinois, Indiana, Ohio, West Virginia, Kentucky, Tennessee, Alabama, and Mississippi).

HENRY B. HAWLEY, Des Moines, Iowa.

Mississippi Valley, West District (Minnesota, North Dakota, South Dakota, Nebraska. Iowa, Kansas, Missouri, Oklahoma, Arkansas, Louisiana, and Texas).

JOHN W. BELL, JR., P. O. Box 1124, Spokane, Washington.

Mountain and Pacific Coast District (Montana, Idaho, Wyoming, Nevada, Utah, Colorado. Arizona, New Mexico, Oregon, Washington, California, Hawaii, and Philippines).

Secretary General:

FRANK BARTLETT STEELE, 183 St. James Place, Buffalo, New York.

Registrar General:

WILLIAM S. PARKS, 900 17th Street N. W., Washington, District of Columbia.

Treasurer General:

JOHN H. BURROUGHS, 1111 Dean Street, Brooklyn, New York.

Historian General:

GEORGE CARPENTER ARNOLD, Arnold Building, Providence, Rhode Island.

Chancellor General:

EUGENE C. BONNIWELL, City Court Building, Philadelphia, Pennsylvania.

Genealogist General:

WALTER K. WATKINS, 9 Ashburton Place, Boston, Massachusetts.

Chaplain General:

REV. LYMAN WHITNEY ALLEN, Newark, New Jersey.

BOARD OF TRUSTEES

The General Officers, together with one member from each State Society, constitute the Board of Trustees of the National Society. The following Trustees for the several States were elected at the Buffalo Congress, May 17, 1921, to serve until their successors are elected at the Congress to be held at Springfield, Mass., in May, 1922:

Alabama, (vacant); Arizona, Clay F. Leonard, Phœnix; Arkansas, George B. Gill, Little Rock; California, Seabury C. Mastick, New York City; Colorado, Malcolm Lindsey, Denver; Connecticut, Horace Wickham, Hartford; Delaware, George Armstrong Elliott, Wilmington; District of Columbia, Albert D. Spangler, Washington; Far Eastern Society, (vacant); Florida, Dr. F. G. Renshaw, Pensacola; Society in France, (vacant); Hawaiian Society, (vacant); Georgia, Allan Waters, Atlanta; Idaho, (vacant); Illinois, Dorr E. Felt, Chicago; Indiana, Charles C. Jewett, Terre Haute; Iowa, Elmer E. Wentworth, State Center; Kansas, John M. Meade, Topeka; Kentucky, George T. Wood, Louisville; Louisiana, Col. C. Robert Churchill, New Orleans; Maine, James O. Bradbury, Saco; Maryland, Hon. Henry Stockbridge, Baltimore; Massachusetts, Samuel Fuller Punderson, Springfield; Michigan, Albert M. Henry, Detroit; Minnesota, Charles E. Rittenhouse, Minneapolis; Mississippi, (vacant); Missouri, George R. Merrill, St. Louis; Montana, Marcus Whritenour, Helena; Nebraska, Benjamin F. Bailey, Lincoln; Nevada, (vacant); New Hampshire, Henry T. Lord, Manchester; New Jersey, Charles Symmes Kiggins, Elizabeth; New Mexico, George G. Klock, Albuquerque; New York, Louis Annin Ames, New York; North Carolina, (vacant); North Dakota, Howard E. Simpson, Grand Forks; Ohio, Moulton Houk, Delaware; Oklahoma, W. A. Jennings, Oklahoma City; Oregon, Wallace McCamant, Portland; Pennsylvania, Col. R. W. Guthrie, Pittsburgh; Rhode Island, Wilfred H. Munro, Providence; South Carolina, (vacant); South Dakota, J. G. Parsons, Sioux Falls; Tennessee, Leland Hume, Nashville; Texas, C. B. Dorchester, Sherman; Utah, Heber M. Wells, Salt Lake City; Vermont, William Jeffrey, Montpelier; Virginia, Arthur B. Clarke, Richmond; Washington, Ernest B. Hussey, Seattle; Wisconsin, Walter H. Wright, Milwaukee; Wyoming, Warren Richardson, Cheyenne.

WALLACE McCAMANT

President General

WALLACE McCAMANT was born at Hollidaysburg, Pa., on the 22d of September, 1867. He is the son of Thomas and Delia (Rollins) McCamant. His father was Auditor General of Pennsylvania from 1888 to 1892.

Wallace McCamant was educated in the public schools of Harrisburg, Pa., and graduated from Lafayette College in 1888. He read law in Lancaster, Pa., and was admitted to the bar of the Second Judicial District of Pennsylvania in 1890. He immediately removed to Portland, Oregon, where he has been engaged in the practice of his profession ever since.

He was Associate Justice of the Supreme Court of Oregon from January 9, 1917, to June 4, 1918. He was a delegate to the Republican National Conventions of 1896, 1900, and 1920. In the latter convention he served on the subcommittee on resolutions, which framed the platform, and he also placed in nomination Hon. Calvin Coolidge, the present Vice-President.

He has been a member of the Sons of the American Revolution since 1891 and served as President of the Oregon Society from 1907 to 1921. He was Vice-President General of the National Society from 1913 to 1914. During his incumbency as President of the Oregon Society this Society entertained the National Society at Portland.

Mr. McCamant married Katherine S. Davis, of Phillipsburg, N. J., in 1893. Mrs. McCamant is a member of the Daughters of the American Revolution and has been State Regent in Oregon.

Mr. McCamant is a 33d-Degree Mason, deeply interested in the work of the Masonic fraternity, and has been for nearly thirty years a member of the Oregon Commandery of the Loyal Legion. Mr. McCamant is a Presbyterian and a member of the Arlington and University Clubs at Portland, Oregon. He is also a member of the Oregon and American Bar Associations. He was President of the Oregon Bar Association from 1919 to 1920.

His Revolutionary ancestors were his great-grandfathers, James McCamant, an ensign in the First Company of the First Battalion of the Pennsylvania Militia, commanded by Lieutenant-Colonel John Gardiner, and Eliphalet Rollins, private in Captain Benjamin Burton's Company, Third Lincoln County Regiment, Massachusetts Troops.

Mr. McCamant has two sons, Davis and Thomas, the former of whom is of age and a member of the Oregon Society. The younger son is a member of the Class of 1922 at Princeton.

GEORGE HALE NUTTING

Vice-President General for New England District

GEORGE HALE NUTTING, President of the Massachusetts Society of the Sons of the American Revolution, was born at Haverhill, Mass., February 27, 1867. He is the oldest son of the late David Hubbard Nutting, M. D., and Mary Elizabeth (Nichols) Nutting.

He is descended from John Nutting, of Chelmsford and Groton, Mass., one of the original proprietors of the town of Groton, who was killed by the Indians in the attack on that frontier town, March 9, 1676, at the opening of King Philip's War.

He is also descended from William Nutting, of Groton, and David Hubbard, of Hancock, N. H., Revolutionary soldiers, and from Deacon Thomas Barrett, of Concord, Mass., who was a member of the Committee of Correspondence and Safety, and a brother of Colonel James Barrett.

Mr. Nutting joined this Society in 1892, and has been a delegate to the National Congresses at Chicago, Newark, Detroit, and Hartford, and has served successively as Manager, Vice-President, and President of the Massachusetts Society, S. A. R.

He is executor and trustee of the J. Howard Nichols estate and is a member of the Boston Chamber of Commerce, Boston City Club, Society of Colonial Wars, Bostonian Society, Prospect Lodge, Mt. Vernon Chapter, and Boston Commandery, K. T., and other Masonic bodies, and also of the Bunker Hill Monument Association, and a proprietor of "The Old North Church" (Christ Church), Boston.

In 1890 Mr. Nutting married Hannah M. Brown, a descendant of old Colonial and Revolutionary stock, by whom he has two children—Nathaniel Hubbard Nutting and Dorothy Barrett Nutting. Her death occurred in 1907. In 1909 he married (second) Gertrude M. Freeman, by which union there have been four children—Elizabeth M., Margaret F., John Freeman (who died in 1918, aged three years), and James Barrett Nutting, who was born in 1919.

In 1919 Mr. Nutting presented the Washington and Franklin medal, for excellence in the study of United States history, to the Massachusetts Society, in memory of his son, John Freeman Nutting, who was enrolled as a member of the Washington Guard at the time of his death. This medal was awarded by the Massachusetts Society in 1920 to one hundred high schools and academies in the Commonwealth, and is to be awarded annually hereafter by the Massachusetts Society.

PHILIP F. LARNER

Vice-President General for Middle and Coast District

PHILIP F. LARNER, elected Vice-President General at Buffalo, N. Y., May 17, 1921, is a native of the City of Washington, D. C., as also were his father and grandfather. His great-grandfather, Jacob Gideon, Jr., removed to Washington from Philadelphia, Pa., about the time the location of the National Capital was established.

Mr. Larner is a graduate of the original Emerson Institute, located in Washington for many years and a well-known educational institution; afterward a graduate of the Law College of the Columbian University and a member of the bar of the Supreme Court of the District of Columbia. Later he has been actively connected for many years with various business organizations in Washington. He is a member of the University Club, as well as several civic and religious organizations.

Mr. Larner became a member of the District of Columbia Society, Sons of the American Revolution, in 1891, his ancestor being his great-great-grandfather, Jacob Gideon, Sr., who enlisted at Valley Forge and served with the Pennsylvania troops in the battles at Guilford, Eutaw Springs, Cowpens, and Yorktown.

Mr. Larner was for a long term of years Treasurer and afterwards President of the District of Columbia Society, and has been a delegate from that Society to numerous annual congresses of the National Society, and was Secretary and Registrar General, 1919-1920. His wife, Fannie D. Larner (deceased), was a charter member of the Daughters of the American Revolution, having the national number 185 in that organization. His daughter, Mrs. Albert J. Gore, is an active member of the Daughters of the American Revolution and the founder and first regent of the Captain Molly Pitcher Chapter, Daughters of the American Revolution, in the City of Washington. His father, Noble D. Larner, at one time President of the District of Columbia Society, died in 1903, while holding the office of Vice-President General in the National Society, Sons of the American Revolution.

MARVIN H. LEWIS

Vice-President General for Mississippi Valley—East District

MARVIN H. LEWIS, stock and bond broker, was born at Elizabethtown, Ky., June 16, 1873, and was educated in the public schools of Louisville and at the South Kentucky College, Hopkinsville. He then engaged in newspaper work and filled various positions on the *Louisville Times* and *Courier-Journal*, having been financial editor of the latter paper for several years. On May 1, 1906, he organized Marvin H. Lewis & Co., which firm does a business in stocks and bonds. He is a member of the Louisville Stock Exchange, Society of Colonial Wars, Sons of the American Revolution, and Pendennis Club. He married, in 1903, Isabel Ambyr Rodgers, of Pittsburgh, Pa. They have one son, Marvin Arthur Lewis, born December 28, 1911. The home address of Mr. Lewis is Weissinger-Gaulbert Apartments; business address, 201 Keller Building, Fifth and Main Streets, Louisville, Ky.

He served in various capacities during the World War, being chairman of the Four-Minute Men, Chairman of State Speakers' Bureau, and member of Executive Committees in the Liberty Loan and other campaigns.

HENRY B. HAWLEY

Vice-President General, Mississippi Valley—West District

HENRY B. HAWLEY, of Des Moines, Iowa, was born on a farm in New York State, near Warsaw. Mr. Hawley began life on his own account as a school teacher, followed later by a short but successful period as a business man, where the field of insurance attracted and held his interest and attention. Aside from insurance, his position in the business, political, and social world of Des Moines is commanding. A man of initiative and with altruistic principles, he has been extremely active along all lines of social betterment, and carried with him from Buffalo, where the first charity organization society in America was established, those ideas of philanthrophy which resulted in the Associated Charities of Des Moines and have permeated the entire group of organizations which are affiliated in the work of human rehabilitation in that community. He was recently made a Life President of the Associated Charities of Des Moines. Mr. Hawley is Past President of the Iowa State Society, having been a member since April, 1898. Among the public spirited personal efforts of Mr. Hawley in the direction of patriotic education we note his presentation of a medal each year to the high school at Warsaw, New York, given to the pupil attaining the highest term mark in American history. This presentation has been made annually since 1911. Mr. Hawley stands high in banking circles in Des Moines and is a member of the Bankers' Club and bank director.

JOHN W. BELL, Jr.

Vice-President General for Mountain and Pacific District

JOHN WILLIAM BELL, JR., of Spokane, Wash., was elected Vice-President General for the Mountain and Pacific District at the Congress held in Hartford, Conn., May 18, 1920. He is the son of John William and Mary Perkins (Horton) Bell, and was born in St. Paul (Merriam Park), Minn., January 30, 1891. Is great-great-great-grandson of Lieut. John Jones, who was a member of General Washington's army. John Jones was descended from Governor Eaton, first governor of Connecticut. On another line he can trace his ancestry back to Joseph Jenckes, from whom Past President General Jenks is descended.

He was admitted to the Washington State Society on January 20, 1914. In 1917 was appointed Secretary-Treasurer *pro tem.* of Spokane Chapter and the following year was elected to the office. In 1919 was President of the Chapter and First Vice-President of the Washington Society. Is now Secretary-Treasurer of the Chapter again, having been elected in January, 1920.

Lived in St. Paul until 1900, when he moved to Tacoma, Wash., and in 1904 to Spokane. Is a member of the Episcopal Church. Married Lillian B. Blakeslee in Spokane, September 2, 1914. Is engaged in the coal business, both wholesale and retail, being assistant to the manager of the Roslyn Fuel Co.'s Spokane branch.

FRANK BARTLETT STEELE

Secretary General

FRANK BARTLETT STEELE, elected Secretary General May 17, 1921, at the Buffalo Congress, was born in Buffalo, New York, March 28, 1864. He is the son of Charles Gould Steele and Harriet Virginia Snyder, and great-grandson of Zenas Barker, who fought in the Revolutionary War with the New York troops in the battle of Oriskany. Mr. Steele was graduated from the State Normal School of Buffalo and studied law in the offices of George Clinton, grandson of De Witt Clinton. Mr. Steele joined the Buffalo Chapter of the Empire State Society in 1897 and became its Secretary in 1901, which office he has held continuously since. He has been a delegate to every National Congress since 1906, except those held at Denver in 1907 and Portland in 1915, and has been on a number of important national committees.

Mr. Steele, in co-operation with the School Department of the City of Buffalo and the Daughters of the American Revolution, has been active in the work of Americanization, the field for this work being almost unlimited in Buffalo, due to its large foreign population.

Mr. Steele, shortly after his admission to the bar, became the Clerk of the Superior Court of Buffalo, and was thereafter transferred into the Supreme

Court of the State of New York. He was at one time clerk of the Board of Supervisors of Erie County.

He is a member of the Society of Mayflower Descendants in line from Governor William Bradford.

During the World War Mr. Steele was made Executive Secretary of the Home Defense Committee of Erie County, a body created by the State of New York, and during this period gave his time unstintedly to the many activities and responsibilities that were placed upon this committee by the National and State Government. Under a statute of the State of New York creating local historians, Mayor Buck appointed Mr. Steele Historian of the City of Buffalo, and in this capacity he assisted in writing and compiling the History of the City of Buffalo and Erie County in the World War; also, at the suggestion of the State Historian, Mr. Steele has made a complete survey of the records and archives of Buffalo and Erie County, and upon his recommendations steps are now being taken by the City Commissioners to improve the conditions under which these records are being preserved.

Mr. Steele married Helen Cleveland Varian, of Titusville, Pa., in 1896. Mrs. Steele is also of Revolutionary ancestry, descending from the Atlees of Pennsylvania, the Varians of New York, and Litchfields of Connecticut. She was a daughter of Col. William Varian, Surgeon on the staff of Gen. Gordon Granger during the Civil War, now buried in Arlington Cemetery.

JOHN HARRIS BURROUGHS

Treasurer General

JOHN HARRIS BURROUGHS was born at Trenton, N. J., April 17, 1849, son of Charles Burroughs, wso served as mayor of Trenton for fifteen consecutive years—from 1832 until 1847—who was also judge of the Court of Common Pleas for Mercer County, N. J., for sixteen years. John Burroughs, the grandfather of the subject of this sketch, was active in the Revolutionary War from the latter part of 1776 until the surrender of Cornwallis at the battle of Yorktown, in 1781. Mr. Burroughs is descended from John Burroughs, who settled in Newtown, Long Island, in 1653, with other English colonists. In the capacity of Treasurer, Vice-President, and President, he has served the Union League Club, Brooklyn. N. Y., in which city he has resided since 1865. He was President of the Empire State Society in 1910 and 1911. From 1874 to 1918 Mr. Burroughs was a dealer in commercial paper and bank stocks in New York City. He is now manager of the Brooklyn Branch of the Corn Exchange Bank of New York.

He was elected Treasurer General at the Baltimore Congress, in 1909, and reelected at each succeeding Congress.

WILLIAM SCOTT PARKS

Registrar General

Compatriot WILLIAM SCOTT PARKS, the Registrar General, was born in Warren. Trumbull County, Ohio, and was educated in the public schools of his native city and Washington, D. C., where he has resided since boyhood. His classical education was received in Columbian College, now George Washington University. He graduated from the Law School in 1881 with the degree of LL. M., and was admitted to the bar after the required examination of the Bar Association, but, with the exception of a few minor cases, has seldom appeared in court. He entered the Treasury Department as a clerk, afterwards a law clerk and accountant, serving in several of the important bureaus.

He is a member of the District of Columbia Society of the Sons of the American Revolution and was its President in 1918, a member of the Sons of the Revolution in the District of Columbia and its present Historian, a member of the Society of Colonial Wars of the District and of its Board of Governors (Council). Mr. Parks is also prominent as a member of the Masonic order, having been Grand Commander of Knights Templar of the District during 1917-1918. He is a member of the National Geographic Society and was a charter member of the Ohio Society of Washington. He was Secretary General of the National Society of the Sons of the American Revolution from January 2, 1919, to May 16 of the same year, and was elected Registrar General of the Society May 17, 1921. His Revolutionary descent is both through his paternal and his maternal ancestry. His great-grandfathers, Reuben Parks and Weait Munson, were soldiers of the Revolutionary War.

Mr. Parks is ninth in direct descent from Robert Parke (1580-1664), who was born in Preston, England, and came to Boston in 1630; was Deputy to the General Court of Connecticut in 1641 and again in 1642, and died February 4, 1664. He also is of the ninth generation of Captain Thomas Munson, who was born in 1612 and died May 7, 1685.

Mr. Parks is married, and has a son and a grandson, his son being a member of the District of Columbia Society of the Sons of the American Revolution.

LIEUT. GEORGE CARPENTER ARNOLD
Historian General

GEORGE CARPENTER ARNOLD, of Providence, R. I., First Lieutenant, Company C, First Regiment of Infantry, Rhode Island Militia, elected Historian General at the Rochester Congress, May 21, 1918, and re-elected at Detroit Congress, in 1919, at Hartford Congress in 1920, and at Buffalo in 1921, was born at Providence July 31, 1868, son of William Rhodes and Sarah Hill (Carpenter) Arnold. His ancestry runs without break back to the Puritan immigration, William Arnold, the immigrant, being mentioned in Lincoln's history of Hingham, Mass. In 1635 William Arnold and family left Somersetshire, England, and came to New England. After residing a short time at Hingham, he became associated, in 1636, with Roger Williams and others in the purchase from the Indian sachems, Canonicus and Miantonomoh, of land at Mooshausic, afterward called Providence, and received grants of land from Williams. His initials, "W. A." are second on the famous Indian deed of Roger Williams. His real estate was mostly in Providence, Pawtuxet, and Warwick, R. I. One hundred and twenty acres of the original grant (including a 27-acre lake) at Warwick, R. I., are now owned by the subject of this sketch, the ancestral home, built in 1771 (by his great²-grandfather, George Arnold), being used by him as a summer residence.

Lieutenant Arnold received his education in the schools of his native city and at the Episcopal Military Academy of Cheshire, Conn., class of 1887.

In November, 1887, he joined Company C, First Regiment of Infantry, Rhode Island Militia; was elected Corporal, 1889; Second Lieutenant, 1890; First Lieutenant, 1891, 1892, 1893, and 1894. For nearly a quarter of a century he was engaged in the worsted yarn business. He is President and Treasurer of the Possnegansett Ice Company; Treasurer and Director of the Arnold Real Estate Company; Treasurer of the Arnold Numismatic Company; Director of the Central Real Estate Company and of the Providence Realty Company; Treasurer of the Motor League of Rhode Island; Treasurer of the Society of Descendants of the Founders of Providence Plantations. He is the author of several books—one treating on Numismatics (of which he is an authority)—and publisher of the "Genealogical Tree of the Arnold Family, embracing nearly thirty generations, from 1100 A. D."

He married Flora Etta Richards December 14, 1892, by whom he has three sons: Lincoln Richards Arnold, Brown University, Class of 1916; Philip Rhodes Arnold, Amherst College, Class of 1918, and Capt. George Carpenter Arnold, Jr., Dartmouth College, Class of 1918, now United States First Vice Consul at Seville, Spain.

EUGENE C. BONNIWELL
Chancellor General

EUGENE C. BONNIWELL was born in Philadelphia, September 25, 1872. He was graduated from the University of Pennsylvania Law School in 1893. He was college champion in pole vaulting and running, a director of the Athletic Association of the University of Pennsylvania, and immediately began the practice of law in his native city. On November 6, 1913, he was elected Judge of the New Municipal Court by an overwhelming majority, a position which he now holds. Five times the firemen of Pennsylvania have conferred upon him the honor of selecting him as president of the Firemen's Association of the State of Pennsylvania. He is a director of the National Security League, President of the Philadelphia Chapter, Sons of the American Revolution; president of the Veteran Athletes of Philadelphia; a director of the Pennsylvania State Chamber of Commerce; vice-director, Committee of Public Safety of Pennsylvania; a member of the Sons of the Revolution; Society of the War of 1812; Friendly Sons of St. Patrick; J. F. Reynolds Camp, No. 4, Sons of Veterans; Registrar of Order of Washington; member of the Historical Society of Pennsylvania; the City Business Club; the City History Club; Order of Eagles; Fraternal Order of Orioles; Order of Moose; Philadelphia Order of Elks, and Chevalier Commander Order of Lafayette.

On June 5, 1900, Judge Bonniwell was married to Madeline H. Cahill. He has seven children, all living.

As a public official, in charge of the mass of misery coming for relief into the great Desertion Court of Philadelphia, during twenty-two months Judge Bonniwell handled 6,000 cases, involving 20,000 children, and collected for deserted wives and infants over half a million dollars. Throughout his public and private life he has always maintained to the fullest degree an untiring interest in the red-blooded activities that make the American youth unsurpassed in their qualities of initiative, resoluteness, and daring, and a public career without blemish has made him one of the foremost citizens of Philadelphia in all the things that relate to indomitable courage, capacity, and interest in civic matters.

WALTER K. WATKINS

Genealogist General

WALTER KENDALL WATKINS was born in Boston, August 5, 1855, and graduated from the Phillips Grammar and English High Schools. Since 1880 he has been engaged in historical and genealogical researches in this country and Great Britain. He has published frequently articles in newspapers and magazines and edited the Colonial Wars Magazine and publications of the Society of Colonial Wars in the Commonwealth of Massachusetts. A specialty has been his works on the early history of Boston and contributions to the publications of the Bostonian Society.

He has been a charter member and director of Boston Chapter, S. A. R.; charter member and historian of Old Suffolk Chapter; charter member and secretary of Malden Chapter. He now holds the office of Historian of the Massachusetts State Society. He was elected Historian General at the National Congresses of 1908 and 1909; a charter member of the Massachusetts Society of Colonial Wars; he has been Genealogist of the State Society since 1896 and Secretary for fifteen years.

He is a charter member of the Massachusetts Society of Mayflower Descendants and Secretary of the Bay State Historical League, composed of seventy-five historical societies in Massachusetts. A member of the New England Historic-Genealogical Society since 1889; he has been on its library committee for several years, and is chairman of the committee on records.

He is also an active and honorary member in several historical societies. He is a resident of Malden, Mass., and Grafton, N. H.

LYMAN WHITNEY ALLEN

Chaplain General

LYMAN WHITNEY ALLEN was born in St. Louis, Missouri, November 19, 1854. He is a son of George Otis Allen and Julia Olds Whitney, of the historic Thornton family of Virginia, conspicuous as officers in the American Revolution. He graduated at Washington University, St. Louis, 1878, receiving the degree of A. B., later A. M.; pursued post-graduate studies in Princeton University and his theological course in Princeton Theological Seminary. He received the degree of D. D. from Wooster University, Ohio, in 1897. He married Myra Irwin, of St. Louis, daughter of Archibald Steele Irwin, an officer in the Civil War. She died in 1900. In 1904 he married Phebeti L. Massena, of Glen Ridge, N. J. She died in 1915. Dr. Allen's ministry was in St. Louis and vicinity from 1882 to 1889, when he was called to the South Park Presbyterian Church of Newark, N. J., where he remained as pastor 27 years.

In October, 1916, he resigned his church to engage in literary work, to which he has given his time and energy up to the present. He has published several volumes of poems, and also miscellaneous poems and prose articles. In 1895 he won the prize of $1,000 offered by the *New York Herald* for the best poem on

American history. His poem, "Abraham Lincoln," was published in the Christmas issues of the *New York Herald*, the *Boston Herald*, and the *St. Louis Republic*. Afterward it appeared in book form and has passed through several editions.

Dr. Allen in 1916 wrote the official Celebration Ode for the 250th Anniversary of the City of Newark, N. J. In 1917 he wrote the official poem for the dedication of the Barnard statue of Lincoln in Cincinnati. May 30, 1917, he delivered the Memorial Day oration in the Soldiers' National Cemetery, Battlefield of Gettysburg. His well-known poem on "Lincoln's Pew" is tableted on the historic pew in the New York Avenue Presbyterian Church (the Church of the Presidents), Washington, D. C. He is connected with several leading clubs and societies in New York, notably the Dickens Fellowship, of which he is President; the Browning Society, the Shakespeare Club, the Dante League, the McDowell Club, the National Arts Club, the Authors' Club, and the Poetry Society of America.

Dr. Allen became a member of the New Jersey Society of the Sons of the American Revolution in 1890. Since then he has been active in the work of the Society, having been Chaplain, First Vice-President, then President. He is now filling his second term as President. At the last meeting of the National Congress, at Buffalo, he was elected Chaplain General. Two of his poems have appeared in recent issues of the National Society's Bulletin, "The New America" and "The Mayflower Pilgrims."

NATIONAL COMMITTEES

Executive Committee:

WALLACE McCAMANT, *Chairman,* Portland, Oregon.
LOUIS ANNIN AMES, 90 Fulton Street, New York, New York.
JAMES H. PRESTON, Munsey Building, Baltimore, Maryland.
CHANCELLOR L. JENKS, 30 North La Salle Street, Chicago, Illinois.
ARTHUR P. SUMNER, 639 Grosvenor Building, Providence, Rhode Island.
GEORGE F. POMEROY, Toledo, Ohio.
W. I. LINCOLN ADAMS, Montclair, New Jersey.

Advisory Committee:

The PAST PRESIDENTS GENERAL.

Credentials:

TEUNIS D. HUNTTING, *Chairman,* 220 Broadway, New York, New York.
WILLIAM J. CONKLING, Orange, New Jersey.
                (Five others to be appointed prior to 1922 Congress.)

Auditing and Finance:

GEORGE D. BANGS, *Chairman,* Huntington, New York.
NORMAN P. HEFFLEY, Brooklyn, New York.
C. SYMMES KIGGINS, Elizabeth, New Jersey.
HENRY VAIL CONDICT, Essex Fells, New Jersey.
ALBERT J. SQUIER, Yonkers, New York.

Memorial:

R. C. BALLARD THRUSTON, *Chairman,* 1000 Columbus Building, Louisville, Kentucky.
GEORGE A. ELLIOTT, Wilmington, Delaware.
MATTHEW PAGE ANDREWS, 849 Park Avenue, Baltimore, Maryland.
CHARLES FRENCH READ, Boston, Massachusetts.
OTIS G. HAMMOND, Concord, New Hampshire.
WILLIAM CHACE GREEN, Providence, Rhode Island.
SEYMOUR W. LOOMIS, New Haven, Connecticut.
CHARLES P. WORTMAN, Syracuse, New York.
GEORGE V. MUCHMORE, Summit, New Jersey.
ALLAN WATERS, Atlanta, Georgia.
CLARENCE A. KENYON, Washington, District of Columbia.
EUGENE C. BONNIWELL, City Hall, Philadelphia, Pennsylvania.

Organization, New England District:

GEORGE HALE NUTTING, Vice-President General, *Chairman,* 53 State St., Boston, Massachusetts.
WILLIAM K. SANDERSON, Portland, Maine.
HARRY T. LORD, Manchester, New Hampshire.
GUY W. BAILEY, Burlington, Vermont.
BURTON H. WIGGIN, Lowell, Massachusetts.
DR. GEORGE T. SPICER, Providence, Rhode Island.
HERBERT H. WHITE, Hartford, Connecticut.

Organization, Middle and Coast District:

PHILIP F. LARNER, Vice-President General, *Chairman,* 918 F Street N. W., Washington, District of Columbia.
HARVEY F. REMINGTON, Rochester, New York.
JAMES A. WAKEFIELD, Pittsburgh, Pennsylvania.
OSBORNE I. YELLOTT, Baltimore, Maryland.
HORACE WILSON, Wilmington, Delaware.
HARRY F. BREWER, Elizabeth, New Jersey.

ARTHUR B. CLARKE, Richmond, Virginia.
SELDEN M. ELY, Washington, District of Columbia.
ALLAN WATERS, Atlanta, Georgia.
FRANK H. BRYAN, Washington, District of Columbia.
PAUL T. HAYNE, Greenville, South Carolina.
DR. F. G. RENSHAW, Pensacola, Florida.

Organization, Mississippi Valley—East:

MARVIN H. LEWIS, Vice-President General, *Chairman*, Keller Building, Louisville, Kentucky.
W. H. BARRETT, Adrian, Michigan.
MOULTON HOUK, Toledo, Ohio.
CREDO HARRIS, South Third Street, Louisville, Kentucky.
CHARLES T. JEWETT, Terre Haute, Indiana.
DORR E. FELT, Chicago, Illinois.
WALTER H. WRIGHT, Milwaukee, Wisconsin.
WILLIAM K. BOARDMAN, Nashville, Tennessee.

Organization, Mississippi Valley—West:

HENRY B. HAWLEY, Vice-President General, *Chairman*, Des Moines, Iowa.
CAPT. FRED A. BRILL, St. Paul, Minnesota.
WALTER E. COFFIN, Des Moines, Iowa.
LINN PAINE, St. Louis, Missouri.
FRANK W. TUCKER, Little Rock, Arkansas.
C. ROBERT CHURCHILL, New Orleans, Louisiana.
C. P. DORCHESTER, Sherman, Texas.
E. G. SPILLMAN, Oklahoma City, Oklahoma.
ARTHUR H. BENNETT, Topeka, Kansas.
DR. BENJAMIN F. BAILEY, Lincoln, Nebraska.
DR. J. G. PARSONS, Sioux Falls, South Dakota.
FRANK D. HALL, Fargo, North Dakota.

Organization, Mountain and Pacific:

JOHN W. BELL, JR., Vice-President General, *Chairman*, Spokane, Washington.
LESLIE BERRY SULGROVE, Helena, Montana.
FRANK G. ENSIGN, Boise, Idaho.
GALEN A. FOX, Cheyenne, Wyoming.
DANIEL S. SPENCER, Salt Lake City, Utah.
EDWARD V. DUNKLEE, Denver, Colorado.
HAROLD BAXTER, 311 Fleming Building, Phœnix, Arizona.
THOMAS F. KELEHER, Albuquerque, New Mexico.
CLAUDE GATCH, Federal Reserve Bank, San Francisco, California.
JESSE MARTIN HITT, Olympia, Washington.
WINTHROP HAMMOND, 127 Sixth Street, Portland, Oregon.

Joint Committee with Descendants of Signers of Declaration of Independence for Historical Research:

R. C. BALLARD THRUSTON, *Chairman*, 1000 Columbus Building, Louisville, Kentucky.
MATTHEW PAGE ANDREWS, 849 Park Avenue, Baltimore, Maryland.
GEORGE A. ELLIOTT, Wilmington, Delaware.

Patriotic Education:

LINN PAINE, *Chairman*, 904 Locust Street, St. Louis, Missouri.
GEORGE B. SAGE, *Vice-Chairman*, 713 Park Avenue, Rochester, New York.
HARRY G. COLSON, Chicago, Illinois.
SAMUEL B. BOTSFORD, Buffalo, New York.
GRENVILLE H. NORCROSS, Boston, Massachusetts.
ASHLEY K. HARDY, Hanover, New Hampshire.
MATTHEW PAGE ANDREWS, 849 Park Avenue, Baltimore, Maryland.

WILLIAM F. PIERCE, Gambier, Ohio.
DR. R. S. HILL, Albuquerque, New Mexico.
WILLIAM P. HUMPHREYS, Holbrook Building, San Francisco, California.
HARRISON G. PLATT, Platt Building, Portland, Oregon.

Naval and Military Records:

REAR ADMIRAL GEORGE W. BAIRD, *Chairman*, 1505 Rhode Island Avenue, Washington, District
    of Columbia.
MAJOR-GENERAL NELSON A. MILES, Washington, District of Columbia.
JAMES D. IGLEHART, Baltimore, Maryland.
C. A. KENYON, Washington, District of Columbia.
CAPT. ALBERT WILBUR SMITH, Bridgeport, Connecticut.
REAR ADMIRAL F. F. FLETCHER, Navy Department, Washington, District of Columbia.
JOSEPH B. DOYLE, Steubenville, Ohio.

Americanization and Aliens:

HARVEY F. REMINGTON, *Chairman*, Wilder Building, Rochester, New York.
COMMANDER JOHN H. MOORE, *Vice-Chairman*, The Wyoming, Washington, District of Columbia.
SAMUEL JUDD HOLMES, *Vice-Chairman*, Burke Building, Seattle, Washington.
THOMAS W. WILLIAMS, East Orange, New Jersey.
HARRY T. LORD, Manchester, New Hampshire.
DR. GEORGE H. BANGS, Swampscott, Massachusetts.
A. McCLELLAN MATHEWSON, 865 Chapel Street, New Haven, Connecticut.
THOMAS STEPHEN BROWN, Pittsburgh, Pennsylvania.
CHANCELLOR L. JENKS, 30 North La Salle Street, Chicago, Illinois.
FREDERICK M. ALGER, Detroit, Michigan.

Flag:

W. V. COX, *Chairman*, Washington, District of Columbia.
BRIGADIER GENERAL OLIVER B. BRIDGMAN, New York, New York.
GENERAL CHARLES A. COOLIDGE, Detroit, Michigan.
COLONEL GEORGE V. LAUMAN, Chicago, Illinois.
COLONEL G. K. HUNTER, St. Louis, Missouri.
LIEUTENANT COLONEL M. W. WOOD, Boise, Idaho.
BRIGADIER GENERAL CHARLES A. WOODRUFF, Berkeley, California.

Investment of Permanent Fund:

The PRESIDENT GENERAL.
The TREASURER GENERAL.
CORNELIUS AMORY PUGSLEY, Peekskill, New York.

National Archives Building:

MAJOR FREDERICK C. BRYAN, *Chairman*, Colorado Building, Washington, District of Columbia
NATHAN WARREN, Waltham, Massachusetts.
JAMES P. GOODRICH, Winchester, Indiana.
AMEDEE B. COLE, St. Louis, Missouri.
EDWARD D. BALDWIN, The Dalles, Oregon.
COMMANDER J. H. MOORE, U. S. N., Washington, District of Columbia.
M. L. RITCHIE, Salt Lake City, Utah.
GENERAL G. BARRETT RICH, Buffalo, New York.
WILLIAM S. PARKS, Washington, District of Columbia.

Increased Membership:

CHANCELLOR L. JENKS, *Chairman*, 30 North La Salle Street, Chicago, Illinois.
LOUIS ANNIN AMES, *Vice-Chairman*, 90 Fulton Street, New York, New York.
ROBERT E. ADRIAN, St. Louis, Missouri.
ARTHUR H. BENNETT, Topeka, Kansas.
HARRY F. BREWER, Elizabeth, New Jersey.

KENNETH C. BRILL, St. Paul, Minnesota.
DR. BENJAMIN F. BAILEY, Lincoln, Nebraska.
FRANK H. BRYAN, Washington, North Carolina.
H. BENNETT, Tulsa, Oklahoma.
GEORGE F. BURGESS, New Haven, Connecticut.
WILLIAM K. BOARDMAN, Nashville, Tennessee.
LEWIS B. CURTIS, Bridgeport, Connecticut.
JOHN HOBART CROSS, Pensacola, Florida.
W. L. CURRY, Columbus, Ohio.
W. E. CHAPLIN, Cheyenne, Wyoming.
H. C. COXE, Paris, France.
T. W. DWIGHT, Sioux Falls, South Dakota.
EMMETT A. DONNELLY, Milwaukee, Wisconsin.
COLONEL GEORGE A. ELLIOTT, Wilmington, Delaware.
ROBERT T. ELLIOTT, Worcester, Massachusetts.
FREDERICK E. EMERSON, Norfolk, Virginia.
FRANK W. GRAHAM, Albuquerque, New Mexico.
H. W. GROUT, Waterloo, Iowa.
DWIGHT B. HEARD, Phœnix, Arizona.
ASHLEY K. HARDY, Hanover, New Hampshire.
FRANK D. HALL, Fargo, North Dakota.
DAVID ARNOLD HENNING, Greenville, South Carolina.
LELAND HUME, Nashville, Tennessee.
JOHN CHARLES HARRIS, Houston, Texas.
I. M. HOWELL, Olympia, Washington.
FAY HEMPSTEAD, Little Rock, Arkansas.
H. LAWRENCE NOBLE, Manila, Philippine Islands.
HARRY KEYSER, Boise, Idaho.
DE MOTT MODISETTE, Cleveland, Ohio.
GEORGE H. NEWHALL, Providence, Rhode Island.
CHAUNCEY P. OVERFIELD, Salt Lake City, Utah.
JOHN M. PARKER, JR., Hartford, Connecticut.
EDMUND L. PARKER, Kokomo, Indiana.
GEORGE E. POMEROY, Toledo, Ohio.
CHARLES N. REMINGTON, Grand Rapids, Michigan.
GEORGE SADTLER ROBERTSON, Baltimore, Maryland.
GEORGE McK. ROBERTS, Schenectady, New York.
E. MONTGOMERY REILY, Kansas City, Missouri.
DONZEL STONEY, San Francisco, California.
WILLIAM H. SEEDS, Denver, Colorado.
WILLIAM K. SANDERSON, Portland, Maine.
LESLIE SULGROVE, Helena, Montana.
B. E. SANFORD, Portland, Oregon.
JOHN B. TORBERT, Washington, District of Columbia.
JAMES T. TAYLOR, Honolulu.
PHILIP S. TULEY, Louisville, Kentucky.
GEORGE N. WRIGHT, Chicago, Illinois.
BIDDLE WILKINSON ALLEN, New Orleans, Louisiana.
A. W. WALL, Pittsburgh, Pennsylvania.

Ceremonies and Colors:

COLONEL GEORGE V. LAUMAN, *Chairman*, 320 Ashland Block, Chicago, Illinois.
CAPTAIN R. W. BROWN, Corry, Pennsylvania.
JOSEPH ATWOOD, Linn, Massachusetts.
JOSEPH M. SHIELDS, Old National Bank Building, Spokane, Washington.
JOSEPH W. HAMMOND, 126 Sixth Street, Portland, Oregon.

Observance of Flag Day:

LEWIS B. CURTIS, *Chairman*, Bridgeport, Connecticut.
W. HOWARD WALKER, Providence, Rhode Island.

MILTON W. GATCH, Baltimore, Maryland.
DR. CHARLES VAN BERGEN, Buffalo, New York.
HERMAN W. FERNBERGER, 1825 North 17th Street, Philadelphia, Pennsylvania.
HENRY B. POLLARD, Richmond, Virginia.
WINFORD LECKY MATTOON, Columbus, Ohio.
FRANK W. GRAHAM, Albuquerque, New Mexico.
LOUIS A. BOWMAN, Northern Trust Company, Chicago, Illinois.
DR. GEORGE D. BARNEY, Brooklyn, New York.

NATIONAL COMMITTEE ON OBSERVANCE OF CONSTITUTION DAY, SEPTEMBER 17

Constitution Day Inaugurated by the Sons of the American Revolution in 1917

Louis Annin Ames, *Chairman*, 99 Fulton Street, New York, New York.
Major W. I. Lincoln Adams, U. S. A., New Jersey.
Hon. George W. Aldridge, New York, New York.
Col. Frederick M. Alger, U. S. A., Grosse Pointe Village, Michigan.
Rev. Lyman Whitney Allen, Newark, New Jersey.
Gen. Francis Henry Appleton, Massachusetts.
Hon. Alfred D. Ayers, Nevada.
Hon. Simeon E. Baldwin, Connecticut.
Thomas F. Bayard, Wilmington, Delaware.
Judge Morris B. Beardsley, Connecticut.
Brig. Gen. Theo. A. Bingham, Connecticut.
William K. Boardman, Tennessee.
Hon. Eugene C. Bonniwell, Pennsylvania.
Louis A. Bowman, Illinois.
John G. Bragaw, Jr., North Carolina.
Brig. Gen. Oliver B. Bridgman, New York.
Austin H. Brown, Indiana.
John H. Burroughs, Treasurer General, New York.
John Bushnell, Nebraska.
Hon. William G. Cody, New York.
Col. Louis R. Cheney, Connecticut.
Rear Admiral Colby M. Chester, U. S. N., Washington, D. C.
Col. C. Robert Churchill, Louisiana.
Arthur B. Clarke, Richmond, Virginia.
Charles Hopkins Clark, Connecticut.
Col. Robert Colgate, New Jersey.
Hon. Calvin A. Coolidge, Vice-President of the United States.
Gen. Charles A. Coolidge, U. S. A., Michigan.
Frank Corbin, Connecticut.
Edwin S. Crandon, Boston, Massachusetts.
John Hobart Cross, Pensacola, Florida.
Hon. Albert B. Cummins, U. S. Senator, Iowa.
Lewis B. Curtis, Bridgeport, Connecticut.
Col. William L. Curry, Ohio.
Hon. Paul Dana, New York.
William C. Demorest, New York.
Hon. Chauncey M. Depew, New York.
Louis H. Dos Passos, New York.
Hon. William P. Dillingham, U. S. Senator, Vermont.
Hon. Ralph D. Earl, New York.
John A. Eckert, New York.
Hon. Walter E. Edge, Senator, New Jersey.
Col. George A. Elliott, Wilmington, Delaware.
Vernon Ashley Field, Massachusetts.
Rear Admiral Frank F. Fletcher, U. S. N., Washington, D. C.

Hon. Joseph Sherman Frelinghuysen, U. S. Senator, New Jersey.
Judge Elbert H. Gary, New York.
Judge J. Howard Gates, Pierre, South Dakota.
Gen. John R. Gibbons, Beauxite, Arkansas.
Hon. Job Hedges, New York.
Hon. James P. Goodrich, Governor of Indiana.
Edward Hagaman Hall, New York.
Hon. James Denton Hancock, Pennsylvania.
Prof. Ashley K. Hardy, New Hampshire.
Credo Fitch Harris, Kentucky.
Dwight B. Heard, Phœnix, Arizona.
Hon. Albert M. Henry, Michigan.
Dr. David Jayne Hill, Washington, D. C.
Major Walter B. Hopping, U. S. A., New York.
Hon. Colgate Hoyt, New York.
Hon. Charles Evans Hughes, New York.
Gen. Willis A. Hulings, Pennsylvania.
Chancellor L. Jenks, Illinois.
Rear Admiral T. F. Jewell, U. S. N., Washington, D. C.
Lieut.-Col. C. T. Jewett, U. S. A., Indiana.
Rear Admiral Albert H. Knight, U. S. N., Massachusetts.
Philip F. Larner, Vice-President General, S. A. R., Washington, D. C.
Judge Eddy Orland Lee, Utah.
Marvin H. Lewis, Vice-President General, Louisville, Kentucky.
Brig. Gen. James Rush Lincoln, Iowa.
Hon. H. Wales Lines, Connecticut.
Hon. Charles Warren Lippitt, former Governor of Rhode Island.
Hon. Henry F. Lippitt, U. S. Senator from Rhode Island.
Hon. Henry Cabot Lodge, U. S. Senator from Massachusetts.
Rev. L. L. Loofbourow, Hawaii.
Hon. Frank O. Lowden, Governor of Illinois.
Judge James Gordon Lyell, Mississippi.
Nelson A. McClary, Illinois.
Hon. William W. McDowell, Montana.
Hon. Wallace McCamant, President General, Sons of the American Revolution, Oregon
Rev. William Gerry Mann, Maine.
William A. Marble, New York.
Dr. Samuel B. McCormack, Pennsylvania.
John M. Meade, Kansas.
Stanwood Menken, New York.
Frank M. Mills, South Dakota.
Edwin P. Mitchell, New York.
Hon. George H. Moses, U. S. Senator, New Hampshire.
Hon. Harry S. New, U. S. Senator from Indiana.
Charles L. Nichols, Colorado.
George Hale Nutting, Massachusetts.
Hon. Carroll S. Page, U. S. Senator from Vermont.
Gen. J. N. Patterson, New Hampshire.
Hon. Thomas A. Perkins, California.
David L. Pierson, New Jersey.
George E. Pomeroy, Ohio.
Dr. Curran Pope.
Hon. James H. Preston, former mayor of Baltimore, Maryland.
Hon. Cornelius A. Pugsley, New York.
Samuel F. Punderson, Massachusetts.
Charles French Read, Massachusetts.
Hon. Harvey F. Remington, New York.
Gen. G. Barrett Rich, Buffalo, New York.
Charles E. Rittenhouse, Minnesota.

John D. Rockefeller, New York.
Hon. Ernest E. Rogers, Connecticut.
Lieut.-Col. Theodore Roosevelt, New York.
Hon. Elihu Root, New York.
Col. Henry W. Sackett, New York.
William K. Sanderson, Maine.
Hon. George H. Shields, Missouri.
Col. Frank S. Sidway, Buffalo, New York.
Judge Ernest C. Simpson, Connecticut.
Hon. George Albert Smith, Utah.
Hon. William Alden Smith, former U. S. Senator from Michigan.
E. G. Spilman, Oklahoma City, Oklahoma.
Vernon P. Squires, North Dakota.
Judge Henry Stockbridge, Maryland.
Hon. William H. Taft, Connecticut.
Col. J. Swigert Taylor, Kentucky.
R. C. Ballard Thruston, Kentucky.
Col. Ralph Emerson Twitchell, New Mexico.
Carl M. Vail, New Jersey.
Col. John Vrooman, New York.
Hon. James W. Wadsworth, U. S. Senator from New York.
Captain Hamilton Ward.
Hon. Francis E. Warren, U. S. Senator from Wyoming.
Dr. William Seward Webb, Vermont.
Elmer Marston Wentworth, Iowa.
Hon. Charles S. Whitman, former Governor of New York.
Prof. William K. Wickes, New York.
Dr. George C. F. Williams, Hartford, Connecticut.
Hon. Robert L. Williams, Governor of Oklahoma.
Henry A. Williams, Ohio.
Thomas Wright Williams, New Jersey.
Col. Elmer E. Wood, U. S. A., Louisiana.
Lieut.-Col. M. W. Wood, U. S. A., Idaho.
Brig. Gen. Charles A. Woodruff, U. S. A., California.
Hon. Rollin S. Woodruff, former Governor of Connecticut.
Newell B. Woodworth, Syracuse, New York.
Prof. Levi Edgar Young, Utah.
Henry A. Williams, Columbus, Ohio.
Walter H. Wright, Milwaukee, Wisconsin.

PRESIDENTS AND SECRETARIES OF STATE SOCIETIES

ARIZONA—President, H. B. Wilkinson, 128 West Adams Street, Phœnix.
  Secretary, Harold Baxter, 311 Fleming Building, Phœnix.
  Treasurer, Kenneth Freeman, Phœnix.

ARKANSAS—President, General Benjamin W. Green, Little Rock.
  Secretary, Fay Hempstead, Little Rock.
  Treasurer, Thomas M. Cory, Little Rock.

CALIFORNIA—President, Frank S. Brittain, Balboa Building, San Francisco.
  Vice-President, Frank S. Britton.
  Secretary and Treasurer, Thomas A. Perkins, Mills Building, San Francisco.

COLORADO—President, Malcolm Lindsey, Denver.
  Secretary, James Polk Willard, Masonic Temple, Denver.
  Treasurer, Walter D. Wynkoop, Denver.

CONNECTICUT—President, Herbert H. White, New Haven.
  Secretary, Frederick A. Doolittle, Bridgeport.
  Treasurer, Charles G. Stone.

DELAWARE—President, Horace Wilson, Wilmington.
  Secretary and Treasurer, Charles A. Rudolph, 900 Vanburen Street, Wilmington.

DISTRICT OF COLUMBIA—President, Selden M. Ely, Gales School Building, Washington.
  Secretary, William Alexander Miller, 911 Monroe Street, Washington.
  Treasurer, Alfred B. Dent.

FAR EASTERN SOCIETY—President-Secretary, H. Lawrence Noble, Post Office Box 940,
    Manila, Philippine Islands.
  Vice-President, Edward B. Copeland.
  Treasurer, Herman Roy Hare.

FLORIDA—President, Dr. F. G. Renshaw, Pensacola.
  Secretary, John Hobart Cross, Pensacola.
  Treasurer, F. F. Bingham.

SOCIETY IN FRANCE—Administered by Empire State Society.

GEORGIA—President, Allan Waters, Post Office Box 361, Atlanta.
  Secretary, Arthur W. Falkinburg, Atlanta.

HAWAII—President, Rev. L. L. Loofbourow, Honolulu.
  Secretary, James T. Taylor, 511 Stangenwald Building, Honolulu.
  Treasurer, Elmer T. Winant.

IDAHO—President, Henry Keyser, Boise.
  Secretary and Treasurer, Frank G. Ensign, Boise.

ILLINOIS—President, Dorr E. Felt, 30 North La Salle Street, Chicago.
  Secretary, Louis A. Bowman, 30 North La Salle Street, Chicago.
  Treasurer, Henry R. Kent.

INDIANA—President, Austin H. Brown, 406 East Fifteenth Street, Indianapolis.
  Secretary and Treasurer, Edmund L. Parker, 208 East Walnut Street, Kokomo.

IOWA—President, Dr. Gershom Hyde Hill, Des Moines.
  Secretary, Captain Elfridge D. Hadley, 409 Franklin Avenue, Des Moines.
  Treasurer, William E. Barrett, Des Moines.

KANSAS—President, John M. Meade, Topeka.
  Secretary, Arthur H. Bennett, Topeka.
  Treasurer, Jonathan A. Norton, Topeka.

KENTUCKY—President, Marvin H. Lewis, Keller Building, Louisville.
  Secretary, George D. Caldwell, Southern Building, Louisville.
  Treasurer, George Tyman Wood, Louisville.

LOUISIANA—President, C. Robert Churchill, 408 Canal Street, New Orleans.
  Secretary, Herbert P. Benton, 403 Whitney Building, New Orleans.
  Treasurer, Harry V. C. Vandercook, New Orleans.

MAINE—President, Hon. James Otis Bradbury, Saco.
    Secretary, Francis L. Littlefield, 291 Brackett Street, Portland.
    Treasurer, Enoch O. Greenleaf, Portland.

MARYLAND—President, Osborne I. Yellott, Baltimore.
    Secretary, George Sadtler Robertson, 1628 Linden Avenue, Baltimore.
    Treasurer, George Goldsborough, Baltimore.

MASSACHUSETTS—President, George Hale Nutting, 53 State Street, Boston.
    Secretary, George S. Stewart, Tremont Building, Boston.
    Treasurer, Lieut.-Col. Charles M. Green, Malden.

MICHIGAN—President, William P. Holliday, Detroit.
    Secretary, Raymond E. Van Syckle, 1729 Ford Building, Detroit.
    Treasurer, Frank G. Smith, Detroit.

MINNESOTA—President, Charles E. Rittenhouse, Minneapolis.
    Secretary, Charles H. Bronson, 48 East Fourth Street, St. Paul.
    Treasurer, Charles W. Eddy, St. Paul.

MISSISSIPPI—President, Judge Gordon Garland Lyell, Jackson.
    Secretary and Treasurer, William H. Pullen, Mechanics' Bank Building, Jackson.

MISSOURI—President, Col. W. D. Vandiver, Columbia.
    Secretary, W. Scott Hancock, 1703 Boatmen's Bank Building, St. Louis.
    Treasurer, I. Shreve Carter.

MONTANA—President, Martin Whritenour, Helena.
    Secretary and Treasurer, Leslie Sulgrove, Helena.

NEBRASKA—President, Benjamin F. Bailey, Lincoln.
    Secretary and Treasurer, Addison E. Sheldon, Lincoln.

NEVADA—President, Rt. Rev. George C. Huntting, 505 Ridge Street, Reno.

NEW HAMPSHIRE—President, Prof. Ashley K. Hardy, Hanover.
    Secretary and Treasurer, Will B. Howe, Concord.

NEW JERSEY—President, Rev. Lyman Whitney Allen, D. D., Newark.
    Secretary, David L. Pierson, 44 Harrison Street, East Orange.
    Treasurer, Earle A. Miller.

NEW MEXICO—President, Edmund Ross, Albuquerque.
    Secretary, Frank W. Graham, Albuquerque.
    Treasurer, Orville A. Matson, Albuquerque.

NEW YORK—President, Harvey F. Remington, Wilder Building, Rochester.
    Secretary, Major Charles A. Du Bois, 220 Broadway, New York.
    Treasurer, James de la Montanye, New York City.

NORTH CAROLINA—President, Frank H. Bryan, Washington.
    Secretary (vacant).
    Treasurer, W. B. Harding, Washington.

NORTH DAKOTA—President, Homer E. Simpson, State University, Grand Forks.
    Secretary, Walter R. Reed, Amenia.
    Treasurer, J. W. Wilkerson, University.

OHIO—President, Walter J. Sherman, The Nasby, Toledo.
    Secretary, W. L. Curry, Box 645, Columbus.
    Treasurer, S. G. Harvey, Toledo.

OKLAHOMA—President, Edward F. McKay, Oklahoma City.
    Secretary, A. B. Galloway, 905 1st National Bank Building, Oklahoma City.
    Treasurer, A. B. Galloway, Oklahoma City.

OREGON—President, Wallace McCamant, Northwestern Bank Building, Portland.
    Secretary, B. A. Thaxter, Post Office Box 832, Portland.
    Treasurer, A. B. Lindsley, Portland.

PENNSYLVANIA—President, James A. Wakefield, 471 Union Arcade, Pittsburgh.
    Secretary, Francis Armstrong, Jr., 515 Wood Street, Pittsburgh.
    Treasurer, A. M. Wall, Pittsburgh.

RHODE ISLAND—President, Francis Eliot Bates, Post Office Box 1254, Providence.
  Secretary, Theodore E. Dexter, Central Falls.
  Treasurer, William L. Sweet.

SOUTH CAROLINA—No report.

SOUTH DAKOTA—President, J. G. Parsons, Sioux Falls.
  Secretary, T. W. Dwight, Sioux Falls.
  Treasurer, B. H. Requa, Sioux Falls.

TENNESSEE—President, William K. Boardman, Nashville.
  Secretary, Frederick W. Millspaugh, Nashville.
  Treasurer, Carey Folk.

TEXAS—President, C. B. Dorchester, Sherman.
  Secretary, Walter S. Mayer, Galveston.

UTAH—President, Heber M. Wells, Dooly Building, Salt Lake City.
  Secretary, Gordon Lines Hutchins, Dooly Building, Salt Lake City.
  Treasurer, Seth Warner Morrison, Jr.

VERMONT—President, William H. Jeffrey, Montpelier.
  Secretary, Walter H. Crockett, Burlington.
  Treasurer, Clarence L. Smith, Burlington.

VIRGINIA—President, Arthur B. Clarke, 616 American National Bank Building, Richmond.
  Secretary and Treasurer, William E. Crawford, 700 Travelers' Building, Richmond.

WASHINGTON—President, Walter Burges Beals, Seattle.
  Secretary, William Phelps Totten, Seattle.
  Treasurer, Chauncey Luther Baxter, Seattle.

WISCONSIN—President, J. Tracy Hale, Jr., Milwaukee.
  Secretary, Emmett A. Donnelly, 1030 Wells Building, Milwaukee.
  Treasurer, William Stark Smith.

WYOMING—President, Warren Richardson, Cheyenne.
  Secretary, Maurice Groshon, Cheyenne.
  Treasurer, James B. Guthrie.

SYNOPSIS OF THE PROCEEDINGS

of the Thirty-second Annual Congress of the National Society, Sons of the American Revolution,

HELD AT LAFAYETTE HOTEL, BUFFALO, N. Y.,

MAY 16 AND 17, 1921

Morning Session, Monday, May 16, 10 a. m.

The President General and other National Officers came forward, escorted by the Color Guard and the Committee on Ceremonies and Colors. The Colors were saluted and the President General, James Harry Preston, assumed the chair.

Chaplain General Rev. Lee S. McCollester, D. D., invoked the Divine blessing.

Addresses of welcome were extended to the Congress by Mayor George S. Buck, Mr. Eugene Tanke, President of the Buffalo Chapter, and Mr. Charles R. Robinson, President of the Chamber of Commerce. These were responded to by Past President General Louis Annin Ames.

The American's Creed was recited by the entire Congress.

The preliminary report of Teunis D. Huntting, Chairman of the Committee on Credentials, was presented and received.

Past President General Woodworth moved that a Committee on Resolutions be appointed by the Chair, to which all resolutions shall be referred without debate. Motion adopted.

The Chairman appointed as a Committee on Resolutions Past President Generals Woodworth and Thruston and Vice-President General Houk.

Mr. Ames moved that the Secretary General send greetings of the Congress to all Past Presidents General not present. Carried.

Annual Address of President General

The custom of our Society requires that before turning over the Society to the incoming President General the retiring President .General shall give a brief résumé of the activities of the Society while under his administration.

It is a matter of regret that the demands of an engrossing profession have prevented me from following the admirable example of the previous Presidents General of the Sons of the American Revolution in making nation-wide tours in the interest of our Society.

Visits, however, have been paid by me to the South and through the Middle West and North during the past year, which I feel have resulted in some good to the Society.

A brief tour through Texas, Oklahoma, Missouri, Illinois, New York, and New Jersey has resulted in pleasant associations with some of the membership in those States and in an interchange of views which I believe has advanced the aims and purposes and activities of the Society.

Perhaps the most definite accomplishment of the year has been the formation of a State Society in Georgia, starting off with an initial number of fifteen members, under the leadership of Mr. Allan Waters, of Atlanta, Georgia. I am glad to be able to report that we have prospects of a very large and flourishing State Society in Georgia.

In addition to the formation of the Society in Georgia, already accomplished, steps are being taken to form a Society in London, through our compatriots of the Sons of the American Revolution now living there, and particularly those connected with the Embassy, and to enlarge the Society in France, now affiliated with the Empire State Society.

We have also under way the formation of a Society in West Virginia and the stimulation of the South Carolina Society.

I feel that by a closer co-operation between the Daughters of the American Revolution and the Sons of the American Revolution a very stimulating influence may be had on both the membership and the activities of each of the Societies. If the various State Societies of the Sons of the American Revolution obtain from the State Societies of the Daughters of the American Revolution the names and addresses of male relatives and circularize these carefully, the result will be a great increase both in the membership and in the usefulness of the Sons of the American Revolution.

In Maryland we have obtained one hundred members by a very brief campaign for membership, addressed particularly to the male relatives of the members of our sister Society, the Daughters of the American Revolution.

The membership of the Sons of the American Revolution throughout the country amounts to 17,113, a net gain of 864 over the previous year, and the indications are that it will have a steady, even rapid, growth.

Three new chapters have been formed in Maryland, of which State Society I was president for the past two years, but I am not informed as to the number of new chapters in the other States.

In common with all our organizations that have been operating under dues and admission charges established before the World War, we find the financial condition of the Society far from encouraging.

I refer you for full particulars on this subject to the reports of the Secretary General and the Treasurer General and to the debate which will doubtless occur on the amendment proposed for increasing the initiation fees or dues.

The expenses of the Society are confined almost exclusively to the Secretary General's office in Washington. There are no charges whatever that fall on the National Society or the State Societies, incident to the National organization, outside of the Secretary General's office. Traveling expenses, hotel bills, postage, printing, and correspondence charges and the details of office administration are borne by the general officers themselves out of their private pockets or are paid by the State Societies. But even this leaves the Society with very slender resources for the administration of a trust which extends over the entire country.

I very sincerely hope that some step will be taken to increase the revenue of the Society, subject to such limitations and restrictions as the Congress may invoke.

In line with economy, it has been suggested by the Executive Committee that we discontinue the Year Book and enlarge very much the scope of the QUARTERLY BULLETIN. This is a matter which should receive the careful consideration of the membership of this Congress.

I am inclined to think that we should issue a quarterly magazine, somewhat similar in scope and design to the magazine of the Daughters of the American Revolution. Being a quarterly magazine, it ought to contain more in detail the activities of the State Societies and the National Society than do either our present BULLETIN or the monthly magazine issued by the Daughters of the American Revolution. In other words, it ought to take the place of the Year Book.

If the dues or initiation fees are increased, as I hope will be done, this increase, if intelligently applied, will furnish a very useful, interesting, and instructive magazine to take the place of the present BULLETIN and Year Book.

May I not say that the aims and purposes of our Society are so lofty and its accomplishments have been already so great, so salutary, that an increase in the revenue of the National Society will, I believe, result in increased membership, increased usefulness, and increased patriotic accomplishment for our splendid Society.

President General Preston's address was received with genuine appreciation.

It was moved and seconded that the minutes of the last Congress as printed in the last Year Book be approved. Motion carried.

The report of Secretary General Larner was read and approved.

The report of Registrar General Larner was read and approved.

The report of the Treasurer General, John H. Burroughs, was received and adopted as read, subject to the approval of the Auditing Committee.

The report of the Genealogist General, Walter K. Watkins, was read and approved.

The report of Chancellor General Remington was read and approved.

The report of Chairman Pugsley, of the Committee on Permanent Investment, was received.

The report of Treasurer General Burroughs on the Permanent Fund was received.

The report of Historian General Arnold was received.

Vice-Presidents General Nutting, of Massachusetts; Williams, of New Jersey; Houk, of Ohio; Paine, of Missouri, and Bell, of Washington, reported from their several districts.

Upon motion, all reports of the officers submitted to the Congress were approved and adopted.

Recess until 2.30 p. m.

(The reports of the Secretary General, Registrar General, and Treasurer General are printed in this BULLETIN; the other reports will be printed in the later Bulletins.)

Afternoon Session, May 16

The President General called the Congress to order at 2.30 p. m.

Mr. Cowart, of New Jersey, presented a resolution in relation to a monument to the memory of Mollie Pitcher; also a resolution in relation to conflicts between capital and labor; also a resolution in regard to an international code of laws for universal peace; all of which were referred to the Committee on Resolutions.

Mr. Nutting, of Massachusetts, presented a resolution for the protection of North Church, Boston. Referred to the Committee on Resolutions.

Mr. Watkins, of Massachusetts, presented a resolution in regard to preserving data at Washington in connection with pension records. Referred to the Committee on Resolutions.

Mr. Ely, of District of Columbia, presented a resolution in regard to the elimination from a pageant in Milwaukee of a float representing the Landing of the Pilgrims. Referred to the Committee on Resolutions. Also a resolution in regard to Bolsheviki propaganda. Referred to the Committee on Resolutions.

Mr. Kenyon, of the District of Columbia, presented a resolution in regard to Socialism in American colleges. Referred to the Committee on Resolutions.

Mr. Sherman, of Ohio, moved that telegrams of greeting be sent to the President and Vice-President of the United States. Motion adopted. .

Judge Remington, of New York, presented a resolution drawn by Col. John W. Vrooman, of Herkimer, New York, in relation to prize essays on patriotic subjects. Referred to the Committee on Resolutions.

Mr. Steele, of New York, presented a resolution in relation to war service medals. Referred to the Committee on Resolutions.

Mr. Fairchild, of Minnesota, presented a resolution in relation to compensation for ex-soldiers. Referred to the Committee on Resolutions.

Past President General Marble presented a resolution in regard to the work of Captain Hugh S. Martin. Referred to the Committee on Resolutions.

All of the above resolutions were referred to the Committee on Resolutions, under the rules.

Reports of committees were then taken up.

Mr. Parks, of the District of Columbia, read the report of Mr. Cox, chairman of the Flag Committee.

Mr. Ely, of the District of Columbia, presented the report of the Committee on War Records, which was read by Admiral G. W. Baird.

Past President General Thruston, chairman of the Committee on Memorials, presented the report of that committee. A rising vote of thanks was tendered to Chairman Thruston.

Mr. Curtis, of Connecticut, made a verbal report of the Committee on Flag Day Celebration.

The Secretary General read the report of the Patriotic Committee, presented by George A. Brennan, of Illinois.

The Chairman presented the reports of the Publicity Committee—Frank L. Stetson, chairman—and the Committee on Increased Membership—Chancellor L. Jenks, chairman.

Mr. Ames, of New York, moved that a committee be appointed by the Chair, to be known as the Committee on Official Reports and Recommendations; this committee to take these reports, take out the vital points at issue in each report, and bring them in at the close of this session and report on which should be printed in the BULLETIN. Motion unanimously carried.

The Chairman appointed Mr. Ames as chairman of this committee and Mr. Jewett, of Indiana—a committee of two.

Mr. Andrews, of Maryland, presented the report of the Committee on the American's Creed.

Mr. Read, of Massachusetts, presented a report in relation to a Memorial to General James Warren, to be erected at Plymouth, Mass. It was moved that the Secretary General be instructed to communicate with the several State Societies and ask them to contribute their proportion of $2,500 for the erection of this memorial. Motion unanimously carried.

Mr. Read, of Massachusetts, gave an interesting description of the gavel used by the President.

The Chairman called upon Mr. Matthew Page Andrews, of Maryland, to make a statement in regard to the book containing the history of the American's Creed.

Mr. Hayward, of Maryland, offered a resolution approving of this history of the American's Creed. This was referred to the Committee on Resolutions.

Mr. Wentworth, of the Committee on Americanization, made a verbal report for this committee.

Mr. Ames, of the Committee on the Celebration of Constitution Day, presented his report.

The Committee on Resolutions was asked to report, and, pending this report, Judge Bonniwell, of Pennsylvania, brought up the matter of the markers for Revolutionary graves, and moved that the matter of proper markers for Revolutionary graves be referred to the incoming Executive Committee, with instructions to consider the matter of markers and report their recommendations. The motion was unanimously adopted.

Chairman Woodworth, of the Committee on Resolutions, read the proposed resolution on immigration, as follows, and moved its adoption:

Whereas our heritage, the heritage from men who lived and wrought and fought and died to safeguard the fundamental institutions of America, depends upon quality of citizenship;

And whereas quality of citizenship depends to a great extent upon a permanent and comprehensive solution of the immigration problem, which since the World War has become especially grave in some of its aspects; therefore be it

Resolved, That the National Congress of the Sons of the American Revolution, in annual session at Buffalo, N. Y., respectfully petitions the Congress of the United States to give to this subject of immigration its careful consideration, with a view to adopting a policy, both selective and restrictive in character, that will aim, first of all, to safeguard the future of the nation for our children and our children's children, and be at the same time, in so far as possible, consistent with our economic needs.

Unanimously adopted.

Chairman Woodworth presented the proposed resolution in regard to amending Article VI of the Constitution of the National Society as follows and moved its adoption:

That Article VI of the Constitution of the National Society be amended to read as follows:

ARTICLE VI.—*Initiation Fee and Dues.*

SEC. 1. In addition to the initiation fee, if any, charged by a State Society, there shall be paid an initiation fee of five dollars for membership in the

National Society, Sons of the American Revolution. Said fee shall be forwarded to the Registrar General with each application for membership. The payment of said fee shall include an engraved certificate of membership for each newly elected compatriot, to be furnished by the National Society.

Sec. 2. Each State Society shall pay annually to the Treasurer General, to defray the expense of the National Society, fifty cents for each member thereof, unless intermitted by the National Congress.

Sec. 3. Such dues shall be paid on or before the first day of April in each year for the ensuing year, in order to secure representation in the Congress of the National Society.

Mr. Cowart, of New Jersey, moved as an amendment to this report of the Committee on Resolutions that each member of the National Society shall be assessed one dollar for his membership in the National Society.

After a full, complete and prolonged discussion, in the course of which several amendments and substitutes were offered, but which were ruled out by the Chair and his decisions sustained by the Congress, the Chairman put the question as follows: The question occurs on the amendment to the amendment, which I understand is, that instead of a five-dollar initiation fee, there be imposed one dollar annual dues instead of fifty cents annual dues to the National Society. The question now occurs on that amendment. All in favor please rise and be counted.

The vote was then taken, the result being 60 in favor of the amendment to the constitutional amendment and 30 opposed.

The CHAIRMAN: The question now occurs on the adoption of the section as amended, which is that the annual dues of the National Society shall be one dollar per year instead of fifty cents per year, as presented in the Constitution. The motion was adopted.

Adjournment taken to Tuesday, May 17, at 9 a. m.

Morning Session, Tuesday, May 17

Congress called to order by the President General.

Rev. Dr. Petty, of Connecticut, invoked the Divine blessing.

The Secretary General read a communication in regard to the death of Dr. Cogswell. Moved by Major Adams that the communication be referred to the Committee on Resolutions for action. Adopted.

While awaiting the report of the Committee on Resolutions, Judge Bonniwell, of Pennsylvania, brought up the question of the Washington Guards, upon which some discussion ensued.

Mr. Bowman, of Illinois, presented a proposed resolution regarding the Society furnishing a certificate of membership without charge. After some discussion, the resolution was lost.

Moved by Major Adams that the discussions of all subjects be limited to three minutes, except by consent of the House. Adopted.

A resolution was offered relative to making the Star-Spangled Banner the National Anthem. Referred to the Committee on Resolutions.

Mr. Woodworth, of the Committee on Resolutions, presented a report of the committee in reference to the several resolutions introduced on the subject of immigration, and moved that the several resolutions be referred to the incoming Committee on Americanization. The motion was adopted.

Mr. Woodworth, of the Committee on Resolutions, reported that the proposed amendment to the Constitution of the Society in reference to creating two societies in a State was not approved by the committee, and moved the adoption of the report of the committee. Motion adopted.

Mr. Woodworth, of the Committee on Resolutions, reported favorably on the following resolutions, which were unanimously adopted:

War Service Medals

Whereas many of our compatriots are veterans of the various wars in which the United States has participated and emerged victorious; and

Whereas due recognition of such valorous services has already been made by the issuance of the War Service Medal of the Sons of the American Revolution; and

Whereas such medal is in such form that it may not be consistently worn in connection with our ceremonial insignia; now, therefore, be it

Resolved, That the National Society, Sons of the American Revolution, authorize and adopt the following decoration to be used in connection with said ceremonial insignia:

Item.—A plain bar to be attached to the ribbon, with the war in which the compatriot has served stamped thereon in relief, one for each such war, the exact design and material thereof to be determined by a committee of three, to be appointed by the President General.

Captain Hugh S. Martin

Whereas Captain Hugh S. Martin, of the Regular Army, having been located in Russia for quite an extended period, has during the past few months, under the auspices and direction of the New Jersey Society, Sons of the American Revolution, delivered various addresses on the subject of the conditions in Russia, especially relating to the Bolsheviki movement, which has attracted the most sincere attention on the part of all who have heard him. He recently delivered the same address at the luncheon of the Members Council of the Merchants Association in New York City, which so aroused the enthusiasm of his hearers that one of the prominent divines of New York City later approached the officers of the Merchants Association and suggested that a fund could be raised to cover the expenses of Captain Martin to have him deliver his address throughout the country, giving his entire time to that work. It was further stated that on a number of occasions when Captain Martin had been making an address some one in the audience asked the question as to who or what organization was behind him in the work he was doing. The suggestion was made that if some patriotic organization of national scope could stand behind him, it would give a greater force to his work and obviate any adverse criticism that might be made unless he could have a backing as above suggested.

We offer the following resolution:

Whereas there is no grander work that the S. A. R. could engage in than to carry the message of Capt. Hugh S. Martin to the public at large; and

Whereas it has been suggested that possibly the necessary funds could be secured to cover the expenses of Captain Martin to enable him to devote his entire time to the carrying on of his message far and wide; now, therefore, be it

Resolved, That the National Society, Sons of the American Revolution, recognizing the merit of the work that can be done by Captain Martin, hereby give its sanction to such work, and that a committee of three, with power, be appointed by the Chair to take under consideration a proposition to give the endorsement of the National Society to Capt. Hugh S. Martin and assume the responsibility for this propaganda, provided the necessary funds are furnished, so that no part of the expense would have to be borne by the National Society.

Star Spangled Banner

Resolved, That the National Society, Sons of the American Revolution, endorse House Bill No. 4391, declaring the Star-Spangled Banner as the National Anthem, and that the proper committees in Congress be notified and the State Societies requested to communicate with their respective Representatives and Senators in Congress.

Archives in Washington

Whereas there is on file in the archives of the Revolutionary War Section of the Bureau of Pensions, at Washington, D. C., a large amount of valuable and interesting material in the form of applications for pensions on the part of officers and soldiers of the American Revolution; therefore be it

Resolved, That the National Society, Sons of the American Revolution, meeting in Buffalo, N. Y., respectfully calls the attention of its representatives in Congress to the desirability of having these pension records made available to the public by having abstracts bearing upon the personal history and war services of each Revolutionary pensioner compiled, arranged, and printed by the Government in a form convenient for ready references, and that an appropriation by Congress be obtained for defraying the expense thereof.

Old North Church, Boston

Whereas Christ Church, Boston, Mass., situated on Salem Street, generally known as "The Old North Church," and beloved throughout the length and breadth of our whole country for its association with the famous "Midnight Ride of Paul Revere," is now menaced constantly with destruction by fire from the fact that a public bake-oven has been erected right next to its easterly side; now, therefore, be it

Resolved by the National Society of the Sons of the American Revolution in Congress assembled at Buffalo, New York, this 17th day of May, in the year 1921, That it shall, and hereby does, go upon record as in favor of the establishment by act of Congress, by right of eminent domain, and by any other powers it thereto enabling, of a small national park, of a size to effectually safeguard the said "The Old North Church," Salem Street, Boston, Mass., from fire hazard, to enclose and surround the said church, to consist of several acres of land from which all buildings except church buildings, including the new "Italian Mission Church," and school and engine houses, shall be entirely removed, and the said tract of land shall be beautified by the setting out of trees and shrubs and the laying of suitable walks and paths therein; to the end that the said "The Old North Church" may be safeguarded, protected, and beautified as a national heritage and a source of patriotic inspiration to the entire country for all time; and be it further

Resolved, That the National Society of the Sons of the American Revolution hereby directs its Secretary General to have these resolutions suitably drawn up and signed by the President General and all the officers of the said National Society of the year 1920-1921 and transmitted to the Congress of the United States as urgent business and with a request for speedy attention. Also, further, that the Secretary General cause these resolutions to be printed in proper form for distribution to each of the State Societies and the District of Columbia Society of the Sons of the American Revolution, with the request that they each shall severally ratify and adopt the same without alteration and forward, with proper attestation of the President and Secretary of each Society, to their representatives in the Senate and House, in Congress at Washington, as urgent business, and with a request that it be given speedy attention.

American Legion Compensation

Whereas the Sons of the American Revolution is essentially a patriotic society, devoted to furthering the highest and best interests of our beloved country in times of peace as in times of war; and

Whereas the American Legion, an association composed of veterans of the late World War, is an organization of similar aims and attributes; and

Whereas all those men who so served in the Army and Navy of the United States of America in the great conflict, and whose valor and unselfish patriotism contributed in such large measure toward the glorious victory won by the Allied Forces overseas, suffered a serious economic loss because of the said services, while those of military qualification who remained at home in commercial pursuits received an utterly disproportionate reward for the performance of such commercial activities; and

Whereas the American Legion has fathered legislation in our National Congress looking toward an adjusted compensation for these ex-soldiers; now, therefore, be it

Resolved, That the National Society, Sons of the American Revolution, in Thirty-second Annual Congress assembled, does here and now, unqualifiedly and without reservation, endorse the American Legion's fourfold plan of adjusted compensation, as exemplified in the bill now pending in the National Congress of the United States; and be it further

Resolved, That a duly attested copy of these resolutions be forwarded to the President of the United States, the Secretary of War, and the Ways and Means Committee of the House of Representatives and Finance Committee of the Senate; and be it further

Resolved, That each and every State Society or Chapter existing under the jurisdiction of the National Society, Sons of the American Revolution, be, and is hereby, requested to endorse the text of these resolutions to their respective congressional delegations, with appropriate recommendations.

Mollie Pitcher

Whereas the Thirty-second Congress of the National Society of the Sons of the American Revolution is informed that the Hon. T. Frank Appleby, Representative of the Third Congressional District of the State of New Jersey, has introduced in the House of Representatives, in the Congress of the United States, now in session at Washington, D. C., a bill to appropriate the sum of $10,000 for the purpose of erecting on the Battlefield of Monmouth a suitable memorial to perpetuate the heroism of Captain Mollie Pitcher in that decisive battle of the American Revolution; therefore be it

Resolved, firstly, That this Congress of the Sons of the American Revolution, now in session in the City of Buffalo, New York, this 16th day of May, A. D. 1921, most heartily commend the patriotic purposes of this bill and recommend its support by the other Representatives and by the Senators of the several States in the present Congress.

Resolved, secondly, That a copy of this resolution, certified to by our President and Secretary, be forwarded to the clerk of the House of Representatives and to the clerk of the Senate, at Washington, D. C., with a request that it shall be read at the earliest convenient date, in a session of each branch of the present Congress.

Book of American Creed

Resolved, That the National Society of the Sons of the American Revolution approves of the use of the American's Creed in school and citizenship work, and that the National Congress of the Sons of the American Revolution endorses the plan proposed for the use of the "Book of the American Creed," issued under the auspices of the National Patriotic Societies, through a committee of which the President General of the Sons of the American Revolution shall be *ex officio* the chairman.

Resolved, further, That this National Congress of the Sons of the American Revolution recommends this book to the attention of all State Societies and local Chapters, to the end that they may endeavor to have the same presented to the graduates of their local grammar and junior high schools in the names of the donors or through a special appropriation of local school boards.

It is suggested that the book be presented to the child upon his or her memorizing the American's Creed, and that the child's name be placed thereon, together with a suitable inscription, signed by the principal of the school or some other school authority.

Intercollegiate Socialism

Whereas the future prosperity of America and the stability of our institutions of government depend in very large measure upon the proper education of the young men and women who are annually graduated from our institutions of higher learning; and

Whereas disclosures recently made have brought to light the existence of an insidious and active campaign on the part of the Intercollegiate Socialist Society and some similar organizations to inoculate the minds of college students with the principles of socialism and eventually to bring them into formal membership in the Communist and Socialist parties; therefore be it

Resolved, That the Congress of the Sons of the American Revolution, held at Buffalo, on May 16, 1921, regards the situation thus disclosed with very grave concern and calls upon the administrative officers and the boards of trustees of American colleges and universities to put forth their utmost efforts not only to eradicate this pernicious propaganda, but also to counteract it by providing for their students thorough instruction in American history and in the fundamental principles of American constitutional government.

Mr. Woodworth, of the Committee on Resolutions, reported that in regard to Section 4, Article V, of the Constitution, giving the Executive Committee authority to discipline its members—members of the Society—the committee would recommend the insertion of these words in the resolution offered: After "the Executive Committee shall have authority" the committee suggests this amendment: "Upon written charges preferred by any State Society, any State Board of Managers, or any local Chapter. With that amendment, the committee recommends the adoption of the resolution offered."

SEC. 4. An Executive Committee of seven, consisting of the President General as Chairman and six members, to be nominated by him and approved by the Board of Trustees, shall in the interim between the meetings of the Board transact such business as may be delegated to it by a Congress of the Society or the Board of Trustees.

The Executive Committee shall have authority, upon written charges preferred by any State Society, any State Board of Managers, or any local Chapter, to discipline or to expel any compatriot who by conduct disloyal to the ideals or prejudicial to the interests of the Sons of the American Revolution shall render himself unworthy of membership therein. Any member who feels himself aggrieved by the action of the committee acting under this power shall have the right of appeal to the next succeeding Congress.

The members of the Executive Committee other than the President General shall be known as Directors General, and by virtue of their office shall be members of the National Congress and entitled to vote at the annual meeting of the National Congress during their terms of office.

(Italic type indicates amendments added.)

Motion adopted.

Mr. Woodworth, of the Committee on Resolutions, reported that the committee took action on the resolution referring to labor and capital and disapproved the same, on the ground that it was not a proper subject for consideration by this Congress. Upon motion, the report of the committee was adopted.

Mr. Woodworth, of the Committee on Resolutions, reported that the committee took action on the resolution referring to the League of Nations and disapproved the same, on the ground that it is not a proper subject for action by this Congress. The report of the committee was adopted.

Mr. Woodworth, of the Committee on Resolutions, reported that the committee approves the reference of the communication and enclosures from Compatriot John W. Vrooman, of the Empire State Society, on the subject of prize essays on patriotic subjects in the schools, to the Committee on Patriotic Education. Recommendation adopted.

Mr. Woodworth, of the Committee on Resolutions, presented the report of the committee in reference to the proposition to amend the Constitution as follows:

4. Proposed by the Connecticut State Society:

You are advised that a committee of seven appointed at a special meeting of the Connecticut Society, Sons of the American Revolution, requests that the Executive Committee of the National Society present, with legal notice of the same, the following proposals, namely, that Article 5, Section 4, of the National Constitution be amended so as to read as follows:

"Sec. 4. An Executive Committee of seven, consisting of the President General as chairman and six members of the Board of Trustees, to be nominated by him and approved by said Board of Trustees, shall in the interim between the meetings of the Board transact such business as may be delegated to it by a Congress of the Society or the Board of Trustees."

Also that Article 13, Section 4, of the By-Laws be amended by striking out from the fourth, fifth, and sixth lines thereof, as shown on page 45, National Year Book, 1920, the words "other than such as may be called during the session or immediately upon the adjournment of an annual or Special Congress of the National Society"; and also by the insertion in line 6 of said Section the word "proposes," between the words "time" and "and".

and asked unanimous consent of this Congress to waive any objections to the technical side of presenting that amendment to this body for consideration. Unanimous consent being given, the Congress proceeded to the consideration of the report of the committee, which was that the committee disapproved of the proposition or proposal, or proposed amendment as offered.

The CHAIRMAN: The question is upon the adoption of the unfavorable report of the committee.

Judge Remington, of New York, moved that the time of President White, of the Connecticut Society, to speak be extended indefinitely. Such consent was granted.

It was moved that the Connecticut resolution be adopted.

The CHAIRMAN: The question is now on the unfavorable report of the committee and whether it shall be received as the judgment of the Congress.

A full, complete, and prolonged discussion then ensued.

Mr. Woodworth then moved the previous question.

The previous question being put by the Chairman, it was stated that the motion appeared to be lost. It was then moved that the resolution of the Connecticut Society be substituted for the report of the committee, and this motion was ruled out of order by the Chair.

Mr. Fairchild appealed from the decision of the Chair, and the decision of the Chair was sustained.

The previous question was again moved and carried.

The CHAIRMAN: The question occurs now upon the recommendation of the committee. Those in favor of sustaining the report of the committee will say aye, those opposed will vote no. I will restate the question in order to make it perfectly clear to you. Those who are in favor of sustaining the report of the committee will vote aye, those opposed to the committee's report will vote no.

The motion being put, the noes seemed to have it.

The CHAIRMAN: The noes seem to have it.

A division was called for, and the report of the committee was sustained by a vote of 66 to 58, and the report of the committee was adopted by the Congress.

President Nutting, of Massachusetts, presented an invitation to hold the next National Congress in Springfield, Mass.

Referred to the incoming Board of Trustees.

It was moved that a vote of thanks be tendered to the National Society of Constitutional Government for having sent pamphlets on socialism in American Colleges. Motion carried.

At this point Colonel Adams, of New Jersey, was called to the chair.

Presentation of Banners

The presentation of the Traveling Banner was made by Col. Arthur B. Clarke, of Virginia, and accepted by President Preston, of Maryland.

Dr. Lyman Whitney Allen, of New Jersey, presented the Syracuse Banner to the New Jersey Society, which was accepted by Major Adams, of New Jersey.

It was moved and seconded that the Year Book be discontinued for the coming year. Motion adopted.

Mr. Sage, of Rochester, New York, invited the members of the Congress to visit the city of Rochester on June 7, to participate in the unveiling of the tablet to Lafayette.

The final report of the Credentials Committee was called for, and Chairman Huntting, of this committee, reported as follows:

General Officers, 12; Past Presidents General, 7; Directors General, 3; Delegates, 136; Total, 158. Ladies, 47.

There being no further business under the head of new business, the Congress proceeded to the election of officers.

Colonel Guthrie nominated John Leonard Merrill, of New Jersey, for President General, whose name was thereafter withdrawn by Major Adams, of New Jersey.

Mr. Edward D. Baldwin, of Oregon, placed in nomination the name of Wallace McCamant for President General and, upon motion, the nominations were closed and the Secretary General was authorized to cast one ballot for Wallace McCamant, of Oregon, for President General. The Secretary having cast the ballot, Judge Wallace McCamant, of Oregon, was duly elected President General of the National Society for the ensuing year.

Judge McCamant was escorted to the platform by Mr. Baldwin, Judge White, and the Rev. Dr. Allen and accepted the office with a short speech of appreciation.

Mr. Wiggin, of Massachusetts, placed in nomination the name of George H. Nutting, of Massachusetts, for Vice-President General of the First District. There being no further nominations, Mr. Nutting was unanimously elected Vice-President General for the First, or New England, District.

Mr. Parks, of the District of Columbia, placed in nomination Mr. Philip F. Larner, of the District of Columbia, for the office of Vice-President General for the Second, or Middle and Coast, District. There being no further nominations, Mr. Larner was unanimously elected Vice-President General for the Second, or Middle and Coast, District.

Mr. Thruston, of Kentucky, placed in nomination the name of Marvin H. Lewis, of Kentucky, for the office of Vice-President General for the Third, or Mississippi Valley, East, District. There being no further nominations, Mr. Lewis was unanimously elected to the office of Vice-President of the Third, or Mississippi Valley, East, District.

Mr. Paine, of Missouri, placed in nomination the name of Mr. Henry B. Hawley, of Iowa, for the office of Vice-President General for the Fourth, or Mississippi Valley, West, District. There being no further nominations, Mr. Hawley was unanimously elected Vice-President General for the Fourth, or Mississippi Valley, West, District.

Mr. Wentworth, of Iowa, placed in nomination the name of Mr. John W. Bell, Jr., of Washington, for the office of Vice-President General for the Fifth, or Mountain and Pacific, District. There being no further nominations, Mr. Bell was unanimously elected to the office of Vice-President General for the Fifth, or Mountain and Pacific, District.

Mr. Shriner, of Maryland, placed in nomination the name of Mr. George Sadtler Robertson, of Maryland, for the office of Secretary General.

At this point Vice-President General Nutting assumed the chair.

Judge Remington, of New York, placed in nomination for the office of Secretary General the name of Frank B. Steele, of New York.

The Chairman appointed Mr. Brewer, of New Jersey; Mr. Barrett, of Michigan, and Mr. Ritchie, of Utah, as tellers, and the Congress proceeded to ballot. Mr. Steele, receiving the majority of ballots cast, was declared duly elected to the office of Secretary General of the National Society.

Mr. Marble, of New York, placed in nomination for the office of Treasurer General the name of John H. Burroughs, of New York. There being no further nominations, Mr. Burroughs was unanimously elected to the office of Treasurer General of the National Society.

Mr. Adams, of New Jersey, placed in nomination the name of the Rev. Lyman Whitney Allen, of New Jersey, for the office of Chaplain General. There being no further nominations, Mr. Allen was unanimously elected to the office of Chaplain General.

The name of Mr. Selden M. Ely, of the District of Columbia, was placed in nomination for the office of Registrar General.

Judge Remington, of New York, placed in nomination for the office of Registrar General the name of Mr. William S. Parks, of the District of Columbia.

There being no further nominations, the Congress proceeded to ballot, and Mr. Parks, having received the majority of votes cast, was declared duly elected to the office of Registrar General of the National Society.

Mr. Bowen, of Illinois, placed in nomination the name of Mr. George A. Brennan, of Illinois, for the office of Historian General.

The name of Mr. George Carpenter Arnold was placed in nomination for the office of Historian General. There being no further nominations, the Congress proceeded to ballot, and Mr. Arnold, receiving the majority of votes cast, was declared duly elected to the office of Historian General of the National Society.

Mr. Read, of Massachusetts, placed in nomination for the office of Genealogist General Mr. Walter Kendall Watkins, of Massachusetts. There being no further nominations, Mr. Watkins was unanimously elected to the office of Genealogist General.

Colonel Guthrie, of Pennsylvania, placed in nomination for the office of Chancellor General the name of Judge Eugene C. Bonniwell, of Pennsylvania. There being no further nominations, Judge Bonniwell was unanimously elected to the office of Chancellor General.

The Congress then proceeded to the election of Trustees from each State. The Secretary General read the list of the nominees for Trustees as follows:

Board of Trustees

Alabama (vacant); Arizona, Clay F. Leonard, Phœnix; Arkansas, George B. Gill, Little Rock; California, Seabury C. Mastick, New York City; Colorado, Malcolm Lindsay, Denver; Connecticut, Clarence Horace Wickham, Hartford; Delaware, George Armstrong Elliott, Wilmington; District of Columbia, Albert D. Spangler, Washington; Far Eastern Society (vacant); Florida, Dr. F. G. Renshaw, Pensacola; Society in France (vacant); Hawaiian Society (vacant); Georgia, Allan Waters, Atlanta; Idaho (vacant); Illinois, Dorr E. Felt, Chicago; Indiana, Charles C. Jewett, Terre Haute; Iowa, Elmer M. Wentworth, State Center; Kansas, John M. Meade, Topeka; Kentucky, George T. Wood, Louisville; Louisiana, Colonel C. Robert Churchill, New Orleans; Maine, James O. Bradbury, Saco; Maryland, Hon. Henry Stockbridge, Baltimore; Massachusetts, Henry Fuller Punderson, Springfield; Michigan, Albert M. Henry, Detroit; Minnesota, Charles E. Rittenhouse, Minneapolis; Mississippi (vacant); Missouri, George R. Merrill, St. Louis; Montana, Marcus Whritenour, Helena; Nebraska, Benjamin F. Bailey, Lincoln; Nevada (vacant); New Hampshire, Henry T. Lord, Manchester; New Jersey, Charles Symmes Kiggins, Elizabeth; New Mexico, George G. Klock, Albuquerque; New York, Louis Annin Ames, New York; North Carolina (vacant); North Dakota, Howard E. Simpson, Grand Forks; Ohio, Moulton Houk, Delaware; Oklahoma, W. A. Jennings, Oklahoma City; Oregon, Wallace McCamant, Portland; Pennsylvania, Colonel R. W. Guthrie, Pittsburgh; Rhode Island, Wilfred H. Munro, Providence; South Carolina (vacant); South Dakota, J. G. Parsons, Sioux Falls; Tennessee, Leland Hume, Nashville; Texas, C. B. Dorchester, Sherman; Utah, Heber M. Wells, Salt Lake City; Vermont, William H. Jeffrey, Montpelier; Virginia, Arthur B. Clarke, Richmond; Washington, Ernest B. Hussey, Seattle; Wisconsin, Walter H. Wright, Milwaukee; Wyoming, Warren Richardson, Cheyenne.

Mr. Wentworth moved the election of the gentlemen whose names have been read to the position of Trustees for the respective State Societies. The motion was carried and the Trustees as read were declared duly elected.

The Congress tendered resolutions of thanks to the Buffalo Chapter for its splendid hospitality, to Mrs. John Miller Horton for her courtesy in opening her house for the beautiful reception, and to the President General for his uniform courtesy and fairness in handling the affairs of the National Society, and especially in his direction of the present Congress. Also to Dr. Lee S.

McCollester for his services as Chaplain General, and a special vote of thanks was given to the Committee of Ladies of Buffalo for the courtesies shown to the visiting ladies of the Congress.

President General Elect McCamant assumed the chair and announced that the Board of Trustees would meet immediately after the adjournment of the Congress.

The Congress then adjourned *sine die*.

REPORT OF THE SECRETARY GENERAL

COMPATRIOTS: In reviewing the affairs of the National Society for the past year, I find that practically every event or matter of interest has been laid before the entire membership of the Society in the quarterly BULLETINS as published during the preceding twelve months. I am hopeful that these BULLETINS, prepared and printed at the result of so much time, labor, and expense, have received the careful attention of our membership, but I have at times been confronted with the inquiry as to whether I believe the membership of the Society do really give these publications the attention which a live interest in the organization would suggest. It may be that the numerous copies returned by the post-office as undelivered and the many changes in address of which notices have not been given to our office, except through the post-office, might indicate a lack of interest in the membership. In the course of a year these items constitute a very large number, and every issue of a BULLETIN requires the preparation of very many slips for changes in the addressograph stencils, which, added to the stencils for new members, call for the making of several thousand new stencils each year.

One of the most conspicuous events of the past year has been the election of the President and Vice-President of the United States as members of our Society.

Another event of great and very hopeful interest has been the organization of a new State Society in Georgia, which was chartered during the month of March. The Society has been regularly organized and officers elected. The President, Compatriot Allan Waters, of Atlanta, has shown a lively and determined interest in the new organization and seems hopeful that at a very early date he will be able to report at least one hundred members on his roll. It is hoped that at a very early date we may have additional encouragement in the revival of interest in our organization in other portions of the Southern States, where the field would seem so ripe for effort.

A very considerable interest has been shown during the past year in the matter of the World War Medals, and nearly two thousand of these have been distributed up to date.

Due notices have been given that four amendments to the Constitution of the National Society have been proposed for consideration at this Congress.

In addition to these amendments, there is a recommendation from the Executive Committee covering the advisability of discontinuing the publication of the Year Book, which has only a very limited circulation, and that in the future the proceedings of the Annual Congress appear in the OFFICIAL BULLETIN.

which reaches the entire membership. It may be added also that the Year Book, containing a very large proportion of material published in the BULLETINS, is a duplication of printing at a very heavy expense. The publication of the Year Book for 1920 was the subject of considerable thought and effort. The cost of printing seemed to have reached its peak. A canvass of the printing business in Washington showed that uniformly there was increase in wages of 35 per cent, binding 50 per cent, and in the cost of paper from 200 to 400 per cent. An investigation of the subject elsewhere showed the same result. We found we could do no better on bids than to allow the printing to remain with the establishment which had done the work for many years, and the cost reached the sum of $2,011.14 for 500 copies, the number of the issue being reduced 100 copies from the usual amount. Let me say here (for I believe the Society at large ought to know a few of these things), we have now on the shelves of our headquarters more than 500 copies of unsalable Year Books covering a period of several years. They have cost much money. Occasionally there is a call for one, but at long intervals. They take up much valuable shelf space and constitute a very doubtful asset.

I have spoken of the excessive cost of printing during the past year. I will state here that for the year ending May, 1919, the usual and ordinary printing of the Society cost $5,264.40. For the past year the cost has been $7,808.34. Owing to increased business, there has probably been an enlargement of our printing supplies, notably in the case of application blanks, for which the demand has been quite heavy. The Year Book has also required an increase in size, in view of the enlarged Genealogical Record and also the extended character of the Proceedings of the Annual Congress, with its large number of official reports. So also in the case of membership certificates, which, as you know, are engraved in the name of and for each separate State. Their cost has increased in recent years from 60 cents each to $1; then $1.25, and now at $1.40. The engrossing costs us 85 cents each. To this must be added the increased cost of mailing tubes, etc. During the past year 642 certificates have been ordered. Some of the State Societies have lessened their orders. We have now on hand, distributed among all the State Societies, awaiting orders, 1,580 certificates, which stand us at the cost of $1,728.35.

Altogether it has been a very busy year. The report of the Registrar General will show the statistics as relating to the membership. Over 1,600 applications have been approved and recorded during the past year and many supplementals also examined and recorded. The past three months have been the most active for several years. In the month of March alone, 220 applications for membership were examined, approved, and recorded. The State official, who in a very few instances handles one hundred applications during a year, will appreciate the work caused by the number received by the National Society in the one month.

The correspondence of all kinds has been very heavy during the year. It relates to many subjects and a multitude of inquiries requiring thought and investigation. It has been my practice to answer every letter personally and to keep a carbon copy of the answer. Unlike our Sister Society of the D. A. R., we do not have among our officials a "Correspondence General," hence I am unable to state accurately just how much mail we have handled. An investigation of the matter, however, convinces me that I have personally dictated not less than 2,200 letters during the past year. In addition to this, there are hundreds of circulars, bills, and advices to State Officials on form sheets which have been mailed.

As an interesting illustration of the pressure which may be experienced in this branch of the work, I will state that about a month ago, on the invitation of our Philadelphia compatriots, I attended the Franklin Statue exercises in that city, held under the auspices of the S. A. R. I was absent from Washington only over Saturday and Sunday, and yet when I returned to my office on Monday morning I found sixty-eight pieces of mail relating to the business of this organization awaiting attention.

I have mentioned a few of these matters of interest simply because I desired to give you some idea of the activity of this office. Such duties require much time and labor; it needs much and competent assistance. The Society is receiving faithful and careful service. The work is being done and I am pleased to say that it is kept well in hand and is now practically up to date.

I am reminded that I have been a member of this organization now for thirty years. I am proud to be of service to it, and I trust that there may be a renewed spirit and united effort in our work which will result in a wide and greatly enlarged strength and influence throughout our country.

Respectfully submitted,

PHILIP F. LARNER,
Secretary General.

WASHINGTON, D. C., *May 12, 1921.*

REPORT OF THE REGISTRAR GENERAL
From March 31, 1920, to April 1, 1921

Your Registrar General has the honor to report that since the formation of the Society, on April 30, 1889, to the end of the present fiscal year, 34,740 members have been enrolled in 52 Societies. The total net membership on April 1 of last year was 16,257. During the present year, ending April 1, 1921, 1,614 new members have been added. The losses by death or from non-payment of dues have amounted to 750, leaving a total net membership in 47 State Societies of 17,121, or net gain of 864. Since that date to the present meeting of the Congress about 200 more applications have been approved. In addition to the 1,614 original claims accepted, 286 supplemental papers have been approved. This shows a steady increase from last year, and the losses, while heavy in some States, are not as great as last year, which immediately followed the World War. Reconstruction was then necessary, but now most of the Societies have settled down with renewed interest to their former active routine. The records show that 642 certificates of membership have been issued. While each member, by the By-Laws, may be entitled to a certificate, the present increased cost of the engraving and labor is such a task upon the Treasury of the States that they are now being ordered for about one-third of the new members.

The State Society showing the largest active membership is Massachusetts, which has 1,800 members; the second highest is the Empire State Society, with 1,701; then New Jersey, with 1,590; Illinois, 1,189, and Connecticut, 1,150.

The State showing the largest number of new members is New Jersey, which enrolled 191 and will again retain the Syracuse Banner. The second largest enrollment was in Massachusetts, 163; then New York, with 145, and Illinois next, with 120. The Traveling Banner, which was presented by the Colorado Society, to be awarded to the State numbering one hundred or more which makes the greatest net percentage of increase, goes this year to the home of the President General, Maryland having added 133 new members to its former roll of 347. The Registrar General here wishes to especially congratulate the Registrars of the States above mentioned upon the high standard of excellence which the applications received from them have invariably shown.

Through the efforts of President General Preston, a new Society, with 16 members, was organized in Georgia and a charter to that effect delivered. There is still much missionary work needed in several of the Southern States, where, as shown by the large membership rolls of our sister organization of Daughters of the American Revolution, thousands of descendents of the heroes of that war now reside and need simply the proper leadership to form an organization of our own.

Through the generosity of the late President General Logan, a large volume, containing the full pedigree and membership of every member, was published in 1901, and since that date the work of enrolling every new member has been continued in the Year Book, with an extract of the pedigree, together with the service, which is published quarterly in the BULLETIN. This method not only places on record a large amount of historical knowledge, but is a help to many seeking aid in joining the Society.

Among the names prominent in the management of the nation's affairs who have been enrolled during the past year are: Hon. Warren G. Harding, President of the United States, who joined the Ohio Society; Hon. Calvin Coolidge, Vice-President of the United States, who became a member of the Massachusetts Society; Hon. Edwin P. Morrow, Governor of Kentucky, and Ex-Governor Folk, of Missouri. Within the past two weeks the papers of Hon. Westmoreland Davis, Governor of Virginia, and Governor Denny, of Delaware, have been approved.

Among the new members from Maine and Rhode Island are two real sons of Revolutionary soldiers.

Among the well-known members who have died since the last report are Lucius P. Deming, First President General of the National Society and First President of the Connecticut Society; Major General Joseph C. Breckenridge, Past President General and Past President of the District of Columbia Society; Dr. John O. Foster, Past Chaplain General of the National Society; Frank W. Rawles, Past Vice-President General of the National Society and Past President of the Arkansas Society; Joseph Ferrant Tuttle, Jr., First President of the Colorado Society; Ex-Governor John Franklin Fort, Past President of the New Jersey Society; Hon. Taylor Beattie, Past President of the Louisiana Society, and William Lowrie March, Past President of the District of Columbia Society. Two real sons of Revolutionary soldiers among our members also passed away.

With the hope that each member of the Congress will return to his home with a determination to do his best in helping to increase the membership in organized States as well as in his own locality, this report is respectfully submitted.

1921 Membership

	March 31, 1920.	Additions.	Losses.	Total April 1, 1921.
Arizona	40	4	6	38
Arkansas	72	4	0	76
California	460	41	19	482
Colorado	334	16	10	340
Connecticut	1,125	55	30	1,150
Delaware	46	53	0	99
District of Columbia	493	33	29	497
Far Eastern	20	0	0	20
Florida	45	2	0	47
Georgia	0	16	0	16
Hawaiian	95	0	0	95
Idaho	138	11	21	128
Illinois	1,152	120	83	1,189
Indiana	217	25	9	233
Iowa	478	20	19	480
Kansas	97	8	2	103
Kentucky	191	29	20	200
Louisiana	257	63	15	305
Maine	313	17	16	314
Maryland	347	133	6	474
Massachusetts	1,770	163	133	1,800
Michigan	637	67	14	690
Minnesota	281	30	5	306
Mississippi	38	3	0	41
Missouri	200	31	20	211
Montana	31	4	2	33
Nebraska	243	..	..	..
New Hampshire	213	13	28	198
New Jersey	1,459	191	60	1,590
New Mexico	64	3	0	67
New York	1,656	145	100	1,701
North Carolina	61	0	0	61
North Dakota	61	3	0	64
Ohio	727	75	37	765
Oklahoma	95	13	1	107
Oregon	258	23	0	281
Pennsylvania	673	38	14	697
Rhode Island	368	36	12	392
South Dakota	78	4	0	82
Tennessee	95	21	9	107
Texas	104	6	0	110
Utah	242	5	20	227
Vermont	212	15	0	227
Virginia	211	46	7	250
Washington	265	14	0	279
Wisconsin	250	9	0	259
Wyoming	37	6	3	40
	16,257	1,614	750	17,121

PHILIP F. LARNER,
Registrar General.

WASHINGTON, D. C., *May* 12, 1921.

REPORT OF THE TREASURER GENERAL

DISBURSEMENTS.

Salary of Secretary General		$900.00
Salary of Registrar General		600.00
Printing and mailing OFFICIAL BULLETIN:		
June, 1920	$1,304.63	
October, 1920	952.15	
December, 1920	817.60	
March, 1921	1,212.91	
		4,287.29
Printing and mailing Year Books		2,011.14
Sundry printing and postage		1,416.47
Envelopes for OFFICIAL BULLETIN		234.50
Sundry expenses of Secretary General's office		1,332.04
Certificates		1,320.00
Engrossing Certificates		547.40
Expenses of Secretary General attending Hartford Congress		73.76
Expenses of Secretary General attending meeting of Executive Committee at Baltimore		10.00
Expenses of Secretary General attending meeting of Executive Committee at New York		43.29
Expenses of Treasurer General attending Hartford Congress		32.09
Expenses of Treasurer General attending meeting of Executive Committee at Baltimore		34.26
Rent of office of Secretary General		480.00
Appropriation toward expenses of Hartford Congress		500.00
Appropriation toward expenses of Buffalo Congress		500.00
Sundry expenses of Treasurer General's office from October 15, 1919, to January 8, 1921		15.66
Pro-rata assessment of expenses of the National Congress for the co-ordination of patriotic and civic work		62.43
Expense of remonstrance to prevent the Connecticut Society from seceding		75.63
Medals		289.03
Ribbons and rosettes		164.16
Reporting proceedings of Hartford Congress		110.00
Safe-deposit rent		6.00
Photographs		2.00
Permanent Fund investment, purchase of $1,000 fourth 4¼ per cent Liberty Loan bond		886.19
Missouri Society refund for certificate		2.00
Bronze tablet to the memory of John Philip Reifsnider		54.00
Wreath for funeral of Past Chaplain General John O. Foster		10.00
Taking up a check of a State Society drawn on a bank that failed before check could be presented		19.00
Register book for Credentials Committee		10.00
Floral wreath placed on statue of General Simon Bolivar		15.00
Collection of out-of-town checks		5.36
Indemnity bond		25.00
Engrossing resolution on the late Past President General Greeley		2.60
Overcredit to a State Society		.06
		$16,076.36
May 12, 1920, balance on hand	$16,076.36	9,328.75

RECEIPTS.

Annual dues:

1919	$138.00	
1920	563.00	
1921	7,606.00	
		$8,307.00
Certificates	1,404.05	
Application and supplemental blanks	289.26	
Interest on balances	198.03	
Interest from investments	535.00	
Interest from Moses Greely Parker Fund	232.42	
Rebates credited to Permanent Fund	380.71	
Medals	749.00	
Supplementals	292.00	
Year Books	138.50	
Ribbon	62.75	
Rosettes	7.22	
Service bars	9.35	
Essay medal	45.00	
Postage	48.89	
Expressage	1.45	
Electrotype	2.40	
Certificate not charged to a State Society	2.00	
		12,705.03
		$22,033.78
Disbursements		16,076.36
Balance on hand May 11, 1921		$5,957.42
In Corn Exchange Bank	$5,551.33	
In Broadway Savings Institution	406.09	
		$5,957.42

JOHN H. BURROUGHS,
Treasurer General.

Audited and found correct.
GEO. D. BANGS.
NORMAN P. HEFFLEY.

Report on the Permanent Fund

President General and Compatriots:

The Treasurer General has the honor to submit the following report on the Permanent Fund:

Since the report of May 12, 1920, there has been received for rebates on insignia, rosettes, and ribbon, $380.71, credited to the Permanent Fund. There has been invested $886.19 for $1,000 fourth 4¼ per cent Liberty Loan bond, leaving on hand $465.72 uninvested. We now hold $14,500, par value, of securities.

Respectfully submitted,

JOHN H. BURROUGHS,
Treasurer General.

List of Delegates to the Thirty-Second Annual Congress of the National Society of the Sons of the American Revolution, Held at Buffalo, N. Y., May 15-18, 1921

NATIONAL SOCIETY OFFICERS

President General, James H. Preston, Maryland; Vice-President General, George Hale Nutting, Massachusetts; Vice-President General, Linn Paine, Missouri; Vice-President General, John W. Bell, Jr., Washington; Secretary and Registrar General, Philip F. Larner, District of Columbia; Chaplain General, Rev. Lee S. McCollester, Massachusetts; Treasurer General, John H. Borroughs, New York; Historian General, George C. Arnold, Rhode Island; Genealogist General, Walter K. Watkins, Massachusetts; Chancellor General, Hon. Harvey F. Remington, New York; Vice-President General, Colonel Moulton Houk, Ohio.

Past Presidents General: William A. Marble, New York; Louis Annin Ames, New York; Elmer M. Wentworth, Iowa; Hon. Morris B. Beardsley, Connecticut; Newell B. Woodworth, New York; R. C. Ballard Thruston, Kentucky; Hon. C. A. Pugsley, New York.

Directors General: Judge Arthur Preston Sumner, Rhode Island; George E. Pomeroy, Ohio; Rev. Lyman W. Allen, D. D., New Jersey.

STATE SOCIETY DELEGATES

CALIFORNIA: Claude Gatch.

COLORADO: Victor E. Keyes.

CONNECTICUT: Orville A. Petty, Herbert H. White, Albert McE. Mathewson, George Holt Starr.

DISTRICT OF COLUMBIA: William S. Parks, Selden M. Ely, Clarence A. Kenyon, Albert D. Spangler, Dr. Mark F. Finley, Claude N. Bennett, George W. Baird.

FLORIDA: Commodore James H. Bull.

GEORGIA: Allan Waters.

ILLINOIS: Colonel George V. Lauman, Harry G. Colson, Henry L. Green, Louis A. Bowman, Dorr E. Felt.

INDIANA: Cornelius F. Posson, Lieutenant Charles T. Jewett.

IOWA: Henry B. Hawley.

KENTUCKY: Marvin H. Lewis.

LOUISIANA: H. Dudley Coleman.

MAINE: James L. Merrick.

MARYLAND: Edward Derr Shriner, Matthew Page Andrews, George Sadtler Robertson, Milton W. Gatch, George C. Thomas, William H. Haywood.

MASSACHUSETTS: T. Julian Silsby, Grenville H. Norcross, Charles F. Read, Joseph H. Gilmore, Burton H. Wiggan, Walter K. Watkins, Walter C. Briggs, Dr. Waldo E. Boardman, Alfred Foster Powers, John Stewart Kirkham, George L. Gould, Richard K. Stacy, Samuel Fuller Punderson, Rev. G. Ernst Merriman.

MICHIGAN: William M. Finck, William H. Holden, William R. Chadwick, Edward C. Parsons, Almon B. Atwater, Dr. Frank Ward Holt, W. H. Barrett.

MINNESOTA: Lambert Fairchild.

MISSOURI: Colonel G. K. Hunter, J. Alonzo Matthews.

NEW JERSEY: W. I. Lincoln Adams, Edward H. Lum, William E. Summers, William J. Conklin, George V. Muchmore, Oscar Stanley Thompson, Samuel Craig Cowart, Richard L. Riker, Joseph Magee Perrine, Samuel Carl Downs, Fred B. Bassett, Harry F. Brewer, Charles Symmes Kiggins, Frederick B. Lovejoy, C. M. McPherson, C. R. McPherson, B. M. Arnold, Henry Vail Condict, Ray A. Miller, Albert L. Miller, Joseph Holmes, Major Bert E. Underwood.

NEW YORK (EMPIRE STATE SOCIETY): T. D. Huntting, George D. Barney, M. D., Lewis B. Curtis, P. Valentine Sherwood, George Royce Brown, W. A. Galpin, George D. Bangs, George L. Walker, Eugene T. Tanke, Brigadier General

Oliver B. Bridgeman, George B. Sage, George McK. Roberts, John C. Wight, Charles H. Wight, Hon. H. F. Remington, Frank B. Steele, O. H. P. Champlin, Rev. Lowell L. Rogers, D. D., Wyman H. A. Spink, Norman P. Heffley, Francis L. Hoff, Hon. Charles E. Ogden, Lewis C. Conant, Captain H. A. Brown, Jesse Peterson, Dr. F. B. Rasbach, Millard H. Dake, Harlan P. Bosworth, Leslie J. Bennett, C. De W. Pugsley, Raymond G. Dann, H. O. Holland, O. P. Benson, D. F. Potter, Dr. Charles Van Bergen, Ellicott Colson, Edgar B. Jewett.

OHIO: S. O. Richardson, Jr., Dudley Watson Moor, Robert P. Boggis, Frank C. Osborn, Winford Lecky Mattoon, W. J. Sherman, Rev. Allen K. Zartman, D. D., Henry A. Williams, Hon. Joseph B. Doyle.

OREGON: Edward D. Baldwin, Wallace McCamant.

PENNSYLVANIA: H. Dudley Coleman, A. C. Shaw, James A. Wakefield, Colonel R. W. Guthrie, Omar S. Decker, Judge Eugene C. Bonniwell, Hon. Isaac B. Brown, Captain R. W. Brown, W. B. Williams.

RHODE ISLAND: Dr. George T. Spicer.

UTAH: Daniel S. Spencer, Levi Edgar Young, Samuel Lorin Powell, Oliver N. Ritchie.

VIRGINIA: Arthur B. Clarke.

WISCONSIN: Walter H. Wright.

Social Functions Incident to the Meeting in Buffalo of the National Congress, May 15-17, 1921

On Sunday evening, May 15, a beautiful and impressive service was held at St. Paul's Cathedral. The delegates and guests marched from the headquarters, preceded by the National Emblem and the flags of the different State Societies. A special musical program had been prepared and was beautifully carried out by the full vested choir of mixed voices. The rector, Dr. Charles H. Jessup, spoke a few impressive words of welcome, and a most eloquent and patriotic sermon was delivered by Chaplain General Lee S. McCollester, D. D. The Right Reverend Charles H. Brent, Bishop of the Diocese of Western New York, also spoke a few words of greeting.

Monday noon, between the sessions of the Congress, a luncheon was served for the gentlemen attending the Congress at the Hotel Lafayette, and a charming luncheon was tendered to the visiting ladies at the Twentieth Century Club, under the direction of a committee of local women, of which Mrs. John Miller Horton was chairman.

On Monday evening a reception in honor of the visiting delegates and ladies and members of Buffalo Chapter and their ladies was given by Mrs. John Miller Horton, Regent of Buffalo Chapter, Daughters of the American Revolution, at her home, in Delaware Avenue. This was a beautiful occasion and attended by over three hundred guests.

Tuesday afternoon an automobile drive was taken around the city of Buffalo and its beautiful parks, with a stop at the Albright Art Gallery and the Buffalo Country Club, where light refreshments were served.

On Tuesday evening the Annual Banquet of the National Society was held in the banquet room of the Lafayette Hotel and attended by the delegates, members of Buffalo Chapter, and ladies to the number of about three hundred. The decorations, carrying out the color scheme of our organization, were most beautiful and appropriate.

Captain Hamilton Ward, of the Buffalo Chapter, acted as toastmaster, a function that he had performed when the National Society met in Buffalo in 1908. The addresses of the evening were made by Past President General James Harry Preston and Samuel B. Botsford, of Buffalo, who spoke impressively on some fads of Americanization; Mr. Charles Francis Adams, former President of Buffalo Chapter, gave several selections from American poets in a manner that charmed and delighted his audience; Mrs. John Miller Horton, Regent of the Buffalo Chapter, Daughters of the American Revolution, gave words of greeting from our sister organization; President General Wallace McCamant made a most thoughtful and eloquent address on the Constitution. After the banquet, dancing was enjoyed by the guests until midnight.

On Wednesday morning the delegates and guests were given a trip to Niagara Falls in special cars and around the Great Gorge Route. A luncheon was served at the Prospect House, and the guests returned to Buffalo some time during the afternoon.

MEETINGS OF TRUSTEES AND EXECUTIVE COMMITTEE

Minutes of the Meeting of the Executive Committee National Society, Sons of the American Revolution, Held May 14, 1921, at Rochester, N. Y.

A meeting of the Executive Committee of the National Society, Sons of the American Revolution, was held, on call by the President General, on Saturday, May 14, 1921, at 11 Livingston Park, Rochester, N. Y. (the D. A. R. House of Rochester Chapter), upon invitation of Compatriot George B. Sage, President of the Rochester Chapter, Sons of the American Revolution.

The meeting was called to order by President General James H. Preston, at 11 o'clock a. m. Those present were President General Preston, Mr. Louis Annin Ames, of New York; Mr. George E. Pomeroy, of Ohio, and Judge A. P. Sumner, of Rhode Island, members of the Executive Committee; also Vice-President General George H. Nutting; Past President General Newell B. Woodworth; Historian General George C. Arnold; Chancellor General Harvey F. Remington; Genealogist General W. K. Watkins; also present Compatriot George B. Sage, President of Rochester Chapter, and Compatriots Frank B. Steele and Millard H. Dake, of the Buffalo Chapter. Of the absent members of the Executive Committee, Past President General Chancellor L. Jenks, of Illinois, was detained by reason of a trial in court in which he was interested as an attorney; Rev. Dr. Lyman Whitney Allen, of New Jersey, by reason of pulpit engagements for Sunday, and Compatriot W. K. Boardman, of Tennessee, on account of an important business engagement at Nashville.

The minutes of the last meeting of the Executive Committee were approved as printed in the BULLETIN.

Letters were read from various compatriots expressing regret at being unable to attend the meeting.

The Secretary General presented several matters deemed of interest to the committee, covering principally the work of the Society during the past year and the present status of the membership, as shown by the annual reports to be submitted to the Congress at Buffalo.

The matter of a careful revision of the list for mailing the Society BULLETIN, covering about 18,000 stencils for the addressograph machine, which had not been revised for several years, was considered and especial reference made to certain States which do not report to the National Society and whose membership still remains on the lists.

On motion, it was ordered that the Secretary General prepare a list of States not reporting, and that the same be referred to the Vice-Presidents General for suitable investigation and report to the Executive Committee, with recommendations.

On motion of Judge Sumner, it was ordered that the matter of obtaining a correct list and the addresses of actual members be referred to the next Executive Committee, with the additional recommendation that steps be taken to obtain a complete roster of the National Society membership.

A letter was submitted from J. E. Caldwell & Co., of Philadelphia, requesting an increase in the contract price for furnishing the Society Insignia. Referred to incoming Executive Committee for action.

The President General reported the organization of a new State Society in Georgia.

On motion, the courtesies of the floor were extended to all present not members of the committee.

Compatriot Frank B. Steele, of Buffalo, was introduced and described the program for the Congress to be held in that city.

The members of the Executive Committee and others present entered upon a general discussion of the proposed amendments to the National Society Constitution to be submitted to the Congress.

The Secretary General was instructed to notify all officers to use India ink on membership certificates.

A letter was submitted from the District of Columbia Society covering a suggestion from the joint committee having charge of the annual meeting held in Washington on February 22, in which it was suggested that the next celebration be undertaken in the names of the National Society of the Daughters of the American Revolution, the General Society of Sons of the Revolution, and the National Society, Sons of the American Revolution, under such arrangements as may be entered into with these respective organizations by the local Societies. The suggestion was approved by the Executive Committee as to the joint annual meeting to be under the auspices of the three Societies, this endorsement not to be considered as carrying a financial obligation.

It was ordered that a representation of the grave-marker manufactured by D. H. Jones Co., of Massachusetts, with a description thereof, should be printed in the BULLETIN for information to the members of the Society.

A letter was presented from the District of Columbia Society containing a resolution adopted by that Society relative to the recognition of the American Flag and opposed to the use of "yellow fringe or frippery of any kind" on the flag. It was suggested by the committee that the District of Columbia Society should consult the regulations of the State and War Departments relative to the flag.

A letter was also presented from J. C. Weight, of Indiana, calling attention to the lack of proper protection from fire of the original drafts of the Constitution of the United States and Declaration of Independence in the State Department at Washington.

The letter was referred to the Secretary General to ascertain the condition of care of these documents at Washington with reference to protection from destruction by fire.

The annual report of Treasurer General John H. Burroughs was presented, showing a balance on hand May 12, 1920, of $9,328.75; receipts, $12,705.03; total, $22,033.78; disbursements, $16,076.36; leaving a balance on hand May 11, 1921, of $5,957.42.

The report was ordered received and filed.

The attention of the committee was called to the decision of the Registrar General with reference to claims for membership based solely upon what is known as the "New Hampshire Association Test," reference being made to the Year Book for 1920, page 110.

Upon consideration of the matter, it was ordered that the question involved be referred to the Chancellor General and Genealogist General for consideration and report. It was further ordered that the Secretary General be directed to procure from the Maine Society a copy of the legal opinion referred to in the report of the Registrar General for 1920.

The President General reported on various matters of interest to the committee and filed several letters for future reference.

A vote of thanks was extended to the Daughters of the American Revolution of Rochester, for their generous hospitality.

The meeting then adjourned.

Secretary General.

Social Functions Incident to the Meeting of the Executive Committee

The members of the Executive Committee and officials attending the meeting in Rochester were entertained at dinner, during a recess in the proceedings, by the Rochester Chapter, S. A. R. In the evening the members of the Rochester Chapter, Daughters of the American Revolution, also entertained the visitors at a very delightful tea at the Chapter House, at which a very cordial greeting was extended by the ladies and a pleasant visit thoroughly enjoyed by all present.

Ladies accompanying the officials present included Mrs. Frank B. Steele and Mrs. Millard H. Dake, of Buffalo, and Mrs. Albert J. Gore, of Washington, D. C.

Minutes of the Board of Trustees of the National Society, Sons of the American Revolution, Held at Buffalo, May 17, 1921, 2.30 p. m.

Present: Wallace McCamant, President General; George Hale Nutting, Vice-President General; Philip F. Larner, Vice-President General; Marvin H. Lewis, Vice-President General; William S. Parks, Registrar General; Frank

B. Steele, Secretary General; George C. Arnold, Historian General; Albert D. Spangler, District of Columbia; Dorr E. Felt, Illinois; Charles T. Jewett, Indiana; Elmer M. Wentworth, Iowa; C. Symmes Kiggins, New Jersey; Louis Annin Ames, New York; Allen Waters, Georgia; Col. C. R. Guthrie, Pennsylvania.

Meeting called to order by the President General, Wallace McCamant. It was moved by Mr. Spangler that the invitation of the Springfield, Mass., Chapter to meet in that city in 1922 be accepted. The motion was adopted.

Moved by Mr. Ames that the sum of $500 be appropriated toward the expenses of the 1922 Congress. The motion was adopted.

It was moved and adopted that the Executive Committee be authorized to transact all necessary business matters of the National Society in the interim between this date and the next meeting of the National Congress.

President General McCamant announced the following as appointed members of the Executive Committee: President General Wallace McCamant, chairman; Mr. James Harry Preston, Maryland; Mr. Arthur Preston Sumner, Rhode Island; Major W. I. Lincoln Adams, New Jersey; Mr. George E. Pomeroy, Ohio; Mr. Louis Annin Ames, New York, and Mr. Chancellor L. Jenks, Illinois. The appointments were confirmed by the Board of Trustees and the meeting of the Board of Trustees then adjourned.

FRANK B. STEELE,
Secretary General.

Minutes of the Executive Committee of 1921-1922 Held at the Residence of Dr. Charles Van Bergen, Buffalo, N. Y., Tuesday, May 17, 1921, at 4 p. m.

Present: Hon. Wallace McCamant, President General, of Oregon; Louis Annin Ames, New York; James Harry Preston, Maryland; George F. Pomeroy, Ohio; Arthur P. Sumner, Rhode Island; W. I. Lincoln Adams, New Jersey; Frank B. Steele, Secretary General, and former Secretary General, Philip F. Larner, District of Columbia.

The President General asked for suggestions from the Executive Committee as to the naming of committees for the ensuing year.

The President General stated that in the matter of keeping in touch with eastern societies he would make at least one trip during the year to the East and visit as many State Societies and local Chapters as possible while on this trip.

The President General further stated that he would correspond with all the State Presidents and also the Vice-Presidents General from the several districts; that he would send out a general letter to State Societies.

The Secretary was instructed to get a list of the State Officers and send to the President General this list, with the National Officers elected at this meeting.

Moved by Mr. Ames that the June BULLETIN shall contain the names of the National Officers, the Presidents and Secretaries of the State Societies, with addresses as far as possible, and a synopsis of the National Congress held in Buffalo, May 15-17, 1921; and also that there be printed five hundred copies of the Constitution and By-Laws, and that this fact be stated in the BULLETIN in conspicuous type, to call attention of the members thereto. Motion adopted.

Motion was made and adopted that the salary of the Secretary General be fixed at $900 for the year, and that the salary of the Registrar General be $600 for the year.

Motion was made and adopted that the sum of $600 be appropriated for the expenses of the offices of Secretary General, Registrar General, and Treasurer General for the next six months, and' that a committee of two be appointed to approve these bills for expenses. The Chairman appointed Mr. Ames and Mr. Adams such a committee.

Moved and adopted that a committee be appointed, consisting of Past President General Woodworth, of New York, Judge Eugene C. Bonniwell, of Pennsylvania, and Judge Arthur P. Sumner, of Rhode Island, who shall have power to revise and accept grave-markers.

It was moved and adopted that the President General and Executive Committee have full authority to settle matters by mail and telegraph.

A vote of thanks was extended to Dr. Charles Van Bergen for his generous hospitality in entertaining the Executive Committee.

On motion, the meeting was adjourned.

FRANK B. STEELE,
Secretary General.

ITEMS OF GENERAL INTEREST

Through the activities of the Flag Day Committee, practically every community in the United States held celebrations on June 14. - Governor Lake, of Connecticut, at the solicitation of Lewis B. Curtis, chairman of the Flag Day Committee, issued a fervent proclamation designating June 14 as Flag Day and urging special observance by schools and communities. Many other communities throughout the country carried on celebrations, either officially or semi-officially, and it is felt that this committee of the Sons of the American Revolution has made its influence felt in a very broad and effective manner.

The National Society, Sons of the American Revolution, presented to the Sulgrave (Washington) Manor, England, the ancestral home of the Washingtons, a handsome silk United States Flag, trimmed and mounted according to United States regulations, on June 21, 1921. The acceptance of the flag was by the Honorary President of the Sulgrave Manor, our Ambassador, Colonel Harvey.

The following telegram was received by Past President General Louis Annin Ames on the occasion of the celebration in New York City of the first inaugural of General Washington as President of the United States:

To the Sons of the American Revolution and other patriotic organizations joining in the celebration of General Washington's inauguration as first President, I want to extend greetings on this anniversary. The establishment of constitutional government under the great leader, in achievement of independence, was the foundation of our national security and power. Let us all join in the hope that this foundation shall never be shaken, and that our future shall be a continuing justification of Washington's faith.

WARREN G. HARDING.

In Memoriam

The following resolution on the death of General Horace Porter, Past President General, has been prepared by a committee representing the National Society, through appointment by President General McCamant:

Whereas the National Society, Sons of the American Revolution, has learned with sincere sorrow that Brigadier-General Horace Porter, a distinguished Past President General of the Society, closed his wonderful career on Sunday, May 29, 1921.

Resolved, That this minute of esteem and affection be inscribed upon the records of the National Society of the Sons of the American Revolution.

General Horace Porter was born at Huntington, Pa., April 15, 1837, the son of a Governor of that State. He was a direct descendant of John Porter, a gallant soldier, who fought at Warwick under William the Conqueror.

The first Porter of this family to settle in America was Robert Porter, whose son Andrew, General Horace Porter's grandfather, distinguished himself as an officer in the American Revolution. With such an ancestry, it was only natural that Horace Porter should leave Harvard for West Point and an army career.

When Fort Sumter was fired upon he was commissioned second lieutenant. His rise in the army was so rapid that at the age of 27 he was commissioned Brigadier-General and Aide-de-Camp to General Grant; then Field Commander of the Union Armies. He won six brevets for bravery. A special act of Congress bestowed the Congressional Medal on him for his bravery at the Battle of Chickamauga.

At the close of the Civil War, when General Grant was Secretary of War, General Porter acted as his assistant. He resigned from the Army at the end of General Grant's first term as President, when he was Executive Secretary to the President, and accepted a vice-presidency of the Pullman Car Company. He was the first president of the West Shore Railroad, later became president of the New York elevated railroads, and during this period he invented the ticket-chopper which is still used at elevated and subway stations.

General Porter raised the sum of $600,000 in a few weeks for the erection in 1892 of a mausoleum on Riverside Drive, New York, where rest the remains of General and Mrs. Grant.

General Porter served with honor the Sons of the American Revolution as President General from 1892 to 1896.

President McKinley, in 1897, appointed General Porter as Ambassador to France, and he remained at that post for eight years. It was while he was Ambassador that General Porter recovered the body of John Paul Jones, the "Father of the American Navy." He spent six years at this task and a large sum of money, for which he refused to be reimbursed, as well as an infinite amount of pains and study to make sure of proper identification of the body, which was in a remarkable state of preservation. The body was brought to this country by an escort of battleships and placed in the crypt of the chapel at the Naval Academy at Annapolis. For this General Porter received the thanks of Congress, which extended to him the privileges of both houses for life.

In 1907, at the age of 70, he represented the United States at the Second Hague Peace Conference.

He closed his career as an earnest advocate of universal peace.

Resolved, That the Society of the Sons of the American Revolution, in paying tribute to the memory of so eminent a compatriot as General Horace Porter, honors itself; for he won the admiration of all as a gallant soldier, a gifted statesman, an able diplomat, a brilliant orator, a fine executive, a successful inventor, and was beloved as a devoted husband, kind father, noble friend, an upright citizen, and earnest patriot. Men of General Horace Porter's character and ability have made America great.

(Signed)   LOUIS ANNIN AMES,
              Past President General, National Society S. A. R.

(Signed)   WILLIAM ALLEN MARBLE,
              Past President General, National Society S. A. R.

(Signed)   CORNELIUS AMORY PUGSLEY,
              Past President General, National Society S. A. R.

The Pilgrimage of the Franklin Statue

Any story of the wonderful pilgrimage of the Franklin Statue from Baltimore, where it was cast, to Waterbury, Conn., its final resting place, would be inadequate unless written by one who accompanied the statue. This meager description, culled from newspapers, programs, and other sources, can give but a mere outline of what took place and especially the part that was played by the Sons of the American Revolution. It is hoped that in the near future a detailed and well-written history of this statue will be in order, that it may be preserved for future records.

The statue, conceived and designed by the famous sculptor, Paul Wayland Bartlett, was to be placed in Waterbury, Conn., through the generosity of the late Elisha Levenworth. It started April 10 from Baltimore, where it was cast in bronze, with a remarkable ovation, in which the Sons of the American Revolution took a most prominent part. Our President General, James Harry Preston, representing the patriotic societies, made the address of the day, and many of our members took an active part in the ceremonies.

In Wilmington, Del., the Sons and Daughters of the American Revolution attended the exercises in a body, and Mr. Edward W. Cooch, a direct descendant of Thomas Cooch, who was a Revolutionary soldier and for whom Cooch's bridge is named, made an address.

In Philadelphia, after stopping at many towns on the way, the ceremonies were in charge of Compatriot Eugene C. Bonniwell, and were most elaborate and impressive. Judge Bonniwell made an address, as did former President General Elmer Wentworth. The story of this ceremony would be worth writing for itself alone.

From Philadelphia the statue was taken to Trenton and Brunswick, stopping at many towns on the way. Arriving in New York, a great demonstration was given and the New York Chapter, Sons of the American Revolution, carried out the program, and members of the Society attended in a body.

After leaving New York it was driven to Boston, Mass., and there at Old South Meeting House, on Sunday, May 8, a most beautiful program was carried out under the auspices of the Sons of the American Revolution, Vice-

President General George Hale Nutting, of our Society, being the general chairman. The Rev. Lewis Wilder Hicks, Chaplain of the Massachusetts Society, and Rev. Lee S. McCollester, Chaplain General of the National Society, gave the invocation and benediction, respectively. Compatriot T. Juloan Silsby was chairman of the Committee on Arrangements.

Before arriving at Waterbury, homage was paid to the statue and the memory of Franklin in New Haven by President Arthur T. Hadley, of Yale, and then by the compatriots at Bridgeport, where it was received with the same enthusiastic and reverent greetings. It finally arrived at Waterbury, its resting-place, and there, after being placed on its foundation, was unveiled by two young collateral relatives of Elisha Levenworth, Mark Levenworth Sperry and Richard Smith Sperry.

The idea of this pilgrimage originated with the Sons of the American Revolution—in fact, it was first suggested by one of our most prominent Past Presidents General and the plans were largely carried out by members of our Society. Compatriot John Henry Smythe accompanied the statue the greater part of the way, and by his presence and knowledge of the subject aided materially in making the pilgrimage the success it achieved.

EVENTS OF STATE SOCIETIES

The Arizona Society joined with the Maricopa Chapter of the Daughters of the American Revolution, on Lexington Day, April 19, 1921, in appropriate exercises upon the occasion of the admission to citizenship of thirty aliens, the successful applicants for final naturalization papers. After swearing in the newly made citizens, United States District Judge Sawtelle, in the Federal Court room at Phœnix, relinquished the bench to the Secretary of the Arizona Society, who presided in the absence of President Wilkinson. Addresses of welcome and congratulation were made by veterans of the Civil War, Spanish-American War, and the World War, followed by representatives of the Sons and Daughters of the American Revolution. The Daughters distributed flags to the new citizens and the Woman's Auxiliary of the American Legion distributed flowers to their wives and sweethearts. Through the efforts of the Arizona Society the Governor issued a proclamation for special observance of Flag Day.

The Arkansas Society held its annual meeting in the parlors of the Marion Hotel, at noon of Washington's Birthday, February 22, 1921. The meeting was well attended and much interest manifested. The following officers were elected for the coming year: President, Gen. Benjamin W. Green; Vice-President, John M. Bracey; Second Vice-President, Frank D. Leaming; Honorary Vice-President, Philander K. Roots; Secretary, Fay Hampstead; Registrar, Ernest C. Newton; Treasurer, Thomas M. Cory; Historian, John O. Blakeney; Chaplain, Dr. John Van Lear.

Resolutions of condolence for the death of Past President Frank W. Rawls and General Jonathan A. Kellogg were adopted. A resolution appointing a committee to confer with the Governor of the State and other State officials with a view of assembling the various historical collections in the State Capitol in one office was adopted. The annual banquet following the meeting was attended by nearly one hundred members and friends. Patriotic addresses were made by Mr. Ally Smith, Gen. B. W. Green, Mrs. Clarence Woodward, State Regent of the Daughters of the American Revolution, and Mr. Fay Hempstead. The latter's address on the "Genesis of the Flag" was especially interesting. Mr. Hempstead has served as State Secretary of the Arkansas Society for over 25 years.

The California Society held its annual meeting and election of officers at the Commercial Club, San Francisco, on Wednesday evening, April 20. After the business meeting the Society commemorated the anniversary of the Battle of Lexington at an informal dinner. Duncan Matthewson, captain of detectives, spoke on "Tong Wars." James A. Johnson, Warden of San Quentin prison, spoke on "Indeterminate Sentence."

The Society presented bronze memorial medals to the following members and sons of members who served in the World War: First Lieutenant S. D. Barnes, Sergeant E. G. Barnum, First Lieutenant J. N. Blood, Second Lieutenant W. V. Empire, Major H. R. Fay, Captain J. B. Frisbee, First Lieutenant W. T. Goldsborough, Captain J. G. Heywood, Second Lieutenant V. D. Lord, First Lieutenant R. H. Lutz, Private J. W. Marsh,

Major J. Mora Moss, Captain G. M. Mott, Major C. D. Y. Ostrom, Private J. R. Perkins, Jr., Commander S. A. Purviance, Major O. H. Sampson, Captain E. T. Thurston.

The Delaware Society held its annual reunion and dinner on Saturday evening, April 16. Reports showed that the organization had largely increased its membership during the last year. Former Mayor Horace Wilson, President of the Society, presided at the meeting and was toastmaster at the dinner. Plans were discussed for the part that the Society is to take in the ceremony relating to the Rodney statue; also the matter of a reunion on the Battlefield of the Brandywine was considered.

The District of Columbia Society held its April meeting at Franklin Square Hotel, on Wednesday evening, the 20th. The address of the evening was delivered by Hon. Wade Hampton Ellis, on the subject "The Enemy Within Our Gates." Mr. Ellis, former Attorney General of Ohio and First Assistant Attorney General of the United States, made a forceful speech and gave first-hand information on his topic, which is so closely related to the purposes of this Society. There was a buffet luncheon and smoker after the meeting.

The Indiana Society held its annual meeting on February 21, at the Lincoln Hotel, Indianapolis, the date being the 143d anniversary of the capture of Fort Sackville (Vincennes) by General George Rogers Clark. The adoption of a program for extensive historical work throughout the State was featured in the afternoon session. The members visited Monument Circle, where President Austin H. Brown placed, in the name of the Society, a wreath upon the monument of General George Rogers Clark. The speakers at the evening session were Hon. Henry J. Ryan, chairman of the National Americanization Committee of the American Legion; Captain W. A. Ketcham, Commander-in-Chief of the G. A. R., and Vice-President Cornelius C. Posson, who spoke feelingly of the neglected graves of some 800 soldiers of the American Revolution which lie in Indiana. At the business meeting the marking of these graves was endorsed.

The Louisiana Society was represented at the State meeting of the Daughters of the American Revolution held at New Orleans, March 31, by Henry Robinson, Historian of the Louisiana Society, S. A. R., who read an address prepared by Colonel C. Robert Churchill, recounting the brilliant exploits in the campaign of young Galvez and his men, who helped the Americans to victory by crushing the British ambitions for control of the Mississippi Valley during the War of the Revolution.

The Maine Society held its annual meeting at the Falmouth Hotel on February 22, 1921. After the election of officers and business meeting the annual banquet took place, the speaker being Hon. Harold E. Cook, who gave a thoughtful address on "Some of the Perils that Confront the Nation." The newly elected President, Hon. James O. Bradbury, also spoke along the same lines.

The Massachusetts Society held its 32d annual meeting at the Municipal Auditorium, at Springfield, Tuesday, April 19. An elaborate program was carried out, continuing throughout the day. At 11 a. m. the ringing of the municipal chimes by Compatriot Ernest Newton Bagg ushered in the ceremonies. At 11.15 the opening business session, with an address of welcome by Compatriot Hon. Edwin F. Leonard, Mayor of Springfield. At 12.15 a band concert, followed by a parade to the Hotel Kimball, where a luncheon was held for the members of the Society and ladies. Here a presentation of World War Service Medals was made. The annual address was given in the afternoon by the Rev. Edward Raymond Hance, of Naugatuck, Conn., who spoke on the "Cavalier and the Puritan." During the session a resolution was passed petitioning the Government to recognize the services of the veterans of the United States Army during the Indian War in New Mexico in 1867, and that a suitable pension be granted these veterans.

The Michigan Society held its annual meeting at Detroit, April 15, at the Detroit Club. Vice-President General Moulton Houk, of Delaware, Ohio, was the guest of honor and speaker. The election of officers and delegates to the National Congress preceded the dinner. Members attended from Grand Rapids, Kalamazoo, Ann Arbor, Pontiac, Adrian, and other Michigan Chapters and made reports of work and progress.

KENT CHAPTER held its annual meeting April 19. Election of officers took place and the following were chosen: H. Parker Robinson, President; Vice-President, Elbert M. Davis; Secretary, Daniel W. Tower; Treasurer, E. D. Winchester; Registrar, Charles N. Remington. Several interesting addresses were made and Mr. Tower acted as toastmaster at the banquet, and the War Service Medals were presented by Mr. Lucius Boltwood to Don W. Ferrant, Lemuel S. Hilman, Clarence R. Lamb, and Ashley C. Leavitt. Representatives also received medals for Arthur R. Hurst, John R. Lamb, Merritt U. Lamb, and Eugene C. Spraker.

The Minnesota Society held a splendid meeting in the Historical Society's building April 19, in commemoration of the Battle of Lexington. A reception was given to the members of the Daughters of the American Revolution, about 125 attending. Prof. A. E. Jenks, of the State University, delivered a fine address on "Materialism." He was introduced by the President, Mr. Charles E. Rittenhouse. Light refreshments were served.

The Missouri Society celebrated Flag Day on June 14 with a program of patriotic exercises in Jefferson Memorial Building. Hon. W. D. Vandiver, President of the Missouri Society, made the address of welcome. Mr. Linn Paine, Chairman of the National Committee on Patriotic Education, made an interesting report of the National Congress held at Buffalo, N. Y., and the Rev. Z. B. T. Phillips, Chaplain of the Missouri Society, made an eloquent address on the American Flag.

The Nebraska Society joined with Lincoln Chapter in placing a commemorative tablet upon the monument of Past President Herbert M. Bushnell in Wyuka Cemetery, at Lincoln, and participated in the Flag Day parade on June 14 by a detachment of the Lincoln Chapter.

The New Hampshire Society held the annual meeting and election of officers on April 19, at Concord. An address on "The United States and World Affairs" was delivered by Prof. Albert H. Washburn, of Dartmouth College. This address was up to the minute in matters pertaining to the country and was full of sane and sound matter.

The New Jersey Society held its annual meeting on April 16 and elected the following officers to carry on its affairs during the fiscal year: President, Rev. Lyman Whitney Allen, D. D.; First Vice-President, Hon. Louis F. Dodd; Second Vice-President, Harry F. Brewer; Secretary, David L. Pierson; Treasurer, Earle A. Miller; Registrar, William J. Conkling; Historian, Rev. Masheim Steck Waters; Genealogist, Samuel C. Worthen; Chancellor, Raymond T. Parrot.

The South Park Presbyterian Church, Newark, was the scene of a very patriotic meeting on Sunday afternoon, April 17, when exercises under the direction of the New Jersey Society were held in remembrance of Lexington and Concord anniversaries. Rev. Dr. Howard Duffield, of New York, preached a stirring sermon on the spirit of the day.

NEWARK CHAPTER has elected Compatriot Sylvester H. M. Agens its President. He hopes to double the membership in the course of the year. Under the auspices of the chapter, Prof. William C. Armstrong, of Elizabeth, gave an historical lecture at the New Jersey Historical Society rooms, Saturday, April 16. A large representation attended.

Plans for the placing of a flag pole at the cemeterial tract owned by the New Jersey Society, on the Battlefield of Springfield, were being completed at the time of sending this report. Passaic Valley Chapter will observe the 141st anniversary of this battle, in the First Presbyterian Church, Springfield, on June 26. Orange Chapter gave a reception to its delegates to the National Congress at the headquarters of the State Society, on Thursday evening, May 26.

ORANGE CHAPTER observed Flag Day June 14, with exercises at the Orange Park, to which foreigners particularly were invited.

Under the auspices of the New Jersey Society, Sons of the American Revolution, a granite boulder was dedicated in the burying ground adjoining the old First Presbyterian Church, Elizabeth, Sunday, June 19, in memory of Rev. Dr. William Force Whitaker, Chaplain General 1913-1915. The address at the exercises held within the edifice was delivered in a masterful and eloquent manner by our Chaplain General, Rev. Dr. Lyman Whitney Allen, President of the New Jersey Society. At the dedicatory exercises, held immediately afterward, David L. Pierson, former Historian General and chairman of the Committee on Monuments and Memorials of the New Jersey Society, delivered an address and the memorial was unveiled by Mrs. George H. Gibson, in whose household Dr. Whitaker spent the greater number of his years. Compatriot Frederick D. Hahn, retiring President of Elizabethtown Chapter, was chairman of the Committee of Arrangements.

A liberty pole forty-five feet in height will be dedicated at the battleground of Springfield, N. J., on Sunday, June 26, by the New Jersey Society, following exercises held in the old First Church of that town, under the direction of

Passaic Valley Chapter. The presiding officer will be David L. Pierson and the pole will be presented by Harry F. Brewer, First Vice-President of the New Jersey Society, and will be accpted by Rev. Dr. Allen, President.

Empire State Society was invited to and attended a patriotic service in the Brooklyn Academy of Music on March 13, 1921, given by the Fort Greene Chapter of the Daughters of the American Revolution.

Compatriot Louis Annin Ames represented the Society at a luncheon held at the Down Town Club to discuss with representatives of other patriotic societies plans for an American Committee of Good-will, the object being to maintain and increase good-will between the people of the English-speaking commonwealths. The Society went on record as protesting against unpatriotic and hostile utterances, such as had recently occurred in New York City, and aims to co-operate with other patriotic and civic societies to suppress such propaganda.

On April 18 a committee represented the Society at the unveiling of the statue to the South American Patriot, General Simon Bolivar. The annual election of officers of the Society took place on April 19, at which the speaker of the evening was Health Commissioner of the City, Compatriot Dr. Royal S. Copeland. Several compatriots represented the Society at the patriotic services held in Carnegie Hall and in Brooklyn on the same date.

The National Society Congress was held at Buffalo, N. Y., on May 16-18, at which the Empire State Society had a full delegation.

THE BUFFALO CHAPTER gave a ladies' night dinner at the Hotel Lafayette on Wednesday evening, April 20, in celebration of the Battle of Lexington. Rev. Robert McAlpin made an eloquent address on "The Shot That Was Heard Around the World." The Chapter and its members gave its time and attention to the entertainment of the delegates and ladies to the National Congress that met in this city from May 15 to May 18. The results of this work were evidently apparent, as was shown by the appreciative words and letters received by the members of the Chapter. The Buffalo members felt honored by the attendance of so many distinguished guests and were well repaid for their efforts. The Chapter feels honored in the recent election by the National body of its long-time local Secretary, Mr. Frank B. Steele, to the office of Secretary General of the National Society.

On Tuesday, June 14, in honor of Flag Day, the Chapter held its annual meeting, election of officers, and banquet. Addresses were made by the Rev. John Sayles and Chauncey J. Hamlin. The following officers were elected: President, Dr. Charles Van Bergen; First Vice-President, Dana Spring; Second Vice-President, Oliver H. Perry Champlin; Secretary, Frank B. Steele; Treasurer, Millard H. Dake; Registrar, William A. Galpuin; Chaplain, Rev. Walter C. Smith, of Dunkirk, N. Y.

THE NEW YORK CHAPTER, Empire State Society, took an active part in receiving and escorting the statue of Benjamin Franklin from the Battery to the City Hall, where exercises were held, on April 23.

A reception was given to President General Hon. James H. Preston by members of the Chapter previous to the annual meeting, April 19, at the "Annex," Broadway and 32d Street, N. Y. City.

There was a large delegation of the compatriots at the services held in St. Paul's Chapel, April 30, in commemoration of the inauguration of President George Washington.

Many compatriots attended the church service given by the Daughters of the Cincinnati, in Trinity Church, April 3, to witness the consecration of their flags.

NEWBURGH CHAPTER, Empire State Society, held its seventeenth annual banquet on the evening of April 18, in the Palatine Hotel, which was attended by about a hundred men and women. Reverend and Compatriot J. Lewis Hartsock, the President, presided. The principal speaker was Hon. Harvey F. Remington, of Rochester, president of the Empire State Society, who delivered a stirring patriotic address. Compatriot A. Elwood Corning, of the Newburgh Chapter, read "Paul Revere's Ride" and a patriotic poem of his own composition.

The following officers were elected at the annual meeting of Newburgh Chapter, held in April: William R. Perkins, President; Charles F. Burnett, First Vice-President; Rev. Joseph W. Babbitt, Second Vice-President; A. E. Layman, Secretary; F. E. Forsyth, Treasurer; Rev. M. Seymour Purdy, Registrar; David W. Jagger, Historian; Rev. F. E. Whitney, Chaplain; Leslie J. White, Color-Bearer. The following standing committees were appointed by the new President: Auditing, J. W. Barnes, W. H. Kelly, Leslie J. White; Entertainment, L. W. Pellett, A. E. Layman, Dr. W. V. Randall; Patriotic Societies, A. E. Corning, Rev. F. E. Whitney, S. L. Stewart.

The Committee on Patriotic Societies will have charge of the arrangements for the annual observance of Independence Day, which will take place largely under the direction of Newburgh Chapter, as usual. There will be a parade of civic and military societies in the forenoon, followed by addresses and singing at Washington's Headquarters.

North Dakota Society.—The annual meeting of the North Dakota Society, S. A. R., was held on the anniversary of Paul Revere's Ride, the evening of April 18, at the Gardner Hotel, Fargo. About thirty were present. The program was, to a large extent, based on the Pilgrim Tercentenary, though the first speaker, Compatriot John H. Reed, had as his subject "The Spirit of Paul Revere," in honor of the anniversary. Compatriot William J. Clapp followed, with the subject "Our Pilgrim Fathers," and Mrs. C. A. Pollock gave a witty supplementary toast on "Our Pilgrim Mothers." The principal address of the evening was by Prof. John Adams Taylor, of the University of North Dakota, on "The Social and Economic Life of the Pilgrims," an instructive and inspiring address on a timely subject.

Hon. Walter L. Stockwell brought fraternal greetings from the Sons of the Revolution. The address of the President, Frank Drew Hall, was based on "The American's Creed." Through the efforts of President Hall a copy of the American's Creed, by William Tyler Page, suitable for framing, has been sent to each public school in the State. It was voted to arrange, if possible, to place a copy of this creed in the hands of each newly made citizen in the State during the coming year.

Authority was granted for the establishment of a local chapter at Grand Forks, which will be the first local chapter in the State.

The officers elected were: Prof. Howard. E. Simpson, of Grand Forks, President; Hon. John O. Hanchett, of Valley City, Vice-President; Walter R. Reed, of Amenia, Secretary and Registrar; J. W. Wilkerson, of Grand Forks, Treasurer; Frank D. Hall, of Fargo, Historian; W. J. Clapp, of Fargo, Chaplain. The next annual meeting will be held at Grand Forks.

The Ohio Society held its annual meeting at Dayton on Lexington Day, April 19, 1921. The members were the guests of the Richard Montgomery Chapter and were royally entertained by the enthusiastic members of that Chapter. The Society has had an increase of 75 members during the past year, and much interest has been manifested among the various chapters in the State in patriotic educational work through the distribution of hundreds of copies of the United States Constitution and the booklet "Information for Immigrants." A general response to these efforts has been noted throughout the State by celebrations in commemoration of Constitution Day, Lexington Day, Memorial Day, and other important anniversaries by the schools. The Society has been active in its efforts for an appropriation by the State to improve the grounds surrounding Fort Laurens, the first fort erected in the territory of Ohio during the War of the Revolution, and in favor of the movement to erect two monuments in memory of Mad Anthony Wayne, one on the battlefield of Fallen Timbers, near Toledo, and one near Greenville, a historical spot, where important treaties were signed by the Indians. The Society is active in the work of identifying and marking the graves of Revolutionary soldiers, over 1,200 having been so far reported. One hundred and forty medals have been presented to soldiers of the World War who are members of the Ohio Society. An elaborate banquet in the evening concluded the gathering for this State meeting and was attended by one hundred and fifty, including many ladies. A message of greeting was sent to President Harding, who replied with a cordial message. The guest of honor was Col. Benson G. Hough, Commander of the famous 106th Regiment, Rainbow Division, now a judge of the Ohio Supreme Court. Other prominent speakers were Rev. E. P. Whallon, of Cincinnati; Dr. W. F. Pierce, and the President of Kenyon College.

WESTERN RESERVE CHAPTER, of Cleveland, celebrated February 22d by holding its annual meeting, and a varied and attractive program was carried out. The annual meeting and luncheon was held at the Cleveland Athletic Club. About sixty were present and the speaker of the occasion was Colonel Hayden Eames, who spoke on the subject of "Radicalism." The election of officers took place and the following were elected: President, Frank C. Osborn; Vice-Presidents, Francis W. Treadway, Mason B. McLaughlin, Robert A. Bishop, E. M. Hall; Secretary, Robert P. Boggis; Assistant Secretary, George E. Rogers; Treasurer, Robert B. Boggis; Registrar, Jesse A. Fenner; Historian, Fred Sylvester Dunham; Chaplain, Rev. F. B. Avery; Honorable Chaplain, Rev. E. W. J. Lindesmith. On the evening of the 22d the Society gave a public reception and ball at the Hotel Statler, which was attended by over three hundred and fifty people. About one hundred attended in Colonial costume. There was a program of patriotic tableaux, songs of Colonial days, and a minuet was danced. The ball-room was decorated by thirty-six Colonial flags loaned by Compatriot Charles R. Putnam.

The Pennsylvania Society held its annual banquet and election of officers at Pittsburgh on February 22. The business session was held at the Pittsburgh Chamber of Commerce, and many interesting matters were taken up and discussed. The Society is receiving many new applications, one member alone, Compatriot John Erlick, having secured eleven. A most interesting and delightful banquet was held in the evening, at McCreery's dining-room, and the addresses were of the highest order. United States Senator J. Thomas Heflin, of Alabama, made the principal address, on "Industrial and Trade Conditions, and the other speakers were Colonel Ned Arden Flood, of New York; Woods N. Carr, and Mrs. J. B. Heron, State Regent of the Daughters of the American Revolution. President James A. Wakefield was toastmaster.

The Rhode Island Society. The annual meeting and election of officers of this Society was held on February 22, at the Rhode Island Historical Society, in Providence. The officers elected were President, Francis Eliot Bates; Vice-President, Clarence Arthur Cotton; Secretary, Theodore Everett Dexter; Treasurer, William Luther Sweet; Registrar, George Thurston Spicer; Historian, Howard Miller Chapin; Chaplain, Rev. Frederick Spies Penford; Poet, George Franklin Weston. Retiring President Clarke made an excellent annual address and Secretary Cotton called attention to the splendid growth of the Rhode Island Society during the past year.

At the noon meeting a simple but impressive ceremony was arranged by President Clarke for the presentation of War Service Medals. The President descended to a place in front of the speakers' table, and, with Secretary Cotton on his right and Registrar Spicer on his left, cordially greeted each compatriot who had served in the World War. In the evening the annual banquet was held at the University Club and every seat was occupied. The principal speeches of the evening following President Clarke's address were given by Rev. Edward Cummings, D. D., of Boston, General Secretary of the World's Peace Foundation; His Excellency Emery J. Sans Souci, Governor of Rhode Island, and Mayor Joseph H. Gainer, of Providence.

The Tennessee Society on May 31 marked Revolutionary graves in Nashville. The ceremony was in charge of Paul Dewitt and the oration was delivered by the Hon. Harvey Hanna, President of the Public Utilities Commission. The Colonial Dames, Daughters of the American Revolution, Daughters of 1812 Confederate Veterans, American Legion, and Boy Scouts all joined in making this occasion a success. On June 12 the Chaplain, Dr. Vance, delivered a Flag Day sermon at the First Presbyterian Church, and Flag Day observances were arranged by the Society to be observed by the Rotary Clubs of Tennessee, the Chamber of Commerce of Chattanooga, and the Commercial Club of Nashville. The Tennessee Society joined with the Daughters of the American Revolution in a joint meeting at Ward-Belmont College.

The Utah Society held its annual meeting December 27, 1920, and elected the following officers: President, Heber M. Wells; Vice-President, Robert E. McConaughy; Secretary, Gordon Lines Hutchins; Treasurer, Seth Warner Morrison, Jr.; Registrar, Chauncey P. Overfield; Historian, Levi Edgar Young; Chaplain, Rev. Hoyt E. Henriques. The President of the Utah Society was the first Governor of the State of Utah and served as Governor for nine years, a longer continuous period than any other executive in the history of the Nation.

The Utah Society awarded patriotic oratory medals at the Agricultural College of Utah at Logan, the High School at Ogden, University of Utah, and Salt Lake High School at Salt Lake City, and prizes to the Boy Scouts at Liberty Park, in Salt Lake City, on Flag Day, June 14, for patriotic essays.

The Vermont Society held its annual meeting on March 16 and the following officers were elected: President, William H. Jeffrey, Montpelier; Vice-President, Charles A. Plumley, Northfield; Secretary, Walter H. Crockett, Burlington; Treasurer, Clarence L. Smith, Burlington; Registrar, Dorman B. E. Kent, Montpelier; Historian, Walter H. Crockett; Chaplain, Rev. I. C. Smart, D. D., Burlington. Admiral Henry T. Mayo, U. S. N., retired, Commander of the Atlantic Fleet during the World War and ranking officer of the American Navy, a native of Vermont, was the guest of the Society on this occasion and was presented by Lieutenant-Governor Foote, who presided. Following the address of Admiral Mayo bronze medals of the Society were awarded, the names being read by the Secretary and presented by Admiral Mayo to the following members: Rev. William J. Ballou, Lieutenant-Colonel William H. Burt, Byron N. Clark, Major John A. Drew, Morris H. Cone, Rear-Admiral W. B. Fletcher, Lieutenant Richard L. Greene, Carl T. Hatch, Commander John F. Hatch, Colonel George J. Holden, Colonel John Howard, William J. Humphrey, J. Milo Jeffrey, Lieutenant A. H. Kidder, Lieutenant-Colonel George E. Nelson, George E. Parker, Stephen K. Perry, Edward R. Presbrey, Major Oliver Presbrey, Lieutenant Mortimer R. Proctor, Captain Redfield Proctor, Lieutenant Albert W. Rutter, William T. Slayton, Walter C. Stevens, Lieutenant William L. Town, Captain J. Watson Webb, Lieutenant W. Seward Webb, Jr., and Lieutenant-Colonel Guy H. Wyman.

The Virginia Society held its annual meeting February 22, at the Westmoreland Club, with 156 present. Former officers were all re-elected and a committee was appointed to work on Americanization of foreigners. The President reported as to the assistance by a committee of the Virginia Society in the reception and entertainment of the members of the Sulgrave Institution last fall, at Williamsburg, Jamestown, and Richmond, in recognition of the Tercentenary celebrations. After the business meeting the Society met in joint session, according to the custom of several years past, with the Society of the Sons of the Revolution in Virginia. A valuable paper on "Washington as a Surveyor" was read by G. Watson James. Further entertainment in lighter vein, followed by supper, completed the meeting.

The Washington Society. Spokane Chapter held a meeting on Friday, June 17, at the Spokane City Club. Luncheon was served at noon and a report of the Annual Congress held at Buffalo, May 15-17, was given by the Secretary, J. W. Bell, Jr.

The Wisconsin Society held its annual meeting in the club-room of the Hotel Pfister on May 26. The President, Walter H. Wright, presided and reported in detail the meeting of the National Congress at Buffalo, which he attended. The Society has instituted an active committee on membership, which is to direct a campaign for the ensuing year. The election of officers, which followed the business session, resulted in the choice of the following: President, J. Tracy Hale, Jr.; First Vice-President, Henry G. Sloan; Second Vice-President, Chalmer B. Traver; Secretary, Emmett A. Donnelly; Treasurer, William Stark Smith; Registrar, William W. Wight; Historian, Charles Stanley Perry; Chaplain, Rt. Rev. William Walter Webb.

ADDITIONS TO MEMBERSHIP.

There have been enrolled in the office of the Registrar General, from March 1, 1921, to June 1, 1921, 577 new members as follows: Arkansas, 4; California, 4; Colorado, 6; Connecticut, 8; Delaware, 19; District of Columbia, 16; Georgia, 15; Idaho, 1; Indiana, 17; Illinois, 16; Iowa, 8; Kansas, 1; Kentucky, 7; Louisiana, 7; Maryland, 37; Massachusetts, 40; Michigan, 25; Minnesota, 5; Missouri, 1; Montana, 2; Nebraska, 3; New Jersey, 125; New Mexico, 2; New York (Empire State), 52; North Dakota, 12; Ohio, 25; Oklahoma, 15; Oregon, 4; Pennsylvania, 50; Rhode Island, 6; Tennessee, 6; Utah, 2; Vermont, 6; Virginia, 9; Washington State, 9; Wisconsin, 4; Wyoming, 1.

In Memoriam

J. SCOTT BALDWIN, Empire State Society, died October 17, 1920.

ABRAHAM BARKER, New Jersey Society, died April 14, 1921.

ANDREW J. BENNETT, New Hampshire Society, died September 30, 1920.

ARTHUR JULIUS BIRDSEYE, Connecticut Society, died April 29, 1921.

THOMAS BALLARD BLAKE, Virginia Society, died April 29, 1921.

DANIEL DINGMAN BRODHEAD, New Jersey Society, died April 25, 1921.

PHILIP F. BROWN, Virginia Society, died March 24, 1921.

T. C. BROWN, Empire State Society, died December 2, 1920.

MILTON H. BURGERT, Ohio Society, died July 4, 1920.

EDWARD B. CAMP, New Jersey Society, died April 6, 1921.

EDWIN CASWELL, Oregon Society, died May 15, 1921.

H. S. CHAMPLIN, Empire State Society, died January 30, 1921.

JOHN L. CHITTENDON, Empire State Society, died April, 1920.

JOHN L. CONUET, New Jersey Society, died January 16, 1919.

EDMUND C. CONVERSE, Empire State Society, died April 4, 1921.

HERVEY H. DORR, Illinois Society, died September 12, 1919.

ALEXIS IRENEE DU PONT, Delaware Society, died May 30, 1921.

HENRY ALLEN HALSEY, Arizona Society, died ——— —, 1920.

G. A. HARMAN, Ohio Society, died March 3, 1919.

EDWARD DWIGHT HENDEE, Connecticut Society, died February 27, 1921.

GEORGE S. HOSMER, Michigan Society, died March 2, 1921.

HARRY W. JAMES, Massachusetts Society, died March 11, 1921.

CHARLES JOHNSON, Pennsylvania Society, died March 29, 1921.

EDWIN T. JONES, Utah Society, died September —, 1920.

NATHANIEL WYETH KENDALL, Connecticut Society, died April 21, 1921.

WILLIAM JAY LANDON, Minnesota Society, died July 18, 1917.

HENRY B. LEDYARD, Michigan Society, died May 24, 1921.

LOUIS N. LEVY, Empire State Society, died April 9, 1921.

WILLIAM M. LITTELL, Captain, A. E. F., Iowa Society, died September, 1918.

WILLIAM S. M. MANDEVILLE, Empire State Society, died April 20, 1921.

ROBERT A. MEEKS, New Jersey Society, died ——— —, 1921.

JAMES G. MERRILL, Tennessee Society, died December 22, 1920.

General Horace Porter, Past President General National Society, Member Empire
    State Society and founder of the Society in France, died May 30, 1921.

SAMUEL THOMPSON PULLIAM, Virginia Society, died May 21, 1921.

GEORGE ROBERTS, Connecticut Society, died May 14, 1921.

MARK ALFRED RODGERS, Arizona Society, died ——— —, 1920.

WOODARD W. SEARS, Empire State Society, died January 20, 1921.

PHILIP W. STANHOPE, Empire State Society, died April 6, 1921.

WILLIAM M. STETSON, Empire State Society, died January 24, 1921.

THOMAS BRINCKERHOFF TRUMBULL, Connecticut Society, died March 27, 1921.

EDWARD HOWARD VAN DYKE, D. D., Delaware Society, died May 21, 1921.

SEYMOUR WALTON, Illinois Society, died June 26, 1920.

J. H. WATTS, Tennessee Society, died December 16, 1918.

GEORGE W. WILLIAMS, Massachusetts Society, died ——— —, 1921.

WALTER C. WINCHESTER, Michigan Society, died ———.

RECORDS OF 577 NEW MEMBERS ENROLLED BY THE REGISTRAR GENERAL FROM MARCH 1, 1921, TO JUNE 1, 1921.

IRVIN ABELL, Louisville, Ky. (34710). Son of Irvin and Sallie Silesia (Rogers) Abell; grandson of Jonathan and Mary Elizabeth (Bard) Rogers; great-grandson of James and Mary (Snider) Rogers; great[2]-grandson of *James Rogers*, private, Virginia Militia, pensioned.

LINCOLN E. ABER, Ingram, Pa. (34341). Son of Jackson and Eliza (Conner) Aber; grandson of William and Margaret (Murdock) Conner; great-grandson of Cornelius and Eliza (Carroll) Conner, Jr.; great[2]-grandson of *Cornelius Conner*, Sergeant, Thirteenth Regt., Virginia Troops.

GEORGE NICHOLAS ACKER, Washington, D. C. (35576). Son of William J. and Jessie (Burgess) Acker; grandson of Johnston Erwin (Edwin) and Martha Ellen (Holt) Burgess; great-grandson of William and Mary Duke (Letton) Holt; great[2]-grandson of Brice and Harriet (Moore) Letton; great[3]-grandson of *Michael Letton*, private, Fifth Regt., Maryland Militia.

RUSH SMITH ADAMS, Lisbon, N. Dak. (33019). Son of Homer and Philanda (Cadwell) Adams; grandson of Ebenezer Smith and Sally (Clark) Cadwell; great-grandson of *Phinias Cadwell*, private and Corporal, 18th Regt., Conn. Militia, pensioned.

SIDNEY DEWITT ADAMS, Lisbon, N. Dak. (33018). Son of Rush Smith and Susan Whitney (Sage) Adams; grandson of Homer and Philinda (Cadwell) Adams; great-grandson of Ebenezer Smith and Sally (Clark) Cadwell; great[2]-grandson of *Phineas Cadwell*, private and Corporal, 18th Regt., Conn. Militia, pensioned.

WILLIS SAGE ADAMS, Lisbon, N. Dak. (33020). Son of Henry Kirke and Frances A. (Sage) Adams; grandson of Henry Dwight and Priscilla (Cadwell) Adams; great-grandson of Ebenezer Smith and Sally (Clark) Cadwell; great[2]-grandson of *Phineas Cadwell*, private and Corporal, 18th Regt., Conn. Militia, pensioned.

WELLINGTON ESTEY AIKEN, Burlington, Vt. (33839). Son of James H. and Mary Frances (Hamley) Aiken; grandson of Simeon and Marietta (Goodrich) Aiken; great-grandson of John and Amelia (Goodrich) Aiken; great[2]-grandson of *John Aiken*, Selectman and Member Advisory and Vigilant Committees, Londonderry, N. H.; great-grandson of John and Amelia (Goodrich) Aiken; great[2]-grandson of *Simeon Goodrich*, Sergeant, Colonel Baldwin's Regt., Mass. Artificers, pensioned.

SEDGWICK RAWLINGS AKIN, Terre Haute, Ind. (35504). Son of Charles Theodore and Mary (S—) Akin; grandson of Ransom W. and Sarah Rawlings (Sedgwick) Akin; great-grandson of Josiah and Rebecca (Stewart) Akin; great[2]-grandson of *James Stewart, Jr.*, private, Westmoreland County, Virginia Rangers.

ETHAN ALLEN, Westfield, N. J. (35178). Son of Walter Howard and Norma (Howland) Allen; grandson of Elihu and Emily (Allen) Howland; great-grandson of Robert and Sarah (Barkalow) Allen; great[2]-grandson of Stephen and Fannie (Height) Allen; great[3]-grandson of *Samuel Allen*, Lieutenant and Captain, Somerset County, New Jersey Militia.

JOHN WENDELL ANDERSON, Detroit, Mich. (35129). Son of Wendell A. and Susan Mary (Small) Anderson; grandson of Abraham W. and Joannah T. (Waterman) Anderson; great-grandson of *John Waterman*, private, Mass. Militia; great-grandson of John and Mary (Harris) Waterman; great[2]-grandson of *William Harris*, Captain, Fourth Regt., Cumberland County, Mass. Militia.

PHILIPS RHODES ARNOLD, Syracuse, N. Y. (35038). Son of George Carpenter and Flora Etta (Richards) Arnold; grandson of William Rhodes and Sarah Hill (Carpenter) Arnold; great-grandson of George Carpenter and Phebe (Rhodes) Arnold; great[2]-grandson of James Utter and Mahetabel (Carpenter) Arnold; great[3]-grandson of George and Ruth (Utter) Arnold; great[4]-grandson of *James Arnold*, Captain, Kent County, Rhode Island Militia, Member Rhode Island Council of War; great[2]-grandson of William and Sarah (Arnold) Rhodes; great[3]-grandson of *Robert Rhodes*, Captain, First Battalion, Kent County, Rhode Island Artillery.

EDMUND TEMPLE ATKINSON, Norfolk, Va. (Md. 34989). Son of Homer and Christiana O. (Pierce) Atkinson; grandson of John Perkins and Mary N. (Christian) Pierce; great-grandson of Oliver and Christiana (Shields) Christian; great[2]-grandson of Robert and Nancy (Brown) Christian; great[3]-grandson of *William Christian*, Lieutenant-Colonel, First Regt., Virginia Troops.

JOHN STARR ATWATER, New Haven, Conn. (34796). Son of John S. and Mary (Miller) Atwater; grandson of Joseph and Sarah (Thomas) Atwater; great-grandson of *Jeremiah Atwater*, Conn. Manufacturer of gunpowder by order of the State.

JOHN FULLER AUSTIN, Westfield, N. J. (35257). Son of Edmund Haines and Hannah (Fuller) Austin; grandson of Abram and Hannah (Duncan) Fuller; great-grandson of Jeremiah and Delly (Stone) Fuller; great^2-grandson of *Abraham Fuller*, Captain, 13th Regt., Conn. Militia.

WILLIAM LAURENS MANNING AUSTIN, Jr., Little Rock, Ark. (31770). Son of William Laurens Manning and Emily (Merrill) Austin; grandson of William Henry and Martha Anne (Hudson) Austin; great-grandson of William Laurens Manning and Elizabeth (Stokes) Austin; great^2-grandson of William and Jennie (Collins) Austin; great^8-grandson of *Nathaniel Austin*, Quartermaster Sergeant and Captain, South Carolina Troops.

AUGUSTUS EMERSON BABCOCK, Brighton, N. Y. (35354). Son of William J. and Eleanore Augusta (Emerson) Babcock; grandson of James M. and Lydia E. (Jackson) Babcock; great-grandson of Isaac and Elizabeth (Wilbur) Babcock; great^2-grandson of Isaiah and Freelove (Briggs) Babcock, Jr.; great^8-grandson of *Isaiah Babcock*, Member Berkshire County, Mass. Committee of Safety; grandson of Amos and Sarah (Lloyd) Emerson; great-grandson of Amos and Polly (——) Emerson; great^2-grandson of *Amos Emerson*, Captain, Colonel Cilley's Regt., New Hampshire Troops, pensioned, Member Committee of Safety.

EDGAR A. BAILEY, Lincoln, Nebr. (33887). Son of William and Harriett A. (Barnes) Bailey; grandson of Bill A. and Mary (Corbin) Barnes; great-grandson of Bill and Esther (Spalding) Barnes; great^2-grandson of *Dyer Spalding*, Colonel, Vermont Militia.

FREDERICK WATSON BAILEY, Tulsa, Okla. (35227). Son of Thomas Stewart and Margaret I. (Eberman) Bailey; grandson of William S. and Isabell (Walker) Eberman, great-grandson of George and Ann (Weaver) Eberman; great^2-grandson of *Jacob Weaver*, Captain, Seventh Co., 10th Regt., Penna. Troops.

KENNETH GROSVENOR BAILEY, Nanuet, N. Y. (35628). Son of Harry E. and Ina Beula (Grosvenor) Bailey; grandson of George E. and Louise M. (Ernst) Bailey; great-grandson of Samuel and Nancy Stiles (Lindsley) Bailey; great^2-grandson of Matthew G. and Abigail (Beers) Lindsley; great^2-grandson of *Joseph Lindsley*, Captain and Major, Morris County, New Jersey Militia and Cont'l Troops; great^2-grandson of Samuel and Sarah (Tappan) Bailey; great^2-grandson of *James Tappan*, private, Somerset County, New Jersey Militia; great^3-grandson of *Jonathan Bailey*, Corporal, Fourth Regt., New Jersey Cont'l Line; grandson of Miram and Martha (Reese) Grosvenor; great-grandson of Amasa and Phœbe (Kenyon) Grosvenor; great^2-grandson of Moses and Dorcas (Sharp) Grosvenor; great^2-grandson of *Caleb Grosvenor*, private, Conn. Light Horse.

ALBERT BREWER BAKER, Pelham, N. Y. (Md. 34991). Son of Henry Fenimore and Cora (W—) Baker; grandson of Milton and Henrietta (A—) Baker; great-grandson of Richard B. and Catharine (———) Baker; great^2-grandson of Samuel Baker; great^8-grandson of *Daniel Baker*, private, Albany and Westchester Counties, New York Militia.

EDWARD EDGAR BAKER, Westfield, N. J. (35301). Son of Francis R. and Charlotte (Radley) Baker; grandson of Hedges and Charlotte (Crane) Baker; great-grandson of Daniel and Margaret (Osborn) Baker; great^2-grandson of Henry and Phebe (Hedges) Baker; great^8-grandson of *Daniel Baker*, Corporal, Sergeant and Ensign, New Jersey Militia, State Troops, and Line.

HENRY FENIMORE BAKER, Jr., Hyde, Md. (34992). Son of Henry Fenimore and Cora (W—) Baker; grandson of Milton and Henrietta (A—) Baker; great-grandson of Richard B. and Catharine (———) Baker; great^2-grandson of Samuel Baker; great^8-grandson of *Daniel Baker*, private, Albany and Westchester Counties, New York Militia.

JEFFERSON WHEELER BAKER, Detroit, Mich. (35150). Son of Charles Whiting and Rebecca Wheeler Baker; grandson of Thomas Jefferson and Mattie Caroline (Whiting) Baker; great-grandson of Thomas and Mary Cummings (Bingham) Baker; great^2-grandson of *Thomas Baker*, Fifer, Colonel Little's Regt., Mass. Militia; great^3-grandson of *John Baker*, Captain, Colonel Little's Regt., Mass. Militia and 12th Cont'l Infty.

WILLIAM ARTHUR BAKER, Tulsa, Okla. (35238). Son of Benjamin Franklin and Sarah Ann (Hurst) Baker; grandson of Charles and Almira (Hunt) Baker; great-grandson of Samuel and Betty (Tiffany) Baker; great^2-grandson of *Heman Baker*.

BUEL BLINN BALDWIN, Burlington, Vt. (33840). Son of Edward J. and Dora Ada (Blinn) Baldwin; grandson of Chester and Mary M. (Hadley) Blinn; great-grandson of Chester and Peggy (Clyde) Blinn; great²-grandson of Simeon and Catherine (Smith) Blinn; great³-grandson of *Billy Blinn*, private, Col. Charles Burrell's Battalion, Conn. Troops.

HARLAN HOGE BALLARD, Pittsfield, Mass. (34969). Son of Addison and Julia Perkins (Pratt) Ballard; grandson of John and Pamelia (Bennett) Ballard; great-grandson of William and Elizabeth (Whitney) Ballard; great²-grandson of *Josiah Ballard*, private, Mass. Militia.

NATHAN BRAINERD BARBER, Waterloo, Iowa (33818). Son of David S. and Louise (Brainerd) Barber; grandson of Nathan Hoyt and Eliza (Hatch) Brainerd; great-grandson of Enoch and Theodate (Hoyt) Brainerd; great²-grandson of Nathan and Meribah Fogg (Perkins) Hoyt; great³-grandson of *Abraham Perkins*, Captain, Col. Pierce Long's Regt., New Hampshire Militia.

HARRY FAY BARDWELL, Westfield, N. J. (35527). Son of Frederick Carew and Laura B. (Fay) Bardwell; grandson of Henry Lombard and Caroline Sloan (Cotton) Bardwell; great-grandson of Josiah and Lucretia Mills (Bishop) Bardwell; great²-grandson of *Joseph Bardwell*, private, Col. Elisha Porter's Regt., Mass. Militia.

CHARLES BARHAM, Nashville, Tenn. (34633). Son of C. W. and Alexine Goldsborough (Ballard) Barham; grandson of Jethro and Martha P. (Wells) Ballard; great-grandson of Thomas Webb and Mary (Roundtree) Ballard; great²-grandson of *Jethro Ballard*, Assessor and Justice, Gates County, North Carolina Court of Pleas; great²-grandson of Jethro and Elizabeth (Sumner) Ballard; great²-grandson of Dempsey Sumner, Justice, Gates County, North Carolina Court of Pleas and Quarter Sessions.

WILLIAM HENRY BARNES, N. Y. (4530). Supplemental. Son of George B. and Nancy Jane (Kingsbury) Barnes; grandson of Levi and Olpha (Barker) Barnes; great-grandson of Benjamin and Abigail (Goodsell) Barnes; great²-grandson of *Daniel Goodsell*, private, Colonel Wylly's Regt., Conn. Militia.

JAMES PERRINE BARNEY, Lieutenant-Colonel, U. S. Army, Washington, D. C. (Ohio 35161). Son of Edward E. and Louise (Perrine) Barney, grandson of Elvain E. and Julia (Smith) Barney; great-grandson of Benjamin and Nancy (Potter) Barney; great²-grandson of Edward and Elizabeth (Beacon) Barney; great³-grandson of *John Barney*, private, Guilford, Vermont Militia.

REUBEN REYNOLDS BARNEY, Corvallis, Ore. (35056). Son of Reuben and Anna (Reynolds) Barney, Jr.; grandson of Reuben and Martha (Prindle) Barney; great-grandson of Hawley and Olive (Audren) Prindle; great²-grandson of Zenas and Hannah (Cogswell) Prindle; great³-grandson of Zalmon and Mary (Williams) Prindle; great⁴-grandson of *Abraham Williams*, private, Phillipsburg Militia, died in British prison.

CHARLES LESLIE BARNUM, New York, N. Y. (35369). Son of Charles and Isadore (White) Knapp; grandson of Noah K. and Mary (Starr) Barnum; great-grandson of Darius and Maria (Knapp) Barnum; great²-grandson of *Seth Barnum*, private, Fifth Regt., Conn. Line.

J. NEILSON BARRY, Spokane, Wash. (34035). Son of Robert Peabody and Julia Kean (Neilson) Barry; grandson of John and Margaret Ann (Fish) Neilson; great-grandson of John and Abigail (Bleecker) Neilson; great²-grandson of *John Neilson*, Brigadier-General, New Jersey Militia; great-grandson of John and Abigail (Bleecker) Neilson; great²-grandson of *Anthony Lispenard Bleecker*, Major, First Regt., New York Militia; great²-grandson of John and Catherine (Voorhees) Neilson; great³-grandson of *Johannes Voorhees*, Captain, First Battlion, Somerset County, New Jersey Militia; grandson of John and Margaret Ann (Fish) Neilson; great-grandson of *Nicholas Fish*, Captain, New York Militia, Major and Brigade Inspector, New York Line; grandson of Samuel Frederick and Martha Lewis (Peabody) Barry; great-grandson of Samuel and Rebecca (Marshall) Barry; great²-grandson of *John Barry*, private, Colonel Vose's Regt., Mass. Troops; great-grandson of Samuel and Rebecca (Marshall) Barry; great²-grandson of *William Marshall*, private, Col. Jacob Gerrish's detachment, Mass. Guards; grandson of Samuel Frederick and Martha Lewis (Peabody) Barry; great-grandson of Samuel and Mrs. Elizabeth (Mansfield) Masury Peabody; great²-grandson of *Moses Peabody*, private, Col. Nicholas Dyke's Regt., Mass. Militia; great-grandson of Samuel and Mrs. Elizabeth (Mansfield) Masury Peabody; great²-grandson of *Andrew Mansfield*, private, Lynn, Mass. Cont'l Troops.

CHARLES RAYMOND BARTON, Tulsa, Okla. (N. J. 35525). Son of Daniel W. and Caroline (Williams) Barton; grandson of Charles Wesley and Isabel (Miller) Barton;

Great-grandson of Lewis and Eliza (Terpenning) Barton; great²-grandson of Jeremiah and Fanny Barton; great³-grandson of *Isaac Barton*, private, Third Regt., Ulster County, New York Militia.

LYSLE WHITESELL BASH, Avonmore, Pa. (35458). Son of William H. and Ada Belle (Whitesell) Bash; grandson of Jonathan and Mary (Smeltzer) Whitesell; great-grandson of Jacob and Susan (Yockey) Smeltzer, Jr.; great²-grandson of Jacob and Mary Smeltzer; great³-grandson of *John Smeltzer*, private, First and Fourth Regts., Penna. Cont'l Line.

THOMAS HUSTON BATEMAN, Philadelphia, Pa. (35288). Son of William H. S. and Ollie Logan (Ennis) Bateman; grandson of William A. and Almeda (Tomlinson) Ennis; great-grandson of Samuel and Lydia (Simpkins) Tomlinson; great²-grandson of William and Phœbe (Harris) Tomlinson; great³-grandson of *James Tomlinson*, private, Cumberland County, New Jersey Militia; great⁴-grandson of *James Tomlinson*, Captain, Col. Enos Seely's Battalion, New Jersey Militia.

WILLIAM H. S. BATEMAN, Philadelphia, Pa. (35288). Son of William H. S. and Ollie Logan (Ennis) Bateman; grandson of William A. and Almeda (Tomlinson) Ennis; great-grandson of Samuel and Lydia (Simpkins) Tomlinson; great²-grandson of William and Phœbe (Harris) Tomlinson; great³-grandson of *Samuel Tomlinson*, private, Cumberland County, New Jersey Militia; great⁴-grandson of *James Tomlinson*, Captain, Col. Enos Seely's Battalion, New Jersey Militia.

ERNEST GRAHAM BATES, Springfield, Mass. (34968). Son of Edward Graham and Sophia Alden (Burr) Bates; grandson of Jonathan and Polly (Beals) Burr; great-grandson of *Israel Burr*, Corporal, Col. John Bailey's Regt., Mass. Militia.

HARRY MURVIN BAXTER, Grand Rapids, Mich. (35126). Son of Frederick C. and Jennie N. (Curtiss) Baxter; grandson of Daniel L. and Abigail Keziah (Baker) Baxter; great-grandson of Daniel and Susan (Robinson) Baxter; great²-grandson of *William Baxter*, private, Fifth Regt., Mass. Militia, pensioned.

EMERY THOMAS BEALL, Xenia, Ohio (35162). Son of E. C. and Rebecca (Smith) Beall; grandson of William T. and Isabella (Alexander) Beall; great-grandson of John Brook and Eleanor (Beatty) Beall; great²-grandson of *Thomas Beall*, Captain, Colonel Rawling's Regt., Maryland Cont'l Troops; great²-grandson of *Thomas Beatty*, Captain, Seventh Regt., Maryland Line.

HARRY CHARLES BEERS, Champaign, Ill. (35428). Son of John and Izora (Nebeker) Beers; grandson of Washington and Susanna (McClain) Nebeker; great-grandson of George and Susanna (Meredith) Nebeker; great²-grandson of *John Nebucher*, private, Col. Thomas Duff's Regt., Delaware Militia.

JOHN OLIVER BELCHER, Springfield, Mass. (34970). Son of John Woodbridge and Abbie (Elder) Belcher; grandson of Oliver Tenney and Betsey (Ellis) Belcher; great-grandson of *Woodbridge Belcher*, private, Col. Timothy Danielson's Regt., Mass. Militia; great-grandson of *John Ellis*, Corporal, Major Eben Allen's Regt., Vermont Militia.

ALDEN BELL, Culpeper, Va. (35086). Son of John Wesley and Maria Champ (Storrow) Bell; grandson of Samuel Appleton and Elizabeth Hill Farley (Carter) Storrow; great-grandson of William Champe and Mary Byrd (Farley) Carter; great²-grandson of *James Parke Farley*, private, Virginia Militia.

STACEY BENDER, Westfield, N. J. (35315). Son of William Howard and Jessie (Hungerford) Bender; grandson of Ephraim H. and Sarah (Whitney) Bender; great-grandson of Wendell and ―― (Millbank) Bender; great²-grandson of *Christian Bender*, Sergeant, 8th Regt., Albany County, New York Militia.

FRANCIS THOMAS BENEDICT, Danbury, Conn. (34788). Son of Thomas Clark and Frances Caroline (Nyonis) Benedict; grandson of Gamaliel Northrop and Sarah (Boughton) Benedict; great-grandson of *Gamaliel Benedict*, Sergeant, Capt. Olmsted's Co., Colonel Beebe's Regt., Conn. Militia, pensioned.

HORACE GUION BENEDICT, Roselle, N. J. (35418). Son of Horace Reid and Helen May (Hume) Benedict; grandson of James Lawrence and Christine Grant (Purdy) Benedict; great-grandson of Joseph and Betsy (Brinckerhoff) Benedict; great²-grandson of Timothy and Phobe (Rockwell) Benedict; great³-grandson of *Joseph Benedict*, Captain, Col. James Holme's Regt., New York Cont'l Troops.

FRANKLIN ALONZO BENJAMIN, Danville, Ill. (34948) Son of Milo Washington and Carrie M. (Sabine) Benjamin; grandson of John and Levirah (Hitchcock) Benjamin;

great-grandson of Rufus Benjamin; great²-grandson of *John Benjamin, Jr.*, private, Conn. Militia, killed in service.

MAHLON BETTS, Wilmington, Del. (35011). Son of Alfred and Esther (Warner) Betts; grandson of Edward Tatnall and Williamina (Young) Warner; great-grandson of William and Esther (Tatnall) Warner; great²-grandson of *Joseph Tatnall*, private, Capt. Paul Raulston's Co., New Castle County, Delaware Militia.

ERNEST H. BEVIER, Cleveland, Ohio (35164). Son of Arthur B. and Jessie M. (Aldrich) Bevier; grandson of Benjamin and Anne (Newkirk) Bevier; great-grandson of Simon and Maria (Bevier) Bevier; great²-grandson of *Cornelius Bevier* (father of Simon), private, Ulster County, New York Militia; great²-grandson of *Johannes Bevier*, Member Ulster County, New York, Committee of Safety; great²-grandson of *Conrad Bevier*, private, Third Regt., New York Troops.

CHARLES DANIEL BIDLEMAN, Dayton, Ohio (35171). Son of John and Evelyne (Phelps) Bidleman; grandson of Henry and Prudence (Darling) Phelps; great-grandson of *Winslow Phelps*, Sergeant and Ensign, Col. Asa Whitcomb's Regt., Mass. Militia.

CLARENCE BIRDSALL, Tome River, N. J. (35526). Son of Amos and Miriah Louisa (Holmes) Birdsall; grandson of Joseph and Anna (Stout) Holmes; great-grandson of *Daniel Stout*, private, Monmouth County, New Jersey Militia.

JOSEPH L. BISHOP, Newton Center, Mass. (35391). Son of Robert R. and Mary Helen (Bullard) Bishop; grandson of Elias and Persis (Daniels) Bullard; great-grandson of Malachi and Polly (Littlefield) Bullard; great²-grandson of *Isaac Bullard*, Sergeant, West Medway Co., Mass. Militia.

WILLIAM BASCOM BISSELL, Lakeville, Conn. (34790). Son of William and Mary G. (Bidleman) Bissell; grandson of Amos and Lydia Bridgman (Hall) Bissell; great-grandson of Benjamin and Esther (Benton) Bissell; great²-grandson of *Zebulon Bissell*, private, 8th Co., Col. Phillip Bradley's Battalion, Conn. Troops, prisoner and died in service.

EDWARD FENNELL BLACKFORD, Westfield, N. J. (35322). Son of John Hancock and Isabella (Greer) Blackford; grandson of William Taylor Blackford; great-grandson of *Jacob Blackford*, private, York County, Penna. Militia, pensioned.

CHARLES KENT BLATCHLY, Rochester, N. Y. (35374). Son of Vernon C. and Mary E. (Kent) Blatchly; grandson of Albert C. and Eliza (Guernsey) Blatchly; great-grandson of Joseph B. and Sarah (Frost) Guernsey; great²-grandson of *Soloman Frost*, private, 13th Regt., Conn. Militia.

PERCY DOUGLAS BOARDMAN, Winston-Salem, N. C. (Tenn. 34634). Son of William Kellogg and Mary Kate (Biddle) Boardman; grandson of Daniel Webster and Mary (Young) Boardman; great-grandson of William S. and Esther (Kilbourn) Young; great²-grandson of Harry and Mary (Mix) Kilbourn; great³-grandson of *Ashbel Kilbourn*, private, Colonel Webb's Regt., Conn. Line, prisoner.

JOHN BEVERLY BOSTWICK, New York (33237). Supplemental. Son of John Newman and Ada La Due (Beverly) Bostwick; grandson of Stephenson Thorne and Martha E. (Newman) Bostwick; great-grandson of Elias and Elizabeth (Hopkins) Newman; great²-grandson of Thomas and Mary (Fairbanks) Hopkins; great³-grandson of *Joseph Hopkins*, Captain, Major Wall's Regt., Rhode Island Militia, and 2d Battalion, Kent County, Rhode Island Militia; great⁴-grandson of *Samuel Hopkins*, Greenwich, R. I., Recruiting Officer and Deputy to General Assembly.

LORIN ALPHONSO BOWER, Chicago, Ill. (34943). Son of Gustavus M. and Minerva Jane (Thrift) Bower; grandson of Andrew Jackson and Minerva Jane (Hawkins) Thrift; great-grandson of Samuel Magruder and Sarah Fleming (Cowan) Thrift; great²-grandson of *Charles Thrift*, private, Col. James Wood's Regt., Virginia Militia.

GRAYSON HUNTER BOWERS, Frederick, Md. (34986). Son of Grayson Eichelberger and Clarisse B. D. (Firestone) Bowers; grandson of Martin Luther and Katherine V. (Galle) Firestone; great-grandson of Joshua and Christiana (Stull) Firestone; great²-grandson of Jacob and Mary M. (Hummell) Firestone; great³-grandson of *Matthias Firestone*, private, York County, Penna. Militia.

RUFUS EMORY BOWLAND, Wilmington, Del. (35024). Son of Rufus D. and Jessie (Purnell) Bowland; grandson of John R. and Indiana (Coulbourne) Bowland; great-grandson of John Nairn and Susan (Dixon) Bowland; great²-grandson of *Thomas Dixon, 3d*, Second Lieutenant, Somerset County, Maryland Militia.

CHARLES EDWARD BOYDEN, Fargo, N. Dak. (33014). Son of John and Eliza Jane (Gunn) Boyden; grandson of Azel and Jane (Stevens) Boyden; great-grandson of Ezekial and Hannah (Cook) Boyden; great²-grandson of *Ezekial Boyden*, Sergeant, Colonel Wheelock's Regt., Mass. Militia.

CLANCY D. BOYNTON, Red Bank, N. J. (35314). Son of Cassimer W. and Eunice (Harrison) Boynton; grandson of Gorham L. and Louisa Bassford Boynton; great-grandson of Joseph and Lucy Cary (Alden) Basford; great²-grandson of Elihu and Lydia (Mitchel) Alden; great³-grandson of *Josiah Mitchel*, private, Colonel Baldwin's Regt., Mass. Troops.

ERNEST HARRIMAN BOYNTON, Woodbridge, N. J. (35416). Son of Cassimer W. and Eunice (Harrison) Boynton; grandson of Gorham L. and Louisa (Bassford) Boynton; great-grandson of Joseph and Lucy Cary (Alden) Bassford; great²-grandson of Elihu and Lydia (Mitchel) Alden; great³-grandson of *Josiah Mitchel*, private, Colonel Baldwin's Regt., Mass. Militia.

CARL ROBERT BRADLEY, Westfield, N. J. (35530). Son of Robert Dwight and Arline (Rathbun) Bradley; grandson of John Alden and Hannah (Ashley) Rathbun; great-grandson of Simeon William and Hannah (Rathbun) Ashley; great²-grandson of Elisha and Lucretia (Packer) Rathbun; great³-grandson of *John Packer, Jr.*, private, Conn. Troops, pensioned.

MALCOLM SIDNEY BRAINARD, East Haven, Conn. (34791). Son of Alvah Sherman and Martha Jane (Morse) Brainard; grandson of Henry Stannard and Ursula Bryant (Brooks) Brainard; great-grandson of Roswell and Laura (Sherman) Brainard; great²-grandson of Ansel and Hannah (Dart) Brainard; great³-grandson of *Josiah Brainard*, Ensign, First Co., 4th Battalion, Wadsworth's Brigade, Conn. Troops.

CLARENCE WILSON BRAZER, Lansdowne, Pa. (N. J. 35316). Son of Christopher and Julia Wilson (Stackhouse) Brazer; grandson of George Washington and Mary Matilda (Thurber) Brazer; great-grandson of Christopher and Elizabeth Ann (Park) Brazer; great²-grandson of Christopher and Nancy (Gault) Brazer; great³-grandson of *Christopher Brazer*, private, Major-General Heath's Regt., Mass. Militia.

HENRY WARD BRIGGS, Wilmington, Del. (26312). Son of Cyrus and Anna Louise (Wilson) Briggs; grandson of Luthar E. and Elmira (Robinson) Briggs; great-grandson of Bradford and Wilhelmenia (Lawyer) Robinson; great²-grandson of *Johannes Lawyer*, private, 15th Regt., New York Militia.

LEON ROYDEN BRIGGS, San Diego, Calif. (34737). Son of Thomas E. and Ella E. (Putney) Briggs; grandson of Lowell and Susan (Haskell) Putney; great-grandson of Amasa and Amanda (Paul) Haskell; great²-grandson of *Stephen Haskell*, private, Mass. Militia.

JOHN HENRY THOMAS BRISCOE, Hollywood, Md. (35332). Son of Walter H. S. and Maria (Ford) Briscoe; grandson of Henry A. and Jane (Thomas) Ford; great-grandson of William and Elizabeth (Tubman) Thomas; great²-grandson of William and Catharine Brooke (Boarman) Thomas, Jr.; great³-grandson of *William Thomas*, Adjutant, 25th Battalion, Maryland Militia, member Maryland First House of Delegates.

JAMES HARDING BROAD, Lynn, Mass. (34971). Son of James Harding and Amberzine Frances (Aymar) Broad; grandson of Francis William and Harriet (Harding) Broad; great-grandson of Timothy and Lucy (Smith) Broad, Jr.; great²-grandson of *Timothy Broad*, private, Mass. Militia.

JOHN PEARSON BRODHEAD, Cape Town, S. A. (Pa. 34344). Son of Wessel and Margaret (Mayes) Brodhead; grandson of Jacob and Sarah Meade (Moore) Mayes; great-grandson of William and Margaret (Meade) Moore; great²-grandson of *David Meade (Mead)*, Ensign, Northumberland County, Penna. Militia.

KARL HENRY BRONSON, Detroit, Mich. (35143). Son of Elfred Aris and Catherine (Kanfield) Bronson; grandson of Frank M. and Lydia L. (Amsden) Bronson; great-grandson of Eleazer Brooke and Lydia (Richardson) Amsden; great²-grandson of *Noah Amsden*, private, Mass. Militia, pensioned.

PAUL FRANCIS BROOKS, Boise, Idaho (35102). Son of Charles E. and Catherine (Hanaford) Brooks; grandson of George Augustus and Catherine (Davlin) Hanaford; great-grandson of John and Abigail (Hunt) Hanaford; great²-grandson of Benjamin and Nancy (Cate) Hanaford; great³-grandson of *Peter Hanaford*, private, Col. Thomas Stickney's Regt., New Hampshire Militia.

CHARLES HENRY BROWN, Hoquiam, Wash. (34040). Son of George M. and Kate (Smith) Brown; grandson of J. W. and Catherine (Walker) Smith; great-grandson of John and Betsey (Stiles) Walker; great²-grandson of *Aaron Stiles*, private, Morris County, New Jersey Militia.

JOHN ASHLEY BROWN, Westfield, N. J. (35251). Son of Joseph A. and Annie L. (Holmes) Brown; grandson of Benjamin F. and Martha Ann (Crammer) Holmes; great-grandson of Joseph and Anna (Stout) Holmes; great²-grandson of Daniel and Annie (Chadwick) Stout; great³-grandson of *Thomas Chadwick*, Captain, Monmouth County, New Jersey Militia and State Troops, Member New Jersey Court-Martial.

JOHN PAULDING BROWN, Montclair, N. J. (35543). Son of J. Stuart and Elizabeth Stow (Brown) Brown; grandson of Peter (father of J. Stuart) and Catherine Linden (Green) Brown; great-grandson of Sebastian and Eliza (Bard) Brown; great²-grandson of Peter and Eleanor (Pawling) Brown; great³-grandson of *John Pawling*, Member Dutchess County, New York Associators.

J. STUART BROWN, Montclair, N. J. (35546). Son of Peter and Catherine Linden (Green) Brown; grandson of Sebastian and Eliza (Bard) Brown; great-grandson of Peter and Eleanor (Pawling) Brown; great²-grandson of *John Pawling*, Member Dutchess County, New York Associators.

NATHAN WORTH BROWN, Toledo, Ohio (35166). Son of Nathan and Mrs. Charlotte Amelia (Worth) Marlett Brown; grandson of Nathan and Betsy (Goldsmith) Brown; great-grandson of *Josiah Brown*, Lieutenant, Col. James Reed's Regt., New Hampshire Troops, Member New Hampshire Committee for Ratification of Constitution.

ROGER STUART BROWN, Montclair, N. J. (35545). Son of J. Stuart and Elizabeth Stow (Brown) Brown; grandson of William Dawes (father of Elizabeth) and Martha (Swan) Brown; great-grandson of John and Sarah (Cogswell) Brown; great²-grandson of *Roger Brown*, Corporal, Mass. Militia; grandson of Peter and Catherine Linden (Green) Brown; great-grandson of Sebastian and Elizabeth (Bard) Brown; great²-grandson of Peter and Eleanor (Pawling) Brown; great³-grandson of *John Pawling*, Member Dutchess County, New York Associators.

WILLIAM HAYS BROWN, Jefferson, Md. (34985). Son of Henry C. and Elizabeth (J——) Brown; grandson of James and Sarah (Hays) Brown; great-grandson of *James Hays*, Lieutenant, Second Battalion, Northumberland County, Penna. Militia.

WILLIAM JORDAN EVERMONT BROWN, Washington, D. C. (35582). Son of Albertius E. and Felicia P. (Jewell) Brown; grandson of Hatton and Sarah D. (Shank) Brown; great-grandson of John A. and Sarah (Holland) Brown; great²-grandson of *Nathan Holland*, Subscriber to Maryland Oath of Fidelity and Allegiance; great²-grandson of Nathan and Sarah (Waters) Holland; great³-grandson of *William Waters*, Purchaser of Provisions for Montgomery County, Maryland Militia.

HARRY CLINTON BROWNE, Flushing, N. Y. (Mass. 35383). Son of Isaac Snell and Elizabeth (Tobin) Browne; grandson of Albert G. and Adaline (Babbitt) Browne; great-grandson of Isaac and Susanna (Bradford) Browne; great²-grandson of *Elisha Bradford*, private, Col. Benj. Simond's Regt., Mass. Militia.

ISAAC SNELL BROWNE, New London, Conn. (Mass. 35382). Son of Albert Gallatin and Adeline L. (Babbitt) Browne; grandson of Isaac and Susanna (Bradford) Browne; great-grandson of *Elisha Bradford*, private, Col. Benj. Simond's Regt., Mass. Militia.

HARRY LINCOLN BRYAN, La Fayette, Ind. (33598). Son of David and Mary Ellen (Bennett) Bryan, Jr.; grandson of David and Caroline Emeline (Norris) Bryan; great-grandson of John and Nancy (Robbins) Bryan; great²-grandson of *John Bryan*, Captain, Penna. Militia, pensioned.

GUY HODGENS BUCHANAN, Westfield, N. J. (35544). Son of Elsworth and Clara (Hodgens) Buchanan; grandson of John and Margaret (McConaughy) Hodgens; great-grandson of Samuel and Margaret (Mitchell) McConaughy; great²-grandson of James and Elizabeth (Irwin) Mitchell; great³-grandson of *Nathaniel Mitchell*, private, 5th Battalion, Cumberland County, Penna. Militia.

WILLIAM T. BUNCE, Milwaukee, Wis. (32670). Son of William C. and Mary (Carpenter) Bunce; grandson of William Montgomery and Mary (Elsworth) Carpenter; great-grandson of *John Ellsworth, Jr.*, private, Col. Lasher's Regt., New York Militia, pensioned.

FRANK BARBER BURDSALL, Wenonah, N. J. (35191). Son of Frances H. and Harriet James (Barber) Burdsall; grandson of Robert and Emily (James) Barber; great-grandson of Lewis Mulford and Harriet (Davis) James; great²-grandson of *David James*, private, Corporal, and Sergeant, New Jersey Militia and Cont'l Line, 6 years' service.

HENRY ALLEN BURLINGAME, Pawtucket, R. I. (34916). Son of *Eseck Burlingame*, Rhode Island Minute-Man, substituting for brother, Nathan Burlingame.

HENRY C. BURROUGHS, Md. (34286). Son of H. Francis and Louisa (Ryan) Burroughs; grandson of John and Mary (Robinson) Burroughs; great-grandson of Samuel and Deborah (Johnson) Burroughs; great²-grandson of *John Burroughs (Burrows)*, private, Col. Joseph Kirkbride's Regt., Bucks County, Penna. Militia.

CLARENCE EDWARD BURT, Mass. (29455). Supplemental. Son of Stephen Albert and Clara Amelia (French) Burt; grandson of William Warren and Adrianna Maybury (Horton) French; great-grandson of Ephraim and Mary Betterly (Carpenter) French, Jr.; great²-grandson of Ephriam and Silence (Hathaway) French; great³-grandson of *James French*, private, Col. Thomas Carpenter's Regt., Mass. Militia; great-grandson of Simeon and Huldah (Chase) Horton; great²-grandson of *Solomon Horton*, Sergeant, Bristol County, Mass. Militia; grandson of Stephen Godfrey and Maria (Burt) Burt; great-grandson of Edmond and Rebecca (Macomber) Burt; great²-grandson of *Abiel Macomber*, Lieutenant, Third Regt., Bristol County, Mass. Militia; great-grandson of Dean (father of Maria) and Polly (Crane) Burt; great²-grandson of *Abner Burt*, private, Col. Thomas Carpenter's Regt., Mass. Militia.

LUDLOW DAY CAMPBELL, Millburn, N. J. (35177). Son of George Washington and Anna (Grier) Campbell; grandson of George W. and Eliza Schuyler (Day) Campbell; great-grandson of Benjamin Ludlow and Harriett Jones (Kipp) Day; great²-grandson of Israel and Elizabeth (Ludlow) Day; great³-grandson of *Cornelius Ludlow*, Major and Lieutenant-Colonel, Eastern Battalion, Morris County, New Jersey Militia.

ROSS LYON CAMPBELL, Wilmington, Del. (35009). Son of William W. and Susan (Belt) Campbell; grandson of Hugh and Rachel (Broome) Lyon; great-grandson of Samuel and Esther Willis (Broome) Lyon; great²-grandson of *Jacob Broome*, Draughtsman of War Maps and Delaware Member Constitutional Convention.

HENRY WARD CANFIELD, Spokane, Wash. (34044). Son of Silas Sprague and Matilda A. (Wetherill) Canfield; grandson of Jared and Phœbe (Dart) Canfield; great-grandson of *Dennis Canfield*, private, First Regt., New York Cont'l Line.

DAVID RANKIN CARNAHAN, Saltsburg, Pa. (35300). Son of David and Isabelle (Fitzgerald) Carnahan; grandson of Mathew and Lillie (Laughlin) Carnahan; great-grandson of *Adam Carnahan*, private, Cumberland County, Penna. Militia.

DEWEY SEWELL CARNAHAN, Salina, Pa. (35451). Son of Robert Dudley and Minnie M. (Cassidy) Carnahan; grandson of Adam and Elizabeth (Kunkle) Carnahan; great-grandson of Mathew and Lillie (Laughlin) Carnahan; great²-grandson of *Adam Carnahan*, private, Cumberland County, Penna. Militia.

JOHN ERBIN CARNAHAN, Saltsburg, Pa. (35298). Son of David and Isabelle (Fitzgerald) Carnahan; grandson of Mathew and Lillie (Laughlin) Carnahan; great-grandson of *Adam Carnahan*, private, Cumberland County, Penna. Militia.

ROBERT DUDLEY CARNAHAN, Saltsburg, Pa. (35299). Son of Adam and Elizabeth (Funkle) Carnahan; grandson of Mathew and Lillie (Laughlin) Carnahan; great-grandson of *Adam Carnahan*, private, Cumberland County, Penna. Militia.

HERBERT CRAIG CARPENTER, Atlanta, Ga. (35216). Son of James Givens and Lillie (Fish) Carpenter; grandson of Hugh Logan and Elizabeth (——) Carpenter; great-grandson of George and Jane (Logan) Carpenter; great²-grandson of *John Carpenter*, private, Col. Nathaniel Gist's Regt., Cont'l Troops.

HERBERT BISHOP CARY, Norwich, Conn. (34792). Son of Charles W. and Nancy Bingham (Bishop) Cary; grandson of Nathan Perkins and Nancy (Lee) Bishop; great²-grandson of *Andrew Lee*, Chaplain, Fourth Regt., Conn. Cont'l Line.

ALBERT HERMON CASE, New York City, N. Y. (35047). Life member. Son of Marion and Mary Sterling (Ladd) Case; grandson of Hermon R. and Paulina (Miner) Case; great-grandson of Aaron Newton and Laura (Roberts) Case; great²-grandson of *Aaron Case*, private, Colonel Enos' Regt., Conn. Militia; great²-grandson of Lemuel and Roxy (Gillet) Roberts; great²-grandson of *Lemuel Roberts*, Captain, Conn. Militia.

ROBERT BRYAN CASSELL, Tenn. (27903). Supplemental. Son of John L. and Phœbe Elizabeth (Bryan) Cassell; grandson of Thomas J. and Polly (Kay) Bryan; great-grandson of *Daniel Bryan*, private, Virginia Cont'l Troops; great²-grandson of William and

Mary (Boone) Bryan; great²-grandson of *Squire Boone*, Member Transylvania House of Representatives of May, '75; great²-grandson of *Morgan Bryan*, Juror and Member Rowan County, North Carolina Committee of Safety.

CHARLES EDWARD CATE, Hammond, La. (34814). Son of Thomas Waterman and Courtney Harvie (Palfrey) Cate; grandson of Edward Augustus and Magdalen Davis (Skillman) Palfrey; great-grandson of Robert Jenkins and Camilla (Davis) Palfrey; great²-grandson of William and Lydia (Cazneau) Palfrey; great²-grandson of *William Palfrey*, Paymaster-General and Aide-de-Camp to Generals Washington and Lee.

ARTHUR BARKER CHAPPELL, Rochester, N. Y. (35032). Son of William and Josephine (Gregg) Chappell; grandson of Benjamin and Gulielma Lester Penn (Carpenter) Gregg; great-grandson of Jonathan and Sylvia (Lewis) Gregg; great²-grandson of *James Gregg*, Captain, First and Third Regts., New York Militia and State Troops.

CHARLES ROBERT CHURCHILL, La. (17463). Supplemental. Son of Charles H. and Martha (Thorn) Churchill; grandson of Robert Herman and Mary Ann (Durando) Thorn; great-grandson of Adam van Slycke and Sara (Grote or Groot) Thorn; great²-grandson of *Samuel Thorn*, Second Lieutenant, Albany County Rangers and First Regt., New York Line.

HENRY FULLER CLAPP, Fargo, N. Dak. (33015). Son of William Joshua and Alice (Stevens) Clapp; grandson of George Leavitt and Harriett (Fuller) Clapp; great-grandson of Joshua and Fanny (Smith) Clapp; great²-grandson of *Joshua Clapp*, Lieutenant, Col. Michael Jackson's Regt., Mass. Militia.

CANTWELL CLARK, Wilmington, Del. (35014). Son of Delaware and Harriette Hooker (Curtis) Clark; grandson of Frederick Agustus and Harriette L. (Hurd) Curtis; great-grandson of William and Sarah Barber (Hooker) Hurd; great²-grandson of *Zibeon Hooker*, Lieutenant, Fifth Regt., Mass. Cont'l Troops.

CHARLES CLARK, Westfield, N. J. (35311). Son of Charles Richard and Irene (Lambert) Clark; grandson of Charles and Mary Ann (Haff) Clark; great-grandson of Samuel Yeomans and Rachel (——) Clark; great²-grandson of *Charles Clark*, Ensign, Essex County, New Jersey Militia and State Troops.

EDWIN CLARK, Minneapolis, Minn. (33519). Son of John and Abigail (Mitchell) Clark; grandson of *John Clark*, private, New Hampshire Militia, widow pensioned.

GEORGE ALBERT CLARK, Westfield, N. J. (35312). Son of Joseph Hines and Mary Elizabeth (French) Clark; grandson of Robert and Phebe (Mooney) French; great-grandson of Isaac and Mary L. (Davis) French; great²-grandson of *Jacob Davis*, private, Essex County, New Jersey Militia, pensioned.

JAMES MONTGOMERY CLARK, Charleston, W. Va. (N. J. 35541). Son of James Lawrence and Hannah Margaret (Johnston) Clark; grandson of Andrew Hetfield and Rebecca (Miller) Clark; great-grandson of *William Clark*, private, Essex County, New Jersey Militia; great²-grandson of *Charles Clark*, Ensign, Essex County, New Jersey Militia.

JAMES OLIVER CLARK, Westfield, N. J. (35194). Son of Mathias and Mary Ann (Miller) Clark; grandson of Samuel Yeomans and Rachel (——) Clark; great-grandson of *Charles Clark*, Ensign, Captain Craig's Co., Essex County, New Jersey Militia.

LINCOLN ROBINSON CLARK, Westfield, N. J. (35409). Son of Abraham Lincoln and Bernetta Boyd (Smucker) Clark; grandson of Amos and Elizabeth Robinson (Hunter) Clark; great-grandson of Luther and Elizabeth (Lincoln) Hunter; great²-grandson of Stephen Lincoln, private, Bristol County, Mass. Militia.

WILLIAM W. CLARK, Riggelsville, Pa. (N. J. 35425). Son of Richmond and Ann (Burk) Clark; grandson of *Jeremiah Clark*, private, Buck's County, Penna. Militia.

JOSEPH THOMAS CLEGG, Siloam Spring, Ark. (31769). Son of Thomas and Rebecca (Lasater) Clegg; grandson of Thomas and Bridget (Polk) Clegg; great-grandson of *William Polk*, Captain, Accomac County, Virginia Militia.

WILLIAM WALLACE COE, Westfield, N. J. (35189). Son of Silas P. and Saphronia (Woodward) Coe; grandson of John Kerr and Isabella (Sinkey) Coe; great-grandson of Silas and Martha (Walters) Coe; great²-grandson of *Ebenezer Coe*, Lieutenant, Col. George Baird's Regt., Penna. Line, pensioned.

EDWIN COFFIN, Boston, Mass. (35381). Son of Edwin and Caroline (Norton) Coffin; grandson of Richard E. and Jane Ann (Cottle) Norton; great-grandson of Thomas and Louisa (Lovisa) (Adams) Norton; great²-grandson of James and Dinah (Adams) Adams; great²-grandson of *Mayhew Adams*.

MORTON CHEESEMAN COGGESHALL, Summit, N. J. (34875). Son of Giles Hosier and Marianna (Walter) Coggeshall; grandson of Caleb and Elizabeth (Hosier) Coggeshall; great-grandson of *Job Coggeshall*, Captain, Rhode Island sloop-of-war "Betsey."

HALMAGH EDSON COLEMAN, Jersey City, N. J. (35367). Son of William Edson and Mary Jane (Van Houten) Coleman; grandson of Louis Edson and Mary Frances (Wells) Coleman; great-grandson of Alfred and Sarah I. (Kirk) Coleman; great²-grandson of *Joel Coleman*, private, Third Regt., Orange County, New York Militia.

THEODORE L. COLEMAN, Milwaukee, Wis. (32667). Son of John Crapser and Ellen R. (Le Fevre) Coleman; grandson of William and Ann (Conkling) Coleman; great-grandson of Nathaniel and Margaret (Bradner) Conkling; great²-grandson of *Nathaniel Conkling*, Lieutenant, Third Regt., Mass. Cont'l Troops.

DANIEL CLEMENT COLESWORTHY, Westfield, N. J. (35325). Son of William Gibson and Eugenie Irene (McIntyre) Colesworthy; grandson of Daniel Clement and Mary Jane (Bowers) Colesworthy; great-grandson of John and Prudence (Richardson) Bowers; great²-grandson of *Asa Richardson*, private, Colonel Baldwin's Regt., Mass. Militia; great³-grandson of *Paul Wyman*, private, Mass. Militia at Lexington Alarm.

GUY ALTON COLT, Harrisburg, Pa. (35276). Son of John Brewer and Flora Alton (Brown) Colt; grandson of Edwin Noyes and Lydia (Brewer) Colt; great-grandson of Henry and Louisa (Burt) Brewer; great²-grandson of *Gaius Brewer*, Sergeant, Mass. Militia.

FREDERICK PIERSON CONDIT, Westfield, N. J. (35254). Son of George Elliott and Mary Davis (Pierson) Condit; grandson of Isaac Howell and Kezia (Clark) Pierson; great-grandson of Abraham and Elizabeth (Pierson) Clark; great²-grandson of *Jesse Clark*, Wagon and Barrackmaster, New Jersey Troops.

CHARLES R. CONLEE, Denver, Colo. (34362). Son of Andrew J. and Laura A. (Ross) Conlee; grandson of James M. and Elizabeth (Sanders) Ross; great-grandson of Robert and Elizabeth H. (Howerton) Ross; great²-grandson of *Reuben Ross*, private, Fourth Regt., Maryland Troops; grandson of John H. and Mary (Crowder) Conlee; great-grandson of William B. and Elizabeth Wise (Bullock) Crowder; great²-grandson of *William Crowder*, private and Commissary, Mecklenburg County, Virginia Militia.

JOSEPH RICHARD CONNOLY, Westfield, N. J. (35404). Son of William Wallace and Ann (Randolph) Connoly; grandson of Joseph F. and Sarah (Clarkson) Randolph; great-grandson of James F. and Keziah (Kelly) Randolph; great²-grandson of *Joseph Fitz Randolph*, Captain, Monmouth County, New Jersey Militia.

ARLAN WILLSHIRE CONVERSE, Chicago, Ill. (34944). Son of Cleros S. and Katherine Taylor (Jones) Converse; grandson of Lucius M. and Cynthia (Sawtelle) Converse; great-grandson of *Solomon Sawtelle*, private and Matross, Mass. Militia and Artillery, pensioned.

EUGENE TRAVIS CONWAY, New York, N. Y. (35625). Son of Harry Elmer and Jessie (McGeorge) Conway; grandson of D. Laird and Ann Elizabeth (Pierson) Conway; great-grandson of Peter and Elizabeth (Laird) Conway; great²-grandson of *William Laird*, Captain, 6th Battalion, Lancaster County, Penna. Militia.

HARRY ELMER CONWAY, New York, N. Y. (35370). Son of D. Laird and Ann Elizabeth (Pierson) Conway; grandson of Peter and Elizabeth (Laird) Conway; great-grandson of *William Laird*, Captain, 6th and 9th Battalion, Lancaster County, Penna. Militia.

EZEKIEL COOPER, Wilmington, Del. (35022). Son of Richard Broadaway and Mary Fletcher (Sherwood) Cooper; grandson of John and Margaret (Hall) Sherwood; great-grandson of *Robert Hall*, private, Col. Henry Neill's Second Regt., Delaware Troops.

HENRY BOYD COOPER, Marion, Ohio (35169). Son of D. W. and Jane Boyd (Skinner) Cooper; grandson of Elias and Hannah (Lovridge) Cooper; great-grandson of *James Cooper*, private, Morris County, New Jersey Militia.

GEORGE WARREN CORNELL, Westfield, N. J. (35265). Son of Robert M. and Hester E. (Warren) Cornell; grandson of Oliver C. and Sarah (Miller) Cornell; great-grandson of Abraham Cornell; great²-grandson of *James Cornell*, private, Sixth Regt., Duchess County, New York Militia.

JOSEPH WILBUR CORY, Westfield, N. J. (35542). Son of Joseph and Margaret (Mooney) Cory; grandson of Benjamin and Susan (Denman) Cory; great-grandson of Christopher and Abigail (Marsh) Denman; great²-grandson of Isaac and Catherine (Terrell) Marsh; great³-grandson of *Isaac Hendricks*, private, Essex County, New Jersey Militia.

JOHN ROWELL COTTON, Chicago Ill. (35433). Son of Alfred Cleveland and Nettie Ustane (MacDonald) Cotton; grandson of Porter and Elvira (Cleveland) Cotton; great-grandson of Melvin and Hannah (Esterbrook) Cotton; great²-grandson of *Thomas Cotton*, private, 11th Regt., Conn. State Troops; great-grandson of Thomas and Anna (Crafts) Cleveland; great²-grandson of *Edward Cleveland*, Sergeant, Colonel Douglass' Regt., Conn. Militia at Siege of Boston, died in service.

ULYSSES GRANT COUFFER, Jr., Edgewood, Pa. (35453). Son of Ulysses Grant and Helen Maria (Newcomb) Couffer; grandson of William and Sarah Ann (Du Bois) Couffer; great-grandson of Tunis Garret Van Derveer and Elizabeth (Smock) Du Bois; great²-grandson of Benjamin and Williampy (Van Dorn) Du Bois; great³-grandson of *Benjamin Du Bois*, Monmouth, N. J., Chaplain and Minute-Man; grandson of George Whitefield and Mary Eliza (Eddy) Newcomb; great-grandson of Asahel and Lucinia (Sykes) Newcomb; great²-grandson of *William Newcomb*, private, Conn. Militia; great-grandson of Azariah and Harriet Maria (Hooker) Eddy; great²-grandson of Jonathan and Rebecca (Rouse) Eddy; great³-grandson of *John Rouse*, Captain, Col. Morris Graham's Regt., Dutchess County, New York Militia; great²-grandson of Thomas Hart and Betsy (Mills) Hooker; great³-grandson of *Thomas Hart Hooker*, private, Col. Joseph Spencer's Regt., Conn. Militia.

JAMES DICKINSON COWAN, Summit, N. J. (35187). Son of Perez Dickinson and Margaret Elizabeth (Rhea) Cowan; grandson of James Hervey and Lucinda (Dickinson) Cowan; great-grandson of Perez and Lucinda (Foster) Dickinson; great²-grandson of *Nathan Dickinson, Jr.*, private, Col. Elisha Porter's Regt., Mass. Militia, Member Mass. Committee of Correspondence and of Mass. General Court.

PEREZ DICKINSON COWAN, Summit, N. J. (35188). Son of James Hervey and Lucinda (Dickinson) Cowan; grandson of Perez and Lucinda (Foster) Dickinson; great-grandson of *Nathan Dickinson, Jr.*, private, Col. Elisha Porter's Regt., Mass. Militia, Member Mass. Committee of Correspondence and of Mass. General Court.

JAMES BURTON CRARY, Grand Rapids, N. Dak. (33012). Son of William Appleton and Mable (McDonald) Crary; grandson of Ezra M. and Margaret (Bell) Crary; great-grandson of Appleton and Roby (Hopkins) Crary; great²-grandson of *Nathan Crary*; private, Conn. and Vermont Militia, pensioned.

LESLIE SEYMOUR CREAL, Terre Haute, Ind. (35503). Son of Herbert Henry and Jessie E. (Simmons) Creal; grandson of Henry Seymour and Hannah Maria (Gray) Creal; great-grandson of Anthony and Malinda (Williams) Creal, Jr.; great²-grandson of Anthony and Hannah (Seymour) Creal; great³-grandson of *Ezra Seymour*, private, 9th Regt., Conn. Militia.

GEORGE RILEY CROSBY, Caldwell, N. J. (35423). Son of John J. and Mary (Dickerson) Riley; grandson of John J. and Emma C. (Dickerson) Riley; great-grandson of Peter and Mary (Leonard) Dickerson; great²-grandson of Joseph and Unice (Pierson) Dickerson; great³-grandson of *Peter Dickerson*, Captain, Third Regt., Maxwell's New Jersey Brigade.

RALPH HUNTER CUMINGS, Baltimore, Md. (34993). Son of Henry Harrison and Charlotte Jane (Sink) Cumings; grandson of Charles and Emily (Amsden) Cumings; great-grandson of Benjamin and Lucy (Whitaker) Cumings; great²-grandson of *Benjamin Cumings*, private, New Hampshire Militia and Cont'l Line.

JOHN ELLSWORTH CUMMINGS, Keokuk, Iowa (33823). Son of Stephen and Amelia P. (Mohn) Cummings; grandson of William and Catharine (Chambers) Cummings; great-grandson of *William Cummings*, Matross, Penna. Artillery, Cont'l Line.

HAROLD STOCKTON CUSTER, Baltimore, Md. (35327). Son of William Augustus and Anna Mary (Stockton) Custer; grandson of Edward and Emily (Thornton) Stockton; great-grandson of Robert and Nancy (Galbraith) Stockton; great²-grandson of *David Stockton*, Captain, Fourth Battalion, York County, Penna. Militia.

ALONZO WILLARD DAMON, Springfield, Mass. (34972). Son of Davis and Lucy (Damon) Damon; grandson of Elijah and Sally (Sears) Damon (father of Davis); great-grandson of *Peter Sears*, Captain-Lieutenant, Mass. Third Cont'l Artillery.

SAMUEL REED DAMON, Kingston, R. I. (34915). Son of Samuel Chester and Elizabeth (Taylor) Damon; grandson of Samuel Reed and Sarah (Bond) Damon; great-grandson of Samuel and Patty (Reed) Damon; great²-grandson of *Benjamin Damon*, private, Mass. militia, pensioned.

WALTER RAINES DARBY, Westfield, N. J. (35181). Son of John Lambert and Hannah E. (Radley) Darby; grandson of Levi and Frances M. (Decamp) Darby; great-grandson of Aaron and Elizabeth (Hatfield) Darby; great²-grandson of *John Darby*, private, Essex County, New Jersey Militia.

JAMES SAMUEL DARNELL, Frankfort, Ky. (34706). Son of William Whittington and Sarah Jane (Taylor) Darnell; grandson of Randolph Railey and Atalanta (Whittington) Darnell; great-grandson of *Aaron Darnell*, Drummer, Virginia Cont'l Line.

JOHN JULIAN DAVIS, Pittsburgh, Pa. (35462). Son of William H. and Minerva (Jones) Davis; grandson of John Leftridge and Ann (Lewis) Jones; great-grandson of John and Mrs. (Leftridge) Tinder Jones; great²-grandson of *John Jones*, Captain, Sixth Regt., Virginia Militia.

WESTMORELAND DAVIS, Richmond, Va. (35088). Son of Thomas Gordon and Annie L. (Morris) Davis; grandson of Christopher Harts and Nancy Harwood Lewis (Thruston) Morris; great-grandson of *Henry Morris*, Assistant Quartermaster-General and private Virginia Militia.

HENRY HOLLISTER DAWSON, East Orange, N. J. (35180). Son of Edwin H. and Julia M. (Hollister) Dawson; grandson of Benjamin F. and Maria V. (Lush) Hollister; great-grandson of Francis and Silence (Richards) Hollister; great²-grandson of *Benjamin Richards*, Lieutenant-Colonel, 28th Regt., Conn. Militia.

EDWARD FREMAUX DE BEIXEDON, Jr., Brooklyn, N. Y. (35629). Son of Edward Fremaux and Olive Douglass (Cantoni) de Beixedon; grandson of Edward Fremaux and Julia Augusta (Rogers) de Beixedon; great-grandson of Samuel Henry and Jane (Kingsland) Rogers; great²-grandson of *David Rogers*, Surgeon, General Silliman's Regt., Conn. Troops.

THOMAS McELRATH DEBEVOISE, Summit, N. J. (35535). Son of George W. and Katherine Price (McElrath) Debevoise; grandson of Thomas and Elizabeth (Price) McElrath; great-grandson of Thompson and Elizabeth (James) Price; great²-grandson of Ephriam and Cloe (Thompson) Price; great²-grandson of *Nathaniel Price*, private and Matross, Gloucester County, New-Jersey Militia and Artillery.

WILLIAM DUHAMEL DENNEY, Dover, Del. (35025). Son of William and Anna (Duhamel) Denney; grandson of William and Rachel (Raymond) Denney; great-grandson of John and Elizabeth (Cummins) Raymond; great²-grandson of *James Raymond*, Member Delaware Privy Council of '79.

WILLIAM AUGUSTUS DENNIS, Maplewood, N. J. (35263). Son of Theodore Augustus and Mary (Sisserson) Dennis; grandson of John C. and Eliza Ann (McCormick) Dennis; great-grandson of Bernard and Sarah (Sandford) McCormick; great²-grandson of *John Sandford*, private, New Jersey Militia and Cont'l Army, seven and one-half years' service, pensioned.

JOHN FRANCIS DENT, Oakley, Md. (35334). Son of Joseph Hugh and Fannie (Dent) Dent; grandson of John Francis and Lillia (Blackistone) Dent; great-grandson of John Benjamin and Catherine (Petrie) Dent; great²-grandson of John Bruver and Priscilla Dent; great²-grandson of *John Dent*, Member Maryland Provincial Convention.

JOSEPH HUGH DENT, Oakley, Md. (35335). Son of William Barton Wade and Sarah Eliza (Hieston) Dent; grandson of Thomas and Sarah (Dent) Dent; great-grandson of William Barton and Margaretta (Smoot) Dent; great²-grandson of *John Dent*, Member Maryland Provincial Convention.

WILLIS ALONZO DEWEY, Ann Arbor, Mich. (35142). Son of Josiah Earl and Eunice Converse (Carpenter) Dewey; grandson of Enoch and Sally (Cushman) Dewey; great-grandson of Stillman and Lurana (Noble) Dewey; great²-grandson of *Enoch Dewey*, private, Captain Root's Co., Colonel Easton's Regt., Mass. Militia.

CHARLES DOBBROW, Jr., Westfield, N. J. (35408). Son of Charles and Martha Jane (Wilbur) Dobbrow; grandson of Nathan Goodwin and Alice M. (Clark) Wilbur; great-grandson of Jesse and Thankful (Barber) Wilbur, Jr.; great²-grandson of *Jesse Wilbur*, private, Rhode Island Troops, pensioned.

ROBERT HOWARD DODSON, Washington, D. C. (35575). Son of Charles Augustus and Emma Elizabeth (Kind) Dodson; grandson of William Beal and Deborah (Starbuck) Dodson; great-grandson of *John Dodson*, private, First Regt., Maryland Cont'l Line.

EDMUND YARD DOUGHERTY, Steubenville, Ohio (35172). Son of William and Zerelda (P——) Dougherty; grandson of John and Debora (Freeman) Dougherty; great-grandson of *John Dougherty*, Captain, First Regt., Penna. Cont'l Line.

WILLIAM LE ROY DOUGHTY, Atlanta, Ga. 35215). Son of Richard Le Roy and Clifford (Jossey) Doughty; grandson of William Johnson and Elizabeth (McWatt) Jossey; great-grandson of Henry and Hulda (Pope) Jossey; great²-grandson of *John Pope*, Captain, Wilkes County, North Carolina Militia.

GEORGE EDWARD DOWDEN, Washington, D. C. (35586). Son of George Augustus and Martha (Anderson) Dowden; grandson of Charles and Susan (Barkalow) Dowden; great-grandson of Christopher and Mary (Beekman) Barkalow; great²-grandson of Christopher and Martha (Veghte) Beekman; great³-grandson of *Garrit Veghte*, Captain, New Jersey Militia.

LESLIE LEE DOYLE, Tulsa, Okla. (35230). Son of George W. and Alice Vories (La Master) Doyle; grandson of William Lamb and Sarah (Scott) Vories; great-grandson of Levi and Letitia (Chilton) Scott; great²-grandson of George and Mary Ellen (Bull) Chilton; great³-grandson of *John Chilton*, Captain, Third Regt., Virginia Militia, killed at Brandywine.

CLYDE INGERSOLL DRAKE, Newton Center, Mass. (35394). Son of Francis Marion and Sarah Elizabeth (Chadwick) Drake; grandson of Samuel and Eliza (Chapman) Drake; great-grandson of Elijah and Abigail (Stoddard) Drake; great²-grandson of *Samuel Drake*, Captain, Fourth Battalion, Penna. Troops; grandson of Samuel and Sally (Ingersoll) Chadwick; great-grandson of *Archelaus Chadwick*, Corporal, Capt. Micah Hamblin's Co., Mass. Militia; great-grandson of *David Ingersoll*, private, Berkshire County, Mass. Militia, Selectman and Treasurer.

FRANCIS JOHN GEORGE DUCK, Scranton, Pa. (35339). Son of George Francis and Martha Jane (Connolly) Duck; grandson of Francis John and Matilda Helen (Welles) Duck; great-grandson of William Alfred and Lucinda (Tenney) Welles; great²-grandson of Noah and Euphemia (Hoog) Welles; great³-grandson of *Noah Welles*, patriot preacher, and private, Conn. Militia at Lexington Alarm.

MUIR BUEL DUFFIELD, Detroit, Mich. (35128). Son of Bethune and Eliza (Muir) Duffield; grandson of Divie Bethune and Mary Strong (Buell) Duffield; great-grandson of George and Isabella Graham (Bethune) Duffield; great²-grandson of George and Rebecca (Slaymaker) Duffield; great³-grandson of *George Duffield*, Chaplain, Pa. Troops, Associate Chaplain, First Cont'l Congress; grandson of Divie Bethune and Mary Strong (Buell) Duffield; great-grandson of Eben Norton and Rebecca (Root) Buell; great²-grandson of Timothy and Olive (Norton) Buell; great³-grandson of *Ebenezer Norton*, Lieutenant Colonel, 17th Reg't, Conn. Militia; great-grandson of Eben Norton and Rebecca (Root) Buell; great²-grandson of *Jesse Root*, Adjutant-Gen'l, Conn. Troops, Delegate to Cont'l Congress.

KENNETH BERNARD DUKE, Leonardtown, Md. (35333). Son of James Roland and Catherine Carroll (Councell) Duke; grandson of George Montgomery and Henrietta Matilda (Price) Councell; great-grandson of Elijah and Martha (Clements) Councell; great²-grandson of *James Clements*, Corporal, Third Regt., Maryland Troops.

EDWIN BROWN DUTCHER, Upper Montclair, N. J. (35310). Son of Charles Henry and Amanda (Story) Dutcher; grandson of Henry and Jane (Mason) Dutcher; great-grandson of Darius and Sarah (Root) Mason; great²-grandson of Aaron and Sarah (Bird) Root, Jr.; great³-grandson of *Aaron Root*, Lieut.-Colonel and Colonel, Berkshire County, Mass. Militia.

RICHARD THOMAS EASTELL, Pittsburgh, Pa. (35283). Son of Eldred Webster and Catherine Lenora (Kellogg) Eastell; grandson of John C. and Sarah Jane (Whitcomb) Kellogg; great-grandson of Elisha and Catherine Lenora (Bent) Whitcomb; great²-grandson of *Reuben Whitcomb*, Captain, Green Mountain Rangers, pensioned.

BENJAMIN MARVIN EELLS, Rock Island, Ill. (34945). Son of Benjamin M. and Rhoda (Collins) Eells; grandson of Benjamin Marvin and Eliza Ann (Brown) Eells; great-grandson of Jeremiah and Mehitabel (Marvin) Eells; great²-grandson of *Jeremiah Beard Eells*, Ensign, General Wooster's Ninth Regt., Conn. Militia, prisoner, pensioned; great²-grandson of *Benjamin Marvin*, Captain, Fourth Regt., New York Troops.

WILLIS JONES EGLESTON, Helena, Mont. (31783). Son of Marvin and Hannah (Jones) Egleston; grandson of Oliver and Lillie (Atwood) Jones; great-grandson of Hiram R.

and Elizabeth (Borland) Jones; great²-grandson of James and Elizabeth (Gray) Borland; great³-grandson of *John Gray*, Captain, Col. Ira Allen's Regt., Vermont Militia.

HOWARD ADOLPHUS ELLIS, Grand Rapids, Mich. (35141). Son of Adolphus A. and Mattie (Nichols) Ellis; grandson of George W. and Sarah L. (Preston) Nichols; great-grandson of Samuel and Rebecca (Sprague) Preston; great²-grandson of Samuel and Louisa (Abbott) Preston; great³-grandson of *Jacob Preston*, Ensign, Col. Latimer's Regt., Conn. Militia.

GEORGE ARMSTRONG ELLIOTT, New York, N. Y. (N. J. 35270). Son of William Brewster and Mary Lang (Cameron) Elliott; grandson of George Fullerton and Kate Augusta (Brewster) Elliott; great-grandson of William Coddington and Elizabeth (Coleman) Brewster; great²-grandson of Nathaniel and Keziah O. (Smedes) Brewster; great³-grandson of Timothy and Phebe (Wood) Brewster; great⁴-grandson of *Samuel Brewster*, Member Second and Third New York Provincial Congresses, and of New Windsor, New York Committee of Safety.

JOHN CAMERON ELLIOTT, Second Lieut., A. E. F., Westfield, N. J. (35304). Son of William Brewster and Mary Lang (Cameron) Elliott; grandson of George Fullerton and Kate Augusta (Brewster) Elliott; great-grandson of William Coddington and Elizabeth (Coleman) Brewster; great²-grandson of Nathaniel and Keziah O. (Smedes) Brewster; great³-grandson of Timothy and Phebe (Wood) Brewster; great⁴-grandson of *Samuel Brewster*, Member of Second and Third New York Provincial Congresses, and of New Windsor, New York Committee of Safety.

WILLIAM BREWSTER ELLIOTT, Jr., N. R. F. C., A. E. F., Westfield, N. J. (35305). Son of William Brewster and Mary Lang (Cameron) Elliott; grandson of George Fullerton and Kate Augusta (Brewster) Elliott; great-grandson of William Coddington and Elizabeth (Coleman) Brewster; great²-grandson of Nathaniel and Keziah O. (Smedes) Brewster; great³-grandson of Timothy and Phebe (Wood) Brewster, great⁴-grandson of *Samuel Brewster*, Member Second and Third New York Provincial Congresses, and New Windsor, New York Committee of Safety.

JAY AGNEW ELLIS, Girard, Pa. (35459). Son of Milton Eugene and Harriet Louise (Alvord) Ellis; grandson of George Riley and Hannah Editha (Sherman) Ellis; great-grandson of Gurdon and Civil (Gordon) Ellis; great²-grandson of William and Ann (Edgerton) Ellis; great³-grandson of *John Ellis*, Chaplain, Col. Jedidiah Huntington's Regt., Conn. Cont'l Troops; grandson of Gad White and Margaret (Bush) Alvord; great-grandson of Gaius and Eunice (Robinson) Alvord; great²-grandson of Gad and Phœbe (White) Alvord; great³-grandson of *Gad Alvord*, private, Hampshire County, Mass. Militia.

ALBERT ELMENDORF, Grantwood, N. J. (35050). Son of John and Augusta (Schall) Elmendorf; grandson of John W. and Susan (Coin) Elmendorf; great-grandson of Wilhelmus and Catherine (Kiersted) Elmendorf; great²-grandson of *Conradt W. Elmendorf*, private, Ulster County, New York Militia, pensioned.

OSCAR ELMENDORF, Brooklyn, N. Y. (35361). Son of John and Augusta (Schall) Elmendorf; grandson of John W. and Susan (Coin) Elmendorf; great-grandson of Wilhelmus and Catherine (Kiersted) Elmendorf; great²-grandson of *Conradt W. Elmendorf*, private, Ulster County, New York Militia, pensioned.

WALTER BOYNTON ERWIN, Chicago, Ill. (35432). Son of Orlando R. and Mary (Parsons) Erwin; grandson of Henry C. and Henrietta (Cook) Parsons; great-grandson of Starr and Elizabeth (Speer) Parsons; great²-grandson of *Abraham Parsons*, private, Gen. Waterbury's Brigade, Conn. State Troops.

LEE WAYLAND ESTERBROOK, Washington, D. C. (35583). Son of Izaac and Harriet Amanda (Wolcott) Easterbrook; grandson of Caleb and Rhoda (Hedges) Wolcott; great-grandson of Norman and Sarah (Cook) Wolcott; great²-grandson of *Justus Wolcott*, private and Corporal, Albany County, New York Militia, and of Second Regt., Cont'l Line.

WILLIAM HENRY EVANS, Nashville, Tenn. (34632). Son of Harry Williamson and Marie (Horton) Evans; grandson of William Henry and Margaret (Williamson) Evans; great-grandson of David Lewis and Mary (Wyche) Evans; great²-grandson of *Elijah Evans*, Lieutenant, Va. Cont'l Troops, prisoner; grandson of John Davis and Maria Graham (Cannon) Horton; great-grandson of Joseph White and Sophia (Western) Davis;

great²-grandson of John and Dorcas (Gleaves) Davis; great³-grandson of *Frederick Davis,* private, Second Battalion, North Carolina Troops.

JOHN TYREE FAIN, Nashville, Tenn. (34637). Son of Richard Walker and Anne Catherine (Walker) Fain; grandson of Henry Jeffries and Elizabeth (Owen) Walker; great-grandson of Henry and Mary Gibson (Spencer) Walker; great²-grandson of *Henry Walker,* private, Sixth and Twelfth Regts., Virginia Militia.

EDWARD W. FAIRFIELD, Peabody, Mass. (35380). Son of Samuel W. and Arabella (B.) Fairfield; grandson of —— and Esther (Foye) Fairfield; great-grandson of *William Foye,* Mass. Seaman on Brigantine "Tyrannacide" and ship "Thomas."

ARTHUR WHITNEY FALKINBURG, Atlanta, Ga. (35210). Son of John O. and Emily Luella (Jacobs) Falkinburg; grandson of Enoch and Electa (Whitney) Jacobs; great-grandson of Solomon and Lucy (Lyman) Whitney; great²-grandson of *Nathaniel Whitney,* private, Vermont Militia.

OLIVER ATKINS FARWELL, Mich. (28129). Supplemental. Son of Oliver Atkins and Charlotte Louise (Brockway) Farwell; grandson of Daniel Dunbar and Lucena (Harris) Brockway; great-grandson of William Calkins and Mrs. Betsey (Hadley) Sumner Brockway; great²-grandson of *Ephraim Brockway,* private, New Hampshire Militia; great²-grandson of *Jacob Hadley,* private, Col. John Stark's Regt., New Hampshire Militia; grandson of Daniel Dunbar and Lucena (Harris) Brockway; great-grandson of James and Sally (Hodge) Harris; great²-grandson of *Champlin Harris,* private, Conn. Militia; great²-grandson of *Solomon Hodge,* private, 16th Regt., New York Militia.

DWIGHT HUMPHREY FEE, Canonsburg, Pa. (35286). Son of William Huston and Julia (Humphrey) Fee; grandson of Robert and Hettie J. (Tanner) Humphrey; great-grandson of Robert and Rachel (Craig) Humphrey; great²-grandson of *Robert Humphrey,* private, Cumberland County, Penna. Militia, pensioned.

WILLIAM HUSTON FEE, Canonsburg, Pa. (35285). Son of John and Hannah (Quinn) Fee; grandson of William and Elizabeth (Hamilton) Fee; great-grandson of *David Hamilton,* private, Cumberland County, Penna. Militia.

FREDERICK ATHERTON FERNALD, Washington, D. C. (35577). Son of James Samuel Neal and Julia Ann (Sanborn) Fernald; grandson of William and Margaret (Thompson) Sanborn; great-grandson of William and Peggy (Cross) Sanborn; great²-grandson of *William Sanborn,* Ensign, Col. Thomas Stickney's Regt., New Hampshire Militia.

ADINO FABRISTER FILES, Maumee, Ohio (35167). Son of Amos W. and Sylvia Ames (Clark) Files; grandson of Robert and Sylvia T. (Wentworth) Clark; great-grandson of *Shubael Wentworth,* private, Mass. Militia and Cont'l Troops.

HIRAM LAFAYETTE FINK, Westfield, N. J. (35272). Son of Solomon and Mary Magdalene (Minsker) Fink; grandson of Moses and Mary F. (Pfluger) Minsker; great-grandson of Ludwick and Mary Cairns (Kearns) Minsker, Jr.; great²-grandson of *Ludwick Minsker,* private, Second Battalion, Penna. Troops.

EDWARD STELLE FITZ RANDOLPH, Westfield, N. J. (35268). Son of Sylvester and Catharine (Elliott) Fitz Randolph; grandson of Edward and Jane M. (Manning) Fitz Randolph; great-grandson of Isaac and Sarah (Morris) Fitz Randolph; great²-grandson of *Joseph Fitz Randolph,* Captain, Monmouth County, New Jersey Militia.

PEYTON FLEMING, Richmond, Va. (35081). Son of Warner Lewis and Katherine Overton (Christian) Fleming; grandson of James D. and Martha (Pryor) Christian; great-grandson of William S. and Joanna (Pollard) Pryor; great²-grandson of Benjamin and Mary (P.) Pollard; great²-grandson of *William Pollard,* Clerk, Hanover County, Va., during Revolutionary period.

STEPHEN CRANE FORDHAM, Westfield, N. J. (35313). Son of Charles William and Jennie Laura (Blossom) Fordham; grandson of Orrin Sears and Maria Louise (Hardin) Blossom; great-grandson of Orrin and Laura (Fellows) Blossom; great²-grandson of *Parker Fellows,* private, Hampshire County, Mass. Militia and Cont'l Troops, pensioned.

CLARENCE LESTER FOSTER, Somerville, Mass. (35396). Son of Herbert Prior and Lamana Caroline (Osborn) Foster; grandson of Carlos and Lamana C. (Makepeace) Osborn; great-grandson of Simeon and Nancy (Lincoln) Makepeace; great²-grandson of William and Lois (Wilbur or Wilbour) Makepeace; great³-grandson of *William Makepeace,* private, Col. Paul Dudley Sargent's Regt., Mass. Militia.

GERALD SARGENT FOSTER, Westfield, N. J. (35269). Son of Jed Smith and Anna Louise (Chapman) Foster; grandson of William H. and Ann Eliza (Hegeman) Chapman; great-grandson of William and Adaline (Bennett) Chapman; great²-grandson of Joseph Chapman, Jr.; great³-grandson of Joseph Chapman; great⁴-grandson of *Phineas Chapman*, Patriot and prisoner at Old Sugar House.

WILLIAM CHAPMAN FOSTER, Westfield, N. J. (35415). Son of Jed Smith and Anna Louise (Chapman) Foster; grandson of William H. and Ann Eliza (Hegeman) Chapman; great-grandson of William and Adaline (Bennett) Chapman; great²-grandson of Joseph Chapman; great³-grandson of *Joseph Chapman*, Lieutenant, Conn. Cont'l Line; great⁴-grandson of *Phineas Chapman*, Carpenter's Mate, ship "Oliver Cromwell," prisoner.

FREDERICK EZRA FOX, Dayton, Ohio (35173). Son of Frederick Coffman and Elizabeth (Brelsford) Fox; grandson of Frederick Chrisman and Hannah (Coffman) Fox; great-grandson of Daniel Booker and Susannah (Chrisman) Fox; great²-grandson of *Frederick Fox*, Drummer and private, Bedford County, Penna. Militia.

GEORGE JACOBY FREEDLEY, Richmond, Va. (35083). Son of Samuel and Sue (Jacoby) Freedley; grandson of Jacob and Susan (Jacoby) Freedley; great-grandson of *Henry Freedley*, private, Penna. Cont'l Troops.

WILLIAM ST. JULIEN FREEMAN, Atlanta, Ga. (35206). Son of James William and Margaret Ellen Boyle (Moore) Freeman; grandson of James Sydney Charles and Elias Susan (Lawrence) Moore; great-grandson of Daniel Robert and Hannah Ainslee (Brailsford) Lawrence; great²-grandson of Edward and Eliza Charlotte (Moultrie) Brailsford; great⁴-grandson of *William Moultrie, Jr.*, Captain, South Carolina Militia; great⁴-grandson of *William Moultrie*, Major-General Cont'l Army, Member South Carolina Provincial Congress and General Assembly.

DUDLEY PAUL FREESE, Helena, Mont. (31784). Son of Paul Dudley and Etta (Youngs) Freese; grandson of George and Margaret Grover (Babbidge) Freese; great-grandson of *Isaac Freese*, private, Mass. Militia.

HOMER MERRILL FRENCH, Westfield, N. J. (35419). Son of Robert Merton and Georgenna (Frances) French; grandson of Robert and Phœbe (Garthwaite) French; great-grandson of Isaac and Mary (Davis) French; great²-grandson of *Jacob Davis*, private, Essex County, New Jersey Militia.

ROBERT WARREN FRENCH, Westfield, N. J. (35540). Son of Robert Merton and Georgenna (Frances) French; grandson of Robert and Phœbe (Garthwaite) French; great-grandson of Isaac and Mary (Davis) French; great²-grandson of *Jacob Davis*, private Essex County, New Jersey Militia.

CHARLES LEONARD FROST, Grand Rapids, Mich. (35137). Son of Alonzo P. and Nellie (Voorheis) Frost; grandson of Josiah and Hannah Morgan (Smith) Frost, Jr.; great-grandson of *Josiah Frost*, private, Hampshire County, Mass. Militia.

NATHAN T. GADD, Broken Bow, Nebr. (33886). Son of Joseph and Susannah (Rush) Gadd; grandson of David and Elizabeth (Truax) Gadd; great-grandson of Samuel and Elizabeth (Palmer) Truax; great²-grandson of *David Palmer*, private, Vermont Militia.

NOEL GAINES, Frankfort, Ky. (34709). Son of John W. and Elizabeth (Noel) Gaines; grandson of Lawson and Mary (Long) Noel; great-grandson of Silas M. and Maria (Waring) Noel; great²-grandson of *Theodoric Noel*, Chaplain, Virginia Militia.

BAYARD GALBRAITH, Carnegie, Pa. (34342). Son of William May and Bertha (Bayard) Galbraith; grandson of Stephen and Lucy Turner (Goff) Bayard; great-grandson of George A. and Anna (Baden) Bayard; great²-grandson of *Stephen Bayard*, Brevet-Colonel, St. Clair's Battalion, Penna. Troops.

CHARLES DUNHAM GARRETSON, Westfield, N. J. (35198). Son of James and Gertrude Elizabeth (Staats) Garretson; grandson of Henry B. and Hannah (Field) Staats; great-grandson of James and Elizabeth (Brokaw) Staats; great²-grandson of Henry and Elizabeth (Baird) Brokaw; great³-grandson of *John Brokaw*, Lieutenant, First Battalion, Somerset County, New Jersey Militia.

PHILIP LEVIS GARRETT, Wilmington, Del. (35013). Son of Samuel H. and Margaret (Redrick) Garrett; grandson of Philip and Mary (Levis) Garrett; great-grandson of Samuel and Rebecca (——) Levis; great²-grandson of *Thomas Levis*, Captain, Chester County, Penna. Militia, Deputy to Philadelphia Conference of '76.

JAMES ALBERT GARY, Jr., Baltimore, Md. (35330). Son of E. Stanley and Mary (Ragan) Gary; grandson of James Albert and Lavinia W. (Corrie) Gary; great-grandson of James Sullivan and Pamelia Ann (Forrest) Gary; great²-grandson of *Ebenezer Forrest*, private, Bristol County, Mass. Militia.

RICHARD DUNCAN GATEWOOD, Commander, U. S. Navy, Washington, D. C. (N. Y. 35366). Son of Richard and Frances Elizabeth Heiskel (Bryan) Gatewood; grandson of Timothy Matlack and Mary (Chambers) Bryan; great-grandson of Timothy Matlack and Frances Elizabeth (Heiskel) Bryan; great²-grandson of Gary and Martha (Matlack) Bryan; great³-grandson of *Timothy Matlack*, Colonel, Philadelphia, Pa., Rifle Battalion and Member Penna. Committee of Safety.

RICHARD EVERETT GEORGE, Ann Arbor, Mich. (35135). Son of Charles H. and Minnie (Spence) George; grandson of David and Barbara Ann (Straw) Spence; great-grandson of Jacob and Pricilla (Garretson) Straw; great²-grandson of George Washington and Hannah (——) Garretson; great³-grandson of *Jacob Garretson*, Sailor and private, New Jersey Militia, pensioned.

JAMES STEWART GIBSON, N. J. (23798). Supplemental. Son of Wilmot Byron and Helen F. R. (Stewart) Gibson; grandson of John and Sarah (Fitz Randolph) Stewart; great-grandson of Taylor and Rebecca (Ohlrey) Fitz Randolph; great²-grandson of *Robert Fitz Randolph*, private, Middlesex County, New Jersey Militia.

ROBERT FITZ RANDOLPH GIBSON, N. J. (25778). Son of Wilmot Byron and Helen Fitz Randolph (Stewart) Gibson; grandson of John and Sarah (Fitz Randolph) Stewart; great-grandson of Taylor and Rebecca (Ohrley) Fitz Randolph; great²-grandson of *Robert Fitz Randolph*, private, Middlesex County, New Jersey Militia.

CHARLES WALKER GIBFORD, Adrian, Mich. (35148). Son of Edward Bacon and Jessie (Walker) Gibford; grandson of Charles Mortimer and Charlotte Jane (Hodgson) Walker; great-grandson of Elihu Stevens and Mary A. (Dexter) Walker; great²-grandson of Solomon and Charity (Stevens) Walker; great³-grandson of *Seth Walker, Jr.*, Sergeant and Ensign, New Hampshire Troops; great⁴-grandson of *Seth Walker, Sr.*, private, Colonel Bellow's Regt., New Hampshire Militia, Member Committee of Safety; great³-grandson of *Elihu Stevens, Jr.*, private, Colonel Bellow's Regt., New Hampshire Militia; great⁴-grandson of *Elihu Stevens, Sr.*, Member New Hampshire Provincial Congress of '76-'78 and Committee of Safety; great²-grandson of Richard and Lydia Dunnell (Perkins) Dexter; great³-grandson of *William Dexter*, Corporal, Col. Eleazer Brook's Regt., Mass. Militia.

FREDERICK BURT GLEASON, Batavia, N. Y. (35362). Son of John Burt and Nancy French (Woolworth) Gleason; grandson of Isaac and Ruth (Burroughs) Gleason; great-grandson of John and Azubah (Hitchcock) Gleason; great²-grandson of *John Hitchcock*, Lieutenant, Mass. Militia at Lexington Alarm.

ISAAC THOMAS GOLDEN, Pawtucket, R. I. (34917). Son of Herman and Eliza Jane (Henry) Golden; grandson of Thomas Lowrey and Phebe (Probasco) Henry; great-grandson of George and Mary (Lowrey) Henry; great-grandson of *Thomas Lowrey*, Colonel, Third Regt., New Jersey State Troops.

ADDISON SPENCER GOODMAN, Grand Rapids, Mich. (35133). Son of Reuben Smith and Mary Elizabeth (Rodgers) Goodman; grandson of Allen and Clarissa (Smith) Goodman; great-grandson of Reuben and Miriam (Goodman) Smith; great²-grandson of *Noah Goodman*, Captain and Major, South Hadley County, Mass. Militia.

JOHN ALBERT GORDON, Hamilton, Ill. (33822). Son of Samuel and Parmelia (Alvord) Gordon; grandson of Samuel and Ursula (Smith) Alvord; great-grandson of *Daniel Alvord*, private, Hampshire County, Mass. Militia, pensioned.

RANDOLPH LEE GOUGH, Wicomico, Md. (35340). Son of Richard and Annie (Sothoron) Gough; grandson of William Henry and Lucinda (Bean) Gough; great-grandson of Thomas O. and Ann (Dent) Bean; great²-grandson of *Hezekiah Dent*, Captain, 12th Battalion, Charles County, Maryland Militia, Member Committee of Observation.

RICHARD GOUGH, Wicomico, Md. (35341). Son of William Henry and Lucinda (Bean) Gough; grandson of Thomas O. and Ann (Dent) Bean; great-grandson of *Hezekiah Dent*, Captain, 12th Battalion, Charles County, Maryland Militia, Member Committee of Observation.

EDGAR FLETCHER GOULD, St. Paul, Minn. (33518). Son of Lucius Thomas and Esther Ann (Whitney) Gould; grandson of John and Mrs. Augusta (Fisk) Brooks Whitney; great-grandson of *John Whitney*, private, New Hampshire Militia.

S. RODNEY GRAGG, Ohio (27742). Supplemental. Son of James C. and Margaret (Shoults) Gragg; grandson of George Washington and Ruth Ann (Gilfillan) Gragg; great-grandson of Alexander and Elizabeth (Munroe) Gilfillan; great²-grandson of *Thomas Gilfillin* (*Gilfillan*), private, Fourth Battalion, Westmoreland County, Penna. Militia; great-grandson of James and Catharine (Devoss) Gragg; great²-grandson of *William Gragg*, private, Augusta County, Virginia Militia; grandson of Alexander and Sarah Elizabeth (Shotts) Shoults; great-grandson of David and Catharine (Long) Shotts; great²-grandson of Jacob and Sarah (Troops) Shotts; great³-grandson of David and Mary (Wagoner) Shotts; great⁴-grandson of *Philip Wagoner*, Second Lieutenant, Second Regt., Penna. Troops.

GUY WILDER GREEN, Lincoln, Nebr. (33885). Son of Jay Gurley and Ellah Belle (Miller) Green; grandson of Ira K. and Lydia Morey (Field) Miller; great-grandson of Robert Westcott and Lydia (Field) Miller; great²-grandson of *Abner Field*, private, Colonel Arnold's Rhode Island Rangers, prisoner on ship "Jersey."

WINFIELD WARDWELL GREENE, Maplewood, N. J. (35185). Son of Winfield Scott and Harriet S. (Wardwell) Greene; grandson of Stephen and Mercy (Hutchings) Wardwell; great-grandson of *William Hutchings*, private, Mass. Militia for sea-coast defense.

ALFRED AYRES GREER, Dormont, Pa. (34348). Son of Thomas Henry and Priscilla Kerr (Ayres) Greer; grandson of John M. and Julia Stebbins (Butler) Greer; great-grandson of John Baker and Harriet Newell (Stebbins) Butler; great²-grandson of Eliger Goodwin and Mary (Marshall) Butler; great³-grandson of *Isaac Butler*, private, Conn. Militia and Cont'l Troops, pensioned; great⁴-grandson of *Samuel Stone Butler*, Second Lieutenant, Conn. Cont'l Troops.

CLINTON PAINE GREER, Baltimore, Md. (34999). Son of William Stansbury and Laura Jane (Yeatman) Greer; grandson of John Randolph and Laura Ann (King) Yeatman; great-grandson of George Wilson and Mary Ann (Gormley) King; great²-grandson of William and Charolotte (Ryland) King; great³-grandson of John and Mary (Pennington) Ryland; great⁴-grandson of *John Pennington*, private, Second Regt., Maryland Troops, died in service.

JOSEPH TRUNDLE GRIFFIN, Frederick, Md. (34983). Son of William H. and Eliza Jane (Thomas) Griffin; grandson of Charles Edward and Eliza Jane (Dutrow) Thomas; great-grandson of Otho and Harriet (Rawlings) Thomas; great²-grandson of *Benjamin Thomas*, Second Lieutenant, 34th Battalion, Frederick County, Maryland Militia.

CHARLES WILFRED GRIMES, Tulsa, Okla. (35228). Son of Wilson W. and Mary (Hizer) Grimes; grandson of George W. and Mary Ann (De Moss) Heizer; great-grandson of George and Margaret (Consort or Wright) Heizer; great²-grandson of Valentine Heizer; great³-grandson of *John Heizer* (*Hizer*), private, Augusta County, Virginia Militia.

ROBERT GRAY GRISWOLD, Westfield, N. J. (35253). Son of Henry Daniel and Jennie Lee (Dudley) Griswold; grandson of John Elliott and Mary D. (Goldsmith) Griswold; great-grandson of Henry and Nancy (Elliott) Griswold; great²-grandson of John and Hannah (Dudley) Griswold; great³-grandson of *John Griswold*, private and Ensign, New Jersey Militia, pensioned; great⁴-grandson of *Thomas Griswold*, private, Conn. Militia.

GEORGE FISK GROSS, Waterford, Mich. (35145). Son of Jonah and Julia A. (Keeler) Gross; grandson of Micah and Elizabeth (Dyer) Gross; great-grandson of *Jonah Gross*, private, Barnstable County, Mass. Militia.

HERBERT LIVINGSTON GRYMES, Baltimore, Md. (34988). Son of Benjamin R. and Mary Olivia (Johnson) Grymes; grandson of Arthur Livingston and Ruth Eugenia (Haslup) Johnson; great-grandson of Arthur Livingston and Margaret (Smith) Johnson; great²-grandson of *Horatio Johnson*, Ensign, Ann Arundel County, Maryland Militia.

GEORGE IRVIN GUNCKEL, Colonel, U. S. Army (retired), Dayton, Ohio (34600). Son of Oliver Irvin and Marriet (Sutphen) Gunckel; grandson of George W. and Julia (Ayers) Gunckel; great-grandson of Michael and Barbara (Shuey) Gunckel; great²-grandson of Philip and Catherine (Schaeffer) Gunckel; great³-grandson of *John Gunckel*, private, First Battalion, York County, Penna. Militia.

JOSEPH SUTPHIN GUNCKEL, Cincinnati, Ohio (35153). Son of Oliver Irvin and Harriet (Sutphin) Gunckel; grandson of George W. and Julia (Ayers) Gunckel; great-grandson of Michael and Barbara (Shuey) Gunckel; great²-grandson of Philip and Catherine (Schaeffer) Gunckel; great³-grandson of *John Gunckel*, private, York County, Penna. Militia.

MILTON GUNCKEL, Dayton, Ohio (35156). Son of William and Mary (A——) Gunckel; grandson of Michael and Barbara (Shuey) Gunckel; great-grandson of Philip and Catherine (Schaeffer) Gunckel; great²-grandson of *John Gunckel (Kunckle)*, private, First Battalion, York County, Penna. Militia.

OLIVER IRVIN GUNCKEL, Dayton, Ohio (35151). Son of George W. and Julia (Ayers) Gunckel; grandson of Michael and Barbara (Shuey) Gunckel; great-grandson of Philip and Catherine (Schaeffer) Gunckel; great²-grandson of *John Gunckel*, private, First Battalion, York County, Penna. Militia.

PEARL L. GUNCKEL, Dayton, Ohio (35158). Son of Philip W. and Mary Ann (Jones) Gunckel; grandson of Philip and Mary Elizabeth (Loehr) Gunckel; great-grandson of Philip and Catherine (Schaeffer) Gunckel; great²-grandson of *John Gunckel (Kunckle)*, private, First Battalion, York County, Penna. Militia.

WILLIAM SAMUEL GUNCKEL, Dayton, Ohio (35157). Son of Lemuel M. and Rachel (B——) Gunckel; grandson of Albert G. and Hannah (Braum) Gunckel; great-grandson of Philip and Catherine (Schaeffer) Gunckel; great³-grandson of *John Gunckel (Kunckle)*, private, First Battalion, York County, Penna. Militia.

VOLNEY C. GUNNELL, Ogden, Utah (32642). Son of Thomas Allen and Marion W. (Thomson) Gunnell; grandson of John Turley and Elizabeth Redd (Major) Gunnell; great-grandson of Thomas and Susanna (Trabue) Major; great²-grandson of *John James Trabue*, Ensign, Virginia Militia.

CLYDE BYRON HAGER, Everett, Wash. (34041). Son of Amos and Allie Belle (Hood) Hager; grandson of Joseph D. and Margaret (Parke) Hood; great-grandson of Joseph and Jane (Thompson) Parke; great²-grandson of John and Mary (Hagerman) Parke; great³-grandson of *Zebulon Parke*, Sergeant, Third Battalion, Second Establishment, New Jersey Cont'l Troops.

J. ALVAN HALL, Chicago, Ill. (34949). Son of Jonathan and Mary Antoinette (Driggs) Hall; grandson of Elihu C. and Caroline (Jones) Driggs; great-grandson of Elliott and Sabrah (Smith) Driggs; great²-grandson of Sherman and Amarilla (Hotchkiss) Smith; great³-grandson of *Richard Smith*, Captain, Colonel Beardsley's Regt., Conn. Militia.

OLIVER WILBUR HALL, Westfield, N. J. (35414). Son of Edward Harrison and Ida Allen (Ketcham) Hall; grandson of Wilbur Thomas and Caroline Ann (Wallace) Hall; great-grandson of William and Ann (Clark) Wallace; great²-grandson of Samuel Yeomans and Rachel (Clark) Clark; great³-grandson of *Charles Clark, Jr.*, Ensign, Essex County, New Jersey Militia and State Troops.

EDWARD CHARLES HALVORSEN, Brooklyn, N. Y. (35044). Son of Thomas and Minnie J. (Spraker) Halvorsen; grandson of Edward and Olive Antoinette (Fluent) Spraker; great-grandson of Rufus and Maria J. (Ross) Fluent; great²-grandson of Jonathan and Mehitable (Dudley) Fluent; great³-grandson of *Jeremiah Dudley*, private, Colonel Frye's and Colonel Whitcomb's Regts., Mass. Militia, pensioned.

MAXWELL CARSON HAMILL, Terre Haute, Ind. (33593). Son of Samuel Rippey and Martha (Wood) Hamill; grandson of George and Mary (Rippey) Hamill; great-grandson of *Samuel Rippey*, private, Col. Samuel Lyon's Regt., Penna. Militia.

CHARLES NEWTON HAMMOND, Elmira, N. Y. (35046). Son of John Griswold and Salome (Lamb) Hammond; grandson of John and Marrilla (Stull) Hammond; great-grandson of *Dudley Hammond*, private, Conn. Militia; great²-grandson of *Amariah Hammond*, private. Col. Zebulon Butler's Regt., Conn. Militia, killed at Wyoming massacre.

SCHUYLER AUGUSTINE HAMMOND, Milwaukee, Wis. (34361). Son of William Browne and Sophia Cosden (Aldridge) Hammond; grandson of Nathan Browne and Mary Ann (King) Hammond; great-grandson of Nathan and Elizabeth (Browne) Hammond; great²-grandson of *Nathan Browne*, Lieutenant, 20th Battalion, Maryland Militia.

BENJAMIN HUGH HANCOCK, Bluefield, W. Va. (Va. 35087). Son of Benjamin Peter and Sarah Frances (Hutchinson) Hancock; grandson of William T. and Agnes (Booth) Hancock; great-grandson of Benjamin and Fannie (Holland) Hancock; great²-grandson of Lewis and Mrs. Celia (Duncan) Oglesby Hancock; great³-grandson of *George Duncan*, Captain, Fluvanna County, Virginia Militia.

JONATHAN HAND, Wildwood, N. J. (35536). Son of Jonathan and Judith S. (Wheaton) Hand; grandson of Jonathan and Sarah (Moore) Hand; great-grandson of *Nathaniel Moore*, Sergeant, Third Regt., Hunterdon County, New Jersey Militia.

THOMAS HENRY HANDY, Manville, R. I. (34913). Son of Russell and Euphremia (Ketcham) Handy; grandson of Ebenezer and Lydia (Rogers) Ketcham; great-grandson of *Timothy Ketcham*, New York Minute-Man, Signer of Association Test; great-grandson of Daniel and Milpah (——) Rogers; great²-grandson of *Richard Rogers*, private, 7th Regt., Dutchess County, New York Militia.

WILLIAM BURNS HANLON, Pittsburgh, Pa. (35277). Son of William B. and Fannie Fulton (Robson) Hanlon; grandson of J. Johnson and Fannie Jane (Cooper) Robson; great-grandson of Hezikiah D. and Mary Jane (Layman) Cooper; great²-grandson of John and Charity (Sparks) Cooper; great³-grandson of *Richard Sparks*, private and Sergeant, Ninth Regt., Penna. Troops.

ASHLEY KINGSLEY HARDY, N. H. (15922). Supplemental. Son of Silas and Joosephine M. (Kingsley) Hardy; grandson of Alonzo and Sophia (Hill) Kingsley; great-grandson of Samuel and Sophia (Ashley) Hill; great²-grandson of Daniel and Mercy (Pratt) Ashley; great³-grandson of *Samuel Ashley*, Colonel, New Hampshire Militia.

JOHN ALEXANDER HARDY, Whitestone, N. Y. (35351). Son of George Fisk and Johnetta (Beall) Hardy; grandson of John Alexander and Maria (Manor) Beall; great-grandson of William Thomas and Isabella Anna (Alexander) Beall; great²-grandson of John Brooke and Eleanor (Beatty) Beall; great³-grandson of Thomas and Verlinda (——) Beall; great⁴-grandson of *Samuel Beall, Jr.*, Colonel, 36th Regt., Maryland Troops, Member Committees of Correspondence and Observation and Delegate to Maryland Provincial Congress.

JOHN IRA HARDY, Albany, N. Y. (Mass. 35379). Son of Lawrence and Mary (Leahy) Hardy; grandson of Ira and Eunice (Langley) Hardy; great-grandson of Jacob and Hannah (Hardy) Hardy; great-grandson of *Joshua Hardy*, Sergeant, Bradford, Mass. Militia at Lexington; great-grandson of Obadiah and Elizabeth (Boody) Langley; great²-grandson of *John Boody*, private, New Hampshire Militia.

HOWARD ENGLER HARMAN, Major, M. C., A. E. F., Chillicothe, Ohio (35152). Son of Howard Beecher and Elizabeth (Engler) Harman; grandson of Othias and Elizabeth (Graybill) Harman; great-grandson of Jacob and Catherine (Diller) Graybill; great²-grandson of Isaac and Susanna (Roland) Diller; great³-grandson of *Jonathin Roland*, Member Lancaster County, Penna., Committee of Safety and Observation.

HAROLD RUSE HARPER, New Orleans, La. (34817). Son of William Yarborough and Lucie (Le Beuf) Harper; grandson of William Yarborough and Margaret A. (Golden) Harper; great-grandson of R. A. and Nancy (Griffin) Golden; great²-grandson of James and Darcus (Watson) Griffin; great³-grandson of *John Watson*, Captain, North Carolina Militia; grandson of Nelvil and Nathalie (Fortier) Le Beuf; great-grandson of Florent and Edwige (Aime) Fortier; great²-grandson of Edmond and Felicite (La Branche) Fortier; great³-grandson of Michel and Marie Rose (Durel) Fortier; great⁴-grandson of *Michel Fortier*, Colonel, Galvez Campaign.

LEWIS WENTWORTH HARRINGTON, Short Hills, N. J. (35547). Son of Stephen and Sarah Bachelder (Holbrook) Harrington; grandson of Wentworth and Rachel Eunice (Hyde) Harrington; great-grandson of *John Harrington*, Sergeant, Colonel Bullard's Co., Mass. Militia.

FRANK M. HARRIS, Des Moines, Iowa (35600). Son of Dwight James and Mary Elvira (Ingham) Harris; grandson of Nathan (Waite) and Charity Emeline (Wadsworth) Harris; great-grandson of Joseph and Lydia (Harris) Wadsworth; great²-grandson of *James Harris*, Corporal and Sergeant, Rhode Island Troops, pensioned.

ELWOOD HARVEY, Wilmington, Del. (35016). Son of Holstein and Eliza (Elliott) Harvey; grandson of Isaac and Sarah (Banning) Elliott; great-grandson of Cloud and Eliza (Stidham) Elliott; great²-grandson of *Benjamin Elliott*, private, New Castle County, Delaware Militia.

MORTON HARVEY, Wilmington, Del. (35017). Son of Holstein and Eliza (Elliott) Harvey; grandson of Isaac and Sarah (Banning) Elliott; great-grandson of Cloud and Eliza (Stidham) Elliott; great²-grandson of *Benjamin Elliott*, private, New Castle County, Delaware Militia.

THEODORE RISLER HARVEY, Westfield, N. J. (35321). Son of William Lytle and Caroline (Gersbacker) Harvey; grandson of Patrick and Rachel Ann (Lytle) Harvey; great-grandson of William and Catherine Van Dyke (Stout) Lytle; great²-grandson of John Van Dyke and Rachel (Rosencrans) Stout; great³-grandson of *Samuel Stout, Jr.*, Captain, Third Regt., Hunterdon County, New Jersey Militia.

EDWARD PRATT HAWKINS, Somerville, Ind. (33596). Son of Edward V. and Margaret (Pratt) Hawkins; grandson of George Passage and Helen (Ferguson) Pratt; great-grandson of David and Margaret (Passage) Pratt; great²-grandson of *David Pratt*, Sergeant and Lieutenant, Col. John Bailey's Regt., Mass. Minute-Men.

ERASSUS STANSBURY HAWKINS, Brooklyn, N. Y. (35373). Son of Charles Wheeler and Mary Elizabeth (Newton) Hawkins; grandson of Mills and Jane (Rose) Hawkins; great-grandson of Zophar and Mary (Hawkins) Hawkins; great²-grandson of *John Hawkins* (son of Zophar), private, New York Militia and Cont'l Line.

ERNEST CLYMER HAWKINS, N. Y. (34880). Supplemental. Son of Charles Wheeler and Mary Elizabeth (Newton) Hawkins; grandson of Samuel and Caroline Jayne (Rhodes) Newton; great-grandson of Caleb and Elizabeth (Lorin) Newton; great²-grandson of *Caleb Newton*, Signer of Association Pledge.

IRA CECIL HAYCOCK, Wilburton, Okla. (35226). Son of William Harrison and Margaret Washington (Le Grand) Haycock; grandson of George Washington and Louisa (Mills) Haycock; great-grandson of John and Janet (Gunnell) Haycock; great²-grandson of Pressley and Ann (Hunter) Gunnell; great³-grandson of John and Jane (Broadwater) Hunter; great⁴-grandson of *Charles Broadwater*, Member Virginia General Assembly from Fairfax County.

WARREN LOWELL HEAP, Washington, D. C. (34098). Son of John Preble and Alta Adeline (—) Heap; grandson of George Washington and Elizabeth Jones (Fisk) Heap; great-grandson of Abraham J. and Artimeta (Hurd) Fisk; great²-grandson of *Robert Fisk*, Sergeant, Ninth Regt., Mass. Troops, 8 years service, pensioned.

JOHN HUNT HENDRICKSON, Portland, Ore. (35054). Son of John David and Louise (Hunt) Hendrickson; grandson of David Boyd and Mary Ann Henshaw (Gorrell) Hunt; great-grandson of William and Isabella Jane (Henshaw) Gorrell; great²-grandson of Levi and Ann (McConnell) Henshaw; great³-grandson of *William Henshaw*, Lieutenant, Col. Stephenson's Virginia Regt., and Morgan's Virginia Riflemen.

NICHOLAS GOLDSBOROUGH HENRY, Washington, D. C. (35581). Son of Francis Jenkins and Willimena E. (Goldsborough) Henry; grandson of John Campbell and Mary (Steele) Henry; great-grandson of *John Henry*, Member Maryland State Council and of Continental Congress.

THOMAS JEFFERSON BARKLEY HERSHEY, Keesport, Pa. (35287). Son of Lewis and liza Adaline (Cunningham) Hershey; grandson of Jacob and Catharine (Wollet) Hershey; great-grandson of *Christian Hershey*, private, Third Battalion Lancaster County, Penna., Militia.

JAMES STARR HEWSON, Newark, N. J. (35192). Son of Theodore Crowell and Elizabeth Woodruff (Donnington) Hewson; grandson of James and Desire (Crowell) Hewson; great-grandson of James and Martha (—) Hewson; great²-grandson of *John Hewson*, Captain, Second Regt., Philadelphia, Penna. Militia.

ALFRED HADLEY HIATT, Peoria, Ill. (35431). Son of Alfred H. and Mary Ann (Bowman) Hiatt; grandson of Amer and Achsah (Willis) Hiatt; great-grandson of Joel and Hannah (Jessop) Willis; great²-grandson of *William Willis*, private, York County, Penna. Militia.

JOHN JAMES HIGH, Westfield, N. J. (35256). Son of Linus and Mary L. (Taylor) High; grandson of Aaron and Jane Dehart (Woodruff) Taylor; great-grandson of Robert and Euphemia (High) Woodruff; great²-grandson of *Josiah Woodruff*, private, Essex County, N. J. Militia; grandson of John and Sarah (Meeker) High; great-grandson of James and Hannah (Foster) Meeker; great²-grandson of *James Meeker*, private, Essex County, New Jersey Militia.

CLARENCE EDWARD HILL, Mass. (34240). Supplemental. Son of William Gilbert and Kate C. (Thompson) Hill; grandson of James and Sarah (Converse) Hill; great-grandson of Ebenezer and Betsey (Whittemore) Hill; great²-grandson of *William Whittemore*, private, Eleventh Regt., Conn. Cont'l Line; great-grandson of Elisha and Betsey (Wheaton) Converse; great²-grandson of Jonathan and Esther (Whipple) Converse; great³-grandson of *Benijah Whipple*, Captain, Gloucester County, Rhode Island Militia.

MALCOLM WESTCOTT HILL, Baltimore, Md. (34980). Son of Thomas and Harriett Louisa (Westcott) Hill; grandson of George Burgin and Mary Ann (Hynson) Westcott; great-grandson of *Samuel Westcott*, Captain, Cumberland County, New Jersey Militia.

LEMUEL SERRELL HILLMAN, Grand Rapids, Mich. (35134). Son of William and Emma Louise (Bell) Hillman; grandson of George Washington and Mary Augusta (Bull) Hillman; great-grandson of James Madison and Rachel Anne (Guion) Bull; great^2-grandson of Monmouth and Anne (Lyon) Guion; great^3-grandson of *Benjamin Lyon*, private, Benedict's Regt., Associated Exempts, New York Militia.

EDWYN WILLIAMS HOBBS, Ogden, Utah (32641). Son of John Frew and Cora (Williams) Hobbs; grandson of George Washington and Abby (Ferguson) Williams; great-grandson of Elisha and Nancy (Whitney) Ferguson; great^2-grandson of *Joshua Whitney*, Ensign, Eighth Regt., Conn. Troops.

CHRISTOPHER ELMER HOBSON, Westfield, N. J. (35424). Son of Christopher and Bertha (Woodruff) Hobson; grandson of Wilford Baker and Mary Elizabeth (Van Nosdall) Woodruff; great-grandson of Robert and Elizabeth (Baker) Woodruff; great^2-grandson of Hedges and Charlotte M. (Crane) Baker; great^3-grandson of *Daniel Baker*, Sergeant and Ensign, New Jersey Militia and State Troops.

RUSSELL HOWARD HOFFMAN, Newark, N. J. (35176). Son of William R. and Eva (Dalrymple) Hoffman; grandson of Isaac A. and Catherine (Kuhl) Hoffman; great-grandson of Peter J. and Sarah Ann (Aller) Hoffman; great^2-grandson of John P. and Jane (Mathias or Matthews) Hoffman; great^3-grandson of Peter and Mary (Willett) Hoffman; great^4-grandson of *John Hoffman*, private, Morris County, New Jersey Militia.

GEORGE VERNON HOGAN, Catonsville, Md. (35329). Son of Robert G. and Cornelia S. (Heslep) Hogan; grandson of Lewis Buckner and Grizelda A. (Seat) Heslep; great-grandson of Robert and Martha (Gilchrist) Seat; great^2-grandson of Allen and Dorothy (Lane) Gilchrist; great^3-grandson of *Joel Lane*, Member North Carolina Provincial Congress of '75 and '76 and of State Senate.

WILLIS HOLIMAN, Martinsville, Ind. (33592). Son of David W. and Mary (Hobson) Holiman; grandson of John W. and Jane (Todd) Hobson; great-grandson of Jonathan and Jane (Dodds) Todd; great^2-grandson of *Thomas Todd*, private, Rowan County, North Carolina Militia, pensioned.

GEORGE H. HOLLISTER, Fargo, N. Dak. (33013). Son of J. Edwin and Lucy A. (Gray) Hollister; grandson of Horace H. and Ruth P. (Rich) Hollister; great-grandson of *Josiah Hollister*, private, Second Battalion, Conn. State Troops, pensioned.

ALFRED C. HOLMES, Portland, Ore. (35055). Son of Christopher Columbus and Emma (Windust) Holmes; grandson of Henry and Mary (Wilder) Holmes; great-grandson of *Nathaniel Wilder*, Sergeant, Mass. Militia.

ROBERT JAMESON HOLMES, Boston, Mass. (34973). Son of Stephen W. and Lulu (Jameson) Holmes; grandson of Lucius and Sophia (Bates) Holmes; great-grandson of Nelson and Lucia (Jacobs) Bates; great^2-grandson of Ira Jacobs; great^3-grandson of *John Jacobs, Jr.*, private, Conn. Militia at Lexington Alarm.

BERTRAM GRIGGS HOLT, New York City, N. Y. (35353). Son of Norman and Catherine Amelia (Griggs) Holt; grandson of Orrim and Eliza (Dunton) Holt; great-grandson of Timothy and Esther (Scripture) Holt; great^2-grandson of *Timothy Holt*, Second-Lieut., Third Battalion, Wadsworth's Brigade, Conn. Troops; great-grandson of *Samuel Dunton*, Sergeant, Sixth Co., Wadsworth's Brigade, Conn. Troops; grandson of Austin and Orilla (Dimock) Griggs; great-grandson of *Shubael Dimock*, private, Col. Johnson's Regt., Conn. Militia; great-grandson of Stephen and Elizabeth (Lathrop) Griggs; great^2-grandson of *Ichabod Griggs, Jr.*, Sergeant, Mass. Militia.

JOSEPH BROWN HOON, New Castle, Pa. (34345). Son of Hugh Beatty and Margaret Elizabeth (Brown) Hoon; grandson of Anthony and Mary Ann (Beatty) Hoon; great-grandson of *Henry Hoone (Hoon)*, private, Lancaster County, Penna. Militia.

GEORGE MELLVILLE HOPE, Jr., Atlanta, Ga. (35209). Son of George Mellville and Kate (White) Hope; grandson of John Calvin and Laura Elizabeth (Farrar) White; great-grandson of Jesse Carter and Sarah Gatewood (Shumate) Farrar; great^2-grandson of Abner and Katie (Malone) Farrar; great^3-grandson of *Thomas Farrar*, Lieutenant and Colonel, South Carolina Troops.

WELLBORN HOPE, Atlanta, Ga. (35208). Son of George Mellville and Kate (White) Hope; grandson of John Calvin and Laura Elizabeth (Farrar) White; great-grandson of Jesse Carter and Sarah Gatewood (Shumate) Farrar; great²-grandson of Abner and Katie (Malone) Farrar; great³-grandson of *Thomas Farrar*, Lieutenant and Colonel, South Carolina Troops.

ABRAM HANCOCK HOPKINS, Richmond, Va. (35084). Son of William Leftwich Turner and Mary Ella (Hancock) Hopkins, Jr.; grandson of William Leftwich Turner and Julia Ann (Muse) Hopkins; great-grandson of John and Mary (Turner) Hopkins; great²-grandson of *James Turner*, private, Bedford County, Virginia Militia; great²-grandson of James and Sally (Leftwich) Turner; great³-grandson of *William Leftwich*, Lieut.-Colonel, Bedford County, Virginia Militia; grandson of Abram Booth and Martha Elizabeth (Walker) Hancock; great-grandson of Moses and Frances E. (Glass) Walker; great²-grandson of Elisha and Judith (Kirby) Walker; great³-grandson of *John Kirby, Jr.*, private, Virginia Militia; great-grandson of Benjamin and Elizabeth (Booth) Hancock; great²-grandson of Lewis and Mrs. Celia (Duncan) Oglesby Hancock; great³-grandson of *George Duncan*, Captain, Fluvanna County, Virginia Militia.

JAMES GARFIELD HOPPES, West New Brighton, N. Y. (35960). Son of Solomon S. and Katherine E. (Stitzer) Hoppes; grandson of John D. and Sarah (Heckaman) Stitzer; great-grandson of *David Statzer (Stitzer)*, Matross, Col. Proctor's Penna. Artillery.

ALBERT AURELIUS HORNOR, Lieut. M. C., A. E. F., Boston, Mass. (35376). Son of Sidney Henry and Betty (Mosby) Hornor; grandson of John Sidney and Elizabeth (Johnson) Hornor; great-grandson of John and Judith M. (Roy) Hornor; great²-grandson of *John Hornor*, fitted out war vessels at own expense.

EDWARD SMITH HOSKINS, Baltimore, Md. (34997). Son of John G. and Esther Louisa (Smith) Hoskins; grandson of Edmund and Elizabeth R. (Herring) Smith; great-grandson of Herry and Eliza (Poe) Herring; great²-grandson of *David Poe*, Assistant Quartermaster General for Baltimore County.

ARTHUR ETHELBERT HOWARD, Jr., Hartford, Conn. (34797). Son of Arthur Ethelbert and Mary Adelaide (Bagley) Howard; grandson of Leverett Smith and Ann Elizabeth (Hallock) Bagley; great-grandson of Augustus and Emeline (Bradley) Bagley; great²-grandson of Cutting and Christiana (Barker) Bagley; great³-grandson of *Jonathan Bagley*, Ensign, Capt. Moses Baker's Co., New Hampshire Volunteers.

HARRY BAGLEY HOWARD, Hartford, Conn. (34798). Son of Arthur Ethelbert and Mary Adelaide (Bagley) Howard; grandson of Leverett Smith and Ann Elizabeth (Hallock) Bagley; great-grandson of Augustus and Emeline (Bradley) Bagley; great²-grandson of Cutting and Christiana (Barker) Bagley; great³-grandson of *Jonathan Bagley*, Ensign, Capt. Moses Baker's Company, New Hampshire Volunteers.

LAWRENCE AUGUSTUS HOWARD, Farmington, Conn. (34799). Son of Arthur Ethelbert and Mary Adelaide (Bagley) Howard; grandson of Leverett Smith and Ann Elizabeth (Hallock) Bagley; great-grandson of Augustus and Emeline (Bradley) Bagley; great²-grandson of Cutting and Christiana (Barker) Bagley; great³-grandson of *Jonathan Bagley*, Ensign, Capt. Moses Baker's Co., New Hampshire Volunteers.

CLARENCE RANDALL HOWE, N. Y. (34886). Supplemental. Son of Clarence Herbert and Helen (Randall) Howe; grandson of Enos Bachelor and Caroline (Rose) Randall; great-grandson of Hiram and Nancy (Hanna) Randall; great²-grandson of Matthew and Catharine (Pierson) Hanna; great³-grandson of Joseph and Sarah (Watrous) Pierson; great⁴-grandson of *Samuel Watrous*, Ensign, Third Co., Thirteenth Regt., Conn. Militia; great⁴-grandson of *Ephraim Pierson, Jr.*, private, Capt. Simmons' Co., Col. Wolcott's Regt., Conn. Militia.

CLAUDE WEAVER HUBBELL, Columbus, Ohio (35165). Son of Saunders and Mary Jane (Weaver) Hubbell; grandson of Saunders and Harriette (Edgette) Hubbell; great-grandson of Bradley and Eliphail (Saunders) Hubbell; great²-grandson of *Abijah Hubbell*, private and Corporal, Fifth Regt., Conn. Cont'l Line.

ROY CHAMPION HUGHES, Tulsa, Okla. (35233). Son of John William and Sarah Alma (Champion) Hughes; grandson of Elias and Sophia Jane (Haugher) Champion; great-grandson of Elias and Esther (Strong) Champion; great²-grandson of *Reuben Champion, Jr.*, private, Sixth Regt., Conn. Militia; great³-grandson of *Reuben Champion*, Surgeon, Mass. Militia, died in service.

HENRY ORLEN HUMMEL, Indianapolis, Ind. (33590). Son of Constantine and Bellsina (Wagoner-Heeb) Hummel; grandson of William and Nancy (Wagoner) Heeb; great-grandson of John and Catharine (Zinn) Wagoner; great[2]-grandson of *George Wagoner*, Lieutenant, Third Battalion, Berks County, Pennsylvania Militia; great-grandson of John and Catharine (Zinn) Wagoner; great[2]-grandson of *Jacob Zinn*, Drummer and Fifer, Lancaster County, Penna. Militia.

FRANKLIN BACHE HUNTINGTON, New York, N. Y. (35043). Son of Charles Lathrop and Elizabeth Franklin (Bache) Huntington; grandson of Benjamin Franklin and Elizabeth H. (Cook) Bache; great-grandson of William and Catharine (Wistar) Bache; great[2]-grandson of Richard and Sarah (Franklin) Bache; great[3]-grandson of *Benjamin Franklin*, Signer of the Declaration of Independence, Minister to France, etc.

CARL B. HUTCHINS, Somerville, Mass. (35378). Son of Bion I. and Hattie (Remick) Hutchins; grandson of John B. and Rebecca (Nason) Remick; great-grandson of Samuel Remick; great[2]-grandson of Jacob Remick; great[3]-grandson of *Nathaniel Remick*, Member Portsmouth, New Hampshire Committee of Safety.

WILLIAM SEELY HUTCHINSON, Pittsburgh, Pa. (34340). Son of Elias Smith and Mary (Seely) Hutchinson; grandson of David and Betsy (Hayward) Hutchinson; great-grandson of Jesse and Polly (Leairth) Hutchinson; great[2]-grandson of *Elisha Hutchinson*, private and Quartermaster Sergeant, Mass. Militia; great-grandson of Jesse and Polly (Leairth) Hutchinson; great[2]-grandson of *Andrew Leairth*, private, New Hampshire Militia, pensioned.

BENJAMIN EDDINS ISBELL, De Queen, Ark. (31768). Son of James B. and Harriett (Eddins) Isbell; grandson of Benjamin Farrar and Elizabeth (McCracken) Eddins; great-grandson of Joseph B. and Elizabeth (Walker) Eddins; great[2]-grandson of *Benjamin Eddins*, private, South Carolina Troops, prisoner.

ALBERT MANDIETT JACKSON, Washington, D. C. (34096). Son of Israel M. and Sarah Elizabeth (Parris) Jackson; grandson of Albert Whitman and Sarah Elizabeth (Smoot) Parris; great-grandson of Albion Keith and Sarah (Whitman) Parris; great[2]-grandson of *Samuel Parris*, Orderly-Sergeant and Lieutenant, Mass. State Troops.

RICHARD TAYLOR JACOB, Oklahoma City, Okla. (35232). Son of Richard Taylor and Sarah McDowell (Benton) Jacob; grandson of John J. and Lucy Donald (Robertson) Jacob; great-grandson of Isaac and Matilda (Taylor) Robertson; great[2]-grandson of *Richard Taylor*, First Lieutenant, Virginia Troops, and Captain, U. S. Navy, wounded, pensioned; great[3]-grandson of *George Taylor*, Member Orange County Com. of Safety and State Convention; great[4]-grandson of *James Taylor*, Colonel, Virginia Militia.

CHARLES HENRY JETT, Richmond, Ky. (34707). Son of Shelby Magoffin and Nancy Margaret (Ogg) Jett; grandson of Curtiss and Nancy (Bryant) Jett; great-grandson of Stephen Jett; great[2]-grandson of *John Jett*, Seaman, Virginia Navy.

ALBERT S. JOHNSON, Wilmington, Dela. (1528). Son of Caleb P. and Martha Bush (Young) Johnson; grandson of John and Margaret (Alexander) Johnson; great-grandson of *John Johnson*, Commissary, Penna. Light Horse.

CARROL PAIGE JOHNSON, Grand Forks, N. Dak. (33016). Son of Samuel Paige and Luna Bell (Bowman) Johnson; grandson of Samuel and Lura S. (Fisher) Johnson; great-grandson of Orsamus R. and Ursula W. (Winslow) Fisher; great[2]-grandson of Asa D. and Louisa (Smith) Fisher; great[3]-grandson of Caleb and Sarah (Reuback) Smith; great[4]-grandson of *Jacob Borhave Reuback*, Surgeon, Vermont Militia; grandson of Daniel P. and Emeline (Rowell) Bowman; great-grandson of Samuel D. and Polly (Moore) Rowell; great[2]-grandson of *Enoch Rowell*, private, New Hampshire Militia, pensioned.

FRED W. JOHNSON, New Harmony, Ind. (33594). Son of William Ludrick and Kate (Highman) Johnson; grandson of Zacariah and Catherine (Staley) Johnson; great-grandson of Samson and —— (Williams) Johnson; great[2]-grandson of *Arthur Johnson*, Corporal and Sergeant, Eighth and Fourth Regts., Virginia Militia.

WILLIAM JOHN JOHNSON, East Berlin, Conn. (34800). Son of George Washington and Margaret (Wall) Johnson; grandson of George Washington and Theodosia (Dunham) Johnson; great-grandson of John and Olive (Morgan) Johnson; great[2]-grandson of *Isaac Morgan*, Conn. Commissary, prisoner.

JOHN FOSTER JOHNSTON, Saltsburg, Pa. (35291). Son of John B. and Catharine (Whitesell) Johnston; grandson of Jonathan and Mary (Smeltzer) Whitesell; great-grandson of Jacob and Susan (Yockey) Smeltzer, Jr.; great²-grandson of Jacob and Mary Smeltzer; great³-grandson of *John Smeltzer*, private, First and Fourth Regts., Penna. Cont'l Line.

PAUL JONATHAN WHITESELL JOHNSTON, Youngstown, Ohio (Pa. 35290). Son of John B. and Catharine (Whitesell) Johnston; grandson of Jonathan and Mary (Smeltzer) Whitesell; great-grandson of Jacob and Susan (Yockey) Smeltzer, Jr.; great²-grandson of Jacob and Mary Smeltzer; great³-grandson of *John Smeltzer*, private, First and Fourth Regts., Penna. Cont'l Line.

THOMAS RUGAN JOHNSTON, Saltsburg, Pa. (35289). Son of John B. and Catharine (Whitesell) Johnston; grandson of Jonathan and Mary (Smeltzer) Whitesell; great-grandson of Jacob and Susan (Yockey) Smeltzer; great²-grandson of Jacob and Mary (——) Smeltzer; great³-grandson of *John Smeltzer*, private, First and Fourth Regts., Penna. Cont'l Line.

EVERETT PECKHAM JONES, Hartford, Conn. (35476). Son of William Frank and Mary Louise (Peckham) Jones; grandson of John Edmund and Myra (Brooks) Jones; great-grandson of Simeon and Lydia (Watrous) Brooks; great²-grandson of *Simeon Brooks*, private, Sixth Regt., Conn. Militia.

CHARLES HIRUNDO KATZENBERGER, Greenville, Ohio (35170). Son of George A. and Grace (Miesse) Katzenberger; grandson of Hirundo and Sarah Elizabeth (Briney) Miesse; great-grandson of Gabriel La Fayette and Mary (Wiest, or Wuest) Miesse; great²-grandson of Jacob and Catherine (Dundore) Miesse; great³-grandson of *Daniel Miesse*, private, Berks County, Penna. Militia.

EVERETT EUGENE KEHEW, Bradford Woods, Penna. (34339). Son of Charles Addison and Julia Ann (Taylor) Kehew; grandson of Avery Peter and Anna (Day) Taylor; great-grandson of *John Taylor*, Lieutenant, Rhode Island Artillery.

CHESTER BURTON KELLOGG, Westfield, N. J. (35318). Son of Charles E. and Alice A. (Park) Kellogg; grandson of Edmund Burke and Nancy Emeline (Avery) Kellogg; great-grandson of Elisha and Nancy (Miner) Avery; great²-grandson of J. O. and Elizabeth (Avery) Miner; great³-grandson of *Ebenezer Avery, Jr.*, Lieutenant, Conn. Militia, killed at Groton Heights.

WALTER YOUNG KEMPER, Franklin, La. (34811). Son of William Peter and Monica Reynolds (Rogers) Kemper; grandson of William Peter and Eliza (Hulick) Kemper; great-grandson of Nathan and Mary (Whitaker) Kemper; great²-grandson of *Peter Kemper*, private, Virginia Militia.

GEORGE McALLASTER KENDALL, Buffalo, N. Y. (35045). Son of James Thompson and Mary Jane (McAllaster) Kendall; grandson of John and Jane (Aiken) McAllaster; great-grandson of *William McAllaster*, private, New Hampshire Militia.

FREDERICK CLARENCE KEPPLER, Elkhart, Ind. (35501). Son of Samuel William and Martha Catherine (Strouse) Keppler; grandson of Jacob and Margaret Anna (Peiffer) Keppler; great-grandson of *John George Peiffer*, private, Col. Oshterman's and Potter's Regts., Penna. Militia.

VINCENT STEINER KERANS, Cambridge, Mass. (35398). Son of R. J. and Hattie (Fairfield) Kerans; grandson of S. H. and Martha Hinman (Burt) Fairfield; great-grandson of Seth and Jennet (Smith) Burt; great²-grandson of Josiah and Polly (Hinman) Smith; great³-grandson of *Seth Smith*, Lieutenant Colonel, Col. Enos' Regt., Mass. Militia.

LEAVENWORTH KERSHAW, Tacoma, Wash. (34036). Son of Charles James and Mary Elizabeth (Leavenworth) Kershaw; grandson of Jesse Henry and Eloise Caroline (Clark) Leavenworth; great-grandson of Henry and Elizabeth Eunice (Morrison) Leavenworth; great²-grandson of *Jesse Leavenworth*, Lieutenant, Conn. Governor's Foot Guards and Quartermaster's Dept.; great³-grandson of *Mark Leavenworth*, Member Conn. State Committee for raising troops.

VICTOR ERNEST KEYES, Greeley, Colo. (20101). Supplementals. Son of Melville and Emma (Bassett) Keyes; grandson of Hervey and Margaret (Marlett) Keyes; great-grandson of Peter and Elizabeth (Evans) Marlett; great²-grandson of *Gideon Marlett*, Adjutant and Ensign, Tryon County, N. Y. Militia; great³-grandson of *John Marlett*, Member New

York Council of Safety and First Provincial Congress; great-grandson of Thompson and Mary (Lane) Keyes; great²-grandson of *Cornelius Lane*, private, New Jersey Militia; great²-grandson of *John Kees*, private, Second Regt., Albany County, New York Militia.

CHARLES FISHER KING, Wilmington, Del. (35018). Son of Sampson Slagle and Jane Clark (Jones) King; grandson of Robert Scott and Susan (Slagle) King; great-grandson of Sampson S. and Mabel (Scott) King; great²-grandson of *Robert King, Jr.*, Lieutenant, Lancaster County, Penna. Militia.

HAROLD AVERY KINGSBURY, Wilmington, Del. (35008). Son of Herbert Nichols and Jane Ellina (Avery) Kingsbury; grandson of Albert Gallatin and Elvira (Carleton) Kingsbury; great-grandson of Lathrop and Samantha (Dimmock) Kingsbury; great²-grandson of *Thomas Kingsbury*, private, Conn. Militia.

JENKINS MIKELL LAWTON, Ridgewood, N. J. (35264). Son of Winborn and Ann Lucas (Maybank) Lawton; grandson of Joseph and Ann Lucas (Pearce) Maybank; great-grandson of David and Mary (Simons) Maybank; great²-grandson of *Joseph Maybank*, Colonel, Berkley County, South Carolina Militia.

HOWARD SEBERN LAYMAN, Springfield, Ill. (35430). Son of Sebern J. and Adelia (Ross) Layman; grandson of Elijah and Sarah Buchanan (Crawford) Ross; great-grandson of John and —— (Smith) Crawford; great²-grandson of *John Crawford*, Ensign and Lieutenant, Second Regt., Virginia Militia, prisoner.

COLUMBUS O'DONNELL LEE, Baltimore, Md. (35342). Son of Thomas Sim and Josephine (O'Donnell) Lee; grandson of William and May Lee (Hollyday) Lee; great-grandson of *Thomas Sim Lee*, second Governor of Maryland, '79.

SAMUEL HANCE LEWIS, Richmond, Va. (35085). Son of Lumford Lomax and Rosalie (Botts) Lewis; grandson of Samuel House and Anna Maria (Lomax) Lewis; great-grandson of Charles and Anna (House) Lewis; great²-grandson of *Thomas Lewis*, member Virginia Convention of '75 and '76.

HARVEY R. LINBARGER, N. J. (15969). Supplemental. Son of John A. and Lena (Gilliand) Linbarger; grandson of Jeremiah and Sarah (Hand) Gilliand; great-grandson of William and Nancy (Terry) Hand; great²-grandson of Thomas and Hannah (Marsh) Terry; great³-grandson of *William Marsh*, private, Essex County, New Jersey Militia.

GEORGE WILSON LOCKWOOD, Tulsa, Okla. (35231). Son of Seymour G. and Annie Laurie (Wilson) Lockwood; grandson of George W. and Emma M. (Potter) Lockwood; great-grandson of Philo D. and Polly (Witley) Lockwood; great²-grandson of Ebenezer and Elizabeth (Seymour) Lockwood; great³-grandson of *Timothy Lockwood*, Captain, Conn. Train band and Coast-guards.

FREDERICK DAVIS LONG, Montpelier, Vt. (33841). Son of Daniel F. and Louisa Clark (Felton) Long; grandson of Artemas and Sally (——) Felton; great-grandson of *Matthias Felton*, private, Mass. Militia.

WILLIAM STOWELL LORING, Dallas, Texas (N. Y. 35375). Son of Prescott and Emma J. (Angellotti) Loring; grandson of David Webster and Susan S. (Leach) Loring; great-grandson of Caleb G. and Harriet (Tuttle) Loring; great²-grandson of Caleb and Mary (Silsbee) Loring; great³-grandson of *Samuel Loring*, private, Independent Co., Mass. Militia.

FRANK CAMPBELL LOVE, Saltsburg, Pa. (35452). Son of Andrew M. and Sarah Jane (Campbell) Love; grandson of Samuel and Hannah (Deery) Campbell; great-grandson of George and Sarah (Carnahan) Campbell; great²-grandson of *Adam Carnahan*, private, Cumberland County, Penna. Militia.

JAMES EDWARD LOVE, Saltsburg, Pa. (35457). Son of Andrew M. and Sarah Jane (Campbell) Love; grandson of Samuel and Hannah (Deery) Campbell; great-grandson of George and Sarah (Carnahan) Campbell; great²-grandson of *Adam Carnahan*, private, Col. Arthur Buchanan's Regt., Cumberland County, Penna. Militia.

EDWARD FARNSWORTH LOW, Westfield, N. J. (35412). Son of Edward Thorndike and Jane Stansbury (Brotherson) Low; grandson of Nathaniel and Ann Elizabeth (Lynde) Low; great-grandson of Nathaniel and Rachel (Oakes) Low; great²-grandson of *Jonathan Oakes*, Captain of Privateers "Hawk," "Thomas," and "Patty;" great-grandson of Nathan and Nancy (Thorndike) Lynde; great²-grandson of Henry and Elizabeth

(Batchelder) Thorndike; great²-grandson of *Larkin Thorndike*, Colonel, Eighth Regt., Essex County, Mass. Militia, Member Com. of Safety and Correspondence.

FREDERICK GORHAM LUCE, Girard, Pa. (34346). Son of Carleton Gorham and Emma (Rockwell) Luce; grandson of Charles Frederick and Eliza Jane (Bessey) Rockwell; great-grandson of Samuel Henry and Esther Mary (Cole) Bessey, Jr.; great²-grandson of Ira and Lydia (Cole) Cole; great³-grandson of *Thomas Cole*, private, Conn. Militia, pensioned.

WILLIAM CARLTON LUCE, Girard, Pa. (34347). Son of Carleton Gorham and Emma (Rockwell) Luce; grandson of Charles Frederick and Eliza Jane (Bessey) Rockwell; great-grandson of Samuel Henry and Esther Mary (Cole) Bessey, Jr.; great²-grandson of Ira and Lydia (Cole) Cole; great³-grandson of *Thomas Cole*, private, Conn. Militia, pensioned.

CHARLES WILLIAM LYMAN, Oklahoma City, Okla. (35237). Son of David C. and Mary (Fitzgerald) Lyman; grandson of Alvin and Margaret (Magee) Lyman; great-grandson of Joseph and Lucinda (Woodworth) Lyman; great²-grandson of *Francis Lyman*, private, Seventh Regt., Conn. Contl. Troops, pensioned.

WILLIAM HEREFORD LYMAN, Chicago, Ill. (34950). Son of William and Martha Louise (Heafford) Lyman; grandson of George Henry and Martha Louise (Bradley) Heafford; great-grandson of Cyrus Parker and Martha Ann (Hodgson) Bradley; great²-grandson of Timothy and Anna (Morrill) Bradley; great³-grandson of *Timothy Bradley*, private, Colonel Gerrish's Regt., New Hampshire Militia.

HENRY WARD LYNDALL, Wilmington, Del. (35650). Son of Henry Ward Beecher and Margaret Matilda (Barnard) Lyndall; grandson of Stephen Flanigan and Catherine Ann (Stoughton) Lyndall; great-grandson of Rowland and Jane (Brady) Stoughton; great²-grandson of John and Jane (McCall) Brady; great³-grandson of *John Brady*, Captain, 12th Regt., Penna. Cont'l Line, killed.

WILLIAM RIDGWAY LYNDE, Westfield, N. J. (35532). Son of Henry and Jennie (Ridgeway) Lynde; grandson of William and Mary (Stimson) Lynde; great-grandson of Henry Bowen and Rebecca (Pond) Simpson; great²-grandson of *George Stimson*, private, Middlesex County, Mass. Militia.

NATHANIEL C. LYON, Marblehead, Mass. (34974). Son of Samuel Merritt and Susan Tucker (Martin) Lyon; grandson of Thomas and Hannah (Tucker) Martin; great-grandson of *Nicholas Tucker*, private, Mass. Militia for sea-coast defense, prisoner.

RALPH McKAY LYTLE, Saltsburg, Pa. (35294). Son of William Calvin and Malinda Jane (Elrick) Lytle; grandson of Samuel Gordon and Eliza Jane (Hunter) Elrick; great-grandson of Frederick and Margaret (Katon) Elrick; great²-grandson of *George Elrick*, private, Count Von Ottendorff's Regt., Penna. Cont'l Line, Member Committee of Inspection and Observation.

HENRY DALLAS McCABE, Pittsburgh, Pa. (34349). Son of James Harvey and Arabella (Sayre) McCabe, Jr.; grandson of James Harvey and Dorcas (Reed) McCabe; great-grandson of James and Jane (Vance) McCabe; great²-grandson of *Robert Vance*, Captain, Ninth Regt., Virginia Troops.

HOWARD H. McCALL, JR., Atlanta, Ga. (35207). Son of Howard H. and Ettie (Tidwell) McCall; grandson of Reuben Westmoreland and Elizabeth Hale (Judson) Tidwell; great-grandson of David M. and Sarah Folsom (Hale) Judson; great²-grandson of Eliphalet and Ann (Stewart) Hale; great³-grandson of *Oliver Hale, Jr.*, Lieutenant, Mass. Militia; great⁴-grandson of *Oliver Hale*, private, Mass. Militia; great⁴-grandson of *Eliphalet Coffin*, private, Mass. Militia at Siege of Boston.

DONALD STEVENSON McCHESNEY, Syracuse, N. Y. (35035). Son of Francis H. and Jenevieve (Stevenson) McChesney; grandson of Alonzo and Emily C. (Lawrence) McChesney; great-grandson of Francis and Mary Angeline (Betts) McChesney; great²-grandson of Joseph and Katherine M. (Shook) McChesney; great³-grandson of *Hugh McChesney*, private, Third Regt., Albany County, New York Militia.

GEORGE BEALL McCLEERY, Frederick, Md. (34984). Son of Perry Beall and Mary Jane (Doub) McCleery; grandson of Robert and Rebecca (Beall) McCleery; great-grandson of *Elisha Beall*, Lieutenant and Captain, First Battalion, Maryland "Flying Camp."

EDWARD DAVISON MacCOLLOM, Boston, Mass. (35377). Son of A. Goodrich and Ann Judson (Davison) MacCollom; grandson of Alexander and Sarah Goodrich (Kimball)

MacCollom; great-grandson of *Samuel Kimball*, Second Lieutenant, Lunenburg, Mass. Militia.

WILLIAM ROSS McCOMMON, Pittsburgh, Pa. (35455). Son of James Henry and Sarah Margaret (Evans) McCommon; grandson of Samuel and Isabella (Ross) McCommon; great-grandson of Abram and Hannah (McConnell) Ross; great²-grandson of Hugh and Rebecca (Whiteside) McConnell; great²-grandson of *Thomas Whiteside*, Captain, Col. Thomas Porter's Battalion, Penna. Militia.

HUNTER McDONALD, Nashville, Tenn. (34639). Son of Angus William and Cornelia (Peake) McDonald; grandson of Angus and Mary (McGuire) McDonald; great-grandson of *Angus McDonald*, Lieutenant-Colonel, Frederick County, Virginia Militia, Member Virginia Committee of Safety; grandson of Humphrey and Ann Linton (Lane) Peake; great-grandson of *William Lane*, Captain, 10th and 14th Regts., Virginia Militia.

JAMES CLARK McGREW, Washington, D. C. (35579). Son of George Harrison and Anna Julia (Lore) McGrew; grandson of James Clark and Persis (Hogans) McGrew; great-grandson of Harrison and Jane (McCullum) Hagans; great²-grandson of *Daniel McCullum*, Ensign, York County, Penna. Associators.

GEORGE T. McHENRY, Indiana, Pa. (34343). Son of Smith M. and Elizabeth (——) McHenry; grandson of John D. and Sophrona (Scott) McHenry; great-grandson of *Oliver Scott*, private, Col. S. B. Webb's Regt., Conn. Militia, pensioned.

IRA HUDSON McKEE, Homestead, Pa. (35456). Son of Joseph P. and Matilda (McFall) McKee; grandson of John and Susan (Ebert) McFall; great-grandson of John and Johanna (Bennett) McFall; great²-grandson of *Hugh McFall*, private, Bucks County, Penna. Militia.

SAMUEL WALLACE McKEE, Grand Rapids, Mich. (35136). Son of James Blaine and Catherine (Patton) McKee; grandson of Thomas and Margaret (Blaine) McKee; great-grandson of *Andrew McKee*, private, Cumberland County, Penna. Militia and Cont'l Line, pensioned; grandson of Thomas and Margaret (Blaine) McKee; great-grandson of *James Blaine*, private and Corporal, Virginia Troops.

CHARLES MOORE McLAUGHLIN, Atlanta, Ga. (35202). Son of Edwin Hall and Ida Lawrence (Moore) McLaughlin; grandson of James Sydney Charles and Eliza Susan (Lawrence) Moore; great-grandson of Robert Daniel and Hannah Ainslee (Brailsford) Lawrence; great²-grandson of Edward and Eliza Charlotte (Moultrie) Brailsford; great³-grandson of *William Moultrie, Jr.*, Captain, South Carolina Militia; great⁴-grandson of *William Moultrie*, Major-General, South Carolina Cont'l Troops, Member South Carolina Provincial Congress and General Assembly.

EUGENE CHAPMAN McLAUGHLIN, Atlanta, Ga. (35203). Son of Edwin Hall and Ida Lawrence (Moore) McLaughlin; grandson of James Sydney Charles and Eliza Susan (Lawrence) Moore; great-grandson of Robert Daniel and Hannah Ainslee (Brailsford) Lawrence; great²-grandson of Edward and Eliza Charlotte (Moultrie) Brailsford; great³-grandson of *William Moultrie, Jr.*, Captain, South Carolina Militia; great⁴-grandson of *William Moultrie*, Major-General, South Carolina Cont'l Army, Member South Carolina Provincial Congress and General Assembly.

LAWRENCE HALL McLAUGHLIN, Atlanta, Ga. (35205). Son of Edwin Hall and Ida Lawrence (Moore) McLaughlin; grandson of James Sydney Charles and Eliza Susan (Lawrence) Moore; great-grandson of Robert Daniel and Hannah Ainslee (Brailsford) Lawrence; great²-grandson of Edward and Eliza Charlotte (Moultrie) Brailsford; great³-grandson of *William Moultrie, Jr.*, Captain, South Carolina Militia; great⁴-grandson of *William Moultrie*, Major-General, Cont'l Army, Member South Carolina Provincial Congress and General Assembly.

MOULTRIE MOORE McLAUGHLIN, Albany, Ga. (35204). Son of Edwin Hall and Ida Lawrence (Moore) McLaughlin; grandson of James Sydney Charles and Eliza Susan (Lawrence) Moore; great-grandson of Robert Daniel and Hannah Ainslee (Brailsford) Lawrence; great²-grandson of Edward and Eliza Charlotte (Moultrie) Brailsford; great³-grandson of *William Moultrie, Jr.*, Captain, South Carolina Militia; great⁴-grandson of *William Moultrie*, Major-General, Cont'l Army, Member South Carolina Provincial Congress and General Assembly.

ROBERTSON BOWIE MAGRUDER, Baltimore, Md. (34994). Son of Robert Bowie and Louise (Robertson) Magruder; grandson of Robert Bowie and Mary (Wise) Magruder; great-grandson of John Reed and Eliza (Waring) Magruder; great²-grandson of John H.

and Elizabeth Margaret (Bowie) Waring; great²-grandson of *Robert Bowie*, Captain, Third Battalion, Maryland "Flying Camp."

DANIEL CARR MAIN, Washington, D. C. (35584). Son of Arthur E. and Lucy E. (Carr) Main; grandson of Daniel Canfield and Harriett (Robbins) Main; great-grandson of James and Susannah (Sheldon) Main; great²-grandson of James and —— (Taylor) Main; great³-grandson of *James Main*, private, 13th Regt., Seventh Brigade, New York State Troops.

VIRGIL SAMPSON MALLORY, North Bergen, N. J. (35317). Son of Eugene Lester and Adele May (Reader) Mallory; grandson of Charles and Lydia Lucina (Sampson) Mallory; great-grandson of Liscum and Cyrene (Davis) Sampson; great²-grandson of *Jacob Sampson*, Sergeant, Col. Samuel Brewer's Regt., Mass. Militia.

RICHARD KIDDER MEADE, Roland Park, Md. (34979). Son of Francis A. and Mattie Benjamin (Mosly) Meade; grandson of Richard K. and Elizabeth (Brown) Meade; great-grandson of William and Mary (Nelson) Meade; great²-grandson of *Richard Kidder Meade*, Captain, Second Regt., Virginia Militia and Aide-de-Camp to Gen. Washington.

FEARSON SAMUEL MEEKS, Washington, D. C. (35580). Son of Samuel Macker and Grace (Fearson) Meeks; grandson of Joseph and Laura (A——) Fearson; great-grandson of Samuel Shaw and Elizabeth (Thecker) Fearson; great²-grandson of James and Sarah (McPherson) Thecker; great³-grandson of *Samuel McPherson*, Captain, Second Regt., Maryland Line.

JOHN LENORD MERRILL, JR., East Orange, N. J. (35401). (Junior member.) Son of John Lenord and Grace (Towner) Merrill; grandson of John Lenord and Elizabeth Tappan (Balch) Merrill; great-grandson of John and Elizabeth (Dodge) Merrill; great²-grandson of Robert and Elizabeth (Dodge) Merrill; great³-grandson of *Robert Dodge*, Lieutenant and Captain, Mass. Militia.

EMMET LEE MERRY, Tulsa, Okla. (31625). Son of David Smith and Jane (Harris) Merry; grandson of David and Margaret (Hale) Merry; great-grandson of Smith and Nancy (Douglas) Hale; great²-grandson of *William Douglas*, Captain, Loudoun County, Virginia Militia.

BURTON WALTUS MELCHER, Milwaukee, Wis. (32668). Son of Frank Robert and Edna Emma (Walters) Melcher; grandson of Louis Christian and Martha Gifford (Dopp) Walters; great-grandson of Henry (Harry) and Eunice Brown (Pike) Dopp, Jr.; great²-grandson of Henry and Martha (Gifford) Dopp; great³-grandson of *Benjamin Gifford*, private, 14th Regt., Albany County, New York Militia.

CHARLES BALDWIN MARBLE, Boston, Mass. (35397). Son of William Crawford and Sarah (Barker) Marble; grandson of Loammi and Harriet (Barnard) Marble; great grandson of *John Marble*, private, Col. Ebenezer Learned's Regt., Mass. Militia; grandson of Biley Gilman and Emeline (Smith) Barker; great-grandson of Noah and Deborah (Gilman) Barker; great²-grandson of *Josiah Barker*, private, Third Regt., New Hampshire Troops.

DAVID JOHN MARKEY, Frederick, Md. (35328). Son of J. Hanshew and Ida M. (Willard) Markey; grandson of Ezra and Laura (Biser) Willard; great-grandson of John and Maria (Shafer) Willard; great²-grandson of *Elias Willialer Willard*, Second Lieut., 34th Battalion, Maryland Militia.

JAMES LAFAYETTE MARKS, Saltsburg, Pa. (35292). Son of Samuel Ferree and Sarah (Fredericks) Marks; grandson of James Turner and Mary (Patterson) Fredericks; great-grandson of Robert and Mary (Linn) Patterson; great²-grandson of James and Guselda (Patterson) Linn; great³-grandson of *Andrew Patterson*, private and Corporal, Cumberland County, Pa. Militia and Artillery.

CLIFFORD DOWNING MARSH, Plainfield, N. J. (35421). Son of George W. and Virginia (Jimerson) Marsh; grandson of Aaron Little and Charlotte (Hand) Jimerson; great-grandson of William and Nancy (Terry) Hand; great²-grandson of Thomas and Hannah (Marsh) Terry; great³-grandson of *William Marsh*, private, Essex County, New Jersey Militia.

CHARLES HALLOWAY MARTIN, Yonkers, N. Y. (35371). Son of Edward and Elizabeth (Albro) Martin; grandson of Edward and Sarah (Fowler) Martin; great-grandson of

Simeon Martin, Captain, Col. Lippitt's Rhode Island Troops, and Rhode Island Adj. Gen.; great²-grandson of *Silvanus Martin*, Captain, Rhode Island Militia.

CHARLES JOHNSTON MARTIN, Jr., Saltsburg, Pa. (35297). Son of Charles Johnston and Sarah Elizabeth (Sipes) Martin; grandson of John and Eliza (Johnston) Martin; great-grandson of John and Ann (Kenley) Johnston; great²-grandson of Charles Jenkins and Cynthia (Geer) Kenley; great³-grandson of *William Kenley*, Penna. Financial Agent.

JOHN BARNETT MARTIN, Pittsburgh, Pa. (35280). Son of Thomas Wilson and Margaret Ella (Penney) Martin; grandson of Jesse Sill and Susan Laughlin (Jackson) Penney; great-grandson of James and Jane (Sill) Penny; great²-grandson of *John Penny*, private, Col. John Daggert's Regt., Mass. Militia at Lexington Alarm.

RALPH EDWARD MARTIN, Westfield, N. J. (35422). Son of Thomas Clifton and Carrie Eugenia (Doane) Martin; grandson of George Wood and Mary Elizabeth (Shattuck) Doane; great-grandson of Leonard and Harriet (White) Doane; great²-grandson of Samuel Dill and Sarah (Sally) (Lombard) Doane; great³-grandson of *Nehemiah Doane*, private, Col. John Crane's Third Regt., Mass. Contl. Artillery.

WILLIAM EMMETT MARTIN, Saltsburg, Pa. (35296). Son of Charles Johnston and Sarah Elizabeth (Sipes) Martin; grandson of John and Eliza (Johnston) Martin; great-grandson of John and Ann (Kenley) Johnston; great²-grandson of Charles Jenkins and Cynthia (Geer) Kenley; great³-grandson of *William Kenley*, Penna. Financial Agent.

HENRY JAMES MASSON, Jr., New York City, N. Y. (35033). Son of Henry James and Sadie (Pancoast) Masson; grandson of Henry James and Fanny Jane (Slawson) Masson; great-grandson of Milton and Prudence (Wood) Slawson; great²-grandson of Elihu and Esther (Case) Slawson; great³-grandson of *Joseph Case*, private and Second Lieutenant, New York Militia and Contl. Line.

FRED CHURCH MASTEN, Pittsburgh, Pa. (35282). Son of Landon and Harriet (Sautee) Masten; grandson of Thomas and Mary (Blackburn) Sautee; great-grandson of *John Blackburn*, Lieutenant, Cumberland County, Pa. Militia.

FRANCIS WELLS MASTIN, Westfield, N. J. (35259). Son of William Francis and Florence Amelia (Wells) Mastin; grandson of James Harvey and Mary Jane (Ripley) Wells; great-grandson of Tyranus and Rebekah (Howe) Ripley; great²-grandson of *Piram Ripley*, private, Conn. and New York Troops and sailor on Conn. Frigate.

REX GEORGE MATTICE, D. C. (34092). Supplementals. Son of George Willard and Emeline Nichols (Fulkerson) Mattice; grandson of Caleb and Julia Ann (Kimble) Fulkerson; great-grandson of Otto and Sara (Ainsley or Ansley) Kimble; great²-grandson of *Able Kimble*, private, Thomas Shreve's Battalion, New Jersey Militia, and 24th Regt., Conn. Militia; great²-grandson of Able and Sybil (Chapman) Kimble; great³-grandson of *Uriah Chapman*, Pike County, Pa., Justice of the Peace; grandson of Freeman Stanton and Nancy (Van Kleek) Mattice; great-grandson of Lawrence and Nancy (Yansen) Mattice; great²-grandson of *Henry Yansen*, private, 15th Regt., Albany County, New York Militia, pensioned.

RAY EDWIN MAYHAM, Captain, A. E. F., Westfield, N. J. (35260). Son of Thomas Creighton and Mary Adaline (Lawyer) Mayham; grandson of Gabriel and Sarah (Durand) Lawyer; great-grandson of Nicholas and Catherine (Bouck) Lawyer; great²-grandson of *Johonus Bouck, Jr.*, private, Col. Peter Vroman's Regt., Albany County, New York Militia; great²-grandson of *Johonus Bouck*, Lieutenant, 15th Regt., Albany County, New York Militia; great²-grandson of *David Lawyer*, Corporal and Sergeant, 15th Regt., Albany County, New York Militia; great³-grandson of *Jacob Frederick Lawyer*, private, Col. Vroman's Regt., Albany County, New York Militia; great²-grandson of David and Catherine (Sternbergh) Lawyer; great³-grandson of *Nicholas Sternbergh*, member Schoharie, New York Committee of Safety; great-grandson of Samuel and Phoebe (Barner) Durand; great²-grandson of *Ebenezer Durand*, private, Col. Meigs' Regt., Conn. Troops, widow pensioned.

ERSKINE BRONSON MAYO, Westfield, N. J. (35306). Son of Warren Spear and Ella Annette (Fuller) Mayo; grandson of Henry and Elizabeth (Eldridge) Mayo; great-grandson of Nathaniel and Hannah (Simonds) Mayo; great²-grandson of *Joseph Mayo*, Lieutenant, Hampshire County, Mass. Militia; great-grandson of Joseph C. and Betsey (Smith) Eldridge; great²-grandson of *Jonathan Eldridge*, Corporal and Sergeant, Col. Parson's Tenth Regt., Conn. Troops.

JOHN TUCKER METCALF, U. S. N., Wickford, R. I. (34912). Son of Harold and Mary Anna (——) Metcalf; grandson of Levi and Georgianna (Tucker) Metcalf; great-grandson of Samuel and Frances (Calder) Metcalf; great²-grandson of *James Calder*, private, Col. Baldwin's 38th Regt., Mass. Militia, pensioned; great-grandson of John and Dorcas (Mathewson) Tucker; great²-grandson of David and Anna (Mowry) Tucker; great³-grandson of *Daniel Mowry*, private, Rhode Island Militia.

WILLIAM PEARSE MICHELL, Jr., Elizabeth, N. J. (35183). Son of William P. and Mary (McIlvaine) Michel; grandson of Albert P. and Anna (Kinzer) McIlvaine; great-grandson of Amos and Elizabeth Shaner (Hurst) Kinzer; great²grandson of George and Anna (Ellmaker) Kinger; great³-grandson of *Nathaniel Ellmaker*, private, Fifth Battalion, Lancaster County, Penna. Militia.

ADONIRAM JUDSON MILLER, Westfield, N. J. (35255). Son of Erastus and Eliza Ann (Badgley) Miller; grandson of Ahijah and Elizabeth (Wilcox) Badgley; great-grandson of *Jonathan Badgley*, private, Essex County, New Jersey Militia, pensioned.

ARTHUR HARRISON MILLER, Major, U. S. Army, Washington, D. C. (34095). Son of Howard and Mary Effie (Akin) Miller; grandson of Anthorny and Jemima (Ackerman) Miller; great-grandson of William and Nancy (Ward) Miller; great²-grandson of *William Miller*, Lieutenant-Colonel, Third Regt., Rhode Island Contl. Troops.

DAVID COCHRANE MILLER, Cleveland, Ohio (35159). Son of William Wightman and Ellen Jane (Cochrane) Miller; grandson of Charles Henry and Martha Elizabeth (Wightman) Miller; great-grandson of William and Elizabeth V. (Hanna) Wightman; great²-grandson of Israel and Demaris (Pendleton) Wightman; great³-grandson of *Joseph Pendleton*, Major, First Regt., Kings County, Rhode Island Militia.

HARRY JONAS MILLER, Westfield, N. J. (35261). Son of Jonas Smith and Ida Linda (Welch) Miller; grandson of John and Peninah Ward (Smith) Miller; great-grandson of *Enoch Miller*, private, Essex County, New Jersey Militia; great-grandson of Jonas and Eliza (Clark) Smith; great²-grandson of *James Smith*, private, Essex County, New Jersey Militia; great²-grandson of *Charles Clark*, Ensign, Essex County, New Jersey Militia.

IRA CARLISLE MILLER, Westfield, N. J. (35271). Son of Adoniram Judson and Sarah Stewart (McFarland) Miller; grandson of Erastus and Eliza Ann (Badgley) Miller; great-grandson of Ahijah and Elizabeth (Wilcox) Badgley; great²-grandson of *Jonathan Badgley*, private, Essex County, New Jersey Militia, pensioned.

JONAS SMITH MILLER, Westfield, N. J. (35190). Son of John and Peninah Ward (Smith) Miller; grandson of *Enoch Miller*, private, Essex County, New Jersey Militia, pensioned; grandson of Jonas and Eliza (Clark) Smith; great-grandson of *James Smith*, private, Essex County, New Jersey Militia; great-grandson of *Charles Clark*, Ensign, Essex County, New Jersey Militia.

EPLER CADWELL MILLS, Virginia, Ill. (35426). Son of Richard W. and Nellie (Epler) Mills; grandson of Chesley L. and Harriet (Cadwell) Mills; great-grandson of George and Pamelia (Lyon) Cadwell; great²-grandson of *Matthew Lyon*, Lieutenant, Vermont Militia, Paymaster of Warner's Contl. Brigade.

DONALD RANSOM MITCHELL, Detroit, Mich. (35127). Son of Ransom Y. and Lydia (Avery) Mitchell; grandson of Amos T. and Sallie E. (Conklin) Mitchell; great-grandson of Benjamin and Mercy (Comfort) Conklin; great²-grandson of *John Conklin*, Sergeant, Col. Luther Baldwin's Regt., New York Contl. Line.

MAURICE LEROY MITCHELTREE, Sharon, Pa. (35454). Son of Charles Irvin and Luella Josephine (Baker) Mitcheltree; grandson of John Irvin and Jane (De Forest) Mitcheltree; great-grandson of Gurshum Vandenburg and Elanor (Dunham) De Forest; great²-grandson of *Abraham De Forest*, Corporal and Ensign, New Jersey Militia, pensioned.

BARRET MONTFORT, Louisville, Ky. (34708). Son of Richard and Henrie (Barret) Montfort; grandson of John G. and Ann E. (Rodes) Barret; great-grandson of Clifton and Amanda (Omsley) Rodes; great²-grandson of *Robert Rodes*, Captain, Virginia Volunteers.

HENRY GEORGE MOONEY, Westfield, N. J. (35531). Son of James H. and Fannie (Hoggett) Mooney; grandson of Elias and Mary (Clark) Mooney; great-grandson of

Andrew Hetfield and Rebecca (Miller) Clark; great^2-grandson of William and Sarah (Hetfield) Clark; great^3-grandson of *Charles Clark*, Ensign and Lieutenant, Essex County, New Jersey Contl. Troops and Militia; great^4-grandson of *William Clark*, private, Essex County, New Jersey Militia, prisoner; great^2-grandson of *Enoch Miller*, private, New Jersey Militia.

HAROLD BRUCE MOORE, Grand Rapids, Mich. (35140). Son of Herman N. and Ellen L. (Deane) Moore; grandson of Gains Shepard and Mary L. (Lyon) Deane; great-grandson of Dwighty and Abigail (——) Dean; great^2-grandson of *Elijah Dean, Jr.*, private, Col. David Brewer's Regt., Mass. Militia.

JOSEPH ROSWELL HAWLEY MOORE, Indianapolis, Ind. (35502). Son of Ezra Lewis and Elizabeth (Bostwick) Moore; grandson of Ezra and Sarah Ann (Lewis) Moore; great-grandson of Ezra and Betsy (Steward) Moore; great^2-grandson of Elisha and Mary (Calkins) Steward; great^3-grandson of *Jonathan Calkins*, Captain, Conn. Militia and State Troops; grandson of Robert and Eliza Jane (Petter) Bostwick; great-grandson of Rufus Hubbell Smith and Elizabeth (Birch) Bostwick; great^2-grandson of *Levi Bostwick*, private, Fifth Regt., Conn. Contl. Troops, widow pensioned.

GEORGE ELGIN MORISON, Lexington, Ky. (34705). Son of George P. and Katie (Elgin) Morison; grandson of J. H. S. and Amanda (Jones) Morison; great-grandson of George and Mary (Wood) Morison; great^2-grandson of *Peter Morison*, private, North Carolina Militia.

WALTER GARY MORISON, Westfield, N. J. (35258). Son of George Lindsay and Ida Ann (Gary) Morison; grandson of James and Susan Jane (Nevius) Morison, Jr.; great-grandson of Martin M. and Mary (Hillyer) Nevius; great^3-grandson of *Simon Hillyer*, private, Monmouth County, New Jersey Militia.

PENDLETON STEWART MORRIS, Grand Rapids, Mich. (La. 34812). Son of Pendleton Stewart and Mary Lillian (Littlefield) Morris; grandson of Harry Innes and Ann Eliza (Stewart) Morris; great-grandson of Isaac and Elizabeth Hugh Tenant (Taylor) Stewart; great^2-grandson of Thompson and Nancy (Oldham) Taylor; great^3-grandson of *Richard Taylor*, Lieutenant, Sixth Regt., Virginia Troops, Commodore Virginia Navy; great-grandson of John and Ann (Innes) Morris; great^2-grandson of *Harry Innes*, Virginia Commissioner of Special Tax and Superintendent of Lead Mines.

ADONIRAM JUDSON MORSE, Wis. Veterans' Home, Wis. (32669). Son of Aaron N. T. and Olivia Abigail (Bass) Morse; grandson of Ziba and Patience (Cady) Bass; great-grandson of Isaac and Polly (Wales) Bass; great^2-grandson of *Edward Bass*, Sergeant, Mass. Militia and Contl. Troops; great^2-grandson of *Jacob Wales*, Captain, Col. Thomas Marshall's Regt., Mass. Contl. Troops.

ORWIN ALLISON MORSE, Sioux City, Iowa (33819). Son of George Warren and Lizzie Jane (Baker) Morse; grandson of Washington and Olive (Buzzell) Morse; great-grandson of Elihu and Betsy (Houghton) Morse; great^2-grandson of *Joseph Morse*, private, Col. John Crane's Regt., Mass. Militia.

WALTER HENRY MORSE, Lawrence, Mass. (34975). Son of William H. and Alice (Ingalls) Morse; grandson of Orlando S. and Sally (Pearly) Morse; great-grandson of *Joseph Morse*, private, Col. Titcomb's Regt., Mass. Militia.

JAMES BENTLEY MULFORD, Washington, D. C. (35578). Son of Theodore L. P. and Bessie Boyd (Bentley) Mulford; grandson of James Victor and Bessie Boyd (Headley) Bentley; great-grandson of Samuel Freeman and Maria Josepha (Boyd) Headley; great^2-grandson of *John Boyd*, Lieutenant and Captain, Penna. Contl. Troops.

CHARLES L. MUNROE, Great Meadows, N. J. (Md. 34990). Son of Ivers and Mary (Thomas) Munroe; grandson of Charles and Lydia (Coun) Munroe; great-grandson of *Ebenezer Munroe*, private, Mass. Militia at Lexington.

IRVING ALONZO NEWELL, Longmeadow, Mass. (35390). Son of Alonzo Burnham and Elvira (Keep) Newell; grandson of John and Sophroina (Bigelow) Newell; great-grandson of *Stephen Newell*, private, Mass. Troops; great^2-grandson of *Abijah Newell*, private, Hampshire County Regt., Mass. Militia.

CLARENCE B. NIXON, Pittsburgh, Pa. (35284). Son of S. S. and Jennie (B——) Nixon; grandson of Samuel and Jane (Steel) Nixon; great-grandson of Thomas and Elizabeth

(Russell) Steel; great²-grandson of *David Steel*, Captain, 13th Regt., Virginia Troops, pensioned.

MARSHALL ALBEE NYE, Minneapolis, Minn. (33522). Son of Wallace George and Henrietta (Rudd) Nye; grandson of Freeman James and Hannah (Pickett) Nye; great-grandson of Jeduthan and Minerva (James) Nye; great²-grandson of Hezekiah and Ansenath (Brill) Nye; great³-grandson of *Samuel Nye*, private, Second Regt., Conn. Troops.

ELLSWORTH ORTON, Pontiac, Mich. (35146). Son of Alvin and Nancy M. (McQueen) Orton; grandson of Zenas and —— (Malott) Orton; great-grandson of Zenas Orton; great²-grandson of *Elida Orton*, private, Conn. Militia, pensioned.

NORRIS WHITLOCK OSBORN, Conn. (32259). Supplemental. Son of G. Edward and Mary Beecher (Riggs) Osborn; grandson of Harpin and Harriet (Upson) Riggs; great-grandson of John and Mary (Beecher) Riggs; great²-grandson of John and Elizabeth (Hawkins) Riggs; great³-grandson of *Zechariah Hawkins*, Member Derby, Conn., Committee of Inspection.

OSCAR EVERETT PAGE, Cambridge, Mass. (34960). Son of Charles Albert and Rebecca (Green) Page; grandson of George Aaron and Mary (Stone) Page; great-grandson of Increase Wilson and Elizabeth (Stone) Page; great²-grandson of *Moses Stone, Jr.*, Sergeant, Mass. Militia.

WALTER MILLARD PALMER, Grand Rapids, Mich. (35149). Son of Walter Atwood and Theodosia (De Puy) Palmer; grandson of Walter Kinney and Harriet Atwood (Baldwin) Palmer; great-grandson of Timothy and Mary (Lathrop) Baldwin; great²-grandson of *David Baldwin*, Captain and Adjutant, Conn. Militia.

RAYMOND EGERY PARKER, Springfield, Mass. (34961). Son of George Lyman and Lillian Eliza (Robinson) Parker; grandson of John and Ruth Hathaway (Egery) Robinson; great-grandson of William and Jane (Bourne) Robinson; great²-grandson of *John Robinson*, private, Second Regt., Mass. Militia.

THOMAS RAYMOND PARKER, Captain, U. S. Army, Seattle, Wash. (34037). Son of Lorrain Sanford and Fannie Matilda (Wasson) Parker; grandson of Riley and Catherine (Marquit) Parker; great-grandson of *Stiles Parker*, private, Col. John Brook's Regt., Mass. Troops.

GORDON HART PARKHILL, Buffalo, N. Y. (35356). Son of James Samuel and Esther (Hart) Parkhill, Jr.; grandson of James Samuel and Julia (Amsdell) Parkhill; great-grandson of Robert and Rachel (Harris) Amsdell; great²-grandson of *Abner Amsdell*, private, Col. Rufus Putnam's Regt., Mass. Troops.

JAMES SAMUEL PARKHILL, Jr., Buffalo, N. Y. (35358). Son of James Samuel and Julia (Amsdell) Parkhill; grandson of Robert and Rachel (Harris) Amsdell; great-grandson of *Abner Amsdell*, private, Col. Rufus Putnam's Regt., Mass. Troops.

DANIEL CHISHOLM PATE, Atlanta, Ga. (35214). Son of John Adams and Jeanette (McCall) Pate; grandson of Travis and Angeline (Adams) Pate; great-grandson of John P. and Julia (Newton) Adams; great²-grandson of William and Mary (Marine) Adams; great³-grandson of *Jonathan Adams*, private, Marlboro County, South Carolina Militia.

ROBERT PATTERSON, Dayton, Ohio (35155). Son of Robert and Mary (Thomas) Patterson; grandson of Jefferson and Juliana (Johnston) Patterson; great-grandson of *Robert Patterson*, private and Captain under George Rogers Clarke, and Captain, Virginia Volunteers.

CLIFFORD EVERSON PEARSALL, Westfield, N. J. (35252). Son of Alfred Everson and Amanda (Terry) Pearsall; grandson of Henry L. and Sarah (Jones) Terry; great-grandson of Hazzard and Annie (Brown) Terry; great²-grandson of *Thomas Terry*, private, Third Regt., New York Minute-men; great³-grandson of *Thomas Terry*, Colonel, Third Regt., Suffolk County, New York Militia.

DONALD MOFFETT PEARSALL, Westfield, N. J. (35275) Son of Clifford Everson and Grace Caroline (Moffett) Pearsall; grandson of Alfred E. and Amanda (Terry) Pearsall; great-grandson of Henry L. and Sarah (Jones) Terry; great²-grandson of Hazzard and Annie (Brown) Terry; great³-grandson of Thomas and Julia (Wiggins) Terry; great⁴-grandson of *Thomas Terry*, Colonel, Third Regt., Suffolk County, New York Militia.

FRANK CARBEE PEARSON, Keokuk, Iowa (33820). Son of Isaiah S. and Hattie (Carbee) Pearson; grandson of John P. and Sarah (Hampton) Carbee; great-grandson of John Hancock and Anna (Powers) Carbee; great²-grandson of *Joel Carbee*, private, Mass. Militia and Contl. Troops, pensioned.

ANDREW BOULDIN PERKINS, Hartsville, Tenn. (34636). Son of Thomas F. and Frankie (Oglesby) Perkins; grandson of Benjamin and Elizabeth (Pursley) Perkins; great-grandson of Benjamin and Saunders Perkins; great²-grandson of *Benjamin Perkins*, Captain, Fourth and 12th Regts., Virginia Contl. Line.

JOHN RUSSELL PERKINS, Jr., Danbury, Conn. (Calif. 34731). Son of John Russell and Mary Whittlesey (Brown) Perkins; grandson of Orlando Middleton and Martha Pomeroy (Whittlesey) Brown; great-grandson of David Chester and Mary Camp (Cogswell) Whittlesey; great²-grandson of David and Martha (Pomeroy) Whittlesey; great³-grandson of Quartus and Phoebe (Sheldon) Pomeroy; great⁴-grandson of *Seth Pomeroy*, Major-General, Mass. Militia, and Delegate to Provincial Congress.

LOUIS HENRY PERKINS, Meriden, Conn. (34793). Son of Solon Benjamin and Roalie A. (Farrell) Perkins; grandson of Lewis and Lois (Peck) Perkins; great-grandson of Amasa and Esther (Hitchcock) Perkins; great²-grandson of *Dan Hitchcock*, private, Conn. Militia at New Haven Alarm.

WILLIAM BANGS WEAVER PERRIN, Lafayette, Ind. (33599). Son of William Henry and Mary Emma Bangs (Weaver) Perrin; grandson of Erasmus Morgan and Fannie Maria (Bangs) Weaver; great-grandson of Washington and Fanny Holbrook (Ball) Bangs; great²-grandson of *Joseph Bangs*, Corporal, Mass. Militia; great³-grandson of *Allen Bangs*, private, Mass. Militia.

ARTHUR DUNTON PERRY, Barnard, Vt. (35392). Son of Zebedee Cushman and Sarah Jane (Dunton) Perry; grandson of Benjamin Fessenden and Christiana (Cushman) Perry; great-grandson of *James Perry*, private and Corporal, Mass. Troops, pensioned.

ELLIOTT PERRY, Westfield, N. J. (35273). Son of Charles L. and Ada (Sherman) Perry; grandson of Nathaniel H. and Mary (Goodwin) Sherman; great-grandson of Nathaniel H. and Phoebe (Adams) Sherman; great²-grandson of Joseph and Lydia (Tifft) Adams; great³-grandson of *Ebenezer Adams*, Captain and Major, Rhode Island Artillery.

WARREN ANDREW PETERS, Westfield, N. J. (35197). Son of James E. and Anna J. (Samson) Peters; grandson of Daniel T. and Jane W. (Sherman) Samson; great-grandson of Thomas H. and Eleanor (Joslyn) Samson; great²-grandson of *Isaiah Samson*, private, Mass. Militia.

GEORGE HOVEY PHELPS, Bowbells, N. Dak. (33011). Son of Simonds Fowler and Susan (Critchett) Phelps; grandson of Seth and Laura (Hovey) Phelps; great-grandson of Joshua and Hanna (Fowler) Phelps; great²-grandson of Joshua and Lois (——) Phelps; great³-grandson of *Samuel Phelps*, private, Mass. Militia at Lexington Alarm.

CALVIN TRACY PIERSON, Orange, N. J. (35402). Son of H. Frank and Maria (Simmons) Pierson; grandson of Calvin D. and Margaretta (Dodd) Pierson; great-grandson of Elijah and Martha (Williams) Pierson; great²-grandson of *Caleb Pierson*, private, Essex County, New Jersey Militia.

OLIVER SQUIER PIERSON, Westfield, N. J. (35319). Son of Everet Marsh and Elizabeth Wood (Williams) Pierson; grandson of Squier and Abby (Marsh) Pierson; great-grandson of Squier and Nancy (De Camp) Pierson; great²-grandson of *David Pierson*, private Essex County, New Jersey Militia.

ALBERT FAWCETT POLK, Wilmington, Del. (35023). Son of Theodore Albert and Sallie E. (Fawcett) Polk; grandson of Charles and Mary Elizabeth (Purnell) Polk, 3rd; great-grandson of Charles and Mary (Manlove) Polk, Jr., Lieutenant, Sussex County, Delaware Militia.

FRED JESSE POMEROY, Batavia, N. Y. (35039). Son of Jesse Levi and Rosamond (Wight) Pomeroy; grandson of Levi and Elnora (Gainyard) Pomeroy; great-grandson of *Simeon Pomeroy*, private, Col. Woolridge's 25th Regt., Mass. Militia, pensioned.

EDWARD HYATT PORTER, Wilmington, Del. (35010). Son of William Frank and Eva Estelle (White) Porter; grandson of Morrison D. and Mary Jane (Hyatt) White; great-grandson of Benjamin Merritt and Mary (Thatcher) Hyatt; great²-grandson of Samuel

and Mary (Stroud) Hyatt; great⁸-grandson of *Peter Hyatt,*.Captain, Fifth Co., Third
Regt., Delaware Militia and Member Delaware State Council.

WILLIAM ALEXANDER POWELL, Richmond, Va. (35082). Son of Jonathan D. and
Annie L. (Hepburn) Powell; grandson of William Alexander and Lucy Peachy (Lee)
Powell; great-grandson of Levin and Susannah Elizabeth (Orr) Powell, Jr.; great²-grand-
son of *Levin Powell,* Major, Virginia Militia, and Lieutenant-Colonel, Grayson's Cont'l
Regt.

WARREN CONE PRATT, Detroit, Mich. (Conn. 34794). Son of Charles Willie and Ella
Barnard (Cone) Pratt; grandson of Sylvanus Franklin and Delia Maria (Barnard) Cone;
great-grandson of John and Sally (Robbins) Barnard, Jr.; great²-grandson of *John
Barnard,* Captain, Colonel Walcott's Regt., Conn. Militia; great-grandson of Joseph Warren
and Mahitable (Swan) Cone; great²-grandson of *Sylvanus Cone,* private and Corporal,
Conn. Militia, prisoner; great²-grandson of Levi and Sarah (Wolcott) Robbins; great²-
grandson of *Elisha Wolcott,* contributed funds for relief of families; great²-grandson of
Levi Robbins, private, Captain Skinner's Co., Sheldon's Conn. Light Horse; grandson of
Charles Augustus and Mary Elizabeth (Randall) Pratt; great-grandson of William
Augustus and Sarah (Lynde) Pratt; great²-grandson of William and Sarah (Kirtland)
Lynde; great³-grandson of *Martin Kirtland,* Captain, Sixth Regt., Conn. Troops.

EDWARD HYDE PRESBREY, New York City, N. Y. (Vt. 33844). Son of Oliver Stetson and
Sarah Maria (Hyde) Presbrey; grandson of John Oliver and Abby Leonard (Godfrey)
Presbrey; great-grandson of William Hodges and Susannah (White) Godfrey; great²-grand-
son of John and Jerusha (Hodges) Godfrey; great³-grandson of *George Godfrey,* Brigadier-
General, Mass. Militia; great²-grandson of *John Godfrey,* Lieutenant, Mass. Militia; great²-
grandson of *Cornelius White, Jr.,* private, Col. Timothy Walker's Regt., Mass. Militia;
great²-grandson of Cornelius and Abigail (Leonard) White; great³-grandson of *Cornelius
White,* Captain, Mass. Cont'l Troops; great³-grandson of *Abiather Leonard,* private,
Colonel Mitchell's Regt., Bristol County, Mass. Militia; great-grandson of John and
Fanny (Soper) Presbrey, Jr.; great²-grandson of *John Presbrey,* private and Corporal,
Col. George Williams' Regt., Mass. Militia; great²-grandson of John and Prudence (Pratt)
Presbrey; great³-grandson of *Nehemiah Pratt,* Captain, Colonel Mitchell's Regt., Bristol
County, Mass. Troops; great²-grandson of *Oliver Soper,* Captain, Col. Timothy Walker's
Regt., Mass. Militia.

JOHN OLIVER PRESBREY, Burlington, Vt. (33842). Son of Oliver Stetson and Sarah
Maria (Hyde) Presbrey; grandson of John Oliver and Abby Leonard (Godfrey) Presbrey;
great-grandson of William Hodges and Susannah (White) Godfrey; great³-grandson of
John Godfrey, Lieutenant, Mass. Militia; great³-grandson of *George Godfrey,* Brigadier-
General, Bristol County, Mass. Militia; great²-grandson of *Cornelius White, Jr.,* private,
Col. Timothy Walker's Regt., Mass. Militia; great²-grandson of Cornelius and Abigail
(Leonard) White, Jr.; great³-grandson of *Cornelius White,* Captain, Mass. Cont'l Troops;
great³-grandson of *Abiather Leonard,* private, Colonel Mitchell's Regt., Bristol County,
Mass. Militia; great-grandson of John and Fanny (Soper) Presbrey, Jr.; great²-grandson
of *John Presbrey,* private and Corporal, Col. George Williams' Regt., Mass. Militia;
great²-grandson of John and Prudence (Pratt) Presbrey; great³-grandson of *Nehemiah
Pratt,* Captain, Colonel Mitchell's Regt., Bristol County, Mass. Troops; great²-grandson of
Oliver Soper, Captain, Col. Timothy Walker's Regt., Mass. Militia.

OLIVER HYDE PRESBREY, Major, U. S. Army, New York City (Vt. 33843). Son of
Oliver Stetson and Sarah Maria (Hyde) Presbrey; grandson of John Oliver and Abby
Leonard (Godfrey) Presbrey; great-grandson of William Hodges and Susannah (White)
Godfrey; great²-grandson of *John Godfrey,* Lieutenant, Mass. Militia; great³-grandson of
George Godfrey, Brigadier-General, Bristol County, Mass. Militia; great²-grandson of
Cornelius White, Jr., private, Col. Timothy Walker's Regt., Mass. Militia; great²-grandson
of Cornelius and Abigail (Leonard) White, Jr.; great³-grandson of *Cornelius White,*
Captain, Mass. Cont'l Troops; great³-grandson of *Abiather Leonard,* private, Colonel
Mitchell's Regt., Bristol County, Mass. Militia; great-grandson of John and Fanny (Soper)
Presbrey, Jr.; great²-grandson of *John Presbrey,* private and Corporal, Col. George Wil-
liams' Regt., Mass. Militia; great²-grandson of John and Prudence (Pratt) Presbrey;
great³-grandson of *Nehemiah Pratt,* Captain,. Colonel Mitchell's Regt., Bristol County,
Mass. Troops; great²-grandson of *Oliver Soper,* Captain, Col. Timothy Walker's Regt.,
Mass. Militia.

ROSWELL S. PRICE, Avalon, Pa. (35278). Son of George H. and Matilda Reed (Pierce) Price; grandson of John and Mary (Ford) Pierce; great-grandson of Theophilus Pierce; great²-grandson of *John Pierce*, Paymaster-General, Continental Army.

HENRY GARRETSON PROVOST, Elizabeth, N. J. (35417). Son of Frederick and Catherine Perrine (Garretson) Provost; grandson of Abram Praa and Catherine Ann (Outcalt) Provost; great-grandson of *Jasper Provost*, private, Middlesex County, New Jersey Militia.

JOSEPH WILTON PUDER, Savannah, Ga. (35213). Son of Joseph Conrad and Florence (Kellogg) Puder; grandson of Henry M. and Eleanor (Quantock) Kellogg; great-grandson of Jeremiah and Eunice (Dodge) Kellogg; great²-grandson of *Benjamin Kellogg*, private, Mass. Militia, pensioned.

JOSEPH ASHLEY PULLING, Hamilton, Ont. (Ind. 35505). Son of William M. and Julia (Hascall) Pulling; grandson of Chauncey S. and Emma Pamelia (Brown) Hascall; great-grandson of Ebenezer and Hannah (Shay) Brown; great²-grandson of Martin and Sarah (Hammond) Brown; great³-grandson of *William Hammond* (*Hammon*), private, Colonel Johnson's Regt., Conn. Militia.

FRANKLIN DELANO PUTNAM, Boston, Mass. (34962). Son of Henry Ware and Mary Nelson (Williams) Putnam; grandson of Franklin Delano and Mary Lane (Nelson) Williams; great-grandson of Samuel and Sarah Fitch (Delano) Williams; great²-grandson of *Gideon Williams*, Second Lieutenant, Bristol County, Mass. Militia; grandson of George and Elizabeth Ann (Ware) Putnam; great-grandson of Andrew and Jerusha (Clapp) Putnam; great²-grandson of *William Putnam*, Member Mass. Constitutional Convention.

ALVAH JOHNSON RAGON, Peoria, Ill. (34946). Son of Daniel Street and Eva (Johnson) Ragon; grandson of Alvah and Jane (Parrett) Johnson; great-grandson of Kelly K. and Elizabeth (Hinman) Johnson; great²-grandson of Samuel and Nancy (Hedges) Hinman; great³-grandson of *Asahel Hinman*, Wagonmaster and Captain, New Jersey Militia.

CHARLES LEMUEL RANDALL, Lowell, Mass. (35389). Son of Alonzo D. and Anna A. (Owen) Randall; grandson of Lemuel and Jerusha (Dwight) Randall; great-grandson of *Ichabod Randall*, private, Col. John Daggett's Regt., Mass. Militia.

JOHN FRANKLIN RANDALL, Falmouth, Mass. (34963). Son of Charles Emery and Adelia Francis (Drake) Randall; grandson of Eliab and Mrs. Mercy (Chandler) Mitchell Randall; great-grandson of Phineas and Jemima (Adams) Randall; great²-grandson of *Hopestill Randall*, private, Mass. Militia.

EDWARD STEVENS RANKIN, Newark, N. J. (35199). Son of William and Ellen Hope (Stevens) Rankin; grandson of Ashbel and Mary (Mead) Stevens; great-grandson of *Elisha Stevens*, private, Col. Jeduthan Baldwin's Regt., Conn. Troops, five years' service.

JAMES ALONZO READ, Arlington, N. J. (35420). Son of Calvin and Catharine (Baxter) Read; grandson of Caleb and Sarah (Richardson) Read; great-grandson of *Eleaser Read*, private, Col. Simeon Spalding's Regt., Mass. Militia.

OSCAR READ, New York City, N. Y. (35037). Son of James M. and Catharine (Garniss) Read; grandson of Thomas W. and Caroline Susan (Rogers) Garniss; great-grandson of David and Esther (Horton) Rogers; great²-grandson of *David Rogers*, Surgeon, New London County, Conn. Militia.

ALFRED REED, Pittsburgh, Pa. (35295). Son of Alfred G. and Mary (B——) Reed; grandson of George W. and Mary Ann (Potts) Reed; great-grandson of George Washington and Catherine (Coontz) Reed; great²-grandson of *Moses Reed*, Captain, First Battalion, Bedford County, Penna. Militia.

EUGENE REESE, Westminster, Md. (35337). Son of William and Sarah Jane (Yingling) Reese; grandson of John and Mary (Zacharias) Reese; great-grandson of *Frederick Rease*, Second Lieutenant, Frederick County, Maryland Troops, Member Committee of Safety.

ABNER D. REEVE, Orange, N. J. (35309). Son of George W. and Laura (Brokaw) Reeve; grandson of Abner D. and Caroline (Baldwin) Reeve; great-grandson of Daniel and Catharine (Meeker) Baldwin; great²-grandson of *Michael Meeker*, private, N. J. Militia, State Troops and Cont'l Line.

RALPH TICHENOR REEVE, Westfield, N. J. (35324). Son of William Edgar and Mamie (Tichenor) Reeve; grandson of Ambrose B. and Ruth A. Lilly (Mather) Reeve; great-grandson of James L. and Catherine (Rogers) Mather; great²-grandson of Noyes and

Catherine (——) Mather; great³-grandson of *Moses Mather*, Conn. patriotic preacher, prisoner.

WILLIAM EDGAR REEVE, Westfield, N. J. (35323). Son of Ambrose B. and Ruth A. Lilly (Mather) Reeve; grandson of James L. and Catherine (Rogers) Mather; great-grandson of Noyes and Catherine (——) Mather; great²-grandson of *Moses Mather*, Conn. patriotic preacher, prisoner.

BERT ERNEST REEVES, Rochester, N. Y. (35352). Son of Thomas H. and Marietta (Hoover) Reeves; grandson of Eli and Katherine (Walrath) Hoover; great-grandson of Peter J. and Gertrude (Seifert) Hoover; great²-grandson of *Jacob Hoover*, private, Tyron County Regt., New York Militia.

EDWARD EVERETT REWICK, Oklahoma City, Okla. (35234). Son of William Orsen and Temperance C. (Hutchinson) Rewick; grandson of William and Sarah (Rice) Rewick (Ruick); great-grandson of *Owen Rewick (Ruick)*, private, Conn. Cont'l Troops.

DON MARTIN RICE, New York, N. Y. (35365). Son of George A. and Emma E. (Macomber) Rice; grandson of Martin Powell and Mary Farrar (Rogers) Rice; great-grandson of Samuel and Electa (Powell) Rice; great²-grandson of *Martin Powell*, Member New Hampshire Committee of Safety and Sequestration Commissioner.

EDWARD LUFF RICE, Jr., Wilmington, Del. (35015). Son of Edward Luff and Mary Ann (Robinson) Rice; grandson of Thomas and Katherine (Naff) Robinson; great-grandson of Hance Naff, Jr.; great²-grandson of *Hance Naff*, private, Major Thomas Duff's Regt., Delaware Militia.

MORRIS EARL RICHARDS, Iron Mountain, Mich. (35131). Son of William J. and Nettie (Hogne) Richards; grandson of Lindsey and Nancy Susan (Taylor) Hogne; great-grandson of Mark and Margaret Amy (——) Taylor; great²-grandson of *George Taylor*, private, Fifth Regt., Virginia Troops.

ARTHUR SYLVESTER RICHARDSON, Mass. (31745). Supplemental. Son of George Henry and Emogene (Gale) Richardson; grandson of William and Emeline (Dodge) Gale; great-grandson of Gibbs and Mary (Wakefield) Dodge; great²-grandson of *Luther Wakefield*, private, Col. Ebenezer Larned's Regt., Mass. Militia.

IRVING HOUGHTON RICHARDSON, Somerville, Mass. (34967). Son of George Parker and Nelly Mabel (Green) Richardson; grandson of Benjamin Houghton and Ella (White) Richardson; great-grandson of Moses Richardson; great²-grandson of *Elias Richardson*, private, Colonel How's and Colonel Webb's Regts., Mass. Militia; great³-grandson of *Moses Richardson*, killed near Lexington.

J. WILSON RICHARDSON, Baltimore, Md. (34996). Son of Elihu Hall and Alice Anna (Wilson) Richardson; grandson of William and Catherine (Hall) Richardson; great-grandson of *Elihu Hall*, Lieutenant-Colonel, Maryland Militia, prisoner.

ALFRED JONES RILEY, N. J. (34674). Supplemental. Son of George Parker and Mary Ella (Jones) Riley; grandson of George M. and Lucy Willard (Parker) Riley; great-grandson of Samuel Stillman and Harriet (Howser) Parker; great²-grandson of Sewell and Sally (Willard) Parker; great³-grandson of *Isaiah Parker*, Surgeon, Mass. Militia; great-grandson of Michael and Julia Ann (Hand) Riley; great²-grandson of Joseph Bonnell and Mary Coe (Gardner) Hand; great³-grandson of *David Hand*, private, Essex County, New Jersey Militia and State Troops.

HAROLD ALBINSON RILEY, East Orange, N. J. (35308). Son of George Parker and Mary Ella (Jones) Riley; grandson of George M. and Lucy Willard (Parker) Riley; great-grandson of Samuel Stillman and Harriet (Howser) Parker; great²-grandson of Sewell and Sally (Willard) Parker; great³-grandson of *Isaiah Parker*, Volunteer Surgeon, Mass. Militia.

ALBERT C. RITCHIE, Annapolis, Md. (35326). Son of Albert and Elizabeth C. (Cabell) Ritchie; grandson of Albert and Catharine Lockland (Davis) Ritchie; great-grandson of Ignatius and Catharine Lynn (Lackland) Davis; great²-grandson of James and Catharine (Lynn) Lackland; great³-grandson of *David Lynn*, Frederick County, Md., Judge who repudiated Stamp Act; grandson of Robert Gamble and Margaret Sophia (Caskie) Cabell; great-grandson of William H. and Agnes Sarah Bell (Gamble) Cabell; great³-grandson of *Nicholas Cabell*, Colonel, Virginia Militia.

GEORGE BARKER ROBB, Newark, N. J. (35534). Son of James Lyman and Caroline Saylor (Zulick) Robb; grandson of Charles B. and Susan (Arnold) Zulick; great-grandson of Anthony and Jane Morton (Cummings) Zulick; great²-grandson of *Thomas Cummings*, private, Penna. Cont'l Line, pensioned.

JONATHAN MAGRUDER ROBBINS, Baltimore, Md. (35336). Son of Orlando Douglas and Fanny Schley (Magruder) Robbins; grandson of Jonathan Willson and Mary Galloway (Lynn) Margruder; great-grandson of David and Mary (Galloway) Lynn, Jr.; great²-grandson of *David Lynn, Jr.*, Captain, Seventh Regt., Maryland Troops, 6½ years' service.

JAMES M. ROBERSON, Covington, Ky. (34704). Son of Adam G. and Louisa (——) Roberson; grandson of William and Hannah (Hutchinson) Roberson; great-grandson of *William Roberson*, Sergeant, Virginia Troops.

LELAND REX ROBINSON, East Orange, N. J. (34874). Son of William O. and Minnie W. (Smith) Robinson; grandson of Octavius Augustus and Hannah (Kleinham) Smith; great-grandson of David and Lomanda (Wright) Smith; great²-grandson of *David Smith*, private, Second Regt., Conn. Line.

LEZLIE CURTIS ROSE, West Orange, N. J. (N. Y. 35030). Son of Charles Henry and Jessie Sherman (Tufts) Rose; grandson of William H. and Mary (Wetherell) Tufts; great-grandson of Henry Putnam and Hannah (Norton) Tufts; great²-grandson of John and Abigail (Wheeler) Tufts; great³-grandson of *John Tufts*, Corporal 37th Regt., Mass. Militia.

DONALD ROSS, Westfield, N. J. (35539). Son of James Samuel and Martha Hulda (Daniels) Ross; grandson of Samuel P. and Sophia (Gould) Daniels; great-grandson of William and Hulda (Gilmore) Gould; great²-grandson of *James Gould*, private, Conn. Cont'l Troops.

GARLAND ROTCH, Lieutenant-Commander, U. S. N., R. F., Seattle, Wash. (34039). Son of Francis and Mary (Garland) Rotch; grandson of Jerome B. and Harriett (Nichols) Garland; great-grandson of Joseph and —— (Starbuck) Garland; great²-grandson of *Moses Garland*, Lieutenant, New Hampshire Militia.

ALVIN FRANKLIN ROTE, Wis. (32661). Supplemental. Son of Lewis and Vashty Cowdery (Hitchcock) Rote; grandson of Tidal and Polly Mary (Cowdery) Hitchcock; great-grandson of *Ambrose Cowdery*, private, Second Regt., Conn. Levies, pensioned.

ROBERT LEWIS ROTE, Wis. (32662). Supplemental. Son of Alvin Franklin and Mary (Krueger) Rote; grandson of Lewis and Vashty Cowdery (Hitchcock) Rote; great-grandson of Tidal (Tidle) and Polly (Cowdery) Hitchcock; great²-grandson of *Ambrose Cowdery*, private, Second Regt., Conn. Militia, pensioned.

ARTHUR BAKER ROWLAND, Westfield, N. J. (35410). Son of Alexander McL. and Carrie L. (Kniffin) Rowland; grandson of Thomas Baker and Elizabeth (Browley) Kniffin; great-grandson of Edgar Logan and Sarah Ann (Green) Kniffin; great²-grandson of Jonathan B. and Harriet (Logan) Kniffin; great³-grandson of *Samuel Logan*, Major, Colonel Du Bois' Regt., New York Troops, prisoner.

CHARLES LESLIE RUMSEY, Baltimore, Md. (35331). Son of Charles and Frances Anna (Sovereign) Rumsey; grandson of Charles and Hannah (Mulford) Rumsey; great-grandson of Benjamin and Mary (Clarke) Rumsey; great²-grandson of *Charles Rumsey*, Colonel, Cecil County, Maryland Militia.

STEPHEN OTIS RUSSELL, Brimfield, Mass. (35388). Son of William H. and Fannie E. (Walker) Russell, Jr.; grandson of William H. and Sophia W. (Ware) Russell; great-grandson of Stephen O. and Mary (McCray) Russell; great²-grandson of Wyllys and Amelia (Wolcott) Russell; great³-grandson of *Roger Wolcott*, Ensign, Capt. Amasa Loomis's Co., Conn. Militia.

CHARLES BURRILL RYAN, Lynnhaven, Va. (35080). Son of Michael and Maria Louisa (Richeson) Ryan; grandson of John Brett and Mildred Ann (Ragsdale) Richeson; great-grandson of *Holt Richeson (Richardson)*, Lieutenant-Colonel, Fifth and Seventh Regts., Virginia Militia, Member Virginia House of Delegates; great-grandson of *Drury Ragsdale*, Captain, First Virginia Regt., Cont'l Artillery.

CHARLES HIRAM SAGE, Batavia, N. Y. (35036). Son of Hiram N. and Josephine T. (Sprague) Sage; grandson of Martin and Mary (King) Sage; great-grandson of John and Hannah (——) Sage; great²-grandson of *Benjamin Sage*, private, Sixth Regt., Albany County, New York Militia.

VICTOR SEWARD SAPPENFIELD, Evansville, Ind. (33597). Son of John Willard and Clara E. (Seward) Sappenfield; grandson of Edwin and Elizabeth M. (Gouterman) Seward; great-grandson of George and Rosina (Venner) Gouterman; great²-grandson of

Peter and Elizabeth Gouterman; great²-grandson of *Henry Gouterman*, Captain, Sussex County, New Jersey Militia.

DUDLEY MORTIMER SARFATY, New York, N. Y. (35364). Son of Moses and Eva (Jacobs) Sarfaty; grandson of Jacob and Corina (Phillips) Jacobs; great-grandson of Moses and Rebecca (Hart) Phillips; great²-grandson of Naphtali and Rachel Mendez (Seixas) Phillips; great³-grandson of *Jonas Phillips,* private, Col. Wm. Bradford's Battalion, Philadelphia Militia.

FRANK HARRY SCHAEFER, Westfield, N. J. (35406). Son of Frank Harry and Blanche (Jahue) Schaefer; grandson of Wellmer and Emma (Clarke) Jahue; great-grandson of Joseph and Dolly (Upham) Clark; great²-grandson of Nathan Clark; great³-grandson of Aaron and Olive (Allen) Clark; great⁴-grandson of *David Clark*, private, Medfield, Mass. Militia.

ISAAC LUDLOW SCUDDER, Westfield, N. J. (35267). Son of Isaac F. and Margaret (Ludlow) Scudder; grandson of John and Mary (Enders) Ludlow (Ludlum); great-grandson of *Jacob Ludlum*, private, Essex County, New Jersey Militia.

HARRY MUMFORD SEABURY, Springfield, Mass. (35387). Son of B. Hammett and Anna (Kelley) Seabury; grandson of George Henry and Betsey Besayade (Pierce) Kelley; great-grandson of Lewis B. and Sarah Ann (Alger) Pierce; great²-grandson of James and Abigail (Kelley) Alger; great³-grandson of Joseph and Elizabeth (Eddy) Kelley; great⁴-grandson of Caleb and Sarah (Cole) Eddy; great⁵-grandson of *Ebenezer Cole*, private, Colonel Carpenter's Regt., Mass. Militia.

CLARENCE DAVEY SELBY, Toledo, Ohio (35168). Son of Sanford Perry and Lizzie Foster (Davey) Selby; grandson of Hines Cone and Sarah (Rardin) Selby; great-grandson of Dyar and Tabitha (Calhoun) Selby; great²-grandson of Jeremiah and Sarah (Cone) Selby; great³-grandson of *William Selby*, Member Conn. Committee for providing clothing for Cont'l Army.

STEELE ROBERTS SELLERS, Pittsburgh, Pa. (35279). Son of Henry Downes and Belinda Steele (Roberts) Sellers; grandson of Robert Emory and Maria Louise (Ward) Sellers; great-grandson of William Benjamin and Amy (Driggs) Ward; great²-grandson of John and Amy (Markham) Driggs; great³-grandson of *Jeremiah Markham*, Sergeant, Conn. Troops, pensioned; great-grandson of Henry Downes and Susan (Emory) Sellers; great²-grandson of Francis and Elizabeth (Downes) Sellers; great³-grandson of *Henry Downes, Jr.*, Lieutenant, Fourth Battalion, Maryland Flying Camp; great²-grandson of William and Rhoda (Bacon) Ward; great³-grandson of William and Mary (Miller) Ward; great⁴-grandson of *William Ward*, Captain, 14th Co., Sixth Regt., Conn. Militia.

CHARLES EDWIN SHEPARD, Batavia, N. Y. (35626). Son of John and Polly (Powers) Shepard; grandson of John and ——— (Marvin) Shepard; great-grandson of *John Shepard*, private, Fourth Regt., Orange County, New York Militia.

ALFRED WATKINS SHIELDS, Toledo, Ohio (35154). Son of Thomas P. and Elizabeth (Ford) Shields; grandson of David and Mary Carrington (Watkins) Shields; great-grandson of *John Shields*, Captain, First Regt., Virginia State Troops, died in service.

FRANCIS EARLE SHRINER, Union Bridge, Md. (34998). Son of Frank J. and Rosa (Grumbine) Shriner; grandson of George Thomas and Josephine (La Motte) Grumbine; great-grandson of William and Comfort (Howells) Grumbine; great²-grandson of *Peter Grumbine*, private, Seventh Battalion, Lancaster County, Penna. Militia, pensioned; great³-grandson of *Leonard Krumbine*, private, Second Battalion, Lancaster County, Penna. Militia.

MILTON RUDOLPH SILANCE, Millburn, N. J. (35537). Son of John Robert and Mary Catherine (Meeker) Silance; grandson of Richard and Esther Bailey (Parcell) Sylands; great-grandson of Enos Baldwin and Catherine Reeves (Smith) Parcell; great²-grandson of *William Smith*, private, Second Regt., Essex County, New Jersey Militia.

ARTHUR BURGETT SLADE, Ridgewood, N. J. (35407). Son of Elmer Stillman and Carrie Lavinia (Smith) Slade; grandson of Stillman and Abbie S. (Keach) Slade; great-grandson of Allen and Nancy (Kingsbury) Slade; great²-grandson of *William Slade*, private and teamster; Conn. Militia, pensioned.

HARRY SPENCER SLOCUM, Spokane, Wash. (34042). Son of Frank E. and Nora (Rogers) Slocum; grandson of Arnold and Elizabeth D. (Hubbard) Slocum; great-grandson of Samuel and Elizabeth (Whitney) Slocum; great²-grandson of *Samuel Slocum*, Captain, Vermont Militia.

DONALD STUART SMITH, Rochester, N. Y. (35031). Son of William Stuart and Minnie Pomeroy (Sackett) Smith; grandson of Daniel Eaton and Mary (Baker) Sackett; great-grandson of Daniel and Abigail (Smith) Sackett; great²-grandson of *Benjamin Sackett*, private, Fourth Regt., Albany County, New York Militia.

FRANK BARTON SMITH, Colusa, Calif. (34735). Son of Ralph R. and Isabella (Marchand) Smith; grandson of George Washington and Isabella (Kerr) Marchand; great-grandson of David and Catherine (Bonnett) Marchand; great²-grandson of *David Marchand*, Captain and Surgeon, Second Battalion, Westmoreland County, Penna. Militia.

HAROLD FLOWER SMITH, Chicago, Ill. (35427). Son of Monroe A. and May Edith (Flower) Smith; grandson of Hiram D. and Mary Cheney (Perry) Flower; great-grandson of Zephon and Margaret Rood (Glazier) Flower; great²-grandson of *Ithuriel Flower*, private and Sergeant, Conn. Militia, prisoner; great³-grandson of *Nathaniel Flower*, private, Sixth Battalion, Wadworth's Brigade, Conn. Troops.

HENRY VILLIERS BROWN SMITH, Santa Rosa, N. Mex. (30091). Son of George H. and Mary Frances (Brown) Smith; grandson of Henry Villiers and Mary Elizabeth (Breed) Brown; great-grandson of Elias and Betsey (Randall) Breed; great²-grandson of Amos and Lucy (Randall) Breed; great³-grandson of *John Breed*, Conn. patriot, giving house for ammunition storage; great³-grandson of *John Randall*, Captain, Rhode Island Militia, Member Conn. Committee of Safety; great-grandson of Hezekiah and Elizabeth (Cole) Brown; great²-grandson of *Thomas Cole*, Captain, First Regt., Rhode Island Militia; grandson of Squire and Prudence (Randall) Smith; great-grandson of Chesebrough and Prudence (Miner) Randall; great²-grandson of *Joshua Randall*, purchasing agent for supplies for soldiers' families; great²-grandson of *Daniel Minor*, private, Conn. Militia; great²-grandson of Elias and Betsey (Randall) Breed; great³-grandson of *Thomas Randall*, private, Colonel Angell's Regt., Rhode Island Militia.

JOHN WALTER SMITH, Batavia, N. Y. (35029). Son of James Warren and Mary F. (Gould) Smith; grandson of John T. and Mary (Thompson) Smith; great-grandson of Henry and Laurinda (Foster) Smith; great²-grandson of Ezekiel and Sally (Smith) Foster; great³-grandson of Ebenezer Smith, Lieutenant, Mass. Militia, Captain, Mass. Cont'l Troops.

LEON E. SMITH, Dayton, Ohio (35174). Son of Hackman A. and Mary E. (Lees) Smith; grandson of John R. and Maria Louise (Gunckel) Lees; great-grandson of Philip and Mary Elizabeth (Lochr) Gunckel; great²-grandson of Philip and Catherine (Schaeffer) Gunckel; great³-grandson of *John Gunckel*, private, First Battalion, York County, Penna. Militia.

MARK HARRISON SMITH, Basin, Wyo. (30018). Son of Edgar C. and Sarah Elizabeth (Ruttan) Smith; grandson of Jacob and Margaret (Clapp) Ruttan; great-grandson of John and Sarah L. (Smith) Clapp; great²-grandson of *Elias Clapp*, private, Second Regt., Westchester County, New York Militia.

MONROE A. SMITH, Ill. (35427). Supplementals. Son of Monroe A. and May E. (Flower) Smith; grandson of Hiram D. and Mary Cheney (Perry) Flower; great-grandson of Amos and Patience (Cheney) Perry; great²-grandson of *William Cheney*, private, Conn. Militia, pensioned; great³-grandson of *Ebenezer Cheney*, Corporal, Col. Samuel Wylly's Regt., Conn. Militia; great⁴-grandson of *William Cheney*, private, Third Regt., Conn. Militia, killed at Bunker Hill; great²-grandson of *Jonas Perry*, private, Mass. Militia; great²-grandson of *Josiah Perry*, private, Worcester County, Mass. Militia; grandson of Lyman and Electa (Jones) Smith; great-grandson of James and Mercy (Dewey) Jones; great²-grandson of *Abner Dewey*, private, Berkshire County, Mass. Militia; great²-grandson of *Elijah Jones*, Sergeant, Mass. Militia.

NELSON LEE SMITH, Ardmore, Pa. (35463). Son of Howard Wayne and Carrie (Heckman) Smith; grandson of William Russell and Emma J. (Moore) Smith; great-grandson of Joseph Ball and Lydia (Russell) Smith; great²-grandson of George and Sarah (Jones) Smith; great³-grandson of *Paul Jones*, private, Philadelphia County, Penna. Militia.

RAYMOND FOSTER SMITH, Chicago, Ill. (35435). Son of James Monroe and Anna Louise (Foster) Smith; Grandson of Christopher C. and Sarah Ann (Van Tuyl) Smith; great-grandson of Daniel and Sarah (Durland) Van Tuyl; great²-grandson of *Abraham Van Tuyl*, Sergeant, Western Battalion, New Jersey Militia, pensioned.

ROBERT HOOPER SMITH, Baltimore, Md. (35338). Son of Robert Ralston and Alberta (Hooper) Smith; grandson of John Colton and Ellen Content (Fox) Smith; great-grandson of Asa and Mary Brainerd (Beckwith) Smith; great²-grandson of *Matthew Smith, 3d,* private, Col. Joseph Spencer's Regt., Conn. Militia.

WALTER ALBERT SMITH, Dunkirk, N. Y. (35042). Son of Joseph Franklin and Emily Day (Haskell) Smith; grandson of Solomon and Eliza (Tarr) Smith; great-grandson of William and Lydia (Mitchell) Tarr; great²-grandson of *Daniel Barber Tarr,* Sergeant, Col. Ebenezer Bridge's Regt., Mass. Militia.

JOHN HENRY SMYTHE, JR., New York, N. Y. (35049). Son of Henry and Ruth Anna (Herrington) Smythe; grandson of John and Ruth Ann (Camburn) Herrington; great-grandson of *John Herrington,* private, Fourth Regt., Penna. Troops.

CHARLES EDWARD SNOW, Marblehead, Mass. (35386). Son of John Hopkins and Annie (Martin) Snow; grandson of Nicholas Tucker and Lydia (Pearson) Martin; great-grandson of Thomas and Hannah (Tucker) Martin; great²-grandson of *Nicholas Tucker,* private, Mass. Militia for sea-coast defense, prisoner.

KENNETH ROWE SNYDER, Lafayette, Ind. (35500). Son of J. Lono and Georgia Blanch (Dunavan) Snyder; grandson of James W. and Caroline (Cooper) Dunavan; great-grandson of William Lair and Eliza (Green) Dunavan; great²-grandson of John and Barbara (Grove) Green; great³-grandson of *Benjamin Green,* private, Loudon County, Virginia Militia, pensioned.

SAM SEATON SPALDING, Montclair, N. J. (35179). Son of Alfred and Rebecca (Seaton) Spalding; grandson of Matthias and Rebecca Wentworth (Atherton) Spalding; great-grandson of *Simeon Spalding,* Colonel, Seventh Regt., Mass. Militia, Chairman Mass. Committee of Safety and Correspondence, and Delegate to Constitutional Convention.

EZRA MERTON SPARLIN, Rochester, N. Y. (35630). Son of Francis T. and Sarah A. (Hovey) Sparlin; grandson of Ebenezer and Nancy A. (Treat) Hovey; great-grandson of *Charles Treat,* Sergeant, Conn. Militia.

EDWIN RUFUS SPAULDING, Springfield, Mass. (35385). Son of Rufus and Ellen Maria (Lawrence) Spaulding; grandson of Phinehas Wright and Rachel (Healey) Spaulding; great-grandson of *Zebulon Spaulding,* private, Colonel Brook's Regt., Mass. Militia.

JOHN W. SPENCER, Grand Junction, Colo. (34366). Son of Samuel S. and Ida Flora (Zimmerman) Spencer; grandson of Isaac and Anna Christianna (Ober) Zimmerman; great-grandson of Jacob and Barbara (Coble) Ober; great²-grandson of *David Coble,* private, Seventh Battalion, Lancaster County, Penna. Militia; great²-grandson of *Christian Ober,* private, Second Battalion, Lancaster County, Penna. Militia.

WYMAN H. A. SPINK, N. Y. (34119). Supplemental. Son of Daniel Whitman and Sarah (Richards) Spink; grandson of Whitman and Cynthia (Weaver) Spink; great-grandson of *John Spink,* private, Rhode Island Militia, pensioned; great²-grandson of *Ishmael Spink,* private, Capt. Joshua Davis' Co., Washington County, Rhode Island Militia; grandson of Peter and Hannah (Olin) Richards; great-grandson of Daniel and Sibyl (Paul) Richards; great²-grandson of *Peter Richards,* Master, Conn. Brigantines "Hancock" and "Marquise de La Fayette."

CHARLES FREDERICK SPINNING, Jersey City, N. J. (35193). Son of Dayton Martin and Eliza Jane (Douglas) Spinning; grandson of Henry B. and Sarah (Comstock) Douglas; great-grandson of Eli and ——— Comstock; great²-grandson of *Caleb Comstock,* private, Conn. Militia.

RONALD MEEKER SPINNING, Nutley, N. J. (35538). Son of Frederick Meeker and Anna Johanna (Eichorn) Spinning; grandson of Benjamin and Sarah Anne (Meeker) Spinning; great-grandson of John and Phoebe (Winters) Spinning; great²-grandson of Benjamin and Charity (Garthwait) Spinning; great³-grandson of *Benjamin Spinning,* private, Essex County, New Jersey Militia.

JOHN SEAMAN SPROWLS, Keokuk, Iowa (33824). Son of Albert and Margaret (Craig) Sprowls; grandson of Alexander K. and Sarah (McLain) Craig; great-grandson of William and Margaret (McClelland) McLain; great²-grandson of Thomas McClelland, private, York County, Penna., and Rowan County, North Carolina Troops, pensioned.

HARRY SIDNEY SQUIRES, Roxbury, Mass. (35384). Son of Sidney F. and Minnie J. (Fetridge) Squires; grandson of Sidney and Sophronia (C———) Squires; great-grandson of Newell and Ruth Squire; great²-grandson of *Saxton Squire,* private and musician, Conn. Militia and Contl. Line.

FRANK DAUGHERTY ST. CLAIR, Saltsburg, Pa. (35293). Son of John Patton and Martha J. (Daugherty) St. Clair; grandson of Thomas and Charlotte Denniston (Patton) St. Clair; great-grandson of James and Jennie (Slemmens) St. Clair, Jr.; great²-grandson of *James St. Clair*, private, Fifth Battalion, Penna. Troops.

GEORGE ACKLEY STEARNS, Pittsburgh, Pa. (35281). Son of Daniel Merrill and Julia (Ackley) Stearns; grandson of John Anson and Miriam (Emerson) Ackley; great-grandson of Asa and Sally (Small) Emerson; great²-grandson of *Asa Emerson*, private. Col. Dikes' Regt., Mass. Militia.

PHILIP WALKER STEVENS, New York, N. Y. (35368). Son of John Walker and Julia Preston (Codding) Stevens; grandson of Ichabod and Hannah Maria (Preston) Codding; great-grandson of Isaac and Lorina Betsey (Walker) Preston; great²-grandson of *Isaac Preston*, Colonel First Battalion, Cumberland County, New Jersey Militia.

EDGAR POE STITZER, New Brighton, N. Y. (35034). Son of Francis A. and Josephine E. (Hause) Stitzer; grandson of John D. and Sarah (Heckaman) Stitzer; great-grandson of *David Statzer*, private, Col. Thomas Proctor's Regt., Penna. Artillery.

BOWMAN FORBES STOCKWELL, Montclair, N. J. (Okla. 35235). Son of E. S. and Addie (Bunnell) Stockwell; grandson of Benjamin L. and Louise E. (Schoonmaker) Bunnell; great-grandson of Charles and Nancy (Lyttle) Bunnell; great²-grandson of Benjamin and Mary Eva (Ozier) Bunnell; great²-grandson of *Benjamin Bunnell*, private, Fifth and Sixth Battalions, Penna. Troops.

LANE KIMBALL STONE, N. Y. (33616). Supplemental. Son of Lane Kimball and Carolyn Marie (Adams) Stone; grandson of Francis Frederick and Maria Clarissa (Spoor) Stone; great-grandson of Sylvanus and Caroline Sophia (Goodrich) Spoor; great²-grandson of Barzillia and Clarissa (Hosford) Goodrich; great³-grandson of *Roger Goodrich*, private, Conn. State Troops.

JOHN MILTON MOBREY STONER, Detroit, Mich. (35130). Son of John Edward and Araminta (Purdy) Stoner; grandson of Milton Bentley and Sarah (Smiths) Purdy; great-grandson of *Jeremiah Purdy*, private, Col. Jonathan Baldwin's Regt., New York Artillery.

ARTHUR MIDDLETON STONG, Denver, Colo. (34365). Son of Henry S. and Sarah A. (Tobias) Stong; grandson of Henry W. and Elizabeth (Schweitzer) Stong; great-grandson of Philip and Barbara (Weatz) Stong; great²-grandson of *Philip Stong*, private, Philadelphia County, Penna. Militia; great³-grandson of *Philip Stong*, private, Philadelphia County, Penna. Militia.

WILLIAM BARTGIS STORM, Frederick, Md. (34987). Son of William Burrows and Fannie E. (Bartgis) Storm; grandson of Peter Leonard and Isabella (Burrows) Storm; great-grandson of John Peter and Mary Magdeline (Haller) Storm; great²-grandson of *Jacob Storm*, private and Wagoner, Seventh Regt., Maryland Troops.

GLENN DAVIES STOTTLEMYER, Burgettstown, Pa. (34336). Son of David D. and Amanda Madora (McNary) Stottlemyer; grandson of William and Letitia (Watt) McNary; great-grandson of William and Margaret (Ramsey) McNary; great²-grandson of *David McNary*, private, Capt. Thomas McNary's Co., York County, Penna. Militia.

ROBERT WILLIAM STOTTLEMYER, Burgettstown, Pa. (34337). Son of David D. and Amanda Madora (McNary) Stottlemyer; grandson of William and Letitia (Watt) (McNary; great-grandson of William and Margaret (Ramsey) McNary; great²-grandson of *David McNary*, private, Capt. Thomas McNary's Co., York County, Penna. Militia.

WADE LINDLEY STOTTLEMYER, Burgettstown, Pa. (34338). Son of David D. and Amanda Madora (McNary) Stottlemyer; grandson of William and Letitia (Watt) McNary; great-grandson of William and Margaret (Ramsey) McNary; great²-grandson of *David McNary*, private, Capt. Thomas McNary's Co., York County, Penna. Militia.

LEON RUSSELL STOW, Grand Rapids, Mich. (35139). Son of Russell J. and Harriet (Henshaw) Stow; grandson of Zebulon and Edytha (Wolcott) Stow; great-grandson of William and Margaret (Gaylord) Stow; great²-grandson of *Jonathan Gaylord*, private and Sergeant, Conn. Militia and Cont'l Line; grandson of Horace and Martha (Montgomery) Henshaw; great-grandson of William and Jerusha (Brace) Henshaw; great²-grandson of *William Henshaw*, Lieutenant, Fifth Regt., Conn. Cont'l Line.

STEVENS DANA STREETER, Washington, D. C. (34097). Son of Theodore and Nancy Pruner (Dana) Streeter; grandson of Stevens and Emeline (Fassett) Dana; great-grandson of Asa Stevens and Nancy (Pruner) Dana; great²-grandson of Anderson and Sarah (Stevens) Dana, Jr.; great³-grandson of *Anderson Dana*, Adjutant, Col. Zebulon Butler's Regt., Conn. Militia, killed at Wyoming.

HARRY JOHNSON STRICKLAND, Hartford, Conn. (34795). Son of George E. and Abbie B. (Coleman) Strickland; grandson of George and Elizabeth (Ranney) Strickland; great-grandson of Joel and Sally (Kilbourn) Strickland; great²-grandson of *Samuel Kilbourn*, private, Conn. Militia.

EDWARD CLARK STRONG, Buffalo, N. Y. (35355). Son of James Clark and Emilie Kennett (Efner) Strong; grandson of Henry P. and Laura (Clark) Strong; great-grandson of *Adonijah Strong*, Lieutenant, First Co., Conn. Artillery.

OZIAS GREGORY STRONG, East Cleveland, Ohio (35160). Son of Jared Steven and Hannah (Shaffer) Strong; grandson of Ozias Gregory and Bethenia Elgin (Pavey) Strong; great-grandson of Ozias and Annis (Gregory) Strong; great²-grandson of *Horatio Strong*, private, Berkshire County, Mass. Militia.

FREDERICK ASA SWAN, Westfield, N. J. (35266). Son of J. Benjamin and Hannah Atkinson (Sutton) Swan; grandson of Frederick and Patience Davis (Mott) Swan; great-grandson of Francis and Abigail (Elliott) Swan; great²-grandson of *Francis Swan*, Sergeant and Ensign, Mass. Militia.

HARMON VEEDER SWART, Westfield, N. J. (35403). Son of Alfred S. and Melvina J. (McGuilvery) Swart; grandson of Anthony R. and Sarah E. (Johnson) McGilvery; great-grandson of Lemuel and Permelia (Bowling) Johnson; great²-grandson of *James Bowling*, private, Virginia Cont'l Line, pensioned.

WALTER CAMPBELL SWEENEY, U. S. Army, Washington, D. C. (Md. 34981). Son of Andrew J. and Maria Elizabeth (Hanna) Sweeney; grandson of Thomas and Jemima (Patterson) Hanna; great-grandson of Robert and Sarah (Van Metre) Patterson; great²-grandson of *John Van Metre*, Captain, Berkeley County, Virginia Militia.

ZACHARY TAYLOR SWEENEY, Columbus, Ind. (35506). Son of Guyrn Emerson and Tabitha (Campbell) Sweeney; grandson of Job and Faith (Edwards) Sweeney; great-grandson of Charles W. and Frances (Shackelford) Sweeney; great²-grandson of *Moses Sweeney*, private, Sixth Regt., Virginia Militia.

IRVING W. SWIFT, Adrian, Mich. (35147). Son of Samuel R. and Sarah C. (Crim) Swift; grandson of Jacob Adam and Christina (Garner) Crim; great-grandson of Adam A. and Elizabeth (Hoover) Crim; great²-grandson of *Paul Crim (Grim)*, private, Fort Herkimer, New York Militia.

CLAUDE P. SYKES, Ann Arbor, Mich. (35138). Son of Pliny P. and Elmie A. (Terry) Sykes; grandson of Zenas and Nancy (Janes) Sikes; great-grandson of *Pliny Sikes*, Captain, Fourth Regt., Hampshire County, Mass. Militia.

FRANCIS MARION TABER, Ill. (27122). Supplemental. Son of Bradford and Hanora (Higgins) Taber; grandson of Jesse and Sarah (Cole) Taber; great-grandson of *John Cole*, private, Col. Jeremiah Olney's Regt., Rhode Island Cont'l Troops, pensioned.

DONALD CAMPBELL TAGGART, Westfield, N. J. (35307). Son of Frank A. and Matilda Marschalk (Sutton) Taggart; grandson of George Thomas and Margaret Dodge (Marschalk) Sutton; great-grandson of Girard Steddiford and Clarissa Mary (Dodge) Marschalk; great²-grandson of John and Sophia (Steddiford) Marschalk; great³-grandson of *Garret Steddiford*, Regimental-Quartermaster and Lieutenant, Third and Fourth Regts., Penna. Troops.

PAUL TANNER, East Aurora, N. Y. (35359). Son of Egbert S. and Helen E. (Barrett) Tanner; grandson of Nelson and Prudence (Lovejoy) Tanner; great-grandson of Benjamin and Rebecca (Fones) Tanner; great²-grandson of *Benjamin Tanner*, private, North Kingston, Rhode Island Militia.

EDMUND HAYNES TAYLOR, Jr., Kentucky (28824). Supplementals. Son of Jacob Swigert and Sadie Bacon (Crittenden) Taylor; grandson of Eugene Wilkinson and Laura (Bacon) Crittenden; great-grandson of John Jordan and Maria Knox (Innes) Todd Crittenden; great²-grandson of *John Crittenden*, Captain-Lieutenant, Virginia Troops, Member Virginia Legislature of 1783; great²-grandson of *Harry Innes*, Superintendent Virginia Powder Mills and Deputy Attorney for Bedford County; great³-grandson of John and Judith (Harris) Crittenden; great⁴-grandson of *John Harris*, Member Cumberland County, Virginia, Com. of Safety; great⁴-grandson of John and Hannah (Stewart) Harris; great⁵-grandson of *Charles Stewart*, private, First Battalion, Bucks County, Penna. Militia; great²-grandson of Harry and Ann (Harris) Sheets Innes; great³-grandson of *John Harris*, private, Second Battalion, Bucks County, Penna. Militia, and Justice for Bucks County; great-grandson of Williamson and Ann (Noel) Bacon; great²-grandson of John and Elizabeth (Ware) Bacon; great³-grandson of *Lydall Bacon*, Captain, New Kent County, Virginia Militia; great²-grandson of Silas M. and Maria (Ware) Noel; great³-grandson of *Theodoris Noel*, Chaplain, Virginia Militia.

GURDON HOYT TAYLOR, Boston, Mass. (35395). Son of William W. and Grace M. (Paine) Taylor; grandson of William W. and Sally Ann (Favor) Taylor; great-grandson of William R. and Nancy T. (Hoyt) Favor; great²-grandson of Joseph and Sally (Tewksbury) Hoyt; great³-grandson of *Zebidiah Hoyt*, Corporal, New Hampshire Militia for coast defense.

HENRY CLAY THATCHER, Detroit, Mich. (35132). Son of Harry C. and Elizabeth (Clapp) Thatcher; grandson of Henry Clay and Mary Elizabeth (Cornelison) Clapp; great-grandson of Nathaniel and Cynthia (Stephen) Clapp; great²-grandson of Ira and Sybil (Ransom) Stephens; great³-grandson of *Samuel Ransom*, Captain, Westmoreland Independent Troops, killed at Wyoming Massacre; grandson of Walter Scott and Helen M. (Sweet) Thatcher; great-grandson of Charles and Rachel (Thayer) Thatcher; great²-grandson of *Asa Thatcher*, private, Conn. Troops, pensioned.

BERT THOMAS, The Dalles, Ore. (35057). Son of Samuel Oliver and Jerusha (Donnell) Thomas; grandson of James and Elizabeth (Fisher) Donnell; great-grandson of *Thomas Donnell*, private, Westmoreland County, Penna. Militia; great²-grandson of *James Donnell*, private, Bedford County, Penna. Rangers.

EDWARD BEVERLY THORNTON, Ridgewood, N. J. (35196). Son of Beverly Edward and Mary Elinor (Smith) Thornton; grandson of John L. and Mary Mills (Hallock) Smith; great-grandson of Samuel and Elinor (Bull) Hallock; great²-grandson of *Daniel Hallock*, private, First Regt., Suffolk County, New York Militia.

EDWARD SHELDON TOWNE, Holyoke, Mass. (34965). Son of James Weld and Cynthia (Gowing) Towne; grandson of Joseph and Elizabeth (Walker) Gowing, Jr.; great-grandson of James and Anna (Harnden) Walker; great²-grandson of *Joshua Harnden*, Lieutenant-Colonel, Jacob Gerrish's Regt., Mass. Militia.

FRANK BECKWITH TOWNE, Holyoke, Mass. (34964). Son of James Weld and Cynthia (Gowing) Towne; grandson of Joseph and Elizabeth (Walker) Gowing; great-grandson of James and Anna (Harnden) Walker; great²-grandson of *Joshua Harnden*, Captain, Col. Fox's Regt., Mass. Militia.

JOSEPH MINOTT TOWNE, Holyoke, Mass. (34966). Son of James Weld and Cynthia (Gowing) Towne; grandson of Joseph and Elizabeth (Walker) Gowing, Jr.; great-grandson of James and Anna (Harnden) Walker; great²-grandson of *Joshua Harnden*, Lieutenant-Colonel, Jacob Gerrish's Regt., Mass. Militia.

RICHARD WATKINS TRAPNELL, Wilmington, Del. (35021). Son of Joseph and Rebecca Holmes (White) Trapnell; grandson of Nathan S. and Fredrica (Mackey) White; great-grandson of John and Rebecca Holmes (McGuire) Mackey; great²-grandson of Edward and Elizabeth (Holmes) McGuire; great³-grandson of *Joseph Holmes*, Colonel, Virginia Militia; great⁴-grandson of *David Hunter*, Captain, South Carolina Militia.

ROBERT MARSH TRASK, Hartford, Conn. (35477). Son of George E. and Ida May (Marsh) Trask; grandson of Leonard and Carrie L. (Brooks) Marsh; great-grandson of Fitch Poole and Mary J. (Chadbourne) Marsh; great²-grandson of *Samuel Marsh*, private, Capt. Jeremiah Eames' Co., New Hampshire Militia.

CHARLES MILTON TREMAINE, Westfield, N. J. (35274). Son of Charles Milton and Marianna Downs (Newhall) Tremaine; grandson of Isaac and Bridget (Bachellor) Newhall; great-grandson of Daniel and Mary (Bailey) Newhall; great²-grandson of John and Mary (Hill) Bailey; great³-grandson of *John Bailey*, Colonel, Second Regt., Mass. Troops and 23rd Cont'l Infantry.

PHILIP FRANCIS TRIPPE, Youngstown, Ohio (Md. 35000). Son of Richard and Sophia Kerr (Thomas) Trippe; grandson of Philip Francis and Sarah Maria (Kerr) Thomas; great-grandson of David and Maria (Perry) Kerr, Jr.; great²-grandson of *William Perry, Jr.*, Quartermaster, Maryland Militia, Delegate to Constitutional Convention and Justice of the Peace.

PERCIVAL HAMMER TROUTMAN, Canon City, Colo. (34364). Son of John Hamilton and Ella Augusta (——) Troutman; grandson of Lewis Wernwag and Anna (Esler) Troutman; great-grandson of George Christian and Sarah (Hamilton) Troutman; great²-grandson of *John Peter Christian Troutman*, private, Penna. Militia.

MILTON ELMO TROWBRIDGE, New Orleans, La. (34813). Son of Roswell Bartholomew and Mary Louise (Walker) Trowbridge; grandson of Isaac and Mary Ann (Willard) Trowbridge; great-grandson of *Newman Trowbridge*, Member of Conn. Committee of Inspection.

HARRY NORMAN TUCKER, Courtenay, N. Dak. (33010). Son of John and Lucina (Whitney) Tucker; grandson of Josiah and Elinor (——) Whitney; great-grandson of *Joshua Whitney*, Ensign, Eighth Regt., Conn. Cont'l Troops, pensioned; great-grandson of Joshua and Sally (Cochrane) Whitney; great²-grandson of *Robert Cochrane*, Lieutenant-Colonel, Second Regt., New York Troops.

FREDERICK JOSEPH TURNER, Westfield, N. J. (35200). Son of Frederick Martin and Emma Delia (Merwin) Turner; grandson of Joseph Mott and Sophia Bingham (Cushman) Turner; great-grandson of Martin and Clarissa (Andrews) Turner; great²-grandson of *Eli Andrews*, private, Col. Heman Swift's Regt., Conn. Cont'l Troops, pensioned.

GEORGE HANCOCK TURNER, New Orleans, La. (34815). Son of Mortimer and Helen (Davidson) Turner; grandson of Richard and Eliza (Pintard) Davidson; great-grandson of *John Pintard*, Deputy Commissary for New York City prisoners.

JAMES WILLIAM TURNER, Shreveport, La. (34816). Son of William Allen and Elizabeth Olivia (Turner) Hall; grandson of Martin Posey and Sarah Delia (Stone) Hall; great-grandson of Thomas Jefferson and Sallie Kendricks (Fox) Stone; great²-grandson of *John Stone*, private, Penna. Cont'l Troops, prisoner.

BERT ALBERT TYLER, Dalton, Ga. (35212). Son of Horace Chamberlin and Abigail (Piper) Tyler; grandson of Asa and Fanny (Tupper) Tyler; great-grandson of Joseph and Esther (Ladd) Tyler; great²-grandson of *Ebenezer Tyler*, private, Col. Jonathan Chase's Regt., New Hampshire Militia.

ROBERT STAFFORD TYSON, Frederick, Md. (34982). Son of Jacob Baer and Amelia (Mause) Tyson; grandson of Jonathan and Elizabeth Worthington Dorsey (Baer) Tyson; great-grandson of Jacob and Elizabeth (Worthington) Baer; great²-grandson of *Henry Baer (Bear)*, private, Capt. Peter Mantz's Co., Maryland "Flying Camp."

LESLIE ARTHUR UNDERWOOD, Brighton, Mass. (35393). Son of Charles S. and Mary Jane (Hill) Underwood; grandson of Charles and Abilene (Bennett) Underwood; great-grandson of *Joseph Bennett*, private, Rhode Island Militia, pensioned.

WILLIAM TAZEWELL UPSHAW, Hartsville, Tenn. (34638). Son of James J. and Violet Racheal (Patterson) Upshaw; grandson of James J. and Eleanor (Benson) Upshaw; great-grandson of Lewis G. Upshaw; great²-grandson of *James Upshaw*, Lieutenant and Captain, Second Regt., Virginia Militia; grandson of John Clendening and Eleanor (Benson) Patterson; great-grandson of William and Rachael Bledsoe (Clendening) Patterson; great²-grandson of James and Betsy (Bledsoe) Clendening; great³-grandson of *Anthony Bledsoe*, Major and Colonel, Virginia Militia.

JAMES MUNROE CRAIG USHER, Tulsa, Okla. (35236). Son of William Henry and Martha Gilbert (Oglesby) Usher; grandson of Garrett Troupe and Narcissa Beasley (Wood) Oglesby; great-grandson of Garrett and Ruth S. (Bradley) Oglesby; great²-grandson of Thomas and Martha (Parties) Oglesby; great³-grandson of *Thomas Oglesby*, private, Virginia Militia.

MARTIN VAN BUREN VAN DE MARK, Concordia, Kans. (33314). Son of Charles Wherry and Addie (Stevens) Van De Mark; grandson of Henry and Lusena (Van Auken) Van De Mark; great-grandson of *John Van Auken*, Drummer, New York Militia, pensioned.

WALTER HAMILTON VAN HOESEN, Fanwood, N. J. (35413). Son of Stephen G. and Eva L. (Hamilton) Van Hoesen; grandson of Frederick T. and Olivia (Gay) Van Hoesen;

great-grandson of Mathias and Susan (Tolle) Van Hoesen; great²-grandson of Francis and Eve (Outt) Van Hoesen; great³-grandson of *Garrett Van Hoesen*, private, Seventh Regt., Albany County, New York Militia.

JOSIAH ALEXANDER VAN ORSDEL, Washington, D. C. (35585). Son of Ralph Lashiel and Margaret (Randolph) Van Orsdel; grandson of Job Fitz and Sarah M. (Morton) Randolph; great-grandson of *John Randolph*, private, Middlesex County, New Jersey Militia .

JOHN NICHOLAS VEDDER, Schenectady, N. Y. (35357). Son of Abram L. and Mary (Vrooman) Vedder; grandson of Cornelia and Maria A. (Lansing) Vedder; great-grandson of Simon Arent and Mary (Bassett) Vedder; great²-grandson of *Arent Simon Vedder*, Lieutenant, Second Regt., Albany County, New York Militia.

ULYSSES SUMNER VILLARS, Aurora, Colo. (34363). Son of Isaiah and Mary Helen (Thompson) Villars; grandson of George and Eleanor Jane (Harris) Villars; great-grandson of James and Mary (Cherry) Harris; great²-grandson of *William Cherry*, Captain, Fourth Regt., Virginia Cont'l Troops.

RODNEY SEAGER VOSE, Spencer, N. Y. (N. J. 35186). Son of Riley A. and Florence May (Davis) Vose; grandson of Thomas and Samaniha (Shepard) Vose; great-grandson of Jacob and Betsey (Bassett) Vose; great²-grandson of *James Vose*, Member New Hampshire Committees of Safety and Enlistment.

CHARLES EDWIN WADE, Detroit, Mich. (35144). Son of John Armstrong and Cecelia Adelaide (Ashcraft) Wade; grandson of Melanethon S. and Eliza (Armstrong) Wade; great-grandson of John and Tabitha (Goforth) Armstrong; great²-grandson of *John Armstrong*, Captain, Penna. Cont'l Line, eight years' service; great²-grandson of *William Goforth*, Lieutenant-Colonel, Fourth Regt., New York Troops.

JOHN V. WAGONER, Indianapolis, Ind. (33591). Son of William and Emelia Ann (Howell) Wagoner; grandson of John and Catharine (Zinn) Wagoner; great-grandson of *George Wagoner*, Lieutenant, Third Battalion, Berks County, Penna. Militia; grandson of John and Catharine (Zinn) Wagoner; great-grandson of *Jacob Zinn*, Drummer and Fifer, Lancaster County, Penna. Militia.

RALPH CAMPBELL WAKEFIELD, Westfield, N. J. (35302). Son of James Campbell and Mary Elizabeth (Higgins) Wakefield; grandson of George Washington and Susan (Campbell) Wakefield; great-grandson of James Archibald and Thirza (Fickett) Campbell; great²-grandson of James and Susanna (Coffin) Campbell; great³-grandson of *Alexander Campbell*, Lieutenant-Colonel, Lincoln County, Mass. Militia.

JOSEPH PATTEN WALES, Wilmington, Del. (35020). Son of John Patten and Ellen (Wood) Wales; grandson of John and Ann (Patten) Wales; great-grandson of *John Patten*, Major, Col. David Hall's Regt., Delaware Troops, prisoner.

GEORGE NELSON WARD, Aurora, Ill. (35429). Son of Daniel S. and Charlotte A. (Irwin) Ward; grandson of Volney James and Matilda (Scott) Ward; great-grandson of Jedediah and Catherine (Gaylord) Ward; great²-grandson of *Jedediah Ward*, Second Major, Berkshire County Regt., Mass. Militia.

WILLIAM HENRY HARRISON WARD, Logansport, Ind. (33595). Son of John and Devrohan (Johnson) Ward; grandson of Samuel and Phœbe (Sutton) Ward; great-grandson of *John Ward*, private, Morris County, New Jersey Militia, pensioned.

CHARLES WARNER, Wilmington, Del. (35012). Son of Alfred du Pont and Emalea (Pusey) Warner; grandson of Charles and Mary Rodman (Richardson) Warner; great-grandson of William and Esther (Tatnall) Warner; great²-grandson of *Joseph Tatnall*, private, Capt. Paul Raulston's Co., New Castle County, Delaware Militia.

CHRISTOPHER SCHENCK WARNER, Westfield, N. J. (35320). Son of Samuel Connor and Elizabeth (Burrows) Warner; grandson of Samuel and Emily Woodland Warner (Connor)*; great-grandson of *Benjamin Connor*, private, Colonel Task's Regt., New Hampshire Militia.

WILLIAM JEWETT WARNER, Hebron, Conn. (35478). Son of William Talcott and Olive Maria (Hutchinson) Warner; grandson of Elijah and Abigail (Buell) Warner; great-grandson of Ichabod Mape and Mary (Talcott) Warner; great²-grandson of *William Talcott*, Lieutenant, Lieut.-Col. Levi Well's Regt., Conn. Militia.

---

*Name of Connor legally changed to Warner.

FRANK J. WASSELL, Little Rock, Ark. (31771). Son of Samuel Spotts and Bettie (Mc-Conaughey) Wassell; grandson of James W. and Albina (McRae) McConaughey; great-grandson of Donald and Margaret (Bracy) McRae; great²-grandson of Jolly and Maria D. (Moore) Bracy; great³-grandson of Isham and Mary (Singleton) Moore; great⁴-grandson of *Mathew Singleton*, Member South Carolina Assembly of '75 and fitted out Militia.

FRANCIS ASBURY WATKINS, Carlton, Minn. (33520). Son of Orick Williams and Susan Thompson (Harlow) Watkins; grandson of Eli and Hulda (Stone) Watkins; great-grand-son of *Elias Watkins*, Captain, New Hampshire Troops.

FREDERICK NICHOLS WATTS, Newark, N. J. (34873). Son of Frank Campbell and Anna M. (Nichols) Watts; grandson of David Augustus and Pamela (Guerin) Nichols; great-grandson of Robert and Elizabeth (Brant) Nichols; great²-grandson of David and Sarah (Rogers) Nichols; great³-grandson of *Robert Nichols*, Captain, Second Regt., Essex County, New Jersey Militia.

JOHN RICHARD WATTS, Jr., Atlanta, Ga. (35211). Son of John Richard and Laura (Copeland) Watts; grandson of Earl Percy and Princess (Norton) Copeland; great-grand-son of Josiah (Snell) and Katherine (Gines) Copeland; great²-grandson of *Elijah Cope-land*, private, Captain Keith's Co., Colonel Daggett's Regt., Mass. Militia.

JOHN KNOWLES WEAVER, Tulsa, Okla. (31624). Son of Charles Henry and Arabella (Fulton) Weaver; grandson of Perry Orson and Mary Jane (Knowles) Weaver; great-grandson of John and Abigail (Hatch) Knowles, Jr.; great²-grandson of John and Sally (Penoyer) Knowles; great³-grandson of *James Knowles, Jr.*, Ensign and Sergeant, Conn. Militia; great²-grandson of *Ede Hatch*, private, Conn. Troops, pensioned; great³-grandson of *Abner Hatch*, private, Conn. Militia and Cont'l Troops; great³-grandson of Ede and Eunice (Chapman) Hatch; great³-grandson of *Simon Chapman;* Ensign, Conn. Militia; great²-grandson of *John Penoyer*, Captain, Colonel Canfield's Regt., Conn. Militia; grand-son of William Henry and Caroline Abigail (Jackson) Fulton; great-grandson of James and Susanna (Trego) Fulton; great²-grandson of *William Fulton*, Lieutenant, Cecil County, Maryland Militia.

WILLIAM ROGERS WESTERFIELD, Montclair, N. J. (35262). Son of William and Mary J. (Rogers) Westerfield; grandson of William and Rachel (Bennett) Westerfield; great-grandson of Job and Hannah (Acarman) Bennett; great²-grandson of *Jacob Bennett*, private, Fourth Regt., New York Line.

WALTER HALL WHEELER, Minneapolis, Minn. (30324). Son of Charles Hall and Frances Spencer (Knowles) Wheeler; grandson of Warren and Catherine Hall (Brewer) Wheeler; great-grandson of John and Betsy (Hall) Brewer; great²-grandson of *Josiah Brewer*, Colonel, Lincoln County, Mass. Militia at Penobscot Expedition.

EDWARD WHITAKER, St. Louis, Mo. (33974). Son of William A. and Letitia (Edwards) Whitaker; grandson of Benjamin Franklin and Elizabeth (Green) Edwards; great-grand-son of *Benjamin Edwards*, Lieutenant, Maryland Cont'l Line; grandson of Benjamin Franklin and Elizabeth (Green) Edwards; great-grandson of *Willis Green*, Second Lieu-tenant, Grayson's Virginia Additional Regt., Member Virginia Assembly of 1783.

CHARLES JARED WHITNEY, Hector, Minn. (33521). Son of Oscar L. and Ann M. (Riley) Whitney; grandson of Lemuel and Fanny M. (Gould) Whitney; great-grandson of John and Mrs. Augusta (Fisk) Brooks Whitney; great³-grandson of *John Whitney*, private, New Hampshire Militia.

GEORGE HAROLD WHITNEY, Westfield, N. J. (35195). Son of George Henry and Henrietta (French) Whitney; grandson of Phineas Mundy and Mary (Oswald) French; great-grandson of David and Margaret (Noe) French, Jr.; great²-grandson of *David French*, private and Minute-Man, Somerset County, New Jersey Militia; great²-grandson of *Lewis Noe*, private, New Jersey Militia and Cont'l Line, Lieutenant in Indian Cam-paign.

AMBROSE SPENCER WIGHT, Iowa (28219). Supplemental. Son of Jay Ambrose and Caroline Elizabeth (Adams) Wight; grandson of Jabez and Mary (Bancroft) Wight; great-grandson of *William Bancroft*, private, Col. Ephraim Doolittle's Regt., Mass. Militia.

HAROLD CASE WILLCOX, Verona, N. Y. (35363). Son of Asel and Isabelle (Faulkner) Willcox; grandson of Franklin A. and Nancy M. (Snell) Willcox; great-grandson of Asel and Hellmeda (Foster) Willcox; great²-grandson of *Samuel Willcox*, private, Col. John Patterson's Regt., Mass. Militia.

CHESTER MONROE WILLIAMS, Sioux City, Iowa (33821). Son of Franklin Pierce and Elizabeth (Kebler) Williams; grandson of Absolom and Melissa (Tiffany) Williams; great-grandson of Absolom and Fanny (Root) Williams; great²-grandson of *Salmon Root*, private and Corporal, Conn. Cont'l Line, pensioned.

WARREN WILLIAMS, Rochester, N. Y. (35627). Son of Nathan Gallup and Helen Clarissa (Dunham) Williams; grandson of Warren and Elizabeth Stanton (Gallup) Williams; great²-grandson of Christopher and Martha E. (Stanton) Gallup; great²-grandson of *Nathan Gallup*, Colonel, Conn. Militia.

WALTER L. WILLIAMSON, Lisbon, N. Dak. (33017). Son of Walter M. and Mary (Raymond) Williamson; grandson of Walter and Mary Matilda (Massey) Williamson; great-grandson of Enos and Sarah (Lewes) Williamson; great²-grandson of *John Williamson*, Lieutenant, Col. Anthony Wayne's Regt., Penna. Troops.

RAYMOND SMITH WILLIS, Glen Ridge, N. J. (35411). Son of Edwin Ethelbert and Mrs. Marcia (Smith) Kitchell Willis; grandson of Thomas Compson and Deborah (Farrand) Willis; great-grandson of *Daniel Ferrand*, private Morris County, New Jersey Militia; great²-grandson of *Bethuel Farrand*, Lieutenant, New Jersey Militia and State Troops; grandson of Hiram and Mary Allen (Osborne) Smith; great-grandson of *Hiram Smith*, Sergeant and Ensign, Morris County, New Jersey Militia; great-grandson of *Thomas Osborne, Jr.*, Lieutenant, Eastern Battalion, Morris County, New Jersey Militia; great-grandson of *Russel Willis*, private, Morris County, New Jersey Militia.

WILLIAM CLIFFORD WILLIS, Milburn, N. J. (N. Y. 35048). Life member. Son of George Emery and Hannah Elizabeth (Winans) Willis; grandson of Nathan Meeker and Mary Ann (Crane) Winans; great-grandson of Elias and Esther (Maxwell) Crane; great²-grandson of *John Crane, 3d*, Essex County, New Jersey Cavalryman and private,, New Jersey Cont'l Line, pensioned.

FRANK BLISS WILSON, Wash. (27229). Supplemental. Son of John Newton and Elmira (Wheaton) Wilson; grandson of John and Mercy (Newton) Wilson; great-grandson of *Nahum Newton*, private, Col. Baldwin's Regt., New Hampshire Militia.

JOHN NEWTON WILSON, Seattle, Wash. (34038). Son of Frank Bliss and Bertha (Kennon) Wilson; grandson of John Newton and Elmira (Wheaton) Wilson, great-grandson of John and Mercy (Newton) Wilson; great²-grandson of *Thomas Wilson*, private, Col. Stark's Regt., New Hampshire Militia; great²-grandson of *Nahum Newton*, private, Col. Baldwin's Regt., New Hampshire Militia.

CHARLES KEELER WINSLOW, Upper Montclair, N. J. (35405). Son of Charles William and Isadore Rebecca (Keeler) Winslow; grandson of Zalmon Gould and Joanna Boyden (Crosby) Keeler; great-grandson of Isaac and Lucy (Barrett) Crosby; great²-grandson of *Israel Barrett*, private, Mass. Militia and Cont'l Troops.

WILLIAM GORDON WOOD, New Rochelle, N. Y. (35372). Son of John and Martha (Bayles) Wood; grandson of Nathaniel and Martha (Hunt) Bayles; great²-grandson of *Jonathan Bayles*, Sergeant, Fifth Regt., New York Militia.

ELMER BENJAMIN WOODRUFF, Westfield, N. J. (35533). Son of Wilford Baker and Mary Elizabeth (Van Nosdall) Woodruff; grandson of Robert and Elizabeth (Baker) Woodruff; great-grandson of Hedges and Charlotte K. (Crane) Baker; great²-grandson of *Daniel Baker*, Sergeant and Ensign, New Jersey Militia and State Troops.

WILLIAM HENRY WOODRUFF, Quincy, Ill. (34947). Son of James and Mary (Dalzell) Woodruff; grandson of Samuel Henry and Eliza Maria (Root) Woodruff; great-grandson of *Samuel Woodruff, Jr.*, private, Col. Prout's Regt., Conn. Militia, pensioned; great²-grandson of *Samuel Woodruff*, private, Col. Noadiah Hooker's Regt., Conn. Militia; great-grandson of Joel and Eleanor (Strong) Root; great²-grandson of *John Strong*, Lieut.-Colonel, 17th Regt., Conn. Troops; great-grandson of Samuel and Esther (Sloper) Woodruff; great²-grandson of *Ambrose Sloper*, Lieutenant, Col. Gay's Regt., Conn. State Troops; great-grandson of Joel and Eleanor (Strong) Root; great²-grandson of *Elisha Root*, Lieutenant, Col. Wolcott's Regt., Conn. Troops.

FRED EDWARD WOODSON, Tulsa, Okla. (35229). Son of Richard Lewis and Mimmie (Hager) Woodson; grandson of Joshua Abel and Mary Elizabeth Jewel (Duke) Woodson; great-grandson of Pryor and Jophine (Ables) Woodson; great²-grandson of *Tarleton Woodson*, Captain, Tenth Regt., Virginia Troops, Major, Second Canadians, prisoner.

HAROLD BURHANS WRIGHT, Westfield, N. J. (35303). Son of Charles F. and Elizabeth (Burhans) Wright; grandson of Barzillia Wood and Minerva (Moon) Wright; great-grandson of David and Sarah (Wood) Wright; great²-grandson of *Barsillia (Basela) Wood*, private and Sergeant, Mass. Militia, pensioned.

JAMES M. WRIGHT, Pacific Grove, Calif. (34732). Son of Alford and Eliza Rebecca (Boyd) Wright; grandson of Isaac and Mahala (Evans) Boyd; great-grandson of *John Boyd*, private, Capt. Gabriel Long's Co., Col. Daniel Morgan's Regt., Virginia Militia.

JAMES MANCHESTER WRIGHT, Jr., Foster Center, R. I. (34914). Son of James Manchester and Tamer E. Wells (Howard) Wright; grandson of Benjamin and Lucy (Wells) Wright, Jr.; great-grandson of James and Lydia (Manchester) Wells; great²-grandson of *James Wells*, Lieutenant, Sixth Co., Scituate, Rhode Island Militia.

JOSEPH ARTHUR YAGER, Toledo, Ohio (35163). Son of Charles Henry and Eliza Ann (Zengler) Yager; grandson of Joseph and Phoebe W. (Palmer) Yager; great-grandson of John and Nancy (Yager) Yager; great²-grandson of Joseph (father of John) and Peggy (Wilhite) Yager; great³-grandson of *John Yager*, private, Culpeper County, Virginia Cont'l Troops.

ADRIAN MONROE YARRINGTON, Brooklyn, N. Y. (35040). Son of Charles W. and Joanna E. (Skinner) Yarrington; grandson of John W. and Sarah (Spears) Yarrington; great-grandson of William and Achsah (Yarrington, cousin) Yarrington; great²-grandson of *William Yarrington*, Corporal and private, New York Troops.

ALBERT HENRY YODER, Grand Forks, No. Dak. (33009). Son of William Henry and Catherine Addie (Buskirk) Yoder; grandson of Isaac S. and Elizabeth (Gabbert) Buskirk; great-grandson of Michael and Elizabeth (Bilderback) Van Buskirk; great²-grandson of *Isaac Van Buskirk*, private, Hampshire County, Virginia Militia, pensioned.

WILLIAM DONALD YOUNG, Montclair, N. J. (35182). Son of Selah and Josephine F. (Young) Young, Jr.; grandson of Selah and Sybil Wiggins (Terry) Young; great-grandson of Joshua and Clarissa (Payne) Terry; great²-grandson of Thomas and Julia (Wiggins) Terry; great³-grandson of *Thomas Terry*, Colonel, Third Regt., Suffolk County, New York Militia; great²-grandson of John and Patience (Van Scoy) Payne; great³-grandson of *John Payne*, private, Col. Marinus Willett's Regt., New York Levies; great-grandson of David and Mary (Petty) Youngs; great²-grandson of *David Youngs*, Sergeant, Eastern Battalion, Morris County, New Jersey Militia.

WALLACE McCAMANT

PRESIDENT GENERAL

OFFICIAL BULLETIN

OF THE

National Society
of the Sons of the American Revolution

Organized April 30, 1889

Incorporated by
Act of Congress, June 9, 1906

President General
WALLACE McCAMANT
Northwestern Bank Building
Portland, Oregon

Published at Washington, D. C., in June, October, December, and March.
Entered as second-class matter, May 7, 1906, at the post-office at Washington, D. C., under the act of July 16, 1894.

Volume XVI   OCTOBER, 1921   Number 2

The OFFICIAL BULLETIN records action by the General Officers, the Board of Trustees, the Executive and other National Committees, lists of members deceased and of new members, and important doings of State Societies. In order that the OFFICIAL BULLETIN may be up to date, and to insure the preservation in the National Society archives of a complete history of the doings of the entire organization, State Societies and local Chapters are requested to communicate promptly to the Secretary General written or printed accounts of all meetings or celebrations, to forward copies of all notices, circulars, and other printed matter issued by them, and to notify him at once of dates of death of members.

GENERAL OFFICERS ELECTED AT THE BUFFALO CONGRESS, MAY 17, 1921

President General:

WALLACE McCAMANT, Northwestern Bank Building, Portland, Oregon.

Vice-Presidents General:

GEORGE HALE NUTTING, 53 State Street, Boston, Massachusetts.

New England (Maine, New Hampshire, Vermont, Massachusetts, Rhode Island, and Connecticut).

PHILIP F. LARNER, 918 F Street N. W., Washington, District of Columbia.

Middle and Coast District (New York, New Jersey, Pennsylvania, Delaware, Maryland, District of Columbia, Virginia, North Carolina, South Carolina, Georgia, and Florida).

MARVIN H. LEWIS, 201 Keller Building, Louisville, Kentucky.

Mississippi Valley, East District (Michigan, Wisconsin, Illinois, Indiana, Ohio, West Virginia, Kentucky, Tennessee, Alabama, and Mississippi).

HENRY B. HAWLEY, Des Moines, Iowa.

Mississippi Valley, West District (Minnesota, North Dakota, South Dakota, Nebraska, Iowa, Kansas, Missouri, Oklahoma, Arkansas, Louisiana, and Texas).

JOHN W. BELL, JR., P. O. Box 1124, Spokane, Washington.

Mountain and Pacific Coast District (Montana, Idaho, Wyoming, Nevada, Utah,, Colorado, Arizona, New Mexico, Oregon, Washington, California, Hawaii, and Philippines).

Secretary General:

FRANK BARTLETT STEELE, 183 St. James Place, Buffalo, New York.

Registrar General:

WILLIAM S. PARKS, 900 17th Street N. W., Washington, District of Columbia.

Treasurer General:

JOHN H. BURROUGHS, 1111 Dean Street, Brooklyn, New York.

Historian General:

GEORGE CARPENTER ARNOLD, Arnold Building, Providence, Rhode Island.

Chancellor General:

EUGENE C. BONNIWELL, City Court Building, Philadelphia, Pennsylvania.

Genealogist General:

WALTER K. WATKINS, 9 Ashburton Place, Boston, Massachusetts.

Chaplain General:

REV. LYMAN WHITNEY ALLEN, 881 S. 7th Street, Newark, New Jersey.

BOARD OF TRUSTEES

The General Officers, together with one member from each State Society, constitute the Board of Trustees of the National Society. The following Trustees for the several States were elected at the Buffalo Congress, May 17, 1921, to serve until their successors are elected at the Congress to be held at Springfield, Mass., in May, 1922:

Alabama, (vacant); Arizona, Clay F. Leonard, Phœnix; Arkansas, George B. Gill, Little Rock; California, Seabury C. Mastick, New York City; Colorado, Malcolm Lindsey, Denver; Connecticut, Clarence Horace Wickham, Hartford; Delaware, George Armstrong Elliott, Wilmington; District of Columbia, Albert D. Spangler, Washington; Far Eastern Society, (vacant); Florida, Dr. F. G. Renshaw, Pensacola; Society in France, (vacant); Hawaiian Society, (vacant); Georgia, Allan Waters, Atlanta; Idaho, (vacant); Illinois, Dorr E. Felt, Chicago; Indiana, Charles C. Jewett, Terre Haute; Iowa, Elmer E. Wentworth, State Center; Kansas, John M. Meade, Topeka; Kentucky, George T. Wood, Louisville; Louisiana, Col. C. Robert Churchill, New Orleans; Maine, James O. Bradbury,* Saco; Maryland, Hon. Henry Stockbridge, Baltimore; Massachusetts, Henry Fuller Punderson, Springfield; Michigan, Albert M. Henry, Detroit; Minnesota, Charles E. Rittenhouse, Minneapolis; Mississippi, (vacant); Missouri, George R. Merrill, St. Louis; Montana, Marcus Whritenour, Helena; Nebraska, Benjamin F. Bailey, Lincoln; Nevada, (vacant); New Hampshire, Henry T. Lord, Manchester; New Jersey, Charles Symmes Kiggins, Elizabeth; New Mexico, George G. Klock, Albuquerque; New York, Louis Annin Ames, New York; North Carolina, (vacant); North Dakota, Howard E. Simpson, Grand Forks; Ohio, Moulton Houk, Delaware; Oklahoma, W. A. Jennings, Oklahoma City; Oregon, Wallace McCamant, Portland; Pennsylvania, Col. R. W. Guthrie, Pittsburgh; Rhode Island, Wilfred H. Munro, Providence; South Carolina, (vacant); South Dakota, J. G. Parsons, Sioux Falls; Tennessee, Leland Hume, Nashville; Texas, C. B. Dorchester, Sherman; Utah, Daniel S. Spencer, Salt Lake City; Vermont, William Jeffrey, Montpelier; Virginia, Arthur B. Clarke, Richmond; Washington, Ernest B. Hussey, Seattle; Wisconsin, Walter H. Wright, Milwaukee; Wyoming, Warren Richardson, Cheyenne.

* Deceased, May, 1921.

PRESIDENTS AND SECRETARIES OF STATE SOCIETIES

ARIZONA—President, H. B. Wilkinson, 128 West Adams Street, Phœnix.
    Secretary, Harold Baxter, 311 Fleming Building, Phœnix.
    Treasurer, Kenneth Freeman, Phœnix.

ARKANSAS—President, General Benjamin W. Green, Little Rock.
    Secretary, Fay Hempstead, Little Rock.
    Treasurer, Thomas M. Cory, Little Rock.

CALIFORNIA—President, Frank S. Brittain, Balboa Building, San Francisco.
    Secretary and Treasurer, Thomas A. Perkins, Mills Building, San Francisco.

COLORADO—President, Victor E. Keyes, 210 Masonic Temple, Denver.
    Secretary, James Polk Willard, 210 Masonic Temple, Denver.
    Treasurer, Walter D. Wynkoop, Denver.

CONNECTICUT—President, Herbert H. White, 76 N. Beacon Street, Hartford.
    Secretary, Frederick A. Doolittle, Bridgeport.
    Treasurer, Charles G. Stone, P. O. Box 847, Hartford.

DELAWARE—President, Horace Wilson, 404 S. Clayton Street, Wilmington.
    Secretary and Treasurer, Charles A. Rudolph, 900 Vanburen Street, Wilmington.

DISTRICT OF COLUMBIA—President, Selden M. Ely, Gales School Building, Washington.
    Secretary, William Alexander Miller, 911 Monroe Street, Washington.
    Treasurer, Alfred B. Dent, 906 A Street S. E., Washington.

FAR EASTERN SOCIETY—President-Secretary, H. Lawrence Noble, Post Office Box 940,
    Manila, Philippine Islands.
    Vice-President, Edward B. Copeland.
    Treasurer, Herman Roy Hare.

FLORIDA—President, Dr. F. G. Renshaw, Pensacola.
    Secretary, John Hobart Cross, Pensacola.
    Treasurer, F. F. Bingham, Pensacola.

SOCIETY IN FRANCE—Administered by Empire State Society.

GEORGIA—President, Allan Waters, Post Office Box 361, Atlanta.
    Secretary, Arthur W. Falkinburg, 624 Forsythe Building, Atlanta.

HAWAII—President, Rev. L. L. Loofbourow, Honolulu.
    Secretary, James T. Taylor, 511 Stangenwald Building, Honolulu.
    Treasurer, Elmer T. Winant.

IDAHO—President, Henry Keyser, Boise.
    Secretary and Treasurer, Frank G. Ensign, Boise.

ILLINOIS—President, Dorr E. Felt, 30 North La Salle Street, Chicago.
    Secretary, Louis A. Bowman, 30 North La Salle Street, Chicago.
    Treasurer, Henry R. Kent, 30 North La Salle Street, Chicago.

INDIANA—President, Austin H. Brown, 406 East Fifteenth Street, Indianapolis.
    Secretary and Treasurer, Edmund L. Parker, 208 East Walnut Street, Kokomo.

IOWA—President, Walter E. Coffin, 902 7th Street, Des Moines.
    Secretary, Captain Elfridge D. Hadley, 409 Franklin Avenue, Des Moines.
    Treasurer, William E. Barrett, 4815 Grand Ave., Des Moines.

KANSAS—President, John M. Meade, Topeka.
    Secretary, Arthur H. Bennett, Topeka.
    Treasurer, Jonathan A. Norton, Topeka.

KENTUCKY—President, Marvin H. Lewis, Keller Building, Louisville.
    Secretary, George D. Caldwell, Southern Building, Louisville.
    Treasurer, George Tyman Wood, Louisville.

LOUISIANA—President, C. Robert Churchill, 408 Canal Street, New Orleans.
   Secretary, Herbert P. Benton, 403 Whitney Building, New Orleans.
   Treasurer, Harry V. C. Vandercook, New Orleans.

MAINE—President, William B. Berry, 42 Pleasant Street, Gardiner.
   Secretary, Francis L. Littlefield, 246 Spring Street, Portland.
   Treasurer, Enoch O. Greenleaf, Portland.

MARYLAND—President, Osborne I. Yellott, Munsey Bldg., Baltimore.
   Secretary, George Sadtler Robertson, 1628 Linden Avenue, Baltimore.
   Treasurer, W. Bernard Duke, 406 Water Street, Baltimore.

MASSACHUSETTS—President, George Hale Nutting, 53 State Street, Boston.
   Secretary, George S. Stewart, Tremont Building, Boston.
   Treasurer, Lieut.-Col. Charles M. Green, Malden.

MICHIGAN—President, William P. Holliday, 68 Davenport Street, Detroit.
   Secretary, Raymond E. Van Syckle, 1729 Ford Building, Detroit.
   Treasurer, Frank G. Smith, 237 Hancock Avenue E., Detroit.

MINNESOTA—President, Charles E. Rittenhouse, 720 Washington Avenue, Minneapolis.
   Secretary, Charles H. Bronson, 48 East Fourth Street, St. Paul.
   Treasurer, Charles W. Eddy, St. Paul.

MISSISSIPPI—President, Judge Gordon Garland Lyell, Jackson.
   Secretary and Treasurer, William H. Pullen, Mechanics' Bank Building, Jackson.

MISSOURI—President, Col. W. D. Vandiver, Columbia.
   Secretary, W. Scott Hancock, 1006 Boatmen's Bank Building, St. Louis.
   Treasurer, I. Shreve Carter, 308 Merchant La Clede Building, St. Louis.

MONTANA—President, Martin Whritenour, Helena.
   Secretary and Treasurer, Leslie Sulgrove, Helena.

NEBRASKA—President, Benjamin F. Bailey, Lincoln.
   Secretary and Treasurer, Addison E. Sheldon, Lincoln.

NEVADA—President, Rt. Rev. George C. Huntting, 505 Ridge Street, Reno.

NEW HAMPSHIRE—President, Prof. Ashley K. Hardy, Hanover.
   Secretary and Treasurer, Will B. Howe, Concord.

NEW JERSEY—President, Rev. Lyman Whitney Allen, D. D., 881 S. 7th Street, Newark.
   Secretary, David L. Pierson, 44 Harrison Street, East Orange.
   Treasurer, Earle A. Miller, 156 William Street, Orange.

NEW MEXICO—President, Edmund Ross, Albuquerque.
   Secretary, Frank W. Graham, Albuquerque.
   Treasurer, Orville A. Matson, Albuquerque.

NEW YORK—President, Harvey F. Remington, Wilder Building, Rochester.
   Secretary, Major Charles A. Du Bois, 220 Broadway, New York.
   Treasurer, James de la Montanye, New York City.

NORTH CAROLINA—President, Frank H. Bryan, Washington.
   Secretary (vacant).
   Treasurer, W. B. Harding, Washington.

NORTH DAKOTA—President, Homer E. Simpson, State University, Grand Forks.
   Secretary, Walter R. Reed, Amenia.
   Treasurer, J. W. Wilkerson, University of North Dakota, Grand Forks.

OHIO—President, Walter J. Sherman, The Nasby, Toledo.
   Secretary, W. L. Curry, Box 645, Columbus.
   Treasurer, S. G. Harvey, Toledo.

OKLAHOMA—President, Edward F. McKay, Oklahoma City.
   Secretary, A. Barritt Galloway, 905 1st National Bank Building, Oklahoma City.
   Treasurer, A. Barritt Galloway, Oklahoma City.

OREGON—President, B. B. Beekman, 601 Platt Building, Portland.
Secretary, B. A. Thaxter, Post Office Box 832, Portland.
Treasurer, A. B. Lindsley, Portland.

PENNSYLVANIA—President, James A. Wakefield, 471 Union Arcade, Pittsburgh.
Secretary, Francis Armstrong, Jr., 515 Wood Street, Pittsburgh.
Treasurer, A. M. Wall, Pittsburgh.

RHODE ISLAND—President, Francis Eliot Bates, Post Office Box 1254, Providence.
Secretary, Theodore E. Dexter, Central Falls.
Treasurer, William L. Sweet.

SOUTH CAROLINA—No report.

SOUTH DAKOTA—President, J. G. Parsons, Sioux Falls.
Secretary, T. W. Dwight, Sioux Falls.
Treasurer, B. H. Requa, Sioux Falls.

TENNESSEE—President, William K. Boardman, Nashville.
Secretary, Frederick W. Millspaugh, Nashville.
Treasurer, Carey Folk, 411 Union Street, Nashville.

TEXAS—President, C. B. Dorchester, Sherman.
Secretary, Walter S. Mayer, Galveston.

UTAH—President, Heber M. Wells, Dooly Building, Salt Lake City.
Secretary, Gordon Lines Hutchins, Dooly Building, Salt Lake City.
Treasurer, Seth Warner Morrison, Jr.

VERMONT—President, William H. Jeffrey, Montpelier.
Secretary, Walter H. Crockett, Burlington.
Treasurer, Clarence L. Smith, Burlington.

VIRGINIA—President, Arthur B. Clarke, 616 American National Bank Building, Richmond.
Secretary and Treasurer, William E. Crawford, 700 Travelers' Building, Richmond.

WASHINGTON—President, Walter Burges Beals, Seattle.
Secretary, William Phelps Totten, Seattle.
Treasurer, Chauncey, Luther Baxter, Seattle.

WISCONSIN—President, J. Tracy Hale, Jr., Wells Building, Milwaukee.
Secretary, Emmett A. Donnelly, 1030 Wells Building, Milwaukee.
Treasurer, William Stark Smith, 373 Lake Drive, Milwaukee.

WYOMING—President, Warren Richardson, Cheyenne.
Secretary, Maurice Groshon, Cheyenne.
Treasurer, James B. Guthrie, Cheyenne.

ACTIVITIES DURING THE SUMMER

Although the summer season is usually a dull one for organizations like ours, the interest of the Sons of the American Revolution has not flagged and in many quarters it has been as strong as at other times of the year. The preparation for Constitution Day, which is now celebrated in so many thousands of places all over the country, and a few other local causes, may have had some effect on this, but the real underlying reason seems to be that this Society is a live one, and that its influence is being felt wherever there is a Chapter that is awake, and also that a splendid lot of men all over the United States are taking deep and active interest in the patriotic work of the Society.

It may interest the members to learn that several of our officers have taken long trips this summer, and though not always primarily in the interests of the Society, yet the officer in every case kept in mind the S. A. R. and made it his business and pleasure to visit Societies and Chapters in the cities where he stopped.

President General McCamant made a trip in September, in the interests of the Society and in celebration of Constitution Day, to Boise, Denver, and Salt Lake City. There was a special meeting of the Utah State Society in honor of this event, and it is hoped a good account of this meeting and the activities of this progressive Society may be published in the December BULLETIN. The President General made a short trip in his own territory earlier in the season to promote the interests of our work.

Director General Adams, of New Jersey, made a trip to the coast in June and met many of the compatriots. He visited President General McCamant in Portland and reported a most delightful time. On his return he was entertained in Salt Lake City and confirms the reports that this Society is most active and up and doing.

The Secretary General visited Chicago early in July and on his way stopped for a few hours with Secretary Van Sycle, of the Michigan Society, who is one of the active workers of our organization. In Chicago the Secretary General met the Board of Managers of the Illinois Society at a luncheon and was delightfully entertained by Secretary Louis Bowman, of that Society.

The President General appointed the Secretary General, who had planned a trip to Plymouth for the Mayflower Congress in September, to represent the National Society, S. A. R., at this meeting and extend our greetings to this Society. This the Secretary did, and when the few inspiring words, as sent by the President General, were spoken at the meeting at Plymouth, September 6th, they were received with enthusiasm by the delegates.

Several of the articles or reports published in this BULLETIN, it would seem, should have special mention. The report of Past President General Thruston, chairman of the Memorial Committee, is one of these and should be read by every compatriot. It is not only adding history to our Society, but is making complete and authentic the history of our country. The amount of time and labor spent on this research work is untold, and it is fortunate that we have a man of Mr. Thruston's aptitude for this work to carry it on. Few others could achieve such results. It is hoped, too, that the articles in this number on the American's Creed and Publicity will be read, digested, and acted upon, and then let every State Society, Chapter, and compatriot strive to make this coming year the greatest in the history of the organization.

᾿η Tuesday, June 21, the Old World Manor House of Sulgrave, the ancestral ι. ᾿f George Washington, which has been restored and furnished as a me- ᾿l f.r peace for more than a century between Great Britain and America, ᾿ꞏ ꞏlc·lirated. The celebration was marked by many interesting ceremonies. ᾿)uꞏing ꞏhe ceremony there was presented a deed, dated 1599, signed by Robert Washington, son of Lawrence Washington, builder of the Manor House, who bought the land in 1539 from Henry VIII. Attached to the deed is the seal, in perfect state of preservation, showing the Washington Arms. There was also unveiled, in the great dining hall, an original Gilbert Stuart portrait of Washington. There was an impressive church service, participated in by representatives of the English and American governments, and after the service a meeting took place on the terrace, and one of the features of the program was the presentation of a beautiful American Flag, the gift of the Sons of the American Revolution. The presentation was made by Mr. Andrew B. Humphrey, representing the American Tercentenary Committee, who will be recalled by the delegates to the Hartford Congress in 1920 as addressing the Convention, most interestingly outlining the plans for the Tercentenary Celebration.

On the Fourth of July Americans in Paris honored the memory of two Frenchmen who represent the close ties between France and America cemented on the battlefields of liberty—Lafayette and the Unknown soldier. At Lafayette's grave our Society was represented by Colonel Thurston Preston, for many years a member of the Sons of the American Revolution, who, at the request of Mr. Cleveland Coxe, Empire State Society of the Sons of the American Revolution, placed a wreath on the tomb in the Picpus Cemetery. Colonel Preston was accompanied by Mrs. Preston, a member of the Daughters of the American Revolution. The Colonel said, in part:

"When General Pershing, speaking at this tomb, said, 'Lafayette, we are here,' he could not have foreseen the numbers of American boys who would remain in France—consecrating the soil with their blood. Yes, Lafayette, we are here still, here in the hearts of France, here side by side with your dead, as we fought side by side for the cause of Liberty and Humanity."

The celebration of the Pilgrim Tercentenary at Plymouth has been a great success. Unfortunately, no adequate provision has been made for the financial burden of the celebration. For the purpose of meeting the legitimate expense connected with the celebration, the Federal Government has issued 300,000 Pilgrim half dollars. The coins are beautiful in design, being the work of Cyrus E. Dallin, the famous sculptor. The Treasury Department officials express the belief that they are the most beautiful coins ever issued by the Government. These coins can be secured from William Carroll Hill, Secretary, Pilgrim Tercentenary Commission, 73 Tremont Street, Boston, or from the National Shawmut Bank of Boston, at one dollar each. They are an appropriate souvenir for distribution at dinners and other functions of our Society. It is hoped that Chapters and State Societies will purchase them in quantities of from 50 to 500, and thus assist in carrying the financial burden incident to this interesting historical celebration.

ANNOUNCEMENTS

All officers, both National and State, are requested to sign the certificates of membership in india ink. Many of the older certificates are fading for lack of proper ink.

The copies of the Constitution and By-Laws ordered printed by the Executive Committee are now ready for distribution and will be sent upon application to the Secretary General.

The Secretary General desires to announce that he is prepared to fill orders from State officers for War Service Medals. Applications for these should come through State officers and not from individuals.

The chairman of the Committee on Observance of Constitution Day, Mr. Louis Annin Ames, desires to announce that a complete report of the recognition of this day will be printed in the December BULLETIN. State Presidents or Secretaries not yet having sent in reports are urged to do so at once, that these may all be incorporated in the general report.

The members of the Society will hear with the greatest regret the news that Mr. Teunis D. Huntting, the faithful and efficient Registrar of the Empire State Society, was most seriously injured by a motorcycle while taking his vacation in Maine this summer. Mr. Huntting lies in a hospital in Portland with a badly fractured leg and it will be some time before he will be back to his duties at 220 Broadway, New York. He has the wishes of his legion of friends in the Sons of the American Revolution that his recovery will be speedy and complete.

The attention of the organization is again called to The American's Creed. This concise and eloquent statement of American principles should be in use in our schools all over the land. Copies of the Creed, tastefully printed, are available for distribution at the price of $4.00 per hundred and $30.00 per thousand. The Book of The American's Creed has been tastefully printed and can be furnished at 35 cents per volume, if ordered in lots of three or more. The book amplifies the teaching of the Creed and explains the circumstances under which it was adopted. Compatriots are requested to co-operate in placing the book in the hands of teachers and the Creed in the hands of students in our schools. Any child who has learned to recite this Creed from day to day as a part of his school curriculum will in all probability be and remain a good American to the end of his life. Full information on the subject can be secured from Compatriot Matthew Page Andrews, at 849 Park Avenue, Baltimore, Md.

The chairman of the Tercentenary Committee, Mr. Charles F. Read, Old State House, Boston, Mass., makes the following appeal in behalf of the Warren Memorial Fund at Plymouth, Mass.:

Contributions for the Warren Memorial Fund, for the memorial to General

James Warren at Plymouth, Mass., should be made promptly, in order that the memorial can be completed in time for the dedication, in May, 1922, when the President General is expected to be present. The State Societies are urged to send in their proportionate shares, as indicated in the request sent out early in June, at as early a date as possible.

Memorials are being placed in Plymouth, Mass., by the Red Men, Colonial Dames, Mayflower Descendants, New England Women of Pennsylvania, the Ancient and Honorable Artillery Company of Boston, the Daughters of the Revolution, Daughters of the American Revolution, the Sons of the Revolution, the Sons of the American Revolution of Massachusetts, the Town of Plymouth, and others. Our National Society is pledged to the completion of this memorial, and surely the State Societies will see that we do not fail in this project.

OPINION OF CHANCELLOR GENERAL EUGENE C. BONNIWELL

Following the Congress of the National Society of the Sons of the American Revolution, held at Buffalo, May 16 and 17, 1921, Mr. John H. Burroughs, Treasurer General of the Society, formally required of the Chancellor General an opinion as to the legality and validity of the amendment adopted at said convention, increasing the dues of the members of the Society.

An examination of the minutes of the proceedings as of the date of May 17, 1921, discloses that the Committee on Resolutions reported an amendment to the Constitution providing for an initiation fee of five ($5.00) dollars upon each member duly elected. Due notice of this amendment, under the Constitution and By-Laws of the Society, had been given, as required by law. Upon a question upon the adoption or rejection of the amendment, the proposed amendment was amended by substituting for the initiation fee annual dues. This amendment to the proposed amendment was duly adopted and thereafter declared carried by the chairman.

Your Chancellor General is of the opinion that an amendment to a constitution must stand or fall upon the original motion. There is no question of parliamentary law herein contained. The constitution is the written charter of rights and privileges of an organization. It is provided that it may be altered or amended by giving due notice in writing of the proposed alteration or amendment. This notice in relation to the original amendment was duly given. The membership of the national organization were able to determine whether they approved or opposed. Those who approved could justly ignore any further activity in the matter, because they did approve, and those who did oppose had the opportunity to present their objections. But the amendment as amended, while it related to the subject of dues, was a complete antithesis of the original amendment; it substituted annual dues for an initiation fee and affects the work of the State Societies in a very marked degree.

Your Chancellor General is of the opinion that the amendment as proposed, and of which notice was duly given, was the only business properly before the meeting at that time, and that it should have been either accepted or rejected. A constitutional amendment could not be amended, in the judgment of your law officer. It might be further pointed out that all amendments to the Constitution require a two-thirds vote. It is true that the amendment to the amendment did receive a two-thirds vote, 60 to 30. There is naught that appears of record that the amendment upon final passage received a majority vote. It does not appear that the necessary two-thirds vote was cast on final passage. This, in the opinion of the Chancellor General, is fatal to its validity, even if the other objection did not exist.

Under all circumstances, I am of the opinion that the amendment as adopted is null and void.

EUGENE C. BONNIWELL,
Chancellor General.

PUBLICITY

For many years it has been felt that our Society has not been given the proper amount of publicity. For the kind of work we are doing, for the amount of time and labor that is expended, and, lastly, because of the kind and caliber of the men who are doing this work in every part of the United States, the amount of space devoted to the interests of the Sons of the American Revolution in our public press is comparatively small.

Of course, in many of the larger communities and in some of the smaller ones, the Society has been given its fair share of notice, but it is well known that many of the functions and meetings get but scant mention compared to the value of the news. Where lies the cause of this and can it be remedied? The fault is no doubt largely due to the members or officers of the local Society, and though it is done unwittingly, it can be easily corrected.

In the very excellent report of Mr. Frank L. Stetson, of Chicago, Chairman of the National Committee on Publicity, is given a most interesting example. He says: "I had the pleasure of attending a meeting of one of the State societies and found that a good deal of newspaper publicity had been given before the meeting. There had not been any provision made to have representatives of the press attend, and, drawing one of the members aside, I spoke to him about it. A telephone call or two and inside of fifteen minutes we had four reporters there with the result that the next morning's papers had exceedingly fine articles on the first page!" This example is so good that it is hardly necessary to say more, but one or two practical suggestions may be given that will help our societies or chapters in this regard.

Today many organizations, business houses, and even individuals have a publicity man to get what they desire before the public. In some cases this may be necessary with the Sons of the American Revolution, but by practical experience it has been found that a goodly amount of space can be obtained by systematic effort, with a committee or a member who will take this work upon himself. The newspapers are being pressed on all sides by many interests for publicity and in most cases they respond to the best of their ability, but they cannot publish reports of or send representatives to all the meetings and events that take place, and it has been found by long experience that if some one who is interested will write a good report for publication and send it in in time, in nine cases out of ten it will be published in full and in a prominent place, because the meetings of the S. A. R. are always of public interest and so recognized by the press of the country.

Why cannot every State Society and every Chapter have a small committee, the smaller the better, who will do this work and take the responsibility of carrying on this publicity? With such a committee in every Society and Chapter working consistently every time a meeting was held, the amount of publicity that the Sons of the American Revolution would get in a year would be tremendous and the results and benefits to the organization would be untold. Past President General Jenks said once at a dinner that, within two days after publishing his photograph in the papers when he was elected President General, greatly to his astonishment four men stopped him in the street and said they wanted to join the Society.

Another suggestion: Every member should constitute himself a publicity agent. There is not a member who has not been asked what the little buff, white, and blue button means. This is your opportunity and if the man asking the question is eligible and desirable it is up to the member to see that a new member is secured. It simply means a proper follow-up, for most men want to join our Society, but many need a little help. Societies, Chapters, and Compatriots, why not try these simple suggestions this year and see how it works out?

Every member should keep in mind the qualifications for membership, which we quote below:

Article III.—Membership.

Section 1. Any man shall be eligible to membership in the Society who, being of the age of twenty-one years or over and a citizen of good repute in the community, is the lineal descendant of an ancestor who was at all times unfailing in his loyalty to and rendered active service in the cause of American Independence, either as an officer, soldier, seaman, marine, militiaman, or minute man in the armed forces of the Continental Congress, or of any one of the several Colonies or States, or as a Signer of the Declaration of Independence, or as a member of a Committee of Safety or Correspondence, or as a member of any Continental, Provincial, or Colonial Congress or Legislature, or as a recognized patriot who performed actual service by overt acts of resistance to the authority of Great Britain.

Provided, however, that any male person above the age of eighteen years and under the age of twenty-one years, whose qualifications in regard to ancestry and personal character are as above prescribed, shall be eligible to a qualified membership to be known and designated as junior membership, said junior membership to permit to each junior member all privileges granted to full membership except those of holding office, of voting, of holding any interest in the property or funds of the Society, or of any Chapter thereof, or of receiving a certificate of membership except as hereinafter provided, or of wearing any insignia of the Society other than the rosette; a special certificate may be issued to such junior member in such form as may be prescribed by the Board of Trustees, providing such junior member shall not be in arrears for dues; on attaining the age of twenty-one years he shall automatically be vested with full membership in the Society.

THE AMERICAN'S CREED FELLOWSHIP

Although the American's Creed belongs to the American people, it must ever be a supreme satisfaction to the Sons of the American Revolution to know that the Creed is essentially an S. A. R. production.

The originator of the Creed idea is a member of the S. A. R. brotherhood, the man who promoted the Creed contest and who managed the publicity is also a member, the man who secured the prize from the city of Baltimore became, two years later, the President General of the National Society, and, above all, the author of the Creed is likewise one of us. Furthermore, the Sons of the American Revolution was the first of the patriotic societies to endorse the Creed, at their convention at Rochester in 1918, and the first patriotic convention to endorse the new plan for its promulgation was that held at Buffalo in May, 1921.

Through the Committee on Resolutions, the Buffalo Convention endorsed the then unpublished proof of "The Book of the American's Creed." This attractive-looking little volume of some sixty-six pages, illustrated in symbolic fashion, has appeared in June, and it contains those expressions explanatory of the twelve phrases of the Creed used by those who have successfully expounded the fundamental principles of American constitutional government to native and foreign-born citizens.

To promote the distribution of this book, *which is not on sale*, The American's Creed Fellowship has been created. Life membership in The American's Creed Fellowship is covered by a subscription of $1.00, in return for which the applicant receives a Founder's Copy of "The Book of the American's Creed," the title page of which announces that it is issued under the auspices of patriotic societies of America.

The Committee on Publication of the book consists of the heads of national patriotic organizations, *and the chairman of that committee is ex officio the President General of the Sons of the American Revolution*, whoever he may be at the time of the issue of the edition. The first edition of this work was sent to press under the presidency of Compatriot James H. Preston, of Maryland, and the second edition will be sent to press under the presidency of Compatriot Wallace McCamant, of Oregon.

It is the purpose of the Fellowship to issue the book in subsequent editions sponsored in this way *so long as the S. A. R. maintains leadership in the matter of promulgating the Creed and in the distribution of the book*. The single requirement of The American's Creed Fellowship is that the applicant endorse The American's Creed as a summary of American political faith and promise that he or she will lend moral support to the use of the Creed throughout the Nation.

Every Son of the American Revolution is cordially invited to join The American's Creed Fellowship and secure a Founder's Copy. Any member of the Fellowship may thereafter obtain additional copies at a cost of publication, if ordered in lots of three or more. Although the book is scarcely off the press, many Sons are already Fellowship members. Compatriot William E. Summers, of Millburn, N. J., writes that he was fortunate enough to have got books in time to give to the public-school graduates of his community, and Compatriot

D. E. Felt, of Chicago, has seen to it that the Illinois Society was supplied with copies for general distribution.

President General McCamant has written of "The Book of the American's Creed," that "the message which it contains is thoroughly wholesome and adapted to present-day conditions."

Applicants for Fellowships should communicate with Compatriot Matthew Page Andrews, Chairman of The American's Creed Committee of the Maryland Society, S. A. R., 849 Park Avenue, Baltimore, Md.

ATTENTION, COMPATRIOTS!

During the last few years a great reform has been effected in the method of naturalizing foreigners. Courts all over the Union have awakened to the value of the privileges conferred when an applicant is admitted to American citizenship. Care is exercised to see that citizenship is granted only to those who have a proper loyalty to our institutions and sufficient intelligence to exercise the right of franchise properly.

The value of this reform is very greatly impaired by the fact that some of the States permit a foreigner to vote before he has received his citizenship papers. The Society took action on this matter at the Syracuse Congress in 1914, strongly recommending that the right of franchise should be limited in all the States to American citizens. This matter is called to the attention of compatriots to the end that steps may be taken to amend the statutes and constitutions which extend the franchise to foreigners who have not yet received their final papers. The Constitution of Oregon was amended in 1914 in accordance with the recommendations of the Syracuse Congress and in that State no one can vote unless he is an American citizen.

WALLACE McCAMANT,
President General.

RESOLUTION PASSED BY EXECUTIVE COMMITTEE, AUGUST 9, 1921.

The following preamble and resolution have been adopted by the Executive Committee:

Whereas the present salaries of the Registrar General's and Secretary General's offices are not sufficient to cover all expenses for clerical help; therefore be it

Resolved, That the salary of the Registrar General of the National Society, Sons of the American Revolution, be $1,200.00 per annum, payable in monthly installments of $100.00 per month, and the salary of the Secretary General of the National Society, Sons of the American Revolution, be $1,800.00 per annum, payable in equal monthly amounts of $150.00; said salaries to date from May 16, 1921, and with the definite understanding that the above-mentioned salaries shall include all expenses for clerical services rendered in connection with these two offices, and there shall be no additional charge submitted by the Registrar General or Secretary General for any expenses save for stationery, printing, engraving and engrossing of certificates, postage, and telegraph charges. Out of the salaries voted to the respective offices shall be paid all expenses for clerical help.

REPORT MEMORIAL COMMITTEE TO NATIONAL CONGRESS, S. A. R.
Buffalo, N. Y., May, 1921

MR. PRESIDENT GENERAL AND COMPATRIOTS:

It is my pleasure to report progress, not as great in volume nor so rapid as I should like to, but what we are doing is being done as carefully and as surely as the circumstances will admit, all expenses being borne by those who are doing it; and in this connection I wish to state that the co-operation, not only of our own members, but also of those of both sexes, whether members of other organizations or not, has been beautiful and most gratifying.

We tried to get certified copies of the wills of all the Signers. Of the 56, we now have 38 of them; of six of those who died intestate, we have obtained information from the reports of their executors or administrators. We have not succeeded in obtaining any information regarding the wills or estates of twelve of the Signers. Any assistance that you, your friends or acquaintances, might render us in this matter will be most gratefully received. Those of whose wills or estates we are lacking in information are the following:

1. Elbridge Gerry, of Mass.	7. Carter Braxton, of Va.
2. James Wilson, of Pa.	8. William Hooper, of N. C.
3. George Clymer, of Pa.	9. Thomas Heyward, Jr., of S. C.
4. Samuel Chase, of Md.	10. Thomas Lynch, Jr., of S. C.
5. George Wythe, of Va.	11. Lyman Hall, of Ga.
6. Thomas Nelson, Jr., of Va.	12. George Walton, of Ga.

We also have tried to locate the burial places of the Signers and obtain copies of the epitaphs on their tombstones and such monuments as are in reasonably close proximity to their remains. Of course, it would be impracticable to attempt to obtain such data regarding the many monuments, tablets, &c., erected to such men as Franklin and Jefferson, for they are almost ubiquitous, so far as our country is concerned.

Of the 56 we have obtained copies of the epitaphs of 43. Most of these have been published and we have compaied some of our copies with the originals. I am sorry to say that we have found a very large percentage of errors, some of them material, but as a rule they are merely such trifles as capitalization, punctuation, or alignment.

Of the 56 Signers,

There was lost at sea... 1

　　Thomas Lynch, Jr., S. C.

The exact spot of their original burial place being known, their remains undisturbed 32

Those whose remains have been removed and reinterred elsewhere.......... 10

Ph. Livingston, N. Y.	Francis L. Lee, Va.
Lewis Morris, N. Y.	Wm. Hooper, N. C.
John Hart, N. J.	John Penn, N. C.
James Wilson, Pa.	Lyman Hall, Ga.
Thos. McKean, Del.	Geo. Walton, Ga.
(Cæsar Rodney?)	

The location of whose graves are known with a close degree of approximation, such as the churchyard or burial ground of Christ Church, in Philadelphia, but the grave unmarked, the marker illegible, or its exact location
unknown 10

Francis Lewis, N. Y.
Francis Hopkinson, N. J.
Rich'd Stockton, N. J.
Geo. Ross, Pa.
Cæsar Rodney, Del.

Rich'd Henry Lee, Va.
George Wythe, Va.
Joseph Hewes, N. C.
Arthur Middleton, S. C.
Thos. Heyward, Jr., S. C.

Those the location of whose graves are unknown or merely surmised........ 3

Carter Braxton, Va.
Benjamin Harrison, Va.

Button Gwinnett, Ga   56

Again we ask the assistance of those who can aid us with citations to or copies
from contemporary newspapers, periodicals, letters or diaries, or even traditional
information coming from one who had contemporary information.

The British made especial efforts to capture men of prominence who had
espoused the cause of the Colonists in that great conflict, and when they suc-
ceeded they persecuted the unhappy prisoner almost unmercifully. Five of our
Signers were thus captured and treated—Stockton, of New Jersey; Heywood, of
North Carolina; Middleton and Rutledge, of South Carolina, and Walton, of
Georgia. Mrs. Francis Lewis, of New York, was also captured and mistreated
because she was the wife of a Signer, and two of the sons of Abraham Clark, of
New Jersey, were captured and similarly treated because their father was a
Signer.

In Philadelphia, Pa., Christ Church is located on Second Street between Arch
and Market. In the churchyard are many graves, including those of Robert
Morris, 1733-1806, and James Wilson, 1742-1798. The "Burial Ground," some
three blocks away, on the corner of 5th and Arch Streets, is crowded with graves,
including those of Benjamin Franklin, 1706-1790, and Benjamin Rush, 1745-1813.
In each of the four above-mentioned cases the remains of Signers lie grouped
along with other members of their families.

Three other Signers, Francis Hopkinson, of New Jersey, 1737-1791; George
Ross, of Pennsylvania, 1730-1778, and Joseph Hewes, of North Carolina, born in
New Jersey in 1730, died in Philadelphia in 1779, were also buried here, but the
church records merely give their names and dates of interment. Search is being
made for the grave of Francis Hopkinson with a good prospect of definitely
locating it.

The grave of John Morton still lies in the cemetery of old St. Paul's Church
in Chester, Pa., in what is today very unfortunate surroundings. People of the
vicinity desire that they remain undisturbed. Of the members of the family who
have been consulted, I am told all have consented to the removal but one influential descendant, who still withholds his consent.

Delaware

Cæsar Rodney, born October 7, 1728; died June 29, 1784. I give the date of
his birth because some authorities erroneously give it as 1730. Rodney's house
was some four miles southeast of Dover and on his plantation. He was buried

there. in his old family burial ground, the site now being occupied by a small clump of trees probably 50 yards in diameter.

In about 1850 an old man named Nicholas Lockerman, who had been present at the burial of Rodney, took a group of men to the place and pointed out the location of the grave, and later one of them (Judge Comegys) is said to have raised a mound over it and placed there a fragment of limestone. In 1884 an association was formed for removing the remains to Dover. Accordingly, Judge Comegys showed them the location. In making the excavation only a few rusty nails were found. Apparently the body, bones and all else, had entirely disintegrated; so the committee removed about 1½ bushels of earth from the spot where they thought the body had lain, and this was placed beneath the handsome granite monument in the burial ground surrounding Christ Church, in Dover, on which is inscribed "Cæsar Rodney."

The late Mr. Ezekiel Cowgill, who subsequently owned the plantation, was also present in 1850 when Nicholas Lockerman showed the location of the Rodney grave. His daughter told me, basing her information on that obtained from her father, that Rodney's grave was lined with brick, that the committee was not taken to the true location, and therefore that Rodney's remains still lie in his old family burial ground.

I have no reason to doubt the sincerity of the statements made to me by those on each side in this controversy.

Virginia

Chancellor Wythe, 1726-1806, was buried in St. John's Churchyard, in Richmond, Va. While the grave is unmarked, its location is known to be in one of two adjoining locations and can probably be determined without any great difficulty. I am glad to be able to report that a concerted effort is being made on the part of some four organizations, of which our Virginia Society is one, to definitely determine its location and erect there a handsome monument to his memory.

In Virginia all the early settlements were made in the tidewater section, and not until after the American Revolution was there any considerable movement to the west of it. It extended from the Atlantic Ocean as far inland as the city of Richmond, a distance of about 100 miles. Within it is the Chesapeake Bay and its many broad arms, each bearing the name of some river. These were broad estuaries, amply deep for the small vessels of that day. Almost none of the land reached a height of 200 feet above tide, the high portions making almost plateaus, with level, flat, lowlands next the streams, occasionally two or more miles in width. It was here that the early planters settled and made their homes, warehouses, stores, and wharves, to and from which their ships, often, if not generally, privately owned, sailed. The first and second generations of our early Virginia families lived in houses so situated, and generally built of logs or frame, preferably the former, because they were more impregnable against Indian weapons, though some of those early homes were of brick. They were often from families of high social standing in England and men of large affairs, who through thrift, energy, and other good qualities rapidly acquired wealth and prominence and became possessed of immense holdings of lands.

Such was the origin of the Lee and Tayloe families in Virginia.

The first of the Lees named Richard settled in Essex County about 1641 and died there in or before 1666. His son Richard (1647-1714), graduate of Oxford, councilor, &c., moved north, into what is now Westmoreland County, and settled on that broad, level, low plain south of the Potomac and east of Machadoc Bay, but his home stood half or three-quarters of a mile from his wharf. It was probably called Stratford, but of that we are not certain. The house was probably of log or frame, as neither stone nor brick is there to mark the site of either foundation or chimney. Here he had his slaves' quarters and his garden, and within the latter his family burial ground. It was a small plot of only about 20 or 21 feet square, surrounded by a brick wall, of which but little more than the foundations are left. Within that there is now but one slab, with inscriptions in both Latin and English to him and his wife, Lettice, daughter of Henry Corbin.

Each of his six children inherited large tracts of land, but the eldest, Richard, the law of primogeniture being then in force, received the larger portion, including the home place, but resided in London, England, though he still retained title to and possession of his father's Virginia home. During his ownership the house caught fire and burned to the ground. It was never rebuilt, not a vestige of it is there today, and its only marker is what remains of the old family burial ground. It soon became known as "The Old Burnt House"; today it is often called "The Old Burnt Field," with the nearest house three-fourths of a mile away, built on much higher ground, by a subsequent generation, and called Mount Pleasant.

A younger brother to Richard Lee (3d), of London, named Thomas (1690-1750), settled some miles to the west, where he built a very handsome residence of brick, said to have been presented to him by Queen Caroline, and which he called "Stratford Hall," today generally known as "Stratford" and celebrated as the birthplace of the great Confederate General, Robert E. Lee.

Here were born three of our Revolutionary patriots, two of whom were signers, namely, Richard Henry Lee, 1732-1794; Francis Lightfoot Lee, 1734-1797, and Dr. Arthur Lee, 1740-1792.

Richard Henry Lee was twice married. He built himself a home to the west of the mouth of Nomini Bay, on high ground, from which he had a wonderfully beautiful view, and named his plantation "Chantilly." The house is long since gone and its site would never be found without a guide who knows its location, for today there is only a slight depression marking the partially filled in cellar and a few of the brick with which it was lined. Seventy-five yards west of it, and evidently within the old garden, is a black walnut tree marking the site of the burial ground where some of the family were interred. It is now a part of a plowed field, with nothing visible to indicate a grave. There was on his plantation a separate burial ground for his slaves.

From the recorded will of Richard Henry Lee I quote:

"First: I desire to be decently privately and frugally buried in the family burying ground at the burnte House as it is called and as neare to my late every deare wife as 'tis possible to place mine without disturbing her remains and upon her left, so that my present dear Mrs. Lee may be laid, when she dyes on my right; and so my body be placed between those of my dear wives;"

There is residing in this section the Rev. Dr. G. W. Beale, a fellow-member of mine in the Virginia Society of the Cincinnati, a man of culture and refinement, who possesses the confidence and commands the respect of the entire community. He has done a vast amount of most valuable genealogical and historical research work, including, of course, that of the Lee family. Some fifteen or twenty years ago he did some magnificent work for me, and, though now very feeble and infirm, he knew of my coming and was kind enough to give me free access to his notes and data. One of his daughters spent several days in acting as my guide and otherwise aiding me in my research work. Dr. Beale told me that Richard Henry Lee was buried at the "Old Burnt Field," as directed in his will. Among his notes was a copy of a letter written in 1851 by a Mrs. Colville Griffith, describing the burial of her grandfather's cousin, Richard Henry Lee, which she had herself witnessed some 57 years before. Dr. Beale called upon and obtained from her her personal recollections, but his physical condition was such that it would not do to hold his attention too long, so I spoke to him of his interview with Mrs. Griffith and said: "The burial ground at the Old Burnt House, as surrounded by the brick wall, was only about 20 feet square and was so filled up with the remains of the early Lees that Richard Henry Lee had to be buried on the outside." He nodded his head in assent and replied, "Yes." I then said: "There are four sides to that burial ground. On which side did she say he was buried—the north, the east, the south, or the west?" To which he replied, "Didn't say; all she said was, He was buried just without the burial ground."

If a stake were driven in the center of that old inclosure and a circle drawn with a radius of 20 feet, it would certainly include the grave of Richard Henry Lee. The ground without has been plowed close up to the brick walls, a foot or more of the surface soil has been washed away, and with proper trenching the graves could be located, but whether or not the identity of the remains could be established I am not prepared to say.

The Tayloe family, into which Francis Lightfoot Lee married, is another with a very similar history. William, the first of the family in America, settled in York County in the first half of the 17th century. His namesake nephew and heir settled on the lowlands, on the north side of the Rappahannock, in what is now Richmond County. I am not certain whether the name of Mount Airy was then applied to this plantation or to adjacent lands which he subsequently patented, but here he built and equipped his home, as was customary in those days, including the family burial ground, which in this case contained then, or at a later date, one or more vaults.

It was his grandson, John Tayloe II, 1721-1779, who in 1747 built the present Mount Airy—a beautiful stone palace, on high ground, some two miles east of "The Old House," as it is called by the Tayloes of today. It was one of his daughters, born in 1752, who married Francis Lightfoot Lee in 1769 and to whom Colonel John Tayloe (II) made a deed of gift in 1778 of 1,000 acres of land, including the still pretty and interesting old stone house called "Menoken," where they lived and died.

Another daughter, Eleanor Tayloe (born in 1756), married, in 1772, the Hon. Ralph Wormeley of Rosegill, the fifth of that name and estate.

Singular as it may seem, they continued to bury their dead in the burying ground at "The Old House" for about a century after building the new. It was there that the remains of the Francis Lightfoot Lee and his wife and Ralph Wormeley and his wife were placed in one of the vaults.

When, owing to the ravages of time, the crown of this vault caved in, the then proprietor of Mount Airy, Colonel Wm. Henry Tayloe (1799-1871), the grandson of Colonel John Tayloe II, concluded it best to establish a new family burial ground on high ground, about 400 yards from his new house and from which there is a grand and extensive view. In furthering this plan, he removed the graves from the old burial ground to the new, bringing with each its own inscribed slab, but when it came to the vault he was not able to identify and separate the remains of the two Tayloe sisters and their husbands, so he placed the remains of all four in one grave in the new burial ground and planted an arbor-vitæ at the head of the grave.

I therefore feel that, through and with the kind assistance of the Tayloe and Beale families, I have succeeded in locating definitely and accurately the resting place of the remains of Francis Lightfoot Lee and a very close approximation to those of his elder brother, Richard Henry Lee.

Had earlier investigators gone on the ground as I did, there is no reason why this information should not have been made public years ago.

R. C. BALLARD THRUSTON,
Chairman.

REPORT OF NATIONAL COMMITTEE ON INCREASED MEMBERSHIP

To the Thirty-second Annual Congress of the National Society of the Sons of the American Revolution:

The numerical growth of the Society during the past year has, on the whole, been gratifying. Despite the lamentable fact that the high inspirations of a war in progress have seemingly subsided in the drab period of materialism which has followed its cessation, interest in patriotism has not wholly died out. Reports from many of the State Societies indicate an alertness to the fact that the safety of our institutions rests on the maintenance of our national ideals.

It is the peculiar function of the Sons of the American Revolution to keep the fires of American idealism alight. In some States the increase in membership is most significant, in each case demonstrating the value of one or two thoroughly enthused compatriots striving untiringly to awaken in the hearts of American citizens a right understanding and appreciation of America's history and principles.

Efforts to increase the membership of our Society are not solely in the interests of the Society. The higher purpose is the strengthening of the morale of the American nation by emphasizing the enduring value of our peculiar national institutions at this time of wide-extended dismemberment of nations.

CHANCELLOR L. JENKS,
Chairman.

REPORT OF COMMITTEE ON MILITARY AND NAVAL WAR RECORDS

To the Congress:

Your Committee on Military and Naval War Records has the honor to report that the Revolutionary War Records, so long kept in Room 512, State, War, and Navy Building, in Washington, have been moved to the building known as the Munitions Building, on B Street, and are still under the custody of the Adjutant General's Office.

It may be that they are of as easy access. The Adjutant General's Office has always been courteous in making searches for us. The Navy Records, also Revolutionary, are still in the Navy Library, in the State, War, and Navy Building. The older records, covering mostly the Colonial period, may be found in the Library of Congress, much scattered, we may say desultory.

Moving of records is usually attended with loss as well as disarrangement of papers.

From the Chief of War Records of the Navy we are informed that many Navy records, which encumbered the corridors of the basement of the Treasury Department, about the year 1855 were destroyed under the belief that they had already served their purpose.

In looking up the records of the naval officers of the original (the Colonial) Navy, your committee has felt some embarrassment in being unable to locate even the final resting place of a number of them. For example, there were three brothers Nicholson, who commanded ships in the War of the Revolution, and we have been able to locate the grave of but one of them, Samuel, who is buried in old Trinity Churchyard, New York City, his grave being marked by a slab; but we cannot locate the graves of his brothers. They were natives of the State of Maryland.

The grave of Captain Thomas Thompson, who commanded the *Raleigh,* is in the North Cemetery, near the city of Portsmouth, N. H., and is not marked. The Grand Army decorates this grave on each Decoration Day. Near the grave of Captain Thompson is that of a Signer, William Whipple, marked by a small slab. Another case is that of Captain Abram Whipple, at Marietta, Ohio, which is unmarked.

The Maryland Society, S. A. R., has set us an example by placing a handsome memorial at the grave of General Smallwood, in Charles County, Maryland, and at the grave of General Mordecai Gist, in old St. Michael's Churchyard, in Charleston, S. C.

While these unmarked graves may not be literally "Military and Naval Records," they surely invite attention to the need of memorials to record the resting place of the men to whom we owe so much.

On the 30th of October, 1920, the District of Columbia Society assembled at the statue of Captain John Paul Jones, in Washington, to dedicate a bronze tablet on which are inscribed the words of the immortal Jones in giving his testimony to the (original) Continental Marine Committee as to the regulations of the Navy and the essential qualifications of an officer.

The Secretary of the Navy ordered the attendance of the Marine Band and a small vessel carrying a light battery to come as near the scene as possible and to fire the salute. The ceremonies were conducted by Rear Admiral Chester, chairman of the committee, who gave a historic address, much of the history of the original Navy, of which Captain John Paul Jones was a central figure or the father.

A classic address was given by the Assistant Secretary of the Navy, the Hon. Gordon Woodbury, and an equally splendid oration by our President General, Mr. James H. Preston.

Not the least of the interesting features was the unveiling of the tablet by the daughter of Rear Admiral John Crittenden Watson, of the Kentucky Society.

The words on the tablet are those which have been impressed on every plebe midshipman on entering the Naval Academy, as well as on every officer entering the service from civil life:

"It is by no means enough that an officer of Navy should be a capable mariner; he should be that, of course, but also a great deal more. He should be, as well, a gentleman of liberal education, refined manner, punctilious courtesy, and the finest sense of personal honor. He should not only be able to express himself clearly and with force in his own language, both with pen and tongue, but should be versed in French and Spanish. He should be the soul of tact, patience, justice, firmness and charity. No meritorious act of a subordinate should escape his attention nor be left to pass without its reward, if even the reward be one word of approval.

"Conversely, he should not be blind to a single fault in any subordinate, though, at the same time, he should be quick and unfailing to distinguish error from malice, thoughtlessness from incompetence, and well-meant shortcoming from heedless or stupid blunder.

"As he should be universal and impartial in his rewards and approval of merit, so should he be judicial and unbending in his punishment or reproof of misconduct."

The thought of placing this enduring tablet on the monument originated with Rear Admiral Watson, at whose request Rear Admiral Chester brought it to the attention of the District of Columbia Society.

The committee appointed by the President of the District of Columbia Society to carry out this scheme was composed of Rear Admirals Chester, Watson, Jewell, and Baird.

Your committee begs leave to place on record some figures n the First Census, from which personages were drawn the first military and naval characters. These figures were given us by Compatriot Albert Johnson, M. C., chairman of the Committee on Immigration and Nationalization House of Representatives. Compatriot Johnson is a member of the (State of Washington Society, S. A. R.:

"According to the First Census, the free population of the United States in 1790, just after the Constitution went into effect, was 3,250,000. Of these 2,345,844 were of British origin. There were 188,589 Scotch people and 44,273 Irish. The Dutch, most of whom lived in New York, numbered 58,6 There were 156,457 Germans, 13,384 French, 1,243 Hebrews, and 3,835 other nationalities."

These figures, from such eminent authority, cannot be disputed. T "Irish" referred to were the Ulster Irish, Presbyterians almost exclusively and the French were mostly the Huguenots, of whom General Francis Mn is an example. These statistics, which seem to us to be of priceless value may, we hope, not be considered out of place.

G. W. Baird, *irman*.

REPORT OF NATIONAL PATRIOTIC COMMITTEE, S. A. R.

The National Patriotic Committee of the Sons of the American Revolution has the honor of submitting to the National Congress its annual report concerning the work of this committee, its aims and its recommendations.

The members of this committee, like all true Americans, are deeply interested in the development of American ideals and are using their utmost power toward their advancement.

They are especially concerned in seeing that the schools of this country secure and retain the best teachers obtainable—men and women of high character and ideals, who are well trained in their profession, teachers who are patriotic Americans, and who will train their pupils to love and cherish American ideals and institutions, that make our country the hope of the world.

These patriotic, trained teachers must be paid a salary befitting their great value to the community and the nation, so that they may be of the greatest service in their great work of training American citizens. Their value has never been realized as now, when they form the greatest bulwark against Bolshevism and anarchy.

Patriotic education is the keynote of the salvation of our country, and it must be well taught in the schools and universities.

In addition to this, the Board of Education in the large cities are doing splendid work in establishing evening schools for adults; classes in factories for adult foreigners; classes for women in schools, field-houses, and other places—in fact, classes of all kinds for native and foreign born, so as to make them patriotic and intelligent Americans.

Chicago, like the other cities, is doing an immense amount of work in all of these patriotic lines. It has distributed many thousands of the American's Creed among its many schools, and this magnificent Creed, born in the famed city of Baltimore, is now a household word in all of the schools of Chicago and in nearly all of its homes, where it has been of the greatest value in teaching the ideals of American government to our foreign born.

The work of the public schools is now becoming more of a public welfare character. Academic work, especially the "three R's," is no longer the sole aim of school work. It is now but one phase of school activity, as so many problems of social and industrial life are now thrust upon the schools. We have now community centers, playgrounds, domestic science, vocational training, etc., under our school system, so as to better develop and train American citizens.

All this takes money, much money. It also becomes a national problem, as well as a State or community problem, and the Government should lend its help. It is doing so and is giving aid to the States in patriotic, agricultural, and vocational lines. This is admirable; but the various acts are not connected, so that their efficiency is impaired through lack of system.

As a result, thinking people from all over the country, who realize the need of an efficient educational system for the good of the whole country, felt strongly that as *good people form* the soul of a nation, a department of education should be formed by the Government, through which education in all its phases should be studied, and aid, both educational and financial, should be extended to the various States.

For this purpose the Smith-Towner Bill was presented to Congress, asking for
the founding of a Department of Education, with a Secretary of Education at its
head. This bill grants great aid to the States, especially in patriotic, agricultural and vocational lines. Some opposition was offered, through fear that the
Government would dominate the teaching in the various States; but a careful
revision of the Smith-Towner Bill has been made, so as to eliminate all possible
danger of the Government interfering with the States in their control of their
own school systems.

The revised Smith-Towner Bill, or Sterling-Towner Bill, which puts all of the
educational bills of the Government under the control of the Department of
Education, would administer aid with much greater efficiency and economy and
deserves the support of every patriotic American.

I would recommend that this bill receive the endorsement and support of the
National Society, Sons of the American Revolution, in Congress here assembled.

GEORGE A. BRENNAN,
Chairman Patriotic Committee.

REPORT OF THE CHANCELLOR GENERAL AT THE MAY CONGRESS

Mr. President General and Compatriots:

Your Chancellor General reports the following matters coming before him for
consideration:

The President General submitted a question which arose between the members
of the Illinois Society and the Registrar General as to the date to be placed upon
certificates to be issued by the National Society, the contention of the Illinois
Society being that the date to be placed upon the certificates should be the date
upon which the compatriot was elected by the State Society, the Registrar General urging that the date should be that upon which the papers were finally
passed upon by the Registrar General.

After careful examination of the Constitution of the National Society and that
of the State Society, the opinion was rendered that the contention of the Illinois
Society should be upheld.

At the request of the Executive Committee, examination was made of the Constitution with reference to the proposed separation of the Connecticut Society
from the National Society, and resolutions and notices prepared by the Connecticut Society were submitted to the Chancellor General for an opinion as to
the validity of action proposed to be taken at a meeting called for February 22,
1921. The opinion rendered was that under the notice presented the proposed
withdrawal of the Connecticut Society could not be accomplished at such meeting, and it is the understanding of this office that further action by the Connecticut Society was deferred until after the present session of the Congress.

At the request of the Executive Committee, several proposed amendments to
the Constitution were submitted to the Chancellor General for drafting, were
duly submitted to the several State Societies, and will be considered by the
present Congress.

At the request of the Registrar of the New York State Society, an opinion was rendered as to the legality of local Chapters admitting to membership members of State Societies from other States.

Your Chancellor General has also had considerable correspondence with the Executive Officers of the National Society with reference to various matters upon which no opinion was formally prepared.

All of which is respectfully submitted.

HARVEY F. REMINGTON,
Chancellor General.

BUFFALO, *May 16, 1921.*

EVENTS OF STATE SOCIETIES

The Arizona Society.—For the purpose of encouraging the spirit of Americanism among the youth of the State, the Arizona Society of the Sons of the American Revolution has instituted a prize oratorical contest open to the members of senior and junior high schools of Arizona. The orations will be on subjects of vital topics of the day—"America's Power to Keep the Peace of the World," "America's Trust to the Western Hemisphere," and "America's Duty to Its Immigrants.'

In announcing the contest, Harold Baxter, Secretary of the Society, said that the plan is similar to that carried on a few years ago and interrupted by the war. It will be conducted as a part of the Americanization work, and copies of the rules of the contest have been forwarded the principals of every high school in the State urging their co-operation.

Elsie Toles, State Superintendent of Public Instruction, approves the plan, the details of which were announced by Mr. Baxter as follows:

In each high school, where there are two or more contestants, a local contest shall be held under the local school authority; the winner of each local contest shall be invited to come to Phœnix for a public State contest, to be held on Tuesday, February 21, 1922. The prizes at this State contest will be $20 and $10 in gold, respectively, each prize to be accompanied by an appropriate medal. All contestants who take part in this State contest will be invited, as special guests, to attend the annual dinner of the Arizona Society, S. A. R., to be held in Phœnix, Wednesday evening, February 22, 1922, and will be entertained while in Phœnix, but car fares must be paid by the schools or cities sending contestants to Phœnix.

The successful contestant in each local contest shall mail, not later than January 14, 1922, to the Secretary of the Arizona Society, S. A. R., one copy of his oration, so that plans may be made for the State contest before the State contest takes place.

The California Society, Sons of the American Revolution, appointed a committee to take action in respect to the memory of Compatriot James L. Cogswell. Said committee reported as follows:

James Lafayette Cogswell was born in the State of Connecticut, November 23, 1830. He died in Alameda County, California, April 13, 1921, at the age of ninety years. Dr. Cogswell, who was of sturdy Revolutionary stock, came to California among the pioneers, coming to this State in 1849. He was a resident for many years of San Francisco. In October, 1875, he issued and had published a call to local eligibles, with a view to forming a Society of Sons of Revolutionary Sires. As an outcome of this, there met at Dr. Cogswell's office in San Francisco, on October 22, 1875, eight men, who organized a temporary society of this nature and arranged to participate in the exercises and march in the parade in San Francisco on July 4, 1876, in celebration of the 100th anniversary of the Signing of the Declaration of Independence. Dr. Cogswell was elected the first president of this society here. The idea was soon taken up in several Eastern States and other societies formed, the result of which was the organization in 1889 of the National Society of the Sons of the American Revolution through delegates from a number of States who met in New York City. The meeting called by Dr. Cogswell in San Francisco has, therefore, the honor of being the beginning of the organization which ultimately became the Sons of the American Revolution.

In respect to the memory of the late James Lafayette Cogswell, we present and move the adoption of the following:

WHEREAS the Supreme Ruler of the Universe called from this earth on April 13, 1921, Compatriot James Lafayette Cogswell, and there is thus taken from our midst our fellow-member, through whose inspiration the Society of the Sons of the American Revolution was founded; therefore be it

Resolved, That the California Society of the Sons of the American Revolution, through its Board of Managers, expresses its regret and respect to the memory of this distinguished compatriot, whose happy thought of so many years ago resulted in the association which we now have and of which we are so proud; and

Resolved, That this Society is a work of which he could well have been proud during his lifetime and constitutes a monument to his memory; and

Resolved, That we extend to the family of the late James Lafayette Cogswell our sympathy and respect, and that the two surviving daughters each be furnished with a copy of these expressions; and further

Resolved, That this action of the Board of Managers of the California Society of the Sons of the American Revolution be made a part of the permanent records of this organization and be bulletined to the members; and further

Resolved, That a copy of this report be forwarded to the office of the National Society of the Sons of the American Revolution, and that we request that our National Society also include these expressions in its permanent records in respect to the memory of our late and honored compatriot and founder.

  (Signed)

HOWARD C. ROWLEY,
Chairman of Committee.

Respectfully submitted.
  H. C. ROWLEY, *Chairman,*
  C. H. BLINN,
  Col. J. C. CURRIER,
  T. A. PERKINS,
        Committee.

The Colorado Society has been making earnest efforts toward the observance of time-honored and historic days and has endeavored particularly to bring to the notice of the authorities a proper recognition of Constitution Day, appealing to churches and schools to institute appropriate exercises on this occasion. The New President of this Society, the Hon. Victor E. Keyes, Attorney General of the State of Colorado, has issued a general letter to the members of his Society, conveying greetings and some of his hopes and aspirations for his Society in devotion to principle, lofty patriotism, and loyalty and pledging his personal influence and support in new consecration to American ideals and American institutions.

The District of Columbia Society celebrated Independence Day with a very fine program, the exercises being held in the large Bureau of Pensions, in the city of Washington. The occasion was full of enthusiasm and the address by Congressman Fred S. Purnell, of Indiana, was most inspiring and appropriate. Beautiful musical numbers and ceremonial reception and salutation of the Flag marked the ceremonies. On September 6 the Society celebrated the 164th anniversary of the birth of Lafayette by a trip to Mt. Vernon by boat, and on September 21 Field Day was celebrated. ·

District of Columbia members of the Sons of the American Revolution and many of their friends met Wednesday, September 21, at Oak Hill Cemetery, to assist in commemorating the placing of gravestone markers on the graves of Lieut. Miah Forrest and Rev. (Capt.) Stephen. B. Balch, soldiers of the Revolutionary War. The invocation was pronounced by Rev. James M. Nourse and President Selden Ely introduced the speaker of the day, William A. Gordon, of Georgetown, who spoke eloquently of the bravery and patriotism of Lieutenant Forrest, and at the grave of Dr. Balch the Rev. James T. Marshall delivered an address of a similar character on this celebrated Georgetown divine.

Empire State Society was active in the ceremonies attending the restoration and erection of a replica of the old Liberty Pole on its former site, in City Hall Park, and its presentation to the City of New York at the annual Flag Day celebration, New York City Hall, Flag Day, June 14, 1921. The Mayor of the City of New York presided.

On Flag Day the S. A. R. sent to England a handsome silk flag of the United States, which was presented to Sulgrave Manor, the ancestral home of the Washingtons. The flag was presented at the Manor House, on June 21, by Compatriot Charles Dumont, of Foxley Lane, Surrey, England, on behalf of the S. A. R., and was accepted by Ambassador Harvey, Honorary President of the Sulgrave Institution.

All schools in Schenectady prepared and executed interesting programs in connection with Flag Day, June 14.

On Independence Day Compatriots of the Empire State Society assembled in front of the barge office, at the Battery, July 4th, and marched with United States troops and the Federation des Veterans Francais de la Grande Guerre to St. Paul's Churchyard, where exercises of international significance were held under the auspices of the New York Chapter, S. A. R., at the tomb of General Bechet (Sieur de Rochefontaine). General Bechet, who was born at Ay, in the Department of the Marne, France, served under Rochambeau in the War for American Independence and later in the United States Army. The Council General of the Department of the Marne and the Municipal Council of the town of Ay joined in sending a bronze palm to be placed on the tomb. The New York Chapter has voted to place a floral wreath on the tomb annually, General Bechet being the most distinguished French officer who both participated in the actual fighting for American Independence and was buried in American soil.

At Mount Vernon, N. Y., the Independence Day celebration was participated in by members of the Empire State Society, S. A. R.

NEW YORK CHAPTER, at a meeting, decided that this Chapter would, by voluntary subscriptions, furnish a room in the new house of the Army and Navy Club of America, Central Park South, as a memorial to those members who made the supreme sacrifice during the World War.

"Uncle Sam Night," arranged by Mrs. Charles R. Scarborough, chairman of the Women's Auxiliary of the New York Port Society, in co-operation with the Sons of the American Revolution, Thursday evening, July 7, at New York Port Society's Building, New York, was a stirring success. The honorary committee was composed of Colonel Louis Annin Ames, Past President-General, Sons of the American Revolution; Brigadier-General Bridgman, President of New York Chapter, S. A. R.; Major Charles A. Dubois, Board of Managers, S. A. R.; Captain Reginald Fay, Board of Managers, S. A. R.; Hon. Felix Cordova Da Vila, Porto Rico Resident Commissioner, Washington, D. C.; Hon. Jaime C. De Veyra, Philippine Islands Resident Commissioner, Washington, D. C.; Frederick

H. Sieberth, Hawaiian Territory Commissioner, New York City, and M. J. De La Roma. A welcome was extended to all seafaring men and their friends by Colonel Louis Annin Ames in the address of welcome.

Constitution Day, the 134th anniversary of the adoption of the Constitution of the United States in Convention, September 17, 1787, was celebrated under the auspices of the New York Chapter, at the site of old Federal Hall, now occupied by the Subtreasury Building, at the corner of Wall and Nassau streets, on Saturday, September 17, 1921, at 12 o'clock noon. Compatriots and their friends assembled at St. Paul's Church at 11:30 a. m. and marched, with a band and detail from the United States Navy and invited delegations from other patriotic societies, to the Subtreasury. A stirring program was gone through with before crowds occupying Broad and Wall streets. The addresses were as follows: Brigadier-General Oliver B. Bridgman, N. G. N. Y. R. L., President of the New York Chapter, S. A. R., presiding. Music by the New York City Police Glee Club. Invocation by Rev. Joseph Fort Newton, D. D., Chaplain of the New York Chapter, S. A. R., and minister of the Church of the Divine Paternity. Address by Brigadier-General Louis W. Stotesbury. Music by the New York City Police Glee Club. Address by Colonel Francis R. Stoddard, Jr. "America" was sung by the audience, led by the Police Glee Club and accompanied by the 22d Regiment Infantry, U. S. A., Band.

The observance of Constitution Day was begun by the Sons of the American Revolution in 1919. Last year there were over 42,000 celebrations of the day throughout the country. Colonel Louis Annin Ames, chairman of the National Committee of the Sons of the American Revolution for the observance of the anniversary this year, reported that about 75,000 celebrations were organized for the anniversary.

The Illinois Society conducted impressive exercises in Chicago on the 17th, of which the special feature was a fine address upon the Constitution by Judge C. S. Cutting, an eminent jurist and member of the present Illinois Constitutional Convention.

The Indiana Society.—It is definitely known that more than 1,000 soldiers of the War of the Revolution are buried on Indiana soil, and it has been estimated that the number would run as high as 1,500 if a complete survey of the subject could be made.

The graves of these patriots are in every county. Off from the main highways of travel, in remote, isolated places, are old, abandoned, bramble-grown cemeteries within whose sacred precincts sleep in peace patriots who fought and endured in order that Independence might be established and that this glorious country might have birth. And they sleep, many of them, in graves that are rapidly becoming obliterated. Time and the ravages of the elements are effacing inscriptions from crude and ancient headstones; moss, leaf-mold, and sediment are burying from sight the very outlines of the graves themselves, and any intended work of reclamation and preservation should not longer be delayed.

The Indiana Society of the Sons of the American Revolution has now made definite arrangement for activity along this line by appointing Cornelius F. Posson, of Brazil, as chairman of a committee to take this task in hand. The task is of large proportions, and Compatriot Posson will need all of the assistance, from all quarters, that he can possibly obtain. Through the medium of the

BULLETIN, the Indiana Society is today making personal appeal to every member of our Society to aid in the work of locating graves of Revolutionary soldiers. Let a survey be made by making inquiry of older citizens, by reference to historical and biographical atlases of your county published in earlier years, and by visits to the older cemeteries and family burying grounds of which you may learn by inquiry. Communicate your findings to Compatriot Posson, who is compiling a record in systematic form, which will enable us to take intelligent and definite action later.

This worthy cause should appeal to every man in whose veins flows the patriotic blood of Revolutionary ancestry. It is a field of endeavor for every Son in every corner of the State and Nation.

In an isolated rural cemetery up in Bartholomew County, Indiana, a compatriot some time ago scraped the moss from an ancient tombstone and uncovered the inscription, which gave the name and the military record of a Revolutionary soldier there buried, followed by these words: "He sleeps in peace in the land he fought to defend." So sleep many today in Indiana soil, many in graves that are entirely unmarked, some almost obliterated.

Compatriots, let us search them out while yet we may. Can we, who pride ourselves in our noble ancestry, engage in a more noble undertaking?

Through co-operation of the officers of the Indiana and Virginia Societies, the war service decoration was conferred on Lieut. Paul O. Meredith, a member of the Indiana Society, now a resident of Norfolk, Virginia. The ceremony, arranged by Hon. Frederick E. Emerson, Second Vice-President of the Virginia Society, was witnessed by 150 members of the United States Shipping Board staff.

When Lieut. Charles Timothy Jewett, of Terre Haute, Ind., Trustee of the National Society, was advised that it would not be convenient for Compatriot Meredith to return to Indiana to receive the decoration, he asked the officers of the Virginia Society to act for Indiana. The decoration was forwarded to Vice-President Emerson, who arranged the presentation. Mr. Meredith's associates of the Shipping Board staff were called together at noon, October 6, by Mr. Emerson. There was a short patriotic address by Judge Ackiss.

The Iowa Society.—The quarterly number of the *Old Continental*, published by the Iowa State Society, brings interesting notices of the activities of that progressive and live organization. It gives a fine detailed report of the annual meeting held April 19, 1921; also the President's address, giving several practical suggestions and urging the members to make "this our Iowa Society of the Sons of the American Revolution a live and useful promoter of true patriotism in the communities of our State." Detailed reports of the several officers are reported in full and show a most excellent condition. This excellent number of the *Continental* shows some splendid work that is being done in the schools and colleges, and gives the medal winners in the contests for colleges and high schools in the State of Iowa that is being carried on by the State Society. A remarkably interesting circumstance in the winning of the medals in the college class was that they were won by William H. Volger and Henry Volger, who are twins and in the same class in college.

The following officers were elected for the ensuing year: President, Walter E. Coffin, Des Moines; First Vice-President, F. D. Harsh, Des Moines; Second

Vice-President, Roger Leavitt, Cedar Falls; Treasurer, William W. Bartlett; Secretary, Captain Eldridge Drew Hadley; Registrar, H. H. Griffiths; Historian, Arthur H. Davidson; Chaplain, William B. Sanford, D. D., all of Des Moines; Additional Managers, H. W. Grout, Waterloo; Francis L. Meredith, Des Moines; J. R. Anderson, Cedar Rapids; Rev. E. M. Vittum, Muscatine; Executive Committee, President, W. E. Coffin, F. D. Harsh, H. H. Griffiths; Trustee of National Society, Elmer Marston Wentworth.

The Kansas Society.—On Friday evening, September 16, the Kansas Society, together with the Daughters of the American Revolution, took part in an interesting and unique affair. Thirty-four foreigners were given their citizenship papers and an interesting program was carried out. Short addresses were made, patriotic music and recitations concluded the program, and light refreshments were served. The new citizens were very much pleased and seemed deeply interested. However, some of the active members of the Society were much affected by some regrettable facts that developed at this meeting. The lack of knowledge of well-known facts on the part of some of the applicants was startling. One had never heard of George Washington and another of Lincoln. Another has lived in Kansas for over forty years and had never taken out anything but first papers and had voted at every election. The Kansas Society expects to bring this matter before the National and State Societies and will urge that the naturalization laws be made more rigid in regard to these matters.

The Kentucky Society.—From Louisville we have word of a mass meeting at one of the large churches on the evening of the 17th, with an address by the Chaplain of the Kentucky Society, Dr. E. L. Powell, attended by over eight hundred people. The occasion was generally recognized throughout the public schools in Louisville and the State at large.

The Maine Society mourns the recent death of its President, Hon. James O. Bradbury, of Saco, who assumed the office only in February last, and who had greatly appreciated the honor bestowed upon him. Compatriot Bradbury was also the Trustee of the National Society for Maine. The Board of Managers elected, on June 9, last, William B. Berry, of Gardiner, to fill out the unexpired term of Mr. Bradbury, and adopted appropriate resolutions upon his death. Compatriot Berry is a direct descendant of Lieutenant Samuel Berry, whose brother, Lieutenant Nathaniel Berry, was the last surviving member of George Washington's Life Guards. A boulder with bronze tablet of inscription suitably commemorates this hero in Gardiner.

On Saturday, September 10, at Auburn, Me., there was unveiled a beautiful tablet to the memory of 357 men who served in the Continental Army during the Revolutionary War. The exercises were conducted by the Mary Dillingham Chapter, Daughters of the American Revolution, and was a most impressive and interesting ceremony. The address of welcome was made by Miss Margaret Wilson, representing the Mary Dillingham Chapter, and was responded to by Miss Maud Myrick, the State Regent of Maine. Judge George C. Wing, President of the Auburn Chapter, Sons of the American Revolution, was the principal speaker and made an eloquent and patriotic address. The event was one of the most significant and memorable in the history of Auburn.

The Massachusetts Society.—The first joint meeting ever held of the Sons and Daughters of the American Revolution of Berkshire County took place at the Red Lion Inn in Stockbridge, June 17, 1921, and was a most enjoyable affair. Representatives of the two organizations were present, about 60 in number, from Williamstown on the north to Stockbridge on the south, representing Berkshire County Chapter, Sons of the American Revolution, of this city; Fort Massachusetts Chapter, Daughters of the American Revolution of North Adams, and the Ausotunnoog Chapter, Daughters of the American Revolution, of Lee and Stockbridge.

The affair was a dinner and outing in connection with the annual meeting of the Sons and celebration of Bunker Hill Day. The dinner was held at 7 o'clock and the speakers included Joseph E. Peirson and William L. Root, of this city, representing Berkshire County Chapter; Miss Seymour, of Stockbridge, representing Ausotunnoog Chapter; Mrs. C. O. Rundell, representing Fort Massachusetts Chapter: Mrs. James R. Savery, representing Peace Party Chapter, and Henry F. Punderson, from George Washington Chapter, Sons of the American Revolution, of Springfield.

Mrs. Savery made a very strong appeal to the members for support for work in the abandoned cemeteries in the smaller hill towns, where graves of Revolutionary War soldiers are in a ruinous condition. Mr. Root stated that it was the purpose of the Berkshire County Chapter to maintain all Revolutionary War markers in the country now existing, in a good condition, and to extend the work and mark all graves of Revolutionary War soldiers so far as possible.

At the business meeting of the Sons, which preceded the dinner, 10 new members were admitted to the Chapter, which now numbers 70.

The past year, it was reported, has been the most successful and prosperous in the history of the Chapter. The following officers were elected:

President, A. J. Witherell, of North Adams; Secretary, William L. Root; Treasurer, Elliot A. Clarke.

In celebration of Flag Day, June 14, the Massachusetts Society, Sons of the American Revolution, met at dinner in the American House, Boston, at 6.30 o'clock P. M., and all members and their ladies were invited to attend.

The speaker was Mr. Melville C. Freeman, of West Roxbury. Past President Vernon A. Field gave a talk on the Evolution of the United States Flag.

Among the invited guests were Major-General David C. Shanks, Major-General Samuel S. Sumner, Brigadier-General William H. Bisbee, and Capt. William B. Clarke.

The annual field day of the Massachusetts Society, Sons of the American Revolution, October 12, 1921, in Lexington, proved a big success. At the luncheon in Masonic Temple, shortly after noon, George Hale Nutting, who presided, read a letter from President Harding expressing his regret at being unable to be the guest of honor.

On the arrival of the visitors at the Munroe Tavern they were received by Edwin B. Worthen, president of the Lexington Historical Society, and by Major Alfred Pierce, of the Lexington Minute Men.

After viewing the tavern they marched to the Lexington Town Hall, escorted by the Minute Men, and "The Spirit of '76." The historical tablets were observed along the way. At the Town Hall the painting of the "Dawn of Liberty," by Sandham, was viewed, and Dr. Fred S. Piper, former president of the Historical Society, gave a short address.

From the Town Hall the visitors went to the battle-green, where, with guides and lecturers, the green, the old cemetery, the Hancock-Clarke, and the Buckman Tavern were visited. Dr. J. Odin Tilton, chairman of the Lexington Park Commissioners, delivered a short address at the Buckman Tavern. After luncheon more sightseeing was enjoyed.

The Michigan Society.—The Board of Governors of the Detroit Chapter, recently elected, held their first meeting in July and outlined a program for the coming year and announced appointments of chairmen of committees. Members attending were the guests of the newly elected President, Carl F. Clarke, at dinner preceding the meeting.

The Chapter took active part in ceremonies in connection with the naturalization of new citizens in June, and Dr. Morgan, Chaplain of the Chapter, presented, on behalf of the Society, to each newly made citizen a silk American Flag. There were 450 fully naturalized new citizens, including many women, and representing about 40 nationalities.

The death, on October 11, of Compatriot George William Bates, Historian General of the National Society from 1901 to 1906 and Vice-President General in 1908, has caused deepest regret among his friends in the Organization and community.

WASHTENAW CHAPTER, of Ann Arbor, observed Independence Day patriotically and pleasantly at the home of its President, Wilbert B. Hinsdale. A patriotic address by Compatriot Junius E. Beal, Regent of the University of Michigan, gave inspiration to the occasion. The Chapter, through its President, has requested the Superintendent of Schools of Ann Arbor to give recognition to Constitution Day by appropriate exercises on September 17th.

The New Hampshire Society, Sons of the American Revolution, in accordance with the request of the National Society and the custom of State Societies throughout the country, formally celebrated the 134th Anniversary of "Constitution Day," on which the Constitution of the United States was finally adopted and signed, at a meeting in the Hall of Representatives, at the State House, in Concord, on Saturday, September 17, 1921, at 11 o'clock a. m., Rumford Chapter, D. A. R., of Concord, co-operating and His Excellency Albert O. Brown, Governor of New Hampshire, presiding. There was an excellent program, with introductory remarks by the President, and an address by Hon. Sherman E. Burroughs, of Manchester, Representative in Congress from the First New Hampshire District, and music.

The New Jersey Society continued its membership campaign through the summer with gratifying results, candidates or inquiries being received daily. The Society will be compelled to move its headquarters in the near future on account of changes in the Lackawanna Railroad tracks, near which the office is located, at 44 Harrison Street, East Orange.

Independence Day was observed by nearly all the Chapters. Orange Chapter held exercises at Orange Park, Compatriot John Leonard Merrill being the speaker, and in the evening he again addressed an audience of several thousand persons at the Watsessing Park, East Orange.

David L. Pierson, Secretary of the State Society, was the speaker at the exercises held in Millburn, on the ground where the Battle of Springfield was fought, June 23, 1780.

MONTCLAIR CHAPTER arranged its program for the forenoon of the day and it was carried out in conjunction with the City Commission. Compatriot Elvord G. Chamberlin, President of the Chapter, was chairman of the meeting. Passaic Valley Chapter took part in the parade in Summit in the morning and Paramus Chapter participated in the public celebration in Ridgewood.

Rev. Dr. Frank Austin Smith, member of the State Board of Managers, delivered an address at Elizabeth, on "The Constitution and its Application to Today's Needs." All told, the day was well remembered in New Jersey. The youngest chapter, West Fields, No. 11, co-operated with the officials of the city of Westfield in an old-fashioned Independence Day remembrance.

At the formal dedication of the Dante House, in Orange, a building devoted to the interests of the Italians of the community, on the anniversary of Constitution Day, September 17, Orange Chapter presented a large bunting flag to the Dante House in the afternoon, when a Liberty Pole was dedicated. An address was delivered by Mayor William A. Lord and David L. Pierson, Secretary of the State Society.

In Orange, Montclair, and other places church bells rang for three minutes at the noon hour and was very beneficial in starting inquiries as to the cause of the commotion.

The headquarters of the New Jersey Society will be removed to Newark at an early day, on account of the taking of the building where the Society is now located for railroad changes on the Lackawanna.

The Ohio Society.—The anniversary of Perry's victory on Lake Erie was duly celebrated by the Western Reserve Society, Sons of the American Revolution, the ceremonial being held at Perry's Monument, overlooking Lake Erie, at Gordon Park, Cleveland, Ohio. The local Chapters of the Daughters of the American Revolution and Daughters of 1812 co-operated in making the occasion a memorable one, there being about 300 representative citizens in attendance. Compatriot Francis W. Treadway, ex-Lieutenant Governor of Ohio, presided, and the address of the day was delivered by Compatriot Rev. George H. Johnson, professor of history at Case School of Applied Science. At the close of the ceremony wreathes were placed on the monument by representatives of the Western Reserve Society, Sons of the American Revolution, and of the Daughters of 1812.

A unique feature of the celebration was a colored guard of boy scouts bearing replicas of the flags used by Perry at this memorable battle, together with the Union Jack and Stars and Stripes used at that date, as well as the flags in use at the present time. These flags were loaned by Compatriot Charles R. Putnam, chairman of the Society's Flag Committee, from his collection of American and Colonial flags, which has become one of the most complete in the United States. Inspiring music was furnished by the full band of the American Steel and Wire Co. and by vocalists who rendered patriotic selections. The occasion furnished a memorable precedent in the patriotic activities of Cleveland, which will doubtless become an annual affair, since Admiral Perry, more truly than any other American hero, was responsible for the preservation of the Northwest Territory to the United States.

This Society also sponsored an active campaign for the general observance of Constitution Day in Cleveland on September 17, a report of which will be given later.

The Tennessee Society will hold its annual meeting October 7, the anniversary of the Battle of King's Mountain, in which the woodsmen of Tennessee bore so prominent a part, and on this occasion there will be exhibited a historic sword of great interest. Daniel Kennedy, ancestor of Rev. M. S. Kennedy, of Pulaski, Tennessee, a member of the Tennessee Society, received this sword from an unknown British officer at the surrender of the British authorities at King's Mountain. His son, John Kennedy, sold the sword on July 25, 1805, to Greenville Lodge, No. 3, F. and A. M. This sword has been used by the tiler of the lodge continuously since 1805, except during the war between the States, when it was carried by Nathan Dodd, a Past Master of the lodge. Daniel Kennedy and his son John were both members of Greenville Lodge and the Tennessee Society is now represented in the lodge by Compatriots R. C. and N. T. Howard, through whose good offices the Society is able to procure the sword for exhibition.

The program of the meeting on October 7 includes an address by the Rev. Dr. Kennedy, and the Society proposes to again surrender the sword to him, the living link between 1780 and 1921. Other Revolutionary relics to be on exhibition at this time include the sash of the British General Ferguson, worn at the time of his death on King's Mountain, and the sword presented by North Carolina to John Sevier in appreciation of his services in this battle. A poem by Mrs. Elizabeth Wilkes Romine, ex-poet laureate of the Tennessee Daughters of the American Revolution and of the United Daughters of the Confederacy, composed especially for the occasion, is also to be a feature of the program.

A monument to the memory of Brig.-Gen. Daniel Kennedy, Greene County's first county clerk, pioneer of Tennessee, soldier, patriot, and statesman, was unveiled Sunday by Capt. Leroy Taylor Chapter, D. A. R., and the American Legion of Greeneville. The unveiling occurred at a little church six miles from Greeneville, known as Mount Zion, and located on the old Kennedy farm, now owned by Judge Dana Harmon. General Kennedy is buried at that place. Mrs. R. C. Howard, Regent of the D. A. R. Chapter, and quite a number of his descendants living in and around Knoxville attended the celebration.

The descendants of Brig.-Gen. Daniel Kennedy have erected a handsome monument to his memory, and Capt. Leroy Taylor Chapter took charge of the unveiling ceremonies, with the co-operation of the American Legion. The monument is a large boulder of Tennessee rock and has a bronze tablet, with the following inscription:

To the Memory
of
Col. Daniel Kennedy
1750-1802
Soldier, Patriot, Statesman
Honored Citizen
Revolutionary Soldier
Pioneer of Tennessee
First Clerk of Court, Greene County
Served under four forms of Government
1783-1802
Supported State of Franklin
Made Peace with Indians
Trustee, Greenville and Washington Colleges
Erected by Descendants
1920

Gen. Daniel Kennedy, who was born in Virginia, was a contemporary of Governor John Sevier. He was a very young man at the breaking out of war with the Indians in Kentucky in 1774, but volunteered in the company of Capt. Evans Shelby and took part in the fierce and bloody battles in which our forefathers of East Tennessee won such fadeless laurels. In 1776 he was at Fort Wautauga under Capt. James Robertson and Lieut. John Sevier. General Rutherford called for the Mountain Brigades in 1780, and Kennedy met Shelby and Sevier at the rendezvous at Sycamore Shoals and was made lieutenant in Colonel Sevier's regiment, which won such immortal glory in the battle. He was promoted to a captaincy for gallantry at King's Mountain and was in this battle.

When Colonel Sevier was made brigadier-general of the Wautauga troop, Captain Kennedy became colonel; so when Sevier became Governor of the State of Franklin (of which Greeneville was the capital), Colonel Kennedy was chosen brigadier-general of the troops of that State.

The Tennessee Society is making progress in increased membership and threatens to win one of the Traveling Banners this year.

Utah Society.—A gavel that is historic and a relic of real value was displayed by Judge Wallace McCamant, President General, who was the guest of honor and principal speaker at a banquet in the Hotel Utah, Salt Lake City, and who detailed its history to the members of the Utah Society of the Sons of the American Revolution, who entertained him.

The gavel is the official instrument of the National Society and was presented to it in May, 1920, as such. The head is made of wood from Faneuil Hall and the handle from the old State-house at Boston. In addition to this, the gavel has twenty-one inserts. One is a piece of Plymouth Rock, one is wood from the home of Paul Revere, one from the home of Asa Pollard, who was the first man killed in the Battle of Bunker Hill; one from the Old North Bridge at Concord, where the shot was fired which was "heard around the world"; one from the man-o'-war *Somerset*, which took part in the Battle of Bunker Hill, and one from the elm tree at Cambridge, Mass., under which Washington took command of the Army of the Revolution.

"The Sons of the American Revolution," Judge McCamant said, "is not just an organization that dwells in the past and hopes to have recognition for what the ancestors of its members did more than 100 years ago. We do a few things, and, as I see it, the fact that we are descended from those who fought in the Revolution only gives us added responsibility. The Society is strictly a patriotic organization. One of the more important things we have been instrumental in bringing about is the general observance of Constitution Day. The prime movers in this work were Elmer Marston Wentworth, of Des Moines, Iowa, and Louis Annin Ames, of New York City."

On his arrival in Salt Lake Judge McCamant was met at the depot by a committee of the local Society. At the banquet the toastmaster, General John Q. Cannon, was introduced by Vice-President Robert E. McCanaughy. The Rt. Rev. Arthur W. Moulton, Episcopal Bishop of Utah, offered the invocation.

In his address Judge McCamant said:

"The Sons of the American Revolution is a patriotic Society. Descent from some one who assisted in establishing American independence is one of the qualifications for membership. We claim no privileges because of our ancestry, but we do think that we have a higher duty than that devolving on most men to serve our country and to protect the political heritage which has come down to us from the fathers.

"Our Society took the initiative in bringing about the nation-wide observance of Constitution Day. At present we are giving a good deal of attention to the matter of patriotic education. We are anxious that the story of our country's past shall be taught in the schools in such a way as to kindle in the students a love for flag and country. Every student in an American school should appreciate the franchises and privileges which are ours as the result of the wisdom and self-sacrifice of the men of the American Revolution. Many of the textbooks on American history in use in our schools are inadequate; some of them are vicious and untruthful.

"We are most anxious to improve conditions in our institutions of higher learning. Our young men and young women go to college at an impressionable age. If they come under the influence of professors who teach destructive political doctrine, they are apt to come out of college with a distorted point of view, which will impair the quality of their citizenship throughout their lives. No one should occupy a chair in the faculty of any American institution unless he is a believer in the principles of the Declaration of Independence and of the Federal Constitution."

The Washington Society.—Spokane Chapter held a meeting at noon on October 17, the members lunching at the Spokane City Club. Compatriot H. W. Canfield addressed the meeting.

ADDITIONS TO MEMBERSHIP.

There have been enrolled in the office of the Registrar-General, from May 31, 1921, to October 1, 1921, 321 new members as follows: California, 14; Colorado, 6; Connecticut, 11; Delaware, 3; Georgia, 4; Idaho, 4; Indiana, 4; Illinois, 14; Iowa, 11; Kansas, 6; Kentucky, 12; Louisiana, 14; Maryland, 7; Maine, 2; Massachusetts, 20; Michigan, 24; Minnesota, 7; Missouri, 5; Nebraska, 5; New Jersey, 71; New Mexico, 1; New York (Empire State), 27; North Dakota, 2; Ohio, 14; Oklahoma, 3; Oregon, 3; Pennsylvania, 1; Rhode Island, 4; South Dakota, 2; Tennessee, 14; Vermont, 2; Virginia, 3; Wisconsin, 1.

In Memoriam

FRANK A. BALL, New Hampshire Society, died November 22, 1920.

WILLIAM A. BLOUNT, Florida Society, died June 15, 1921.

JAMES O. BRADBURY, Maine Society, died May —, 1921.

FRED E. BUTLER, Michigan Society, died August 29, 1920.

JAMES L. COGSWELL, California Society, died April 13, 1921.

GEORGE D. COPLEY, Connecticut Society, died January 7, 1921.

AUGUSTUS C. CORBY, New Jersey Society, died July 26, 1921.

FREDERICK H. DOREMUS, New Jersey Society, died July 4, 1921.

WILLIAM FAITOUTE, New Jersey Society, died July 6, 1921.

FREDERICK WEED FLINT, Empire State Society, died September 24, 1921.

IRA F. HARRIS, First Vice-President New Hampshire Society, died September 18, 1921.

GEORGE W. KETCHAM, New Jersey Society, died July 22, 1921.

ALONZO P. LENOX, New Jersey Society, died July 5, 1921.

ROBERT W. McCLAUGHRY, Major, A. E. F., Illinois Society, died November 9, 1920.

ALLEN B. MORSE, Michigan Society, died July 1, 1921.

ROBERT MOSBY PULLIAM, Virginia Society, died July 26, 1921.

JAMES HALL REED, Pennsylvania Society, died June 27, 1919.

JESSE C. REMICK, Michigan Society, died April 9, 1919.

JEREMIAH SMITH, New Hampshire Society, real son of Revolutionary soldier, died September 3, 1921.

HARRY F. TAYLOR, M. D., Michigan Society, died March 17, 1921.

ALBERT TUTTLE, Vermont Society, died —— —, 1921.

CHARLES L. WEIL, Michigan Society, died July 16, 1921.

GEORGE M. WILLIAMS, New Jersey Society, died June 25, 1921.

JOHN P. WILLIAMS, Charter Member Tennessee Society, died June 20, 1921.

CHARLES H. WOOSTER, Wisconsin Society, died May 20, 1921.

WALTER H. WRIGHT, JR., Wisconsin Society, died December 22, 1920.

RECORDS OF 321 NEW MEMBERS AND 82 SUPPLEMENTALS AP-
PROVED AND ENROLLED BY THE REGISTRAR-GENERAL, FROM
MAY 31, 1921, TO OCTOBER 1, 1921.

JOHN MATTHEWS ABERNATHY, Pulaski, Tenn. (34645). Son of Jerome Clayton and
Elizabeth (Eslick) Abernathy; grandson of Newton Green and Arkansas Dorothy (Franklin) Eslin; great-grandson of Benjamin and Frances Dorothy (Lee) Franklin; great²-
grandson of John and Susanna (Short) Lee; great³-grandson of *Thomas Short*, Captain,
Amelia County, Virginia Militia.

MILTON PRAY ADAMS, Grand Rapids, Mich. (35702). Son of William M. and Catharine
A. (Pray) Adams; grandson of Esek and Alvina F. (Torrey) Pray; great-grandson of
Oliver and Anar (Churchill) Torrey; great²-grandson of *Samuel Torrey*, Lieutenant, Ver-
mont Militia, pensioned.

WASHINGTON IRVING LINCOLN ADAMS, Jr., Montclair, N. J. (35727). Son of
Washington Irving Lincoln and Grace (Wilson) Adams; grandson of Washington Irving
and Marion Lydia (Briggs) Adams; great-grandson of Barnabas Soureman and Elizabeth
(Carhart) Adams; great²-grandson of Jesse and Mary (Secard, or Secor) Adams; great³-
grandson of *Jesse Adams*, private, Second and Fourth Regts., New York Line.

WILLIAM ALDEN, Decatur, Ga. (35220). Son of John Tolman and Sarah H. (Tilton)
Alden; grandson of John Tolman and Mehitable (Tolman) Alden; great-grandson of *John
Tolman*, Corporal and Sergeant, Mass. Militia.

JAMES WALTER ALLEN, Nashville, Tenn. (36053). Son of John and Sarah Louisa (Harwood) Allen; grandson of John and Nancy C. (Morton) Allen; great-grandson of Vincent
and Mary (Bowdon) Allen; great²-grandson of *Charles Allen*, Captain, Second and Fifth
Regts., North Carolina Militia.

POPE WALKER ALLEN, Topeka, Kans. (33320). Son of Walter N. and Jeannette E.
(Walker) Allen; grandson of James V. and Eliza (Mason) Allen; great-grandson of *John
Allen*, Lieutenant, North Carolina Troops.

THEODORE THOMPSON ALLEN, Detroit, Mich. (35858). Son of Theodore Shepherd and
Florence (Newman) Allen; grandson of Stephen Thompson and Sarah Elizabeth (Martin)
Allen; great-grandson of Elijah and Rhoda (Thompson) Allen; great²-grandson of Silas
and Esther (Hastings) Allen; great³-grandson of *Jonathan Hastings*, Major, Fifth Regt.,
Hampshire County, Mass. Militia.

WILLIAM PRESTON ALLEN, Jackson, Miss. (La. 34821). Son of William Colier and Clara
Cynthia (Preston) Allen; grandson of Eli Victor and May (Stewart) Preston; great-grand-
son of Ira Luman and Cynthia Ann (Allen) Preston; great²-grandson of Ira and Deborah
(Goff) Preston; great³-grandson of *Charles Goff*, private, Conn. Militia, pensioned; great²-
grandson of Samuel and Lucy (Johnson) Preston; great³-grandson of *Amos Johnson*,
Ensign, Nineteenth Regt., Conn. Cont'l Infantry.

JOHN McDOUGAL ATHERTON, Louisville, Ky. (34712). Son of Peter and Elizabeth
(Mayfield) Atherton; grandson of John and Sarrah (McDougal) Mayfield; great-grandson
of *Alexander McDougal*, Lieutenant, South Carolina Troops.

CHARLES MORTON ATKINS, Hastings, Mich. (35703). Son of Augustus Wolcott and
Maria Louisa (Johnson) Atkins; grandson of Ashbel and Sophia (Cole) Atkins; great-
grandson of *Samuel Atkins*, private and Ensign, Conn. Militia and State Troops.

JEAN L. AUXIER, Pikeville, Ky. (34713). Son of Nathaniel John and Olive (Leslie) Auxier;
grandson of Andrew and Elizabeth (Scott) Auxier; great-grandson of Nathaniel and Hester
Ann (Mayo) Auxier; great²-grandson of Samuel and Rebecca (Phillips) Auxier; great³-
grandson of *Samuel Auxier (Oxer)*, private, Colonel Montgomery's Regt., Virginia Militia,
pensioned.

ELLIS BENJAMIN BAKER, Jr., New Haven, Conn. (35485). Son of Ellis Benjamin and
Mary Gorham (Frost) Baker; grandson of John Fletcher and Clara (Benjamin) Baker;
great-grandson of Asa and Deborah (Keeler) Baker; great²-grandson of Scott and Sarah
(Loveland) Baker; great³-grandson of *Asa Loveland*, private, Second Regt., Conn. Militia,
died in service.

LUTHER STRONG BAKER, Plad, Mo. (Nebr. 33888). Son of Daniel C. and Ábigail M.
(Strong) Baker; grandson of Luther and Abigail (Woodruff) Strong; great-grandson of
Joseph Strong, private, Fifth Regt., Conn. Line.

WALTER CLAYTON BANISTER, New York, N. Y. (N. J. 35745). Son of Isaac and
Luella (Clayton) Banister; grandson of James A. and Lydia Slater (Birdsall) Banister;
great-grandson of Isaac and Cynthia (Baird) Banister; great²-grandson of William and
Elizabeth (Vail) Baird; great³-grandson of *Benjamin Vail*, Captain, Orange County, New
York Militia, killed in battle.

ROY VOORHEES BARNES, Royal Oak, Mich. (35704). Son of William M. and Carrie M.
(Voorheis) Barnes; grandson of William S. and Alma M. (Cook) Voorheis; great-grandson
of Aaron and Nancy (Coon) Cook; great²-grandson of *Joseph Coon* (*Koon*), private,
Harrison County, Virginia Militia.

ROLAND BENNER BARRETT, Michigan. Supplemental. Son of Wilbert Hamilton and
Elizabeth (Benner) Barrett; grandson of William E. and Sarah S. (Riggans) Benner;
great-grandson of Henry L. and Elizabeth G. (Dowdney) Benner; great²-grandson of
Henry and Jane (Boyd) Benner; great³-grandson of *Martin Benner*, private, Tenth Regt.,
Penna. Cont'l Troops.

AUBREY BARTLETT, New Orleans, La. (35978). Son of Franklin Adams and Emma Marie
(Gagnet) Bartlett; grandson of Casam Emir and Sarah Evalina (Melhada) Bartlett; great-
grandson of Stephen and Abigail (Bayley) Bartlett; great²-grandson of *Asa Bailey*, private,
Col. Timothy Bedell's Regt., New Hampshire Militia.

SAMUEL HASKELL BASS, Springfield, Mass. (35859). Son of William Seth and Fannie
Agnes (Howe) Bass; grandson of Seth and Ann Lovett (Harmon) Bass; great-grandson
of Seth and Mary (Jones) Bass; great²-grandson of *Samuel Bass, Jr.*, Lieutenant, Mass.
Militia and Cont'l Line.

LELAND FLINT BEAN, Adrian, Mich. (35705). Son of Seth and Jennie (Flint) Bean;
grandson of Charles C. and Delucia J. (Brach) Flint; great-grandson of Cyril and Mary
(Bacon) Flint; great²-grandson of *Josiah Bacon, Jr.*, private, Mass. Militia and Cont'l
Troops; great²-grandson of *Josiah Bacon*, Sergeant, Colonel Brewer's Regt., Mass. Militia,
killed at Bunker Hill.

WILLIAM HENRY BEARDEN, Auburn, Ill. (35436). Son of Simeon and Lucinda (Young)
Bearden; grandson of John and Nellie (Calhoon) Bearden; great-grandson of *John Bearden*, private, South Carolina Militia, pensioned.

LOVICK PIERCE BELLAH, Madison, Tenn. (34646). Son of Samuel Zere (Steele) and
Martha Ann (Stokes) Bellah; grandson of S. S. and Elizabeth Caroline (Middlebrook)
Bellah; great-grandson of Jere and Sophia Weston (Shell) Middlebrook; great²-grandson
of *John Middlebrook, Jr.*, private, Colonel Lytle's Regt., North Carolina Cont'l Troops.

RUFUS ALBERT BERRY, Berkeley, Calif. (34742). Son of Campbell Palson and Roann
Quillen (Davis) Berry; grandson of Blackburn Henderson and Eliza (Palson) Berry;
great-grandson of Thomas and Elizabeth (McFerrin) Berry; great²-grandson of *William
McFerrin*, private, Augusta County, Virginia Cont'l Troops, pensioned.

ISAAC S. BLACKWELDER, Illinois (1305). Supplemental. Son of Peter and Mrs. Nellie
(Scherer) Wagoner Blackwelder; grandson of Frederick and Margaret (Clapp) Scherer;
great-grandson of *Frederick Scherer* (*Shurer*), private, Tenth Regt., North Carolina
Militia.

HENRY HARRISON BLINN, St. Paul, Minn. (35679). Son of William Harrison and
Margaret (Dustin) Blinn; grandson of Chester and Sally (Clyde) Blinn; great-grandson
of Simon and Catherine (Smtih) Blinn; great²-grandson of *Billy Blinn*, private, Colonel
Burrell's Regt., Conn. Troops.

JOHN BEVERLEY BOSTWICK, New York (33237). Supplemental. Son of John Newman
and Ada La Due (Beverley) Bostwick; grandson of Stephenson Thorne and Martha
Elizabeth (Newman) Bostwick; great-grandson of Elias and Elizabeth (Hopkins) Newman; great²-grandson of Thomas and Mary (Fairbanks) Hopkins; great³-grandson of
William Fairbanks, private, Rhode Island Militia.

HAROLD KING BOWEN, Fort Dodge, Iowa (35608). Son of William Walker and Lydia
May (King) Bowen; grandson of David Wood and Lydia Ann (Hall) King; great-grand-
son of Phinneas and Lydia (Huntley) Hall; great²-grandson of James and Lydia (Caulkins)
Huntley, Jr.; great³-grandson of *James Huntley*, Captain, Lieutenant-Colonel Storr's Regt.,
Conn. Militia.

THOMAS HOPKINS BRADFORD, Detroit, Mich. (35725). Son of James C. and Sarah Polk (Jones) Bradford; grandson of Robinap Cadwallader and Sarah Rochel (Polk) Jones; great-grandson of Lucius J. and Mary (Eastin) Polk; great²-grandson of *William Polk*, Colonel, North Carolina Militia.

WOODWARD HAROLD BRENTON, Dallas Center, Iowa (35602). Son of Charles Richmond and Caroline A. (Woodward) Brenton; grandson of William Henry and Mary Elizabeth (Richmond) Brenton; great-grandson of James Blaird and Eliza (St. John) Brenton; great²-grandson of Henry and Esther (Barrie) Brenton; great²-grandson of *James Brenton*, Major and Captain, Virginia Militia.

HAL KINGSBURY BROWN, San Augustine, Texas (La. 34822). Son of James Hunter and Katherine (Kingsbury) Brown; grandson of Andrew J. and Elizabeth Lewis (Minor) Brown; great-grandson of Samuel Overton and Lydia Laurie (Lewis) Minor; great²-grandson of Thomas Walter and Elizabeth (Meriwether) Lewis; great²-grandson of *Nicholas Lewis*, Colonel, Albemarle County, Virginia Militia.

PHILIP F. BROWN, Jr., Richmond, Va. (35092). Son of Ben R. and Mary Elizabeth (Taylor) Brown; grandson of Edward I. and Martha Susan (Rucker) Brown; great-grandson of Isaac and Mary (Christian) Rucker; great²-grandson of *Ambrose Rucker*, Captain, Amherst County, Virginia Militia, Member Special War Committee.

NEWELL CUTLER BULLARD, North Attleboro, Mass. (35860). Son of Herbert Cutler and Anna Louise (Hayward) Bullard; grandson of Joseph Newell and Sarah (Cutler) Bullard; great-grandson of Simon and Nabby (Brewer) Cutler, Jr.; great²-grandson of *David Brewer, Jr.*, Captain, Hampshire County, Mass. Militia; great²-grandson of *David Brewer*, Colonel, Ninth Regt., Hampshire County, Mass. Militia; great²-grandson of *Simon Cutler*, private, Mass. Militia.

JOHN FITZHARRIS BURLESON, Grand Rapids, Mich. (35706). Son of Charles and Elizabeth (Spaulding) Burleson; grandson of Erastus and Eliza (Walker) Spaulding; great-grandson of George Washington and Elizabeth (Palmer) Spaulding; great²-grandson of *William Spaulding*, private, Colonel Hinman's Regt., Conn. Militia.

JOHN BURNAM, New Orleans, La. (34823). Son of Anthony Rollins and Margaret Alexander (Summers) Burnam; grandson of Curtis Field and Sarah Helen (Rollins) Burnam; great-grandson of Thompson and Lucinda (Field) Burnam; great²-grandson of John and Mary Ann (Fort) Burnam; great²-grandson of *Henry Burnam*, private, South Carolina Cont'l Troops; great²-grandson of John and Diana (Field) Field; great²-grandson of *Henry Field, Jr.* (father of Diana Field), Member Virginia Conventions of 1775-76; great²-grandson of *John Field* (father of John Field), Colonel, Virginia Militia, killed at Point Pleasant; great-grandson of Anthony Wayne and Sarah Harris (Rodes) Rollins; great²-grandson of *Henry Rollins*, private, Penna. Cont'l Troops; great²-grandson of *Robert Rodes*, Captain, Albemarle County, Virginia Militia; grandson of George and Esther (Alexander) Summers; great²-grandson of Samuel and Margaret (Stucker) Alexander; great²-grandson of *Peter Alexander*, private, Virginia Militia.

COLIN CLARK BURR, Jersey City, N. J. (N. Y. 35640). Son of Frank L. and Josephine A. (Clark) Burr; grandson of Harris R. and Clarinda (Blatchley) Burr; great-grandson of Stephen and Cynthia (Hubbard) Burr; great²-grandson of *Jonathan Burr*, private, Colonel Wolcott's Regt., Conn. Militia.

HAROLD BERNHARD BUSE, Lieutenant, U. S. N. R., A. E. F., Westville, Conn. (35486). Son of Bernhard and Etta (Graves) Buse; grandson of Lewis Wakeman and Rhoda S. (Henderson) Graves; great-grandson of Matthew Royce and Sarah W. (Tyrrell) Henderson; great²-grandson of Reuben and Mehetable (Royce) Henderson; great²-grandson of *James Henderson, Jr.*, Corporal, Col. Job Cushman's Regt., Mass. Militia.

EUGENE H. BUSH, Tecumseh, Nebr. (33891). Son of David R. and Sarah (Ross) Bush; grandson of James M. and Elizabeth A. (Sanders) Ross; great-grandson of Robert and Elizabeth (Howerton) Ross; great²-grandson of *Reuben Ross*, private, Maryland and Virginia Troops, pensioned.

GEORGE DEWEY BUSHNELL, Chicago, Ill. (Nebr. 33889). Son of Herbert M. and Elsie N. (Campbell) Bushnell; grandson of Martin and Charlotte P. (Clark) Bushnell; great-grandson of Stephen and Charlotte (Lovejoy) Clark; great²-grandson of *Paul Clark*, Corporal and Sergeant, Rhode Island Troops, 8 years' service, pensioned.

CHESTER LAWRENCE CALDWELL, St. Paul, Minn. (33523). Son of William Wallace and Maria (De Yonge) Caldwell; grandson of Thomas and Jane (Beasley) Caldwell; great-grandson of *Stephen Beasley*, Captain, Penna. armed gun-boat "Viper."

JAMES ALEXANDER CAMPBELL, Decatur, Ga. (35221). Son of John and Catherine Celia (Hooks) Campbell; grandson of Marshall and Tabitha (Fitzpatrick) Hooks; great-grandson of Joseph and Sally (Baldwin) Fitzpatrick; great²-grandson of *William Baldwin*, Lieutenant, Col. Elijah Clark's Regt. of Minute Men; great²-grandson of *David Baldwin*, Captain, Col. John Steveworth's Regt. of Minute Men.

JOHN W. CAMPBELL, JR., New York, N. Y. (35636). Son of John W. and Emma (Alston) Campbell; grandson of John and Eliza (Strother) Alston; great-grandson of James Wade and Margaret French (McConickie) Strother; great²-grandson of James Robert and Susan (Slaughter) McConickie; great³-grandson of *Philip Slaughter*, Captain and Regimental Quartermaster, Virginia State Troops, pensioned; grandson of Alexander W. and Anni Dixon (Allen) Campbell; great-grandson of Dixon and Louise (Gibbs) Allen; great²-grandson of George W. and Lu Anne (Dibrell) Gibbs; great³-grandson of *Charles Dibrell*, Ensign, Virginia Militia, pensioned.

ADELBERT JEWETT CANFIELD, Cambridge, Mass. (35861). Son of William S. and Catherine (Waltermire) Canfield; grandson of William Jewett and Sarah (Sconton) Canfield; great-grandson of Asahel and Jerusha (Hamlin) Canfield; great²-grandson of *Nathan Canfield*, private, Westchester County, New York Militia.

ARCHIE BLAINE CANFIELD, Duluth, Minn. (33524). Son of Stephen Nathaniel and Larenia (Barnes) Canfield; grandson of Henry Montfort and Angeline (Williams) Canfield; great-grandson of Stephen and Esther (Adsit) Canfield; great²-grandson of *James Canfield, Jr.*, private, Colonel Brinkerhoff's and Colonel Du Bois's Regts., New York Militia.

CHARLES ARTHUR CARLISLE, South Bend, Ind. (35441). Son of Meade Woodson and Emma (Barr) Carlisle; grandson of John H. and Isabella (McKee) Barr; great²-grandson of *Hugh McKee*, private, Delaware Militia.

DOUGLAS WILDEY CAULKINS, Cleveland, Ohio (35175). Son of Daniel Douglas and Emma (Wilder) Caulkins; grandson of William W. and Catherine Ann (Baker) Caulkins; great-grandson of Daniel Douglas and Ann (Baker) Caulkins; great²-grandson of *Enoch Baker*, Corporal and Sergeant, Conn. Militia, pensioned.

JAMES HENRY CAUSEY, Denver, Colo. (34367). Son of William Winfield and Susanna May (Johnston) Causey; grandson of Uriah Fookes and Maria (Dobbins) Causey; great-grandson of William and Nancy (Livingston) Causey; great²-grandson of Stephen Causey; great³-grandson of *Patrick Causey*, private, Wicomico County, Maryland Militia.

WILLIAM WINFIELD CAUSEY, Baltimore, Md. (35343). Son of William Winfield and Susanna May (Johnston) Causey; grandson of Uriah Fookes and Maria (Dobbins) Causey; great-grandson of William and Nancy (Livingston) Causey; great²-grandson of Stephen Causey; great³-grandson of *Patrick Causey*, private, Wicomico County, Maryland Militia.

WILLARD De WITT CHAMBERLIN, Dayton, Ohio (35885). Son of Samuel and Caroline (Swan) Chamberlin; grandson of Samuel and Ruby (Whitcomb) Chamberlin; great-grandson of William and Mary (Wilcox) Chamberlin; great²-grandson of Peleg and Jane (Higgins) Chamberlin; great³-grandson of *William Chamberlin*, private, Colonel Elmore's Regt., Conn. Militia, pensioned.

CHARLES CLARENCE CHAPMAN, Portland, Ore. (35058). Son of L. A. I. and Emma (Keyes) Chapman; grandson of Stephen Paine and Amelia (Darsett) Keyes; great-grandson of Frederick and Rachel (Jacobs) Keyes; great²-grandson of *William Keyes*, Captain, Sixteenth Regt., New Hampshire Militia.

RAYMOND ROGERS CHATFIELD, Westfield, N. J. (35736). Son of Horace F. and Sarah Louise (Prime) Chatfield; grandson of Claudius Buchanan and Mary (Cotrel) Prime; great-grandson of Ebenezer and Experience (Conklin) Prime; great²-grandson of *Benjamin Youngs Prime*, writer and speaker; great³-grandson of *Ebenezer S. Prime*, patriot preacher.

WILLIAM H. CHILDS, Adrian, Mich. (35707). Son of Edmund and Ida J. (Todd) Childs; grandson of John Henry and Susan M. (Hoxter) Todd; great-grandson of Gabriel and Mary P. (Ireland) Todd; great²-grandson of John Todd, Jr.; great³-grandson of *John Todd*, Sergeant, Ninth Regt., Conn. Militia.

FRANK ELMER CHURCHILL, Jacksonville, Texas (La. 35982). Son of Luther Bernard and Jane (Hawkins) Churchill; grandson of John and Experience (Hale) Churchill; great-grandson of William and Eunice (Badger) Churchill; great²-grandson of *Ichabod Churchill*, Sergeant, Middleboro County, Mass. Militia.

WALTER CORWIN CLARK, Berkeley, Calif. (34743). Son of Charles Kittridge and Harriett (Howell) Clark; grandson of Ephraim Wesson and Mary (Kittridge) Clark; great-grand-son of *Edward Clark*, private, New Hampshire Militia; great-grandson of Edward and Elizabeth (Wesson) Clark; great²-grandson of *Ephraim Wesson*, private, New Hampshire Militia, Member New Hampshire Provincial Congress and Committee of Safety.

THOMAS ROSSER CLARKSON, St. Louis, Mo. (35555). Son of Joseph Goodman and Mary Lizzie (Covington) Clarkson; grandson of Walter G. and Lucy Evelona (Clarkson) Covington; great-grandson of *Richard Covington*, private, Virginia Militia.

CLAURICE ALVEREL GODFREY CLOSSON, Independence, Mo. (35556). Son of Andrew Valentine and Mary Alida (Brown) Closson; grandson of James Byron and Mary Annie (Godfrey) Brown; great-grandson of John Warren and Louisa Nye (Barlow) Godfrey; great²-grandson of Solomon Nye and Anna (Barlow) Barlow; great²-grandson of *Obed Barlow*, private, Mass. Militia.

LESLIE NORMAN CONGER, Captain U. S. Army, Yuma, Ariz. (Mich. 35722). Son of Norman B. and Eliza R. (Lotspeich) Conger; grandson of Seymour Beach and Mary A. (Barker) Conger; great-grandson of Enoch and Esther (West) Conger; great²-grandson of *Ussiah Conger*, private, Albany County, New York Militia.

CHEEVER CLINTON CONLEE, Dayton, Ohio (35876). Son of Alexander W. and Augusta (Pauline) Conlee; grandson of John H. and Mary (Crowder) Conlee; great-grandson of William B. and Elizabeth Wise (Bullock) Crowder; great²-grandson of *William Crowder*, private, Mecklenberg County, Virginia Militia, pensioned.

ELMER HOWARD CONWAY, New York City, N. Y. (35645). Son of Harry Elmer and Jessie (McGeorge) Conway; grandson of Dennis Laird and Ann Elizabeth (Pierson) Conway; great-grandson of Peter and Elizabeth (Laird) Conway; great²-grandson of *William Laird*, Captain, Lancaster County, Penna. Militia.

ALFRED RICHARDS CORY, Jamestown, R. I. (34918). Son of Alfred R. and Elizabeth Stanhope (Watson) Cory; grandson of Andrew J. and Lucy Maria (Almy) Cory; great-grandson of Andrew and Jane Gray (Seabury) Cory; great²-grandson of *Philip Cory*, Captain, Tiverton, Rhode Island Militia.

ERSKINE HOWARD COURTENAY, Ensign, U. S. N., R. F., Louisville, Ky. (34716). Son of William Howard and Isabel Stevenson (Clark) Courtenay; grandson of Robert Graham and Annie Christian (Howard) Courtenay; great-grandson of John and Annie Christian (Bullitt) Howard; great²-grandson of Alexander Scott and Priscilla (Christian) Bullitt; great³-grandson of *William Christian*, Lieutenant-Colonel, Virginia Militia and Commander-in-Chief against Cherokees in '76.

JAMES CLARK COURTENAY, A.C., U. S. N., A. E. F., Louisville, Ky. (34717). Son of William Howard and Isabel Stevenson (Clark) Courtenay; grandson of Robert Graham and Annie Christian (Howard) Courtenay; great-grandson of John and Annie Christian (Bullitt) Howard; great²-grandson of Alexander Scott and Priscilla (Christian) Bullitt; great³-grandson of *William Christian*, Lieutenant-Colonel Virginia Militia and Commander-in-Chief against Cherokees in '76.

CHARLES INMAN CRAIG, Denver, Colo. (34373). Son of Henry J. and Ada (J. ——) Craig; grandson of George and Arilda Jane (Tenneson) Craig; great-grandson of Thomas and Susan (——) Craig; great²-grandson of *Thomas Craig*, Colonel, Third Regt., Penna. Cont'l Line.

MOSES COULTER CRAIG, Wilmington, Del. (35653). Son of John Euster and Euphemia Susan (Coulter) Craig; grandson of Alexander K. and Sarah (McLain) Craig; great-grandson of William and Margaret (McClelland) McLain; great²-grandson of *Thomas McClelland*, private, Penna. Troops, pensioned.

HENRY CROWELL CROSBY, Paterson, N. J. (35962). Son of John Henry and Mary Harriet (Crowell) Crosby; grandson of Joseph Tucker and Electa Montelle (Vanderhoven) Crowell; great-grandson of Nathan and Harriet (Tucker) Crowell; great²-grandson of *Joseph Crowell*, private, New Jersey Militia and Cont'l Troops, pensioned.

JOHN H. CROSBY, Paterson, N. J. (35961). Son of Henry Barrett and Paulina Fairfield (Hathorn) Crosby; grandson of Thomas Welling and Anna Barton (Hinchman) Hathorn; great-grandson of *John Hathorn*, Colonel, Orange County, New York Militia.

JOSEPH ADDISON CROSBY, Paterson, N. J. (36006). Son of John Henry and Mary Harriet (Crowell) Crosby; grandson of Joseph Tucker and Electa Montelle (Van der

Hoven) Crowell; great-grandson of Nathan and Harriet (Tucker) Crowell; great²-grandson of *Joseph Crowell*, private, Middlesex County, New Jersey Militia and Cont'l Troops, prisoner.

WHITFIELD MORRIS CULBERSON, Morristown, N. J. (36007). Son of Albert M. and Mary L. (Heckel) Culberson; grandson of Noah Morris and Hannah M. (Van Gilder) Culberson; great-grandson of Henry Whitfield and Phebe (Baldwin) Culberson; great²-grandson of Noah and Catharine (Sayre) Baldwin; great²-grandson of *Jonathan Baldwin*, private, Essex County, New Jersey Militia.

FRANCIS OTIS DART, San Diego, Calif. (34744). Son of John Luke and Rhoda Ann (Smith) Dart; grandson of Eli and Eleanor (Farrer) Dart; great-grandson of John and Elishaba (Briggs) Darte (Dart); great²-grandson of *Eliphalet Darte*, Recognized Patriot and Signer of Association Test.

EDWARD SEWARD DEAN, Batavia, N. Y. (35638). Son of Charles Holmes and Olive (Seward) Dean; grandson of Charles Fitz Allen and Pamelia Eugenia (Dykeman) Seward; great-grandson of Leverett and Olive (Riddle) Seward; great²-grandson of John and Olive (Blodget) Riddle; great²-grandson of *Thomas Riddle*, private, Colonel Brewer's Regt., Mass. Militia.

GEORGE L. DENNIS, Newark, N. J. (35728). Son of Eugene E. and Louise M. (Mauer) Dennis; grandson of John C. and Eliza Ann (McCormick) Dennis; great-grandson of Bernard and Sarah (Sandford) McCormick; great²-grandson of *John Sandford*, private, New York Militia and Cont'l Troops, pensioned.

GEORGE VERNON DENNIS, Newark, N. J. (35729). Son of George L. and Pauline (Thier) Dennis; grandson of Eugene E. and Louise M. (Mauer) Dennis; great-grandson of John C. and Eliza Ann (McCormick) Dennis; great²-grandson of Bernard and Sarah (Sandford) McCormick; great²-grandson of *John Sandford*, private, New York Militia and Cont'l Troops, pensioned.

EDWARD CLARE DODGE, Oakfield, N. Y. (35906). Son of Lorenzo Dow and Delia C. (Mantor) Dodge; grandson of Harry C. and Betsey (Baker) Dodge; great-grandson of *Henry Dodge*, Musician, Fourth Regt., Dutchess County, New York Militia.

WILLIAM J. DOREMUS, Paterson, N. J. (36003). Son of Walter J. and Anna (——) Doremus; grandson of Jacob W. and Sophia E. (Van Diean) Doremus; great-grandson of John Berdan and Margaret (Westervelt) Doremus; great²-grandson of *George Doremus*, private, Bergen County, New Jersey Militia.

VIRGIL ZARTMAN DORFMEIER, Dayton, Ohio (35877). Son of William F. and Myrta (Zartman) Dorfmeier; grandson of Solomon King and Malinda (Vogt) Zartman; great-grandson of Isaac and Rebecca (King) Zartman; great²-grandson of Peter and Mary Magdalene (Whitmer) King; great²-grandson of Peter and Mary Magdalene (Overmyer) Whitman; great⁴-grandson of *John George Overmyer*, Captain, Northumberland County, Penna. Militia.

ALBERT WESTCOTT DRIVER, Bridgeport, Conn. (35479). Son of Samuel and Helen Jane (Westcott) Driver; grandson of William and Henry Mae (Perry) Westcott; great-grandson of Valarous and Charlotte (Perry) Westcott; great²-grandson of *Jonathan W. Westcott*, private, Mass. Troops.

THOMAS BRUCE DRUMMOND, San Diego, Calif. (34745). Son of Fitz-Henry Warren and Morrell (Stevenson) Drummond; grandson of Thomas and Kate Ann (Barnes) Drummond; great-grandson of Homer and Almira (Ludington) Barnes; great²-grandson of Stephen Russell and Catherine (Slayton) Ludington; great⁴-grandson of *Reuben Slayton*, Captain, Fourth Regt., Mass. Cont'l Troops.

LOUIS Du BOIS, New Jersey (34860). Supplementals. Son of Clarence Mulford and Nettie (Cole) Du Bois; grandson of William and Sarah (Williams) Du Bois; great-grandson of William and Sarah (Mulford) Du Bois; great²-grandson of *Jeremiah Du Bois*, private, Salem County, New Jersey Militia, pensioned; great²-grandson of Jeremiah and Sarah (Shute) Du Bois; great³-grandson of *William Shute*, Colonel, Second Regt., Salem County, New Jersey Militia.

FRED DON DYSINGER, Montclair, N. J. (35919). Son of George and Minnie Sophia (Williams) Dysinger; grandson of George and Anna Marie (Miller) Dysinger, Jr.; great-grandson of George and Elizabeth (Hollenback) Dysinger; great²-grandson of *Nicholas Deisinger*, Corporal, Sixth Battalion, Berks County, Penna. Militia.

HENRY GARDNER EARLE, Edgewood, R. I. (34919). Son of Alfred Gardner and Nora Niobe (Almy) Earle; grandson of Albert Sidney and Cornelia (Knight) Almy; great-grandson of Isaac Cook and Alice (Bateman) Almy; great^2-grandson of Cook and Charlotte (Cook) Almy; great^3-grandson of *Isaac Cook*, Captain, First Company, Tiverton, Rhode Island Militia.

JOHN MILTON ELDER, Cœur d'Alene, Idaho (35103). Son of John and Betsey Hutchins (Boynton) Elder; grandson of Isaac and Mary (Quint) Elder, Jr.; great-grandson of *Isaac Elder*, Lieutenant, Colonel Wheaton's Regt., Mass. Militia.

RICHMOND BULLOCK ELLIOTT, Upper Montclair, N. J. (35726). Son of Richmond Bullock and Letitia (Hassert) Elliott; grandson of Jason and Ruth B. (Martin) Elliott; great-grandson of Joseph and Betsey (Towne) Elliott; great^2-grandson of Roger and Betsey (Prince) Elliott; great^3-grandson of *Joseph Elliott*, Captain, Col. Israel Putnam's Conn. Militia at Bunker Hill.

IRVIN H. ELLSWORTH, Orrville, Ohio (35882). Son of E. D. and N. J. (Overmeier) Ellsworth; grandson of Jacob and M. M. (Honnuel) Overmeier; great-grandson of David and B. (Hockacker) Overmeier; great^2-grandson of *John George Overmeier*, Captain, Northumberland County, Penna. Militia.

PRESLEY KITTREDGE EWING, New Orleans, La. (34818). Son of Fayette Clay and Frances Martha (MacDonald) Ewing; grandson of Fayette Clay and Eliza Josephine (Kittredge) Ewing; great-grandson of Ephraim McLean and Jane Pope (McIntyre) Ewing; great^2-grandson of *Robert Ewing*, Member Virginia Militia.

THOMAS REED EWING, Louisville, Ky. (34721). Son of David Henry and Arzilla Ann (Weldon) Ewing; grandson of James and Sally (Clarke) Ewing; great-grandson of *John Clarke*, private, Virginia Militia.

CHESTER HAROLD FARTHING, Missouri (32566). Son of William Dudley and Sarah Boyd (Phillips) Farthing; grandson of Thomas and Eliza Mildred (Chadwell) Phillips; great-grandson of George and Nancy (Johnston) Caldwell; great^2-grandson of *William Johnston*, private, Colonel Marion's Regt., South Carolina Militia; great^3-grandson of *Gideon Johnston*, Captain, State Regt., Virginia Troops.

WILLIAM DUDLEY PAUL FARTHING, East St. Louis, Ill. (35557). Same as Chester Harold Farthing, Missouri (32566).

HENRY BARKER FERNALD, Upper Montclair, N. J. (35963). Son of James Champlin and Nettie (Barker) Fernald; grandson of Charles Luther and Rachel (Maxwell) Barker; great-grandson of Luther Dana and Maria (Devol) Barker; great^2-grandson of Joseph and Elizabeth (Dana) Barker; great^3-grandson of *William Dana*, Captain-Lieutenant, Mass. Militia.

LUTHER DANA FERNALD, Montclair, N. J. (35548). Same as Henry Barker Fernald, New Jersey (35963).

HENRY MASTEN FINE, Fort Bayard, N. Mex. (30092). Son of Andrew and Mary (Masten) Fine; grandson of Henry Van Warren and Clarissa (Gurnett) Masten, Jr.; great-grandson of Henry Van Warren and Hannah (Nichols) Masten; great^2-grandson of *Cornelius C. Masten*, private, First Regt., Ulster County, New York Militia.

CHARLES CLEMENT FISHER, Marion, Ohio (35879). Son of Timothy Bruen and Elenora P. (Bennett) Fisher; grandson of *Isaac Fisher*, private, First Regt., Bergen County, New Jersey State Troops.

ALANSON AUGUSTUS FLINT, San Francisco, Calif. (34739). Son of Alanson Augustus and Ella Mary (Bradley) Flint; grandson of Alanson and Hannah (Griffin) Flint; great-grandson of John and Ruth (Upton) Flint; great^2-grandson of *Samuel Flint*, Captain, Essex County, Mass. Militia.

NATHAN BEMAN FLOOD, North Adams, Mass. (35855). Son of Roger Alexander and Maria (Pierson) Flood; grandson of Luke and Leucene (Alexander) Flood; great-grandson of *Roger Alexander*, private, Colonel Peck's Regt., Rhode Island Troops and Sailor, Rhode Island privateers.

EDWARD RICHARD FOLSOM, Irvington, N. J. (36016). Son of Frederick Lewis and Mrs. Martha (Layton) Mott Folsom; grandson of Otis W. and Harriet (Holley) Folsom; great-grandson of Araspus and Susan (Pendleton) Folsom; great^2-grandson of *Zebulon Pendleton*, private, Rhode Island Militia and Artillery, pensioned.

GEORGE KEELER FOLSOM, Hilton, N. J. (36017). Son of Edward Richard and Sara Elizabeth (Keeler) Folsom; grandson of Frederick Lewis and Mrs. Martha (Layton) Mott Folsom; great-grandson of Otis W. and Harriet (Holley) Folsom; great²-grandson of Araspus and Susan (Pendleton) Folsom; great³-grandson of *Zebulon Pendleton*, private, Rhode Island Militia and Artillery, pensioned.

LOUIS LAYTON FOLSOM, Irvington, N. J. (36018). Same as George Keeler Folsom, New Jersey (36017).

HENRY PLEASANT FOWLKES, Nashville, Tenn. (34641). Son of Henry Pleasant and Lucy T. Fowlkes; grandson of Henry Robinson and Susan Ann (Russell) Fowlkes; great-grandson of Pleasant and Doria (——) Russell; great²-grandson of *James Russell*, Sergeant of Artillery, Virginia Cont'l Line.

FREDERICK EZRA FOX, Ohio (35173). Supplementals. Son of Frederick Coffman and Elizabeth (Brelsford) Fox; grandson of Frederick Crissman and Hannah (Coffman) Fox; great-grandson of John and Rachael (Shoemaker) Coffman; great²-grandson of *Jacob Coffman*, private, Virginia Militia; grandson of Ezra and Jane (Watkins) Brelsford; great-grandson of Joshua and Nancy (Colvin) Watkins; great²-grandson of *Henry Colvin*, private, First Regt., Virginia State Troops; great²-grandson of *William Watkins*, Drummer, Third Regt., Maryland Troops.

WILLIAM MOORHOUSE FRANCIS, Atlanta, Ga. (35219). Son of Charles Dayton and Hannah (Sykes) Francis; grandson of John and Mary (Camp) Francis; great-grandson of John and Saphrona (Lusk) Francis; great²-grandson of *Justus Francis*, private, Col. Roger Eno's Regt., Conn. Militia, widow pensioned.

BENJAMIN ROBERT FRANKLIN, New Orleans, La. (34819). Son of Robert Morris and Sarah (Francis) Franklin; grandson of Benjamin Cromwell and Eliza Cleveland Franklin; great-grandson of John and Mary (Graves) Cleveland; great²-grandson of John and Mrs. Catherine (Montgomery) Cleveland; great²-grandson of *Ben. Cleveland*, Colonel, North Carolina Militia.

BENJAMIN HOBSON FRAYSER, Boston, Mass. (Vt. 35089). Son of Benjamin Hobson and Anne Rebecca (Finch) Frayser; grandson of Albert R. and Martha (Hobson) Frayser; great-grandson of Benjamin and Sally Woodson (Hatcher) Hobson; great²-grandson of *John Hatcher*, Lieutenant, Col. Richard Parker's Regt., Virginia Militia.

DWIGHT WOODBURY FROST, Summit, N. J. (35969). Son of Alfred A. and Elizabeth E. (Stockwell) Frost; grandson of John A. and Phœbe J. (Murray) Stockwell; great-grandson of Robert and Olive (Bancroft) Murray; great²-grandson of Alpheus and Phœbe (Woodbury) Bancroft; great³-grandson of *Robert Bancroft*, Matross, Mass. Cont'l Artillery, pensioned.

HERBERT HUME GADSBY, North Adams, Mass. (35854). Son of James T. and Thankful M. (Cook) Gadsby; grandson of Samuel Cook; great-grandson of *John Cook*, Lieutenant and Regimental Quartermaster, First Regt., Rhode Island Troops.

JOHN BEEBE GIBSON, West Orange, N. J. (35741). Son of William A. and Diadama (Beebe) Gibson; grandson of John W. and Sarah Fay (St. John) Beebe; great-grandson of William and Maria (Van Zandt) Beebe; great²-grandson of John and Jane (Abbott) Beebe; great³-grandson of *Thomas T. Beebe*, Ensign, Seventh Regt., New York Militia.

ALLEN ARTHUR GILBERT, Chicago, Ill. (35442). Son of Allen Alling and Sarah Allen (Flowers) Gilbert; grandson of Amos Alling and Emily (Thornton) Gilbert; great-grandson of *Amos Gilbert*, private, Conn. Militia, pensioned.

HENRY CURTIS GILBERT, Terre Haute, Ind. (35508). Son of Curtis and Mary Caroline (King) Gilbert; grandson of *Benjamin Gilbert*, private, Col. Henry Shurburne's Regt., Conn. Line, pensioned.

WILLIAM HENRY GILBERT, Hrtford, Conn. (35487). Son of Henry Still and Emily Louisa (Miller) Gilbert; grandson of Elijah and Louisa Matilda (Gildersleeve) Miller; great-grandson of Sylvester and Rebecca (Dixon) Gildersleeve; great²-grandson of *Philip Gildersleeve*, private, Col. James Clinton's Regt., New York Cont'l Line.

WILLIAM SYDNOR GILBREATH, Detroit, Mich. (35708). Son of Erasmus Corwin and Susan Sinclare (Corse) Gilbert; grandson of Fortunatus Sydner and Rachel Moore (Lansing) Gilbreath; great-grandson of Robert and Mary Taylor (Sydnor) Gilbreath; great²-grandson of *Robert Gilbreath*, Sergeant, Virginia Cont'l Troops; great²-grandson of *Fortunatus Sydnor*, private, Lancaster County, Virginia Cont'l Troops.

JOHN TOWNSEND GILL, New Haven, Conn. (35480). Son of John T. and Calista E. (Hopkins) Gill; grandson of Aaron Townsend and Betsey (Eastman) Hopkins; great-grandson of Robert H. Hopkins; great-grandson of *James Hopkins*, Ensign, Ebenezer Allen's Regt., Vermont Militia.

NESBIT GAMALIEL GLEASON, Cambridge, Mass. (35862). Son of Benjamin Gamaliel and Elizabeth Hindle (Grovenor) Gleason; grandson of Gamaliel and Hannah (Morse) Gleason; great-grandson of Benjamin and Rhoda (Gleason) Gleason, Jr.; great²-grandson of *Benjamin Gleason*, private, Mass. Militia; great²-grandson of *Jonas Gleason*, Minute Man at Lexington Alarm.

STEPHEN DOUGLAS GLINES, Baltimore, Md. (35344). Son of Eben K. and Maggie E. (Barton) Glines; grandson of David and Matilda (Rowe) Glines; great-grandson of *Benjamin Glines*, private, Major Wm. Scott's Battalion, New Hampshire Cont'l Troops.

JOEL WHITNEY GOFF, Madison, S. Dak. (30662). Son of Edward and Elizabeth (Spaulding) Goff; grandson of Edward and Hannah (Dill) Goff; great-grandson of *James Goff*, Corporal and Sergeant, Mass. Troops, pensioned.

MAURICE GOLDSMITH, New York, N. Y. (35901). Son of Nomar and Eva (Maas) Goldsmith; grandson of Abraham Alexander and Rose (Hilzein) Goldsmith; great-grandson of Moses and Ellen (Alexander) Goldsmith; great²-grandson of Abraham and Hannah (Aaron) Alexander, Jr.; great²-grandson of *Abraham Alexander*, Lieutenant, General Sumter's Regt., South Carolina Militia.

BYRON H. GOODRICH, Hudson, Mich. (35709). Son of Henry and Esther (Mason) Goodrich; grandson of George and Clamania (Lee) Goodrich; great-grandson of *Daniel Goodrich*, private, Col. Erastus Wolcott's Regt., Conn. Militia.

FLETCHER B. GOODRICH, Hudson, Mich. (35710). Son of Byron H. and Lois (Gooder) Goodrich; grandson of Henry and Esther (Mason) Goodrich; great-grandson of George and Clamania (Lee) Goodrich; great²-grandson of *Daniel Goodrich*, private, Col. Erastus Wolcott's Regt., Conn. Militia.

MARSHALL L. GOODRICH, Hudson, Mich. 35711). Same as Fletcher B. Goodrich, Mich. (35710).

GEORGE SIDNEY GOODSPEED, Cowesett, R. I. (34920). Son of George Edward and Addy Isabel (Turner) Goodspeed; grandson of Nathan Brown and Georgianna (Van Dyke) Turner; great-grandson of Francis and Emmeline (Dole) Van Wyke; great²-grandson of Elihu and Lydia (Pierce) Dole; great²-grandson of Amos and Mathilda (Hewes) Dole; great⁴-grandson of *Amos Dole*, private, Col. John Robinson's Regt., Mass. Militia.

ARTHUR JAMES GOSNELL, Rochester, N. Y. (35902). Son of James and Sylvia (Foote) Gosnell; grandson of Lemuel Thomas and Emily Augusta (Whitney) Foote, Jr.; great-grandson of Lemuel Thomas and Lucy (Clark) Foote; great²-grandson of *Reuben Clark*, private, Berkshire County, Mass. Militia, pensioned.

HARRY NICOL GRAHAM, Paterson, N. J. (35964). Son of Nichol and Lydia Ann (Johnston) Graham; grandson of Mahlon and Mary (Evans) Johnston; great-grandson of John and Elizabeth (Farrar) Evans; great²-grandson of *Obadiah Evans*, private, New Jersey Militia, State and Cont'l Troops.

JOSEPH H. GRANT, Oklahoma City, Okla. (35241). Son of William D. and Samantha (J——) Grant; grandson of Asa and Elizabeth (——) Grant; great-grandson of *William Grant, Jr.*, Lieutenant, South Carolina Militia, pensioned; great²-grandson of *William Grant*, Captain, Col. Thomas Brandon's Regt., South Carolina Militia.

MICHAELS HUFFAKER GRASSLY, Illinois (31893). Supplemental. Son of Adam Fred and Fannie Meriwether (Huffaker) Grassly; grandson of Michaels Lee and Frances Jane (Smith) Huffaker; great-grandson of Edwin Bathurst and Sallie Shelton (Monroe) Smith; great²-grandson of *John Monroe*, private, Third Regt., Virginia Troops.

GEORGE HOLDRIDGE GREENE, Adrian, Mich. (35712). Son of George Olin and Mary M. (Holdridge) Greene; grandson of Eleazer and Mehitable (Stone) Holdridge; great-grandson of Felix and Deborah (Slocum) Holdridge; great²-grandson of *Eleazer Slocum*, private, Albany County, New York Militia.

ERVIN GURNSEY GRINNELL, Batavia, N. Y. (35635). Son of Paul and Sarah Maria (Butler) Grinnell, grandson of John and Praxana (Tinkham) Grinnell; great-grandson of Isaiah and Jane (Crane) Grinnell; great²-grandson of *Amasa Grinnell*, private, Col. James Holmes' Fourth Regt., New York Militia.

LLOYD GARRISON GRINNELL, Highland Park, Mich. (35713). Son of Ervin G. and Mary (Timmerman) Grinnell; grandson of Paul and Sarah (Butler) Grinnell; great-grandson of John and Praxana (Tinkham) Grinnell; great²-grandson of Isaiah and Jane (Crane) Grinnell; great³-grandson of *Amasa Grinnell*, private, Col. James Holmes' Regt., New York Militia, pensioned.

HARRY WALTER HABERMAN, Marion, Ohio (35880). Son of Christian Frederick and Cora (Clark) Haberman; grandson of John Walter and Elizabeth (Turney) Clark; great-grandson of Joseph and Margaret (Weber) Turney; great²-grandson of *John Turney*, private, Second Battalion, Northampton County, Penna. Militia.

ORVILLE REED HAGAN, Paterson, N. J. (36008). Son of Joseph Jones and Sarah (Reed) Hagan; grandson of Orville and Elizabeth (Allen) Reed; great-grandson of Kitchell and Sarah (Dibble) Reed, Jr.; great²-grandson of *Kitchell Reed*, private, Third Regt., New York Troops.

EZRA ANDREWS HALE, Rochester, N. Y. (35904). Son of William Barton and Clara Louise (Andrews) Hale; grandson of Abner Cable and Sally Ann (Barton) Hale; great-grandson of Ozias and Sally (Lanison) Barton; great²-grandson of *Jonathan Barton*, private, Mass. Cont'l Troops, pensioned.

WILLIAM HARMON HALL, San Diego, Calif. (34746). Son of James P. and Myra (Bradley) Hall; grandson of Harmon and Harriet (Bishop) Bradley; great-grandson of *Abraham Bradley*, private, Mass. Militia.

FREDERICK HANNA, Captain, U. S. Army, retired, Detroit, Mich. (35724). Son of John and Blanche (Odell) Hanna; grandson of James Albert and Roxana (Palmer) Odell; great-grandson of Nehemiah and Elizabeth (Boyle) Palmer; great²-grandson of *Nehemiah Palmer*, Seaman and gunner, Conn. Sloops "Renage" and "Randolph."

HAROLD RUSE HARPER, New Orleans, La. (34820). Son of William Yarborough Harper; grandson of William Yarborough and Margaret A. (Golden) Harper; great-grandson of R. A. and Nancy (Griffin) Golden; great²-grandson of James and Dorcus (Watson) Griffin; great³-grandson of *John Watson*, Captain, North Carolina Militia.

EARL ALEXANDER HARRIS, Newark, N. J. (35916). Son of Charles M. and Alice (Hopewell) Harris; grandson of Francis and Hannah (Alexander) Harris; great-grandson of John and Hannah (Boyd) Alexander; great²-grandson of *James Boyd*, private, Ulster County, New York Militia and Artillery, pensioned.

ROBERT ALEXANDER HARTRICK, Decatur, Ill. (35443). Son of Henry and Nancy Emily (Taylor) Hartrick; grandson of Matthew McElroy and Elizabeth (Cohenouer) Taylor; great-grandson of Robert and Mary (McElroy) Taylor; great²-grandson of Alexander and Mary (Donaldson) McElroy; great³-grandson of *Adam McElroy*, private, Second Battalion, Penna. Militia.

LEDYARD ELY HASTINGS, New Haven, Conn. (35481). Son of Frederick G. and Katharine Ledyard (Ely) Hastings; grandson of William B. and Elizabeth S. (Morgan) Ely; great-grandson of William H. and Margaret (Chevenard) Morgan; great²-grandson of John nd Julia (Seymour) Chevenard; great³-grandson of Thomas S. Seymour; great⁴-grandson of *Thomas Youngs Seymour*, Captain, Second Regt., Conn. Cont'l Dragoons.

WILLIAM DILL HATHAWAY, New York, N. Y. (35634). Son of William Eberman and Myra (Chamberlain) Hathaway; grandson of John J. and Sarah J. (Kile) Chamberlin; great-grandson of Joseph Fitch and Rebecca (Montgomery) Chamberlin; great²-grandson of James and Sarah (Hills) Montgomery; great³-grandson of *John Montgomery*, private, Mass. Militia.

RALPH CLYMER HAWKINS, New York (34560). Supplemental. Son of Ernest Clymer and Ada Sanford (Hallock) Hawkins; grandson of Charles Wheeler and Mary Elizabeth (Newton) Hawkins; great-grandson of Mills and Jane (Rose) Hawkins; great²-grandson of Zopher and Mary (Hawkins) Hawkins; great³-grandson of *Simeon Hawkins* (father of Mary), Suffolk County, New York refugee and signer of several petitions; great⁴-grandson of *Alexander Hawkins*, Signer of Suffolk County, N. Y., Association and petitions; great²-grandson of Simeon and Elizabeth (Hawkins) Hawkins; great⁴-grandson of *David Hawkins* (father of Elizabeth), Signer of Suffolk County, N. Y., Association; grandson of Henry Webb and Alice Estelle (Miller) Hallock; great-grandson of Sylvester and Emily (Tuthill) Miller; great²-grandson of Zophar Mills and Betsy (Davis) Miller; great³-grandson of *David Davis*, private and Sergeant, New York Militia and Cont'l Line; great⁴-grandson of Bartley Fanning and Fanny (Miller) Tuthill; great⁴-grandson of

Nathaniel and Martha (Miller) Miller; great⁴-grandson of *Ebenezer Miller* (father of Martha), Captain, Colonel Floyd's Regt., New York Minute Men and Sailor on Frigate "Trumbull"; great-grandson of Samuel and Caroline Jayne (Rhodes) Newton; great²-grandson of Caleb and Elizabeth (Lorin) Newton, Jr.; great²-grandson of *Caleb Newton (Nuton)*, Signer of Suffolk County, N. Y., Association.

LOUIS CLAUDE SWANSON HAYNES, Captain, A. E. F., Flint Hill, Va. (35091). Son of William Daniel and Frances (James) Haynes; grandson of John O. W. and Elizabeth Ann (Keen) Haynes; great-grandson of Stephen and Nancy (Oglesby) Haynes; great²-grandson of Shadrack and Celia (Duncan) Oglesby; great²-grandson of *George Duncan*, Captain, Fluvanna County, Virginia Militia.

WILLIAM B. HEARTWELL, Auburn, N. Y. (34368). Son of Oscar Fitzallen and Julia Ann (Webster) Heartwell; grandson of Benjamin and Jane (Burnett) Heartwell; great-grandson of *Joseph Heartwell*, Captain, New Hampshire Militia and Cont'l Troops.

ALBERT EDWARD HECKMANN, New Harmony, Ind. (35509). Son of Louis and Ella (Johnson) Heckman; grandson of William Ludrick and Kate (Highman) Johnson; great-grandson of Zachariah and Catharine (Staley) Johnson; great²-grandson of Samson and ———— (Williams) Johnson; great²-grandson of *Arthur Johnson*, Corporal and Sergeant, Eighth and Fourth Regts., Virginia Cont'l Troops.

GEORGE WASHINGTON HESTON, Pacific Beach, Calif. (34744). Son of George Washington and Sarah Jane (Bender) Heston; grandson of Edward and Mary (Pugh) Heston; great-grandson of Abraham and Hannah (Supplee) Heston; great²-grandson of *Edward Heston (Heeston)*, Lieutenant-Colonel, Penna. Militia, prisoner.

ALBERT HENRY HEUSSER, Paterson, N. J. (35972). Son of Albert and Emma A. (Tier) Heusser; grandson of George and Hannah Jane (Bartine) Tier, Jr.; great-grandson of George and Elenor (O'Neil) Tier; Great²-grandson of *John O'Neil*, private, Maxwell's Brigade, N. J. Cont'l Troops.

BEVERLY B. HOBBS, Keokuk, Iowa (35607). Son of John W. and Susan (Summerville) Hobbs; grandson of James and Susan (Stover) Summerville; great-grandson of James and Ruth (Holliday) Summerville; great²-grandson of *William Holliday*, Paymaster, Bedford County, Penna. Militia.

CHARLES HOLDEN, Grand Rapids, Mich. (35723). Son of Ebenezer Gregg Danforth and Melissa Eliza (Smith) Holden; grandson of Samuel and Mary (Hastings) Smith; great-grandson of Thomas and Hannah (Billings) Hastings; great²-grandson of *Thomas Hastings*, Lieutenant, Hampshire County, Mass. Militia.

FRANK WARD HOLT, Michigan (9095). Supplemental. Son of Ira Farnsworth and Perla M. (Ward) Holt; grandson of Lorenzo and Abigail (Cleveland) Ward; great²-grandson of *Solomon Cleveland*, private, Conn. Cont'l Line, pensioned.

ALBERT WILLIAM HONEYWILL, Jr., Hartford, Conn. (35484). Son of Albert W. and Grace (Dykeman) Honeywill; grandson of Elisha Peter and Annie E. (Phelps) Dykeman; great-grandson of Hezekiah and Esther (Warren) Dyckman; great²-grandson of Daniel and Susanna (Knapp) Warren; great²-grandson of *Israel Knapp*, Captain, Col. Henry Luddington's Regt., New York Militia; great²-grandson of Peter and Ruth (Carl) Dykeman; great²-grandson of *Joseph (Johan) Dyckman*, Captain, Dutchess County, New York Militia.

GILES PARKER HOWARD, Denver, Colo. (34371). Son of Cyrus Greeley and Nancy (Kneeland) Howard; grandson of Silas and Martha (Laws) Kneeland; great-grandson of *Timothy Kneeland*, Lieutenant, Col. Nathan Sparhawk's Regt., Mass. Militia.

CLAUDE FERRY HOWELL, Chicago, Ill. (35444). Son of Charles Herbert and Orill Eliza (Ferry) Howell; grandson of Enos Dexter and Sylvia Amelia (Nichols) Ferry; great-grandson of Asher and Asenath (Nichols) Ferry; great²-grandson of Jabez and Sarah (Brown) Nichols; great²-grandson of *Jonathan Brown*, Lieutenant, Mass. Militia.

OREN HOWES, Hudson, Mich. (35714). Son of Jeremiah and Catharine (Stark) Howes; grandson of Enos and Priscilla (Howes) Howes; great-grandson of *John Howes*, private, Colonel Freeman's Regt., Mass. Militia.

JAMES LINDSAY HOYT, Stamford, Conn. (35488). Son of William Griffin and Ella (Lindsay) Hoyt; grandson of Ira Ford and Mary Pell (Uixon) Hoyt; great-grandson of Aaron Gregory and Hannah Smith (Bouton) Hoyt; great²-grandson of *John Hoyt, Jr.*, private, Col. John Meade's Regt., Conn. Militia, pensioned.

HARVEY HUGG, Cranford, N. J. (35923). Son of William Henry and Lydia Dutton (Pyle' Hugg; grandson of Benjamin Flintham and Dorsey (Ashley) Hugg; great-grandson of *Robert Ashley*, private, North Carolina Militia, prisoner, widow pensioned.

HENRY CHRISTIAN HUISKAMP, Keokuk, Iowa (35606). Son of H. W. and Eckstein (Norton) Huiskamp; grandson of Elijah H. and Melinda Clark (Wilson) Norton; great-grandson of John and Elizabeth Trigg (Clark) Wilson; great²-grandson of Robert P. and Malinda (Trigg) Clark; great²-grandson of *Robert Clark*, private, Bedford County, Virginia Militia.

GUY R. HUNT, Lincoln, Nebr. (33892). Son of Lewis V. and Celia F. (Ross) Hunt; grandson of James M. and Elizabeth A. (Sanders) Ross; great-grandson of Robert and Elizabeth (Howerton) Ross; great²-grandson of *Reuben Ross*, private, Maryland and Virginia Troops, pensioned.

ROBERT THOMAS HUSTON, Connersville, Ind. (35507). Son of John Van Winkle and Mary Adelaide (Davis) Huston; grandson of Josiah Alden and Harriet Jane (Gale) Davis; great-grandson of Solomol and Salome (Alden) Davis; great²-grandson of *Josiah Davis*, Lieutenant, Mass. Militia and Cont'l Line; great²-grandson of *Josiah Alden*, private, York County, Mass. Militia; great-grandson of John and Abigail (Smith) Gale; great²-grandson of *John Gale*, private, Col. Thomas Stickney's Regt., New Hampshire Militia; great²-grandson of *Robert Smith*, Lieutenant, Colonel Stickney's Regt., New Hampshire Militia; great²-grandson of *Austin Alden*, Lieutenant, Mass. Cont'l Troops; great²-grandson of Austin and Salome (Lombard) Alden; great⁴-grandson of *Solomon Lombard*, Chairman, Judge Advocate and Mass. Committee of Safety; great²-grandson of John and Rebecca (Webster) Gale; great²-grandson of *John Webster*, Selectman and Member Salisbury, N. H., War Committees.

JOSEPH P. HUTCHISON, Illinois (34428). Supplemental. Son of James E. and Susan (Hopkins) Hutchison; grandson of Thomas and Orpha (Pierce) Hopkins; great-grandson of Abizur and Jane (Hopkins) Pierce; great²-grandson of *Daniel Pierce*, private, Albany County, New York Militia.

MILES BREWTON HUTSON, New Orleans, La. (35983). Son of Charles Woodward and Mary Jane (Lockett) Hutson; grandson of William Ferguson and Sophronia Lucia (Palmer) Hutson; great-grandson of Richard Woodward and Martha O'Reilly (Ferguson) Hutson; great²-grandson of *Thomas Hutson*, Captain, South Carolina Militia, wounded.

JOHN WILBUR JACOBY, Marion, Ohio (35887). Son of Michael and Catharine (Emery) Jacoby, Jr.; grandson of Michael and Elizabeth (Worline) Jacoby; great-grandson of Henry and Catharine (Cline) Worline; great²-grandson of *Conrad Cline*, private, Penna. Militia and Cont'l Troops.

ALLEN FOURESTIER JAQUITH, Elizabeth, N. J. (35549). Son of Joseph Fourestier and Harriet Warren (Allen) Jaquith; grandson of Nathaniel Crosby and Emma Stokes (Simpson) Jaquith; great-grandson of Nathaniel and Eleanor (Stimpson) Jaquith; great²-grandson of Nathan and Anna (Crosby) Jaquith; great²-grandson of *Benjamin Jaquith*, private, Mass. Militia in Lexington Alarm.

FREDERIC HORNER JOHNSON, San Francisco, Calif. (34748). Son of Theodore Horner and Ida Marcia (Errette) Johnson; grandson of Thomas and Ruth Amelia (Wing) Errette; great-grandson of Amos Orange and Sarah (Cameme) Wing; great²-grandson of *Thomas Wing*, private, Conn. Militia at Lexington Alarm.

FRED LYNN JOHNSON, Adrian, Mich. (35715). Son of Alfred and Glendora (Mason) Johnson; grandson of John G. and Amanda D. (Carter) Mason; great-grandson of Norman B. and Mentha M. (Bradish) Carter; great²-grandson of Calvin and Nancy (Post) Bradish; great²-grandson of *John Bradish*, private, Col. Ezra May's Regt., Mass. Militia.

EDWIN BROADDUS JONES, Wilmington, Del. (35655). Son of William D. and Virginia Frances (Broaddus) Jones; grandson of Edwin and Eliza (Montague) Broaddus; great-grandson of Philip and Elizabeth (Williams) Montague; great²-grandson of *Philip Montague*, Colonel, Middlesex County, Virginia Militia.

FREDERIC MARSHALL JONES, Springfield, Mass. (35863). Son of Marshall and Mary Ann (Roberts) Jones; grandson of Marshall and Wealthy C. (Sarvin) Jones; great-grandson of *Amos Jones*, private, Col. Thomas Gardner's Regt., Mass. Militia, pensioned.

HARRY RANDALL JONES, Farmington, Iowa (35611). Son of Henry and Eliza Jane (Randall) Jones; grandson of Leonard L. and Maria L. (Warren) Randall; great-grandson of Porter and Lydia (Howard) Warren; great²-grandson of Peter and Judith (Adams) Warren; great²-grandson of *Thomas Warren*, Captain, Mass. Militia at Bunker Hill.

JOSEPH CABELL JONES, Frankfort, Ky. (34722). Son of Lewis R. and Emily B. (Coffey) Jones; grandson of Thomas Jefferson and Rachel (Coffey) Jones; great-grandson of John and Margaret Ann (——) Jones; great²-grandson of *Joshua Jones*, private, Virginia Militia.

CALVIN NICOLAS JOYNER, Baton Rouge, La. (35979). Son of Nicolas Everett and Sarah Baker (Austin) Joyner; grandson of William McRae and Mary R. (Holcombe) Austin; great-grandson of Armistead R. and Emma (Spencer) Holcombe; great²-grandson of Richard and Anna (Baker) Spencer; great²-grandson of *Perry Spencer*, private, Talbot County, Maryland Militia.

MARION SAWYER KENNEDY, Pulaski, Tenn. (36052). Son of James Foster and Hannah Catherine (McGaughey) Kennedy; grandson of Daniel and Margaret (——) Kennedy; great-grandson of John and Patience (D. ——) Kennedy; great²-grandson of *Daniel Kennedy*, Adjutant and Ensign, Penna. Troops, prisoner.

CHARLES SANFORD KING, New Rochelle, N. Y. (35900). Son of Jabe Otis and Ella (Mason) King; grandson of George and Naomi (Otis) King; great-grandson of Belah and Miranda (Hatch) King; great²-grandson of *Douglas King*, private, Hampshire County, Mass. Militia; grandson of Benjamin L. and Delia (Fairchild) Mason; great-grandson of Samuel and Elizabeth (Lucas) Mason; great²-grandson of *Benjamin Mason*, private, New Hampshire Militia.

FRANK MORTON KING, Boston, Mass. (35864). Son of Francis D. and Mary Ann (Maloy) King; grandson of Artemas and Sally (Byram) King; great-grandson of Nathan and Prudence (Dean) King; great²-grandson of *John King*, Captain, Col. Timothy Walker's Regt., Mass. Militia.

HARRY ANABLE KNIFFIN, Westfield, N. J. (35737). Son of George Green and Harriet Isabel (Sheldon) Kniffin; grandson of Edgar Logan and Sarah (Green) Kniffin; great-grandson of Jonathan B. and Harriet (Logan) Kniffin; great²-grandson of *Samuel Logan*, Major, New York Militia and Cont'l Line.

LEWIS ABBERLEY KNIFFIN, Westfield, N. J. (35735). Son of Sidney L. and Minnie (Walker) Kniffin; grandson of Thomas B. and Elizabeth (Brownley) Kniffin; great-grandson of Edgar Logan and Sarah Ann (Green) Kniffin; great²-grandson of Jonathan B. and Harriet (Logan) Kniffin; great²-grandson of *Samuel Logan*, Major, New York Militia and Cont'l Line, prisoner.

ALBERT HOWARD KNIGHT, Riverpoint, R. I. (34921). Son of Albert Waterman and Ada Frances (Crandall) Knight; grandson of Richard Bowers and Eliza Abby (Hill) Knight; great-grandson of Elder Richard and Rebecca (Brayton) Knight; great²-grandson of Stephen and Mary (Manchester) Knight; great²-grandson of *Matthew Manchester*, Member Rhode Island Committee of Safety.

ARTHUR CANFIELD KNIGHT, Cleveland, Ohio (35888). Son of Charles Marshall and Ivie (Canfield) Knight; grandson of Charles Thomas and Pheba Adelma (Miner) Canfield; great-grandson of Daniel Anderson and Sarah Francis (——) Miner; great²-grandson of *John Miner*, private, Conn. State Troops, pensioned.

HOWARD WAGGONER KNIGHT, Chicago, Ill. (35445). Son of Samuel Edwin and Mary E. (Waggoner) Knight; grandson of Daniel and Elizabeth (Shisler) Waggoner; great-grandson of John B. and Mary (Bowman) Waggoner; great²-grandson of *John Waggoner*, private, Penna. Dragoons, pensioned.

ROBERT LOCHLAN KNOWLES, Grand Junction, Colo. (34369). Son of Charles Carroll and Ida May (——) Knowles; grandson of George Wilson and Jennie Rebecka (Mays) Knowles; great-grandson of George Anson and Sarah Avery (Meader) Knowles; great²-grandson of Joseph and Hannah (Haines) Knowles; great²-grandson of *Joseph Knowles*, private, Chester, New Hampshire Militia.

JOSEPH LALLANDE, New Orleans, La. (35981). Son of Joseph Gustave and Leonide (Bouligney) Lallande; grandson of Joseph and Caroline (Roche) Lallande de Ferriere; great-grandson of *Nicolas Louis Lalande de Ferriere*, Cadet under General Galvez at siege of Baton Rouge and taking of Pensacola.

THEODORE BURGER LATHROP, Branford, Conn. (35482). Son of Stanley Edwards and Elizabeth (Littell) Lathrop; grandson of Alfred Crafts and Stella (Hough) Lathrop;

great-grandson of Erastus and Judith (Crafts) Lathrop; great²-gandson of *Ebenezer Lathrop*, Captain, Conn. Militia.

DONALD CURTIS LEACH, Portland, Me. (26028). Supplementals. Son of Convers Edward and Gertrude E. (Lang) Leach; grandson of Caleb Norris and Ellen A. (Cummings) Lang; great-grandson of Joseph Brackett and Betsey (Libby) Lang; great²-grandson of Dennis and Elizabeth (McKenney) Libby; great²-grandson of *Ichabod Libby*, Sergeant Thirty-first Regt., Mass. Militia; great²-grandson of *Samuel McKenney*, private. Cumberland County, Mass. Militia; great-grandson of Nathaniel G. and Dorcas A. (Colby) Cummings; great²-grandson of Cyrus and Elizabeth (Curtis) Cummings; great²-grandson of Nathaniel and Mary (Crawford) Cummings; great⁴-grandson of *Jonathan Crawford*, private, New Hampshire Militia.

WILSON BLAKE LEECH, Charlotte, Tenn. (34643). Son of Leonard L. and Sarah Ann (Hardin) Leech; grandson of Joab and Zany (Dillahunta) Hardin; great-grandson of Joseph and Sarah (Drake) Hardin; great²-grandson of *John Hardin*, private and Captain, Penna. Militia.

WILLARD EUGENE LELAND, Baltimore, Md. (35345). Son of Walter Fisk and Addie Lee (Moreland) Leland; grandson of Herbert S. and Mary Helen (Fisk) Leland; great-grandson of Chauncey and Eliza (Aldrich) Fisk; great²-grandson of Hezekiah and Eleanor (Cooley) Fisk; great²-grandson of *Asa Fisk*, Lieutenant, Mass. Minute Men and Captain Cont'l Troops.

GEORGE ARMSTRONG LIGGETT, Springfield, N. J. (35746). Son of John Albert and Mary Boyd (Armstrong) Liggett; grandson of Caleb and Jane (Cowan) Liggett; great-grandson of George and Rachel (McKinley) Liggett; great²-grandson of *John Liggett*, private, Chester County, Penna. Militia.

GEORGE BLANCHARD LITTLEFIELD, Portland, Me. (34514). Son of Henry and Ellen Blanchard (Lyman) Littlefield; grandson of Sylvanus Ripley and Christiana (Blanchard) Lyman; great-grandson of Eliphalet and Abigail (Ripley) Lyman; great²-grandson of Sylvanus and Abigail (Wheelock) Ripley; great²-grandson of *Eleazer Wheelock*, Member New Hampshire Committees of Correspondence and of Public Safety.

BENJAMIN WALTER LOVELAND, Hartford, Conn. (35483). Son of Francis H. and Harriet Preston (Doolittle) Loveland; grandson of Jesse and Lucretia (Paine) Loveland; great-grandson of *Lazarus Loveland*, private, Col. Erastus Wolcott's Regt., Conn. Militia.

DONALD BEARDSLEY LOW, Ridgewood, N. J. (36009). Son of Frank Eliot and Mary (Doremus) Low; grandson of Peter and Eliza Ann (Wandle) Doremus; great-grandson of John Berdon and Margret (Westervelt) Doremus; great²-grandson of *George Doremus*, private, Bergen County, New Jersey Militia.

CHARLES WESLEY LYON, Brooklyn, N. Y. (35903). Son of Charles Wesley and Eunice (Smith) Lyon; grandson of Samuel Allen and Pamelia Howell (Cramer) Lyon; great-grandson of John and Elizabeth Medlas (Allen) Lyon; great²-grandson of *Samuel Allen*, Artificer and Ensign, New Jersey Militia, pensioned.

ELIOT GROSVENOR LYON, Oklahoma City, Okla. (35239). Son of Charles Huntington and Ruth McClellan (Botham) Lyon; grandson of Samuel Walter and Maria Jane (Grosvenor) Lyon; great-grandson of Samuel Huntington and Maria (Warner) Lyon; great²-grandson of Walter and Mary (Huntington) Lyon; great³-grandson of *William Huntington*, Fifer and Corporal, Col. Israel Putnam's Regt., Cont'l Line.

WILLIAM CLIFTON MACFADDEN, South Fargo, N. Dak. (33022). Son of William and Emma Barnes (Ward) Macfadden; grandson of Levi Barnes and Mary Spencer (Freeman) Ward; great-grandson of *Rufus Ward*, private, Mass. Militia, pensioned.

WILLIAM HARRY MAGILL, Fargo, N. Dak. (33021). Son of Henry E. and Louise Dilworth (Richardson) Magill; grandson of Williams Meyers and Sarah Jane (Zehring) Richardson; great-grandson of Philip and Anna Barbara (Zeller) Zehring; great²-grandson of *Christian Zehring*, private, Lancaster County, Penna. Militia.

WILLIAM AUGUSTUS MARSH, New York (32611). Supplemental. Son of Benjamin F. and Mary Ardelia (Gregory) Marsh; grandson of Evert and Mary D. (Chandler) Marsh; great-grandson of *Charles Marsh*, private, Essex County, New Jersey Militia.

JOSEPH HENRY MARSHALL, Ross, Calif. (34749). Son of Joseph Whippy and Anna Barnard (Coffin) Marshall; grandson of Henry and Phœbe (Barnard) Coffin; great-grandson of Benjamin and Anna (Folger) Barnard; great²-grandson of *Thomas Barnard*, Commander, Mass. privateer "Poffet."

THOMAS DAYTON MARTIN, New Jersey (29361). Supplemental. Son of John Dayton and Elizabeth (Marshall) Jones Martin; grandson of Thomas and Rebekah (Spinning) Martin; great-grandson of Benjamin and Charity (Garthwait) Spinning; great²-grandson of *Benjamin Spinning*, private, Essex County, New Jersey Militia.

JOSIAH SMITH MAXCY, Gardiner, Me. (34515). Son of Josiah and Eliza Jane (Crane) Maxcy; grandson of Smith and Clarissa (——) Maxcy; great-grandson of Josiah and Sally (Pickering) Maxcy; great²-grandson of *Benjamin Maxcy*, Second Lieutenant, Colonel Daggett's Regt., Mass. Militia.

MARSHALL MINTER MAYS, Denver, Colo. (34370). Son of Daniel W. and Susan Manning (Minter) Mays; grandson of Jeremiah A. and Sarah (McDowell) Minter; great-grandson of Samuel and Anne (Irvine) McDowell; great²-grandson of *Samuel McDowell*, Colonel, Virginia Militia.

HIRAM ULYSSES GRANT McADAMS, Carrollton, Ill. (35551). Son of Joseph and Mary (Silkwood) McAdams; grandson of William and Rebecca (Cashen) McAdams, Jr.; great-grandson of *William McAdams*, private, North Carolina Militia, pensioned.

PLINY WRIGHT McALLISTER, Minneapolis, Minn. (35678). Son of Joshua O. and Alvira A. (Wright) McAllister; grandson of James McAllister; great-grandson of *William McAllister*, private, New York Militia and State Troops, pensioned.

HOWARD F. McCONNELL, Montclair, N. J. (35920). Son of John E. and Annie (Fulmer) McConnell; grandson of John E. and Sarah (Chalfant) McConnell; great-grandson of Matthew and Ruth Hall (Davis) McConnell; great²-grandson of *Matthew McConnell*, Corporal, Penna. Troops.

ROBERT CLARK McCORNACK, Sioux City, Iowa (35605). Son of Fletcher A. and Mary (Clark) McCornack; grandson of Theodore Frelinghuysen and Lucia Jane (Tuller) Clark; great-grandson of Henry and Mary (Wilcox) Tuller; great²-grandson of Zachues and Tempa (Case) Wilcox; great³-grandson of *Darius Case*, private, Col. Thomas Baldwin's Regt., Conn. Troops.

LEE HARVEY McDILL, Nashville, Tenn. (34644). Son of Andrew Thomas and Elizabeth Emmeline (Gowdy) McDill; grandson of William and Elsie (Brown) Gowdy; great-grandson of James M. and Mary (Stewart) Brown; great²-grandson of *William Brown*, private, Col. Samuel Culbertson's Regt., Cumberland County, Penna. Militia.

BENTLEY MATTHEWS McMULLIN, Denver, Colo. (34372). Son of Samuel G. and Rella (H——) McMullin; grandson of Samuel H. and Belle (Matthews) McMullin; great-grandson of Thomas J. and Isabel (Brown) Matthews; great²-grandson of *William Brown*, Corporal and Sergeant, Eighth Regt., Conn. Cont'l Line.

FREDERICK McSHANE, New Orleans, La. (34825). Son of Edward and Lydia Ann (Chapman) McShane; grandson of Jeremiah and Mary Ann (Prevost) Chapman, Jr.; great-grandson of Jeremiah and Ann Osborne (Page) Chapman; great²-grandson of *Daniel Chapman, Jr.*, private, Essex County, Mass. Militia.

JOHN WILLIAMS McSHANE, New Orleans, La. (35980). Son of Frederick and Catherine (Williams) McShane; grandson of Edward and Lydia Ann (Chapman) McShane; great-grandson of Jeremiah and Mary Ann (Prevost) Chapman, Jr.; great²-grandson of Jeremiah and Ann Osborne (Page) Chapman; great³-grandson of *Daniel Chapman*, private, Essex County, Mass. Militia.

GEORGE NICHOLAS MECHAM, Omaha, Nebr. (33890). Son of Harrison Alexander and Ruth Alice (Coyle) Mecham; grandson of John Wesley and Ruth Prudence (Kallier) Mecham; great-grandson of Joseph and Hannah Ladd (Tyler) Mecham; great²-grandson of Joseph and Sarah (Bradford) Mecham (Meacham); great³-grandson of *Samuel Meacham*, private, Colonel Chase's Regt., New Hampshire Militia.

BRADFORD MORSE MELVIN, San Francisco, Calif. (34738). Son of Henry Alexander and S. Louise (Morse) Melvin; grandson of Samuel Houston and Sarah Amanda (Slemmons) Melvin; great-grandson of Samuel and Sarah (Osborn) Slemmons; great²-grandson of *William Slemmons*, private, Lancaster County, Penna. Militia.

RUSSELL HYDE MERRILL, Floriston, Calif. (Iowa 35609). Son of Samuel A. and Fanny Raney (Hyde) Merrill; grandson of Jeremiah Hill and Ann Elizabeth (Dearborn) Merrill; great-grandson of Abel and Abigail (Hill) Merrill; great²-grandson of Abel and Elizabeth (Page) Merrill; great³-grandson of *Samuel Merrill*, Lieutenant, Colonel Seammon's Regt., York County, Mass. Militia.

DICK A. MITCHELL, Mountain Iron, Minn. (35675). Son of Jackson Gates and Sarah Elizabeth (Hubbell) Mitchell; grandson of Anderson and Elzira (Whitlock) Mitchell; great-grandson of Charles and Patsy (Wilson) Whitlock; great²-grandson of *Moses Wilson,* private, Madison County, Virginia Militia.

PERCY G. MORGAN, Paris, Texas (Kans. 33317). Son of Morris James and Mary R. (Wagner) Morgan; grandson of John Rittenhouse and Susanna (Bicknell) (2nd wife) Morgan; great-grandson of Benjamin and Tacy (Stroud) Morgan; great²-grandson of Morgan and Ann (Roberts) Morgan; great³-grandson of *John Roberts,* Lieutenant and Captain, Colonel Nelson's Regt., Penna. Troops.

GEORGE CARRINGTON MOSEBY, Richmond, Va. (35090). Son of Bennett Williamson and Louisa Jane (Venable) Moseby; grandson of Paul Carrington and Emily Eaton (Carrington) Venable; great-grandson of Samuel (Woodson) and Mary Carrington) Venable; great²-grandson of *Paul Carrington,* Member, Virginia House of Delegates and Committee of Safety.

FRED ADAMS DEAN MOULTON, Boston, Mass. (35865). Son of Alpheus Windsor and Harriet (Dean) Moulton; grandson of John and Clarissa (Belknap) Moulton; great-grandson of Windsor and Mary (Loker) Moulton; great²-grandson of *Caleb Moulton,* Captain, Col. Thomas Poor's Regt., Mass. Militia.

STANLEY WINDSOR MOULTON, Boton, Mass. (35866). Son of Herbert and Lizzie Delaney (Lunt) Moulton; grandson of Alpheus Windsor and Harriet (Dean) Moulton; great-grandson of John and Clarissa (Belknap) Moulton; great²-grandson of Windsor and Mary (Loker) Moulton; great³-grandson of *Caleb Moulton,* Captain, Col. Thomas Poor's Regt., Mass. Militia.

WILLARD STURGIS MUCHMORE, Newark, N. J. (35732). Son of David Brant and Mary Jane (Miller) Muchmore; grandson of David Morehouse and Clarissa D. (Sturgis) Muchmore; great-grandson of Samuel and Sarah (Carter) Muchmore; great²-grandson of *John Muchmore,* private, Essex County, New Jersey Militia.

WILLIAM NEER, Paterson, N. J. (35970). Son of David and Ellen (Passage) Neer, grandson of Samuel and Lucinda (Morrison) Neer; great-grandson of *Charles (Carl) Neer,* Scout and Sharpshooter, Dutchess and Albany Counties, New York Militia, pensioned.

MARTIN REMINGTON NELSON, Des Moines, Iowa (35610). Son of Henry H. and Mary E. (Arnold) Nelson; grandson of James and Abigail (Snyder) Arnold; great-grandson of John and Catherine (Cortelyou) Snyder; great²-grandson of *George Snyder,* private, Albany and Dutchess Counties, New York Militia.

ALBERT RODMAN NICHOLS, Rhode Island (25961). Supplemental. Son of John Robinson and Arabella (Rodman) Nichols; grandson of Isaac and Elizabeth Robinson (Brown) Nichols; great-grandson of John and Mary E. (Robinson) Brown; great²-grandson of *George Brown,* private, Newport County, Rhode Island Militia, pensioned.

WILLIS CLARKE NOBLE, Jr., Montclair, N. J. (35742). Son of Willis Clarke and Willa J. (Gibson) Noble; grandson of Jacob Augustus and Minerva Grilly (Clarke) Noble; great-grandson of Jacob Mosely and Eliza (Alderman) Noble; great²-grandson of *Jacob Noble,* Sergeant, Hampshire County, Mass. Militia.

DENNIS LUKE NORTHWAY, East Cleveland, Ohio (35889). Son of Dwight I. and Therissa Amanda (May) Northway; grandson of Samuel and Abigail Taylor (Hillman) May; great-grandson of Charles and Dorcas (Osborn) May; great²-grandson of *Joshua Osborn,* private, Conn. Militia, pensioned.

ELMER ELLSWORTH NORTHWAY, East Cleveland, Ohio (35886). Son of Dwight T. and Therissa Amanda (May) Northway; grandson of Samuel and Abigail Taylor (Hillman) May; great-grandson of Charles and Dorcas (Osborn) May; great²-grandson of *Joshua Osborn,* private, Conn. Militia, pensioned.

NATHANIEL HUBBARD NUTTING, Massachusetts (33275). Supplemental. Son of George Hale and Hannah Maria (Brown) Nutting; grandson of Edmund Quincy and Sarepta Ann (Coffin) Brown; great-grandson of Nathaniel and Catherine (Nichols) Brown; great²-grandson of John and Mary (Mitchell) Brown; great³-grandson of *Josiah Brown,* Sergeant, Mass. Militia at Lexington Alarm.

EMMET O'NEAL, Louisville, Ky. (34719). Son of Joseph T. and Lydia (Wright) O'Neal; grandson of Merit Singleton and Elizabeth (Arnold) O'Neal; great-grandson of George and Lucy (Singleton) O'Neal; great²-grandson of *George O'Neal,* private, Virginia and Kentucky Troops.

JOSEPH THOMAS O'NEAL, Louisville, Ky. (34718). Son of Joseph T. and Lydia (Wright) O'Neal; grandson of Merit Singleton and Elizabeth (Arnold) O'Neal; great-grandson of George and Lucy (Singleton) O'Neal; great²-grandson of *George O'Neal*, private, Virginia and Kentucky Troops.

FRANK LOW OTTMAN, Schenectady, N. Y. (35643). Son of Jeremiah and Mary Jane (Low) Ottman; grandson of Peter and Hannah (Ballinger) Ottman; great-grandson of David and Mary (King) Ballinger; great²-grandson of *Ludwig Kling*, Sergeant, First Regt., Tryon County, New York Militia.

FRANK HERBERT PAGE, Longmeadow, Mass. (35399). Son of Thomas Clark and Charlotte (Wheeler) Page; grandson of James and Eliza (Woodman) Page; great-grandson of Moses and Abigail (Leavitt) Woodman; great²-grandson of *Nathan Woodman*, private and Corporal, Mass. Cont'l Line.

CAMPBELL PALFREY, New Orleans, La. (35976). Son of Herbert and Jessie (Campbell) Palfrey; grandson of George and Gertrude Elizabeth (Wendell) Palfrey; great-grandson of Henry William and Mary Bloomfield (Inskeep) Palfrey; great²-grandson of *William Palfrey*, Aide-de-Camp to Washington and Paymaster-General.

HERBERT PALFREY, New Orleans, La. (35977). Son of George and Gertrude Elizabeth (Wendell) Palfrey; grandson of Henry William and Mary Bloomfield (Inskeep) Palfrey; great-grandson of *William Palfrey*, Aide-de-Camp to Washington and Paymaster-General.

CHARLES ADAMS PATTERSON, Wilmington, Del. (35652). Son of George and Eleanor (Campbell) Geer Patterson; grandson of Frederick and Elizabeth (Loser) Patterson; great-grandson of George Patterson; great²-grandson of George and Jane (Burd) Patterson; great³-grandson of *James Burd*, Colonel, Fourth Battalion, Lancaster County, Penna. Militia.

CHARLES LEROY PEARSON, Rochester, N. Y. (35639). Son of Charles Albert and Amelia (Loomis) Pearson; grandson of Charles and Mary Adams (Young) Pearson; great-grandson of Jonathan and Olive (Coffin) Pearson; great²-grandson of *Jonathan Pearson*, private, Essex County, Mass. Militia; great²-grandson of *Lemuel Coffin*, private, Mass. Militia and Cont'l Troops.

STEPHEN KINGSBURY PERRY, Vermont (33830). Supplemental. Son of Charles Lucius and Ada Lauretta (Sherman) Perry; grandson of Nathaniel Havens and Mary Ann (Goodwin) Sherman; great-grandson of Martin Norton and Sylvia (Cushing) Goodwin; great²-grandson of *Daniel Goodwin*, Scout and Guard, Colonel Alcott's and Colonel Johnson's Regts., Vermont Militia.

WINTHROP SCOTT PERRY, Buenos Aires, Argentina (Vt. 33845). Son of Charles Lucius and Ada Lauretta (Sherman) Perry; grandson of Nathaniel Havens and Mary Ann (Goodwin) Sherman; great-grandson of Nathaniel Harcus and Phebe (Adams) Sherman; great²-grandson of Joseph and Lydia (Tifft) Adams; great³-grandson of *Ebenezer Adams*, Captain, R. I. Artillery.

ALBERT HOVEY PEYTON, Dalton, Ga. (35222). Son of Thomas West and Mary T. (Hovey) Peyton; grandson of Thomas West and Sarah O. (Dowd) Peyton; great-grandson of Thomas West Peyton; great²-grandson of *Francis Peyton*, Paymaster, Prince William County, Virginia Militia.

GEORGE WASHINGTON PIERSON, Westfield, N. J. (35734). Son of William Cory and Carrie Louise (Drake) Pierson; grandson of George Washington and Abigail (Cory) Pierson; great-grandson of Moses and Elizabeth (Martin) Pierson; great²-grandson of *David Pierson*, private, Essex County, New Jersey Militia.

CHARLES TIMOTHY PLUNKETT, Adams, Mass. (35853). Son of William C. and Louisa (Brown) Plunkett; grandson of Timothy and Betsey (Monroe) Brown; great-grandson of *Caleb Brown*, private, Mass. Militia.

THEODORE ROBINSON PLUNKETT, Adams, Mass. (35856). Son of William B. and Lyda (French) Plunkett; grandson of William C and Lovisa (Brown) Plunkett; great-grandson of Timothy and Betsey (Munroe) Brown; great²-grandson of *Caleb Brown*, private, Mass. Militia.

WILLIAM HOWARD POWERS, South Dakota (30663). Supplementals. Son of Charles and Lydia Ann (Banks) Powers; grandson of Peter and Altana (Davis) Powers; great-grandson of *John Davis*, Captain and Major, Fourth Regt., New York Troops; grandson of David Bradley and Pamelia (Phillips) Banks; great-grandson of Bradley and Sally

(Gold) Banks; great²-grandson of *Thaddeus Banks*, private, Conn. Militia; great²-grandson of *Talcott Gold*, private, Conn. Militia and Midshipman on Frigate "Alliance," pensioned; great-grandson of Elisha and Mary (Lewis) Phillips; great²-grandson of *Esquire Phillips*, private, Conn. Militia; great-grandson of Elisha and Mary (Lewis) Phillips; great²-grandson of *Augustus Lewis*, private, Vermont Militia; great-grandson of *William Powers*, private and Surgeon, Albany County, New York Militia.

WILFRID TUDOR PRATT, New York, N. Y. (35637). Son of William Tudor and Clara Lyman (Forsyth) Pratt; grandson of John Morrison and Mary Watson (Tudor) Pratt; great-grandson of Harry and Susan (Cleveland) Pratt; great²-grandson of *James Pratt*, private, Colonel Webb's Regt., Conn. Militia.

STEWART MOORE PRICE, Chestertown, Md. (35346). Son of Lewis Stewart and Ida (Moore) Price; grandson of Thomas Roberts and Martha Ann (Stewart) Price; great-grandson of John Evans and Elizabeth (Rochester) Stewart; great²-grandson of *Edward Stewart*, private, Kent County, Maryland Militia.

WILLIAM ALBERT PRIME, JR., New York City, N. Y. (35641). Son of William Albert and Marion (Dutton) Prime; grandson of Clarence Edward and Emeline (Babcock) Dutton; great-grandson of Samuel Henry and Emily (Curtis) Dutton; great²-grandson of Amos and Hannah (Douglas) Dutton; great³-grandson of *William Douglas*, Colonel, Sixth Regt., Conn. State Troops, wounded.

ALBERT QUACKENBUSH, Paterson, N. J. (36004). Son of David P. and Charity Ann (Van Houton) Quackenbush; grandson of Peter and Hester (Demarest) Quackenbush; great-grandson of John and Hannah (Ackerman) Quackenbush; great²-grandson of *Reynier Quackenbush*, Captain, New York Militia.

JOHN D. QUACKENBUSH, Paterson, N. J. (35966). Son of David P. and Charity Ann (Van Houton) Quackenbush; grandson of Peter and Hester (Demarest) Quackenbush; great-grandson of John and Hannah (Ackerman) Quackenbush; great²-grandson of *Reynier Quackenbush*, private, Orange County, New York Militia.

PETER C. QUACKENBUSH, Paterson, N. J. (36010). Son of David P. and Charity Ann (Van Houton) Quackenbush; grandson of Peter and Hester (Demarest) Quackenbush; great-grandson of John and Hannah (Ackerman) Quackenbush; great²-grandson of *Reynier Quackenbush*, Captain, New York Militia.

WILLIAM H. RAUCHFUSS, Paterson, N. J. (35968). Son of L. H. T. William and Leah Margaret (Quackenbush) Rauchfuss; grandson of Peter and Hester (Demarest) Quackenbush; great-grandson of John and Hannah (Ackerman) Quackenbush; great²-grandson of *Reynier Quackenbush*, private, Orange County, New York Militia; great-grandson of David D. and Hannah (Van Saun) Demarest; great²-grandson of *David P. Demarest*, private, Bergen County, New Jersey State Troops.

EUGENE HOWARD RAY, Louisville, Ky. (34711). Son of Samuel and Ellen Thomas (Howard) Ray; grandson of Jesse and Lucy (Mayfield) Howard; great-grandson of John and Sarrah (McDougal) Mayfield; great²-grandson of *Alexander McDougal*, Lieutenant, South Carolina Troops.

CHARLES BABBIDGE RAYNER, Austin, Texas (N. J. 35917). Son of Edwin A. and Ella Holmes (Marvin) Rayner; grandson of Warren G. and Catharine (Babbidge) Rayner; great-grandson of Thomas and Mary (Parker) Rayner; great²-grandson of *John Rayner*, private, Mass. Militia, prisoner.

STANLEY FORMAN REED, Maysville, Ky. (34715). Son of John and Frances (Forman) Reed; grandson of Samuel and Anna Frances (Soward) Forman; great-grandson of Alfred and Elizabeth (Chiles) Soward; great²-grandson of David and Frances (Craig) Chiles; great³-grandson of Lewis and Elizabeth (Saunders) Craig; great⁴-grandson of *Tolliver Craig*, Lieutenant, Virginia Militia.

GEORGE OTIS REVERE, New York City, N. Y. (35647). Son of George Brigham and Elizabeth Frances (Kingsbury) Revere; grandson of George and Mary Coffin (Smith) Revere; great-grandson of Paul and Sally (Edwards) Revere, Jr.; great²-grandson of *Paul Revere*, Lieutenant-Colonel, Mass. Artillery.

JOSEPH CAMPBELL RHEA, Pulaski, Tenn. (34647). Son of David and Bettie (Buford) Rhea; grandson of Joseph C. and Catherine (Reynolds) Rhea; great-grandson of William and Elizabeth (Brodin) Rhea; great²-grandson of *Joseph Rhea*, Chaplain, Virginia Militia and Cont'l Troops.

LAWRENCE HOWARD ROBLEE, Chicago, Ill. (35437). Son of Henry Scott and Alma L. (Partridge) Roblee; grandson of Frederick H. and Mary E. (Root) Partridge; great-grandson of Stephen Eastman and Hannah (Moxley) Root; great²-grandson of *John Root*, private, Conn. Militia, pensioned.

HENRY WILSON ROGERS, Maplewood, N. J. (35905). Son of Silas Oscar and Henrietta E. (Underhill) Rogers; grandson of Alanson T. and Perlina (Marshall) Underhill; great-grandson of *Zaccheus Marshall*, Lieutenant, Dutchess County, New York Militia.

LEON FOLLET ROLLINS, Keokuk, Iowa (35603). Son of Charles H. and Martha (Follett) Rollins; grandson of Enoch W. and Pamela (Lyford) Rollins; great-grandson of Ebenezer Newel and Sarah Winslow (Church) Rollins; great²-grandson of *Nathaniel Rollins*, private, New Hampshire Militia.

WILLIAM BETHEL ROMINE, Pulaski, Tenn. (34648). Son of J. A. and Sarah E. (Fullwood) Romine; grandson of Samuel Marion and Ann Belle (Howard) Fullwood; great-grandson of William and Elizabeth (Banning) Fullwood; great²-grandson of *Benoni Banning*, private, Campbell's Regt., Virginia Militia.

DURANT ROSE, New City, N. Y. (N. J. 35918). Son of Charles H. M. and Heloise H. (Durant) Rose; grandson of Thomas Clark and Heloise H. (Timbrell) Durant; great-grandson of Thomas and Sybil (Wright) Durant; great²-grandson of *Thomas Durant*, Captain, Mass. Militia; great³-grandson of *Edward Durant*, Delegate to Mass. Provincial Congress, Chairman, Committee of Correspondence.

CUSTER E. ROSS, Silverton, Ore. (35059). Son of Enoch M. and Charlotte (Porter) Ross; grandson of John R. and Emily Ann (Baker) Ross; great-grandson of Daniel and Ann (McClintock) Ross; great²-grandson of *John Ross*, private, Fourteenth and Tenth Regts., Virginia Cont'l Line; great-grandson of Joseph and Wealthey (Harding) Baker; great²-grandson of *Ebenezer (Ebanasor) Baker*, private, Albany County, New York Militia.

GRANDISON DELANEY ROYSTON, St. Louis, Mo. (35553). Son of Charles Edward and Mary M. (Andrews) Royston; grandson of William Wright and Elizabeth Littlejohn (Jones) Andrews; great-grandson of Isaac Newton and Mary (Jones) Jones; great²-grandson of *Daniel Jones*, Captain, Third Regt., North Carolina Troops.

CLYDE IRWIN RUSH, Mesa, Idaho (35105). Son of Clarence Irwin and Edna L. (Jones) Rush; grandson of William and Abi (Irwin) Rush; great-grandson of Job and Anna (Rinehart) Rush; great²-grandson of Christian and Mary (Douglass) Rinehart; great³-grandson of *Aaron Douglass*, private, N. J. Militia.

HOWARD LEVI RUSH, Mesa, Idaho (35104). Same as Clyde Irwin Rush, Idaho (35105).

FRANKLIN JASON RUSSELL, Adrian, Mich. (35716). Son of Ebbert Emerson and Margaret (Angell) Russell; grandson of Benjamin Franklin and Elizabeth Gilman (Colby) Russell; great-grandson of Jason and Elizabeth (Thorp) Russell; great²-grandson of Noah and Eunice (Bemis) Russell; great³-grandson of *Jason Russell*, private, Mass. Militia, killed on retreat from Lexington.

LLOYD MELVILLE SACKETT, Oklahoma City, Okla. (35240). Son of Samuel J. and Emma A. (Melville) Sackett; grandson of Samuel B. and Lucinda (Preston) Sackett; great-grandson of David Filer and Martha (Milliken) Sackett; great²-grandson of *Samuel Sackett*, Surgeon Westmoreland County, Penna. Militia.

ALBERT WILLIAM SANBERN, Brooklyn, N. Y. (35646). Son of Jeremiah S. and Martha A. (Loomis) Sanbern; grandson of Henry and Elizabeth (Utley) Loomis; great-grandson of *Nathaniel Loomis*, Ensign, Twelfth Regt., Conn. Militia.

FRANK RAYMOND SANDT, Paterson, N. J. (36011). Son of Jacob and Annie (Frey) Sandt; grandson of Leonard and Anna (Correll) Sand(t); great-grandson of John Adam and Anna Maria (Fucks) (Fux) Sand; great²-grandson of *Adam Sand*, private, Northampton County, Penna. Militia.

JAMES EVERETT SANNER, Baltimore, Md. (35347). Son of Joseph H. and Emma C. (Bridgett) Sanner; grandson of James Arthur and Anne Elizabeth (Sanner) Bridgett; great-grandson of Jeremiah and Margaret (Bohanan) Sanner; great²-grandson of Jonathan and Mary (Richardson) Bohanan; great³-grandson of *George Bohanan*, private, St. Mary's County, Maryland Militia.

CROSBY MILLER SARGEANT, Paterson, N. J. (35974). Son of Ide Gill and Katie Mabel (Lamb) Sargeant; grandson of Joseph and Esther Maria (Moses) Sargeant; great-grandson of Joseph and Eleanor (Pearl) Moses; great²-grandson of Silvanus and Sallie

(Barden) Moses; great²-grandson of *Samuel Moses*, private, Colonel Gerrish's Regt., Mass. Militia, and Signer New Hampshire Association Test.

JOSEPH LAMB SARGEANT, Paterson, N. J. (35973). Same as Crosby Miller Sargeant, New Jersey (35974).

HARRY SCHAEFER SCHANK, Brooklyn, N. Y. (35633). Son of James Hill and Clara (Johnston) Schank; grandson of Elijah Combs and Emilie (Dashiell) Schank; great-grandson of Rulef R. and Easter (Combs) Schank; great²-grandson of Elijah and Rebecca (Reid, or Reed) Combs; great²-grandson of *Thomas Combs, Jr.*, Captain, Middlesex County, New Jersey Rangers; great³-grandson of *Aaron Reid (Reed)*, private, Monmouth County, New Jersey Militia.

LOUIS CRANE SCHERMERHORN, Hawthorne, N. J. (35922). Son of Jonathan Crane and Elizabeth Moore (Lee) Schermerhorn; grandson of William B. and Sarah (Kelley) Schermerhorn; great-grandson of *Bartholomew Schermerhorn*, private, Albany County, New York Militia.

DAVID WERT SCHICK, San Diego, Calif. (34750). Son of John Lawrence and Sarah Jane (Welty) Schick; grandson of Henry and Eva (Wert) Welty; great-grandson of *John Welty*, private, York County, Penna. Militia.

ANSELL JULIUS SCHLOSS, San Francisco, Calif. (35936). Son of Louis and Rachel (Lang) Schloss; grandson of Moses Ansel and Rachel (Jackson) Schloss; great-grandson of James Jackson; great²-grandson of *Solomon Jackson*, private, pensioned.

WASHINGTON GRANT SCOTT, Freeport, Ill. (35446). Son of Joseph and Jemima (McClentick) Scott; grandson of Isaac and Persis (Latham) Scott; great-grandson of *Isaac Scott*, private, Col. Morris Graham's Regt., New York State Troops.

CHARLES H. SCRIBNER, Paterson, N. J. (36012). Son of William and Mary E. (Hill) Scribner; grandson of Joseph and Sarah (Kellogg) Scribner; great-grandson of *Enoch Scribner*, Clerk, Sergeant and Ensign, Conn. Militia.

FREDERICK LYLE SEARING, Mankato, Minn. (35680). Son of Edward and Mary Louisa (Lattin) Searing; grandson of John P. and Mehitable (Requa) Searing; great-grandson of *James Requa*, private, Westchester County, New York Militia and Justice of the Peace.

JOHN HENRY SEARING, Carbondale, Ill. (35447). Son of Harry Ramsey and Nellie (Sprague) Searing; grandson of George Henry and Ella Nora (Denning) Sprague; great-grandson of Zebediah and Athela S. (Gillett) Sprague; great²-grandson of *Philip Sprague*, private, Vermont Militia, pensioned; great³-grandson of *Jesse Sprague*, Sergeant, Vermont Militia; great²-grandson of Israel and Mary (Sanborn) Gillette; great²-grandson of *Israel Gillette*, private, Vermont Militia.

WILLIAM PERSONETTE SEDDON, Paterson, N. J. (35747). Son of William D. and Sarah (Gould) Seddon; grandson of Encrease Personette and Mary Jane (Douglass) Gould; great-grandson of Moses E. and Rebecca Van Gieson (Gould) Gould; great²-grandson of John (father of Rebecca) and Sophia (Van Gieson) Gould; great³-grandson of *Joseph Gould*, private, Second Regt., Essex County, New Jersey Militia.

JAMES WILBUR SHANKLAND, Captain, Medical Corps, A. E. F., St. Louis, Mo. (35552). Son of James Mason and Elizabeth G. (Hare) Shankland; grandson of James Wilmuth and Henrietta (Round) Shankland; great-grandson of *Rhoads Shankland*, Captain, Col. Henry Neill's Regt., Delaware Militia.

WILLIAM SYLVANUS SHIELDS, Chicago, Ill. (35448). Son of John and Myrtilla (Stewart) Shields; grandson of Joseph and Isabella (McKnight) Shields; great-grandson of *John Shields*, private, Penna. Militia, pensioned; grandson of Alexander and Susan (Sutton) Stewart; great-grandson of Garvin and Jane (Ward) Sutton; great²-grandson of *Peter Sutton*, private, New Jersey Militia and Light Horse; great²-grandson of *John Ward*, private, Morris County, New Jersey Militia, pensioned.

MARK OWINGS SHRIVER, Jr., Baltimore, Md. (35348). Son of Mark O. and Katharine (Dietrich) Shriver; grandson of William and Mary Margaret (Owings) Shriver; great-grandson of Andrew and Elizabeth (Shultz) Shriver; great²-grandson of *David Shriver*, Member First Maryland Constitutional Convention and Committee of Safety.

FREDERIC POND SIMONDS, Brookline, Mass. (35867). Son of William Henry and Susan Breed (Perkins) Simonds, Jr.; grandson of William Henry and Julia Ann (Goldsmith)

Simonds; great-grandson of Nathaniel and Nancy Corning (Taylor) Goldsmith; great²-grandson of *John Goldsmith*, private, Col. Thomas Stickey's Regt., New Hampshire Militia.

JESSE ROY SIXX, Totowaboro, N. J. (35967). Son of Scott and Alice L. (Sager) Sixx; grandson of Henry and Laura S. (Christian) Sager; great-grandson of John B. and Bolnia (Hamilton) Christian; great²-grandson of Daniel and Christina (Auspeger) Christian; great³-grandson of *Daniel Christian*, private, Berks County, Penna. Militia and Cont'l Troops, pensioned.

ADDISON TAYLOR SMITH, Washington, D. C. (Idaho 35106). Son of Isaac and Jane (Forsythe) Smith; grandson of Elijah and Susannah (Griffith) Forsyth; great-grandson of *John Forsyth*, private, York County, Penna. Militia, pensioned.

HAWLEY LESTER SMITH, Evanston, Ill. (35439). Son of Weldon Charles and Allie Mary (Colby) Smith; grandson of Charles White and Lucy Ball (Gage) Smith; great-grandson of Leonard and Alsena (Ball) Gage; great²-grandson of James and Polly (Drury) Gage, Jr.; great³-grandson of *Ebenezer Drury*, private, Colonel Scammell's Regt., New Hampshire Troops; great⁴-grandson of *Zedekiah Drury*, private, New Hampshire Militia; great³-grandson of Ebenezer and Miriam (Goodale) Drury; great⁴-grandson of *Enos Goodale*, private, Colonel Scammell's Regt., New Hampshire Troops; grandson of John Bigsby and Mary (Lester) Colby; great-grandson of Timothy and Sarah (Weed) Lester; great²-grandson of Amos and Hannah (Kirkham) Weed; great³-grandson of *Jacob Weed*, private, Mass. Militia; great-grandson of Ira and Mary Caroline (Stocker) Colby; great²-grandson of *Thomas Colby*, private, New Hampshire Militia and Cont'l Troops, pensioned.

KENNETH PROCTER SMITH, Brookline, Mass. (35400). Son of Bryant G. and Anna (Procter) Smith; grandson of George H. and Sarah (Steele) Procter; great-grandson of Francis Epes and Ann (Allen) Procter; great²-grandson of Daniel Epes and Lydia (Gould) Procter; great³-grandson of *Joseph Procter*, Member, Gloucester, Mass. Committee of Safety.

LEWIS TYLER SMYSER, Louisville, Ky. (34720). Son of Harry Lee and Rebecca (Gwathmey) Smyser; grandson of Isaac H. and Jennie Louise (Owen) Tyler; great-grandson of Henry S. and Rebecca Ann (Gwathmey) Tyler; great²-grandson of Samuel and Mary (Booth) Gwathmey; great³-grandson of *William Aylette Booth*, Colonel, Virginia Militia and Member Virginia House of Delegates of '79.

WATSON BALLARD SNELL, Toledo, Ohio (35883). Son of Oliver Ballard and Mary (Watson) Snell; grandson of Andrew Jay and Lillian (Ballard) Snell; great-grandson of Levi and Jane (Clyde) Snell; great²-grandson of Matthew and Jane (Clark) Clyde; great³-grandson of *Samuel Clyde*, Lieutenant-Colonel, New York Militia.

DANIEL E. SQUIER, Battle Creek, Mich. (35717). Son of Charles Albert and Julia Elizabeth (Hickman) Squier; grandson of Daniel and Patience Yard (Simpson) Squier; great-grandson of Daniel and Sarah Ann (Litle) Squier; great²-grandson of *Daniel Squier*, private, Col. Andrew Ward's Regt., Conn. Troops, pensioned.

THEODORE LOUIS SQUIER, Battle Creek, Mich. (35718). Same as Daniel E. Squier, Michigan (35717).

JAMES MADISON STANLEY, Fort Scott, Kans. (33318). Son of John O. and Dolly (Flansburg) Stanley; grandson of *John Flansburg*, Corporal, Albany County, New York Militia.

JOHN SHERMAN STANLEY, Pittsburgh, Pa. (Kans. 33319). Son of James Madison and Tacy Stroud (Morgan) Stanley; grandson of John Rittenhouse and Rachel Elizabeth (Bicknell) Morgan; great-grandson of Benjamin and Tacy (Stroud) Morgan; great²-grandson of Morgan and Ann (Roberts) Morgan; great³-grandson of *John Roberts*, Lieutenant and Captain, Colonel Nelson's Regt., Penna. Troops.

FRANCIS UPHAM STEARNS, Adams, Mass. (35868). Son of Charles Augustus and Mary E. (Burnham) Stearns; grandson of Edward Roy and Elizabeth Tyler (Barker) Stearns; great-grandson of Elijah and Polly (Rawlins) Stearns; great²-grandson of *John Stearns*, private, New Hampshire Cont'l Line.

ROGER STEPHENS, Westfield, N. J. (35739). Son of George Francis and Caroline (Eakins) Stephens; grandson of Henry Lewis and Charlotte Anne (Weville) Stephens; great-grandson of George and Harriet (Cozens) Weville; great²-grandson of William and Charlotte (Nicola) Cozens; great³-grandson of *Lewis Nicola*, Colonel and Brevet Brigadier-General Penna. Invalid Corps.

HARRY THOMAS STEVENS, Alameda, Calif. (35937). Son of John Henry and Mary Meiggs (Hamlin) Stevens; grandson of Thomas and Mary Ann (Chadwick) Stevens; great-grandson of Daniel and Almira (——) Stevens; great²-grandson of *Thomas Stevens*, Corporal, Worcester County, Mass. Militia and Cont'l Troops.

MOSES CORNELIUS STONE, Wellesley, Mass. (35852). Son of Moses and Harriet (Parker) Stone; grandson of Moses and Elizabeth (Brown) Stone; great-grandson of *Moses Stone, Jr.*, Lieutenant, First Regt., Mass. Militia.

CHARLES BARR STOWELL, Hudson, Mich. (35719). Son of Josiah and Charlotte (Barr) Stowell; grandson of Samuel and Anne (Frye) Barr, Jr.; great-grandson of *Timothy Frye*, Lieutenant, Mass. Militia.

GEORGE HALSEY STURGES, Newark, N. J. (35731). Son of Joseph Gordon and Anna Adele (Taylor) Sturges; grandson of Joseph Halsey and Jane Eliza (Jillson) Sturges; great-grandson of Thompson and Abby (Halsey) Sturges; great²-grandson of *John Halsey*, private, Morris County, New Jersey Militia and Cont'l Troops.

SAMUEL HOWARD SWIFT, Adrian, Mich. (35720). Son of Irving W. and Estelle (Hughes) Swift; grandson of Samuel R. and Sarah C. (Crim) Swift; great-grandson of Jacob Adam and Christina (Garner) Crim; great²-grandson of Adam A. and Elizabeth (Hoover) Crim; great³-grandson of *Paul Crim (Grim)*, private, New York Militia at Fort Herkimer.

EDGAR JOHN TANDY, Westfield, N. J. (35738). Son of John and Susan (Julia) Tandy; grandson of John and Dotha (Cook) Julia; great-grandson of Martin and Clara (Rossiter) Cook; great²-grandson of *Oliver Cook*, private, Conn. Militia, pensioned.

FREDERICK STANDMORE TANDY, Newark, N. J. (35748). Son of Edgar John and Ella Standmore (Kelley) Tandy; grandson of John and Susan (Julia) Tandy; great-grandson of John and Dotha (Cook) Julia; great²-grandson of Martin and Clara (Rossiter) Cook; great³-grandson of *Oliver Cook*, private, Conn. Militia, pensioned.

RUSSELL HAVILAND TANDY, Westfield, N. J. (35850). Same as Frederick Standmore Tandy, New Jersey (35748).

WILLIAM HENRY TANDY, Rahway, N. J. (35748). Same as Frederick Standmore Tandy, New Jersey (35748).

GRANT STANBERY TAYLOR, Toledo, Ohio (35881). Son of John B. and Sarah Jane (Stanbery) Taylor; grandson of Joseph and Sarah (Beard) Stanbery; great-grandson of *Samuel Stanbery (Stanbury)*, private, Morris County, New Jersey Militia and State Troops.

JOHN BYRON TAYLOR, Watertown, N. Y. (35631). Son of John Lorien and Magdalanah M. (Fox) Taylor; grandson of Christopher and Nancy (Snell) Fox; great-grandson of John Jacob and Mary (Empie) Snell; great²-grandson of *Jacob Snell*, private, Tryon County, New York Militia.

EDWARD ULREY THATCHER, Toledo, Ohio (35884). Son of Horace Edward and Mary (Ulrey) Thatcher; grandson of Edward A. and Ada (Webb) Ulrey; great-grandson of Nathaniel and Mary Jane (Angel) Webb; great²-grandson of Nathan and Margaret (Albright) Webb; great³-grandson of Nathaniel and Charlotte (Cleveland) Webb; great⁴-grandson of *Stephen Webb*, private, Colonel Waterbury's Regt., Conn. State Troops.

EDWIN RICE THURSTON, Toledo, Ohio (35878). Son of Johnson and Katherine (Thrift) Thurston; grandson of Robert Wilson and Angerona (Rice) Thrift; great-grandson of Clark Hammond and Katherine (Morous) Rice; great²-grandson of Ebenezer and Martha (Hamon) Rice; great³-grandson of *Samuel Rice*, private and Fifer, Fifth Regt., Mass. Cont'l Line.

EUGENE THWING, Ridgewood, N. J. (35743). Son of Edward Payson and Susan Maria (Waite) Thwing; grandson of Thomas and Grace Welch (Barnes) Thwing; great-grandson of *Nicholas Thwing*, private and Corporal, Mass. Militia and Cont'l Troops.

NORMAN EDWIN TITUS, New York City, N. Y. (35642). Son of Edward Coddington and Fanny (Gibson) Titus; grandson of Delos Edwin and Isabel Gray (Hunt) Titus; great-grandson of William and Judith (Husted) Titus; great²-grandson of *David Titus*, Captain, Albany County, New York Militia.

JAMES RALPH TOBIN, Springfield, Ill. (35440). Son of John Franklin and Mary Ella (Hillman) Tobin; grandson of James and Eleanore Jane (Marlow) Tobin; great-grandson of Isaac and Matilda Anne (Benton) Tobin; great²-grandson of Edward Willett and Hannah (Duvall) Benton; great³-grandson of *Benjamin Duvall*, private and Sergeant, Sixth Regt., Maryland Cont'l Troops, pensioned.

NICHOLAS MURRAY TOWNLEY, Jr., Paterson, N. J. (36013). Son of Nicholas Murray and Amelia Davis (Woodhull) Townley; grandson of John Hamilton and Cornelia Clark (Seariny) Townley; great-grandson of Edward and Ann (Hamilton) Townley; great²-grandson of *Matthias Townley*, private, Essex County, New Jersey Militia.

HERBERT DANIEL TUNIS, Morris Plains, N. J. (35730). Son of Daniel W. and Charlotte (Davis) Tunis; grandson of Silas D. and Ellen (Bailey) Tunis; great-grandson of Daniel and Phœbe (Lindsley) Tunis; great²-grandson of *John Lindsley*, Captain, Eastern Battalion, Morris County, New Jersey Militia.

ALBERT ACKERMAN VAN BLARCOM, Paterson, N. J. (36002). Son of Walter G. and Hannah Elizabeth (Bolton) Van Blarcom; grandson of Albert J. and Helena (Ackerman) Van Blarcom; great-grandson of David D. and Rachel (Tallman) Ackerman; great²-grandson of Harmon T. and Hester (Bogart) Tallman; great²-grandson of *Theunis Talema (Tallman)*, private, Col. A. Hawkes Hay's Regt., Orange County, New York Militia.

JOHN HERBERT VAN BLARCOM, Paterson, N. J. (36201). Son of Albert J. and Helena (Ackerman) Van Blarcom; grandson of David D. and Rachel (Tallman) Ackerman; great-grandson of Harmon T. and Hester (Bogart) Tallman; great²-grandson of *Theunis Talema, (Tunis Tallman)*, private, Orange County, New York Militia.

WALTER G. VAN BLARCOM, Paterson, N. J. (35975). Same as John Herbert Van Blarcom, New Jersey (36201).

ROBERT LOWRY VAN DYKE, Westfield, N. J. (35740). Son of James Cole and Frances Anne (Lowry) Van Dyke; grandson of Frederick Augustus and Anna (Herberton) Van Dyke, Jr.; great-grandson of Frederick Augustus and Eliza (Anderson) Van Dyke; great²-grandson of Frederick and Lydia (Cole) Van Dyke; great²-grandson of *John (Jan) Van Dyke*, private, Somerset County, New Jersey Militia.

AUGUSTUS VAN GIESON, Paterson, N. J. (35965). Son of Henry and Jane (Williams) Van Gieson; grandson of Isaac and Maria (Vanderbeek) Van Gieson; great-grandson of *Hendrick (Henry) Van Gieson*, private, Bergen County, New Jersey Militia.

GLENN ALFRED VAN SYCKLE, Battle Creek, Mich. (35721). Son of Morgan H. and Justine (Wilson) Van Syckle; grandson of George Washington and Sarah (Hulick) Van Syckle; great-grandson of Henry and Phœbe (Morgan) Hulick; great²-grandson of *Derrick Hulick*, private, New Jersey Militia, pensioned.

GEORGE FRANK VINCENT, Lynn, Mass. (35857). Son of Frank Elmer and Emma Brizilas (Mills) Vincent; grandson of George Albert and Susie (Richardson) Vincent; great-grandson of Aaron and Sarah (Brown) Richardson; great²-grandson of *Herbert Richardson*, private, General Gates' Division, Mass. Guards.

JOHN READ VOIGT, North Chattanooga, Tenn. (34650). Son of Henry N. and Eliza (Read) Voigt; grandson of John Franklin and Eliza Ann (Pratt) Read; great-grandson of James Gray and Mary (Mahon) Read; great²-grandson of William and Agnes (Venable) Mahon; great³-grandson of James and Judith (Newton) Venable; great⁴-grandson of *Joseph Newton*, Member Charlotte County, Virginia Committee of Safety.

CARL VAN VOORHIS, Newark, N. J. (35733). Son of Charles H. and Elsie (Rudolph) Van Voorhis; grandson of William and Sophia E. (De La Ru) Van Voorhis; great-grandson of Daniel Cornelius and Sarah (Varian) Van Voorhis; great²-grandson of *Daniel Van Voorhis*, private, Dutchess County, New York Militia.

FRANK H. VREELAND, Paterson, N. J. (36005). Son of John E. and Alice (Van Orden) Vreeland; grandson of Dayton B. and Susan (Sisco) Vreeland; great-grandson of Elias and Catharine (Yorke) Vreeland; great²-grandson of *Garrett G. Vreeland*, private, New Jersey Militia, widow pensioned.

FRANK H. VREELAND, Paterson, N. J. (35924). Son of Dayton B. and Susan (Sisco) Vreeland; grandson of Elias and Catharine (Yorke) Vreeland; great-grandson of *Garret Vreeland*, Corporal and Sergeant, New Jersey Militia.

FREDERICK JOHN VREELAND, Paterson, N. J. (35925). Son of Nehemiah and Louisa (Klein) Vreeland; grandson of John E. and Ann Louise (Post) Vreeland; great-grandson of Elias and Catharine (Yorke) Vreeland; great²-grandson of *Garret Vreeland*, Corporal and Sergeant, New Jersey Militia.

JOHN E. VREELAND, Paterson, N. J. (36014). Son of Dayton B. and Susan (Sisco) Vreeland; grandson of Elias and Catharine (Yorke) Vreeland; great-grandson of *Garre Vreeland*, private, New Jersey Militia, widow pensioned.

NEHIMIAH VREELAND, Paterson, N. J. (35921). Son of John E. and Ann Louise (Post) Vreeland; grandson of Elias and Catharine (Yorke) Vreeland; great-grandson of *Garret Vreeland*, Corporal and Sergeant, Bergen County, New Jersey Militia, pensioned.

HERBERT P. WALKER, Clarion, Iowa (35604). Son of William E. and Kate L. (Woolford) Walker; grandson of George and Polly (Countryman) Walker; great-grandson of Peter and Charlotte (——) Walker; great²-grandson of *Jacob Walker*, Second Lieutenant, Bedford County, Penna. Militia.

MARCUS WALKER, New Orleans, La. (34824). Son of Edward M. and Katherine (Wood) Walker; grandson of Marcus and Sarah (Trowbridge) Walker; great-grandson of Isaac and Elizabeth (Pardee) Trowbridge; great²-grandson of *Newman Trowbridge*, Selectman and Member Conn. Committee of Inspection.

RALPH EMERSON WALKER, Minneapolis, Minn. (35676). Son of Wellington Jason and Leila Ada (Hawkes) Walker; grandson of Elijah and Caroline (Walker) Walker; great-grandson of Jason and Betsey (McIntosh) Walker; great²-grandson of *James Adair Walker*, Lieutenant, Hampshire County, Mass. Militia.

CHARLES CRESOP WARD, San Francisco, Calif. (35938). Son of Jacob Loman and Elizabeth Hutton (Crouch) Ward; grandson of Jonathan and Delilah (Haigler) Crouch; great-grandson of Andrew and Elizabeth (Hutton) Crouch; great²-grandson of Jonathan and Mary (Troutwine) Hutton; great²-grandson of *Moses Hutton*, Captain, Virginia Militia.

EDWIN WARNER, Nashville, Tenn. (34640). Son of James C. and Mary T. (Williams) Warner; grandson of Jacob L. and Elizabeth (Cartwright) Warner; great-grandson of James and Sallie (——) Cartwright; great²-grandson of *Robert Cartwright*, fighter on Tennessee frontier.

SAMUEL SHELTON WATKINS, Kentucky (25349). Supplementals. Son of Henry Colston and Letitia Todd (Griffith) Watkins; grandson of Daniel Moseley and Virginia Shelby (Todd) Griffith; great-grandson of William Ridgeley and Arria (Moseley) Griffith; great²-grandson of Joshua and Elizabeth (Ridgeley) Griffith; great⁶-grandson of *Henry Griffith*, Member Frederick County Committee of Observation and Maryland General Assembly; great²-grandson of *Thomas Moseley*, Sergeant, Thirteenth Regt., Virginia Militia; great²-grandson of Thomas and Judith (Finney) Moseley; great²-grandson of *John Finney*, private, Col. John Gibson's Regt., Virginia Militia; great³-grandson of *William Ridgeley*, Lieutenant, Maryland Militia; great-grandson of Charles Stewart and Letitia (Shelby) Todd; great²-grandson of Isaac and Susanna (Hart) Shelby; great²-grandson of *Nathaniel Hart*, Captain, North Carolina Rangers, killed by Indians; great³-grandson of *Evan Shelby, Jr.*, Major, Virginia Militia, killed by Indians; great⁴-grandson of *Evan Shelby*, Brigadier-General, Virginia Militia; great²-grandson of *Thomas Todd*, private, Virginia Cavalry; great²-grandson of Thomas and Elizabeth (Harris) Todd; great³-grandson of *Hannah Stewart Harris*, who gave house as headquarters for General Washington; grandson of Samuel Shelton and Mary Elizabeth (Thomas) Watkins; great-grandson of Anslem and Maria (McClanahan) Watkins; great²-grandson of *Thomas McClanahan*, Captain, Virginia Militia; great²-grandson of Thomas and Elizabeth (Field) McClanahan; great³-grandson of *Henry Field, Jr.*, Delegate, Virginia Convention for Culpeper County; great-grandson of Joshua Howard and Lucy Landon Carter (Colston) Thomas; great²-grandson of William Traverse and Elizabeth B. (Armistead) Colstron; great²-grandson of William and Lucy Landon (Carter) Colstron; great⁴-grandson of *Landon Carter*, Member Virginia War Committees; great⁵-grandson of Henry and Winifred (Peachy) Armistead; great⁴-grandson of *William Peachy*, Colonel, Fifth Regt., Virginia Militia.

LUCIUS FREDERICK WATSON, New York City, N. Y. (35644). Son of William Miner and Pauline E. (Ferry) Watson; grandson of Lucius and Harriet (Dusenbury) Ferry; great-grandson of Thomas and Harriet (Costegan) Dusenbury; great²-grandson of *Lewis Johnston Costigan*, Lieutenant, First Battalion, New Jersey Cont'l Troops, prisoner.

JOHN REX WEAVER, Woonsocket, S. Dak. (Wyo. 30020). Son of William Kean and Margaret C. (Griffit) Weaver; grandson of John Girt and Margaret (Alter) Weaver; great-grandson of Joseph and Jane (Girt) Weaver; great²-grandson of *Henry Weaver*, Captain, Lancaster County, Penna. Militia and Committeeman.

CLIFFORD SIMS WEEKS, East Orange, N. J. (35971). Son of Henry Martin and Mary Malvina (Fairchild) Weeks, Jr.; grandson of David Day and Rebecca R. (Richardson)

Fairchild; great-grandson of Joseph and Elizabeth (Hoppock) Fairchild; great²-grandson of *Peter Fairchild*, private, Morris County, N. J. Militia and State Troops, pensioned.

MERLE HAZZARD WEIBLE, Coffeyville, Kans. (33316). Son of Harry C. and Paula (Hazzard) Weible; grandson of John and Helen (Latham) Hazzard; great-grandson of Joseph and Polly (Crosby) Latham; great²-grandson of Arthur Latham; great³-grandson of *Nehemiah Latham*, Lieutenant, Mass. Militia.

CHARLES EDWIN WELLS, North Adams, Mass (35851). Son of Daniel M. and Mary M. (Sly) Wells; grandson of Orsen and Zernah (Phillips) Wells; great-grandson of Charles and Sarah (Warren) Wells; great²-grandson of *John Warren*, Corporal, Mass. Militia.

KINGSLEY BARBOUR WHITE, Sioux City, Iowa (35601). Son of Willard and Emma Frances (Nightingale) White; grandson of Selden and Diadama Hanna (Barbour) White; great-grandson of Giles and Mary (Garrett) Barbour; great²-grandson of John and Mary (Case) Garrett, Jr.; great³-grandson of *John Wait Garrett*, Major, Twenty-sixth Regt., Conn. Troops, killed at Wyoming Massacre.

NEWTON HARRIS WHITE, Wales, Tenn. (36051). Son of Newton and Courtney Scivila (Gordon) White; grandson of Thomas Kennedy and Elizabeth (Lane) Gordon; great-grandson of *Martin Lane*, private, North Carolina Militia.

BRET HARTE WHITMAN, Jr., New York City, N. Y. (35649). Son of Bret Harte and Mary Rosalaen (Delamatu) Whitman; grandson of William and Maria (Smith) Delamatu; great-grandson of James F. and Sarah (Phillips) Smith; great²-grandson of *Enoch Smith*, private, Conn. Troops, pensioned.

JOHN WESLEY WHITNEY, Bruce, Wis. (35677). Son of Lemuel and Fanny M. (Gould) Whitney; grandson of John and Augusta Fisk (Brooks) Whitney; great-grandson of *John Whitney*, private, New Hampshire Militia.

MARCUS WHRITENOUR, Montana (31777). Supplemental. Son of Edward and Hylinda (Earl) Whritenour; grandson of Edward and Phœbe (Green) Whritenour; great-grandson of *Peter Whritenour*, private, Northampton County, Penna. Militia.

EDWIN HOWARD WILCOX, Chicago, Ill. (35438). Son of Josiah Case and Frances Adelaide (Shaler) Wilcox; grandson of Ephraim and Emma Corbit (Wilson) Shaylor (Shaler); great-grandson of *Joseph Shaylor*, Ensign and Lieutenant, Conn. Troops.

WILLIAM THOMAS WILKINS, Olive Branch, Miss. (Tenn. 34642). Son of Aaron W. and Hester (A. ——) Wilkins; grandson of Aaron and Elina (Jeffries) Wilkins; great-grandson of *John Jeffries*, Captain, South Carolina Militia.

ERNEST CLIFFORD WILLARD, Portland, Ore. (35060). Son of Henry Whitcomb and Mary Sophia (Bardeen) Willard; grandson of Henry and Mary Ann (Houghton) Willard; great-grandson of Phineas and Mary (Whitcomb) Houghton; great²-grandson of *John Whitcomb*, Major-General, Mass. Militia and Brigadier-General, Cont'l Line.

JOHN PHILLIP WILLIAMS, Jr., Nashville, Tenn. (34649). Son of John Philip and —— (——) Williams; grandson of John Philip and Mildred (Hopson) Williams; great-grandson of George B. and Eliza (Read) Hopson; great²-grandson of *Joseph Hopson*, Lieutenant, Seventh Regt., Virginia Militia, pensioned.

WALTER EVERETT WILSON, Topeka, Kans. (33315). Son of Charles L. and Garrie Mohalibut (Sanborn) Wilson; grandson of William Frederick and Mary Ann (Rowe) Sanborn; great-grandson of Benjamin and Rebecca (Smith) Sanborn; great²-grandson of *William Sanborn*, Chairman of Kingston, New Hampshire Committee for payment of Militia.

ALBAN MORLEY WOOD, Frederick, Md. (35349). Son of J. E. R. and Anna O. (Shreve) Wood; grandson of Benjamin F. and Mary E. (Trundle) Shreve; great-grandson of Daniel and Esther (Belt) Trundle; great²-grandson of Carlton and Anne (Campbell) Belt; great³-grandson of *Aeneas Campbell*, Captain, First Battalion, Maryland Flying Camp.

JOHN L. WOODBURY, Louisville, Ky. (34714). Son of Charles Leonard and Elizabeth Hamilton (Brown) Woodbury; grandson of Leonard and Louisa (Cummings) Woodbury; great-grandson of *John Woodbury*, Lieutenant, Mass. Militia.

WALTER WOOLSEY, Elizabeth, N. J. (35744). Son of Moses and Cornelia Maria (Wynkoop) Woolsey; grandson of Jacob R. and Blandina (Delamater) Wynkoop; great-grandson of Evert C. and Rachel (Hardenburgh) Wynkoop; great²-grandson of *Cornelius E. Wynkoop*, Second Major, Ulster County, New York Militia.

EDWARD DALY WRIGHT, New York City, N. Y. (35648). Son of Samuel and Aurelia (Fleming) Wright; grandson of Henry and Caroline (Wells) Fleming; great-grandson of Henry and Letitia (Parke) Fleming; great²-grandson of John and Mary (Slaymaker) Fleming, Jr.; great³-grandson of *Amos Slaymaker*, private, Lancaster County, Penna. Militia; great⁴-grandson of *Henry Slaymaker*, Member Fifth Battalion, Lancaster County, Penna. Militia, Delegate to State Constitutional Convention of '76.

ALVIN LESKE WYNNE, Philadelphia, Penna. (35464). Son of Samuel and Nettie N. (J——) Wynne, Jr.; grandson of Samuel Wynne; great-grandson of James Wynne; great²-grandson of *Jonathan Wynne*, private, Chester County, Penna. Militia.

THOMAS YOUNG, New York City, N. Y. (35632). Son of Thomas McKeen and Ida May (Baker) Young; grandson of William and Rebecca (Goodrich) Baker; great-grandson of Elijah and Rachel (Lloyd) Goodrich; great²-grandson of *John Lloyd*, Lieutenant, New York Militia and Cont'l Line; great²-grandson of *Michael Goodrich*, private, Conn. Militia and Cont'l Troops.

THOMAS RINEK ZULICH, Paterson, N. J. (36015). Son of Henry B. and Emma R. (Hesser) Zulich; grandson of Henry and Margaret (Shoemaker) Hesser; great-grandson of *Frederick Hesser*, drummer and private, Penna. Militia, pensioned.

OFFICIAL BULLETIN

OF THE

National Society
of the Sons of the American Revolution

Organized April 30, 1889

Incorporated by
Act of Congress, June 9, 1906

President General
WALLACE McCAMANT
Northwestern Bank Building
Portland, Oregon

Published at Washington, D. C., in June, October, December, and March.
Entered as second-class matter, May 7, 1906, at the post-office at Washington, D. C., under the act of July 16, 1894.

Volume XVII   DECEMBER, 1921   Number 3

The OFFICIAL BULLETIN records action by the General Officers, the Board of Trustees, the Executive and other National Committees, lists of members deceased and of new members, and important doings of State Societies. In order that the OFFICIAL BULLETIN may be up to date, and to insure the preservation in the National Society archives of a complete history of the doings of the entire organization, State Societies and local Chapters are requested to communicate promptly to the Secretary General written or printed accounts of all meetings or celebrations, to forward copies of all notices, circulars, and other printed matter issued by them, and to notify him at once of dates of death of members.

GENERAL OFFICERS ELECTED AT THE BUFFALO CONGRESS, MAY 17, 1921

President General:

WALLACE MCCAMANT, Northwestern Bank Building, Portland, Oregon.

Vice-Presidents General:

GEORGE HALE NUTTING, 53 State Street, Boston, Massachusetts.

New England (Maine, New Hampshire, Vermont, Massachusetts, Rhode Island, and Connecticut).

PHILIP F. LARNER, 918 F Street N. W., Washington, District of Columbia.

Middle and Coast District (New York, New Jersey, Pennsylvania, Delaware, Maryland, District of Columbia, Virginia, North Carolina, South Carolina, Georgia, and Florida).

MARVIN H. LEWIS, 201 Keller Building, Louisville, Kentucky.

Mississippi Valley, East District (Michigan, Wisconsin, Illinois, Indiana, Ohio, West Virginia, Kentucky, Tennessee, Alabama, and Mississippi).

HENRY B. HAWLEY, Des Moines, Iowa.

Mississippi Valley, West District (Minnesota, North Dakota, South Dakota, Nebraska, Iowa, Kansas, Missouri, Oklahoma, Arkansas, Louisiana, and Texas).

JOHN W. BELL, JR., P. O. Box 1124, Spokane, Washington.

Mountain and Pacific Coast District (Montana, Idaho, Wyoming, Nevada, Utah, Colorado, Arizona, New Mexico, Oregon, Washington, California, Hawaii, and Philippines).

Secretary General:

FRANK BARTLETT STEELE, 183 St. James Place, Buffalo, New York.

Registrar General:

WILLIAM S. PARKS, 900 17th Street N. W., Washington, District of Columbia.

Treasurer General:

JOHN H. BURROUGHS, 1111 Dean Street, Brooklyn, New York.

Historian General:

GEORGE CARPENTER ARNOLD, Arnold Building, Providence, Rhode Island.

Chancellor General:

EUGENE C. BONNIWELL, City Court Building, Philadelphia, Pennsylvania.

Genealogist General:

WALTER K. WATKINS, 9 Ashburton Place, Boston, Massachusetts.

Chaplain General:

REV. LYMAN WHITNEY ALLEN, 881 S. 7th Street, Newark, New Jersey.

BOARD OF TRUSTEES

The General Officers, together with one member from each State Society, constitute the Board of Trustees of the National Society. The following Trustees for the several States were elected at the Buffalo Congress, May 17, 1921, to serve until their successors are elected at the Congress to be held at Springfield, Mass., in May, 1922:

Alabama, (vacant); Arizona, Clay F. Leonard, Phœnix; Arkansas, George B. Gill, Little Rock; California, Seabury C. Mastick, New York City; Colorado, Malcolm Lindsey, Denver; Connecticut, Clarence Horace Wickham, Hartford; Delaware, George Armstrong Elliott, Wilmington; District of Columbia, Albert D. Spangler, Washington; Far Eastern Society, (vacant); Florida, Dr. F. G. Renshaw, Pensacola; Society in France, (vacant); Hawaiian Society, (vacant); Georgia, Allan Waters, Atlanta; Idaho, (vacant); Illinois, Dorr E. Felt, Chicago; Indiana, Charles C. Jewett, Terre Haute; Iowa, Elmer E. Wentworth, State Center; Kansas, John M. Meade, Topeka; Kentucky, George T. Wood, Louisville; Louisiana, Col. C. Robert Churchill, New Orleans; Maine, William B. Berry, Gardiner; Maryland, Hon. Henry Stockbridge, Baltimore; Massachusetts, Henry Fuller Punderson, Springfield; Michigan, Albert M. Henry, Detroit; Minnesota, Charles E. Rittenhouse, Minneapolis; Mississippi, (vacant); Missouri, George R. Merrill, St. Louis; Montana, Marcus Whritenour, Helena; Nebraska, Benjamin F. Bailey, Lincoln; Nevada, (vacant); New Hampshire, Henry T. Lord, Manchester; New Jersey, Charles Symmes Kiggins, Elizabeth; New Mexico, George G. Klock, Albuquerque; New York, Louis Annin Ames, New York; North Carolina, (vacant); North Dakota, Howard E. Simpson, Grand Forks; Ohio, Moulton Houk, Delaware; Oklahoma, W. A. Jennings, Oklahoma City; Oregon, Wallace McCamant, Portland; Pennsylvania, Col. R. W. Guthrie, Pittsburgh; Rhode Island, Wilfred H. Munro, Providence; South Carolina, (vacant); South Dakota, J. G. Parsons, Sioux Falls; Tennessee, Leland Hume, Nashville; Texas, C. B. Dorchester, Sherman; Utah, Daniel S. Spencer, Salt Lake City; Vermont, William Jeffrey, Montpelier; Virginia, Arthur B. Clarke, Richmond; Washington, Ernest B. Hussey, Seattle; Wisconsin, Walter H. Wright, Milwaukee; Wyoming, Warren Richardson, Cheyenne.

PRESIDENTS AND SECRETARIES OF STATE SOCIETIES

ARIZONA—President, H. B. Wilkinson, 128 West Adams Street, Phœnix.
  Secretary, Harold Baxter, 311 Fleming Building, Phœnix.
  Treasurer, Kenneth Freeman, Phœnix.

ARKANSAS—President, General Benjamin W. Green, Little Rock.
  Secretary, Fay Hempstead, Little Rock.
  Treasurer, Thomas M. Cory, Little Rock.

CALIFORNIA—President, Frank S. Brittain, San Francisco.
  Secretary and Registrar, Thomas A. Perkins, Mills Building, San Francisco.
  Treasurer, John C. Currier, 713 Merchants' Exchange Bldg., San Francisco.

COLORADO—President, Victor E. Keyes, 210 Masonic Temple, Denver.
  Secretary, James Polk Willard, 210 Masonic Temple, Denver.
  Treasurer, Walter D. Wynkoop, Denver.

CONNECTICUT—President, Herbert H. White, 76 N. Beacon Street, Hartford.
  Secretary, Frederick A. Doolittle, 117 Middle Street, Bridgeport.
  Treasurer, Charles G. Stone, P. O. Box 847, Hartford.

DELAWARE—President, Horace Wilson, 404 S. Clayton Street, Wilmington.
  Secretary and Treasurer, Charles A. Rudolph, 900 Vanburen Street, Wilmington.

DISTRICT OF COLUMBIA—President, Selden M. Ely, Gales School Building, Washington.
  Secretary, William Alexander Miller, 911 Monroe Street, Washington.
  Treasurer, Alfred B. Dent, 906 A Street S. E., Washington.

FAR EASTERN SOCIETY—President-Secretary, H. Lawrence Noble, Post-office Box 940.
    Manila, Philippine Islands.
  Vice-President, Edward B. Copeland.
  Treasurer, Herman Roy Hare.

FLORIDA—President, Dr. F. G. Renshaw, Pensacola.
  Secretary, John Hobart Cross, Pensacola.
  Treasurer, F. F. Bingham, Pensacola.

SOCIETY IN FRANCE—Administered by Empire State Society.

GEORGIA—President, Allan Waters, Post-office Box 361, Atlanta.
  Secretary, Arthur W. Falkinburg, 1301 Atlanta Trust Co. Bldg., Atlanta.
  Treasurer, Dan C. Pate, 1264 Winter Avenue, Atlanta.

HAWAII—President, Donald S. Bowman, Honolulu.
  Secretary, James T. Taylor, 511 Stangenwald Building, Honolulu.
  Treasurer, L. M. Judd.

IDAHO—President, Henry Keyser, Boise.
  Secretary and Treasurer, Frank G. Ensign, Boise.

ILLINOIS—President, James M. Eddy, 30 North La Salle Street, Chicago.
  Secretary, Louis A. Bowman, 30 North La Salle Street, Chicago.
  Treasurer, Henry R. Kent, 30 North La Salle Street, Chicago.

INDIANA—President, Austin H. Brown, 406 East Fifteenth Street, Indianapolis.
  Secretary and Treasurer, Edmund L. Parker, 208 East Walnut Street, Kokomo.

IOWA—President, Walter E. Coffin, 902 7th Street, Des Moines.
  Secretary, Captain Elbridge D. Hadley, 409 Franklin Avenue, Des Moines.
  Treasurer, William E. Barrett, 4815 Grand Ave., Des Moines.

KANSAS—President, John M. Meade, Topeka.
  Secretary, Arthur H. Bennett, Topeka.
  Treasurer, Jonathan A. Norton, Topeka.

KENTUCKY—President, E. T. Hutchings, Columbia Building, Louisville.
  Secretary, George D. Caldwell, Inter-Southern Building, Louisville.
  Treasurer, Alexander W. Tippett, U. S. Trust Co. Building, Louisville.

LOUISIANA—President, C. Robert Churchill, 408 Canal Street, New Orleans.
  Secretary, Herbert P. Benton, 403 Carondelet Building, New Orleans.
  Treasurer, S. O. Landry, 616 Maison Blanche Building, New Orleans.

MAINE—President, William B. Berry, 42 Pleasant Street, Gardiner.
Secretary, Francis L. Littlefield, 246 Spring Street, Portland.
Treasurer, Enoch O. Greenleaf, Portland.

MARYLAND—President, Osborne I. Yellott, 931 Calvert Building, Baltimore.
Secretary, George Sadtler Robertson, 1628 Linden Avenue, Baltimore.
Treasurer, W. Bernard Duke, 406 Water Street, Baltimore.

MASSACHUSETTS—President, George Hale Nutting, 53 State Street, Boston.
Secretary, George S. Stewart, 539 Tremont Building, Boston.
Treasurer, Lieut.-Col. Charles M. Green, 78 Marlboro Street, Boston.

MICHIGAN—President, William P. Holliday, 68 Davenport Street, Detroit.
Secretary, Raymond E. Van Syckle, 1729 Ford Building, Detroit.
Treasurer, Frank G. Smith, 237 Hancock Avenue E., Detroit.

MINNESOTA—President, Charles E. Rittenhouse, 720 Washington Avenue, Minneapolis.
Secretary, Charles H. Bronson, 48 East Fourth Street, St. Paul.
Treasurer, Charles W. Eddy, 302 Pittsburg Building, St. Paul.

MISSISSIPPI—President, Judge Gordon Garland Lyell, Jackson.
Secretary and Treasurer, William H. Pullen, Mechanics' Bank Building, Jackson.

MISSOURI—President, Col. W. D. Vandiver, Columbia.
Secretary, J. Alonzo Matthews, 901 Pontiac Building, St. Louis.
Treasurer, I. Shreve Carter, 308 Merchant La Clede Building, St. Louis.

MONTANA—President, Martin Whritenour, Helena.
Secretary and Treasurer, Leslie Sulgrove, Helena.

NEBRASKA—President, Benjamin F. Bailey, Lincoln.
Secretary and Treasurer, Addison E. Sheldon, 1319 South 23d Street, Lincoln.

NEVADA—President, Rt. Rev. George C. Huntting, 505 Ridge Street, Reno.

NEW HAMPSHIRE—President, Prof. Ashley K. Hardy, Hanover.
Secretary and Treasurer, Will B. Howe, Concord.

NEW JERSEY—President, Rev. Lyman Whitney Allen, D. D., 881 S. 7th Street, Newark.
Secretary, David L. Pierson, 33 Lombardy Street, Newark.
Treasurer, Earle A. Miller, 156 William Street, Orange.

NEW MEXICO—President, Edmund Ross, Albuquerque.
Secretary, Frank W. Graham, Albuquerque.
Treasurer, Orville A. Matson, Albuquerque.

NEW YORK—President, Harvey F. Remington, Wilder Building, Rochester.
Secretary, Major Charles A. Du Bois, 220 Broadway, New York City.
Treasurer, James de la Montanye, 220 Broadway, New York City.

NORTH CAROLINA—President, Frank H. Bryan, Washington.
Secretary (vacant).
Treasurer, W. B. Harding, Washington.

NORTH DAKOTA—President, Howard E. Simpson, University of North Dakota, Grand Forks.
Secretary, Walter R. Reed, Amenia.
Treasurer, J. W. Wilkerson, University of North Dakota, Grand Forks.

OHIO—President, Walter J. Sherman, The Nasby, Toledo.
Secretary, W. L. Curry, Box 645, Columbus.
Treasurer, S. G. Harvey, Toledo.

OKLAHOMA—President, Edward F. McKay, Oklahoma City.
Secretary-Treasurer, A. Barritt Galloway, 905 1st National Bank Bldg., Oklahoma City.

OREGON—President, B. B. Beekman, 601 Platt Building, Portland.
Secretary, B. A. Thaxter, Post-office Box 832, Portland.
Treasurer, A. B. Lindsley, Henry Building, Portland.

PENNSYLVANIA—President, James A. Wakefield, 471 Union Arcade, Pittsburgh.
Secretary, Francis Armstrong, Jr., 515 Wood Street, Pittsburgh.
Treasurer, A. M. Wall, Pittsburgh.

RHODE ISLAND—President, Francis Eliot Bates, Post-office Box 1254, Providence.
Secretary, Theodore F. Dexter, Central Falls.
Treasurer, William L. Sweet, Box 1515, Providence.

SOUTH CAROLINA—No report.

SOUTH DAKOTA—President, Amos E. Ayres, Sioux Falls.
Secretary, T. W. Dwight, Sioux Falls.
Treasurer, B. H. Requa, Sioux Falls.

TENNESSEE—President, William K. Boardman, Nashville.
Secretary, Frederick W. Millspaugh, Nashville.
Treasurer, Carey Folk, 411 Union Street, Nashville.

TEXAS—President, C. B. Dorchester, Sherman.
Secretary, Walter S. Mayer, Galveston.

UTAH—President, Heber M. Wells, Dooly Building, Salt Lake City.
Secretary, Gordon Lines Hutchins, Dooly Building, Salt Lake City.
Treasurer, Seth Warner Morrison, Jr.

VERMONT—President, William H. Jeffrey, Montpelier.
Secretary, Walter H. Crockett, Burlington.
Treasurer, Clarence L. Smith, Burlington.

VIRGINIA—President, Arthur B. Clarke, 616 American National Bank Building, Richmond.
Secretary and Treasurer, William E. Crawford, 700 Travelers' Building, Richmond.

WASHINGTON—President, Walter Burges Beals, Seattle.
Secretary, William Phelps Totten, 653 New York Building, Seattle.
Treasurer, Chauncey Luther Baxter, Seattle.

WISCONSIN—President, J. Tracy Hale, Jr., Wells Building, Milwaukee.
Secretary, Emmett A. Donnelly, 1030 Wells Building, Milwaukee.
Treasurer, William Stark Smith, 373 Lake Drive, Milwaukee.

WYOMING—President, Warren Richardson, Cheyenne.
Secretary, Maurice Groshon, Cheyenne.
Treasurer, James B. Guthrie, Cheyenne.

Special Announcement of the Springfield Chapter, Massachusetts Society, Sons of the American Revolution, in Reference to the Next Congress, That Will Be Held in That City the Third Monday in May, 1922

The following are the names of the Executive Committee and Board of Managers, together with the chairmen of the various committees who will conduct the affairs of the Congress:

EXECUTIVE COMMITTEE

Board of Managers.—Charles F. Warner, President; Frank P. Forbes, Vice-President; Henry A. Booth, Secretary; George B. Joslyn, Treasurer; Rev. John H. Lockwood, D. D., Chaplain; Henry N. Bowman, Historian; Allen W. Hopkins, Registrar.

Finance Committee.—Chairman, Henry C. Haile.
Reception Committee.—Chairman, Henry F. Punderson.
Program and Printing.—Chairman, Dr. John Mac Duffie.
Banquet Committee.—Chairman, John K. Joy.
Automobile Committee.—Chairman, Seth H. Clark.
Decorations.—Chairman, James H. Bigelow.
Registration.—Chairman, Edwin G. Rude.
Publicity.—Chairman, Ernest N. Bagg.
Colors.—Chairman, Andrew S. Bryant.

ANNOUNCEMENTS

The itinerary of the President General will be: Chicago, February 11 and 12; Washington, February 15; Montclair, February 19; Boston, February 22, with possible stops at Toledo, Baltimore, Hartford, and Providence.

Members are herewith advised that, by approved action of the Executive Committee, the request of J. E. Caldwell & Company, of Philadelphia, that a reasonable increase in the price of the insignia of the Society be allowed is granted, and the following schedule of prices will go into effect after January 1: 14-carat Large Insignia, $25.00; silver-gilt Large Insignia, $12.00; 14-carat gold Miniature Insignia, $14.00; the silver-gilt Miniature Insignia, $5.50; the present war tax of 5 per cent, or any other tax hereafter imposed, to be paid in addition to the prices above quoted.

The Secretary General desires to call the attention of State Officers to the ruling of the Executive Committee with regard to presentation of the War Service Medal, namely, that this medal should be presented for active military or naval service rendered by compatriots in the late war. The State Secretaries should satisfy themselves of the eligibility of the recipient, and not include civil service in this, before giving orders and arranging for the presentation of the medals.

Supplementary to the report of Past President General Thruston in the October BULLETIN, the latter desires to add the following interesting information:

"Soon after the Congress, through those who heard the reading of this report, we have succeeded in obtaining the administration upon the estate of Elbridge Gerry, of Massachusetts, and a copy of the will of Thomas Nelson, Jr., of Virginia."

Director General Adams, of New Jersey, made an official visit to Washington, D. C., in October to arrange with Senator Frelinghuysen, who is chairman of the Senate Committee on Military Affairs, to amend our National Charter so as to permit of one hundred instead of sixty (as at present) National Trustees.

Director General Adams was appointed by the Executive Committee chairman of a committee to attend to this business. While in Washington he called also upon Senator Edge, of New Jersey, who, like Senator Frelinghuysen, is a member of the Sons of the American Revolution.

Director General Adams paid his respects, likewise, to Compatriot Charles Evans Hughes, Secretary of State, and was later received in private conference by the President, who is also a distinguished member of our patriotic Organization.

On account of an unavoidable delay in receiving from the foundry the historical markers which the Oregon Society had caused to be made for the battlefield at Princeton, the committee in charge, of which Maj. W. I. Lincoln Adams, Director General, from New Jersey, is chairman, decided to postpone the dedicatory exercises on the battlefield until the warmer weather of next spring. Comprehensive plans for very interesting exercises at that time are being completed. President Hibben has promised to participate, as well as Professor Wertenbaker, who is the highest authority living on the battle itself. The Princeton

Battery will escort the columns to the battlefield and fire a salute of honor there at the conclusion of the exercises. It is hoped that the President General can himself attend, as well as several other of our National Officers and Past Officers.

The President General has recently appointed two special committees, namely, a Committee on Amendment of National Charter, of which Major W. I. Lincoln Adams, of New Jersey, is chairman, with the Hon. Joseph S. Frelinghuysen, Hon. James W. Wadsworth, Hon. Harry S. New, Hon. William P. Dillingham, Hon. C. N. McArthur, and Mr. John H. Cowles. This committee is to take up the matter of amendment of the National Charter with reference to increasing the number of National Trustees.

Another special committee is that authorized by the last National Congress, to provide a special Service Bar, to be worn on ceremonial occasions with the National Insignia, to indicate service in the various wars. Capt. Henry H. Brown, of New York, is chairman of this committee, with Col. George V. Lauman, of Illinois, and Gen. Oliver B. Bridgeman, of New York. This committee announces that the Service Bar will be ready for distribution on and after January 15. Information may be obtained from the Secretary General.

Mr. George A. Brennan, Historian of the Illinois Society, Sons of the American Revolution, has ready for publication a most interesting book describing the beauties of the "Dunes," its rare plants, birds, and animals and its wonderful history, from the Mound Builders to the present time, including the discovery, near Waverly Beach, of the site of the old French Fort Petite, 1750-1800; and also the correct location of the Revolutionary battle of December 5, 1780, which was fought at Michigan City instead of South Chicago. The book is called "The Wonders of the Dunes," and is especially appealing to lovers of nature and history. It will be published by Bobbs-Merrill Co., Indianapolis, and those interested may get further information by corresponding with that firm.

THE YEAR BOOK OF THE LOUISIANA SOCIETY

Nothing could show the spirit of our organization more than the remarkably complete and interesting 1921 Year Book of the Louisiana Society, Sons of the American Revolution. It is, without doubt, the best thing that has been issued by this Society, and no other Society in the National Organization has even approached the scope and completeness that is shown in this book. Beginning with a complete roster of the officers, committees, and members, with authentic addresses, it then gives an interesting history of the Louisiana Society, and, further, something that should be in every year book or pamphlet issued by other societies, a few paragraphs telling the purposes and objects of our Organization and reasons for membership, and what the Society has accomplished, with much other valuable information along these lines. Then there is a short report of the National Congress held at Buffalo and a most interesting address by Colonel Churchill, as given before the State meeting of the Daughters of the American Revolution, in which he gives the history of Louisiana in the Revolutionary War. Then there are the Galvez records and letters, which "are really remarkable finds that were made in the records of the Galvez Expedition, uncovered in Seville, Spain, through the efforts of the Louisiana Society, and many new lights have been thrown on the history of Louisiana of that period." All this, together with a roster of the militia and fixed Louisiana Spanish regiments and companies, make this book a most valuable addition not only to the Society's archives, but a real contribution to history. The credit for this work is due to the untiring energy and capacity of Col. C. Robert Churchill, President of the Louisiana Society, who has done so much to promote the interests of the Sons of the American Revolution in his city and State.

"HERE LIES POOR BUT HONEST DUST"

By Cornelius F. Posson

The rude sandstone slab had been broken off near its base and lay flat upon the ground. Similar was the fate of the headstone upon the grave next to this one. Of the graves themselves, no trace remained, nor could their location ever have been determined by any man, but for the fact that the stubs of the two headstones still showed just above the ground, not being entirely eroded by the elements as yet; but I doubt not that by another autumn all traces of the last resting places of this patriot and his wife would be entirely lost. But we shall not permit it so to be.

There was evidence of there having been another grave or two near by, and the spot was evidently a family burial plot during the years around 1840. Over there on the knoll, about forty rods distant the old homestead used to stand, and over here, under the shade of these four or five friendly trees, they used to come and bury their family dead. Scarcely any trace of the old home remains, and the little burial plot is now a part of a hillside pasture, and cattle graze wantonly over the place.

I came upon this spot one recent morning, being directed thither by a great-grandson of the man whose "poor but honest dust" lies buried there. It is in an out-of-the-way place in Vigo County, Indiana.

The inscription, cut in the inartistic fashion of eighty years ago, with uneven spacing and some misspelled words, was much worn away and seemed to baffle complete interpretation; but earnestly and with great patience we traced, with moistened finger-tip, each faint letter, and so, word by word, gradually we were able to reconstruct the ancient epitaph. Here it is:

Here lies
POOR BUT HONEST DUST.
WILLIAM RAY
Was Born in Ireland
Nov. 26th, 1740,
and Died July 28th, 1840,
a Vetron
who fought in the
War of the Revolution.

Raising the broken slab to a vertical position and propping it up against some stones, a snapshot of it was taken; also a picture of wider range was taken, embracing that part of the field where the grave is located.

There are many graves like this in Indiana, graves within whose sacred confines repose the dust of soldiers of the Revolutionary war (1775-1783). Some are in family burial plots of the earlier days, like the one described; some are in old, abandoned, bramble-grown graveyards, off from the main highways of travel, and a few are located in cemeteries which are still used as burial places.

All of these graves the Indiana Society of the Sons of the American Revolution is seeking to definitely locate, with a view to reclaiming them before it is too late, and marking them for permanent preservation. The work throughout the State is in charge of a committee of which I am chairman. I earnestly invite correspondence from any one who can afford any authentic information concerning the Indiana grave of a Revolutionary soldier.

The grave of William Ray, in Vigo County, has been located just in time to save it, and the Sons of the American Revolution, with appropriate ceremony, will place a permanent marker on the spot this fall. The military service of this patriot is shown by the United States Pension Rolls. He lived to the age of 99 years and 8 months. And as regards his dust, it was not poor. Count no dust poor that had a mortal part in the struggle of the American Colonies for their independence. Not *poor,* but *rich* is the dust of those who suffered

VIEW OF THE SANDSTONE SLAB   FIELD WHERE GRAVE IS LOCATED

and endured that independence might be established, and that this glorious country might have birth.

And so it is that William Ray is not forgotten, and eighty years and more after his mortal body was laid away to rest his lonely grave is sought out and visited by those who seek to honor him. Thus it is that the Society of the Sons of the American Revolution aims to perpetuate the memory of the men who by their services and sacrifies during the War of the American Revolution achieved the independence of the American people.

· NOTE.—Since the foregoing was written it has been learned that William Ray was not merely a soldier of the Revolution, but was a Revolutionary officer. The U. S. Bureau of Pensions, under date of October 17, 1921, affords me the following information:

Enlisted '775; length of service, 3 years 2 months; rank, lieutenant in Captain Anthony Wayne's Company and also lieutenant in Captain Mordecai Chaffin's Company, Colonel Anthony Wayne's Regiment, Pennsylvania Militia.

Also served short terms as private against British and Indians during the Revolution and afterwards; no officers stated; dates not given.

Revolutionary battles engaged in: White Plains, Brandywine, Germantown, Monmouth, Stony Point.

Residence at date of enlistment, Chester County, Pa., with the above Anthony Wayne.

Date of application for pension, May 8, 1834. His claim was allowed. Residence at date of application, Vigo County, Indiana.

He was born in 1740, in Ireland. He emigrated to America in 1772, and lived with Isaac Wayne, father of Anthony, until he "volunteered." His pension was paid until July 28, 1840. No family data on file.

Very commendable indeed is the endeavor of this patriotic Society to locate and to reclaim the graves of these patriots, and no one who is in possession of any information on the subject should fail to communicate with Cornelius F. Posson, Brazil, Indiana.

REPORT OF COMMITTEE ON THE OBSERVANCE OF CONSTITUTION DAY, SEPTEMBER 17, 1921

DECEMBER 1, 1921.

Mr. President General and Members of the National Executive Committee:

The campaign made this year by the Sons of the American Revolution for the celebration of Constitution Day resulted in a nation-wide observance. Space will not permit of a detailed description of the thousands of meetings, yet the story would be far from complete unless mention were made of the part played by the leading men of the nation and the assistance rendered by many other organizations and the deep interest manifested by the patriotic citizens everywhere.

Upon the request of the Sons of the American Revolution, our distinguished compatriot, President Warren G. Harding, wrote letters to the chairman of the National Committee and chairman of the Ohio State Committee heartily endorsing the movement.

Proclamations calling for the observance of the day were issued by the governors of the following States:

Arkansas, Colorado, Indiana, Kentucky, Louisiana, Maryland, Minnesota, Nebraska, Nevada, New Hampshire, North Dakota, Ohio, South Dakota, Oregon, Tennessee, Utah, Virginia, Wyoming.

Hearty co-operation was rendered by the National Security League, Constitutional League, State and local bar associations, State, county, and city boards of education, Masonic bodies, Order of Elks, Rotary and Kiwanis clubs, theatrical profession, community centers, boards of trade, and chambers of commerce. The newspapers were generous in according space, not only recording the celebrations, but in editorial articles, using over 200,000 newspaper columns.

The New York Chapter of the Sons of the American Revolution achieved great success in its effort to have the day fittingly observed in New York City. The procession, under command of Major Charles A. Du Bois, marshal, composed of an escort of mounted police, the band and a company of the 22d Regiment of Infantry, U. S. A., from Governor's Island, under command of Capt. Paul R. Knight, the color guard and compatriots of the Sons of the American Revolution, and delegations from the Society of the Cincinnati, the Founders and Patriots of America, the Veteran Corps of Artillery, and other patriotic organizations, formed at S. A. R. headquarters, on Broadway opposite St. Paul's Church, at 11:45, and marched through a heavy rain to the Subtreasury, at the corner of Wall and Nassau streets, the site of the old Federal Hall, where Washington was inaugurated first President of the United States. Addresses were made by Brig.-Gen. Louis W. Stotesbury and Col. Francis R. Stoddard, Jr. Music was furnished by the New York City Police Glee Club, accompanied by the 22d Infantry, U. S. A., Band.

Upon the request of the Sons of the American Revolution, the Fifth Avenue Association circularized its members, requesting the display of the United States flag on September 17 and using of patriotic decorations in their windows. This request was complied with by all the merchants on Fifth Avenue.

Agreeable to the Sons of the American Revolution, the Interborough Rapid Transit Co., which is composed of all the elevated railroads and subways in Greater New York, carrying over two million passengers daily, displayed in each car, for the week from September 10 to September 17, a placard designating September 17 as Constitution Day and calling upon the people to hold in loving remembrance the Constitution of the United States, as under its protection we enjoy all the advantages of free government.

The Department of Education, in the grammar schools, high schools, and city colleges in the city of New York, on Friday afternoon, held closing exercises in honor of Constitution Day.

Masonic bodies of the State, bar associations, moving-picture houses, State and county boards of education all contributed their part toward an intellectual understanding of the day.

Arizona.—Reports from this State all tell that Constitution Day was generally observed. The proclamation of the Governor, Thomas E. Campbell, tells not only the story of the Constitutional Conference, at which George Washington, of Virginia, was present, but refers to the Constitution as embodying the basic spirit of Americanism, the foundation of free and supreme law of our land. Arizona made a great record for itself in its first year of the observance of Constitution Day, and credit is due to the State Society, Sons of the American Revolution, under whose auspices the ceremonies were inaugurated.

Colorado.—Under the leadership of President Victor C. Keyes, the Colorado Society took the initiative in organizing celebrations throughout the State. Much credit is due to the Superintendent of Schools for the part played by the Department of Education in the observance of the day. The Colorado Society observed its 25th anniversary on Constitution Day by holding, at Denver, a patriotic meeting including all patriotic societies of Colorado, with the Opportunity School and boards of education of the State. It was a great educational as well as patriotic occasion. President Keyes is the State's Attorney-General, and he had four district judges throughout the State as coworkers in the movement for the observance of Constitution Day.

Connecticut.—A large patriotic meeting was held at New Haven, under the auspices of the General David Humphrey Chapter, S. A. R. There were present representatives from the D. A. R. and other patriotic organizations.

District of Columbia Society.—The Sons of the American Revolution observed the day by holding a Field Day meeting at Oak Hill Cemetery, Georgetown, and placed two Revolutionary gravestone markers—one on the grave of Lieut.-Col. Uriah Forrest and the other on the grave of Capt. Stephen Bloomer Balch, Revolutionary Army Chaplain. Addresses were made by William A. Gordon, prominent historian, and Rev. James T. Marshall, present pastor of the church founded by Dr. Balch.

Georgia.—The Sons of the American Revolution interested all patriotic and civic societies of the State, and through the press of the State outlined an observance of the day, requesting all churches on September 18 to have a fitting program in grateful memory of the adoption of the Constitution and the request met with a generous response. The Georgia Society itself held a special service in the Central Congregational Church, at Atlanta, and a wonderful patriotic and historic address was delivered by Dr. William Stuehell, at which were in attendance patriotic and civic bodies, led by the S. A. R.

Indiana.—The Indiana Society, Sons of the American Revolution, issued a Constitution Day Bulletin to the superintendents of schools throughout the State, calling for the observance in the schools on the Friday preceding Constitution Day, and offered to furnish as speakers members of the Sons of the American Revolution and the Bar Association of the State. The response was most encouraging. Some of the school programs were formulated by the Sons of the American Revolution, and in Terre Haute and in West Terre Haute special mention was made of the Society in the school program. The John Morton Chapter held its annual meeting on September 4 and then arranged to have its members serve as speakers in co-operation with the Bar Association and members of the Department of Education. The mayors of the principal cities of Indiana issued formal proclamations on Constitution Day. The observance of the day in Indiana this year was more general than ever before. Press reports record a much larger number of celebrations this year than last.

Illinois.—The Illinois Society, Sons of the American Revolution, held its annual celebration on Constitution Day, in commemoration of the anniversary of the adoption of the United States Constitution, at Morrison Hotel, Chicago. An address was delivered by Judge C. S. Cutting, member of the Illinois Constitutional Convention. His theme was "The Constitution." Throughout the State the departments of education held exercises in observance of the day.

Iowa.—The Sons of the American Revolution of Iowa were very active not alone in stimulating celebrations throughout the State, in the public schools, by bar associations, but reported the following meetings held entirely under the auspices of the Sons of the American Revolution:

Lexington Chapter, Keokuk, Iowa, held a patriotic meeting on September 17. A very able address was delivered by Judge W. S. Hamilton.

Alexander Hamilton Chapter, Sheldon, held their annual meeting on Constitution Day, with a very attractive program.

Valley Forge Chapter, Nevada, Iowa, held a patriotic meeting, discussing the events that led to the signing of the Constitution.

Ben Franklin Chapter, Des Moines, held a banquet, and addresses were delivered by Past President-General Elmer M. Wentworth and Henry H. Griffiths.

Kentucky.—Last year the Kentucky Society, Sons of the American Revolution, outdistanced the other patriotic societies in the number of people in attendance at its celebration, namely, 65,000. Constitution Day, September 17, in the State of Kentucky, this year conflicted with the State Fair, and the Sons of the American Revolution were asked to postpone their Constitution Day celebration for a week later, as the State Fair had a large investment and would have difficulty in paying expenses and meeting interest on its investment if the Sons of the American Revolution held its Constitution Day observance at Louisville on that date. However, the public schools of the State, on Friday afternoon, September 16, celebrated Constitution Day, and on Sunday, September 18, the Sons of the American Revolution held a mass meeting in the evening, at the First Christian Church, in Louisville. The address was made by the Chaplain of the S. A. R., Dr. E. L. Powell, and 800 people were present.

It is through the Vice-President General, Marvin H. Lewis, that we obtained an account of this meeting and a report that the State Superintendent of Schools of Chicago, Illinois, issued instructions to all school superintendents to have brief exercises regarding Constitution Day in the various public schools in the State and city; he also furnished an account of the celebration held by the Illinois Society.

Minnesota.—The Minnesota Society, Sons of the American Revolution, observed Constitution Day by a patriotic service Sunday evening, September 18, in Minneapolis and St. Paul, at both of which there was a large attendance. The addresses at Minneapolis were delivered by Rev. Dr. Marion D. Shutter and Hon. Walter H. Newton. The speaker at the St. Paul meeting was Rev. J. W. Holland, and his subject was "We, the People." A meeting was also held at Duluth on the same evening, under the auspices of the Bar Association.

The Governor of the State issued a proclamation for the observance of the day. A celebration was held in Minneapolis, at Gateway Park, at which addresses were made by the Governor, Mayor of the City, Congressman Walter H. Newton, and Judge Torrence. The Commissioner of Education listed Constitution Day for observance each year in the schools throughout the State. The event was an occasion of appropriate exercises in the Minneapolis schools on the Friday preceding the anniversary.

Proclamations were issued by the Governor of the State and the mayors of Minneapolis and St. Paul. The newspapers of the State gave wide publicity to the observance of the day.

Constitution Day was observed in Minneapolis and St. Paul. Mayor George E. Leach, of St. Paul, appointed a committee, with James F. Ellis as chairman. Mr. Ellis and his committee co-operated with the Sons of the American Revolution, American Legion, and other patriotic organizations in arranging a program for the day.

Missouri.—Celebrations were held in all the high schools of the State during the school hours on September 16. The Sons of the American Revolution furnished a visiting committee of speakers to call at these meetings. Three public meetings were held in Columbia—one at the city high school, one at the State university and one at the Methodist Church, on the evening of Sunday, September 18. The Sons of the American Revolution had the co-operation of the Bar Association, Department of Education, and other literary organizations.

New Hampshire.—The celebration of the 134th anniversary of the adoption of the Constitution was held by a meeting at the Hall of Representatives, State House, Concord, September 17, 1921, at 11 o'clock a. m., the Rumford Chapter, D. A. R., co-operating. His Excellency Albert O. Brown, Governor of New Hampshire, presided. The program consisted of prayer by the Chaplain; music, furnished by the Rumford Chapter, D. A. R.; introductory remarks by the President of the S. A. R.; address by Hon. Sherman E. Burroughs, of Manchester, Representative in Congress from the First New Hampshire District; singing of "America" by the audience. Other observances of the day were held under the auspices of the Department of Education.

New Jersey.—As usual, New Jersey observed the day most fittingly. Through the overtures made by the New Jersey Society, many of the mayors of New Jersey issued proclamations, calling upon the people to display the flag and to observe the anniversary of the adoption of the Federal Constitution. Orange Chapter observed the anniversary by presenting a large flag of Stars and Strips to the Dante House, Orange, opened by enterprising citizens of Italian lineage for the purpose of Americanizing the Sons of Italy coming to the city. In the absence of Compatriot John Lenord Merrill, President of the Chapter, the presentation was made by David L. Pierson, Secretary of the New Jersey Society and former President of the Chapter. The flag was drawn to the top of the staff by Capt. John R. Williams, a member of the Chapter and a Civil War veteran. Compatriot Pierson also made an address on the Constitution. Compatriot William A. Lord, mayor of Orange, delivered the principal address of the afternoon. All of the schools of the Oranges held exercises on September 16, the day preceding the anniversary, which fell upon Saturday. Church bells were rung at noon, on the anniversary, for three minutes, and this was a forceful reminder to the people that the day was worthy of celebration.

Mayor Howard F. McConnell, of Montclair, a member of Montclair Chapter, issued a proclamation, which was printed on posters and distributed through the city, calling the people's attention to the anniversary. Church bells were rung at 12 o'clock noon and again at 6 o'clock in the evening, each time for five minutes. By request of Montclair Chapter, the Board of Education arranged for a program, to be followed in remembrance of the day on Friday, September 16. On the evening of September 17 a band concert was given on the lawn of the high school, and Elvord G. Chamberlin, President, read extracts from the Constitution to an audience of about 2,000 persons.

Paramus Chapter, located at Ridgewood, dedicated a tablet in the Ridgewood High School on Constitution Day, upon which are engraved the names of students winning the annual prize offered by the Chapter on a subject pertaining to the Revolutionary War.

All the Chapters, with one or two exceptions, called upon the people to observe the day and a large number of the members were engaged in delivering addresses at the schools and other places where exercises were held.

Ohio.—The Ohio Society has observed Constitution Day generally ever since the day was inaugurated by the Sons of the American Revolution, and they have co-operated especially with the departments of education, furnishing the superintendents of public schools with copies of the United States Constitution and our little booklet, "Information for Immigrants." The schools have cordially responded to the request and suggestions of the S. A. R. and each succeeding year have enlarged the number of celebrations. The Sons of the American Revolution have interested other patriotic societies in observing the day, and the State Society sent out to all of its members a copy of a letter written to the Secretary of the Ohio Society by President Harding, an Ohio compatriot. The letter reads as follows:

THE WHITE HOUSE,
WASHINGTON, *August* 18, 1921.

MY DEAR MR. CURRY:

It is a pleasure to address a word of greeting and encouragement to those who will unite this year in celebrating Constitution Day, September seventeenth. I have always thought of Constitution Day as marking the real birth of our Nation. In speaking on September seventeenth last year, I said:

"I know that we date our independence to the memorable July day in 1776 when the bell of Independence Hall 'rang out liberty' to all the peoples of the world. I know that the confederation of colonies was the great, the essential step toward the consolidation of victories of the Revolution, but it was the ratification of the inspired Constitution of 1787 that first established us as a nation. I want it to abide; I want it to impel us onward; I want the Republic for which it was conceived; and I want the Republic governed in America, under the Constitution."

With all sincerity and with a conviction that has been strengthened by the events of the past year, I can now repeat this expression. The trying times of the last seven years have supremely tested the governmental systems of all the world; and I feel that we of America may well felicitate ourselves and give thanks to Divine Providence, that in this test no governmental system has demonstrated a greater capacity to meet and bear the utmost stresses of human crisis than our own. This knowledge cannot but enhearten us, as we look to the future, with its many and difficult problems still to be met.

Once more we may remind ourselves that the Constitution is strong enough for every requirement, elastic enough to adapt itself to changing conditions and developing evolutions. So, on this anniversary we may well dedicate ourselves to the supreme purpose of maintaining our institutions under it, and of making them in the future, as they have been in the past, a beacon light to illumine the way of progress for men seeking freedom everywhere.

Most sincerely yours,

WARREN G. HARDING.

Mr. W. L. CURRY,
Secretary, Sons of the American Revolution, Columbus, Ohio.

The Governor of the State issued a proclamation and the mayors of the principal cities issued proclamations. Exercises were held throughout the State, in the public and parochial schools and most of the churches, with the result that the day was more generally observed than in any preceding year. The newspapers co-operated by publishing this letter and editorials, calling attention to the observance which this anniversary commemorated.

Oregon.—The Oregon Society began early their plans for the observance of Constitution Day. A committee was formed on August 3, 1912, and a typewritten historical sketch of the inauguration of the observance of Constitution Day in 1917 by the Sons of the American Revolution was published by the newspapers of the State on Sunday, August 21. A statement was prepared by the City Superintendent of Schools, D. A. Groat, and was published in an early issue of the *Portland School Bulletin,* a publication of official character, which is mailed to all grammar school and high school principals and teachers in the city of Portland.

Compatriot Harrison G. Platt, President of the Bar Association, planned for the observance of the day in the courts of the State and took the matter up with the various local bar associations in the several counties. The result of this work was that a proclamation, calling for the general observance by the people of Oregon, was issued by Governor Benjamin W. Olcott. Numerous observances were held in the high schools of the State and in the eight high schools in the city of Portland, and instructive addresses were delivered on Friday morning, September 16. With one exception, all the speakers were provided from the County Bar Association. In three of the high schools, owing to the large attendance and inadequate seating capacity, second assemblies were held and addresses were repeated. In the high school at Roseburg the address was made by Compatriot O. P. Coshow. At the high school at Burns, Oregon, the address was made by A. W. Gowan. At the high school at La Grande the speaker was Compatriot Walter M. Pierce. At the Corvallis High School the speaker was Compatriot C. R. Ingalls. Patriotic meetings were held at Marshfield, Union, Hillsboro, and several other towns.

The seven departments of the Circuit Court of Oregon for this county held a joint meeting in Portland on the morning of September 17. Two admirable addresses were delivered, one by Martin L. Pipes, on "The Meaning and Application of the Constitution," and the other by Judge John McCourt, on "The Retention or Extension of War-time Provisions of the Constitution."

At Salem, the capital of the State, a very successful celebration was held, on September 17, under the auspices of the Circuit Court and the Marion County Bar Association. Mr. George M. Brown, justice of the Supreme Court of Oregon, delivered the address of the day, on "The Constitution," which the press reported as being unusually able and instructive. A joint meeting was also held in Salem in the afternoon of that day by the Daughters of the American Revolution and the Women's Relief Corps.

At Roseburg a public celebration was held on the evening of September 15, the arrangements therefor having been made by the Circuit Court of Douglas County. Judge J. W. Hamilton delivered an appropriate address.

The Circuit Court for Washington County also reports that it held exercises on the morning of September 17, on which occasion a number of addresses were made by members of the local bar.

An exceedingly gratifying and successful feature of the celebration of the anniversary in Portland was a series of programs at the luncheons of the leading civic organizations of the city during the week of September 12-17. Beginning with the luncheon of the Forum of the Chamber of Commerce on Monday, these programs continued daily during the week. The speakers at the Forum luncheon were Judge John Kavanaugh, who delivered an eloquent address on "Some Basic Principles of the Constitution," and Hugh Montgomery, who closed with a stirring address on "American Ideals." The Chamber of Commerce dining-room was crowded and the business men present evinced a great interest in the occasion. On Tuesday, September 13, occurred the luncheon of the Rotary Club. Judge Robert C. Tucker delivered the address on that occasion, his subject being "The Constitution and Service." On Wednesday, September 14, the Portland Ad Club observed the day at its luncheon, with Mr. Hugh Montgomery delivering an address on "The Constitution." The Kiwanis Club observed the day with appropriate exercises on September 15. On Saturday, September 17, the Oregon Civic League and Daughters of the American Revolution gave a joint luncheon, to which members of the Oregon Society, S. A. R., were invited as guests. At this luncheon Judge John Kavanaugh repeated the address on "Some Basic Principles of the Constitution," which he had delivered at the Chamber of Commerce Forum luncheon on Monday.

On the evening of September 22 Mr. Hugh Montgomery addressed the East Side Business Men's Club on the subject of "American Ideals." The Progressive Business Men's Club and the City Club also assured me that they would observe the day at their luncheons during that week, but I have not received any report thereon up to this time.

A number of the Oregon chapters of the Daughters of the American Revolution observed the day by appropriate gatherings, and several other organizations held meetings in honor of the anniversary.

Through Superintendent of Schools D. A. Grout, of Portland, teachers in the seventh and eighth grades of the grammar schools were requested to observe the day on the morning of September 16, devoting five minutes thereto, with a short talk on the Constitution and a recital of the American's Creed. This request was made through the official school publication and was generally complied with.

Pennsylvania.—Under the able leadership of our Chancellor General, Eugene C. Bonniwell, a meeting was held at Independence Hall, Philadelphia, carrying out work of high distinction and merit. Other observances were held throughout the State.

Maryland.—While no report has come from the Maryland Society direct, it was most active in arranging celebrations in the leading cities of the State and furnished free, to the moving-picture theaters, sets of 12 slides, as follows:

A 1. Picture—The Capitol (vignette).

> Text: *We, the people, and our Constitution.*
> The Constitution of the United States was adopted on September 17, 1787. It has been the "supreme law of the land" for 134 years.

A 2. "Star Spangled Banner" (one stanza).

A 3. The Preamble of the Constitution.

A 4. *The Constitution.*

> Drafted by a convention which was called by a conference of five States, recommended by Congress, and attended by delegates from 12 of the 13 States. Approved by 52 of the 55 delegates to this convention. Ratified by 11 States in special conventions and later accepted by the other two.
> *The Constitution is indeed a document of the people.*

A 5. Picture—James A. Garfield.

> Quotation: The sovereign of this nation, the God-crowned and Heaven-anointed sovereign, in whom resides "the State's collective will," and to whom we all owe allegiance, is the people themselves.

A 6. Picture—Theodore Roosevelt.

> Quotation: A good Constitution and good laws under the Constitution and fearless and upright officials to administer the laws—all these are necessary; but the prime requisite in our national life is, and must always be, the possession by the average citizen of the right kind of character.

A 7. Picture—Voter Casting Ballot.

> Text: In no sense is citizenship a reward that has been given to you because you have lived in the United States a certain number of years. It is a job that has been given to you. Keep this truth in mind. Never lose sight of the fact that you have been admitted to full partnership in the greatest enterprise that the world has ever seen.—CHARLES SEYMOUR WHITMAN.

A 8. Picture—Abraham Lincoln.

> Quotation: As the patriots of seventy-six died to support the Declaration of Independence, so to the support of the Constitution and laws

let every American pledge his life, his property, and his sacred honor; let every man remember that to violate the law is to trample on the blood of his father and tear the charter of his own and his children's liberty.

A 9. Quotation: The basis of our political systems is the right of the people to make and to alter their constitutions of government. But the Constitution which at any time exists, till changed by an explicit and authentic act of the whole people, is sacredly obligatory upon all.—GEORGE WASHINGTON.

A 10. Picture—George Washington.
Caption: Commander-in-Chief of the American Army throughout the Revolution; presiding officer of the Convention which drafted the Constitution; first President of the United States.

A 11. The American's Creed.

A 12. Picture—United States Flag.
Quotation: Accept it, then, in all its fullness of meaning. It is not a painted rag; it is a whole national history. It is the Constitution; it is the Government; it is the free people that stand in the Government. Forget not what it means, and for the sake of its ideas, rather than its mere emblazonry, be true to your country's flag.—HHERY WARD BEECHER.

Tennessee.—Like the Maryland Society, the Tennessee Society used series of colored slides telling the story of the Constitution in pictorial fashion.

South Dakota.—South Dakota appointed on September 16 a State Committee to organize patriotic celebrations throughout the State in honor of the anniversary of the signing of the Constitution. The committee is as follows: Hon. Doane Robinson, Pierre; R. E. Cone, Huron; Dr. E. L. Perkins, Sioux Falls; Dr. E. S. Adams, Yankton; R. L. Slagle, Vermilion; R. F. Kerr, Brookings; Dr. J. G. Parsons, Sioux Falls; Mark Slaymaker, Pipestone, Minn.; Hon. Howard Gates, Pierre; J. E. Mather, Watertown; Fred A. Reynolds, Chamberlain; Tad A. Bailey, Pipestone, Minn.; Clyde & McGinatie, Hecla; Col. A. B. Sessions, Sioux Falls; Rev. Guy P. Squires, Brookings; J. W. Goff, Madison; F. M. Mills, chairman, Sioux Falls.

The committee interested other patriotic associations and civic societies, clubs, chambers of commerce, boards of education, schools, colleges, fraternal and bar associations, State and county authorities, and all good citizens generally and solicited the support of the press of the State. Circulars were mailed throughout the State. Personal letters were written to the members of the committee, patriotic organizations, regents of the Daughters of the American Revolution, heads of colleges and principals of high schools. Circulars were sent to all the newspapers, and prominent men throughout the State were asked to co-operate so as to promote the observance of the day. The Governor issued a proclamation. A public meeting at Sioux Falls was very largely attended. The President of the State Society presided. The music was furnished by the Sioux Falls Band. The singing was led by the Community Society, and there was an address, "The Constitution Then and Now," by Rev. L. Wendell Fifield. The meeting closed by the audience singing the "Star Spangled Banner."

Utah.—Throughout the State of Utah the Sons of the American Revolution held patriotic services commemorating Constitution Day, in which participated members of the Sons of the American Revolution. On Monday evening, September 19, at Hotel Utah, Salt Lake City, Utah, the Sons of the American Revolution observed the day by tending a banquet in honor of our President General, Wallace McCamant. At this banquet the presiding officer used a gavel that was presented to the National Society in May, 1920, the head made of wood from Faneuil Hall and the handle from the old State House of Boston. In addition to this, the gavel has twenty-one inserts. One is a piece of Plymouth Rock, one is wood from the home of Paul Revere, one from the home of Asa Pollard, who was the first man killed in the Battle of Bunker Hill; one from the Old North bridge at Concord, where the shot was fired which was "heard around the world"; one from the man-o'-war *Somerset*, which took part in the Battle of Bunker Hill, and one from the elm tree at Cambridge, Mass., under which Washington took command of the army of the Revolution. President General McCamant was the principal speaker.

Your committee regrets exceedingly that this is only a partial report, as many State Directors have failed to send in their reports of meetings in their respective States. The committee, however, thank those State directors who have aided the committee in making up this report. Unfortunately, the committee has had to rely upon outside information, such as newspaper clippings and accounts sent in by departments of education, chambers of commerce, boards of trade, and other patriotic and civic organizations. As far as possible, the committee reports the number of celebrations as follows:

Alabama	24
Alaska	102
Arkansas	17
Arizona	321
California	211
Connecticut	1
Colorado	107
Delaware	27
District of Columbia	1
Florida	161
Georgia	22
Idaho	41
Illinois	2,874
Indiana	707
Iowa	811
Kansas	83
Kentucky	69
Maine	183
Maryland	1,300
Massachusetts	1,424
Michigan	809
Missouri	1,144
Montana	63
New Hampshire	302
New Jersey	12,042
New York	11,418
North Carolina	217
Ohio	1,642
Oklahoma	246
Oregon	3,100
Panama Canal Zone	1
Pennsylvania	2,449

Porto Rico..   2
Tennessee   81
South Dakota..   92
Utah   7
Vermont   30
Virginia   17
Washington   410
Wisconsin   103
West Virginia..   3
                                                                      _____
    Total.. 42,664

Respectfully submitted,

LOUIS ANNIN AMES,

Chairman, Committee on the Observance of Constitution Day.

PRESENTATION BY CHANCELLOR GENERAL BONNIWELL OF THE ORDER OF LAFAYETTE TO MARSHAL FOCH

During the great reception given to Marshal Foch in Philadelphia on November 16, Judge Bonniwell, Chancellor General of the National Society, Sons of the American Revolution, presented to the great French leader the order of Lafayette. This ceremony was carried out at the Washington statue, Judge Bonniwell speaking as follows:

"We, who are descendants of the American patriots who fought for liberty under the direct command of Lafayette, eternally grateful to heroic France for her fearless aid at the hour of our Nation's birth, ask for the supreme honor of enrolling you a member of the Order of Lafayette.

"The succor which the youthful, the gallant, the intrepid Marquis brought the thirteen Colonies, you brought the world.

"You have confounded the enemies of France, not merely by your incomparable military tactics, but by your humility, and your allegiance to Almighty God. You have inspired the lovers of France. You have reanimated the cause of real Christianity.

"Therefore, in pledge of an undying amity, we make you a Comrade of the Order of Lafayette, saying to you, and to your land, that the affection between the immortal Washington and Lafayette shall always endure between America and France.

"Your enemies will be our enemies, your grief our sorrow, your triumph our pride."

WHAT SHALL WE DO ABOUT IT?

An appeal comes from one of our most active compatriots in the South, suggesting a possible reorganization of our Society on a basis similar to that of our sister Society, the Daughters of the American Revolution, which, it is pointed out, has a membership of over one hundred thousand, while our Society, the predecessor and progenitor of the other, has less than twenty thousand. The compatriot goes on to say that if the Society of Sons of the American Revolution was run on the same business plan as the Daughters, the membership could be quadrupled in a short time.

There is, no doubt, some truth in what our enthusiastic compatriot says, and it might be well for our members to stop and consider for a moment what are the possibilities of a society such as ours. When the Congress met in Buffalo last May, the proprietor of the headquarters hotel said to several of the members that in all his convention experience, and that had been large, he had never seen a finer body of men attending a convention. This was not a mere perfunctory remark, but made with sincere feeling and honesty. When we realize that men of this stamp from all parts of the country are giving of their time and abilities to carry on the work of patriotism and the achievement of American ideals, we must believe that some lasting results have been obtained, and the history of our Society and its work bears this out. Now, if these results could be multiplied by three or four, by increasing our membership to that extent, the potentialities of what could be attained for good in this nation are untold. That this sort of work is needed in the present crisis of our country's history goes without saying; that the unrest that is being fomented not only in Europe, but in this country, by sinister influences needs a counterbalance of the kind that an organization like ours can give goes without saying, and it is easy to appreciate that one hundred thousand men with ideals and traditions that are bred in the bone, like ours, scattered from Maine to California, and from the Great Lakes to the Gulf, and working in harmony with one hundred thousand or more women with similar ideals and traditions, could wield an influence that would be a bulwark against the menace of Bolshevism and radicalism and all the other evil influences that are confronting us at this time.

The trouble with our organization seems to be that too few of our members are doing the real work of the organization. In every Society or Chapter there are one or two, or just a small group, who are active and enthusiastic, and the rest seem satisfied to trail along and concur in everything that suits them and object to the things that do not, but take no active part in the work.

It is not quite fair to compare our organization to that of the Daughters, for the social side appeals to these women more than it does to the men, and their organization being on a chapter basis, with an active centralized governing body in their Board of Management, has been the real reason for their remarkable growth in the first place; and, now that they have become such a national power, the advantage of membership has become so apparent that new members come to them without having to be urged, as is the case with many of our applicants.

Concretely, what can be done to overcome this attitude, not only of our own members, but of those whom we are seeking as desirable compatriots? To ascertain this, let us stop to consider what has been done and what is being done at the present time by some of our State Societies, Chapters, and individuals.

The Louisiana Society, under the leadership of Colonel Churchill, not only won the traveling banner a year or so ago, but has lately made wonderful strides in membership and activities; the Tennessee Society, through the influence of past President General Thruston and the leadership of Mr. Boardman and its present remarkably able and enthusiastic Secretary, Frederick Millspaugh, is going ahead by leaps and bounds, and many of our larger societies will have to look to their laurels if they wish to keep up with Tennessee; the results in New Jersey and Maryland, which won the banners last year, speak for themselves; in the West we have a splendid and growing Society in Utah. These are the glowing instances, though there are many others that could be named. What has done this? Hard, earnest, and sincere *personal* work by enthusiastic members who have the interest of the Society at heart. If such results can be accomplished in some States, why not in the whole Society? The plan that was devised a few years ago, of dividing the country into sections, under the direction of the Vice-Presidents General, is a most practical and complete one; but, lacking a central head or directing power, has it accomplished as great results as might have been expected?

Our President General is elected for one year, under the custom that has grown up. His Executive Committee is scattered from one end of the country to the other. They are men, generally, of unusual abilities and attainments, who give much of their time and attention to the workings of the Society, but from the very fact of their living so far apart, they cannot give that attention and direction to details that is needed to carry out what is necessary to bring the best results.

The Daughters of the American Revolution have a central head and managing board, meeting monthly, and, because of their great membership, a much larger income with which they can carry out their splendid plans for patriotic work. Is it not possible for the Sons of the American Revolution to work out some plan that will put us on a similar basis, so that we shall go forward with these noble women in a mutual effort to make America keep the ideals that were our ancestors' and should be kept alive for the centuries to come?

EVENTS OF STATE SOCIETIES

The District of Columbia Society, upon invitation of the War Department, took part in the parade accompanying the body of the "Unknown Soldier" to Arlington, and a delegation of good size was present. Several members of other State Societies came to Washington and joined in the parade with the local organization. These included Vice-President General, George Hale Nutting, and Burton H. Wiggin, Vice-President of the Massachusetts Society, of Massachusetts, and the following representatives from the Pennsylvania Society: Col. R. W. Guthrie, National Trustee; Hon. Samuel B. McCormick, Hon. W. C. Lyne, and O. S. Decker. The visitors marched the entire distance to Arlington, and were provided with seats in the Amphitheater during the ceremonies. The National Society presented a wreath, which was carried by the District of Columbia delegation and which was given a place of honor before the altar in the Amphitheater preceding the ceremonies, in spite of the hundreds of other floral offerings which came from all parts of the country.

The District of Columbia Society, S. A. R., in co-operation with the Sons of the Revolution of the District of Columbia, are offering a gold medal for the best essay upon the subject "The Expedition of George Rogers Clark, 1778," to pupils of public and private schools in the District of Columbia. The committee of judges, of which our Registrar General, Mr. William S. Parks, is chairman, has issued a circular announcing the contest and rules to be observed. The presentation of this medal will be made on February 22, and will be a notable event, as President Harding will personally present the reward.

The Hawaiian Society held its annual business meeting at Cook's Hall, Y. M. C. A. Building, at noon on Tuesday, October 4, the President, Rev. Henry P. Judd, presiding. New officers were elected for the ensuing year, as follows: President, Donald S. Bowman; Vice-President, Dr. C. B. Cooper; Treasurer, L. M. Judd; Registrar, Gerrit P. Wilder; Secretary, James T. Taylor; C. S. Carlsmith, Eben P. Low, and H. B. Penhallow, managers. By request, a delegation to represent the Sons of the American Revolution at the meeting of the American Legion on Thursday, October 6, was appointed to arrange plans for a celebration of Armistice Day. An invitation from the local Chapter of the Daughters of the American Revolution to co-operate with them in a proper celebration of Lexington Day, April 17, 1922, was unanimously accepted.

The newly elected President, Mr. Bowman, expressed his appreciation of the honor conferred and his expectation that renewed interest and activity for the coming year would be greatly in evidence.

The officers and Board of Managers of the Society held a meeting at Cooke's Hall on Tuesday, November 22. President Donald S. Bowman presided. The Secretary, James T. Taylor, reported verbally on the activities of the Society in the Armistice Parade. The new banner was displayed to the public view for the first time and was carried by the Secretary. The President appeared in Colonial costume and led this section of the parade.

The Society made a very creditable showing and was subject of much favorable comment. President Bowman appointed the following committee of arrangements to act with the Daughters of the American Revolution in the celebration of Lexington Day: Charles Atherton, chairman; Gerrit P. Wilder and Eben P. Low. The following resolution was unanimously adopted:

Whereas the shortage of labor is seriously affecting the agricultural and all other industries in Hawaii; and

Whereas each and every other person in Hawaii will be seriously affected if not relieved,

We therefore, in meeting assembled, pray the United States Congress to give us relief by passing House Joint Resolution No. 171.

The Illinois Society held its annual meeting and election of officers on Friday evening, December 2, at the Central Y. M. C. A. café. An informal dinner was held at 6:30, and after the election of officers and reports of the Society for the year were read, an address on "Our Soldiers at the Front" was given by Brigadier-General Abel Davis, who inspired us by his wonderful tribute to the heroism of our boys at the front.

The following officers were elected for the ensuing year: President, James M. Eddy; First Vice-President, Jesse A. Baldwin; Second Vice-President, James Edgar Brown; Secretary, Louis A. Bowman; Treasurer, Henry R. Kent; Historian, George A. Brennan; Registrar, John D. Vandercook; Chaplain, William W. Johnstone, D. D.; Sergeant-at-Arms, Cil R. Boman; Additional Board of Managers, Burton J. Ashley, I. S. Blackwelder, Chancellor L. Jenks, William P. Reed, Carroll H. Sudler, David V. Webster; Delegate at Large, Dorr E. Felt. Colonel Eddy, who was elected President, represented Illinois, by appointment of the War Department, at the Armistice Day services in Washington, November 11, 1921. He was retired after forty years' service of continuous military duty in Illinois National Guard. He served on the border and throughout the World War as Lieutenant-Colonel of the 131st Regiment, United States Army, formerly the 1st Illinois Regiment, National Guard. Since the election of officers the Society has had the great misfortune to lose by death two of its officers elected at the annual meeting. First Vice-President Jesse A. Baldwin passed away December 8 and Burton J. Ashley, member of the Board of Managers, December 4.

Indiana Society.—The John Morton Chapter of the Indiana Society of Terre Haute, Ind., observed Indiana Day December 12 with a dinner and informal program at Memorial Hall. The new Chapter officers elected at the annual meeting, September 4, assumed their duties. Judge George Addison Scott, President of the Chapter, gave a short review of the steps taken by the Congress, the territorial government, and the constitutional convention in erecting the State of Indiana out of the Northwest Territory and the admission of the State into the Union, December 11, 1816.

Prof. Herbert Briggs reported encouraging progress in the undertaking of the Chapter to provide for the regular study of Indiana history in the public schools. This movement was launched by the Chapter following the observance of the centennial of the Battle of Fort Harrison in 1912. The program has now enlisted the support of the State Board of Education and other patriotic and historical societies. In addition to an accepted text-book on Indiana history, there will be provided a questionnaire to develop the study of history in the various counties.

Report was made on the progress of the Indiana Society committee on the marking of graves of soldiers of the War of Independence. Compatriot Dalton B. Shourds was appointed chairman of a committee to locate appropriate places along the old Indian boundary provided in the treaty between General William Henry Harrison and the Indians. This boundary, known as "The 10 o'clock Line," crosses the Wabash River near Montezuma and intersects the National Highway, the Dixie Bee Line Highway, and other old trail roads. The Chapter will co-operate with the Indiana State Highway Commission in erecting the markers.

The new officers of John Morton Chapter are Judge George Addison Scott, President; Will W. Adamson and Leslie Seymour Creal, Vice-Presidents; Oscar Rankin, Chaplain; Prof. Herbert Briggs, Historian; Horace E. Tune, Treasurer, and National Trustee Charles Timothy Jewett, Secretary. It is the purpose of the Chapter to erect in Memorial Hall a bronze tablet bearing the names of the soldiers of the War of Independence buried in Vigo County.

The annual meeting of the Indiana Society will be held in Indianapolis, on February 25, 1922, in celebration of the anniversary of the capture of Fort Sackville, Vincennes, by George Rogers Clark.

The Kentucky Society celebrated the surrender of Cornwallis at Yorktown with a dinner at the Pendennis Club on October 19. Preceding the dinner the annual election of officers was held and the following were elected for the ensuing year: President, E. T. Hutchings; Vice-Presidents, J. Swigert Taylor, Curran Pope, Raymond Grant, and E. S. Woosley; Secretary, George D. Caldwell; Registrar, Ben La Bree; Historian, James H. Richmond; Chaplain, E. L. Powell; Surgeon, Richard H. Coke.

The retiring President, Mr. Marvin H. Lewis, epitomized the reports of the various committees which had been at work during the past year and spoke, among other things, of the committee which is preparing to place a bronze tablet in or on the Louisville Public Library to record the fact that the 57 trees planted in the library grounds in memory of Louisville soldiers who lost their lives in the World War were placed there under the auspices of this Society, in co-operation with 56 other civic and patriotic organizations, each having contributed a sum sufficient to pay for one tree, at the request of the Kentucky Society, S. A. R. The Committee on Immigration is working hard to promote a law restricting immigration. He stated that 80 per cent of all memorials received by Congress came from organizations with which our organization had corresponded; that the service records of 52 members who saw armed service in the World War had been collected by the Committee on Patriotic Service, this number being about 25 per cent of the membership; spoke of the successful prize-essay contest conducted by the Committee on Patriotic Education among the schools of Louisville; the appropriate celebration of Constitution Day in the Louisville and State schools and churches at the instigation of the Kentucky Society, and the giving of a scholarship of $125 in either the Louisville University or Kentucky University, to be awarded to one of five students of the senior classes of the high schools of the State having best average on competitive examination.

Another feature of the evening was the address by Compatriot James H. Richmond on the engrossing subject of disarmament. At the request of the Society, the address was printed in full in the Louisville papers.

The Maine Society held an interesting meeting of its Board of Managers on November 28, at which a report from the committee appointed by the State Society in February, 1920, to request an appropriation for a new bronze tablet to be placed on the marker at Valley Forge was received. The committee of three, comprising Hon. A. M. Spear, Hon. Oliver B. Clason, and Mr. M. Converse Leach, appeared before the Maine Legislature to request the appropriation desired, and were successful in securing an appropriation of $600. At the recent meeting in November, Compatriots William B. Berry, President of the Maine Society; William K. Sanderson, Hon. A. M. Spear, and Charles L. Hutchinson were appointed a committee to obtain sketches and prices for the tablet and submit the same to Governor Percival P. Baxter and Council for their formal approval. Compatriot E. Leander Higgins, architect, of Portland, is preparing sketches.

The State Society reports encouraging progress in the matter of securing increased membership, and plans for more extended publicity of its activities, which will be of direct aid to this increase. At the November meeting the election of a National Trustee to fill the vacancy caused by the death of the Hon. James O. Bradbury resulted in the selection of William B. Berry, of Gardiner, the new President of the State Society.

The Maryland Society held an interesting meeting on October 19, which was addressed by the Hon. William Miles Maloy, chairman of the Public Service Commission of the State of Maryland, on the Irish question. Mr. Maloy spent the summer traveling through Ireland, getting first-hand information on the Sinn Fein and Ulster questions. The Society is forging ahead with the work on the American's Creed and hopes that after the good start made this year they will be able to have the School Board of Maryland furnish copies of the American's Creed Book to the graduates each year. The Society held a meeting on November 23 in Frederick, Maryland, as the guests of the Laurence Everhart Chapter, celebrating the anniversary of the "Repeal of the Frederick County Stamp Act."

The Massachusetts Society.—In August last Francis Lewis Chapter, Walpole, celebrated the fifth anniversary of its organization with appropriate and highly interesting ceremonies, it having been organized by its present President on August 13, 1916. Its present officers are: President, Isaac Newton Lewis; First Vice-President, Louis E. Vose; Second Vice-President, Percyval Lewis; Third Vice-President, William A. Millard; Secretary, Walter B. Allen; Treasurer, George A. Plimpton; Registrar, John H. Allen; Historian and Librarian, Isaac Newton Lewis.

Although the ancestor for whom the Chapter was named was from New York, the members often gather at his grave in the old Trinity Churchyard, near the Schuyler, Livingston, and Hamilton families. The headstone is quite humble, but clearly legible, much more so than the 140 graves annually honored with a Betsy Ross flag here on Memorial Day by the members. A service with full publicity of all events is deemed a duty by the Chapter. The Chapter is organized for the good it can do; not for a good time. But one member has been lost by death and two from resignation. Being the only Chapter in the country which gave two Presidents to the Nation, it has tried to arouse a commensurate loyalty and interest in patriotic things.

THE GEORGE WASHINGTON CHAPTER, of Springfield, is making plans for the entertainment of the National Society when it holds its Congress in that city, in May, 1922. There is no city in the country so well fitted to care for conventions as is Springfield. It has an auditorium unsurpassed by any in the country, with a seating capacity for over four thousand and an organ costing $20,000. There is a Mahogany Room in the building which reminds one of stories from the Arabian Nights. The hotel accommodations of the city are equal to a city three times its size. It has one park of about 700 acres and sixty or seventy smaller ones. A United States armory and arsenal is located there, and railroads run north, east, south, and west, there being over 200 trains each day entering and leaving the Union Station. There are two colleges in the city, the International Y. M. C. A. College and the American International College, and three others, Amherst, Smith, and Mount Holyoke, but a few miles away. For newspapers it has the *Springfield Republican, Springfield Union,* and *Springfield Daily News* and the different farm papers published by the Phelps Publishing Company, among which being the *Farm and Home* and the *New England Homestead.* The Nayasset Club, one of the best-known clubs in New England, is located in the city in its own building and the Colony Club owns and occupies the mansion built by the late D. B. Wesson. Webster's Dictionary is published in the city.

Michigan Society.—Constitution Day was observed generally in Michigan. William P. Holliday, President of Michigan Society, S. A. R., acting as General Chairman of the committee for Michigan, invited the participation of the several Chapters and other patriotic and public organizations and the schools. In Detroit appropriate exercises were arranged in the public schools by Superintendent Frank Cody, following the suggestions of the S. A. R. Washtenaw Chapter, at Ann Arbor, and Oakland Chapter, at Pontiac, also observed the day.

DETROIT CHAPTER, at a reception tendered newly admitted citizens by the Board of Commerce, presented each new citizen with a silk United States flag. Dr. Minot C. Morgan, Chaplain, Michigan Society, S. A. R., made the presentations.

The members of Detroit Chapter were invited to the reception tendered by the Detroit and Highland Park Chapters of the D. A. R. to the delegates attending their annual State conference held at Detroit.

Detroit Chapter, S. A. R., was honored by the American Legion, in that President Carl F. Clarke was invited to assist in the reception of Marshal Foch during his recent visit to Detroit.

Detroit Chapter held its first meeting of the season November 22, at the University Club. Judge Fred H. Aldrich was the guest and spoke on "Efforts to Maintain the Peace of the World by Limitation of Armaments." Judge Aldrich is professor of international law at the Detroit College of Law and author of a book upon the subject indicated. Buffet lunch and cigars were served. Service medals were presented.

Detroit Chapter gave a dinner at the Hotel Statler, December 6, in honor of its guest, Rear-Admiral William Snowden Sims, U. S. N. President Carl F. Clarke presided. Dr. James W. Inches, Commissioner, welcomed the Admiral in the absence of the mayor. Rev. Minot C. Morgan, Chaplain, Sons of the American Revolution, gave the invocation. Compatriot Dr. Earl C. Barkley, Chairman of the Committee on National Defense, under the auspices of which the meeting was held, sang. Rear-Admiral Fullam, U. S. N., also participated. Four hundred guests were present, including ladies. Compatriot Harold F. Emmons was chairman of the Committee of Arrangements and was assisted by Rufus H. Knight, George E. Bushnell, John W. Starrett, C. E. Frazer Clark, Allen Ludington, E. M. Bosley, and the Secretary, Raymond E. Van Syckle.

OAKLAND CHAPTER held its annual banquet at Pontiac in November. George E. Bushnell, Vice-President of Detroit Chapter, was invited to give the address. William P. Holliday, President of the State Society, S. A. R., and Carl F. Clarke, President of Detroit Chapter, also attended and spoke. Lieutenant Patterson, of Pontiac, participated. Clarence K. Redfield, President of Oakland Chapter, presided. Service medals were presented.

LENAWEE CHAPTER enjoyed a dinner at the Adrian Club during November, at which Service medals were presented to those entitled. President Wilbert H. Barrett presided.

KENT CHAPTER held a meeting December 6 at Grand Rapids.

The Missouri Society.—The annual banquet of the Missouri Society was held October 19, commemorating the 140th Anniversary of the Surrender of Cornwallis at Yorktown. W. D. Vandiver, President of the Missouri Society, Sons of the American Revolution, presided and made a brief address, reviewing the activities of the State organization. Linn Paine, Registrar of the Society and chairman of the National Committee on Patriotic Education, told of the work that was being done by the National Society to insure accuracy in histories supplied for text-books in our public schools. Col. John H. Parker, Commandant at Jefferson Barracks, delivered the chief address of the evening, reviewing the events of the land and naval forces leading to Cornwallis' surrender. Music was furnished by Dr. Allan A. Gilbert, accompanied by Miss Carmichael.

In the afternoon, preceding the banquet, the Board of Managers held a special meeting at the Planters' Hotel for the purpose of accepting the resignation of W. Scott Hancock, Secretary of the Society, caused by ill health. J. Alonzo Matthews was elected his successor for the unexpired term.

Nebraska Society.—Armistice Day is becoming the chief patriotic holiday and was observed by a patriotic parade in which all societies joined. Lincoln Chapter and the D. A. R. chapters took part in our parade November 11.

Dr. Benjamin F. Bailey, President of the State Society, was elected president of the Lincoln Commercial Club for the ensuing year. George Alvin Dana, Vice-President of the Nebraska Society, died at his home, in Lincoln, October 27, 1921. He was born in Camden, New York, in 1864 and has been a resident of Lincoln since 1866. Mr. Dana was quiet, efficient, active in the Methodist Church and in all patriotic causes, and universally beloved. He was a charter member of Lincoln Chapter. Joseph Leeper Codington, of Omaha, has the best record for new membership secured for the Nebraska Society during the past year. He is an enthusiastic worker for both the principles and membership of the Sons of the American Revolution.

Rev. W. F. Eyster, D. D., a member of Crete Chapter, Nebraska, died June 18, 1921, making him 99 years and five months old. He was the oldest college graduate in the United States at the time of his death. He was born in Gettysburg, January 20, 1822. Entered Penn College at the age of 11 and graduated at the age of 17, in 1839. Spent two years in the Lutheran Theological School. In 1841 he became principal of the school at Jefferson, Md. He was ordained the following year, at Frederick, Md., and served Lutheran congregations until 1858, when he became principal of the Hagerstown Female Seminary. He was married in 1850, to Lucretia Gibson, in Philadelphia, Pa. Dr. Eyster had many thrilling and interesting experiences in giving aid and comfort to the Union soldiers as they crossed and recrossed the Mason and Dixon Line. He heard Lincoln deliver his famous address at Gettysburg. Dr. Eyster became professor of English language and literature in the college at Rock Island in 1873, but resigned in 1883 on account of his impaired hearing. He built a home in Crete, Nebr., where he spent the remaining years of his life, in almost perfect health, with the companionship of his unmarried son and daughter. He retained his brilliant mind and interest in people and events to the very last.

Invitation has been received from Genoa, Nebraska, to organize a local chapter, S. A. R. Genoa is one of the important historical places in Nebraska, former site of the Pawnee Nation and of many Indian battles. The D. A. R. Chapter at Genoa is active in promoting a S. A. R. Chapter.

The New Jersey State Society, with characteristic enterprise, has purchased a three-story and basement brick house in a desirable part of Newark for its permanent headquarters. It has formed a Real Estate Holding Company to take title to the property and issue first-mortgage, 6 per cent sinking fund bonds to pay for the same. The bonds have been promptly subscribed for and the Society has taken possession of the property. The house is attractively located at No. 33 Lombardy Street, facing a small city park. Lombardy Street runs east from Broad Street, opposite the famous Washington Monument. The building, which is to be occupied as the headquarters of the New Jersey Society, Sons of the American Revolution, as well as by one or two other patriotic societies, is in excellent repair; has running water on all floors, good heating plant, and light; also kitchen in basement. The lot, being 150 feet deep, will allow space for the erection later of an auditorium seating 400. Besides being ideally located for headquarters of the Society, it is situated in that part of Newark which is fast enhancing in value. New Jersey is the first State Society in the country to own its own headquarters.

CAPTAIN ABRAHAM GODWIN CHAPTER, No. 12, was organized in Paterson on Saturday, October 22, by Rev. Dr. Lyman Whitney Allen, President of the State Society. An automobile trip was first taken to the headquarters of Lafayette, at Preakness, and also the headquarters of General Washington, in the famous Dey House, both in the vicinity of Paterson. The officers of the new Chapter are: President, Albert Lincoln Wyman; Vice-President, Ide Gill Sergeant; Recording Secretary, Major Augustus Van Gieson; Corresponding

Secretary, Dr. William H. Rauchfuss; Treasurer, Nicholas M. Townley, Jr.; Registrar, Dr. Frank R. Sandt; Chaplain, Rev. George L. Labaw; Historian, Louis C. Schermerhorn. Eighty members were placed on the roster at roll-call, and the Chapter bids fair to become most active in the patriotic work in the city founded by Alexander Hamilton in 1792. It was Hamilton's expectation to there found a great industrial city, and his expectations, though frustrated during his life, have been brought to a complete realization in 1920.

MONTCLAIR CHAPTER held a very interesting meeting in the Art Museum, in that city, November 10. The principal address was delivered by Bishop Wilson R. Stearly, Chaplain of the State Society, in consonance with the spirit of Armistice Day (it being the eve). He claimed that the Conference on the Limitation of Armaments should appeal to every earnest, patriotic citizen. Mayor McConnell, one of the new twenty-five members, also delivered an address. The Eagle Rock Chapter, D. A. R., and Rev. Dr. Lyman Whitney Allen, State President, were the guests of honor.

ORANGE CHAPTER has been presented with a handsome silk flag of buff, white, and blue by its President, John Lenord Merrill. The presentation took place on the night of October 20, and the Chapter was very pleasantly surprised. Mr. Merrill is serving his second term as President, having occupied the office in 1906 and 1907. Thomas W. Williams, past Vice-President General, who was in the chair during the ceremonies, has written a letter to Compatriot Merrill, by direction of the Chapter, expressing its appreciation for his generous act.

PASSAIC VALLEY CHAPTER held a patriotic meeting on Armistice Day, in connection with the G. A. R., American Legion, and Veterans of Foreign Wars, in the town of Summit, where the Chapter is located. Compatriot Oliver B. Merrill, Mayor, presided, and addresses were made by Hon. Ruford Franklin and Irving Bacheller, the noted novelist.

WEST FIELDS CHAPTER, No. 11, New Jersey Society, Sons of the American Revolution, held forth on the evening of December 15 at the Congregational Church in Westfield in an old-fashioned patriotic rally. The occasion marked the presentation of the charter by the State Society to the Chapter. H. Donald Holmes, chairman of the Committee on Chapters, was master of ceremonies. Rev. Dr. Lyman Whitney Allen, Chaplain General and President of the New Jersey Society, presented the charter, and made an address upon the work of the National, State, and Chapter organizations. The beautiful flag of stars and stripes and the one of buff, white, and blue were also presented during the evening by Compatriot Pearsall, of the West Fields Chapter. The occasion was graced by the West Fields Chapter of the D. A. R. and the evening was very happily spent in a program of addresses and music. The State Board of Managers was largely represented. The charter for the Captain Abraham Godwin Chapter of Paterson will be presented on a date to be fixed in February.

ELIZABETHTOWN CHAPTER met at the new headquarters of the State Society, 33 Lombardy Street, Newark, on December 12, and listened to an address by Captain W. B. Estes, of New York, formerly a United States Army intelligence officer, on what communism really is and how it affects the liberties of the American people. Richard S. Earl, President of the Chapter, presided.

The Board of Managers, at its meeting on December 9, elected Col. Charles A. Andrews Assistant Registrar, the office being created on account of the increasing number of members being appreciated and of the many inquiries being made of a genealogical character.

The New Jersey Society is preparing to receive President General Wallace McCamant in February. He will be met in New York and escorted to New Jersey, where a reception will be given him at headquarters on February 18, and on the following day he will speak at a patriotic service in Montclair.

Empire State Society.—The regular meeting of the New York Chapter was held on Monday, October 31, 1921, at 8 p. m., the anniversary of the organization of the Sons of Liberty, at the new home of the Army and Navy Club of America, 112 West 59th Street, New York City. The New York Chapter has furnished the "directors' room" there. This date being also the 40th anniversary of the death of President Garfield, Henry C. Quimby, Esq., Vice-President of the Union League Club, talked on "The Marvelous Career of Our Martyr President." It was a rare treat to hear Mr. Quimby and a large number availed themselves of the opportunity. Hon. Harvey F. Remington, President of the Empire State Society, was present. The usual collation was served at the close of the meeting. Oliver B. Bridgman, President, presided.

The annual banquet was planned for November, contingent upon the ability of Marshal Foch, of France, to be the guest of honor. His itinerary prevented him from fixing on a suitable date and the banquet has therefore been deferred until 1922.

The American Legion, in connection with New York Chapter, Sons of the American Revolution, and other patriotic societies, had a service at Madison Square Garden on Armistice Day at 11 a. m. The ceremonies at Arlington were reproduced by amplifier, so that all the Garden was able to hear the President's oration and the other services. The great hall was more than filled, and overflowed into Madison Square, where amplifiers also reproduced the Washington ceremonies so all could hear them.

Rochester Chapter elected the following officers October 17th at a regular meeting: President, Raymond G. Dann; Vice-President, William B. Boothby; Secretary, Charles A. Brady; Treasurer, John B. Howe; Registrar, Edward R. Foreman; Historian, Fred L. Yates; Chaplain, Rev. James T. Dickinson. The following were elected to the Board of Managers: The officers and Charles E. Ogden, *ex officio;* George B. Sage, *ex officio;* Charles H. Wiltsie, Harvey F. Remington, Colonel Samuel C. Pierce, and Judge Arther E. Sutherland. George W. Aldridge was elected to the Board of Managers of the State Society. The principal speaker was Edward R. Foreman, who outlined the plans for compiling a history of Rochester during the World War.

The work to be undertaken by this Chapter for the coming year is as follows: Americanization work in connection with the Daughters of the American Revolution and the Rochester Chamber of Commerce, under the direction of Past President Sage. The commemoration and marking of historical spots in and about Rochester, in co-operation with the Rochester Historical Society and the Daughters of the American Revolution. The carrying forward of marking the graves of American Revolutionary soldiers buried in Monroe County. Drive to increase membership.

THE COL. CORNELIUS VAN DYCK CHAPTER, in co-operation with the Schenectady Chapter of the Daughters of the American Revolution and the Beukendaal Chapter of the Daughters of the American Revolution, on November 15 heard Mr. James O. Fagan, curator of the famous Old South Meeting House, Boston, speak on "The Romance of Early New England History." He spread the wonderful story, from its beginnings into its wider significance, with fascinating interest. The regular December meeting was held December 5th.

GENESEE CHAPTER, BATAVIA, had a large attendance at its regular meeting, on October 29. It was decided to co-operate with Deo-on-go-wa Chapter, D. A. R., in the search for the graves of all Revolutionary soldiers in Genesee County. A committee, consisting of F. M. Richards, D. L. Wilkinson, and Fred J. Pomeroy, was appointed. At the monthly meeting, November 26, favorable reports were made. Charles R. Loomis will speak at the December meeting on "The Causes of the American Revolution." The officers of the Chapter are: W. H. A. Spink, President; G. G. Dexter, Vice-President; C. Randall Howe, Secretary; G. H. Paddock, Treasurer.

NEWTOWN BATTLE CHAPTER, ELMIRA.—At a special meeting of the Chapter at the Neighborhood House, a social settlement center for the youth of all creeds and nationalities, with over 500 enrolled in their various clubs and classes, a portrait of George Washington, given by the State Society, was unveiled with appropriate ceremonies. The annual meeting was held in the Chapter rooms November 5. It was voted to discontinue rental of separate rooms and unite with the local D. A. R. Society in the upkeep and use of Chapter rooms.

Officers for the ensuing year were elected as follows: President, Jesse L. Churchill; Vice-President, H. H. Bickford; Second Vice-President, H. S. Chapman; Secretary, G. M. Diven, 615 Hoffman Street; Treasurer, Chas. L. Hart; Registrar, H. C. Millspaugh; Historian, J. A. Olmstead; Chaplain, J. H. Pierce.

SYRACUSE CHAPTER held its annual dinner at the University Club, Syracuse, on the 14th of November. About forty members attended the dinner. After the dinner the annual meeting of the Chapter was held and the officers elected for the ensuing year were: President, Newell B. Woodworth; Vice-President, William W. Wiard; Secretary, Charles C. Cook; Treasurer, Willis E. Gaylord; Registrar, J. Frank Durston; Historian, Prof. Frederick F. Moon; Chaplain, Rev. Dr. Walter R. Ferris.

BUFFALO CHAPTER is planning a series of meetings, beginning in December and continuing for the following three or four months. The Chapter will be entertained by Dr. Van Bergen, the President, in January.

The Ohio Society.—The members of the Ohio Society have been very active in Americanization work during the summer and fall months by encouraging naturalization of foreigners and observance of Constitution Day in the public schools of the State.

A letter was prepared by the President and Secretary of the State Society and forwarded to the superintendents of schools in every county of the State, 88 in number, appealing to them to observe Constitution Day. A copy of a very interesting patriotic letter received by the Secretary of the Society from President Warren G. Harding, who is a member of the Society, was also enclosed to the school superintendents above noted. Copies of these letters were sent to all the Chapter officers, to several patriotic organizations, and notices were also published in many of the daily newspapers in the State, calling attention to observance of the day. Patriotic services were held in many of the schools, and in fact the observance was general, and there have been received a number of interesting letters from superintendents, giving the programs and expressing appreciation for copies of the Constitution and the booklet, "Information for Immigrants," many copies of which were distributed to the schools by the Society.

In the cities, members of the Chapter took an active interest in naturalization of foreigners. Two public meetings were held by our members in Columbus, at which a reception was held for newly naturalized citizens, during the summer, and their final papers were delivered. The D. A. R. joined in these meetings, and the families of the new citizens were all invited. There was a patriotic program of music, addresses by members, and the visitors were presented with small American flags. These were very happy occasions and there was much rejoicing by the new citizens and their families.

The members of all the Chapters have been busy in Americanization work, and, summing up results in the public schools and in service assisting in naturalization of foreigners, feel well repaid for the time thus devoted to this patriotic work, and propose to continue in this good service with renewed energy. Upward of thirty members have been added to the rolls of the Ohio Society since the annual meeting in April last.

The Oregon Society held a smoker Wednesday evening, October 19, which was very enjoyable and quite largely attended. Mr. Hugh Montgomery, of Portland, read an exceptionally instructive paper upon "The Participation of the French in the American Revolution," which was greatly appreciated and enjoyed by the members present. After tracing the incidents and events leading up to and accompanying French participation in the Revolution, and referring to the too common belief that the aid given by France was due entirely to selfish national motives and policies and actuated by a revengeful spirit toward England, Mr. Montgomery developed at considerable length the idea that from the time of Louis XIV down to the outbreak of the French Revolution there existed in France an undercurrent of social and political progress, reflected in the writings of their philosophers and men of letters, typifying that force which in ages past had been the vanguard of all social and political progress. The concrete effort of the American Colonies to put this force into practical effect, Mr. Montgomery insisted, invited from the French a sympathy which was reflected in their own corresponding desires. This, he maintained, was the real underlying cause for the French assistance to the American Colonies. It was the common cause of human progress.

The Society was honored with the presence of President General McCamant, who followed Mr. Montgomery in an extremely entertaining and instructive address, in which he commented upon and supplemented the matters contained in Mr. Montgomery's paper and referred to several things of special local interest.

The President General had with him the gavel of the National Society, which, with its souvenir insets from numerous historic places, proved to be an object of decided interest to the members present.

In August the Oregon Society raised a special fund by voluntary subscription among its members for the purpose of providing and erecting three bronze tablets upon the Princeton battlefield. President General McCamant has been greatly interested in this activity and has given material aid and co-operation in making it a success. He enlisted the interest and co-operation of Prof. T. J. Wertenbaker, of Princeton University, who has made a careful study of the Princeton battle and is thoroughly familiar with the topography of the battle-field. Professor Wertenbaker has very kindly prepared the inscriptions for the tablets. The tablets are now being cast, and it is expected that they will be erected either late in October or early in November. Professor Wertenbake-has advised President General McCamant that it is likely that dedicatory cere-monies will be held on the battlefield. The Oregon Society has designated Thomas McCamant, son of President General McCamant and a student of Princeton University, to be the official representative of the Oregon Society at such dedicatory ceremonies as may be held.

The Pennsylvania Society was represented at the services on Armistice Day at Washington for the Unknown Soldier by a special committee of the Pennsyl-vania Society appointed by President James A. Wakefield, who attended the burial service and took part in the exercises with the special committee of the National Society, composed of representatives from every State. The committee of the Pennsylvania Society was composed of Col. R. W. Guthrie, National Trustee; Dr. Samuel B. McCormick, Chancellor Emeritus of the University of Pittsburgh; A. C. Shaw, 1st Vice-President; W. C. Lyne, Chairman of the Memorial Committee; Omar S. Decker and S. E. Gill, of Pittsburgh, and Clarence P. Wynne, of Scranton, Vice-President. A large floral piece of im-mortelles in buff, white, and blue, a replica of the Society's Recognition Button, was placed by the Pennsylvania Committee upon the grave at the close of the services. The Pennsylvania Society celebrated Armistice Day with a dinner and smoker at the Hotel Chatham, Pittsburgh, Dr. William M. Davidson, super-intendent of Pittsburgh public schools, being the principal speaker, his topic "Lafayette." About 150 attended.

South Dakota Society held an appropriate observance of Constitution Day at the Colliseum in Sioux Falls, a meeting which was well attended and most enthusi-astic. The President of the State Society, Mr. Amos E. Ayres, presided and, in addition to inspiring music augmented by community singing, the feature of the evening was an address on "The Constitution Then and Now," by Rev. L. Wen-dell Fifield. President Ayres, who is also President of the Board of Education of Sioux Falls, arranged with the superintendents of schools to have fitting observances in the schools of the city on Friday, September 16. A State-wide committee was also appointed by President Ayres, which succeeded in having suitable ceremonies held in several of the larger cities and towns throughout the State. South Dakota was one of the many States of the Union whose governors issued proclamations calling for appropriate recognition of this day.

Tennessee Society.—A relic recently presented to the Ladies' Hermitage, President Andrew Jackson's old home, is a candle that was burning in Cornwallis' tent at the surrender of Yorktown. It was taken as a souvenir by an American officer and later given to Jackson while President. The candle is about four inches long and age has stained it a deep brown. Since Jackson's death it has been lighted twice, on anniversaries of the Battle of New Orleans.

The Virginia Society, in September, 1921, issued invitations to several civic societies to send delegations to the launching of the scout cruiser *Richmond* at Cramps' ship yards at Philadelphia, which event took place September 29. The Virginia Society, Sons of the American Revolution, was represented by Compatriots Frederick W. Scott, E. D. Hotchkiss, Admiral William Strother Smith, U. S. N., and Arthur B. Clarke, President of the Virginia Society. The customary bottle of wine was hurled and broken by Miss Elizabeth Strother Scott, the beautiful daughter of Compatriot Frederick W. Scott, and Admiral Strother Smith represented also the Secretary of the Navy. After the most successful event, a most inviting lunch was served to the invited guests. There were great crowds present to witness the first ceremonial launching in Cramps' ship yards in six years.

On October 19, the 140th anniversary of the surrender of Lord Cornwallis, took place the formal installation of Dr. J. A. C. Chandler as President of William and Mary College, at Williamsburg, Va., which is near both Yorktown and Jamestown. The President of the United States and four of his Cabinet were present. He spoke at Yorktown, later at William and Mary College, and after lunch drove to Jamestown, the first permanent English settlement on this continent. At the ceremonies at the college were about four thousand visitors, among whom were representatives of all colleges in the United States more than 100 years old.

William and Mary College was founded in 1693 and is the logical successor of the first college, which was established in 1619 and destroyed by the Indians in 1622. Many patriotic societies were represented and participated in the college parade and occupied seats on the large platform erected adjacent to the old college, which was designed by Sir Christopher Wren. By invitation, the President of the Virginia Society represented the Society and presented S. A. R. rosettes to Governor Westmoreland Davis and President Warren G. Harding, both of whom have recently become compatriots. Possibly there were more people present than were ever before in this quaint old colonial town.

The Washington State Society has been actively interested through the latter months in locating graves of Revolutionary Ancestors of the members of that Society, where this has proved possible, and satisfactory progress has been made in this work. The Spokane Chapter has been especially active. The Society has recently presented twenty War Service Medals to members of the Society eligible to receive these because of their active military or naval service in the late war.

ADDITIONS TO MEMBERSHIP.

There have been enrolled in the office of the Registrar-General, from September 30, 1921, to December 1, 1921, 244 new members as follows: California, 20; Colorado, 2; Connecticut, 6; Delaware, 4; District of Columbia, 13; Florida, 1; Georgia, 1; Idaho, 1; Indiana, 4; Illinois, 10; Iowa, 16; Kentucky, 1; Louisiana, 4; Maryland, 6; Maine, 6; Massachusetts, 15; Michigan, 13; Minnesota, 3; Missouri, 1; Nebraska, 2; New Hampshire, 1; New Jersey, 41; New York (Empire State), 26; North Dakota, 1; Ohio, 4; Oregon, 5; Pennsylvania, 14; South Dakota, 2; Tennessee, 6; Texas, 2; Utah, 1; Virginia, 3; Washington State, 4; Wisconsin, 3; Wyoming, 2.

In Memoriam

JAMES EVERETT ALDEN, Connecticut Society, died November 26, 1921.

FRANCIS BURKE ALLEN, Connecticut Society, died July 27, 1921.

DAVID ROYAL ALLING, Connecticut Society, died June 7, 1921.

FREDERICK FISK ANDREWS, Connecticut Society, died March 23, 1921.

JOHN C. AVERILL, Connecticut Society, died August 13, 1919.

THOMAS DE WITT BARLOW, Connecticut Society, died September 16, 1921.

GEORGE WILLIAM BATES, Michigan Society, died October 11, 1921.

MELVILLE M. BIGELOW, Life Member Massachusetts Society, died May 4, 1921.

HOWELL W. BONAWITZ, Massachusetts Society, died May 14, 1921.

EDWIN J. BONETTE, Massachusetts Society, died July 9, 1921.

JAMES O. BRADBURY, Maine Society, died May —, 1921.

FRANK CHAPMAN BUSHNELL, Connecticut Society, died November 24, 1921.

CLAYTON H. CASE, Connecticut Society, died June 24, 1921.

WILLIAM HOPKINS CATLIN, Connecticut Society, died October 28, 1921.

CLINTON L. CONKLING, Illinois Society, died October 12, 1920.

FRANK COWLES, Connecticut Society, died November 24, 1921.

FREDERICK JENNINGS DANIELS, Connecticut Society, died June 15, 1921.

COLONEL FREDERICK W. GALBRAITH, Massachusetts Society, Commander of the American Legion, died June 8, 1921.

CHARLES GRISWOLD, Connecticut Society, died November 6, 1921.

FRANK C. HAYWARD, Massachusetts Society, died September 9, 1921.

EDWARD STEVENS HENRY, Connecticut Society, died October 10, 1921.

ALLEN REID JOBES, Oregon Society, died November 23, 1921.

EMERY W. JOHNSON, Life Member Massachusetts Society, died July 29, 1921.

SEYMOUR CRANE LOOMIS, Connecticut Society, died October 19, 1921.

ALBERT ORRIN MILLER, New Jersey Society, died September 2, 1921.

HENRY B. MILLER, Oregon Society, died November 28, 1921.

ANDREW NICHOLS, Massachusetts Society, died September 18, 1921.

CHARLES W. NOYES, Empire State Society, died December 20, 1921.

GEORGE WAKEMAN OSBORN, Connecticut Society, died October 25, 1921.

FRANK S. PERKINS, Massachusetts Society, died June —, 1921.

WILLARD S. REED, Empire State Society, died ——, 1921.

JESSE C. REMICK, Michigan Society, died April 9, 1919.

AMOS W. RIDEOUT, Massachusetts Society, died October 15, 1921.

FRANK L. SAWYER, Massachusetts Society, died October 16, 1921.

JOHN H. SAWYER, Massachusetts Society, died December 21, 1920.

THOMAS W. SELLORDS, Michigan Society, died October 20, 1921.

ALBERT SHUMWAY, New Jersey Society, died November 14, 1921.

EDWIN ERNEST SIBLEY, Massachusetts Society, died October 13, 1921.

CHARLES LUTHER SPENCER, Connecticut Society, died September 21, 1921.

ALBERT H. STEARNS, Massachusetts Society, died June 5, 1921.

WILLIAM ANDREW STRITMATER, Past President Newcastle, Chapter, Pennsylvania Society, died September 19, 1921.

HARRY F. TAYLOR, Michigan Society, died March 17, 1921.

FRANK V. THOMPSON, Massachusetts Society, died October 23, 1921.

S. EVERETT TINKHAM, Massachusetts Society, died April 21, 1921.

HON. WILLIAM D. TREFRY, Massachusetts Society, died April 11, 1921.

JOHN ROBERT WILLIAMS, New Jersey Society, died November 16, 1921.

FRANK ERNEST WOODWARD, Past President Massachusetts Society, died August 5, 1921.

RECORDS OF 244 NEW MEMBERS AND 59 SUPPLEMENTALS APPROVED AND ENROLLED BY THE REGISTRAR-GENERAL, FROM SEPTEMBER 30, 1921, TO DECEMBER 1, 1921.

ENOCH BOOTHE ABELL, Leonardtown, Md. (35350). Son of James F. and Maria James (Nuthall) Abell; grandson of Enoch B. and Ann (Norris) Abell; great-grandson of John Booth and Elizabeth (——) Abell; great²-grandson of *Enoch Abell*, Lieutenant, St. Marys County, Maryland Militia.

KEMP GIRARD ACKER, Sharon, Pa. (D. C. 35587). Son of William J. and Jessie (B——) Acker; grandson of Johnston Erwin (Edwin) and Martha Ellen (Holt) Burgess; great-grandson of William and Mary Duke (Letton) Holt; great²-grandson of Brice and Harriet (Moore) Letton; great²-grandson of *Michael Letton*, private, Fifth Regt., Maryland Militia.

ROYAL McCOY ALDERMAN, Cleveland, Ohio (35892). Son of Alva Dean and Elizabeth (McCoy) Alderman; grandson of William Ware and Elizabeth (Davis) McCoy; great-grandson of Ransom Briscoe and Nancy (Lusby) Davis; great²-grandson of Hugh and Elizabeth (Smith) Davis; great²-grandson of *Frederick Davis*, private, Second Battalion, North Carolina Troops.

NATHAN EVERETT HERDMAN ALLEN, Brooklyn, N. Y. (35907). Son of Samuel Curtis and Margaret E. (Herdman) Allen; grandson of George and Jane (Bronson) Allen; great-grandson of Otis and Lucy (Ide) Allen; great²-grandson of *Samuel Allen*, Ensign, Seventeenth Regt., New York Militia.

GORDON BARBOUR AMBLER, U. S. N., A. E. F., Richmond, Va. (35093). Son of John Nicholas and Anna Rockwell (Neal) Ambler; grandson of Philip Barbour and Willie Harrison (Nicholas) Ambler; great-grandson of John Jaquelin and Elizabeth (Barbour) Ambler; great²-grandson of *John Ambler*, private, Virginia Militia.

A. LESTER ANDRUS, Portland, Ore. (35064). Son of Wallace R. and Annie (Mead) Andrus; grandson of Marcus and Harriet (Sturges) Mead; great-grandson of *Calvin Mead*, private, Ninth Regt., Conn. Militia, pensioned.

MORTIMER STACY ASHTON, Corry, Penna. (35465). Son of Amos Turner and Amelia Huntington (Sill) Ashton; grandson of Job and Abby Stacy (Turner) Ashton; great-grandson of Amos Reed and Sarah Jarsey (Stacy) Turner; great²-grandson of *Thomas Stacy*, Captain, Rhode Island Privateer "Diamond,' died on "Jersey" prison ship; grandson of Frederick and Margaret Ann (Cocks) Sill; great-grandson of Thomas and Clarissa (Treadway) Sill; great²-grandson of *Micah Sill*, private, Colonel Parson's Regt., Conn. Cont'l Troops.

HARRY HOWARD ATKINSON, Brookline, Mass. (36102). Son of George Washington and Eliza (Allen) Atkinson; grandson of Samuel and Abigail (March) Atkinson; great-grandson of John and Abigail (Hodgdon) March; great²-grandson of *James March*, private, Col. Pierse Long's Regt., New Hampshire Artillery.

THEODORE MAYO ATKINSON, Brookline, Mass. (36103). Son of Harry Howard and Catherine Olivia (Mayo) Atkinson; grandson of George Washington and Eliza (Allen) Atkinson; great-grandson of Samuel and Abigail ((March) Atkinson; great²-grandson of John and Abigail (Hodgdon) March; great²-grandson of *James March*, private, Col. Pierse Long's Regt., New Hampshire Militia.

EDWARD ALLISON ATWOOD, Paterson, N. J. (36171). Son of Hedges and Gussie M. (Allison) Atwood; grandson of Anthony Dunbar and Nancy Maria (Hedges) Atwood; great-grandson of Edward and Phoebe (Doty) Hedges; great²-grandson of *James Doty*, private, New Jersey Militia and State Troops.

EUGENE ROSS BAKER, Keokuk, Iowa (35615). Son of Eugene S. and Mary (Cochran) Baker; grandson of Silas F. and Weltha (Griswold) Baker; great-grandson of Nathaniel Baker; great²-grandson of *Thomas Baker*, Sergeant, Colonel Woodbridge's Regt., Mass. Militia, pensioned.

MYRLE F. BAKER, Keokuk, Iowa (35614). Same as Eugene Ross Baker, Keokuk, Iowa (35615).

JOHN McHENRY BARNEY, Milwaukee, Wis. (32671). Son of Samuel Stebbins and Ellen Sybil (McHenry) Barney; grandson of John and Adeline Augusta (Knox) Barney; great-grandson of *William Barney,* private, Colonel Bradford's Regt., Mass. Militia.

HENRY BAILEY BARRY, Major, U. S. Army, Camp Bragg, N. C. (Mass. 36107). Son of Frederick A. and Henrietta M. (Bailey) Barry; grandson of Henry L. and Mary E. (Patterson) Bailey; great-grandson of James and Olive (Hopkins) Patterson; great²-grandson of *Solomon Hopkins,* Quartermaster, Mass. Cont'l Sloop of War "Ranger," pensioned.

ELMER J. BARTHOLD, Olyphant, Penna. (35466). Son of Thomas F. and Frances (Dorsheimer) Barthold; grandson of Jacob and Barbara (Brong) Dorsheimer; great-grandson of *Manuel Dorsheimer,* private, Second Battalion, Penna. "Flying Camp."

STANLEY LOGAN BATEMAN, Philadelphia, Penna. (36301). Son of William H. S. and Ollie Logan (Ennis) Bateman; grandson of William Atkinson and Almeda (Tomlinson) Ennis; great-grandson of Samuel and Lydia (Simpkins) Tomlinson; great²-grandson of William and Phobe (Harris) Tomlinson; great³-grandson of *Samuel Tomlinson,* private, Colonel Seely's Battalion, New Jersey Militia; great⁴-grandson of *James Tomlinson,* Captain, Colonel Seeley's Battalion, New Jersey Militia.

JACK HENSON BEACHLEY, Hagerstown, Md. (36080). Junior number. Son of Harry Knode and Alice (Taylor) Beachley; grandson of Jacob H. and Anna (Knode) Beachley; great-grandson of Simon and Louisa (Humrickhouse) Knode; great²-grandson of Frederick and Hanny (Harry) Humrickhouse; great³-grandson of *Peter Humrickhouse,* Captain, Philadelphia County, Penna., Militia.

ARTHUR CLIFFORD BELLOWS, Brooklyn, N. Y. (35908). Son of Charles and Mary Ellen (Delano) Bellows; grandson of Orlando and Maria (Blauvelt) Bellows; great-grandson of *Theodore Bellows,* Sergeant, Col. Moses Nichols' Regt., New Hampshire Militia; great-grandson of Theodore and Sarah (Hutchins) Bellows; great²-grandson of *Phineas Hutchins,* private, New Hampshire Militia at Ticonderoga; great²-grandson of Phineas and Abigail (Reed) Hutchins; great²-grandson of *James Reed,* Colonel, New Hampshire Militia, and Brigadier-General, Cont'l Line.

CHARLES CLIFFORD BELLOWS, Cleveland, Ohio (36181). Son of Arthur Clifford and Katherine (Strang) Bellows; grandson of Charles and Mary Ellen (Delano) Bellows; great-grandson of Orlando and Maria (Blauvelt) Bellows; great²-grandson of *Theodore Bellows,* Sergeant, Colonel Nichols' Regt., New Hampshire Militia; great²-grandson of Theodore and Sarah (Hutchins) Bellows; great³-grandson of *Phineas Hutchins,* private, New Hampshire Militia; great³-grandson of Phineas and Abigail (Reed) Hutchins; great⁴-grandson of *James Reed,* Colonel, New Hampshire Militia, and Brigadier-General, Cont'l Line.

BARD SHERMAN BERRY, San Francisco, Calif. (Iowa 35612). Son of Able Sherman and Mabel (Moore) Berry; grandson of John P. and Mary Catherine (Campbell) Moore; great-grandson of Stewart Marks and Eliza Jean (Bard) Campbell; great²-grandson of Richard and Elizabeth (Dunlap) Bard; great³-grandson of David and Elizabeth (Deimer) Bard; great⁴-grandson of *Richard Bard,* private, Cumberland County, Penna. Militia.

HENRY EDMUND BITTINGER, Washington, D. C. (35588). Son of Michael Henry and Martha (Moffett) Bittinger; grandson of John and Mary (Coskery) Bittinger; great-grandson of Joseph and Anna Elizabeth (Baugher) Bittinger; great²-grandson of *Nicholas Beittinger,* Captain, Third Battalion, York County, Penna. Minute Men, prisoner.

EDWIN BEDFORD BLAIR, Blue Lick, Mo. (Ill. 35449). Son of John and Nancy (Garrard) Blair; grandson of James Coleman and Catherine (Sterns) Garrard; great-grandson of Thomas Lewis and America Grace (Coleman) Garrard; great²-grandson of James and Nancy (Lewis) Garrard; great³-grandson of *James Garrard,* Captain, Virginia Militia; great⁴-grandson of *William Garrard,* Colonel, Stafford County, Virginia Militia.

HERBERT HOLLING BLAKE, Berkeley, Calif. (35939). Son of Sherman Tecumseh and Clara (Holling) Blake; grandson of Charles Edward and Laura (Hands) Blake; great-grandson of Ebenezer and Petromella (——) Blake; great²-grandson of *Ebenezer Blake,* private, Suffolk County, Mass. Militia.

SHERMAN TECUMSEH BLAKE, Berkeley, Calif. (35940). Son of Charles Edward and Laura (Hands) Blake; grandson of Ebenezer and Petromella (——) Blake; great-grandson of *Ebenezer Blake,* private, Suffolk County, Mass. Militia.

FERDINAND A. BOARD, Keokuk, Iowa (35619). Son of Thomas R. and Nellie (Sawyer) Board; grandson of Iram Allen and Mary C. (Irwin) Sawyer; great-grandson of Allen and Clarissa (Hazen) Sawyer; great²-grandson of *Ephraim Sawyer, Jr.*, Captain, Mass. Cont'l Troops; great²-grandson of *Ephraim Sawyer*, Lieutenant-Colonel, Mass. Militia.

MATHEW H. BORLAND, Burgettstown, Penna. (35467). Son of Matthew H. and Martha (Miller) Borland; grandson of Cornelius and Rebecca (Kelso) Borland; great-grandson of Benjamin and Martha (Murdock) Kelso; great²-grandson of *John Kelso*, Sergeant, First Regt., Penna. Cont'l Line, pensioned.

SAMUEL BOOTH BOTSFORD, Buffalo, N. Y. (36182). Son of Cyrus and Julia (Warner) Botsford; grandson of Henry W. and Anna (Wilmarth) Warner; great-grandson of Samuel and Betsy (Wooster) Warner; great²-grandson of *Benjamin Warner*, private, Captain Hanchet's Company, Conn. Militia at Quebec.

EDWIN AUGUSTUS BRAINERD, Westfield, N. J. (36277). Son of Augustus James and Ann Eliza (Knowles) Brainerd; grandson of Chauncey and Narcissa B. (Post) Brainerd; great-grandson of Silas and Lucinda (Brainerd) Brainerd; great²-grandson of Josiah and Lois (Hurlburt), Jr.; great²-grandson of *Josiah Brainerd*, Lieutenant, Colonel Cook's Regt., Conn. Militia, prisoner.

CHARLES ALLEN BRISTOL, Cheyenne, Wyo. (30021). Son of Samuel Allen and Ellen (Lee) Bristol; grandson of Leverett and Sarah N. (Field) Bristol; great-grandson of Anson and Achsah (Benton) Field; great²-grandson of Benjamin and Lucy (Murray) Field; great²-grandson of *David Field*, private, Colonel Talcott's Regt., Conn. Militia.

DETLER WULF BRONK, Ann Arbor, Mich. (Mass. 35874). Son of Mitchell and Marie (Wulf) Bronk; grandson of Abram and Cynthia (Brewster) Bronk; great-grandson of Stephen and Anna (Pierce) Brewster; great²-grandson of *Joseph Brewster*, private, Conn. Militia and Cont'l Troops, pensioned.

JAMES RUSH BRONSON, San Francisco, Calif. (35941). Son of James Cathcart and Hannah Melinda (Pennington) Bronson; grandson of Nathan and Martha (Yates) Pennington; great-grandson of William and Elizabeth (Wolford) Pennington; great²-grandson of *Nathan Pennington*, private, New Jersey Cont'l Troops; great²-grandson of Nathan and Mrs. Margaret (Wescott) Lonard Pennington; great²-grandson of *Richard Wescott*, Major, New Jersey Militia.

ANDREW DOBBIE BROWN, Central City, Nebr. (33893). Son of Charles Lybrand and Sarah Elizabeth (Mosier) Brown; grandson of Joseph and Rebecca Loraine (Foster) Brown; great-grandson of Job and Hannah (Packard) Foster; great²-grandson of James and Hannah (Stetson) Foster; great²-grandson of *Joseph Foster*, private, New Hampshire Militia and Artillery.

EDWARD AMENT BROWN, Rochester, N. Y. (35933). Son of John H. and Henrietta (Ament) Brown; grandson of Edward and Mary (Barnhart) Ament; great-grandson of *Eldert (Evert) Ament*, private, Second Regt., Albany County, New York Militia.

CHARLES RICHARD BRYSON, Pittsburgh, Penna. (35473). Son of Charles H. and Isabell (Cuddy) Bryson; grandson of John and Katherine (Beisel) Cuddy; great-grandson of *Jacob Beisel*, private, Third Regt., Penna. Troops.

CHARLES BULL, Upper Montclair, N. J. (36174). Son of Jabez Benedict and Sarah Elizabeth (Butler) Bull; grandson of James and Sarah (Cooke) Butler; great-grandson of Henry and Chloe (Hinsdale) Butler; great²-grandson of *Barnabas Hinsdale*, Ensign, Conn. Minute Men and Militia.

WILLIAM BUCHANAN BURKE, Danville, Ky. (Tenn. 36056). Son of Jerome Buchanan and Mary Elizabeth Chapman (Elliston) Burke; grandson of Samuel and Mary (Hurley) Burke; great-grandson of William and Sallie (Scott) Burke; great²-grandson of *Thomas Burke*, Corporal, Seventh Regt., Virginia Cont'l Troops.

WALTER DANFORTH BUSH, Jr., Wilmington, Del. (35658). Son of Walter Danforth and Rebecca Gibbons (Tatnall) Bush; grandson of Henry Lea and Caroline (Gibbons) Tatnall; great-grandson of Edward and Margery (Papson) Tatnall; great²-grandson of *Joseph Tatnall*, patriot miller for Cont'l Army.

JOSEPH THOMPSON CARPENTER, Blissfield, Mich. (36026). Son of James Leslie and Susan M. E. (Thompson) Carpenter; grandson of Joseph P. and Lydia (Wright) Carpenter; great-grandson of *William Carpenter*, private, New Hampshire Militia, pensioned.

JOSEPH MEAD CASE, Mendham, N. J. (35927). Son of Joshua and Fannie Anna (Jenks) Case; grandson of John and Mary (Mead) Case; great-grandson of *Joseph Case*, Second Lieutenant, Orange County, New York Militia.

FREDERICK WILLIAMS CHAMBERLIN, Ridgewood, N. J. (36159). Son of Eugene and Kate Elizabeth (Tucker) Chamberlin; grandson of Wesley and Annis C. (Williams) Chamberlin; great-grandson of Henry and Francis (Wilson) Chamberlin; great²-grandson of *Godfrey Chamberlin*, private, Colonel Phillips' Regt., Hunterdon County, New Jersey Militia.

ALBERT DESMOND CHESTON, Clifton, N. J. (36159). Son of Wilmot Mortimer and Mary (Osmond) Cheston; grandson of Elijah and Mary L. (Pryor) Cheston; great-grandson of *John Cheston*, private, First Battalion, First Establishment, New Jersey Cont'l Line.

JAMES BENNETT CHILDS, Chicago, Ill. (35450). Son of Trall Bennett and Mary Catherine (Michener) Childs; grandson of James B. and Mary (Dunbar) Michener; great-grandson of Aaron and Jennette (Doolittle) Dunbar; great²-grandson of Aseph and Polly (Ives) Dunbar; great³-grandson of *Aaron Dunbar*, private, Tenth Regt., Conn. Militia.

MARLBOROUGH CHURCHILL, U. S. Army, Washington, D. C. (La. 35986). Son of John Wesley and Mary Jane (Donald) Churchill; grandson of John Emery and Eliza Ann (Coburn) Churchill; great-grandson of *Francis Churchill*, Fifer, Mass. Militia for seacoast defense.

ARTHUR JAY CLARK, Pennsburg, Pa. (N. J. 36173). Son of Josiah and Isabell (Jewell) Clark; grandson of Smith and Catharine (Strouse) Clark; great-grandson of William and Margaret (Smith) Clark; great²-grandson of *Jeremiah Clark*, private, First Regt., Bucks County, Penna. Militia.

FRANK B. CLARK, Quakerstown, Pa. (N. J. 36172). Same as Arthur Jay Clark, Pennsburg, Pa. (N. J. 36173)

IRVIN LEMUEL CLARK, New Castle, Pa. (36303). Son of Charles Lemuel and Margaret (Earl) Clark; grandson of Mahlon and Lizzie (Baughman) Clark; great-grandson of Richard and Ann (Burk) Clark; great²-grandson of *Jeremiah Clark*, private, First Regt., Bucks County, Penna. Militia.

JEWELL STANLEY CLARK, Cleveland, Ohio (N. J. 36166). Son of Josiah and Isabel (Jewell) Clark; grandson of Smith and Catherine (Strouse) Clark; great-grandson of William and Margaret (Smith) Clark; great³-grandson of *Jeremiah Clark*, private, Colonel Keller's Regt., Bucks County, Penna Militia.

JOSIAH CLARK, Quakertown, Pa. (36165). Son of Smith and Catherine (Strouse) Clark; grandson of William and Margaret (Smith) Clark; great-grandson of *Jeremiah Clark*, private, Colonel Keller's Regt., Bucks County, Penna. Militia.

ARTHUR BELL CLARKE, Richmond, Va. (1752). Supplemental. Son of Augustus Burfort and Emma Bullington (Kusee) Clarke; grandson of Jesse Frayser and Cynthia (Bullington) Kusee; great-grandson of Josiah and Maria (Hobson) Bullington; great²-grandson of Josiah and Sarah (Bailey) Bullington; great²-grandson of *Joseph Bailey*, private, Henrico County, Virginia Militia.

THOMAS BENEDICT CLARKE, Jr., New York City, N. Y. (35934). Son of Thomas Benedict and Fanny Eugenia (Norris) Clarke; grandson of John Jacob and Charlotte (Harrison) Norris; great-grandson of Hiram and Nasy (Farrell) Harrison; great²-grandson of *Adonijah Harrison*, private, Essex County, New Jersey Militia.

TURLEY COBURN, Washington, D. C. (35589). Son of James Munroe and Irene (Turley) Coburn; grandson of John D. and Martha (Galloway) Coburn; great-grandson of *Alpheus Coburn*, Corporal, Colonel Ward's Regt., Mass. Militia.

RALPH JAMES CODE, Dorchester, Mass. (35875). Son of Abram John and Cynthia Anne (Austin) Code; grandson of Leslie Winfield and Mary Charlotte (Pardee) Austin; great-grandson of William H. and Susan Berry (De Wolfe) Pardee; great²-grandson of Joseph and Mary H. (Berry) De Wolfe; great³-grandson of *Samuel De Wolfe*, private and Corporal, Conn. Militia.

ALONZO COLE, Roseburg, Ore. (35065). Son of Chancy and Eliza (Morgan) Cole; grandson of Evans and Nancy (Popino) (Popineau) Morgan; great-grandson of *Peter Popino (Popineau)*, private, Monongolia County, Virginia Militia.

LESTER WEEDEN COLE, Titusville, Penna. (35910). Son of William Weedon and Agnes (Barker) Cole; grandson of William and Mary Jane (Hensen) Cole; great-grandson of

Benjamin and Jane (Porter) Cole; great²-grandson of Samuel and Lucy (Skillings) Cole; great²-grandson of *Samuel Cole*, Lieutenant, Essex County, Mass. Militia.

DAVID McELROY COLLISSON, Keokuk, Iowa (35623). Son of Henry Rix and Margaret (McElroy) Collisson; grandson of David White and Mary (Bailey) McElroy; great-grandson of Walter Scott and Ann Jane (Horshaw) Bailey; great²-grandson of Calvin Porter and Sibyl (Hatch) Bailey; great²-grandson of *Charles Bayley*, private, Col. Timothy Bedell's Regt., New Hampshire and Vermont Militia.

CHESTER INGALLS CONN, Portland, Ore. (35063). Son of Horace N. and Marion I. (Smith) Conn; grandson of George H. and Mary E. (Nichols) Conn; great-grandson of Horace and Martha (Fox) Conn; great²-grandson of William and Arithusa (Munroe) Fox; great²-grandson of *Jonathan Fox*, Colonel, Middlesex County, Mass. Militia.

WILLIAM MALCOLM CORSE, Westfield, N. J. (36160). Son of William A. and Genevieve H. (Alexander) Corse; grandson of William and Eliza P. (Williams) Corse; great-grandson of Thomas Russel and Ruth (Abbot) Williams; great²-grandson of *Henry Williams*, Commander of Mass. privateer "Salem."

THEODORE ALEXANDER CRAIG, Keokuk, Iowa (35617). Son of John Henderson and Alice (Read) Craig; grandson of Daniel and Alice (Brice) Read; great-grandson of Ezra and Nancy (Clark) Read; great²-grandson of *Daniel Read*, private, Corporal and Clerk, Colonel Whitney's and Colonel Tyler's Regts., Rhode Island Troops.

HERBERT ROYAL CRANE, New Jersey (20340). Supplemental. Son of Charles G. and Marie E. (Dickinson) Crane; grandson of William Henry and Mary Jane (Gillen) Crane; great-grandson of John and Hanah (Tidd) Gillen; great²-grandson of *Thomas Gillen*, member Washington's Life Guard.

FRANK CRESSY, Concord, N. H. (36251). Son of William P. and Mary C. (Gould) Cressy; grandson of Edward and Sarah (Sawyer) Cressy; great-grandson of *Daniel Cressy*, private, New Hampshire Militia and Cont'l Troops.

WILLIAM WILLARD CROCKER, Burlingame, Calif. (35954). Son of William Henry and Ethel Willard (Sperry) Crocker; grandson of Charles and Mary Ann (Deming) Crocker; great-grandson of John Jay and Emily (Read) Deming; great²-grandson of Charles John and Rachel (Miller) Read; great²-grandson of *Seth Read (Reed)*, Lieutenant-Colonel, Mass. Fifteenth Cont'l Infantry.

HADLEY M. CROSBIE, Newton Centre, Mass. (35873). Son of John M. and Matilda (Frazer) Crosbie; grandson of Thomas and Margaret (Hadley) Crosbie; great-grandson of Isaac and Ruth (Marshall) Hadley; great²-grandson of *Joseph Hadley*, Captain, North Carolina Militia.

EVAN R. CULLINGS, Schenectady, N. Y. (35912). Son of Archibald Buchanan and Hannah Brown (Bradshaw) Cullings; grandson of John and Christiana (Buchanan) Cullings; great-grandson of Archibald and Margaret (Ferguson) Buchanan; great²-grandson of *John Ferguson*, private, Fifteenth Regt., Albany County, New York Militia.

LEONARD CUTLER, San Francisco, Calif. (35942). Son of Alfred Dennis and Emma Isordora (——) Cutler; grandson of Leonard and Maria (——) Cutler; great-grandson of *Thomas Cutler*, private, Mass. Militia.

ALLEN CHARLES DAMON, Passaic, N. J. (N. Y. 36179). Son of Joel Goulding and Pamelia (Strong) Damon; grandson of George W. and Eunice (Goulding) Damon; great-grandson of Isaac and Diademia (Phelps) Damon; great²-grandson of Judd and Ruth (Putnam) Damon; great³-grandson of *Josiah Putnam*, Captain, Col. Jedadiah Foster's Regt., Mass. Militia.

RAYMOND GOODRICH DANN, New York (27219). Supplemental. Son of John E. and Mary Caroline (Goodrich) Dann; grandson of Sellish and Isabella Sophia (Hall) Dann; great-grandson of Hiland Bishop and Caroline Sophia (Hamlin) Hall; great²-grandson of Amos and Phebe (Coe) Hall; great³-grandson of *Stephen Hall*, Captain, Col. Herman Swift's Regt., Conn. Cont'l Line.

ALLEN RUSSELL DAVIS, Harriman, Tenn. (36057). Son of L. Tyler and Virginia (Russell) Davis; grandson of Simon Pierce and Emily (Banks) Russell; great-grandson of Sumner and Phebe (Pierce) Russell; great²-grandson of William and Dolly (Clark) Russell; great³-grandson of *Ephraim Russell*, private, Colonel Prescott's Regt., Mass. Militia.

GEORGE SELLS DAVIS, Newton, Iowa (Ill. 36301). Son of John McCleary and Mary Catherine (Christy) Davis; grandson of Joshua and Rebecca (McCleary) Davis; great-grandson of *Robert McCleary*, Sergeant, Lancaster County, Penna. Militia.

LEE HENRY DAVIS, Chicago, Ill. (36202). Same as George Sells Davis, Ill. (36201).

WALTER ALAN DAVIS, Ithaca, N. Y. (35931). Son of Goodman Richard and Benveneda (Brickner) Davis; grandson of Michael Marks and Miriam (Piexotto) Davis; great-grandson of Daniel Maduro and Rachel (Seixas) Piexotto; great²-grandson of *Benjamin Mendes Seixas*, Officer, New York Militia.

BERNARD DIBBLE, Camden, N. J. (Pa. 35468). Son of Theodore Savage and Nina (Da Costa) Dibble; grandson of Theodore Hoyt and Mary Shelly (Reilly) Dibble; great-grandson of Timothy Taylor and Esther (Taylor) Dibble; great²-grandson of *Joshua Taylor*, Sergeant, Colonel Swift's Regt., Conn. Cont'l Troops.

JOHN V. DRIPS, Belvidere, So. Dak. (30664). Son of Joseph H. and Hannah (Hawkins) Drips; grandson of William and Martha Ann (Clark) Drips; great-grandson of *Robert Clark*, private, Cumberland County, Penna. Militia.

JAMES STRODE ELSTON, Elmwood, Conn. (35489). Son of Jacob Tice and Anna Mary (Strode) Elston; grandson of Claudius Reynolds and Martha (Tice) Elston; great-grandson of Jacob and Harriet (Moore) Tice; great²-grandson of *Henry Tice*, private, Ulster County, New York Militia and State Troops, pensioned.

GEORGE FREDERICK ESCHBACH, Melbourne, Fla. (D. C. 35590). Son of Frederick A. and Rebecca Virginia (Lupton) Eschbach; grandson of Cyrus and Susan H. (Eichelberger) Lupton; great-grandson of William Boyer and Martha (Ladue) Lupton; great²-grandson of *Joseph Lupton*, Sergeant, Col. Edward Steven's Regt., Virginia Troops.

LEO BUCHANAN ESCHBACH, Melbourne, Fla. (D. C. 35591). Same as George Frederick Eschbach (D. C. 35590).

ALBERT GRANT EVANS, Minneapolis, Minn. (35683). Son of George Brayton and Rhoda Gertrude (Leonard) Evans; grandson of John Sessions and Philinda Sabina (Brown) Evans; great-grandson of Parley and Submit (Farwell) Brown; great²-grandson of *Ebenezer Brown*, private, Fifth Regt., Conn. Cont'l Line.

JONATHAN A. EVANS, Ellwood City, Penna. (36304). Son of John Ralston and Mary (——) Evans; grandson of Jonathan and Christina (King) Evans; great-grandson of John and Isabella (Hays) Ralston; great²-grandson of *John Hays*, Captain, Northampton County, Penna.° Militia.

EDGAR BRUCE FERGUSSON, Richmond, Va. (35094). Son of Mellville Bruce and Carrie (Batcheler) Fergusson; grandson of John Wesley and Evilina Godwin (Shelton) Fergusson; great-grandson of George and Ann Ursula (——) Fergusson; great²-grandson of *Robert Fergusson, Jr.*, private, First Regt., Virginia Light Dragoons.

HERBERT WORTH FILLMORE, Nanking, China (Ind. 35510). Son of Fred. A. and Laura (Moore) Fillmore; grandson of William Roper and Mary (Wooden) Moore; great-grandson of Solomon and Ann (Beekley) Moore; great²-grandson of *Anthony Moore*, private, Maryland and Virginia Troops.

CHARLES IRWIN FLYNN, Cleveland, Ohio (35893). Son of Henry and Mary Louisa (Miller) Flynn; grandson of Charles Meredith and Louisa (Frederickson) Miller; great-grandson of Godfrey and Catharine (Hester) Frederickson; great²-grandson of *Conrad Hester*, private, Philadelphia, Penna. Militia.

EDWARD WEST FOSTER, Nashville, Tenn. (36055). Son of Robert Coleman and Julia H. (Woods) Foster; grandson of Robert Coleman and Louisa Turner (Saunders) Foster; great-grandson of Robert Coleman and Ann Hubbard (Slaughter) Foster; great²-grandson of *Antony Foster, Jr.*, private, Colonel Christian's First Regt., Virginia Troops and Keeper of Supplies.

JOHN GORDON FOSTER, Lynn, Mass. (36104). Son of William Dennison and Phebe Ann (Godfrey) Foster; grandson of Samuel and Phebe (Henshaw) Godfrey; great-grandson of John and Jerusha (Hodges) Godfrey; great²-grandson of *George Godfrey*, Brigadier-General, Bristol County, Mass. Militia, Chairman, Committee of Safety and Correspondence and Member Mass. General Court, 1770-84.

ROBERT COLEMAN FOSTER, Nashville, Tenn. (36058). Son of Edward West and Susan (Cockrill) Foster; grandson of Robert Coleman and Julia H. (Woods) Foster;

great-grandson of Robert Coleman and Louisa T. (Saunders) Foster, Jr.; great²-grandson of Robert Coleman and Ann Hubbard (Slaughter) Foster, Sr.; great³-grandson of *Antony Foster, Jr.,* private, Colonel Christian's Regt., Virginia Militia, later in charge of supplies, pensioned; grandson of Benjamin Franklin and Sarah C. (Foster) Cockrill; great-grandson of Mark Robertson and Susan (Collinsworth) Cockrill; great²-grandson of *John Cockrill, Jr.,* private, Tenth Regt., Virginia Troops; great²-grandson of John Cockrill, Jr., and *Ann Robertson Cockrill,* defender of Nashville, Tenn., Fort; great-grandson of Ephraim H. and Jean Mebane (Lytle) Foster (father of Sarah C. Foster); great²-grandson of *William Lytle,* Captain, North Carolina Troops.

NORTON ELMER FRANK, Brooklyn, N. Y. (35911). Son of Elmer D. and Mary E. (Burbank) Frank; grandson of Joseph Henry and Sara Jane (Norris) Burbank; great-grandson of Isaac and Mary E. (Troxell) Burbank; great²-grandson of *Eleazor Burbank,* private, Mass. Militia, pensioned.

ALBERT E. FULLER, Madison, So. Dak. (30665). Son of Frank and Esther Ann (——) Fuller; grandson of William H. and Mary (W——) Fuller; great-grandson of *John Fuller,* Sergeant, Conn. Militia, pensioned.

JAMES McQUEEN FULTON, Keokuk, Iowa (35620). Son of William and Lizzie '(Dalzell) Fulton; grandson of William and Nancy (Peairs) Fulton; great-grandson of *Robert Fulton,* private, Westmoreland County, Penna. Militia.

WILLIAM JEWETT FULTON, Keokuk, Iowa (35622). Son of William Jewett and Jessie (Fisher) Fulton; grandson of Robert and Harriet (Trussell) Fulton; great-grandson of William and Nancy (Peairs) Fulton; great²-grandson of *Robert Fulton,* private, Westmoreland County, Penna. Militia.

HARRISON WARD GARDNER, Walla Walla, Wash. (34045). Son of Herbert A. and Nancy Elizabeth (Hungate) Gardner; grandson of Amos and Louisa (Jackman) Gardner; great-grandson of Warren and Mary (Lincoln) Gardner; great²-grandson of Warren and Mary (Dunbar) Gardner; great³-grandson of *Stephen Gardner, Jr.,* private, Colonel Lovell's Regt., Mass. Militia.

LESTER DURAND GARDNER, New York City, N. Y. (35935). Son of Harry and Frances (Scott) Gardner; grandson of Boris Fahenestock and Ann (Rogers) Gardner; great-grandson of William and Mary (Sweetser) Rogers; great²-grandson of Jacob and Elizabeth (Simes) Rogers; great³-grandson of *William Rogers,* private, First Regt., Maryland Militia, prisoner.

SHEPHERD MILLS GASTON, Keokuk, Iowa (36226). Son of Alexander and Ruth (Shaw) Gaston; grandson of Joseph and Elizabeth (Mills) Shaw; great-grandson of *John Mills,* Second Lieutenant, Virginia Cont'l Line.

GEORGE BLAKE GOODALE, Bangor, Me. (34516). Son of Thomas and Sally Hayes (Blake) Goodale; grandson of *Thomas Goodale,* private, Essex County, Mass. Cont'l Troops.

HAZARD KNOWLES GRIFFITH, Washington, D. C. (35592). Son of Charles Greenberry and Frances (Knowles) Griffith; grandson of Greenberry and Prudence (Jones) Griffith; great-grandson of Howard and Jemima (Jacob) Griffith; great²-grandson of *Greenberry Griffith,* private, Baltimore County, Maryland Militia, Member Committee of Observation.

DAVID BASSETT GROSVENOR, Roswell, Idaho (35107). Son of Lemuel Conant and Naomi Josephine (Bassett) Grosvenor; grandson of Silas Newton and Mary Angelina (Conant) Grosvenor; great-grandson of David Hall and Martha (Newton) Grosvenor; great²-grandson of *Daniel Grosvenor,* Captain and Chaplain, Mass. Militia at Lexington Alarm.

B. EGBERT GURNEY, Newburgh, N. Y. (35909). Son of Edgar Benedict and Julia Ann (Kenwill) Gurney; grandson of William Benedict and Ann (Robeson) Gurney; great-grandson of Joseph Hoag and Abigail (Hazard) Gurney; great²-grandson of *Tiddeman Hazard,* private, Rhode Island Militia.

SMITH HAMILL, Keokuk, Iowa (35616). Son of David Brown and Maria Louise (——) Hamill; grandson of Smith and Nancy (McCandless) Hamill; great-grandson of John M. and Mary (Young) McCandless; great²-grandson of *William Young,* private, Cumberland County, Penna. Militia.

BENJAMIN MILES HAMMOND, San Francisco, Calif. (35943). Son of Giroud Evans and Virginia Esther (Evans) Hammond; grandson of Benjamin Franklin and Mary

Catherine (Miles) Hammond; great-grandson of Dudley and Nancy (Jenkins) Hammond; great[2]-grandson of Job and Lucy Eager (Howard) Hammond; great[3]-grandson of *Samuel Hammond*, Captain, Virginia Cont'l Line.

JOHN CLIFFORD HANNA, Detroit, Mich. (36027). Son of John and Blanche (Odell) Hanna; grandson of James Albert and Roxana (Palmer) Odell; great-grandson of Nehemiah and Elizabeth (Boyle) Palmer; great[2]-grandson of *Nehemiah Palmer*, Seaman and Gunner, Conn. sloops "Revenge" and "Randolph."

CHARLES JOHNSON HANSELL, Narberth, Penna. (35469). Son of George W. and Sue (Johnson) Hansell; grandson of Charles and Sarah Ann (Venai) Johnson; great-grandson of Peter and Ann (Zell) Johnson; great[2]-grandson of *Joseph Johnson*, Corporal and Sergeant, Penna. Invalid Regt., Cont'l Line.

JOHN W. HARDING, Paterson, N. J. (36168). Son of William Baldwin and Cynthia (Ward) Harding; grandson of John and Mary (Slocum) Harding; great-grandson of John and Mrs. Affa (Baldwin) Jenkins Harding; great[2]-grandson of *Stephen Harding*, Captain, Penna. Militia, prisoner at Wyoming Massacre.

JAMES ROBERTSON HARNEY, Milwaukee, Wis. (32672). Son of Ben Mills and Margaret Wellington (Drappen) Harney; grandson of John Hopkins and Martha C. (Wallace) Harney; great-grandson of Selby and Hannah (Hopkins) Harney; great[2]-grandson of *Jonathan Harney*, Lieutenant, Colonel Haslet's Regt., Delaware Militia, prisoner.

JOSEPH WESLEY HARTSHORN, Lynn, Mass. (36106). Son of Curtis Hamilton and Delia C. (Klin) Hartshorn; grandson of Curtis and Catharine (Wenzell) Hartshorn; great-grandson of John and Hepzibah (Bigelow) Wenzell; great[2]-grandson of *Joseph Bigelow*, private, Mass. Militia.

WILLIAM EDWARD HARVEY, Springfield, Mass. (36108). Son of John Edward and Harriet Ferry (Strong) Harvey; grandson of William Wales and Lestina T. (Stacy) Harvey; great-grandson of John and Chloe (Shan) Stacy; great[2]-grandson of Nymphlus and Sarah (Gibbs) Stacy; great[3]-grandson of *William Stacy (Stacey)*, Lieutenant-Colonel, Seventh and Fourth Regts., Mass. Cont'l Troops, prisoner.

ELWOOD HAUSMANN, Washington, D. C. (35593). Son of Alfred Emile and Josephine (Campbell) Hausmann; grandson of Bernard Moore and Emily Jane (Moore) Campbell; great-grandson of Walter Lewis and Sarah (Moore) Campbell; great[2]-grandson of Archibald and Catherine (Lewis) Campbell; great[3]-grandson of *John Campbell*, Captain, Virginia Militia.

HARRY WILLIAM HEINE, Greenup, Ky. (Mich. 36028). Son of Henry William and Clara M. (Hoop) Heine; grandson of James and Sarah Anne (Williams) Hoop; great-grandson of Henry B. and Jean (Anderson) Williams; great[2]-grandson of James and Sarah (Brower) Williams; great[3]-grandson of *Hendrick Brower*, private, Col. Jacobus Swartwout's Regt., New York Militia.

ELDRIDGE HENDERSON, Brooklyn, N. Y. (36176). Son of James Neely and Mary Louise (Grafton) Henderson; grandson of Nathan and Barba (——) Grafton; great-grandson of Martin and Hannah (——) Grafton; great[2]-grandson of *William Grafton*, private, Hartford County, Maryland Militia.

CLARENCE EDWARD HILL, Massachusetts (34240). Supplemental. Son of William Gilbert and Kate C. (Thompson) Hill; grandson of Charles Gage and Elizabeth (Wallwork) Thompson; great-grandson of Ebenezer and Hannah (Gage) Thompson; great[2]-grandson of *Isaac Gage*, private, Col. Jacob Gerrish's Regt., Mass. Guards.

JAMES BRENTS HILL, Nashville, Tenn. (36054). Son of James A. and Mary (Lowry) Hill, grandson of Winkfield and Patsy (Anderson) Hill; great-grandson of *Thomas Hill*, private, Col. James Martin's Regt., North Carolina Troops, pensioned.

ROBERT GARRETT HILLER, Keokuk, Iowa (36227). Son of Charles and Mary Morse (Thompson) Hiller; grandson of Hiram Milliken and Sarah Fulton (Bell) Hiller; great-grandson of William and Charlotte (Milliken) Hiller; great[2]-grandson of John and Harned (Roberts) Milliken; great[3]-grandson of *James Milliken*, private, Colonel Hale's Regt., New Hampshire Militia.

DAVID C. HILTON, Lincoln, Nebr. (33894). Son of John B. W. and Mary Elizabeth (Redgate) Hilton; grandson of Edmund and Lydia Ann (Miller) Redgate; great-grandson of Stephen and Elizabeth (Weeks) Miller; great[2]-grandson of *Stephen Weeks (Wickes)*, private, Westchester County, New York Militia.

JOHN GALETTE HINES, Brooklyn, N. Y. (35932). Son of John F. and Minnie (Place) Hines; grandson of John Galette and Eliza (Lewis) Place; great-grandson of Robert and Elizabeth (Williams) Place; great²-grandson of *Enoch Miles Place*, Sergeant, Brevet Ensign and Standard Bearer, Rhode Island Militia and State Troops, widow pensioned.

HARVEY DANIEL HOOVER, Carthage, Ill. (36203). Son of Samuel Enoch and Joana Jane (Gable) Hoover; grandson of Daniel and Catherine (Ditzler) Hoover; great-grandson of *Ulrich Hoover*, private, York and Lancaster Counties, Penna. Militia.

EDWIN NOTT HOPSON, Jr., Paterson, N. J. (36153). Son of Edwin Nott and Louise M. (Bush) Hopson; grandson of John and Hannah Elenor (Seeny) Bush; great-grandson of Owen and Eliza Ann (Tiers) Seeny; great²-grandson of George and Elenor (O'Neil) Tiers; great²-grandson of *John O'Neil*, private, Maxwell's Brigade, New Jersey Militia, pensioned.

NORMAN BRADISH HORTON, Fruit Ridge, Mich. (36029). Son of George B. and Mentha Amanda (Bradish) Horton; grandson of Norman F. and Caroline M. (Caton) Bradish; great-grandson of Calvin and Nancy (Post) Bradish; great²-grandson of *John Bradish*, private, Col. Ezra May's Regt., Mass. Militia.

CLARENCE OTIS STEPHEN HOWE, Upper Montclair, N. J. (36278). Son of Leslie L. and Elizabeth J. (Sweeny) Howe; grandson of James Otis and Amelia O. (Hitchcock) Howe; great-grandson of Lyman and Annie P. (Perry) Howe; great²-grandson of *Gardner Howe*, private, Shrewsbury, Mass. Militia.

THOMAS HUBBARD, Toledo, Ohio (35890). Son of Amos Fisk and Ursula (Graves) Hubbard; grandson of Josiah Dwight and Abigail (Pomeroy) Graves; great-grandson of Elihu and Lydia (Barber) Pomeroy; great²-grandson of *Benjamin Pomeroy*, Chaplain, Third Regt., Conn. Line.

WILLIAM EDWARD HUGHEY, Clifton, N. J. (36151). Son of Robert McKean and Rose (Rhea) Hughey; grandson of Joseph and Margaret (Cavet) Hughey; great-grandson of *John Hughey*, private, Lancaster County, Penna. Militia.

CHARLES MAGEE IRWIN, Narberth, Penna. (35474). Son of Edward Gwinn and Annie Hall (Magee) Irwin; grandson of Noah Wiltbank and Patience (Kellum) Magee; great-grandson of Thomas and Mary (Mason) Kellum; great²-grandson of *Charles Mason*, Bombardier, Col. Benjamin Flower's Regt., Penna. Artillery.

ARTHUR COPELAND JACKSON, District of Columbia (33262). Supplemental. Son of Arthur G. and Donnie May (Copeland) Jackson; grandson of Samuel and Maggie (Beal) Copeland; great-grandson of Stephen D. and Eliza A. (Kiser) Beal; great²-grandson of Peter and Frances (McDonald) Beal; great²-grandson of *Philip Beal*, private, Col. Jacob Cook's Regt., Lancaster County, Penna Militia.

EVERETT E. JACKSON, Baltimore, Md. (36077). Son of Elihu E. and Annie Frances (Rider) Jackson; grandson of William H. and Margaret (A——) Rider; great-grandson of Noah and Elizabeth (Byrd) (Bird) Rider; great²-grandson of John and Mrs. Margaret (Law) Handy Byrd (Bird); great²-grandson of *Benjamin Byrd (Bird)*, private, Somerset County, Maryland Militia; grandson of Hugh and Sarah McBryde (Humphreys) Jackson; great-grandson of John and Eleanor (Hammond) Jackson; great²-grandson of *Zedekiah Hammond*, private, Worcester County, Maryland Militia; great²-grandson of *William Hammond*, private, Worcester County, Maryland Militia; great-grandson of Joshua and Elizabeth (McBryde) Humphreys; great²-grandson of *Joseph Humphreys (Humphries)*, private, Salisbury Battalion, Somerset County, Maryland Militia.

HUGH WILLIAM JACKSON, Pelham Manor, N. Y. (Md. 36076). Same as Everett E. Jackson, Jr., Maryland (36077).

PAUL FREDERICK JACKSON, Maplewood, N. J. (36283). Son of John Collins and Viola (Chase) Jackson; grandson of Israel and Catherine Ann (Collins) Jackson; great-grandson of John Anderson and Sarah (Sites) Collins; great²-grandson of *James Collins*, Sergeant, Second Regt., Maryland Militia.

RICHARD NEWTON JACKSON, Baltimore, Md. (36078). Same as Everett E. Jackson, Jr., Maryland (36077).

FREDERICK T. F. JOHNSON, Washington, D. C. (35594). Son of Thomas S. J. and Margaret Ann (Stuck) Johnson; grandson of Hezekiah and Catherine Henrietta (McGonnegle) Johnson; great-grandson of *Hezekiah Johnson*, private, Charles County, Maryland Militia.

HARRIS HANCOCK JOHNSTON, St. Louis, Mo. (35558). Son of Josiah Stoddard and Eliza Woolfolk (Johnson) Johnston; grandson of John Harris and Eliza Ellen (Davidson) Johnston; great-grandson of John and Abigail (Harris) Johnston; great²-grandson of *Archibald Johnston*, Captain, Dutchess County, New York Militia.

CALVIN IRA KEPHART, California (29964). Supplemental. Son of George Elwood and Anna Catherine (Weisel) Kephart; grandson of Samuel and Catherine Ann (Kober) Weisel; great-grandson of John M. and Mary (Conver) Kober; great²-grandson of *Jacob Conver (Convear)*, private, Philadelphia and Northampton Counties, Penna. Militia; great²-grandson of Jacob and Elizabeth (Reed) Conver; great³-grandson of *Jacob Reed*, Lieutenant-Colonel, First Battalion, Philadelphia County, Penna. Militia.

SAMUEL WEISEL KEPHART, San Francisco, Calif. (35955). Son of George Elwood and Anna Catherine (Weisel) Kephart; grandson of Henry Harmon and Amy T. (Hyde) Kephart; great-grandson of Jacob and Magdalena (Ruth) Kephart; great²-grandson of *John Kephart*, private, Philadelphia, Penna. German Cont'l Regt.

RUSSELL ELWOOD KEPHART, San Francisco, Calif. (35956). Same as Samuel W. Kephart, Calif. (35955).

FREDERICK CLARENCE KEPPLER, Indiana (35501). Supplemental. Son of Samuel William and Martha Catherine (Strouss) Keppler (Kepler); grandson of Ruben and Anna Johanna (Doll) Strouss; great-grandson of Abraham and Magdalene (Knauss) Doll; great²-grandson of *Henrich (Henry) Knauss*, Captain, Fifth Battalion, Berks County, Penna. Militia.

FRANK MORTON KING, Massachusetts (35864). Supplementals. Son of Francis Dane and Mary Ann (Maloy) King; grandson of Artemas and Sally (Byram) King; great-grandson of *Nathan King*, private, Mass. Militia; great²-grandson of *John King*, Lieutenant, Mass. Cont'l Infantry; great²-grandson of *Philip King*, Captain, Bristol County Regt., Mass. Militia; great-grandson of Nathan and Prudence (Dean) King; great²-grandson of *Ebenezer Dean*, Captain, Bristol County, Mass. Militia and Cont'l Troops; great-grandson of William and Mary (Williams) Byram; great²-grandson of *Abiel Williams*, Second Lieutenant, Bristol County, Mass. Militia.

HOWARD DODSON KLINE, Chicago, Ill. (36204). Son of Henry Clay and Alice Janet (Dodson) Kline; grandson of Charles Augustus and Emma Elizabeth (Kind) Dodson; great-grandson of William Beal and Deborah (Starbuck) Dodson; great²-grandson of *John Dodson*, private, First Regt., Maryland Cont'l Line.

ALBAH BENJAMIN KNOWLTON, Seattle, Wash. (34046). Son of Israel Stone and Hepsebeth Card (Fisk) Knowlton; grandson of Benjamin and Olive (Stone) Knowlton; great-grandson of *Nathan Knowlton*, private and Corporal, Mass. Militia, pensioned.

GEORGE SHARP LANNOM, Jr., Tullahoma, Tenn. (36059). Son of George Sharp and Mary Narcissa (Chappel) Lannom; grandson of Joseph N. and Sarah Ann (Sharp) Lannom; great-grandson of Theophilis Alexander and Mary Jane (Clay) Sharp; great²-grandson of Joshua and Sarah (Jennings) Clay; great³-grandson of *John Clay*, private, Col. William Davies' Regt., Virginia Cont'l Troops.

FRED M. LEE, Belleville, N. J. (36284). Son of Daniel Lee and Ellen Elizabeth (Cottrell) Lee; grandson of John and Mittie (Baker) Lee; great-grandson of Daniel and Mollie B. (Olmstead) Lee; great²-grandson of *Daniel Olmstead*, private, Fairfield County, Conn. Militia, pensioned.

ROLAND WINTHROP LEFAVOUR, Beverly, Mass. (35872). Son of Howard Richards and Rebecca Ober (Perry) Lefavour; grandson of Winthrop E. and Augusta (Brazil) Perry; great-grandson of John W. and Mary Ann (Standley) Brazil; great²-grandson of James and Eunice (Raymond) Brazil; great³-grandson of Jonathan and Mary (Twiss) Raymond; great⁴-grandson of *Robert Twiss*, private and Corporal, Mass. Cont'l Line, pensioned.

IRVING BOWEN LINCOLN, Portland Ore. (35064). Son of Fred L. and Julia (Gleason) Lincoln; grandson of Daniel S. and Harriet Eliza (Leonard) Lincoln; great-grandson of Charles and Amanda (Scovill) Lincoln; great²-grandson of *Charles Lincoln*, private, Mass. Militia.

WALTER LORD, Brooklyn, N. Y. (35913). Son of James Sprout and Emily (Puffer) Lord; grandson of Joseph Lyman and Fannie (Gates) Lord; great-grandson of *Lemuel Gates*, Captain, Mass. Artillery and Engineers.

WILLIAM RUPERT LORING, Hadley, Mass. (36105). Son of Horace Parsons and Mary Ann Francis (Atkinson) Loring; grandson of Chester Owen and Ann E. (Stanton) Loring; great-grandson of Isaac and Caroline (Owen) Loring; great²-grandson of *Ignatius Loring*, Captain, Mass. Militia and Justice of the Peace.

LESLIE CLIFFORD LOVE, Montclair, N. J. (36161). Son of John James Hervey and Frances Jane (Crane) Love; grandson of Robert and Ann Thompson (Fair) Love; great-grandson of James and Mary (Guthrie) Love; great²-grandson of *Thomas Love*, Second Lieutenant, Chester County, Penna. Militia.

PIERRE WALDO LYON, Chicago, Ill. (36205). Son of Frank Emory and Jennie C. (Vredenburg) Lyon; grandson of John and Mary Ann (Child) Vredenburg; great-grandson of Obadiah and Charity (Thompson) Child; great²-grandson of *Timothy Child*, private, Conn. Militia, widow pensioned.

NOEL DUNHAM LUDLOW, Westfield, N. J. (36282). Son of Alfred Dunham and Morgiana (Holt) Ludlow; grandson of William Wellesley and Maria (Fanning) Holt; great-grandson of Lester and Katherine (Clyde) Holt; great²-grandson of *Samuel Clyde*, Lieutenant-Colonel, New York Militia and Chairman, Tyron County, New York Committee of Safety.

ALFRED SIDNEY MACFARLANE, Jacksonville, Fla. (Va. 35095). Son of Charles W. and Annie (Peticolas) Macfarlane; grandson of William and Elizabeth Ella (Day) Macfarlane; great-grandson of Stephen and Anne Hay (Brooke) Macfarlane; great²-grandson of *Lawrence Brooke*, Surgeon on "Bon Homme Richard."

WARD BEECHER MANCHESTER, Batavia, N. Y. (36180). Son of Hiram Benson and Mary (Hill) Manchester; grandson of Hezekiah and Delia (Burross or Barrows) Manchester; great-grandson of Benson and Thankful (Sanford) Manchester; great²-grandson of *James Manchester*, private, Second Regt., Bristol County, Mass. Militia.

JOHN LLEWELLYN MATTHEWS, Paterson, N. J. (36155). Son of George T. and Sarah F. (Gibbs) Matthews; grandson of Samuel M. and Betsy (Fletcher) Matthews; great-grandson of Samuel and Mamie (Catlin) Matthews; great²-grandson of *Aaron Matthews*, Sergeant and Ensign, Conn. Cont'l Troops.

CHARLES HENRY MAULL, Lewes, Del. (35657). Son of George Hickman and Hannah (Clifton) Maull; grandson of Asa and Elizabeth (——) Clifton; great-grandson of *Whittington Clifton*, private, Sussex County, Delaware Militia.

WILLIAM BURTT McCAIN, San Francisco, Calif. (35944). Son of Thomas Benton and Elsie (Montgomery) McCain; grandson of James and Mazula (Gaskill) McCain; great-grandson of Budd and Hannah (Davis) Gaskill; great²-grandson of *Samuel Gaskill*, Lieutenant, Burlington County, New Jersey Militia.

WILLIAM L. McCAULEY, Chicago, Ill. (36206). Son of George D. and Nancy Adaline (Albright) McCauley; grandson of William and Manurvy (Doughton) McCauley; great-grandson of *James McCauley*, Captain, Marion's Brigade, South Carolina Troops.

HENRY RAY MEAD, Omer, Mich. (36030). Son of Justin Kellogg and Margaret Duncan (Ray) Mead; grandson of Henry Bascom and Sybil (Duncan) Ray; great-grandson of Charles Spicer and Adaline (Watts) Duncan; great²-grandson of Charles F.' and Susan H. (Camden) Duncan; great²-grandson of *William Camden*, Sergeant, Col. John Pope's Regt., Virginia Militia; great-grandson of Luke E. and Marietta (Drown) Ray; great²-grandson of Benjamin and Joanna (Davis) Brown; great²-grandson of *Daniel Davis*, private, Virginia Militia, pensioned; grandson of James Howe and Mary Ann (Kellog) Mead; great-grandson of Squire and Nancy (Ambler) Mead; great²-grandson of Edward and Mary (Finch) Mead; great²-grandson of *Thaddeus Mead*, private, Third Regt., Westchester County, New York Militia.

LOUIS CHESTER MELCHER, Madison, Wis. (32673). Son of Frank Robert and Edna Emma (Walters) Melcher; grandson of Louis Christian and Martha Gifford (Dopp) Walters; great-grandson of Henry and Eunice Brown (Pike) Dopp, Jr.; great²-grandson of Henry and Martha (Gifford) Dopp; great²-grandson of *Benjamin Gifford*, private, Albany and Dutchess Counties, New York Militia.

LEONARD JOHNSON MERCHANT, St. Joseph, Mo. (35490). Son of George and Eunice (Johnson) Merchant; grandson of Amos and Sally (Hubbard) Johnson; great-grandson of *Jonathan Johnson*, Captain and Lieutenant-Colonel, Conn. State Troops, pensioned.

CLEMENT HARVEY MILLER, Oakland, Calif. (35945). Son of Clement Finley and Mary (More) Miller; grandson of Henry and Betsy Ann (Farrington) More, Jr.; great-grandson of March and Pauline (Fitch) Farrington; great²-grandson of Thomas and Joanna (Frye) Farrington, Jr.; great³-grandson of *Thomas Farrington*, Lieutenant-Colonel, Rufus Putnam's Regt., Mass. Cont'l Troops.

HARVEY DAVIS MILLER, California (34177). Supplemental. Son of Clement Harvey and Alice (Davis) Miller; grandson of Thomas Chiles and Rebecca Fifield (Rutherford) Davis; great-grandson of Thomas Chiles and Elizabeth (Chiles) Davis; great²-grandson of *Richard Davis*, Sergeant, First Regt., Virginia Light Dragoons.

THOMAS RUTHERFORD MILLER, California (34178). Supplemental. Same as Harvey Davis Miller, California (34177).

JOHN ENSIGN MITCHELL, Keokuk, Iowa (35624). Son of Ira and Jane (Rhodes) Mitchell; grandson of *Ensign Mitchell*, private, New York Militia and Second Regt., Cont'l Line.

CHARLES MORTON MOADINGER, Flushing, N. Y. (35914). Son of Charles Oliver and Carrie J. (Morton) Moadinger; grandson of William S. and P. Jane (Charles) Morton; great-grandson of John Langdon and Ann Evelyn (Clark) Morton; great²-grandson of Thomas and Ann (Mosely) Morton; great³-grandson of *Bryant (Briant) Morton*, Captain, Mass. Militia for seacoast defense.

JASON BELL MOODY, Houston, Tex. (29500). Son of William Anderson and Betty (Bell) Moody; grandson of Jason and Lydia (Bray) Bell; great-grandson of James and Elizabeth (Tuxton) Bell; great²-grandson of Arthur and Sarah (Ferebee) Tuxton; great³-grandson of *Joseph Ferebee*, Captain, North Carolina Militia and Marshall of Court of Admiralty.

COURTNEY LEE MOORE, San Francisco, Calif. (35946). Son of John Courtney and Pauline (Harris) Moore; grandson of John Sydney and Susan A. (Morrison) Moore; great-grandson of Daniel L. Morrison; great²-grandson of *Isaac Morrison*, Captain, First Regt., New Jersey Cont'l Troops.

JAMES JOHNSTON MORSE, New Orleans, La. (35984). Son of Irving Haskell and Alice (Johnston) Morse; grandson of Grosvenor Clark and Abby (Barber) Morse; great-grandson of Horace and Emeline (Perry) Barber; great²-grandson of Abel and Subinet (Morse) Perry; great³-grandson of Dea Abel and Aseneth (Haven) Perry; great⁴-grandson of *Abel Perry*, Lieutenant, Mass. Militia at Siege of Boston.

GEORGE CARRINGTON MOSELEY, Richmond Va. (35090). Son of Bennett Williamson and Louisa Jane (Venable) Moseley; grandson of Paul Carrington and Emily Eaton (Carrington) Venable; great-grandson of Samuel (Woodson) and Mary (Carrington) Venable; great²-grandson of *Paul Carrington*, Member, Virginia House of Delegates and Committee of Safety.

FREDERICK ALLEN MUNGER, Newburgh, N. Y. (36177). Son of Charles D. and Sarah F. (Crist) Munger; grandson of Isaac S. and Mary A. (Van Vlack) Munger; great-grandson of John and Catherine (Devine) Munger; great²-grandson of *John Munger*, private, Dutchess County, New York Militia.

ROY GARLAND MUNROE, Denver, Colo. (34374). Son of Charles Micajah and Clara Elizabeth (Garland) Munroe; grandson of Jesse Beers and Ann Fosgate (Gowing) Munroe; great-grandson of Andrew and Mary (Beers) Munroe; great²-grandson of *Andrew Munroe*, private, Mass. Militia.

FRANK ERSKINE MURRAY, Salt Lake City, Utah (32643). Son of Thomas and Margaret (Parrett) Murray; grandson of James and Mary (Mitchell) Murray; great-grandson of *Thomas Murray*, Lieutenant-Colonel, Lancaster County, Penna, Associators and Militia.

STEPHEN MORTIMER NASH, Auburn, Me. (34517). Son of Charles Jellerson and Eunice Loring (Buck) Nash; grandson of Ammi Reed and Julia Ann (Sleeper) Nash; great-grandson of Nathan and Mary (Ham) Sleeper; great²-grandson of *David Sleeper*, private, New Hampshire Militia.

RAYMOND NEER, Paterson, N. J. (36154). Son of John and Gertrude (Moot) Neer; grandson of Samuel and Lucinda (Morrison) Neer; great-grandson of *Charles Neer*, private, scout and sharpshooter, Duchess and Albany Counties, New York Militia, pensioned.

MARTIN REMINGTON NELSON, Iowa (35610). Supplemental. Son of Henry H. and Mary E. (Arnold) Nelson; grandson of Lester and Polly (Hanchett) Nelson; great-grandson of Calvin and Ruth (Remington) Nelson; great^2-grandson of Younglove Nelson; great^3-grandson of *John Younglove Nelson*, Captain, Col. Ira Allen's Regt., Vermont Militia.

LESLIE EVERETT NORWOOD, South Portland, Me. (34520). Son of Everett Walter and Annie (Griggs) Norwood; grandson of Robie M. and Aljava (Carver) Norwood; great-grandson of Oliver Mann and Mary (Norton) Norwood; great^2-grandson of Lemuel and Mary (——) Norton; great^3-grandson of *Noah Norton*, private and Corporal, Mass. Militia for seacoast defense.

ROBIE MELVIN NORWOOD, Southwest Harbor, Me. (34518). Son of Robie M. and Aljava (Carver) Norwood; grandson of Oliver Mann and Mary (Norton) Norwood; great-grandson of Lemuel and Mary (Norton) Norwood; great^2-grandson of *Noah Norton*, private and Corporal, Mass. Militia for seacoast defense.

SETH WADEMERE NORWOOD, Portland, Me. (34519). Same as Robie Melvin Norwood, Southwest Harbor, Me. (34518).

JOHN DAVIDSON OLIVER, South Amboy, N. J. (36022). Son of Thomas W. L. and Mary J. (Davison) Oliver; grandson of Charles and Ann (Longstreet) Oliver; great-grandson of William and Sarah (Runyon) Longstreet; great^2-grandson of *Aaron Longstreet, Jr.*, Captain, Middlesex County, New Jersey Militia.

EDWIN WINTHROP OSBORN, Minnesota (25316). Supplemental. Son of Samuel H. and Cynthia (Nutt) Osborn; grandson of Samuel and Sophia (Harding) Osborn; great-grandson of Jabez and Hannah (Hibbard) Osborn; great^2-grandson of *Jeremiah Osborn*, private, Conn. Militia and Artillery, pensioned.

JAMES LYLE OSBORNE, Oakland, Calif. (35958). Son of James Stuart and Blanche (McCormick) Osborne; grandson of Egbert Haywood and Cynthia A. (Crisp) Osborne; great-grandson of Edwin Jay and Margaret (Bell) Osborne; great^2-grandson of *Green Bell*, Captain, Seventh Regt., North Carolina Cont'l Troops.

JAMES STUART OSBORNE, San Francisco, Calif. (35957). Son of Egbert Haywood and Cynthia A. (Crisp) Osborne; grandson of Edwin Jay and Margaret (Bell) Osborne; great-grandson of *Green Bell*, Captain, Seventh Regt., North Carolina Cont'l Troops.

HARRY LUKE OWEN, York, Pa. (35470). Son of Henry Fry and Maria (Reeves) Owen; grandson of Jonathan and Catherine (Hubley) Owen; great-grandson of Thomas and Providence (Schroeder) Owen; great^2-grandson of Abraham and Mary (Dunn) Owen; great^3-grandson of *Thomas Owens*, private, Lancaster County, Penna. Militia.

ROBERT JENKINS PALFREY, New Orleans, La. (35985). Son of George Washington and Sarah Elizabeth (Harrison) Palfrey; grandson of Robert Jenkins and Cavilla (Davis) Palfrey; great-grandson of William and Lydia (Cazneau) Palfrey; great^2-grandson of *William Palfrey*, Aide-de-Camp to General Washington, Paymaster-General and appointed Consul General to France.

CHARLES LOESER PATTERSON, Wilmington, Dela. (35656). Son of Frederick and Elizabeth (Burleigh) Patterson; grandson of George and Maria (Shinkle) Patterson; great-grandson of George and Jane (Burd) Patterson; great^2-grandson of *James Burd*, Colonel, Penna. Militia.

WALTER BROWN PATTERSON, Washington, D. C. (35595). Son of John Bartlett and Mary Jane (Brown) Patterson; grandson of William and Frances Mary (Shepard) Patterson; great-grandson of *Joseph Patterson*, Sergeant, New Hampshire Militia, pensioned; great^2-grandson of *Alexander Patterson*, private, Colonel Stark's Regt., New Hampshire Troops, wounded at Bunker Hill; grandson of Hiram and Mary (White) Brown; great-grandson of William and Sarah (Buntin) Brown; great^2-grandson of *Andrew Buntin*, Captain, Colonel John Waldron's Regt., New Hampshire Militia, killed at White Plains; great-grandson of James and Polly (Alexander) White; great^2-grandson of Isaac and Mary (Moore) White; great^3-grandson of *John Moore*, Lieutenant, Col. Joseph Cilley's Regt., New Hampshire Militia, prisoner.

EDWARD HUGUENIN PEARCE, Major, U. S. Army, San Francisco, Calif. (35947). Son of Webb Nicholson and Nellie Theodora (Trowbridge) Pearce; grandson of Theodore Francis and Sarah Eliza (Hugunin) Trowbridge; great-grandson of Alvah and Marcia (Birch) Trowbridge; great^2-grandson of Reuben and Susannah (Benedict) Trowbridge; great^3-grandson of *John Trowbridge*, Sergeant, Conn. Militia and Cont'l Troops, pensioned.

LEIGH MORGAN PEARSALL, Westfield, N. J. (36024). Son of Alfred Everson and Amanda (Terry) Pearsall; grandson of Henry L. and Sarah (Jones) Terry; great-grandson of Hazzard and Annie (Brown) Terry; great²-grandson of Thomas and Julia (Higgins) Terry; great³-grandson of *Thomas Terry*, Colonel, Third Regt., Suffolk County, New York Militia.

RALPH CORNISH PEARSALL, Westfield, N. J. (36021). Son of Alfred Everson and Amanda (Terry) Pearsall; grandson of Henry L. and Sarah (Jones) Terry; great-grandson of Hazzard and Annie (Brome) Terry; great²-grandson of Thomas and Julia (Higgins) Terry; great³-grandson of *Thomas Terry*, Colonel, Third Regt., Suffolk County, New York Militia.

PHILIP COOMBS PEARSON, Naugatuck, Conn. (35491). Son of John Francis and Lillie Bradshaw (Coombs) Pearson; grandson of Augustus and Catherine De Ford (Davenport) Pearson; great-grandson of Anthony and Sarah Jackson (Little) Davenport, Jr.; great²-grandson of Anthony and Catherine (Greenleaf) Davenport; great³-grandson of *Jonathan Greenleaf*, private, Mass. Militia at Lexington Alarm, Member Committee of Safety and Correspondence.

JOHN HYREN PECK, Des Moines, Iowa (35618). Son of La Forest Henry and Anna Elizabeth (Bartley) Peck; grandson of Hyren Henry and Alma M. (Hill) Peck; great-grandson of Welcome and Harriett G. (Hayford) Peck; great²-grandson of Barney and Elizabeth (Colgrove) Peck; great³-grandson of *Peleg Peck*, private, Colonel Craig's Regt., Rhode Island Militia.

CHARLES FLOYD PERKINS, Brookline, Mass. (36101). Junior member. Son of Charles Brooks and Mary Louise (Floyd) Perkins; grandson of Charles Brooks and Eleanor Elizabeth (Bisbee) Perkins; great-grandson of Thomas Spencer and Betsey Bartlett (Sampson) Perkins; great²-grandson of Samuel and Abigail (Bartlett) Sampson; great³-grandson of *Samuel Sampson (Samson)*, private, Middleborough, Mass. Militia; great⁴-grandson of *John Samson*, private, Mass. Minute Men and Militia; great³-grandson of *Solomon Bartlett, Jr.*, Corporal and Sergeant, Mass. Cont'l Troops; grandson of Charles Octavius and Maria Eliza (Johnson) Floyd; great-grandson of Daniel and Catherine (Poor) Floyd; great²-grandson of Lemuel and Elizabeth (Richardson) Poor; great³-grandson of *Peter Poor*, Lieutenant, Mass. Militia at Lexington Alarm; great³-grandson of *Eleazer Richardson*, private, Mass. Minute Men at Lexington Alarm; great²-grandson of Daniel and Mary (Dampney) Floyd; great²-grandson of *Joseph Dampney*, private, Colonel Mansfield's Regt., Mass. Militia; great-grandson of Thomas and Elizabeth Manning (Magnoni) Bisbee; great²-grandson of Zebulon and Sally (Samson) Bisbee; great³-grandson of *George Bisbee*, private, Mass. Militia, pensioned.

ALBERT HOVEY PEYTON, U. S. Army, Dalton, Ga. (35222). Supplemental. Son of Thomas West and Mary Thornburg (Hovey) Peyton; grandson of William Marshall and Ellen Eliza (Thornburg) Hovey; great-grandson of Thomas and Margaret Catherine (Miller) Thornburg; great²-grandson of John and Sophia (Clendenin) Miller; great³-grandson of *Christian Miller*, Sergeant, Shenandoah County, Virginia Militia, pensioned.

HENRY BYRON PHILLIPS, Berkeley, Calif. (35959). Son of Albert Alexander and Almira (Rice) Phillips; grandson of George and Rebecca (Corpe) Phillips; great-grandson of Joseph and Nancy (Williams) Phillips; great²-grandson of *David Phillips*, private, Rhode Island Militia.

LOUIS MOREAU PORTER, Summit, N. J. (36167). Son of Joseph Moore and Hannah F. (Veale) Porter; grandson of Fletcher G. and Margater (Shepard) Porter; great-grandson of Joseph and Frances (Pritchard) Porter; great²-grandson of *William Porter*, Lieutenant, Eighth Regt., Virginia Cont'l Line.

CLARENCE ARTHUR POWELL, Chicago, Ill. (36207). Son of William Clarence and Agnes (Bate) Powell; grandson of Josiah S. and Martha (Hess) Powell; great-grandson of Henry and Mary (Alspaugh) Powell; great²-grandson of Peter and Catherine (Fellers) Powell; great³-grandson of *Philip Powell*, private, First Battalion, Philadelphia, Penna. Militia.

LEIGH WELLS PRENTICE, Philadelphia, Pa. (36302). Son of Levi Wells and Emma Roseline (Sparks) Prentice; grandson of Samuel Wells and Rhoda S. (Robbins) Prentice; great-grandson of John and Olive (Kibbe) Prentice, Jr.; great²-grandson of *John Prentice*, Corporal, Conn. Militia.

AUGUSTUS SIDNEY PRESCOTT, St. Paul, Minn. (35681). Son of Charles Abbott and Martha (Sargant) Prescott; grandson of Asa and Sophia (Derby) Prescott; great-grandson of Ebenzer and Lydia (Wood) Prescott; great²-grandson of *Ebeneser Prescott*, private, Mass. Militia.

EDMUND BROWN RANDALL, Paterson, N. J. (36279). Son of Thomas William and Jennie Sarah (Perry) Randall; grandson of George W. and Margaret Melvina (——) Perry; great-grandson of Bethuel and Sarah (Pierson) Williams; great²-grandson of *Samuel Williams*, private, Second Regt., Essex County, New Jersey Light Horse.

GROVER REES, Houston, Tex. (29499). Son of Charles and Ophelia (Hardy) Rees, Jr.; grandson of Charles and Artemise (Breaux) Rees; great-grandson of David and Anastasia (Guidry) Rees; great²-grandson of *John Reese*, Captain, Second and Third Battalions, Penna. Troops.

LATIMER COOK REEVES, Keokuk, Iowa (36228). Son of David E. and Cora (Clark) Reeves; grandson of Obed H. and Elizabeth Fisher (Cook) Clark; great-grandson of John W. and Ester (Westbrook) Fisher; great²-grandson of Joseph I. and Sarah Ann (Ennis) Westbrook; great³-grandson of *Daniel Ennis*, Ensign, Third Regt., Sussex County, New Jersey Militia.

CLARENCE EDGAR RICE, Springfield, Mass. (35870). Son of Luther and Mary (Skinner) Rice; grandson of Amon and Phila (Tolles) Rice; great-grandson of *Isaac Rice*, private, Mass. Cont'l Line.

OSCAR NELSON RICE, Adrian, Mich. (36031). Son of Alvin D. and Lydia Jane (Drown) Rice; grandson of Joseph and Mary (Burnell) Rice; great-grandson of *Joseph Rice*, private, Colonel Doolittle's Regt., Mass. Militia.

JOHN BYRD RIDER, Riderwood, Ala. (Md. 36079). Son of William H. and Margaret (A——) Rider; grandson of Noah and Elizabeth (Byrd) (Bird) Rider; great-grandson of John and Mrs. Margaret (Law) Handy Byrd; great²-grandson of *Benjamin Byrd (Bird)*, private, Somerset County, Maryland Militia.

FRANKLIN RIGHTMIRE, Paterson, N. J. (36281). Son of Voorhees T. and Mary L. (Britton) Rightmire; grandson of Dean and Mary S. (Dey) Britton; great-grandson of John Wetherill and Catharine (Rue) Dey; great²-grandson of Nehemiah and Rachel (Wetherill) Dey; great³-grandson of *John Wetherill*, Colonel, New Jersey Militia, Member Provincial Congress and Committee of Safety and Correspondence.

GEORGE McKENZIE ROBERTS, New York (29209). Supplemental. Son of George Simon and Florence Loise (McKenzie) Roberts; grandson of George Clapp and Elizabeth Cogswell (Hewett) Roberts; great-grandson of Thomas and Sophia (Spear) Roberts; great²-grandson of *John Roberts*, private, Col. Samuel Wylly's Regt., Conn. Cont'l Infantry.

WILLIAM V. ROSENCRANS, Paterson, N. J. (36280). Son of Martin and Martha (Van Blarcom) Rosenkrans; grandson of Avert (Everitt) and Mary (Buss) Rosenkrans; great-grandson of Benjamin and Margaret (Schoonover) Rosenkrans; great²-grandson of *John Rosenkrans*, Colonel, New Jersey Militia.

KENNETH BISHOP ROWLEY, Swampscott, Mass. (36109). Son of Frederick H. and Lillian J. (Bishop) Rowley; grandson of George A. and Josephine (Fay) Bishop; great-grandson of Lysander and Priscilla E. (Chamberlain) Fay; great²-grandson of Salmon and Deborah (Merriam) Chamberlain; great³-grandson of John and Gratia (Goodale) Chamberlain; great⁴-grandson of *Ebeneser Goodale (Goodall)*, Captain, Mass. Minute Men and Militia.

FREDERICK CROMWELL ROYCE, Brooklyn, N. Y. (35915). Son of Thomas Cromwell and Anna Louisa (Sweet) Royce; grandson of Halstead and Sarah Ann (Sears) Sweet; great-grandson of *Benoni Sweet*, private, Col. James Holmes' Regt., New York Cont'l Line.

WILLIAM FRANKLIN RUBY, La Fayette, Ind. (35511). Son of John Ochiltree and Deborah (Faile) Ruby; grandson of Peter and Nancy (Polk) Ruby; great-grandson of *Charles Polk*, Captain in Gen'l George Rogers Clark Campaign.

EDWARD W. RUSSELL, Paterson, N. J. (36162). Son of John W. and Josephine H. (Dale) Russell; grandson of Ebenezer and Mary (Stone) Russell; great-grandson of Daniel and Sarah (Sutton) Russell; great²-grandson of *Richard Sutton*, Second Lieutenant, Essex County, Mass. Militia.

MATHIAS WILLIAM SAMPLE, Iowa City, Iowa (35621). Son of Hamilton S. and Ruhama (Zimmerman) Sample; grandson of Mathias and Sarah (Sample) Zimmerman; great-grandson of Ezekiel and Sarah (Hutchinson) Sample; great²-grandson of *Ezekiel Sample,* Corporal, Col. William Irvine's Regt., Sixth Battalion, Penna. Troops.

FRANK SANBERN, Brooklyn, N. Y. (35928). Son of Albert William and Hattie (Congdon) Sanbern; grandson of Jeremiah S. and Martha A. (Loomis) Sanbern; great-grandson of Henry and Elizabeth (Utley) Loomis; great²-grandson of *Nathaniel Loomis,* Ensign, Twelfth Regt., Conn. Militia.

OLIVER SANDREUTER, Stamford, Conn. (35493). Son of Edward and May (Potter) Sandreuter; grandson of Robert Perce and Katharine (Beaker) Potter; great-grandson of George Muirheid and Mary (Van Cleve) Beaker; great²-grandson of William and Elizabeth (Muirheid) Beaker; great²-grandson of *Jonathan Muirheid,* private, Hunterdon County, New Jersey Militia; great²-grandson of Charles and Sarah (Waters) Van Cleve; great²-grandson of *John Van Cleve,* private, First Regt., Hunterdon County, New Jersey Militia; great-grandson of Charles Oliver and Sally Maria (Bennett) Potter; great²-grandson of Elisha Williams and Huldah (Lewis) Bennett; great³-grandson of *Valentine Lewis,* private, Conn. Militia, pensioned; great⁴-grandson of Aaron and Lucy (Williams) Bennett; great⁴-grandson of *Elisha Williams,* private, Conn. Militia and Member State Finance Committee; great⁴-grandson of Elisha and Lucy (Denison) Williams; great⁵-grandson of *George Denison,* private, Conn. Militia, pensioned.

STUART SANDREUTER, Stamford, Conn. (35492). Same as Oliver Sandreuter, Connecticut (35493).

HAZEN IRWIN SAWYER, Keokuk, Iowa (35613). Son of Iram Allen and Mary C. (Irwin) Sawyer; grandson of Allen and Clarissa (Hazen) Sawyer; great-grandson of *Ephraim Sawyer, Jr.,* Captain, Col. Timothy Bigelow's Regt., Mass. Militia; great²-grandson of *Ephraim Sawyer,* Lieutenant-Colonel, Whitcomb's Regt., Mass. Militia.

JAMES SAWYER, Cleveland, Ohio (35894). Son of James F. and Nancy (Coston) Sawyer; grandson of Isaac B. and Mary Kelly Mills (Edney) Sawyer; great-grandson of Samuel and Eleanor (Mills) Edney; great²-grandson of *William Mills,* private, North Carolina Militia, and Member Pitt County Committee of Safety.

GEORGE PENROSE SCHMUCKER, Washington, D. C. (35596). Son of George P. and Annie Elizabeth (Snyder) Schmucker; grandson of Rueben and Cecila (Roth) Snyder; great-grandson of Jacob and Annie (Schrieber) Roth; great²-grandson of Jacob and Eva (Leisering) Schrieber; great²-grandson of *Jacob Schrieber,* private, Northampton County, Penna. Militia.

HARRY BLAUVELT SCHOONMAKER, Paterson, N. J. (36152). Son of Henry and Stella (Bush) Schoonmaker; grandson of John and Hannah Elenor (Feeney) Bush; great-grandson of Owen and Eliza Ann Tier(s) (Monroe) Feeney; great²-grandson of George and Elenor (O'Neil) Tier(s); great²-grandson of *John O'Neil,* private, Colonel Maxwell's Brigade, New Jersey Troops, pensioned.

SAMUEL VAIL SCHOONMAKER, Newburgh, N. Y. (35926). Son of John and Mary Adelaide (Vail) Schoonmaker; grandson of John Adriance and Rachel (Sammons) Schoonmaker; great-grandson of *Abraham Schoonmaker,* Adjutant, Colonel Hardenburgh's Regt., Ulster County, New York Militia.

WILLIAM DAVIS SEABROOK, Paterson, N. J. (36175). Son of Thomas and Josephine (Adams) Seabrook; grandson of Thomas and Evaline (Barber) Seabrook; great-grandson of James and Merriam (Lambert) Seabrook; great²-grandson of John and Mrs. Hannah (Little) Dennis Lambert; great²-grandson of *John Little, Jr.,* Member Shrewsbury, New Jersey Committee of Observation.

URIAH SEELY, Newark, N. J. (36170). Son of James and Amanda (Mason) Seely; grandson of *John Seely (Seeley),* private, New Jersey Militia, State and Cont'l Troops.

FRED ROMAYNE SEGER, Adrian, Mich. (36032). Son of Fred Romayne and Margaret (Sweet) Seger; grandson of Myron W. and Margaret (Mettler) Sweet; great-grandson of Daniel and Nancy (Mickley) Mettler; great²-grandson of Daniel and Tamer (Evans) Mickley; great²-grandson of *John Jacob Mickley,* private, Philadelphia, Penna. Militia and preserver of bells of Christ Church.

ISAAC A. SERVEN, Clifton, N. J. (36019). Son of Oliver and Mary Anne (O'Neill) Serven; grandson of Isaac and Nancy (Scudder) Serven; great-grandson of *Garret Serven*, private, Orange County, New York Militia.

CHARLES WILLIAM SHAW, Springfield, Mass. (35871). Son of Charles L. and Lucy H. (Barton) Shaw; grandson of Elkanah and Fidelia (Rindge) Barton, Jr.; great-grandson of *Elkanah Barton*, private, Mass. and Conn. Militia, pensioned.

TIMOTHY WALLACE SHERWOOD, Fort Wayne, Ind. (35512). Son of Thomas Russell and Anna Maria (Wallace) Sherwood; grandson of Timothy and Olive (Sherman) Wallace; great-grandson of *Ebenezer Wallace (Wallis)*, private, Mass. Militia, pensioned.

WILLAM THOMAS SHERWOOD, Washington, D. C. (35599). Son of Clarkson R. and Ella N. (Larman) Sherwood; grandson of John Quincy and Mary Jane (———) Larman; great-grandson of John and Margaret (Lauman) Larman; great²-grandson of *Jacob Lauman*, private, Penna. Militia.

CHARLES UPTON SHREVE, 3RD, Detroit, Mich. (36033). Son of Leven Lawrence and Elizabeth (Mitchell) Shreve; grandson of Charles Upton and Sallie Benbridge (McCandless) Shreve; great-grandson of James and Sarah T. (Benbridge) McCandless; great²-grandson of Henry and Sarah (Truxton) Benbridge; great³-grandson of *Thomas Truxton*, Commander ship "Constellation"; great-grandson of Thomas Talliferro and Eliza (Rogers) Shreve; great²-grandson of *William Shreve*, private, Maryland Militia.

MARTIN ELLIOTT SHULTZ, Fort Myers, Fla. (29918). Son of George Renton and Josephine (Smith) Shultz; grandson of Benjamin and Deborah (Bittenbender) Shultz; great-grandson of Samuel and Mary Wagner (Deshler) Bittenbender; great²-grandson of John Adam and Deborah (Wagner) Deshler; great³-grandson of *David Deshler*, Member Northampton County, Penna. Committee of Correspondence and Commissary of Supplies.

EARL LEO SIXX, Paterson, N. J. (36020). Son of Scott and Alice L. (Sager) Sixx; grandson of Henry and Laura S. (Christian) Sager; great-grandson of John B. and Bolina (Hamilton) Christian; great²-grandson of Daniel and Christiann (Anspiger) Christian, Jr.; great³-grandson of *Daniel Christian*, private, Penna. Militia and Cont'l Troops, pensioned.

HAROLD S. SIXX, Clifton, N. J. (36025). Same as Earl Leo Sixx, New Jersey (36020).

HERBERT SUMNER SLEEPER, Lewiston, Me. (34521). Son of Sumner and Amelia Miller (Pratt) Sleeper; grandson of Nathan and Mary (Ham) Sleeper; great-grandson of *David Sleeper*, private, New Hampshire Militia.

ELMER MENZO SMITH, San Francisco, Calif. (35948). Son of Zenas Watson and Helen Martha (Hurd) Smith; grandson of Silas Reeves and Mary Ann (Bellows) Hurd; great-grandson of Ebenezer and Sarah (Reeves) Hurd; great²-grandson of *Abraham Hurd*, private, Conn. Militia.

JOHN ABDIEL SMITH, Major, U. S. Army, Washington, D. C. (35597). Son of John George and Mary Ann (McLure) Smith; grandson of Abdiel and Mary (Shearer) McLure; great-grandson of Robert and Agnes (McLeod) McLure; great²-grandson of *Abdiel McLure, Jr.*, Lieutenant, Penna. "Flying Camp."

McNEIR SMITH, Bethlehem, Penna. (D. C. 35598). Son of James Edgar and Emma (McNeir) Smith; grandson of George Alexander Randall and Margaret Emma (Henning) McNeir; great-grandson of William and Mary Ann (Maccubbin) McNeir; great²-grandson of Thomas and Elizabeth (Coberth) McNeir; great³-grandson of *Thomas McNeir*, Sergeant, Frederick, Maryland German Artillery; great³-grandson of Thomas and Nancy (Burgess) McNeir; great⁴-grandson of *Edward Burgess*, Captain, Maryland "Flying Camp," Member Maryland Committee of Observation and House of Delegates.

ROY UNDERWOOD SMITH, Paterson, N. J. (36156). Son of William Henry and Jennie Van (Houten) Smith; grandson of Hiram Judson and Sarah Elizabeth (Underwood) Smith; great-grandson of Jonas and Mary (Stiles) Underwood; great²-grandson of *Jonas Underwood*, private, Col. Rufus Putnam's Regt., Mass. Militia, pensioned.

STERLING WALLACE SMITH, Oakland, Calif. (35949). Son of Loyal and Mary Lovina (Speer) Smith; grandson of Harvey and Maria (Sacket) Smith; great-grandson of *Amos Smith*, private, Col. John Fellow's Regt., Mass. Militia.

FRANK ATWELL SOMERVILLE, Fort Collins, Colo. (34375). Son of Samuel Wilson and Jennie (Farish) Somerville; grandson of James and Mary (Atwell) Somerville; great-grandson of *Francis Atwell*, Captain, Fauquier County, Virginia Militia.

LEO JOHN STAFFORD, Adrian, Mich. (36034). Son of John W. and Edith (McCurty) Stafford; grandson of Thomas and Catherine (Doty) McCurty; great-grandson of Michael and Rachel (Rouse) Doty; great²-grandson of *Peter Doty*, private, Fourteenth Regt., Albany County, New York Militia.

PAUL HAROLD STAFFORD, Adrian, Mich. (36035). Son of Ernest B. and Bessie May (Pentecost) Stafford; grandson of John W. and Edith (McCurty) Stafford; great-grandson of Thomas and Catharine (Doty) McCurty; great²-grandson of Michael and Rachel (Rouse) Doty; great²-grandson of *Peter Doty*, private, Fourteenth Regt., Albany County, New York Militia.

JAMES MADISON STANLEY, Kansas (33318). Supplemental. Son of John O. and Dolly (Flansburg) Stanley; grandson of John and Catherine (Becker) Flansburg; great-grandson of *Matthew Flansburg*, Lieutenant, Colonel Quackenboss' Regt., Albany County, New York Militia.

JOHN PRICE STARKS, Louisville, Ky. (34723). Son of James Madison and Susan (Crutcher) Starks; grandson of Richard and Parmelie (Berry) Crutcher; great-grandson of Samuel and Susannah (Hieatt) Berry; great²-grandson of *Benjamin Berry*, private, Virginia Cont'l Line, pensioned.

LEWIS THOMAS STERLING, Iron Mountain, Mich. (36036). Son of William Erastus and Octavia (Parsons) Sterling; grandson of William and Jerusha (Ely) Sterling; great-grandson of *William Sterling*, Captain, Third Regt., Conn. Militia and Member Army Purchasing Committee.

ARCHIE STEVENSON, Arthur, No. Dak. (33023). Son of Thomas and Sophia Glass (Spinning) Stevenson; grandson of George Burnett and Elizabeth Cassatt (Monfort) Spinning; great-grandson of *Isaac Spinning*, private, First Regt., Essex County, New Jersey Militia.

JAMES A. GARFIELD STITZER, East Orange, N. J. (N. Y. 36178). Son of William T. and Emma (Hammes) Stitzer; grandson of John D. and Sarah (Heckaman) Stitzer; great-grandson of *David Stitzer (Statzer)*, private, Col. Thomas Proctor's Regt. Penna. Artillery.

GAILLARD STONEY, San Francisco, Calif. (35950). Son of Thomas Porcher and Kate Maria (Allen) Stoney; grandson of Joseph and Katharine (Walker) Allen; great-grandson of Isaac and Rebecca (Dakin) Allen; great²-grandson of *Abijah Allen*, Sergeant, New Hampshire Militia.

BOYD J. TALLMAN, Seattle, Wash. (34047). Son of John and Ruth Carnahan (Boyd) Tallman; grandson of William and Jane (Carnahan) Boyd; great-grandson of John and Elizabeth (Elliott) Carnahan; great²-grandson of *James Carnahan*, Captain, Penna. Militia and Cont'l Line.

WILLIAM THORPE TAPLEY, St. Paul, Minn. (35682). Son of George Arthur and Helen A. (Pickering) Tapley; grandson of George A. and Parnell Munroe (Thorpe) Tapley; great-grandson of Ira and Catherine (Munroe) Thorpe; great²-grandson of *Eliphalet Thorpe*, Captain, Col. John Brook's Regt., Mass. Cont'l Troops; great²-grandson of *Philemon Munroe*, private, Col. Eleazer Brook's Regt., Mass. Militia.

HENRY RUMSEY TATNALL, Wilmington, Del. (35660). Son of Thomas and Margaret Conarroe (Rumsey) Tatnall; grandson of Joseph and Sarah (Richardson) Tatnall; great-grandson of Edward and Margery (Paxson) Tatnall; great²-grandson of *Joseph Tatnall*, patriotic miller and home given to General Wayne as headquarters.

ARTHUR SAMUEL TAYLOR, Olympia, Wash. (34048). Son of Samuel Mason and Georgia (Smith) Taylor; grandson of Samuel and Almira (Green) Taylor; great-grandson of George and Martha (Hulett) Taylor; great²-grandson of *Nathan Taylor*, Lieutenant, Major Whitcomb's Regt., New Hampshire Rangers.

CHURCHILL TAYLOR, Oakland, Calif. (35951). Son of James Magarr and Laura Montague (Montell) Taylor; grandson of John L. and —— (Magarr) Taylor; great²-grandson of *James Magarr*, private, Col. Timothy Bigelow's Regt., Mass. Militia.

EDWARD WYLLYS TERRY, San Francisco, Calif. (35952). Son of Lucius Hall and Mary Elizabeth (——) Terry; grandson of Roderick and Harriet (Taylor) Terry; great-grandson of John and Elizabeth (Terry) Taylor; great²-grandson of *Nathaniel Terry*, Colonel, Nineteenth Regt., Conn. Militia.

WALTER KIEFFER THRUSH, Harrisburg, Penna. (35471). Son of Ambrose W. and Mary (Kieffer) Thrush; grandson of Cyrus Thompson and Lydia Ann (Britton) Kieffer; great-grandson of Dewald and Rebecca (Bard) Kieffer; great²-grandson of *William Bard (Baird)*, private, Cumberland County, Penna. Militia.

RALPH CLARENCE TILLSON, Portland, Ore. (35061). Son of Clarence Dee and Kittie (Hill) Tillson; grandson of Josiah Pierce and Olive (Lucas) Tillson; great-grandson of Horace and Elizabeth (Hinkson) Lucas; great²-grandson of Eber and Eunice (Woolworth) Lucas; great³-grandson of *Phineas Woolworth*, private, Second Regt., Conn. Militia, pensioned; grandson of James Henry and Rebecca Scott (Moore) Hill; great-grandson of William and Eleanor (Hughes) Moore; great²-grandson of John and Margaret (Logan) Hughes; great³-grandson of *Samuel Logan*, private, Lancaster County, Penna. Militia, pensioned.

HARRY LORENCE TOPPING, Kankakee, Ill. (36208). Son of Nelson Seversen and Louise (Fieber) Topping; grandson of Edward and Elizabeth R. (Gardenier) Topping; great-grandson of John S. and Jane (Van Hoevenberg) Gardenier; great²-grandson of *Rudolph Van Hoevenbergh*, Lieutenant, Fourth Regt., New York Cont'l Troops.

PORTER VAN RIPER, Paterson, N. J. (36169). Son of Laurence A. and Carrie (E——) Van Riper; grandson of William S. and Mary (O'Brian) Porter; great-grandson of John and Emily (McNeil) O'Brian; great²-grandson of John and Polly (Catlin) O'Neil; great³-grandson of *Archibald O'Neil*, Captain, Conn. Militia.

STANLEY CHAUNCEY VAUGHAN, Cheyenne, Wyo. (30022). Son of Frank Hawkins and Lilla D. (Pratt) Vaughan; grandson of Chauncey W. and Luvia (Perrin) Vaughan; great-grandson of Oliver and Elpha (Hawkins) Perrin; great²-grandson of *Dexter Hawkins*, private, Colonel Cary's Regt., Rhode Island Militia.

JOHN READ VOIGT, North Chattanooga, Tenn. (34650). Son of Henry N. and Eliza (Read) Voigt; grandson of John Franklin and Eliza Ann (Pratt) Read; great-grandson of James Gray and Mary (Mahon) Read; great²-grandson of William and Agnes (Venable) Mahon; great³-grandson of James and Judith (Newton) Venable; great⁴-grandson of *Joseph Morton*, Member Charlotte County, Virginia Committee of Safety.

JOHN LUCIUS WALKER, Pittsburgh, Penna. (35472). Son of John William and Florence Edna (Sanderson) Walker; grandson of Lucius and Lucretia Marland (Prentiss) Sanderson; great-grandson of Joseph and Rhoda Maria (Hill) Prentiss; great²-grandson of Festus G. and Rhoda (Torrance) Hill; great³-grandson of *Robert Torrance*, Salisbury, Conn. Artificer.

WILLIAM ELLIOTT RAMSDEN WARNER, California (26756). Supplemental. Son of John Elliott and Florence Daisy (Ramsden) Warner; grandson of Jerry Bradley and Mary Ann (Brown) Warner; great-grandson of Stephen Thurston and Anna (Davis) Brown; great²-grandson of *Malachi Davis*, private, Colonel Stickney's Regt., New Hampshire Militia.

PHILIP KIMBALL WATSON, Detroit, Mich. (36037). Son of Joseph Sumner and Mabel (Stevens) Watson; grandson of Noah S. and Lucy M. (Quimby) Watson; great-grandson of Johnson D. and Mary (Collins) Quimby; great²-grandson of *Aaron Quimby (Queenbi)*, Sergeant and Captain, New Hampshire Militia.

DAVID FAIRCHILD WEEKS, Skillman, N. J. (36023). Son of Henry Martin and Mary Malvina (Fairchild) Weeks; grandson of David Day and Rebecca R. (Richardson) Fairchild; great-grandson of Joseph and Elizabeth (Hoppock) Fairchild; great²-grandson of *Peter Fairchild*, Minute Man and private, Morris County, New Jersey Militia and State Troops, pensioned.

CHARLES WILLIAM WENTWORTH, Westfield, N. J. (36163). Son of Charles Hiram and Mary Evelyn (Greene) Wentworth; grandson of Hiram David and Lucy Frothingham (Wead) Wentworth; great-grandson of Thomas and Rebecca (Blackman) Wentworth; great²-grandson of *Jedediah Wentworth*, private and Corporal, Mass. Militia and Cont'l Troops.

FRANK WEYANT, Ridgewood, N. J. (35929). Son of Wilbur Fisk and Mary Elizabeth (Hunter) Weyant; grandson of George Washington and Amanda (Decker) Weyant; great-grandson of Francis and Abbie (Rider) Weyant; great²-grandson of Tobias and Jerusha (Smith) Weyant; great³-grandson of *John Weiant (Wygant)*, private, Fourth Regt., Orange County, New York Militia, Signer of Association Test.

CHARLES A. WHITMAN, Newark, N. J. (36276). Son of Samuel B. and Elizabeth (Symons) Whitman; grandson of Jacob and Emeline (Hayward) Whitman; great-grandson of *Isaac Whitman*, private, Suffolk County, New York Militia, prisoner.

SAMUEL RAYMOND WILLIAMS, Detroit, Mich. (36038). Son of William Brown and Lucy Hubbard (White) Williams; grandson of Enoch J. and Elizabeth Worthington (Gaylord) White; great-grandson of Enoch and Martha (Lamb) White, Jr.; great²-grandson of *Enoch White*, Lieutenant, Mass. Militia; great²-grandson of *Daniel Gad Lamb*, private, Mass. Militia; great-grandson of Chester and Sidney (Dickinson) Gaylord; great²-grandson of *Samuel Gaylord*, private, Mass. Militia at Lexington Alarm; grandson of William and Phœbe Ann (Brown) Williams; great-grandson of William and Mary Magdalene (Young) Brown; great²-grandson of George and Alice (Hardesty) Brown; great²-grandson of *William Brown*, Lieutenant, Captain Robb's Company, Westmoreland County, Penna. Rangers.

JULIUS EDGAR WILLOUGHBY, Wilmington, N. C. (La. 35987). Son of John Paul and Mary Jane (Cosby) Willoughby; grandson of John Hinchy and Amanda Melvina (Tyler) Willoughby; great-grandson of Willis and Mrs. Mary (Hinchy) Collins Willoughby; great²-grandson of *Edlyne Willoughby*, private, Seventh Regt., Virginia Troops, prisoner, pensioned.

BENJAMIN HEDGES WOODRUFF, Westfield, N. J. (36164). Son of Robert and Elizabeth (Baker) Woodruff; grandson of Hedges and Charlotte K. (Crane) Baker; great-grandson of *Daniel Baker*, Sergeant and Ensign, Essex County, New Jersey Militia and Corporal, Cont'l Line.

GRANT FRANKLIN WRIGHT, Salem, Ind. (35513). Son of Philbird Marion and Barbara Elizabeth (Wiseman) Wright; grandson of Jacob and Mary Magdalene (Ratts) Wiseman; great-grandson of Henry T. and Barbara (Winkler) Ratts; great²-grandson of Francis and Catherine (Bott) Winkler; great³-grandson of *Rheinhard Bott*, Captain, First Company, Third Battalion, York County, Penna. Militia.

JAMES FREDERICK WRIGHT, New Haven, Conn. (35494). Son of Charles F. and Elizabeth (Burhans) Wright; grandson of Barzillai Wood and Minerva (Moon) Wright; great-grandson of David and Sarah (Wood) Wright; great²-grandson of *Barzillai Wood*, Corporal and Sergeant, Mass. Militia, pensioned.

DAVID DUDLEY FIELD YARD, New York City, N. Y. (35930). Son of Wesley Sterling and Annie Macfarlan (Wood) Yard; grandson of Joseph Ashton and Mary Woodward (Sterling) Yard; great-grandson of John Wesley and Ann (Woodward) Sterling; great²-grandson of *James Sterling*, Major, First Regt., Burlington County, New Jersey Militia.

HARRY VREELAND YOUNGMAN, Montclair, N. J. (36158). Son of Vreeland H. and Mary E. (Shaw) Youngman; grandson of Nicholas and Margaret H. (Burbank) Youngman; great-grandson of *John Youngman*, private, Colonel Cilley's Regt., New Hampshire Cont'l Troops.

DINNER OF NEW YORK CHAPTER, EMPIRE STATE SOCIETY, FEBRUARY 21, 1922

OFFICIAL BULLETIN

OF THE

National Society
of the Sons of the American Revolution

Organized April 30, 1889

Incorporated by
Act of Congress, June 9, 1906

President General
WALLACE McCAMANT
Northwestern Bank Building
Portland, Oregon

Published at Washington, D. C., in June, October, December, and March.
Entered as second-class matter, May 7, 1906, at the post-office at Washington, D. C., under the act of July 16, 1894.

Volume XVI   MARCH, 1922   Number 4

The OFFICIAL BULLETIN records action by the General Officers, the Board of Trustees, the Executive and other National Committees, lists of members deceased and of new members, and important doings of State Societies. In order that the OFFICIAL BULLETIN may be up to date, and to insure the preservation in the National Society archives of a complete history of the doings of the entire organization, State Societies and local Chapters are requested to communicate promptly to the Secretary General written or printed accounts of all meetings or celebrations, to forward copies of all notices, circulars, and other printed matter issued by them, and to notify him at once of dates of death of members.

GENERAL OFFICERS ELECTED AT THE BUFFALO CONGRESS, MAY 17, 1921

President General:

WALLACE McCAMANT, Northwestern Bank Building, Portland, Oregon.

Vice-Presidents General:

GEORGE HALE NUTTING, 53 State Street, Boston, Massachusetts.

New England (Maine, New Hampshire, Vermont, Massachusetts, Rhode Island, and Connecticut).

PHILIP F. LARNER, 918 F Street N. W., Washington, District of Columbia.

Middle and Coast District (New York, New Jersey, Pennsylvania, Delaware, Maryland, District of Columbia, Virginia, North Carolina, South Carolina, Georgia, and Florida).

MARVIN H. LEWIS, 201 Keller Building, Louisville, Kentucky.

Mississippi Valley, East District (Michigan, Wisconsin, Illinois, Indiana, Ohio, West Virginia, Kentucky, Tennessee, Alabama, and Mississippi).

HENRY B. HAWLEY, Des Moines, Iowa.

Mississippi Valley, West District (Minnesota, North Dakota, South Dakota, Nebraska, Iowa, Kansas, Missouri, Oklahoma, Arkansas, Louisiana, and Texas).

JOHN W. BELL, JR., P. O. Box 1124, Spokane, Washington.

Mountain and Pacific Coast District (Montana, Idaho, Wyoming, Nevada, Utah, Colorado, Arizona, New Mexico, Oregon, Washington, California, Hawaii, and Philippines).

Secretary General:

FRANK BARTLETT STEELE, 183 St. James Place, Buffalo, New York.

Registrar General:

WILLIAM S. PARKS, 900 17th Street N. W., Washington, District of Columbia.

Treasurer General:

JOHN H. BURROUGHS, 1111 Dean Street, Brooklyn, New York.

Historian General:

GEORGE CARPENTER ARNOLD, Arnold Building, Providence, Rhode Island.

Chancellor General:

EUGENE C. BONNIWELL, City Court Building, Philadelphia, Pennsylvania.

Genealogist General:

WALTER K. WATKINS, 9 Ashburton Place, Boston, Massachusetts.

Chaplin General:

REV. LYMAN WHITNEY ALLEN, 881 S. 7th Street, Newark, New Jersey.

BOARD OF TRUSTEES

The General Officers, together with one member from each State Society, constitute the Board of Trustees of the National Society. The following Trustees for the several States were elected at the Buffalo Congress, May 17, 1921, to serve until their successors are elected at the Congress to be held at Springfield, Mass., in May, 1922:

Alabama, (vacant); Arizona, Clay F. Leonard, Phœnix; Arkansas, George B. Gill, Little Rock; California, Seabury C. Mastick, New York City; Colorado, Malcolm Lindsey, Denver; Connecticut, Clarence Horace Wickham, Hartford; Delaware, George Armstrong Elliott, Wilmington; District of Columbia, Albert D. Spangler, Washington; Far Eastern Society, (vacant); Florida, Dr. F. G. Renshaw, Pensacola; Society in France, (vacant); Hawaiian Society, (vacant); Georgia, Allen Waters, Atlanta; Idaho, (vacant); Illinois, Dorr E. Felt, Chicago; Indiana, Charles C. Jewett, Terre Haute; Iowa, Elmer E. Wentworth, State Center; Kansas, John M. Meade, Topeka; Kentucky, George T. Wood, Louisville; Louisiana, Col. C. Robert Churchill, New Orleans; Maine, William B. Berry, Gardiner; Maryland, Hon. Henry Stockbridge, Baltimore; Massachusetts, Henry Fuller Punderson, Springfield; Michigan, Albert M. Henry, Detroit; Minnesota, Charles E. Rittenhouse, Minneapolis; Mississippi, (vacant); Missouri, George R. Merrill, St. Louis; Montana, Marcus Whritenour, Helena; Nebraska, Benjamin F. Bailey, Lincoln; Nevada, (vacant); New Hampshire, Henry T. Lord, Manchester; New Jersey, Charles Symmes Kiggins, Elizabeth; New Mexico, George G. Klock, Albuquerque; New York, Louis Annin Ames, New York; North Carolina, (vacant); North Dakota, Howard E. Simpson, Grand Forks; Ohio, Moulton Houk, Delaware; Oklahoma, W. A. Jennings, Oklahoma City; Oregon, Wallace McCamant, Portland; Pennsylvania, Col. R. W. Guthrie, Pittsburgh; Rhode Island, Wilfred H. Munro, Providence; South Carolina, (vacant); South Dakota, J. G. Parsons, Sioux Falls; Tennessee, Leland Hume, Nashville; Texas, C. B. Dorchester, Sherman; Utah, Daniel S. Spencer, Salt Lake City; Vermont, William Jeffrey, Montpelier; Virginia, Arthur B. Clarke, Richmond; Washington, Ernest B. Hussey, Seattle; Wisconsin, Walter H. Wright, Milwaukee; Wyoming, Warren Richardson, Cheyenne.

PRESIDENTS AND SECRETARIES OF STATE SOCIETIES

ARIZONA—President, Lloyd B. Christy, 116 N. 1 Avenue, Phœnix.
    Secretary, Clarence P. Woodbury, 1509 Grand Avenue, Phœnix.
    Treasurer, Kenneth Freeland, Phœnix.
ARKANSAS—President, General Benjamin W. Green, Little Rock.
    Secretary, Fay Hempstead, Little Rock.
    Treasurer, Thomas M. Cory, Little Rock.
CALIFORNIA—President, Frank S. Brittain, 80 Cerritos Avenue, San Francisco.
    Secretary and Registrar, Thomas A. Perkins, Mills Building, San Francisco.
    Treasurer, John C. Currier, 713 Merchants' Exchange Building, San Francisco.
COLORADO—President, Victor E. Keyes, 210 Masonic Temple, Denver.
    Secretary, James Polk Willard, 210 Masonic Temple, Denver.
    Treasurer, Walter D. Wynkoop, Mt. States T. & T. Co., Denver.
CONNECTICUT—President, Herbert H. White, 76 N. Beacon Street, Hartford.
    Secretary, Frederick A. Doolittle, 117 Middle Street, Bridgeport.
    Treasurer, Charles G. Stone, P. O. Box 847, Hartford.
DELAWARE—President, Horace Wilson, 404 S. Clayton Street, Wilmington.
    Secretary and Treasurer, Charles A. Rudolph, 900 Vanburen Street, Wilmington.
DISTRICT OF COLUMBIA—President, Selden M. Ely, Gales School Building, Washington.
    Secretary, Kenneth S. Wales, Washington.
    Treasurer, Hilleary F. Offcut, Jr., 1501 Crittenden Street N. W., Washington.
FAR EASTERN SOCIETY—President-Secretary, H. Lawrence Noble, P. O. Box 940, Manila,
    Philippine Islands.
    Vice-President, Edward B. Copeland.
    Treasurer, Herman Roy Hare.
FLORIDA—President, Dr. F. G. Renshaw, Pensacola.
    Secretary, John Hobart Cross, Pensacola.
    Treasurer, F. F. Bingham, Pensacola.
SOCIETY IN FRANCE—Administered by Empire State Society.
GEORGIA—President, Allen Waters, P. O. Box 361, Atlanta.
    Secretary, Arthur W. Falkinburg, 1301 Atlanta Trust Co. Building, Atlanta.
    Treasurer, William Alden, Box 172, Decatur.
HAWAII—President, Donald S. Bowman, Honolulu.
    Secretary, James T. Taylor, 511 Stangenwald Building, Honolulu.
    Treasurer, L. M. Judd.
IDAHO—President, Albert H. Conner, Boise.
    Secretary and Treasurer, Frank G. Ensign, Boise.
ILLINOIS—President, James M. Eddy, 30 North La Salle Street, Chicago.
    Secretary, Louis A. Bowman, 30 North La Salle Street, Chicago.
    Treasurer, Henry R. Kent, 30 North La Salle Street, Chicago.
INDIANA—President, Cornelius F. Posson, Brazil.
    Secretary and Treasurer, Edmund L. Parker, 208 East Walnut Street, Kokomo.
IOWA—President, Walter E. Coffin, 902 7th Street, Des Moines.
    Secretary, Captain Elbridge D. Hadley, 409 Franklin Avenue, Des Moines.
    Treasurer, William E. Barrett, 4815 Grand Avenue, Des Moines.
KANSAS—President, John M. Meade, Topeka.
    Secretary, Arthur H. Bennett, Topeka.
    Treasurer, Walter E. Wilson, Topeka.
KENTUCKY—President, E. T. Hutchings, Columbia Building, Louisville.
    Secretary, George D. Caldwell, Inter-Southern Building, Louisville.
    Treasurer, Alexander W. Tippett, U. S. Trust Co. Building, Louisville.
LOUISIANA—President, C. Robert Churchill, 408 Canal Street, New Orleans.
    Secretary, Herbert P. Benton, 403 Carondelet Building, New Orleans.
    Treasurer, S. O. Landry, 616 Maison Blanche Building, New Orleans.
MAINE—President, William B. Berry, 42 Pleasant Street, Gardiner.
    Secretary, Francis L. Littlefield, 246 Spring Street, Portland.
    Treasurer, Enoch O. Greenleaf, Portland.

MARYLAND—*President, Osborne I. Yellott, 931 Calvert Building, Baltimore.
    Secretary, George Sadtler Robertson, 1628 Linden Avenue, Baltimore.
    Treasurer, W. Bernard Duke, 406 Water Street, Baltimore.
MASSACHUSETTS—President, George Hale Nutting, 53 State Street, Boston.
    Secretary, George S. Stewart, 9 Ashburton Place, Boston.
    Treasurer, Lieut.-Col. Charles M. Green, 78 Marlboro Street, Boston.
MICHIGAN—President, William P. Holliday, 68 Davenport Street, Detroit.
    Secretary, Raymond E. Van Syckle, 1729 Ford Building, Detroit.
    Treasurer, Frank G. Smith, 237 Hancock Avenue E., Detroit.
MINNESOTA—President, Kenneth G. Brill, 43 South Hamline Avenue, St. Paul.
    Secretary, Charles H. Bronson, 48 East Fourth Street, St. Paul.
    Treasurer, Charles W. Eddy, 302 Pittsburg Building, St. Paul.
MISSISSIPPI—President, Judge Gordon Garland Lyell, Jackson.
    Secretary and Treasurer, William H. Pullen, Mechanics' Bank Building, Jackson.
MISSOURI—President, Col. W. D. Vandiver, Columbia.
    Secretary, J. Alonzo Matthews, 901 Pontiac Building, St. Louis.
    Treasurer, I. Shreve Carter, 308 Merchant La Clede Building, St. Louis.
MONTANA—President, Paris B. Bartley, Helena.
    Secretary and Treasurer, Leslie Sulgrove, Helena.
NEBRASKA—President, Benjamin F. Bailey, 506 1st National Bank Building, Lincoln.
    Secretary, Addison E. Sheldon, 1319 South 23d Street, Lincoln.
    Treasurer, C. E. Bardwell, 522 Terminal Building, Lincoln.
NEVADA—President, Rt. Rev. George C. Huntting, 505 Ridge Street, Reno.
NEW HAMPSHIRE—President, Prof. Ashley K. Hardy, Hanover.
    Secretary and Treasurer, Will B. Howe, Concord.
NEW JERSEY—President, Rev. Lyman Whitney Allen, D. D., 881 S. 7th Street, Newark.
    Secretary, David L. Pierson, 33 Lombardy Street, Newark.
    Treasurer, Earle A. Miller, 156 William Street, Orange.
NEW MEXICO—President, C. C. Manning, Gallup.
    Secretary, Frank W. Graham, Albuquerque.
    Treasurer, Orville A. Matson, Albuquerque.
NEW YORK—President, Harvey F. Remington, Wilder Building, Rochester.
    Secretary, Major Charles A. Du Bois, 220 Broadway, New York City.
    Treasurer, James de la Montanye, 220 Broadway, New York City.
NORTH CAROLINA—President, Frank H. Bryan, Washington.
    Secretary (vacant).
    Treasurer, W. B. Harding, Washington.
NORTH DAKOTA—President, Howard E. Simpson, University of North Dakota, Grand Forks.
    Secretary, Walter R. Reed, Amenia.
    Treasurer, J. W. Wilkerson, University of North Dakota, Grand Forks.
OHIO—President, Walter J. Sherman, The Nasby, Toledo.
    Secretary, W. L. Curry, Box 645, Columbus.
    Treasurer, S. G. Harvey, 290 E. Gay Street, Columbus.
OKLAHOMA—President, George L. Bowman, Kingfisher.
    Secretary-Treasurer, Edward F. McKay, 536 West 31st Street, Oklahoma City.
OREGON—President, B. B. Beekman, 601 Platt Building, Portland.
    Secretary, B. A. Thaxter, Post Office Box 832, Portland.
    Treasurer, A. A. Lindsley, Henry Building, Portland.
PENNSYLVANIA—President, W. C. Lyne, Farmers' Bank Building, Pittsburgh.
    Secretary, Francis Armstrong, Jr., 515 Wood Street, Pittsburgh.
    Treasurer, A. M. Wall, Farmers' Bank Building, Pittsburgh.
RHODE ISLAND—President, Herbert A. Rice, 809 Hospital Trust Building, Providence.
    Secretary, Theodore E. Dexter, 104 Clay Street, Central Falls.
    Treasurer, William L. Sweet, Box 1515, Providence.
SOUTH CAROLINA—No report.
SOUTH DAKOTA—President, Amos E. Ayres, Sioux Falls.
    Secretary, T. W. Dwight, Sioux Falls.
    Treasurer, B. H. Requa, Sioux Falls.

---

* Deceased, March 20, 1922.

TENNESSEE—President, William K. Boardman, Nashville.
    Secretary, Frederick W. Millspaugh, Nashville.
    Treasurer, Carey Folk, 411 Union Street, Nashville.
TEXAS—President, C. B. Dorchester, Sherman.
    Secretary, Walter S. Mayer, Galveston.
    Treasurer, P. R. Markham, Sherman.
UTAH—President, Robert E. McConaughy, 1079 E. 2d South Street, Salt Lake City.
    Secretary, Gordon Lines Hutchins, Dooly Building, Salt Lake City.
    Treasurer—Seth Warner Morrison, Jr., 32 S. 7th East Street, Salt Lake City.
VERMONT—President, William H. Jeffrey, Montpelier.
    Secretary, Walter H. Crockett, Burlington.
    Treasurer, Clarence L. Smith, Burlington.
VIRGINIA—President, Arthur B. Clarke, 616 American National Bank Building, Richmond.
    Secretary and Treasurer, William E. Crawford, 700 Travelers' Building, Richmond.
WASHINGTON—President, Walter Burges Beals, Haller Building, Seattle.
    Secretary, Henry J. Gorin, 322 Central Building, Seattle.
    Treasurer, Kenneth P. Hussey, 917 North 34th Ave., Seattle.
WISCONSIN—President, J. Tracy Hale, Jr., Wells Building, Milwaukee.
    Secretary, Emmett A. Donnelly, 1030 Wells Building, Milwaukee.
    Treasurer, William Stark Smith, 373 Lake Drive, Milwaukee.
WYOMING—President, David A. Haggard, Cheyenne.
    Secretary, Maurice Groshon, Cheyenne.
    Treasurer, James B. Guthrie, Cheyenne.

THE SPRINGFIELD CONGRESS

The committee in charge of the Springfield Congress makes the following announcement:

The headquarters will be at the Hotel Kimball, on Chestnut Street, five minutes' walk from the station. One hundred and fifty rooms have been set aside for the delgates. The prices for rooms are as follows: Single rooms, without bath, $2.50 and $3.00; with bath, $3.50 to $5.00; double rooms, without bath, $5.00; with bath, $7.00 to $8.50. The other hotels in the city are the Hotel Bridgeway, $2.75 to $3.50, with bath; Hotel Worthy, $2.00 to $6.00; Clinton Hall, $2.00 and up.

The tentative program is as follows:

Sunday evening—Church service at 7.30 p. m., at South (Congregational) Church. Sermon by the Chaplain General. Delegates will march to the Church in a body, escorted by the local Chapter. Municipal chimes will play.

Monday forenoon—Meeting of Congress.

Monday noon—Luncheon.

Monday afternoon—Session of Congress.

Tuesday morning—Final session of Congress and election of officers.

Tuesday noon—Luncheon, the place under consideration being the Country Club.

Tuesday afternoon—Automobile trip around the city and surrounding country.

Tuesday evening—Complimentary banquet to the delegates.

All inquiries of the local committee (except for hotel reservations) should be addressed to *Charles F. Warner, Principal, Technical High School, Springfield, Mass.*

NATIONAL COMMITTEE ON ARRANGEMENTS

Mr. Burton H. Wiggin, chairman, Boston, Mass.

Mr. William B. Berry, Gardiner, Maine.

Mr. Charles F. Read, Boston, Mass.

Dr. George T. Spicer, Providence, R. I.

FOR YOUR FAVORABLE CONSIDERATION

I regret the necessity of again taking up with the membership the troublesome question of finances. The conditions which have operated to increase expenses in our homes and in our business undertakings have unavoidably increased the expenses of the National Society. The enormous volume of work in the Registrar General's office is most inadequately compensated. The services of the Secretary General, if rendered in the business world, would command a much larger remuneration than the Society is able to pay him. I doubt if there is any other organization in which so many individuals expend money for the benefit of the organization without rendering expense bills therefor. Even so, the revenues of the National Society do not now cover its necessary and minimum expenses. We have dispensed with the Year Book, but we cannot give up the BULLETIN. It is the organ by which the National Society maintains touch with the individual compatriots, wheresoever dispersed. We were under no expense for rent during the lifetime of A. Howard Clark. He stored our records for us in the Smithsonian Institution. Since his death it has been necessary for us to rent quarters in Washington.

I bespeak favorable consideration of the amendments proposed by the Executive Committee for the relief of the treasury. The National Society, Daughters of the American Revolution, now collects an initiation fee of $5.00 and a per capita tax of $1.00 for the use of the National Society. These exactions have not checked the growth or diminished the usefulness of our sister Society. Can we not profit by their experience?

Wallace McCamant

Minutes of the Meeting of the Executive Committee of the National Society, Sons of the American Revolution, Held at the Union League Club, New York City, February 17, 1922.

There were present the President General, Hon. Wallace McCamant; Directors General James Harry Preston, Louis Annin Ames, Arthur P. Sumner, and Major W. I. Lincoln Adams; also Secretary General Frank B. Steele and Treasurer General John H Burroughs.

The meeting was called to order by the President General as chairman, and the Secretary General read the minutes of the former meeting of the Executive Committee, held in Buffalo, on May 18, 1921, and also the minutes of the Executive Committee business that was carried on by mail in the interim, as designated by the Board of Trustees.

The Report of the Treasurer General was received and ordered filed.

The Report of the Registrar General was received, accepted, and ordered filed.

It was moved by Director General Preston that the future BULLETINS contain a brief statement of purposes and objects of the Society and a statement of the requirements for eligibility to membership in the Society. This was adopted.

Director General Adams reported upon the work of the special committee appointed to take up the matter of enlarging the Board of Trustees, made necessary by the increased number of General Officers. It was moved and adopted that this committee should continue its work until after the meeting of the National Congress in Springfield in May.

It was moved by Judge Sumner that the Executive Committee propose the following amendment to the Constitution and recommend its adoption:

That Article VI of the Constitution of the National Society be amended to read as follows:

ARTICLE VI.—*Initiation Fee and Dues.*

SEC. 1. *In addition to the initiation fee, if any, charged by a State Society, there shall be paid an initiation fee of five dollars for membership in the National Society, Sons of the American Revolution. Said fee shall be forwarded to the Registrar General with each application for membership. The payment of said fee shall include an engraved certificate of membership for each newly elected compatriot, to be furnished by the National Society.*

SEC. 2. Each State Society shall pay annually to the Treasurer General, to defray the expense of the National Society, fifty cents for each member thereof, unless intermitted by the National Congress.

SEC. 3. Such dues shall be paid on or before the first day of April in each year for the ensuing year, in order to secure representation in the Congress of the National Society.

(Italics indicate amendments added.)

This resolution was adopted

It was moved by Judge Sumner that the Executive Committee propose the following amendment to the Constitution as an alternative to the amendment proposed above, as follows:

That Article VI of the Constitution of the National Society be amended to read as follows:

Each State society shall pay annually to the Treasurer General to defray the expense of the National Society, *one dollar* for each member thereof, unless intermitted by the National Congress.

Such dues shall be paid on or before the first day of April for the ensuing year, in order to secure representation in the Congress of the National Society.

(Italics indicate amendments added or changed.)

This resolution was adopted

Director General Adams moved that one of the National Society War Medals be sent to the Numismatic Society of New York. This was adopted.

Director General Adams moved that the following amendment be proposed by the Executive Committee and its adoption recommended:

That Section 1 of Article VII of the Constitution be amended to read as follows:

The annual Congress of the National Society, for the election of General Officers and for the transaction of business, shall be held on the *fourth Monday of August* in each year. The place of such meeting shall be designated by the Board of Trustees.

(Italics indicate words changed or added.)

This motion was adopted.

A letter was read from Vice-President General George Hale Nutting suggesting and recommending that a complete index of the membership of the National Society and ancestors be printed and distributed.

It was moved by Director General Ames that the President General appoint a committee to report to the National Congress on this subject, with reference to the cost of publishing such an index, and that only such number be printed, if decided upon, as may be subscribed for.

This resolution was adopted.

The President General appointed Vice-President General Nutting, Secretary General Steele and Genealogist General Watkins as this committee.

Upon motion, the meeting adjourned subject to the call of the Chair.

Respectfully submitted,

Frank B Steele

Secretary General.

SPECIAL ANNOUNCEMENT

At a meeting of the Connecticut Society held at Bridgeport, February 22, 1922, the following amendment to the Constitution of the National Society, S. A. R., was presented, unanimously adopted, and recommended for adoption by the Congress of the National Society at Springfield, Mass., May 15-16, 1922:

That Article V, Section 4, of the Constitution be amended to read as follows:

An Executive Committee of seven, consisting of the President General as chairman and six members to be nominated by him *from the Board of Trustees* and approved by *said* Board [ ], shall in the interim between the meetings of the Board transact such business as may be delegated to it by a Congress of the Society or *by* the Board of Trustees. *Said committee shall furnish the members of the Board, at regular periods, at least semi-annually, an explicit statement of the business transacted by said committee in the interim between such periods.*

(Italics indicate amendments added, and brackets, words omitted.)

Such amendment will be presented at the meeting of the Congress of the National Society at Springfield, May 15-16, 1922.

PURPOSES AND OBJECTS OF THE S. A. R.

(Extracts from Constitution)

The purposes and objects of this Society are declared to be patriotic, historical, and educational, and shall include those intended or designed to perpetuate the memory of the men who, by their services or sacrifices during the war of the American Revolution, achieved the independence of the American people; to unite and promote fellowship among their descendants; to inspire them and the community at large with a more profound reverence for the principles of the government founded by our forefathers; to encourage historical research in relation to the American Revolution; to acquire and preserve the records of the individual services of the patriots of the war, as well as documents, relics, and landmarks; to mark the scenes of the Revolution by appropriate memorials; to celebrate the anniversaries of the prominent events of the war and of the Revolutionary period; to foster true patriotism; to maintain and extend the institutions of American freedom, and to carry out the purposes expressed in the preamble of the Constitution of our country and the injunctions of Washington in his farewell address to the American people.

Qualifications for Membership

Any man shall be eligible to membership in the Society who, being of the age of twenty-one years or over, and a citizen of good repute in the community, is the lineal descendant of an ancestor who was at all times unfailing in his loyalty to, and rendered active service in, the cause of American Independence, either as an officer, soldier, seaman, marine, militiaman or minute man, in the armed forces of the Continental Congress, or of any one of the several Colonies or States, or as a Signer of the Declaration of Independence, or as a member of a Committee of Safety or Correspondence, or as a member of any Continental, Provincial, or Colonial Congress or Legislature, or as a recognized patriot who performed actual service by overt acts of resistance to the authority of Great Britain.

Fees and dues are regulated by the State Societies.

Application for membership is made on standard blanks furnished by the State Societies. These blanks call for the place and date of birth and of death of the Revolutionary ancestor and the year of birth, of marriage, and of death of ancestors in intervening generations. Membership is based on one original claim; additional claims are filed on supplemental papers. The applications and supplementals are made in duplicate.

ANNOUNCEMENTS

Major Washington Irving Lincoln Adams, of New Jersey, Director General of the National Society, made the Washington's Birthday address, on "Washington." at the Westinghouse Radio Station in Newark, speaking to an audience from two to three hundred thousand, it is estimated.

The fact that Major Adams bears the name of Washington and was also born on February 22 gave a personal significance to his selection as the orator on this occasion. He was perfectly heard as far south as Texas, as far north as New Brunswick, and west to the Mississippi.

The Daughters of the American Revolution have caused to be introduced in Congress a bill to make Yorktown, Va., a military park. The importance of the events which took place at Yorktown in 1781 is obvious to all compatriots. It is remarkable that the site of these events has remained in private ownership all of these years. Notwithstanding this fact, the breastworks which were stormed by the armies of Washington and Rochambeau are still very largely intact. The acquisition of the land and its preservation as a patriotic shrine will involve the expenditure of a comparatively small amount of money. The purpose is in every respect praiseworthy and in line with the objects for which our Society is organized. Each compatriot is requested to write to his representatives in both branches of Congress, requesting their support for this bill. The bill has been introduced in the Senate by Senator Frank Kellogg and in the House by Representative Walter R. Newton.

President General.

Compatriot Admiral George W. Baird, of the District of Columbia Society, has been appointed by President Harding a member of the Perry Monument Commission, which holds its annual meeting at Put-in-Bay in August.

WAR DEPARTMENT,
THE ADJUTANT GENERAL'S OFFICE,
November 29, 1921.

To the Secretary National Society, Sons of the American Revolution:

Acknowledgment is made of the tribute placed by you on the bier of the unknown American soldier who lost his life during the World War and whose burial took place November 11, 1921.

The War Department is deeply grateful for this evidence of sympathetic reverence to the spirit of those who made the supreme sacrifice for a great ideal.

Very respectfully,

(Signed)

P. C. HARRIS,
The Adjutant General.

The new Service Bars to be worn with the Insignia are now available. The illustration below will give an idea of its appearance on the ribbon.

These may be had in silver gilt at $1.50, or in solid gold at $2.65. Compatriots should apply for these directly to the Secretary General, with a copy of service discharge or commission. A permit to purchase the Bar will upon receipt of such proof of service be issued.

Compatriot Cornelius F. Posson, of Indiana, chairman of the Indiana Society's Committee on Patriots' Markers, writes: "I was much pleased to note in the October BULLETIN, under Indiana Society notes, the mention of the activity in which our Indiana Society is engaged. As a result of this bit of publicity quite a little correspondence has come to me from other States, from men who were formerly Indianians, affording me information concerning the location of some Revolutionary graves. I have been able definitely to locate three graves directly as a result of that article." The article in the December BULLETIN by Compatriot Posson gave the story of the finding of one of these graves. Publicity helps!

MOUNT VERNON

By W. L. CURRY, OF THE OHIO SOCIETY

O ripple of Potomac's stream, break gently where the tread
Of thousands press the hallowed sod about our greatest dead;
Mount Vernon, freedom's dearest shrine, guard well thy sacred trust,
Locked in thy royal heart of hearts, we keep the patriot's dust.

I see him glide among the huts that dot a cheerless gorge,
The Joshua of a struggling band, the man of Valley Forge;
Where'er he goes his smile illumes the shades that thickly lie,
And all who hear his words resolve with him "to do or die."

The pilgrim comes from lands enslaved beyond the restless sea,
To meditate where sleeps the man who taught men to be free;
The glitter of the blade he drew makes bright the world today,
And hands unborn will crown its hilt with laurel and with bay.

He needs no granite shaft to tell of glorious actions done;
His monument the fairest land that lies beneath the sun;
Tonight with swelling pride we seek the banquet board once more
And drink to him whose fame goes far beyond Virginia's shore.

Thus back to Washington tonight our thoughts like eagles fly;
'Twas he that gave our flag the stars that shine in Glory's sky;
Wrapped in his cloak, he calmly sleeps upon Mount Vernon's breast,
Of liberty's immortal sons the greatest and the best.

WASHINGTON, THE GENTLEMAN

A Brief Outline of the Address Given by the President General Before Many of the State Societies on His Recent Trip

Washington was so many-sided that it is not possible to do justice on any one occasion to his life, work, and character. It is a good plan to emphasize some one thought on each occasion when we meet to do him honor. I suggest as a suitable theme for consideration by our Society this year, on his birthday, "George Washington, the Gentleman."

He was well born. He came of a long line of high-spirited, self-respecting men and women. He had the affiliations of a gentleman; his friendships were with such men as Philip Schuyler, Anthony Wayne, Alexander Hamilton, Gouverneur Morris, Henry Lee, and Lafayette. He had the dignity and the delicacy of feeling of a gentleman. He was modest, thoughtful of the feelings of others, kindly, courteous, and self-effacing.

Washington was the soul of honor; scrupulous, punctual, and exact in the fulfillment of his obligations, pecuniary and otherwise. He was generous and mindful at all times of the debt owing by a man of means to the community. He was chivalric in his treatment of women.

Washington had the presence of a gentleman. He enjoyed the comradeships of a gentleman. As a friend, he was staunch, loyal, helpful, and dependable. His devotion to his comrades in arms was one of the marked characteristics of his later life.

As a public man, he was respectful to those who differed with him. He was always mindful of the ethics of controversy. On all occasions he was tactful and mindful of the little things which mark the well-bred.

Washington lived the life of a gentleman. His tastes and pleasures were those of a gentleman. He was unfailing in his hospitality. He was a hero even to his private secretary.

We have felt a pride that the commander under whom our forefathers fought was the purest of all patriots, the noblest of military chieftains, and the master builder of the American Commonwealth. Let us be mindful that he was also the first gentleman of his time.

THE INSPIRATION OF NEW JERSEY

When any of our State Societies or any of our Chapters achieve some success or accomplish a particular object, it is the policy of the officers of the Society and the Editors of the BULLETIN to feature this achievement in a fitting manner and give to this Society or Chapter all the credit that is due to it.

To show how one Society or Chapter has accomplished its endeavor should be an inspiration to all of our other bodies and help them to go forward to similar ends. We are one big, splendid, patriotic organization, working for the betterment of our country and its citizenship, and the utmost harmony should prevail among our several State Societies and Chapters. There should be no jealousies and no recrimination and the *esprit de corps* of the whole Society should be of the highest and noblest.

Therefore, when we look at the results that have been accomplished by New Jersey and her remarkable body of men, who have worked together during this past year so successfully, it is only fair to give that progressive State full credit for its achievements.

Starting this year with encouragement because of the success of the year previous, this State has gone forward with renewed vigor, and today New Jersey, if not actually at the head of the list of States in numbers, is so near that pinnacle that it may take the official count at the annual Congress to determine if she has not reached this much-desired place.

The details of what has been accomplished would take more space than can be given in this number of the BULLETIN, but some of the outstanding results may be named: Two splendid new Chapters, Westfield and Paterson, have been chartered. These Chapters, having a large membership to start with, are going ahead with the others of the State with every prospect of further increase. Probably the achievement which best demonstrates the energy and progressiveness of the State is the purchase of a building in Newark for the headquarters of the State Society. Having been almost literally thrown out in the streets by the encroachment of a railroad, the resourceful compatriots of New Jersey were not daunted, and by good luck were able to purchase a building in the down-town section of Newark and now are fully established and running their business from 33 Lombardy Street. This alone is a great accomplishment. The activities during the year of the State and the many Chapters have been the best in the history of the Society, and the results in increased membership have shown this.

How has all this been done? First and foremost, by the hard, persistent, and determined *personal* work of the officers and members of the State Society and its several Chapters, who have given liberally of their time. As has been said before, the general rule in any Society like ours is to leave the work or running of the organization to a few men, and the rest simply do not function. In New Jersey, though the burden of the detail of this work has fallen upon the most efficient, untiring, and energetic Secretary of that Society, men deeply interested in the growth and welfare of the work of our organization have put their shoulders to the wheel and have succeeded in putting this State in the enviable position in which she stands today.

That there is no jealousy over what New Jersey has done, and that only the best of spirit exists with her sister State across the Hudson, was shown while the President General was the guest of both of these Societies, on his recent visit to the East. At all the meetings held compatriots from both States were present, and the interchange of kindly greetings and sincere congratulations were heard on all sides. It was a remarkable illustration of the spirit of our organization, and if our Societies in other parts of the country will adopt this same splendid spirit our great organization will hold its splendid place as one of the most powerful organizations for good American citizenship which our dear country maintains. Let us take New Jersey's example to our hearts and let her inspire us to similar effort and endeavor!

THE PRESIDENT GENERAL'S TRIP

On the 2d of February the President General left Portland on a trip of visitation to the different State Societies. On the 5th of February he met with the California Society at the Commercial Club, in San Francisco, and called the attention of the membership to the fact that a highly objectionable school history is in general use in the public schools of California. Assurances were given that the California Society would give this matter its immediate attention.

On the 9th of February he visited the Louisiana Society, lunching with the board of managers and dining with the membership generally. The Louisiana Society was found to be live, active, and aggressive. Under the leadership of Col. C. Robert Churchill, it is measuring up to all its responsibilities. The only regret is that the compatriots in this Society are not better known to our membership in other States.

On the 11th of February the President General was in Chicago, speaking at a dinner given in honor of Gen. John J. Pershing and in commemoration of Lincoln's Birthday. The Illinois Society is also active, aggressive, and ably led.

On the 13th of February the President General visited the Anthony Wayne Chapter of the Ohio Society, at Toledo. The annual meeting of the Chapter was held on this date and Hon. O. S. Brumback was elected President for the ensuing year. He presided at an exceedingly interesting dinner.

February 15th was Ladies' Day night in the District of Columbia Society and Vice-President and Mrs. Coolidge dignified the occasion by their presence. The President General was greatly favored in being able to meet the compatriots at Washington on this occasion. While in Washington he called at Continental Hall, but was unable to see Mrs. Minor, President General of the Daughters of the American Revolution, because of her absence on a trip in the West. He did confer with Vice-President General Larner and with Registrar General Parks.

On the evening of February 16 the President General met with the Maryland Society at a dinner given at the Maryland Club, in Baltimore. The hospitality of Baltimore is well known, and this occasion measured up to the reputation of the city.

On the 17th of February the President General entertained the Executive Committee and Past Presidents General at luncheon at the Union League Club, in New York City, and after luncheon a meeting of the Executive Committee was held.

On the 18th of February Director General W. I. Lincoln Adams and a number of the officers and members of the New Jersey Society escorted the President General to Washington's Headquarters at Morristown. After an hour spent in this most interesting shrine, the party went to Newark, where a dinner of the New Jersey Society was held in the evening.

On the afternoon of Sunday, February 19, the President General spoke in the First Congregational Church at Montclair. The service was largely attended, not only by our own membership, but by representatives of the Daughters of the American Revolution and many other organizations. The meeting was interesting and inspiring.

On the 20th of February the President General appeared before Commissioner Hirshfield, in the Municipal Building, at New York City, and made known the interest of this Society in the matter of school text-books on American history. Disclaiming any desire to punish the present generation of Englishmen for the sins of George III, he insisted that the story of the American Revolution should be told in our school histories with emphasis on the righteousness of our fore-fathers' cause and with colorful portrayal of the sacrifices and achievements by which our liberties were won. The municipal authorities of New York City have directed an inquiry into the matter of text-books on American history, and Commissioner Hirshfield has the hearing in hand. It is believed that the public attention which has been focused on the subject will result in great good.

On the evening of February 20 the President General dined with the Connecticut Society at Hartford. There was an excellent attendance, and the Connecticut Society was found to be active and deeply interested in the perpetuation of the memories of the great men of Revolutionary times.

On the 21st of February the President General returned to New York City and spoke on the evening of that day at a dinner of the New York Chapter given at the Army and Navy Club. He amplified his views on the school-book question as above outlined.

On the 22d of February the President General was in Boston and had the privilege of attending the annual meeting of the Massachusetts Society. The meeting was in all respects in harmory with the best traditions of this important branch of our organization.

On the 25th of February the President General completed his tour by attending a dinner at Louisville, Ky., given jointly in honor of Washington and George Rogers Clark. The Kentucky Society was found to be flourishing, well led, and alive to its opportunities.

Every Society and Chapter visited was found to be composed of gentlemen and of genuine Americans. The trip was one of great privilege, and acknowledgment is made of the courtesy and hospitality which were everywhere extended.

REPORT OF GENEALOGIST GENERAL AT BUFFALO CONGRESS, MAY 16, 1921

The Genealogist General has received several requests for information on genealogical questions and service records, and among other matters of interest had the pleasure of preparing the papers of Vice-President Calvin Coolidge.

Correspondence has shown the need of a more complete form of application paper, a blank with spaces for localities as well as dates. These are necessary for more ready verification of the data filed. A locality serves to identify an individual in the period previous to the middle of the last century, when the majority of names had no middle initial.

Another advantage could be obtained to future applicants by the compilation of abstracts of the war service of Revolutionary pensions and its publication by the Federal Government.

I would be glad to present, as a supplement of this report, a compilation of the printed works giving the lists of Revolutionary soldiers, issued by the original States of the Union. In this I refer to the omission by the majority of the printed lists of pensioners given in three volumes (Vols. XII, XIII, XIV) of the report of Secretary of War Lewis Cass, in 1834, on the Pension List.

WALTER K. WATKINS,
Genealogist General.

REPORT OF THE HISTORIAN GENERAL AT BUFFALO CONGRESS, MAY 16, 1921

HISTORY OF THE CITY OF BUFFALO

Buffalo, the "City of Homes," lies on the outlet of Lake Erie, at the head of the Niagara River and on Buffalo Creek, which constitutes its harbor. It was formerly occupied by the Eries, a most powerful and warlike tribe of Indians, who resided on the south side of the great lake which bears their name.

In 1655 the Eries were exterminated by the Iroquois, or Five Nations, a confederation formed between the Mohawks, Oneidas, Onondagas, Cayugas, and Senecas (of the Huron family), the most important tribes in New York State. Later the Tuscaroras migrated from North Carolina, joining the Union for their own protection, which thus came to be known as the Six Nations.

The occupation of this locality by the Senecas, the most powerful of the Six Nations, followed these events, and from the fact that large herds of buffalo formerly visited the salt lick or spring on the banks of the creek in this vicinity, they called it Buffalo Creek, from which Buffalo takes its name. History records that Buffalo Creek was the name by which this locality was known as early as 1784, as it is used in the treaty made with the Six Nations at Fort Stanwix in that year.

In a letter of General Irvine (who commanded the Western Department from 1781 to 1783) to General George Washington, in 1788, this place is spoken of as Buffalo.

In 1792 a Mr. Winney is said to have been the first white man to reside in Buffalo. He was an Indian trader, his house being well stocked with rum, whiskey, Indian knives, and trinkets peculiar to the times. John Palmer was the first innkeeper, building his house there in 1794, and remained in Buffalo until 1802, as it appears from the public records that a road led "from Batavia to the mouth of Buffalo Creek, near John Palmer's house," at that time.

Buffalo was originally laid out by the Holland Land Co. in 1801 and was entirely burned by the British in 1813, with the exception of two buildings; but the commencement of the rapid growth and great importance of the "City of Homes" may be dated from the opening of the Erie Canal, in 1825. The head of the Erie Canal, which connects Lake Erie with the Hudson River and ocean traffic, is at Buffalo, and the immense concentration of railroad lines is drawn here largely by the Lake traffic.

Buffalo stands in the full glow of the electrical sunrise, the reservoir of this marvelous force being Niagara Falls, at Buffalo's very door, and the time will come when at the foot of Lake Erie and along the shores of the Niagara River will flourish a city of such large proportions that it will rank among the greatest in the world.

BURNING OF THE "GASPEE"

One of the most famous and decisive acts which marked the prelude of the Revolutionary War was the burning of His Majesty's armed schooner *Gaspee*, of eight guns, as she lay aground at Namquit Point (now Gaspee Point), which runs off from the farm of the late Governor John Brown Frances on Narragansett Bay, one mile below Pawtuxet and six miles south of Providence, Rhode Island.

The first appearance of the *Gaspee* in the waters of the bay was in March, 1772, being dispatched here by the commissioners of customs to prevent breaches of the revenue laws. The *Gaspee* had become exceedingly obnoxious by the indiscreet zeal with which its commander, Lieutenant William Duddingston, strove to enforce the revenue laws. He had seized twelve hogsheads of rum, a quantity of sugar, the property of Jacob Green & Co., of Warwick, sending it all to Boston for condemnation, instead of libelling it at the vice-admiralty court of the colony at Newport. This was directly contrary to the law.

Duddingston had made it a practice to stop and board all vessels entering or leaving the ports of Rhode Island or leaving Newport for Providence, a course which created much annoyance and irritation to the whole population, as it was at a time when commercial intercourse between the different parts of the colony was very largely carried on by small craft upon the waters of Narragansett Bay.

On the 9th of June, 1772, Captain Benjamin Lindsey, of the sloop *Hannah*, left Newport for Providence, and soon after the *Gaspee* was underway in pursuit, continuing the chase as far as Namquit Point.

Lindsey was well acquainted with the waters of the bay and hove about at the end of the point, standing to the westward. Though Duddingston changed his course, it was too late, for his vessel, being of a greater draft, grounded. Lindsey continued his way to Providence, and upon his arrival informed Mr. John Brown, one of the leading merchants, of the *Gaspee's* situation.

Soon after sunset Daniel Pearce passed along Main Street, beating his drum, informing the inhabitants, and at midnight eight of the largest long-boats, with muffled oars, embarked from Fenner's wharf, directly opposite the dwelling of James Sabins, on South Main Street, who kept a house of board and entertainment for gentlemen, being the same house purchased a few years after by the late Welcome Arnold. The party proceeded down the bay, and between the hours of 12 and 1 o'clock, on the morning of June 10, 1772, the *Gaspee* was boarded and captured before resistance could be made.

Lieutenant Duddingston was wounded, his being the first Tory blood shed in connection with the Revolutionary War. The officers and crew were ordered to collect their clothing, etc., after which all were removed and the vessel set on fire, which consumed her to the water's edge. Duddingston was landed at the old Still House wharf at Pawtuxet and placed in the house of Joseph Rhodes, on Still House Lane (now Ocean Street), where his wounds were dressed by Dr. John Mawney.

The bold enterprise excited much interest and the news made a tremendous stir, both in the Colonies and in Great Britain. A court of inquiry was instituted, and it was proposed to send the offenders to England for trial, if they could be caught; but, like the Boston Tea Party, a year later (1773), the secret was closely kept until it was too late to punish the offenders.

The sword had been drawn, and undoubtedly this tended to hasten the separation of the Colonies from the mother country and bring on the storm that was soon to break forth in fury over the land.

Respectfully submitted,

GEORGE CARPENTER ARNOLD,
Historian General.

May 16, 1921.

SUPPLEMENTARY TO THE REPORT ON OBSERVANCE OF CONSTITUTION DAY IN DECEMBER, 1921, "BULLETIN"

Some time prior to September 17 the Secretaries of all the Chapters in the State were requested to take steps to secure the observance of Constitution Day in their respective localities by their own Societies and by other organizations and public boards, and that they report as to what recognition was paid to the day.

Mr. E. R. Whitney, Superintendent of Public Instruction of the City of Schenectady, reported that the day was observed in the public schools of Schenectady on Friday, the 16th of September, and in his letter stated that his department found it a very valuable means of Americanization, especially with a large foreign-born population.

Frank B. Steele, Secretary General, reported that the Mayor of Buffalo issued a special proclamation for the observance of the day, and that the Superintendent of Schools of the City of Buffalo made a special request for its observance and recognition in the schools. He also reported that it was generally brought to the attention of the community, although no special celebration was had by the Buffalo Chapter.

Constitution Day was observed in Rochester by the welcoming of three hundred newly naturalized citizens by the Council for Better Citizenship of the Chamber of Commerce. This Council for Better Citizenship has done remarkable work in the city of Rochester during the past year. It has been financed through an appropriation from the Chamber of Commerce and also from private contributions, and about four times a year dinners are given to the newly naturalized citizens. The one this year was fixed on September 17 and special stress was laid upon the day upon which this function was held. A fine five-course dinner was served and the program was one which would inspire both the native and the foreign-born. The day was also observed in the public schools of Rochester and programs appropriate to the day were given in many of these schools.

It is a matter of regret that I cannot give you a detailed report from other cities, but I know that celebrations were held in many localities.

Very respectfully submitted,

HARVEY F. REMINGTON,
Empire State Society.

EVENTS OF STATE SOCIETIES

The Arizona Society held its 26th annual meeting on the morning of February 22, at which Lloyd B. Christy was elected President; Harold Baxter, Vice-President; Clarence P. Woodbury, Secretary; Kenneth Freeland, Treasurer; Evan S. Stallcup, Registrar; Rt. Rev. J. W. Atwood, Historian, and Rev. J. Rockwood Jenkins, Chaplain. A dinner in the evening followed, with retiring President H. B. Wilkinson presiding as toastmaster. The speakers of the evening were Harold Baxter and W. P. Sims. Presentation was made of the prizes won in an oratorical contest which was held at the high school the preceding evening. Floyd Holdren, of Chandler, was awarded a silver medal and twenty dollars in gold for his address on "America's Power to Keep the Peace of the World," and Gleeson Northcroff received a bronze medal and ten dollars in gold as second winner for his address on "America's Duty to Our Immigrants." The Society voted to continue the prize essay and oratorical contests in the high schools of the State for the ensuing year. The Society also voted to co-operate with the Arizona D. A. R. in raising funds for a memorial to the Oatman Family, Arizona pioneers.

The California Society had the privilege of being the first State Society to receive and entertain the President General, as he started out for his long tour of the States, early in February. Judge McCamant arrived in San Francisco on February 4, where the California Society held a luncheon and reception in his honor at the San Francisco Commercial Club, and were addressed by him. Members were privileged to bring guests. The State Society of California is about to award three prizes, of $25, $15, and $10 each, to high-school pupils of the State for the best essays on the following subject: "The Origin of the Ideas in the Declaration of Independence as Written by Jefferson." This is an annual offering of the California Society, the contest closing March 1. On February 22 the compatriots joined with the Daughters of the American Revolution in a George Washington memorial program at the San Francisco Museum of Art, in the Palace of Fine Arts.

San Diego Chapter, No. 2, of the California Society held an annual meeting at the San Diego Hotel on Tuesday evening, November 15. This was ladies' night and a large attendance resulted. The date marked the 144th anniversary of the adoption of the Articles of Confederation by Congress. The speaker of the evening was Brigadier General John McClellan, U. S. A., retired, who had as his topic "The Political Future of the Hawaiian Islands." The Chapter now has forty-one members, seven new members being presented at this meeting. War Service medals were presented to four members. The newly elected officers of the Chapter are Dr. Fred Baker, President; James C. Elms, Jr., and George W. Heston, Vice-Presidents; Allen H. Wright, Secretary; Franklin P. Reed, Treasurer; David W. Schick, Historian; Kenneth McKenzie, Registrar; Dr. W. Harmon Hall, Marshal; Rev. Alfred H. Haines, Chaplain.

The Connecticut State Society held its annual banquet February 22 at the Stratfield Hotel, Bridgeport, with President White, of the Connecticut Society, presiding as toastmaster. President White, after calling for a silent toast to

George Washington, addressed the members, making a special plea for more active interest and more members, and spoke of the traditions of Connecticut in the organization of the S. A. R., receiving its charter on January 13, 1889, and contributing three Presidents General to the National Society, the first one, Lucius P. Deming, recently deceased; the second, the late Gen. Edwin S. Greeley, and the third being Judge Morris B. Beardsley. Prof. Charles M. Bakewell, of Yale University, made a fine address on "America's Idealism," followed by an address by Rev. William Horace Day, who spoke optimistically of the "New Spirit of America."

THE DAVID HUMPHREYS BRANCH, of New Haven, has recently issued an interesting leaflet describing the interesting career of David Humphreys, "Soldier, Statesman, Poet, and Manufacturer," for whom the Branch is named, and also the lake recently created by the dam built by the Connecticut Light and Power Company across the Housatonic River, thus perpetuating the name of one of Connecticut's Revolutionary sires, who also did much for his community and his country, both at home and in diplomatic circles abroad.

COL. JEREMIAH WADSWORTH BRANCH, of Hartford, held its annual meeting on February 20 at the Hartford Club, having the President General as special honor guest for the occasion. President Herbert H. White, of the State Society, was also a guest and addressed the Society, taking some of the early colonial families of Connecticut as his theme, while the President General made a splendid address on George Washington. The President of the Hartford Branch, George S. Godard, presided and spoke of an interesting document, believed to be the first edition of the Declaration of Independence, prepared by a woman, Mary Catherine Godard. Copies of Col. Francis Parson's article on "The British Attack at Bunker Hill" were distributed, the booklet being published through the kind offices of Clarence Horace Wickham, National Trustee for Connecticut.

District of Columbia Society held a Ladies' Night reception and banquet on the occasion of the visit of President General McCamant to Washington, February 15. The Society also had as its special guests Vice-President and Mrs. Coolidge, for whom a special reception committee was appointed. Following the formal reception a ceremony attending the presentation of two new flags, which included the formal salute, the repetition of "The America's Creed," and the singing of the "Star-Spangled Banner," was held. Then, under the direction of President Selden M. Ely, new members were installed. An entertainment of music and esthetic dancing followed, after which refreshments and social dancing were indulged in.

On February 22 the eighth joint celebration of the Sons of the Revolution in the District of Columbia, the Daughters of the American Revolution, and the Sons of the American Revolution of the District of Columbia took place. This was a formal program of patriotic music and addresses, the principal speaker being Dr. Thomas Edward Green, of the American Red Cross. This was the occasion upon which a gold medal was awarded by these Societies jointly for an historical essay by a high-school pupil, Registrar General William S. Parks being the chairman of committee of judges for this award. The title of the prize essay was "The Expedition of George Rogers Clark," which was written by Karl G. Pearson, of the Eastern High School.

Illinois Society held, on February 11, in Chicago, the largest banquet in the history of the Society when its honor guests were General Pershing and President General McCamant. Past President General Elmer Wentworth was also a guest, and all three of these gentlemen delivered inspiring and splendid addresses on Lincoln. General Pershing greeted personally 352 guests. On Sunday, February 12, President General McCamant spoke at the Fourth Presbyterian Church. The Illinois Society has presented six victrolas to the Hines Hospital, where the wounded soldiers will much enjoy and appreciate them. One thousand copies of the "American's Creed" book have been presented to the Chicago schools, and this action has been highly commended by Superintendent Mortison.

SPRINGFIELD CHAPTER held a celebration in honor of Washington's Birthday, at the St. Nicholas Hotel, with a banquet, at which the President, Mr. Charles S. Andrus, presided as toastmaster. The speakers were Hon. Len Small, Governor of Illinois, and Hon. Oliver H. Shoup, Governor of Colorado. The feature of the evening was the presentation of eleven War Service medals, ten of these being for World War service and one for Spanish-American War service. The recipients of the medals were Compatriots Ben B. Boynton, Frank L. Hatch, Henry R. Helmle, Philo B. Kane, William J. Leaverton, David Lockie, Charles P. Power, John G. Ruckel, Earl B. Searcy, John M. Tipton, and Herman H. Tuttle. The presentation was made by Mrs. James B. Searcy, of the Springfield Chapter, Daughters of the American Revolution, whose three sons and son-in-law were in the World War. The Springfield Chapter has started active efforts for 100 new members.

The Indiana Society.—The board of managers of the Indiana Society of the Sons of the American Revolution accepted the invitation of John Morton Chapter to hold the 1922 annual meeting in Terre Haute, Saturday and Sunday, February 25 and 26. The annual business meeting was held Saturday afternoon and the banquet Saturday evening. The Sunday program included a motor-car pilgrimage to the grave of Patriot William Ray, near Riley, Ind., where the official marker was erected.

Members were to plan their trip so as to arrive in Terre Haute as early Saturday as possible, to meet some of the more than fifty new members who have registered in the Society this year and to see at first hand some of the big work Compatriot Posson has been doing in locating the graves of soldiers of the War of Independence.

JOHN MORTON CHAPTER planned some special entertainment. One session was held in the recently restored Memorial Hall, now used by all patriotic societies. This building housed the first chartered bank in Indiana and is opposite the court-house, where hangs the great bell, made possible through the bequest of Colonel Francis Vigo to the county which bears his name.

The program also provided for a visit to the new Indiana Theater, the most beautiful show-house in the country, and in which Compatriot Raymond Townsley, World War band leader, directs a great orchestra of selected musicians.

The Society adopted a permanent bronze marker to place on graves of Revolutionary soldiers, and directed that the setting of each marker be attended by appropriate ceremonies. It pledged its co-operation to the State Board of Education in developing the study of Indiana history in the schools of the State—a work which has been persistently urged by the committee of the S. A. R. since

1908 and which is now definitely assured. Resolutions were adopted expressing the appreciation of the achievements of the Indiana History Committee; indorsing the adjusted compensation advocated by the American Legion for soldiers of the World War; urging continued activities in the work of marking historic places in Indiana; appealing to the State to make a permanent memorial of the site of Fort Sackville, Vincennes; and thanking the Knights of Columbus for perpetuating the name of the patriot-priest Father Pierre Gibault in establishing its State home for dependent boys in Vigo County. Charles T. Jewett, Trustee for Indiana, read a message of greeting from the Hon. George A. Gordon, 101 years old, of Eureka, Kansas, the last surviving member of the Indiana Constitutional Convention of 1850. Mr. Gordon is a grandson of George Gordon, a soldier of the War for Independence, and the Society elected him to honorary membership and made him Honorary Vice-President for life. The meeting was in all respects considered the most successful in the thirty-three years of the Society's existence. Compatriot Cornelius F. Posson, of Brazil, is the newly elected president.

The Society mourns the loss by death this month of Compatriot Edward Gilbert, of Tampa, Florida, Honorary Vice-President of the John Morton Chapter, of Terre Haute. Mr. Gilbert was a brother of Compatriot Henry Curtis Gilbert and their father was the first postmaster of Terre Haute and the first clerk of the circuit court. Edward Gilbert moved to Florida several years ago to live with his daughters. In recognition of services he rendered to the Society as Secretary of the Fort Harrison Centennial Association, he was voted an Honorary Vice-President of the Chapter.

The Kansas Society held its annual dinner and business meeting on February 22, at the Elks Club, in Topeka. Addresses were made by Dr. Edmund J. Kulp, of the First Methodist Church, and Judge Henry F. Mason, of the Supreme Court, interspersed with a musical program. Amendments to the constitution and by-laws were adopted, permitting an increased number of vice-presidents, to be selected from various portions of the State. Much is hoped by this action toward an increase of interest and activity in the organization. Activities for the year will be centered upon securing for Kansas a bronze replica of the Houdon Statue of General George Washington. The Society has offered to co-operate with the State of Idaho in doing honor to the memory of a former Governor of Idaho, who recently died in poverty in Kansas. The Society will join this year as previously, with the local D. A. R. in providing instructive entertainment to newly naturalized citizens periodically through the year, a service greatly enjoyed and appreciated both by those for whom it is arranged and by the officials in charge of naturalization.

Maryland Society.—This Society deeply mourns the sudden and tragic death, on March 20, of its honored President, Osborne I. Yellott. Mr. Yellott was killed in an automobile accident, and details are not at hand at this writing. The sympathy of the National Society is extended to the Maryland Society in this shocking event.

Massachusetts Society celebrated Washington's Birthday in a noteworthy manner, having as its guest of honor the President General, Judge Wallace

McCamant. The exercises were held at the Hotel Victoria, and were opened with an informal reception at 11 o'clock, followed by luncheon. The receiving committee was composed of the President of the Massachusetts Society, George Hale Nutting, assisted by Past Presidents of the Society, General Francis Henry Appleton, Nathan Warren, Edwin S. Crandon, Luther Atwood, Vernon A. Field, Charles French Read, and Henry Fuller Punderson. Vice-President Burton H. Wiggin was chairman of the committee of arrangements. The President General addressed the compatriots on "George Washington the Gentleman," an extract of which address is given elsewhere in this issue of the BULLETIN. After the addresses the ceremony of presentation of World War Service Medals took place. Four Medals were awarded to members of the Society who had given World War service.

GEORGE WASHINGTON CHAPTER, of Springfield, held its annual meeting at the Nyasset Club, and reported a membership of 237. A fine address by Representative C. L. Brier, of Boston, in which he outlined and demonstrated the foresight shown by George Washington, as evidenced by many of his utterances and policies. He instanced, among other points Washington's advocacy of the right of self-determinism, or the right of every group or of States to determine which way they should go, and his views on the problem of taxation. Washington's belief, that "our obligation with the rest of the world is that of consultation," was pointed out, and his stand with reference to the maintenance of a reasonably sized army and navy, although a well-known upholder of peace, were characterized as similar, if not identical, with the aims of the Washington Limitation of Armaments Conference. His attitude on the problem of immigration, too, believing in selected types of immigrants and an enlarged consular service in order to properly care for this important matter, were among the points of Washington's character and policies brought out by the speaker. A report of progress in the plans for the coming National Congress of the Sons of the American Revolution, to be held at Springfield in May, was made by the President, Mr. Charles F. Warner, the tentative program for which is to be found on another page of this BULLETIN.

Michigan Society.—WASHTENAW CHAPTER (Ann Arbor) held a meeting on Thursday evening, December 29, to which members were privileged to invite guests. President W. B. Hinsdale entertained the Chapter with an address, illustrated with lantern slides of pictures taken by himself last summer, showing Indian remains in Ohio and elsewhere.

KENT CHAPTER (Grand Rapids) held a meeting on January 10, at which an address was given by Compatriot John S. Lawrence on "The Constitution." At their meeting on February 7 Compatriot Mark Norris gave an address entitled "A Forgotten Revolutionary General."

DETROIT CHAPTER held a meeting on January 31, at the Hotel Statler, Detroit, at which the members of the Daughters of the American Revolution were invited guests. The principal guest and speaker was Superintendent Frank Cody, of the Detroit public schools, who spoke on "Patriotic Education." His account of the activities in the public schools in Detroit was illustrated by an exhibition of moving pictures showing the pupils at play and work. The progress made in musical instruction was evidenced by the playing of an orchestra of fifty-four pieces from the Cass Technical High School, of which Compatriot Benjamin

F. Comfort is the principal. President Carl F. Clark, of the Detroit Chapter, presided at this meeting. This Chapter held a unique historical meeting at the Detroit Public Library on February 23. Clarence M. Burton, past President of Michigan Society, was the first speaker and introduced William L. Jenks, of Port Huron, Historian of Michigan Society, Sons of the American Revolution, who read a most interesting paper on "William Hull, First Territorial Governor of Michigan." Mr. Jenks presented the career of Governor Hull in a more favorable light than commonly recalled and gave many hitherto-unpublished details of his life, and asserted that he had been punished during his court-martial for results due to the inefficiency of his superiors and the departments at Washington rather than for his own fault.

Miss Krum, librarian of the Burton Historical Collection, spoke of Mr. Burton's magnificent contribution to the people of Detroit, of the historical and genealogical collection acquired by him through years of effort, and described its invaluable worth. Those present were then taken into the adjoining rooms, where the Burton Historical Collection is beautifully housed.

Mr. Burton pointed out particular priceless treasures of early manuscripts and Indian deeds, maps, and diaries, and related how possession of these had been obtained, and their destruction prevented.

Secretary Raymond E. Van Syckle announced that the new Year Book of the Chapter disclosed that 30 per cent of the membership of Detroit Chapter served in the Army and Navy of the United States during the late war. Of the 378 members enrolled, 117 received Service Medals from the Chapter in recognition of their services in the war.

Anthony Wayne Chapter held its annual meeting for the election of officers February 13, at the Toledo Club, with Hon. Wallace McCamant, President General, as guest of honor and speaker of the evening. His address on the life and character of Lincoln was scholarly and eloquent. Another guest was Dr. Martin, of Grand Rapids, who while a young man occupied desk room in Lincoln's Springfield office. Still another guest was Rev. Robert Lincoln Long, of Toledo, pastor of Collingwood Avenue Presbyterian Church, born in Kentucky and named after the son of the great emancipator. A committee was appointed for marking historic sites in northwestern Ohio and another committee on American history in the public schools of Ohio.

The Minnesota Society has made a notable advance by issuing for the first time a charter to a local Chapter, namely, Minneapolis Chapter, No. 1. The Chapter was organized on December 14, 1921, due to the energy of Mr. Charles E. Rittenhouse, then President of the State Society, who at that time delivered the charter to Dr. Douglas P. Wood, the President of the Minneapolis Chapter, and fifteen members, who had originally petitioned for the same, and the charter roll has now been signed by about fifty-four, and will be held open until the next meeting, to be held on Lexington Day, April 19, thus affording an opportunity to others to come in as charter members. A great deal of interest has been aroused by this organization, and there is every evidence that the State Society will be built up locally through this action. The membership is limited to Hennepin County, in which Minneapolis is situated. The new President of the Minnesota State Society, Kenneth G. Brill, at a meeting on Washington's Birthday, emphasized the importance of this movement in the annals of the

State Society. Upon this occasion Dr. Wood offered a prize of $50, to be divided among the junior high and upper grades of the schools of Minneapolis, for the best four essays on the Battle of Lexington and Concord.

The Montana Society held its twenty-eighth annual meeting on Wadnesday evening, February 22, in the Y. M. C. A. banquet room. President Marcus Whritenour presided over the business session, using an historical cherry-wood gavel. Five new members were admitted to the Society and applications from nine others were announced. A report from the special committee having charge of a State-wide prize essay contest for pupils of high schools was made by Mr. Charles L. Clark, chairman, and the winning four, two girls and two boys, will receive the S. A. R. medals shortly. Officers for the ensuing year were elected, as follows: President, Paris B. Bartley; Vice-President, Lyman H. Bennett; Secretary-Treasurer, Leslie Sulgrove; Registrar, Willis Jones Egleston; Historian, Marcus •Whritenour; Chaplain, William R. Burroughs; Librarian, Ranney Y. Lyman. Addresses were made by the retiring President, Mr. Whritenour and the newly elected officers, and later a reception, arranged by the Oro Fino Chapter, Daughters of the American Revolution, took place, with an enjoyable program of music and dancing.

The New Jersey Society.—Threefold ceremonies under the auspices of the New Jersey Society, Sons of the American Revolution, marked the observance of Washington's Birthday, and which covered a period of four days. Beginning with Saturday, February 18, when Judge Wallace McCamant, President General, was the guest of the New Jersey Society, the final number on the program occurred at noon on the natal of the Father of His Country.

First of all the functions was a luncheon given in honor of the President General by Major Washington Irving Lincoln Adams, Director General and Past President of the State Society, the others present being Frank B. Steele, Secretary General; Rev. Dr. Lyman Whitney Allen, Chaplain General and President of the New Jersey Society; Louis Annin Ames, Past President General; David L. Pierson, Past Historian General and Secretary of the New Jersey Society; Past Vice-President General Thomas W. Williams; Harry F. Brewer, Vice-President New Jersey Society; Carl M. Vail, Past President of the New Jersey Society; Judge Adrian Lyon, and Elvord G. Chamberlin, President of the Montclair Chapter. A number of toasts were proposed, and after the very delightful affair Judge McCamant and Secretary General Steele were escorted to the Ford Mansion at Morristown, where Washington made his headquarters in 1779-1780. After an inspection of the large number of colonial relics gathered there, including the original commission issued to Washington by the Continental Congress as the Commander-in-Chief, the party returned to Newark and to the Robert Treat Hotel, where a banquet was tendered the President General by the New Jersey Society, at 7.30 in the evening.

Major Adams, who presided, announced Sylvester H. M. Agens, President of the Newark Chapter, as the toastmaster. Tribute to the State of New Jersey for its heroic part in the War for American Independence was paid by the President General in the only speech delivered, after the one of welcome by the toastmaster. Toasts were drunk to the President of the United States, the

Army, the Navy, and the Sons of the American Revolution. The benediction was offered by Rev. Dr. Allen, Chaplain General.

NEW HEADQUARTERS OF THE NEW JERSEY SOCIETY
Photograph taken after placing wreath on the Washington Statue on
February 22, 1922

Then the party adjourned to the headquarters of the New Jersey Society, at 33 Lombardy Street, Newark, which was then given its official housewarming. The building, of brownstone, three stories in height, was occupied on October

27, 1921, the anniversary of Roosevelt's birthday, and in less than two months, the purchase price amounting to many thousands of dollars, was paid, and the property is now held free and clear by the Sons of the American Revolution Realty Company. There was no speechmaking at the headquarters, the reception committee of the house committee being Chester N. Jones, chairman; William J. Conkling, and Russell B. Rankin.

On Sunday afternoon the Montclair Chapter held its annual service, in memory of Washington's Birthday, at the First Congregational Church, on Fullerton Avenue, in that city. The handsome church, nearly filled, has a seating capacity of 1,200. President General McCamant was the speaker of the afternoon, and thrilled the large congregation with an illuminating address on the life and character of the First American. The procession as it entered the church from the chapel was one of the most inspirational scenes connected with the New Jersey Society, in its nearly third of a century of existence. Nearly every Chapter, of which there are twelve, carried its colors, and other societies also were well represented. "Onward Christian Soldiers" was the processional hymn, following which came the invocation offered by President General Dr. Lyman Whitney Allen; the pledge to the Flag by President Elvord G. Chamberlin, of the Montclair Chapter; the singing of the Star Spangled Banner, and an address of welcome by President Chamberlin. Prayer was offered by Rev. Frederick P. Young. Rev. Dr. Allen introduced the President General, as the President of the New Jersey Society, and Major Adams, in behalf of Montclair Chapter.

Another event in the series of celebrations of Washington's Birthday remembrances was the presentation of a charter to the Captain Abraham Godwin Chapter, at Paterson, on Tuesday night, February 21. The Chapter was instituted on October 22, with eighty members. Compatriot Albert Lincoln Wyman, President, and who presided, presented the national colors and Compatriot Peter Quackenbush the S. A. R. colors to the Chapter. Rev. Dr. Lyman Whitney Allen, President, made the address of presenting the charter and then called upon David L. Pierson, Secretary, to make the formal presentation as the one who had suggested and assisted in perfecting the organization. Congressman Walter M. Chandler, of New York, delivered a glowing address on "The Republic of the Fathers." The G. A. R. and the D. A. R. were largely represented in the meeting.

Compatriots of the New Jersey Society gathered at the headquarters in the forenoon of Washington's Birthday, and at 11 o'clock held informal exercises in remembrance of the day. Sylvester H. M. Agens, chairman of the committee of arrangements, made an address of welcome; the invocation was offered by Rev. M. S. Waters, Historian of the State Society, and an address on "Individual Responsibility" was delivered by David L. Pierson, Secretary. Chester N. Jones, master of ceremonies, then formed a procession, led by the chairman and State Secretary, which proceeded to the Washington statue, in Washington Park, and just at 12 noon a large wreath of calix and other leaves, surmounted with the national and S. A. R. colors, was placed thereon by Robert Osborne Washington, eight years old, a direct descendant of the family of which Washington was a member. Returning to headquarters, a picture of the building and of the colors and official party was taken.

PASSAIC VALLEY CHAPTER held a very interesting meeting at the Summit Y. M. C. A. on Friday, February 24. The speaker of the evening was John

Lenord Merrill, Past President of the State Society and twice President of Orange Chapter, now occupying the office.

THE SECOND RIVER CHAPTER has elected new officers as follows: John N. Klein, President; Edward C. Axtell, Vice-President; Henry L. Denison, Secretary; Brewster H. Jones, Treasurer; Edwin R. Ackerman, Historian; W. W. Draper, Registrar; Chaplain, Rev. J. Garland Hamner. The Chapter enjoyed a dinner on January 27, at the Second Reformed Church, Belleville, the speakers including Compatriots Rev. Dr. Frank A. Smith, of Elizabeth, and Chester N. Jones, Past President of the State Society.

NEWARK CHAPTER met at the headquarters on January 27 and listened to a very able address by Colonel James W. Howard, on "The Citizens' Duty." Russell B. Rankin is the Registrar of the Chapter, a recently created office. He has been instrumental in adding a number of compatriots to the roster.

Rev. Charles L. Reynolds, Chaplain of the Newark Chapter, was the speaker at the February meeting, held at the home of Colonel James W. Howard, on February 27. An address by Rev. Dr. Lyman Whitney Allen, Chaplain General and President of the New Jersey Society, was expected, but he was seized with an attack of laryngitis during the day and was unable to attend. President Sylvester H. M. Agens presided, and others who spoke were Chester N. Jones, Past President, and David L. Pierson, Secretary of the New Jersey Society. Russell B. Rankin, Registrar, reminded the Chapter that its tenth anniversary will occur on March 29 and it will be observed with a meeting at the State headquarters, as now planned.

ORANGE CHAPTER met at the headquarters on January 23, and, with the genial manners and resourcefulness of President Merrill, the meeting was, with the address on Americanization by Compatriot Harry F. Brewer, Jr., First Vice-President of the State Society, made very delightful.

Francis Edwin Elwell, member of the New Jersey Society, died suddenly at Noroton, Conn., on January 23, while waiting for a trolley car. He was descended from forebears who battled at Concord Bridge and he was a friend of Emerson, Thoreau, Louisa Alcott, and others of the intellectual group gathered at Concord in the period of half a century ago. Compatriot Elwell designed innumerable memorials, but of them all the one at Orange, in the old burying-ground, showing the Dispatch Rider in almost lifelike pose, is considered one of his best. His unusual ability to portray real life and give warmth and glow to bronze makes his work stand out pre-eminently as among the leaders of artistic merit. Mr. Elwell was also a member of Orange Chapter.

Compatriots Major Adams and Albert Lincoln Wyman have both delivered addresses over the radio, the Major on the night of Washington's Birthday, which is also his.

Empire State Society.—The State Society has been active and represented on many important occasions during 1922. It was represented by Compatriot Louis Annin Ames, Director General of the National Society, who spoke before the Montclair Chapter of the S. A. R. on the evening of February 7, at the New Jersey headquarters, Newark, N. J., and attended on Friday, February 17, at the Union League Club, New York, the meeting of the National Executive Board and a luncheon tendered the President General, at the Union League Club, on February 18; also a banquet tendered the President General by the New Jersey

Society at the Robert Treat Hotel, Newark, N. J.; also at the meetings of the Daughters of the Cincinnati and the Dames of the Loyal Legion.

NEW YORK CHAPTER.—Washington's Birthday observances of the New York Chapter were extensive and successful as usual this year and included the regular Chapter meeting on the eve of Washington's Birthday, Tuesday, February 21, 1922, at the Army and Navy Club. Preceding the meeting a dinner was served and largely attended. The Chapter had as its honored guest Hon. Wallace McCamant, Portland, Oregon, President General of the National Society, who spoke eloquently of the need of active and constructive work by the National Society and all its chapters and members. He spoke of the important need of Americanization work in our schools and gave quotations to prove that many teachers and even text-book histories needed the true Revolutionary Americanization spirit. Such work was pointed out as extremely appropriate and practical for those in the S. A. R. who sought activities of real benefit to the "men of tomorrow."

A patriotic mass meeting was largely attended by members of the S. A. R. at Carnegie Hall, Wednesday morning, February 22, 1922. The annual church service was held on Sunday afternoon, February 26, at the Church of the Divine Paternity, and an eloquent appeal for Americanization was made by Compatriot Joseph Fort Newton, D. D., Chaplain of the Chapter. The cadets of the New York State Nautical School were the escort of honor. The following patriotic societies were represented: Daughters of the American Revolution, Daughters of the Revolution, Sons of the Revolution, Colonial Dames of America, Colonial Dames of State of New York, Patriotic Women of America, United States Daughters of 1812, Daughters of the Cincinnati, Society of Colonial Wars, Military Order of the Loyal Legion, Founders and Patriots of America, Society of American Wars, Saint Nicholas Society, Saint Andrews' Society, Canadian Society, Huguenot Society, National Security League, The Union Society of the Civil War, and Veterans of the World War.

ROCHESTER CHAPTER.—On December 18, 1921, the South Congregational Church of this city conducted a special Forefathers' Day patriotic service, in which the members of this Chapter participated. The pastor, Rev. Joseph B. Kettle, delivered an address upon "The Pilgrim Fathers." On January 20 the regular quarterly meeting of the Chapter was held in the D. A. R. Chapter House, at which the wives of the members, the officers of the Irondequoit Chapter, D. A. R., and many new or eligible members attended. Compatriot Charles Francis Adams, Past President of the Buffalo Chapter, S. A. R., gave a unique and delightful monologue, both in poetry and prose. A luncheon was served in the dining-room of the Chapter House, at which the President of the Empire State Society, Hon. Harvey F. Remington, and wife were present. At the Board of Managers' meeting in December a committee was appointed to co-operate with the Rochester Historical Society in erecting a tablet upon the site of the home of Col. Nathaniel Rochester, founder of the city. This committee includes compatriot Rochester H. Rogers, a descendant of Colonel Rochester. On Sunday evening, February 12, the Chapter members attended a special Abraham Lincoln service at the First Methodist Episcopal Church. On the 28th of February Judge McCamant, President General of the National Society, S. A. R., visited the Rochester Chapter and was entertained by the officers and many compatriots.

THE COL. CORNELIUS VAN DYCK CHAPTER.—This Chapter, in co-operation with the Schenectady Chapter of the Daughters of the American Revolution and the Beukendaal Chapter of the Daughters of the American Revolution, had a very interesting meeting on March 7. Mr. Harry V. Bush, of Canajoharie, spoke on "The Mohawk Valley," which address was illustrated with stereopticon pictures of historical places in the valley. The speaker was introduced by E. R. Whitney, President of the Chapter.

PAINTED POST CHAPTER.—At the annual election of officers of the Painted Post Chapter the following were chosen: Hon. Alanson B. Houghton, newly appointed ambassador to Germany, President; E. Stuart Underhill, Jr., of Corning, Vice-President; John L. Chatfield, of Painted Post, Secretary; William J. Heermans, of Corning, Treasurer; Uri Mulford, of Corning, Historian; Arthur A. Houghton, of Corning, Dr. Byron Pierce, of Coopers Plains, and Hon. Delmar M. Darrin, of Addison, Board of Managers. The Chapter has had an active season.

GENESEE CHAPTER.—This Chapter is co-operating with Deo-on-go-wa Chapter, D. A. R., in a search for the graves of men who fought in the Revolution and who are buried in this county. Many have been located. When one is found, the man's service record is looked up in the rosters of the Revolutionary regiments and tabulated, along with all matters concerning his life. Regular meetings have been held the fourth Friday in each month, which have been well attended and at which important historical matters have been treated. The membership included compatriots in Batavia, Warsaw, Oakfield, Elba, Medina, and Alexander.

THE BUFFALO CHAPTER held a most interesting meeting on the evening of Saturday, February 11, at the Touraine Hotel. The occasion was a dinner, which was attended by about fifty members. The speaker of the evening was Mr. Frederick J. Libby, Executive Secretary of the National Council for the Limitation of Armaments. Mr. Libby gave a most illuminating and eloquent address on the workings of the Conference in Washington and made a plea for the influence of our members toward the early ratification of the treaties.

North Dakota.—This Society has been making very encouraging gains in membership this year, so that it dares to look with envy upon one of the Traveling Banners. Whether successful or not in securing either of these, North Dakota hopes to give other contestants cause to look carefully to their laurels in this important matter. A local Chapter has been organized at Grand Forks, the first one in this State to be authorized by the State Society. The organization meeting was held February 27, local members and ladies attending a dinner presided over by Past President Vernon P. Squires and addressed by Compatriot Prof. John Adams Taylor, of the State University, on "The Social and Economic Life of the Pilgrims." The charter of the new Chapter will be presented at the annual meeting and dinner of the State Society to be held in Grand Forks on Patriots' Day, April 19, at which time the new Chapter will entertain the State Society. The officers of the new Chapter elected at this organization meeting are: President, Vernon P. Squires; Vice-President, John Adams Taylor; Secretary-Registrar, George F. Rich; Treasurer, F. F. Burchard; Historian, A. H. Yoder, and Chaplain, Dr. S. Paige Jordan.

Ohio Society.—Members of Anthony Wayne Chapter, Sons of the American Revolution (Toledo), were delightfully entertained in the home of Compatriot A. M. Woolson, on Parkwood Avenue, Tuesday evening, November 22, 1921. The evening was arranged by Dudley Watson Moor, President of the local Chapter, and Walter J. Sherman, President of the Ohio Society, assisted by Compatriots George E. Pomeroy, O. S. Brumback, George Seney, Whitney, Gardiner, Nye, and Middleton. Prof. Josef Martin, who has lately come from New York to make Toledo his home, gave several splendid piano selections, and an impromptu talk by Dr. Allen A. Stockdale was also an interesting feature of the program.

The Oklahoma Society held its annual meeting on February 22, at which time new officers were elected, Mr. George L. Bowman, of Kingfisher, being the new President of the Society and Mr. Edward Ferris McKay, retiring President, assuming the office of Secretary. Features of the program were patriotic readings and music, including "A Letter of 1748" and the recently issued brochure on Fort McHenry. Mr. Barritt Galloway, the retiring Secretary, spoke on "Fort McHenry Today," having had ten months of service there during the World War. Resolutions were adopted petitioning Congress to make a permanent memorial of Fort McHenry. An address on "Washington" was given by Rev. E. D. Salkeld. Resolutions were adopted requesting the next Oklahoma Legislature to commemorate in some suitable way the centennial of the establishing of Fort Gibson and Fort Towson in Oklahoma, which anniversary occurs in 1924.

The Oregon Society held its annual meeting on February 22, at which the following officers were elected: President, B. B. Beekman; Vice-President, Winthrop Hammond; Secretary, B. A. Thaxter; Treasurer, A. A. Lindsley; Registrar, Alfred Parker; members of Board of Managers, Charles F. Beebe, B. E. Sanford, P. P. Dabney, and J. S. Cooper, Jr. A resolution was passed endorsing the movement to secure congressional action setting aside Fort McHenry as a national memorial park, and a special committee was appointed to confer with Oregon Senators and Representatives relative thereto. The action of the Board of Managers in electing Wallace McCamant President General and Dr. John H. Boyd, now deceased, honorary life members of the Oregon Society was unanimously ratified. The annual dinner on the evening of the same day was an exceptionally pleasant event and was enjoyed by a large number of members and guests. Dr. Richard F. Scholz, President of Reed College, delivered a very scholarly and forceful address upon the subject "Washington and the American Tradition"; Prof. Alfred E. Zimmern, formerly of Oxford University, more recently of the University of Wales, who attended the Washington Conference on Limitation of Arms as observer and is now engaged in lecturing in American colleges on international relations, spoke instructively on "The Present International Situation"; the closing address, given by Dr. William Hung, Professor of History in the University of Pekin, on "Washington's Influence on the Chinese," was very pleasing and informative. The three addresses furnished a most interesting review of Washington's service and far-reaching influence from American, British, and Chinese viewpoints.

The Pennsylvania Society held its annual meeting February 22, with election of officers in the afternoon, at the Chamber of Commerce, in Pittsburgh, and a banquet in the evening, at which addresses were heard by ex-Gov. Andrew J. Montague, of Virginia; Congressman A. W. Barkley, of Paducah, Ky.; Bishop Charles B. Mitchell, of Minnesota, and Dr. Dorsey C. Murphy, dean of Slippery Rock Normal School. The new President of the Pennsylvania Society is Mr. W. C. Lyne, of Pittsburgh, senior member in point of service of the State Board of Managers, and represents an old colonial Revolutionary family, distinguished for service in the English Parliament, the American Congress, the President's Cabinet, and during the Revolutionary period was represented on Washington's staff and the House of Virginia Burgesses, and also furnished, in William Lyne, the chairman of the famous Committee of Safety of King and Queen County, Virginia.

President Lyne has been active in the work of Americanizing foreign citizens, and during the war was on the Executive National Committee, of which Theodore Roosevelt was the advisory head. He also was a delegate to the Win-the-War Convention, held in Philadelphia, presided over by ex-President Taft, and served on the Executive Council of the Four Minute Men, organized by Woodrow Wilson, and was a member of the Intercollegiate Bureau, acting in an advisory relation with the Administration in Washington.

McKeesport Chapter, the newest chapter of the Pennsylvania Society, was formally organized on February 10 with a charter membership of twenty-five and about fifteen others pending. About fifty attended the organization meeting, at which the charter was presented by officers of the State Society. The charter is dated January 19, 1922. The first officers chosen were: President, A. E. Leffler; Vice-President, A. B. Holmes; Secretary, John A. Kelso; Treasurer, Gilbert F. Myer; Historian, J. C. Miller; Registrar, Marion M. Ginn; Chaplain, Rev. George R. Phillips. The formation of this new Chapter is largely due to the efforts and enthusiasm of the late Dr. J. P. Blackburn, former Vice-President of the Pennsylvania Society and resident of McKeesport.

The Pennsylvania Society deeply mourns the death, on January 22, of Dr. James Power Blackburn, of McKeesport. Dr. Blackburn was Vice-President of the Pennsylvania State Society and member of the Board of Managers. He was deeply beloved by all who knew him and highly respected and regarded among the members of the medical profession. He was always deeply interested in S. A. R. matters and was instrumental in organizing a Chapter at McKeesport, which held its initial meeting on February 10 with twenty-five charter members. Dr. Blackburn was a member of the American Medical Association and the Pennsylvania State and Allegheny County Medical Societies. He was instrumental in forming the McKeesport Academy of Medicine and served as its first President and was on the staff of the local hospital since its inception. He was chief surgeon for the Pittsburgh and Lake Erie Railroad and consulting surgeon for the Pittsburgh Railway Company. Dr. Blackburn was also interested in Masonic affairs, being actively associated with McKeesport Lodge, F. and A. M., Royal Arch Masons, Commandery, Knights Templar, and Mystic Shrine. He traced his lineage far back of his American Revolutionary ancestry, of which he was justly proud, to that of William the Conqueror. The Society at large joins with Pennsylvania in a sincere sense of loss in the death of Dr. Blackburn.

The Rhode Island Society annual meeting took place on February 22, the business session being held at noon in the rooms of the Rhode Island Historical Society and a banquet in the evening at the Turks Head Club. The new President of the Society is Mr. Herbert Ambrose Rice. The speaker at the banquet was the Hon. Alexander Monro Grier, K. C., of Toronto, Ontario, who made an eloquent and charming address.

The Tennessee Society.—One more than twice the number ever present prior to this year attended the meeting of the Tennessee Society in Nashville on the evening of February 22, when twenty-two new members took the obligation of the ritual. The Society was addressed, on "George Washington, the Gentleman," by Dr. Edwin Mims, of Vanderbilt University, who said: "It is always a very fine thing to renew the ideals of our country, and if we keep before us always these ideals, this same unselfishness, this same love of country that we were all lifted to four years ago, we have solved the problem of citizenship."

W. K. Boardman, F. W. Millspaugh, John C. Brown, J. Tyree Fain, and Capt. Douglas Henry were elected delegates to the Springfield Congress, with Edward West Foster, Robert C. Foster, Leland Hume, and L. E. Gates as alternates. Tennessee is planning to send a full delegation.

On February 25 the Society presented the patriotic play "America First" in the Ryman Auditorium, in Nashville, before an audience of several thousands. The curtain raiser was "A Colonial Tea Party," a tableau presented by the Colonial Dames, the D. A. R., and the Girls' Cotillion Club. The entire proceeds were given to the 114th Machine-Gun Battalion toward their fund for a marker in honor of the many Tennessee boys who gave up their lives in France in 1918.

On March 12 the Tennessee Society joined with the Colonial Dames in presenting Americanization films, which were seen with great interest by recently naturalized citizens and by those who have applied for naturalization. The series of films will be displayed in local theaters for five weeks by the patriotic organizations of the city.

Tennessee expects to announce to the National Congress the formation of four live chapters in the State.

The Tennessee Society expects to go before the 1922 Congress with an urgent invitation for the Congress of 1923 to be held in Nashville. The Society feels that a great and much-needed impetus will be given to the organization in Tennessee if this invitation be accepted, and that it would also be of benefit to the visiting delegates in familiarizing them with points of historical interest in that section and with its commercial and social aspects.

The Utah Society had a large attendance at its annual meeting, held in Salt Lake City, December 27, 1921. Much enthusiasm was displayed and a resolution was unanimously adopted to invite the holding of the Thirty-fourth Annual Congress of the National Society in Salt Lake City in the summer of 1923, and measures have been taken to, if possible, secure this Congress of the National Society for the Rocky Mountain West, but one meeting of the National Society having ever been held on the western side of the Continental Divide. Hon. Robert E. McConaughy, of Salt Lake City, was chosen as President in succession to former Governor Heber M. Wells, retiring President, now residing in Washington, D. C., and General John Q. Cannon was chosen as Vice-

President. The twenty-eighth annual banquet will be held at the Weber Club, Ogden, Utah, on April 19, the anniversary of the Battle of Lexington, Hon. Stuart P. Dobbs, of Ogden, being chairman of the banquet committee. This is the first time the annual banquet has been held outside of Salt Lake City, and the Salt Lake members and their ladies will make the thirty-seven-mile trip by automobile over the boulevard connecting these very beautiful cities.

Vermont Society.—The annual meeting of this Society was held in Burlington, on the afternoon of February 22. The officers of 1921-22 were, without exception, re-elected to serve for the ensuing year. In the evening a joint meeting with other patriotic organizations was held, including a banquet at the Hotel Sherwood. The speaker of the evening was President Paul D. Moody, of Middlebury College, and Compatriot Walter H. Crockett, Secretary of the Vermont Society, spoke for the S. A. R.

The Washington State Society.—SEATTLE CHAPTER.—The Chapter has held five meetings during the year, all well attended. The outstanding effort of the year was the Pageant, which held first place in the Independence Day cerebration of the city of Seattle. The Spirit of '76, a Bunker Hill Phalanx of thirteen members in Continental costume, a large American Flag carried by the members of the Chapter, followed by a beautiful historical float showing an Indian man and maid, two Pilgrims and Priscilla, George Washington, a Minute Man, Abraham Lincoln, a Civil War Veteran, and the Goddess of Liberty made a really fine display, which was given much space in the local press and created much favorable comment. The Seattle Chapter felt great encouragement over the success of this effort and the impetus given the Chapter generally as a result of this public demonstration. The annual meeting held on the 21st resulted in the election of new officers, with the exception of the President, Mr. Walter Burgis Beals, who was unanimously re-elected.

ADDITIONS TO MEMBERSHIP.

There have been enrolled by the Registrar-General, from November 30, 1921, to March 1, 1922, 441 new members as follows: Arizona, 4; California, 14; Colorado, 5; Connecticut, 17; Delaware, 1; District of Columbia, 12; Florida, 2; Georgia, 3; Idaho, 1; Illinois, 19; Indiana, 18; Iowa, 19; Kansas, 7; Kentucky, 6; Louisiana, 13; Maine, 15; Maryland, 10; Massachusetts, 24; Minnesota, 10; Missouri, 6; Nebraska, 5; New Hampshire, 1; New Jersey, 87; New Mexico, 3; New York (Empire State), 35; North Dakota, 1; Ohio, 24; Oklahoma, 2; Oregon, 4; Pennsylvania, 27; Rhode Island, 10; South Dakota, 4; Tennessee, 17; Texas, 1; Vermont, 4; Virginia, 6; Washington State, 2; Wyoming, 2.

In Memoriam

FRANK ABBOTT, District of Columbia Society, died July 15, 1921.
FREDERICK GIRARD AGENS, New Jersey Society, died December 2, 1921.
FRANK E. ALFRED, Vermont Society, died September 20, 1921.
BURTON J. ASHLEY, Illinois Society, died December 4, 1921.
JESSE A. BALDWIN, First Vice-President, Illinois Society, died December 8, 1921.
MERRICK REIMER BALDWIN, New Jersey Society, died February 17, 1922.
LEWIS E. BEITLER, Pennsylvania Society, died January 22, 1922.
JAMES POWER BLACKBURN, Pennsylvania Society, died January 23, 1922.
FREDERICK BOSTWICK, Registrar, Connecticut Society, died January 22, 1922.
HERBERT BOWEN, Michigan Society, died December 17, 1921.
ORLANDO BOWMAN, New Hampshire Society, died May 5, 1918.
JOHN H. BOYD, Oregon Society, died January 12, 1922.
CHARLES HENRY BRADBURY, Life Member Massachusetts Society, died January 30, 1922.
NEWTON MAY BROOKS, District of Columbia Society, died July 2, 1921.
GEORGE VANDERHOFF BROWER, Empire State Society, died October 14, 1921.
HON. EMORY ALBERT CHASE, Empire State Society, died June 25, 1921.
GRACEY CHILDERS, District of Columbia Society, died March 18, 1921.
WILLIAM FRANKLIN CLARK, District of Columbia Society, died January 24, 1922.
MILON OSCAR CLUFF, Massachusetts Society, died November 21, 1921.
WILLIAM BROWN COGSWELL, Empire State Society, died June 7, 1921.
CHARLES WILLIAM COOMBS, District of Columbia Society, died January 16, 1922.
AARON BALDWIN CURRY, North Dakota Society, died March 13, 1921.
GEORGE ALVIN DANA, Vice-President Nebraska Society, died October 27, 1921.
JOSEPH DORR, Massachusetts Society, died December 15, 1921.
JOHN ELRICK, Pennsylvania Society, died November 6, 1921.
FRANCIS EDWIN ELWELL, New Jersey Society, died January 23, 1922.
REV. W. E. EYSTER, Nebraska Society, died June 18, 1921.
JEROME T. FLINT, Vermont Society, died April 21, 1921.
CHARLES FLOWERS, Michigan Society, died October 27, 1921.
OSCAR B. FRYE, Iowa Society, died July 9, 1921.
CLINTON BURT GIBBS, Empire State Society, died September 24, 1921.
GEORGE LAMBERT GOULD, Massachusetts Society, died October 30, 1921.
CHARLES F. GREENE, Vermont Society, died November 15, 1921.
DAVID ALLSTON GURNEY, Massachusetts Society, died June 6, 1921.
FRANK HANFORD, Washington State Society, died November 20, 1921.
ROSSLYN JOSEPH HANSON, North Dakota Society, died October 18, 1921.
WILLIAM P. HARRIS, Michigan Society, died February 5, 1922.
BERNARD HOOE HARRISON, District of Columbia Society, died September 19, 1921.
CLIFFORD CYRUS HAYNES, Massachusetts Society, died November 13, 1920.
PAUL T. HAYNE, South Carolina Society, died September 14, 1921.
G. WARREN HAYWOOD, Massachusetts Society, died January 23, 1922.
NATHANIEL W. HOBBS, New Hampshire Society, died August 2, 1921.
ALEXANDER MARTIN HOLDEN, Empire State Society, died May 31, 1921.
BENJAMIN PROCTOR HOLMES, New Jersey Society, died January 20, 1922.
CHARLES FRED JENNINGS, Utah Society, died December 27, 1921.
A. R. JOBES, Oregon Society, died November 23, 1921.
JOSEPH TABER JOHNSON, District of Columbia Society, died March 12, 1921.
WALLACE LOWE KIMBALL, Massachusetts Society, died December 7, 1921.
THEODORE G. LEWIS, Empire State Society, died September 28, 1920.
WILLIAM WILSON LIGHTHIPE, Empire State Society, died August 7, 1921.
WILLIAM ELIAS LITCHFIELD, Massachusetts Society, died November 19, 1921.
MAXWELL BUNDY LLEWELLYN, Minnesota Society, died September 29, 1921.
JAMES EDWARD McDOWELL, Pennsylvania Society, died September 3, 1921.

WILLIAM E. MARTIN, Pennsylvania Society, died November 4, 1921.

HENRY B. MILLER, Oregon Society, died November 28, 1921.

WILLIAM JOHN NEVINS, New Jersey Society, died February 11, 1922.

GEORGE W. ORR, Michigan Society, died January 23, 1922.

E. SOUTHARD PARKER, District of Columbia Society, died October 21, 1921.

JESSE PETERSON, Empire State Society, died October 12, 1921.

FRANCIS MOHUN PHELPS, District of Columbia Society, died March 17, 1921.

HENRY BLACKMAN PLUMB, District of Columbia Society, died May 27, 1921.

FRANKLIN CHASE POPPLETON, Ohio Society, died November 18, 1921.

CHARLES ALLEN RICE, Pennsylvania Society, died January 30, 1922.

MASON NOBLE RICHARDSON, District of Columbia Society, died November 12, 1921.

WILLIAM W. RITER, Utah Society, died January 17, 1922.

GEORGE P. RUST, Oklahoma Society, died January 31, 1920.

JAMES F. SEAVEY, New Hampshire Society, died August 15, 1920.

WILLIAM SHERER, Empire State Society, died November 20, 1921.

WILLIAM SHERER, JR., Empire State Society, died November 5, 1921.

Daniel Howe Simmons, real son of a Revolutionary soldier, member Oregon Society, died January 12, 1922.

ADDISON HENRY SMITH, Massachusetts Society, died October 18, 1921.

GEORGE W. SPARKS, Delaware Society, died November 27, 1921.

WELTON STANFORD, Empire State Society, died January 17, 1922.

E. R. SULLIVAN, Pennsylvania Society, died February 3, 1922.

HON. DAVID A. TAGGERT, New Hampshire Society, died February 9, 1922.

MAJOR HENRY SHERMAN VAIL, Illinois Society, died February 16, 1919.

JOHN T. VAN ORSDALE, Colonel, U. S. Army, Empire State Society, died October 18, 1921.

REUBEN E. WALKER, New Hampshire Society, died January 1, 1922.

FREDERICK M. WELLS, Vermont Society, died May 19, 1921.

HERMAN JOHN WESTWOOD, Empire State Society, died November 22, 1921.

CHARLES WHITE WHITTLESEY, Massachusetts Society, died November 26, 1921.

DORVIL MILLER WILCOX, Massachusetts Society, died January 24, 1922.

NATHAN GALLUP WILLIAMS, Empire State Society, died July 30, 1921.

JOSEPH CLARK WINANS, New Jersey Society, died August 9, 1921.

HENRY C. WINSOR, New Jersey Society, died February 6, 1922.

EDWARD CAZNEAU WYETH, Massachusetts Society, died January 19, 1922.

OSBORNE I. YELLOTT, President Maryland Society, died (suddenly) March 19, 1922.

RECORDS OF 441 NEW MEMBERS AND 130 SUPPLEMENTALS APPROVED AND ENROLLED BY THE REGISTRAR-GENERAL, FROM NOVEMBER 30, 1921, TO MARCH 1, 1922.

ENOCH BOOTH ABELL, Md. (35350). Supplemental. Son of James F. and Maria James (Nuthall) Abell; grandson of Enoch B. and Ann (Norris) Abell; great-grandson of John Booth and Elizabeth (——) Abell; great²-grandson of *John Abell*, Lieutenant, St. Mary's County, Maryland Militia.

FRED DEAN ADAMS, Warren, Ohio. (36480). Son of Fred W. and Olive (Palmeter) Adams; grandson of Whittlesey and Margaret (Smith) Adams; great-grandson of Asael and Lucy (Mygat) Adams; great²-grandson of *Asahel Adams*, private, Connecticut Line and "Guards."

FRED WHITTLESEY ADAMS, Warren, Ohio. (36478). Son of Whittlesey and Margaret (Smith) Adams; grandson of Asael and Lucy (Mygatt) Adams; great-grandson of *Asahel Adams*, private, 7th Regt., Connecticut Line and "Guards."

GUILFORD JONES ADAMS, Humboldt, Tenn. (36072). Son of John Jeremiah Robert and Jennie (Webb) Adams; grandson of Jeremiah Mitchell and Ann (Hampton) Adams; great-grandson of Jeremiah and Elizabeth (Griggs) Adams; great²-grandson of Richard Adams, Jr.; great³-grandson of *Richard Adams*, member Virginia Convention of 1775.

NORMAN WHITTLESEY ADAMS, Warren, Ohio. (36479). Same as Fred Dean Adams, Ohio (36480).

SYLVESTER HALSEY MOORE AGENS, N. J. (32374). Supplemental. Son of Frederick Girard and Emma Louise (Moore) Agens; grandson of Sylvester Halsey and Henrietta Malvina (Peshine) Moore; great-grandson of Jacob and Prussia Alling (Ball) Peshine; great²-grandson of *Pierre Abraham Péchin*, French patriot, house burned by Hessians and young son taken prisoner.

WILLIAM HENRY ALEXANDER, Columbus, Ohio. (36476). Son of Thomas Carroll and Martha Ann (Banta) Alexander; grandson of Henry and Susan (Winniford) Banta; great-grandson of Isaac and Eliza (Barker) Banta; great²-grandson of David and Mary (De Mott) Banta; great³-grandson of *Hendrick (Henry) Banta*, private, York County, Pennsylvania Militia and Associators, member Committee of Observation.

FRANK GILMAN ALLEN, Norwood, Mass. (36122). Life Member. Son of Frank (Mitchell) and Abbie L. (Gilman) Allen; grandson of Isaac M. and Diana (Page) Allen; great-grandson of Isaac and Susanna (Mitchell) Allen; great²-grandson of Asa and Abigail (Blunt) Allen; great³-grandson of *Samuel Allen*, private, Senior Class, Col. Cravy's Regt., Massachusetts Militia, Member Com. of Correspondence, Rhode Island Legislature and Justice of Court of Common Pleas.

FREDERICK CRANE ALLING, New York, N. Y. (36385). Son of Charles and Harriet (Scovile) Alling; grandson of John and Jane (Robinson) Alling; great-grandson of John and Sally Fulton (Hamilton) Alling; great²-grandson of *John Alling*, Lieutenant, Baldwin's New Jersey Regt., Artillery Artificers.

WIRT HIMES ALLISON, Sioux Falls, So. Dak. (30669) Son of James and Dorothy A. (Himes) Allison; grandson of William and Nancy Ann (Feeter) Himes; great-grandson of William and Elizabeth (Bellinger) Feeter; great²-grandson of *Adam Bellinger*, private, scout and guide, Tryon County, New York Militia.

EARLE HOLMES AMOS, Indianapolis, Ind. (35515). Son of James Oliver and Beulah Mary (Holmes) Amos; grandson of Francis Marion and Eunice Ann (Cisne) Amos; great-grandson of Emanuel and Sarah (Girard) Cisne (Cessna); great²-grandson of Stephen and Mary (Rose) Cessna; great³-grandson of Jonathan and Rebecca (Worley) Cessna; great⁴-grandson of *John Cessna*, Major, Bedford County, Pennsylvania Militia.

JAMES OLIVER AMOS, Terre Haute, Ind. (35514). Son of Francis Marion and Eunice Ann (Cisne) Amos; grandson of Emanuel and Sarah (Girard) Cisne (Cessna); great-grandson of Stephen and Mary (Rose) Cessna; great²-grandson of Jonathan and Rebecca (Worley) Cessna; great³-grandson of *John Cessna*, Major, Bedford County, Pennsylvania Militia.

SPENCER ELWELL ANDERSON, Seattle, Wash. (34049). Son of Wendell A. and Susan M. (Small) Anderson; grandson of Abraham W. and Joannah T. (Waterman) Anderson; great-grandson of *John Waterman*, private, Col. Theophilas Cotton's Regt., Massachusetts Militia; great-grandson of John and Mary (Harris) Waterman; great²-grandson of *William Harris*, Captain, Cumberland County, Massachusetts Militia.

JESSE CHARLES ANDREW, West Point, Ind. (36430). Son of Thomas M. and Lida (Atkins) Andrew; grandson of Jesse and Sarah Warwick (Nichol) Andrew; great-grandson of *John Andrew*, Surgeon, New Jersey Militia; grandson of Joseph and Loretta (Hooper) Atkins; great-grandson of Pontius and Lydia (Clark) Hooper; great²-grandson of *Samuel Clark*, Captain and Major, New York Troops; great²-grandson of Samuel and Elizabeth (Fowler) Clark; great³-grandson of *Samuel Fowler*, private, Ulster County, New York Militia.

JOSEPH ATKINS ANDREW, La Fayette, Ind. (36429). Same as Jesse Charles Andrew, Indiana. (36430).

THOMAS MOORE ANDREW, Jr., Boston, Mass. (Ind. 36428). Same as Jesse Charles Andrew, Indiana. (36430).

A. LESTER ANDRUS, Portland, Ore. (35063). Son of Wallace R. and Annie (Mead) Andrus; grandson of Marcus and Harriet (Sturges) Mead; great-grandson of *Calvin Mead*, private, Ninth Regt., Connecticut Militia, pensioned.

ALFRED WEBSTER ANTHONY, San Diego, Calif. (36409). Son of Charles Elam and Lucy M. (Elmar) Anthony; grandson of Elam and Nancy (Hunt) Anthony; great-grandson of *Humphrey Hunt*, private and Corporal, New Hampshire Troops.

ROBERT SILL APPLETON, Peoria, Ill. (36218). Son of Edward Everett and Ellen Maria (Sill) Appleton; grandson of Thomas Gilman and Almira (Phelps) Sill; great-grandson of Thomas and —— (Gilman) Sill; great²-grandson of *Thomas Sill*, Captain, Warner's Conn. Additional Cont'l Regt., killed.

BRENT ARNOLD, Jr., Louisville, Ky. (34724). Son of Brent and Elizabeth Mills (Jones) Arnold; grandson of James Madison and Lucy Jane (Thompson) Arnold; great-grandson of Foster and Polly (Williams) Thompson; great²-grandson of *Roger Thompson*, Captain, Albemarle County, Virginia Minute-Men; great²-grandson of *David Williams*, Lieutenant, Eighth Regt., Virginia Troops.

HERBERT TRUMAN AYERS, East Providence, R. I. (34922). Son of Henry Thomas and Susan Melissa (——) Ayers; grandson of Thomas L. and Sarah Ann (Wilson) Ayers; great-grandson of John and Sarah Orne (Bellamy) Wilson; great²-grandson of John and Tamesia (Haley) Bellamy; great³-grandson of *John Bellamy*, Sergeant, York County, Massachusetts Militia.

GEORGE WILLIAM AYRES, Kimberly, Minn. (N. J. 36390). Junior Member. Son of Horace B. and Ida (——) Ayres; grandson of George H. and Sarah Bray (Shaw) Ayres; great-grandson of Robert Cummins and Keziah (Johnson) Shaw; great²-grandson of John and Mrs. Sarah (Bray) Cox Shaw; great³-grandson of *Andrew Bray*, private, Hunterdon County, New Jersey Militia, and 2nd Battalion, 2nd Establishment Cont'l Line.

J. BUCHER AYRES, McKeesport, Pa. (36308). Son of William and Ellen (Criswell) Ayres; grandson of William and Mary Elizabeth (Bucher) Ayres; great-grandson of *John Ayres*, private, Lancaster County, Pennsylvania Militia.

JOSEPH JAMES AYRES, Keokuk, Iowa. (36245). Son of Thomas Robinson Jameson and Sarah Ann (Smith) Ayres; grandson of Nathaniel Ruggles and Margery (Smith) Smith; great-grandson of *Ralph Smith Gentleman*, private, Massachusetts Militia for defense of Boston Harbor.

CLARENCE EVERETT BACON, Montclair, N. J. (36386). Son of Clarence Everett and Katharine Sedgwick (Whiting) Bacon; grandson of Gurdon Saltonstall and Catherine (Sedgwick) Whiting; great-grandson of Albert and Mary Lucy (Hunt) Sedgwick; great²-grandson of John Andrews and Nancy (Buel) Sedgwick; great³-grandson of *John Sedgwick*, Major, Connecticut Cont'l Troops, and Lieutenant-Colonel, Connecticut Militia.

FRED L. BAKER, Topeka, Kans. (36727). Son of Cassius Newell and Adelia (Bogart) Baker; grandson of Harris Porter and Emily *(Holcomb) Baker; great-grandson of Zumri and Rumah (Porter) Baker; great²-grandson of *Elijah Baker*, Corporal, Col Chapman's Regt., Connecticut Militia.

PAUL HOLTON BALLOU, Chester, Vt. (33846). Son of Henry Lincoln and Carrie May (Hubbard) Ballou; grandson of William Sabin and Esther Amanda (Andrews) Ballou; great-grandson of John and Sophia (Sabin) Ballou; great²-grandson of John and Elizabeth (Pickering) Ballou; great³-grandson of *Seth Ballou*, private, Col. Ashley's Regt., New Hampshire Militia; grandson of Charles Leonard and Abby Elizabeth (Hoit) Hubbard; great-grandson of Leonard Clark and Caroline Phillips (Maynard) Hubbard; great²-grandson of Daniel and Catharine (Griffin) Hubbard; great³-grandson of *Levi Hubbard*, private, Col. Luke Drury's Regt., Massachusetts Militia; great⁴-grandson of *Samuel Hubbard*, Captain, First Regt., Worcester County, Massachusetts Militia; great-grandson of Theophilus and Mary Damon (Chandler) Hoit; great²-grandson of Theophilus and Sabrina (Shaw) Hoit; great³-grandson of *Abiathar Shaw*, private and Fifer, Massachusetts Militia; great²-grandson of Abel and Mary (Burrell) Chandler; great³-grandson of *Benjamin Burrell*, private, Col. Josiah Whitney's Regt., Massachusetts Militia for sea-coast defense.

CLIFFORD AUGUSTUS BANTLEON, Kansas City, Kans. (33322). Son of Henry Augustus and Mary (McNally) Bantleon; grandson of Graham P. and Elizabeth (Kent) McNally; great-grandson of James and Elizabeth (Hammer) Kent; great²-grandson of Joel and Hannah (Otty) Hammer; great³-grandson of *William Otty*, Sergeant, Third Regt., Pennsylvania Troops.

JONATHAN MARSHALL BARTON, St. Louis, Mo. (35561). Son of Jonathan M. and Louisa (Hutson) Barton; grandson of William and Sarah (Dunning) Barton; great-grandson of David and Hannah (Hill) Barton; great²-grandson of *Joshua Barton*, private, Col. Sevier's and Col. Shelby's Regts., South Carolina Troops.

WALTER HAYWOOD BEARDSLEY, Bartley, Neb. (33899). Son of Truman Charles and Alice (Maurer) Beardsley; grandson of Oliver Augustus and Mary Eliza (Miller) Beardsley; great-grandson of James and Elizabeth (Darby) Miller; great²-grandson of *Benjamin Beardsley (Beardslee)*, private, Fourth Regt., Connecticut Militia.

JAMES EVERETT BEEBE, Warren, Ohio. (36481). Son of Robert McEwan and Hulda (Case) Beebe; grandson of James and Abi (McEwan) Beebe; great-grandson of *Bezaleel Beebe*, Lieutenant-Colonel, 17th Regt., Connecticut Militia.

EDWARD LE HERON BEECHER, Buffalo, N. Y. (36193). Son of James Curtis and Josephine (Heron) Beecher; grandson of Hiram Sylvester and Elsie Maria (Curtis) Beecher; great-grandson of Sylvester and Hanna (Stedman) Beecher; great²-grandson of *Joseph Beecher*, Captain, First Co., Farmington, Connecticut Militia.

ELDRIDGE MARTIN BEECHER, New Britain, Conn. (35495). Son of William Eldridge and Mary (Barnes) Beecher; grandson of Martin and Lois Adeline (Parker) Barnes; great-grandson of Leman and Lois (Augur) Parker; great²-grandson of *Daniel Parker*, private and Sergeant, Connecticut Militia.

ALFRED HANSON BENJAMIN, Montclair, N. J. (36682). Son of Alfred Benjamin and Eleanor Savery (Hanson) Benjamin; grandson of David and Cornelia (Smith) Benjamin; great-grandson of Elijah Benjamin; great²-grandson of *David Benjamin*, private, Connecticut Militia.

ARTHUR HARRY BENNETT, Topeka, Kans. (33323). Son of Arthur Henry and Allicia Sophia (McIlravy) Bennett; grandson of Fayette Henry and Mary Eliza (Merriman) Bennett; great-grandson of Ashley Cooper and Charlotte Sophia (Cooper) Bennett; great²-grandson of Zebulon and Sarah (Cooper) Bennett, Jr.; great³-grandson of *Zebulon Bennett*, private, Col. Huntington's Regt., Connecticut Militia, killed.

ARTHUR NORTON BENNETT, Fort Collins, Colo. (36336). Son of Elisha Wood and Carrie Nason (Dana) Bennett; grandson of N. H. and Lois C. (Tolman) Dana; great-grandson of Thomas and Jane (Cook) Tolman; great²-grandson of Charles and Elizabeth (Burbeck) Cook; great³-grandson of Edward and Jane (Milk) Burbeck; great⁴-grandson of *William Burbeck*, Lieutenant-Colonel, Massachusetts Artillery and Superintendent of Laboratory.

FAY ASHLEY BENNETT, Topeka, Kans. (36728). Same as Arthur Harry Bennett, Kans. (33323).

LUTHER WILLIAM BENSON, Chicago, Ill. (36219). Son of Luther William and Anna Collord (Slade) Benson; grandson of George Washington and Mary Amande (Towner)

Slade; great-grandson of Abel and Emeline (Collord) Towner; great²-grandson of Thomas Bradbury Chandler and Catherine (Tremper) Collord; great²-grandson of *Michael Tremper*, private, Dutchess County, New York Militia.

BARTLETT T. BENT, Newington, Conn. (35496). Son of Thomas B. and Hattie M. (Johnson) Bent; grandson of E. Emory and Ann Josephine (Calkins) Johnson; great-grandson of Emory and Elizabeth Ann (Card) Johnson; great²-grandson of Jared and Sarah (Ransom) Johnson; great³-grandson of *John Johnson*, private, Connecticut Militia, pensioned.

JAMES EDGAR BENTON, Fairbury, Nebr. (33895). Son of Herman Osceola and Carrie Emma (Sanderson) Benton; grandson of Lucius and Lucretia Marland (Prentiss) Sanderson; great-grandson of Joseph and Rhoda Maria (Hill) Prentiss; great²-grandson of Festus G. and Rhoda (Torrance) Hill; great²-grandson of *Robert Torrance*, Salisbury, Connecticut Artificer.

JEROME BENTON, Batavia, N. Y. (36461). Son of John Pheat and Betsey (Townsend) Benton; grandson of Daniel and Abigail (——) Benton; great-grandson of *Joel Benton*, private, Vermont Militia.

THURLOW WEED BERGEN, Washington, D. C. (36126). Son of George B. and Isserella (Winner) Bergen; grandson of Isaac and Mary Ann (Freeman) Winner; great-grandson of William and Mary (Swayzee) Freeman; great²-grandson of *William Freeman*, private, Middlesex County, New Jersey Militia.

RICHARD CONSTABLE BERNARD, Baltimore, Md. (36089). Son of Alfred Duncan and Martha Hanson (Constable) Bernard; grandson of Richard and Frances A. (Duncan) Bernard; great-grandson of Johnsie and Julia A. (Gore) Duncan; great²-grandson of William and Ann (Shipley) Duncan; great²-grandson of *John Duncan*, private, Third Regt., Maryland Militia.

FLOYD BISHOP BOTHWELL, Utah. (32632). Son of Glenn R. and Jessie E. (Glenn) Bothwell; grandson of Henry Hartsock and Elizabeth (Grasier) Glenn; great-grandson of George Knox and Sarah (Hartsock) Glenn, Jr.; great²-grandson of George Knox and Rachel (Adams) Glenn; great³-grandson of *Alexander Adams*, Pennsylvania Gunner, U. S. Navy.

ROY CLAYTON BOTHWELL, Utah. (32211). Supplemental. Same as Floyd Bishop Bothwell, Utah. (32632).

JAMES HARKNESS BOWMAN, Hawthorn, N. J. (36368). Son of James Harkness and Martha L. (Watson) Bowman; grandson of John H. and Eliza Jane (Hopper) Bowman; great-grandson of Cornelius P. and Leah (Ryerson) Hopper; great²-grandson of *Peter A. Hopper*, private, Bergen County, New Jersey Militia.

MURRAY SWETT BRADISH, Portland, Me. (34522). Son of Walter Foster and Frances (Swett) Bradish; grandson of Martin and Louisa Ann (Gilson) Bradish; great-grandson of David and Amelia Maria (Colville) Bradish; great²-grandson of *David Bradish*, Major and Captain, Col. Bigelow's and Col. Phinney's Regts., Massachusetts Militia.

ROGER DE WITT BROADBENT, Upper Montclair, N. J. (36685). Son of De Witt and Ella (Kierstead) Broadbent; grandson of Edward and Electa (Messler) Broadbent; great-grandson of Abraham C. and Gertrude (Garrabrant) Messler; great²-grandson of *Garrabrant N. Garrabrant*, private, Essex County, New Jersey Militia, State Troops, Artillery and Cont'l Line, pensioned.

LOUIS L'ECLUSE BROWNE, Morristown, N. J. (36689). Son of Thomas Quincy and Juliet Frances (Wheildon) Browne; grandson of Thomas and Mary Ann (Thompson) Browne; great-grandson of Timothy and Sarah (Calder) Thompson, Jr.; great²-grandson of *Timothy Thompson*, Sergeant, Col. Bond's Regt., Massachusetts Militia.

MONMOUTH SELA GEDNEY BUCKBEE, White Plains, N. Y. (36183). Son of Monmouth Samuel and Mabel Francis (Keyser) Buckbee; grandson of Sela and Martha Ann (Smith) Buckbee; great-grandson of Monmouth Hart Guion and Sally (Avery) Buckbee; great²-grandson of Henry and Hannah (Rockefeller) Avery; great³-grandson of *William Rockefeller*, Lieutenant, Col. Henry Livingston's Regt., New York Militia; great⁴-grandson of *Simeon Rockefeller*, private, Col. Livingston's Regt., New York Militia; great⁵-grandson of *Diel Rockefeller*, Captain, Col. Livingston's Regt., New York Militia; great²-grandson of Edward and Elizabeth (Lyon) Buckbee; great³-grandson of

John Buckbee, private and Sergeant, Westchester County, New York Militia; great-grandson of *Benjamin Lyon*, private, New York Militia; great³-grandson of *Solomon Avery*, private, Connecticut Troops at Wyoming; great-grandson of Samuel Ferris and Susan (Barger) Smith; great²-grandson of Lemuel and Charity (Kirkham) Smith; great³-grandson of *Philemon Smith*, private, Connecticut Militia and State Troops, pensioned; great²-grandson of Nathaniel and Susan (Crawford) Barger; great³-grandson of *John Barger*, private, New York Cont'l Troops and Militia.

WILLIAM J. BULLEIT, Congdon, Ind. (35516). Son of Victor Henry and Mahala (Johnson) Bulleit; grandson of Amos and Charlotte (Shuck) Johnson; great-grandson of *Henson Johnson*, private, Virginia Militia, pensioned.

WILLIAM BUCHANAN BURKE, Tenn. (36056). Son of Jerome Buchanan and Mary Elizabeth Chapman (Elliston) Burke; grandson of *Samuel Burke*, Sergeant, Fifth Regt., Virginia Cont'l Line; grandson of Samuel and Mary (Hurley) Burke; great-grandson of *Thomas Hurley*, private, Third and Seventh Regts., Virginia Line, killed; great-grandson of *William Burke*, private, Seventh Regt., Virginia Cont'l Line, pensioned; grandson of Robert and Sally (Mountjoy) Elliston; great-grandson of *John Mountjoy*, Captain, Third, Sixth and Tenth Regts., Virginia Troops; great²-grandson of *William Mountjoy*, Quartermaster and Paymaster, Third Virginia Regt.; great-grandson of John and Mary Anne (Garrard) Mountjoy; great³-grandson of *William Garrard*, County-Lieutenant, Stafford County, Virginia Militia.

CLARENCE BURLEIGH, Pittsburgh, Pa. (36313). Son of Thomas Dearborn and Mary L. (Cook) Burleigh; grandson of Jonathan and Charlotte Fifield (Wyatt) Burleigh; great-grandson of *Jonathan Burleigh*, private, Col. Tash's Regt., New Hampshire Militia.

CLARENCE BURLEIGH, Jr., Pittsburgh, Pa. (36314). Son of Clarence and Ida May (Weir) Burleigh; grandson of Thomas Dearborn and Mary L. (Cook) Burleigh; great-grandson of Jonathan and Charlotte Fifield (Wyatt) Burleigh; great-grandson of *Jonathan Burleigh*, private, Col. Tash's Regt., New Hampshire Militia.

JULIAN ASHBY BURRUSS, Blacksburg, Va. (35097). Son of Woodson Cheadle and Cora Emmett (McDowell) Burruss; grandson of Jacob and Lucinda (Collins) Burruss; great-grandson of Pleasant and Nancy (Cheadle) Burruss; great²-grandson of William and Susanna (Terrell) Burruss; great³-grandson of *Jacob Burruss*, private, Col. Alexander Spottswood's Regt., Virginia Troops.

ORVILLE O. BUTCHER, Kokomo, Ind. (35521). Son of John Bryant and Sarah J. (Thomas) Butcher; grandson of William and Sidonie (Hancock) Butcher; great-grandson of Francis and Elizabeth (Poore) Hancock; great²-grandson of John G. and Avis (Turpin) Hancock; great³-grandson of *William Hancock*, private, Col. Alden's Regt., Massachusetts Cont'l Line.

JOSEPH WELLINGTON BYRNS, Nashville, Tenn. (36074). Son of James H. and Mary Emily (Jackson) Byrns; grandson of John and Elizabeth (Long) Byrns; great-grandson of John and Margaret (Johnson) Long; great²-grandson of Henry and Mary (Karr) Johnson, Jr.; great³-grandson of *Henry Johnson*, private, Second Regt., North Carolina Troops.

EDWARD THOMPSON CAIRUS, Montclair, N. J. (36353). Son of James Robert and Nellie (Thompson) Cairus; grandson of Hiram Cook and Sarah (Richards) Thompson; great-grandson of Asa and Emily (Roberts) Thompson, Jr.; great²-grandson of Asa and Sarah (Cook) Thompson; great³-grandson of *Ephraim Cook*, Captain, Tenth Regt., Connecticut Militia.

KENYON STAFFORD CAMPBELL, Columbus, Ohio. (36489). Son of Thomas Huffman and Lulu (Stafford) Campbell; grandson of Jehu Bennetta and Alzina (Huffman) Campbell; great-grandson of Armstead and Nancy (Button) Huffman; great²-grandson of *Ambrose Huffman*, private, Virginia Cont'l Troops.

EDWARD NORRIS CARPENTER, Cranston, R. I. (34923). Son of Edward Everett and Maria (Hamblin) Carpenter; grandson of Joseph and Nancy Mason (Bullock) Carpenter; great-grandson of James and Lucy (Bliss) Carpenter; great²-grandson of *Thomas Carpenter*, Colonel, Massachusetts Militia.

ARTURO YNOCENCIO CASANOVA, Jr., Washington, D. C. (36127). Son of Arturo Ynocencio and Jenie (McCausland) Casanova; grandson of William Hervey and Laura

Bell (Hoop) McCausland; great-grandson of Thomas and Charlotte (Piersol) McCausland; great²-grandson of *William McCausland*, Major, First Battalion, Lancaster County, Pennsylvania Militia.

KELLOGG KENNON VENABLE CASEY, Wilmington, Del. (35662). Son of Joseph James and Mary Calloway (Martin) Casey; grandson of Charles C. Venable and Fannie Holder (Williams) Martin; great-grandson of Richard and Catherine (Holder) Williams; great²-grandson of *John Holder*, Captain, Virginia and Kentucky Militia; great²-grandson of John and Frances (Calloway) Holder; great³-grandson of *Richard Calloway*, Justice of the Peace and Delegate to Virginia Assembly of '77.

ELBERT HOWARD CATLIN, Houston, Tex. (Conn. 36706). Son of John Howard and Josephine Aurilla (Wooster) Catlin; grandson of John and Laura (Humision) Catlin; great-grandson of Levi and Anna (Landon) Catlin; great²-grandson of *Thomas Catlin*, Ensign, First Regt., Connecticut Militia, Member of Clothing Committee.

ARTHUR BEEBE CHAPIN, Boston, Mass. (36123). Son of Edward Whitman and Mary Lavinia (Beebe) Chapin; grandson of Whitman and Theodosia (McKinstry) Chapin; great-grandson of Moses and Kezia (Chapin, dau. of Ephraim) Chapin; great²-grandson of *Ephraim Chapin*, Captain, Hampshire County, Massachusetts Militia.

HENRY AARON CHAPIN, St. Louis, Mo. (35560). Son of Charles Henry and Sarah Ann (Nettleton) Chapin; grandson of Henry and Catherine (Fisher) Chapin; great-grandson of *Phineas Chapin*, private, Col. Webb's Regt., Connecticut Cont'l Line.

JOHN CARROLL CHASE, Derry, N. H. (Mass. 36124). Son of Charles and Caroline (Chase) Chase; grandson of Joseph (father of Charles) and Mehitable (Hall) Chase; great-grandson of Stephen and Rhoda (Blake) Chase; great²-grandson of *Jacob Chase*, private, Col. Thomas Stickney's Regt., New Hampshire Militia, Member Com. of Safety, and other committees, and Representative State Convention of 1780.

LEON WILLIAM CHUMLEA, Lafayette, Ind. (35522). Son of William David and Imogene Roselle (Collins) Chumlea; grandson of William and Elizabeth Ann (Woodmansee) Collins; great-grandson of Lorenzo Dow and Hannah Maria (Van Gorden) Woodmansee; great²-grandson of Daniel and Rachel (Cushman) Woodmansee; great³-grandson of *James Woodmansee*, Lieutenant, Monmouth County, New Jersey Militia.

CARROLL LINDLEY CHURCH, Gardiner, Me. (36577). Son of James and Susan (Noyes) Church; grandson of Manthano and Lydia (Stuart) Noyes; great-grandson of *Thomas Noyes*, private, Cumberland County, Massachusetts Militia.

HARRY MANTHANO CHURCH, Gardiner, Me. (36576). Son of James and Susan (Noyes) Church; grandson of Manthano and Lydia (Stuart) Noyes; great-grandson of *Thomas Noyes*, private, Cumberland County, Massachusetts Militia.

ROGERS PLATT CHURCHILL, Elmira, N. Y. (38184). Son of Jesse L. and Maud (Platt) Churchill; grandson of Charles and Esther Jane (Rogers) Churchill; great-grandson of William and Bathsheba (Williams) Churchill; great²-grandson of *Joseph Churchill*, private, Massachusetts Militia.

IRA BENTON CLARK, Nashville, Tenn. (36070). Son of John W. and Maria (Stowbaugh) Clark; grandson of Amos and Elizabeth (Leakey) Clark; great-grandson of Abraham and Nancy (White) Clark; great²-grandson of *Daniel Clark*, private, First Regt., New Jersey Militia, died at Valley Forge.

JEROME BORDEN CLARK, Foxcroft, Me. (36578). Son of Albert W. and Eunice Hammond (Cleaves) Clark; grandson of Joshua and Susan (Haskell) Cleaves; great-grandson of *Zebulon Haskell*, Corporal and Sergeant, Massachusetts Militia.

DANIEL ALFRED CLARKE, Jr., North Scituate, R. I. (34924). Son of Daniel A. and Mary E. (Harrington) Clarke; grandson of Simeon and Waite (Angell) Harrington; great-grandson of *Simeon Harrington*, Captain, Second Co., Scituate, Rhode Island Militia.

JOSEPH BURT CLOUGH, Cleveland Heights, Ohio. (35898). Son of Ansel Bennett and Lucinda (McBonney) Clough; grandson of Joseph Blaney and Lepha Ann (Tewksberry) Clough; great-grandson of Richard and Peggy (Chase) Clough; great²-grandson of *Winthrop Clough*, private, Col. Bedell's Regt., New Hampshire Militia.

CLARENCE B. CLUFF, Westfield, N. J. (36690). Son of Milon O. and Elizabeth (Wardman) Cluff; grandson of Daniel B. and Lucy A. (Webster) Cluff; great-grandson of John and Hannah (Cummings) Webster; great²-grandson of *Ebenezer Webster*, private, Col. William Grigg's Regt., New Hampshire Cont'l Troops.

SIDNEY WALTER COAN, Muskogee, Okla. (35243). Son of Peter and Helena Maria (Cox) Coan; grandson of David A. and Amy (Fleming) Cox; great-grandson of Peter and Sarah (Caughey) Fleming; great²-grandson of *James Fleming*, private, Rowena County, North Carolina Militia, pensioned.

PAUL COCKERILLE, Washington, D. C. (36132). Son of Samuel Johnstone and Hevila Ruter (Dufour) Cockerille; grandson of Richard Henry and Anne (Coleman) Cockerille; great-grandson of James and Hannah (Cleveland) Coleman; great²-grandson of *James Cleveland*, Captain, Second Regt., Loudoun County, Virginia Militia.

JOHN BRIDGER COFFIN, Rochester, N. Y. (36185). Son of Henry Fosdick and Hepsibeth (Coffin) Coffin; grandson of John Bridger and Phœbe (Gardner) Coffin; great-grandson of Benjamin and Judith (Coffin) Gardner; great²-grandson of *Josiah Coffin, 3rd.*, private, Massachusetts Militia, died on prison ship "Jersey."

IRA GORDON COLBY, Claremont, N. H. (36253). Son of Ira and Louisa Mehitable (Way) Colby; grandson of Ira and Polly (Foster) Colby; great-grandson of Zebulon and Polly (Story) Foster; great²-grandson of *Aaron Foster*, private and Clerk, Massachusetts Militia; grandson of Gordon and Abigail (Perley) Way; great-grandson of George and Sarah (Douglas) Way; great²-grandson of *George Douglas*, Member New London, Conn., Committee on supplies for soldiers' families and guardian of town records; great²-grandson of William and Mary (Lathrop) Way; great³-grandson of *Jedediah Lathrop*, private, Norwich, Connecticut, State Troops; great-grandson of Edmund and Abigail (Bailey) Perley; great²-grandson of *Nathan Perley*, Sergeant, Massachusetts Militia at Lexington Alarm.

FRANK BEACH COLE, Tacoma, Wash. (36231). Son of William and Lucetta (Webster) Cole; grandson of William and Nancy (Stratton) Cole; great-grandson of John and Katherine (Bryan) Cole; great²-grandson of *Phillip Cole*, Colonel, Fourth Battalion, Northumberland County, Pennsylvania Associators.

JAMES EDGAR COLE, Delavan, Minn. (35692). Son of Edgar II. and Eva (Sharply) Cole; grandson of George Horatio and Clementine Erphilia (Rorman) Cole; great-grandson of Richard and Emily (Morgan) Cole; great²-grandson of *William Cole*, Corporal, Col. Paul Sargent's Regt., Massachusetts Militia; great²-grandson of *Benjamin Morgan*, Surgeon's Mate, Col. Joseph Vose's Regt., Massachusetts Troops.

RICHARD SINCLAIR COLFAX, Pompton, N. J. (36375). Son of William and Adelia (Roome) Colfax; grandson of William W. and Esther (Mandeville) Colfax; great-grandson of *William Colfax*, Lieutenant, Washington's Guards, and Captain, Col. Swift's Regt., Connecticut Cont'l Line.

WILLIAM SCHUYLER COLFAX, Pompton Lakes, N. J. (36362). Son of William and Adelia (Roome) Colfax; grandson of William W. and Esther (Mandeville) Colfax; great-grandson of *William Colfax*, Captain, Gen'l Swift's Regt., Connecticut Troops.

ALBERT COMSTOCK, Paterson, N. J. (36364). Son of Albert and Anne (Colfax) Comstock; grandson of William W. and Ester (Mandeville) Colfax; great-grandson of *William Colfax*, Lieutenant, Washington's Guards, and Captain, Col. Swift's Regt., Connecticut Cont'l Line.

DICK COOK, Chicago, Ill. (36220). Son of Walter and Helen (Dick) Cook; grandson of Herman M. and Mary (Swarner) Dick; great-grandson of John and Agnes (Waugh) Swarner; great²-grandson of Samuel and Jean (Grayson) Waugh; great³-grandson of *James Waugh*, private, Second Battalion, Cumberland County, Pennsylvania Militia.

HILLIARD DUNNING COOK, Gardiner, Me. (36579). Son of Harold Elijah and Alberta Fayette (Parkhurst) Cook; grandson of George Delwin and Helen Melvina (Dunning) Cook; great-grandson of Reuben and Lucy (Holden) Dunning; great²-grandson of *Samuel Holden*, private and drummer, Sixth Regt., Massachusetts Cont'l Line.

HENRY BECKER COOKE, East Orange, N. J. (36091). Son of Augustus Gambrill and Ida (Gillard) Cooke; grandson of John and Mary Ann (Logan) Cooke, great-grandson of John and Sarah (Root) Cooke; great²-grandson of Daniel and Elizabeth (Crowell) Root; great³-grandson of *Henry Crowell*, Signer of the Maryland Association Agreement.

WARREN PATTEN COON, Captain-Chaplain, A. E. F., Newark, N. J. (36387). Son of George Washington and Emily Elizabeth (Le Van) Coon; grandson of Stephen Potter and Maryette (Drake) Coon; great-grandson of Alexander Coon; great²-grandson of *William Coon*, private, Albany County, New York Militia.

WARD CHARLES COOPER, Kokomo, Ind. (35517). Son of Charles Edwin and Ida (McCool) Cooper; grandson of Gabriel W. and Martha M. (Kennedy) McCool; great-grandson of Robert and Elizabeth (King) Kennedy; great²-grandson of *George King*, private and Orderly Sergeant, Berkeley County, Virginia Militia, pensioned.

JOHN S. P. COPLAND, Portland, Ore. (35066). Son of Walter and Emma S. (Pickering) Copland; grandson of John (Starbird) and Emily (Wood) Pickering; great-grandson of Henry and Sarah (Adams) Wood; great²-grandson of *Josiah Adams*, Paymaster Twelfth Regt., Massachusetts Cont'l Troops.

HARRY HAWES COREY, Newark, N. J. (36298). Son of Ashley Spencer and Lettie Thirza (Hawes) Corey; grandson of William C. and Olive Arvilla (Cady) Hawes; great-grandson of Eleazor and Olivia (Hyde) Hawes; great²-grandson of *William Hawes,* private, Col. Thomas Nixon's Regt., Massachusetts Cont'l Troops.

HUBERT RAY CORNISH, Paterson, N. J. (36289). Son of Demmon and Mary Catherine (Haner) Cornish; grandson of Benjamin and Lucy (Deming) Cornish; great-grandson of *Benjamin Cornish*, private, Vermont Militia.

GEORGE GRISWOLD COTTON, Syracuse, N. Y. (36465). Son of Sandford Dennis and Jane Ellen (Terry) Cotton; grandson of George Holbrook and Clarissa (Earll) Cotton; great-grandson of *Willard Cotton*, private, Windsor County, Vermont Militia; great²-grandson of *Thomas Cotton, Jr.*, private, Connecticut Militia.

JAMES DICKINSON COWAN, N. J. (35187). Supplementals. Son of Perez Dickinson and Margaret Elizabeth (Rhea) Cowan; grandson of Samuel and Martha (Lynn) Rhea; great-grandson of Joseph and Frances (Breden) Rhea; great²-grandson of *Joseph Rhea,* Chaplain, Col. William Christian's Regt., Virginia Troops; grandson of James Hervey and Lucinda (Dickinson) Cowan; great-grandson of James and Margaret Christie (Russell) Cowan; great²-grandson of *Andrew Russell,* Captain, Fifth Regt., Virginia Troops; great²-grandson of Andrew and Margaret (Christian) Russell; great²-grandson of *William Christian,* Captain, Col. William Christian's Regt., Virginia Troops; great-grandson of Perez and Lucinda (Foster) Dickinson; great²-grandson of *Nathaniel Foster, Jr.,* private, Col. Ebenezer White's Regt., Massachusetts Militia; great²-grandson of Nathaniel and Lydia (Barnaby) Foster, Jr.; great²-grandson of *Samuel Barnaby*, Member Massachusetts First Const'l Convention and Committee of Correspondence, also Massachusetts Militia.

WILLIAM CRAIG, Blue Springs, Nebr. (33898). Son of Thomas and Catharine (——) Craig; grandson of *Thomas Craig*, Colonel, Pennsylvania Cont'l Troops.

HERBERT ROYAL CRANE, N. J. (20340). Supplemental. Son of Charles G. and Marie E. (Dickinson) Crane; grandson of Philemon and Mary E. Roll (De Camp) Dickinson; great-grandson of Philemon and Hetty (Paradise) Dickinson; great²-grandson of *Brainard Dickinson*, private, New Jersey State Troops.

CHARLES LOUIS CRISS, Pittsburgh, Pa. (36306). Son of Rittenhouse and Eliza Jane (Stewart) Criss; grandson of Robert and Margaret (Wilson) Stewart; great-grandson of Samuel and Elizabeth (McCarty) Stewart; great²-grandson of *George Stewart*, Colonel, Lancaster County, Pennsylvania Militia, widow pensioned.

NICHOLAS RITTENHOUSE CRISS, Pittsburgh, Pa. (36309). Same as Charles Louis Criss, Pa. (36306).

FRED WILDER CROSS, South Royalston, Mass. (36118). Son of Wilder and Roxanna A. (Knight) Cross; grandson of Peter and Lucy (Hammond) Cross; great-grandson of Benjamin and Sarah (Fiske) Hammond; great²-grandson of *Joseph Hammond*, Lieutenant-Colonel, New Hampshire Militia.

STANLEY MORGAN CROWELL, Bloomfield, N. J. (36397). Son of Levi Howes and Alice May (Morgan) Crowell; grandson of Levi and Angeline (Baker) Crowell, Jr.; great-grandson of Levi and Julia Ann (Baker) Crowell; great²-grandson of Thomas and Anna (Howes) Crowell; great²-grandson of *Edward Crowell*, private, Massachusetts Militia at Lexington Alarm.

JOHN PERKINS CRUIKSHANK, Fort Madison, Iowa. (36233). Son of Alexander and Keziah (Perkins) Cruikshank; grandson of Stephen and Catherine (Summe) Perkins; great-grandson of *George Perkins*, private, South Carolina Militia, pensioned.

MYRON EATON CURTISS, Virginia, Minn. (N. Y. 36186). Son of Myron Roys and Sarah Ann (Owen) Curtiss; grandson of Milton and Harriet (Doolittle) Curtiss; great-grandson of Joseph and Ruth (Roys) Curtiss; great²-grandson of *Jonathan Curtiss*, private, Col. John Ashly's Regt., Berkshire County, Massachusetts Militia.

ISAAC NEWTON CUSHMAN, Chula Vista, Calif. (36410). Son of Clark and Abigail (Tucker) Cushman; grandson of *Holmes Cushman*, private, Plymouth County, Massachusetts Militia and Cont'l Troops.

FRANK HOWARD CUSTER, Summitville, Ind. (35518). Son of William F. and Ella F. (Howard) Custer; grandson of James F. and Harriet (Foster) Howard; great-grandson of John and Margaret (Jones) Howard; great²-grandson of *Adam Howard*, private, Virginia Militia, pensioned.

LEVITT LUZERN CUSTER, Dayton, Ohio. (35897). Son of Levitt Ellsworth and Effie Jane (Zimmerman) Custer; grandson of Isaac and Anna (Ober) Zimmerman; great-grandson of Jacob and Barbara (Coble) Ober; great²-grandson of *David Coble*, private, Col. Lowry's Regt., Lancaster County, Pennsylvania Militia.

WILLIAM EDWARD DALLAS, Longmont, Colo. (36339). Son of William Albert and Sarah Lucinda (McLaran) Fallas; grandson of William and Wealthy (Winslow) Fallas; great-grandson of William and Hannah (Stone) Fallas; great²-grandson of *Silas Stone*, private, Col. Nathan Sparhawk's Regt., Massachusetts Militia.

LYNN BOARDMAN DANA, Warren, Ohio. (36482). Son of William Henry and Emma Jane (Tuttle) Dana; grandson of Junius and Martha (Potter) Dana; great-grandson of Anderson and Ann (Dennison) Dana; great²-grandson of Daniel and Dollie (Kibbe) Dana; great³-grandson of *Anderson Dana*, Delegate to Connecticut Assembly, private, Connecticut Militia at Wyoming, killed.

HECTOR DAWES, Chicago, Ill. (36209). Son of George and Elizabeth (Ames) Dawes; grandson of William Mears and Abby (Nabby) Kendall (Holden) Dawes; great-grandson of *William Dawes*, 2nd Major, Col. Henry Bromfield's Boston Regt., and assistant to Paul Revere.

WILLIAM RUGGLES DAWES, Evanston, Ill. (36210). Son of Hector and Jane Augusta (Ruggles) Dawes; grandson of George and Elizabeth Johnson (Ames) Dawes; great-grandson of William Mears and Abby (Nabby) Kendall (Holden) Dawes; great²-grandson of *William Dawes*, 2nd Major, Col. Henry Bromfield's Boston Regt., and assistant to Paul Revere.

ARTHUR DEAN, Nevada, Iowa. (36243). Son of Moses and Rachel (Evens) Dean; grandson of Ruben and Elizebeth (Divine) Dean; great-grandson of *Solomon Dean*, private, Ulster County, New York Militia, and Col. Baldwin's Regt., New York Cont'l Line.

MYSTRU VAUDRUBURG DE FORREST, Sharon, Pa. (36318). Son of William Coon and Elizabeth (Locke) De Forest; grandson of Gurshum V. and Elanor (Dunham) De Forest; great-grandson of *Abraham De Forest*, Corporal and Ensign, Somerset and Hunterdon Counties, New Jersey Militia.

WILFRID THEODORE DEMERS, Gardiner, Me. (34523). Son of Theodore H. and Gertrude (Higgins) Demers; grandson of William and Henrietta (McCausland) Higgins; great-grandson of William H. and Eliza A. (Berry) McCausland; great²-grandson of Andrew and Mary H. (Bates) McCausland; great³-grandson of *Henry McCausland*, private, Col. Sherborn's Regt., Massachusetts Cont'l Line, wife pensioned.

FRED FAY DEXTER, Longmeadow, Mass. (36125). Son of John P. and Myra A. (Fay) Dexter; grandson of William and Independence (Root) Fay; great-grandson of Timothy and Hannah (Jones) Fay, Jr.; great²-grandson of *Timothy Fay*, private, Massachusetts Militia and Connecticut Cont'l Troops, 6 years service.

AQUILLA GIBBS DIBRELL, Sparta, Tenn., Commander, U. S. Navy. (36073). Son of Frank and Louisa (Rhea) Dibrell; grandson of George Gibbs and Mary E. (Leftwich) Dibrell; great-grandson of Anthony and Milly (Carter) Dibrell; great²-grandson of *Charles Dibrell*, Ensign, Virginia Militia, pensioned.

JOHN LINCOLN DICKEY, Ohio. (14877). Supplemental. Son of John Parsons Alexander and Hannah Caroline (Peterson) Dickey; grandson of Alexander Brown and Jane (Henry) Dickey; great-grandson of *Robert Dickey*, member Col. Wm. Bratton's Regt., South Carolina Light-horse, and member Second South Carolina Provincial Congress.

JOHN NEWTON DRUMMOND DICKINSON, Keokuk, Iowa. (36238). Son of Benesly Waugh and Manetta (Miller) Dickinson; grandson of John and Susan (Mellinger) Miller; great-grandson of John and Barbara (Roahland) Mellinger; great²-grandson of *John Jacob Mellinger*, private, Col. Lambert Cadwalader's Third Regt., Pennsylvania Militia.

GEORGE FRANK DIPPELL, Fargo, N. Dak. (33024). Son of George Washington and Clara Adell (Fleming) Dippell; grandson of John Luther and Esther Hazen (Bush) Dippell; great-grandson of Luther and Eunice (Cornish) Bush; great²-grandson of *Jonathan Bush*, Captain, Eighth Co., Nineteenth Regt., Connecticut Trained Band.

ALSON M. DOAK, Ligonier, Pa. (36322). Son of William and Margaret Jane (Lockhart) Doak; grandson of Moses and Rachel (Stephens) Doak; great-grandson of *Robert Doak*, private, Third and Fourth Battalions, Pennsylvania Troops.

FREDERICK RUSSELL DOLBEARE, Hartford, Conn. (35497). Son of Frederick Lewis and Eleanor Leigh (Russell) Dolbeare; grandson of Frederick William and Armenia (Lewis) Dolbeare; great-grandson of John and Alathea (Overton) Lewis; great²-grandson of Benjamin and Zintha (Muntt) Lewis; great³-grandson of *Eleazer Lewis*, private, Fourth Regt., Connecticut Cont'l Line.

ALBERT E. DOREMUS, East Orange, N. J. (36691). Son of James Martin and Mary T. (Sawyer) Doremus; grandson of Jacob G. and Rachel (Berry) Doremus; great-grandson of Goline and Hester (Mead) Doremus; great²-grandson of *Thomas Doremus*, private, New Jersey State Troops.

LOUIS B. DORR, New Rochelle, N. Y. (36454). Son of Charles Bartlett and Priscilla (Rogers) Dorr; grandson of Joseph and Mary (Barto) Dorr; great-grandson of Joseph and Sabrina (Bartlett) Dorr; great²-grandson of *William Dorr*, Fifer and private, Massachusetts Militia and Heath's Cont'l Infantry.

WILLIS GIFFORD DOWDEN, Maplewood, N. J. (36694). Son of George Augustus and Martha (Anderson) Dowden; grandson of Charles and Susan (Barkalow) Dowden; great-grandson of Christopher and Mary (Beekman) Barkalow; great²-grandson of Christopher and Martha (Veghte) Beekman; great³-grandson of *Garrit Veghte (Vedder)*, Captain, New Jersey Militia.

ROBERT HAROLD DOWNING, Meadville, Pa. (36310). Son of James Davis and Angie (——) Downing; grandson of Andrew G. and Leanah (Walters) Downing; great-grandson of Philip and Catherine (Tracy) Walters; great²-grandson of *John Walters*, private, Fourth and Third Regts., Pennsylvania Troops.

JOHN SMITH DRAKE, Crafton, Pa. (36687). Son of William Henry and Emma Lambert (Smith) Drake; grandson of John Stout and Abigail P. (Hunt) Drake; great-grandson of William and Achsah (Weart) Drake; great²-grandson of Enoch and Catharine (Stout) Drake; great³-grandson of *Thomas Drake*, Lieutenant, Hunterdon County, New Jersey Militia.

WILBUR ARTHUR DRAKE, Plainfield, N. J. (36684). Son of Charles M. and Elizabeth (Antea) Drake; grandson of John D. and Susan (Mundy) Drake; great-grandson of Daniel and Margery (Reynolds) Drake; great²-grandson of *Jeremiah Drake*, private, Somerset County, New Jersey Militia.

GEORGE IRVING DREW, San Francisco, Calif. (35960). Son of Loraine Judkins and Louisa Elvira (Tyler) Drew; grandson of Rowland and Sally (Ginn) Tyler; great-grandson of *Ebenezer Tyler*, Lieutenant, Massachusetts Militia.

JOHN BOYD DUFF, Jr., Pittsburgh, Pa. (36311). Son of John Boyd and Alice Ellsworth (Vance) Duff; grandson of John Felix and Mary Jane (Burtt) Duff; great-grandson of Joseph Smith and Rebecca (Bougher) Burtt; great²-grandson of *Abraham Bougher (Booker or Bugher)*, private, Ninth and Thirteenth Regts., Virginia Troops.

WILLIAM GRAY DUFF, Bellevue, Pa. (36312). Same as John Boyd Duff, Jr., Pa. (36311).

WAYNE DUMONT, Paterson, N. J. (36377). Son of John Finley and Anna Eliza (Klein) Dumont; grandson of John and Mary (Finley) Dumont; great-grandson of *John Finley*, private and Wagon-Master, Hunterdon County, New Jersey Militia, Corporal, New Jersey Cont'l Troops, widow pensioned.

JOHN ANTHONY DUNLAP, Keokuk, Iowa. (36235). Son of David Riddle and Harriet Ann (Wilkins) Dunlap; grandson of John and Jean (Nesmith) Dunlap; great-grandson of Jonathan and Elenor (Dickey) Nesmith; great²-grandson of *James Nesmith, Jr.*, private, New Hampshire Militia and Cont'l Troops.

LOUIS ALLEN DUNLAP, Stewart, Minn. (35690). Son of Walter Clarence and Minnie Briggs) Dunlap; grandson of Nathan Draper and Harriet (Doud) Dunlap; great-grandson of Josiah and Mary (Draper) Dunlap; great²-grandson of *William Dunlap*, Sergeant, Lancaster County, Pennsylvania Militia, pensioned.

JAMES AMBROSE EASLEY, Springfield, Ill. (36212). Son of Robert Henry and Mary (Frances) Easley; grandson of James B. and Margaret (Dodds) Easley; great-grandson of Joseph and Mattie (Drennan) Dodds; great²-grandson of William and Mary (Thomas) Drennan; great³-grandson of *William Drennan*, private, Cumberland County, Pennsylvania Militia.

SAMUEL WILLIS ELLIOTT, Batavia, N. Y. (36459). Son of Jesse and Phœbe (Yeomans) Elliott; grandson of *William Elliott*, private, New Hampshire Militia and member Mason, New Hampshire, Committee of Safety.

GUSTAV H. EMERY, Washington, D. C. (36133). Son of William O. and Augusta (Roetzal) Emery; grandson of Ira and Emmaline Melissa (Stearns) Emery; great-grandson of John and Sarah (Waldo) Stearns; great²-grandson of Elijah and Betsey (Augier) Waldo; great³-grandson of *Edward Waldo*, Second Lieutenant, Col. Hobert's Regt., New Hampshire Militia, pensioned.

CHARLES OTTO ERNEST, Paterson, N. J. (36299). Son of Otto and Florence I. (Westervelt) Ernest; grandson of Cornelius and Eleanora J. (Young) Westervelt; great-grandson of William II. and Cornelia Eleanor (Archer) Young; great²-grandson of *James Archer*, Lieutenant, Westchester County, New York Militia.

GEORGE WASHINGTON ERNEST, Paterson, N. J. (36300). Same as Charles Otto Ernest, New Jersey. (36299).

ARCHIE LEWIS ERWIN, Nashville, Tenn. (36075). Son of Joseph Boyd and Frances Caldonia (Smith) Erwin; grandson of William Pryor and Louisa Andrews (Dean) Smith; great-grandson of Greenberry and Eleanor (Wilson) Dean; great²-grandson of *Joseph Wilson*, private, Virginia Cont'l Troops.

TRUMAN PEEBLES ETTELE, Harrisburg, Pa. (36324). Son of Henry and Mary Catherine (Peebles) Ettele; grandson of Philip and Sarah (Radabach) Ettele; great-grandson of *David Ettele (Atley)*, private, Eighth Battalion, Lancaster County, Pennsylvania Associators; great²-grandson of *Gottlieb David Ettele*, Signer of Oath of Allegiance and Contributor of Supplies to the Army.

HARRY BOMBERGER ETTER, Middletown, Pa. (36325). Son of Henry Augustus and Mary Elizabeth (Schreiner) Etter; grandson of Henry and Christiana (Bomberger) Schreiner; great-grandson of John and Rachel (Blattenberger) Bomberger, Jr.; great²-grandson of *John Bomberger*, private, Ninth and Third Battalions, Lancaster County, Pennsylvania Militia.

DAVID RICHARD FAIN, Nashville, Tenn. (36062). Son of Richard Walker and Anne Catherine (Walker) Fain; grandson of Henry Jeffries and Elizabeth (Owen) Walker; great-grandson of Henry and Mary Gibson (Spencer) Walker; great²-grandson of *Henry Walker*, private, Tenth and Sixth Regts., Virginia Troops.

MOSES WILFORD FAITOUTE, Summit, N. J. (36354). Son of Aaron H. and Sarah M. (Winans) Faitoute; grandson of Moses and Elizabeth (Higgins) Faitoute; great-grandson of *James Higgins*, private, Capt. Nixon's Troop, Middlesex County, New Jersey Light-Horse.

PHILO TAYLOR FARNSWORTH, Jr., Utah. (24359). Son of Philo Taylor and Julia P. (Murdock) Farnsworth, Jr.; grandson of Philo Taylor and Margaret (Yates) Farnsworth; great-grandson of Reuben and Lucinda (Kent) Farnsworth; great²-grandson of

Reuben Farnsworth, private, Col. Gideon Warren's Regt., Vermont Militia; great²-grandson of Cephas and Lydia (Sheldon) Kent; great³-grandson of *Cephas Kent*, member Vermont Committee of Safety and private Col. Ira Allen's Regt., Vermont Militia; grandson of John Riggs and Almira (Lott) Murdock; great-grandson of Cornelius P. and Permelia (Darrow) Lott; great²-grandson of Joseph and Mary (Ward) Darrow; great³-grandson of *George Darrow*, Captain, New York Militia.

IRVING LORD FARR, Montclair, N. J. (36376). Son of Mortimer Ives and Henrietta Rose (Lord) Farr; grandson of William and Elizabeth (Alden) Lord, Jr.; great-grandson of *William Lord*, private, Col. Thaddeus Cook's Regt., Connecticut Militia.

FREDERICK O. FAYERWEATHER, Paterson, N. J. (36391). Son of W. O. and Lavinia (Cooke) Fayerweather; grandson of John Somerville and Abigail (Oakley) Fayerweather; great-grandson of Curtis and Sally (Johnson) Fayerweather; great²-grandson of Joseph and Rachel (Beers) Fayerweather; great³-grandson of John and Abigail (Curtis) Fayerweather; great⁴-grandson of *Jonas Curtis*, private, Col. Waterbury's Regt., Connecticut Militia.

JOHN ARTHUR FEE, Albuquerque, N. Mex. (30095). Son of Lee Moore and Grace (Ward) Fee; grandson of John S. and Abigail Almira (Moore) Fee; great-grandson of William and Mary (Curry) Moore; great²-grandson of *Robert Curry*, private, Fourth Regt., Virginia Light Dragoons.

GERALD BATTELLE FENTON, Columbus, Ohio. (36477). Son of Clarence M. and Cora (Battell) Fenton; grandson of Benjamin and Julia A. (Sagnaish) Fenton; great-grandson of Solomon and Sarah H. (Sturges) Fenton; great²-grandson of Aaron Burr and Selima (Wakeman) Sturges; great³-grandson of *William Wakeman*, Sergeant, Fairfield County, Connecticut Militia.

THADDEUS CLAY FERRELL, Humboldt, Tenn. (36066). Son of Thaddeus Newton and Louisa (Clay) Ferrell; grandson of Samuel and Louisa (Edward) Clay; great-grandson of Joshua and Sarah (Jennings) Clay; great²-grandson of *John Clay*, private, Virginia Militia.

COLIN SPANGLER FEW, Middletown, Pa. (36751). Son of Kirk and Mary (McCurdy) Few; grandson of Colin Kurtz and Louisa M. (Spangler) McCurdy; great-grandson of Zachariah and Sarah (Gardner) Spangler; great²-grandson of *John Spangler*, private, Third Battalion, York County, Pennsylvania Militia.

FREDERICK WORTMAN FLETCHER, Freeport, N. Y. (36199). Son of Theodore Comings and Carrie E. G. (Simonds) Fletcher; grandson of Edward P. and Isabella (Wortman) Fletcher; great-grandson of Comings and Sally (Wheeler) Fletcher; great²-grandson of *Ebenezer Fletcher*, Fifer, Col. Nathan Hale's Regt., New Hampshire Cont'l Troops, prisoner.

CARLOS M. FLOWER, Los Angeles, Calif. (La. 35990). Son of Charles Mulholland and Caroline (Merrill) Flower; grandson of Oliver Saunders and Emma Louise (Trimble) Merrill; great-grandson of Misgate and Hannah (Chapman) Merrill; great²-grandson of Aaron and Mercy (Levitt) Merrill; great³-grandson of *Stephen Merrill*, Captain, Massachusetts Militia at Lexington Alarm.

HERBERT CLARENCE FOOKS, Baltimore, Md. (36090). Son of George W. and Sarah Emily (Causey) Fooks; grandson of Irving and Charlotte J. (Coulbourn) Fooks; great-grandson of Uriah and Eliza Jane (Johnson) Fooks; great²-grandson of *Jesse Fooks (Fooke)*, private, Wicomico Company, Maryland Militia; grandson of Josiah and Sallie (Nutter) Causey; great-grandson of Patrick and Polly (Cropper) Causey; great²-grandson of *Patrick Causey*, private, Wicomico Company, Maryland Militia.

HERBERT MERRILL FORRISTALL, Saugus, Mass. (36110). Son of Alpheus Merrill and Sarah M. (Adams) Forristall; grandson of Joseph Mellen and Fanny (Grigham) Forristall; great-grandson of *Joseph Forristall*, private and Corporal, Massachusetts Militia, pensioned.

RUFUS EDWARD FOSTER, New Orleans, La. (35994). Son of Gustavus and Catherine (Moore) Foster; grandson of Isaac and Elizabeth (Smith) Foster; great-grandson of *Isaac Foster*, Lieutenant, Gloucester County, Virginia Militia.

SIDNEY A. FOSTER, Des Moines, Iowa. (36247). Son of Austin and Sarah (Stout) Foster; grandson of Peter L. and Waite (Luther) Stout; great-grandson of *Jesse Stout*, private, Hunterdon County, New Jersey Militia.

GEORGE HERBERT FOX, Mansfield, Ohio. (36485). Son of Edward L. and Ida (Sharp) Fox; grandson of George Alexander and Martha (Howse) Sharp; great-grandson of Robert and Mary (Beaty) Howse; great²-grandson of *William Beaty*, Captain, Brunswick County, Virginia Militia.

EDWARD LUDLOW FREELAND, Phœnix, Ariz. (36602). Son of Henry Randin and Caroline Steel (Walker) Freeland; grandson of William and Caroline (Steel) Walker; great-grandson of Thomas and Mary (Eaton) Walker; great²-grandson of *Abel Walker*, private, Col. Thomas Carpenter's Regt., Massachusetts Militia.

CHARLES McNAUGHTON FROST, Jamul, Calif. (36411). Son of Josiah Bent and Ellen Cornelia (Mills) Frost; grandson of Calvin Paine and Sarah (Rice) Frost; great-grandson of *Josiah Frost*, private, Hampshire County, Massachusetts Militia.

WALTER BLISS FROST, Providence, R. I. (34925). Son of William F. and Lois Maria (Bliss) Frost; grandson of George and Lois (Martin) Bliss; great-grandson of *James Bliss*, Surgeon's Mate, Col. Thomas Carpenter's Regt., Massachusetts Militia.

GEORGE H. FRYE, Windsor, Colo. (36340). Son of Benjamin Abbot and Ellen (Wallace) Frye; grandson of Jesse and Susannah Manning (Abbot) Frye; great-grandson of Benjamin and Dorcas (Noyes) Abbot; great²-grandson of *Benjamin Abbot*, Sergeant, Col. Stark's Regt., New Hampshire Militia.

CHARLES GRANT FRYER, Schenectady, N. Y. (36468). Son of John May and Harriet (Brackett) Fryer; grandson of John Adams and Abigail M. (Sturges) Brackett; great-grandson of James and Anna Watson (Flower) Brackett; great²-grandson of *Nathan Brackett, Jr.*, private, Col. Jonathan Bass' Regt., Massachusetts Militia.

FRANK CHARLES FULLER, Madison, So. Dak. (30667). Son of Albert E. and Esther O. (Buck) Fuller; grandson of Frank and Esther Ann (Aldrich) Fuller; great-grandson of William H. and Mary W. (Blackmarr) Fuller; great²-grandson of *John Fuller*, Sargeant, Litchfield County, Connecticut Militia, pensioned.

LOUIS WEAVER GABELL, West Philadelphia, Pa. (36307). Son of Cromwell Pearce and Louise (Gross) Gabell; grandson of Columbus W. and Mary Francis (Weaver) Gabell; great-grandson of Cromwell Pearce and Charity Cooper (Richardson) Weaver; great²-grandson of Isaac and Frances Brassington (Pearce) Weaver; great³-grandson of *Cromwell Pearce*, Colonel, Chester County, Pennsylvania Militia.

HARRY EZEKIEL GAVITT, Topeka, Kans. (36726). Son of William Wellington and Rejina L. (Spangle) Gavitt; grandson of Ezekiel Stanton and Elizabeth (Miller) Gavitt; great-grandson of *William Gavitt, Jr.*, privateer, Brig "Favorita," Sloops "Randolph" and "De Grasse," prisoner on "Jersey" prison-ship.

CHARLES HARDEN GAY, Gardiner, Me. (36581). Son of Charles Martel and Catherine Maria (Harden) Gay; grandson of Charles and Almira (Stevens) Gay; great-grandson of *Seth Gay*, private, Massachusetts Militia at Lexington Alarm; great²-grandson of *William Gay*, private at Lexington Alarm.

WILLIAM RUFUS GAY, Gardiner, Me. (36580). Same as Charles Harden Gay, Me. (36581).

ANTHONY WAYNE GEISSINGER, Columbus, Ohio. (36491). Son of James and Henrietta A. (Dorsey) Geissinger; grandson of Alfred Warfield and Charlotte (Heckrotte) Dorsey; great-grandson of Allen and Elizabeth (Smith) Dorsey; great²-grandson of *Ely Dorsey*, member Anne Arundel County, Maryland, Committee of Observation.

EDWARD TINKHAM GIBSON, Brooklyn, N. Y. (36197). Son of Edward Griswold and Sarah Emily (Tinkham) Gibson; grandson of Solomon Donald and Nancy Ann (Martin) Gibson; great-grandson of *David Gibson*, Corporal, Col. Josiah Whitney's Regt., Massachusetts Militia.

LOUIS SYLVESTER GILBERT, Hartford, Conn. (35498). Son of Henry S. and Emily L. (Miller) Gilbert; grandson of Elijah and Louisa Matilda (Gildersleeve) Miller; great-grandson of Sylvester and Rebecca (Dixon) Gildersleeve; great²-grandson of *Philip Gildersleeve*, private, Third Regt., New York Cont'l Line.

HENRY MILTON GOODNOW, Clifton, N. J. (36369). Son of Richard and Clara (Brown) Goodnow; grandson of Milton W. and Matilda (Williams) Goodnow; great-grandson of James and Sarah (Hunt) Williams; great²-grandson of *David Hunt*, Regimental Quartermaster, Fifth Regt., New York Line.

WILLIAM WALLACE GOODRICH, Winchester, Ind. (35523). Son of John B. and Elizabeth Putnam (Edgar) Goodrich; grandson of Edward and Jane Gray (Putnam) Edger; great-grandson of Ernestus and Elizabeth (Gray) Putnam; great²-grandson of *Aaron J. Putnam*, private, Second Regt., Albany County, New York Militia.

HAROLD GORDON, Westfield, N. J. (36295). Son of William Henry and Margaret Ursula (Voorhees) Gordon, Jr.; grandson of William Henry and Sarah E. (Disbrow) Gordon; great-grandson of Samuel and Abigail (Buckelew) Gordon, Jr.; great²-grandson of *Samuel Gordon*, private, Middlesex County, N. J. Militia.

CHARLES ALLISON GREENE, New Orleans, La. (35988). Son of Allison Lawson and Susan Cary (Rosenbury) Greene; grandson of Charles Edward and Charlotte (Storrs) Rosenbury; great-grandson of Lucina and Susan Young (Caryl) Storrs; great²-grandson of *Dan Storrs*, Clerk, Col. Experience Storr's Regt., Conn. Militia at Lexington Alarm.

RICHARD THURSTON GREENE, Montclair, N. J. (36357). Son of James Gardner and Mary Helen (Rice) Greene; grandson of Appleton and Mary (Meacham) Rice; great-grandson of *Martin Rice*, private and Fifer, Massachusetts Militia.

WILLIAM MORSE GRISWOLD, London, Eng. (Conn. 35499). Son of Charles and Irene (Morse) Griswold; grandson of Edward and Laura (Hubbard) Griswold; great-grandson of Daniel W. and Esther (Case) Griswold; great²-grandson of *White Griswold*, private, Eighth Regt., Connecticut Line, prisoner.

CORNELIUS JAMES GWYNNE, Wood Ridge, N. J. (N. Y. 36471). Son of Alexander and Emily (Bishop) Gwynne; grandson of Cornelius and Hannah (Winchell) Bishop; great-grandson of Henry and Rebecca (Ladieu) (Ladew) Winchell; great²-grandson of *James Winchell*, private, Fourth Regt., New York Cont'l Line.

WHITMAN CATLIN HAFF, Stamford, Conn. (36701). Son of Edward Payson and Frances (Wright) Haff; grandson of John Bascom and Caroline Matilda (Henderson) Wright; great-grandson of George R. and Margaret (Hallenbeck) Hendrickson; great²-grandson of Hendrick and Rachel (Winne) Hallenbeck; great³-grandson of *Bernardus Hallenbeck*, Second Lieutenant, First Regt., Albany County, New York Militia.

ARTHUR ANDREWS HALL, Adams, Mass. (36801). Son of Andrews and Susan Harkness (Anthony) Hall; grandson of Alanson and Rebecca (Walker) Hall; great-grandson of Erastus and Polly (Moss) Hall; great²-grandson of *Benjamin Hall*, private, Col. Roger Enos' Battalion, Connecticut Militia, member Wallingford Com. of Inspection.

STEPHEN LOW ARNOLD HALL, Adams, Mass. (36802). Same as Arthur Andrews Hall (Mass., 36801).

JAMES MADISON HAMILTON, Rutland, Vt. (33849). Son of Jamin Hannibal and Ellen Mariah (Goff) Hamilton; grandson of Hannibal Charles and Julia Emily (Thompson) Hamilton; great-grandson of Nathan and Phebe (Ballard) Hamilton; great²-grandson of *Elisha Hamilton*, private, Massachusetts and Vermont Militia.

DANIEL STANTON HAMMOND, Paterson, N. J. (36290). Son of Daniel Stanton and Helyne Myra (Scott) Hammond; grandson of Daniel Stanton and Sophia Augusta (Blakslee) Hammond; great-grandson of Pardon Tillinghast and Roby Hopkins (Stanton) Hammond; great²-grandson of William and Alice (Tillinghast) Hammond, Jr.; great³-grandson of *William Hammond*, Rhode Island Commissary-General for recruits and supplies.

WILLIAM L. F. HARDHAM, Newark, N. J. (36679). Son of Lawrence J. and Mary B. (Hiscox) Hardham; grandson of Freeman H. and Nancy (Westerfield) Hiscox; great-grandson of David and Anna (Thompson) Hiscox, Jr.; great²-grandson of *David Hiscox*, Lieutenant, Col. Samuel McClellan's Regt., Connecticut Militia.

EDWIN MORTIMER HARRISON, Montclair, N. J. (36383). Son of Edwin M. and Mary Frances (Hamilton) Harrison; grandson of Jared Erwin and Catharine (Egbert) Harrison; great-grandson of *Moses Harrison*, private, Essex County, New Jersey Militia.

HENRY TURNER HARRISON, Worcester, Mass. (Md. 36082). Son of Joseph Nathan and Julia Anne (Turner) Harrison; grandson of Thomas Edward and Cecelia (Dent) Harrison; great-grandson of *Gideon Dent*, private, Charles County, Maryland Militia.

JAMES EDWARD HARRISON, Baltimore, Md. (36085). Son of Spencer and Wilhelmina Augusta (Byns) Harrison; grandson of Theophilus and Martha Elizabeth (Turner)

Harrison; great-grandson of Thomas Edward and Cecelia (Dent) Harrison; great²-grandson of *Gideon Dent*, private, Charles County, Maryland Militia.

ROLAND LEE HARRISON, Washington, D. C. (Md. 36083). Same as Henry Turner Harrison (Md., 36082).

THEOPHILUS KENOLEY HARRISON, Baltimore, Md. (36084). Same as James Edward Harrison (Md., 36085).

THOMAS CHAPMAN HARRISON, Charlotte Hall, Md. (36081). Same as Henry Turner Harrison (Md., 36082).

JOHN ROCHAMBEAU HAUDENSHIELD, Carnegie, Pa. (36315). Son of John Edward and Mary Holmes (Burk) Haudenshield; grandson of William Henry and Susan (Steel) Burk; great-grandson of Samuel and Nancy (Detrich) Steel; great²-grandson of Andrew and Mary (Stitt) Steel; great³-grandson of *John Steel*, Captain, Pennsylvania Independent Co. of Foot.

AARON B. HAVILAND, Hillside, N. J. (36400). Son of Aaron and Hannah Morris (Blair) Haviland; grandson of Aaron and Eliza (Brant) Haviland; great-grandson of Jacob and Eliza (Freeman) Brant; great²-grandson of *David Brant*, Teamster, Wagonmaster General's Department, New Jersey Militia.

JOHN FENTON HAWKEN, St. Louis, Mo. (35562). Son of Otis R. and Lily Boggs (Long) Hawken; grandson of John Fenton and Frances Elizabeth (Pipkin) Long; great-grandson of William Lindsay and Elizabeth (Sappington) Long; great²-grandson of *John Long*, Captain, Virginia Troops.

ELBERT DANIEL HAYFORD, Hallowell, Me. (36582). Son of Daniel and Virginia Ellen (Brown) Hayford; grandson of Samuel and Charlotte (Pompilly) (Pumpelly) Hayford; great-grandson of William and Philena (French) Hayford, Jr.; great²-grandson of *William Hayford*, private, Massachusetts Militia.

CHESTER BARRETT HEAL, New York City, N. Y. (36187). Son of George Albert and Emma L. (Griffith) Heal; grandson of Joseph H. and Mary Van Pelt (Smith) Heal; great-grandson of James and Eliza (Barrett) Heal; great²-grandson of Reuben and Sarah (Thorndike) Barrett; great³-grandson of Nathan and Miriam (Hunt) Barrett; great⁴-grandson of *James Barrett*, Colonel, Concord Massachusetts Militia, member State Convention and Provincial Congress.

DOUGLAS SELPH HENRY, Captain, A. E. F., Nashville, Tenn. (36064). Son of Robert A. and Emily (James) Selph; grandson of Iley Nunn and Nancy Thomas (Brown) Selph; great-grandson of Henry Hill and Nancy Ellington (Marshall) Brown; great²-grandson of Jeremiah and Martha (Hill) Brown; great³-grandson of *Green Hill*, member North Carolina Assembly and Congress, and Major, North Carolina Militia.

ROBERT SELPH HENRY, Captain, A. E. F., Nashville, Tenn. (36063). Same as Douglas Selph Henry (Tenn., 36064).

JOSEPH DWEN HIGGINS, Brooklyn, N. Y. (36194). Son of Francis Taylor and Henrietta Josephine (Stockton) Higgins; grandson of Samuel Wesley and Mary Ann (Seeley) Stockton; great-grandson of W. H. and Mary Ann (Pendleton) Seeley; great²-grandson of *Joseph Pendleton*, Captain and Major, Westerly and Kings County, Rhode Island Militia.

CHARLES HILL, Harriman, Tenn. (36065). Son of Isaac Alexander and Margaret (Kendrick) Hill; grandson of Barney and Nancy Green (Millican) Hill; great-grandson of Joab and Elizabeth (Lane) Hill; great²-grandson of *William Hill, Jr.*, member North Carolina Com. of Safety; great³-grandson of *William Hill*, member Hillsboro, North Carolina Provincial Congress; great²-grandson of Isaac and Sarah (Russell) Lane; great³-grandson of *George Russell*, Lieutenant, Col. Sevier's Regt., North Carolina Militia; grandson of John and Martha (Owens) Kendrick; great-grandson of Samuel Sumpter and Sarah (Randolph) Owens; great²-grandson of Edward and Elizabeth (Sumpter) Owens; great³-grandson of *William Sumpter*, Captain, Burke County, North Carolina Militia; great-grandson of *Samuel Kendrick*, private, Virginia State Troops; great²-grandson of *Edom Kendrick*, private, Virginia Militia; grandson of Barney and Nancy G. (Millican) Hill; great-grandson of Joab and Elizabeth (Lane) Hill; great²-grandson of *Isaac Lane*, Lieutenant, Col. John Sevier's Regt., North Carolina Militia, pensioned; great³-grandson of *Tidence Lane*, patriot preacher.

GEORGE ALBERT HILL, Jr., Ridgewood, N. J. (36380). Son of George Albert and Josephine Lyon (Hazleton) Hill; grandson of Edmund F. and Sarah (Garfield) Hazleton; great-grandson of Josiah and Sarah (Emerson) Hazleton; great²-grandson of *John Emerson*, private, Col. Moses Nichols' Regt., New Hampshire Militia.

HAROLD DYER HILL, Paterson, N. J. (36351). Son of Robert Clark Hutchinson and Elizabeth (MacChesney) Hill; grandson of Samuel and Ann (Capner) Hill; great-grandson of *Smith Hill*, Quartermaster, First Regt., Burlington County, New Jersey Militia.

JEREMIAH FRANCIS HILL, Newark, N. J. (36696). Son of Charles Freeman and Lavinia Ann (Parker) Hill; grandson of Jeremiah and Lucinda (Libby) Hill; great-grandson of Joshua and Mary (Gilpatrick) Hill; great²-grandson of *Joseph (Gose) Hill*, private, Col. Moses Kelley's Regt., New Hampshire Militia.

ROBERT SHERRARD HILL, Steubenville, Ohio. (36494). Son of Joseph Welsh and Mary Ann (Sherrard) Hill; grandson of *Robert Hill*, private, Third Battalion, Washington County, Pennsylvania Militia.

JOHN WILLIAM HILTON, Betheny, Nebr. (33896). Son of John B. W. and Mary Elizabeth (Redgate) Hilton; grandson of Edmund and Lydia Ann (Miller) Redgate; great-grandson of Stephen and Elizabeth (Weeks) Miller; great²-grandson of *Stephen Weeks*, private, Col. Drake's Regt., Westchester County, New York Militia.

LESLIE ROBERTS HIMES, New Bethlehem, Pa. (36317). Son of John Rutherford and Mary (Roberts) Himes; grandson of Joseph C. and Margaret (Rutherford) Himes; great-grandson of John and Sylvina (Space) Himes; great²-grandson of Zephaniah and Katie (Armstrong) Space; great³-grandson of *John Space*, private, Second Regt., New Jersey Cont'l Line.

ARTHUR GARFIELD HOLLIS, Oklahoma City, Okla. (35242). Son of Alonzo K. and Minnie Field (Harris) Hollis; grandson of George and Sarah (Field) Harris; great-grandson of Joseph and Lucretia (Lord) Harris; great²-grandson of *Israel Harris*, Captain, Col. Benjamin Simond's Regt., Massachusetts Militia, pensioned.

REUBEN R. HOLMES, Dayton, Ohio. (36486). Son of Samuel A. and Virginia (Rose) Holmes; grandson of Samuel B. and Catharine (Shafor) Holmes; great-grandson of William and Jane (Ryerson) Shafor; great²-grandson of *Peter Shafor*, private, Somerset County, New Jersey Militia.

FRANK WARD HOLT, Mich. (18318). Supplemental. Son of Ira Farnsworth and Perla M. (Ward) Holt; grandson of Nicholas Mosher and Ann (Reynolds) Holt; great-grandson of Abiel and Mary (Mosher) Holt; great²-grandson of *Abiel Holt*, private, Connecticut Militia.

FREDERICK SHERMAN HOPKINS, Springfield, Mass. (36117). Son of Frederick Eugene and Harriet Ann (Sherman) Hopkins; grandson of William Fay and Laura (Campbell) Hopkins; great-grandson of Herman and Miriam (Blaisdell) Hopkins; great²-grandson of Henry and Sarah (Fay) Hopkins; great³-grandson of *Weight Hopkins*, Major and Captain, Seth Warner's Regt., Vermont Militia.

CRAFT ACKERMAN HOPPER, Paterson, N. J. (36291). Son of Charles Craft and Louisa (Ackerman) Hopper; grandson of Abram and Charity Ann (Romaine) Ackerman; great-grandson of John and Catherine (Post) Ackerman; great²-grandson of Abram A. and Mary (Manning) Ackerman; great³-grandson of *Abraham Manning*, private, Bergen County, New Jersey Militia, 7 years' service.

EDWIN NOTT HOPSON, Paterson, N. J. (36355). Son of Charles R. and Mary Elizabeth (May) Hopson; grandson of John and Mary (Doremus) May; great-grandson of Pieter and Catharine (——) Doremus; great²-grandson of *Thomas Doremus*, private, Second Regt., Essex County, New Jersey Militia.

ROY MARTIN HOUGHTON, New Haven, Conn. (36707). Son of David and Amanda H. (Smith) Houghton; grandson of Daniel and Lydia (Cutler) Houghton; great-grandson of James and Mary (——) Houghton; great²-grandson of *Jonathan Houghton*, Captain, Worcester County, Massachusetts Militia.

CARL CLIFFORD HOWARD, Glasgow, Ky. (34725). Son of Thomas S. and Queen (Langford) Howard; grandson of Harmon P. and Cansada (Morehead) Howard; great-grandson of Jesse and Lucy (Mayfield) Howard; great²-grandson of John and Sarrah

(McDougal) Mayfield; great³-grandson of *Alexander McDougal*, Lieutenant, South Carolina Troops.

JOHN LUTHER HOWLAND, Providence, R. I. (36501). Son of Amasa W. and Rebecca Adelaide (Emerson) Howland; grandson of Oliver Ackley and Sarah Ann (Cothrane) Emerson; great-grandson of *Theodore Emerson*, private, Massachusetts Militia.

CLIFFORD BURTON HOYT, East Orange, N. J. (36680). Son of Charles Wesley and Artemisia V. (Bull) Hoyt; grandson of Ezra Dibble and Sarah M. (White) Bull; great-grandson of Horace and Mary (Dibble) Bull; great²-grandson of *Asa Bull*, private, Col. Charles Webb's Regt., Connecticut Militia.

PHILIP HUBBELL, Pajarito, N. Mex. (30096). Son of J. Filipe and May Helene (——) Hubbell; grandson of James L. and Julianita (G——) Hubbell; great-grandson of John L. and Sophia (Morse) Hubbell; great²-grandson of John and Parrillas (Foote) Hubbell; great³-grandson of *Comfort Hubbell*, member Connecticut Committee of Safety and Inspection.

JOSEPH FRANCIS HUGGINS, Portland, Ore. (35067). Son of James Francis and Alice (Patterson) Huggins; grandson of Joseph Stillman and Elizabeth Grimes (Murdough) Huggins; great-grandson of Joseph and Hannah (Bingham) Huggins; great²-grandson of *Elias Bingham*, Corporal, Seventh Regt., Connecticut Militia.

CHURCHILL HUNGERFORD, Wenonah, N. J. (36286). Son of Henry and Mary Elizabeth (Churchill) Hungerford; grandson of William and Mary Myrick (Haden) Churchill; great-grandson of *Solomon Churchill*, private, Massachusetts Militia for coast defense, pensioned; grandson of Henry and Jeannette (Northrup) Hungerford; great-grandson of Benjamin and Zadde (Newell) Hungerford; great²-grandson of *Benjamin Hungerford*, and Lieutenant, Col. Benjamin Hinsman's Regt., Connecticut Militia; grandson of William and Mary Myrick (Haden) Churchill; great-grandson of Solomon and Elizabeth (Bartlett) Churchill; great²-grandson of *Thomas Bartlett*, private, Massachusetts Coast Guards.

RALPH BENJAMIN HUNTER, Cleveland Heights, Ohio. (36493). Son of Thomas Edwin and Jennie (Oman) Hunter; grandson of Benjamin and Sarah (Jump) Hunter; great-grandson of Samuel and Jane (Paul) Hunter; great²-grandson of *George Hunter*, private, Cumberland County, Pennsylvania Militia.

FRANK B. HUTCHENS, Los Angeles, Calif. (36401). Son of Charles Tanner and Angeline (Chadwick) Hutchens; grandson of Noah and Phœbe (Tanner) Hutchens; great-grandson of *Noah Hutchens*, private and Corporal, Massachusetts Militia.

ROBERT PARKE HUTCHINSON, Bethlehem, Pa. (36316). Son of Elias Smith and Mary (Seely) Hutchinson; grandson of David and Betsey (Hayward) Hutchinson; great-grandson of Jesse and Polly (Searitt) Hutchinson; great²-grandson of *Andrew Searitt*, private, New Hampshire and Massachusetts Militia, pensioned.

ALBERT ICKSTADT, Jr., Chicago, Ill. (36213). Son of Albert and Mildred (Quimby) Ickstadt; grandson of John Bartlett and Sarah Eliza (Leland) Quimby; great-grandson of Cyrus and Sarah (Howard) Leland; great²-grandson of Cyrus and Betsey (Kimball) Leland; great³-grandson of Noah Brooks and Persis (Brigham) Kimball; great⁴-grandson of *Aaron Kimball*, Captain, Worcester County, Massachusetts Militia.

KENNETH CARR INGRAHAM, Seattle, Wash. (36651). Son of Edward Sturgis and Myra A. (Carr) Ingraham; grandson of W. F. and Jane (Whipple) West; great-grandson of Jeremiah R. and Nancy A. (Pelton) Whipple; great²-grandson of Ezra and Cleo (Wright) Pelton; great³-grandson of *Ithmar Pelton*, Ensign, Twenty-third Regt., Connecticut Train Band.

CHARLES WESLEY JACOBY, Waldo, Ohio. (35895). Son of Michael and Catharine (Emery) Jacoby, Jr.; grandson of Michael and Elizabeth (Worline) Jacoby; great-grandson of Henry and Catharine (Cline) Worline; great²-grandson of *Conrad Cline*, private, Sixth Regt., Pennsylvania Cont'l Line.

EDWIN LE ROY JACOBY, East Orange, N. J. (36488). Son of John and Eliza (Van Brimmer) Jacoby; grandson of Michael and Elizabeth (Worline) Jacoby; great-grandson of Henry and Catharine (Cline) Worline; great²-grandson of *Conrad Cline*, private, Sixth Regt., Pennsylvania Cont'l Line.

JOHN JACOBY, Marion, Ohio. (36487). Son of Michael and Elizabeth (Worline) Jacoby; grandson of Henry and Catharine (Cline) Worline; great-grandson of *Conrad Cline*, private, Sixth Regt., Pennsylvania Cont'l Line.

SAMUEL LAWRENCE JAMES, New Orleans, La. (35992). Son of Samuel Lawrence and Emma Dorothy (Hart) James; grandson of James Lawrence and Beulah Biddle (Arney) James; great-grandson of Samuel Lawrence and Mary (Hall) James; great²-grandson of *Edward Hall*, Major, First Battalion, Salem County, New Jersey Militia.

HOLDER MORGAN JAMESON, Watertown, Mass. (36119). Son of John Alexander and Theodora Parker (Holder) Jameson; grandson of Nathaniel and Hannah Dodge (Morgan) Holder; great-grandson of Andrew and Rachael (Safford) Morgan, Jr.; great²-grandson of *Andrew Morgan*, private, Massachusetts sea-coast defense; Seaman and mate Massachusetts brigantine "Tyranniside" and privateer "Junius Brutus," prisoner.

CHARLES CHAMBERLAIN JOHNSON, Brooklyn, N. Y. (36464). Son of William and Angeline (Chamberlain) Johnson; grandson of Jacob Payson and Catherine (Kuney) Chamberlain; great-grandson of John and Mary (Lee) Chamberlain; great²-grandson of *Jacob Chamberlain*, member Boston Committee for purchasing ammunition and of other war committees.

CLINTON HERBERT JOHNSON, Jr., Prividence, R. I. (36502). Son of Clinton H. and Claribel (Bentley) Johnson; grandson of John and Miranda (Chaplin) Bentley; great-grandson of Moses and Betsey (Smith) Chaplin; great²-grandson of Moses and Lucy (Page) Chaplin; great³-grandson of *Jonas Page*, Sergeant, Col. Brooks' Regt., Massachusetts Militia.

FRANCIS HOPKINS JOHNSON, N. J. (36388). Son of Thomas M. and Fanny (Speddued) Johnson; grandson of James and Anne Matthews (Richards) Johnson; great-grandson of *James Johnson*, Colonel, Frederick County, Maryland Militia.

HARRY BISHOP JOHNSON, Providence, R. I. (36506). Son of Lyman Humiston and Mary Lucinda (Bishop) Johnson; grandson of David Chittenden and Lucinda (Baldwin) Bishop; great-grandson of Jonathan Chittenden and Julia (Tyler) Bishop; great²-grandson of *James Bishop*, private, Connecticut Militia, widow pensioned.

ROBERT NELSON JOHNSON, Fort Madison, Iowa. (36237). Son of Nelson and Nancy Ann (Porter) Johnson; grandson of Seth and Lavina (Adams) Johnson; great-grandson of Daniel and Lucretia (Prout) Johnson; great²-grandson of *Seth Johnson*, private, Middlesex County, Connecticut Militia; great-grandson of Reuben and Rozillah (Hoodley) Adams; great²-grandson of *Nathaniel Hoodley*, private, Col. William Douglas' Regt., Connecticut Militia, pensioned; grandson of William and Catherine (Pollock) Porter; great-grandson of William and Sarah (Fruit) Pollock; great²-grandson of *Robert Fruit*, private, Pennsylvania Militia and chairman Committee of Safety.

LESTER ALEXANDER JOHNSTON, Paterson, N. J. (36692). Son of Wesley S. B. and Rose (Edwards) Johnston; grandson of John T. and Martha (Tredwell) Johnston; great-grandson of Levereth and Martha (Tredwell) Treadwell (son of Jacob); great²-grandson of John and Phebe (Pell) Tredwell (father of Martha); great³-grandson of *Samuel Tredwell*, Captain, Westchester County, New York Light Horse.

GEORGE ELWOOD JONES, Newark, N. J. (36392). Son of Charles Bines and Annie Elizabeth (Onderdonk) Jones; grandson of Gerrard and Mary Ann (Carhart) Jones; great-grandson of Joel and Ann (Van Pelt) Carhart; great²-grandson of *Thomas Carhart*, private and Corporal, New Jersey Militia and Cont'l Troops.

EDWIN BLACK JUDD, Hartford, Conn. (36702). Son of John Dwight and Frances Barbara (Black) Judd; grandson of Willard and Sophia (Searle) Judd; great-grandson of Allen and Sarah (Snow) Judd; great²-grandson of *Thomas Judd*, private, Col. Woodbridge's Regt., Massachusetts Militia; grandson of Archibald and Eleanor (Wooden) Black; great-grandson of *John Black*, private, Col. Wynkoop's Regt., Massachusetts Militia; great-grandson of James and Elizabeth (Towsend) Wooden, Jr., great²-grandson of *James Wooden*, Corporal and Bombardier, Massachusetts Artillery.

SAMUEL GILBERT JUMP, Muncie, Ind. (36431). Son of Samuel Vaughn and Mary Sophia (Gilbert) Jump; grandson of Othniel Jedithan and Seraph (Webster) Gilbert: great-grandson of Uri and Mercy (Ashley) Webster; great²-grandson of *Daniel Ashley*. Lieutenant, Col. Baldwin's Regt., New Hampshire Militia; great³-grandson of *Samuel Ashley*, Colonel, Thirteenth Regt., New Hampshire Militia.

ROBERT FULTON KEIPER, Middletown, Pa. (36752). Son of Edw. Smith and Annie Margaret (Detweiler) Keiper; grandson of Joseph and Cordelia (Smith) Keiper; great-grandson of Jacob and Susanna (Grise) Keiper; great²-grandson of *John Grise*, private, Lancaster County, Pennsylvania Militia.

DAVID HENRY KELLER, Pineville, La. (35998). Son of James E. M. and Laura A. (Whitesell) Keller; grandson of David and Ellen (Brown) Keller; great-grandson of Jacob and Susanna (Overpeck) Brown; great²-grandson of *John Brown*, Captain, Fifth Battalion, Northampton County, Pennsylvania Militia.

GEORGE MARTIN KELLOGG, Jr., Chicago, Ill. (36214). Son of George Martin and Mary Edna (Jackson) Kellogg; grandson of George Washington and Mary (McMillan) Kellogg; great-grandson of Otis and Priscilla (Gibson) Kellogg; great²-grandson of Martin and Patty (Gibson) Kellogg; great³-grandson of *Eliphalet Kellogg*, private, Albany County, New York Militia.

WILLIAM SETON KENT, Washington, D. C. (36134). Son of Jonathan Yates and Ellen Victoria (Belt) Kent; grandson of William J. and Ellen Ursula (Bowie) Belt; great-grandson of *J. Sprigg Belt*, Second Lieutenant, Maryland Militia; great-grandson of John B. and Catherine (Hall) Bowie; great²-grandson of *Benjamin Hall*, member Maryland Constitutional Convention and Major, Middle Battalion, Maryland Troops.

HOWARD NATHANIEL KENYON, Lieut. U. S. M. C., Quantico, Va. (D. C. 36128). Son of Nathaniel C. and Ella Eugenie (Scofield) Kenyon; grandson of Archibald and Juliana (Pratt) Kenyon; great-grandson of Samuel R. and Clarissa (Miller) Kenyon; great²-grandson of David and Mary (Rogers) Kenyon; great³-grandson of *William Kenyon*, Ensign, Colonel Dyer's Regt., Rhode Island Militia, pensioned; grandson of Aaron and Mary (Hay) Scofield; great-grandson of William and Mary (Hays) Hay; great²-grandson of *James Hays*, Lieutenant, Second Battalion, Northumberland County, Pennsylvania Militia; great-grandson of Sylvanus and Martha (Lyon) Scofield; great²-grandson of *Hait Scofield*, private, Fairfield County, Connecticut Militia, pensioned.

RALPH CLAUDE KEPHART, U. S. Navy, Calif. (36402). Son of George Elwood and Anna C. (Weisel) Kephart; grandson of Henry (Harmon) and Amy T. (Hyde) Kephart; great-grandson of Jacob and Magdalena (Puth) Kephart; great²-grandson of *John Kephart*, private, Philadelphia German Regt., Cont'l Line.

JOSEPH AUSTIN KILBOURN, Hartford, Conn. (36708). Son of Horace and Mary (Young) Kilbourn; grandson of Joseph and Hannah (Sellew) Kilbourn; great-grandson of *Philip Sellew*, member Connecticut Cont'l Army Clothing Committee, Tax Collector, and member Connecticut General Assembly of '83.

JOSEPH BIRNEY KILBOURN, Hartford, Conn. (36703). Son of Joseph Austin and Sarah Alacoque (Dooley) Kilbourn; grandson of Horace and Mary (Young) Kilbourn; great-grandson of Joseph and Hannah (Sellew) Kilbourn; great²-grandson of *Philip Sellew*, member Clothes Purchasing Committee for Cont'l Army, and member Connecticut General Assembly of '83.

HARRY DONLY KIRKOVER, Eggertsville, N. Y. (36188). Son of Henry D. and Emma J. (Barnard) Kirkover; grandson of Robert and Hannah C. (Manning) Barnard; great-grandson of Joseph and Margaret (Wafel) Barnard; great²-grandson of *Henry Wafel*, private, New York Militia.

PHILIP GORDON KITCHEN, Wynewood, Pa. (36305). Son of James G. and Margaret Amelia (Webb) Kitchen; grandson of James Lamborn and Susan Rapp (Graeff) Webb; great-grandson of Daniel and Margaret (Rapp) Graeff, Jr.; great²-grandson of *Daniel Graeff*, Captain, Berks County, Pennsylvania Militia.

PHAON SILAS KOHLER, Glassport, Pa. (36319). Son of Edward and Lydia (Remely) Kohler; grandson of John Peter and Susanna (Kern) Kohler; great-grandson of *Jacob Kohler*, private, Northampton County, Pennsylvania Militia.

GEORGE WARNE LABAW, Paterson, N. J. (36287). Son of John Chamberlain and Mary (Warne) Labaw; grandson of George and Sarah (Fulmer) Warne; great-grandson of *John Warne*, private, Middlesex County, New Jersey Militia.

ALBERT WALSH LANG, Boston, Mass. (36111). Son of Albert Seavey and Mary Ann (Walsh) Lang; grandson of Alfred and Susan (Burley) Lang; great-grandson of Samuel and Lydia (Furber) Lang; great²-grandson of *Thomas Lang*, private, New Hampshire

Militia; great-grandson of Ezra and Lucy (Hyde) Burley; great^2-grandson of *Jacob Burley (Burleigh)*, private, Col. Stephen Evans' Regt., New Hampshire Troops; great^3-grandson of *Josiah Burly (Burleigh)*, private, Col. Joshua Wingate's Regt., New Hampshire Militia.

GLENN BURNELL LANTZ, New Brighton, N. Y. (36462). Son of Stephen P. and Martha Catherine (Myers) Lantz; grandson of John and Nancy Priscilla (Hoback) Myers; great-grandson of William K. and Martha Esther (Herrick) Hoback; great^2-grandson of Samuel and Katherine (Malloy) Herrick; great^3-grandson of *Joseph Herrick*, private, Col. Johnson's Regt., Massachusetts Militia; great^4-grandson of *Israel Herrick*, private, Col. Frye's Regt., Massachusetts Militia.

HAROLD FOWLER LARKIN, West Hartford, Conn. (36709). Son of James Edwin and Adella Hannah (Fowler) Larkin; grandson of Perez Marshall and Lois Elvira (Miller) Fowler; great-grandson of Chauncey Burritt and Apphia (Twining) Fowler; great^2-grandson of *Titus Fowler*, Sergeant, Col. John Moseley's Regt., Massachusetts Militia.

HAROLD EMERSON LAWRENCE, Paterson, N. J. (36288). Son of Will Francis and Jennie Lord (Verry) Lawrence; grandson of Thomas Reed and Polly Barnes (Litchfield) Lawrence; great^2-grandson of Thaddeus and Joa (Oakes) Lawrence; great^3-grandson of *Timothy Lawrence*, private, Massachusetts Militia.

WILLIAM KEMP LEMON, Jr., Middletown, Pa. (36753). Son of James Henry and Emma Minerva (Shaffer) Lemon; grandson of William Kemp and Catherine (Heckert) Lemon; great-grandson of Simon and Jane (Sweigart) Lemon; great^2-grandson of *George Leamon (Lemon)*, private, First Battalion, Lancaster County, Pennsylvania Militia.

CLAUDE FREDERICK LESTER, Wash. (28935). Supplemental. Son of Fred Volney and Eva M. (Conklin) Lester; grandson of Volney and Mary Jane (Smith) Lester; great-grandson of Martin and Esther (Bronson) Smith; great^2-grandson of Simeon and Chloe (Smith) Smith; great^3-grandson of *Eldad Smith*, private, Connecticut Militia at Lexington Alarm.

ROBERT KENDALL LEWIS, Jr., Chicago, Ill. (36215). Son of Robert Kendall and Annabella Whaley (Jones) Lewis; grandson of John Bayley and Anna America (Follin) Jones; great-grandson of James and Mary Ann (Cross) Follin; great^2-grandson of *John Follin*, sailor, Virginia Navy, prisoner.

HENRY PETER LEWMAN, Louisville, Ky. (36529). Son of George and Adeline (Peter) Lewman; grandson of John and Mary (Grisamore) Lewman; great-grandson of Moses and Elizabeth (Cash) Lewman; great^2-grandson of *John Lewman*, Sergeant, Sixth Regt., Pennsylvania Cont'l Line; great^2-grandson of *John Cash*, private, Lancaster County, Pennsylvania Militia.

JOHN BUREL LEWMAN, Prather, Ind. (Ky. 36528). Son of Moses T. and N. L. (Conover) Lewman; grandson of John and Mary (Grisamore) Lewman; great-grandson of Moses and Elizabeth (Cash) Lewman; great^2-grandson of *John Lewman*, Sergeant, Sixth Regt., Pennsylvania Cont'l Line; great^2-grandson of *John Cash*, private, Lancaster County, Pennsylvania Militia; grandson of Garrett and Susanna (Monteith) Conover; great-grandson of *William Conover*, private, First Regt., Monmouth County, New Jersey, Militia.

DAVID SPECHT LING, Sheldon, Iowa. (36242). Son of Henry and Mary (Specht) Ling; grandson of David and Priscilla (Bissel) Specht; great-grandson of *Christian Specht*, private, Pennsylvania Militia, pensioned.

PAUL BRADNER LITTLEHALE, Cranford, N. J. (36683). Son of Wilbur Stearns and Etta E. (House) Littlehale; grandson of Daniel Stearns and Joanna B. (Davis) Littlehale; great-grandson of Daniel Stearns and Joanna B. (Davis) Littlehale; great^2-grandson of Roger Langdon and Mary (Griffin) Littlehale; great^3-grandson of *Abraham Littlehale*, private, Middlesex County, Massachusetts Militia.

RICHARD CARPENTER LOCKWOOD, N. Y. (26471). Supplemental. Son of Jeremiah Talcott and Louise (Carpenter) Lockwood; grandson of Jeremiah Talcott and Jane (Shurrager) Lockwood; great-grandson of James and Nancy Vorhies (Albin) Lockwood; great^2-grandson of *Jacob Lockwood*, Drummer, Third Regt., Connecticut Troops; great-grandson of Simeon and Annie Ekert (Ackert) Shurger (Shurrager); great^2-grandson of *Andres Shurger*, Ulster County, New York patriot, killed by Indians and Tories.

FRANK OTEY LONG, Mt. Pleasant, Tenn. (36776). Son of Henry and Frances Burton (Scurlock) Long; grandson of T. P. and Anne (Huntsman) Scurlock; great-grandson of Adam and Sarah Wesley (Quarles) Huntsman; great²-grandson of *William Quarles*, Ensign and Second Lieutenant, First Regt., Virginia Troops.

LEON MILNER LONG, Mt. Pleasant, Tenn. (36777). Same as Frank Otey Long, Tenn. (36776).

CHARLES LAWRENCE LONGLEY, Boise, Idaho. (35108). Son of Alfred and Julia M. (Read) Longley; grandson of Thomas and Martha Arms (Taylor) Longley; great-grandson of *Edmund Longley*, Captain, Middlesex County, Massachusetts Militia.

ANDREW J. LOOMIS, Santa Fe, New Mex. (30093). Son of Thompson and Laura (A——) Loomis; grandson of Solomon and Hannah (Armstrong) Loomis; great-grandson of *Simon Loomis*, private, Connecticut Militia, Col. Sheldon's Light Dragoons and Putnam's Cont'l Troops, pensioned.

MILTON E. LOOMIS, Westfield, N. J. (36693). Son of L. Rood and Mary W. (Early) Loomis; grandson of Charles H. and Julia Ann (Rood) Loomis; great-grandson of Anson and Highly (Hitchcock) Loomis; great²-grandson of *Michael Loomis*, Ensign, Col. John Fellows' Regt., Connecticut Militia.

HAROLD CLARENCE LOUNSBERRY, Marshalltown, Iowa. (36246). Son of Harvey Wellington and Sarah Agnes (Gonsley) Lounsberry; grandson of Joshua Whitney Hillman and Priscilla M. (Gager) Lounsberry; great-grandson of Joseph and Mary (Whitney) Lounsberry; great²-grandson of *Michael Lounsberry*, private, Ninth Regt., New York Militia.

ROBERT ADDISON LUSE, Sharon, Pa. (36320). Son of Robert and Calista Freelove (Slater) Luce; grandson of Nathan and Freelove (Crossman) Slater; great-grandson of *Benjamin Slater*, private, Connecticut Militia.

ROBERT WILLIAM LUSE, Sharon, Pa. (36321). Son of Robert Addison and Henrietta Marvin (Fell) Luse; grandson of Robert and Calista Freelove (Slater) Luse; great-grandson of Nathan and Freelove (Crossman) Slater; great²-grandson of *Benjamin Slater*, private, Connecticut Militia.

DONALD FISHER LYBARGER, Ohio. (34598). Supplementals. Son of Jesse James and Margaret Shuler (Fisher) Lybarger; grandson of Elijah Crum and Julydia Workman (Winterringer) Lybarger; great-grandson of James Thompson and Amelia Eagle (Crum) Lybarger; great²-grandson of Andrew and Naomi (Thompson) Lybarger; great³-grandson of *Ludwick Lybarger*, private, Bedford County, Pennsylvania Militia; great²-grandson of Lewis Crum; great³-grandson of *John Crum*, private, Eleventh and Seventh Regts., Virginia Troops.

EDWARD CANFIELD LYON, Caldwell, N. J. (36381). Son of Edward Thomas and Mary Waynman (Canfield) Lyon; grandson of Thomas and Abigail Parmelia (Mead) Lyon; great-grandson of *Caleb Lyon, Jr.*, private, Westchester County, New York Militia; great²-grandson of *Caleb Lyon*, private, Fourth Regt., Westchester County, New York Militia; grandson of Abraham C. and Sarah C. (Waynman) Canfield; great-grandson of Jacob and Eunice (Munson) Canfield; great²-grandson of *Abraham Canfield*, Express Rider, New Jersey Light Horse; great²-grandson of *Moses Munson*, Captain, Morris County, New Jersey Militia, Captain and Foragemaster Team Brigade.

OLIVER CRANE LYON, Montclair, N. J. (36285). Son of Edward Canfield and Caroline H. (Crane) Lyon; grandson of Edward T. and Mary Waynman (Canfield) Lyon; great-grandson of Thomas and Abigail Parmelia (Mead) Lyon; great²-grandson of *Caleb Lyon, Jr.*, private, Fourth Regt., Westchester County, New York Militia; grandson of Oliver and Marion Dunn (Turnbull) Crane; great-grandson of Stephen Fordham and Matilda Howell (Smith) Crane; great²-grandson of *Peter Smith*, Lieutenant, Third and Fifth Regts., Pennsylvania Troops and Private Secretary to General Washington.

LOUIS BLALOCK McCARTHY, West Roxbury, Mass. (36803). Son of Louis and Theodosia (Blalock) McCarthy; grandson of Samuel W. and Nancy S. (Young) Blalock; great-grandson of Tilman and Sarah Ainsworth (Wilson) Blalock; great²-grandson of *John Blalock*, Lieutenant, Col. Downman's Regt., and Captain of Guards, North Carolina Militia, pensioned.

DAVID McCONAUGHY, Montclair, N. J. (36382). Son of David and Leana (Mathews) McConaughy; grandson of James Burroughs and Catherine (Griffith) Mathews; great-grandson of *Samuel Griffith*, Captain, Maryland Cont'l Troops.

FRANK KELLY McCUTCHEN, Dalton, Ga. (35225). Son of Cicero Decatur and Frances Cornelia (Kelly) McCutchen; grandson of Thomas Davis and Phœbe Caroline (Bryan) Kelly; great-grandson of Andrew and Delphie Garnett (Jones) Bryan; great²-grandson of *Andrew Bryan*, private, Chester County, Pennsylvania Militia.

COREY FULLER McFARLAND, Keokuk, Iowa. (36239). Son of Jacob Corey and Mary (Woodcock) McFarland; grandson of David and Polly (Stevens) MacFarlin; great-grandson of Elijah and Sarah (Marshall) MacFarlin, Jr.; great²-grandson of *Elijah MacFarling*, private, Plympton County, Massachusetts Troops, died in service.

CLEMENT L. McKEE, Washington, Pa. (36323). Son of Finley and Eliza Ann (Harper) McKee; grandson of Henry and Susanna (Hornbeck) McKee; great-grandson of *John McKee*, private, Fayette County, Pennsylvania Militia, pensioned; grandson of Daniel and Margery (Huston) Harper; great-grandson of William and Mary (Morrison) Huston; great²-grandson of *Joseph Huston*, private, Capt. George Vance's Co., Pennsylvania Rangers and Frontiersmen.

NEWTON FELCH McKEON, Paterson, N. J. (36393). Son of Marcus James and Parthenea Dow (Felch) McKeon; grandson of Isaac Newton and Margaret Holmes (Dow) Felch; great-grandson of Nathan and Rebecca (Shepard) Felch, Jr.; great²-grandson of *Nathan Felch*, private, Middlesex County, Massachusetts Militia, pensioned.

JOHN HOWARD McLAUGHLIN, Westfield, N. J. (36292). Son of Alexander and Amanda (Spayde) McLaughlin; grandson of Archibald and Rebecca (Wells) McLaughlin; great-grandson of Samuel and Hannah (Barnes) Wells; great²-grandson of *Samuel Wells*, private, Col. Charles Armand's Regt., Virginia Cont'l Line.

WILLIAM HENRY McMASTER, Alliance, Ohio. (36484). Son of James Nelson and Susan Elizabeth (Neff) McMaster; grandson of Samuel and Sarah Ann (Gregory) McMaster; great-grandson of Robert and Sarah (Meek) McMaster; great²-grandson of *William McMaster*, private, Westmoreland County, Pennsylvania "Associators."

HENRY W. McMILLAN, West Burlington, Iowa. (36241). Son of Charles and Mary E. (Woodworth) McMillan; grandson of Samuel and Mary (Sample) Woodworth; great-grandson of John and Ann (Taylor) Sample; great²-grandson of Henry and Mary (Blackburn) Taylor; great²-grandson of *Robert Taylor*, private, Fifth Regt., Virginia Militia.

STEPHEN YERKES McNAIR, Brooklyn, N. Y. (36452). Son of Stephen Yerkes and Mattie E. (Knowles) McNair; grandson of John and Mary (Yerkes) McNair; great-grandson of Stephen and Alice (Watson) Yerkes; great²-grandson of *Harman Yerkes*, private, Bucks County, Pennsylvania Militia.

EARL CLEVELAND MAIN, Sioux Falls, So. Dak. (30666). Son of Gilbert S. and Alice Maria (Brainerd) Main; grandson of Alfred Kellogg and Hannah Merritt (Small) Brainerd; great-grandson of Halsey and Rachelua (Kellogg) Brainerd; great²-grandson of Joshua and Hannah (Fuller) Brainerd; great³-grandson of *Abner Brainerd*, Lieutenant, Capt. Holmes' Co., Connecticut State Troops and Cont'l Line.

BENJAMIN BROWN MANCHESTER, Providence, R. I. (36505). Son of Silas Henry and Ellen Frances (Munroe) Manchester; grandson of Jonas and Julia Ann (Smith) Munroe; great-grandson of Abraham and Sarah (Knight) Munroe; great²-grandson of *Nathaniel Munroe*, private, Massachusetts Militia at Lexington Alarm.

HENRY FRANCIS MANCHESTER, Providence, R. I. (36504). Same as Benjamin Brown Manchester (R. I., 36505).

HENRY IRELAND MARBLE, Ridgewood, N. J. (36360). Son of W. Irving and Caroline B. (Ireland) Marble; grandson of James Frederick and Eliza (Monell) Marble; great-grandson of James and Charlotte (Smith) Monell, Jr.; great²-grandson of *James Mounell*, Lieutenant, Ulster County, New York Militia.

WASHINGTON IRVING MARBLE, Ridgewood, N. J. (36359). Son of James Frederick and Eliza (Monell) Marble; grandson of James and Charlotte (Smith) Monell, Jr.; great-grandson of *James Mounell*, Lieutenant, Ulster County, New York Militia.

WILLIAM GUY MARKHAM, Rush, N. Y. (36470). Son of Guy and Eliza Emma (Williams) Markham; grandson of *William Markham*, private and Sergeant, Col. Nichols' Regt., New Hampshire Militia.

LE ROY HARRISON MARKLEY, Middletown, Pa. (36754). Son of Abram Ackerman and Rebecca Sparks (Kennard) Markley; grandson of William Grover and Hannah Matilda (Simmons) Kennard; great-grandson of William and Rachel Ann (Giffing) Kennard; great²-grandson of *John Kennard, Jr.*, private, Thirteenth Battalion, Kent County, Maryland Militia.

WILLIAM F. MARSH, Pelham, N. H. (36252). Son of Enoch M. and Mary E. (Hobbs) Marsh; grandson of Moody and Elizabeth P. (Spofford) Hobbs; great-grandson of Dudley and Mary (Atwood) Spofford; great²-grandson of *Thomas Spofford*, Ensign and Sergeant, New Hampshire Militia.

JOHN W. MARSHALL, Richmond, Va. (35098). Son of Eleazer and Rebecca (Wilson) Marshall; grandson of *Isaac Marshall*, private, Fourteenth and Tenth Regts., Virginia Troops, prisoner, pensioned.

GEORGE D. MARTIN, Merchantville, N. J. (36394). Son of Julius C. and Mary (D——) Martin; grandson of Samuel and Mary (Willett) Martin; great-grandson of *Samuel Willett*, private, New Jersey Militia.

WILLIAM BLOOMFIELD PEPPER MARTS, Montclair, N. J. (36398). Son of Warren and Lillian (Pepper) Marts; grandson of William Bloomfield and Emeline Louretta (Stithams) Pepper; great-grandson of Daniel and Elizabeth (Tubman) Stithams; great²-grandson of Nehemiah and Ann (Peirce) Tubman; great³-grandson of *Abel Peirce*, drummer and private, Col. Rufus Putnam's Regt., Massachusetts Militia.

JAMES PLEASANTS MASSIE, Richmond, Va. (36551). Son of Eugene Carter and Laura Roy (Ellerson) Massie; grandson of Henry and Susan Elizabeth (Smith) Massie, Jr.; great-grandson of Henry and Susan Preston (Lewis) Massie; great²-grandson of *Thomas Massie*, Major, Eleventh and Second Regts., Virginia Cont'l Line; great-grandson of Thomas Bolton and Caroline S. R. (Thomson) Smith; great²-grandson of William Russell and Elizabeth (Sabb) Thomson; great³-grandson of *William Thomson*, Colonel and Brevet Brig.-General, South Carolina Rangers and member First Provincial Congress, prisoner.

HENRY JEFFREY MATCHETT, Fort Leavenworth, Kans. (33321). Son of Abraham J. and Amelia (Warwick) Matchett; grandson of Frederick and Eliza (Helm) Warwick; great-grandson of George M. and Catherine (Wolfe) Helm; great²-grandson of Woodhull and Eliza (McDonald) Helm; great³-grandson of Thomas Helm; great⁴-grandson of William and Dorothy (Woodhull) Helm; great⁵-grandson of *Nathaniel Woodhull*, Brigadier-General, New York Militia, President Provincial Congress, died of wounds.

GEORGE NICHOLAS MECHAM, Nebr. (33890). Supplementals. Son of Harrison Alexander and Ruth Alice (Coyle) Mecham; grandson of John Wesley and Ruth Prudence (Vallier) Mecham; great-grandson of Joseph and Hannah Ladd (Tyler) Mecham; great²-grandson of Joseph and Sarah (Bradford) Mecham; great³-grandson of Samuel and Phœbe (Main) Mecham (Meacham); great⁴-grandson of *Samuel Meacham*, Selectman, Enfield, New Hampshire, in charge of Association Test; great²-grandson of Joseph and Mehitable Esther (Ladd) Tyler; great³-grandson of *Ebenezer Tyler*, private, Col. Chase's Regt., New Hampshire Militia.

ROBERT THORNHILL MESSLER, Westfield, N. J. (36296). Son of David Nevins and Lounetta (Opdycke) Messler; grandson of William S. and Margaret M. (Van Zandt) Messler; great-grandson of Peter and Esther (Smith) Messler; great²-grandson of *Cornelius Messler*, private, Hunterdon and Middlesex Counties, New Jersey Militia.

BENJAMIN CLEMENT MINER, Summit, N. J. (36397). Son of Champlin Clement and Anna E. (Sturdevant) Miner; grandson of Clement and Sally (Crane) Miner; great-grandson of *Benjamin Miner*, Captain, Morris County, New Jersey Militia, pensioned.

CLAXTON MONRO, Burlington, Vt. (33847). Son of Hezekiah Usher and Harriet M. (Barnes) Monro; grandson of George Thomas and Emily A. (Berry) Monro; great-grandson of Thomas B. and Clarissa (Sanford) Monro; great²-grandson of Thomas and Sybil (Borden) Monro; great³-grandson of *Thomas Monro*, Surgeon, prisoner on Prison Ship "Jersey."

THOMAS HUNTINGTON MONROE, Atlanta, Ga. (35223). Son of Alonzo Judson and Lucretia Anna (Huntington) Monroe; grandson of Charles Andrew and Lucretia Atwood (Waterman) Huntington; great-grandson of Thomas and Eleanor (Dodge) Waterman; great^2-grandson of *Arannah Waterman*, Connecticut Minute-Man and Assistant Commissary; grandson of Alonzo Welton and Anna Maria (Albee) Monroe; great-grandson of Joseph Porter and Caltha (Putnam) Albee; great^2-grandson of Dan. Baldwin and Maria Louise (Ensign) Putnam; great^2-grandson of *Israel Putnam*, Major-General Cont'l Army.

JOSEPH MONTGOMERY, 2nd., Harrisburg, Pa. (36755). Son of James B. and Emma Lynn (Buchecker) Montgomery; grandson of James and Sarah Ann (Peipher) Montgomery, Jr.; great-grandson of James and Susan (Fedder) Montgomery; great^2-grandson of *Robert Montgomery*, clerk Fourth Battalion, Lancaster County, Pennsylvania Militia.

BENJAMIN LUCIAN MOORE, Springfield, Tenn. (36071). Son of Jerome Egbert and Rebecca (Litzy) Moore; grandson of Risdon Dent and Mary Arseneth (Mitchell) Moore; great-grandson of *Smith Moore*, Second Lieutenant, Fifth Regt., Maryland Troops.

GEORGE GIDEON MORRIS, Washington, D. C. (36129). Son of James B. and Kezia (Way) Morris; grandson of Levi and Lucretia (Stevens) Morris; great-grandson of *George Morris*, private, Third Regt., Pennsylvania Cont'l Line, pensioned.

CLARENCE RAYMOND NEIDENGARD, Steubenville, Ohio. (36490). Son of Henry and Julia Emilie (Odell) Neidengard; grandson of John Valentine and Jane (Fisher) Odell; great-grandson of *John Fisher*, private, Second Regt., Virginia Militia.

WILLIAM WASHINGTON NEIFERT, Conn. (27344). Supplementals. Son of William and Lucinda (Luidner) Neifert; grandson of Jacob and Elizabeth (Faust) Neifert; great-grandson of John and Mary Rosina (Huntzinger) Faust; great^2-grandson of *Johannes Faust*, private, Berk's County, Pennsylvania Militia; great^2-grandson of *John G. Huntzinger*, private, Northampton County, Pennsylvania Militia.

SAMUEL BROOKS NEWMAN, East Orange, N. J. (36370). Son of Samuel Brooks and Mattie O. (Lonsdale) Newman; grandson of Samuel Brooks and Jane (Miller) Newman; great-grandson of Joseph and Dolly (Brooks) Newman; great^2-grandson of *Thomas Newman*, Sergeant, Essex County, Massachusetts Militia.

JASON HOWARD NEWTON, Springfield, Mass. (36112). Son of Frank H. and Emma Reed (Morton) Newton; grandson of George W. and Ellen Butler (Boynton) Morton; great-grandson of John Alden and Sophronia (Thayer) Morton; great^2-grandson of *Enoch Thayer*, private, Hampshire County, Massachusetts Militia.

NORMAN THOMAS NEWTON, Wyoming, N. Y. (D. C. 36130). Son of John P. and Jessie (King) Newton; grandson of George Oscar and Amanda Elvira (Vance) King; great-grandson of Hollis and Sally (Babcock) King; great^2-grandson of Levi and Lydia (Sartwell) King; great^3-grandson of *Adonijah King*, private, Col. Josiah Whitney's Regt., Massachusetts Militia; great^4-grandson of *William King*, private, Third Regt., New Hampshire Cont'l Troops; great-grandson of John Henderon and Mary Ann (Carnes) Vance; great^2-grandson of Robert and Margaret (Moore) Vance; great^3-grandson of *Robert Vance*, Captain, Col. John Gibson's Ninth Regt., Virginia Militia.

RALPH WALDO NICKERSON, Hillside, N. J. (36399). Son of George F. and Mary Maria (Springer) Nickerson; grandson of Thomas and Mary Ann (Manchester) Springer; great-grandson of *Knight Springer*, private, Rhode Island Militia and Cont'l Troops, pensioned.

LIONEL GRENELLE NIGHTINGALE, Brooklyn, N. Y. (36467). Son of Lionel Bridges and Julia Stuart (Grenelle) Nightingale; grandson of William Henry and Julia Porter (Huntington) Grenelle; great-grandson of Joseph Carew and Julia Stewart (Dodge) Huntington; great^2-grandson of Joseph and Eunice (Carew) Huntington; great^3-grandson of Andrew and Lucy (Coit) Huntington; great^4-grandson of *Jabez Huntington*, Major-General, Connecticut Militia.

WILLIAM NORRIS OCHILTREE, Cleveland, Ohio. (36426). Son of William E. and Estelle May (Norris) Ochiltree; grandson of John Jasper and Elizabeth C. (Ellis) Norris; great-grandson of Aquilla and Sarah (Sargent) Norris, Jr.; great^2-grandson of *Aquilla Norris*, Captain, Harford County, Maryland Militia.

MYLES POWERS O'CONNOR, Nashville, Tenn. (36068). Son of Jerome St. John and Henrietta (Blackman) O'Connor; grandson of Albert Washington and Elizabeth Hardway (Andrews) Blackman; great-grandson of Bennett and Anna (Clinton) Blackman; great²-grandson of *Richard Clinton*, private, South Carolina Militia, pensioned.

PAUL Q. OLIVER, Westfield, N. J. (36688). Son of William Henry and Katharine Minturn (Baker) Oliver; grandson of Nehemiah and Jane Dearman (Minturn) Baker; great-grandson of *Allen Baker*, Essex County, Massachusetts, Minute-Man at Lexington Alarm.

HAROLD DEMENT PADGETT, San Francisco, Calif. (36412). Son of Benjamin H. and Eliza Belle (Dement) Padgett; grandson of William Edward and Eliza E. (Wolfe) Dement; great-grandson of John Edward and Rebecca Dent (Briscoe) Dement; great²-grandson of Edward and Sarah Marshall (Wilkinson) Briscoe; great³-grandson of William Mackall and Asa Herbert (Dent) Wilkinson; great⁴-grandson of *John Dent*, Brigadier-General, Maryland Militia.

THOMAS ALEXIS PAINTER, Upper Montclair, N. J. (36293). Son of Thomas Alexis and Adelaide Elizabeth (Lockwood) Painter; grandson of Alexis and Thalia Maria (McMahon) Painter; great-grandson of *Thomas Painter*, private, Connecticut State Troops, prisoner.

PAUL BARBOUR PARKER, Kokomo, Ind. (35520). Son of Edmund L. and Elizabeth (Barbour) Parker; grandson of Edmund A. and Laura (Hubbard) Parker; great-grandson of Lemuel and Eliza (Hosley) Parker, 3rd.; great²-grandson of *Lemuel Parker, Jr.*, musician and drum-major, Massachusetts Militia.

HENRY HERBERT PARMELEE, Paterson, N. J. (36371). Son of William Smith and Mary Elizabeth (Butterworth) Parmelee; grandson of John Edwin and Catherine (Smith) Parmelee; great-grandson of Linus and Priscilla (Handy) Parmelee; great²-grandson of *Samuel Parmelee*, private, Thirteenth Regt., Connecticut Militia.

OWEN C. PEARCE, Manasquan, N. J. (36363). Son of Benjamin B. and Annie (Curtis) Pearce; grandson of Robert and Rebecca (Newbury) Pearce; great-grandson of Benjamin and Elizabeth (Newbury) Pearce; great²-grandson of *William Pearce*, private, New Jersey Cont'l Line and Monmouth County Militia.

JOHN CALDER PEARSON, Ohio. (34140). Supplementals. Son of John Keeling and Mary Frances (Perkins) Pearson; grandson of Orren and Sarah M. (Clinton) Perkins; great-grandson of Joel and Mary (Matthewson) Clinton; great²-grandson of John and Mary (Scribner) Clinton, Jr.; great³-grandson of *Zacheus Scribner*, private, Connecticut Militia and Cont'l Line; great-grandson of William and Parthenia (Miller) Perkins; great²-grandson of *Samuel Miller*, Corporal, Col. Thomas Carpenter's Regt., Massachusetts Militia; great³-grandson of *John Clinton, Sr.*, New York patriot and signer Petition to Committee of Safety; great²-grandson of *William Matthewson*, private, Massachusetts and Rhode Island Militia, pensioned; great²-grandson of *David Perkins*, private, Plymouth County, Massachusetts Militia; grandson of John and Rebecca (Lewis) Pearson; great²-grandson of *John Lewis*, Sergeant, Third Regt., Tryon County, New York Militia, prisoner; great³-grandson of *Peter Lewis*, Tryon County, New York, patriot, who had all property destroyed; great²-grandson of John and Sarah (Putnam) Lewis; great²-grandson of *Teunis Putman*, private, Second Regt., Albany County, New York Militia.

EDWARD HARRISON PENCE, Chicago, Ill. (36221). Son of Winfield Scott and Lillian Woods (Grafton) Pence; grandson of Ambrose and Rebecca Ellen (Woods) Grafton; great-grandson of Joseph Hamilton and Sarah (Hevering) Woods; great²-grandson of Andrew and Mary (Stephenson) Woods; great³-grandson of *Joseph Woods*, delegate, Pennsylvania Provincial Congress.

VALENTINE R. PENNEY, Los Angeles, Calif. (36403). Son of Rufus and Elosia (Parker) Penney; grandson of Valentine and Polly (——) Parker; great-grandson of *Nathaniel Parker*, private, Col. Gideon Warren's Regt., Vermont Militia.

CHARLES EDWARD PERKINS, New Orleans, La. (35993). Son of Edward Henry and Hannah (Boyce) Perkins; grandson of Henry W. and Harriet C. (Smith) Perkins; great-grandson of Willis and Laura (Dickerman) Perkins; great²-grandson of David and Lola (Todd) Perkins; great³-grandson of *Reuben Perkins*, private, Derby, Connecticut Militia.

ROBERT MERRITT PERKINS, Newark, N. J. (36372). Son of Merritt Greenwood and Matilda Drake (Riker) Perkins; grandson of John and Lucia Willis (Greenwood) Perkins; great-grandson of Asa and Huldah (Hayward) Perkins; great²-grandson of Timothy and Huldah (Ames) Hayward; great²-grandson of Sylvanus and Huldah (Johnson) Ames; great⁴-grandson of *Isaac Johnson*, Major, Plymouth County, Massachusetts Militia.

ARTHUR PERRIN, Brookline, Mass. (36804). Son of Franklin and Louisa Charlotte (Gage) Perrin; grandson of Augustus and Harriet (Child) Perrin; great-grandson of *Abraham Perrin*, private, Connecticut Light Horse.

HARRY AMBROSE PERRIN, Jacksonville, Ill. (36211). Son of Daniel A. and Achsah Rebecca (Perrine) Perrin; grandson of James William and Deborah Ann (Dey) Perrine; great-grandson of William I. and Catherine (Davis) Perrine; great²-grandson of *James Perrine*, private, Monmouth County, New Jersey Militia.

OSCAR HOYT PERRY, Portland, Me. (36583). Son of Albert and Jane Salmon (Hart) Perry; grandson of William and Keziah (Drury) Perry; great-grandson of Abel and Asenah (Haven) Perry, Jr.; great²-grandson of *Abel Perry*, Lieutenant, General Ward's Regt., Massachusetts Militia.

ALBERT HOVEY PEYTON, Georgia. (35222). Supplementals. Son of Thomas West and Mary Thornburg (Hovey) Peyton; grandson of William Marshall and Ellen Eliza (Thornburg) Hovey; great-grandson of Thomas and Margaret Catherine (Miller) Thornburg; great²-grandson of John and Sophia (Clendennin) Miller; great³-grandson of *Christian Miller*, Sergeant, Shenandoah Co., Virginia Militia, pensioned; great³-grandson of *William Clendennin*, Captain, Virginia Militia.

JOHN NEWTON PHARR, Olivier, La. (35989). Son of Henry Newton and Anna Jane (Smith) Pharr; grandson of John Newton and Henrietta Clara (Andrus) Pharr; great-grandson of Elias and Martha Caroline (Orr) Pharr; great²-grandson of Henry and Margaret (Bain) Pharr; great³-grandson of *Walter Pharr*, private, General Horatio Gates' Regt., Cont'l Troops, wounded.

LEWIS EUGENE PIERSON, Brooklyn, N. Y. (36451). Son of Edgar L. and Anna B. (Southard) Pierson; grandson of James Washington and Sarah Ann (Peshine) Southard; great-grandson of Gilbert and Anna (Wey) Southard; great²-grandson of *Thomas Southard*, private, Dutchess County, New York Militia; great-grandson of Jacob and Prussia Alling (Ball) Peshine; great²-grandson of *Edward Ball*, private, Essex County, New Jersey Militia and Sergeant, Col. Sheldon's Cont'l Troops.

WILLIAM BARTLEY PIRTLE, Louisville, Ky. (36526). Son of James Speed and Emily Mathusa (Bartley) Pirtle; grandson of William Thompson and Emily Mathusa (Johnson) Bartley; great-grandson of Henry and Elizabeth Julia (Flournoy) Johnson; great²-grandson of *Robert Johnson*, Captain under George Rogers Clark, and member Virginia Legislature of '82.

WINTHROP PIZZINI, Lieut., A. E. F., New York City, N. Y. (36453). Son of William B. and Florence A. (Webber) Pizzini; grandson of Andrew and Anna Gertrude (Davis) Pizzini, Jr.; great-grandson of Benjamin and Burronsinia (Solis) Davis; great²-grandson of Daniel and Sarah Helm (Norris) Solis; great³-grandson of Eden and Anna (Hiers) Norris; great⁴-grandson of Henrick and Sarah (Whitlock) Hiers; great⁵-grandson of *John Whitlock*, Lieutenant, Monmouth County, New Jersey Militia, killed.

WILLIAM NORRIS PLUMMER, San Jose, Calif. (36404). Son of Thomas and Sally Jane (Norris) Plummer; grandson of John Boyd and Elizabeth (Craig) Plummer; great-grandson of *Samuel Craig, Jr.*, Lieutenant, Captain Orr's Co., Pennsylvania Troops, pensioned; great²-grandson of *Samuel Craig*, Captain, First Regt., Pennsylvania Troops.

EDWARD FOUNTAIN PORTER, Keokuk, Iowa. (36236). Son of Edward S. and Mary Frances (Moody) Carter; grandson of Benjamin Franklin and Anna Maria (Porter) Moody; great-grandson of Julius Risley and Elizabeth K. (Berry) Porter; great²-grandson of *Ezekiel Porter*, private, Massachusetts Militia.

HOMER BAIR POSTLETHWAITE, St. Paul, Minn. (35684). Son of William Perry and Elizabeth Catherine (Means) Postlethwaite; grandson of David and Jane Minor (Bell) Postlethwaite; great-grandson of John and Sarah (Ross) Postlethwaite, Jr.; great²-grandson of *John Postlethwaite (Postlewait)*, private, Lancaster County, Pennsylvania Militia.

IRA WARREN POSTLETHWAITE, Keokuk, Iowa. (36229). Son of William Perry and Elizabeth Catherine (Means) Postlethwaite; grandson of David and Jane Minor (Bell) Postlethwaite; great-grandson of John and Sarah (Ross) Postlethwaite, Jr.; great²-grandson of *John Postlethwaite*, private, Fourth Battalion, Lancaster County, Pennsylvania Militia.

PAUL ADAMS POTTER, Ames, Iowa. (36240). Son of Ezra Cornelius and Minnie (Adams) Potter; grandson of Cornelius Seabury and Desdemonia (Barden) Potter; great-grandson of Cornelius and Hannah (Barber) Potter; great²-grandson of Eseck and Sarah (Stoddard) Potter; great²-grandson of *Eseck Potter*, private, Col. Pope's Regt., Massachusetts Militia, died in service.

WILLIAM GLENN PRATHER, Pensacola, Fla. (29920). Son of William Vaughan and Elizabeth Jane (Ewing) Prather; grandson of William and Sarah Jane (Glenn) Ewing; great-grandson of Moses Ferguson and Elizabeth (Cowan) Glenn; great²-grandson of *Archibald Glenn*, private, Bedford County, Cont'l Troops.

WILLIAM PALMER PYLE, Keokuk, Iowa. (36234). Son of N. H. and Grace E. (Brown) Pyle; grandson of James Samuel and Emma Rose (Bowlus) Brown; great-grandson of Abraham and Lucretia (Grey) Brown; great²-grandson of Levi and Tryphemia (Baker) Grey; great³-grandson of *Samuel Baker*, private, Col. Marinus Willett's Regt., New York Levies.

CHARLES STRONG QUINN, Rochester, N. Y. (36455). Son of Arthur Hughes and Henrietta Louise (Strong) Quinn; grandson of David and Zilpha (Cady) Strong; great-grandson of *Josiah Strong*, private, Connecticut Cont'l Line, wounded, pensioned.

FRANK PERRY RAILSBACK, McComb City, Miss. (La. 35991). Son of William P. and Viola (Staples) Railsback; grandson of David and Mary (Smith) Railsback; great-grandson of David and Sarah (Stevens) Railsback; great²-grandson of *David Railsback*, private, North Carolina Militia.

EDWARD STEVENS RANKIN, Jr., Newark, N. J. (36365). Son of Edward Stevens and Julie S. J. (Russell) Rankin; grandson of William and Ellen Hope (Stevens) Rankin; great-grandson of Ashbel and Mary (Mead) Stevens; great²-grandson of *Elisha Stevens*, private, Col. Wolcott's and Col. Baldwin's Regts., Connecticut Troops, five years' service.

ROBERT PATTISON RAYMOND, Middletown, Pa. (36756). Son of Seymour and Anna Ford (Kennard) Raymond; grandson of William and Rachel Ann (Giffing) Kennard; great-grandson of *John Kennard, Jr.*, private, Thirteenth Battalion, Kent County, Maryland Militia.

CHARLES F. READ, Portland, Ore. (35068). Son of Gilbert E. and Mary Ann (——) Read; grandson of Rufus and Rhoda (K——) Read; great-grandson of Peter and Lydia (Gilbert) Read; great²-grandson of *John Gilbert*, Captain, Connecticut Militia, killed at defense of New Haven.

HARRY JAMES REDFIELD, Washington, D. C. (36135). Son of William Douglas and Catherine (Carley) Redfield; grandson of Darius Oliver Griswold and Sarah Amanda (Boughton) Redfield; great-grandson of John A. and Abigail (Bulkley) Redfield; great²-grandson of *James Redfield*, private, Connecticut Militia.

WARREN GARDNER REED, Morgan City, La. (36000). Son of Warren Bettison and Grace (Gardner) Reed; grandson of Lyman (Coleman) and Kate ((Bettison) Reed; great-grandson of Warren Atherton and Louisa (Lyman) Reed; great²-grandson of Warren and Mary (Atherton) Reed; great³-grandson of *Benjamin Reed*, Corporal, Col. Sproal's Regt., Massachusetts Militia, pensioned.

SAMUEL WALLACE REYBURN, New York, N. Y. (36466). Son of Joseph Woods and Arkansas Elvira (Lawson) Reyburn; grandson of Samuel Wallace and Eliza Ann (Woodward) Reyburn; great-grandson of Samuel Wallace and Catherine (Bryan) Reyburn; great²-grandson of *George Raiborne (Reyburn)*, fifer, Col. John Neville's Regt., Virginia Troops, prisoner.

CHARLES RHINEHART, Dallas Center, Iowa. (36244). Son of George L. and Orilla Adaline (Albin) Rhinehart; grandson of Andrew and Margaret (Oldshoe) Rhinehart; great-grandson of Andrew and Christiana (Shuey) Rhinehart; great²-grandson of *John Ludwig Shuey*, private, Second Battalion, Lancaster County, Pennsylvania Militia;

great²-grandson of *Ludwig Henrich Shuey*, chairman, Lancaster County, Pennsylvania Committee of Safety; grandson of William W. and Mary (Burns) Albin; great-grandson of John and Catharine (Moreland) Albin; great²-grandson of *John Moreland*, private, Chester County, Pennsylvania Militia; great²-grandson of *William Albin*, private, Westmoreland County, Pennsylvania Militia; great-grandson of Thomas and Martha (Sears) Burns; great²-grandson of *John Burns*, private, Washington County, Pennsylvania Militia.

HALSON WHITTIER RICHARDS, HOULTON, Me. (36584). Son of George W. and Jennie F. (Pattee) Richards; grandson of David and Frances Parker (Richards) Pattee; great-grandson of Eliphalet and Sally (McQuesten) Richards; great²-grandson of *Eliphalet Richards*, private, New Hampshire Militia.

JOHN KEMP GOODLOE RIDGELY, New Orleans (La. 35995). Son of Frederick W. and Harriet Lucretia (Isette) Ridgely; grandson of William S. and Sarah (Graham) Ridgely; great-grandson of *Frederick Ridgely*, Surgeon, Fourth Regt., Maryland Troops.

EDWIN CLIFFORD ROBINSON, Marshall, Minn. (35691). Son of William Charles and Ella W. (Clark) Robinson; grandson of George McCook and Rhozina E. (Grow) Robinson; great-grandson of Jonah and Sarah (Morrison) Robinson; great²-grandson of *Jonah Robinson*, private, Lancaster County, Pennsylvania Associators.

SAMUEL SCOTT ROBINSON, St. Louis, Mo. (35559). Son of Samuel Scott and Isabel (McLanahan) Robinson; grandson of Robert and Nancy (Moorhead) McLanahan; great-grandson of Joseph and Jane (McElhoes) Moorhead; great²-grandson of *Fergus Moorhead*, private, Westmoreland County, Pennsylvania Militia.

WALTER ALFRED ROBINSON, Columbus, Ohio. (36492). Son of George F. and Lavina Day (Bramble) Robinson; grandson of Ayres L. and Deborah (Stites) Bramble; great-grandson of Benjamin Stites, Jr.; great²-grandson of *Benjamin Stites*, Captain, Washington County, Pennsylvania Militia.

WALTER RALPH ROCKHOLD, Glen Ridge, N. J. (36367). Son of Leonidas C. and Phebe Ann (Potter) Rockhold; grandson of Amos and Phebe (Denman) Potter; great-grandson of *Jacob Potter*, private and Wagon-Master, Essex County, New Jersey Militia, pensioned.

WALTER KING ROSS, Washington, D. C. (36136). Son of George F. and Lucy A. (King) Ross; grandson of John A. and Jeannette Eliza (Witherow) Ross; great-grandson of Samuel and Elizabeth (Macklin) Witherow; great²-grandson of *James Macklin*, private, Fourth Battalion, Cumberland County, Pennsylvania Militia.

EDGAR LEOPOLD ROSSELOT, Evansville, Ind. (35519). Son of William Jasper and Emily E. (Rider) Rosselot; grandson of Edgar Monroe and Isabelle (Orr) (Seely) Rider; great-grandson of Adam Curry and Elizabeth A. (McCullough) Rider; great²-grandson of John and Barbara (Akins) McCullough; great²-grandson of *James McCullough*, Second Lieutenant and Quartermaster, Fifth Regt., Pennsylvania Cont'l Line.

JAMES WEBB SAFFOLD, Cleveland, Ohio. (35899). Son of Starke Selbert and Harriet (W——) Saffold; grandson of Milton Jefferson and Martha (Harrison) Saffold; great-grandson of Reuben and Mary (Phillips) Saffold, Jr.; great²-grandson of *Reuben Saffold*, Captain, Col. Elijah Clark's Regt., Georgia Militia.

CHESTER RAY SAMMIS, Huntington, N. Y. (36460). Son of Theodore and Florine (Fernald) Sammis; grandson of Edgar and Jane Place (Titus) Sammis; great-grandson of Jacob and Esther (Douglas) Titus; great²-grandson of William and Susan (Conklin) Douglas; great³-grandson of *Thomas Conklin*, private, First Suffolk County Regt., New York Militia.

FRANK RAYMOND SANDT, N. J. (36011). Supplemental. Son of Jacob and Annie (Frey) Sandt; grandson of Leonard and Anna (Correll) Sandt; great-grandson of John George and Susanna (Young) Correll; great²-grandson of *Philip Correll*, private, Bucks County, Pennsylvania Associators.

GEORGE ELLERY SANFORD, Humboldt, Nebr. (33897). Son of Edwin and Margueret (Cockrell) Sanford; grandson of Ellery and Mary (Brook) Sanford; great-grandson of John Usher and Charlot (Bourne) Sanford; great²-ggrandson of Shearjeshub and Rachel (Kent) Bourne, Jr.; great³-grandson of *Shearjeshub Bourne*, member Rhode Island Legislature that ratified the Declaration of Independence and first Chief Justice Supreme Court.

FRED W. SCOFIELD, Cannon Falls, Minn. (35685). Son of Wilbur H. and Lucy A. (Oakes) Scofield; grandson of Luther and Roxanna (Damon) Scofield; great-grandson of Amos Scofield; great²-grandson of *Silas Scofield*, private and Corporal, Westchester County, New York Militia.

HUGH DOGGETT SCOTT, Jr., Fredericksburg, Va. (35099). Son of Hugh Doggett and Jennie Lee (Lewis) Scott; grandson of Louis and Jane Elizabeth (Owen) Lewis; great-grandson of Arthur Benjamin and Mary Susan (Taylor) Owen; great²-grandson of John and Catherine (Montague) Owen; great³-grandson of *William Montague*, private, Middlesex County, Virginia Militia.

EDWARD JAY SEEBER, Rochester, N. Y. (36200). Son of Jacob and Lavina (Coppernoll) Seeber; grandson of Abram and Nancy (Young) Seeber; great-grandson of Adolph and Sally (Yates) Seeber; great²-grandson of William and Elizabeth (Schneer) Seeber; great³-grandson of *William Seeber*, Lieutenant-Colonel, Tryon County, New York Militia, killed.

JAMES PRIMROSE SEELY, Upper Montclair, N. J. (36395). Son of Uriah and Nancy (Hopping) Seely; grandson of James and Amanda (Mason) Seely; great-grandson of *John Seely*, private, New Jersey Militia, State Troops and Cont'l Line.

WILLIAM HOPPING SEELY, Newark, N. J. (36396). Same as James Primrose Seely, N. J. (36395).

EDGAR CALVIN SEIBERT, Orange, N. J. (36384). Son of George C. and Alice Seachrist (Orth) Seibert; grandson of Adam Godlove and Frances (Seachrist) Orth; great-grandson of Godlove and Sarah (Steiner) Orth; great²-grandson of *Balser Orth*, Major, Second Battalion, Lancaster County, Pennsylvania Militia.

LUCIUS VINTON SELLEEK, Pueblo, Colo. (36338). Son of Myron Phelps and Elizabeth Evelyn (——) Selleek; grandson of William Henry and Catherine (Phelps) Selleek; great-grandson of Thomas and Sabrina (Johnson) Selleek; great²-grandson of Deodate and Madeline (Poupoir) Selleek; great³-grandson of *John Selleek*, Vermont patriot at battle of Hubbardton.

EDWIN JAMES SERVEN, Lakeview, N. J. (36378). Son of Oliver and Mary Ann (O'Neill) Serven; grandson of Isaac and Nancy (Scudder) Serven; great-grandson of *Garret Serven*, private, Orange County, New Jersey Militia.

LEWIS ALBERT SEXTON, Hartford, Conn. (36710). Son of William Robert and Mary Eliza (——) Sexton; grandson of James G. and Delana (——) Sparkman; great-grandson of *William Sparkman*, private, North Carolina Cont'l Line.

JOHN BROOKE SHAUGHNESSY, Chicago, Ill. (36216). Son of Thomas Henry and Mary Elizabeth (Supplee) Shaughnessy; grandson of Hiram Rambo and Mary Julia (Brooke) Supplee; great-grandson of John Hunter and Matilda (Milton) Brooke; great²-grandson of David and Hannah (Jones) Brooke; great²-grandson of *Benjamin Brooke*, Captain, Sixth Battalion, Philadelphia Militia; great-grandson of William and Elizabeth (Jarrett) Supplee; great²-grandson of John and Catherine (Weber) Supplee; great³-grandson of *Isaac Supplee*, private, Pennsylvania Militia.

GEORGE LEWIS SHORTMAN, Ripley, N. Y. (36189). Son of William L. and Evelyn (Beatly) Shortman; grandson of John and Annie (Newton) Beatly; great-grandson of Timothy and Polly (Hillsgrove) Newton; great²-grandson of *John Hillsgrove*, private, Col. Sargent's and Col. Reed's Regts., New Hampshire Militia.

BOYD LINCOLN SLOANE, West Paterson, N. J. (36686). Son of Lemuel P. and Clare Lincoln (Fleetwood) Sloane; grandson of George and Sarah Ann (Gandy) Fleetwood; great-grandson of Ephriam and Sarah (Lee) Gandy; great²-grandson of *Thomas Gandy*, private, Cumberland County, New Jersey Militia.

FREDERICK KINSMAN SMITH, Warren, Ohio. (36483). Son of Edward A. and Laura E. (Furman) Smith; grandson of Weed and Laura M. (Lyon) Furman; great-grandson of James and Phila (Risley) Lyon; great²-grandson of *Matthew Lyon*, Colonel and Paymaster-General, Vermont Troops, member State Legislature of '79.

HARRY FOWLER SMITH, Portland, Me. (36585). Son of William Henry and Marcia Hodsdon (Smith) Smith; grandson of Gilbert and Betsey (Harnden) Smith; great-grandson of Jacob and Mary (Rotter) Smith; great²-grandson of *James Smith*, private, Third and Seventeenth Regts., Massachusetts Militia.

HENRY LOSSON SMITH, Dalton, Ga. (35224). Son of William F. C. and Euphiny Smith (McNair) Smith; grandson of Samuel and Mary (Miller) McNair; great-grandson of *Daniel McNair*, private, Col. James McNeil's Regt., Georgia Troops.

HUNTER IMBODEN SNYDER, Denver, Colo. (36337). Son of Henry Wilkerson and Jennie Crawford (Imboden) Snyder; grandson of John Daniel and Eliza Allen (McCue) Imboden; great-grandson of George and Isabella (Wunderlick) Imboden; great²-grandson of John Daniel and Susanna (Saunders) Wunderlick; great³-grandson of *Daniel Wunderlick*, private, Lancaster County, Pennsylvania Militia.

JOHN F. SOULE, Alameda, Calif. (36405). Son of Joseph T. and Frances Schuyler (Fensley) Soule; grandson of Thomas and Sally Currier (Follansbee) Soule; great-grandson of James and Keziah (Currier) Follansbee; great²-grandson of *Daniel Currier*, private, Col. Jacob Gerrish's Regt., Massachusetts Guards.

JOHN GLOVER SOUTH, Frankfort, Ky. (36527). Son of Samuel and Malvry Blackwell (Jett) South; grandson of Jerry Weldon and Mary (Cockrel) South; great-grandson of Samuel and Patsy (Glover) South; great²-grandson of *John South, Jr.*, Lieutenant, Lincoln County, Virginia Militia.

LOUIS CARVER SOUTHARD, Brookline, Mass. (36805). Son of William Lewis and Lydia Carver (Dennis) Southard; grandson of John Paul and Joanna (Carver) Dennis; great-grandson of Nathaniel and Joanna (Godfrey) Carver; great²-grandson of *George Godfrey*, Brigadier-General, Bristol County, Massachusetts Militia, chairman Com. of Correspondence and Safety, and County Treasurer.

HENRY GRANGER SPEED, Washington, D. C. (36137). Son of Joshua and Anna (Granger) Speed; grandson of Henry William and Laura E. (Thompson) Granger; great-grandson of Anston and Rhoda (Bostwick) Granger; great²-grandson of Elijah and Sarah (Buckley) Bostwick, Jr.; great²-grandson of *Elijah Bostwick*, Captain, Albany County, New York Militia.

ELON PERRY SPINK, Attica, N. Y. (36190). Son of David A. and Mary S. (Jones) Spink; grandson of Whitman and Cynthia (Weaver) Spink; great-grandson of *John Spink*, private, Rhode Island Militia, pensioned; great²-grandson of *Ishmael Spink*, private, Washington County, Rhode Island Militia; great-grandson of *Nicholas Weaver*, private, Vermont Militia; great-grandson of Nicholas and Nathan (Matteson) Weaver; great²-grandson of *Nathan Matteson*, private, Col. Kasson's Regt., Rhode Island Militia.

ALBERT CLINTON SPOONER, Brooklyn, N. Y. (36463). Son of Walter Clinton and Ida Frances (Hall) Spooner; grandson of Isaac and Sarah Sophia (Phelps) Hall; great-grandson of Asa Hosmer and Margery (McCoun) Phelps; great²-grandson of Eliphalet and Mehitable (Dodge) Phelps, Jr.; great³-grandson of *Eliphalet Phelps*, private, Eighteenth Regt., Connecticut Militia; great⁴-grandson of *Silas Phelps*, private, Col. Samuel B. Webb's Regt., Connecticut Cont'l Troops.

RITCHIE SHERVAN START, Watertown, Mass. (36114). Son of Philip S. and Elizabeth A. H. (Shervan) Start; grandson of Romeo Hoyt and Frances Juliette (Reynolds) Start; great-grandson of Moses Barnard and Laura (Griswold) Start; great²-grandson of Moses and Margaret (Gould) Start; great³-grandson of *Simeon Gould*, Sergeant-Major, New Hampshire Militia and Cont'l Troops.

GUY ELLSWORTH STAY, New York City, N. Y. (36191). Son of Willard Ellsworth and Sarah Margaret (Cole) Stay; grandson of Daniel Baher and Maria Slater (Brown) Cole; great-grandson of Benjamin and Sally (Wright) Cole; great²-grandson of Ebenezer and Pricilla (Salisbury) Cole; great³-grandson of *Curtis Cole*, Captain, Rhode Island Militia.

JOHN HECKMAN STEWART, Watertown, Mass. (36120). Son of George Sawin and Mary Alice (Heckman) Stewart; grandson of John Brigham and Nancy Abigail (Parker) Stewart; great-grandson of Thomas Carlisle and Emily (Brigham) Stewart; great²-grandson of Amherst and Anne (Carlisle) Stewart; great³-grandson of *David Carlisle (Carlile)*, Captain, Worcester County, Massachusetts Militia and Cont'l Troops.

RAYMOND HOWARD STILLMAN, Eatontown, N. J. (36356). Son of William Howard and Elizabeth B. (Dingwell) Stillman; grandson of Lewis Mortimer and Sarah C. (Moores) Stillman; great-grandson of Ebenezer and Rhoda (Francis) Stillman; great²-grandson of *Joseph Stillman*, Connecticut Minute-man at Lexington Alarm.

HENRY WALLACE STOCK, Albany, N. Y. (36195). Son of Walter and Martha (Brandmaehl) Stock; grandson of Henry and Lavina (McKinney) Stock; great-grandson of James and Lavina (Pangburn) McKinney; great²-grandson of *Andrew McKinney*, private, Pennsylvania State Troops and Artificers Corps, Cont'l Line.

LYMAN C. STOCKING, St. Louis, Mo. (35563). Son of Charles H. and Adella M. (Wilkins) Stocking; grandson of Lyman and Elizabeth (Hendrickson) Stocking; great-grandson of Hezekiah and Lois (Carter) Stocking; great²-grandson of *Reuben Stocking*, Lieutenant on privateer "Sampson," prisoner; great³-grandson of *George Stocking*, private, Connecticut Militia, at Lexington Alarm.

CHARLES LOGAN STONE, St. Louis, Mo. (35564). Son of William C. and Belle (Railey) Stone; grandson of Logan and Harriet M. (Rowland) Railey; great-grandson of Charles and Mary (Mayo) Railey; great²-grandson of *William Mayo*, Captain, Virginia Militia.

FERNAN FRAY STONE, Toledo, Ohio. (35896). Son of Marshall and Elizabeth (Ballinger) Stone; grandson of Samuel and Nancy (Burton) Stone; great-grandson of *James Burton*, Captain, Col. Francis Taylor's Regt., Virginia Convention Guards, pensioned.

JOHN WEST STONE, Minneapolis, Minn. (35689). Son of John Denniston and Martha (Allen) Stone; grandson of Gardner and Sally Ann (Denniston) Stone; great-grandson of *Windsor Stone*, private, Massachusetts Cont'l Line, pensioned.

ROBERT STONE, Topeka, Kans. (33324). Son of Jesse and Sarah Caroline (Packard) Stone; grandson of Cyrus and Sarah (Barrows) Packard; great-grandson of *William Barrows*, private and guard, Massachusetts Militia.

JOHN DUMONT STOUT, Roselle, N. J. (36361). Son of John Fisher and Ida (Williams) Stout; grandson of John Batiste Dumont and Susan Van Dorn (Fisher) Stout; great-grandson of Richard and Elizabeth (Van Ness) Stout; great²-grandson of *Thomas Stout*, Major, Hunterdon County, New Jersey Militia.

ROBERT LEE STRICKLER, Frankfort, Ind. (36427). Son of William Lewis and Mary Margurite (Swink) Strickler; grandson of Daniel A. and Mary Jane (Brown) Strickler; great-grandson of Jacob and Elizabeth (Lewis) Brown; great²-grandson of *Thomas Lewis*, Lieutenant, 11th Regt., Virginia Cont'l Troops.

EDWORD ANDREWS STUDLEY, Falmouth, Me. (34524). Son of Edword Andrew and Laura A. (Goodrich) Studley; grandson of Horcey and Pamelia (Andrews) Studley; great-grandson of *Isaac Andrews*, Captain, New Hampshire Militia, Selectman and Justice of the Peace; great-grandson of *Consider Studley*, private and Corporal, Massachusetts Militia.

HORACE SUMNER, Hyde Park, Mass. (36113). Son of William Ford and Ruth Ann (Weeks) Sumner; grandson of William and Abigail (Ford) Sumner; great-grandson of *William Sumner*, Ensign, Thirty-sixth Regt., Massachusetts Militia; great-grandson of *Jazaniah Ford*, private and Corporal, Massachusetts Militia.

JESSE FORD SUMNER, Hyde Park, Mass, (36115). Son of William Ford and Ruth Ann (Weeks) Sumner; grandson of William and Abigail (Ford) Sumner; great-grandson of *William Sumner*, Ensign, 36th Regt., Massachusetts Militia; great-grandson of *Jazaniah Ford*, Lieutenant and Captain, Massachusetts Militia.

GEORGE BLAIR SWORTFIGUER, Oakland, Calif. (36413). Son of Arthur Claghorn and Grace (Smart) Swortfiguer; grandson of David and Mary Emily (Jett) Smart; great-grandson of Hezekiah and Margaret (Hinkston) Smart; great²-grandson of Samuel and Nancy (Wilson) Hinkston; great²-grandson of *John Hinkston*, Major, Virginia Militia.

CHARLES HOWARD TALL, Jr., Newport News, Va. (35100). Son of Charles Howard and Annie M. (Shew) Tall; grandson of Harry and Annie (Vinson) Shew; great-grandson of James Thomas Robinson and Ann (Stewart) Vinson; great²-grandson of *David Stewart*, private, Maryland Militia.

JOHN B. TANNER, Portland, Ore. (35069). Son of John and Harriet Gertrude (Woodcock) Tanner; grandson of Sylvanus Green and Jeanette (Shaw) Woodcock; great-grandson of David and Aphia (Peabody) Woodcock, Jr.; great²-grandson of *David Woodcock*, Sergeant, Col. Carpenter's Regt., Massachusetts Militia.

CHARLES GILMAN TARBELL, Champaign, Ill. (36222). Son of Clarence Lyle and Sarah O. (Morse) Tarbell; grandson of Robert E. and Caroline (Humphrey) Morse; great-grandson of William and Sarah (Stocker) Humphrey; great²-grandson of Squire and Sallie (Sweet) Humphrey; great³-grandson of *William Humphrey*, Lieutenant and Brevet-Major, Rhode Island Troops, prisoner.

LOUIS JOHN TAYLOR, Phœnix, Ariz. (36603). Son of Thomas Blaine and Nellie (Van Sant) Taylor; grandson of J. W. and Lydia (Anderson) Van Sant; great-grandson of Nicholas and Mercy (Davis) Van Sant; great²-grandson of —— and —— (Westcott) Davis; great³-grandson of *Richard Westcott*, Major, Third Battalion, Gloucester County, New Jersey Militia.

MONTE BURR TAYLOR, Wheaton, Ill. (36223). Son of Linus Gibbs and Mary (Potter) Taylor; grandson of Enos Smith and Adelia Jane (Kellogg) Taylor; great-grandson of Jonathan and Anna (Smith) Taylor; great²-grandson of *Jasher Taylor*, private, Col. Fellows' Regt., Massachusetts Militia; great²-grandson of *Jonathan Taylor*, private, Col. Whitcomb's Regt., at Lexington Alarm and member War Committees; great-grandson of Hiram Tyre and Emeline (Fiske) Kellogg; great²-grandson of *Joel Kellogg, Jr.*, private, Col. John Ashley's Regt., Massachusetts Militia; great²-grandson of *Joel Kellogg*, private, Col. John Brown's Regt., Massachusetts Militia; great²-grandson of Henry and Mary (Slater) Fiske; great³-grandson of *William Fiske (Fisk)*, private, Albany County, New York Militia.

ROLAND HERBERT TAYLOR, Phœnix, Ariz. (23325). Son of Marvin Merchant and Henrietta Emilie (Reuter) Taylor; grandson of Hector J. and Polly Maria (Merchant) Taylor; great-grandson of William and Nancy (Rickney) Taylor, 3rd; great²-grandson of *William Taylor, Jr.*, private, Connecticut Militia at Lexington Alarm; great³-grandson of William Taylor, Sr., Sergeant, Connecticut Militia, pensioned.

PAUL TEAGARDEN, Dallas, Texas. (36326). Son of Joseph Oswin and Cornelia Rudd (Birdsong) Teagarden; grandson of Oswin and Mehettable (Baker) Teagarden; great-grandson of John B. and Rose (McClure) Teagarden; great²-grandson of *William Teagarden*, private, "Invalid Regt.," Pennsylvania Troops; great-grandson of Artemas and Mehettable (Conant) Baker; great²-grandson of Thatcher and Elizabeth (Manley) Conant; great³-grandson of *George Conant*, private, Massachusetts Militia; great²-grandson of *Asa Manley*, private, Connecticut Militia at Lexington Alarm.

CARLYLE W. THOMAS, Bridgeport, Conn. (Mass. 36116). Son of Joseph and Eliza (Woodbury) Thomas; grandson of Isaac and Dolly (Woodbury) Woodbury; great-grandson of *Jonathan Woodbury*, (father of Dolly), private, Sixth Regt., Worcester County, Massachusetts Cont'l Troops.

CHARLES OSCAR THOMAS, Jr., U. S. Army, Fort Brown, Texas. (Tenn. 36061). Son of Charles Oscar and Elizabeth Read (Williams) Thomas; grandson of John Phillip and Mildred (Hopson) Williams; great-grandson of George B. and Eliza (Read) Hopson; great²-grandson of *Joseph Hopson (Hobson)*, Lieutenant, Seventh Regt., Virginia Troops.

HARVEY C. THOMAS, Md. (25571). Supplemental. Son of Richard Pierce and Harriet (Cowman) Thomas; grandson of Edward and Lydia S. (Gilpin) Thomas; great-grandson of William and Martha (Patrick) Thomas; great²-grandson of *John Patrick*, Captain, Harford County, Maryland Militia, signer of Harford Declaration of Independence.

WALTER OWEN TIBBLES, Chicago, Ill. (36224). Son of Charles Edwin and Ada (Owen) Tibbles; grandson of William and Martha (Cooley) Tibbles; great-grandson of Jabez and Lucy (Frost) Cooley, Jr.; great²-grandson of *Jabez Cooley*, private, Col. Timothy Danielson's Regt., Massachusetts Militia.

WILLIAM GILMER TIMBERLAKE, Jackson, Tenn. (36069). Son of William Poindexter and Susan Josephine (Gilmer) Timberlake; grandson of Nicholas Johnson and Ellen (Barnett) Gilmer; great-grandson of John and Lucy (Johnson) Gilmer; great²-grandson of Thomas Meriwether and Elizabeth (Lewis) Gilmer; great³-grandson of *Thomas Lewis*, member Augusta County, Virginia, "Sons of Liberty" and delegate to Virginia State Convention of '75 and '76.

FRANCIS HARRISON TODD, Paterson, N. J. (36352). Son of Theron Alfred and Hattie Emeline (Webster) Todd; grandson of Charles and Jennette Maria (Clark) Webster; great-grandson of Levi and Sarah M. (Gilbert) Clark; great²-grandson of *Lyman Clark*, private, Col. Samuel Wyllys' Regt., Connecticut Cont'l Troops, pensioned.

ROBERT GARDNER TOLMAN, Champaign, Ill. (36225). Son of Robert Francis and Winnifred (Atkins) Tolman; grandson of Robert Francis and Martha Ann (Hart) Tolman; great-grandson of Robert Pierce and Mary (Walker) Tolman; great²-grandson of Jonas and Mary (Pierce) Tolman; great³-grandson of *Naphthali Pierce*, private, Col. Robinson's Regt., Massachusetts Militia; grandson of Sullivan Homan and Frances (Wilkins) Atkins; great-grandson of Thomas and Lucinda (Fairbanks) Atkins; great²-grandson of Thomas and Betsy (Dudley) Atkins; great²-grandson of *Nathaniel Dudley*, private, Col. Gales' Regt., New Hampshire Militia; great⁴-grandson of *John Dudley*, New Hampshire Muster and Paymaster, member Committee of Safety and Speaker of House of Representatives.

OSCAR J. TOMLINSON, St. Cloud, Fla. (Vt. 33848). Son of Gidon and Lovna (Greeley) Tomlinson; grandson of *Eliphalet Tomlinson*, private, Connecticut Cont'l Line, pensioned.

ROY EVERETT TOMLINSON, Montclair, N. J. (36677). Son of Everett S. and Genevieve (Rush) Tomlinson; grandson of Abijah and Marion (Wright) Tomlinson; great-grandson of Philo and Harriet (Atwell) Tomlinson; great²-grandson of Dan and Susannah (Hotchkiss) Tomlinson; great²-grandson of *Noah Tomlinson*, member Derby, Connecticut Com. of Inspection, Recruiting and other war committees.

WALTER ALANSON TOWNE, New London, Conn. (36704). Son of Alanson and Rosanna (Skinner) Towne; grandson of Nathan and Elizabeth (Russell) Towne; great-grandson of *John Towne, Jr.*, Captain, Fifth Regt., Worcester County, Massachusetts Militia.

ROGER ALLEN TOWNSEND, New Haven, Conn. (36705). Son of Alonzo Augustus and Emma (Bouton) Townsend; grandson of Allen and Susan (Blackman) Townsend; great-grandson of *Timothy Townsend*, private, Second Regt., Connecticut Militia.

JOHN CHAPLAIN TRAVERS, Baltimore, Md. (36087). Son of William Dove and Hattie Keene (Spilman) Travers; grandson of Robert Lee and Anne Hooper (Pattison) Spilman; great-grandson of Jeremiah Le Compte and Ann Le Compte (Hooper) Pattison; great²-grandson of James and Elizabeth (Le Compte) Pattison; great³-grandson of *Moses Le Compte*, Lieutenant, Maryland Militia.

WILLIAM M. TRAVERS, Baltimore, Md. (36086). Same as John Chaplain Travers, Md. (36087).

JAMES BENJAMIN TURRITTIN, St. Paul, Minn. (35687). Son of Frank E. and Helen L. (McLeod) Turrittin; grandson of Madison Ira and Louisa (Wood) McLeod; great-grandson of Frederick and Electa (Russell) Wood; great²-grandson of *Ebenezer Wood*, private, Connecticut Cont'l Line, pensioned.

EDWIN STEWART UNDERHILL, Jr., Corning, N. Y. (36456). Son of Edwin S. and Minerva (Allen) Underhill; grandson of William W. and Helen (Gansvoort) Allen; great-grandson of John R. and Rebecca (Irwin) Gansevoort; great²-grandson of *Conrad Gansevoort*, Second Lieutenant, First Regt., Albany County, New York Militia.

LANCE UNDERHILL, Schenectady, N. Y. (36458). Son of William Ely and Mary Louise (——) Underhill; grandson of John P. and Harriet (Barhydt) Underhill; great-grandson of John S. M. and Hannah (Lighthall) Barhydt; great²-grandson of *John Lighthall*, private, First Regt., New York Troops.

WILLIAM ALLEN UNDERHILL, Corning, N. Y. (36457). Same as Edwin Stewart Underhill, Jr., N. Y. (36456).

SYLVESTER VAN GIESON, Paterson, N. J. (36379). Son of Augustus A. and Elizabeth (Hawrey) Van Gieson; grandson of Isaac and Maria (Vanderbeek) Van Gieson; great-grandson of *Hendrick Van Gieson*, private, Col. Theunis Dey's Regt., New Jersey Militia.

WILLIAM OSCAR VINCENT, Jr., Newark, N. J. (36681). Son of William Oscar and Helen Esther (——) Vincent; grandson of George Eliphlet and Julia A. (——) Vincent; great-grandson of Peter Sayre and Eliza (Lyon) Vincent; great²-grandson of Amos and Sarah (Mason) Vincent; great³-grandson of Peter and Sarah (Quimby) Vincent; great⁴-grandson of *John Vincent*, private, Second Regt., Essex County, New Jersey Militia.

BERT WADDELL, Moorcroft, Wyo. (30024). Son of Daniel and Henrietta Iodoma (Strine) Waddell; grandson of Samuel and Catherine (Jacoby) Waddell; great-grandson of Michael and Elizabeth (Worline) Jacoby; great²-grandson of —— and Catherine

(Cline) Worline; great²-grandson of *Conrad Cline*, private, Sixth Regt., Pennsylvania Cont'l Line.

FREDERIC LINDSEY WALDRON, Edgewood, R. I. (36503). Son of Charles A. and Caroline (Luther) Waldron; grandson of Hiram and Abigail (Lindsey) Luther; great-grandson of Jonathan W. and Hannah (Easterbrooks) Lindsey; great²-grandson of *Aaron Easterbrooks*, private and Corporal, Col. Thomas Carpenter's Regt., Massachusetts Militia, pensioned.

KENNETH SANFORD WALES, D. C. (34088). Supplementals. Son of Frank Adelbert and Minie Webster (Taylor) Wales; grandson of Milo A. and Sophronia D. (Benton) Taylor; great-grandson of Timothy and Minerva (Webster) Benton; great²-grandson of *Timothy Benton*, Captain, Connecticut Artillery; great²-grandson of *Simeon Webster*, private, Second Regt., Connecticut Cont'l Line; great-grandson of Levi and Eunice (Burnham) Taylor, Jr.; great²-grandson of *James Burnham*, private, Col. Baldwin's Regt., Connecticut Artificers; great²-grandson of Levi and Sarah (Smith) Taylor; great²-grandson of *Nathan Smith*, private, Col. Elisha Porter's Regt., Massachusetts Militia.

CHARLES FRANCIS WALKER, Gardiner, Me. (34525). Son of James and Julia (Douglas) Walker; grandson of Joshua and Hannah S. (Potter) Walker; great-grandson of Lemuel and Hannah (Allen) Walker; great²-grandson of *John Walker*, Second Lieutenant, Capt. Littlefield's Co., Massachusetts Militia, for sea-coast defense.

CLAUDE FREDERIC WALKER, Brooklyn, N. Y. (36711). Son of Charles Swan and Alice (Morehouse) Walker; grandson of Charles G. and Emeline (——) Morehouse; great-grandson of Henry and Lydia (Mather) Morehouse; great²-grandson of Moses and Sally (Bishop) Mather; great²-grandson of *Joseph Mather*, Captain, Connecticut Militia, pensioned.

JAMES HERVEY WALKER, South Orange, N. J. (36366). Son of William Hervey and Ella Maria (Hillman) Walker; grandson of James Hervey and Sarah (McClintock) Walker; great-grandson of William and Eunice (Powers) Walker; great²-grandson of *Abel Walker*, private, Col. Thomas Carpenter's Regt., Massachusetts Militia.

RALPH BOWLES WARD, Newark, N. J. (36294). Son of Robert Smith and Selina A. (Freeman) Ward; grandson of Caleb Smith and Deidamia (Bowles) Ward; great-grandson of Caleb Smith and Abigail (Nichols) Ward; great²-grandson of *Robert Nichols*, Captain, Essex County, New Jersey Militia and State Troops.

RALPH McPHERSON WARD, San Diego, Calif. (36414). Son of Butler and Jane (McPherson) Ward; grandson of Jabez and Aurilla (Tufts) Ward; great-grandson of Ralph and Lovain (Butler) Ward; great²-grandson of *Jabez Ward*, Corporal and Sergeant, Berkshire County, Massachusetts Cont'l Troops.

TRACY BRONSON WARREN, Conn. (7770). Supplemental. Son of David Hard and Louisa (Bronson) Warren; grandson of William and Almira (Tyler) Bronson; great-grandson of Roswell and Susannah (Easton) Tyler; great²-grandson of *Eliphalet T. Easton*, private, Col. Chandler's Regt., Connecticut Militia.

WILLIAM HUNTER WASHINGTON, Nashville, Tenn. (36067). Son of Francis Whiting and Sarah Catherine (Crockett) Washington; grandson of Fontaine Posey and Eliza (Smith) Crockett; great-grandson of *Anthony Crockett*, Lieutenant, Virginia Troops; grandson of Francis Whiting and Eliza (Hall) Washington; great-grandson of Warner and Mary (Whiting) Washington; great²-grandson of *Francis Whiting*, Lieutenant, Virginia Cont'l Dragoons.

PAUL WATERMAN, Hartford, Conn. (36712). Son of James Henry and Maria Louise (Clark) Waterman; grandson of Abijah Stone and Clara (Revan) Clark; great-grandson of Abijah and Betsy (Heald) Clark; great²-grandson of *Samuel Clark*, Lieutenant, Fifth Regt., Middlesex County, Massachusetts Militia.

MALVIN HARRY WEEKS, Collingswood, N. J. (36373). Son of Henry Martin and Mary Malvina (Fairchild) Weeks; grandson of David Day and Rebecca R. (Richardson) Fairchild; great-grandson of Joseph and Elizabeth (Hoppock) Fairchild; great²-grandson of *Peter Fairchild*, private, Morris County, New Jersey Militia and State Troops, pensioned.

ARTHUR KENDRICK WELLS, Wellesley, Mass. (36807). Son of John Thomas and Mary Alice (Claflin) Wells; grandson of John Thomas and Sarah (Bartlett) Wells;

great-grandson of Henry and Mrs. Elizabeth (Atkins) Gilbert Bartlett; great²-grandson of *Israel Bartlett, Jr.,* Lieutenant, Essex County, Massachusetts Militia.

WELLINGTON WELLS, Boston, Mass. (36806). Son of Henry Jackson and Maria Adelaide (Goodnow) Wells; grandson of Gideon Parker and Susanna (Wellington) Wells; great-grandson of *Thaddeus Wellington,* private and drummer, Massachusetts Militia and Cont'l Troops.

WALTER HALL WHEELER, Minneapolis, Minn. (30324). Supplementals. Son of Charles Hall and Frances Spencer (Knowles) Wheeler; grandson of Warren and Catherine Hall (Brewer) Wheeler; great-grandson of Warren and Ellis (Harmon) Wheeler; great²-grandson of *Zenas Wheeler,* Captain, Berkshire County, Massachusetts Militia and Cont'l Troops and member of Committee of Correspondence and Inspection; great²-grandson of Zenas and Elizabeth (Dodge) Wheeler; great³-grandson of *Abraham Dodge,* private, Berkshire County, Massachusetts Militia.

HORACE MANLEY WHITE, Alexandria, La. (35997). Son of Horace Henry and Fannie Andrews (Blythe) White; grandson of Richard Anderson and Bethenia Andrews (Lavender) Blythe; great-grandson of Richard and Elizabeth (Anderson) Blythe; great²-grandson of William C. and Jane (Williams) Anderson; great²-grandson of *James Anderson,* private, Col. Nathaniel Gist's Regt., North Carolina Cont'l Troops.

LORING QUINCY WHITE, Cohasset, Mass. (36121). Son of Loring Quincy and Mary (Bradford) White; grandson of George Washington and Betsey (Burrell) White; great-grandson of Jonathan and Polly (Loud) White; great²-grandson of *Benjamin White,* private and drummer, Massachusetts Militia.

RICHARD FRANKLIN WHITE, Alexandria, La. (35996). Son of Horace Henry and Fannie Andrews (Blythe) White; grandson of Richard Anderson and Bethenia Andrews (Lavendar) Blythe; great-grandson of Richard and Elizabeth (Anderson) Blythe; great²-grandson of William C. and Jane (Williams) Anderson; great³-grandson of *James Anderson,* private, Col. Nathaniel Gist's Regt., North Carolina Cont'l Troops.

CHARLES LE ROY WHITMAN, Newark, N. J. (36297). Son of Charles A. and Carrie (Parker) Whitman; grandson of Samuel B. and Elizabeth (Symons) Whitman; great-grandson of Jacob and Emeline (Hayward) Whitman; great²-grandson of *Isaac Whitman,* private, Suffolk County, New York Militia, prisoner.

ROY RILEY WHITNEY, Montevideo, Minn. (35686). Son of Oscar L. and Ann M. (Riley) Whitney; grandson of Lemuel and Fanny M. (Gould) Whitney; great-grandson of John and Mrs. Agusta (Fisk) Brooks Whitney; great²-grandson of *John Whitney,* private, New Hampshire Militia.

GEORGE ARTHUR WHITTEMORE, Phœnix, Ariz. (36604). Son of Henry Sargent and Mary (Norton) Whittemore; grandson of Amasa and Sonty (Rice) Whittemore; great-grandson of Asa and Lucy (Muzzy) Whittemore; great²-grandson of *Jeremiah Whittemore,* member Spencer, Massachusetts Committee of Safety and Correspondence.

EDGAR WHRITENOUR, Paterson, N. J. (36358). Son of Edward and Hylinda (Earle) Whritenour; grandson of Edward and Phobe (Green) Whritenour; great-grandson of *Peter Whritenour (Reittenauer),* private, Northampton County, Pennsylvania Militia.

BENJAMIN FRANKLIN WIGGINTON, Jr., San Diego, Calif. (36407). Son of Benjamin Franklin and Martha Jane (Twyman) Wigginton; grandson of James and Matilda (Robertson) Twyman, Jr.; great-grandson of *James Twyman,* Orderly Sergeant and Guard, Albemarle County, Virginia Militia.

JAMES WILLIAM WIGGINTON, Chula Vista, Calif. (36406). Same as Benjamin Franklin Wigginton, Jr., Calif. (36407).

WILLIAM ADAMS WIGHT, Chicago, Ill. (36217). Son of Jay Ambrose and Caroline Elizabeth (Adams) Wight; grandson of Jabez and Mary (Bancroft) Wight; great-grandson of *William Bancroft,* private, Col. Doolittle's and Col. Porter's Regts., Massachusetts Militia.

NORMAN TRYON WILCOX, Keokuk, Iowa. (36230). Son of Edmund North and Frances Emilia (Tryon) Wilcox; grandson of Elisha Bacon and Hepzibah (Cornwell) Wilcox; great-grandson of Daniel and Lucy (Hamlin) Cornwell; great²-grandson of William and Hepzibah (Savage) Hamlin, Jr.; great³-grandson of *William Hamlin,* private, Connecticut Cont'l Line, pensioned.

FRANK JONES WILDER, Somerville, Mass. (36808). Son of Charles and Mary E. (Jones) Wilder; grandson of Mark and Eliza (Thayer) Wilder; great-grandson of Abel and Deborah (Perry) Wilder, Jr.; great²-grandson of *Abel Wilder*, private, Massachusetts Militia.

FRANK BURTT WILDRICK, Paterson, N. J. (36374). Son of Edward A. and Jennie H. (Burtt) Wildrick; grandson of Robert J. and Cynthia Goodyear (Bateman) Burtt; great-grandson of Stephen and Maria (Benham) Bateman; great²-grandson of Elihu and Esther (Griffin) Benham, Jr.; great²-grandson of *Elihu Benham*, private, First Regt., Connecticut Militia, pensioned.

ARTHUR MORTON WILLIAMS, Excelsior, Minn. (35688). Son of Orland George and Cora E. (Hathaway) Williams; grandson of Charles W. and Addie (Biglow) Hathaway; great-grandson of George and Amy (Learned) Biglow; great-grandson of Gershom and Nabby (Learned) (his cousin) Learned; great²-grandson of *Samuel Learned*, private, Middlesex County, Massachusetts Militia; great²-grandson of *Edward Learned, Jr.*, (father of Nabby), private, Massachusetts Militia, at Lexington Alarm.

CHARLES ALBERT WILLIAMS, Batavia, N. Y. (36198). Son of James M. and Mary Angeline (Cornwell) Williams; grandson of Robert and Phœba (Taggart) Cornwell; great-grandson of Alexander and Persis (Capwell) Taggart; great²-grandson of *William Capwell*, Corporal and Sergeant, Rhode Island Militia, pensioned.

EDWARD STETSON WILLIAMS, Elizabeth, N. J. (36676). Son of Amzi Frost and Harriet (Baxter) Williams; grandson of Aaron and Sarah (Frost) Williams; great-grandson of *Aaron Williams*, private, Essex County, New Jersey Militia.

SAMUEL STANHOPE WILLIAMSON, Duluth, Minn. (D. C. 36131). Son of Joseph A. and Frances (M——) Williamson; grandson of William and Jane W. (Balch) Williamson; great-grandson of *Stephen Bloomer Balch*, Captain, Calvert County, Maryland Militia, pensioned.

WILLIAM WILLOUGHBY, Blount Springs, Ala. (La. 35999). Son of Julius Edgar and Mary Alice (Byars) Willoughby; grandson of John Paul and Mary Jane (Cosby) Willoughby; great-grandson of John Hinchy and Amania Melvina (Tyler) Willoughby; great²-grandson of Willis and Mrs. Mary (Hinchy) Collins Willoughby; great²-grandson of *Edlyne Willoughby*, private, Seventh Regt., Virginia Troops, prisoner, pensioned.

DAVID WILLIS WILMORE, Winchester, Ind. (35524). Son of John Love and Mary (Lesley) Wilmore; grandson of Willis Clayton and Sarah (Love) Wilmore; great-grandson of William and Nancy (Harrison) Wilmore; great²-grandson of *John Wilmore*, private, Col. Daniel Morgan's Regt., Virginia Riflemen.

JOSEPH PORTER WILSON, Dothan, Ala. (Fla. 29919). Son of William S. and Addie (Anderson) Wilson; grandson of John Porter and Ella (Smith) Wilson; great-grandson of William C. and Roxana (Paramore) Wilson; great²-grandson of William and Mrs. Susan (Cawthon) McCullock Wilson; great³-grandson of *William Wilson*, Captain, Norfolk, Virginia Militia.

WARDEN McKEE WILSON, Indianapolis, Ind. (36433). Son of Henry Lane and Alice (Vajen) Wilson; grandson of James and Emma (Ingersoll) Wilson; great-grandson of John and Margaret (Cochran) Wilson; great²-grandson of James and Agnes (McKee) Wilson; great³-grandson of *William McKee*, Captain, Virginia Militia and member Virginia Convention to ratify the Constitution.

FRANCIS SIMON WINFIELD, Asbury Park, N. J. (36678). Son of Frank E. and Minnie K. (Sofield) Winfield; grandson of Charles and Frances (Larkin) Sofield; great-grandson of John Bloodgood and Sarah (Mallory) Larkin; great²-grandson of Jacob and Hannah (Foote) Mallory; great³-grandson of *David Foote*, private, General Wooster's Regt., Connecticut Militia.

WALTER LESLIE WISE, Newark, N. J. (36389). Son of Edwin Borden and Emma E. (Holmes) Wise; grandson of William Martin and Martha (Collins) Holmes; great-grandson of James and Catharine (Rinesmith) Collins; great²grandson of *John Collins*, private, Capt. Mills' Co. of Artificers, Ass't Commissary of Issues and Captain of Team Brigade.

RICHARD CLAUDE WOLFE, Chicago, Ill. (36626). Son of Hartwig Cohen and Clara Leah (Yatter) Wolfe; grandson of Saling and Sarah (Cohen) Wolfe; great-grandson of

Hartwig and Deborah (Marks) Cohen; great²-grandson of Samuel Mendez and Sarah (Harris) Marks; great²-grandson of *Isaac Marks*, private, Albany County, New York Militia.

SALING HENRY WOLFE, Chicago, Ill. (36627). Same as Richard Claude Wolfe, Ill. (36626).

WALTER ALBERT WOOD, Gardiner, Me. (36586). Son of William M. and Rose H. (Follansbee) Wood; grandson of William and Harriet Emmeline (Harley) Follansbee; great-grandson of James and Sally Hooper (Woodbridge) Follansbee; great²-grandson of Benjamin and Ann (Hodge) Woodbridge, Jr.; great³-grandson of *Benjamin Woodbridge*, sentinel, Col. Wm. Jones' Regt., Lincoln County, Massachusetts Militia at recapture of ship "Grout" and delegate to Provincial Congress.

CHARLES THOMPSON WOODRUFF, Sparrow's Point, Md. (36092). Son of Jerome Joseph and Myra Blanchard (Wheat) Woodruff; grandson of Orris and Eliza Ann (Caldwell) Woodruff; great-grandson of *Gurdon Woodruff*, private, Col. Erastus Wolcott's Regt., Connecticut Militia.

HUGH BECHTELL WOODS, Des Moines, Iowa. (36232). Son of William Harrison and Lucretia Neff (Bechtell) Woods; grandson of Martin Marshall and Elizabeth (Neff) Bechtell; great-grandson of John and Lucretia (Webster) Neff; great²-grandson of *John Bateman Webster*, Captain-Lieutenant, Fourth Pennsylvania Artillery, Cont'l Troops.

WILLIAM ROBERT WOODS, Custer, So. Dak. (30668). Son of Newton and Sarah M. (Copeland) Woods; grandson of William John and Sarah Lyon (Mann) Woods; great-grandson of Robert and Mary (Patten) Mann; great²-grandson of *John Mann*, first-class private, Delaware Christeen Company.

THOMAS CHEW WORTHINGTON, 3d, Baltimore, Md. (36088). Son of Thomas Chew and Mary Kate (Walker) Worthington, Jr.; grandson of Thomas Chew and Louisa (Davis) Worthington; great-grandson of Rezin Hammond and Rachel Owings (Shipley) Worthington; great²-grandson of *Thomas Worthington*, member Baltimore County, Maryland, Committee of Safety.

CHARLES F. WRIGHT, Jr., Glen Ridge, N. J. (36695). Son of Charles F. and Elizabeth (Burham) Wright; grandson of Barzillai Wood and Minerva (Moon) Wright; great-grandson of David and Sarah (Wood) Wright; great²-grandson of *Barzillai Wood*, private and Corporal, Hampshire County, Massachusetts Militia and Cont'l Troops, pensioned.

ALBERT HENRY YODER, N. Dak. (33009). Supplemental. Son of William Henry and Katharine Adelaide (Buskirk) Yoder; grandson of Henry and Ruth Ann (Rader) Yoder; great-grandson of Jacob and Catherine (Dellinger) Yoder; great²-grandson of *John Dellinger*, member Tryon County, North Carolina, Committee of Safety and Captain, Tryon County, North Carolina Militia, pensioned; grandson of Isaac Shelby and Elizabeth (Gabbert) Buskirk; great-grandson of Henry and Catherine (Holsapple) Gabbert; great²-grandson of *Michael Gabbert*, private, Shenandoah County, Virginia Militia, pensioned.

Index of Ancestors to be Found in Bulletins June, October, and December, 1921, and March, 1922

Bayley, Charles, Dec., 47
Beal, Philip, Dec., 51
Beall, Elisha, June, 94
Beall, Samuel, Jr., June, 87
Beall, Thomas, June, 71
Beard, Jeremiah, June, 80
Bearden, John, Oct., 40
Beardslee, Benjamin, March, 42
Beasley, Stephen, Oct., 41
Beatty, Thomas, June, 71
Beaty, William, March, 52
Beebe, Bezaleel, March, 42
Beebe, Thomas T., Oct., 46
Beecher, Joseph, March, 42
Beisel, Jacob, Dec., 45
Beittinger, Nicholas, Dec., 44
Belcher, Woodbridge, June, 71
Bell, Green, Dec., 55
Bellamy, John, March, 41
Bellows, Theodore, Dec., 44
Belt, J. Sprigg, March, 57
Bender, Christian, June, 71
Benedict, Gamaliel, June, 71
Benedict, Joseph, June, 71
Benham, Elihu, March, 75
Benjamin, David, March, 42
Benner, Martin, Oct., 40
Bennett, Jacob, June, 114
Bennett, Joseph, June, 112
Bennett, Zebulon, March, 42
Benton, Joel, March, 43
Benton, Timothy, March, 73
Berry, Benjamin, Dec., 60
Bevier, Johannes, June, 72
Bigelow, Joseph, Dec., 50
Bingham, Elias, March, 56
Bisbee, George, Dec., 56
Bishop, James, March, 57
Bissell, Zebulon, June, 72
Black, John, March, 57
Blackburn, John, June, 97
Blackford, Jacob, June, 72
Blackman, Elijah, March
Blaine, James, June, 95
Blake, Ebenezer, Dec., 44
Blalock, John, March, 60
Bledsoe, Anthony, June, 112
Bleecker, Anthony Lispenard, June, 70
Blinn, Billy, Oct., 40; June, 70
Bliss, James, March, 52
Bohanan, George, Oct., 57
Bomberger, John, March, 50
Boody, John, June, 87
Boone, Squire, June, 76
Booth, William Aylette, Oct., 59
Bostwick, Elijah, March, 69
Bostwick, Levi, June, 99
Bott, Rheinhard, Dec., 62
Bouck, Johonus, Jr., June, 97

Bougher, Abraham, March, 49
Bourne, Shearjeshub, March, 67
Bowie, Robert, June, 96
Bowling, James, June, 110
Boyd, James, Oct., 48
Boyd, John, June, 99, 115
Boyden, Ezekiel, June, 73
Brackett, Nathan, Jr., March, 52
Bradford, Elisha, June, 74
Bradish, David, March, 43
Bradish, John, Oct., 50; Dec., 51
Bradley, Abraham, Oct., 48
Bradley, Timothy, June, 94
Brady, John, June, 94
Brainard (Brainerd), Josiah, June, 73; Dec., 45
Brainerd, Abner, March, 61
Brant, David, March, 54
Bray, Andrew, March, 41
Brazer, Christopher, June, 73
Breed, John, June, 107
Brenton, James, Oct., 41
Brewer, David, Oct., 41
Brewer, Gains, June, 77
Brewer, Josiah, June, 114
Brewster, Joseph, Dec., 45
Brewster, Samuel, June, 81
Broad, Timothy, June, 73
Brockway, Ephraim, June, 82
Brokaw, John, June, 83
Brooke, Benjamin, March, 68
Brooke, Lawrence, Dec., 53
Brooks, Simeon, June, 92
Broome, Jacob, June, 75
Brower, Hendrick, Dec., 50
Brown, Caleb, Oct., 55
Brown, Ebenezer, Dec., 48
Brown, George, Oct., 54
Brown, John, March, 57
Brown, Jonathan, Oct., 49
Brown, Josiah, June, 74; Oct., 54
Brown, Roger, June, 74
Brown, William, Oct., 53; Dec., 62
Browne, Nathan, June, 86
Buckbee, John, March, 44
Bull, Asa, March, 56
Bullard, Isaac, June, 72
Bunnell, Benjamin, June, 109
Buntin, Andrew, Dec., 55
Burbank, Eleazer, Dec., 49
Burbeck, William, March, 42
Burd, James, Oct., 55; Dec., 55
Burgess, Edward, Dec., 59
Burke, Samuel, March, 44
Burke, Thomas, Dec., 45
Burke, William, March, 44
Burleigh, Jacob, March, 59
Burleigh, Jonathan, March, 44
Burleigh, Josiah, March, 59

Burlingame, Ezeck, June, 75
Burnam, Henry, Oct., 41
Burnham, James, March, 67, 73
Burns, John, March, 67
Burr, Israel, June, 71
Burr, Jonathan, Oct., 41
Burrell, Benjamin, March, 42
Burroughs, John, June, 75
Burruss, Jacob, March, 44
Burt, Abner, June, 75
Burton, James, March, 70
Bush, Jonathan, March, 49
Bush, Moses, March
Butler, Isaac, June, 85
Butler, Samuel Stone, June, 85
Bryan, Andrew, March, 60
Bryan, Daniel, June, 75
Bryan, John, June, 74
Byrd (Bird), Benjamin, Dec., 51, 57

Cabell, Nicholas, June, 104
Cadwell, Phineas, June, 68
Calder, James, June, 98
Calkins, Jonathan, June, 99
Calloway, Richard, March, 45
Camden, William, Dec., 53
Campbell, Aeneas, Oct., 63
Campbell, Alexander, June, 113
Campbell, John, Dec., 50
Canfield, Abraham, March, 60
Canfield, Dennis, June, 75
Canfield, James, Jr., Oct., 42
Canfield, Nathan, Oct., 42
Capwell, William, March, 75
Carbee, Joel, June, 101
Carhart, Thomas, March, 57
Carlisle, David, March, 69
Carnahan, Adam, June, 75, 93
Carnahan, James, Dec., 60
Carpenter, John, June, 75
Carpenter, Thomas, March, 44
Carpenter, William, Dec., 45
Carrington, Paul, Oct., 51; Dec., 54
Carter, Landon, Oct., 62
Cartwright, Robert, Oct., 62
Case, Aaron, June, 75
Case, Darius, Oct., 53
Case, Joseph, June, 97; Dec., 46
Cash, John, March, 59
Catlin, Thomas, March, 45
Causey, Patrick, Oct., 42; March, 51
Cessna, John, March, 40
Chadwick, Archelaus, June, 80
Chadwick, Thomas, June, 74
Chamberlain, Jacob, March, 57
Chamberlin, Godfrey, Dec., 46
Chamberlin, William, Oct., 42
Champion, Reuben, Jr., June, 90
Chapin, Ephraim, March, 45

Chapin, Phineas, June, 83; March, 45
Chapman, Daniel, Sr. & Jr., Oct., 53
Chapman, Joseph, June, 83
Chapman, Simon, June, 114
Chase, Jacob, March, 45
Cheney, Ebenezer, June, 107
Cheney, William, June, 107
Cherry, William, June, 113
Cheston, John, Dec., 46
Child, Timothy, Dec., 53
Chilton, John, June, 80
Christian, Daniel, Oct., 59; Dec., 59
Christian, William, June, 68; Oct., 43;
    March, 47
Churchill, Francis, Dec., 46
Churchill, Ichabod, March, 42
Churchill, Joseph, March, 45
Churchill, Solomon, March, 56
Clapp, Elias, June, 107
Clapp, Joshua, June, 76
Clark, Charles, June, 76, 86, 98
Clark, Daniel, March, 45
Clark, David, June, 106
Clark, Edward, Oct., 43
Clark, Jeremiah, June, 76; Dec., 46
Clark, Jesse, June, 77
Clark, John, June, 76; Oct., 45
Clark, Lyman, March, 71
Clark, Paul, Oct., 41
Clark, Reuben, Oct., 47
Clark, Robert, Oct., 50; Dec., 48
Clark, Samuel, March, 41, 73
Clark, William, June, 76, 99
Clay, John, Dec., 52; March
Clements, James, June, 80
Clendennin, William, March, 51, 65
Cleveland, Ben., Oct., 46
Cleveland, Edward, June, 78
Cleveland, James, March, 46
Cleveland, Solomon, Oct., 49
Cline, Conrad, Oct., 50; March, 56, 57, 72
Clinton, John, March, 64
Clinton, Richard, March, 64
Clifton, Whittington, Dec., 53
Clough, Winthrop, March, 45
Clyde, Samuel, Oct., 59; Dec., 53
Coble, David, June, 108; March, 48
Coburn, Alpheus, Dec., 46
Cochrane, Robert, June, 112
Cockrill, Ann Robertson, Dec., 49
Cockrill, John, Dec., 49
Coe, Ebenezer, June, 76
Coffin, Eliphalet, June, 94
Coffin, Josiah, 3d, March, 46
Coffin, Lemuel, Oct., 55
Coffman, Jacob, Oct., 46
Coggeshall, Job, June, 77
Colby, Thomas, Oct., 59
Cole, Curtis, March, 69

Dorsheimer, Manuel, Dec., 44
Dorr, William, March, 49
Doty, James, Dec., 43
Doty, Peter, Dec., 60
Dougherty, John, June, 80
Douglas, George, March, 46
Douglas, William, June, 96; Oct., 56
Douglass, Aaron, Oct., 57
Downes, Henry, Jr., June, 106
Drake, Jeremiah, March, 49
Drake, Samuel, June, 80
Drake, Thomas, March, 49
Drennan, William, March, 50
Drury, Ebenezer, Oct., 59
Drury, Zedekiah, Oct., 59
Du Bois, Benjamin, June, 78
Du Bois, Jeremiah, Oct., 44
Dudley, Jeremiah, June, 86
Dudley, John, March, 72
Dudley, Nathaniel, March, 72
Duffield, George, June, 80
Dunbar, Aaron, Dec., 46
Duncan, George, June, 86, 90; Oct., 49
Duncan, John, March, 43
Dunlap, William, March, 50
Durand, Ebenezer, June, 97
Durant, Edward, Oct., 57
Duvall, Benjamin, Oct., 60
Dyckman, Joseph (Johan), Oct., 49

Easterbrooks, Aaron, March, 73
Easton, Eliphalet, March, 73
Eddins, Benjamin, June, 91
Edwards, Benjamin, June, 114
Elder, Isaac, Oct., 45
Eldridge, Jonathan, June, 97
Elliott, Benjamin, June, 87
Elliott, Joseph, Oct., 45
Elliott, William, March, 50
Ellis, John, June, 71, 81
Ellmaker, Nathaniel, June, 98
Ellsworth, John, Jr., June, 74
Elmendorf, Conradt W., June, 81
Elrick, George, June, 94
Emerson, Amos, June, 69
Emerson, Asa, June, 109
Emerson, John, March, 55
Emerson, Theodore, March, 56
Ennis, Daniel, Dec., 57
Ettele (Atley), David, March, 50
Ettele (Atley), Gottleib D., March, 50
Evans, Elijah, June, 81
Evans, Obadiah, Oct., 47
Ewing, Robert, Oct., 45

Fairbanks, William, Oct., 40
Fairchild, Peter, Oct., 63; Dec., 61; March, 73
Farley, John Parke, June, 71

Farnsworth, Reuben, March, 51
Farrand, Bethuel, June, 115
Farrar, Thomas, June, 89, 90
Farrington, Thomas, Dec., 54
Faust, Johannes, March, 63
Fay, Timothy, March, 48
Felch, Nathan, March, 61
Fellows, Parker, June, 82
Felton, Matthias, June, 93
Ferebee, Joseph, Dec., 54
Ferguson, John, Dec., 47
Fergusson, Robert, Jr., Dec., 48
Ferrand, Daniel, June, 115
Field, Abner, June, 85
Field, David, Dec., 45
Field, Henry, Jr., Oct., 41, 62
Field, John, Oct., 41
Finley, John, March, 50
Finney, John, Oct., 62
Firestone, Matthias, June, 72
Fish, Nicholas, June, 70
Fisher, Isaac, Oct., 45
Fisher, John, March, 63
Fisk, Asa, Oct., 52
Fisk, Robert, June, 88
Fisk, William, March, 71
Fitz Randolph, Joseph, June, 77, 82
Flansburg, John, Oct., 59
Flansburg, Matthew, Dec., 60
Fleming, James, March, 46
Fletcher, Ebenezer, March, 51
Flint, Samuel, Oct. 45
Flower, Ithuriel, June, 107
Flower, Nathaniel, June, 107
Follin, John, March, 59
Fooks (Fooke), Jesse, March, 51
Foote, David, March, 75
Ford, Jazaniah, March, 70
Forrest, Ebenezer, June, 84
Forristall, Joseph, March, 51
Forsyth, John, Oct., 59
Fortier, Michel, June, 87
Foster, Anson, March
Foster, Antony, Jr., Dec., 48, 49
Foster, Isaac, March, 51
Foster, Joseph, Dec., 45
Foster, Nathaniel, Jr., March, 47
Fowler, Samuel, March, 41
Fowler, Titus, March, 59
Fox, Frederick, June, 83
Fox, Jonathan, Dec., 47
Foye, William, June, 82
Francis, Justus, Oct., 46
Franklin, Benjamin, June, 91
Freedley, Henry, June, 83
Freeman, William, March, 43
Freese, Isaac, June, 83
French, David, June, 114
French, James, June, 75

Harney, Jonathan, Dec., 50
Harrington, John, June, 87
Harrington, Simeon, March, 45
Harris, Hannah Stewart, Oct., 62
Harris, Israel, March, 55
Harris, John, June, 111
Harris, James, June, 87
Harris, William, June, 68; March, 41
Harrison, Adonijah, Dec., 46
Harrison, Moses, March, 53
Hart, Nathaniel, Oct., 62
Haskell, Stephen, June, 73
Haskell, Zebulon, March, 45
Haskins, Edward, March, 53
Hastings, Jonathan, Oct., 39
Hastings, Thomas, Oct., 49
Hatch, Abner, June, 114
Hatch, Ede, June, 114
Hatcher, John, Oct., 46
Hathorn, John, Oct., 43
Hawes, William, March, 47
Hawkins, Alexander, Oct., 48
Hawkins, David, Oct., 48
Hawkins, Dexter, Dec., 61
Hawkins, John, June, 88
Hawkins, Simeon, Oct., 48
Hawkins, Zechariah, June, 100
Hayford, William, March, 54
Hays, James, June, 74; March, 58
Hays, John, Dec., 48
Heartwell, Joseph, Oct., 49
Heizer (Hizer), John, June, 85
Henderson, James, Jr., Oct., 41
Hendricks, Isaac, June, 77
Henry, John, June, 88
Henshaw, William, June, 88, 109
Herrick, Israel, March, 59
Herrick, Joseph, March, 59
Herrington, John, June, 108
Hershey, Christian, June, 88
Hesser, Frederick, Oct., 64
Hester, Conrad, Dec., 48
Heston (Heeston), Edward, Oct., 49
Hewson, John, June, 88
Higgins, James, March, 50
Hill, Green, March, 54
Hill, Joseph, March, 55
Hill, Robert, March, 55
Hill, Smith, March, 55
Hill, Thomas, Dec., 50
Hill, William, Sr. & Jr., March, 54
Hillsgrove, John, March, 68
Hillyer, Simon, June, 99
Hinkston, John, March, 70
Hinman, Asahel, June, 103
Hinsdale, Barnabas, Dec., 45
Hiscox, David, March, 53
Hitchcock, Dan, June, 101
Hitchcock, John, June, 84

Hodge, Solomon, June, 82
Hoffman, John, June, 89
Holden, Samuel, March, 46
Holder, John, March, 45
Holland, Nathan, June, 74
Holliday, William, Oct., 49
Hollis, Arthur Garfield, March
Hollister, Josiah, June, 89
Holmes, Joseph, June, 111
Holt, Abiel, March, 55
Holt, Timothy, June, 89
Hoodley, Nathaniel, March, 57
Hooker, Thomas Hart, June, 78
Hooker, Zibeon, June, 76
Hoone, Henry, June, 89
Hoover, Jacob, June, 104
Hoover, Ulrich, Dec., 51
Hopkins, James, Oct., 47
Hopkins, Samuel, June, 72
Hopkins, Solomon, Dec., 44
Hopkins, Weight, March, 55
Hopper, Peter A., March, 43
Hoppins, Joseph, June, 72
Hopson, Joseph, Oct., 63; March, 71
Hornor, John, June, 90
Horton, Samuel, June, 75
Horton, Solomon, June, 75
Houghton, Jonathan, March, 55
Howard, Adam, March, 48
Howe, Gardner, Dec., 51
Howes, John, Oct., 49
Hoyt, John, Jr., Oct., 49
Hoyt, Zebidiah, June, 111
Hubbard, Levi, March, 42
Hubbard, Samuel, March, 42
Hubbell, Abijah, June, 90
Hubbell, Comfort, March, 56
Huffman, Ambrose, March, 44
Hughey, John, Dec., 51
Hulick, Derrick, Oct., 61
Humphrey, Robert, June, 82
Humphrey, William, March, 71
Humphreys (Humphries), Joseph, Dec., 51
Humrickhouse, Peter, Dec., 44
Hungerford, Benjamin, March, 56
Hunt, David, March, 52
Hunt, Humphrey, March, 41
Hunter, David, June, 111
Hunter, George, March, 56
Huntington, Jabez, March, 63
Huntington, William, Oct., 52
Huntley, James, Oct., 40
Huntzinger, John G., March, 63
Hurd, Abraham, Dec., 59
Hurley, Thomas, March, 44
Huston, Joseph, March, 61
Hutchens, Noah, March, 56
Hutchings, William, June, 85
Hutchins, Phineas, Dec., 44

Hutson, Thomas, Oct., 50
Hutton, Moses, Oct., 62
Hyatt, Peter, June, 102

Ingersoll, David, June, 80
Innes, Harry, June, 99, 110

Jackson, Solomon, Oct., 58
Jacobs, John, Jr., June, 89
James, David, June, 75
Jaquith, Benjamin, Oct., 50
Jeffries, John, Oct., 63
Jett, John, June, 91
Johnson, Amos, Oct., 39
Johnson, Arthur, June, 91; Oct., 49
Johnson, Henry, March, 44
Johnson, Henson, March, 44
Johnson, Hezekiah, Dec., 51
Johnson, Horatio, June, 85
Johnson, Isaac, March, 65
Johnson, James, March, 57
Johnson, John, June, 91; March, 43
Johnson, Jonathan, Dec., 53
Johnson, Joseph, Dec., 50
Johnson, Robert, March, 65
Johnson, Seth, March, 57
Johnston, Archibald, Dec., 52
Johnston, Gideon, Oct., 45
Johnston, William, Oct., 45
Jones, Amos, Oct., 50
Jones, Daniel, Oct., 57
Jones, Elijah, June, 107
Jones, John, June, 78
Jones, Joshua, Oct., 51
Jones, Paul, June, 107
Judd, Thomas, March, 57

Kees, John, June, 93
Kellogg, Benjamin, June, 103
Kellogg, Eliphalet, March, 58
Kellogg, Joel, Jr., March, 71
Kelso, John, Dec., 45
Kemper, Peter, June, 92
Kendrick, Edom, Sr., March, 54
Kendrick, Samuel, March, 54
Kenley, William, June, 97
Kennard, John, Sr. & Jr., March, 62, 66
Kennedy, Daniel, Oct., 51
Kent, Cephas, March, 51
Kenyon, William, March, 58
Kephart, John, Dec., 52; March, 58
Ketcham, Timothy, June, 87
Keyes, William, Oct., 42
Kilbourn, Ashbel, June, 72
Kilbourn, Samuel, June, 110
Kimball, Aaron, March, 56
Kimball, Samuel, June, 95
Kimble, Able, June, 97
King, Abonijah, March, 63

King, Douglas, Oct., 51
King, George, March, 47
King, John, Oct., 51; Dec., 52
King, Nathan, Dec., 52
King, Philip, Dec., 52
King, Robert, Jr., June, 93
King, William, March
Kingbury, Thomas, June, 93
Kirtland, Martin, June, 102
Kling, Ludwig, Oct., 55
Knapp, Israel, Oct., 49
Knauss, Henrich (Henry), Dec., 52
Kneeland, Timothy, Oct., 49
Knowles, James, Jr., June, 114
Knowles, Joseph, Oct., 51
Knowlton, Nathan, Dec., 52
Kohler, Jacob, March, 58
Krumbine, Leonard, June, 106

Laird, William, June, 77; Oct., 43
Lallande de Ferriere, Nicolas Louis, Oct., 51
Lamb, Daniel Gad, Dec., 62
Lane, Cornelius, June, 93
Lane, Isaac, March, 54
Lane, Joel, June, 89
Lane, Martin, Oct., 63
Lane, Tidence, March, 54
Lane, William, June, 95
Lang, Thomas, March, 58
Latham, Nehemiah, Oct., 63
Lathrop, Ebenezer, Oct., 52
Lathrop, Jedediah, March, 46
Lawman, Jacob, Dec., 59
Lawrence, Timothy, March, 59
Lawyer, David, June, 97
Lawyer, Jacob Frederick, June, 97
Lawyer, Johannes, June, 23
Leairth, Andrew, June, 91
Leamon, George, March, 59
Learned, Edward, Jr., March, 75
Learned, Samuel, March, 75
Leavenworth, Mark, June, 92
Le Compte, Moses, March, 72
Lee, Andrew, June, 75
Lee, Thomas Sim, June, 93
Leftwich, William, June, 90
Leonard, Abiather, June, 102
Letton, Michael, June, 68; Dec., 43
Levis, Thomas, June, 83
Lewis, Augustus, Oct., 56
Lewis, Eleazer, March, 49
Lewis, John, March, 64
Lewis, Nicholas, Oct., 41
Lewis, Peter, March, 64
Lewis, Thomas, June, 93; March, 70, 71
Lewis, Valentine, Dec., 58
·Lewman, John, March, 59
Libby, Ichabod, Oct., 52
Liggett, John, Oct., 52

Lighthall, John, March, 72
Lincoln, Charles, Dec., 52
Lincoln, Stephen, June, 76
Lindsley, John, Oct., 61
Lindsley, Joseph, June, 69
Little, John, Jr., Dec., 58
Littlehale, Abraham, March, 59
Lloyd, John, Oct., 64
Lockwood, Jacob, March, 59
Lockwood, Timothy, June, 93
Logan, Samuel, June, 105; Oct., 51; Dec., 61
Lombard, Solomon, Oct., 50
Long, John, March, 54
Longley, Edmund, March, 60
Longstreet, Aaron, Jr., Dec., 55
Loomis, Michael, March, 60
Loomis, Nathaniel, Oct., 57; Dec., 58
Loomis, Simon, March, 60
Lord, William, March, 51
Loring, Ignatius, Dec., 53
Loring, Samuel, June, 93
Lounsberry, Michael, March, 60
Love, Thomas, Dec., 53
Loveland, Asa, Oct., 39
Loveland, Lazarus, Oct., 52
Lowrey, Thomas, June, 84
Ludlow, Cornelius, June, 75
Ludlum, Jacob, June, 106
Lupton, Joseph, Dec., 48
Lybarger, Ludwick, Sr., March, 60
Lyman, Francis, June, 94
Lynn, David, June, 104
Lynn, David, Jr., June, 105
Lyon, Benjamin, June, 89; March, 44
Lyon, Caleb, Sr. & Jr., March, 60
Lyon, Matthew, June, 98; March, 68
Lytle, William, Dec., 49

McAdams, William, Oct., 53
McAllaster (McAllister) William, June, 92; Oct., 53
McCauley, James, Dec., 53
McCausland, Henry, March, 48
McCausland, William, March, 45
McChesney, Hugh, June, 94
McClanahan, Thomas, Oct., 62
McCleary, Robert, Dec., 48
McClelland, Thomas, June, 108; Oct., 43
McConnell, Matthew, Oct., 53
McCullough, James, March, 67
McCullum, Daniel, June, 95
McDonald, Angus, June, 95
McDougal, Alexander, Oct., 39, 56; March, 56
McDowell, Samuel, Oct., 53
McElroy, Adam, Oct., 48
McFall, Hugh, June, 95
MacFarling, Elijah, Sr., March, 61
McFerrin, William, Oct., 40

McKee, Andrew, June, 95
McKee, Hugh, Oct., 42
McKee, John, March
McKee, William, March, 75
McKenney, Samuel, Oct., 52
McKinney, Andrew, March, 70
McLure, Abdiel, Jr., Dec., 59
McMaster, William, March, 61
McNair, Daniel, March, 09
McNary, David, June, 109
McNeir, Thomas, Dec., 59
McPherson, Samuel, June, 96
Macklin, James, March, 67
Macomber, Abiel, June, 75
Magarr, James, Dec., 60
Main, James, June, 96
Makepeace, William, June, 82
Mann, John, March, 76
Manchester, James, Dec., 53
Manchester, Matthew, Oct., 51
Manley, Asa, March, 71
Manning, Abraham, March, 55
Mansfield, Andrew, June, 70
Marble, John, June, 96
March, James, Dec., 43
Marchand, David, June, 107
Markham, Jeremiah, June, 106
Markham, William, March
Marks, Isaac, March, 76
Marlett, Gideon, June, 92
Marlett, John, June, 92
Marsh, Charles, Oct., 52
Marsh, Samuel, June, 111
Marsh, William, June, 93, 96
Marshall, Isaac, March, 62
Marshall, William, June, 70
Marshall, Zaccheus, Oct., 57
Martin, Silvanus, June, 97
Marvin, Benjamin, June, 80
Mason, Benjamin, Oct., 51
Mason, Charles, Dec., 51
Massie, Thomas, March, 62
Masten, Cornelius C., Oct., 45
Mather, Joseph, March, 73
Mather, Moses, June, 104
Matlack, Timothy, June, 84
Matteson, Nathan, March, 69
Matthews, Aaron, Dec., 53
Matthewson, William, March, 64
Maxcy, Benjamin, Oct., 53
Maybank, Joseph, June, 93
Mayo, Joseph, June, 97
Mayo, William, March, 70
Meacham, Samuel, Oct., 53; March, 62
Mead, Calvin, Dec., 43; March, 41
Mead, Thaddeus, Dec., 53
Meade, David, June, 73
Meade, Richard Kidder, June, 96
Meeker, James, June, 88

Meeker, Michael, June, 103
Mellinger, John Jacob, March, 49
Merrill, Samuel, Oct., 53
Merrill, Stephen, March, 51
Messler, Cornelius, March, 62
Mickley, John Jacob, Dec., 58
Middlebrook, John, Jr., Oct., 40
Miesse, Daniel, June, 92
Miller, Christian, Dec., 56; March, 65
Miller, Ebenezer, Oct., 49
Miller, Enoch, June, 99
Miller, Samuel, March, 64
Miller, William, June, 98
Milliken, James, Dec., 50
Mills, John, Dec., 49
Mills, William, Dec., 58
Miner, John, Oct., 51
Minor, Benjamin, March, 62
Minor, Daniel, June, 107
Minsker, Ludwick, June, 82
Mitchell, Ensign, Dec., 54
Mitchell, Josiah, June, 73
Mitchell, Nathaniel, June, 74
Monroe, John, Oct., 47
Monro, Thomas, March, 62
Montague, Philip, Oct., 50
Montague, William, March, 68
Montgomery, John, Oct., 48
Montgomery, Robert, March, 63
Moore, Anthony, Dec., 48
Moore, John, Dec., 55
Moore, Nathaniel, June, 86
Moore, Smith, March, 63
Moorhead, Fergus, March, 67
Moreland, John, March, 67
Morgan, Andrew, March, 57
Morgan, Benjamin, March, 46
Morgan, Isaac, June, 91
Morison, Peter, June, 99
Morris, George, March, 63
Morris, Henry, June, 79
Morrison, Isaac, Dec., 54
Morse, Joseph, June, 99
Morton, Bryant (Briant), Dec., 54
Morton, Joseph, Dec., 61
Moseley, Thomas, Oct., 62
Moses, Samuel, Oct., 58
Moulton, Caleb, Oct., 54
Moultrie, William, June, 83, 95
Mountjoy, John, March, 44
Mountjoy, William, March, 44
Mounell, James, March, 61
Mowry, Daniel, June, 98
Muchmore, John, Oct., 54
Muirheid, Jonathan, Dec., 58
Munger, John, Dec., 54
Munroe, Andrew, Dec., 54
Munroe, Ebenezer, June, 99
Munroe, Nathaniel, March, 61

Munroe, Philemon, Dec., 60
Munson, Moses, March, 60
Murray, Thomas, Dec., 54

Naff, Hance, June, 104
Nebucher, John, June, 71
Neer, Charles (Carl), Oct., 54; Dec., 54
Neilson, John, June, 70
Nelson, John Younglove, Dec., 55
Nesmith, James, Jr., March, 50
Newcomb, William, June, 78
Newell, Abijah, June, 99
Newell, Stephen, June, 99
Newman, Thomas, March, 63
Newton, Caleb, June, 88; Oct., 49
Newton, Joseph, Oct., 61
Newton, Nahum, June, 115
Nichols, Robert, June, 114; March, 73
Nicola, Lewis, Oct., 59
Noble, Jacob, Oct., 54
Noe, Lewis, June, 114
Noel, Theodoris, June, 83
Norris, Aquilla, Sr., March, 63
Norton, Ebenezer, June, 80
Norton, Noah, Dec., 55
Noyes, Thomas, March, 45
Nye, Samuel, June, 100

Oakes, Jonathan, June, 93
Ober, Christian, June, 108
Oglesby, Thomas, June, 112
Olmstead, Daniel, Dec., 52
O'Neal, George, Oct., 54
O'Neil, Archibald, Dec., 61
O'Neil, John, Oct., 49; Dec., 51, 58
Orth, Balzer, March, 68
Orton, Elida, June, 100
Osborn, Jeremiah, Dec., 55
Osborn, Joshua, Oct., 54
Osborne, Thomas, Jr., June, 115
Otty, William, March, 42
Overmyer, John George, Oct., 44, 45
Owens, Thomas, Dec., 55

Packer, John, Jr., June, 73
Page, Jonas, March, 57
Painter, Thomas, March, 64
Palfrey, William, June, 76; Oct., 55; Dec., 55
Palmer, David, June, 83
Palmer, Nehemiah, Oct., 48; Dec., 50
Parke, Zebulon, June, 86
Parker, Daniel, March, 42
Parker, Isaiah, June, 104
Parker, Nathaniel, March, 64
Parker, Lemuel, Jr., March, 64
Parker, Stiles, June, 100
Parmelee, Samuel, March, 64
Parris, Samuel, June, 91
Parsons, Abraham, June, 81

Patten, John, June, 113
Patterson, Alexander, Dec., 55
Patterson, Andrew, June, 96
Patterson, Joseph, Dec., 55
Patterson, Robert, June, 100
Patrick, John, March, 71
Pawling, John, June, 74
Payne, John, June, 116
Peabody, Moses, June, 70
Peachy, William, Oct., 62
Pearce, Cromwell, March, 52
Pearce, William, March, 64
Péchin, Pierre Abraham, March, 40
Peck, Peleg, Dec., 56
Peirce, Abel, March, 62
Peiffer, John George, June, 92
Pelton, Ithmar, March, 56
Pendleton, Joseph, June, 98; March, 54
Pendleton, Zebulon, Oct., 45
Pennington, John, June, 85
Pennington, Nathan, Dec., 45
Penny, John, June, 97
Penoyer, John, June, 114
Perkins, Abraham, June, 70
Perkins, Benjamin, June, 101
Perkins, David, March, 64
Perkins, George, March, 48
Perkins, Reuben, March, 64
Perley, Nathan, March, 46
Perrin, Abraham, March, 65
Perrine, James, March, 65
Perry, Abel, Dec., 54; March, 65
Perry, James, June, 101
Perry, Jonas, June, 107
Perry, Josiah, June, 107
Perry, William, Jr., June, 112
Peyton, Francis, Oct., 55
Pharr, Walter, March, 65
Phelps, Eliphalet, March, 69
Phelps, Samuel, June, 101
Phelps, Silas, March, 69
Phelps, Winslow, June, 72
Phillips, David, Dec., 56
Phillips, Esquire, Oct., 56
Phillips, Jonas, June, 106
Pierce, Daniel, Oct., 50
Pierce, John, June, 103
Pierce, Napthali, March, 72
Pierson, Caleb, June, 101
Pierson, David, June, 101; Oct., 55
Pierson, Ephraim, Jr., June, 90
Pintard, John, June, 112
Place, Enoch Miles, Dec., 51
Poe, David, June, 90
Polk, Charles, Dec., 57
Polk, Charles, Jr., June, 101
Polk, William, June, 76; Oct., 41
Pollard, William, June, 82
Pomeroy, Benjamin, Dec., 51

Pomeroy, Seth, June, 101
Pomeroy, Simeon, June, 101
Poor, Peter, Dec., 56
Pope, John, June, 80
Popino (Popineau), Peter, Dec., 46
Porter, Ezekiel, March, 65
Porter, William, Dec., 56
Postlethwaite, John, March, 65, 66
Potter, Esek, March, 66
Potter, Jacob, March, 67
Powell, Levin, June, 102
Powell, Martin, June, 104
Powell, Philip, Dec., 56
Powers, William, Oct., 56
Pratt, David, June, 88
Pratt, James, Oct., 56
Pratt, Nehemiah June, 102
Prentice, John, Dec., 56
Presbrey, John, June, 102
Prescott, Ebenezer, Dec., 57
Preston, Isaac, June, 109
Preston, Jacob, June, 81
Price, Nathaniel, June, 79
Prime, Benjamin Youngs, Oct., 42
Prime, Ebenezer S., Oct., 42
Procter, Joseph, Oct., 59
Provost, Jasper, June, 103
Purdy, Jeremiah, June, 109
Putman, Aaron J., March, 53
Putman, Teunis, March, 64
Putnam, Israel, March
Putnam, Josiah, Dec., 47
Putnam, William, June, 103

Quackenbush, Reynier, Oct., 56
Quarles, William, March, 60
Quimby (Queenbi), Aaron, Dec., 61

Ragsdale, Drury, June, 105
Raiborne, George, March, 66
Railsback, David, March, 66
Randall, Hopestill, June, 103
Randall, Ichabod, June, 103
Randall, John, June, 107
Randall, Joshua, June, 107
Randall, Thomas, June, 107
Randolph, John, June, 113
Randolph, Robert Fitz, June, 84
Ransom, Samuel, June, 111
Raymond, James, June, 79
Rayner, John, Oct., 56
Read, Daniel, Dec., 47
Read, Eleazer, June, 103
Read (Reed), Seth, Dec., 47
Rease, Frederick, June, 103
Redfield, James, March, 66
Reed, Benjamin, March, 66
Reed, Jacob, Dec., 52
Reed, James, Dec., 44

Sill, Thomas, March, 41
Singleton, Mathew, June, 114
Slade, William, June, 106
Slater, Benjamin, March, 60
Slaughter, Philip, Oct., 42
Slaymaker, Amos, Oct., 64
Slaymaker, Henry, Oct., 64
Slayton, Reuben, Oct., 44
Slemmons, William, Oct., 53
Sleeper, David, Dec., 54, 59
Slocum, Eleazer, Oct., 47
Slocum, Samuel, June, 106
Sloper, Ambrose, June, 115
Smeltzer, John, June, 71, 92
Smith, Amos, Dec., 59
Smith, David, June, 105
Smith, Ebenezer, June, 107
Smith, Eldad, March, 59
Smith, Enoch, Oct., 63
Smith, Hiram, June, 115
Smith, James, June, 98; March, 68
Smith, Matthew, June, 108
Smith, Nathan, March, 60, 73
Smith, Peter, March, 60
Smith, Philemon, March, 44
Smith, Ralph, March, 41
Smith, Richard, June, 86
Smith, Robert, Oct., 50
Smith, Seth, June, 92
Smith, William, June, 106
Snell, Jacob, Oct., 60
Snyder, George, Oct., 54
Soper, Oliver, June, 102
South, John, March, 69
Southard, Thomas, March, 65
Space, John, March, 55
Spalding, Dyer, June, 69
Spalding, Simeon, June, 108
Spangler, John, March, 51
Sparkman, William, March, 68
Sparks, Richard, June, 87
Spaulding, William, Oct., 41
Spaulding, Zebulon, June, 108
Specht, Christian, March, 59
Spencer, Perry, Oct., 51
Spink, Ishmael, March
Spink, John, June, 108; March, 69
Spinning, Benjamin, June, 108; Oct., 53
Spinning, Isaac, Dec., 60
Spofford, Thomas, March, 62
Sprague, Philip, Oct., 58
Springer, Knight, March, 63
Squier, Daniel, Oct., 59
Squire, Saxton, June, 108
St. Clair, James, June, 109
Stacy, Thomas, Dec., 43
Stacy (Stacey), William, Dec., 50
Stanbery, Samuel, Oct., 60
Statzer, David, June, 90

Stearns, John, Oct., 59
Steddiford, Garret, June, 110
Steel, David, June, 100; March
Steel, John, March, 54
Sterling, James, Dec., 62
Sterling, William, Dec., 60
Sternbergh, Nicholas, June, 97
Stevens, Elihu, Sr. & Jr., June, 84
Stevens, Elisha, June, 103; March, 66
Stevens, Thomas, Oct., 60
Stewart, Charles, June, 111
Stewart, David, March, 70
Stewart, Edward, Oct., 56
Stewart, George, March, 47
Stewart, James, Jr., June, 68
Stiles, Aaron, June, 74
Stillman, Joseph, March, 69
Stimson, George, June, 94
Stites, Benjamin, March, 67
Stitzer (Statger), David, Dec., 60
Stocking, George, March, 70
Stocking, Reuben, March, 70
Stockton, David, June, 78
Stone, John, June, 112
Stone, Moses, Jr., June, 100; Oct., 60
Stone, Silas, March, 48
Stone, Windsor, March, 70
Stong, Philip, June, 109
Storm, Jacob, June, 109
Storrs, Dan, March, 53
Stout, Daniel, June, 72
Stout, Jesse, March, 51
Stout, Samuel, Jr., June, 87
Stout, Thomas, March, 70
Strong, Adonijah, June, 110
Strong, Horatio, June, 110
Strong, John, June, 115
Strong, Joseph, Oct., 40
Strong, Josiah, March, 66
Studley, Consider, March, 70
Sumner, Dempsey, June, 70
Sumner, William, March, 70
Sumpter, William, March, 54
Supplee, Isaac, March, 68
Sutton, Peter, Oct., 58
Sutton, Richard, Dec., 57
Swan, Francis, June, 110
Sweeney, Moses, June, 110
Sweet, Benoni, Dec., 57
Sydnor, Fortunatus, Oct., 46

Talcott, William, June, 113
Talema (Tallman), Thennis, Oct., 61
Tanner, Benjamin, June, 110
Tappan, James, June, 69
Tarr, Daniel Barber, June, 108
Tatnall, Joseph, June, 72, 113; Dec., 45, 60
Taylor, George, June, 91, 104
Taylor, James, June, 91

Taylor, Jasher, March, 71
Taylor, John, June, 92
Taylor, Jonathan, March, 71
Taylor, Joshua, Dec., 48
Taylor, Nathan, Dec., 60
Taylor, Richard, June, 91, 99
Taylor, Robert, March, 61
Taylor, William, Sr. & Jr., March, 71
Teagarden, William, March, 71
Teddeman, Hazard, Dec., 49
Terry, Nathaniel, Dec., 61
Terry, Thomas, June, 100, 116; Dec., 56
Thatcher, Asa, June, 111
Thayer, Enoch, March, 63
Thompson, Roger, March, 41
Thomas, Benjamin, June, 85
Thomas, William, June, 73
Thompson, Timothy, March, 43
Thomson, William, March, 62
Thorn, Samuel, June, 76
Thorndike, Larkin, June, 94
Thorpe, Eliphalet, Dec., 60
Thrift, Charles, June, 72
Thwing, Nicholas, Oct., 60
Tice, Henry, Dec., 48
Titus, David, Oct., 60
Todd, John, Oct., 42
Todd, Thomas, June, 89
Tolman, John, Oct., 39
Tomlinson, Eliphalet, March, 72
Tomlinson, James, June, 71; Dec., 44
Tomlinson, Noah, March, 72
Tomlinson, Samuel, June, 71; Dec., 44
Torrance, Robert, Dec., 61; March, 43
Torrey, Samuel, Oct., 39
Towne, John, March, 72
Townley, Matthias, Oct., 61
Townsend, Timothy, March, 72
Trabue, John James, June, 86
Treat, Charles, June, 108
Tredwell, Samuel, March, 57
Tremper, Michael, March, 43
Troutman, John Peter Christian, June, 112
Trowbridge, John, Dec., 55
Trowbridge, Newman, June, 112; Oct., 62
Truxton, Thomas, Dec., 59
Tucker, Nicholas, June, 94, 108
Tufts, John, June, 105
Turney, John, Oct., 48
Tuyman, James, March, 74
Twiss, Robert, Dec., 52
Tyler, Ebenezer, June, 112; March, 49, 62

Underwood, Jonas, Dec., 59
Upshaw, James, June, 112

Vail, Benjamin, Oct., 40
Van Auken, John, June, 112
Van Buskirk, Isaac, June, 116

Van Cleve, John, Dec., 58
Van Dyke, John, Oct., 61
Van Geison, Hendrick, Oct., 61; March, 72
Van Hoesen, Garrett, June, 113
Van Hoevenbergh, Rudolph, Dec., 61
Van Metre, John, June, 110
Van Tuyl, Abraham, June, 107
Van Voorhis, Daniel, Oct., 61
Vance, Robert, June, 94; March, 63
Vedder, Arent Simon, June, 115
Veghte, Garrit, June, 80; March, 49
Vincent, John, March, 72
Vose, James, June, 113
Vreeland, Garrett G., Oct., 61

Wafel, Henry, March, 58
Waggoner, John, Oct., 51
Wagoner, George, June, 113
Wagoner, Philip, June, 85
Wakefield, Luther, June, 104
Wakeman, William, March, 51
Waldo, Edward, March, 50
Wales, Jacob, June, 99
Walker, Abel, March, 52, 73
Walker, Henry, June, 82; March, 50
Walker, Jacob, Oct., 62
Walker, James Adair, Oct., 62
Walker, John, March, 73
Walker, Seth, Sr. & Jr., June, 84
Wallace (Wallis), Ebenezer, Dec., 59
Walters, John, March, 49
Weaver, Henry, Oct., 62
Ward, Jabez, March, 73
Ward, Jedediah, June, 113
Ward, John, June, 113; Oct., 58
Ward, Rufus, Oct., 52
Ward, William, June, 106
Warne, John, March, 58
Warner, Benjamin, Dec., 45
Warren, John, Oct., 63
Warren, Thomas, Oct., 51
Waterman, Arannah, March, 63
Waterman, John, June, 68; March, 41
Waters, William, June, 74
Watkins, Elias, June, 114
Watkins, William, Oct., 46
Watrous, Samuel, June, 90
Watson, John, June, 87; Oct., 48
Waugh, James, March, 46
Weaver, Jacob, June, 69
Weaver, Nicholas, March, 69
Webb, Stephen, Oct., 60
Webster, Ebenezer, March, 46
Webster, John, Oct., 50
Webster, John Bateman, March, 76
Webster, Simeon, March, 73
Weed, Jacob, Oct., 59
Weeks, Stephen, March, 55
Weeks (Wickes), Stephen, Dec., 50

Weiant (Wygant), John, Dec., 62
Welles, Noah, June, 80
Wellinger, John Jacob, March
Wellington, Thaddeus, March, 74
Wells, James, June, 116
Wells, Samuel, March, 61
Welty, John, Oct., 58
Wentworth, Jedediah, Dec., 61
Wentworth, Shubael, June, 82
Wescott, Richard, Dec., 45; March, 71
Wesson, Ephraim, Oct., 43
Westcott, Jonathan W., Oct., 44
Westcott, Samuel, June, 89
Wetherill, John, Dec., 57
Wheeler, Zenas, March, 74
Wheelock, Eleazer, Oct., 52
Whipple, Benijah, June, 88
Whitcomb, John, Oct., 63
Whitcomb, Reuben, June, 80
White, Benjamin, March, 74
White, Cornelius, June, 102
White, Enoch, Dec., 62
Whiteside, Thomas, June, 95
Whiting, Francis, March, 73
Whitlock, John, March, 65
Whitman, Isaac, Dec., 62; March, 74
Whitney, John, June, 84, 114; Oct., 63; Mar.,
    74
Whitney, Joshua, June, 89
Whitney, Nathaniel, June, 82
Whittemore, Jeremiah, March, 74
Whittemore, William, June, 88
Whritenour, Peter, Oct., 63; March, 74
Wilbur, Jesse, June, 79
Wilder, Abell, March, 75
Wilder, Nathaniel, June, 89
Willard, Elias Willialer, June, 96
Willett, Samuel, March, 62
Williams, Aaron, March, 75
Williams, Abraham, June, 70
Williams, David, March, 41
Williams, Elisha, Dec., 58
Williams, Gideon, June, 103
Williams, Henry, Dec., 47
Williams, Samuel, Dec., 57
Williamson, John, June, 115

Willcox, Samuel, June, 114
Willis, Russel, June, 115
Willis, William, June, 88
Willoughby, Edlyne, Dec., 62; March, 75
Wilmore, John, March, 75
Wilson, Joseph, March, 50
Wilson, Moses, Oct., 54
Wilson, Thomas, June, 115
Wilson, William, March, 75
Winchell, James, March, 53
Wing, Thomas, Oct., 50
Wolcott, Elisha, June, 102
Wolcott, Justus, June, 81
Wood, Ebenezer, March, 72
Wolcott, Roger, June, 105
Wood, Barzillai (Bazela), June, 116; Dec., 62;
    March, 76
Woodbridge, Benjamin, March, 76
Woodbury, John, Oct., 63
Woodbury, Jonathan, March, 71
Woodcock, David, March, 70
Wooden, James, March, 57
Woodhull, Nathaniel, March, 62
Woodman, Nathan, Oct., 55
Woodmansee, James, March, 45
Woodruff, Gurdon, March, 76
Woodruff, Josiah, June, 88
Woodruff, Samuel, Sr. & Jr., June, 115
Woods, Joseph, March, 64
Woodson, Tarleton, June, 115
Woolworth, Phineas, Dec., 61
Worthington, Thomas, March, 76
Wunderlick, Daniel, March, 69
Wyman, Paul, June, 77
Wynne, Jonathan, Oct., 64

Yager, John, June, 116
Yansen, Henry, June, 97
Yarrington, William, June, 116
Yerkes, Harman, March, 61
Young, William, Dec., 49
Youngman, John, Dec., 62
Youngs, David, June, 116

Zehring, Christian, Oct., 52
Zinn, Jacob, June, 91, 113

Washington I. L. Adams

OFFICIAL BULLETIN

OF THE

National Society
of the Sons of the American Revolution

Organized April 30, 1889

Incorporated by
Act of Congress, June 9, 1906

President General
W. I. LINCOLN ADAMS
Montclair, New Jersey

Published at Washington, D. C., in June, October, December, and March.
Entered as second-class matter, May 7, 1906, at the post-office at Washington, D. C., under the act of July 16, 1894.

Volume XVII	JUNE, 1922	Number 1

The OFFICIAL BULLETIN records action by the General Officers, the Board of Trustees, the Executive and other National Committees, lists of members deceased and of new members, and important doings of State Societies. In order that the OFFICIAL BULLETIN may be up to date, and to insure the preservation in the National Society archives of a complete history of the doings of the entire organization, State Societies and local Chapters are requested to communicate promptly to the Secretary General written or printed accounts of all meetings or celebrations, to forward copies of all notices, circulars, and other printed matter issued by them, and to notify him at once of dates of death of members.

FOREWORD TO OUR COMPATRIOTS

The Officers of the National Society and the Editors of the BULLETIN, following the direction of the National Congress and the Executive Committee, have discontinued the Year Book and instead have enlarged the BULLETIN to cover, to a certain extent at least, the information that was contained in the Year Book, which reached but a small proportion of our members. On account of the shortness of the time between the National Congress, held in Springfield, Mass., May 15 and 16, and the issuance of this BULLETIN, which, under the postal regulations, must be mailed before the end of June, this issue must necessarily be somewhat hastily compiled, and no doubt some errors have been made. However, it will be the endeavor of the Officers and Editors in the remaining issues of this year to make the BULLETIN a complete, interesting, and live record of all the matters pertaining to the best that is in this Society. The co-operation of compatriots is cordially invited to assist the Editors in this work, and our members are assured that it will be the endeavor of those in charge to give space and prominence to all matters that affect the best interests of the Society of the Sons of the American Revolution.

PURPOSES AND OBJECTS OF THE S. A. R.

(Extracts from Constitution)

The purposes and objects of this Society are declared to be patriotic, historical, and educational, and shall include those intended or designed to perpetuate the memory of the men who, by their services or sacrifices during the war of the American Revolution, achieved the independence of the American people; to unite and promote fellowship among their descendants; to inspire them and the community at large with a more profound reverence for the principles of the government founded by our forefathers; to encourage historical research in relation to the American Revolution; to acquire and preserve the records of the individual services of the patriots of the war, as well as documents, relics, and landmarks; to mark the scenes of the Revolution by appropriate memorials; to celebrate the anniversaries of the prominent events of the war and of the Revolutionary period; to foster true patriotism; to maintain and extend the institutions of American freedom, and to carry out the purposes expressed in the preamble of the Constitution of our country and the injunctions of Washington in his farewell address to the American people.

Qualifications for Membership

Any man shall be eligible to membership in the Society who, being of the age of twenty-one years or over and a citizen of good repute in the community, is the lineal descendant of an ancestor who was at all times unfailing in his loyalty to, and rendered active service in, the cause of American Independence, either as an officer, soldier, seaman, marine, militiaman or minute man, in the armed forces of the Continental Congress, or of any one of the several Colonies or States, or as a Signer of the Declaration of Independence, or as a member of a Committee of Safety or Correspondence, or as a member of any Continental, Provincial, or Colonial Congress or Legislature, or as a recognized patriot who performed actual service by overt acts of resistance to the authority of Great Britain.

Application for membership is made on standard blanks furnished by the State Societies. These blanks call for the place and date of birth and of death of the Revolutionary ancestor and the year of birth, of marriage, and of death of ancestors in intervening generations. Membership is based on one original claim; additional claims are filed on supplemental papers. The applications and supplementals are made in duplicate.

GENERAL OFFICERS ELECTED AT THE SPRINGFIELD CONGRESS, MAY 16, 1922

President General:

W. I. LINCOLN ADAMS, Montclair, New Jersey.

Vice-Presidents General:

HARRY T. LORD, Manchester, New Hampshire.

New England (Maine, New Hampshire, Vermont, Massachusetts, Rhode Island, and Connecticut).

PHILIP F. LARNER, 918 F Street N. W., Washington, District of Columbia.

Middle and Coast District (New York, New Jersey, Pennsylvania, Delaware, Maryland, District of Columbia, Virginia, North Carolina, South Carolina, Georgia, and Florida).

LOUIS A. BOWMAN, 30 North La Salle Street, Chicago, Illinois.

Mississippi Valley, East District (Michigan, Wisconsin, Illinois, Indiana, Ohio, West Virginia, Kentucky, Tennessee, Alabama, and Mississippi).

HENRY B. HAWLEY, Des Moines, Iowa.

Mississippi Valley, West District (Minnesota, North Dakota, South Dakota, Nebraska, Iowa, Kansas, Missouri, Oklahoma, Arkansas, Louisiana, and Texas).

GEORGE ALBERT SMITH, Utah Savings & Trust Building, Salt Lake City, Utah.

Mountain and Pacific Coast District (Montana, Idaho, Wyoming, Nevada, Utah, Colorado, Arizona, New Mexico, Oregon, Washington, California, Hawaii, and Philippines).

Secretary General:

FRANK BARTLETT STEELE, 183 St. James Place, Buffalo, New York.

Registrar General:

FRANCIS BARNUM CULVER, 2203 North Charles Street, Baltimore, Maryland; 918 F Street N. W., Washington, District of Columbia.

Treasurer General:

GEORGE McK. ROBERTS, Room 2126, 120 Broadway, New York City.

Historian General:

JOSEPH B. DOYLE, Steubenville, Ohio.

Chancellor General:

EUGENE C. BONNIWELL, City Court Building, Philadelphia, Pennsylvania.

Genealogist General:

WALTER K. WATKINS, 9 Ashburton Place, Boston, Massachusetts.

Chaplain General:

Rev. FREDERICK W. PERKINS, D. D., 27 Deer Cove, Lynn, Massachusetts.

BOARD OF TRUSTEES

The General Officers, together with one member from each State Society, constitute the Board of Trustees of the National Society. The following Trustees for the several States were elected at the Springfield Congress, May 16, 1922, to serve until their successors are elected at the Congress to be held at Nashville, Tenn., in May, 1923:

Alabama, (vacant); Arizona, W. B. Twitchell, Phœnix; Arkansas, George W. Clark, Little Rock; California, Seabury C. Mastick, New York City; Colorado, Victor E. Keyes, Denver; Connecticut, Herbert H. White, Hartford; Delaware, Hon. Horace Wilson, Wilmington; District of Columbia, Albert D. Spangler, Washington; Far Eastern Society, H. Lawrence Noble, Manila; Florida, Dr. F. G. Renshaw, Pensacola; Society in France, (vacant); Hawaiian Society, Donald S. Bowman, Honolulu; Georgia, Allan Waters, Atlanta; Idaho, M. A. Wood, Boise; Illinois, Dorr E. Felt, Chicago; Indiana, Charles C. Jewett, Terre Haute; Iowa, Elmer E. Wentworth, State Center; Kansas, John M. Meade, Topeka; Kentucky, George T. Wood, Louisville; Louisiana, Col. C. Robert Churchill, New Orleans; Maine, William B. Berry, Gardiner; Maryland, Hon. Henry Stockbridge, Baltimore; Massachusetts, George Hale Nutting, Boston; Michigan, Albert M. Henry, Detroit; Minnesota, Charles E. Rittenhouse, Minneapolis; Mississippi, Hon. Gordon G. Lyell, Jackson; Missouri, George R. Merrill, St. Louis; Montana, Marcus Whritenour, Helena; Nebraska, Benjamin F. Bailey, Lincoln; Nevada, (vacant); New Hampshire, Hon. Harry T. Lord, Manchester; New Jersey, Charles Symmes Kiggins, Elizabeth; New Mexico, George G. Klock, Albuquerque; New York, Louis Annin Ames, New York; North Carolina, (vacant); North Dakota, Howard E. Simpson, Grand Forks; Ohio, Hon. Warren G. Harding, Washington, D. C.; Oklahoma, W. A. Jennings, Oklahoma City; Oregon, Wallace McCamant, Portland; Pennsylvania, Col. R. W. Guthrie, Pittsburgh; Rhode Island, Hon. Arthur P. Sumner, Providence; South Carolina, (vacant); South Dakota, F. M. Mills, Sioux Falls; Tennessee, Leland Hume, Nashville; Texas, C. B. Dorchester, Sherman; Utah, Daniel S. Spencer, Salt Lake City; Vermont, William Jeffrey, Montpelier; Virginia, Arthur B. Clarke, Richmond; Washington, Ernest B. Hussey, Seattle; Wisconsin, Walter H. Wright, Milwaukee; Wyoming, Warren Richardson, Cheyenne.

WASHINGTON IRVING LINCOLN ADAMS

President General

Our newly elected President General, Major WASHINGTON IRVING LINCOLN ADAMS, of Montclair, N. J., was born in New York City on Washington's Birthday.

He is a direct descendant of Henry Adams, of Braintree, who came from England, with his eight sons, in 1630, and who gave to the country two Presidents, and Samuel Adams, the patriot. Major Adams' ancestor in England was related to the Washington family there before General Washington's ancestor came to this country. He is a member of the Sons of the American Revolution by virtue of descent from five qualifying ancestors.

Major Adams was President of the New Jersey State Society for two terms, and it was during one of his terms as President that the National Society held its large and very successful Congress in Newark in 1916. He was one of the founders and for two years was President of the Montclair Chapter, in his home town. Last year he served the National Society most faithfully as a Director General, making an official trip cross the continent last summer and acting as chairman of important national committees. He made the address on "Washington," by means of the Westinghouse radio apparatus, on Washington's Birthday, this year, to an audience estimated at over three hundred thousand listening countrymen.

Major Adams has been active in various patriotic and public organizations for many years. He was elected Governor of the Society of Colonial Wars, in the State of New Jersey, at its annual court, in Lakewood, last May, and he was one of the founders and for two years Governor of the New Jersey State Society of the Order of the Founders and Patriots of America. He is Treasurer General of the Huguenot Society of America, a trustee of the New Jersey Historical Society, and a hereditary member of the Washington Association of New Jersey. He is also a member of the Society of the War of 1812, the New England Society, and the St. Nicholas Society.

In 1916 Major Adams attended the military training camp at Plattsburg, and, passing the examination of the War Department, was commissioned a major in the Officers' Reserve Corps of the United States Army on January 8, 1917. When America entered the World War he was called to the colors and served actively for more than a year. For a number of months he was officer-in-charge of the Finance Division of the Department of the East, and as such he daily disbursed millions of dollars in the purchase of supplies for our troops overseas.

Major Adams had two sons and a son-in-law in active service. One son, Lieutenant Briggs Kilburn Adams, of the Royal Flying Corps, who was killed in France, was the author of a remarkable series of letters, which were published in the *Atlantic Monthly* for October, 1918, under the title "The American Spirit," and subsequently were collected in book form, in which they created a deep and widespread impression.

He is a member of the Society of Foreign Wars, the Society of American Officers, the American Legion, and the Army and Navy Club of America. He was chairman of the New Jersey delegation of the American Legion at its first national convention, held in Minneapolis in 1919.

In business Major Adams is a banker and a printer; in politics, a lifelong Republican. He was a Presidential Elector in New Jersey in 1916 and has been a delegate to the National Republican Convention. He was his party's nominee for Congress in the Tenth District of New Jersey in 1912.

Major Adams is a Thirty-second Degree Mason and an Elk. He is a director and officer in a number of banks and business corporations, and has held many positions of honor and trust in his home town of Montclair and in the State of New Jersey.

HARRY TRUE LORD

Vice-President General for New England District

HARRY TRUE LORD, elected Vice-President General for New England District at the Springfield Congress, May 16, 1922, was born at Manchester, N. H., May 7, 1863. He is the son of Harrison Dearborn Lord and Juliaette True Lord and a descendant of Hosea Sturtevant, a pensioner of the Revolutionary War, and of Edward Dearborn, who fought at Bunker Hill. He was educated in the public schools of Manchester, N. H., and was graduated from Dartmouth College in the class of '87, after which he read law in Manchester and was admitted to the New Hampshire bar in 1894.

Mr. Lord has represented his ward in the New Hampshire Legislature several times, was President of the New Hampshire State Senate in 1909 and 1910, and member of the Governor's Council in 1911 and 1912. He served as a member of the local board under the selective service law, during the World War, from June, 1917, to April, 1919, for the most of that period devoting his whole time and giving the use of his office to the service. He is a member of the Masonic bodies, Calumet Club, and treasurer of the Manchester Historic Association. He joined this Society in 1914, was a delegate to the National Congress at Hartford, Conn., in 1920, and Springfield, Mass., in 1922, and is a Past President of the New Hampshire Society. His wife, Florence M. Lord, is a member of Molly Stark Chapter, Daughters of the American Revolution.

PHILIP F. LARNER

Vice-President General for Middle and Coast District

PHILIP F. LARNER, after the service of two terms in 1919 and 1920 as Secretary General and Registrar General, was elected Vice-President General at Buffalo, N. Y., May 17, 1921, and re-elected at Springfield, Mass., May 16, 1922, and is a native of the City of Washington, D. C., as also were his father and grandfather. His great-grandfather, Jacob Gideon, Jr., removed to Washington from Philadelphia, Pa., about the time the location of the National Capital was established.

Mr. Larner is a graduate of the original Emerson Institute, located in Washington for many years and a well-known educational institution; afterward a graduate of the Law College of the Columbian University and a member of the bar of the Supreme Court of the District of Columbia. Later he has been actively connected for many years with various business organizations in Washington. He is a member of the University and City Clubs, as well as several civic and religious organizations.

Mr. Larner became a member of the District of Columbia Society, Sons of the American Revolution, in 1891, his ancestor being his great-great-grandfather, Jacob Gideon, Sr., who enlisted at Valley Forge and served with the Pennsylvania troops in the battles at Guilford, Eutaw Springs, Cowpens, and Yorktown.

Mr. Larner was for a long term of years Treasurer and afterwards President of the District of Columbia Society, and has been a delegate from that Society to numerous annual congresses of the National Society. His wife, Fannie D. Larner (deceased), was a charter member of the Daughters of the American Revolution, having the national number 185 in that organization. His daughter, Mrs. Albert J. Gore, is an active member of the Daughters of the American Revolution and the founder and first regent of the Captain Molly Pitcher Chapter, Daughters of the American Revolution, in the City of Washington. His father, Noble D. Larner, at one time President of the District of Columbia Society, died in 1903, while holding the office of Vice-President General in the National Society, Sons of the American Revolution.

LOUIS A. BOWMAN

Vice-President General, Mississippi Valley, East District

Louis A. Bowman, elected Vice-President General for the Mississippi Valley, East District, at the Springfield Congress, May 16, 1922, is a native of Rock Island, Ill., removing to Chicago while still a boy and becoming actively identified with the civic, patriotic, and moral forces of the city at an early age. He became a member of the Sons of the American Revolution in 1903 and was elected Secretary of the Illinois Society in 1909, serving continuously since. During this time he has attended every National Congress of the Society save one and has served on various national committees. He was admitted to the bar in 1901 and is assistant attorney for the Northern Trust Company of Chicago.

In the Association of Commerce he served three years as chairman of the Banking Section and four years as a member of the Illinois Committee. He is Secretary of the Lions Club of Chicago, member of the Union League, Hamilton, and other clubs and treasurer of several civic and educational organizations. He has been an officer in the Young Men's Christian Association for many years, serving for nineteen years as Secretary of the State Association of Illinois and for fifteen years a director of the Central Association of Chicago. He is actively identified with the Presbyterian denomination, serving as elder and treasurer in his home church at Oak Park and as a director of various denominational institutions and as a commissioner to the General Assembly.

His associates in the Illinois Society have referred to his work there as characterized by zeal, courage, initiative, enthusiasm, and efficient leadership.

HENRY B. HAWLEY

Vice-President General, Mississippi Valley, West District

Henry B. Hawley, of Des Moines, Iowa, elected at Buffalo, 1921, and re-elected at Springfield, Mass., May 16, 1922, was born on a farm in New York State, near Warsaw. Mr. Hawley began life on his own account as a school teacher, followed later by a short but successful period as a business man, where the field of insurance attracted and held his interest and attention. Aside from insurance, his position in the business, political, and social world of Des Moines is commanding. A man of initiative and with altruistic principles, he has been extremely active along all lines of social betterment, and carried with him from Buffalo, where the first charity organization society in America was established, those ideas of philanthropy which resulted in the Associated Charities of Des Moines and have permeated the entire group of organizations which are affiliated in the work of human rehabilitation in that community. He was recently made a Life President of the Associated Charities of Des Moines. Mr. Hawley is Past President of the Iowa State Society, having been a member since April, 1898. Among the public-spirited personal efforts of Mr. Hawley in the direction of patriotic education we note his presentation of a medal each year to the High School at Warsaw, New York, given to the pupil attaining the highest term mark in American history. This presentation has been made annually since 1911. Mr. Hawley stands high in banking circles in Des Moines, is a member of the Bankers' Club and a bank director.

GEORGE ALBERT SMITH

Vice-President General

GEORGE ALBERT SMITH, member of the Utah Society, was elected Vice-President General at Springfield, Mass., May 16, 1922. Born in Salt Lake City, April 4, 1870. He is the son of John Henry and Sarah Farr Smith. His grandfather, George A. Smith, was one of the leaders in the first company of pioneers to settle in the Rocky Mountain region. This group was composed of one hundred and forty-three men, three women, and two children. They were the first Anglo-Saxons in America to raise crops by irrigation. This little group was the nucleus from which has come the settlement of the Commonwealths of Utah, Idaho, Nevada, California, and Arizona.

George Albert Smith is a descendant of Edward Winslow, of the *Mayflower*, who later became Governor of the Plymouth Colony. Among his ancestors are also the original families of Libbey, Freeman, Hovey, and Lord, all of New England. Some of the Revolutionary ancestors of George Albert Smith are: Samuel Smith, Chairman of the Committee of Safety at Topsfield, Mass.; Asahel Smith, son of Samuel Smith, who was also of Topsfield, Mass.; Jonathan Farr, private; Timothy Chase, aid to General Washington, and Richard Lyman, orderly sergeant to General Putnam.

Having grown up in a pioneer country, George Albert Smith has witnessed much of the development of western America, in which, with many of his kindred, he has taken a very prominent part. While his scholastic training was received in the common schools of Utah and in the State University, his education has also been greatly enlarged by travel, taken extensively, both in Europe and America.

Mr. Smith was appointed Receiver of Public Money and Disbursing Agent for Utah by President McKinley, and later he was reappointed to this same position by President Roosevelt. During the World War he was a member of the Utah State Council of Defense and he was also Chairman of the Armenian and Syrian Relief.

Mr. Smith has served as Chaplain of the Utah Society of the Sons of the American Revolution, has served repeatedly as a member of the Board of Managers, and has been twice elected President. In the Congresses of the National Society he has frequently been Utah's representative.

Mr. Smith is president, vice-president, or director of some of Utah's largest banking and commercial enterprises. One of these institutions is the Zion's Co-operative Mercantile Institution, the first department store in America and today the largest wholesale and retail house in the Rocky Mountain region. Mr. Smith is Chairman of the Executive Committee of the *Deseret News,* the oldest newspaper west of the Rocky Mountains.

George Albert Smith has served as both president and vice-president of the International Irrigation Congress, as president of the International Dry Farm Congress, as president of the International Farm Congress, and at this writing he is vice-president of the Western States Reclamation Association, which organization comprises the thirteen Western States which are so greatly interested in the work of the United States Reclamation Service.

In the Church of Jesus Christ of Latter-Day Saints, of which Mr. Smith is a member, he has served in many important capacities. At the close of the World War he was made president of the Latter-Day Saints European Mission, with headquarters in England. Belonging to this mission, there are conferences or church organizations in nearly all of the European countries. Mr. Smith is a member of the Council of the Twelve of his church, which means he is one of the fifteen men who stand at the head of this organization, and he is also General Superintendent of the Young Men's Mutual Improvement Association of the same church, which organization has a membership of nearly fifty thousand young men, most of whom are in America.

FRANK BARTLETT STEELE

Secretary General

FRANK BARTLETT STEELE, elected Secretary General May 17, 1921, at the Buffalo Congress, and re-elected at Springfield, Mass., May 16, 1922, was born in Buffalo, New York, March 28, 1864. He is the son of Charles Gould Steele and Harriet Virginia Snyder, and great-grandson of Zenas Barker, who fought in the Revolutionary War with the New York troops in the battle of Oriskany. Mr. Steele was graduated from the State Normal School of Buffalo and studied law in the offices of George Clinton, grandson of De Witt Clinton. Mr. Steele joined the Buffalo Chapter of the Empire State Society in 1897 and became its Secretary in 1901, which office he has held continuously since. He has been a delegate to every National Congress since 1906, except those held at Denver in 1907 and Portland in 1915, and has been on a number of important national committees.

Mr. Steele, in co-operation with the School Department of the City of Buffalo and the Daughters of the American Revolution, has been active in the work of Americanization, the field for this work being almost unlimited in Buffalo, due to its large foreign population.

Mr. Steele, shortly after his admission to the bar, became the Clerk of the Superior Court of Buffalo, and was thereafter transferred into the Supreme Court of the State of New York. He was at one time clerk of the Board of Supervisors of Erie County.

He is a member of the Society of Mayflower Descendants in line from Governor William Bradford.

During the World War Mr. Steele was made Executive Secretary of the Home Defense Committee of Erie County, a body created by the State of New York, and during this period gave his time unstintedly to the many activities and responsibilities that were placed upon this committee by the National and State Governments. Under a statute of the State of New York creating local historians, Mayor Buck appointed Mr. Steele Historian of the City of Buffalo, and in this capacity he assisted in writing and compiling the History of the City of Buffalo and Erie County in the World War; also, at the suggestion of the State Historian, Mr. Steele has made a complete survey of the records and archives of Buffalo and Erie County, and upon his recommendations steps are now being taken by the City Commissioners to improve the conditions under which these records are being preserved.

Mr. Steele married Helen Cleveland Varian, of Titusville, Pa., in 1896. Mrs. Steele is also of Revolutionary ancestry, descending from the Atlees of Pennsylvania, the Varians of New York, and Litchfields of Connecticut. She was a daughter of Col. William Varian, Surgeon on the staff of Gen. Gordon Granger during the Civil War, now buried in Arlington Cemetery.

GEORGE McKENZIE ROBERTS

Treasurer General

GEORGE McKENZIE ROBERTS, of New York City, elected Treasurer General at the Springfield Congress, May 16, 1922, is the son of George Simon and Florence Loise (McKenzie) Roberts, and was born December 28, 1886, in Vergennes, Vt. He is assistant treasurer of the International General Electric Company, Inc., 120 Broadway, New York City, and has been connected with the General Electric Company and its subsidiary company since 1901, except for the period from 1907 to 1913, when he was with the Bradstreet Company, in New Haven, Conn. He is a member of the Empire State Society, Sons of the American Revolution, and a former Third Vice-President thereof. He is now on its Board of Managers and a member of the Finance Committee. He was originally a member of the Colonel Cornelius Van Dyck Chapter, Schenectady, N. Y., of which he was Second and later First Vice-President and is now an honorary member of that Chapter. He is Secretary of the New York Chapter, the largest Chapter in the National organization, and was a delegate to the National Congresses of 1920, 1921, and 1922 from that Chapter. His Revolutionary ancestors were Sergeant Joseph Convers and Private Daniel Cummings, of Massachusetts; Sergeant Daniel Tallmadge, Corporal George McKenzie, and Privates John Roberts and Eli Denslow, of Connecticut.

Mr. Roberts is also a member of the Sons of the Revolution in the State of New York and of its Philip Livingston Chapter of Albany, N. Y.; also of the Society of Colonial Wars, in the State of New York, and of the Governor Thomas Dudley Family Association of Boston, Mass., membership in both of these being through descent from Governor Thomas Dudley, of Massachusetts Bay Colony. He is also a member of the New England Society in the City of New York, the Vermont Society of New York City, the New York State Historical Association, the National Geographic Society, and the Denslow Family

Association; also of the Schenectady County (N. Y.) Historical Society, of which he is a trustee and former recording secretary. He is also a member of the National Association of Credit Men and of the Supervisory Committee of its Foreign Credit Interchange Bureau, as well as a member of the New York Credit Men's Association.

He is interested in historical and genealogical subjects and has prepared a genealogy of the Denslow Family which will soon be published. All of the living members of his family are members of either the S. A. R. or the D. A. R., his father being a member of the New York Chapter, Empire State Society; his brother, Wilson Burr Roberts, of the General David Humphreys Branch, No. 1, Connecticut Society, and his grandmother, Mrs. Helen Rebecca (Denslow) McKenzie, of the Mary Clap Wooster Chapter, D. A. R., of New Haven, Conn.

FRANCIS BARNUM CULVER

Registrar General

FRANCIS BARNUM CULVER, author and publisher, elected Registrar General at the National Congress at Springfield, Mass., in May, 1922, was born at Baltimore, Md., on November 12, 1868.

He is the son of the late William Edward Culver, a private banker and capitalist of Louisville, Ky., for many years prior to the Civil War, by his second wife, Jane McClintock, a native of Pennsylvania.

The father of the Registrar General was born near Wilkes-Barre, Pa., in 1803, and removed with his parents to Ohio in 1809, but on attaining his majority took up his residence in Bourbon County, Kentucky, and was appointed by Postmaster General John McLean, in 1825, postmaster at Centerville, being, perhaps, the youngest postmaster at that time in the service.

On the paternal side Mr. Culver traces back to the Puritan ancestor, Edward Culver (grandson of Rev. Edward Culver, Episcopal rector of St. Mary's, Harmondsworth, Middlesex, under Queen Elizabeth), who came to Boston in 1635, but shortly afterward signed the Dedham Covenant of 1636, and married, at Dedham, Mass., Ann Ellyce, this marriage being the second, in order, to be entered upon the First Church Register of Dedham by the Rev. John Allyn. Subsequently the family removed to Roxbury, Mass., and in 1652 to New London County, Connnecticut.

Mr. Culver's paternal grandfather was Solomon Culver, born at Litchfield, Conn., in 1760, who removed with his elder brother, Captain Nathaniel Culver, to New York shortly before the Revolution. At the age of seventeen years Solomon Culver was enrolled in Colonel William Bradford Whiting's (17th New York) Regiment of King's District, Albany (now Columbia) County, which was attached to the Division of General Schuyler, embracing Berkshire County, Massachusetts, and Albany County, New York, militia. He served at Fort George and Fort Edward and was in the American retreat from General Burgoyne's advance toward Saratoga, where the battle took place that resulted in the capitulation of Burgoyne. Solomon Culver married Lodamia Burr, of Farmington, Conn., and through these two families the Registrar General is descended from such New England forebears as Backus, Burr, Pratt, Hibberd, Hinman, Stiles, Cadwell, Stebbins, Butler; and from Hon. John Clarke, Royal Charterer of Connecticut in 1662, and from Rev. Samuel Stone, who, along with

Rev. Thomas Hooker, emigrated from England to Cambridge, Mass., and in 1636 removed to Hartford, Conn., founding the First Church in that settlement. Through his mother Mr. Culver is a descendant of William Sheild, of Kent County, Md., who was one of the famous "Maryland 400" at the battle of Long Island.

Francis Barnum Culver was graduated from the Johns Hopkins University in the class of 1889, receiving the degree of B. A. He has devoted a great part of his life to genealogical and historical pursuits, has contributed numerous articles on these subjects to magazines, and is the author of certain books, such as "Blooded Horses of Colonial Days, or Classic Horse Matches in America before the Revolution" and a "Historical Sketch of the Militia of Maryland."

Mr. Culver is a member and officer in several patriotic societies, including the Scions of Colonial Cavaliers, Colonial Wars, Sons of the American Revolution, War of 1812, Order of Washington, Order of La Fayette, Knights of the Golden Horseshoe, as well as of the English-speaking Union and the Johns Hopkins Club, and represents his class as chairman in the Alumni Association of the Johns Hopkins University. He is Registrar of the Maryland Society, Sons of the American Revolution.

JOSEPH B. DOYLE

Historian General

JOSEPH B. DOYLE, elected Historian General at the 33d National Congress, at Springfield, Mass., on May 16, 1922, is a descendant of Benjamin Doyle who was born in Loudoun County, Va., in 1762. The latter's wife, Patience, born in 1771, was the daughter of John McGuire, of Winchester, Va., a member of the George Rogers Clark Expedition to the Ohio country in 1778-9, which secured the Northwest Territory to the Union.

The family were among the pioneer settlers of Steubenville, Ohio, going there from West Middletown, Pa., in 1798. John B. Doyle, son of Benjamin, was then four years of age; his son, Joseph C., was born at Steubenville on September 26, 1823, and the subject of this sketch dates from September 10, 1849. His life has been comparatively uneventful. Graduating from the Steubenville High School in his sixteenth year, a commercial college in Pittsburgh a few months later, he studied law and was admitted to the bar on September 29, 1870, being then just past 21 years of age. Shortly after he took up journalism, which he followed closely for thirty-four years. After a season of rest and travel abroad, he was appointed County Law Librarian, which position he still holds, to a certain extent keeping up his journalistic and other literary work. His leading productions have been: Memorial Life of Hon. Edwin M. Stanton, General Frederick William Von Steuben and the American Revolution, The Church in Eastern Ohio, Twentieth Century History of Jefferson County, with numerous minor publications.

Mr. Doyle has been a participant in local activities, such as Red Cross, Chamber of Commerce, Chairman of Soldiers Bonus Board, Public Library, Union Cemetery, Past President and Historian of the Ohio Society, S. A. R., etc. He is a member of St. Paul's Church, Steubenville, and has been a vestryman in that organization for many years.

EUGENE C. BONNIWELL
Chancellor General

EUGENE C. BONNIWELL, elected at Buffalo, N. Y., in 1921, and re-elected at Springfield, Mass., May 16, 1922, was born in Philadelphia, September 25, 1872. He was graduated from the University of Pennsylvania Law School in 1893. He was college champion in pole vaulting and running, a director of the Athletic Association of the University of Pennsylvania, and immediately began the practice of law in his native city. On November 6, 1913, he was elected Judge of the New Municipal Court by an overwhelming majority, a position which he now holds. Five times the firemen of Pennsylvania have conferred upon him the honor of selecting him as president of the Firemen's Association of the State of Pennsylvania. He is a director of the National Security League, Past President of the Philadelphia Chapter, Sons of the American Revolution; president of the Veteran Athletes of Philadelphia; a director of the Pennsylvania State Chamber of Commerce; vice-director, Committee of Public Safety of Pennsylvania; a member of the Sons of the Revolution; Society of the War of 1812; Friendly Sons of St. Patrick; J. F. Reynolds Camp, No. 4, Sons of Veterans; Registrar of Order of Washington; member of the Historical Society of Pennsylvania; the City Business Club; the City History Club; Order of Eagles; Fraternal Order of Orioles; Order of Moose; Philadelphia Order of Elks, and Chevalier Commander, Order of La Fayette. On behalf of this last society, during the great reception given to Marshal Foch in Philadelphia on November 16, Judge Bonniwell presented to the great French leader the order of La Fayette. This ceremony was carried out at the Washington statue.

On June 5, 1900, Judge Bonniwell was married to Madeline H. Cahill. He has seven children, all of whom are living.

As a public official, in charge of the mass of misery coming for relief into the great Desertion Court of Philadelphia, during twenty-two months Judge Bonniwell handled 6,000 cases, involving 20,000 children, and collected for deserted wives and infants over half a million dollars. Throughout his public and private life he has always maintained to the fullest degree an untiring interest in the red-blooded activities that make the American youth unsurpassed in their qualities of initiative, resoluteness, and daring, and a public career without blemish has made him one of the foremost citizens of Philadelphia in all the things that relate to indomitable courage, capacity, and interest in civic matters.

WALTER K. WATKINS
Genealogist General

WALTER KENDALL WATKINS, elected at Buffalo, N. Y., in 1921, and re-elected at Springfield, Mass., in 1922, was born in Boston, August 5, 1855, and graduated from the Phillips Grammar and English High Schools. Since 1880 he has been engaged in historical and genealogical researches in this country and Great Britain. He has published frequently articles in newspapers and magazines and edited the *Colonial Wars Magazine* and publications of the Society of Colonial Wars in the Commonwealth of Massachusetts. A specialty has been his works on the early history of Boston and contributions to the publications of the Bostonian Society.

He has been a charter member and director of Boston Chapter, S. A. R.; charter member and historian of Old Suffolk Chapter; charter member and secretary of Malden Chapter. He now holds the offices of Secretary and Historian of the Massachusetts State Society. He was elected Historian General at the National Congresses of 1908 and 1909; a charter member of the Massachusetts Society of Colonial Wars; he has been Genealogist of the State Society since 1896 and Secretary for fifteen years.

He is a charter member of the Massachusetts Society of Mayflower Descendants and Secretary of the Bay State Historical League, composed of seventy-five historical societies in Massachusetts. A member of the New England Historic-Genealogical Society since 1889; he has been on its library committee for several years, and is chairman of the committee on records.

He is also an active and honorary member in several historical societies. He is a resident of Malden, Mass., and Grafton, N. H.

REV. FREDERIC WILLIAMS PERKINS, D. D.

Chaplain General

FREDERIC WILLIAMS PERKINS, who was elected Chaplain General at the National Congress in Springfield, Mass., in May, 1922, was born in Boston, Mass., on June 16, 1870. He was fitted for college in the Roxbury Latin School and entered Tufts College, from which he was graduated in 1891. He served as pastor of the Church of the Redeemer, in Hartford, Conn., from 1894 to 1901; of the First Universalist Church of Haverhill, Mass., from 1901 to 1905, and of the First Universalist Church, in Lynn, Mass., from that time to the present. Dr. Perkins has served as a trustee of the Universalist General Convention and is at present president of the Lynn Associated Charities and vice-chairman of the Lynn Chapter, American Red Cross, having special oversight of the home service during the World War. He is a member of Old Essex Chapter, in Lynn, of the Sons of the American Revolution and is a lineal descendant of Robert Williams, one of the first settlers of Roxbury, Mass. He married Mary Sherman Thayer, of Somerville, Mass., on June 21, 1894, and they have one son, Sherman Thayer Perkins. Dr. Perkins is a member of the Oxford, Whiting, and Rotary Clubs of Lynn, Mass.

NATIONAL COMMITTEES

Executive Committee:

W. I. LINCOLN ADAMS, *Chairman*, Montclair, New Jersey.
WALLACE McCAMANT, Northwestern Bank Building, Portland, Oregon.
LOUIS ANNIN AMES, 99 Fulton Street, New York, New York.
ARTHUR P. SUMNER, County Court House, Providence, Rhode Island.
GEORGE E. POMEROY, 19 Spitzer Arcade, Toledo, Ohio.
MARVIN H. LEWIS, Keller Building, Louisville, Kentucky.
HARRY T. LORD, Manchester, New Hampshire.

Advisory Committee:

The PAST PRESIDENTS GENERAL.

Credentials:

TEUNIS D. HUNTTING, *Chairman*, 220 Broadway, New York, New York.
WILLIAM J. CONKLING, Orange, New Jersey.
                    (Five others to be appointed prior to 1922 Congress.)

Auditing and Finance:

GEORGE D. BANGS, *Chairman*, Huntington, New York.
NORMAN P. HEFFLEY, Brooklyn, New York.
C. SYMMES KIGGINS, Elizabeth, New Jersey.
HENRY VAIL CONDICT, Essex Fells, New Jersey.
ALBERT J. SQUIER, Yonkers, New York.

Memorial:

R. C. BALLARD THRUSTON, *Chairman*, 1000 Columbus Building, Louisville, Kentucky.
GEORGE A. ELLIOTT, Wilmington, Delaware.
MATTHEW PAGE ANDREWS, 849 Park Avenue, Baltimore, Maryland.
CHARLES FRENCH READ, Boston, Massachusetts.
OTIS G. HAMMOND, Concord, New Hampshire.
WILLIAM CHACE GREEN, Providence, Rhode Island.
GEORGE C. ARNOLD, Providence, Rhode Island.
CHARLES P. WORTMAN, Syracuse, New York.
GEORGE V. MUCHMORE, Summit, New Jersey.
CLARENCE A. KENYON, Washington, District of Columbia.
EUGENE C. BONNIWELL, City Hall, Philadelphia, Pennsylvania.

Organization, New England District:

HARRY T. LORD, Vice-President General, *Chairman*, Manchester, New Hampshire.
WILLIAM K. SANDERSON, Portland, Maine.
GUY W. BAILEY, Burlington, Vermont.
BURTON H. WIGGIN, Lowell, Massachusetts.
DR. GEORGE T. SPICER, Providence, Rhode Island.
HERBERT H. WHITE, Hartford, Connecticut.

Organization, Middle and Coast District:

PHILIP F. LARNER, Vice-President General, *Chairman*, 918 F Street N. W., Washington, District of Columbia.
HARVEY F. REMINGTON, Rochester, New York.
W. C. LYNE, Pittsburgh, Pennsylvania.
HERBERT B. FLOWERS, Baltimore, Maryland.
HORACE WILSON, Wilmington, Delaware.

HARRY F. BREWER, Elizabeth, New Jersey.
JOHN F. JONES, Blacksburg, South Carolina.
ARTHUR B. CLARKE, Richmond, Virginia.
SELDEN M. ELY, Washington, District of Columbia.
FRANK H. BRYAN, Washington, District of Columbia.
PAUL T. HAYNE, Greenville, South Carolina.
DR. F. G. RENSHAW, Pensacola, Florida.

Organization, Mississippi Valley—East:

LOUIS A. BOWMAN, Vice-President General, *Chairman*, 30 N. La Salle Street, Chicago, Illinois.
W. H. BARRETT, Adrian, Michigan.
MOULTON HOUK, Toledo, Ohio.
CREDO HARRIS, South Third Street, Louisville, Kentucky.
CHARLES T. JEWETT, Terre Haute, Indiana.
DORR E. FELT, Chicago, Illinois.
WALTER H. WRIGHT, Milwaukee, Wisconsin.
WILLIAM K. BOARDMAN, Nashville, Tennessee.

Organization, Mississippi Valley—West:

HENRY B. HAWLEY, Vice-President General, *Chairman*, Des Moines, Iowa.
CAPT. FRED A. BRILL, St. Paul, Minnesota.
WALTER E. COFFIN, Des Moines, Iowa.
LINN PAINE, St. Louis, Missouri.
FRANK W. TUCKER, Little Rock, Arkansas.
C. ROBERT CHURCHILL, New Orleans, Louisiana.
C. P. DORCHESTER, Sherman, Texas.
E. G. SPILLMAN, Oklahoma City, Oklahoma.
ARTHUR H. BENNETT, Topeka, Kansas.
DR. BENJAMIN F. BAILEY, Lincoln, Nebraska.
DR. J. G. PARSONS, Sioux Falls, South Dakota.
HOWARD E. SIMPSON, Grand Forks, North Dakota.

Organization, Mountain and Pacific:

GEORGE ALBERT SMITH, Vice-President General, *Chairman*, Salt Lake City, Utah.
LESLIE BERRY SULGROVE, Helena, Montana.
FRANK G. ENSIGN, Boise, Idaho.
GALEN A. FOX, Cheyenne, Wyoming.
DANIEL S. SPENCER, Salt Lake City, Utah.
EDWARD V. DUNKLEE, Denver, Colorado.
HAROLD BAXTER, 311 Fleming Building, Phœnix, Arizona.
THOMAS F. KELEHER, Albuquerque, New Mexico.
CLAUDE GATCH, Federal Reserve Bank, San Francisco, California.
JESSE MARTIN HITT, Olympia, Washington.
WINTHROP HAMMOND, 127 Sixth Street, Portland, Oregon.

Joint Committee with Descendants of Signers of Declaration of Independence for Historical Research:

R. C. BALLARD THRUSTON, *Chairman*, 1000 Columbus Building, Louisville, Kentucky.
MATTHEW PAGE ANDREWS, 849 Park Avenue, Baltimore, Maryland.
GEORGE A. ELLIOTT, Wilmington, Delaware.

Patriotic Education:

WALLACE McCAMANT, *Chairman*, Northwestern Bank Building, Portland, Oregon.
GEORGE B. SAGE, *Vice-Chairman*, 713 Park Avenue, Rochester, New York.
HARRY G. COLSON, Chicago, Illinois.
SAMUEL B. BOTSFORD, Buffalo, New York.

GRENVILLE H. NORCROSS, Boston, Massachusetts.
ASHLEY K. HARDY, Hanover, New Hampshire.
MATTHEW PAGE ANDREWS, 849 Park Avenue, Baltimore, Maryland.
MARVIN H. LEWIS, Louisville, Kentucky.
HERBERT P. WHITNEY, Toledo, Ohio.
WILLIAM F. PIERCE, Gambier, Ohio.
DR. R. S. HILL, Albuquerque, New Mexico.
WILLIAM P. HUMPHREYS, Holbrook Building, San Francisco, California.
HARRISON G. PLATT, Platt Building, Portland, Oregon.

Naval and Military Records:

REAR ADMIRAL GEORGE W. BAIRD, *Chairman*, 1505 Rhode Island Avenue, Washington, District of Columbia.
MAJOR-GENERAL NELSON A. MILES, Washington, District of Columbia.
JAMES D. IGLEHART, Baltimore, Maryland.
C. A. KENYON, Washington, District of Columbia.
CAPT. ALBERT WILBUR SMITH, Bridgeport, Connecticut.
REAR ADMIRAL F. F. FLETCHER, Navy Department, Washington, District of Columbia.
JOSEPH B. DOYLE, Steubenville, Ohio.
COMMANDER THOMAS W. HARRIS, Buffalo, New York.

Americanization and Aliens:

HARVEY F. REMINGTON, *Chairman*, Wilder Building, Rochester, New York.
COMMANDER JOHN H. MOORE, *Vice-Chairman*, The Wyoming, Washington, District of Columbia
SAMUEL JUDD HOLMES, *Vice-Chairman*, Burke Building, Seattle, Washington.
THOMAS W. WILLIAMS, East Orange, New Jersey.
CORNELIUS DOREMUS, Ridgewood, New Jersey.
DR. GEORGE H. BANGS, Swampscott, Massachusetts.
A. McCLELLAN MATHEWSON, 865 Chapel Street, New Haven, Connecticut.
THOMAS STEPHEN BROWN, Pittsburgh, Pennsylvania.
CHANCELLOR L. JENKS, 30 North La Salle Street, Chicago, Illinois.
FREDERICK M. ALGER, Detroit, Michigan.

Flag:

W. V. COX, *Chairman*, Washington, District of Columbia.
BRIGADIER GENERAL OLIVER B. BRIDGMAN, New York, New York.
GENERAL CHARLES A. COOLIDGE, Detroit, Michigan.
COLONEL GEORGE V. LAUMAN, Chicago, Illinois.
COLONEL J. SWIGERT TAYLOR, Frankfort, Kentucky.
COLONEL G. K. HUNTER, St. Louis, Missouri.
LIEUTENANT COLONEL M. W. WOOD, Boise, Idaho.
BRIGADIER GENERAL CHARLES A. WOODRUFF, Berkeley, California.
MAJOR GILBERT MAXWELL, Montclair, New Jersey.

Investment of Permanent Fund:

The PRESIDENT GENERAL.
The TREASURER GENERAL.
CORNELIUS AMORY PUGSLEY, Peekskill, New York.

National Archives Building:

MAJOR FREDERICK C. BRYAN, *Chairman*, Colorado Building, Washington, District of Columbia.
JAMES P. GOODRICH, Winchester, Indiana.
AMEDEE B. COLE, St. Louis, Missouri.
EDWARD D. BALDWIN, The Dalles, Oregon.
COMMANDER J. H. MOORE, U. S. N., Washington, District of Columbia.
M. L. RITCHIE, Salt Lake City, Utah.

GENERAL G. BARRETT RICH, Buffalo, New York.
WILLIAM S. PARKS, Washington, District of Columbia.
CHARLES N. K. HALSEY, Elizabeth, New Jersey.

Ceremonies and Colors:

COLONEL GEORGE V. LAUMAN, *Chairman,* 320 Ashland Block, Chicago, Illinois.
CAPTAIN R. W. BROWN, Corry, Pennsylvania.
JOSEPH ATWOOD, Lynn, Massachusetts.
JOSEPH M. SHIELDS, Old National Bank Building, Spokane, Washington.
JOSEPH W. HAMMOND, 126 Sixth Street, Portland, Oregon.

Observance of Flag Day:

LEWIS B. CURTIS, *Chairman,* Bridgeport, Connecticut.
W. HOWARD WALKER, Providence, Rhode Island.
MILTON W. GATCH, Baltimore, Maryland.
CAPTAIN HENRY A. BROWN, Kenmore, New York.
HERMAN W. FERNBERGER, 1825 North 17th Street, Philadelphia, Pennsylvania.
HENRY B. POLLARD, Richmond, Virginia.
WINFORD LECKY MATTOON, Columbus, Ohio.
FRANK W. GRAHAM, Albuquerque, New Mexico.
LOUIS A. BOWMAN, Northern Trust Company, Chicago, Illinois.
DR. GEORGE D. BARNEY, Brooklyn, New York.

NATIONAL COMMITTEE ON OBSERVANCE OF CONSTITUTION DAY, SEPTEMBER 17

Constitution Day Inaugurated by the Sons of the American Revolution in 1917

Louis Annin Ames, *Chairman,* 99 Fulton Street, New York, New York.
Major W. I. Lincoln Adams, Montclair, New Jersey.
Col. Frederick M. Alger, U. S. A., Grosse Pointe Village, Michigan.
Rev. Lyman Whitney Allen, Newark, New Jersey.
Gen. Francis Henry Appleton, Massachusetts.
Hon. Alfred D. Ayers, Nevada.
Hon. Simeon E. Baldwin, Connecticut.
Thomas F. Bayard, Wilmington, Delaware.
Judge Morris B. Beardsley, Connecticut.
Brig. Gen. Theo. A. Bingham, Connecticut.
William K. Boardman, Tennessee.
Hon. Eugene C. Bonniwell, Pennsylvania.
Louis A. Bowman, Illinois.
John G. Bragaw, Jr., North Carolina.
Brig. Gen. Oliver B. Bridgman, New York.
Austin H. Brown, Indiana.
John H. Burroughs, New York.
John Bushnell, Nebraska.
Hon. William G. Cody, New York.
Col. Louis R. Cheney, Connecticut.
Rear Admiral Colby M. Chester, U. S. N., Washington, D. C.
Col. C. Robert Churchill, Louisiana.
Arthur B. Clarke, Richmond, Virginia.
Charles Hopkins Clark, Connecticut.
Col. Robert Colgate, New Jersey.
Hon. Calvin A. Coolidge, Vice-President of the United States.
Gen. Charles A. Coolidge, U. S. A., Michigan.
Frank Corbin, Connecticut.

Edwin S. Crandon, Boston, Massachusetts.
John Hobart Cross, Pensacola, Florida.
Hon. Albert B. Cummins, U. S. Senator, Iowa.
Lewis B. Curtis, Bridgeport, Connecticut.
Col. William L. Curry, Ohio.
Hon. Paul Dana, New York.
William C. Demorest, New York.
Hon. Chauncey M. Depew, New York.
Louis H. Dos Passos, New York.
Hon. William P. Dillingham, U. S. Senator, Vermont.
Hon. Ralph D. Earl, New York.
John A. Eckert, New York.
Hon. Walter E. Edge, Senator, New Jersey.
Col. George A. Elliott, Wilmington, Delaware.
Vernon Ashley Field, Massachusetts.
Rear Admiral Frank F. Fletcher, U. S. N., Washington, D. C.
Hon. Joseph Sherman Frelinghuysen, U. S. Senator, New Jersey.
Judge Elbert H. Gary, New York.
Judge J. Howard Gates, Pierre, South Dakota.
Gen. John R. Gibbons, Beauxite, Arkansas.
Hon. Job Hedges, New York.
Hon. James P. Goodrich, Governor of Indiana.
Edward Hagaman Hall, New York.
Hon. James Denton Hancock, Pennsylvania.
Prof. Ashley K. Hardy, New Hampshire.
Credo Fitch Harris, Kentucky.
Dwight B. Heard, Phœnix, Arizona.
Hon. Albert M. Henry, Michigan.
Dr. David Jayne Hill, Washington, D. C.
Major Walter B. Hopping, U. S. A., New York.
Hon. Colgate Hoyt, New York.
Hon. Charles Evans Hughes, New York.
Gen. Willis A. Hulings, Pennsylvania.
Chancellor L. Jenks, Illinois.
Rear Admiral T. F. Jewell, U. S. N., Washington, D. C.
Lieut.-Col. C. T. Jewett, U. S. A., Indiana.
Rear Admiral Albert H. Knight, U. S. N., Massachusetts.
Philip F. Larner, Vice-President General, S. A. R., Washington, D. C.
Judge Eddy Orland Lee, Utah.
Marvin H. Lewis, Louisville, Kentucky.
Brig. Gen. James Rush Lincoln, Iowa.
Hon. H. Wales Lines, Connecticut.
Hon. Charles Warren Lippitt, former Governor of Rhode Island.
Hon. Henry F. Lippitt, U. S. Senator from Rhode Island.
Hon. Henry Cabot Lodge, U. S. Senator from Massachusetts.
Rev. L. L. Loofbourow, Hawaii.
Hon. Frank O. Lowden, Illinois.
Judge James Gordon Lyell, Mississippi.
Nelson A. McClary, Illinois.
Hon. William W. McDowell, Montana.
Hon. Wallace McCamant, Oregon.
Rev. William Gerry Mann, Maine.
William A. Marble, New York.
Dr. Samuel B. McCormack, Pennsylvania.
John M. Meade, Kansas.
Stanwood Menken, New York.
Frank M. Mills, South Dakota.
Edwin P. Mitchell, New York.
Hon. George H. Moses, U. S. Senator, New Hampshire.

Hon. Harry S. New, U. S. Senator from Indiana.
Charles L. Nichols, Colorado.
George Hale Nutting, Massachusetts.
Hon. Carroll S. Page, U. S. Senator from Vermont.
Gen. J. N. Patterson, New Hampshire.
Hon. Thomas A. Perkins, California.
David L. Pierson, New Jersey.
George E. Pomeroy, Ohio.
Dr. Curran Pope.
Hon. James H. Preston, Maryland.
Hon. Cornelius A. Pugsley, New York.
Samuel F. Punderson, Massachusetts.
Charles French Read, Massachusetts.
Hon. Harvey F. Remington, New York.
Gen. G. Barrett Rich, New York.
Charles E. Rittenhouse, Minnesota.
John D. Rockefeller, New York.
Hon. Ernest E. Rogers, Connecticut.
Lieut.-Col. Theodore Roosevelt, New York.
Hon. Elihu Root, New York.
Col. Henry W. Sackett, New York.
William K. Sanderson, Maine.
Hon. George H. Shields, Missouri.
Col. Frank S. Sidway, Buffalo, New York.
Judge Ernest C. Simpson, Connecticut.
Hon. George Albert Smith, Utah.
Hon. William Alden Smith, former U. S. Senator from Michigan.
E. G. Spilman, Oklahoma City, Oklahoma.
Vernon P. Squires, North Dakota.
Judge Henry Stockbridge, Maryland.
Hon. William H. Taft, Connecticut.
Col. J. Swigert Taylor, Kentucky.
R. C. Ballard Thruston, Kentucky.
Col. Ralph Emerson Twitchell, New Mexico.
Carl M. Vail, New Jersey.
Col. John Vrooman, New York.
Hon. James W. Wadsworth, U. S. Senator from New York.
Captain Hamilton Ward, Buffalo, New York.
Hon. Francis E. Warren, U. S. Senator from Wyoming.
Dr. William Seward Webb, Vermont.
Elmer Marston Wentworth, Iowa.
Hon. Charles S. Whitman, former Governor of New York.
Prof. William K. Wickes, New York.
Dr. George C. F. Williams, Hartford, Connecticut.
Hon. Robert L. Williams, Governor of Oklahoma.
Henry A. Williams, Ohio.
Thomas Wright Williams, New Jersey.
Col. Elmer E. Wood, U. S. A., Louisiana.
Lieut.-Col. M. W. Wood, U. S. A., Idaho.
Brig. Gen. Charles A. Woodruff, U. S. A., California.
Hon. Rollin S. Woodruff, former Governor of Connecticut.
Newell B. Woodworth, Syracuse, New York.
Prof. Levi Edgar Young, Utah.
Henry A. Williams, Columbus, Ohio.
Walter H. Wright, Milwaukee, Wisconsin.

PRESIDENTS AND SECRETARIES OF STATE SOCIETIES

ARIZONA—President, Lloyd B. Christie, 116 N. 1 Avenue, Phœnix.
Secretary, Clarence P. Woodbury, 1509 Grand Avenue, Phœnix.
Treasurer, Kenneth Freeland, Phœnix.

ARKANSAS—President, John M. Bracey, Little Rock.
Secretary, Fay Hempstead, Little Rock.
Treasurer, Thomas M. Cory, Little Rock.

CALIFORNIA—President, Charles E. Hale, 51 Main Street, San Francisco.
Secretary-Registrar, Thomas A. Perkins, Mills Building, San Francisco.
Treasurer, John C. Currier, 713 Merchants' Exchange Building, San Francisco.

COLORADO—President, Hon. George H. Bradfield, Greeley.
Secretary, James Polk Willard, 210 Masonic Temple, Denver.
Treasurer, Walter D. Wynkoop, Mt. States T. & T. Co., Denver.

CONNECTICUT—President, Herbert H. White, 76 N. Beacon Street, Hartford.
Secretary, Frederick A. Doolittle, 117 Middle Street, Bridgeport.
Treasurer, Charles G. Stone, P. O. Box 847, Hartford.

DELAWARE—President, Robert H. Richards, 1415 Delaware Avenue, Wilmington.
Secretary-Treasurer-Registrar, Charles A. Rudolph, 900 Vanburen Street, Wilmington.

DISTRICT OF COLUMBIA—President, Selden M. Ely, Gales School Building, Washington.
Secretary, Kenneth S. Wales, 110 Florence Court, E., Washington.
Treasurer, Hilleary F. Offcut, Jr., 1501 Crittenden Street N. W., Washington.

FAR EASTERN SOCIETY—President-Secretary, H. Lawrence Noble, P. O. Box 940, Manila,
Philippine Islands.
Treasurer, Herman Roy Hare.

FLORIDA—President, Dr. F. G. Renshaw, Pensacola.
Secretary, John Hobart Cross, Pensacola.
Treasurer-Registrar, F. F. Bingham, Pensacola.

SOCIETY IN FRANCE—Administered by Empire State Society.

GEORGIA—President, Allen Waters, P. O. Box 361, Atlanta.
Secretary-Registrar, Arthur W. Falkinburg, 1301 Atlanta Trust Co., Building, Atlanta.
Treasurer, William Alden, Box 172, Decatur.

HAWAII—President, Donald S. Bowman, Honolulu.
Secretary, James T. Taylor, 207 Kauikeolani Building, Honolulu.
Treasurer, L. M. Judd.

IDAHO—President, Albert H. Conner, Boise.
Secretary and Treasurer, Frank G. Ensign, Boise.

ILLINOIS—President, James M. Eddy, 30 North La Salle Street, Chicago.
Secretary, Louis A. Bowman, 30 North La Salle Street, Chicago.
Treasurer, Henry R. Kent, 30 North La Salle Street, Chicago.

INDIANA—President, Cornelius F. Posson, Box 331, Brazil.
Secretary and Treasurer, Edmund L. Parker, 208 East Walnut Street, Kokomo.

IOWA—President, Walter E. Coffin, 902 7th Street, Des Moines.
Secretary, Captain Elbridge D. Hadley, 409 Franklin Avenue, Des Moines.
Treasurer, William E. Barrett, 4815 Grand Avenue, Des Moines.

KANSAS—President, John M. Meade, Topeka.
Secretary, Arthur H. Bennett, 434 Woodlawn Avenue, Topeka.
Treasurer-Registrar, Walter E. Wilson, Topeka.

KENTUCKY—President, E. T. Hutchings, Columbia Building, Louisville.
Secretary, George D. Caldwell, Inter-Southern Building, Louisville.
Treasurer, Alexander W. Tippett, U. S. Trust Co. Building, Louisville.

LOUISIANA—President, C. Robert Churchill, 408 Canal Street, New Orleans.
Secretary, Herbert P. Benton, 403 Carondelet Building, New Orleans.
Treasurer, S. O. Landry, 616 Maison Blanche Building, New Orleans.

MAINE—President, William B. Berry, 42 Pleasant Street, Gardiner.
    Secretary, Francis L. Littlefield, 246 Spring Street, Portland.
    Treasurer, Enoch O. Greenleaf, Portland.

MARYLAND—President, Herbert Baker Flowers, 3008 N. Calvert Street, Baltimore.
    Secretary, George Sadtler Robertson, 1628 Linden Avenue, Baltimore.
    Treasurer, Benson Blake, Jr., Baltimore.

MASSACHUSETTS—President, Dr. Charles Bangs, Swampscott.
    Secretary, Walter K. Watkins, 9 Ashburton Place, Boston.
    Treasurer, Lieut.-Col. Charles M. Green, 78 Marlboro Street, Boston.

MICHIGAN—President, William P. Holliday, 68 Davenport Street, Detroit.
    Secretary, Raymond E. Van Syckle, 1729 Ford Building, Detroit.
    Treasurer, Frank G. Smith, 237 Hancock Avenue E., Detroit.

MINNESOTA—President, Kenneth G. Brill, 43 South Hamline Avenue, St. Paul.
    Secretary, Charles H. Bronson, 48 East Fourth Street, St. Paul.
    Treasurer, Charles W. Eddy, 302 Pittsburg Building, St. Paul.

MISSISSIPPI—President, Judge Gordon Garland Lyell, Jackson.
    Secretary and Treasurer, William H. Pullen, Mechanics' Bank Building, Jackson.

MISSOURI—President, Linn Paine, 904 Locust Street, St. Louis.
    Secretary, J. Alonzo Matthews, 901 Pontiac Building, St. Louis.
    Treasurer, I. Shreve Carter, 308 Merchant La Clede Building, St. Louis.

MONTANA—President, Paris B. Bartley, Helena.
    Secretary and Treasurer, Leslie Sulgrove, Helena.

NEBRASKA—President, Benjamin F. Bailey, 506 1st National Bank Building, Lincoln.
    Secretary, Addison E. Sheldon, 1319 South 23d Street, Lincoln.
    Treasurer, C. E. Bardwell, 522 Terminal Building, Lincoln.

NEVADA—President, Rt. Rev. George C. Huntting, 505 Ridge Street, Reno.

NEW HAMPSHIRE—President, Prof. Ashley K. Hardy, Hanover.
    Secretary and Treasurer, Charles L. Mason, Concord.

NEW JERSEY—President, Hon. Adrian Lyon, Perth Amboy.
    Secretary, David L. Pierson, 33 Lombardy Street, Newark.
    Treasurer, Frank E. Quinby.

NEW MEXICO—President, C. C. Manning, Gallup.
    Secretary, Frank W. Graham, Albuquerque.
    Treasurer, Orville A. Matson, Albuquerque.

NEW YORK—President, Gearge D. Bangs, Tribune Building, New York City.
    Secretary, Major Charles A. Du Bois, 220 Broadway, New York City.
    Treasurer, James de la Montanye, 220 Broadway, New York City.

NORTH CAROLINA—Special Organizer for North and South Carolina, Maj. John F. Jones,
    Blacksburg, S. C.

NORTH DAKOTA—President, Howard E. Simpson, University of North Dakota, Grand Forks.
    Secretary-Registrar, Walter R. Reed, 407 7th Avenue, Fargo.
    Treasurer, Willis E. Fuller, Northern National Bank, Grand Forks.

OHIO—President, Walter J. Sherman, 302 Produce Exchange Building, Toledo.
    Secretary-Registrar, W. L. Curry, Box 645 Columbus.
    Treasurer, S. G. Harvey, 650 Oakwood Avenue, Toledo.

OKLAHOMA—President, George L. Bowman, Kingfisher.
    Secretary-Treasurer, Edward F. McKay, 536 West 31st Street, Oklahoma City.

OREGON—President, B. B. Beekman, 601 Platt Building, Portland.
    Secretary, B. A. Thaxter, Post Office Box 832, Portland.
    Treasurer, A. A. Lindsley, Henry Building, Portland.

PENNSYLVANIA—President, W. C. Lyne, Farmers' Bank Building, Pittsburgh.
    Secretary, Francis Armstrong, Jr., 515 Wood Street, Pittsburgh.
    Treasurer, A. W. Wall, Farmers' Bank Building, Pittsburgh.

RHODE ISLAND—President, Herbert A. Rice, 809 Hospital Trust Building, Providence.
    Secretary, Theodore E. Dexter, 104 Clay Street, Central Falls.
    Treasurer, William L. Sweet, Box 1515, Providence.

SOUTH CAROLINA—Special Organizer for North and South Carolina, Maj. John F. Jones, Blacksburg.

SOUTH DAKOTA—President, Col. A. B. Sessions, Sioux Falls.
Secretary, T. W. Dwight, Sioux Falls.
Treasurer, B. H. Requa, Sioux Falls.

TENNESSEE—President, William K. Boardman, Nashville.
Secretary, Frederick W. Millspaugh, Nashville.
Treasurer, Carey Folk, 411 Union Street, Nashville.

TEXAS—President, C. B. Dorchester, Sherman.
Secretary, Walter S. Mayer, 1404 39th Street, Galveston.
Treasurer, P. R. Markham, Sherman.

UTAH—President, Robert E. McConaughy, 1079 E. 2d South Street, Salt Lake City.
Secretary, Gordon Lines Hutchins, Dooly Building, Salt Lake City.
Treasurer—Seth Warner Morrison, Jr., 32 S. 7th East Street, Salt Lake City.

VERMONT—President, William H. Jeffrey, Montpelier.
Secretary, Walter H. Crockett, Burlington.
Treasurer, Clarence L. Smith, Burlington.

VIRGINIA—President, Arthur B. Clarke, 616 American National Bank Building, Richmond.
Secretary and Treasurer, William E. Crawford, 700 Travelers' Building, Richmond.

WASHINGTON—President, Walter Burges Beals, Haller Building, Seattle.
Secretary, Henry J. Gorin, 322 Central Building, Seattle.
Treasurer, Kenneth P. Hussey, 903 Boylston Avenue, Seattle.

WISCONSIN—President, Henry S. Sloan, 216 W. Water Street, Milwaukee.
Secretary, Emmett A. Donnelly, 1030 Wells Building, Milwaukee.
Treasurer, William Stark Smith, 480 Clinton Street, Milwaukee.

WYOMING—President, David A. Haggard, Cheyenne.
Secretary, Maurice Groshon, Cheyenne.
Treasurer, James B. Guthrie, Cheyenne.

A CALL FOR VOLUNTEERS

Do you live in a town or city where there is no Chapter of the Sons of the American Revolution? If so, will you volunteer to investigate and see if it is not possible to organize a Chapter in that city? If yes again, will you write at once to your State Secretary, whose name appears in this BULLETIN, and give him your name and address, and any other information that you may have?

If you do not get a ready response from your State Secretary, write to the Secretary General of the National Society. He will assist you, and if you desire will give you the names of our compatriots' who live in your city or town.

If you live in a city where there is a Chapter already established, perhaps you know of some near-by city or town that has no Chapter; if so, will you volunteer to assist in organizing one in that place? If so, do the same thing as above stated.

The possibilities of Chapter organization throughout the country are very great, and it can only be done by the co-operation of our members everywhere. If you are interested in our great Society and its growth, just do this little bit of work in your locality.

HISTORY AND PATRIOTISM

It is a great pity that the proper teaching of American history from well-written and truthful text-books, which can be a most effective means of fostering a true love for country, is so largely neglected in our schools and colleges; or, what is much worse, is too often improperly done.

Real patriotism is a reverence for the past and a hope and faith for the future. Those who are ignorant of our true history, and who consequently have no ambition for our future, as well as those who are living in the present alone, are incapable of the noble sentiment of true patriotism.

For this reason many of our foreign born and a large part of the so-called laboring classes, who have little or no interest in and knowledge of our glorious past, can and do have slight ambition for our future, while those who most highly value their historical heritage, as they usually do who are most familiar with it, are naturally desirous of transmitting its noble traditions, undiminished and unimpaired, to their own descendants.

Many of our present social and industrial problems, therefore, which are so perplexing in this difficult period of reconstruction after the upheavals of the great World War, might be largely solved by a knowledge of our inspiring history and of the great men who helped to make it. An elevated love of country is stimulated by a study of its true history, and a nation whose population loves its country and reveres its heroes need have no fears for its future.

The Jews have always very wisely made their national history a large part of the education of their youth, and even of their religion, with the result that few races have preserved through adversity and various unfavorable vicissitudes their national consciousness to so great a degree.

Ignorance of the past and indifference to the future usually go hand in hand. What a mistake, then, to neglect the proper teaching of our history to our youth, at the time when they can be most influenced by it, for their and our common good. The knowledge of certain outstanding facts of our history and the form of our government should legally be required, I think, before those of our foreign-born population who seek citizenship in our country are given the franchise; and our own American-born youth should be qualified to at least the same degree of proficiency in our history and the knowledge of our form of government before they are permitted to exercise the franchise now granted them on merely attaining the age of twenty-one years.

And in this connection it must be borne in mind that many of our American-born population are quite as much in need of "Americanization" as those who come to us from foreign shores. This is partly due to lack of interest on the part of their parents and partly due to the fact that the history which is taught them in our public schools is from faulty text-books and by unsympathetic, or worse, instructors.

The Sons of the American Revolution are very greatly interested in the proper teaching of American history in our schools and colleges, together with a much needed censorship of the text-books employed in them. We have a National Committee, under the chairmanship of Judge Wallace McCamant, of Portland, Oregon, former President General of the National Society, on Patriotic Education, which expects to be very active in this constructive patriotic work during the present year; and I confidently hope that Judge McCamant and his important committee will receive the helpful co-operation of our entire membership.

Washington I. L. Adams

President General.

CARD FROM TENNESSEE SOCIETY

"The Tennessee Society deeply appreciates the honor of entertaining the 1923 Congress. It is particularly pleasing that we shall meet in May, when the fragrance of the honeysuckle, the magnolia, and the rose fills the air and Nature will join in welcoming our friends.

"Nashville is a beautiful old city of homes, noted throughout the South for hospitality, and its people are mainly sprung from the old Revolutionary stock of Virginia and the Carolinas. A cordial welcome is extended to our compatriots, and especially to the ladies, as in Nashville they will find waiting them the whole-hearted friendship of the Old South."

(Signed)   WILLIAM KELLOGG BOARDMAN,
                                                    President.

ANNOUNCEMENTS

The Secretary General respectfully requests all State Secretaries and others sending in material for publication in the BULLETIN, to kindly get all copy to the office of the Secretary General on or before the 15th of the month of publication, namely, October, December, March, and June.

Our Chancellor General, Judge Eugene C. Bonniwell, of Philadelphia, has been appointed by the Hon. John Frederick Lewis, President of the Philadelphia Sesqui-Centennial Committee, chairman of the Membership Committee of the forthcoming exposition.

President General Adams participated by invitation, as the representative of our National Society, in the exercises at Princeton, N. J., June 9, when the President of the United States, Compatriot Warren G. Harding, National Trustee for Ohio, dedicated the memorial with a notable address.

The Special Committee on Charter Revision, appointed by President General Adams, of which Hon. Cornelius A. Pugsley, of New York, is chairman, will soon go to Washington for a conference with U. S. Senator J. S. Frelinghuysen, chairman of the Committee on Military Affairs, with regard to amending our National Charter in accordance with the resolution unanimously adopted at the Springfield Congress.

The Hon. Louis Annin Ames, Director General and former President General, together with Major Washington Irving Lincoln Adams, President General, will represent our National Society on the committee to arrange for the joint service on Sunday, December 17, at 4 o'clock, in the Cathedral of St. John the Divine, in New York, in recognition of world amity and the brotherhood of the English-speaking nations.

One of the statements made by the President General in his address at the annual banquet in Springfield, which met with widespread approval, was the hope he expressed that opportunities might be found by which he could confer with representatives of "the other great Revolutionary Society, with mutual respect and friendliness, with a view to forming one powerful National organization for the advancement of constructive and progressive patriotic work in this Republic."

The National Society was represented at the Congress of the Daughters of the American Revolution in Washington last April by Past President General James Harry Preston, of Baltimore, who represented President General Mc-Camant. Judge Preston reported it a most impressive and inspiring meeting, with fine speakers and music. Mrs. George Maynard Minor, the President General of the D. A. R., was the guest of the National Society, Sons of the American Revolution, at our recent Congress at Springfield, Mass., and made a most pleasing impression and address.

.

One of the interesting features of the Congress at Springfield was the presence, as a delegate from the Massachusetts Society, of Dr. CROSBY A. PERRY, a *real* Son of the American Revolution. Dr. Perry was presented to the Congress by President Bangs, of the Massachusetts Society, and accorded an ovation by the Congress. President General McCamant invited Dr. Perry to a seat upon the platform during the sessions.

The President General attended the annual church service of the Elizabethtown Chapter, in Elizabeth, N. J., on the afternoon of June 4, and made a short address on that occasion. He was the guest of the Buffalo Chapter, in Buffalo, N. Y., on the eve of Flag Day, June 13, and addressed the meeting.

The compatriots of Montclair, N. J., where the President General resides, tendered him a complimentary banquet on the evening of June 12, which was a largely attended and very successful affair. Officials of the New Jersey State Society and the Springfield delegates from New Jersey were present.

The President General, in his speech of acceptance at the Springfield Congress, which was most cordially received, said, among other things, that he would "expect a co-operation from all, in accordance with the unanimity of his election"; that "the great States of Massachusetts, New York, and Connecticut would look the same to him as his own home State of New Jersey," and that he would "be the President General of the entire National Society." He expressed his great interest in the reform of our school and college histories and in the Americanization work of our Society, and pledged his hearty support and co-operation in continuing "the splendid work of his brilliant predecessor" along these important lines.

The Secretary General desires to call the attention of compatriots to eligibility requirements for receiving the Service Medals or Service Bars of the Society. Either or both of these awards are given for *active* service in the *military, naval,* or *marine* branches of the United States Service. This announcement is repeated because of apparent misunderstandings that have occurred. The *medal* is awarded by State Societies and should be applied for to *State officers.* The new Service *Bar,* illustrated in the March, 1921, BULLETIN, should be applied for directly to the Secretary General. In applying for either, copies of discharge papers or commissions should accompany applications. The Executive Committee has been obliged, very regretfully, to refuse to confer the new Service Bar in a few special instances, because the applicants, while most loyal and devoted in our country's service during the late World War, in certain capacities did not come under the above requirements.

Major John F. Jones, of Blacksburg, S. C., appointed at the Springfield Congress Special Organizer for the Society in North and South Carolina, is already bending his efforts toward carrying on this work. The newspapers of Columbia, S. C., have printed articles in reference to the matter and Major Jones has had a number of inquiries. It is hoped that compatriots in this section of the country will lend every possible assistance to Major Jones in his efforts to build up the Society.

THE ACCOMPLISHMENT OF SPRINGFIELD CONGRESS

There is no doubt that for real accomplishment the Springfield Congress was one of the best ever held by the National Society. The dominating note was harmony, and not for years has a Congress moved with such a spirit of co-operation, such a desire to iron our differences, such a feeling that the organization was on a higher and better plane than ever before, and that from now on this Society would go forward with renewed vigor to achieve greater and better things than it has ever before attempted.

When men of the type that attend our congresses can get together on a common ground, can come face to face and without fear or favor talk matters over, only the best of results will come forth. Our membership is of too high an order to allow small or petty feeling to stand in the way of greater accomplishment, and whenever we have had differences they have been frank and credit given for the honesty of opinions. This was demonstrated in the Springfield Congress when on the floor of the Congress several delegates gave utterance to their views in a perfectly frank and fearless manner with but one idea in mind, and that for the best interests and good of our organization.

The resolutions that were adopted were all of a nature that showed the lofty and patriotic spirit of the Society and its members. The other work was accomplished with clearness and dispatch, and it is felt that a new era of good feeling will ensue that will make this patriotic Society the best of its kind in the United States.

There were several things that stood out as movements toward greater things, the most notable being the stand taken by the Society on the teaching of history in the public schools of our country. This is a matter that needs serious consideration and practical, concrete attention, and the fact that the chairman of that committee for the coming year is our former President General, who worked so hard upon this during his administration, will assure greater success during the coming year.

The passing by an almost unanimous vote of the amendment that will increase the finances of the Society and the hearty acquiescence of those who sincerely opposed this change will help to make the Society stronger and better. It was recognized by all that this great Society should be put upon a sound financial basis and not have the ignominy of having to face financial stress in everything we undertake.

The desire to assist those that are ready and willing to take hold and build up the Society in places where it is dormant was illustrated in the appointment of a special representative in the South, where the seed of a live organization is greatly to be desired. What can be done in some of our States can be done in others, and if the right man or men will take hold splendid results will be accomplished.

Many other matters were taken up and discussed and every member should read the proceedings of the Springfield Congress, published in this BULLETIN, and get the spirit and inspiration that was engendered there.

It would not be just to him or to the rest of the organization if we did not recognize that much of this spirit of co-operation and harmony received its inspiration from the retiring President General. His high ideals, his wonderful gift of oratory, his gift of clear statement, his magnetic personality, and his unselfishness probably did more to lift the ideals of our Society above the mediocre than anything else, and though many others took part in the proceedings that made toward a better feeling and harmony of interests, there can be no doubt but that to a large extent the influence of the strong character of our President General was deeply felt in achieving the harmonious results that were finally accomplished.

Minutes of the Meeting of the Executive Committee, Held at the Hotel Kimball, Saturday Evening, May 13, 1922, at 7 o'clock.

There were present President General Wallace McCamant, Directors General Ames, of New York; Adams, of New Jersey; Jenks, of Illinois; Pomeroy, of Ohio; also Secretary General Steele, Registrar General Parks, and Past President General Marble.

The meeting was called to order by the President General.

The minutes of the meeting of the Executive Committee held on February 17, 1922, in the city of New York, were read and approved. A short report was made by the Secretary General of routine work of the Society since that date.

The question of eligibility of compatriots for the new Service Bars to be worn on the ribbon of the Official Insignia was brought up for discussion, and it was moved by Mr. Ames that only those compatriots who have served in the Army, Navy, or Marine Corps of the United States of America in time of war shall be entitled to receive and wear the Service Bar on the Insignia.

The question of buying back insignia from members who have resigned or been dropped was referred to the State Societies.

All matters taken up by the Executive Committee by mail since the last meeting in February were confirmed.

After a general discussion of the affairs of the Society, the meeting adjourned.

Frank B. Steele

Secretary General.

Minutes of the Meeting of the Trustees of the National Society, Sons of the American Revolution, Held at the Hotel Kimball, on Saturday Evening, May 13, 1922.

Present: The President General, Wallace McCamant. General officers: Vice-President General Nutting, Vice-President General Lewis, Vice-President General Larner, Secretary General Steele, Registrar General Parks, Chancellor General Bonniwell, Genealogist General Watkins, Historian General Arnold, Chaplain General Allen, Past President General Ames; Wickham, of Connecticut; Punderson, of Massachusetts; Mastick, of California; Spencer, of Utah; Kiggins, of New Jersey.

The meeting was called to order by the President General.

The minutes of the last meeting of the Board of Trustees having been heretofore published in the BULLETIN, upon motion it was decided to dispense with the reading thereof.

It was moved and seconded that the Trustees ratify and confirm all of the acts and proceedings of the Executive Committee that have taken place during the fiscal year beginning May 16, 1921, and ending this day. Motion adopted.

It was moved by Mr. Watkins that the State of Massachusetts or any other State be allowed to change the form of the application blanks by adding the location of the birth, death, or marriage of the ancestors of the applicant. Carried.

It was moved by Mr. Ames that a committee of three be appointed to carry out the provisions of the resolution in relation to changing the blank in regard to adding the location of the birth, death, and marriage of ancestors of the applicant for membership, and this committee to have power to prepare such blank for general use of the Society. That upon such blanks there shall be appended a footnote stating that lack of such information shall not be a bar to the admission of the applicant to the Society. Carried.

The President General appointed Genealogist General Watkins, Secretary General Steele, and Registrar General Parks as such committee.

Upon motion, the meeting adjourned.

Frank B. Steele

Secretary General.

SYNOPSIS OF THE PROCEEDINGS

of the Thirty-third Annual Congress of the National Society, Sons of the American Revolution,

HELD AT HOTEL KIMBALL, SPRINGFIELD, MASS.,

MAY 15 and 16, 1922

Morning Session, Monday, May 15, 10 a. m.

The session was called to order by President General Wallace McCamant. The colors were borne to the platform and received with the customary flag salute.

Chaplain General Rev. Lyman Whitney Allen, D. D., invoked the divine blessing.

Mr. Charles Franklin Warner, President of the George Washington Chapter of Springfield and Chairman of the local Committee on Arrangements, welcomed the Congress and introduced His Excellency Channing Cox, Governor of Massachusetts.

Governor Cox gave a most inspiring address of welcome to the delegates and was received with enthusiasm.

It was moved by Genealogist General Watkins that Governor Cox be made a member of the Sons of the American Revolution through the Massachusetts Society, the papers to take the usual course. The question was put and the motion prevailed by a unanimous rising vote.

Addresses of welcome were made by His Honor Mayor Leonard, of the city of Springfield, a compatriot, and by Dr. Charles H. Bangs, President of the Massachusetts Society.

The President General invited all Past Presidents General in attendance at the Congress to occupy seats on the platform. The following responded: Past Presidents General William A. Marble, Morris B. Beardsley, R. C. Ballard Thruston, Elmer M. Wentworth, Chancellor L. Jenks, Louis Annin Ames, Cornelius A. Pugsley, and Newell B. Woodworth.

The following letters from the President and Vice-President of the United States were then read:

THE WHITE HOUSE, *May 8, 1922.*

MY DEAR MR. McCAMANT:

I note the approaching National Congress of the National Society of the Sons of the American Revolution and am writing just a word to indicate my interest in the effort the organization has been making in behalf of improved teaching of history in American schools. I feel that the subject is one which particularly deserves the attention of persons who are competent to contribute something to improvement in this direction. Your own organization has been among the leaders in this matter, as it has for many years in behalf of every patriotic cause. I trust you will not weary in well-doing, and that your efforts in behalf of a better presentation and understanding of the truths of our national history may produce the good results that we all so much desire.

Very sincerely,
(Signed)

WARREN G. HARDING.

Mr. WALLACE McCAMANT,
President General of the National Society of the
Sons of the American Revolution,
Hotel Kimball, Springfield, Mass.

THE VICE-PRESIDENT'S CHAMBER,
WASHINGTON, *May* 9, 1922.

MY DEAR JUDGE MCCAMANT:

It would be very gratifying if I could be at your Massachusetts meeting, but it is impossible for me to consider it, as I have engagements in Ohio at that time. You will find no lack of interesting topics and historical associations coming from the American Revolution in Massachusetts. They are so much in the mind of each of you that they need no rehearsal.

It is always helpful, however, to contemplate the sacrifices which the Fathers made to establish our institutions and to revere their memory by following their example. Our institutions need the same self-sacrificing loyalty for their support which it was necessary to make for their establishment. The attack rarely comes in the form of an army with banners, but it is always present in the more insidious form of opposition to constituted authority and the selfish expectation of personal advantage at the expense of the public welfare. The higher our state of development, the more intricate our civilization, the greater sacrifices are necessary and the more patriotism is needed. Our Society represents that sacrifice and that patriotism and a determination to contribute to its continuation. In that great cause there will never be wanting an opportunity for service.

Very truly yours,
(Signed)   CALVIN COOLIDGE.

Hon. WALLACE MCCAMANT,
    President General, National Society,
        Sons of the American Revolution,
            Hotel Kimball, Springfield, Mass.

Greetings were also read from the Mercy Warren Chapter, D. A. R., of Springfield, and a night letter from Compatriot C. Robert Churchill, of Louisiana, advocating several suggestions for action by the Congress.

The President General then addressed the Congress.

THE ADDRESS OF THE PRESIDENT GENERAL

Compatriots, I would very grossly violate the proprieties if I should burden you with any lengthy discourse at this time. I want to express on behalf of the Congress our appreciation of all these greetings which we have received. Surely, if the good wishes of our compatriots throughout the nation mean anything, we shall have a very prosperous and agreeable time.

During the year I have traveled over the country and have visited some seventeen of the State Societies. The trips which I have taken have been a source of very great privilege to me. I have found the compatriots differing in the types and activities of their work, but wherever I have gone I have found them gentlemen and Americans (applause), and I desire to make official acknowledgment of the many personal courtesies which I have received.

Now, just a few words about an item of business which will come before the Society. The most unpleasant subject is the one I had better discuss first and get it behind me, and that is the condition of the finances of the Society. I have alluded to it in the BULLETIN, and I think all of you who are here are familiar with the situation. I feel very uncomfortable at the inadequate compensation which the Society is paying to those of its officers who receive any compensation at all. The work of the Secretary General, the work of the Registrar General, is burdensome in the extreme; the preparation of these BULLETINS, which go out to every member of the Society, the editing of the matter, the reading of the proof, and the handling of the enormous correspondence and great work of hte Society, assigned to the Secretary General, constitute a burden of which I had no conception until I became President General. And the work of the Registrar General is also exceedingly burdensome. It is with the utmost difficulty that Mr. Parks has been able to carry on this work, and I desire to make my personal acknowledgment of the fidelity and loyalty to the organization of these two outstanding officers. But, even with the inadequate compensation which is paid to the men who hold these offices, the revenues of the National Society are inadequate to the expenses. There has been no change in the matter of providing for the revenues of the Society for many, many years, and in the interim the cost of everything has increased way out of sight. We undoubtedly in our own household economic conditions have recognized the necessity for enlargement, and the National Society was obliged some time ago to borrow $5,000 to carry on its work until the remittances from the individual State Societies should be received. Some relief is absolutely necessary, unless the Society is to become insolvent. The recommendations of the Executive Committee appeared in the BULLETIN, and they will be undoubtedly the subject of debate here. All that I desire to say, in calling the Congress together, is that the situation is one which is very critical, and it is very necessary that some relief be given the National Society, and I hope there may not be such division of opinion among those who are willing to give the relief as will result in the unfortunate situation which obtained at the end of the Congress last year, when we found that by reason of irregularities in the action of the Society no relief had been granted, although the Congress intended to grant relief. I trust that, not for that reason or any other, will there be a failure to meet this issue squarely.

One of the State Societies has seen fit to circularize the National Society in criticism of the Directors General in one of the actions taken by the Board. I refer to the proposed amendment of the charter of the National Society providing for the increase in the number of Trustees of the Society to 80. We are now limited to 60 Trustees, and the provision of our Constitution is that our General Officers provided for in section 1 of article 5, together with one member from each State Society, shall constitute the Board of Trustees of the National Society. There are 48 States. We have been in the habit of treating the District of Columbia, the Far East Society, and the Society in France as State Societies, making in all 52. I am aware that some of these Societies are moribund and can scarcely be said to exist. Nevertheless, we have nominally 52 State Societies and 13 General Officers, making a total of 65 entitled to be members of the Board of Trustees, whereas the Charter limits us now to a maximum of 60. In the opinion of the Executive Committee, that was a situation which called for the only method of relief which was in our power to seek, namely, the amendment of our Charter by an act of Congress, and the Executive Committee saw fit to endeavor to put that through Congress. When objection was made by a State Society, further action was postponed, and I recommend that the National Society take action on that subject.

Another amendment has been proposed at the instance of some of the Far West Societies. I am able to speak positively as to the views of California, Utah, and Oregon Societies. The time set, under the present Constitution, for holding the annual meeting is extremely inconvenient for Societies located in the other extreme of the country. The great majority of you who are here today are able to reach Springfield by one day's journey from your homes. A man cannot come from one of those Pacific Coast Societies to the meeting and attend the Congress on much less than three weeks' absence from home, and he will nearly always find that things which he wants to do here occupy other time; so that in making the trip it involves about a month's absence from his desk in order to attend a Congress.

Now, compatriots, you can readily understand the burden which is involved in coming here at a time when business is still active. And if the Constitution remains as it is now, you will find that the Far West Societies will continue to be inadequately represented at this Congress. If any one thinks that the Societies in that part of the Union are not active, he has another guess coming. My suggestion is that we make an amendment to the Constitution which would bring the holding of the Congress nearer to the vacation period. My own suggestion was that it be held the last week in June. Many times we have members of the Society who want to come on to an eastern college for some class reunion, to see a son or daughter graduate at an eastern college, and if the time for holding the Congress was fixed at about that period of the year, it could be combined to advantage and it would be possible for us more frequently to be adequately represented. However, I am mindful of the fact that, under any and all conditions, the largest number of members in attendance at the Society will be from this section of the country, and I do not wish to press anything which will be inconvenient to the greater number.

I have presumed to speak at greater length than I intended because I am well aware that the amendment will not carry. I have sounded the sentiment here and all I want is to present the viewpoint of the members of our section of the country who, for the reason that I have stated, are unable to be adequately represented at the Congress, unless you come to our territory, which I hope you will frequently do.

The most important piece of work which the Society has had in hand since I have been your presiding officer has been the review of the school books of American history. Any one who has not looked into that subject can have no adequate idea of the kind of teaching which the young men and women are receiving in our public schools on the subject of American History. It is only here and there that you find any one who acquires after he leaves school any considerable knowledge of American history in addition to that which he gets at school in his school course, while a young man. And these school books are introduced under a system which is radically and fundamentally wrong. The text-books, as a matter of practice, are introduced on the personality of the selling agent much more than on the merits of the books themselves. The boards who select them are made up mostly of school teachers and people of small means, undoubtedly well meaning, and they are undoubtedly often swept off their feet by the courtesies and attentions which are extended to them by the smooth-talking, slick young men who are allowed almost unlimited expense accounts by the publishers. The books are more offensive than you would have any idea if you have not looked into them. Some of them almost entirely exclude the history of the American Revolution, devoting in one case out of 627 pages 17 pages to the Revolution, and five of those are devoted to the frontier fighting. There are sins of omission and sins of commission. Some of them malign the reputation of our institutions, some are sympathetic in one sense and opposed in another, and in one instance they are apologetic for Benedict Arnold and exceedingly critical of the people of Philadelphia with whom Arnold had acquaintance, and in many respects the publications are open to substantial criticisms. And there are at least two of them that are out-and-out socialistic. The influence of many of them will be very bad and tend to make students Bolshevistic and Communistic, and I earnestly recommend that the National Society take action on this subject, and that it follow up the work already started. There has been a great deal done throughout the Union, a great deal of attention has been focused on this matter, and it is quite possible in all of the States throughout the Union for a review to be effected which will react favorably throughout the next generation. (Applause.)

Now, just a few words more. We have a large mass of business to transact and a short time in which to transact it. I earnestly recommend that all compatriots who take part in the debates of the Congress weigh their words carefully, remember that the time is precious, and keep the discussion in as narrow compass as will admit of the fair presentation of your views, and remember that one of the purposes of this Society is to promote fellowship among the descendants of the soldiers who fought in the War of the Revolution. Let us leave here in the spirit of brotherhood, and let us remember that we are all gentlemen; and, however much me may differ, let us always discuss questions with the kindliness of spirit and courtesy which is becoming this great organization. (Applause.)

Past President General Woodworth moved that a Committee on Resolutions be appointed by the Chair, to which all resolutions shall be deferred without debate. The motion was adopted.

Past President General Ames moved that the Committee on Resolutions be considered a Committee on Official Reports, including the subject-matter of the President General's Report, together with the recommendations which he made, the committee to report upon these matters to the Congress. The motion was adopted.

The President General appointed as Committee on Resolutions Newell B. Woodworth, of New York; George Hale Nutting, of Massachusetts; George Albert Smith, of Utah; Joseph B. Doyle, of Ohio, and Lieutenant-Colonel Isaac B. Brown, of Pennsylvania.

Mr. Ames moved to extend the greetings of the Congress to all Past Presidents General not present, and also to Mr. Albert M. Henry, of Detroit, and Mr. Teunis D. Huntting, of Brooklyn, who were detained and prevented from attending the Congress by illness. The motion was adopted.

The President General then asked that resolutions be presented at this time, that they might be referred to the Committee on Resolutions. The following resolutions were then presented:

By Vice-President General Lewis: A resolution with respect to revision of text-books.

By Mr. Brewer, of New Jersey: A resolution relative to the correction of the Charter.

By Dr. Bangs, of Massachusetts: A resolution relative to the National Archives Building.

By Mr. Vail, of New Jersey: A resolution with respect to the observance of the 150th anniversary of Revolutionary events.

By Mr. Ely, of District of Columbia Society: Respecting immigration.

By Mr. Warner, of Massachusetts: A resolution in regard to the Lexington Memorial.

By Mr. Brewer, of New Jersey: A resolution favoring the National Society publishing a magazine.

By Judge Bonniwell, of Pennsylvania: A resolution relative to the 150th anniversary of the Signing of the Declaration of Independence.

By Mr. Arnold, of New Jersey: A resolution relative to respect for the flag.

Mr. Wiggin, of Massachusetts, offered the following resolution and moved its adoption:

Resolved, That the National Society of the Sons of the American Revolution hereby authorizes the appointment of Campatriot John F. Jones, of the Massachusetts Society, for thirty-eight years a resident of South Carolina, as Special Organizer of the Sons of the American Revolution for the States of North and South Carolina, under a commission to run for one year, which shall bear the signatures of the President General and the Secretary General and the seal of the National Society.

The President General stated that if there was no objection the rules would be suspended and this resolution acted upon at once. There being no objection, the resolution was unanimously adopted.

A resolution by Mr. North, of California, with regard to the revision of text-books was referred to the Committee on Resolutions.

The report of Secretary General Frank B. Steele was read and approved.

The report of Registrar General Parks was read and approved.

The report of Treasurer General John H. Burroughs was adopted as read, subject to the approval of the Auditing Committee.

The Secretary General read the report of Cornelius A. Pugsley in behalf of the Trustees of the Permanent Fund.

Upon motion of Admiral Baird, of the District of Columbia, it was voted that all reports be received and spread upon the record.

Vice-Presidents General Nutting of Massachusetts, Larner of the District of Columbia, Lewis of Kentucky, and Hawley of Iowa (given by Mr. Wentworth) presented reports from their several districts. There was no report at this time from Vice-President General Bell, of Washington.

Recess until 2:30 p. m.

Afternoon Session, May 15

The President General called the session to order at 2:30 p. m.

The report of Historian General George C. Arnold was received.

The report of Chaplain General Lyman Whitney Allen was received.

The report of Chancellor General Eugene C. Bonniwell was received.

The report of Genealogist General Walter K. Watkins was received.

A resolution was offered by Mr. Bowman, of Illinois, relative to issuing cards of membership. This was referred to the Committee on Resolutions.

An invitation to join the National American Council in their meeting on May 17 was received and accepted.

The report of the Committee on Memorials—Mr. R. C. Ballard Thruston, of Kentucky, chairman—was received.

The report of the Committee on Patriotic Education—Mr. Linn Paine, of Missouri, chairman—was received.

Mr. Woodworth, chairman of the Committee on Resolutions, presented the following:

Resolved, That the Sons of the American Revolution, in National Congress assembled, express their deep interest in the subject of text-books on American history in use in our public schools. We protest against the use of any text-book which lauds the Tories and censures the patriots, which maligns the memory of any of the great men of the Revolutionary period or undervalues the services and sacrifices by which our national independence was won. Text-books on American history should be written only by those who are in sympathy with the principles for which our forefathers fought. Every such history should adequately stress the story of the American Revolution, portray in colorful outline the heroic incidents of the struggle, and teach the priceless value of the institutions which we inherit from our forefathers. We protest against any text-book which teaches socialism, bolshevism, or class hatred. The Committee on Patriotic Education is instructed to carry this resolution into effect and is authorized to take all needful measures to eliminate from our schools all text-books objectionable on the above grounds.

Mr. Woodworth moved the adoption of the resolution.

The motion was seconded, the question was put, and the resolution was unanimously adopted.

Mr. Woodworth offered as a substitute resolution, in reference to the proper saluting of the flag by civilians, the following:

Resolved, That the report of the Joint Committee of the Patriotic Societies in the District of Columbia in reference to the proper civilian salute to the flag and the proper manner of the display of the flag be printed in full in the BULLETIN during the ensuing year.

Mr. Woodworth moved the adoption of the resolution, the motion was seconded, the question put, and the resolution was unanimously adopted.

At this point in the proceedings the delegates were advised of the arrival of Mrs. George Maynard Minor, President General of the Daughters of the American Revolution, and the President General appointed Past Presidents General Pugsley and Beardsley a committee to escort Mrs. Minor to the platform. Mrs. Minor was accorded a prolonged ovation and made a most graceful and pleasing address, bringing greetings and assurances of co-operation from her sister Society.

The chairman of the Committee on Resolutions then continued to report:

Mr. Woodworth presented the following resolution, offered by the Pennsylvania Society:

Resolved, That we unreservedly commend the purpose of the city of Philadelphia to fittingly commemorate the 150th anniversary of the Signing of the Declaration of Independence by the great exposition devoted to the arts of peace. This Society declares that every patriotic citizen and every patriotic society should unite in this reaffirmation of the nation's loyalty to the immortal principles enunciated in that great document, so that the spirit which animated the founders of the Republic should blaze afresh in the hearts of their descendants and of the new comers to this land of liberty.

Mr. Woodworth moved the adoption of the resolution, the motion was seconded, the question put, and the resolution was unanimously adopted.

Mr. Woodworth presented the following resolution:

Resolved, That the telegraphic suggestion of Compatriot C. Robert Churchill, President of the Louisiana Society, regarding issuing annual membership cards to paid up members, be approved, and that the completion and execution of the plan be referred to the Secretary General, to be carried out either through his own office or that of the various State Societies as may be found most convenient, after full consideration.

Mr. Woodworth moved the adoption of the resolution, the motion was seconded, the question put, and the resolution was unanimously adopted.

Mr. Woodworth presented the following resolution:

Resolved, That the National Society of the Sons of the American Revolution, in Congress assembled, memorialize the Congress of the United States to amend the charter of the National Society of the Sons of the American Revolution by omitting from section 4, line 2, of an act passed by the 59th Congress of the United States of America, "to incorporate the National Society of the Sons of the American Revolution," the words "more than sixty nor," making the section read: "That the property and affairs of said corporation shall be managed by not less than forty trustees," etc., and that the incoming Executive Committee shall, and hereby is, empowered and instructed to take such steps as may be necessary to carry out this action of the Congress.

Mr. Woodworth moved the adoption of the resolution, the motion was seconded, and, after considerable discussion, upon a rising vote the resolution was adopted.

Moved by Mr. White, of Connecticut, that the resolution as reported by the Committee on Resolutions be amended at a proper place, so as to provide for a memorial to Congress for a number of Trustees which shall not exceed 100. Upon vote this amendment was lost and the resolution as reported by the committee was adopted.

The report of the chairman of the Committee on Naval and Military Records, Admiral Baird, of the District of Columbia, was received.

The report of the chairman of the Committee on Americanization and Aliens, Judge Harvey F. Remington, of New York, was received.

The report of the Committee on the Flag was read by the Registrar General in the absence of Chairman Cox, of the District of Columbia.

The report of the Committee on National Archives Building was read by the Secretary General.

The report of the Committee on Increased Memberbership—Hon. Chancellor L. Jenks, of Illinois, chairman—was received.

The report of the chairman of the Committee on Observance of Flag Day, Mr. Lewis B. Curtis, of Connecticut, was received.

The report of the chairman of the Committee on Observance of Constitution Day—Mr. Louis Annin Ames, chairman—was received.

The report of the Committee on General James Warren Memorial—Mr. Charles Read, chairman—was received.

The report of the Special Committee on new Service Bars was made by the Secretary General in lieu of the chairman, Captain Henry A. Brown, of New York.

The presentation of Traveling Banners then took place.

The presentation of the Syracuse Banner, for greatest numerical increase of membership, was made by Past President General Jenks to the New Jersey Society and accepted by Past President Carl Vail for the New Jersey Society.

The presentation of the Traveling Banner, for the largest percentage of increase, was made by Judge Harvey F. Remington, of New York, to the Tennessee Society, and accepted for this Society by Vice-President General Marvin H. Lewis.

Mr. Ames, of New York, moved that the Committee on Resolutions bring in a resolution relative to the Cuban Memorial to the Maine. This motion was adopted.

The chairman of the Committee on Resolutions, Mr. Woodworth, brought in a further report, as follows:

Resolved, That we favor the erection by the Federal Government, on Lexington Common, of a suitable memorial, to be unveiled and dedicated on the hundred and fiftieth anniversary of the battle; and be it further *Resolved,* That we recommend that this memorial record the names of the seventy-seven Minute Men who there ushered in the American Revolution; and also the names of the twenty-six towns whose citizens took part in the battle which followed.

Mr. Woodworth moved the adoption of the resolution, the motion was seconded, the question put, and the resolution was unanimously adopted.

Mr. Woodworth presented the following resolution, offered by the District of Columbia Society:

Be it resolved by the Congress of the Sons of the American Revolution, at Springfield, Mass., on May 16, 1922, That we heartily endorse the report and recommendation of Lillian Russell in relation to the arrest of immigration, and we urge its unqualified adoption, and that a copy of this resolution be presented to the President of the United States.

Mr. Woodworth moved the adoption of the resolution, the motion was seconded, the question put, and the motion was unanimously adopted.

Judge Remington, of New York, moved that we proceed to the consideration of the proposed amendment in regard to changing Article VII, section 1, of the Constitution with respect to change of date for the annual Congress. This motion was seconded and adopted.

The Secretary General read the proposed amendment, as follows:

That section 1 of Article VII of the Constitution be amended so as to read as follows:

The annual Congress of the National Society for the election of General Officers and for the transaction of business shall be held on the *fourth Monday of August* in each year. The place of such meeting shall be designated by the Board of Trustees.

(Words in italics indicate words changed or added.)

After full discussion, Mr. Woodworth, of New York, moved that the amendment be laid on the table. The motion was seconded, the question put, and the motion to lay on the table was adopted.

Recess was declared until 9 a. m. Tuesday, May 16.

Tuesday Morning Session, May 16

The President General called the Congress to order at 9 o'clock.

Prayer was offered by the Chaplain General.

A telegram of greeting was read from Speaker Gillette, of the House of Representatives.

Mr. Woodworth, chairman of the Committee on Resolutions, reported for his committee as follows:

Mr. Woodworth presented the following resolution, offered by the Abraham Godwin Chapter of Paterson, N. J.:

WHEREAS the one hundred and fiftieth anniversary of the historical events of the American Revolution is in the near future; therefore be it

Resolved, That a special committee be appointed by the President General to arrange for appropriate celebrations by State Societies and local Chapters, and for the observance in the public schools of the country of these near approaching anniversaries.

Mr. Woodworth moved the adoption of the resolution, the motion was seconded, the question put, and the resolution was unanimously adopted.

Mr. Woodworth presented the following resolution:

WHEREAS it is understood that the Government of Cuba is to erect a monument to the dead of the battleship *Maine*, destroyed in the Harbor of Havana; therefore be it

Resolved, That the delegates to the 33d Annual Congress of the Sons of the American Revolution, in Congress assembled, formally express their appreciation of this proposed tribute to be erected by the Government of Cuba, and that the Secretary General convey this expression to the proper authorities, and that the President General be authorized to appoint any committee in connection with this subject that he may deem wise.

Mr. Woodworth moved the adoption of this resolution, the motion was seconded, the question put, and the resolution was unanimously adopted.

Further amendments to the Constitution were then considered.

The Secretary General read the amendment to Article VI with reference to initiation fee and dues, as follows:

That Article VI of the Constitution of the National Society be amended to read as follows:

ARTICLE VI.—*Initiation Fees and Dues.*

SEC. I. *In addition to the initiation fee, if any, charged by a State Society, there shall be paid an initiation fee of five dollars for membership in the National Society, Sons of the American Revolution. Said fee shall be forwarded to the Registrar General with each application for membership. The payment of said fee shall include an engraved certificate of membership for each newly elected compatriot, to be furnished by the National Society.*

SEC. 2. Each State Society shall pay annually to the Treasurer General, to defray the expense of the National Society, fifty cents for each member thereof, unless intermitted by the National Congress.

SEC. 3. Such dues shall be paid on or before the first day of April in each year for the ensuing year, in order to secure representation in the Congress of the National Society.

(Italics indicate amendments added.)

In order to improve the phraseology, it was moved by Mr. Rice, President of the Rhode Island Society, to amend the amendment as follows:

In section I, after the word "Revolution," substitute for the remainder of said section the following:

"Said fee shall be forwarded to the Registrar General with each application for membership and shall entitle the newly elected compatriot to receive from the National Society an engraved certificate of membership."

After some discussion, the question upon the amendment to the proposed amendment of the Constitution, Article VI, was adopted.

The question then recurred upon the adoption of the amendment to the Constitution of Article VI as amended, and after full discussion this amendment to the Constitution was adopted by a vote of 142 in favor to 9 against.

Section I will now read as follows:

ARTICLE VI.—*Initiation Fees and Dues.*

SEC. 1. *In addition to the initiation fee, if any, charged by a State Society, there shall be paid an initiation fee of five dollars for membership in the National Society, Sons of the American Revolution. Said fee shall be forwarded to the Registrar General with each application for membership and shall entitle the newly elected compatriot to receive from the National Society an engraved certificate of membership.*

At this point the Committee on Credentials made its report, which was read by Mr. Weeks, of New Jersey, showing 195 delegates present, accompanied by 69 ladies.

Mr. Brewer, of New Jersey, moved that the National Society, Sons of the American Revolution, waive all initiation fees on applications received prior to October 1, 1922.

This was seconded, the question was put, and upon a standing vote it appeared that 100 having voted in favor of the motion and 26 against it, the motion was adopted, and it was so declared by the Chair.

The amendment to section 2 of Article VI of the Constitution was then discussed, and it was moved by Mr. Rice, of Rhode Island, that this proposed amendment to the Constitution be laid upon the table.

The question being put, upon a rising vote it was found that 44 voted in favor of the motion and 82 against, and the motion was declared lost.

The question then recurred upon the amendment as proposed by the Executive Committee to section 2 of Article VI.

Mr. Brewer, of New Jersey, asked the President General if this amendment was properly before the Congress.

The President General ruled that, in his opinion, it was properly before the Congress.

Mr. Brewer respectfully appealed from the decision of the Chair.

The President General put the motion as follows: All in favor of sustaining the decision of the Chair will rise and remain standing until counted by the Secretary General.

The SECRETARY GENERAL: Twenty-two are in favor of sustaining the Chair.

The PRESIDENT GENERAL: All contrary minded will rise and remain standing until counted.

The SECRETARY GENERAL: One hundred against.

The PRESIDENT GENERAL: The appeal is sustained by the Congress. The point of order appears to be well taken and the second amendment is not before the Congress for consideration.

The Secretary General then read the amendment to Article V, section 4, of the Constitution, as follows:

An Executive Committee of seven, consisting of the President General as chairman and six members to be nominated by him *from the Board of Trustees* and approved by *said* Board [ ], shall in the interim between the meetings of the Board transact such business as may be delegated to it by a Congress of the Society or *by the Board of Trustees. Said committee shall furnish the members of the Board, at regular periods, at least semi-annually, an explicit statement of the business transacted by said committee in the interim between such periods.*

(Italics indicate amendments added, and brackets, words omitted.)

Mr. White, of Connecticut, after stating that "this amendment was proposed with a clear conscience, without any selfish motive by the State Society, having in mind purely and simply what it believed to be for the best interests of the National Society as a whole, and that after having discussed the matter freely with other members of the Society," moved that this amendment be laid upon the table.

This was seconded, the question was put, and the motion to lay on the table was adopted.

Mr. WHITE (of Connecticut): Mr. President, I move that a committee, consisting of five members from the National Society, shall be selected by the President General in office—the incoming President General—and five members to be selected by the Connecticut Society, be formed, and that this committee meet and go over the whole matter of this difference of opinion which the Connecticut Society has had, in the hope that an agreement can be arrived at, and that a report be made to the Executive Committee, so that said report may be published in the December BULLETIN, and that the State Societies can be notified in the usual and proper way, in order to get the matter properly before the next Congress.

The motion being seconded, the question was put and the motion was adopted.

Mr. White, of Connecticut, moved that the incoming President General and the incoming Chancellor General be a committee charged with the duty to examine the Charter, Constitution, and By-Laws and make such recommendations as shall harmonize the three documents, one with the other; they to report to the Society through the BULLETIN at the earliest possible date.

This motion was seconded, the question was put, and the motion adopted.

Mr. Wiggin, of Massachusetts, moved the adoption of the following resolution:

Resolved, That the Massachusetts Society, Sons of the American Revolution, instruct its delegates to the next National Congress of the Sons of the American Revolution to urge that body to pass a resolution calling on the Congress to appropriate funds and pass the necessary legislation looking to the immediate erection of an archives building where the national records may be conveniently stored and their safety assured.

There being no objection, the resolution of the Massachusetts Society was unanimously endorsed.

Mr. Ames moved that the following amendment to the Constitution be proposed by this Congress for consideration by the Society, for action at the next National Congress.

That Section 2, Article VI of the Constitution of the National Society be amended to read as follows:

Each State Society shall pay annually to the Treasurer General to defray the expense of the National Society, *one dollar* for each member thereof, unless intermitted by the National Congress.

Such dues shall be paid on or before the first day of April for the ensuing year, in order to secure representation in the Congress of the National Society.

(Italic indicates amendments added or changed.)

This motion being seconded, the question was put and the motion was adopted.

Mr. Woodworth presented the following preamble and resolution:

WHEREAS the Armament Conference called together by the President of the United States of America at Washington, in November, 1921, is recognized as an important step in the advance of civilization, the outstanding weakness of our government, as shown by its history, having been its lack of a military policy, with its resultant invariable failure to be ready when war has come; and

WHEREAS this Society deems it to be as essential today as it was in the time of the days of the Revolution, to "provide for the common defense" of our country, in order that we may continue to preserve the heritage of liberty and independence for ourselves and our posterity; therefore be it

Resolved by the Society of the Sons of the American Revolution in Congress assembled at Springfield, Mass., That the Congress of the United States be asked to support the National Defense Act of 1920, which for the first time in our history gave the country a military policy and provided for a system of organization and training of the Regular Army, National Guard, and Organized Reserves as one co-ordinated army; and also that Congress be asked to comply with the recommendation of the President and the Secretaries of War and of the Navy in determining the size and strength of the Army and Navy; copies of these resolutions to be furnished to the President, members of his Cabinet, and to each member of the Congress of the United States, and also be given to the press.

Mr. Woodworth moved the adoption of the resolution, the motion was seconded, the question put, and the resolution was unanimously adopted. .

Mr. Woodworth, for the Committee on Resolutions, moved that the telegram of the Delaware Society, suggesting the adoption of a smaller and less expensive Certificate of Membership be referred to the incoming Executive Committee with power.

The motion was seconded, the question put, and the resolution adopted unanimously.

Mr. Woodworth presented the following resolution on immigration:

WHEREAS our heritage, the heritage from men who lived and wrought and fought and died to safeguard the fundamental institutions of America, depends upon quality of citizenship; and

WHEREAS quality of citizenship depends to a great extent upon a permanent and comprehensive solution of the immigration problem, which since the World War has become especially grave in some of its aspects; therefore be it.

Resolved, That the National Congress of the Sons of the American Revolution, in annual session at Springfield, Mass., respectfully petitions the Congress of the United States to give to this subject of immigration its careful consideration, with a view to adopting a policy, both selective and restrictive in character, that will aim, first of all, to safeguard the future of the nation for our children and our children's children, and be at the same time, in so far as possible, consistent with our economic needs.

Mr. Woodworth moved the adoption of the resolution, the motion was seconded, the qustion put, and the resolution was unanimously adopted.

Mr. WOODWORTH: Mr. President General, the Committee on Resolutions has prepared a formal resolution of thanks to the local Chapter and would move that this resolution be spread upon the minutes and the Secretary General be instructed to furnish a copy to the local Chapter:

The National Society of the Sons of the American Revolution, in Congress assembled, May 16, 1922, in grateful appreciation of the kindness, courtesy, and generous hospitality of our compatriots of Massachusetts and the George Washington Chapter, do hereby extend to them our sincere thanks. Our visit has been most delightful, from the splendid opening address of Governor Cox, throughout the entire proceedings. Everything has been done to make our stay enjoyable. Our visit to Springfield will be long remembered by all who have been privileged to enjoy it.

The motion was seconded, the question put, and the resolution adopted unanimously.

Mr. WOODWORTH: The Committee on Resolutions has now concluded its duties and moves for its discharge.

The PRESIDENT GENERAL: The committee will be discharged, unless there is objection, and will receive the thanks of the Congress.

Invitations for the next session of the Congress were then received.

Dr. Robert Foster, of Tennessee, was recognized and presented the invitation of the Tennessee Society for the National Congress to meet at Nashville, Tenn., in 1923. This was supplemented by telegrams and letters; also by remarks from Mr. Thruston, Mr. Lewis, Admiral Baird, and others.

Mr. George Albert Smith, of the Utah Society, was recognized and presented the invitation of the Utah Society for the next Congress to meet at Salt Lake City. His address was supplemented by telegrams and letters and remarks by Mr. North, of California.

Mr. Herbert Flowers, of Maryland, was recognized and presented the invitation of the Maryland Society for the Congress to meet at Frederick, which was supplemented by endorsements from others.

In accordance with the requirements of the Constitution, the invitations were referred to the incoming Board of Trustees

There being no further business under the head of "New Business," the Congress proceeded to the election of officers.

Judge Adrian Lyon, President of the New Jersey Society, placed in nomination for the office of President General of the National Society Major Washington Irving Lincoln Adams, of New Jersey, and upon motion the nominations were closed and the Secretary General instructed to cast one ballot for Washington Irving Lincoln Adams, of New Jersey, for President General. The Secretary General having cast the ballot, Mr. Adams was duly elected President General of the National Society for the ensuing year.

Major Adams was escorted to the platform by Past Presidents General Woodworth and Pugsley and accepted the office with a few words of deep appreciation.

Prof. Ashley K. Hardy, President of New Hampshire Society, placed in nomination for the office of Vice-President General for the New England District the name of Harry T. Lord, of New Hampshire. There being no further nominations, Mr. Lord was unanimously elected Vice-President General for the First, or New England District.

Mr. Selden M. Ely, President of the District of Columbia Society, placed in nomination for the office of Vice-President General for the Second, or Middle and Coast District, the name of Mr. Philip F. Larner, of the District of Columbia. There being no further nominations for this office, Mr. Larner was unanimously re-elected for the office of Vice-President General for the Second, or Middle and Coast District.

Mr. Marvin H. Lewis, of Kentucky, placed in nomination for the office of Vice-President General for the Third, or Mississippi Valley, East District, the name of Louis A. Bowman, of Illinois. There being no further nominations for this office, Mr. Bowman was unanimously elected to the office of Vice-President General for the Third, or Mississippi Valley, East District.

Mr. Wentworth, of Iowa, placed in nomination for the office of Vice-President General for the Fourth, or Mississippi Valley, West District, the name of Mr. Henry B. Hawley, of Iowa. There being no further nominations for this office, Mr. Hawley was unanimously re-elected to the office of Vice-President General for the Fourth, or Mississippi Valley, West District.

Mr. Abbot R. Heywood, of Utah, placed in nomination for the office of Vice-President General for the Fifth, or Mountain and Pacific District, the name of Mr. George Albert Smith, of Utah. There being no further nominations, Mr. Smith was unanimously elected to the office of Vice-President General for the Fifth, or Mountain and Pacific District.

Mr. George D. Bangs, President of the Empire State Society, placed in nomination for the office of Secretary General the name of Mr. Frank Bartlett Steele, of New York. There being no further nominations for this office, Mr. Steele was unanimously re-elected to the office of Secretary General.

Mr. John H. Burroughs, of New York, placed in nomination for the office of Treasurer General the name of Mr. George McKenzie Roberts, of New York. There being no further nominations, Mr. Roberts was unanimously elected to the office of Treasurer General.

It was moved by Mr. Curtis, of Connecticut, that a rising vote of thanks be tendered Mr. John H. Burroughs for his fifteen years of devoted service as Treasurer General of the National Society. The motion was adopted by a unanimous rising vote.

Mr. Herbert B. Flowers, of Maryland, placed in nomination for the office of Registrar General the name of Mr. Francis Barnum Culver, of Maryland. There being no further nominations for this office, Mr. Culver was unanimously elected to the office of Registrar General.

Mr. Robert P. Boggis, of Ohio, placed in nomination for the office of Historian General the name of Mr. Joseph B. Doyle, of Ohio. There being no further nominations for this office, Mr. Doyle was unanimously elected to the office of Historian General.

Mr. Chancellor L. Jenks, of Illinois, placed in nomination for the office of Chancellor General the name of Hon. Eugene C. Bonniwell, of Pennsylvania. There being no further nominations for this office, Judge Bonniwell was unanimously re-elected to the office of Chancellor General.

Mr. Luther W. Atwood, of Massachusetts, placed in nomination for the office of Genealogist General the name of Walter K. Watkins, of Massachusetts. There being no further nominations for this office, Mr. Watkins was unanimously re-elected to the office of Genealogist General.

Mr. Burton H. Wiggin, of Massachusetts, placed in nomination for the office of Chaplain General the name of Rev. Frederic W. Perkins, D. D., of Massachusetts. There being no further nominations, Dr. Perkins was unanimously elected to the office of Chaplain General.

Mr. Pugsley, of New York, moved that a rising vote of thanks be tendered the retiring President General because of his abilities as a presiding officer, his eloquent addresses throughout the year in which he has been President General, and his fine judgment and impartial administration. The motion was unanimously adopted by a rising vote.

Mr. Ely, of the District of Columbia, moved a rising vote of thanks to Mr. William S. Parks for his services as Registrar General during the past year. The motion was put and the members responded unanimously by a rising vote.

Mr. Ely, of the District of Columbia, moved that nominations of State Societies for Trustees of the National Society be accepted and that the nominees be declared Trustees of the National Society, and where there are no nominees the Presidents of State Societies be the Trustees for such States. This motion was put and adopted.

The names of the Board of Trustees will be found on page 4.

Whereupon, there being no further business, upon motion, duly made and seconded, the Congress was adjourned *sine die*.

Minutes of the Meeting of the Board of Trustees, National Society, Sons of the American Revolution, Held at the Hotel Kimball, Springfield, Mass., Tuesday, May 16, 1922, at 12.45 p. m.

The meeting was called to order by President General W. I. Lincoln Adams.

Upon roll call the following members responded: President General Adams; General Officers: Vice-Presidents General Larner, Lord, Bowman, Smith, Secretary General Steele, Registrar General Culver, Treasurer General George McK. Roberts, Chancellor General Bonniwell, Genealogist General Watkins; Trustees: Ames, of New York; Wentworth, of Iowa; Nutting, of Massachusetts; McCamant, of Oregon; White, of Connecticut; Kiggins, of New Jersey; Spencer, of Utah. There were also present Mr. Flowers, of Maryland; Mr. Ely, of the District of Columbia, and Mr. Lewis, of Kentucky.

The President General presented his nominations for the Executive Committee as follows: Wallace McCamant, of Oregon; Louis Annin Ames, of New York; Arthur Preston Summer, of Rhode Island; George E. Pomeroy, of Ohio; Marvin H. Lewis, of Kentucky, and Harry T. Lord, of New Hampshire. Upon motion, these nominations were unanimously confirmed.

The matter of deciding upon the location for the next Congress was then discussed, and, upon vote being taken, the city of Nashville, Tenn., was fixed upon as the meeting place of the National Congress, Sons of the American Revolution, in 1923. It was moved by Mr. Wentworth that the Trustees appropriate $500 toward the expense of holding the Congress for 1923 at Nashville. This was carried.

It was moved by Mr. Ames that the Executive Committee be empowered to carry on the work of the Society for the ensuing year. Carried.

It was moved by Mr. White that the salary of the Registrar General of the National Society, Sons of the American Revolution, be $1,200 per annum, payable in monthly installments of $100 per month, and the salary of the Secretary General of the National Society, Sons of the American Revolution, be $1,800 per annum, payable in equal monthly amounts of $150, with the definite understanding that the above-mentioned salaries shall include all expenses for clerical services rendered in connection with these two offices, and there shall be no additional charge submitted by the Registrar General or Secretary General for any expenses save for stationery, printing, engraving and engrossing of certificates, postage, and telegraph charges. This motion was duly seconded and adopted.

It was moved by Mr. Wentworth that the traveling expenses of the Secretary General be paid for his attendance at meetings of the Executive Committee and the National Congress, and that the expenses of the Registrar General, Treasurer General, and Chairman of the Committee on Credentials be paid for attendance at the National Congress. Carried.

It was moved by Mr. White that the Secretary General should submit a brief report of the proceedings of the Executive Committee to each Trustee in advance of publication thereof in any issue of the BULLETIN. Carried.

Upon motion, the meeting adjourned.

Frank B. Steele
Secretary General.

Minutes of the Meeting of the Executive Committee, Held Tuesday, May 16, 1922, at Country Club, Springfield, Mass.

Present: President General Adams, Past President and Director General McCamant, Past President and Director General Ames, Director General Sumner, Director General Lewis, Director General Lord, Secretary General Steele; also Past President General Jenks, Past President General Woodworth, Past President General Thruston, Past President General Wentworth, Past President General Pugsley, Past President General Beardsley, Past President General Marble, Mr. Francis Barnum Culver, Registrar General, and Vice-President General Larner.

The meeting was called to order by the President General.

It was moved by Mr. Ames that the Secretary General edit and condense the reports of the Congress, and when so edited and condensed they be published in the BULLETIN. Carried.

It was moved by Past President General McCamant and duly seconded that the matter of changing the size and form of the certificates of membership to be presented to the members be left to the President General, Director General Ames, and the Secretary General, with power to provide a more convenient and less expensive certificate than that now in use. Carried.

It was moved by Director General Sumner that the Executive Committee be empowered to carry on the business of the Society during the year, either by letter or telegram. Carried.

It was moved by Mr. Lord that the President General and the Registrar General be empowered to rent rooms for the archives of the Society in Washington, D. C. Carried.

The President General appointed Mr. Pugsley, Mr. Roberts, and the President *ex officio* as Committee on Permanent Fund.

It was moved by Mr. Ames that, in order to carry out the direction of the National Congress held on May 15 and 16, 1922, the President General appoint a committee of five, including himself as *ex officio* member, as a Committee on Charter Revision. Carried.

The President General appointed upon this Committee on Charter Revision Hon. Cornelius A. Pugsley, of Peekskill, N. Y., chairman; Adrian Lyon, of Perth Amboy, N. J.; Past President General James H. Preston, of Baltimore, Md.; Hon. Rollin S. Woodruff, of New Haven, Conn., and the President General, W. I. Lincoln Adams.

Frank B. Steele
Secretary General.

SOCIAL FEATURES OF THE CONGRESS AT SPRINGFIELD

On Sunday evening, May 14, a special patriotic service was held at the South Congregational Church. The delegates, led by the local committee, marched in a body to the church, headed by the national colors and our own standards. A most beautiful service was held—lovely music sung by a remarkably fine choir, an impressive ritual and prayer by the pastor of the church, Rev. James Gordon Gilkie, and an eloquent address by our beloved Chaplain General, Rev. Lyman Whitney Allen—and all left a deep impression upon those who attended this service.

Luncheon was served to the delegates and ladies at the Hotel Kimball at noon, between the sessions of the Congress on Monday, and on that evening a charming reception was given by former President of the George Washington Chapter, Dr. John MacDuffie and Mrs. MacDuffie, at the MacDuffie School, in Central Street. Nothing could have been more delightful than the visit to this famous institution, which was thrown open for inspection, to feel the warmth of Doctor and Mrs. MacDuffie's greetings, and realize in the students that were present what a fine result he is achieving. This was best illustrated in the charming little Oriental girl who made such an impression on every one who met her.

The drive around Springfield's beautiful streets, with the subsequent stop and luncheon at the Country Club, was most interesting and further demonstrated to the delegates and guests that the hospitality of this remarkably fine city was unbounded.

The banquet at the Hotel Kimball, in the evening, was attended by several hundred delegates and guests and was a brilliant occasion. Past President General McCamant made a masterly address and carried his audience to the highest pinnacle of patriotism with his eloquence and fervor. Major W. l. Lincoln Adams, the newly elected President General, spoke in his usual happy vein and told of his desire to make the Society larger and better during his coming term of office. Other addresses were made by Mrs. Albert Calder, 2d, of Providence, R. I., representing the Daughters of the American Revolution as Vice-President General; Dr. Charles H. Bangs, representing the Massachusetts State Society; Captain John S. Barrows, of the Governor's Staff, representing the Commonwealth of Massachusetts, and Honorable Charles Wilder Bosworth, of Springfield. The banquet was most delightfully presided over by the accomplished and genial President of the George Washington Chapter, Mr. Charles F. Warner.

One of the interesting and enjoyable features of this entertainment was a living tableau of "The Spirit of '76," truthfully posed by three young men of the Junior Society, who marched from the banquet hall after the tableau with as proud a tread as any battle-scarred veterans could, to their fife and drums. At this banquet was also conferred one of the Society's bronze War Service Medals for distinguished military service, upon Mr. Robert Foster, of Nashville, Tenn., a delegate from that State and the young man who extended the invitation to the Congress to meet in his city in 1923, at the morning session. Altogether when the good-byes were said after this final function all felt that it was a most fitting close to a series of very delightful hospitalities.

OFFICERS AND DELEGATES PRESENT AT THE 33d ANNUAL CONGRESS OF THE NATIONAL SOCIETY, SONS OF THE AMERICAN REVOLUTION.

President General, Wallace McCamant.
Vice-President General, George Hale Nutting.
Vice-President General, Philip F. Larner.
Vice-President General, Marvin H. Lewis.
Secretary General, Frank Bartlett Steele.
Registrar General, William S. Parks.
Treasurer General, John H. Burroughs.
Historian General, George Carpenter Arnold.
Chancellor General, Eugene C. Bonniwell.
Genealogist General, Walter K. Watkins.
Chaplain General, Rev. Lyman Whitney Allen, D. D.

Past Presidents General

Hon. C. A. Pugsley
William A. Marble
Newell B. Woodworth
Louis Annin Ames

Hon. Morris B. Beardsley
Roger C. Ballard Thruston
Elmer M. Wentworth
Chancellor L. Jenks

Directors General

Washington I. L. Adams   George E. Pomeroy   Arthur F. Sumner

Delegates

CALIFORNIA

Lt.-Com. Seabury C. Mastick, U. S. N.   Arthur W. North

CONNECTICUT

Edward W. Beardsley
Leverett Belknap
Frank E. Blakeman
O. H. Broyhwell
Frederick A. Doolittle
George S. Goddard
Joseph C. Gorton
Wilson H. Lee
A. McC. Mathewson
Dr. Frederic J. Murless, Jr.
John M. Parker, Jr.

Edgar L. Pond
Hon. Ernest E. Rogers
George H. Sage
Edwin W. Schultz
Charles G. Stone
Col. Tracy B. Warren
Martin Welles
Herbert H. White
Clarence Horace Wickham
Harry R. Williams
Arthur E. Woodruff

DISTRICT OF COLUMBIA

Rear-Admiral George W. Baird
John S. Barker
John I. Brown
Selden Marvin Ely

George R. Ide
Orlando W. Goodwin
Clarence A. Kenyon
J. McD. Stewart

ILLINOIS

Louis A. Bowman   Michaels H. Grassly   William Reed

IOWA

Vincent Arthur Lagen   William B. Sanford

KENTUCKY

J. Swigert Taylor

LOUISIANA

H. Dudley Coleman

MAINE

William B. Berry
James L. Merrick

William Kennedy Sanderson
Philip F. Turner

MARYLAND

Francis B. Culver
Major Herbert C. Fooks
Herbert B. Flowers
Milton W. Gatch

J. Monroe Holland
George Sadtler Robertson
Edward D. Shriner

MASSACHUSETTS

Capt. Charles B. Appleton
Luther Atwood
Col. Alvin R. Bailey
Thomas W. Baldwin
Charles H. Bangs, M. D.
James H. Bigelow
Dr. Waldo E. Boardman
Henry N. Bowman
Henry A. Booth
Cheney H. Calkins
Seth H. Clark
Edward J. Cox
J. Morton Davis
Horace A. Edgecomb
David L. Fiske
Frank P. Forbes
Henry Chapin Halle
Harrison Loring Hamilton
Lincoln C. Haynes

Rev. Lewis W. Hicks
George B. Joslyn
John K. Joy
John Stuart Kirkham
Dr. John MacDuffie
Grenville H. Norcross
Alfred F. Powers
Henry F. Punderson
Samuel F. Punderson
Charles French Read
Edwin G. Rude
Thomas M. Shepherd
T. Julien Silsby
Richard H. Stacy
Luke S. Stowe
Lt.-Col. Walter C. Sweeney, U. S. A.
Arthur O. Taylor
Charles Franklin Warner
Burton H. Wiggin

Dr. Crosley A. Perry (son of a Revolutionary soldier)

MICHIGAN

Almon B. Atwater
Wilbert H. Barrett
Dr. Frank Ward Holt

Edward C. Parsons
Daniel W. Tower

MISSOURI

J. Alonzo Matthews

Linn Paine

NEW HAMPSHIRE

Prof. Ashley Kingsley Hardy

Hon. Harry T. Lord

NEW JERSEY

Bridgewater M. Arnold
Frederick B. Bassett
Harry F. Brewer
J. Stuart Brown
Elvord G. Chamberlin
Henry Vail Condict
William J. Conkling
Moses Miller Crane
Dwight P. Cruikshank
Samuel C. Downs

Hon. Edward R. Folsom
Joseph Holmes
Charles Symmes Kiggins
Frederick B. Lovejoy
Edward H. Lum
Hon. Adrian Lyon
Gilbert D. Maxwell
Chauncey R. McPherson
Albert L. Miller
Ray Acken Miller

George V. Muchmore
Thomas A. Painter
William E. Summers
Louis Sherwood
William Henry Sutton, Jr.
Oscar S. Thompson

Major Bert E. Underwood
Carl Montaigne Vail
John Randell Weeks
Thomas W. Williams
Edward Winslow

NEW YORK (Empire State)

Col. William P. Alexander
Robert M. Anderson
George D. Bangs
George D. Barney, M. D.
Leslie J. Bennett
Brig.-Gen. Oliver B. Bridgman
George Royce Brown
Lewis B. Curtis
Louis B. Dorr
Norman P. Heffley

Walter C. Morris
George McK. Roberts
Hon. Harvey F. Remington
P. Valentine Sherwood
Samuel L. Stewart
Eugene F. Tanke
George L. Walker
Charles H. Wight
John C. Wight

NORTH DAKOTA

Rev. Charles C. Creegan, D. D.

Rev. Casherie DeW. Dowling, D. D.

OHIO

Robert P. Boggis

Joseph B. Doyle

OREGON

Frederick A. Ross

Irving Rand

PENNSYLVANIA

Rev. Mortimer S. Ashton
I. B. Blain
Capt. R. W. Brown

Lt.-Col. Isaac B. Brown
Henry W. Fernberger
William Bronson Williams

RHODE ISLAND

Albert L. Calder, 2d
Henry Clinton Dexter
Mahlon M. Gowdy

Charles Warren Lippett, Jr.
Herbert Ambrose Rice
George Thurston Spicer, M. D.

TENNESSEE

Robert C. Foster

UTAH

Rev. Hoyt E. Henriques
Abbot Rodney Heywood
Edmund Ross Leis

Samuel Lorin Powell
Hon. George Albert Smith
Daniel S. Spencer

VIRGINIA

William E. Crawford

RECAPITULATION

National Officers 11
Past Presidents General....................................... 8
Directors General 3
Delegates 175
                                                            ———
    Total.. 197

SECRETARY GENERAL'S REPORT TO THE NATIONAL CONGRESS AT SPRINGFIELD, MAY 14, 1922

To make a complete report of the work of the Secretary General during any one year would take more time and space than would be either in good taste or your patience would allow. The many and diversified details that are constantly coming up in this office would fill several volumes.

The outlines of the work are, as you know, published in the BULLETIN from time to time, but there are many, too, that are of general interest, and when one has a chance to survey the work of this great organization from a broad standpoint and national outlook, it is easily comprehended that this Society of the Sons of the American Revolution is a body of earnest, patriotic men who are devoting time and money to the best interests of our Nation.

It is the desire of the Secretary General in this report to touch upon some of the most salient incidents of his work and let the report of the States and committees tell the further story of our achievements.

Besides the voluminous correspondence that must be kept up to the minute or the accumulation will be too great to overcome (1,350 letters have been written this year, exclusive of notices, bills, etc.), the most important and interesting work of the Secretary General is the editing of the BULLETIN. As the compatriots are aware, it was decided at the last Congress to cut out the Year Book, which was very expensive and reached but comparatively few of our members, and in place of this enlarge the scope of the BULLETIN, which reaches all members and gives them, to a certain extent, an insight into the workings of the National and State Societies and information concerning activities throughout the country.

Following along these lines, it has been the endeavor of the Secretary General to make the BULLETIN this year a more attractive and readable publication. The compilation and editing of these volumes has been most interesting. The editor has tried to emphasize certain phases of the work of the organization, and the interest and activities shown in many parts of our country, and the co-operation of the National, State, and local Chapter officers has all assisted in giving, it is hoped, a more interesting and a wider view of what the Society is doing, both as a whole and in local matters.

Without the co-operation of the State Societies and local Chapters, these results would be small and the editor urges every delegate to this Congress to see to it that his State or Chapter will lend assistance toward making the BULLETIN carry our message, by sending in at regular intervals items of local activities that pertain to the work of the several States and Chapters in the promotion of any patriotic endeavor or even social gatherings.

It has also been the endeavor of the Secretary General to give credit where credit is due, and when any one Society makes a forward step it has been the policy to give that Society commendation and publicity, in order that others may, perhaps, be inspired to carry out a similar plan or inaugurate another. Nothing that has been sent to the editor along such lines has been kept from the pages of the BULLETIN, and special prominence and notice has been given any Society that has sent word of its special efforts and achievements. From letters that have come into this office, there is no doubt that this has been appreciated by the Society thus noticed, and that the publicity given has been an inspiration to others to do something along similar lines.

The special mention of the remarkable work of New Jersey in increasing membership and acquiring a new home of its own; the splendid increase in membership of the Tennessee Society and the spirit shown there; the continued progress of Louisiana and the fine Year Book issued by that Society this year; the fine work in locating and marking graves that Indiana has done; and the progress all along the line in the old-time leading States of New England, New York, Pennsylvania, Maryland, as well as Middle and Far Western Societies, all demonstrate how we are working toward bigger and better ends, and the publicity given these States in the BULLETIN has been a factor in arousing and promoting interest everywhere and among individuals.

From officers and members have come suggestions as to the betterment of the Society, inspired in many cases by what has been printed in the BULLETIN, one instance being from one of our most energetic secretaries, who has brought up again the long-discussed question of more and better Chapters. His argument is that the formation of local Chapters tends to create local interest in the organization as a whole, and that the Sons of the American Revolution will have much more rapid growth if the emphasis is laid upon this feature of our work. His recommendation is backed up with very definite and convincing arguments and seems to be borne out by the results that have been achieved in those States that have made the greatest increase in local Chapters. It might be well for the Society to consider a well-directed plan along these lines.

Probably the next most important work that has been handled by the Secretary General is the revision of the entire mailing list of the National Society. Former Secretary General Larner made a strong recommendation for this in his last year's report and the Executive Committee authorized the Secretary General to undertake the matter of revision. What seemed even at first to be no small undertaking has turned out to be a stupendous task.

Hardly a day has passed that the present Secretary or an assistant has not worked for hours on this list, and, although the end seems to be in sight, still after each BULLETIN is issued the returns from the post-office come, in surprisingly large quantities, showing the non-delivery of BULLETINS to compatriots. It really seems at these periods as though our membership was a migratory one and only a few of our number stay put for more than four months at a time!

However, this has decreased with each issue, and it is hoped in time there will be a fairly accurate list.

It may surprise some of you to learn that the actual number of cancellations to date of stencils for members who have died, resigned, or been dropped is 1,855. Much of this "dead-wood" has been carried on the list for years. One State Secretary wrote, in answer to an urgent appeal for his State list, that it had not been revised since the organization of his Society, over thirty years ago. This hardly seems credible; but, from the number weeded out of many of the lists, it looks as if this might be literally true in several of the other States. Figures are dry, but one or two other items like the above might be of interest and possibly inspire the delegates, when they return home, to assist the Secretary General to get these lists in better shape. There have been 1,354 changes in addresses on old stencils and several hundred new stencils ordered which were missing on the list, aside entirely from those made out for the regular increase of new members. There are still a few delinquent States from whom the Secretary General has been able to get no response to the requests for the State lists, but in the large majority of cases the response has been hearty and prompt, and this co-operation has been very greatly appreciated. I appeal to the delegates present to carry back an urgent message for continued co-operation along these lines and where no lists have been sent in, to endeavor to have this done. With constant effort alone can this list be kept in any kind of good order, but it is hoped it will never be allowed to drop back into the condition into which it had fallen.

The demand for War Service Medals has kept up steadily through the year and about 150 have been distributed. The new Service Bar that was prepared under the direction of the special committee appointed by the President General, following the resolution of last year's Congress, seems to have met with most hearty approval. Many applications have already been received for them since they were issued, in February, and those who have received them have written, expressing great satisfaction. The question of eligibility to receive both of these rewards is one which should be permanently settled at this meeting.

The observance of Constitution Day was wonderfully successful this year and detailed reports of this celebration were published in the BULLETIN of December and March. It is one of the outstanding features of the Society and gives us excellent publicity throughout the country.

In the matter of publicity, it would seem that many of our Societies have followed the suggestions contained in one of the early BULLETINS of this year, and from clippings that have come into this office from all parts of the country it would appear that our local organizations have awakened to the fact that proper newspaper publicity works great results for the Society. In this connection there came to the Secretary a few days since a most interesting and pleasant incident. A letter was received from the Vice-President and Editor of the California Society of the Sons of the Revolution, inclosing newspaper clippings relating to our Society, as well as our kindred organization of the Sons of the Revolution. These had been received by him through a clipping bureau. This pleasant spirit of co-operation and good fellowship was much appreciated and duly acknowledged. The number of articles was remarkably large and goes to show that we are alive in that part of the country.

Our work along the lines of patriotic education has progressed as usual and will be shown in the report of that committee. In the matter of censorship of school histories, the Society at large and in various localities has evinced great interest and influence, and this is a work in which our President General personally has taken great interest and wielded much influence.

The tour of the President General in February, which was written up by himself, all too modestly, in the March issue of the BULLETIN, was a great success, and all the Societies so fortunate as to have a visit from him were truly delighted, not only in the opportunity to meet him face to face, but in the unquestioned inspiration which his splendid addresses gave. This personal visiting of National Officers to local organizations is an immense help, and many of the smaller local Chapters would find it so if they could afford to invite them to come. Only the other day I had a letter asking if there were any funds provided for this purpose by the National Society and wishing that something of this sort were possible.

There has been most pleasant co-operation and team-work between the Registrar General and the Secretary General, and I desire here to testify to my personal appreciation of this on the part of the Registrar General, without which the conduct of my office with any degree of smoothness would be almost impossible. Certificates to the number of 410 have been signed, sealed, and distributed to the several State Societies within a few days—hours, almost—of receipt in this office. Of course, the great distance these certificates have had to travel this year has caused some delay, but I believe they have been handled as expeditiously as possible under the circumstances.

This pleasant spirit of co-operation between other officers with the Secretary General has not been absent in any instance, but has been particularly apparent in the case of the President General and the Treasurer General, with whom, naturally, next to that of Registrar General, the Secretary General has the greatest correspondence. Incidentally, it might be noted that a large percentage of the "office expense" attributed to the Secretary General in the report of the Treasurer General could be properly charged to other offices, as the Secretary General is expected to issue all bills and other notices on behalf of other offices and committees.

In the March BULLETIN there was printed a complete list of ancestors for all new members elected this year. There had been a constant demand for this from our hard-working registrars and genealogists, and since the publication of the index many letters expressing gratification and commendation have been received. It is recommended that such an index be published at least twice a year.

The one discouraging matter that the Secretary General has had to face is the lack of response from certain States to letters and requests. This lack of co-operation makes the work in some quarters very difficult, and it is hard to believe that any State officer will ignore correspondence addressed to him in his official capacity. When this repeats itself it looks like a deliberate lack of interest or desire to co-operate in the efficient working of the organization as a whole. Happily, instances of this kind are few and are well atoned for by the very cordial response received elsewhere. It is with pleasure that the Secretary reports that several of the Societies which have been in a more or less inactive or at least sluggish condition have come to life this year and now seem to be in the hands of active and enthusiastic men. It is hoped that in another year this spirit will spread to the laggard States and they will awaken to their responsibilities and a need of team-work and co-operation with the National Officers.

Naturally, on account of the many and diversified matters that come to the office of the Secretary General, including numerous problems with which a new Secretary must familiarize himself, mistakes have been made. The Secretary General has endeavored to be careful and conscientious, and if errors have crept in it has not been for any lack of effort or attention to the duties of the office, but on account of multiplicity of details constantly arising. It is believed that any mistakes made have been of slight importance. The one idea of the Secretary General this year has been for the best interests of our great Society, and to put himself at the service of his compatriots for this purpose.

Respectfully submitted,

FRANK B. STEELE,
Secretary General.

May 15, 1922.

REPORT OF TREASURER GENERAL, MAY 10, 1922

Balance on hand May 11, 1921 .... $5,957.42

RECEIPTS

Annual Dues:

1920	$39.00	
1921	725.50	
1922	8,265.50	
		$9,030.00
Blanks	268.00	
Certificates	882.24	
Supplementals	396.00	
Medals	185.10	
Interest on balances...................................	114.87	
Interest on investments...............................	558.75	
Rebates on insignia, ribbons, and rosettes...............	271.06	
Postage	11.59	
Year Books	6.77	
Electro insignia.......................................	1.25	
Transfer blanks.......................................	4.40	
Rosettes	18.30	
Service Bars..	7.75	
Loan from Corn Exchange Bank.......................	5,000.00	
Interest received from Moses Greeley Parker Fund.......	232.06	
Oklahoma Society.....................................	84.46	
Sash ribbon..	18.67	
		17,091.27
		$23,048.69
Disbursements		19,656.68
Balance on hand May 10, 1922.............................		$3,392.01
In Corn Exchange Bank...................................		$2,289.87
In Broadway Savings Bank.................................		747.55
Checks on hand...		354.59
		$3,392.01

JOHN H. BURROUGHS,
Treasurer General.

Audited and found correct.
     GEO. D. BANGS.
     NORMAN P. HEFFLEY.

DISBURSEMENTS

Salary of Philip F. Larner from May 1 to 15, 1921...............	$62.50
Sundry expenses of Philip F. Larner, attending Buffalo Congress and Executive Committee meeting at Rochester.....................	84.73

Sundry expenses of preparing index for 1920 Year Books.......... 65.00
Sundry expenses as Secretary General............................ 190.24
Indemnity bond for Treasurer General............................ 25.00
Sundry printing 1,263.71
Salary of Secretary General to May 1, 1922...................... 1,725.00
Salary of Registrar General to May 1, 1922...................... 1,150.00
Sundry expenses of Secretary General's office—supplies, postage,
    covers for certificates..................................... 170.72
Sundry expenses of Registrar General's office—postage, expressage,
    porterage, telegrams 136.17
Sundry expenses of Registrar General for services of Mrs. A. Howard
    Clark (this was before salary was raised)................... 78.67
Sundry expenses of Treasurer General, attending Buffalo Congress.. 58.66
Sundry expenses of Treasurer General from January 28, 1921, to
    July 9, 1921.. 12.56
Reporting proceedings of Buffalo Congress....................... 230.30
Rent of offices of the Society at Washington to May 1, 1922....... 630.00
Engrossing certificates 262.80
Certificates 700.00
Safe-deposit rent 6.00
Silk flag presented to Sulgrave Institute....................... .70.00
Rosettes and ribbons.. 133.85
Wreath for funeral of General Horace Porter..................... 15.00
Wreath for services at Arlington for the "Unknown Soldier"....... 20.00
Wreath for Washington Monument at Washington.................... 10.00
Office supplies for Secretary General's office.................. 93.93
Collection of out-of-town checks................................ 5.05
Multigraphing letters for Constitution Day...................... 8.25
Multigraphing letters for North Church.......................... 3.50
Medals 117.15
Printing and mailing OFFICIAL BULLETINS:
    June $1,937.35
    October 1,501.69
    December 1,220.07
    March 1,800.70
                                                        ———————
                                                        6,459.81
The Corn Exchange Bank, payment of demand loan.............. 5,000.00
Interest on above loan... 57.00
Appropriation for Springfield Congress......................... 500.00
BULLETIN envelopes... 124.50
Oklahoma Society for protested check........................... 56.06
Ribbon and flag-pole... 56.75
Silvered Service Bars.. 6.00
Silver plates for flag-pole.................................... 15.00
Expenses of Secretary General, attending meeting of Executive Com-
    mittee in New York... 44.75
Montclair Herald... 5.75
Rhode Island Society, amount overpaid on dues.................. 1.00
Kentucky Society, amount overpaid on blanks.................... .25

Revenue stamp on demand note given Corn Exchange Bank........   1.00
To balance cash, error in last year's statement...................   .02

$19,656.68

REPORT ON PERMANENT FUND

MAY 10, 1922.

President General and Compatriots:

The Treasurer General has the honor to submit the following report on the Permanent Fund:

Since the report of May 11, 1921, there has been received $365.72 from rebates on insignia, rosettes, and ribbons, making the amount uninvested $736.78. The amount of securities now held is $14,500, par value.

A special report on these securities will be made by Hon. Cornelius A. Pugsley, of the Permanent Fund Investment Committee.

Respectfully submitted,

JOHN H. BURROUGHS,
Treasurer General.

REPORT OF COMMITTEE ON INVESTMENT OF PERMANENT FUNDS

MAY 5, 1922.

Mr. FRANK B. STEELE, *Secretary General,*
 183 *St. James Place, Buffalo, N. Y.*

MY DEAR SECRETARY GENERAL:

I have examined the securities in the safe-deposit vault in New York held by the National Society of the Sons of the American Revolution and find the securities are as follows:

> $1,000 4¼ per cent Liberty bonds (4th).
> 2,500 4¼ per cent Liberty bonds (3d).
> 1,000 3½ per cent Liberty bonds (1st).
> 1,000 Keokee Consolidated Coke Co. 5 per cent bonds.
> 1,000 Atchison, Topeka and Santa Fe 4 per cent.
> 2,000 State of New York 4 per cent
> 4,000 4 per cent bonds City of New York.
> 1,000 4½ per cent City of New York.
> 1,000 New York Railway Adjustment 5's.

Making a total of $14,500

I am forwarding you this report upon these securities in order that the same may be presented, as required, at the National Congress at Springfield, Mass.

Very sincerely yours,

C. A. PUGSLEY,
Chairman of Committee.

REPORT OF THE REGISTRAR GENERAL

MAY 15, 1922.

COMPATRIOTS:

The Registrar General has the honor to report that during the official year ending March 31, 1922, 1,523 new members were enrolled in forty-three State Societies. The losses by death, transfer, and other causes were 848. The present membership is 17,703, a gain of 873 during the year. Since the close of the Society's year a total of 250 applications have been received and registered.

(Membership May 15, about 18,000.)

The State Society showing the largest membership at the close of the year is New Jersey, with a total membership of 1,852, a net gain over the previous year of 262. The State Society showing the largest percentage of gain is Tennessee; the membership of this Society on the first of April, 1921, was 107. The additions during the year just closed were 57; the losses were 5, showing a net gain of 52, or 48½ per cent. It will be seen from these figures that the New Jersey Society retains the Syracuse Banner, and to the Tennessee Society will be awarded the Traveling Banner of the National Society.

Other Societies that have been industrious in securing new members are the Empire State, with 131; Pennsylvania, 105; Massachusetts, 97; Illinois, 68; California, 57; District of Columbia, 45; Ohio, 57; Iowa, 62, and California, 56.

During the year just passed a Son of a Revolutionary soldier has been admitted to the Massachusetts Society and duly registered by the National Society. He is Dr. Crosby A. Perry, of Pittsfield, Mass., 84 years of age, active physically, and mentally as sound as if he were twenty or thirty years younger. His National number is 36809 and his State number 4287. This unusual registration was made on March 21, 1922. Dr. Perry is a delegate to this Congress.

Among the well-known members of the Society who have died during the year are General Horace Porter, Past President General of the National Society, Ambassador to France, one of the founders of the Sons of the American Revolution, and a member of the staff of General U. S. Grant during the Civil War, his Secretary for many years, and during his whole life a tower of strength to every patriotic impulse and interest. Others who have died are Dr. Edward Van Dyck, of the Delaware Society; Col. Frederic W. Galbraith, of the Massachusetts Society, Commander of the American Legion; Osborne I. Yellott, President of the Maryland Society; Frank Ernest Woodward, Past President of the Massachusetts Society; Jesse A. Baldwin, First Vice-President of Illinois Society; George Alvin Dana, Vice-President, Nebraska Society; Frederick Bostwick, Registrar of the Connecticut Society, and Ira F. Harris, First Vice-President of the New Hampshire Society. Compatriots George S. Stewart, Secretary of the Massachusetts Society, and Will B. Howe, Secretary of the New Hampshire Society, also, have passed to their final reward.

Two real Sons of Revolutionary soldiers have passed away during the year, Jeremiah Smith, of the New Hampshire Society, a son of Jeremiah Smith, who was a private in Captain Steven Parker's New Hampshire Company, who joined the Continental Army under General Gates, and Daniel Howe Simmons, a member of the Oregon Society, 93 years of age, who was a son of John Simmons, a private in Colonel Hayes' New York Militia. The elder Simmons was born in 1761, enlisted from Clarkstown, N. Y., and died in 1843.

It is not necessary to dwell in detail upon the work of the Registrar General. The card index of every ancestor, as well as the name of each member enrolled, has been continued and aggregates now about 50,000 names. This list of soldiers of the American Revolution is not only of value to us in our research work and in verifying the statements in applications received, but i . invaluable as a reference record for those seeking necessary data to compile or complete applications for admission to the Society through the State Society.

As no Year Book was published during the year, a complete pedigree of each new member, as well as the military service of the ancestors, have been prepared in this office and printed in the quarterly BULLETIN. A paragraph upon the new members from each State and a list of the deceased members is furnished quarterly for publication in the BULLETIN.

The records of the office are in very good condition and the reference books available cover quite fully all the necessary ancestral history required. Should, however, information desired be unavailable, it can in almost every case be supplied upon application to the Adjutant General of the United States Army, War Department, Washington, D. C., or to the U. S. Bureau of Pensions. The registration books of the Society are handled so frequently that some of the older ones should be rebound in order that their preservation may be assured.

The volume of correspondence incident to the office of Registrar General has largely increased and letters not strictly pertaining to the registration itself have been received in large numbers. Inquiries on almost every subject, and particularly on Americanization and information as to immigrants and aliens, the Flag and the Constitution, have been answered through this office. About 2,500 pieces of mail have been handled, and over 2,000 letters, including notices of registry, etc., have been written.

.   .   .   .   .

In conclusion, I cannot speak too highly of the courtesies I have received from the officers and members of the National Society, particularly President General McCamant and Secretary General Steele. At all times during the year the Secretary General and Registrar General have been as one in their endeavors to conduct the business of the Society and I owe not a little to this spirit of cooperation which has so completely prevailed during the year that ends today.

WM. S. PARKS,
Registrar General.

1922 MEMBERSHIP REPORT OF THE REGISTRAR GENERAL

	March 31, 1921.	Additions.	Losses.	March 31, 1922.	Net gain.	Net loss.	New members.
Arizona	37	12	1	48	11	...	5
Arkansas	66	2	...	68	2	...	2
California	482	68	21	529	47	...	56
Colorado	340	21	33	328	...	12	20
Connecticut	1,150	43	21	1,172	22	...	43
Delaware	99	21	13	107	8	...	17
Dist. of Columbia	497	55	37	515	18	...	45
*Florida	47	4	8	43	...	4	4
Georgia	16	12	...	28	12	...	6
Idaho	128	10	13	125	...	3	10
Illinois	1,189	99	68	1,220	31	...	68
Indiana	232	43	10	265	33	...	39
Iowa	480	62	52	490	10	...	62
Kansas	103	24	3	124	21	...	16
Kentucky	200	24	4	220	20	...	23
Louisiana	305	40	10	335	30	...	37
Maine	329	30	13	346	17	...	28
Maryland	474	42	20	496	22	...	42
Massachusetts	1,811	116	92	1,835	24	...	96
Michigan	690	45	33	702	12	...	43
Minnesota	250	23	6	267	17	...	22
Missouri	211	17	8	220	9	...	15
Montana	33	3	2	34	1	...	2
Nebraska	247	18	15	250	3	...	17
New Hampshire	198	5	18	185	...	13	4
New Jersey	1,590	318	56	1,852	262	...	312
New Mexico	66	7	9	64	...	2	7
New York	1,701	149	80	1,770	69	...	131
North Dakota	64	22	3	83	19	...	21
Ohio	765	90	2	853	88	...	57
Oklahoma	107	13	1	119	12	...	13
Oregon	259	15	14	260	1	...	14
Pennsylvania	697	112	46	763	66	...	105
Rhode Island	392	20	32	380	...	12	20
South Dakota	82	6	10	78	...	4	6
Tennessee	107	57	5	159	52	...	50
Texas	95	7	4	98	3	...	6
Utah	227	7	22	212	...	15	4
Vermont	212	8	24	196	...	16	6
Virginia	250	21	8	263	13	...	20
*Washington	279	16	...	295	16	...	16
Wisconsin	164	7	31	140	...	24	7
Wyoming	37	7	...	44	...	...	6
Total	16,708	1,721	848	17,581	971	105	1,523

*Far East	20	
*France	...	
*Mississippi	41	
*Nevada	...	
*North Carolina	61	
*South Carolina	...	
	16,830	17,703

* No report.

DEDICATION OF MARKERS AT PRINCETON BATTLEFIELD

DEDICATION OF MARKERS AT PRINCETON BATTLEFIELD, APRIL 29, 1922

On Saturday, April 29, 1922, the exercises were held for the unveiling of the markers of the Princeton battlefield. Major Washington Irving Lincoln Adams, Director General of the Sons of the American Revolution, now President General, presided over the ceremonies. After prayer by Dr. Waters, President Hibben was called on to make a few remarks before the unveiling of the tablet, as he had to be excused early for another engagement. His address was in part as follows:

MR. CHAIRMAN AND LADIES AND GENTLEMEN:

It hardly seems possible that we are standing today upon a battlefield. It is a great burden upon our imagination to conceive that here, almost 150 years ago, our ancestors were fighting for liberty. The battle was not a great battle, measured by the number of men who were engaged, or the number killed and wounded, or the amount of powder that was burned. Almost every hour of the great World War saw more killed and wounded, more ammunition fired, than this battle of Princeton. Why, therefore, do we meet here to celebrate so small an event? While in itself small, yet it was great in its consequences, because it came at a time which, the historians now are all agreed, marked the turning point of the fortunes of the Colonies. The War of the Revolution, if it had not been for the Battle of Princeton, would doubtless have been referred to in history as the Rebellion of the Colonies or the Revolt of the Colonies, and we would have remained a colony of Great Britain to this day. It was the Battle of Princeton which gave the United States to America and gave us our liberty. And yet liberty, my friends, is never a gift, something secure for all time. It is something, rather, that every generation must win for itself, maintain it, and enlarge it in its scope to all men of all races, of all peoples the world over. Our fathers fought through the Civil War in order that there might be a new interpretation of this word "liberty," and there has been given a new significance to it. And as today we rejoice in our glorious heritage, we must not feel that this heritage is a privilege merely. It is not that; it is an obligation, it is a responsibility resting upon each generation, and particularly upon the young men and women of the coming generation.

In yonder field, as I look at it, directly in front of me, lie the American and the British soldiers in one common grave. They fought fiercely for mastery here; they fought but yesterday as comrades in the great war that we hope eventually will bring universal peace to the world. There is this symbol in the nature and in the very soil of this grave that forever must remain before us, and its significance is this: that Great Britain and America, once foes upon this place where we stand, must forever be united together, in order that we may maintain liberty, not for our two nations merely, but liberty for the whole world; and such an occasion as this emphasizes to our minds our obligation that we in turn may serve our day and generation in times of peace as our fathers served their day and generation in times of war. (Applause.)

Chairman Adams then introduced Thomas McCamant, "a student of Princeton University, a member of the graduating class this year, who is the son of Wallace McCamant, the President General of our National Society. Young Mr. McCamant is, of course, eligible to our order and will become a member as soon as he is old enough. He is, however, old enough to receive the Phi Beta Kappa key which is dangling from his chain. I have pleasure in introducing Mr. McCamant, who will actually unveil the tablet."

Mr. McCamant's speech in part is as follows:

MARKER UNVEILED APRIL 29, 1922

LADIES AND GENTLEMEN:

You have been told that these markers have been given by the Oregon Society of the Sons of the American Revolution. As the representative of that Society, I wish, in so far as I can, to state the purpose of that gift and, in a measure, to interpret its significance.

Most of the societies and organizations with which we are familiar face, as it were, in two directions: They have their origin in the past and, without forgetting that origin, they look to the future for the consummation of their purposes. This is pre-eminently true of the greatest and most permanent of all the organizations which we know in our day, the Christian Church. It looks ever forward to the conversion of humanity and the coming of the kingdom of God; and yet, at the same time, its eyes are always fixed upon the past, upon the life of its founder, and it is always fondly reading the accounts of its inception. By looking back it feels that it gains power to move forward.

In its smaller way, this is exactly true of the Society of the Sons of the American Revolution. Its interest is in every forward-looking patriotic movement and all of its activities are directed with a view to the furtherance of those things which make for the improvement of our national life. And yet, in an equally true sense, this Society is always looking back; it is cherishing the memory of those years which saw the birth of our nation and of the ideals which are the mainstay of our higher national life. It believes that in the memory of that glorious past we can move forward to a yet more glorious future.

The Oregon Society of the Sons of the American Revolution has no ground in its own State which it may consider as sacred because of its Revolutionary associations. The first permanent white settlement was not made in Oregon until more than twenty years after the close of the Revolutionary War.

It is for these reasons that Oregon looks all the way across the continent and seeks to do what it can that the memory of the battle which was fought here on this ground, and of the brave men who by their lives or by their deaths made possible its success, shall not perish. It wishes that all of those who pass by on these roads may see that they are passing through fields on which was written in blood one of the most heroic pages of our Nation's history. It wishes that some of those who pass by on these roads may stop and consider the hardships under which these men fought, and the high idealism of their purpose, and the heroic grandeur of their actions, and that, thinking of these things, they may turn again to think of our present Nation with more seriousness and more devotion. It wishes that those who have read the pages of this history and been thrilled by its heroism may be able to come here, as to a shrine, and let the events of that great day live over again in the setting of the spots on which they took place.

I think that the men in the Oregon Society feel that there is a certain significance simply in the fact that this marking is being done by fellow-patriots on the other side of the continent. This battle was not New Jersey's battle only, nor the battle of the Eastern States. It was the battle of the whole United States. Those few fought then for the many of today, and East and West and North and South now join in doing honor to those few who fought that we many might live as a free nation. The Oregon Sons of the American Revolution give these markers in order that the memory of their forefathers and the forefathers of our whole Nation, who fought here, may be eternally preserved. (Applause.)

(Here the actual unveiling of the marker by Mr. McCamant took place.)

Chairman Adams then introduced Prof. T. J. Wertenbaker, the man who composed the inscription on the markers, who has made a special study of this significant Battle of Princeton, and who, therefore, very properly may be considered as an authority on this subject.

Professor Wertenbaker gave a brief but vivid story of the Battle of Princeton, showing how Washington not only extricated his army from a most precarious position, but also won a notable victory. To use Professor Wertenbaker's closing words:

The results of this battle were very momentous indeed. Washington saved his own army from a very perilous position which threatened its complete destruction. It destroyed a very important division of the British troops. It revived the spirits of the little colony as nothing else had done. It broke the prestige of the British troops. It was the first time that the British had been beaten. It recovered for the American forces a large part of New Jersey; so that I think it is not too much to say that the battle which occurred on the exact spot where we are standing saved the American Revolution.

EVENTS OF STATE SOCIETIES

The California Society.—The anniversary of the battle of Lexington was not forgotten by a loyal band, the California Society of the Sons of the American Revolution. Seventy-six descendants of the men who fought to free the colonies in '76 attended the annual meeting and banquet of the Society at the Commercial Club on April 19. A program of patriotic oratory and songs was given, following the business meeting. Colonel Robert H. Noble was the speaker of the day. A short address was made by Thomas M. Shepard, of Massachusetts, a guest of honor. Marion Vecki and Miss Mabel Turner sang.

Election of officers was the chief event of the business meeting, which opened the celebration. Charles E. Hale was elected President.

The Society offered prizes to the pupils in the high schools of California for the three best essays written on "The Origin of the Ideas in the Declaration of Independence, as Written by Thomas Jefferson," to be submitted by March 1, 1922.

The committee, composed of E. De Los Magee, W. H. Jordan, and L. E. Stoddard, awarded first prize, of $25, to Mary Motter, Covina High School; second prize, of $15, to Lewis Dobbins, Colusa High School; third prize, of $10, to Minnie Pittillo, Covina High School. She also took a prize in 1921 in the Society's essay contest. The first prize was donated by Compatriot B. M. Newcomb, of Berkeley.

War Service Medals have been presented to fifty-two, as published heretofore, and to the following: R. H. Baker, first lieutenant, U. S. S. *New Hampshire;* F. W. Brittain, private, S. A. T. C., University of California; J. C. Elms, Jr., second lieutenant, Army Transport Service; R. G. Fernald, first lieutenant, Air Service; H. W. Gibson, private, Medical Department, A. E. F.; K. S. Gray, corporal, New Zealand Rifle Brigade, N. Z. E. F.; C. H. Hoffman, private, Air Service, A. E. F.; E. H. Pierce, major, Adjutant General's Department, N. A.

San Diego Chapter, California Society, observed the anniversary of the birth of George Washington with a dinner at the San Diego Hotel. The main address was by Rear-Admiral Guy H. Burrage, U. S. N., commanding officer of the destroyer division of the Pacific fleet. Colonel William D. Beach, U. S. A., retired, who was a general officer overseas during the World War, also spoke.

Major Ira Hobart Evans, United States Volunteers, of this Chapter, died at his home in San Diego, Calif., April 19, 1922. He was a native of New Hampshire and was aged 78 years. He received his education in Vermont and joined the troops from that State during the Civil War, rapidly advancing to the rank of major at the age of 21. Major Evans was awarded the Congressional Medal of Honor for distinguished bravery at Hatchers Run, Va., in 1865. Major Evans was originally a member of the Vermont Society of the Sons of the American Revolution, later transferring to the Texas Society, and in 1922 became a member of the California Society by transfer. He was also a member of the Society of Colonial Wars, of the Military Order of the Loyal Legion of the United States, and of the Medal of Honor Legion. He belonged to the Congregationalist Church.

The Connecticut Society.—Former Gov. Rollin S. Woodruff, of New Haven, was elected president of the Connecticut Society, Sons of the American Revolution, at the annual meeting at Hartford, June 14.

Other officers were elected as follows: Vice-Presidents, Orlando H. Brothwell, Bridgeport; H. Wales Lines, Meriden; Ernest E. Rogers, New London; Secretary, Frederick A. Doolittle, Bridgeport; Treasurer, Charles G. Stone, Hartford; Registrar, Lawrence E. Bostwick, New Haven; Historian, Frank B. Gay, Hartford; Chaplain, Rev. Orville A. Petty, New Haven; Necrologist, Leverett Belknap, Hartford.

The new president will have the appointment of a committee of five from the State Society to confer with a similar committee of the National Society regarding certain amendments and revisions proposed by Connecticut at the last congress of the National Society, S. A. R., held at Springfield.

The retiring president, Mr. White, whose administration has shown singular ability, was elected to have in charge the Lebanon war office and other properties of the society.

The General David Humphreys Branch, of New Haven, decorated the graves of 288 soldiers and patriots on Sunday, June 18. This Chapter has taken a definite step with regard to forming an association for the purpose of co-operating with the local post of the American Legion in its civic and patriotic work and to provide an opportunity for the residents of New Haven to show practical appreciation of the services rendered in the World War by the enlisted men from New Haven. The S. A. R. Chapter is associated in this commendable step with other patriotic and civic organizations of the city—thirteen in all. The David Humphreys Branch has presented 6 silver and 15 bronze Essay Medals to the children of the schools of New Haven for meritorious work in American History.

The Hawaiian Society held a regular business meeting on May 2, at which reports of progress and activity were presented. The joint meeting with the Daughters of the American Revolution on Lexington Day, April 18, was reported as a great success, concluding with a banquet and entertainment. Arrangements for the annual meeting on June 17 and for an appropriate celebration of Independence Day were made and committees appointed. The Society mourns the death, on April 23, of Compatriot Peter Cushman Jones, who was the first President and a life member of the Hawaiian Society.

The Illinois Society celebrated Lexington Day, April 19, with a dinner, at Chicago, addressed by Mr. Dorr E. Felt, former President of the Society, upon "Observations of the Battlefields of Europe." He described his experiences visiting the industrial centers and battlefields, as a member of the United States Industrial Commission to Europe. General Nathan William MacChesney, formerly Judge Advocate, General Headquarters, France, delivered an intensely interesting address upon his experiences in France and at the Peace Conference. Flag Day was observed June 14, in co-operation with the Chicago Association of Commerce, with an address, upon the history and significance of the Flag, by James Edgar Brown, Vice-President of the Society. Some twenty members of the Board of Managers have during recent weeks been systematically visiting the naturalization courts, making observations preparatory to future recommendations for adding to the dignity, solemnity, and patriotic spirit of these occasions.

SPRINGFIELD CHAPTER, Sons of the American Revolution, heard an interesting account of a real Son at the Lexington Day program Wednesday evening, April 19, when they celebrated with a dinner at the Pollyanna Grill.

Dr. H. H. Tuttle told of Peter Millington, a Son of the American Revolution, buried in Sangamon County. Sangamon County is the burial place of many distinguished soldiers. It is rare to find a family that furnished distinguished officers in three great wars—the Revolution, Mexican, and Civil wars.

Peter Millington was born July 6, 1737, in Vermont, when George Washington was but five years of age. He lived throughout the period of Washington's lifetime and forty years beyond. His birth, no doubt, dates earlier than any other person buried in Sangamon County. From the time of his birth to the present lacks just fifteen years of being two centuries.

He ranked as captain in the Revolutionary Army and accompanied Ethan Allen and Benedict Arnold on their Canadian expedition. He was captured at Quebec and held a prisoner until the close of the War. He died and was buried in Cotton Hill township, Zion Cemetery, Sangamon County, in 1839, in his 102d year.

Dr. H. S. Layman spoke on the subject "The Fight of the Anglo-Saxon Race for Democracy." Many new angles on the relation of the United States and England were presented and a discussion followed.

The Sons of the American Revolution are considering the proposition of purchasing a joint Chapter house here with the Daughters of the American Revolution. The President, Charles S. Andrus, appointed a committee of three to go with a committee appointed by the regent of the D. A. R. to inspect the Ferguson Home with the view of buying it.

On Decoration Day the Chapter marked the grave of Moses Broadwell, a Revolutionary patriot buried in this county, in Oak Ridge Cemetery, where the National Lincoln Monument is located.

The Indiana Society issues a small bulletin from time to time for the purpose of keeping the members in touch with the Society's activities in the State throughout the year. The effort of the Society, launched in 1908, to have regular study of Indiana history in the public schools has brought results. The co-operation of the Society is pledged to insure the accuracy of such books, and programs for history study, as are provided. Very great credit is due Prof. Herbert Briggs, of Terre Haute, present Historian of the Indiana Society, for his labors along this line, extending through a period of nearly twelve years. His efforts have put the Indiana Society in the forefront of the forces that have been contending for the teaching of local history in the schools. He made the Indiana Society a pioneer in the work, and since Indiana took it up at his behest and urging, other State Societies have followed the example we have set and are pursuing a similar activity in their respective States. The Society during the year will be especially active along two lines of endeavor: An intensive membership campaign will be conducted. The retiring President, Austin H. Brown, has been appointed chairman of a membership committee made up of "live-wire" members in various parts of the State. In addition to their efforts, each present member will endeavor to secure a new member during the year. The work begun last year, of compiling an historical record of Indiana Revolutionary soldiers and the locating and marking of their graves, will continue unabated. The new President, Mr. Cornelius Posson, continues as chairman of the committee and is hoping to have a good, live committeeman in each county of the State.

The Iowa Society.—W. G. Blood was re-elected President of Lexington Chapter, No. 4, Sons of the American Revolution, at the annual meeting, held in the Tiffany Room of the Hotel Iowa. Under his administration the Chapter goal of fifty members was reached and surpassed by three, and now the Chapter is trying for the century mark in membership.

Resolutions of respect for the late L. A. Hamill were presented by the committee.

Edward F. Carter divided honors with Dr. H. D. Hoover as the speaker of the evening, and he gave his version of Paul Revere's ride, which was received with acclaim by the members.

President Blood presided as toastmaster, and in introducing Mr. Carter gave a number of quotations from Emerson and Longfellow concerning the momentous days in April, 1775, the one hundred and forty-seventh anniversary of which the sons were celebrating.

A letter was read from Walter E. Coffin, president of the State Society, complimenting the local Chapter on its membership growth. Reports on activities of the Chapter in membership were made by Chairman Long of that committee and by Chairman Howell on Americanization efforts, who announced another naturalization day ceremony soon.

The Secretary read a letter of regret from Captain E. D. Hadley, State Secretary of the S. A. R., who was invited to attend the meeting of the Chapter, but who, on account of the work connected with the State Society meeting, could not get away in time to get to Keokuk. Letters and messages were read from members not able to be present, among them Dr. E. B. Newcomb, who said this was the first time that he had not been able to be present at an S. A. R. ceremony. He and James B. Diver are the only ones of the Chapter left who were present at its organization.

The Kansas Society.—Largely through the efforts of the Kansas Society, public recognition of Flag Day was very generally given throughout the city of Topeka. Lincoln Post, G. A. R., with the Ladies' Circle, held appropriate and elaborate exercises at Garfield Park, followed by a basket supper. Patriotic music and addresses marked the program. Exercises at the First Unitarian Church, under the auspices of the Women's Relief Corps, included the presentation of a flag in memoriam to the late Samuel T. Howe. The Daughters of the American Revolution conducted a fine memorial meeting, as did also the Spanish American Veterans and the members of the Jewish Synagogue and other churches and public schools generally throughout the city.

The Louisiana Society.—Probably the most interesting event in the history of the Louisiana Society for 1922 was the visit and entertainment by the Society of President General Wallace McCamant early in February. President McCamant was the guest at a banquet on the evening of February 9, at which a distinguished representation of the Society was present and gave cordial greeting to the distinguished visitors. President McCamant spoke on "Washington, the Gentleman," and his address was a masterly and patriotic tribute to the Father of his Country. A number of speakers were on the program, which included a welcome from Mayor McShane and addresses by U. S. Judge Rufus Foster, who praised the Boy Scouts; Captain James Dinkins, who praised the Confederate soldier; Colonel Elmer E. Wood, veteran of the Spanish-American War; Colonel James D. Edmonds, veteran of the World War, and numerous others. The attendance was upward of seventy-five (75) and the occasion one that will live in the annals of the Louisiana Society. Earlier in the day President General McCamant was the guest at lunch of the officers of the State Society.

The annual meeting and election of officers of the Louisiana Society was held January 17, at the Grunewald Hotel. The annual reports of President Churchill, Secretary Benton, and Treasurer Landry were read and approved. In his report, President Churchill referred to the gratifying increase shown in membership since the last annual meeting. The need was stressed for a more centralized scheme of work for building up the Society and the suggestion was made that the growth of the Society now made paid help almost necessary. The initiation fee was increased to $5 and arrangements were made for quarterly luncheons, to be held with special programs and speakers.

The Society's 1921 Year Book, with its wealth of historical material bearing on the early history of the Galvez expeditions, came in for much favorable comment. A resolution was introduced and adopted, calling upon the National Society, in the interests of greater efficiency, to elect a paid Registrar General and a paid Secretary General. The election of officers took place and the Society's gold medal was voted President Churchill as a token of appreciation for the labor involved in compiling the 1921 Year Book.

The Maine Society boasts among its members Osborne T. Allen, the only real son of the American Revolution now living in Maine, who was born when his father, James Allen, was 74 years old. He was the youngest of 14 children. The eldest Allen did not die until he was nearly 105, so that Osborne T. Allen was about 30 years old at the time of his father's death.

Mr. Allen has heard his father tell of incidents of the Battle of Trenton, of fighting at Fort Griswold, and of a seven days' march when he was forced to go without shoes during the latter part of the distance, his feet swollen and bleeding from the hardships of the journey; also of the War of 1812, in which he fought.

His father was born in New London, Conn., and was only 14 years old when he went into George Washington's army. When he first came to Maine he settled in Scarboro, where he married Abigail Berry, his first wife. He then lived eight years in Portland, and from that city moved to Canton, where he has spent the greater part of his life.

From his father he acquired some musical training and inherited in no small degree his musical talent. He learned to play the violin when a boy and played the horn in an army band during the Civil War, in which he saw active service.

Mr. Allen was at Antietam, Gettysburg, Saint Marys Heights, Fredericksburg, Missionary Ridge, and Chancellorsville. On the march from Gettysburg to Rappahanock Station he sustained a sunstroke, which sent him to the hospital and finally home. Two brothers, Charles D. and Lorenzo W., also served in the war with him.

Some two years ago the Maine Sons of the American Revolution appointed Justice A. M. Spear, of Gardiner; E. Converse Leach, of Portland, and O. B. Clason, of Gardiner, as a committee to go before the Legislature and obtain an appropriation of $600 from the State for the purpose of erecting a bronze tablet on the Maine marker at Valley Forge in commemoration of the Maine soldiers who lost their lives in the Revolutionary War, to replace the old one, the funds at the time the first was erected not being sufficient to place a satisfactory one there. The committee was successful and the money was appropriated. The Maine Society then appointed a committee to attend to all the details, and the result is a beautiful memorial, bearing the seal of Maine, a pine and a cone, together with a suitable inscription written by ex-Governor Cobb.

Governor Baxter has authorized Chairman Berry to proceed with the work, provided it does not cost more than the amount appropriated, $600. The metal to be used is regulation U. S. statuary bronze, which is the highest grade that can be produced for the work. It is expected that the memorial will be placed in position some time in July.

This year the Sons of the American Revolution and the Daughters of the American Revolution participated in the Memorial Day Exercises. The following members of the former order have been selected as a committee to assist in the plans for the observance of the day: James M. L. Bates, William R. Gay, and Walter Wood.

The Massachusetts Society has suffered severe losses recently in the deaths of their late State Secretary, George S. Stewart, on April 17, and the late Registrar Emeritus, Herbert W. Kimball, on April 10. The latter officer had filled the office of Registrar for 26 years and the office of Secretary for a large part of this time. Compatriot Nathan Warren died on April 11, at the age of 84 years, and is deeply mourned by the Society. He was Registrar for two years and President of the Society in 1901-2. Resolutions of respect and sympathy have been drafted by the Society and spread upon its records. The Society has a membership of 1,851, having had a net increase of 151 members in the last two years. The newly elected officers of the Society, of whom Dr. Charles H. Bangs is the President, are hopeful of a still larger increase during the coming year and have started an active campaign to pull the membership up to 2,000 or more before the next annual Congress. Each member of the Society is urged to personally present the name of at least one new member at an early date.

Boston Chapter held its annual meeting on May 19, at the State Headquarters, in Ashburton Place. William C. Comstock was re-elected president. J. C. Staton, of the California Raisin Growers' Association, gave an illustrated talk on the raisin industry.

The Michigan Society.—The annual meeting of this Society was held at the Detroit Club, Detroit, Saturday, April 15, 1922, at 6:30 p. m., at which time the visiting members were the guests of Detroit Chapter at dinner. The election of officers and delegates to the National Congress preceded the dinner.

The President, Mr. William P. Holliday, presided. Invocation was pronounced by Rev. Joseph A. Vance, D. D., Chaplain. Secretary Raymond E. Van Syckle reported the growth of the Society during the past year, and its financial condition was set forth by Treasurer Frank G. Smith. Reports of the progress of the organization throughout the State were made by Wilbert H. Barrett, President of Lenawee Chapter, Adrian; Clarence K. Redfield, President, and George H. Kimball, Sr., Historian, of Oakland Chapter, Pontiac; Dr. Wilbert B. Hinsdale, President, and Milton E. Osborn, Secretary, Washtenaw Chapter, Ann Arbor; Ward F. Davidson, Upper Peninsula; Dr. Wilfrid Haughey, Battle Creek; and Carl F. Clarke, President of Detroit Chapter. Service medals were presented to Dr. Wilfrid Haughey, of Battle Creek, major, Base Hospital No. 36, A. E. F., and William S. Gilbreath, Jr., Detroit, sergeant, Camp Beauregard, for their service in the World War. The presentation was made by Compatriot General Charles A. Coolidge, U. S. A. Dr. Wilfrid Haughey, Battle Creek, called attention to the booklet recently issued by the Sons of the Revolution at Los Angeles, Calif., entitled "Treason to American Tradition," by Charles Grant Miller, and pointed out the tendency in some recent compilations of textbooks on American history to omit many of the vital principles, heroes, and incidents of the Revolution hitherto held sacred in American history. A stirring account of bolshevistic and communistic movements inimical to American institutions was delivered by Dr. F. E. Perry, Secretary of the Coalition Committee for the State of Michigan.

The annual meeting of KENT CHAPTER was held Tuesday evening, April 18, in the parlors of Park Congregational Church, at 6 p. m., with the ladies in attendance. At 8 o'clock the meeting adjourned to the auditorium of the parish house, where an interesting talk, illustrated with colored slides, was given by Compatriot Daniel W. Tower, upon "Revolutionary and Literary Shrines of the Eastern States." The Daughters of the American Revolution and their escorts were also invited to attend.

The following officers were elected: President, Elvert M. Davis; Vice-President, William R. Shelby; Secretary, Daniel W. Tower; Registrar, Charles N. Remington; Board of Managers: Waldo M. Ball, Frank A. Stone, Addison S. Goodman, and the officers *ex officio*.

The LENAWEE CHAPTER, at Adrian, Lenawee County, held its annual meeting on the evening of Tuesday, April 4. The officers reported that twenty-one new members had been added during the last year. The election resulted in the choice of the following officers to serve for the ensuing year: President, W. H. Barrett; Vice-President, Ladd J. Lewis, Jr.; Secretary-Treasurer, W. Herbert Goff; Registrar, Franklin J. Russell; Chaplain, Irving W. Swift; Historian, Ladd J. Lewis. The members listened to a very instructive and entertaining address by the Rev. Dr. F. A. Perry on the subject, "Movements Subversive to American Ideals."

OAKLAND COUNTY CHAPTER, Pontiac, held its annual meeting on March 23, at which time Clarence K. Redfield was re-elected President for his third term. Miss Florence Pangborn and Miss Ruth Rowe, of Milford, were declared winners of the historical essay contest recently conducted by the Oakland County Chapter of the Sons of the American Revolution. The Pontiac contestants wrote on the subject, "England During the American Revolution." The out-of-town contestants wrote on "George Rogers Clark in the Northwest." The winners received their prizes and had an opportunity to read their essays at a public meeting held in the high school auditorium. At this meeting also, Frank Cody, superintendent of Detroit schools, gave an address. Mr. Cody closed his address with a fine tribute to the Sons of the American Revolution, under whose auspices the program was given, and then presented a motion picture depicting in detail the work that is being done for American and foreign children in Detroit's 156 schools.

The Nebraska Society.—The annual meeting of the Nebraska Society, Sons of the American Revolution, was held February 22, 1922. It was voted that the State Society invite the State and Local D. A. R. organizations in Nebraska to join with it in the celebration of Washington's Birthday on February 22, 1923. A noted speaker is planned for and a fine patriotic and fraternal celebration.

The plan of printing a year book to contain historical and patriotic matter, the constitution, a list of all members in good standing, with names of their Revolutionary ancestors and services rendered in the Revolution and program of work for the coming year, was agreed to. Preparation of this year book involves considerable labor and it will appear in the early summer.

The State Office has completed the assembling, indexing, and binding into three handsome volumes of all the applications for membership in the Nebraska Society since its organization, April 26, 1890, to the present date. These volumes are now at the State Historical Society rooms, where they may be consulted by any persons. They will be of great convenience in securing new members.

LINCOLN CHAPTER will hold regular monthly meetings during the coming year, with program, reports on new members and patriotic work. Among the things planned are services in night school, Americanization, and marking historical sites in Nebraska. The first meeting was held March 20. The second meeting April 17. Each member is urged to secure a new member for the year 1922.

The desk of the Nebraska Society has been placed in a convenient niche in the State Historical Society rooms, with a silver plate showing its ownership. A large engraving, 30 x 70 inches, of "Washington Crossing the Delaware" has recently been placed by the Society in the office of the Nebraska Masonic Home at Plattsmouth. Compatriot Chester C. Wells, of Omaha, national number 36978, enjoys the distinction of entering the Society with ten supplementals, showing that many ancestors in the Revolution. Registrar General Parks adds this notation: "This number of supplementals exceeds any I have before registered."

April 19, anniversary of the Battle of Lexington, was celebrated by Lincoln Chapter with a dinner and address by President Calvin H. French, of Hastings College. President French has recently transferred his membership from Florida to the Nebraska Society.

Charles J. Bowlby died at Crete, April 23, aged 75. Compatriot Bowlby was President of the Nebraska Society in 1917. For forty years he was editor of the *Crete Democrat,* a close personal friend of William J. Bryan, and leader in State politics.

Historical sites in Nebraska have engaged the attention of the Society. The Secretary recently made a journey to Massacre Canyon, in Hitchcock County, location of the last battle between the Sioux and Pawnee Indian tribes, August 5, 1873. The Pawnees were defeated with a loss of 156 killed and never again made their annual tribal hunt for buffalo. Plans for marking the site of this battle with a granite monument are under way.

The New Jersey Society elected officers for the new year on April 22, as follows: President, Judge Adrian Lyon, Perth Amboy; First Vice-President, Harry F. Brewer, Jr., Elizabeth; Second Vice-President, Elvord G. Chamberlin, Montclair; Secretary, David L. Pierson, East Orange; Treasurer, Frank E. Quinby, East Orange; Registrar, William J. Conkling, Orange; Assistant Registrar, Col. Charles A. Andrews, East Orange; Genealogist, Samuel C. Worthen, East Orange; Historian, Rev. M. S. Waters, Newark; Chaplain, Rev. Dr. Frank A. Smith, Elizabeth; Chancellor, Raymond T. Parrot, Elizabeth; Trustee of National Society, C. Symmes Kiggins, Elizabeth; Librarian, Russell B. Rankin, Newark.

Services in memory of the battles of Lexington and Concord were held at the Trinity Church Cathedral, Newark, on Sunday, April 23, under the auspices of the State Society. The sermon, preached by the Rev. Luke M. Wight, Chaplain of Montclair Chapter, pictured two scenes—"The Aftermath of Calvary, or the Birth of Human Freedom," and "The Aftermath of Lexington, or the Birth of American Liberty." The Society and a number of the D. A. R. and other organizations marched to the church from the headquarters, at 33 Lombardy Street.

On Saturday, April 29, exercises were held at Princeton, marking the battlefield of January 3, 1777. Major Washington Irving Lincoln Adams, Past President of the New Jersey Society, presided at the ceremonies, at the request of the Oregon Society, which provided the memorials. President John Grier Hibben, of the University, in the opening address, called upon the boys and girls of today to be prepared to carry on the responsibility of maintaining inviolate the idea of liberty for which the forefathers fought. Mr. McCamant, son of President General Wallace McCamant, delivered the address in behalf of the Oregon Society, and Professor T. J. Wortenbaker, professor of history at the University, reviewed the story of the Battle. A band of music was in attendance and the exercises concluded with the singing of America and discharge of a salute of eleven guns by the Princeton Battery. A large delegation of the New Jersey Society attended.

The first meeting of the Board of Managers was held on the evening of April 29, when committee assignments were announced by the new President, Judge Adrian Lyon, and the plans for the year's activities were discussed.

Under the direction of President Lyon a new Chapter was organized at Haddonfield on Saturday evening, May 6, which has been christened the South Jersey Chapter. Its new officers are: President, Rear Admiral Reynold T. Hall; Vice-President, Edward C. Geehr; Secretary and Treasurer, J. Sterling Stockton; Registrar and Historian, Colonel Winfield S. Price.

At the meeting of the Board of Managers on May 19 an executive committee was elected, which will take care of the business of the Society during the interim of board meetings.

Judge Lyon and a number of the members of the New Jersey Society, Sons of the American Revolution, attended the exercises of dedication of the $300,000 battle monument at Princeton, marking the battle fought there, on January 3, 1777. President and Mrs. Harding graced the occasion, which occurred on Friday, June 9.

ORANGE CHAPTER held its annual meeting on Monday, April 24, the following officers being elected: President, James L. Garabrant; Vice-President, Isaac W.

Faulks; Secretary, Elbert L. Sloat; Treasurer, O. Stanley Thompson, Jr.; Chaplain, Rev. George P. Eastman; Historian, Rev. Charles B. Bullard.

PASSAIC VALLEY CHAPTER, of Summit, visited the headquarters of the State Society, at Newark, on April 27, and after the business had been transacted listened to an address by David L. Pierson, Secretary of the State Society, on "The Call to Service."

NEWARK CHAPTER, at a very largely attended meeting at the State headquarters on April 19, observed the anniversary of the Battle of Lexington and the Battle of Concord. The speaker of the evening was former Congressman Edward W. Gray. The occasion also marked the tenth anniversary of the Chapter, and a paper on the rise and development of the organization was read by Compatriot John Willis Weeks, Historian. It was reported that the Chapter had doubled its membership during the year.

MONTCLAIR CHAPTER held its annual meeting on Tuesday, May 9, at the home of former President Major W. I. Lincoln Adams, 32 Llewellyn Road, Montclair. Under the auspices of the Chapter a subscription banquet was tendered to Major Washington Irving Lincoln Adams, President General, upon his election to the high office by the Congress at Springfield. Over 100 prominent members of the Sons of the American Revolution from various parts of New Jersey attended the affair, which was held in the Montclair Club on the evening of June 12. President J. Stewart Gibson was toastmaster, and the speakers were Judge Adrian Lyon, State President; John Lenord Merrill, former President of the New Jersey Society: Mayor Howard F. McConnell, and former Mayor Louis F. Dodd, both members of the Chapter. President General Adams was greeted with an ovation lasting several minutes, when he arose to speak. It was one of the most delightful occasions in the history of the New Jersey Society.

Flag Day, June 14, was featured by Orange and Newark Chapters with specially arranged programs. The former was addressed by Judge Adrian Lyon, on "Americanization and the Flag," and also by Dr. Lillian Garabrant, Regent of the Lexington (Mass.) Chapter, D. A. R. An orchestra of ten pieces added zest to the occasion. A supper was served. The exercises of the Newark Chapter were delightfully carried out, and included an address by David L. Pierson, State Secretary, on "Sacrifices for the Flag," during which he advocated the placing of a tablet in the City Hall, upon which are to be inscribed the names of men and women who have given of themselves for the uplift of the community. A subscription of generous proportions was immediately forthcoming at the conclusion of the address. Sylvester H. M. Agens, President of Newark Chapter, delivered an address on the Flag, at the Third Presbyterian Church, Newark, on Sunday, June 11. All of the 112 churches in Paterson observed Flag Day on this Sunday, June 11, by request of Captain Abraham Godwin Chapter.

Major Bert E. Underwood, of Summit, has presented a handsome framed portrait of Chester N. Jones, former President, to the State Society, and large contributions of books are being made daily in response to a circular sent out by Russell B. Rankin, librarian.

Orange Chapter will hold a mass meeting at 9 o'clock on the morning of July 4, on Military Common, Orange. An automobile pilgrimage will be run from Elizabethtown on Bunker Hill Day, June 17, through various historical points of interest in Union County, concluding at Summit, where State President Lyon will deliver an address.

The fifteenth anniversary of the dedication of the Dispatch Rider Statue in Orange, erected in memory of the men and women of the community who assisted in establishing American Independence, was observed on the morning of Flag Day. David L. Pierson, State Secretary, and President of the Old Burying Ground Association, secured the co-operation of Superintendent W. Burton Patrick, of the Orange Schools. A procession of school children marched from the high school to the statue, where a wreath was placed in the name of the Orange Chapter, an address was given by the Secretary, "America" was sung, and all marched around the statue, saluting. It was a memorable occasion.

Passaic Valley Chapter decorated graves of soldiers on Memorial Day in Springfield and other cemeteries near Summit, where the Chapter is stationed. Secretary David L. Pierson delivered two addresses—one to Uzal Dodd Post, G. A. R., of Orange, at Rosedale Cemetery, and another at a luncheon given in honor of the post by the Ladies' Auxiliary.

Sunday afternoon, June 4, in the old historic Third Presbyterian Church of Elizabeth, N. J., the Sons of the American Revolution commemorated the one hundred and forty-second anniversary of the Battle of Elizabethtown.

The exercises were conducted by the Elizabethtown Chapter, and both Major W. I. Lincoln Adams, President General of the National Society, and Judge Adrian Lyon, President of the New Jersey State Society, made addresses.

The President General pointed out the appropriateness of holding the celebration in "the House of God; for," said he, "our patriotic forefathers were God-fearing and God-loving men, and they established this Republic in the fear and the love of God."

He then went on to say of "Washington, the great commander of our ancestors," that "it was not so much as the great military chieftain, mounted on his famous white charger, and with sword unsheathed, at the head of his gallant army" that he liked most to think, as it was of him "as the Christian gentleman, kneeling in the snow at Valley Forge and praying there alone to the Great God of battles for his suffering and heroic soldiers."

Major Adams concluded his impressive address by saying it was his belief that "in serving God with sincerity and devotion we serve, in the highest and best sense, our country; and that in the true service of our country we serve not only our countrymen and humanity, but also the God of our forefathers, our own Heavenly Father and our King."

New York (Empire State Society).—The annual meeting of the Society was held on April 19, the anniversary of the Battle of Lexington, in the handsome home of the Army and Navy Club, New York City. The meeting was preceded by an elaborate dinner given under the auspices of the local Chapter. Officers for the ensuing year were elected, the regular ticket being unanimously chosen, as follows: President, George D. Bangs; First Vice-President, Col. Henry W. Sackett; Second Vice-President, Brig.-Gen. Oliver B. Bridgman; Third Vice-President, Jabin A. Secor; Secretary, Major Charles A. Du Bois; Treasurer, James de la Montanye; Registrar, Teunis D. Huntting; Historian, Hon. James B. Laux; Chaplain, Rev. Joseph Fort Newton, D. D.

At the National Congress of the Sons of the American Revolution the Empire State Society was honored by having Louis Annin Ames appointed as a Director General on the staff of the President General; Frank B. Steele, of Buffalo, elected as Secretary General; George McK. Roberts, New York City Chapter, elected as Treasurer General; Mr. Pugsley appointed chairman of the Finance Committee; Louis Annin Ames, chairman of the National Committee on the Observance of Constitution Day; Lewis B. Curtis, chairman of the Committee on the Observance of Flag Day.

NEW YORK CHAPTER.—The annual meeting of the Chapter was held on the same date and in the same place as that of the State Society. After the dinner, which was attended by over one hundred compatriots, the ticket of the nominating committee was unanimously chosen.

After the election an extremely interesting illustrated lecture was given by Rev. Henry V. P. Darlington, of Brooklyn, N. Y. His pictures and talk graphically portrayed the devastation and ruin of war on the battle fronts of France, with which his chaplaincy in the A. E. F. had made him extremely familiar. His vivid portrayal of his subject was vigorously applauded.

On Sunday, April 30, there was a special service, under the auspices of New York Chapter, in St. Paul's Chapel, Broadway and Fulton Street, to commemorate the 133d anniversary of the inauguration of Washington, who, accompanied by Congress, went to St. Paul's Chapel to worship immediately after taking the oath of office. The Right Rev. Bishop Thomas F. Gailor preached. A feature of the service was the placing of a wreath in the pew where Washington sat. Compatriots assembled in front of the Sons of the American Revolution headquarters and proceeded with the colors to the church at 3:45 p. m.

Memorial Day was fittingly observed by the Chapter in various ways, including the placing of a wreath upon the grave of a French officer buried in St. Paul's churchyard, by a special committee composed of Compatriots George McK. Roberts, James B. Laux, and William Hagaman Hall.

The Sons of the American Revolution, New York Chapter, accepted the invitation of the Sons of the Revolution in New York State to be their guests on Flag Day, Wednesday, June 14, 1922, and marched with them to City Hall Park and attended the ceremonies connected with the rededication of the Nathan Hale statue on its present site, the unveiling of the Liberty Pole Tablet, and the Annual Flag Day celebration.

A recent letter from the Committee of the National Society of the Sons of the American Revolution on the observance of Flag Day says that "the general display of the National Flag on that day from our homes, automobiles, et cetera, in the opinion of your committee, would do more for Americanization and the promotion of patriotism than could be accomplished in any other way."

It also says that "last year June 14th was celebrated more widely than ever before, and this year we look for even greater success. Many of the governors of the States issued special proclamations and thousands of meetings, with patriotic addresses, were held by schools, local Chapters of the Sons of American Revolution, and other organizations. Your committee have had many letters from all over the country telling them of the success of these meetings."

The New York Chapter appointed a committee to represent the Sons of the American Revolution at the Americanization Court July 4th; as also for the observance of Constitution Day at the Sub-Treasury Building, September 17th.

COL. CORNELIUS VAN DYCK CHAPTER held its annual meeting Wednesday, June 7, in the Education Building, Schenectady. The following officers were elected for the ensuing year: President, Charles H. Huntley; 1st Vice-President, H. F. Condict; 2d Vice-President, E. J. Hand; Secretary, Hanford Robison; Treasurer,

H. S. Stedman; Registrar, H. T. Williams; Historian, George M. Betts; Chaplain, Heber Williams; Executive Committee, John C. Van Voast, E. S. Vrooman, A. L. Stevens, Jesse L. Patton, F. L. Ottman.

On Saturday, June 10, the Chapter made a pilgrimage to Saratoga battleground in autos. Mr. Percy M. Van Epps, an authority on the Saratoga campaign, described the points of interest.

On Wednesday, June 14, Flag Day, the Society, in conjunction with the Mohawk Valley Historic Association, assisted in the celebration of the two hundreth anniversary of the settlement of the Palatines in the Mohawk Valley. The exercises were held at the Old Stone Church, at Stone Arabia. The speakers, Dr. Sullivan, State Historian, and William Pierrepont White, of Utica, made eloquent addresses.

NEWBURGH CHAPTER.—Independence Day will be fittingly observed in Newburgh, as usual, under the lead of Newburgh Chapter, Sons of the American Revolution. Public exercises will be held at Washington's Headquarters in the forenoon, with patriotic addresses, reading of the Declaration of Independence, and patriotic songs. A national salute will be fired at sunrise at Washington's Headquarters and the bells of the city will be rung at that time, at noon, and at sunset.

The nineteenth annual banquet of Newburgh Chapter was held in the Palatine Hotel on Wednesday evening, April 19, the anniversary of the Battle of Lexington. The President of the Chapter, W. R. Perkins, presided as toastmaster. The principal address was delivered by the Rev. J. J. Henry, of Poughkeepsie, and was of a brilliant and patriotic character. The Reverend and Compatriot Babbitt gave a reading of "Paul Revere's Ride." Both men and women attended. Officers were elected by the Chapter at this meeting and it was decided that Mayor Leonard be requested to proclaim Wednesday, June 14, as Flag Day; also to urge the people of the City of Newburgh to display the American flag on that day.

Through the Board of Education, Newburgh Chapter is to award five dollars as a prize to the pupil of the Newburgh Academy who has the highest standing for the past year in American history.

At a meeting of Newburgh Chapter, held on Tuesday evening, June 13, at the summer residence of the President, William R. Perkins, at Orange Lake, a resolution was unanimously adopted stating that it is the sentiment of the Chapter that the movement to secure the amalgamation into one organization of the Sons of the American Revolution and the Sons of the Revolution be encouraged. This is in accordance with the recent recommendation of President General Adams, of the S. A. R., to the same effect.

Compatriot Stewart gave an extended report of the recent annual session of the National Congress of the Sons of the American Revolution, held in Springfield, Mass.

THE BUFFALO CHAPTER.—The Buffalo Chapter held a most enjoyable meeting on Friday evening, April 7, at the Buffalo Club. The speaker of the evening was Alexander Monro Grier, Esq., King's Councillor, of Toronto, Ontario. Mr. Grier, who is a prominent lawyer and president of the Canadian Niagara Power Company, made a most eloquent address and charmed his hearers with his force and diction. There was a large attendance of the members and much enthusiasm.

On Tuesday evening, June 13, the eve of Flag Day, the Buffalo Chapter was fortunate to have as their guest of honor Major W. I. Lincoln Adams, the newly elected President General of the National Society. It was the occasion of the annual meeting and banquet and the chapter felt itself honored that the President General came to Buffalo to attend this meeting. The dinner was held at the Country Club and the ladies were invited to join the members at dinner after the business meeting. President General Adams made a fine address on some of the aims and work of the Society. He spoke particularly of the text-books on history in the United States and also of the uprooting of unpatriotic teachers who are known to be carrying on socialistic ideas in our schools. The members of the Buffalo Chapter were greatly impressed with the clean-cut Americanism of Major Adams. The other speakers were Mrs. John Miller Horton, Regent of the Buffalo Chapter, Daughters of the American Revolution, who gave greetings from her chapter; the Rev. Orville B. Swift, of Niagara Falls, who made an eloquent address on the ideals represented by the Flag, and several other members spoke briefly. The officers elected for the ensuing year were: President, Commander Thomas W. Harris; First Vice-President, William W. Reilley; Second Vice-President, Captain Henry A. Brown; Secretary, Frank B. Steele; Treasurer, Millard H. Dake; Registrar, William A. Galpin; Chaplain, Rev. Walter A. Smith, of Dunkirk, N. Y. About one hundred were present.

The Ohio Society.—The annual meeting of the Ohio Society was held in Columbus, Ohio, May 3, 1922. Headquarters were at the Chittenden Hotel and members convened for the business session at 10 o'clock. Luncheon was served at 12 o'clock, with an informal program of patriotic music and short talks by prominent speakers, arranged by members of the Benjamin Franklin Chapter, and the glad hand was extended to all members and their invited guests. The business session was continued immediately after the luncheon. So many societies hold their sessions in Columbus and other cities in which members are interested that it seemed advisable to postpone the annual meeting to this date and also omit the banquet this year.

The new Register of the Ohio Society, just published, shows that the members have been active in Americanization work, especially in the public schools, during the past year, as well as in the naturalization of foreigners. It has been a busy year and, as evidenced by the addition of 65 members, the results have been very satisfactory, and the general response of members to service along patriotic lines is most gratifying. This Society is known as the "Original Americanization Society." Plans for increased activity during the coming year were made at this meeting.

The Pennsylvania Society signally observed Memorial Day at Pittsburgh by decorating the graves of Revolutionary officers and soldiers in Allegheny Cemetery, among whom are such well-known patriots as Major John Irwin, who bore on his body the marks of 18 thrusts of the British bayonets at Paoli; General John Neville, of Virginia, who has given his name to Neville Street, Pittsburgh, and Neville Island, and who not only took active part under Washington at Trenton and Princeton during the Revolution, but back in 1753 marched with the ill-fated Braddock and with General Washington in the campaign against Fort Duquesne. In this section also rest the remains of Major Isaac Craig.

Major Ebenezer Denny, General James O'Hara, General Adamson Tannehill, and others, while in another section rest Ensign Johnston, Captain John Guthrie, and Colonel John Gibson, and others, while in Homewood Cemetery the remains of Colonel John Wilkins and Colonel John Wilkins, Jr., are interred. Over the graves of these men in section 11 were placed "Old Glory," and beneath was placed the war flower—the scarlet poppy.

Some of the graves decorated were those of men who had fought in the three wars—the American Revolution, War 1812, and far back in the French and Indian wars. This remembrance in connection with Memorial Day was the first of its kind in local history.

The Society established a new Chapter at Middletown on June 9.

NEWCASTLE CHAPTER, as well as the entire State Society, deeply mourns the death, on April 27, of J. Smith Dushane, member of the Board of Management of the Pennsylvania Society and the eldest member of the Lawrence County bar and former district attorney. Mr. Dushane was 84 years of age and had filled all the offices of New Castle Chapter, being at the time of his death the Registrar. A veteran of the Civil War with a wonderful record, he was prominent in the G. A. R.

SHENANGO CHAPTER. Patriotism and service were made the keynote of the addresses at the tenth anniversary dinner of Shenango Chapter, Sons of the American Revolution, on Saturday, April 29, and it was made plain that while the members have a pardonable pride in the part their ancestors played in the making of the nation, their purpose today is to spread Americanism and to keep alive the ideals of the founders of our country. Shenango Chapter, which started ten years ago with less than ten members, now has a large and growing roster and is to be heartily congratulated upon its expansion. In bringing United States Senator George Wharton Pepper and State officers of the organization there for the event, officers of the Chapter made the gathering one of the most notable in the history of the community. The illuminating reference made by several of the speakers to the remarkable part played in the Revolution by General Hugh Mercer, after whom our county was named, were of exceptional interest to every resident. Delegations of members from Pittsburgh and New Castle attended the celebration, including a number of the officers of the State Society.

McKEESPORT CHAPTER held a meeting on April 29, at which reports of progress were made, nine new applications being favorably acted upon, while several others are pending. This new Chapter, which only received its charter since January 1, is ambitious to become one of the largest in the State and hopes to accomplish this before the charter roll closes, in June. Tentative plans for duly observing Flag Day with appropriate ceremonies were outlined.

The Tennessee Society.—Through the efforts of this Society the Nashville Chamber of Commerce sent out the following letter to every organization in the city—civic, religious, and educational, urging observance of Flag Day, and this was productive of fine results, the suggestions contained therein being adopted very generally throughout the city.

The letter reads:

At the request of the local branch of the Society of the Sons of the American Revolution, I am calling your attention to the National Flag Day, June 14.

During the war we each of us learned to revere the flag. I am afraid that we are gradually losing the interest that we acquired during those dark days, or at least we do not show our appreciation as we did during the World War. This should not be. Love of the flag should go hand in hand with love of our country, and the effect upon the coming generation of a display of the flag cannot be measured.

I am, therefore, writing to ask that you bring this matter to the attention of your members, and ask them, as far as possible, to fly the flag on Flag Day, June 14.

While we have no large foreign element to be influenced by this action, we can influence our own children, who might otherwise never acquire the love and respect for the flag that is so necessary to good citizenship. It would be a great thing if every business house and residence in Nashville displayed "Old Glory," and every automobile carried our flag on its windshield on June 14.

I trust that you will co-operate with the Sons of the American Revolution in making a success of Flag Day.

The Tennessee Society is very jubilant over its success in securing the Traveling Banner of the National Society for the greatest percentage of increase, presented at the late Congress at Springfield, and also over the prospect of holding the next National Congress at Nashville, the Board of. Trustees having accepted the invitation of Tennessee.

The Utah Society.—Enlivened by friendly tilts over the League of Nations and by interesting discussions of foreign relations, the first banquet of the Utah Society, Sons of American Revolution, the twenty-eighth annual gathering of its kind of that organization, was held at the Weber Club, Ogden, April 19. The affair marked one of the two occasions in American history most sacred to the Society, the anniversary of the Battle of Lexington, the other occasion being the birthday of George Washington. The banquet was attended by members of the Society from Salt Lake, Ogden, Brigham City, and Payson, and the visiting guests left well pleased with Ogden hospitality.

In the afternoon the third annual contest between representatives of the Ogden High School and of the Weber Normal College was held at the Tabernacle. The prize was a medal offered for patriotic oratory by the Utah Society to the winners of such contests, not only in Ogden, but also at the Utah Agricultural College, at the University of Utah, and at a contest between representatives of the two Salt Lake City high schools. Leonard Wright, of the Weber Normal College, was the successful contestant, Miss Helen Cleveland, of the Ogden High School being given second honors on a very close decision. The chairman at the contest was the Rev. Hoyt E. Henriques, of Salt Lake. Mr. Wright's topic was "Law Enforcement the Guardian of American Government."

At the banquet, after a musical program, the President of the Society, Robert M. McConaughy, of Salt Lake, made a short address, reporting upon the prospects favoring the bringing of the 1923 National Convention of the Sons of the American Revolution to Utah. He then introduced the chairman of the banquet committee, Stuart P. Dobbs, of Ogden, who briefly welcomed the visiting members of the Society to Ogden and in turn introduced Abbot R. Heywood,, of Ogden, as the toastmaster. Mr. Heywood, before introducing the first speaker, briefly touched upon the functions of the Society as commemorative of the efforts of the ancestors of its members in securing American liberty, and then gave way to George Albert Smith, of Salt Lake, who spoke upon "America's World Position."

The Utah Society, on June 14th, tendered a complimentary banquet, at the Hotel

Utah, to their compatriot, the Hon. George Albert Smith, recently elected Vice-President General for the Mountain and Pacific District. This was a brilliant affair, largely attended, the program including addresses by Gen. John Quale Cannon, Hon. Abbott R. Heywood, the Hon. Ross Beason, Mayor C. Clarence Nelson, the Hon. Stuart P. Dobbs, and the guest of honor, Mr. Smith.

ADDITIONS TO MEMBERSHIP

There have been enrolled in the office of the Registrar General from February 28, 1922, to June 1, 1922, 462 new members, as follows: Arkansas, 2; California, 12; Colorado, 5; Connecticut, 15; Delaware, 6; District of Columbia, 13; Florida, 1; Georgia, 3; Idaho, 5; Illinois, 27; Indiana, 5; Iowa, 16; Kansas, 8; Kentucky, 3; Louisiana, 10; Maine, 5; Maryland, 9; Massachusetts, 36; Michigan, 20; Minnesota, 23; Missouri, 3; Montana, 3; Nebraska, 13; New Hampshire, 9; New Jersey, 73; New Mexico, 4; New York, 33; North Dakota, 17; Ohio, 14; Oklahoma, 1; Oregon, 3; Pennsylvania, 33; South Dakota, 2; Tennessee, 13; Texas, 6; Utah, 2; Virginia, 1; Washington State, 1; Wisconsin, 6; Wyoming, 1.

In Memoriam

OBEDIAH E. ARMSTRONG, New Jersey Society, died November --, 1920.

WILLIAM ALDEN AUSTIN, Rhode Island Society, died September 21, 1921.

CHARLES ALFRED BAHRENBURG, New Jersey Society, died February 9, 1922.

CHARLES J. BOWLBY, Past President Nebraska Society, died April 23, 1922.

ROBERT A. BRONSON, Connecticut Society, died May 1, 1922.

FRANK W. BUSWELL, Oregon Society, died April 9, 1922.

JUSTIN DAVID CALL, Utah Society, died May 20, 1922.

IRA BENTON CLARK, Tennessee Society, died May 17, 1922.

WILLIAM ELIJAH COVEY, Connecticut Society, died February 3, 1922.

ALPHONSE CRANE, California Society, died September 9, 1921.

THOMAS POSEY CRAIG, Colorado Society, died September 13, 1921.

HENRY D. CROW, California Society, died December 27, 1921.

J. SMITH DUSHANE, Member Board of Management, Pennsylvania Society, died April 26, 1922.

WILLIAM J. EGLESTON, Montana Society, died March 9, 192.

IRA HOBART EVANS, Past President Texas Society, died April 19, 1922.

CHARLES EDWIN FAIRBANKS, New Jersey Society, died December 4, 1920.

THOMAS G. GIBSON, Wyoming Society, died April 26, 1922.

CHARLES FREDERICK GLADDING, Connecticut Society, died May 4, 1922.

L. A. HAMILL, Iowa Society, died February 15, 1922.

JEROME C. HOSMER, Massachusetts Society, died March 17, 1922.

WILL B. HOWE, Secretary New Hampshire Society, died April 1, 1922.

FREDERICK LAMBER HUNTINGTON, Connecticut Society, died May 8, 1922.

PETER CUSHMAN JONES, Hawaii Society, died April 23, 1922.

HERBERT W. KIMBALL, Secretary-Registrar Massachusetts Society, 1894-1921, died April 10, 1922.

GEORGE N. KREDIER, Illinois Society, died January 4, 1922.

HENRY ALEXANDER LAUGHLIN, Pennsylvania Society, died ——, 1922.

GEORGE F. LONG, Illinois Society, died April 18, 1922.

GEORGE WILLIAM PECK, Connecticut Society, died February 1, 1922.

WILLIAM HENRY RICHMOND, Connecticut Society, died March 14, 1922.

LEWIS FRANKLIN SALLEE, Nebraska Society, died May 4, 1921.

H. B. SCOTT, Iowa Society, died February 22, 1922.

WILLIAM CONVERSE SKINNER, Connecticut Society, died March 8, 1922.

FRANK B. SPALTER, Massachusetts Society, died March 15, 1922.

GEORGE S. STEWART, Secretary-Registrar Massachusetts Society, died April 17, 1922.

WILLIAM WALCOTT STRONG, Wisconsin Society, died January 3, 1922.

WILLIAM E. WARNER, California Society, killed at Washington, D. C. January 28, 1922.

NATHAN WARREN, Past President Massachusetts Society, died April 11, 1922.

JEROME A. WATROUS, Wisconsin Society, died June 5, 1922.

HARVEY LEE VANBENSCHOTEN, North Dakota Society, died September 15, 1918.

ARTHUR I. VESCELIUS, New Jersey Society, died February 19, 1922.

ARTHUR J. WELD, Connecticut Society, died February 7, 1922.

RECORDS OF 462 NEW MEMBERS AND 155 SUPPLEMENTALS APPROVED AND ENROLLED BY THE REGISTRAR GENERAL FROM FEBRUARY 28, 1922, TO JUNE 1, 1922.

PORTER HARTWELL ADAMS, Brookline, Mass. (36823). Son of Charles Albert and Jeannie H. (Porter) Adams; grandson of Albert and Lucy Ann (Gibson) Adams; great-grandson of Stephen and Mary (Hartwell) Gibson; great^2-grandson of Thomas and Lucy (Martin) Gibson; great^3-grandson of *Abraham Gibson*, private Col. Asa Whitcomb's Regt., Mass. Militia.

CLARENCE HENRY ALEXANDER, South Orange, N. J. (37002). Son of William H. and Esmerelda Alice (Waldron) Alexander; grandson of Henry P. and Mary Ann (Harris) Waldron; great-grandson of Russell D. and Rebecca (Carl) Harris; great^2-grandson of *Squire Harris*, private, N. J. State Troops, pensioned.

NATHANIEL FLINT ALLARD, Fryeburgh, Me. (36587). Son of Joel T. and Phoebe Chandler (Elliott) Allard; grandson of James and Mary (Chandler) Elliott; great-grandson of *John Elliott*, private, Lieutenant-Colonel, Loammie Baldwin's Regt., Mass. Militia and Cont'l Infantry.

EDWARD GRANT ALLEN, Grand Forks, No. Dak. (36930). Son of Nelson Elisha and Sarah Clarissa (Botsford) Allen; grandson of Cyrus and Amanda (Durkee) Allen; great-grandson of Elisha and Betsy (Gore) Durkee; great^2-grandson of *Obediah Gore*, private, Conn. Troops at Wyoming Massacre.

FRANK CAMPBELL ALLEN, Nashville, Tenn. (36782). Son of B. F. and Maria Louisa (Trousdale) Allen; grandson of William and Mary (Bugg) Trousdale; great-grandson of *James Trousdale*, Captain, Gen'l Francis Marion's Regt., North Carolina Troops.

HARVEY IRVIN ALLEN, Dayton, Ohio (36495). Son of Frank L. and Anna Josephine (Snowden) Allen; grandson of William and Eliza (Irvin) Snowden; great-grandson of William and Martha (Brooks) Irvin; great^2-grandson of *Samuel Irwin (Irvin)*, Lieutenant-Colonel, Third Battalion, Cumberland County, Penna. Militia.

ROGER ALLING, Sault St. Marie, Mich. (N. J. 36875). Son of Stephen Howard and Margaret N. (Threlkeld) Alling; grandson of James Morrison and Eliza Richwood (Spencer) Alling; great-grandson of Stephen Young and Sarah Maria (McKay) Alling; great^2-grandson of Young Stephen and Patty (Cory) Alling; great^3-grandson of *John Alling*, Third Lieutenant, Captain Wheeler's Co., Newark, N. J., Minute-men, and private, Baldwin's Cont'l Artificers.

ALBERT FAY ALLISON, New York, N. Y. (So. Dak. 30670). Son of Wirt Heines and Harriet (M—) Allison; grandson of James and Dorothy A. (Heines) Allison; great-grandson of William and Nancy Ann (Feeter) Heines; great^2-grandson of *William Feeter*, private Scout and Guide, New York Troops.

EDWARD JOHN ANGLE, Nebraska (26393). Supplemental. Son of John Bouslough and Jane (Bell) Angle; grandson of James and Catherine (Young) Bell; great-grandson of *William Young*, Lieutenant, Ninth Battalion, Lancaster County, Penna. Militia; grandson of Daniel and Elizabeth (Bouslough) Angle; great-grandson of John and Susanna (Miller) Angle; great^2-grandson of *Henry Angle (Engle)*, Captain, Seventh Battalion, Lancaster County, Penna. Militia.

MAXEY APPLEGATE, Freehold, N. J. (37020). Son of Edwin Forrest and Mary Lucinda (French) Applegate; grandson of William and Elizabeth (Price) Applegate; great-grandson of *William Applegate*, private and Quartermaster, Middlesex County, New Jersey Militia.

WILBERFORCE EWING ARCHIBALD, Springfield, Ill. (36629). Son of Thomas Henry and Susan Wadleigh (Tuck) Archibald; grandson of Henry and Rebecca (Marshall) Archibald; great-grandson of *Thomas Marshall*, private, Col. Samuel Webb's Regt., Conn. Militia, pensioned.

BRIDGEWATER MEREDITH ARNOLD, JR., Orange, N. J. (36872). Son of Bridgewater Meredith and Margaret (Hunter) Arnold; grandson of John Ford and Rebecca (Campbell) Arnold; great-grandson of *Lewis Arnold*, private, Middlesex County, New Jersey militia.

ERNEST FLAGG AYRES, Boise, Idaho (35112). Son of Branch F. and Edora (Cady) Ayres; grandson of James F. and Martha (Flagg) Ayres; great-grandson of Josiah and Lucretia (Hull) Ayres; great²-grandson of *Moses Ayres*, private, Colonel Brewer's Regt., Mass. Militia.

ALFRED GOODRICH BADGER, Billings, Mont. (31785). Son of Charles Henry and Etta (Pack) Badger; grandson of Alfred Goodrich and Adeline (Van Sice) Badger; great-grandson of Ebenezer and Harriet (Brigden) Badger; great²-grandson of *Michael Brigden*, private, Conn. Militia.

FRANKLIN WOODRUFF BAILEY, Newark, N. J. (37014). Son of Samuel Fred and Emma Augusta (Flagg) Bailey; grandson of William Francis and Mary (Woodruff) Bailey; great-grandson of Samuel and Nancy Stiles (Lindsley) Bailey; grea²-grandson of Samuel and Sarah (Tappan) Bailey; great²-grandson of *Jonathan Bailey*, Corporal, Essex County, New Jersey Militia and private, Cont'l Troops.

SAMUEL TERRY BAILEY, Ogden, Utah (32645). Son of John Franklin and Mary E. (Fulton) Bailey; grandson of Dan and Mary (Taylor) Bailey; great-grandson of *Samuel Bailey*, Lieutenant, Ninth Company, Sixteenth Regt., Conn. Militia.

LELAND VINCENT BAKER, Summit, N. J. (36852). Son of Walter S. and Martha A. (Sparrow) Baker; grandson of David and Betsy M. (Higgins) Baker; great-grandson of *Eleazer Higgins*, private, Colonel Marshall's Regt., Mass. Militia, prisoner.

JOSEPH WILBUR BALDERSTON, Elizabeth, N. J. (37142). Son of Marcellus and Margaret Hall (Haislett) Balderston; grandson of William Valentine and Mary Ann (Cadle) Haislett; great-grandson of William and Mary (Hall) Cadle; great²-grandson of *Richard Hall*, Corporal, Third Regt., Maryland Line.

JOHN NEHEMIAH BALDWIN, Omaha, Nebr. (36986). Son of John Nehemiah and Lilla Gray (Holcomb) Baldwin; granson of George and Sarah Ann (Gorton) Holcomb; great-grandson of Solomon and Sarah (Scott) Gorton; great²-grandson of John and Opha (Boone) Gorton; great³-grandson of *Samuel Gorton*, Captain and Quartermaster, Kent County, Rhode Island Militia; grandson of Caleb and Jane (Barr) Baldwin; great-grandson of Nehemiah and Patience (Tunis) Baldwin; great²-grandson of *Caleb Baldwin*, private, New Jersey Militia; great²-grandson of John and Sarah (Harris) Tunis; great²-grandson of *George Harris*, Minute-man, New Jersey State Troops; great-grandson of Thomas and Ann (Emmett) Barr; great²-grandson of *Alexander Barr*, Colonel, Westmoreland County, Penna. Militia.

SAMUEL HASKELL BASS, Massachusetts (35859). Supplemental. Son of William Seth and Fannie Agnes (Howe) Bass; grandson of Abel and Eunice R. (Brown) Howe; great-grandson of Guy C. and Eunice (Robinson) Brown; great-grandson of *Joshua Brown*, Captain, Col. Timothy Bigelow's Regt., Mass. Militia; great²-grandson of Zacheus and Bridget (Winchester) Robinson; great²-grandson of *William Winchester*, Lieutenant, Thirteenth Regt., Mass. Militia.

RANSOM HAZELIP BASSETT, Louisville, Ky. (36531). Son of Edmund Ruffin and Myrtle (Hazelip) Bassett; grandson of James Harvey and Georgia (Houston) Bassett; great-grandson of Jeremiah and Tryphena (Birch) Bassett; great²-grandson of *Thomas Erskine Birch*, Ensign, Virginia Navy, wounded.

NATHANIEL HORTON BATCHELDER, Windsor, Conn. (36715). Son of Henry Morrill and Martha Osgood (Horton) Batchelder, grandson of Samuel Lang and Mary (Brown) Batchelder; great-grandson of David and Mehitable (Lang) Batchelder; great-grandson of Stephen and Abigail (Weare) Lang; great³-grandson of *Mescheh Weare*, Chairman of New Hampshire Com. of Safety and Justice of the Peace; grandson of Nathaniel Augustus and Harriet Maria (Symonds) Horton; great-grandson of Nathaniel and Martha (Very) Horton; great²-grandson of *Lemuel Horton*, private, Milton, Mass. Militia, pensioned.

DAVID CARSON BAYLESS, Baltimore, Md. (36095). Son of Albert Jessop and Sarah Tilden (Carson) Bayless; grandson of James Pritchard and Mary Ann (Jessop) Bayless; great-grandson of *Nathaniel Bayless*, Second Lieutenant, Third Regt., Maryland Militia.

FRANK WILLIAM BAYLEY, Jamaica Plains, Mass. (36811). Son of William Henry and Lucy (Chase) Bayley, grandson of Luther Rogers and Lucy Demond (Follansbee) Chase; great-grandson of Nathan and Judith (Rogers) Chase; great²-grandson of *Edmund Chase*, private, Capt. Moses Little's Co., at Lexington Alarm.

ALBERT CLINE BAYLIS, New York City, N. Y. (36888). Son of Franklin and Harriet (Cline) Baylis; grandson of Abiah P. and Mary J. (Gregory) Baylis; great-grandson of Joseph and Rachael (Bullock) Gregory; great^2-grandson of *Ebenezer Gregory*, private, Conn. Militia; great ^{3}-grandson of *Joseph Gregory*, Ensign, Seventh Regt., Dutchess County, New York Militia; great-grandson of William and Polly (Culver) Baylis; great^2-grandson of *John Baylis*, private, Colonel Van Schaick's Regt., New York Line.

LELAND PORTER BEAL, Hudson, Mich. (36039). Son of Eli A. and Lois A. (Wilcox) Beal; grandson of Porter and Susan (Brownell) Beal; great-grandson of Joseph and Elizabeth (Cleghorn) Beal; great^2-grandson of *Seth Beal*, private, Weymouth, Mass. Militia.

EDWARD HEWLETT BENJAMIN, San Francisco, Calif. (36415)). Son of Erastus Mapes and Ruth Slocum (Mahon) Benjamin; grandson of Michael and Susanna (Bailey) Benjamin, great-grandson of *Judah Benjamin*, private, Colonel Moseley's Regt., Conn. Militia.

PAUL REVERE BENSON, Havana, Cuba (Ill. 36646). Son of Luther William and Anna Collord (Slade) Benson; grandson of George Washington and Mary Amande (Towner) Slade; great-grandson of Abel and Emeline (Collord) Towner; great^2-grandson of Thomas Bradbury Chandler and Catherine (Tremper) Collord; great^3-grandson of *Michael Tremper*, private, Dutchess County, New York Militia.

PHILIP EDMUNDS BESSOM, Swampscott, Mass. (37109). Son of Philip Bessom and Sarah Elizabeth (Bartlett) Bessom, Jr.; grandson of Joseph E. and Nancy T. (Thompson) Bartlett; great-grandson of John and Sarah Grush (Tewksbury) Thompson; great^2-grandson of James and Mrs. Nancy (——) Goodwin Tewksbury, Jr.; great^3-grandson of *James Tewksbury*, private, Marblehead, Mass. Militia.

WILLIAM BLANEY BESSOM, Lynn, Mass. (37116). Son of Richard V. and Rachel (Gill) Bessom; grandson of William Bubier and Maria (Van Blunk) Bessom Jr.; great-grandson of William Bubier and Anna Martin (Harris) Bessom; great^2-grandson of *Robert Harris*, Lieutenant, Col. John Glover's Regt., Mass. Militia.

LEWIS LEMUEL BINGHAM, Estherville, Iowa (36909). Son of Lemuel R. and Martha E. (Tracy) Bingham; grandson of Samuel and Emeline (Newton) Tracy; great-grandson of Joseph and Ruth (Carter) Tracy; great^2-grandson of *Thomas Tracy*, private, Colonel Wood's Regt., Vermont Militia.

WALTER IRVIN BEAM, Wilmette, Ill. (36628). Son of Henry Francis and Margaret Elizabeth (Irvin) Beam; grandson of Joseph Clifford and Margaret (Burns) Beam; great-grandson of Thomas Lemon and Rachel (Clifford) Beam; great^2-grandson of *Henry Beam*, private, Westmoreland and Lancaster Counties, Penna. Militia.

HENRY FRANKLIN BEARDSLEY, Danbury, Conn. (36716). Son of John H. and Melinda R. (Osborne) Beardsley; grandson of Alfred and Emeline (Burchard) Beardsley; great-grandson of Josiah and Catherine (Abbott) Beardsley; great^2-grandson of *Josiah Beardsley*, private, Col. Samuel Whiting's Regt., Conn. Militia.

W. A. RUSSELL BELL, Frederick, Md. (36096). Son of Albert and Elizabeth C. (Cashman) Bell; grandson of Jonas and Catherine A. (Mickley) Bell; great-grandson of Frederick and Maria (Emerick) Bell; great^2-grandson of *Peter Bell* (*Beall*), Captain, Col. John Stull's Regt., Maryland Troops.

CORWIN RUTHVEN BENNETT, Des Moines, Iowa (36911). Son of Jasper Corrington and Loine (Dooley) Bennett; grandson of Phineas and Semira Arminta (Codding) Bennett; great-grandson of Joseph and Lydia (Birdsall) Bennett; great^2-grandson of Isaac and Anna (Losee) Bennett; great^3-grandson of *Simeon Losee*, private, Second Regt., New York Militia.

JOHN WARD BERETTA, San Antonio, Texas (36327). Son of John King and Sallie Mills (Ward) Beretta; grandson of John R. and Louisa Nicholas (Hartsook) Ward; great-grandson of Daniel J. and Elizabeth Hannah (Carrington) Hartsook; great^2-grandson of Benjamin and Mary Ann (Cabell) Carrington; great^3-grandson of *Nicholas Cabell*, Colonel, Amherst County, Virginia Militia.

RALPH EMERSON BICKNELL, Swampscott, Mass. (36824). Son of Francis A. and Nancy Maria (Torrey) Bicknell; grandson of Lemuel and Nancy Star (Bicknell) Torrey; great-grandson of James and Hannah (Holbrook) Torrey; great^2-grandson of *Lemuel Torrey*, private and Sergeant, Weymouth, Mass. Militia.

GARRET VINSON BILLINGS, Upper Montclair, N. J. (37135). Son of Richard Nelson and Clarissa (Van Reipen) Billings; grandson of Garret Daniel and Caroline (Westervelt) Van Reipen; great-grandson of Daniel and Elizabeth (——) Van Reipen; great²-grandson of Cornelius and Elizabeth (Vreeland) Van Reipen; great³-grandson of *Daniel Van Reipen*, Lieutenant, New Jersey Militia.

JOHN CARROLL BLACKMAN, Cheyenne, Wyo. (30023). Son of John Clark and Nettie (Greenlese) Blackman; grandson of Horace Granger and Amelia (Clark) Blackman; great-grandson of Isaac Newton and Henrietta (Granger) Blackman; great²-grandson of Samuel and Esther (Hamilton) Blackman; great³-grandson of *Elijah Blackman*, Captain, Col. Henry Sherburne's Regt., Conn. Cont'l Line, pensioned.

CHARLES KENT BLATCHLY, New York (35374). Supplementals. Son of Vernon C. and Mary Emma (Kent) Blatchly; grandson of Eri and Amanda B. (Howell) Kent, Jr., great-grandson of Samuel and Betsey D. (Olmstead) Howell; great²-grandson of Lewis and Sarah (Bennett) Olmstead; great³-grandson of *Jared Olmstead*, Conn. Minute-man at Tyron's Invasion; great⁴-grandson of *Samuel Olmstead*, Fairfield County, Conn. Justice of the Peace and Member of Conn. General Assembly of 1778-'79; grandson of Albert C. and Eliza (Garnsey) Blatchly; great-grandson of Joseph B. and Sarah (Frost) Garnsey; great²-grandson of *Joel Garnsey (Guernsey)*, private, Conn. Militia and Cont'l Troops; grandson of Albert C. and Eliza Guernsey (Garnsey) Blatchly; great-grandson of Daniel and Amy (Bristol) Blatchly; great³-grandson of *Bazaliel (Bisaleel) Bristol*, Captain, Bristol County, Conn. Militia.

FRANKLIN SUMMERS BOLLES, Newark, N. J. (37001). Son of Ezra Baldwin and Adaline Hunt (Summers) Bolles; grandson of George W. and Hannah Riggs (Terrill) Summers; great-grandson of *Amos Terrill*, private, Essex County, New Jersey Militia.

LAURENCE RAYMOND BOLLES, Nutley, N. J. (37146). Son of Franklin Summers and Laura Virginia (Reeve) Bolles; grandson of Ezra Baldwin and Adaline (Hunt) Summers; great-grandson of George W. and Hannah (Riggs) Terrill; great²-grandson of *Amos Terrill*, private, Essex County, New Jersey Militia.

CLARENCE HAVELOCK BOLTON, New Haven, Conn. (36720). Son of James R. and Fannie (Sheldon) Bolton; grandson of Joseph and Abby (Barker) Sheldon; great-grandson of Joseph and Hepsibah (Richardson) Sheldon; great²-grandson of *Tilley Richardson*, private, Col. Josiah Whitney's Regt., Mass. Militia.

KENNETH WILLIAMSON BOND, Cheyenne, Wyo. (30025). Son of Fred and Clara (Williamson) Bond; grandson of Avery J. and Sabra A. (Dennis) Bond; great-grandson of James and Lindemina (Avery) Bond; great²-grandson of Benjamin and Merriam (Manter) Bond; great³-grandson of *John Bond*, private, Col. Ephraim Doolittle's Regt., Mass. Militia.

JAMES SINCLAIR BOYD, Brooklyn, N. Y. (37177). Son of Charles and Isabella (Smith) Boyd; grandson of William D. and Harriet (Parent) Boyd; great-grandson of Ebenezer and Sarah (Merritt) Boyd, Jr.; great²-grandson of *Ebenezer Boyd*, Captain, Third Regt., Westchester County, New York Militia.

COURTLANDT VAN BEUREN BOYDEN, Elmhurst, N. Y. (37176). Son of Elias W. and Julia Eliza (Van Beuren) Boyden; grandson of Elias W. and Sylvia (Adams) Boyden; great-grandson of Barnard and Abigail (Barnes) Whitney Boyden; great²-grandson of *Richard Boyden*, private, Col. Ephraim Wheelock's Regt., Mass. Militia.

GALBRAITH MURRAY BRAWNER, Frankfort, Ky. (36532). Son of Alexander G. and Hannah C. (Morgan) Brawner; grandson of Robert A. and Mary C. (Murray) Brawner; great-grandson of James Galbraith and Mary C. (Schneider) Weinbrinner Murray; great²-grandson of *Leckey Murray*, Surgeon, Fifth Battalion, Lancaster County, Penna. Militia.

JAMES MALCOLM BRECKENRIDGE, St. Louis, Mo. (35566). Son of George and Julia (Clark) Breckenridge, grandson of James and Elizabeth Ann (Bryan) Breckenridge; great-grandson of George and Elizabeth (Cowan) Breckenridge; great²-grandson of *Alexander Breckenridge*, private, Virginia Militia at King's Mountains; great³-grandson of *George Breckenridge*, private, Virginia Militia at King's Mountain; great-grandson of *James Bryan*, private, Col. Otho Williams' Regt., Virginia Cont'l Troops.

SAMUEL BARRON BREWSTER, Woodbridge, N. J. (37133). Son of George and Eliza Case (Barron) Brewster; grandson of George Youngs and Elizabeth (Mundy) Brewster;

great-grandson of Timothy and Sarah (Youngs) Brewster; great²-grandson of *Samuel Brewster*, Member Com. of Safety and Provincial Congress, Ulster County, N. Y.; great-grandson of Ezra and Catharine (Prall) Mundy; great-grandson of *Samuel Mundy*, private, Middlesex County, New Jersey Militia and State Troops.

EARLE SPENCER BRINSMODE, New Haven, Conn. (36717). Son of Herman Stanley and Francis Maria (Benham) Brinsmode; grandson of Charles Spencer and Mary Elizabeth (Frisbie) Brinsmode; great-grandson of Abraham and Betsy (Beach) Brinsmode; great²-grandson of Daniel and Mary (Beebe) Brinsmode; great³-grandson of *Abraham Brinsmode*, Captain, Conn. Militia at Tryon's Raid.

WALTER LINCOLN BRINSMODE, Bridgeport, Conn. (36718). Same as Earle Spencer Brinsmode, Conn. (36717).

EDWARD DUNHAM BRISTER, Summit, N. J. (36699). Son of Joseph E. and Isabella B. (Meeker) Brister; grandson of William B. and Mary (Bishop) Meeker, great-grandson of Nathaniel and Betsy (Dobbs) Bishop; great²-grandson of William and Urania (Hoyt) Dobbs; great³-grandson of *William Dobbs*, Captain, in New York Marine Service.

JOSEPH FRANCIS BROADBENT, McKeesport, Penna. (37081). Son of Henry Augustus and Margaret (Anderson) Broadbent; grandson of Ammon and Emma Almira (Wadsworth) Broadbent; great-grandson of *Joseph Wadworth*, Captain, Fourteenth Regt., Mass. Troops.

WALTER BELDING BROCKWAY, Portland, Me. (36588). Son of Marcus and Adaline M. (Pond) Brockway; grandson of Prescott and Eliza (Palmer) Pond; great-grandson of *Elijah Pond*, Captain, Mass. Minute-men at Lexington Alarm.

HAROLD GRISWOLD BROWN, Minneapolis, Minn. (35694). Son of Theron G. and Harriet O. (Griswold) Brown; grandson of Lester and Fanny (Gates) Griswold; great-grandson of Henry W. and Samantha (——) Gates; great²-grandson of *Luther Gates*, Musician, Fourth Regt. Conn. Line, pensioned.

JAMES ARTHUR BROWN, Lebanon, Ind. (36435). Son of James A. and Sarah Jane (Watkins) Brown; grandson of Jacob B. and Elizabeth (Lewis) Brown; great-grandson of *Thomas Lewis*, Lieutenant, Fifteenth Regt., Virginia Cont'l Troops.

MARTIN M. BROWN, North Adams, Mass. (36815). Son of Russell D. and Eliza C. (Millard) Brown; grandson of Harvey and Lucinda (Fuller) Brown; great-grandson of Jonas and Lois (Russell) Brown; great²-grandson of *Josiah Brown*, Captain, Col. Enoch Hale's Regt., New Hampshire Militia.

ROBERT JAMES BROWN, Little Rock, Ark. (31773). Son of Robert Joseph and Annie (Parker) Brown; grandson of Leveret R. and Catherine A. (Ostrander) Brown; great-grandson of Joseph P. and Lura (Russell) Brown; great²-grandson of Joseph P. and Experience (Stafford) Brown; great³-grandson of *Abraham Brown*, Captain, Stockbridge, Mass. Militia.

RUFUS L. BROWN, North Adams, Mass. (36814). Same as Martin M. Brown, Mass. (36815).

HARRY FLEMING BUCKLIN, Brazil, Ind. (36436). Son of James John and Mary (Fleming) Bucklin; grandson of James Magee and Mary Ann (Beckwith) Bucklin; great-grandson of John Williams and Polly Floyd (Smith) Beckwith; great²-grandson of *John Beckwith*, Sergeant, Captain Post's Maryland Co., General Hazen's Cont'l Regt.

EDWARD BUMGARDNER, Lawrence, Kans. (36732). Son of Andrew and Sophia Elizabeth (Straight) Bumgardner; grandson of Jesse Bales and Adah (Henry) Straight; great-grandson of Peter and Elizabeth (Bales) Straight; great²-grandson of *Jacob Straight*, private, Virginia Militia.

JESSE DESMAUX BURKS, Berkeley, Calif. (D. C. 36139). Son of Jesse Herring and Sabina (Dismukes) Burks; grandson of Marcus L. and Delia (Watkins) Dismukes; great-grandson of *Paul Dismukes*, private, Spottsylvania County, Virginia Troops, pensioned.

ROBERT RAY BURKS, Knoxville, Tenn. (36791). Son of Robert L. and Eliza (Jakes) Burks; grandson of Willis and Lucinda (——) Burks; great-grandson of *Samuel Burks*, private, North Carolina Militia, pensioned.

OSCAR CALKINS, Brockton, Mass. (36825). Son of Samuel I. and Chloe Walker (Harvey) Calkins; grandson of Otis and Anna (Leach) Harvey, great-grandson of *Nathan Harvey*, private and drummer, Bridgewater, Mass. Militia.

DAVID WOODWARD CANNON, Salt Lake City, Utah (32644). Son of John Q. and Annie (Wells) Cannon; grandson of George Quayle and Elizabeth (Hoagland) Cannon; great-grandson of Abraham L. and Margaret (Quick) Hoagland; great²-grandson of James and Maria (Hoagland) Quick; great²-grandson of *Jacobus Quick*, Captain, Second Battalion, Somerset County, New Jersey Militia.

SAMUEL EWING CARNEY, Nashville, Tenn. (36785). Son of Walter Overton and Nannie (Jones) Carney; grandson of William Joseph and Laura Maria (Bertha) Carney; great-grandson of Le Grand Hargis and Catherine Wells (Lytle) Carney; great²-grandson of John and Tabitha (Morton) Lytle; great²-grandson of *William Lytle*, Captain, North Carolina Cont'l Line.

HOWELL CARTER, JR., New Orleans, La. (36959). Son of Howell and Dora Long (Johnston) Carter; grandson of Albert Gallatin and Frances Priscilla (Howell) Carter; great-grandson of Charles Burr and Priscilla (Kirkland) Howell; great²-grandson of *Richard Howell*, Major, Second Regt., New Jersey Militia.

WOODBRIDGE GEORGE CARY, Highland Park, Ill. (36630). Son of William Miller and Caroline (George) Carr; grandson of James and Mercy (Weaver) Cary; great-grandson of *Jabez Weaver*, Sergeant, Vermont Militia.

HARLAND DONALD CASLER, East Orange, N. J. (36857). Son of William H. and Alice (De Witt) Casler; grandson of Levi and Lany M. (McChesney) Casler; great-grandson of Jacob and Rachel (Fetterly) Casler, Jr.; great²-grandson of Jacob Casler, private, Tryon County, New York Militia.

DANIEL DOUGLAS CAULKINS, Cleveland, Ohio (36499). Son of William W. and Catherine Ann (Baker) Caulkins; grandson of Daniel Douglas and Ann (Baker) Caulkins; great-grandson of *Enoch Baker*, Corporal and Sergeant, Conn. Militia, pensioned.

SIDNEY MARCH CHASE, Minneapolis, Minn. (35697). Son of Clement Caleb and Rose T. (March) Chase; grandson of Samuel and Sally A. (Gile) Chase; great-grandson of David and Sally (Ayer) Gile; great²-grandson of *Esekill (Ezekiel) Gile*, Captain, Col. Stephen Peabody's Regt., New Hampshire Militia.

CHARLES EDISBURY CHERRINGTON, Grand Junction, Colo. (36345). Son of Homer Clark and Emily Sarah (Wynne) Cherrington, grandson of James W. and Happy (Weed) Cherrington; great-grandson of William and Olive (Branch) Weed; great²-grandson of *Asa Branch*, private, Capt. John Strong's Co., Pittsfield, Mass. Militia.

SAMUEL CORNELIUS CISSEL, JR., Washington, D. C. (36141). Son of Samuel Cornelius and Martha (Lemon) Cissel; grandson of David Thomas and Sarah Sinclair (Young) Cissel; great-grandson of William and Rachel Sarah (Williams) Cissel; great²-grandson of Humphrey and Sarah (Beall) Williams; great³-grandson of *Richard Beall*, Captain, Prince George County, Maryland Militia; grandson of William Henry and Belle (Warwick) Lemon; great-grandson of Charles and Lucy Augusta (Ward) Lemon; great²-grandson of John and Lucy (Howe) Ward; great³-grandson of *Andrew Ward*, private, Essex County, Mass. Militia for Sea-coast Defense.

ADDISON HOLMAN CLARK, Westfield, N. J. (37004). Son of Addison Scudder and Rebecca Holman (Woodbury) Clark; grandson of Thomas Woodruff and Abby (Clark) Clark; great-grandson of Abraham and Elizabeth (Pierson) Clark; great²-grandson of *Jesse Clark*, Wagon and Barrack Master, New Jersey Militia.

GEORGE EDSON CLARK, Farmingdale, Me. (36589). Son of Edson Porter and Virginia (Pettis) Clark; grandson of Nathan and Polly (Jenks) Clark; great-grandson of John and Kezia (Smith) Clark; great²-grandson of *John Clark*, private, Mass. Cont'l Troops.

WALDO APPLETON CLARK, Washington, D. C. (36146). Son of Appleton Prentiss and Florence (Perry) Clark; grandson of Appleton P. and Elizabeth (W—) Clark; great-grandson of George and Charlotte (Prentiss) Clark; great²-grandson of *Isaac Clark*, Lieutenant, Mass. Militia.

RICHARD WARNER CLARKE, New York City, N. Y. (36881). Son of Charles Patrick and Agnes Sinclair (Warner) Clarke; grandson of George Harvey and Margaret (Campbell) Warner; great-grandson of Austin and Phebe (Griswold) Warner; great²-grandson of Ambrose and Annie (Smith) Griswold; great³-grandson of *Caleb Smith*, private, Second Regt., Essex County, New Jersey Militia.

CHARLES GRESSINGER CLAYLAND, Pittsburgh, Penna. (37085). Son of Harry M. B. and Nancy (Magill) Clayland; grandson of Charles and Catherine (Grove) Magill; great-grandson of *Charles Magill*, Major and Colonel, Virginia State Troops, widow pensioned.

KENNETH R. COBB, JR., New York, N. Y. (36887). Son of Kenneth R. and Marie (Pizzini) Cobb; grandson of Andrew and Anna Gertrude (Davis) Pizzini; great-grandson of Benjamin and Burronsinia (Solis) Davis; great²-grandson of Daniel and Sarah Helen (Norris) Solis; great³-grandson of Eden and Anna (Hiers) Norris; great⁴-grandson of Heurick and Sarah (Whitelock) Hiers; great⁵-grandson of *John Whitlock*, Lieutenant, Mommouth County, New Jersey Militia, killed.

FREDERICK SEARS COE, Newark, N. J. (37138). Son of James Aaron and Mary Louise (Sears) Coe; grandson of Aaron and Julia (Baldwin) Coe; great-grandson of Sayers and Sally (Davis) Coe; great²-grandson of *Joseph Davis*, private, Essex County, New Jersey Militia.

WILLIAM PENNINGTON COE, Newark, N. J. (37015). Son of George V. and Mary A. (Blair) Coe; grandson of Isaac and Catherine (Pierson) Coe; great-grandson of Sayers and Sally (Davis) Coe; great²-grandson of *Joseph Davis*, private and Wagonmaster, Essex County, New Jersey Militia.

MAYNARD COPELAND COLE, Omaha, Nebr. (36976). Son of Ansel Orlester and Martha Louise (Copeland) Cole; grandson of George Carpenter and Mary Anne (Rounds) Cole; great-grandson of Simeon and Olive (Carpenter) Cole; great²-grandson of Simeon and Margaret (Capron) Cole; great³-grandson of *Simeon Cole*, Captain, Col. Thomas Carpenter's Regt., Bristol County, Mass. Militia.

JAMES RETZER COMLY, San Diego, Calif. (36417). Son of Harry Retzer and Beatrice (Seykova) Comly; grandson of James M. and Sarah L. (Retzer) Comly; great-grandson of Henry and Rebecca (Worrell) Comly; great²-grandson of *Isaac Worrell*, Captain, Second Battalion, Philadelphia County, Penna. Militia.

ARCHIBALD WOODRUFF CONKLIN, Newark, N. J. (37012). Son of Nathaniel and Elizabeth J. (Woodruff) Conklin; grandson of Archibald and Catherine (Johnson) Woodruff; great-grandson of Parsons and Mary (Mulford) Woodruff; great²-grandson of *Seth Woodruff*, Sergeant, First Regt., Essex County, New Jersey Militia.

FREDERICK MILLER CONKLING, New Jersey (26106). Supplementals. Son of William Johnson and Mary Irene (Perry) Conkling; grandson of Joshua and Charlotte Augusta (Meeks) Conkling; great-grandson of John Johnson and Hannah (Tuttle) Conkling; great²-grandson of *Joshua Conkling*, Teamster, Essex County, New Jersey Militia; great-grandson of John and Elizabeth (Lewis) Meeks; great²-grandson of John and Susanne Helene Marie (de Moulinar) Meeks; great²-grandson of *Joseph Meeks*, New York City Associator and patriot.

HAROLD WILLIAM CONNOLLY, Dorchester, Mass. (37101). Son of Fred William and Ellen Louise (Meade) Connolly; grandson of Fayette Clark and Mary Jane (Wolcott) Meade; great-grandson of Henry Bissell and Mary (Shepherd) Wolcott; great²-grandson of Gideon and Huldah (Bissell) Wolcott; great³-grandson of *Hezekiah Bissell*, Captain, Col. Erastus Wolcott's Regt., Conn. Militia and of North Parish Alarm List.

JOHN GILBERT CUTLER CONSTABLE, Cleveland, Ohio (36496). Son of Robert Thomas and Elizabeth (Cutler) Constable; grandson of Alvin and Ruth (Thomas) Cutler; great-grandson of Nathaniel and Betsy (Plimpton) Cutler; great²-grandson of *Elisha Cutler*, private, Colonel Wheelock's Regt., Mass. Militia.

GEORGE STEELE COOK, Springfield, Mass. (37102). Son of William Frederick and Florence Gertrude (Steele) Cook; grandson of Asahel and Emeline Melissa (Field) Cook; great-grandson of Ezekiel and Polly (Woodbury) Cook; great²-grandson of *Daniel Cook (Cooke)*, private, Colonel Sear's Regt., Hampshire County, Mass. Militia.

KARL RUTHVEN COOK, Mexico City, Mex. (Ill. 36648). Son of Willis Curtis and Mary Ellen (Williams) Cook; grandson of Curtis and Betsy Snow (Brown) Cook; great grandson of *Lemuel Cook*, private, Conn. Militia, pensioned.

LAWRENCE HARVEY COOK, Palo Alto, Calif. (36418). Son of Harvey and Adella Oneta (Winters) Cook; grandson of George Washington and Sarah Catharine (Westervelt) Winters; great-grandson of Silas and Harriet (Kimball) Westervelt; great²-grandson of *Casparus Westervelt*, private, Dutchess and Orange Counties, New Jersey Militia, pensioned.

PHILIP COOK, Wilmington, Del. (35665). Son of John Darwin Shepard and Rosalie Elvira (Barlow) Cook; grandson of Joseph and Phebe (Phillips) Barlow; great-grandson of Joseph and Sarah (Reading) Phillips; great²-grandson of *Thomas Reading*, Captain Sixth Co., Third Battalion, New Jersey Troops.

HORACE CRIBBS COPE, McKeesport, Penna. (37082). Son of Cyrus P. and Sarah Jane (Cribbs) Cope; grandson of George A. and Jane (Skelly) Cribbs; great-grandson of William and Mary Elizabeth (Byerly) Skelly; great²-grandson of *Jacob Byerly*, private, Virginia and Penna. Cont'l Troops, pensioned; great-grandson of Christopher and Mary (Silvis) Cribbs; great²-grandson of *John Cribbs*, private, Eighth Regt., Penna. Cont'l Troops.

HARRISON CORBIN, New Haven, Conn. (36719). Son of Frank Addison and Frances (Harrison) Corbin; grandson of James Booth and Mary Ann (Mitchell) Smith; great-grandson of Thaddeus and Candace (Dutton) Smith; great²-grandson of *Theophilus Miles Smith*, Matross, Milford, Conn. Militia; grandson of Henry Augustus and Sarah Rebecca (Robbins) Harrison; great-grandson of Oliver and Rebecca (Woodhouse) Robbins; great²-grandson of Robert and Abigail (Hanmer) Robbins; great³-grandson of *Samuel Hanmer*, private, Military Company on sloop "Anne."

EPES HARVEY MOSES CORY, Omaha, Nebr. (36987). Son of Samuel Baker and Frances Mary (Savage) Cory; grandson of Benjamin W. and Hannah (Perin) Coshon Savage; great-grandson of John and Rachel (Rice) Perin; great²-grandson of *Lemuel* and Martha (Nasil) *Perin*, Sergeant, Colonel Carpenter's Regt., Mass. Militia; great³-grandson of *Jesse Perrin* (*Perin*), Sergeant, Col. John Daggett's Regt., Mass. Militia and Town Clerk; grandson of Benjamin and Abigail (Bryant) Cory, Jr.; great-grandson of Benjamin and Susanna (Denman) Cory; great²-grandson of *Christopher* and Abigail (Hendricks) *Denman*, private, New Jersey Militia; great³-grandson of *Isaac Hendricks*, private, Essex County, New Jersey Militia.

ULYSSES GRANT COUFFER, JR., Pennsylvania (35453). Supplementals. Son of Ulysses Grant and Helen Maria (Newcomb) Couffer; grandson of William and Sarah Ann (Du Bois) Couffer; great-grandson of Benjamin and Williampy (Van Dorn) Du Bois; great²-grandson of *Peter Van Dorn*, Purveyor to New Jersy Troops; great³-grandson of *Jacob Van Dorn*, Miller who donated flour to American troops; great²-grandson of Aaron and Saran Conover (Schenck) Smock; great³-grandson of *Hendrick Smock*, Captain, Monmouth County, New Jersey Militia; great⁴grandson of *John Smock*, Colonel, First Regt., New Jersey Militia; great³-grandson of *Garret Schenck*, Dragoon, First Regt., Monmouth County, New Jersey Militia.

HAROLD EELLS COVERT, Ann Arbor, Mich. (36048). Son of Jesse and Stella (Eells) Covert; grandson of James Adalbert and Mary (MacGregory) Eells; great-grandson of Aaron Gregory and Huldah (Heath) Eells; great²-grandson of Jeremiah and Thankfull (——) Eells; great³-grandson of *Jeremiah Beard Eells*, Captain, Ninth Regt., Conn. Troops, prisoner.

MARCUS EUCLID COVINGTON, Valdosta, Ga. (Va. 36552). Son of Thomas H. and Sarah Frances (Woodson) Covington; grandson of Matthew and Mariella (Leake) Woodson; great-grandson of Richard and Sophie (Anderson) Leake; great²-grandson of *Elisha Leake*, Captain, Goochland County, Virginia Militia.

WILLIAM T. A. CRAIG, New Bethlehem, Penna. (36763). Son of William H. H. and Mary Jane (Henderson) Craig; grandson of George W. and Mary M. (Conrad) Craig; great-grandson of *John Craig*, private, Fourth and Fifth Battalions, Penna. Troops.

CHARLES GEORGE CRANE, Newark, N. J. (37137). Son of Charles George and Marie E. (Dickinson) Crane; grandson of William Henry and Mary Jane (Gillen) Crane; great-grandson of *Josiah Crane*, Captain, Eastern Battalion, Morris County, New Jersey Militia.

WILLIAM APPLETON CRARY, Grand Forks, No. Dak. (36934). Son of Ezra and Margaret (Bell) Crary; grandson of Appleton and Roby (Hopkins) Crary; great-grandson of *Nathan Crary*, private, Conn. and Vermont Militia.

EDWARD E. CRAWFORD, Brooklyn, N. Y. (36899). Son of John F. and Mary Annie (Moriarty) Crawford; grandson of Benjamin and Charlotte (Selleck) Crawford; great-grandson of *Nathan (Nathaniel) Selleck*, Captain, Eli Reed's Regt., Conn. Militia.

HOWARD READ CRONK, Omaha, Nebr. (36979). Son of Hubert Henry and Ida Marie (Banter) Cronk; grandson of Harvey and Ellen (Read) Cronk; great-grandson of Richard and Cynthia (Anderson) Read; great²-grandson of *Jonathan Read*, private and Corporal, Rehoboth, Mass. Militia, pensioned; great³-grandson of *Nathan Read*, private, Col. Thomas Carpenter's Regt., Mass. Militia.

GEORGE SAMUEL CROSBY, Maplewood, N. J. (36700). Son of Harrison Woodhull and Charlotte Augusta (Andrews) Crosby; grandson of John P. and Eunice (Candee) Andrews; great-grandson of *Benjamin Andrews*, private, Conn. Militia, pensioned.

DE WITT SMITH CROW, Springfield, Ill. (36649). Son of Oliver P. and Emma L. (Smith) Crow; grandson of John and Elizabeth (Trumbo) Smith; great-grandson of Adam and Mildreth (Foster) Trumbo; great²-grandson of *Henry Foster*, private, Virginia Cont'l Line, pensioned.

KEITH GOODRICH CROWTHER, Waterloo, Iowa (36248). Son of Richard E. and Frances (Goodrich) Crowther; grandson of John Franklin and Marion (Coates) Goodrich; great-grandson of Allen and Mercy (Emerson) Goodridge; great²-grandson of *Allen Goodridge*, Sergeant, Col. Moses Nichol's Regt., New Hampshire Militia; great²-grandson of Allen and Sarah (Crosby) Goodridge; great³-grandson of *Josiah Crosby*, Captain, Third Regt., New Hampshire Troops.

ALEXANDER (SASHA) CULBERTSON, New York City, N. Y. (36893). Son of Almon Elias and Xenia (Rogoznaia) Culbertson; grandson of Elias and Harriet (Marsh) Culbertson; great-grandson of William and Nancy (Mohr) Culbertson; great²-grandson of Robert and Elizabeth (Thomas) Culbertson; great³-grandson of *Alexander Culbertson*, private, Cumberland County, Penna. Militia; great-grandson of Ira and Caroline (Forquhar) Marsh; great²-grandson of Benjamin and Elsa (Snyder) Marsh; great³-grandson of *Simeon Marsh*, private, Sussex County, New Jersey Militia, pensioned.

ALMON ELIAS CULBERTSON, New York City, N. Y. (36891). Son of Elias and Harriet (Marsh) Culbertson; grandson of William and Nancy (Mohr) Culbertson; great-grandson of Robert and Elizabeth (Thomas) Culbertson; great²-grandson of *Alexander Culbertson*, private, Cumberland County, Penna. Militia; grandson of Ira and Caroline (Farquhar) Marsh; great-grandson of Benjamin and Elsa (Snyder) Marsh; great²-grandson of *Simeon Marsh*, private, Sussex County, New Jersey Militia, pensioned.

ELY CULBERTSON, New York City, N. Y. (36892). Same as Alexander (Sasha) Culbertson, New York (36893).

EUGENE KING CUMMINGS, New York City, N. Y. (36895). Son of William Augustus and Emma L. (King) Cummings; grandson of David Codwise and Emeline (Peck) King; great-grandson of William and Rachel (Starr) King; great²-grandson of *Ezra* and Elizabeth (Codwise) *Starr*, Captain and Major, Third Regt., Conn. Light Horse; great³-grandson of *George Codwise*, private, Fifth Co., Third Regt., New York Militia; great³-grandson of *Daniel Starr*, Major, Third Regt., Conn. Light Horse and Member Conn. Assembly of 1775; great-grandson of Jared B. and Maria A. (Northrop) Peck; great²-grandson of *Nathan Peck*, Fifer, Col. David Waterbury's Regt., Conn. Militia.

JOHN EDWARD CUMMINGS, Springfield, Mass. (37103). Son of Chauncey Edward and Delia M. (Hemenway) Cummings; grandson of Andrew and Almira (Taylor) Cummings; great-grandson of *Abraham Cummings*, private, Col. Thomas Carpenter's Regt., Mass. Militia.

LYLE RAYMOND CURTISS, Jackson, Tenn. (36779). Son of Lewis L. and Cornelia (Raymond) Curtiss; grandson of George L. and Matilda J. (Smith) Curtiss; great-grandson of Lewis and Mary (Goodwin) Curtiss; great²-grandson of Abel and Olive (Sorry) Goodwin; great³-grandson of *William Goodwin*, private and Corporal, Conn. Militia; grandson of Charles Harvey and Mary Jane (Underwood) Raymond; great-grandson of John and Christiana (Dugle) Underwood; great²-grandson of Robert and Jane (Wigton) Underwood; great³-grandson of *John Wigton*, Lieutenant and Paymaster, Third Regt., Penna. Cont'l Line.

RICHARD WIGGIN DAKE, Nashville, Tenn. (36780). Son of William Church and Adelaide (Wiggin) Dake; grandson of Jabez P. and Elizabeth (Church) Dake; great-grandson of Jabez and Sophia (Brown) Dake; great²-grandson of *William Gould Dake*, private, Sixteenth Regt., Albany County, New York Militia, pensioned.

GORDON WEBSTER DALY, Brookline, Mass. (36819). Son of Franklin P. and Gertrude (Walker) Daly; grandson of Charles Benjamin and Harriet N. (Merrill) Walker; great-grandson of Benjamin and Sarah A. (Cross) Walker; great²-grandson of Ebenezer and Abigail (Webb) Cross; great³-grandson of *Ralph Cross*, Lieutenant-Colonel and Colonel, Second Regt., Essex County, Mass. Militia.

GEORGE WARREN DANIELS, Tallula, Ill. (36637). Son of Veering and Sarah Virginia (English) Daniels; grandson of Veerin and Nancy Webster (Barton) Daniels; great-grandson of Titus Theodore and Ruth Huse (Wood) Barton; great²-grandson of *David Barton*, Lieutenant and Captain, Hampshire County, Mass. Militia.

BRUCE JORDAN DAVIDSON, Marseilles, Ill. (36650). Son of Frank Bruce and Eva Leona (Jordan) Davidson; grandson of Edwin Shoup and Julia Adeline M. (Le Pitre) Jordan; great-grandson of Pierre and Eliza Ann (Chatfield) Le Pitre; great²-grandson of Sherman and Deborah (Wood) Chatfield; great³-grandson of Eli and Lois (Mallary) Chatfield; great⁴-grandson of *Oliver Chatfield*, private, *Conn. Militia;* great-grandson of David Jefferson and Julia Ann (Cady) Jordan; great²-grandson of Joseph Cleveland and Mary (Williamson) Rosencrantz Cady; great³-grandson of *David Cady, Jr.*, Captain, Conn. Militia at Lexington Alarm.

IRVING HENRY DAVIS, Manchester, Ga. (Mass. 36818). Son of Orlando J. and Rebecca Ann (Fiske) Davis; grandson of Jonathan Stowe and Georgiana Maria (Keith) Fiske; great-grandson of David and Sarah (Stowe) Fiske; great²-grandson of *William Fiske*, Lieutenant, Upton, Mass. Militia.

WARREN TRUE DAVIS, Swampscott, Mass. (37113). Son of Warren Johnson and Emily Elizabeth (Chatwin) Davis; grandson of Warren Washington and Eliza (Reed) Davis; great-grandson of Ezekiel and Ednah (Wilkins) Davis; great²-grandson of *Aquilla Wilkins*, Corporal and Sargeant, Mass. Cont'l Troops.

WALTER M. DAY, Worcester, Mass. (36821). Son of Rufus Larned and Mary Eliza (Bugbee) Day; grandson of John Hancock and Martha A. (Kidder) Day; great-grandson of *Jonathan Day*, Musician, Colonel Larned's Regt., Mass. Militia, Member Committee of Inspection, Correspondence, and Safety, Selectman and Delegate to County Convention.

WINDSOR BOYDEN DAY, Springfield, Mass. (37104). Son of Robert W. and Ida L. (Boyden) Day; grandson of William Waite and Emeline Eunice (Russell) Day; great-grandson of Major and Maletha (Manderville) Day; great²-grandson of Nehemiah and Teizah (Alvord) Day, Jr.; great³-grandson of *Nehemiah Day*, private, Conn. Militia at Lexington Alarm.

CHARLES TAYLOR DEATS, Flemington, N. J. (36860). Son of Hiram Edmund and Eva Augusta (Taylor) Deats; grandson of James Graves and Elizabeth Ely (Perrine) Taylor; great-grandson of James William and Deborah Ann (Dey) Perrine; great²-grandson of David Baird and Elizabeth (Ely) Dey; great³-grandson of *John Dey*, Captain, Second Regt., Middlesex County, New Jersey Militia; great²-grandson of William I. and Catharine (Davis) Perrine; great³-grandson of *James Perrine*, private First Regt., Monmouth County, New Jersey Militia; grandson of Hiram and Elmira (Stevenson) Deats; great-grandson of John and Ursilla (Barton) Deats; great²-grandson of *Elisha Barton*, Captain, Morris County, New Jersey Militia.

CASPER DAVID DECKER, South Orange, N. J. (36858). Son of Maurice Shultz and Ulilla May (Lockwood) Decker; grandson of Richard Caton and Susannah (Feshler) Lockwood; great-grandson of Edmund and Mary Ann (Cash) Russell Lockwood; great²-grandson of Isaac and Sally (Gore) Cash; great³-grandson of *Obadiah Gore, Jr.*, Lieutenant, Westmoreland County, Penna. Militia and Cont'l Troops; great-grandson of Obadiah and Anna (Avery) Gore, Jr.; great⁴-grandson of *Richardson Avery*, private, Penna. Militia at Wyoming Valley, prisoner.

HOWARD GRANT DECKER, Greenville, Texas (36332). Son of Le Roy and Ida (Hayes) Decker; grandson of John Wright and Martha Axtell Hayes; great-grandson of Samuel Loree and Nancy (Sanders) Axtell; great²-grandson of Silas and Elizabeth (Loree) Axtell; great³-grandson of *Henry Axtell*, Major, Eastern Battalion, Morris County, New Jersey Militia.

WILLIAM THEODORE DELAPLAINE, Frederick, Md. (36093). Son of William T. and Fannie (Birely) Delaplaine; grandson of Theodore C. and Hannah Ann (Edmonstone) Delaplaine; great-grandson of Eden and Lucretia (Waters) Edmonstone; great²-grandson of *Thomas Edmondstone*, Lieutenant, Montgomery County, Maryland Militia.

THOMAS COLLINS DENNY, Des Moines, Iowa (36912). Son of Barton S. and Mary (Massie) Denny; grandson of John Collins and Susan (Johnson) Massie; great-grandson of Nathaniel and Alice (Collins) Massie; great²-grandson of *Nanthaniel Massie,* Captain, Goochland County, Virginia Militia.

CHARLES ALFRED DE SAUSSURE, Memphis, Tenn. (36789). Son of Louis McPherson and Jane Hay (Hutson) De Saussure; grandson of Henry William and Eliza (Ford) De Saussure; great-grandson of *John Daniel Hector De Saussure,* Captain, Beaufort, South Carolina Volunteer Co.; grandson of William Maine and Martha (Hay) Hutson; great-grandson of *Thomas Hutson,* Colonel, General Marion's Regt., South Carolina Militia and Member South Carolina Constitutional Convention.

GEORGE CLINTON DICE, Hutchinson, Kans. (36734). Son of Hiram W. and Clara M. (Johnson) Dice; grandson of Richard and Frances Cordelia (Harrison) Johnson; great-grandson of Tom and Lucy (Earnest) Harrison; great²-grandson of *Silas Harrison,* private, Conn. Militia, pensioned.

WILLIAM BUFORD DICKERSON, Nashville, Tenn. (36783). Son of Jones W. and Vashti (Gordon) Dickerson; grandson of Thomas Martin and Sallie (McLaurine) Gordon; great-grandson of Thomas Kennedy and Elizabeth (Lane) Gordon; great²-grandson of *Martin Lane,* private, North Carolina Militia.

ROBERT GEORGE DIECK, Portland, Oreg. (35071). Son of Herman Louis and Adelaide Howard (Boyer) Dieck; grandson of Peter and Ann (Jones) Burklebach Boyer, great-grandson of *John Boyer,* Sergeant, Penna. Militia.

WILLIAM HUGHES DILLER, Springfield, Ill. (36631). Son of Isaac R. and Addie May (Hughes) Diller; grandson of Roland Weaver and Esther Coates (Ridgway) Diller; great-grandson of Jonathan and Ann (Weaver) Diller; great²-grandson of Isaac and Susanna (Roland) Diller; great³-grandson of Jonathan and Catherine (Huber) Roland; great⁴-grandson of *John Huber,* private, First Regt., Penna. Cont'l Troops.

SAMUEL RAYMOND DOBBS, Camden, N. J. (37143). Son of Samuel B. and Emily (Anderson) Dobbs; grandson of Edward Harrison and Emily (Ferguson) Anderson; great-grandson of John W. and Catherine (Benner) Anderson; great²-grandson of Edward and Catherine (Highley) Anderson; great³-grandson of *Isaac Anderson,* Lieutenant, Fifth Battalion, Chester County, Penna. Militia.

EARL LOUIS DOBEAS (WORTHING) Adopted. Cedar River, Mich. (37019). Son of Alonzo and Georgiana O. (Camb) Worthing; grandson of Nathan and Rebecca (Hall) Worthing; great-grandson of Isaac and Judith (Currier) Worthen (Worthing); great² grandson of Jacob and Mary (Brown) Worthen (Worthing); great³-grandson of *Ezekiel Worthen,* Major, New Hampshire Troops and Member New Hampshire Constitutional Convention.

GOLINE DOREMUS, Newark, N. J. (36851). Son of James Martin and Mary T. (Sawyer) Doremus; grandson of Jacob G. and Rachel (Berry) Doremus; great-grandson of Goline and Hester (Mead) Doremus; great²-grandson of *Thomas Doremus,* private, Essex County, New Jersey Militia.

EGBERT CARY DOUGHTY, Hackensack, N. J. (37018). Son of Egbert Cary and Susan (Reynolds) Doughty; grandson of Thomas Joseph and Cecelia (Cary) Doughty; great-grandson of Egbert and Tamer (Flagler) Cary; great²-grandson of *Ebenezer Cary,* Adjutant Muster Master, New York Militia.

BENJAMIN DAWSON DOWDEN, Montclair, N. J. (37010). Son of George Augustus and Martha (Anderson) Dowden; grandson of Charles and Susan (Boskalow) Dowden; great-grandson of Christopher and Mary (Beekman) Boskalow; great²-grandson of Christopher and Martha (Vegthe) Beekman; great³-grandson of *Garrit Vegthe (Vetter),* Captain, New Jersey Militia.

WILLIAM HENRY DULEY, Chicago, Ill. (36632). Son of Henry Harrison and Gertrude Anna (Atchley) Duley; grandson of William Henry and Sarah Jane (Baldwin) Duley; great-grandson of Philander and Paulina (Greene) Baldwin; great²-grandson of *Eleazer Baldwin,* private, Second Regt., Conn. Line, pensioned; great³-grandson of *Caleb Baldwin,* Captain, Second Regt., Conn. Cont'l Line.

GEORGE W. DUNCAN, Philadelphia, Penna. (37080) Son of Edward and Amanda F. (Matlack) Duncan; grandson of Guy Bryan and Sarah (Corliss) Matlack; great-grandson of William and Hannah (Carmalt) Matlack; great²-grandson of *Timothy Matlack,* Colonel, Rifle Battalion, Philadelphia City Militia.

ROBERT ELLIS DUNLAP, Oakland, Calif. (36422). Son of George Thomas and Emma May (Ellis) Dunlap; grandson of Robert Rankin and Agnes Harriet (Maddux) Dunlap; great-grandson of Wesley and Esther (Gaston) Maddux; great²-grandson of *Stephen and Mary (Davidson) Gaston*, private, Captain McClure's Co., South Carolina Militia; great²-grandson of *James* and Catharine (Creighton) *Gaston*, private, South Carolina Militia; great⁴-grandson of *John Gaston*, South Carolina Patriot.

JOSEPH AVERY DUNN, East Orange, N. J. (37023). Son of Frank A. and Rosanna B. (Stringer) Dunn; grandson of David D. and Martha (Williams) Dunn; great-grandson of Jeptha and Grace (——) Dunn; great²-grandson of Jeremiah and Mary (Fitz Randolph) Dunn; great³-grandson of *Jeremiah Dunn*, Lieutenant, Middlesex County, New Jersey Militia.

ROLAND HAS-BROUCK DUNN, Newark, N. J. (37025). Son of Frank A. and Rosanna B. (Stringer) Dunn; grandson of David D. and Martha (Williams) Dunn; great-grandson of Jeptha and Grace (——) Dunn; great²-grandson of Jeremiah and Mary (Fitz Randolph) Dunn; great³-grandson of *Jeremiah Dunn*, Lieutenant, Middlesex County, New Jersey Militia.

SAMUEL M. DUNN, Newark, N. J. (37017). Son of Jeptha W. and Sarah (Mason) Dunn; grandson of David D. and Martha (Williams) Dunn; great-grandson of Jeptha and Grace (——) Dunn; great²-grandson of *Jeremiah Dunn*, private, Middlesex County, New Jersey Militia.

CHARLES DANA DUNTON, West Medford, Mass. (37105). Son of Charles D. and Ellen M. (Wheeler) Dunton; grandson of Charles and Susan (Sanderson) Wheeler; great-grandson of Isreal and Rebecca (Rice) Wheeler; great²-grandson of Israel and Lucy (Ingersoll) Wheeler; great³-grandson of *Elisha Wheeler*, Lieutenant, Col. How's Regt., Mass. Militia at Lexington Alarm.

JOHN FRANK DUNTON, Auburndale, Mass. (37106). Same as Charles Dana Dunton, Massachusetts (37105).

HERBERT WILBUR DUTCH, Montclair, N. J. (37141). Son of Marshall Holly and Charlotte Herrick (Hill) Dutch; grandson of Joshua and Caroline Freeman (Herrick) Hill; great-grandson of Jedidiah and Mehitabel (Thompson) Herrick; great²-grandson of Joseph and Mercie (Preston) Herrick; great³-grandson of *Israel Herrick*, private, Essex County, Mass. Militia.

GEORGE LAWRENCE DUTTON, Portland, Oreg. (35072). Son of George C. and Ida (Beckwith) Dutton; grandson of Chester and Mary Anne (Mellen) Dutton; great-grandson of Daniel P. and Nancy (Matthews) Dutton; great²-grandson of Thomas and Thankful (Punderson) Dutton; great³-grandson of *Thomas Dutton*, Second Lieutenant, Conn. Militia and Member of War Committees.

VICTOR M. EARLE, Yonkers, N. Y. (36890). Son of Ferdinand Pinney and Lillie Y. (Smith) Earle; grandson of William P. and Elizabeth (Pinney) Earle; great-grandson of Benjamin and Sarah (McKinney) Pinney; great²-grandson of *Eleazer Pinney*, Sergeant, Conn. Militia.

RALPH MASON EASTMAN, Dorchester, Mass. (36820). Son of Charles Mason and Emilie Dean (Bailey) Eastman; grandson of Charles Francis and Sarah Dillingham (Dean) Bailey; great-grandson of Luther and Betsy (Abercrombie) Bailey; great²-grandson of *Abijah Bailey*, private, New Hampshire Cont'l Line, pensioned.

FREDERIC BENJAMIN EATON, Rochester, N. H. (N. Y. 36877). Son of Henry True and Julia A. (Doe) Eaton; grandson of True and Elizabeth (York) Eaton; great-grandson of Henry True and Elizabeth (Emerson) Eaton; great²-grandson of *Nathaniel Emerson*, Lieutenant-Colonel, New Hampshire Militia and Cont'l Troops, Member, Committee of Safety, State Legislature and Delegate to State Constitutional Convention.

LAMBOURN A. EDWARDS, Stone Lake, Wis. (37276). Son of Hamilton B. and Allie (Coats) Edwards, grandson of David and Rebecca (Lamborn) Edwards; great-grandson of Ezra and Elizabeth (Baily) Lamborn; great²-grandson of Jacob and Elizabeth (Webb) Baily; great³-grandson of *Ezekiel Webb*, private, Third Battalion, Chester County, Penna. Militia.

WILLIS JONES EGLESTON, Helena, Mont. (31783). Supplemental. Son of Marvin and Hannah (Jones) Egleston; grandson of Nelson and Livonia (Jacobs) Egleston; great-grandson of *Simeon Jacobs*, Sergeant and Corporal, Mass. Militia, widow pensioned.

EDGAR ELY, Middletown, Penna. (37087). Son of Aaron Baker and Elizabeth (E.) Ely; grandson of Benjamin W. and Henrietta F. (Baker) Ely; great-grandson of Frederick and Elizabeth (Fertig) Baker; great²-grandson of *Peter Becker*, private, Lancaster Co., Penna. Militia.

CHARLES EDWARD EMERY, Chicago, Ill. (37201). Son of Livingston and Polly Clapp (Pratt) Emery; grandson of Charles Edward and Susan Symmes (Livingston) Emery; great-grandson of Essex Ridley and Orphelia Maria (Mead) Livingston; great²-grandson of *William Livingston, Jr.*, New Jersey volunteer at capture of ship "Blue Mountain Valley"; great³-grandson of *William Livingston*, Member Cont'l Congress, Brigadier General of Militia and Governor of New Jersey; great-grandson of Moses Little and Minerva (Prentiss) Emery; great²-grandson of Josiah and Susannah (Little) Emery; great²-grandson of *Moses Little*, Lieutenant, Col. Jacob Gale's Regt., New Hampshire Militia.

WILLIAM ORRIN EMERY, Washington, D. C. (36150). Son of Ira and Emmaline Melissa (Stearns) Emery; grandson of John and Sarah (Waldo) Stearns; great-grandson of Elijah and Betsy (Angier) Waldo; great²-grandson of *Edward Waldo*, Second Lieutenant, New Hampshire Troops, wounded, pensioned.

SAMUEL LYMAN EUSTIS, Onaga, Kans. (36736). Son of John and Susan Wheat (Howard) Eustis; grandson of Samuel Wheat and Ester (Hog) Eustis; great-grandson of *Thomas Eustis*, Captain, Mass. Minutemen at Lexington Alarm.

GLENN BLACKMER EWELL, Rochester, N. Y. (36882). Son of Jirah Blackmer and Mary Florine (Mallory) Ewell; grandson of Henry Bancroft and Fanny (Blackmer) Ewell; great-grandson of Henry and Betsy (Bancroft) Ewell; great²-grandson of James and Sarah (Holbrook) Ewell great³-grandson of *John Ewell*, private, Seventh Regt., Mass Militia.

BYRON FRANCIS EWERS, Sacramento, Calif. (36423). Son of Thomas A. and Lulu (Adams) Ewers; grandson of John George and Elvira (Bradley) Adams; great-grandson of George and Jamima (Collard) Adams; great²-grandson of *Samuel Adams*, private, Charles County, Maryland Militia.

DORR EUGENE FELT, Illinois (24595). Son of Eugene Kincaid and Elizabeth (Morris) Felt; grandson of Asa George and Harriet (Foster) Felt; great-grandson of Abram and Patience (Woodhull) Foster; great²-grandson of *Jedidiah Foster*, Corporal, Col. Thomas Bartlett's Regt., New Hampshire Militia.

CALVIN FENTRESS, Chicago, Ill. (36638). Son of James and Mary Tate (Perkins) Fentress; grandson of Joseph Warren and Mary Ridgely (Talbot) Perkins; great-grandson of Eli and Delia (Waters) Talbot; great²-grandson of Thomas and Ruth (Greer) Talbot; great³-grandson of *Matthew Talbot, Jr.*, Sergeant and Ensign, Virginia Militia.

ROBERT SOLON FISK, Minneapolis, Minn. (35699). Son of Solon and Ellen M. (Funk) Fisk; grandson of Leonard and Julia (Colt) Fisk; great-grandson of *Stephen Fisk*, private, Col. Thomas Marshall's Regt., Mass. Militia.

WALTER TUTTLE FLORENCE, Plain City, Ohio (37030). Son of John and Blanche (Morgridge) Florence; grandson of Joshua Bailey Emerson and Harriet Hoyt (Tuttle) Morgridge; great-grandson of Richard and Sally (Emerson) Morgridge; great²-grandson of *Jonathan Emerson*, Lieutenant, First Regt., New Hampshire Cont'l Troops, pensioned.

ROGERS FLYNN, JR., East Orange, N. J. (36871). Son of Oscar Rogers and Florence (James) Flynn; grandson of Theodore David and Cornelia (Ferguson) James; great-grandson of Amos Square and Eliza (Underwood) Ferguson; great²-grandson of James Gaylord and Christianna (Day) Ferguson; great³-grandson of Samuel and Memory (Gaylord) Ferguson; great⁴-grandson of Jotham and Esther (——) Gaylord; great⁵-grandson of *David Gaylord*, private, Col. Joseph Spencer's Second Regt., Conn. Troops.

OTIS WILLIAM FOLLETT, Des Moines, Iowa (36908). Son of Henry Webster and Delta (Kellogg) Follett; grandson of William H. and Sarah (Brooks) Kellogg; great-grandson of James and Bets (Canfield) Brooks; great²-grandson of Cornelius and Mary (Hyndshaw) Brooks; great³-grandson of *James Brooks*, private, First Regt., New Jersey Cont'l Line.

CLAUD MARSHALL FOSTER, Atlanta, Ga. (36828). Son of W. R. and Nelly (Miller) Foster; grandson of Bass and Ellen (McHenry) Miller; great-grandson of J. B. and

Sidney (Edgar) McHenry; great²-grandson of J. M. and Julia (Breedlove) Edgar; great³-grandson of *William Breedlove*, private, Colonel Gaskin's Regt., Virginia Troops, pensioned.

SILAS SEVERANCE FOWLER, Keosauqua, Iowa (36342). Son of Lewis and Meribah Weldon) Fowler; grandson of Royal and Rebecca (Severance) Fowler; great-grandson of *Samuel Fowler*, Lieutenant, Col. Timothy Bedell's Regt., New Hampshire Militia.

WILLIAM ERIC FOWLER, Washington, D. C. (36147). Son of John Calhoun and Emma Smith (Peden) Fowler; grandson of Riley and Susan (Crane) Fowler; great-grandson of John and Nancy Agnes (Peden) Fowler; great²-grandson of *Thomas Peden*, private, Col. Thomas Clarke's Regt., North Carolina Cont'l Line.

WILLIAM WALLACE POX, Chicago, Ill. (36633). Son of Franklin Skinner and Beatrice (Armstrong) Fox; grandson of William Wallace and Harriet (Johnston) Armstrong; great-grandson of Harrison and Margaret (Cox) Armstrong; great²-grandson of Thomas and Jane (Cook) Armstrong; great³-grandson of *William Armstrong*, Corporal, Sixth Regt., Penna. Troops.

CLYDE HAROLD FULLER, Milwaukee, Wis. (37279). Son of Oliver Clyde and Kate (Caswell) Fuller; grandson of Henry Alexander and Martha Caroline (Wyly) Fuller; great-grandson of Oliver Cromwell and Lucy (Eddins) Wyly; great²-grandson of James Rutherford and Sarah (Hawkins) Clark; great³-grandson of James and Jemina (Cleveland) Wyly; great⁴-grandson of *Benjamin Cleveland*, Colonel, Wilkes County, North Carolina Militia; great³-grandson of William and Elizabeth (Sevier) Clark; great⁴-grandson of *John Sevier*, Colonel, North Carolina Militia.

MARSHALL GANTT, Wilmington, Del. (35663). Son of John Gibson and Laura (Smith) Gantt; grandson of Richard Hall and Ann Elizabeth (Gibson) Gantt; great-grandson of Thomas and Mary Smith (Hall) Gantt; great²-grandson of Thomas and Barbara (Blake) Gantt; great³-grandson of *Edward Gantt*, Captain, Maryland Cont'l Troops, Member Maryland Provincial Congress and of the Committee of Safety.

LESTER DURAND GARDNER, New York (35935). Supplementals. Son of Harry and Frances (Scott) Gardner; grandson of Robert and Catherine (Gannett) Scott; great-grandson of Thomas J. and Nancy (Thomson) Gannett; great²-grandson of *Henry Gannett*, Captain, Louisa County, Virginia Militia and Member Committee of Safety; great²-grandson of Rodes and Sally (Vivian) Thomson; great³-grandson of *William Thomson*, Captain, Virginia State Troops.

WILLIAM SYDNOR GILBREATH, JR., Detroit, Mich. (37053). Son of William Sydnor and Minnie (Schaff) Gilbreath; grandson of Erasmus C. and Susan (Corse) Gilbreath; great-grandson of Fortunatus Sydnor and Rachel Moore (Lansing) Gilbreath; great²-grandson of Robert and Mary Taylor (Sydnor) Gilbreath; great³-grandson of *Robert Galbreath (Gilbreath)*, Sergeant, Hanover County, Virginia Cont'l Line.

WILLIAM HERBERT GOFF, Adrian, Mich. (36041). Son of Leslie Timothy and Carrie D. (Kellogg) Goff; grandson of Sewell Stillman and Lucy (Frary) Goff; great-grandson of *Ezra Goff*, Fifer, drummer and private, Mass. Militia.

LE ROY WILLARD GOODWATER, Grand Forks, N. Dak. (33028). Son of William Henry and Mary Louise (Coss) Goodwater; grandson of Benjamin and Helen (Coss) Goodwater; great-grandson of Warren and Edith (Powers) Coss; great²-grandson of Nathaniel and Esther (Johnson) Powers; great³-grandson of *Josiah Powers*, private, Col. James Reed's Regt., New Hampshire Troops, pensioned.

GEORGE BLACKHAM GRAFF, Boise, Idaho (35109). Son of John K. and Elizabeth (Blackham) Graff; grandson of George B. and Margaret A. (Stormont) Graff; great-grandson of Joseph and Sarah (Kausler) Graff; great²-grandson of *George Graff*, Captain, First Battalion, Penna. Flying Camp.

JOHN DANIEL GRAY, Chicago, Ill. (36634). Son of John Alexander and Sarah J. Henninger) Gray; grandson of Alexander and Sarah (Tempest) Gray; great-grandson of William and Eliza (Morton) Tempest; great²-grandson of Robert and Deborah Shelly) Tempest; great³-grandson of *Robert Tempest*, private, Sixth Philadelphia Battalion, Penna. Troops.

MARTIN ARVINE GREGORY, Valparaiso, Ind. (36434). Son of William Homer and Sarah Alice (Watson) Gregory; grandson of Martin Amos and Sarah Place (Card)

Gregory; great-grandson of Amos and Clarissa M. (Ford) Gregory; great²-grandson of Noah and Sarah (Nash) Gregory; great³-grandson *Nathan Gregory*, private and Lieutenant, Conn. Militia, pensioned.

PAUL BARTLETT GRIFFITH, Grand Forks, N. Dak. (36938). Son of Robert Burton and Minnie Celestia (Webster) Griffith; grandson of Henry Milo and Adeline (Bartlett) Webster; great-grandson of Justus and Hannah (Wentworth) Webster; great²-grandson of *Daniel Wentworth*, private, Mass. Militia; great²-grandson of *Constant Webster*, Lieutenant, Second Regt., Hampshire County, Mass. Militia.

EARNEST GRILL, Boulder, Colo. (36344). Son of Henry H. T. and Mary Susan (Holland) Grill; grandson of John and Elizabeth (Woodridge) Holland; great-grandson of *Richard Holland*, Captain, Tenth Regt., Virginia Militia.

SHERMAN WHITACRE GRISELLE, Chicago, Ill. (36639). Son of Joseph W. and Grace E. (Brunner) Griselle; grandson of Lewis A. and Jane E. (Sherman) Brunner; great-grandson of Horace and Lucinda (Harris) Sherman; great²-grandson of Abel and Orinda (Bricknell) Sherman; great³-grandson of *Thomas Sherman*, private, Col. Timothy Danielson's Regt., Mass. Militia.

JAMES RUSSELL GUILD, Albuquerque, N. Mex. (30099). Son of Rufus C. and Susan (B.) Guild; grandson of Elias Cornelius and Alice (Blair) Guild; great-grandson of Israel and Rachael (Kellogg) Guild; great²-grandson of *Jesse Guild*, private, Hampshire County, Mass. Militia and Cont'l Troops; great²-grandson of *Phineas Kellogg*, private, Col. Thomas Marshall's Regt., Mass. Cont'l Troops.

WILLIAM HARDIN GUTHRIE, Nashville, Tenn. (36778). Son of Frank C. and Virginia (Hardin) Guthrie; grandson of Isaac Newton and Martha Ann (Montgomery) Guthrie; great-grandson of James and Elizabeth (Gibbs) Guthrie; great²-grandson of *Julius Gibbs*, private, Virginia Militia, pensioned.

ARCHIBALD H. HAMILTON, Pittsburgh, Penna. (36764). Son of Archibald G. and Gertrude Van R. (Henderson) Hamilton; grandson of Harvey and Harriet Jane (Hogeboom) Henderson; great-grandson of John Lawrence and Harriet (Yates) Hogeboom; great²-grandson of Peter Lawrence and Helena (Van Woert) Hogeboom; great³-grandson of *Lawrence Hogeboom*, private and Sergeant, Albany County, New York Militia; great³-grandson of Johannes (John) *Van Woert*, Second Lieutenant, Third Regt., Albany County, New York Troops, and Deputy Commissary of Purchases, pensioned; great³-grandson of Johannes and Cathalyna (Lansing) Van Woert; great⁴-grandson of *Jacob Jacoke Lansing*, Captain, Fourth Co., Third Regt., Albany County, New York Militia.

HOWARD ENGLER HARMAN, Ohio (35152). Supplemental. Son of Howard Beecher and Elizabeth (Engler) Harman; grandson of Othias and Elizabeth (Graybill) Harman; great-grandson of *George Harman*, private, Virginia Militia.

CHARLES NORMAN HARRINGTON, La Crosse, Wis. (32675). Son of Norman Slade and Eliza Jane (Davenport) Harrington; grandson of Ira and Arabella (Sperry) Harrington; great-grandson of Ammi and Pamma (McClellan) Harrington; great²-grandson of *Thaddeus Harrington*, private, Shirley, Mass. Militia and Cont'l Troops.

GEORGE WENTZ HARRIS, Montclair, N. J. (37006). Son of William J. and Phoebe L. (Baldwin) Harris; grandson of William H. and and Phoebe H. (Baldwin) Harris; great-grandson of Robert and Mary (Gould) Baldwin; great²-grandson of *William Gould*, private, New Jersey Militia.

RICHARD HARTSHORNE, East Orange, N. J. (37003). Son of William Sydney and Margaret Bentley (Harrison) Hartshorne; grandson of John and Caroline (Smith) Hartshorne; great-grandson of Moses and Phebe (Ward) Smith; great²-grandson of *Moses Smith*, private, Second Regt., Essex County, New Jersey Militia, killed.

REX WHIPPLE HEALD, Minneapolis, Minn. (35700). Son of Henry Prescott and Hannah M. (Taylor) Heald; grandson of Prescott and Mary H. (Whipple) Heald; great-grandson of Amos and Lydia (Edwards) Heald; great²-grandson of *Daniel Heald*, private, Col. Jonathan Reed's Regt., Mass. Militia.

HENRY HERBERT HEALY, Grand Forks, N. Dak. (36928). Son of Henry Wilkinson and Lucy (Dales) Healy; grandson of Almon and Lucy (Woods) Healy; great-grandson of Ezra and Polly (Shipman) Healy; great²-grandson of *Jabez Healy*, private, Hampshire County, Mass. Militia.

HERBERT GAYLORD HEATH, Lake City, Colo. (36341). Son of Henry Preston and Emma (Dennis) Heath; grandson of Andrew and Mary (Corwin) Dennis; great-grandson of Nathaniel and Elizabeth (Biles) Corwin; great²-grandson of *Joseph Corwin*, private, Morris County, New Jersey Militia.

WILLIAM GRAHAM HEINER, Pittsburgh, Pa. (36767). Son of Daniel Brodhead and Belle Tod (Acheson) Heiner; grandson of Daniel Brodhead and Mary (Graham) Heiner; great-grandson of John and Mary (Haines) Heiner; great²-grandson of Casper and Anne Garton (Brodhead) Heiner; great²-grandson of *Daniel Brodhead*, Brevet, Brigadier-General, Penna. Troops.

GEORGE M. HENDEE, Suffield, Conn. (Mass. 36810). Son of William G. and Emma (Upton) Hendee; grandson of Abel and Cynthia (Eaton) Hendee; great-grandson of *Caleb Hendee, Jr.*, Sergeant and Ensign, Conn. Militia, Cont'l Infantry and Dragoons, five years service, pensioned.

JOHN FAIRMAN HENDRICKOM, New York City, N. Y. (36886). Son of Gilbert Bailey and Mary Jane (Fairman) Hendrickom; grandson of John and Maria Reed (Bailey) Hendrickom; great-grandson of Gilbert and Nancy (Reed) Bailey; great²-grandson of *Joseph Bailey*, private, Suffolk County, New York Militia and Cont'l Line.

JACOB LEWIS HERSHEY Youngwood, Penna. (36757). Son of Lewis and Eliza Adaline (Cunningham) Hershey; grandson of Jacob and Catharine (Wollet) Hershey; great-grandson of *Christian Hershey*, private, Third Battalion, Lancaster County, Penna. Militia.

CHARLES GERALDUS HILL, Baltimore, Md. (36097). Son of Daniel Shines and Susan Irwin (Toole) Hill; grandson of Charles Applewhite and Rebecca (Long) Hill; great-grandson of William Hill; great²-grandson of *Green Hill*, Second Major, North Carolina Militia, Member Newbern, Hillsboro, and Halifax Congresses; great-grandson of Gabriel and Sarah (Richmond) Long; great²-grandson of *Nicholas Long*, Colonel, North Carolina Militia, Deputy Quartermaster General and Member Provincial Congresses.

DUDLEY SLOAN HILL, Baltimore, Md. (36098). Son of Charles Geraldus and Isabel (Painter) Hill; grandson of Daniel Shines and Susan Irwin (Toole) Hill; great-grandson of Charles Applewhite and Rebecca (Long) Hill; great²-grandson of William Hill; great²-grandson of *Green Hill;* Major, North Carolina Militia and Member Newbern, Hillsboro, and Halifax Congresses; great²-grandson of Gabriel and Sarah (Richmond) Long; great²-grandson of *Nicholas Long*, Colonel, North Carolina Militia, Deputy Quartermaster General and Member Provincial Congresses.

MILTON PAINTER HILL, Baltimore, Md. (36099). Same as Dudley Sloan Hill, Baltimore, Md. (36098).

ROBERT SHERRARD HILL, Ohio (36494). Supplementals. Son of Joseph Welsh and Mary Ann (Sherrard) Hill; grandson of Robert and Rosamond (Welsh) Hill; great-grandson of *George Hill*, private, Washington County, Penna. Militia; grandson of Robert Andrew and Mary (Kithcart) Sherrard; great-grandson of *Joseph Kithcart*, private, Lancaster County, Penna. Militia; great-grandson of Joseph and Elizabeth (Cunningham) Kithcart; great²-grandson of *Barnett Cunningham*, private, Westmoreland County, Penna. Militia; great-grandson of *John Welsh*, private, Fifth Battalion, Washington County, Penna. Militia.

JOHN RUTHERFORD HIMES, New Bethlehem, Penna. (36765). Son of Joseph C. and Margaret (Rutherford) Himes; grandson of John and Sylvina (Space) Himes; great-grandson of Zephaniah and Katie (Armstrong) Space; great²-grandson of *John Space*, private, Second Establishment, New Jersey Cont'l Line.

WALTER PAYNE HIMES, Philadelphia, Penna. (36768). Son of John Rutherford and Mary (Roberts) Himes; grandson of Joseph C. and Margaret (Rutherford) Himes; great-grandson of John and Sylvina (Space) Himes; great²-grandson of Zephaniah and Katie (Armstrong) Space; great³-grandson of *John Space*, private, Second Regt., New Jersey Cont'l Line.

W. EDGAR HIMES, New Bethlehem, Penna. (36766). Same as John Rutherford Himes, Pennsylvania (36765).

MORGAN V. S. HINCHMAN, New Brunswick, N. J. (36898). Son of William H. and Lucretia W. (Oram) Hinchman; grandson of Johnson and Cornelia (Van Tine) Oram; great-grandson of *Darby Oram*, private, Colonel Barton's Regt., Rhode Island Militia, Carpenter's Mate U. S. S. "Alliance," and Seaman on Whale Boats, pensioned.

LOUIS CHAPIN HINCKLEY, Springfield, Mass. (36816). Son of Louis D. and Myrtie (Ballou) Hinckley; grandson of Rufus and Lois A. (Kellog) Hinckley; great-grandson of John and Laura (Chapin) Kellog; great²-grandson of Moses and Keziah (——) Chapin; great³-grandson of *Ephraim Chapin*, Captain, Eighth Co., First Regt., Hampshire County, Mass. Militia.

CHARLES ARTHUR HOLDEN, Hanover, N. H. (36255). Son of Charles William and Martha Stearns (Willard) Holden; grandson of William Parker and Lydia (Brigham) Holden; great-grandson of Nathan and Esther (Damon) Holden; great²-grandson of *John Holden*, Lieutenant, Middlesex County, Mass. Militia, pensioned.

FRANK LUDLOW HOLT, Plainfield, N. J. (36884). Son of Chauncy and Elizabeth A. (Ludlow) Holt; grandson of Henry Dobbs and Elizabeth (Hawley) Holt; great-grandson of Charles and Mary (Dobbs) Holt; great²-grandson of *William Holt*, private, Col. Jeremiah Mason's Regt., Conn. Militia.

RALPH MARSHALL HUESTON, Keokuk, Iowa (36250). Son of John Newton and Sallie (Fretwell) Hueston; grandson of Ralph and Eliza (Peck) Hueston; great-grandson of Matthew and Catherine (Davis) Hueston; great²-grandson of *William Hueston*, Captain, Penna. Associators.

CHARLES SEAVER HURD, Newark, N. J. (37008). Son of Charles Corbin and Louisa (Adams) Hurd; grandson of Samuel and Mary Ann (Corbin) Hurd; great-grandson of Samuel and Anna (Thurston) Hurd; great²-grandson of *Samuel Hurd*, Captain, Fifth Co., Sixteenth Regt., New Hampshire Militia.

CLARENCE PARKER HURD, Newark, N. J. (36869). Same as Charles Seaver Hurd, New Jersey ()7008).

SPENCER VAN SYCKLE HURD, Newark, N. J. (37009). Son of Clarence Parker and Kate K. (Van Sykle) Hurd; grandson of Charles Corbin and Louisa (Adams) Hurd; great-grandson of Samuel and Mary Ann (Corbin) Hurd; great²-grandson of Samuel and Anna (Thurston) Hurd; great³-grandson of *Samuel Hurd*, Captain, Fifth Co., Sixtenth Regt., New Hampshire Militia.

WILLIAM WALLACE HURD, East Orange, N. J. (37144). Same as Charles Seaver Hurd, New Jersey (37008).

CLAIRE ELWOOD HUTCHIN, Chicago, Ill. (36640). Son of Walter and Anna C. (Dillehunt) Hutchin; grandson of Isaac Wallace and Mianda (Monson) Hutchin; great-grandson of Thomas and Sarah (Brelsford) Hutchin; great²-grandson of *William Hutchin*, private, New Jersey Militia; great-grandson of Bushrod W. and Sabra (Bates) Monson; great²-grandson of Jared and Elizabeth (Peck) Munson; great³-grandson of *Walter Munson*, private, Col. Andrew Ward's Regt., Conn Militia.

HENRY BUSH HUTCHISON, McKeesport, Penna. (37090). Son of Philip and Lucetta (——) Hutchison; grandson of Philip Hutchison; great-grandson of *Cornelius Hutchison*, private, Col. Walter Stewart's Regt., Penna. Cont'l Line, pensioned.

WILLIAM J. HUTCHISON, Kittanning, Penna. (36769). Son of Joseph H. and Mary Ellen (Foster) Hutchison; grandson of Joseph Cunningham and Eliza (Mathews) Hutchison; great-grandson of Joseph and Anna (Cunningham) Hutchison; great²-grandson of *Barnet Cunningham*, private, Westmoreland County, Penna. Rangers.

EDWARD STURGIS INGRAHAM, Seattle, Wash. (36652). Son of Samuel and Almira (Davenport) Ingraham; grandson of Moses and Abigail (Sturgis) Ingraham; great-grandson of *Jeremiah Ingraham*, private, Mass. Minute Men.

HAROLD RAY IRISH, Silverton, Oreg. (35070). Son of Edgar Walton and Helen (Coon) Irish; grandson of George and Maria (Potter) Irish, Jr.; great-grandson of George and Betsy (Babcock) Irish; great²-grandson of *Benjamin Irish*, private and Sergeant, Conn. Militia and Cont'l Troops.

WILLIAM EUGENE IRONS, Brooklyn, N. Y. (37179). Son of William Eugene and Charlotte Augusta (Fuller) Irons; grandson of Nathaniel and Almira (Pendleton) Fuller; great-grandson of Philo and Rachel (Palmer) Fuller; great²-grandson of *Amos Fuller*, private, Fourteenth Co., Sixth Brigade, Conn. Militia.

JAMES ROSSITER IZANT, Warren, Ohio (36500). Son of Robert T. and Sadie (King) Izant; grandson of James M. and Lucy C. (Christie) King; great-grandson of John and Hannah B. (Andrews) Christie; great²-grandson of John and Hannah (Reen) Andrews; great³-grandson of *John Andrews*, Ensign, Sixteenth Regt., Conn. Militia.

ROBERT JACKSON, Concord, N. H. (36256). Son of James Robert and Lydia (Drew) Jackson; grandson of William and Prucia (Morrill) Jackson; great-grandson of Joseph and —— (Mason) Morrill; great^2-grandson of *Joseph Morrill*, private, Methuen, Mass. Militia, pensioned.

WILLIAM WARREN JACKSON, Augusta, Me. (36590). Son of James Myrick and Emeline Holt (Boynton) Jackson; grandson of Isaac and Mary Jane (Rice) Jackson; great-grandson of *William Rice*, private, Mass. Militia.

HOWARD PARKE JONES, Newark, N. J. (37140). Son of George Washington and Julia Charlotte (Pratt) Jones; grandson of Evan and Caroline (Parke) Jones; great-grandson of George Washington and Mary (Fleming) Parke; great^2-grandson of *Joseph Parke*, private, Chester County, Penna. Militia and Light Dragoons, and Member of War Committees.

WILLIE PARKER JONES, Washington, D. C. (36145). Son of James A. and Mary Evelyn (Hill) Jones; grandson of Amos and Mary S. (Gould) Hill; great-grandson of Jacob and Phebe Catherine (Parker) Gould; great^2-grandson of Thomas and Hanna (Hill) Gould; great^3-grandson of *Jacob Gould*, private, Captain Sprague's Co., Mass. Minute Men at Lexington.

ZACHARY TAYLOR JONES, Toledo, Ohio (36497). Son of George Washington and Jane O. Nan (Tibbats) Jones; grandson of John W. and Anne W. (Taylor) Tibbats; great-grandson of James and Keturah (Moss) Taylor; great^2-grandson of *James Taylor*, Colonel, Virginia Militia, Member Virginia Legislature and Chairman Committee of Public Safety.

CULLOM WELLS KAY, Louisiana (17452). Supplemental. Son of Benoist Willing and Eveline Enid (Cullom) Kay; grandson of Richard Wioatte and Emily (Wells) Kay; great-grandson of William Willing and Rosalie (Meullion) Wells; great^2-grandson of *Ennemond Meullion*, Second Lieutenant, Capt. Jean Francois Allain's Co., Louisiana Militia.

WILLARD KEEN, Huntsville, Tenn. (36787). Son of James Marion and Virginia Richmond (Mabry) Keen; grandson of John G. and Jane (Johnson) Keen; great-grandson of John and Mary (Webb) Johnson; great^2-grandson of *John Boswell Johnson*, Paymaster and Captain, First Regt., Virginia Troops.

JESSET DENNIS KELEHER, Realton, N. Mex. (30096). Son of Thomas F. and Jessie (——) Keleher; grandson of Daniel and Julia (Welcocks) Scannell; great-grandson of William and Charity (Broomfield) Welcocks; great^2-grandson of Ezra and Sarah (Friend) Welcocks; great^3-grandson of *William Welcocks*, private, Fifteenth Regt., Virginia Militia.

GEORGE TROXELL KELLER, Easton, Penna. (37078). Son of William H. and Emma Florence (Kinsey) Keller; grandson of John I. and Mary Chambers (Ashmore) Kinsey; great-grandson of William and Frances D. (Chambers) Ashmore; great^2-grandson of Clark and Mary (Guild) Chambers; great^3-grandson of *David Chambers*, Colonel, New Jersey Militia and State Troops.

FRANKLIN MINER KELLOGG, Short Hills, N. J. (36870). Son of Charles E. and Alice A. (Park) Kellogg; grandson of Edmund Burke and Nancy Emeline (Avery) Kellogg; great-grandson of Elisha and Nancy (Miner) Avery; great^2-grandson of J. O. and Elizabeth (Avery) Miner; great^3-grandson of *Ebenezer Avery, Jr.*, Lieutenant, Conn. Militia, killed at Groton Heights.

WILLIAM THURSTON KELLY, East Orange, N. J. (36853). Son of George Rembrandt and Margaret Augusta (Sperbeck) Kelly; grandson of William and Hannah Barnard (Davis) Kelly; great-grandson of Samuel Barnard and Esther (Sloane) Davis; great^2-grandson of Aaron and Hannah (Barnard) Davis; great^3-grandson of *Samuel Barnard*, Captain and Major, Middlesex County, Mass. Militia.

WALTER HARRISON KELSEY, Hutchinson, Kans. (36735). Son of James Milton and Margaret (Pierson) Kelsey; grandson of Harrison and Mary (Brown) Kelsey; great-grandson of Joseph Kelsey; great^2-grandson of *Thomas Kelsey*, private, Ulster County, New York Militia, pensioned.

WILLIAM RANDOLPH CURRY KENDRICK, Des Moines, Iowa (36249). Son of Americus Vespucius and Martha Ann (——) Kendrick; grandson of Daniel B. and Oliva (Curry) Kendrick; great-grandson of *Williamm Kendrick*, private, Culpepper County, Virginia Militia,

MARION SAWYER KENNEDY, Pulaski, Tenn. (36052). Son of James Foster and Hannah Catherine (McGaughey) Kennedy; grandson of Daniel and Margaret (——) Kennedy; great-grandson of John and Patience (Davis) Kennedy; great²-grandson of *Daniel Kennedy*, Colonel, Greene County, Tenn. Militia.

JONATHAN FRANCIS KILBOURN, Brooklyn, N. Y. (36878). Son of Joseph Austin and Sarah Alacoque (Dooley) Kilbourn; grandson of Horace and Mary (Young) Kilbourn; great-grandson of Joseph and Hannah (Sellew) Kilbourn; great²-grandson of *Philip Sellew*, Delegate, Conn. State Assembly of '83, Member Purchasing Committee and State War-Tax Collector.

ORRIN PAUL KILBOURN, Hartford, Conn. (36721). Son of Joseph Austin and Sarah Alacoque (Dooley) Kilbourn; grandson of Horace and Mary (Young) Kilbourn; great-grandson of Joseph and Hannah (Sellew) Kilbourn; great²-grandson of *Phillip Sellew*, Member Committee on Purchasing Clothing for Cont'l Army, Collector of State Tax, and Representative to Conn. General Assembly.

DAVID PIERSON KILPATRICK, Alexandria, La. (36951). Son of Ralph and Alice (Pierson) Kilpatrick; grandson of Milton and Margery (Cushman) Kilpatrick; great-grandson of Ralph and Esther Rebecca (Brashears) Cushman; great²-grandson of Clark and Katherine (Grout) Cushman; great²-grandson of *Elijah Grout*, Muster-Master, Commissary and Member New Hampshire Commmittee of Safety.

EVERETT AUGUSTUS KIMBALL, Springfield, Mass. (36817). Son of Elijah and Susan E. (Hakness) Kimball; grandson of Elijah and Augusta (King) Kimball; great-grandson of Leonard and Patty (Baird) Kimball; great²-grandson of *Aaron Kimball*, Captain, Worcester County, Mass. Militia.

ARTHUR FRANK KING, Marion, Ohio (37026). Son of Frank H. and Minnie (Jacoby) King; grandson of John and Eliza (Van Brimmer) Jacoby; great-grandson of Michael and Elizabeth (Worline) Jacoby; great²-grandson of Henry and Catharine (Cline) Worline; great²-grandson of *Conrad Cline*, private, Sixth Regt., Northampton County, Penna. Cont'l Line.

GEORGE NOAH KINGSBURY, Boise, Idaho (35110). Son of Hiram and Fanny (Starr) Kingsbury; grandson of George and Lora (Southworth) Kingsbury; great-grandson of *Daniel Kingsbury*, Ensign, Second Battalion, Conn. State Troops.

FREDERIC ELLSWORTH KIP, Montclair, N. J. (36865). Son of Nicholas J. and and Susan Pinkham (Worcester) Kip; grandson of John and Jane (Van Winkle) Kip; great-grandson of *Cornelius Kip*, private, Bergen County, New Jersey Militia and State Troops.

LESTER HOWARD KNAPP, Keokuk, Iowa (36905). Son of Francis B. and Nellie E. Snow) Knapp; grandson of Benjamin F. and Ruth D. (Harris) Snow; great-grandson of Fileston and Nancy (Heath) Snow; great²-grandson of *Benjamin Snow*, Ensign, Second Regt., New Hampshire Troops.

WILLIAM WARNER KNOX, Wilmington, Del. (35664). Son of John and Margaret Ann (McIlhenny) Knox; grandson of Hugh and Ann (Taughinbaugh) McIlhenny; great-grandson of Robert and Martha (King) McIlhenny; great²-grandson of *Robert McIlhenny*, private, Eighth Battalion, Lancaster County, Penna. Militia.

FREDERICK MANNING KREINER, Newark, N. J. (36874). Son of Conrad H. and Josephine Esther (Fisher) Kreiner; grandson of William Bishop and Elizabeth (Scudder) Fisher; great-grandson of Thomas and Elizabeth (Ayres) Scudder; great²-grandson of *Richard Scudder*, private, Essex County, New Jersey Militia.

EDWARD BROWN LADD, Winchester, Mass. (37114). Son of Edward Alzamond and Almira Baldwin (Brown) Ladd; grandson of John Manson and Sarah Ann (Baldwin) Brown; great-grandson of Cyrus and Rachel Walker (Revere) Baldwin; great²-grandson of Paul and Sally (Edwards) Revere; great²-grandson of *Paul Revere*, Lieutenant-Colonel, Col. Thomas Craft's Mass. Artillery and Cont'l Troops.

HARRY FOSS LAKE, Concord, N. H. (36257). Son of Moses R. and Mary Jane (Batchelder) Lake; grandson of Edmund and Nancy (Smith) Batchelder; great-grandson of David and Lydia (Scribner) Batchelder; great²-grandson of *David Batchelder*, Member Deerfield, N. H., Committee of Safety.

MILES KRAUSE LANDER, Grand Forks, No. Dak. (36929). Son of Edward John and Jessie King (Krause) Lander; grandson of Ustick Onderdonk and Mary (King) Krause;

great-grandson of Jesse and Emma (Fitch) King; great²-grandson of Asa and Sophronia (Olcott) Fitch; great³-grandson of *Elisha Fitch*, Corporal, Third Regt., New York Levies, and private, New York Militia.

ROBERT McKEE LAPSLEY, Keokuk, Iowa (36913). Son of David Nelson and Margaret Jane (Jerkins) Lapsley; grandson of John A. and Mary Wear (McKee) Lapsley; great-grandson of *John Lapsley*, Ensign, First and Second Lieutenants, Seventh Regt., Virginia Militia, pensioned.

ELMER HERBERT LAWSON, Eudora, Kans. (36733). Son of James Spencer and Louise (Pilla) Lawson; grandson of John Strawbridge and Elizabeth (Finney) Lawson; great-grandson of James and Elizabeth (Johnson) Finney; great²-grandson of *Lazarus Finney*, Lieutenant, Second Battalion, Chester County, Penna. Associators.

JESSE CHAUNCY NELSON LAY, Nampa, Idaho (35113). Son of Charles F. and Sarah (Garner) Lay; grandson of Chauncy and Elvira (——) Garner; great-grandson of James and Jane (Nelson) Garner; great²-grandson of *Robert Nelson*, Corporal, Ninth Regt., Virginia Militia, pensioned.

LEWIS BENJAMIN LEEDS, Pittsburgh, Penna. (37088). Son of William H. S. and Sarah M. (Shubert) Leeds; grandson of Lewis and Phoebe (Baker) Leeds; great-grandson of John and Margaret (Adams) Baker; great²-grandson of Daniel and Mary (Badcock; Baker; great³-grandson of Joseph and Phoebe (Mackey) Badcock; great⁴-grandson of *John Mackey*, Colonel, Cape May, Battalion, New Jersey Troops.

W. H. SEWARD LEEDS, Bellevue, Penna. (37089). Same as Lewis Benjamin Leeds, Pittsburgh, Penna. (37088).

CAMPFIELD LEONARD, Syracuse, N. Y. (37178). Son of Edwin Jerome and Cynthia (Ames) Leonard; grandson of Henry Griffin and Catharine (Campfield) Leonard; great-grandson of Solomon and Mary Ann (Waldo) Leonard; great²-grandson of *Asa Leonard*, private, Conn. Militia and Cont'l Line.

MORTON LIEBSCHUTZ, Belleville, N. J. (36861). Son of Felix and Fanny (Levy) Liebschutz; grandson of Morton and Rebecca Annette (Phillips) Levy; great-grandson of Michael and Rachel (Phillips) Levy; great²-grandson of *Jonas Phillips*, private, Col. William Bradford's Battalion, Philadelphia Militia.

LEWIS EDWARD LIMBERT, Dayton, Ohio (37032). Son of Thomas Howard and Stella (——) Limbert; grandson of Thomas Jefferson and Margaret (I.—) Limbert; great-grandson of John T. Limbert; great²-grandson of Thomas and Sarah (Huston) Limbert; great³-grandson of *William Huston*, Adjutant and Lieutenant, Colonel Hartley's Regt., Penna. Cont'l Line.

ARTHUR CLARK LISCOM, Detroit, Mich. (36049). Son of Lucius Grey and Susie Emerson (Clark) Liscom; grandson of Samuel Daniel and Sarah Elizabeth (Emerson) Clark; great-grandson of Daniel and Amy (Davis) Clark; great²-grandson of *William Clark*, private, Townsend, Mass. Militia and Colonel Bailey's Regt., Cont'l Line.

ELWIN LITTLE, New York City, N. Y. (36889). Son of Elwin and Alice (Hart) Little; grandson of Bitfield Plummer and Lydia Adelaide (Manson) Little; great-grandson of Richard and Priscilla (Plummer) Little; great²-grandson of *Benjamin Little*, private, New Hampshire Militia; great²-grandson of Benjamin and Rhoda (Bartlett) Miller; great²-grandson of *Simeon Bartlett*, Chairman New Hampshire Committee of Safety; great²-grandson of *Bitfield Plummer*, private, New Hampshire Cont'l Line; grandson of William Taylor and Chloe Lion (Barbour) Hart; great-grandson of Gideon Blackburn and Hetty Alexander (Taylor) Hart; great²-grandson of *Joseph Hart*, private, Fourth Regt., Virginia Militia.

JOHN FRANKLIN LITTLE, Washington, D. C. (37151). Son of Frank L. and Mary Elizabeth (Sasnett) Little; grandson of Richard Phelps and Mary Ann (Harris) Sasnett; great-grandson of Henry and Mary Elizabeth (Harris) Harris; great²-grandson of Absalom (father of Henry) and Elizabeth (Lane) Tarver; great³-grandson of *Benjamin Harris*, Lieutenant, Second Regt., Virginia Cont'l Line.

JOHN WILDER LITTLE, Madison, Nebr. (36977). Son of John Wilder and Mary (Loomis) Little; grandson of Jonathan Colton and Electa (Stockbridge) Loomis; great-grandson of *Abner Loomis*, private, Conn. Militia.

JOHN W. LOCKHART, Galveston, Tex. (36331). Son of William Browning and Esther (Gresham) Lockhart; grandson of Walter and Josephine (Mann) Gresham; great-grandson of William and Esther Steele (Baskin) Mann; great^2-grandson of Thomas Stewart and Mary (Noble) Baskin; great^3-grandson of *William* and Ann (Reid) *Baskin*, Captain, South Carolina Militia; great^3-grandson of *George Reid*, Captain, South Carolina Militia at Camp Ninety.

FRANK OTEY LONG, Tennessee (36776). Supplemental. Son of Henry and Francis Burton (Scurlock) Long; grandson of Timothy Pickering and Anne (Huntsman) Scurlock; great-grandson of Joseph and Mrs. Martha (Glascoe) Sheppard Scurlock; great^2-grandson of *Mial Scurlock*, Major, Chatham County, North Carolina Minute Men, Member North Carolina Assembly and Provincial Congress.

LEON MILNER LONG, Tennessee (36777). Supplemental. Same as Frank Otey Long, Tennessee (36776). Supplemental.

RICHARD FOSTER LUMBARD, Dallas, Tex. (Calif. 36419). Son of La Mont C. and Fannie Adell (Breck) Lumbard; grandson of Orson Allen and Ermina M. (Rogers) Breck; great-grandson of John Baldwin and Jemima Allen (Spalding) Breck; great^2-grandson of Jacob and Lucy (Ward) Spalding; great^3-grandson of Isaac and Mercy (Knapp) Spalding; great^4-grandson of *Jacob Spalding*, private, Capt. Andrew Backus's Co., Conn. Militia at Lexington Alarm.

HAROLD MARTIN LYCAN, Indianapolis, Ind. (36438). Son of Clark S. and Anna (Martin) Lycan; grandson of William T. and Elizabeth (Payne) Martin; great-grandson of James and Barbara (Sigafoos) Martin; great^2-grandson of Benjamin and Margaret (Mann) Martin; great^3-grandson of *Andrew Mann*, Captain, Eighth Penna. Regt., Cont'l Line; great^3-grandson of *James Martin*, Captain, Second Battalion, Bedford County, Penna. Militia.

GEORGE EDGAR McALLISTER, Minneapolis, Minn. (35698). Son of Joshua Odell and Almira (Wright) McAllister; grandson of James McAllister; great-grandson of *William McAllister*, private, Fourth and Second Regts., New York Troops, pensioned.

LEE ADRIAN McCARDELL, Braddock Heights, Md. (36100). Son of Edgar Stonebraker and Abby Gertrude (Barnes) McCardell; grandson of Adrian Calfred and Alforetta Rebecca (Stonebraker) McCardell; great-grandson of Wilfred and Catherine (Humrickhouse) McCardell; great^2-grandson of Frederick and Hannah (Harry) Humrickhouse; great^3-grandson of *Peter Humrickhouse*, Lieutenant, Second Battalion, Philadelphia County Militia.

ROBERT JACKSON McCAULEY, Leeds, Md. (37326). Son of John and Emma L. (Campbell) McCauley; grandson of James and Sarah (Beard) McCauley; great-grandson of John and Elizabeth (McCauley) McCauley; great^2-grandson of Daniel and Francina (Baker) McCauley; great^3-grandson of *Jethro Baker*, Maryland Commissary, died in service.

ALEXANDER McCOLL, Grand Rapids, Mich. (37051). Son of John Alexander and Ella Kate (Swain) McColl; grandson of Charles Freeman and Lucy Marilla (Knight) Swain; great-grandson of Charles Putnam and Harriet (Bryant) Swain; great^2-grandson of Johnathan and Mary (Freeman) Bryant; great^3-grandson of *Samuel Freeman*, Member Mass. Com. of Correspondence Provincial Congress and of General Court.

ARCHIBALD TWINE McCOLL, Grand Rapids, Mich. (37052). Same as Alexander McColl, Michigan (37051).

HALLE DAVID McCULLOUGH, Brookings, S. Dak. (30671). Son of John Henry and Maybelle Dottie (Holloway) McCullough; grandson of David and Lois (De Maranville) McCullough; great-grandson of Nehemiah De Maranville, Jr.; great^2-grandson of Nehemiah De Maranville; great^3-grandson of *Louis De Maranville*, private, Col. Timothy Davidson's Regt., Mass. Militia.

HARRY CHARLES McDERMOTT, Milwaukee, Wis. (32674). Son of Charles and Maria M. (Simpson) McDermott; grandson of Henry W. and Esther (Baldwin) Simpson; great-grandson of Morgan and Catherine (Cameron) Simpson; great^2-grandson of *Peter Simpson, Jr.*, private, Dutchess, Orange, and Ulster Counties, New York Militia.

HARRY LEWIS McKAIN, Pittsburgh, Penna. (36770). Son of William James and Josephine (Lightcap) McKain; grandson of John Jacob and Rebecca (Bell) McKain; great-grandson of William and Catharine (Huff) McKain; great^2-grandson of *Jacob Huff*, private, Thirteenth Regt., Penna. Cont'l Line, pensioned.

DANIEL H. McKEE, Wilkinsburg, Penna. (36773). Son of Finley and Eliza Ann (Harper) McKee; grandson of Henry and Susanna (Hornbake) McKee; great-grandson of *John McKee*, private, Penna. Militia and Cont'l Troops, pensioned; grandson of Daniel and Margery (Huston) Harper; great-grandson of William and Mary (Morrison) Huston; great²-grandson of *Joseph Huston*, private, Westmoreland County, Penna. Rangers.

HAMILTON BIGGER McNAIR, Brooklyn, N. Y. (36896). Son of Stephen Yerkes and Mattie E. (Knowles) McNair; grandson of John and Mary (Yerkes) McNair; great-grandson of Stephen and Alice (Watson) Yerkes; great²-grandson of *Harman Yerkes*, private, Bucks County, Penna. Associators.

JAMES FRANKLIN McNAUL, Pittsburgh, Penna. (36771). Son of Robert Way and Melissa Lowrie (Wilson) McNaul; grandson of George and Lydia (Packer) Wilson; great-grandson of *Job E. Packer*, private, First Battalion, Chester County, Penna. Militia.

GEORGE DALLAS MACKAY, JR., Newark, N. J. (36873). Son of George Dallas and Grace M. (Bellows) Mackay; grandson of Thorn M. and Jane M. (Rhodes) Mackey; great-grandson of Levi and Rebecca (Scott) Mackey; great²-grandson of *John Mackey*, Drummer, Fifth Regt., New York Cont'l Line; grandson of Frederick and Maria (Perkins) Bellows; great-grandson of Theodore and Elizabeth (Davis) Bellows, Jr.; great²-grandson of *Theodore Bellows*, Sergeant, Col. Moses Nichols' Regt., New Hampshire Militia.

HARRY DENNY MAGAW, McKeesport, Penna. (36774). Son of Truxton Van Lear and Mary McPherson (Reed) Magaw; grandson of William Aston Van Lear and Sophia Cochrane (Porter) Magaw; great²-grandson of *William Magaw*, Surgeon, First Regt., Penna. Cont'l Line.

CARLETON MOORE MAGOUN, Sioux City, Iowa (36903). Son of John A. and Elizabeth A. (Moore) Magoun, Jr.; grandson of John Adams and Ella C. (Woodbury) Magoun; great-grandson of John Calvin and Sarah Ann (Adams) Magoun; great²-grandson of Joseph and Sally (Tufts) Adams; great³-grandson of *Joseph Adams*, Sergeant, Col. Jacob Gerrish's Regt., Mass. Militia.

CHARLES ELMER MAGOUN, Sioux City, Iowa (36901). Same as Carleton Moore Magoun, Iowa (36903).

GEORGE MAGOUN, Sioux City, Iowa (36902). Same as Charles Elmer Magoun, Iowa (36901).

WILL RUCKER MANIER, JR., Nashville, Tenn. (36788). Son of Will Rucker and Mary (Owsley) Manier; grandson of John Samuel and Susan Malinda (Miller) Owsley; great-grandson of Thomas W. and Mary Jane (Hocker) Miller; great²-grandson of Daniel and Susannah (Woods) Miller; great³-grandson of *Robert Miller, Jr.*, Lieutenant and Captain, Orange County, Virginia Militia.

JOHN ALBERT BARNETT MANSFIELD, West Haven, Conn. (36714). Son of John J. and Louise C. (Barnett) Mansfield; grandson of Albert E. and Martha C. (Peckham) Barnett; great-grandson of Jeremiah and Rebecca (Gilbert) Barnett; great²-grandson of Elijah and Esther (Dodd) Gilbert; great³-grandson of *Bishop Dodd*, private, Conn. Militia, pensioned.

CHARLES CAPRON MARSH, East Orange, N. J. (37024). Son of John Edward and Caroline A. (Capron) Marsh; grandson of Seth M. and Caroline A. (Scofield) Capron; great-grandson of *Seth Capron*, Corporal and Sergeant, Mass. Militia and Coxswain of General Washington's barge, widow pensioned.

FRANK PALMER MASON, Taunton, Mass. (37107). Son of Daniel Hale and Hannah Balcolm (Wilmarth) Mason; grandson of Learned and Priscilla (Balcolm) Wilmarth, Jr.; great-grandson of Learned and Betsey (Lane) Wilmarth; great²-grandson of Ephraim and Elizabeth (Copeland) Lane, Jr.; great³-grandson of *Ephraim Lane*, Lieutenant-Colonel, Col. Thomas Carpenter's Regt., Mass. Militia.

LEROY ALLEN MATTHEWS, Montclair, N. J. (37136). Son of Granville A. and Fanny A. (Whitmarsh) Matthews; grandson of Fordyce and Eliza (Allen) Whitmarsh; great-grandson of Jacob and Olive (Packard) Whitmarsh; great²-grandson of Jacob and Anna (Pool) Whitmarsh; great³-grandson of *Samuel Pool*, Lieutenant, Col. J. Jacob's Regt., Mass. Militia; great²-grandson of *Jacob Whitmarsh*, private, Colonel Hawes'

Regt., Mass. Militia; great-grandson of Josiah and Sarah (Kingsbury) Allen; great-grandson of Zebulon and Priscilla (Atwood) Allen; great²-grandson of *Wait Atwood*, private, Mass. Militia, 1775.

CHARLES HENRY MAXSON, St. Paul, Minn. (35693). Son of Sandford L. and Nancy Jane (Coon) Maxson; grandson of William R. and Abby (Langworthy) Maxson; great-grandson of Benjamin C. and Martha (Crandall) Maxson; great²-grandson of *Zacheus Maxson*, Ensign, Colonel Richmond's Regt., R. I. Militia, pensioned.

CHARLES JONES MAXWELL, Merchantville, N. J. (37129). Son of John Gordon and Emme Staton (Laws) Maxwell; grandson of John and Jane Maria (Castner) Laws; great-grandson of Jacob and Hannah (Wilson) Castner; great²-grandson of *Samuel Castner*, private, Philadelphia County, Penna. Militia.

GEORGE MANDESLEY MAYNARD, Washington, D. C. (36148) Son of George Colton and Lucy (Warner) Maynard; grandson of Charles Mosely and Sophronia (Colton) Maynard; great-grandson of Henry and Lydia (Booth) Colton; great²-grandson of *Joseph Booth*, Captain, Nineteenth Regt., Conn. Militia; great-grandson of Ezra and Raney (Moseley) Maynard; great²-grandson of *Malachi Maynard*, private, Mass. Minute Men at Lexington Alarm; great²-grandson of *Joseph Moseley*, private, Mass. Militia.

FRED JEROME MEAD, Newark, N. J. (36866). Son of Jerome Lewis and Lucinda (Woodward) Mead; grandson of Joel E. and B. Ann (Lewis) Mead; great-grandson of Abraham and Deborah (Barker) Mead; great²-grandson of *Ethan Mead*, private, Third Regt., Westchester County, New York Militia.

BURTON WALTERS MELCHER, Wisconsin (32668). Supplemental. Son of Frank Robert and Edna Emma (Walters) Melcher; grandson of Louis Christian and Martha Gifford (Dopp) Walters; great-grandson of Henry (Harry) and Eunice Brown (Pike) Dopp, Jr.; great²-grandson of Artemas and Marion (Parker) Pike; great²-grandson of *Benjamin Pike*, Sergeant, Mass. Militia.

LOUIS CHESTER MELCHER, Wis. (32673). Supplemental. Same as Burton Walters Melcher (32668). Supplemental.

CAP EARL MILLER, North Fargo, N. Dak. (36933). Son of David Wesley and Margaret Ruth (McWilliams) Miller; grandson of William and Lucy Ann (Noffsinger) McWilliams; great-grandson of John and Lydia (Ferguson) McWilliams; great²-grandson of *William McWilliams*, private, Penna. Militia, pensioned; great-grandson of Daniel and Lucy Ann (Vantreese) Noffsinger; great²-grandson of *Joseph Vantreese*, private, Frederick County, Maryland Militia.

HERMAN FOSGATE MILLER, Estherville, Iowa (36906). Son of Joseph W. and Ada (Wilson) Miller; grandson of G. C. and Sarah (Holcomb) Wilson; great-grandson of James H. and Lucy (Woolworth) Holcomb; great²-grandson of Asahel and Sarah (Enie) Holcomb; great³-grandson of *Asahel Holcomb*, Captain, Eighteenth Regt., Conn. Militia, pensioned.

PERCY KAY MILLER, Montclair, N. J. (37005). Son of Charles G. and Marietta (Folts) Miller; grandson of Henry and Mary Elizabeth (Hess) Folts; great-grandson of George and Mary (Chapsattle) Hess; great²-grandson of *Han Jost Hess*, private, Col. Peter Gansvort's Regt., New York Troops, 6 years' service, pensioned.

SIDNEY TROWBRIDGE MILLER, JR., Detroit, Mich. (37055). Son of Sidney Trowbridge and Lucy Trumball (Robinson) Miller; grandson of Sidney Davey and Kate Sproat (Trowbridge) Miller; great-grandson of Charles Christopher and Catharine (Whipple) Sibley; great²-grandson of Solomon and Sarah Whipple (Sproat) Sibley; great³-grandson of *Ebenezer* and Catharine (Whipple) *Sproat*, Colonel, Twelfth Regt., Mass. Troops; great⁴-grandson of *Abraham Whipple*, Commodore, Cont'l Navy; great²-grandson of *Luther S.* and Elizabeth (Tillman) *Trowbridge*, Major, Mass. Cont'l Troops; great²-grandson of *John Tillman*, Major, Second Regt., New York Line.

CARL SHIELDS MILLIKEN, Denver, Colo. (36343). Son of William B. and Josephine (Shields) Milliken; grandson of George Washington and Martha Esther (Freeman) Shields; great-grandson of Jordan Lewis and Sarah (Shipman) Freeman; great²-grandson of William and Mary (Massie) Freeman; great³-grandson of *Thomas Massie*, private, Col. John Lynch and Major William Lewis's Regts., Virginia Militia.

CHARLES BAYARD MITCHELL, St. Paul, Minn. (36772). Son of Daniel Patrick and Eliza Ann (Baker) Mitchell; grandson of George and Mary (McCann) Mitchell; great-grandson of *John Mitchell*, private, Virginia Militia and Cont'l Artillery, pensioned.

FRANCIS JOSEPH ROSS MITCHELL, Montclair, N. J. (36862). Son of George Dyson and Mary Charlotte (Driskell) Mitchell; grandson of William and Margaret (Clayton) Mitchell; great-grandson of *William Mitchell*, private, and drummer, Second Regt., Penna. Troops.

ORVILLE BARKLEY MITMAN, Detroit, Mich. (36045). Son of L. C. and Letticia F. (Barkley) Mitman; grandson of Nathan and Sarah Ann (Dennis) Barkley; great-grandson of *John Dennis*, private, Gloucester County, New Jersey Militia and sailor on whaleboat service.

JOSEPH MONTGOMERY, 2nd, Pennsylvania (36755). Supplemental. Son of James B. and Emma Lynn (Buchecker) Montgomery; grandson of Edward E. and Rebecca (Lynn) Buchecker; great-grandson of Jonathan and Elizabeth (Thomas) Lynn; great²-grandson of *Felix Lynn*, private, Northampton County, Penna. Militia.

ROYAL JASPER MOULTON, Cando, N. Dak. (36939). Son of Jasper and Lora E. (Dorrance) Moulton; grandson of Royal and Debora (Thomas) Moulton; great-grandson of Lewis and Clara (Lathrop) Moulton; great²-grandson of Royal Moulton; great²-grandson of *Joseph* and Hannah (Fuller) *Moulton*, Sergeant, Monson, Conn. Militia; great⁴-grandson of *Freeborn Moulton*, Captain, Mass. Minute. Men at Lexington Alarm.

CHARLES S. MORLEY, East Orange, N. J. (37126). Son of Charles Sheriff and Hallie (Myers) Morley; grandson of Henry and Rosanna (Duffy) Myers; great-grandson of Hugh and Eliza Ann (Keffer) Duffy; great²-grandson of Anthony and Sarah (Shillingsford) Keffer; great²-grandson of *Martin Keffer*, private, First Battalion, Northampton County, Penna. Militia.

ALBERT SWIFT MORSE, Summit, N. J. (36854). Son of Joseph Gibbs and Abigail (Le Baron) Morse;- grandson of James and Lucinda (Morton) Le Baron; great-grandson of Lazurus and Abigail (Maxim) Le Baron; great²-grandson of *James Le Baron*, private, Col. Abijah Stern's Regt. Mass. Guards.

BURR LOVE MOULTHROP, San Francisco, Calif. (36424). Son of Howland King and Marie (Lonideck) Moulthrop; grandson of John Lankton and Sarah A. (Smith) Moulthrop; great-grandson of Josiah and Sophia (——) Moulthrop; great²-grandson of *John Moulthrop*, private, Col. Thomas Webb's Regt., Conn. Militia.

FRANK JOTHAM MOULTON, Boston, Mass. (36812). Son of James Gardner and Sarah J. (McCorrison) Moulton; grandson of Jotham Moulton, Jr.; great-grandson of *Jotham Moulton*, Brigadier-General, York County, Mass. Militia.

JAMES GARDNER MOULTON, Boston, Mass. (36813). Son of Frank Jotham and Abbie L. (Heuff) Moulton; grandson of James Gardner and Sarah J. (McCorrison) Moulton; great-grandson of Jotham Moulton, Jr.; great-grandson of *Jotham Moulton*, Brigadier-General, York County, Mass. Militia.

WILLIAM MACY MUNROE, Dorchester, Mass. (36822). Son of George and Annie E. (Hubbard) Munroe; grandson of William M. and Rebecca C. (Swain) Munroe; great-grandson of John and Lydia (Macy) Munroe; great²-grandson of *Nathan Munroe*, Minute Man and private, Mass. Militia.

FREDERIC EMIL NAGEL, Chicago, Ill. (36647). Son of Emil N. and Jennie Irwin (Patton) Nagel; grandson of Harry D. and Mathilda Elizabeth (McEnally) Patton; great-grandson of John and Susan (Antés) Patton; great²-grandson of *John Patton*, Colonel, Penna. Additional Cont'l Regt.; great²-grandson of *Philip Antes*, private, Northumberland County, Penna. Militia; great²-grandson of *Henry Antes*, Captain and Lieutenant-Colonel, Northampton County, Penna. Associators.

FRANKLYN DANA NASH, St. Louis, Mo. (35567). Son of James E. and Mary Adelia (Patrick) Nash; grandson of Reuben (Woodworth) and Emeline (Droughou) Patrick; great-grandson of William and Esther (Woodworth) Patrick, Jr., great²-grandson o. *William Patrick*, private, Thirteenth Regt., Albany County, New York Militia and Member Committee of Safety.

WILLIAM JOSEPH NEHER, Springfield, Ill. (36641). Son of Benjamin Franklin and Isabella (Hardcastle) Neher; grandson of Nelson and Amanda (Swartwout) Neher; great-grandson of John and Jemima (Rosekrans) Swartwout; great²-grandson of *Jacobus Rosekrans*, Captain, Dutchess County, New York Militia and Cont'l Line.

ROBERT M. NELSON, Memphis, Tenn. (36786). Son of William J. and Carrie (Croft) Nelson; grandson of George N. and Charlotte Elmore (Cherry) Croft; great-grandson of

Robert M. and Carolin (Crenshaw) Cherry; great²-grandson of Samuel and Susan Polk (Reese) Cherry; great³-grandson of *Thomas* and Jane (Harris) *Reese*, Chaplain, Fourth Regt., North Carolina Troops; great⁴-grandson of *David Reese*, Signer of Mecklenburg Declaration of Independence.

CHARLES PIERCE NEWBERRY, Detroit, Mich. (36047). Son of William Elihu and Mary Louise (Coates) Newberry; grandson of Henry L. and Margaret (Moore) Newberry; great-grandson of Elihu and Rhoda (Phelps) Newberry; great²-grandson of *Amasa Newberry*, Corporal and Sergeant, Conn. Militia.

THOMAS NEWBILL, Nashville, Tenn. (36781). Son of George and Grace (Meredith) Newbill; grandson of Thomas H. and Jane (Hodge) Meredith; great-grandson of Thomas H. and Jane (Jordan) Meredith; great²-grandson of *David Meredith*, private, Virginia Militia.

GEORGE FRED NEWELL, San Anselmo, Calif. (36416). Son of George Baker and Sarah Stafford (Lewis) Newell; grandson of Elizah B. and Harriet B. (Baker) Newell; great-grandson of William and Marcia (Andrus) Baker; great²-grandson of William and Sarah (Fletcher) Baker; great³-grandson of *Daniel Fletcher*, Major, Col. Jonathan Reed's Regt., Mass. Militia.

HAROLD HERBERT NILES, Concord, N. H. (36258). Son of Charles H. and Henrietta (Parkhurst) Niles; grandson of Jonathan Granville and Sarah E. (Spofford) Parkhurst; great-grandson of Horace and Rebecca (Baldwin) Parkhurst; great²-grandson of *Jonathan Parkhurst*, private, New Hampshire Militia and Cont'l Troops.

JEROME ANTHONY O'CONNELL, Springfield, Ill. (36635). Son of William and Ellen (Fitzgerald) O'Connell, grandson of John and Elizabeth Given (Malloy) O'Connell; great-grandson of James and Jane (Given) Malloy; great²-grandson of *David Given*, Corporal, Col. Jonathan Mitchell's Regt., Mass. Militia.

EDWIN WINTHROP OSBORN, Minnesota (25316). Supplemental. Son of Samuel H. and Cynthia (Nutt) Osborn; grandson of James and Sarah (Brown) Nutt; great-grandson of William and Hannah (Glidden) Nutt; great²-grandson of *William Nutt*, private, New Hampshire Cont'l Troops, 1781, Signer of Association Test.

RAYMOND STORMS OSBORN, Sewickley, Penna. (N. Y. 36879). Son of George W. and Josephine (Storms) Osborn; grandson of Joseph and Sarah (Sypher) Storms; great-grandson of Edward and Rachael (Willey) Sypher; great²-grandson of *Edward Willey*, private, Col. Philip Van Cortland's Regt., New York Cont'l Line.

ALFRED ALAN OVERBAGH, Evanston, Ill. (36956). Son of Franklin and Annie Louise (Cameron) Overbagh; grandson of William and Jane Eliza (Hommell) Overbagh; great-grandson of William and Eve (Rockerfeller) Overbagh; great²-grandson of *John Jurry Overbagh, Jr.*, private and Sergeant, New York Militia, widow pensioned.

DONALD CAMERON OVERBAGH, Chicago, Ill. (36957). Same as Alfred Alan Overbagh, Illinois (36956).

FRANKLIN OVERBAGH, Evanston, Ill. (36955). Son of William and Jane Eliza (Hommel) Overbagh; grandson of William and Eve (Rockefeller) Overbagh; great-grandson of *John Jurry Overbagh, Jr.*, private and Sergeant New York Militia, widow pensioned.

WILLIAM FRANKLIN OVERBAGH, Evanston, Ill. (La. 36952). Son of Franklin and Annie Louise (Cameron) Overbagh; grandson of William and Jane Eliza (Hommel) Overbagh; great-grandson of William and Eve (Rockefeller) Overbagh; great²-grandson of *John Jurry Overbagh, Jr.*, private, Col. Marinus Willett's Regt., New York Levies; great³-grandson of *Johan Jurry Overbagh*, private, Col. Marinus Willett's Regt., New York Levies.

ALBERT MacFARLAND OWEN, York, Penna. (37083). Son of Thomas and Kate (Schall) Owen; grandson of Thomas and Providence (Schroeder) Owen; great-grandson of Abraham and Mary (Dunn) Owen; great²-grandson of *Thomas Owens*, private, Lancaster County, Penna. Militia.

GEORGE COMFORT PARKHURST, Colmbus, Ga. (Conn. 36722). Son of Charles Dyer and Carrie (Starr) Parkhurst; grandson of George Edgar and Sarah Isabelle (Mallory) Starr; great-grandson of Nathan and Sarah Wignall (Stockman) Mallory; great²-grandson of Jacob and Susan (Spooner) Stockman; great³-grandson of *Charles Spooner*, Lieutenant, Newport, Rhode Island Light Infantry.

GEORGE CLARK PARSONS, Detroit, Mich. (36040). Son of Edward Colt and Frances Mary (Penniman) Parsons; grandson of Jonathan and Mary (Colt) Parsons; great-grandson of Oliver P. and Mary (Brewer; Colt; great²-grandson of *Gaius Brewer*, Sergeant, Col. Charles Pynchon's Regt., Mass. Militia.

MONTGOMERY HOWARD PARSONS, Detroit, Mich. (37054). Son of Howard H. and Aurora M. (Pratt) Parsons; grandson of Williams Riley and Caroline C. (Hough) Parsons; great-grandson of Josiah Van Vechton and Dolly (Cotton) Hough; great²-grandson of *Justus Hough*, private, Hampshire County, Mass. Militia; great²-grandson of Justus and Sarah (Whitney) Hough; great²-grandson of *Jonathan Whitney*, Corporal, Col. Dike's Regt., Mass. Militia; grandson of Charles B. and Emeline Hope (Smith) Pratt; great-grandson of Abner and Eliza (Norton) Montgomery Pratt; great²-grandson of *Jonathan Norton*, Lieutenant, First Regt., Berkshire County, Mass. Militia.

WILLIAM SCOTT PARKS, D. C. (19353). Supplemental. Son of Reuben Sylvester and Emmeline Ann (Scott) Parks; grandson of Sylvester and Laura (Andrus) Parks; great-grandson of Reuben and Betty (Clark) Parks; great²-grandson of *James Clark*, private and Second Lieutenant, Mass. Militia; Member Committees of Inspection, Safety, Recruiting, and Declaration of Rights.

WESLEY ENNIS PATTON, Memphis, Tenn. (36790). Son of Percy Hoyt and Hannah Coolidge (Ennis) Patton; grandson of John Wesley and Lurona (Coolidge) Ennis; great-grandson of Charles and Caroline (McCartney) Coolidge; great²-grandson of Samuel and Lurona (Cook) Coolidge; great²-grandson of *Samuel Coolidge*, private, Mass. Militia; grandson of Thomas Newton and Mollie (Terry) Patton; great-grandson of James Henry and Nancy (Hart) Patton; great²-grandson of Gilbert and Nancy (Moore) Hart; great²-grandson of *James* and Nancy (Strayhorn) *Hart*, private, Orange County, North Carolina Militia; great⁴-grandson of *John Strayhorn*, private, North Carolina Militia.

ROBERT WESTLY PEACH, Newark, N. J. (37134). Son of Samuel Westley and Anna Robertson (Wiggins) Peach; grandson of William and Elizabeth Grotts (Gregory) Peach; great-grandson of William and Sarah (Pearce) Peach; great²-grandson of *William Peach*, Matross, Marblehead, Mass. Militia, pensioned.

GEORGE MANN PECK, Princeton, N. J. (37016). Son of Ezra Jones and Annie Lingan (Bartlett) Peck; grandson of Enock and Julietta Ann (Jones) Peck; great-grandson of Darius and Lydia (Mack) Peck, Jr.; great²-grandson of *Darius Peck*, Second Lieutenant, Conn. Militia.

LUTHER PECK, Plymouth, Mich. (37056). Son of Carlos L. and Ellen E. (Sedgwick) Peck; grandson of Martin and Mary G. (Boyden) Sedgwick; great-grandson of Azel and Amelia (Stevens) Boyden; great²-grandson of Ezekiel and Hannah (Cook) Boyden, Jr.; great³-grandson of *Ezekiel Boyden*, Sergeant, Col. Wheelock's Regt., Mass Militia.

HERMAN K. PECKHAM, Nebraska (33884). Supplemental. Son of Joshua Stetson and Ann (Atkinson) Peckham; grandson of Abel and Adah (Brown) Peckham; great-grandson of Joshua and Sarah (Stetson) Peckham; great²-grandson of *Stephen Stetson* (*Stutson*), private, Colonel Angell's Regt., Rhode Island Militia.

HENRY CARMICHAEL PENINGTON, Wilmington, Del. (35666). Son of Henry Rowan and Henrietta (Carmichael) Penington; grandson of John Barr and Rebecca A. (Rowan) Penington; great-grandson of Thomas MacDonough and Henrietta (Barr) Penington; great²-grandson of James and Hannah (MacDonough) Penington; great³-grandson of *Thomas MacDonough*, Major, Colonel Haslet's Regt., Delaware Troops.

HOWARD DELVON PERKINS, New Haven, Conn. (36723). Son of Edwin Charlton and Harriet Eliza (Haskins) Perkins; grandson of Franklin and Eliza (Lathrop) Haskins; great-grandson of Enoch and Phebe (Weeks) Haskins; great²-grandson of *Joshua Haskins*, private, Mass. Militia and First Regt., Cont'l Line.

ARTHUR PERRIN, Massachusetts (36804). Supplemental. Son of Franklin and Louisa Charlotte (Gage) Perrin; grandson of Augusta and Harriet Child) Perrin; great-grandson of Abraham and Rachael (——) Perrin; great²-grandson of *David Perrin*, private, Conn. Militia at Lexington alarm; Selectman and Member Com. of Inspection, etc.; great-grandson of Stephen and Sarah (Weld) Child; great²-grandson of *David Weld*, private, Suffolk County, Mass. Militia and Member of Roxbury, Mass., Com. of Correspondence; great²-grandson of David and Sarah (Davis) Weld; great³-grandson of

Aaron Davis, Colonel, Suffolk County, Mass. Militia, Member Mass. Provincial Congress, General Court, and Committee of Correspondence; grandson of Nathaniel and Abby Richardson (Gardner) Gage; great-grandson of Stephen Partridge and Achsah (Moore) Gardner; great²-grandson of *Aaron Gardner*, Captain and Major, Middlesex County, Mass. Militia; great-grandson of Nathaniel and Betsy (Kimball) Gage; great²-grandson of *Nathaniel Gage*, Captain, Essex County, Mass. Militia and Member local War Committees; great²-grandson of *Daniel Kimball, Jr.*, Selectman and Member of Bradford, Mass., War Committees; great²-grandson of Daniel and Elizabeth (Tenney) Kimball, Jr.; great²-grandson of *John Tenney*, Lieutenant, Col. Timothy Pickering, Jr.'s Regt., Mass. Militia; great²-grandson of *Josiah Moore*, private, Col. John Whitcomb's Regt., Mass. Militia at Lexington Alarm.

CROSBY A. PERRY, Pittsfield, Mass. (36809). Son of *Micah Perry*, private, Capt. James Berry's Co., Col. Thomas Poor's Regt., Mass. Militia, pensioned.

JUSTUS HOLMES PERSHING, Greensburg, Penna. (37086). Son of Isaac and Frances (Truxell) Pershing; grandson of Daniel and Christina (Milliron) Pershing; great-grandson of *Frederick Pershing*, private, Penna. "Frontier Rangers."

FRANK ANDREW PETTIT, Byron, Ill. (36636). Son of Gilbert Wick and Ella (Banist r) Pettit; grandson of Francis M. and Mary (Stanhope) Banister; great-grandson of Hiram S. and Lovina (Bliss) Stanhope; great²-grandson of Joseph and Zibiah (Nutting) Stanhope; great³-grandson of *Joseph Stanhope*, private, Hampshire County, Mass. Militia; great²-grandson of Porter and Lucinda (Lamb) Bliss; great³-grandson of David and Polly (Elmore) Bliss; great⁴-grandson of *David Bliss*, private, Col. Joseph Marsh's Regt., Vermont Militia; great³-grandson of *Joseph Lamb*, private, Mass. Cont'l Troops.

HARRY PERCY PHILLIPS, Mahnomen, Minn. (35695). Son of Oliver H. and Marietta (Walkup) Phillips; grandson of Israel and Fidelia (Goodale) Phillips; great-grandson of *Samuel Phillips, Jr.*, private, Bristol County, Mass. Militia.

LIONEL FELIX PHILLIPS, Livingston, N. J. (36863). Son of Morton and Carrie Josephine (Wittman) Liebschutz; grandson of Felix and Fanny (Levy) Liebschutz; great-grandson of Morton and Rebecca (Phillips) Levy; great²-grandson of Michael and Rachel (Phillips) Levy; great³-grandson of *Jonas Phillips*, private, Col. William Bradford's Battalion, Philadelphia Militia.

ARTHUR SOUTHARD PIERSON, Sansalito Calif. (36420). Son of Edgar Le Bar and Anna Burnett (Southard) Pierson; grandson of James Washington and Sarah Ann (Peshine) Southard; great-grandson of Gilbert and Anna (Wey) Southard; great²-grandson of *Thomas Southard*, private, Second Regt., Dutchess County, New York Militia.

JAMES TOPPING PIERSON, Glen Ridge, N. J. (36859). Son of James Willis and Cornelia (Dodge) Pierson; grandson of James Topping and Catherine (Clark) Pierson; great-grandson of Squire and Abigail (Marsh) Pierson; great²-grandson of Squire and Nancy (De Camp) Pierson; great³-grandson of *David Pierson*, private, Essex County, New Jersey Militia.

HERBERT EUSEBIUS PILGRAM, Pittsburgh, Penna. (37076). Son of Frederick and Elizabeth Hester (Moore) Pilgram; grandson of William and Mary Ann (Doll) Moore; great-grandson of Conrad and Maria Magdalena (Graff) Doll; great²-grandson of *Andrew Graff*, Captain and Quartermaster, Lancaster County, Penna. Militia, Member Committee of Observation and Delegate to "Associator's" Conference.

BARD BURGE PLUMMER, Milton, N. H. (36260). Son of Bard B. and Eliza D. (Wentworth) Plummer; grandson of Enoch W. and Orinda (Ayres) Plummer; great-grandson of Joseph and Sally (Brown) Plummer; great²-grandson of *Beard Plummer*, priva.e, Milton, New Hampshire Militia.

JOSEPH LYM PLUMMER, Milton, N. H. (36261). Son of Moses B. and Elizabeth J. (Hussey) Plummer; grandson of Joseph and Adaline F. (Baker) Plummer; great-grandson of Joseph and Sally (Brown) Plummer; great²-grandson of *Beard Plummer*, private, Milton, New Hampshire Militia.

JULIAN ADDISON POLLARD, Omaha, Nebr. (36980). Son of James Addison and Josephine (Hall) Pollard; grandson of Moses and Abigail (Boynton) Pollard; great-grandson of *Joseph Pollard*, private and Corporal, New Ipswich, New Hampshire Militia.

FRANK POPE, Evanston, Ill. (37203). Son of William and Cornelia Rochester (Waring) Pope; grandson of Perry and Hannah (Webster) Pope; great-grandson of Benjamin and Margaret (Foster) Pope; great²-grandson of Richard and Innocent (Head) Pope; great³-grandson of *Seth Pope*, Colonel for Bristol County, Mass. Militia.

HENRY POPE, Chicago, Ill. (37202). Same as Frank Pope, Evanston, Ill. (37203).

WINFIELD SCOTT PRICE, Camden, N. J. (36868). Son of Joseph Collins and Anna Rebecca (Chew) Price; grandson of Arthur H. and Rebecca C. (Swift) Chew; great-grandson of Andrew and Rebecca (Cattell) Chew; great²-grandson of *Jonas Cattell*, private, Gloucester County, New Jersey Militia and State Troops, pensioned.

HARRY H. PRITCHARD, Bridgeport, Conn. (36724). Son of Henry Hall and Mary Swan) Pritchard; grandson of Samuel Holland and Jannet (Hall) Pritchard; great-grandson of David and Anna (Hitchcock) Pritchard; great²-grandson of Benjamin and Eunice (Hotchkiss) Hitchcock; great³-grandson of *Benjamin Hitchcock*, private, Tenth Regt., Conn. Militia.

FRANK S. PRUDEN, Dalten, Ga. (36826). Son of William Henry and Susan (Smith) Pruden; grandson of Joseph and Nancy (Strong) Pruden; great-grandson of *Newton Prudden*, Corporal, Col. Joseph Thompson's Regt., Conn. Militia.

ISRAEL LOUIS PUTNAM, Grass Range, Mont. (31786). Son of Henry Clay and Amanda (Webster) Putnam; grandson of Lewis John Pope and Eliza (Kidwell) Putnam; great-grandson of Israel Putnam, Jr.; great²-grandson of *Israel Putnam*, Major-General, Cont'l Army, 1777-'81 .

ROBERT CARLYLE RECK, Minneapolis, Minn. (35696). Son of Robert Harrison and Nellie Emolyn (Pauley) Reck; grandson of James S. and Ella D. (Chappell) Pauley; great-grandson of Chester B. and Fannie (Allen) Chappel; great²grandson of Ransford and Rachel (Babcock) Allen; great³-grandson of *Nathaniel Babcock*, private, Capt. Black's Co., Colonel Moseley's Regt., Mass. Troops.

LYMAN C. REED, Morgan City, La. (36953). Son of Warren Bettison and Grace (Gardner) Reed; grandson of Lyman Coleman and Kate (Bettison) Reed; great-grandson of Warren Atherton and Louisa (Lyman) Reed; great²-grandson of Warren and Mary (Atherton) Reed; great³grandson of *Benjamin Reed*, Corporal, Colonel Carey's and Colonel Sproal's Regts., Mass. Militia, pensioned.

STANLEY FORMAN REED, Kentucky (34715). Suplementals. Son of John and Frances (Forman) Reed; grandson of Samuel and Ann Frances (Soward) Forman; great-grandson of Alfred and Elizabeth (Chiles) Soward; great-grandson of David and Frances (Craig) Chiles; great³-grandson of *Lewis Craig*, Virginia volunteer defender of Bryant Station; great³-grandson of Lewis and *Elizabeth Sanders Craig*, patriot who carried water to Bryant Station during attack; great⁴-grandson of Tolliver and *Polly Hawkins Craig*, Virginia patriot who assisted in defense of Byrant Station.

WILLIAM PHELPS REED, Illinois (17306). Supplemental. Son of William and Marie Dening (Hawley) Reed; grandson of Nelson and Elizabeth Phelps (Swearingen) Hawley; great-grandson of *Amos Hawley*, private, Captain Galusha's Co., Vermont Militia.

LUTELLUS LINDLEY ROBBINS, McKeesport, Penna. (36775). Son of William N. and Flavia Clarissa (Woods) Robbins; grandson of Moses and Rebecca (Woods) Robbins; great-grandson of *Brintinel Robins*, Ensign, Westmoreland County, Penna. Militia, pensioned.

WILLIAM HOSLER RHOADES, Toledo, Ohio (37028). Son of Edward Henry and Maude (Hosler) Rhoades, Jr.; grandson of Edward Henry and Hannah Sophia (——) Rhoades; great-grandson of Lewis Hunt and Rachel Parsons (Williams) Rhoades; great²-grandson of *Samuel Rhoades*, Captain, Mass. Militia.

EDWIN JAMES RHODES, Estherville, Iowa (36907). Son of Franklin Henry and Hattie (Culver) Rhodes; grandson of Levi Merryman and Amelie (Lillie) Culver; great-grandson of Abram and Polly (Spears) Lillie; great²-grandson of Henry and Aminta (Williams) Lillie; great³-grandson of *David Lillie*, Ensign, Col. Charles Webb's Regt., Conn. Cont'l Troops.

CHARLES W. RHULE, Wickes, Montana (31787.) Son of William and Delilah (Cree) Rhule; grandson of Samuel Power and Ann (Brandt) Cree; great-grandson of Daniel and Elizabeth (Waggoner) Brandt; great²-grandson of *John Wagonner*, Sergeant, First Battalion, Cumberland County, Penna. Militia.

LINVILLE WADSWORTH ROBBINS, Stoughton, Mass. (37117). Son of Edward Everett and L. Augusta (Gatchell) Robbins; grandson of Charles Averson and Mary (Edgecomb) Robbins; great-grandson of Charles Robbins; great²grandson of *Luther Robbins,* Quartermaster Sergeant, Plymouth County, Mass. Militia.

HEWITT GRIGGS ROBERTSON, Washington, D. C. (36143). Son of William Turner and Kate Paulina (Griggs) Robertson; grandson of Clark Hewitt and Sarah Smith (Nicholls) Griggs; great-grandson of Isaac Smith and Johanna Maria (Rind) Nicholls; great²-grandson of *William Nicholls,* Lieutenant, Maryland Militia.

STANLEY BARNES ROBERTSON, Detroit, Mich. (36042). Son of Harley Dayton and Nellie Gertrude (Barnes) Robertson; grandson of Nathaniel Harrison and Sarah Elizabeth (Ladd) Barnes; great-grandson of Nathaniel and Levina (Forbush) Barnes; great²-grandson of Jonathan and Betsey (Hayden) Forbush; great²-grandson of *David Forbush,* private, Col. Artemus Ward's Regt., Mass. Militia, Member Committee of Safety.

TOM HOWARD ROBERTSON, Detroit, Mich. (36043). Same as Stanley Barnes Robertson, Michigan (36042).

EDWIN WALTEN ROBINSON, Atlanta, Ga. (36827). Son of Robert Edwin and Estelle (Walton) Robinson; grandson of John Evans and Isadore (Burch) Robinson; great-grandson of John Evans and Sarah Ann (Ramley) Robinson; great²-grandson of *Randall Robinson,* private, Captain Water's Co., South Carolina Troops.

RAMEAL DUDLEY ROBINSON, Toledo, Ohio (36498). Son of Elihu Douglas and Emily F. (Hoyt) Robinson; grandson of Phineas Chapman and Lula Mareer (Elliot) Robinson; great-grandson of Simeon and Lucy (Putnam) Elliott; great²-grandson of *David Putnam,* Second Lieutenant, Third Regt., Mass. Cont'l Artillery.

ALLEN HIGGINS RODES, El Paso, Tex. (36329). Son of William and Mary Ford (Higgins) Rodes; grandson of Joseph Waller and Sarah Evans (Marshall) Rodes; great-grandson of Robert and Elizabeth (Evans) Marshall; great²-grandson of Richard and Sarah (Pulliam) Evans; great²-grandson of *Peter Evans,* Captain, Colonel Wheedon's Regt., Prince William County, Virginia Militia.

AMBROSE WHITNEY ROSE, Huntington, N. Y. (36474). Son of Jeremiah Clark and Jane Frances (Millikin) Rose; grandson of Archibald and Mary Otis (Rose) Millikin; great-grandson of Archibald and Hannah (Rathbun) Millikin; great²-grandson of Walter and Hannah (Rose) Rathbun; great²-grandson of *Samuel Rathbun, Jr.,* Lieutenant, Rhode Island Militia.

GEORGE RUPLEY, Minnesota (25303). Supplemental. Son of George Gilbert and Wilhelmina (Baxter) Rupley; grandson of Simon and Sarah (Gilbert) Rupley; great-grandson of George and Elizabeth (Ritter) Knouse Gilbert; great²-grandson of *Casper Ritter,* private and "Clarck," Second Battalion, Northampton County, Penna. Militia.

ARTHUR MERRIAM ROWLEY, Springfield, Mass. (37112). Son of H. Curtis and Thirza J. (Merriam) (Rowley; grandson of Warren Dunham and Harriet M. (Curry) Rowley; great-grandson of Asher and Mehitable (Dunham) Rowley; great²-grandson of *Jonathan Dunham,* Corporal, Col. Jonathan Latimer's Regt., Conn. Militia.

GUY MONSLAVE RYDER, Newark, N. J. (36856). Son of Henry Wines and Laura Evangeline (Bown) Ryder; grandson of William Seddon and Laura Ann (Mount) Bown; great-grandson of James Roosevelt and Laura Johanna (——) Mount; great²-grandson of *Adam Dobbs Mount,* private, Second Regt., New Jersey Artillery, Cont'l Troops.

AUGUSTUS HAWS SANDS, New York City, N. Y. (36883). Son of Augustus Hewlett and Charlotte E. (Haws) Sands; grandson of Augustus Hewlett and Ann Amelia (Brooks) Sands; great-grandson of John and Jane (Hewlett) Sands; great²-grandson of *John Sands,* Colonel, Second Regt., Queens County, New York Militia.

JOHN KUHN SCOTT, Pittsburgh, Penna. (37077). Son of James Herron and Frances Ramsay (Kuhn) Scott; grandson of James Smith and Mary (Cubbage) Scott; great-grandson of Josiah and Jane (Darragh) Scott; great²-grandson of *Hugh Scott,* Major, Second Battalion, Washington County, Penna. Militia.

PHILIP BOYER SCOTT, New York City, N. Y. (36880). Son of Edwin Livingston and Lotta Marie (Person) Scott; grandson of Abram McLean and Julia Ann (Boyer) Scott; grandson of *Hugh Scott, Jr.,* private, Second Battalion, Washington County, Penna. Militia; great²grandson of *Hugh Scott,* Major, Second Battalion, Washington County, Penna. Militia.

CHARLES KEEN SEAMAN, JR., Perth Amboy, N. J. (37022). Son of Charles Keen and Mary Frances Seaman; grandson of Anthony and Ann (Hadden) Seaman; great-grandson of Jacob and Sally (Ayres) Hadden; great²-grandson of *Thomas Hadden, Jr.*, private, First Regt., Middlesex County, New Jersey Militia; great²-grandson of *Thomas Hadden*, Lieutenant-Colonel, First Regt., Middlesex County, New Jersey Militia; great-grandson of Henry and Isabel (Hansell) Seaman; great²-grandson of *Anthony Hansell*, private, Second Regt., Middlesex County, New Jersey Militia.

EDWARD JAY SEEBER, New York (36200). Supplementals. Son of Jacob and Lavina (Copperwell) Seeber; grandson of James and Nancy (Strayer) Copperwell; great-grandson of John and Margaret (Diefendorf) Strayer; great²-grandson of *John Strayer*, private, Tryon County, New York Militia; grandson of Abram and Nancy (Young) Seeber; great-grandson of Adolph and Sally (Yates) Seeber; great²-grandson of *Christopher P. Yates*, Lieutenant-Colonel, Tryon County, New York Militia; Quartermaster General, Member Committee of Safety and of Provincial Congress.

FRED LOVING SEELY, Asheville, N. C. (N. J. 36867). Son of Uriah and Nancy (Hopping) Seely; grandson of James and Amanda (Mason) Seely; great-grandson of *John Seely*, private, New Jersey Militia, State and Cont'l Troops.

WALTER HOFF SEELY, Pleasantville, N. Y. (N. J. 36855). Son of Uriah and Nancy (Hopping) Seely; grandson of James and Amanda (Mason) Seely; great-grandson of *John Seely*, private, New Jersey Militia, State and Cont'l Troops.

BURTON ALEXANDER SELLEW, Hartford, Conn. (36725). Son of De Forest and Annie J. (Thuer) Sellew; grandson of Horace B. and Eliza A. (Treat) Sellew; great-grandson of Russel and Polly (Loveland) Sellew; great²-grandson of *Phillip Sellew*, Member Committee on Purchasing Clothing for Cont'l Army, Collector of State Tax and Representative to Conn. General Assembly.

HARRY CLARK SHEDD, Brooklyn, N. Y. (36897). Son of George F. and Eugenia I. (——) Shedd; grandson of George F. and Lucinda (——) Shedd; great-grandson of Jeptha and Fanny (——) Shedd; great²-grandson of *Oliver Shedd*, private, Col. Jonathan Reed's Regt., Mass. Militia.

ALEXANDER HAMILTON SHERMAN, JR., Brooklyn, N. Y. (36894). Son of Alexander Hamilton and Isabelle (Newkirk) Sherman; grandson of Hamilet Bodine and Emma Virginia (Harrington) Newkirk; great-grandson of Daniel and Rachel (Christ) Newkirk; great²-grandson of Adam and Amietje (Hannah) (Shafer) Newkirk; great³-grandson of Adam and Magdelina (Grinberg) Newkirk; great⁴-grandson of *John Newkirk*, Captain, Second Regt., Ulster County, New York Militia.

TIMOTHY WALLACE SHERWOOD, Ind. (35512). Supplemental. Son of Thomas Russell and Anna Maria (Wallace) Sherwood; grandson of Timothy and Olive (Sherman) Wallace; great-grandson of Nathan and Mary (Carpenter) Sherman; great²-grandson of *George Sherman*, Sergeant and Corporal, Berkshire County, Mass. Militia; great³-grandson of *George Sherman*, Captain, Colonel Stafford's Independent Company, Mass. Volunteers; great-grandson of Ebenezer and Anna (Snow) Wallace; great²-grandson of *Silas Snow*, Second Lieutenant, Eighth Regt., Worcester County, Mass. Militia.

CHARLES SHEWMON, Kokomo, Ind. (36437). Son of Joseph and Mary M. (Shaffer) Shewmon; grandson of Benjamin and Elizabeth Ann (Huff) Shaffer; great-grandson of *Frederick Shaffer*, private, Colonel Campbell's Company, Virginia Militia.

ABEL VAIL SHOTWELL, Omaha, Nebr. (36983). Son of Hudson Burr and Emma Jane (Noe) Shotwell; grandson of George Tharp and Sarah Jane (Doty) Noe; great-grandson of John and Elizabeth (Ustick) Doty; great²-grandson of *John* and Esther (Hunt) *Doty*, 2d., private, First Battalion, Somerset County, New Jersey Militia; great²-grandson of *John Doty*, private, First Battalion, Somerset County, New Jersey Militia; grandson of Edward Randolph and Margaret (Hart) Shotwell; great-grandson of Peter and Phoebe (Vail) Shotwell; great²-grandson of *Isaiah* and Constant (Lippincott) *Shotwell*, Quaker who aided by contributions of money; great³-grandson of *John Shotwell*, Quaker who assisted by contributing money.

FRANKLIN ALBERT SHOTWELL, Omaha, Nebr. (36982). Same as Abel Vail Shotwell, Nebraska (36983).

FREDERICK WILLIAM SHOTWELL, Omaha, Nebr. (36985). Same as Abel Vail Shotwell, Nebraska (36983).

ROSS LEE SHOTWELL, Omaha, Nebr. (36984). Same as Abel Vail Shotwell, Nebraska (36983).

WILLIAM H. SHULZ, Grand Forks, N. Dak. (36940). Son of Charles E. and Margaret (Gregg) Shulz; grandson of Israel and Roxcey (Olds) Gregg; great-grandson of Joseph and Sally (Whitney) Olds; great²-grandson of *Benjamin Olds*, private, Hampshire County, Mass. Militia.

CHARLES SANDFORD SKILTON, Lawrence, Kans. (36731). Son of Otis Avery and Adeline (Sanford) Skilton; grandson of Henry and Maria (Marshall) Skilton; great-grandson of Avery and Parthenia (Judd) Skilton; great²-grandson of *Henry Skilton*, Physician Mass. Militia.

ARTHUR WHITMORE SMITH, Ann Arbor, Mich. (36044). Son of Francis Egerton and Eliza Ann (Currier) Smith; grandson of Ambrose and Cynthia Maria (Egerton) Smith; great-grandson of Ariel and Abigail Proctor (Keyes) Egerton; great²-grandson of *Ariel Egerton*, private, Conn. Militia, pensioned.

EDWARD JOHN SMITH, Prospect Heights, Ill. (37204). Son of Clark Cicero and Melissa (Robinson) Smith; grandson of James and Harriet (Goodrich) Smith; great-grandson of John I. and Katherine (McLeod) Smith; great²-grandson of *John Smith*, private, First Regt., New Jersey Cont'l Line.

FRANK HILL SMITH, Washington, D. C. (36144). Son of James Rembert and Elizabeth (Crafton) Smith; grandson of *Isaac Smith*, private, Williamsburg County, Virginia Militia and Cont'l Troops, pensioned.

GEORGE HOLCOMBE SMITH, Pittsburgh, Penna. (36762). Son of Clark McDowell and Leona (Holcombe) Smith; grandson of George Augustus and Fidelia Clairbel (Dobson) Smith; great-grandson of Thomas Davenport and Rachel (Lockey) Barnet (Marsh) Smith; great²-grandson of Frances (Fanny) (Morse) Marsh; great³-grandson of *Amos Morse*, Lieutenant and Captain, First Regt., Essex County, New Jersey Militia; great⁴-grandson of Amos and Frances (Clark) Morse; great⁴-grandson of *Abraham Clark*, New Jersey Signer of the Declaration of Independence.

JOHNSON SCHOLL BRUNER SMITH, San Francisco, Calif. (36425). Son of D. Sidney T. and Mary Elizabeth (Bruner) Smith; grandson of Andrew and Mary (Weaver) Smith; great-grandson of *Michael Smith*, Drummer, Third, Fourth, and Fifth Regts., Maryland Militia.

WILLIAM EMERSON SMITH, Fairfield, Conn. (37301). Son of Edwin Banks and Catherine (Remer) Smith; grandson of Edmund Banks and Julia Burr (Craft) Smith; great-grandson of John Lockwood and Jane (Banks) Smith; great²-grandson of *Joseph Banks*, private and Sergeant, Conn. Militia, pensioned.

HAROLD ALFRED SONN, Newark, N. J. (36864). Son of George C. and Ada (Dusenberry) Sonn; grandson of Benjamin Fritts and Elizabeth (Probasco) Honness; great-grandson of Michael and Elizabeth (Fritts) Honness; great²-grandson of George and Martha (Beavers) Fritts; great³-grandson of *Joseph Beavers*, Colonel, Second Regt., Hunterdon County, New York Militia.

JAMES KNOX SPANGLER, McKeesport, Penna. (36760). Son of Louis and Polly (Shank) Spangler; grandson of Abraham and Margaret (Stoy) Spangler; great-grandson of *Daniel Stoy*, private, Somerset County, Penna. Militia, pensioned.

DAVID GRAHAM SPINDLER, Swissvale, Penna. (37084). Son of David W. and Mary A. (Wilkinson) Spindler; grandson of William and Catherine (Richie) Spindler; great-grandson of Jacob and Liddie (Friend) Spindler; great²-grandson of *Tobias Friend*, private, Washington County, Penna. Militia.

ORA MORRIS SPINK, Painesville, Ohio (37031). Son of Albert M. and Mary Ann (Hemens) Spink; grandson of Elijah and Wilhelmina (Vincent) Spink; great-grandson of —— and Cynthia (Castor) Spink; great²-grandson of *John Casterer (Castor)*, Ensign, Colonel McNistry's and Colonel Hogeboone's Regts., New York Militia, pensioned.

FRED SPINNING, JR., Baltimore, Md. (N. J. 37013). Son of Frederick (Meeker) and Anna (J——) Spinning; grandson of Benjamin and Sarah Ann (Meeker) Spinning; great-grandson of John and Phoebe (Winters) Spinning; great²-grandson of Benjamin and Charity (Garthwait) Spinning; great³-grandson of *Benjamin Spinning*, private, Essex County, New Jersey Militia.

FREDERICK ALONZO STEBBINS, Coudersport, Penna. (37079). Son of Charles Alonzo and Rebecca Ann (Glassmire) Stebbins; grandson of Pierre Alonzo and Almira (Brundage) Stebbins; great-grandson of Lewis and Sarah (Delevan) Stebbins; great^2-grandson of *Nehemiah Stebbins*, private, Second Regt., Weschester County, New York Militia.

WILLIAM CLYDE STEBBINS, Grand Forks, N. Dak. (36931). Son of John and Ida M. (Brokaw) Stebbins; grandson of Dwight and Rosina (Freeland) Stebbins; great-grandson of Consider and Esther (Farnsworth) Stebbins; great^2-grandson of *Gershom Farnsworth*, Coporal, Col. Samuel William's Mass. Regt. at Lexington Alarm; grandson of William Custard and Haty Braw (Myers) Brokaw; great-grandson of William and Agnes (Gilcrest) Brokaw; great^2-grandson of *George Brokaw*, private, Somerset County, New Jersey Militia.

CHARLES McCLARY STEELE, Epsom, N. H. (36254). Son of Charles A. and Hannah P. (Cilley) Swain Steele; grandson of Samuel P. and Hannah W. (Critchett) Cilley; great-grandson of Daniel and Hannah (Plummer) Cilley; great^2-grandson grandson of *Joseph Cilley*, Member New Hampshire Committee of Safety and Colonel, First Regt., New Hampshire Militia; grandson of Jonathan and Elizabeth H. (McClary) Steele; great-grandson of *Michael McClary*, Member New Hampshire Committee of Safety and Captain, Fifth Co., Third Battalion, New Hampshire Troops.

FRANK FLETCHER STEPHENS, Columbia, Mo. (35565). Son of Thomas White and Mary E. (Tyler) Stephens; grandson of George Washington and Caroline (Park) Tyler; great-grandson of *Asa Tyler*, private, Conn. Militia and Ensign, New York State Guards; grandson of John and Sarah Jane (Shultz) Stephens; great-grandson of John and Elizabeth (Dunbar) Shultz; great^2-grandson of Andrew and Deborah (Mitchell) Dunbar; great^2-grandson of *Hamilton Dunbar*, Sergeant, Virginia Cont'l Line.

BERTRAM SHEARER STEPHENSON, Detroit, Mich. (37057). Son of Hiram and Marga (Gellilard) Stephenson; grandson of John Harrison and Sarah (Shearer) Stephenson; great-grandson of Patrick and Sarah (Paine) Shearer; great^2-grandson of *David Paine*, private, Seventh Regt., Mass. Cont'l Troops.

ALBERT EDWARD STEVENS, Montclair, N. J. (37021). Son of James Coffin and Ellen (Sandford) Stevens; grandson of William Henry and Cornelia Jane (Casslaer) Stevens; great-grandson of Isaac and Rachel (——) Stevens; great^2-grandson of *Stephen A. Stevens*, private, Second Regt., Orange County, New York Militia.

DONALD BARTLETT STEVENS, Springfield, Mass. (37115). Son of Everett L. and Bessie A. (Rhodes) Stevens; grandson of Cyrus P. and Harriet N. (Bartlett) Stevens; great-grandson of David and Eunice (Marsh) Bartlett, Jr.; great^2-grandson of David and Joanna (Haseltine) Bartlett; great^3-grandson of *Edmund Bartlett*, private, Mass. Militia and Member Newburyport, Mass., Committee of Safety.

ORIN ALVA STEVENS, Fargo, N. Dak. (36926). Son of Phineas Revillo and Elsie (Johnson) Stevens; grandson of Benjamin Franklin and Olive (Dudley) Johnson; great-grandson of Caleb and Thirza (Treadway) Johnson; great^2-grandson of *Daniel Johnson*, private, Colonel Bigelow's Regt., Worcester County, Mass. Millitia.

CHARLES HARRINGTON STEWART, U. S. Army, Camp Eustis, Va. (D. C. 36140). Son of J. McDonald and Helen J. (Gooddard) Stewart; grandson of James Muir and Susan A. (Swett) Stewart; great-grandson of Samuel and Rebecca (Clark) Swett; great^2-grandson of *Greenleaf Clark*, Captain, Newburg, Mass. Militia, widow pensioned.

JOHN CARTER STEWART, Louisville, Ky. (36530). Son of Joseph Adger and Anna (Carter) Stewart; grandson of Joseph Alexander and Carrie Julia (Robinson) Stewart; great-grandson of James Hardwick and Martha Ann Elizabeth (Webb) Robinson; great^2-grandson of John and Ann (Thomason) Webb; great^3-grandson of *Francis Webb*, Midshipman, Virginia Navy; great-grandson of John Lewis and Julia Ann (Hollingsworth) Stewart; great^2-grandson of Alexander and Sarah (Striplin) Stewart; great^3-grandson of *Alexander Stewart*, private, South Carolina Militia; grandson of John Allen and Albana Caroline (Carson) Carter; great-grandson of Caswell and Levinnia (Jones) Carter; great^2-grandson of Allen and Jane (McClanahan) Jones; great^2-grandson of *Thomas McClanahan*, private, Virginia Cont'l Troops and Colonel Boylor's Cavalry.

JOSEPH ADGER STEWART, Kentucky (13326). Supplemental. Son of Joseph Alexander and Carrie Julia (Robinson) Stewart; grandson of John Lewis and Julia Ann (Hollingsworth) Stewart; great-grandson of Alexander and Sarah (Striplin) Stewart; great²-grandson of *Alexander Stewart*, private, South Carolina Militia.

WALDRON EARLE STEWART, Adrian, Mich. (37058). Son of Francis M. and Elizabeth M. (Henry) Stewart; grandson of Simon J. and Almira B. (Whipple) Henry; great-grandson of Wesley and Elvira (Hudson) Whipple; great²-grandson of *Jonathan Whipple*, private, Mass. Militia.

HENRY HOWARD STILES, Altoona, Penna. (36330). Son of William and Margaret (Dickehut) Lyford Stiles; grandson of Henry Frederick and Margaret Mitchell (Lyford) Dickehut; great-grandson of William Gilman and Margaret (Mitchell) Lyford; great²-grandson of *Francis Lyford*, private, Col. Stephen Evan's Regt., New Hampshire Militia.

CHARLES HENRY STINAFF, Akron, Ohio (37027). Son of Charles Henry and Vernie Estelle (Smith) Stinaff; grandson of Henry William and Lydia (Button) Stinaff; great-grandson of William and Sally (Babcock) Stinaff; great²-grandson of Perry H. and Cynthia (Hiscox) Babcock; great²-grandson of *Jonathan Babcock*, Member Rhode Island "Sons of Liberty," erecting "Liberty Pole" on his premises.

JOHN ESCHER STOLL, Chicago, Ill. (36645). Son of John Jacob and Eva (Escher) Stoll; grandson of Martin E. and Louise Ellen (Mertz) Escher; great-grandson of Solomon and Lucy Ann (Butts) Mertz; great²-grandson of Henry and Hannah (Dorney) Mertz; great³-grandson of *George Henry Mertz*, private, Second Battalion, Northampton County, Penna. Militia.

HARRIS GARY STOWE, Grafton, Mass. (37110). Son of Silas Edward and Lucy Arminda (Gary) Stowe; grandson of Jonathan Warren and Mary (Hunt) Stow; great-grandson of Jonathan and Elizabeth (Eames) Stow, Jr.; great²-grandson of *Jonathan Stow*, Lieutenant, Col. Abijah Stearn's Regt., Mass. Militia.

RAYMOND THOMAS STOWE, Elizabeth, N. J. (36698). Son of Joseph Albert and Minnie Carolyn (Thomas) Stowe; grandson of Joseph Fulton and Mary Ann (Handy) Stowe; great-grandson of Asa and Mary (Wheaton) Handy; great²-grandson of *Ebenezer Handy*, Corporal and Sergeant, Col. Christopher Lippett's Regt. Rhode Island Militia, pensioned.

HENRY LEWIS STREETER, Boise, Idaho (35111). Son of William H. and Alice Margaret (Lewis) Streeter, Jr.; grandson of Richard and Sarah Delia (Perkins) Lewis; great-grandson of Ralph Cranby and Polly (Gaines) Perkins; great²-grandson of Roger and Betsy (Candee) Perkins; great³-grandson of *Ithial Perkins*, private, Conn. Militia, wounded.

HARVEY DOUGLAS STURGES, Neawrk, N. J. (37139). Son of Joseph Gordon and Anna Adele (Taylor) Sturges; grandson of Joseph Halsey and Jane Eliza (Jillson) Sturges; great-grandson of Thompson and Abby (Halsey) Sturges; great²-grandson of *John Halsey*, private, Morris County, New Jersey Militia and Cont'l Troops, 7 years' service.

EVERETT NOYES SULLIVAN, Dolliver, Iowa (36910) Son of Charles E. and Louie (Rackliffe) Sullivan; grandson of Eli N. and Mary (Neal) Rackliffe; great-grandson of Benjamin and Rachel (Oliver) Rackliffe; great²-grandson of *John Oliver*, private, Twelfth Regt., Mass. Militia.

FRANK FOSTER SUMNEY, Dravosburg, Penna. (37091). Son of Isaac and Elizabeth (Foster) Sumney; grandson of David and Nancy (Hand) Sumney; great-grandson of Isaac and Magdelena (Turney) Sumney; great²-grandson of *Jacob Sumney*, private, Fifth and Tenth Battalions, Penna. Troops.

FREDERICK AUGUSTUS SWANBERG, San Francisco, Calif. (36421). Son of Charles Olaf and Ione Sophia (Wirt) Swanberg; grandson of Augustus Cæsar and Susan Marie (Kimball) Wirt; great-grandson of Nathan S. and Harriet (Sanborn) Kimball; great²-grandson of Josiah and Sally (Shepherd) Sanborn, Jr.; great³-grandson of *Josiah Sanborn*, Lieutenant, New Hampshire Militia.

CHARLES BRADFORD SYLVESTER, Portland, Me. (36591). Son of Samuel C. and Rebecca B. (Mayberry) Sylvester; grandson of Francis and Susanna (Stuart) Mayberry; great-grandson of *William Mayberry*, Adjutant, Eleventh Regt., Mass. Militia; great²-grandson of *Richard Mayberry*, Captain, Eleventh Regt., Mass. Militia.

RICHARD SYLVESTER, Wilmington, Del. (35668). Son of Richard and Martha (Woods) Sylvester; grandson of Henry H. and Elizabeth (Hubbard) Sylvester; great-grandson of Ezra and Hannah (Henry) Sylvester; great²-grandson of *Peter Sylvester*, private, Mass. Militia, killed at Fort Stanwix.

MARSTIN EDGAR TALLANT, Minneapolis, Minn. (37226). Son of Frank Edgar and Susan Amanda (Drew) Tallant; grandson of George Winslow and Mary Amand (Webster) Drew; great-grandson of Albert and Mary (Beard) Webster; great²-grandson of George Washington and Dorcas (Wilson) Webster; great³-grandson of *David Webster*, Colonel, New Hampshire Militia and State Troops.

WEBSTER TALLANT, Mound, Minn. (37227). Same as Marstin Edgar Tallant, Minnesota (37226).

GEORGE ALBERT TAYLOR, Boston, Mass. (37118). Son of James Truman and Helen Frances (Peters) Taylor; grandson of John Rogers and Abby (Covell) Peters; great-grandson of *Absalom Peters*, Captain, New Hampshire Militia and Aide-de-Camp to General Bailey, pensioned.

JAMES TAYLOR, Washington, D. C. (36149). Son of Milton F. and Ella R. (McNaughton) Taylor; grandson of David Young and Deborah (Ashbrook) McNaughton; great-grandson of Thomas and Rebeka (Young) McNaughton; great²-grandson of *David Young*, Matross, Colonel Harrison's Regt., Maryland Artillery.

CHARLES M. THOMPSON, Elizabeth, Penna. (36761). Son of Charles C. and Malinda (Michener) Thompson; grandson of Milton and Sarah (Morgan) Michener; great-grandson of Andrew and Elizabeth (Kinsell) Morgan; great²-grandson of William and Priscilla (——) Morgan; great³-grandson of George and Priscilla (Swearengen) Morgan; great⁴-grandson of *William Morgan*, Captain, Penna. Militia.

JOSEPH M. THRALLS, Wellington, Kans. (36730). Son of Johnson and Luvina (Davis) Thralls; grandson of Isaac and Elizabeth (Johnson) Thralls; great-grandson of *Richard Thralls*, private, Colonel Gibson's Regt., Virginia Troops, pensioned.

WARREN HARRINGTON THRALLS, Wellington, Kans. (36729). Son of Joseph M. and Fannie Katharine (Harrington) Thralls; grandson of Johnson and Luvina (Davis) Thralls; great-grandson of Isaac and Elizabeth (Johnson) Thralls; great²-grandson of *Richard Thralls*, private, Colonel Gibson's Regt., Virginia Troops, pensioned.

FLOYD R. TODD, Moline, Ill. (36642). Son of Luzerne A. and Marien D. (Rogers) Todd; grandson of Zervah and Eliza Jane (Silliman) Todd; great-grandson of Zervah and Almira (McKee) Todd; great²-grandson of *Jehiel Todd*, private, Conn. Militia, pensioned; great²-grandson of *Joseph McKee*, Sergeant, Conn. Militia at Lexington Alarm; great²-grandson of Joseph and Irene (Marsh) McKee; great²-grandson of *Daniel Marsh*, Lieutenant, Conn. Militia.

FRANK TODD, Chicago, Ill. (36643). Son of Joseph Franklin and Lois L. (Eastman) Todd; grandson of Zerah and Almira (McKee) Todd; great-grandson of *Jehiel Todd*, private, Conn. Militia, pensioned; grandson of Enos and Charity (Woodward) Eastman; great-grandson of *Enoch Eastman*, Lieutenant and Captain, New Hampshire Militia.

EARLE HERBERT TOSTEVIN, Mandan, N. Dak. (36932). Son of Edwin A. and Florence Gertrude (Clemens) Tostevin; grandson of Hosea and Abby Jane (Dodge) De Groat Clemens; great-grandson of Oliver Hazard and Temperance (Gallys) Dodge; great²-grandson of Jacob and Rebecca (Morgan) Gallup; great³-grandson of *Nathan Gallup*, Colonel, Conn. Militia.

JUDD TUMBRIDGE, Brooklyn, N. Y. (36472). Son of John William and Mary Louise (Judd) Tumbridge; grandson of Edson Amos and Katherine (Everitt) Judd; great-grandson of Amos Murray and Elizabeth Ann (Titus) Judd; great²-grandson of Eri and Rhoda (Titus) Judd; great³-grandson of Amos and Loly (Dayton) Titus; great⁴-grandson of *Michael Dayton*, Captain, Conn. Militia; great²-grandson of Joseph and Polly (West) Titus, Jr.; great³-grandson of *Joseph Titus*, private, Conn. Militia, pensioned; great-grandson of Abraham Brownson and Sarah Concurance (Stone) Everitt; great²-grandson of *Abner Everitt*, private, Colonel Moseley's and Colonel Canfield's Regts., Conn. Militia, pensioned; great²-grandson of Hervey and Sarah (Castle) Judd; great⁴-grandson of *Noah Judd*, private, Conn. Militia.

JAY TURLEY, Turley, N. Mex. (30097). Son of Jacob Omner and Louisa Ann (Woodhouse) Turley; grandson of Theodore and Ruth Jane (Giles) Turley; great-grandson of *Samuel Giles*, Chief-Gunner, Captain Fettyplace's Co., Mass. Seacoast Defense, and Pilot on ship "Tartar."

WALTER GUY TURLEY, Santa Fe, N. Mex. (30098). Son of Jacob Omner and Louisa Ann (Woodhouse) Turley; grandson of Theodore and Ruth Jane (Giles) Turley; great-grandson of *Samuel Giles*, Chief-Gunner, Captain Fettyplace's Co., Mass. Seacoast Defense and Pilot on ship "Tartar."

HARRY HORTON TUTTLE, Grand Forks, N. Dak. (36937). Son of Myron W. and Emily (Race) Tuttle; grandson of Charles and Caroline (Griswold) Tuttle; great-grandson of David and Sarah (Richards) Tuttle; great^2-grandson of John and Abigail (Olmstead) Richards, Jr.; great^2-grandson of *John Richards*, private, Ninth Regt., Conn. Militia.

CHARLES WILLIS TYLER, Laconia, N. H. (36259). Son of Charles and Lucy Farrer (Russell) Tyler; grandson of Gideon G. and Sarah (Plant) Russell; great-grandson of *Aquilla Russell*, private, Col. Paul Dudley Sargent's Regt., Mass. Militia.

ARTHUR PALMER VAN HORN, San Antonio, Tex. (36328). Son of John Hastings and Ella (Palmer) Van Horn; grandson of James Devine and Sarah Jane (Taylor) Van Horn; great-grandson of John and Thirza (Hastings) Van Horn; great^2-grandson of *Isaiah Van Horn*, Lieutenant, Fourth Battalion, Bucks County, Penna. Militia; great^2-grandson of *Henry Van Horn*, Captain, Bucks County, Penna. Militia.

JOSIAH ALEXANDER VAN ORSDEL, District of Columbia (35585). Supplemental. Son of Ralph Lashiel and Margaret (Randolph) Van Orsdel; grandson of Job and Sarah M. (Morton) Fitz Randolph; great-grandson of John and Elizabeth (Vance) (Fitz) Randolph; great^2-grandson of *William Vance*, private, Penna. Militia and Cont'l Troops.

HORACE SILLIMAN VAN VOAST, JR., Schenectady, N. Y. (36475). Son of Horace S. and Mary Wakeman (Salter) Van Voast; grandson of Albert and Mary (Vedder) Van Voast; great-grandson of Albert and Maria (Benson) Van Voast; great^2-grandson of Joachim and Neeltje (Vedder) Van Voast; great^3-grandson of *Johannes Jacobus Van Vorst (Voast)*, Wagonmaster, First Regt., New York Cont'l Line, pensioned.

LESLIE CASPER VAN WOERT, Athens, N. Y. (36876). Son of Edward N. and Mary F. (Spoor) Van Woert; grandson of Edward and Helena (Spoor) Van Woert; great-grandson of Nicholas I. and Rebecca (Warner) Van Woert; great^2-grandson of Isaac and Hannah (Bunt) Van Woert; great^3-grandson of Nicholas and Mary (Staats) Van Woert; great^4-grandson of *Jacob R. Van Woert*, private, Third Regt., Albany County, New York Militia.

JOHN WESLEY VAUGHAN, Washington, D. C. (36142). Son of William Ellegood and Mary Idalene (Johnson) Vaughan; grandson of William Ellegood and Claudia (Morris) Vaughan; great-grandson of Thomas and Claudia (Ellegood) Vaughan; great^2-grandson of William and Sarah G. (Matthews) Ellegood; great^3-grandson of *Thomas Matthews*, Lieutenant-Colonel, Virginia Militia.

WILLIAM LIPPINCOTT WADDELL, Minneapolis, Minn. (35701). Son of Charles William and Lucie (Harris) Waddell; grandson of Ephriam Eddy and Ester Jane (Grayum) Waddell; great-grandson of William and Eliza (Eddy) Waddell, Jr.; great^2-grandson of Nathan and Rebecca (Safford) Eddy, Jr.; great^3-grandson of *Nathan Eddy*, private, Col. Ebenezer Sproat's Regt., Mass. Militia.

HALSTED H. WAINWRIGHT, Manasquan, N. J. (37130). Son of Halsted and Elizabeth (Bedle) Wainwright; grandson of Halsted H. and Catherine (Little) Wainwright; great-grandson of Halsted and Catherine (Buck) Wainwright; great^2-grandson of *Thomas Wainwright*, Captain, Third Regt., Monmouth County, New Jersey Militia, prisoner on prison ship "Jersey."

BENJAMIN TAYLOR WALDO, New Orleans, La. (36954). Son of James Curtis and Margaret Mary (Woods) Waldo; grandson of James Elliott and Eveline Almira (Cobb) Waldo; great-grandson of Shubael and Rebeckah (Crosby) Waldo; great^2-grandson of *Daniel* and Hannah (Carlton) *Waldo*, private, Colonel Bellon's Regt., New Hampshire Militia; great^2-grandson of *John Carlton*, private, Second Regt., Conn. Troops.

EDWARD HOWE WALES, Hyde Park, N. Y. (36473). Son of Salem Howe and Frances Elizabeth (Johnson) Wales; grandson of Oliver and Lucy (Tiffany) Wales; great-grandson of *Oliver Wales*, private, Conn. Militia and Member Committee on provisions for soldiers' families.

JOHN ALLEN WALKER, Brownwood, Tex. (Md. 36094). Son of John Allen and Caledonia (Pruitt) Walker; grandson of Joel and Mary (Motheral) Walker; great-grandson of Allen and Esther (McCrory) Walker; great²-grandson of *Thomas McCrory*, Captain, Ninth Regt., North Carolina Cont'l Line.

WELLINGTON JASON WALKER, Springfield, Mass. (37108). Son of Elijah and Caroline (——) Walker; grandson of Jason and Betsey (McIntosh) Walker; great-grandson of *James Walker*, Mass. Minute Man at Lexington and Bennington.

GEORGE E. WALLACE, Bismark, N. Dak. (36941). Son of William J. and Mary J. (Lightbody) Wallace; grandson of James and Marella (Wade) Lightbody; great-grandson of Joseph and Polly (Baldwin) Wade; great²-grandson of *John Baldwin*, private, Frederick County, Maryland Flying Camp.

LEW EDWARD WALLACE, San Francisco, Calif. (37251). Son of William Jasper and Sarah Eunice (Washburn) Wallace; grandson of Alfred Finney and Eunice (Maxwell) Washburn; great-grandson of Hercules M. and Sarah (Evarts) Washburn; great²-grandson of *Jonah Washburn, Jr.*, private, Middleboro, Mass. Militia; great²-grandson of *Jonah M. Washburn*, Lieutenant, Fourth Regt., Mass. Militia.

ROBERTSON SAYRE WARD, East Orange, N. J. (37145). Son of Elias Sayre and Anna Dickerson (Bonnell) Ward; grandson of Joel M. and Julia (Dickerson) Bonnell; great-grandson of Peter and Martha (Condit) Dickerson; great²-grandson of *Abner Condit*, private, Third Regt., New Jersey Cont'l Line.

TRACY BRONSON WARREN, Connecticut (7770). Supplementals. Son of David Hard and Louisa (Bronson) Warren; grandson of Adamson and Sarah M. (Hickox) Warren; great-grandson of Caleb and Ruth (Scoville) Hickox; great²-grandson of Edward and Ruth (Norton) Scoville; great³-grandson of *Edward Scoville*, Captain, Tenth Regt., Conn. Militia; grandson of William and Almira (Tyler) Bronson; great-grandson of Asahael and Esther (Upson) Bronson; great²-grandson of *James Bronson*, Captain, Conn. Militia; great-grandson of Roswell and Susannah (Easton) Tyler; great³-grandson of *James Tyler*, private, Seventh Regt., Conn. Militia.

GEORGE ARNOLD WASHBURN, Bridgeport, Conn. (37302). Son of William and Susan (Woodin) Washburn; grandson of Absalom and Charity Elizabeth (Carrigan) Washburn; great-grandson of William and Margaret (Hunt) Carrigan; great²-grandson of *Gilbert Carrigan*, private, New York Militia.

HIRAM WATSON, Peoria, Ill. (36644). Son of George and Sophia (White) Watson; grandson of *Thomas Watson*, Captain, Colonel Butler's Regt., Conn. Militia, pensioned.

HORACE GRIFFITH WEBSTER, Grand Forks, N. Dak. (36935). Son of Oscar Almeron and Lydia Maud (Griffith) Webster; grandson of Henry Milo and Adeline (Bartlett) Webster; great-grandson of Justus and Hannah (Wentworth) Webster; great²-grandson of *Constant Webster*, Lieutenant, Hampshire County, Mass. Militia.

WALTER HARVEY WEED, JR., Ensign, U. S. Navy, Connecticut (36713). Son of Walter Harvey and Helena Charlotte (Hill) Weed; grandson of Ebenezer J. and Mary Ellen (Mosman) Hill; great-grandson of Moses and Charlotte Illsley (McLellan) Hill; great²-grandson of Ebenezer and Sarah (Barlow) Hill; great³-grandson of *Ebenezer Hill*, Captain, First Co., Seventh Regt., Conn. Line.

WILLIAM HARPER WEEKS, New York City, N. Y. (37128). Son of William Thatcher and Amanda (Lury) Weeks; grandson of Hiland B. and Allura (Camp) Weeks; great-grandson of David and Cornelia (Conklin) Weeks; great²-grandson of *Andrew Weeks*, private, Albany County, New York Militia and Cont'l Line.

FREDERICK LEWIS WEIS, Rhode Island (32488). Supplementals. Son of John Peter Carl and Georgina (Lewis) Weis; grandson of Abiel Smith and Harriet Phipps (Richardson) Lewis; great-grandson of George and Harriet Newell (Phipps) Richardson; great²-grandson of William and Prudence (Burpee) Richardson; great³-grandson of *Moses Burpee*, private, Col. Josiah Whitney's Regt., Mass. Militia; great³-grandson of Benjamin and Abigail (Whitcomb) Richardson; great⁴-grandson of *John Whitcomb*, Brigadier-General, Mass. Militia.

HERBERT RUSSELL WELCH, Westfield, N. J. (37007). Son of William S. and Mary I. (Woodruff) Welch; grandson of Robert and Elizabeth (Baker) Woodruff; great-grandson of Hedges and Charlotte K. (Crane) Baker; great²-grandson of *Daniel Baker*, Sergeant and Ensign, First Regt., Essex County, New Jersey Militia.

CHESTER CAMERON WELLS, Omaha, Nebr. (36978). Son of Walter Woodworth and Lydia Jane (Cameron) Wells; grandson of Alanson and Mary Ann (Woodworth) Wells; great-grandson of Isham and Mahala (Anderson) Wells; great²-grandson of *James Wells,* private, Vermont Militia; great-grandson of Walter and Apie (Harrington) Woodworth; great²-grandson of Gersham and Clarissa (Heath) Woodworth; great²-grandson of *William* and Mary (Lott) *Wentworth,* Captain, Col. Lewis Van Woert's Regt., New York Militia; great⁴-grandson of *Caleb Woodworth,* private, Conn. Militia at Lexington Alarm; great²-grandson of *Daniel Heath,* Lieutenant, Sixteenth Regt., Albany County, New York Militia; great⁴-grandson of *John Lott,* private, Eighth Regt., Albany County, New York Militia; grandson of Wallen and Sarah Jane (Woods) Cameron; great-grandson of Alexander and Lydia (Miller) Cameron, Jr.; great²-grandson of *Alexander* and Elizabeth (Simmerman) *Cameron,* private, Eighth Battalion, Cumberland County, Penna. Militia; great²-grandson of *John Cameron,* private, Lancaster County, Penna. Militia; great-grandson of Horace Potter and Jane Wright (Mumford) Woods; great²-grandson of *Joseph* and Sarah (Peterson) *Woods,* patriot boy; great²-grandson of *Jacob Woods,* patriot farmer; great²-grandson of James and Catherine (Wright) Mumford; great²-grandson of *David Mumford,* Corporal, Fourth Regt., New Jersey Militia; great²-grandson of *Aaron Wright,* Second Lieutenant, First Battalion, Bedford County, Penna. Militia; great²-grandson of David and Abigail (Turrill) Mumford; great⁴-grandson of *James Turrill,* Member New Milford, Conn., Committee of Inspection and Correspondence.

GEORGE BLISS WELLS, Detroit, Mich. (36046). Son of George Lee and Sybil Florilla (Bliss) Wells; grandson of Samuel Butler and Sally Clarisa (Cadwell) Bliss; great-grandson of Henry and Sybil Florilla (Butler) Bliss; great²-grandson of *Peletiah Bliss, Jr.,* Minute Man and private, Vermont Militia.

FRANK WEST, Colonel, U. S. Army, retired, Mohawk, N. Y. (36885). Son of Harley and Mary Ann (Loveridge) West; grandson of William and Elizabeth (Cady) West, 3rd; great-grandson of William and Nancy (Williams) West, Jr.; great²-grandson of *William West,* Colonel and Brigadier-General, Rhode Island Militia.

JAMES CAMPBELL WHICKER, Oklahoma City, Okla. (36245). Son of James and Theresa (Weaver) Whicker; grandson of Berry and Lillian (Campbell) Whicker; great-grandson of *William Whicker,* Sergeant, North Carolina Militia, pensioned.

ALBERT RAY WHITE, Marinette, Wis. (37277). Son of Albert Zerah and Lucinda Jane (Nicholson) White; grandson of Ransom James and Hannah (Barnum) White; great-grandson of Harris and Mary (Sinclair) White; great²-grandson of Zerah and Mary (Polly) (Sanders) Sinclair; great²-grandson of *John Sanders,* Sergeant, Col. Timothy Bedell's Regt., New Hampshire Militia.

ALBERT ZERAH WHITE, Marinette, Wis. (37278). Son of Ransom James and Hannah (Barnum) White; grandson of Harris and Mary (Sinclair) White; great-grandson of Zerah and Mary (Polly) (Sanders) Sinclair; great²-grandson of *John Sanders,* Sergeant, Col. Timothy Bedell's Regt., New Hampshire Militia.

GEORGE MORRIS WHITESIDE, 2d, Wilmington, Del. (35667). Son of Frank Rush and Margaret (Custer) Whiteside; grandson of Rush James and Margaret Amanda (Stout) Whiteside; great-grandson of John and Elizabeth (Zehrfuss) Whiteside; great²-grandson of *Thomas Whiteside (Whitesides),* Captain, Colonel Porter's Battalion, Penna. Militia.

JOHN EDEN WHITTEN, Lincoln, Nebr. (36981). Son of Walter S. and Lilian (Potter) Whitten; grandson of William H. and Paul (Parr) Potter; great grandson of Andrew H. and Lucina (Donaldson) Parr; great²-grandson of Robert and Isabella (Clendenin) Robertson; great³-grandson of *James Clendenin,* private, Second Regt., Penna. Riflemen, pensioned.

CALEB H. WICKERSHAM, Marshalltown, Iowa (36904). Son of Joseph S. and Rachel Edward (Brogan) Wickersham; grandson of Caleb and Rachel (Edwards) Brogan; great-grandson of *John Brogan,* private, Eighth Battalion, Chester County, Penna. Militia.

JOHN WILCOX, Detroit, Mich. (36050). Son of Melvin Alfred and Mary Rebecca (Cook) Wilcox; grandson of Alfred and Ann (Davis) Wilcox; great-grandson of Lemuel and Rhoda (North) Wilcox; great²-grandson of *Josiah Wilcox,* Fifer, Conn. Militia.

EDMOND RICHARDSON WILES, Little Rock, Ark. (31772). Son of William Warren and Jane (Anderson) Wiles; grandson of Timothy and Tunsey Jane (Dikes) Anderson; great-grandson of Henry and Jane (Coffee) Anderson, Jr; great²-grandson of *Henry Anderson*, Captain, Colonel Casey's Regt., South Carolina Troops.

SAMUEL STANHOPE WILLIAMSON, District of Columbia (36131). Supplemental. Son of Joseph A. and Frances M. (Woods) Williamson; grandson of James Sterret and Marianne (Witherspoon) Woods; great-grandson of *John Witherspoon*, Member of Cont'l Congress and Signer of the Declaration of Independence.

CYRIL LATIMORE WILLOUGHBY, Lakeland, Fla. (29921). Son of John Hinchy and Amand Melvina (Tyler) Willoughby; grandson of Willis and Mary (Hinchy) Collins Willoughby; great-grandson of *Edlyne Willoughby*, private, Seventh Regt., Virginia Cont'l Troops, pensioned.

WILLIAM HORACE WITHERSTINE, Grand Forks, N. Dak. (36936). Son of Horace and Amelia (Hatfield) Witherstine; grandson of David and Margaret (Petrie) Witherstine; great-grandson of Frederick and Catherine (Thumb) Petrie; great²-grandson of *William Petrie*, (*Petry*), Surgeon, New York Troops.

PETER TORBOSS WOOD, Newark, N. J. (37011). Son of John and Charlotte Ann (Torboss) Wood; grandson of Daniel Smith and Nancy (Baldwin) Wood, Jr.; great-grandson of *Daniel Smith Wood*, Captain, Essex County, New Jersey Militia.

BENJAMIN MARSH WOODRUFF, Springfield, N. J. (37132). Son of John S. and Phoebe (Compton) Woodruff; grandson of David Crane and Sally (Marsh) Woodruff; great-grandson of Asher and Jemima (Roll) Woodruff; great²-grandson of *Daniel Woodruff*, private, Essex County, New Jersey Militia.

SAMUEL BAYARD WOODWARD, Worcester, Mass. (37111). Son of Samuel and Lucy R. (Treadwell) Woodward; grandson of Moses and Lydia B. (Parker) Treadwell; great-grandson of *Moses Treadwell*, Lieutenant, Third Regt. Essex County, Mass. Militia.

WILLIAM WOODWARD, New Orleans, La. (36958). Son of Erastus Marion and Maria (Carpenter) Woodward; grandson of Wooster and Lovina (Brown) Carpenter; great-grandson of *Ashabel Carpenter*, private, Col. Thomas Carpenter's Regt., Mass. Militia.

CHARLES SPRAGUE WRAGG, Toledo, Ohio (37029). Son of William H. and Cecelia (Sprague) Wragg; grandson of James B. and Sarah (Chamberlain) Sprague; great-grandson of James and Polly (Bailey) Sprague; great²-grandson of *James Sprague*, private, Col. Thomas Tash's Regt., New Hampshire Militia.

HENRY WILLIAM YATES, Omaha, Nebr. (36988). Son of Henry Whitfield and Eliza Barr (Samuels) Yates; grandson of George Warren and Rebecca Tilton (Todd) Samuels; great-grandson of David and Eliza (Barr) Todd; great²-grandson of *Levi* and Jane (Briggs) *Todd*, Major at Blue Licks and aide to Col. George Rogers Clarke; great²-grandson of *Samuel Briggs*, private, Capt. Benjamin Logan's Co. at Fort Araph.

LEVERETT GRIGGS YODER, Lieutenant, U. S. Army, Camp Lewis, Wash. (N. Dak. 36927). Son of Albert Henry and Susan Norton (Griggs) Yoder; grandson of William Henry and Catharine Adeline (Van Buskirk) Yoder; great-grandson of Isaac Shelby and Elizabeth (Gabbert) Van Buskirk; great²-grandson of Michael and Elizabeth (Bilderback) Van Buskirk; great³-grandson of *Isaac Van Buskirk*, private, Daniel Morgan's Regt., Virginia Militia, pensioned; great-grandson of Henry and Catharine (Halsapple) Gabbert; great²-grandson of *Michael Gabbert*, private, Colonel Boyer's and Colonel Vance's Regts., Virginia Troops, pensioned; great-grandson of Henry and Ruth Ann (Rader) Yoder; great²-grandson of Jacob and Catharine (Dellinger) Yoder; great³-grandson of *John Dellinger*, Ensign and Captain, North Carolina Militia; pensioned; member Lincoln County Committee of Safety and Signer of Delaration of Rights; grandson of Joseph Emerson and Mary Ellen (Little) Griggs; great-grandson of Leverett and Catharine (Stearns) Griggs; great²-grandson of Stephen and Elizabeth (Lathrop) Griggs; great³-grandson of *Ichabod Griggs*, Ensign, Tolland, Conn. Militia, died in service; great-grandson of Henry and Susan Norton (Smith) Little; great²-grandson of Jesse and Martha (Gerrish) Little; great³-grandson of *Henry Gerrish*, Lieutenant-Colonel, Stickney's Regt., New Hampshire Militia.

ROBERT MAUJER YOUNG, Brooklyn, N. Y. (36900). Son of William Robert and Mary Lihou (Maujer) Young; grandson of Robert and Elizabeth (Davis) Young; great-grandson of Jesse and Phoebe (Hallock) Davis; great^2-grandson of David and Dinah (——) Hallock; great^2-grandson of *Richard Hallock*, private, New York Militia and Signer of Association Test.

ROGER YOUNG, Newark, N. J. (37127). Son of Henry and Margaret Anna (Hitchcock) Young; grandson of James Kent and Mary Artemesia (Kellogg) Hitchcock; great-grandson of Spencer and Margaret Stuart (Palmer) Kellogg; great^2-grandson of *Levi Kellogg*, private and Sergeant, Mass. Militia and Cont'l Troops, pensioned.

STUART ADAMS YOUNG, Newark, N. J. (37131). Son of Henry and Margaret Anna (Hitchcock) Young; grandson of James Kent and Mary Artemesia (Kellogg) Hitchcock; great-grandson of Spencer and Margaret Stuart (Palmer) Kellogg; great^2-grandson of *Levi Kellogg*, private and Sergeant, Northampton, Mass. Militia and Cont'l Troops.

CEREMONIES ON LAFAYETTE-MARNE DAY, NEW YORK

Colonel Sackett and Past President General Ames with the vessels of earth and water. The third gentleman from the left of the picture is Marquis de Chambrun, great-grandson of Marquis de Lafayette. The fifth gentleman from the left, front row, is Consul-General Liebert.

OFFICIAL BULLETIN

OF THE

National Society
of the Sons of the American Revolution

Organized April 30, 1889

Incorporated by
Act of Congress, June 9, 1906

President General
W. I. LINCOLN ADAMS
Montclair, New Jersey

Published at Washington, D. C., in June, October, December, and March.
Entered as second-class matter, May 7, 1906, at the post-office at Washington, D. C., under the act of July 16, 1894.

| Volume XVII | OCTOBER, 1922 | Number 2 |

The OFFICIAL BULLETIN records action by the General Officers, the Board of Trustees, the Executive and other National Committees, lists of members deceased and of new members, and important doings of State Societies. In order that the OFFICIAL BULLETIN may be up to date, and to insure the preservation in the National Society archives of a complete history of the doings of the entire organization, State Societies and local Chapters are requested to communicate promptly to the Secretary General written or printed accounts of all meetings or celebrations, to forward copies of all notices, circulars, and other printed matter issued by them, and to notify him at once of dates of death of members.

PURPOSES AND OBJECTS OF THE S. A. R.

(Extracts from Constitution)

The purposes and objects of this Society are declared to be patriotic, historical, and educational, and shall include those intended or designed to perpetuate the memory of the men who, by their services or sacrifices during the war of the American Revolution, achieved the independence of the American people; to unite and promote fellowship among their descendants; to inspire them and the community at large with a more profound reverence for the principles of the government founded by our forefathers; to encourage historical research in relation to the American Revolution; to acquire and preserve the records of the individual services of the patriots of the war, as well as documents, relics, and landmarks; to mark the scenes of the Revolution by appropriate memorials; to celebrate the anniversaries of the prominent events of the war and of the Revolutionary period; to foster true patriotism; to maintain and extend the institutions of American freedom, and to carry out the purposes expressed in the preamble of the Constitution of our country and the injunctions of Washington in his farewell address to the American people.

Qualifications for Membership

Any man shall be eligible to membership in the Society who, being of the age of twenty-one years or over and a citizen of good repute in the community, is the lineal descendant of an ancestor who was at all times unfailing in his loyalty to, and rendered active service in, the cause of American Independence, either as an officer, soldier, seaman, marine, militiaman or minute man, in the armed forces of the Continental Congress, or of any one of the several Colonies or States, or as a Signer of the Declaration of Independence, or as a member of a Committee of Safety or Correspondence, or as a member of any Continental, Provincial, or Colonial Congress or Legislature, or as a recognized patriot who performed actual service by overt acts of resistance to the authority of Great Britain.

Application for membership is made on standard blanks furnished by the State Societies. These blanks call for the place and date of birth and of death of the Revolutionary ancestor and the year of birth, of marriage, and of death of ancestors in intervening generations. Membership is based on one original claim; additional claims are filed on supplemental papers. The applications and supplementals are made in duplicate.

GENERAL OFFICERS ELECTED AT THE SPRINGFIELD CONGRESS, MAY 16, 1922

President General:

W. J. LINCOLN ADAMS, Montclair, New Jersey.

Vice-Presidents General:

HARRY T. LORD, Manchester, New Hampshire.
    New England (Maine, New Hampshire, Vermont, Massachusetts, Rhode Island, and Connecticut).

PHILIP F. LARNER, 918 F Street N. W., Washington, District of Columbia.
    Middle and Coast District (New York, New Jersey, Pennsylvania, Delaware, Maryland, District of Columbia, Virginia, North Carolina, South Carolina, Georgia, and Florida).

LOUIS A. BOWMAN, 30 North La Salle Street, Chicago, Illinois.
    Mississippi Valley, East District (Michigan, Wisconsin, Illinois, Indiana, Ohio, West Virginia, Kentucky, Tennessee, Alabama, and Mississippi).

HENRY B. HAWLEY, Des Moines, Iowa.
    Mississippi Valley, West District (Minnesota, North Dakota, South Dakota, Nebraska, Iowa, Kansas, Missouri, Oklahoma, Arkansas, Louisiana, and Texas).

GEORGE ALBERT SMITH, Utah Savings & Trust Building, Salt Lake City, Utah.
    Mountain and Pacific Coast District (Montana, Idaho, Wyoming, Nevada, Utah, Colorado, Arizona, New Mexico, Oregon, Washington, California, Hawaii, and Philippines).

Secretary General:

FRANK BARTLETT STEELE, 183 St. James Place, Buffalo, New York.

Registrar General:

FRANCIS BARNUM CULVER, 2203 North Charles Street, Baltimore, Maryland; 918 F Street N. W., Washington, District of Columbia.

Treasurer General:

GEORGE McK. ROBERTS, Room 2126, 120 Broadway, New York City.

Historian General:

JOSEPH B. DOYLE, Steubenville, Ohio.

Chancelor General:

EUGENE C. BONNIWELL, City Court Building, Philadelphia, Pennsylvania.

Genealogist General:

WALTER K. WATKINS, 9 Ashburton Place, Boston, Massachusetts.

Chaplain General:

Rev. FREDERICK W. PERKINS, D. D., 27 Deer Cove, Lynn, Massachusetts.

BOARD OF TRUSTEES

The General Officers, together with one member from each State Society, constitute the Board of Trustees of the National Society. The following Trustees for the several States were elected at the Springfield Congress, May 16, 1922, to serve until their successors are elected at the Congress to be held at Nashville, Tenn., in May, 1923:

Alabama, (vacant); Arizona, W. B. Twitchell, Phœnix; Arkansas, George W. Clark, Little Rock; California, Seabury C. Mastick, New York City; Colorado, Victor E. Keyes, Denver; Connecticut, Herbert H. White, Hartford; Delaware, Hon. Horace Wilson, Wilmington; District of Columbia, Albert D. Spangler, Washington; Far Eastern Society, H. Lawrence Noble, Manila; Florida, Dr. F. G. Renshaw, Pensacola; Society in France, (vacant); Hawaiian Society, Donald S. Bowman, Honolulu; Georgia, Allan Waters, Atlanta; Idaho, M. A. Wood, Boise; Illinois, Dorr E. Felt, Chicago; Indiana, Charles C. Jewett, Terre Haute; Iowa, Elmer E. Wentworth, State Center; Kansas, John M. Meade, Topeka; Kentucky, George T. Wood, Louisville, Louisiana, Col. C. Robert Churchill, New Orleans; Maine, William B. Berry, Gardiner; Maryland, Hon. Henry Stockbridge, Baltimore; Massachusetts, George Hale Nutting, Boston; Michigan, Albert M. Henry, Detroit; Minnesota, Charles E. Rittenhouse, Minneapolis; Mississippi, Hon. Gordon G. Lyell, Jackson; Missouri, George R. Merrill, St. Louis; Montana, Marcus Whritenour, Helena; Nebraska, Benjamin F. Bailey, Lincoln; Nevada, (vacant); New Hampshire, Hon. Harry T. Lord, Manchester; New Jersey, Charles Symmes Kiggins, Elizabeth; New Mexico, George G. Klock, Albuquerque; New York, Louis Annin Ames, New York; North Carolina, (vacant); North Dakota, Howard E. Simpson, Grand Forks; Ohio, Hon. Warren G. Harding, Washington, D. C.; Oklahoma, W. A. Jennings, Oklahoma City; Oregon, Wallace McCamant, Portland; Pennsylvania, James A. Wakefield,* Pittsburgh; Rhode Island, Hon. Arthur P. Sumner, Providence; South Carolina, (vacant); South Dakota, F. M. Mills, Sioux Falls; Tennessee, Leland Hume, Nashville; Texas, C. B. Dorchester, Sherman; Utah, Daniel S. Spencer, Salt Lake City; Vermont, William Jeffrey, Montpelier; Virginia, Arthur B. Clarke, Richmond; Washington, Ernest B. Hussey, Seattle; Wisconsin, Walter H. Wright, Milwaukee; Wyoming, Warren Richardson, Cheyenne.

* Elected to fill vacancy caused by death of Col. Robert W. Guthrie, July, 1922.

PRESIDENTS AND SECRETARIES OF STATE SOCIETIES

ARIZONA—President, Lloyd B. Christie, 116 N. 1 Avenue, Phœnix.
    Secretary, Clarence P. Woodbury, 1509 Grand Avenue, Phœnix.
    Treasurer, Kenneth Freeland, Phœnix.
ARKANSAS—President, John M. Bracey,* Little Rock.
    Vice-President, Frank D. Leaming.
    Secretary, Fay Hempstead, Little Rock.
    Treasurer, Thomas M. Cory, Little Rock.
CALIFORNIA—President, Charles E. Hale, 51 Main Street, San Francisco.
    Secretary-Registrar, Thomas A. Perkins, Mills Building, San Francisco.
    Treasurer, John C. Currier, 713 Merchants' Exchange Building, San Francisco.
COLORADO—President, Hon. George H. Bradfield, Greeley.
    Secretary, James Polk Willard,* 210 Masonic Temple, Detroit.
    Assistant Secretary, Charles B. Toppan.
    Treasurer, Walter D. Wynkoop, Mt. States T. & T. Co., Denver.
CONNECTICUT—President, Hon. Rollin S. Woodruff, 210 Edwards Street, New Haven.
    Secretary, Frederick A. Doolittle, 117 Middle Street, Bridgeport.
    Treasurer, Charles G. Stone, P. O. Box 847, Hartford.
DELAWARE—President, Robert H. Richards, 1415 Delaware Avenue, Wilmington.
    Secretary-Treasurer-Registrar, Charles A. Rudolph, 900 Vanburen Street, Wilmington.
DISTRICT OF COLUMBIA—President, Selden M. Ely, Gales School Building, Washington.
    Secretary, Kenneth S. Wales, 110 Florence Court, F., Washington.
    Treasurer, Hilleary F. Offcut, Jr., 1501 Crittenden Street N. W., Washington.
FAR EASTERN SOCIETY—President-Secretary, H. Lawrence Noble, P. O. Box 940, Manila, Philippine Islands.
    Treasurer, Herman Roy Hare.
FLORIDA—President, Dr. F. G Renshaw, Pensacola.
    Secretary, John Hobart Cross, Pensacola.
    Treasurer-Registrar, F. F. Bingham, Pensacola.
SOCIETY IN FRANCE—Administered by Empire State Society.
GEORGIA—President Allen Waters, P. O. Box 361, Atlanta.
    Secretary-Registrar, Arthur W. Falkinburg, 1301 Atlanta Trust Co. Building, Atlanta.
    Treasurer, William Alden, Box 172, Decatur.
HAWAII—President, Donald S. Bowman, Honolulu.
    Secretary, James T. Taylor, 207 Kauikeolani Building, Honolulu.
    Treasurer, Elmer T. Winant, Honolulu.
IDAHO—President, Abert H. Conner, Boise.
    Secretary and Treasurer, Frank G. Ensign, Boise.
ILLINOIS—President, James M. Eddy, 30 North La Salle Street, Chicago.
    Secretary, Louis A. Bowman, 30 North La Salle Street, Chicago.
    Treasurer, Henry R. Kent, 30 North La Salle Street, Chicago.
INDIANA—President, Cornelius F. Posson, 538 East Drive, Woodruff Place, Indianapolis.
    Secretary and Treasurer, Edmund L. Parker, 511 East Walnut Street, Kokomo.
IOWA—President, Frank D. Harsh, Des Moines.
    Secretary, Captain Elbridge D. Hadley, 409 Franklin Avenue, Des Moines.
    Treasurer, William E. Barrett, 4815 Grand Avenue, Des Moines.
KANSAS—President, John M. Meade, Topeka.
    Secretary, Arthur H. Bennett, 434 Woodlawn Avenue, Topeka.
    Treasurer-Registrar, Walter E. Wilson, Topeka.
KENTUCKY—President, E. T. Hutchings, Columbia Building, Louisville.
    Secretary, George D. Caldwell, Inter-Southern Building, Louisvile.
    Treasurer, Alexander W. Tippett, U. S. Trust Co. Building, Louisville.
LOUISIANA—President, C. Robert Churchill, 408 Canal Street, New Orleans.
    Secretary, Herbert P. Benton, 403 Carondelet Building, New Orleans.
    Treasurer, S. O. Landry, 616 Maison Blanche Building, New Orleans.
MAINE—President, William B. Berry, 42 Pleasant Street, Gardiner.
    Secretary, Francis L. Littefield, 246 Spring Street, Portland.
    Treasurer, Enoch O. Greenleaf, Portland.
MARYLAND—President, Herbert Baker Flowers, 3008 N. Calvert Street, Baltimore.
    Secretary, George Sadtler Robertson, 1628 Linden Avenue, Baltimore.
    Treasurer, Benson Blake, Jr., Baltimore.

MASSACHUSETTS—President, Dr. Charles H. Bangs, Swampscott.
   Secretary, Walter K. Watkins, 9 Ashburton Place, Boston.
   Treasurer, Lieut.-Col. Charles M. Green, 78 Marlboro Street, Boston.
MICHIGAN—President, Carl F. Clarke, 92 Peterboro Street, Detroit.
   Secretary, Raymond E. Van Syckle, 1729 Ford Building, Detroit.
   Treasurer, Frank G. Smith, 1183 W. Boston Boulevard, Detroit.
MINNESOTA—President, Kenneth G. Brill, 43 South Hamline Avenue, St. Paul.
   Secretary, Charles H. Bronson, 48 East Fourth Street, St. Paul.
   Treasurer, Charles W. Eddy, 302 Pittsburg Building, St. Paul.
MISSISSIPPI—President, Judge Gordon Garland Lyell, Jackson.
   Secretary and Treasurer, William H. Pullen, Mechanics' Bank Building, Jackson.
MISSOURI—President, Linn Paine, 904 Locust Street, St. Louis.
   Secretary, J. Alonzo Matthews, 901 Pontiac Building, St. Louis.
   Treasurer, I. Shreve Carter, 308 Merchant La Clede Building, St. Louis.
MONTANA—President, Paris B. Bartley,* Helena.
   Secretary and Treasurer, Leslie Sulgrove, Helena.
NEBRASKA—President, Benjamin F. Bailey, 506 1st National Bank Building, Lincoln.
   Secretary, Addison E. Sheldon, 1319 South 23d Street, Lincoln.
   Treasurer, C. E. Bardwell, 522 Terminal Building, Lincoln.
NEVADA—President, Rt. Rev. George C. Huntting, 505 Ridge Street, Reno.
NEW HAMPSHIRE—President, Prof. Ashley K. Hardy, Hanover.
   Secretary and Treasurer, Rufus H. Baker, 12 Liberty Street, Concord.
NEW JERSEY—President, Hon. Adrian Lyon, Perth Amboy.
   Secretary, David L. Pierson, 33 Lombardy Street, Newark.
   Treasurer, Frank E. Quinby, 33 Lombardy Street, Newark.
NEW MEXICO—President, C. C. Manning, Gallup.
   Secretary, Frank W. Graham, Albuquerque.
   Treasurer, Orville A. Matson, Albuquerque.
NEW YORK—President, George D. Bangs, Tribune Buiding, New York City.
   Secretary, Major Charles A. Du Bois, 220 Broadway, New York City.
   Treasurer, James de la Montanye, 220 Broadway, New York City.
NORTH CAROLINA—Special Organizer for North and South Carolina, Maj. John F. Jones,
      Blacksburg, S. C.
NORTH DAKOTA—President, Howard E. Simpson, University of North Dakota, Grand Forks.
   Secretary-Registrar, Walter R. Reed, 407 7th Avenue So., Fargo.
   Treasurer, Willis E. Fuller, Northern National Bank, Grand Forks.
OHIO—President, Edward L. Shuey, Dayton.
   Secretary-Registrar, W. L. Curry, Box 645, Columbus.
   Treasurer, S. G. Harvey, 650 Oakwood Avenue, Toledo.
OKLAHOMA—President, George L. Bowman, Kingfisher.
   Secretary-Treasurer, Edward F. McKay, 536 West 31st Street, Oklahoma City.
OREGON—President, B. B. Beekman, 601 Platt Building, Portland.
   Secretary, B. A. Thaxter, Post Office Box 832, Portland.
   Treasurer, A. A. Lindsley, Henry Building, Portland.
PENNSYLVANIA—President, W. C. Lyne, Farmers' Bank Building, Pittsburgh.
   Secretary, Francis Armstrong, Jr., 515 Wood Street, Pittsburgh.
   Treasurer, A. W. Wall, Farmers' Bank Building, Pittsburgh.
RHODE ISLAND—President, Herbert A. Rice, 809 Hospital Trust Building, Providence.
   Secretary, Theodore E. Dexter, 104 Clay Street, Central Falls.
   Treasurer, William L. Sweet, Box 1515, Providence.
SOUTH CAROLINA—Special Organizer for North and South Carolina, Maj. John F. Jones,
      Blacksburg.
SOUTH DAKOTA—President, Col. A. B. Sessions, Sioux Falls.
   Secretary-Registrar, T. W. Dwight, Sioux Falls.
   Treasurer, B. H. Requa, Sioux Falls.
TENNESSEE—President, William K. Boardman, Nashville.
   Vice-President-at-Large, U. P. Millspaugh, Nashville.
   Secretary-Registrar, J. Tyree Fain, Nashville.
   Treasurer, Carey Folk, 411 Union Street, Nashville.
TEXAS—President, C. B. Dorchester, Sherman.
   Secretary-Treasurer, Walter S. Mayer, 1404 39th Street, Galveston,

UTAH—President, Robert E. McConaughy, 1079 E. 2d South Street, Salt Lake City.
    Secretary, Gordon Lines Hutchins, Dooly Building, Salt Lake City.
    Treasurer, Seth Warner Morrison, Jr., 32 S. 7th East Street, Salt Lake City.
VERMONT—President, William H. Jeffrey, Montpelier.
    Secretary, Walter H. Crockett, Burlington.
    Treasurer, Clarence L. Smith, Burlington.
VIRGINIA—President, Arthur B. Clarke, 616 American National Bank Building, Richmond.
    Secretary and Treasurer, William E. Crawford, 700 Travelers' Building, Richmond.
WASHINGTON—President, Walter Burges Beals, Haller Buiding, Seattle.
    Secretary, Henry J. Gorin, 322 Central Building, Seattle.
    Treasurer, Kenneth P. Hussey, 903 Boylston Avenue, Seattle.
WISCONSIN—President, Henry S. Sloan, 216 W. Water Street, Milwaukee.
    Secretary, Emmett A. Donnelly, 1030 Wells Building, Milwaukee.
    Treasurer, William Stark Smith, 373 Lake Drive, Milwaukee.
WYOMING—President, David A. Haggard, Cheyenne.
    Secretary, Maurice Groshon, Cheyenne.
    Treasurer, James B. Guthrie, Cheyenne.

STATE SOCIETIES AND CHAPTERS

(Membership based on Annual Reports of April, 1922)

ALABAMA SOCIETY

Organized June 27, 1903; Admitted into National Society November 18, 1903

(No report received; Society inactive.)

ARIZONA SOCIETY

48 MEMBERS

Organized June 13, 1896; Annual Meeting, February 22

Officers Elected 1922

President, Lloyd B. Christy; Vice-President, Harold Baxter; Secretary, Clarence P. Woodbury; Treasurer, Kenneth G. Freeland; Registrar, Evan S. Stallcup; Historian, Rt. Rev. J. W. Atwood; Chaplain, Rev. J. Rockwood Jenkins, all of Phœnix.

ARKANSAS SOCIETY

66 MEMBERS

Organized April 29, 1889; Annual Meeting, February 22

Officers Elected 1922

President, John M. Bracey*; Vice-Presidents, Frank B. Leaming and J. O. Blakeney; Secretary, Fay Hempstead; Treasurer, Thomas M. Cory; Registrar, Ernest C. Newton; Historian, Sam S. Wassell, all of Little Rock.

CALIFORNIA SOCIETY

529 MEMBERS

Instituted October 22, 1875, as Sons of Revolutionary Sires; Constitution Adopted August 7, 1876; Name Changed to Sons of the American Revolution March 22, 1890; Annual Meeting, April 19.

* Deceased.

Officers Elected 1922

President, Charles E. Hale; Vice-Presidents, Fred L. Berry and E. Delos Magee; Secretary-Registrar, Thomas A. Perkins; Treasurer, John C. Currier; Historian, Howard C. Rowley, all of San Francisco.

Chapter Officers

San Diego Chapter.—Annual meeting, November. Officers elected 1921: President, Dr. Fred Baker; Vice-Presidents, James C. Elms, Jr., George W. Heston; Secretary, Allen Henry Wright; Treasurer, Franklin P. Reed; Historian, David W. Schick; Registrar, Kenneth McKenzie; Marshal, Dr. W. Harmon Hall; Chaplain, Rev. Alfred H. Haines.

COLORADO SOCIETY

328 Members

Organized July 4, 1896; Annual Meeting, February 22

Officers Elected 1922

President, Hon. George H. Bradfield, Greeley; Vice-Presidents, Victor E. Keyes, Denver; Samuel Le Nord Caldwell, Colorado Springs; Richard H. Arms, Grand Junction; Asa D. Holt, Longmont; Walter L. Wilder, Pueblo; George C. McCormick, Fort Collins, and George H. Horne, Greeley; Secretary-Registrar, Dr. James Polk Willard,* Denver; Assistant Secretary, Charles B. Toppan, Denver; Treasurer, Walter D. Wynkoop, Denver; Historian, Lathrop M. Taylor, Fort Collins; Chaplain, Rev. F. A. Hatch, Pueblo.

Chapter Officers

Colorado Springs Chapter.—President, Samuel Le Nord Caldwell; Secretary, Frank R. Rothrock.
 Denver Chapter.—President, Dr. L. C. Wheeler; Secretary, A. F. Tingle.
 Fort Collins Chapter.—(No report.)
 Grand Junction Chapter.—President, Richard H. Arms; Secretary, John C. Page.
 Greeley Chapter.—President, George E. Horn; Secretary, Charles E. Littell.
 Longmont Chapter.—President, E. L. Montgomery; Secretary, C. W. Boynton.
 Pueblo Chapter.—President, Wardner Williams; Secretary-Registrar, Norval W. Wall.

CONNECTICUT SOCIETY

1,172 Members

Organized April 2, 1889; Annual Meeting, June 14, Anniversary of Connecticut's Declaration of Independence

Officers Elected 1922

President, Hon. Rollin S. Woodruff, New Haven; Vice-Presidents, Orlando H. Brothwell, Bridgeport; Hon. H. Wales Lines, Meriden, and Hon. Ernest E. Rogers, New London; Secretary, Frederick A. Doolittle, 117 Middle Street, Bridgeport; Treasurer, Charles G. Stone, Hartford; Registrar, Lawrence E. Bostwick, New Haven; Historian, Frank B. Gay, Hartford; Chaplain, Rev. Orville A. Petty, New Haven; Necrologist, Leverett Belknap, Hartford; Auditors, Frederick W. Hall, Bridgeport, and Charles E. P. Sanford, New Haven.

Branch Officers

Gen. David Humphreys Branch, No. 1, New Haven.—245 members; annual meeting, May. President, Ernest C. Simpson; Vice-President, Clarence Blakeslee; Secretary-Treasurer, George F. Burgess; Historian, Albert McC. Mathewson; Chaplain, Rev. Harris E. Starr.
 Capt. John Couch Branch, No. 2, Meriden.—President, H. Wales Lines.

---

* Deceased, September, 1922.

General Silliman Branch, No. 3, Bridgeport.—President, Col. T. B. Warren; Secretary, Frederick A. Doolittle.

Israel Putnam Branch, No. 4, Norwich.—16 members; annual meeting, April 20. President, Charles E. Chandler; Vice-President, William H. Allen; Secretary-Treasurer, Henry F. Parker.

Norwalk Branch, No. 5.—Secretary, Charles A. Quintard.

Nathan Hale Branch, No. 6, New London.—President, Hon. Ernest E. Rogers.

Col. Jeremiah Wadsworth Branch, No. 7, Hartford.—300 members; annual meeting, October. President, George S. Godard; Vice-President, F. Clarence Bissell; Secretary-Treasurer, Charles G. Stone; Historian, Frank B. Gay; Chaplain, Rev. Arthur Adams, Ph. D.; Necrologist, Leverett Belknap; Auditor, Edward W. Beardsley.

Col. Elisha Sheldon Branch, No. 8, Salisbury.—35 members; annual meeting, November. President, Donald T. Warner; Vice-President, Leonard J. Nickerson; Secretary, Malcolm D. Rudd; Treasurer, William B. Perry, Jr.; Historian, Donald J. Warner; Necrologist, Richard K. Miles; Auditor, William P. Russell.

DELAWARE SOCIETY

107 MEMBERS

Organized January 29, 1889; Annual Meeting, April 19

Officers Elected 1922

President, Robert H. Richards, Wilmington; Vice-Presidents, James H. Hughes, Dover, and Edwin C. Marshall, Lewes; Secretary-Treasurer-Registrar, Charles A. Rudolph, 900 Van Buren Street, Wilmington; Chaplain, Rev. Richard W. Trapnell, Wilmington.

DISTRICT OF COLUMBIA SOCIETY

(Washington, D. C.)

515 MEMBERS

Organized April 19, 1890; Annual Meeting, February 22

Officers Elected 1922

President, Selden Marvin Ely; Vice-Presidents, Samuel Herrick, Rear Admiral Frank F. Fletcher, and Justice Josiah A. Van Orsdel; Secretary, Kenneth Sanford Wales; Treasurer, Hilleary L. Offcutt, Jr.; Registrar, Capt. Overton C. Luxford; Assistant Registrar, Charles M. Bryant; Historian, Henry White Draper; Librarian, William L. Boyden, all of Washington; Chaplain, Rev. James M. Nourse, Westminster, Md.

FAR EASTERN SOCIETY, MANILA, P. I.

19 MEMBERS (1920)

Charter Granted February, 1911; Organization Perfected October, 1911

President-Secretary, H. Lawrence Noble, Manila; Treasurer, Herman Roy Hare, Manila.

SOCIETY IN FRANCE

15 MEMBERS (1920)

Organized in Paris, September 16, 1897; Administered by Empire State Society

FLORIDA SOCIETY

40 MEMBERS

Organized March 14, 1896; Annual Meeting, April 19

Officers Elected 1922

President, Dr. F. G. Renshaw, Pensacola; Vice-Presidents, R. M. Cary, Pensacola; F. M. Hudson, Miami; Peter O. Knight, Tampa; G. M. West, Panama City; Charles J. Williams, Jr., Jacksonville; W. S. Branch, Orlando; Secretary, John Hobart Cross, Pensacola; Treasurer-Registrar, F. F. Bingham, Pensacola; Chaplain, Rt. Rev. Edward G. Weed, Jacksonville.

Chapter Officers

Miami Chapter.—Organized 1922. (No report.)

GEORGIA SOCIETY

28 MEMBERS

Organized March 14, 1921; Annual Meeting, June 17

Officers Elected 1921

President, Allen Waters, Mt. Vernon, Illinois; Vice-President, H. C. Carpenter, Atlanta; Secretary-Registrar, Arthur W. Falkinburg, Atlanta; Treasurer, William Alden, Decatur.

HAWAIIAN SOCIETY

95 MEMBERS (1920)

Organized June 17, 1896; Annual Meeting, October 4

Officers Elected 1921

President, Donald S. Bowman; Vice-President, C. B. Cooper; Secretary, James T. Taylor; Treasurer, Elmer T. Winant; Registrar, Gerrit P. Wilder, all of Honolulu.

IDAHO SOCIETY

125 MEMBERS

Organized April 8, 1909; Annual Meeting, February 22

Officers Elected 1922

President, Albert Holmes Conner, Boise; Vice-Presidents, E. H. Sherman, Boise; M. H. Brownell, Hailey, and D. W. Church, Pocatello; Geo. N. Osborne, Black Lake; Bowen Curley, Idaho Falls; S. A. Easton, Kellogg; Wm. H. Eldridge, Twin Falls; Asher A. Getchell, Silver City; W. H. Gibson, Mountain Home; Rev. W. S. Hawkes, Caldwell; Miles S. Johnson, Lewiston; J. M. Elder, Cœur d'Alene, and Samuel H. Hays, Boise; Secretary-Treasurer-Registrar, Frank G. Ensign, Boise; Chaplain, R. B. Wright, D. D., Boise.

ILLINOIS SOCIETY

1,220 MEMBERS

Organized January 14, 1890; Annual Meeting, December 3, Commemorating Admission of Illinois into the Union

Officers Elected 1922

President, James M. Eddy, Chicago; Vice-Presidents, James Edgar Brown, Chicago, and William G. Adkins, Chicago; Secretary, Louis A. Bowman, Chicago; Treasurer, Henry R. Kent, Chicago; Registrar, John D. Vandercook, Lombard; Historian, George A. Brennan, Chicago; Chaplain, William W. Johnstone, D. D., Chicago; Sergeant-at-Arms, Cecil R. Bonfan, Chicago.

Chapter Officers

Oak Park Chapter.—President, J. C. Miller; Secretary, Frank L. Stetson.
Peoria Chapter.—President, Philip H. Gregg; Secretary, Bruce E. Dwinnell.
Springfield Chapter.—Organized February, 1897. President, Charles S. Andrus; Secretary-Treasurer, Isaac R. Diller.

INDIANA SOCIETY

265 MEMBERS

Organized January 15, 1890; Annual Meeting, February 25

Officers Elected 1922

President, Cornelius F. Posson, Indianapolis; Vice-Presidents, H. Louis Mauzy, Rushville; Dr. C. I. Fleming, Terre Haute; Mason J. Niblack, Vincennes, and Hon. Louis B. Eubank, Indianapolis; Secretary-Treasurer, Edmund L. Parker, Kokomo; Registrar, William C. Royse, Terre Haute; Historian, Herbert Briggs, Terre Haute; Chaplain, Rev. Augustus C. Wilmore, Winchester.

John Morton Chapter, Terre Haute.—President, George A. Scott; Vice-Presidents, Will W. Adamson and Leslie S. Creal; Secretary, Charles T. Jewett; Treasurer, Horace E. Tune; Historian, Herbert E. Briggs; Chaplain, Oscar Rankin.

Gen. Pleasant A. Hackleman Chapter, Rushville.—President, Dr. Frank G. Hackleman (Report of 1920).

IOWA SOCIETY

490 MEMBERS

Organized September 5, 1893; Annual Meeting, April 19

Officers Elected 1922

President, F. D. Harsh, Des Moines; First Vice-President, Roger Leavitt, Cedar Falls; Second Vice-President, George C. White, Nevada; Secretary, Capt. Elbridge Drew Hadley, Des Moines; Assistant Secretary, Francis L. Meredith, Des Moines; Treasurer, William E. Barrett, Esq., Des Moines; Registrar, H. H. Griffiths, Esq., Des Moines; Historian, Rev. E. M. Vittum, Muscatine; Chaplain, William B. Sanford, D. D., Des Moines.

Chapter Officers

Ben Franklin Chapter, Des Moines.—President, Elbridge D. Hadley; Secretary, Gershom H. Hill.
Bunker Hill Chapter, Waterloo.—President, Roger Leavitt, Cedar Falls; Secretary, Thomas M. Buchanan.
Lexington Chapter, Keokuk.—President, W. G. Blood; Secretary, Frederic C. Smith.
Washington Chapter, Ames.—President, —— ——; Secretary, E. C. Potter.
Woodbury County Chapter, Sioux City.—President, Alphaeus B. Beall; Secretary, A. E. Line.
Poweshiek Chapter, Grinnell.—President, —— ——; Secretary, F. P. Marvin.
Alexander Hamilton Chapter, Sheldon.—President, F. H. Wilsey; Secretary, George T. Wellmas.

Lew Wallace Anderson Chapter, Cedar Rapids.—President, L. W. Mansfield; Secretary, D. R. Holden.

Valley Forge Chapter, Nevada.—President, A. C. Allen; Secretary, Francis S. Smith.

KANSAS SOCIETY

124 Members

Organized March 31, 1892; Annual Meeting, February 22

Officers Elected 1922

President, John M. Meade, Topeka; Vice-Presidents, Henry W. McAfee, Topeka; William S. Thompson, Hutchinson; John Stout Maxwell, Pittsburg; Charles L. Davidson, Wichita; Dr. Arthur W. Clark, Lawrence; Jason R. Austin, Emporia; Amzie E. Jordan, Beloit, and Pratt Barndollar, Coffeyville; Secretary-Registrar, Arthur H. Bennett, Topeka; Treasurer, Walter Everett Wilson, Topeka; Historian, Daniel Wert Nellis, Topeka.

KENTUCKY SOCIETY

220 Members

Organized April 8, 1889; Annual Meeting, October 19

Officers Elected 1921

President, E. T. Hutchings, Louisville; Vice-Presidents, J. Swigert Taylor, Frankfort; Curran Pope, Louisville, Raymond Grant, Louisville, and Elbert S. Woosley, Louisville; Secretary, George D. Caldwell; Treasurer, Alex. W. Tippett; Registrar, Ben La Bree; Historian, James H. Richmond; Chaplain, E. L. Powell; Surgeon, Richard H. Coke, all of Louisville.

LOUISIANA SOCIETY

335 Members

Organized May 16, 1893; Annual Meeting in December

Officers Elected 1921

President, Col. C. Robert Churchill, New Orleans; Vice-Presidents, W. S. Lewis, New Orleans; Joseph B. Blatterman, Shreveport, and Carl C. Friedrichs, New Orleans; Secretary, Herbert P. Benton, New Orleans; Financial Secretary, George A. Treadwell, New Orleans; Treasurer, S. O. Landry, New Orleans; Registrar, Melvin B. Griffin, New Orleans; Historian, H. W. Robinson, New Orleans; Chaplain, Rev. Wm. S. Slack, Maringouin; Genealogist, Wallace Trowbridge, New Orleans.

MAINE SOCIETY

346 Members

Organized March 14, 1891; Annual Meeting, February 22

Officers Elected 1922

President, William B. Berry, Gardiner; Vice-President, —— ——; Secretary, Francis L. Littlefield, Portland; Treasurer, Enoch O. Greenleaf, Portland; Registrar, James C. Woolley, Portland; Historian, John F. Sprague, Foxcroft; Librarian, William T. Cousens, Portland; Chaplain, Rev. Edmund A. Laine, Jr., Portland.

MARYLAND SOCIETY

496 Members

Organized April 20, 1889; Annual Meeting, April 19

Officers Elected 1922

· President, Herbert Baker Flowers, Baltimore; Vice-Presidents, T. Murray Maynadier, Baltimore; John H. K. Shannahan, Sparrows Point, and Albion J. Corning, Jr., Baltimore; Secretary, George Sadtler Robertson; Treasurer, Benson Blake, Jr.; Registrar, Francis B. Culver; Historian, George W. Ward; Chaplain, Rev. Henry Branch, all of Baltimore.

Chapter Officers

Sergt. Lawrence Everhart Chapter, Frederick.—President, Albert S. Brown; Secretary, Edward D. Shriner, Jr.

MASSACHUSETTS SOCIETY

1,848 Members

Organized April 19, 1889; Annual Meeting, April 19

Officers Elected 1922

President, Charles H. Bangs, M. D., Swampscott; Vice-Presidents, Burton H. Wiggin, Lowell; J. Morton Davis, Salem, and Samuel F. Punderson, Springfield; Secretary-Registrar, Walter Kendall Watkins, 9 Ashburton Place, Boston; Treasurer, Lieut.-Col. Charles M. Green, Boston; Historian, Walter Kendall Watkins, Malden; Chaplain, Rev. Lewis Wilder Hicks, Wellesley.

Chapter Officers

Old Salem Chapter, Salem.—President, Isaac H. Sawyer, Topsfield; Secretary, Osborne Leach, Danvers.
Boston Chapter.—President, William O. Comstock; Secretary, Charles C. Littlefield.
George Washington Chapter, Springfield.—President, Charles F. Warner; Secretary, Henry A. Booth.
Old Middlesex Chapter, Lowell.—President, Dr. George L. Van Deusen; Secretary, C. B. Livingston.
Old Essex Chapter, Lynn.—President, Benjamin N. Johnson; Secretary, Luther Atwood.
Old Colony Chapter, Whitman.—President (vacant); Secretary, Charles E. Lovell.
Worcester Chapter.—President-Secretary, Richard T. Elliott.
Berkshire County Chapter, Pittsfield.—President, A. J. Witherell, North Adams; Secretary, William L. Root.
Robert Treat Paine Chapter, Taunton.—President, Enos D. Williams; Secretary, Louis B. Walker.
Malden Chapter—President, Horace Chester; Secretary, Walter K. Watkins.
Cambridge Chapter—President, John Amee; Secretary, Shepard Howland.
Seth Pomeroy Chapter, Northampton.—President, Rev. H. G. Smith; Secretary, George H. Sergeant.
Roxbury Chapter.—President, J. H. Richardson; Secretary (vacant).
Dukes County Chapter, Edgartown.—President, E. H. Pease; Secretary, A. W. Dean.
Francis Lewis Chapter, Walpole.—President, Isaac N. Lewis; Secretary, H. Raymond Lewis.
Old Suffolk Chapter, Chelsea; *Newtowne Chapter,* Newton, and *Fall River Chapters* have charters, but are at present unorganized.

MICHIGAN SOCIETY

702 MEMBERS

Organized January 18, 1890; Annual Meeting, April 15

Officers Elected 1922

President, William P. Holliday, Detroit; Vice-Presidents, Lee M. Hutchins, Grand Rapids, and Clarence K. Redfield, Pontiac; Secretary, Raymond E. Van Syckle, Detroit; Treasurer, Frank G. Smith, Detroit; Registrar, Franklin S. Dewey, Detroit; Historian, William L. Jenks, Port Huron; Chaplain, Rev. Minot C. Morgan, D. D., Detroit.

Chapter Officers

Detroit Chapter.—378 members; chartered May 2, 1913. President, Carl F. Clarke; Vice-President, George E. Bushnell; Second Vice-President, Julius E. Thatcher; Secretary, Raymond E. Van Syckle; Treasurer, Frank G. Smith; Historian, Allen G. Ludington; Chaplain, Rev. Jos. A. Vance, D. D.

Kalamazoo Chapter.—4 members; chartered December 31, 1915. President, Edward C. Parsons; Secretary, Dr. William A. Stone.

Kent Chapter, Grand Rapids.—104 members; chartered March 27, 1914. President, H. Parker Robinson; Vice-President, Elvert M. Davis; Secretary, Daniel W. Tower; Treasurer, ———— ————; Registrar, Charles N. Remington.

Washtenaw Chapter, Ann Arbor.—45 members; chartered March 27, 1914. President, Dr. Wilbert B. Hinsdale; Vice-President, Henry W. Newkirk; Secretary, Wolcott H. Butler; Treasurer, Milton E. Osborn; Historian, Harlan H. Johnson; Chaplain, Lucius L. Clarke.

Kalamazoo Chapter.—Chartered December 31, 1915. President, Edward C Parsons; Secretary, Dr. William A. Stone.

Mt. Pleasant Chapter.—Chartered January 22, 1915. Secretary, Sheridan E. Gardiner.

St. Clair Chapter, Port Huron.—18 members; chartered December 28, 1917. President, Burt D. Cady; Vice-President, Sydney G. McClouth; Secretary, William R. Chadwick; Treasurer, Albert D. Bennett; Historian, William L. Jenks; Chaplain, Alfred L. Chamberlain.

Lenawee Chapter, Adrian.—33 members; chartered July 9, 1920. President, Wilbert H. Barrett; Vice-President, Franklin D. Teachout; Secretary-Treasurer, W. Herbert Gott; Registrar, Irwin A. Dewey; Historian, Ladd J. Lewis.

Oakland Chapter, Pontiac.—23 members; chartered November 6, 1920. President, Clarence K. Redfield; Vice-President, Charles I. Shattuck; Secretary, Alfred L. Smith; Treasurer, John Eugene Church; Registrar, Charles V. Taylor; Historian, George Henry Kimball; Chaplain, Henry J. Simpson.

MINNESOTA SOCIETY

267 MEMBERS

Organized December 26, 1889; Annual Meeting in January

Officers Elected 1922

President, Kenneth G. Brill, St. Paul; Vice-Presidents, Dr. Douglas F. Wood, Minneapolis, and Grier M. Orr, St. Paul; Secretary, Charles H. Bronson; Treasurer, Charles W. Eddy; Registrar, Charles Stees; Historian, Rev. M. D. Edwards; Chaplain, Rev. S. W. Dickinson, all of St. Paul.

Chapter Officers

Minneapolis Chapter, No. 1.—54 members; organized December 14, 1921. President, Dr. Douglas F. Wood; Vice-Presidents, Charles P. Schouten; Walter H. Wheeler; Secretary, Louis P. Chute, 2325 Pleasant Avenue; Treasurer, Albert J. Robertson; Historian, Arthur H. Benton.

Duluth Chapter, No. 2.—Organized 1922.

MISSISSIPPI SOCIETY

38 MEMBERS

Organized May 10, 1909 (Report of 1918)

President, Hon. Gordon Garland Lyell; Secretary-Registrar, William H. Pullen; Treasurer, Philip S. Merrill, all of Jackson.

MISSOURI SOCIETY

220 MEMBERS

Organized April 23, 1889; Annual Meeting, March 4

Officers Elected 1922

President, Linn Paine; Vice-Presidents, Charles W. Bates, Samuel McK. Green, Charles M. Hay, and Harry S. Hawes; Honorary Vice-Presidents, George H. Shields, W. B. Homer, James E. Withrow, L. D. Kingsland, and Harmon J. Bliss; Secretary, J. Alonzo Matthews; Treasurer, I. Shreve Carter; Registrar, Homer Hall; Historian-Genealogist, W. H. H. Tainter; Chaplain, Rev. Z. B. T. Philips, D. D., all of St. Louis.

Chapter Officers

Kansas City Chapter.—(Inactive.)

MONTANA SOCIETY

34 MEMBERS

Organized June 5, 1894; Annual Meeting, February 22

Officers Elected 1922

President, Paris B. Bartley,* Helena; Vice-President, Lyman Hakes Bennett, Virginia City; Secretary-Treasurer, Leslie Sulgrove, Helena; Historian, Marcus Whritenour, Helena; Chaplain, William Rush Burroughs, Helena; Librarian, Ranney Yale Lyman, Helena.

NEBRASKA SOCIETY

250 MEMBERS

Organized April 26, 1890; Annual Meeting, February 22

Officers Elected 1922

President, Benjamin F. Bailey, Lincoln; Vice-Presidents, J. L. Codington, and John M. Banister, Omaha; Secretary-Registrar, Addison E. Sheldon, Lincoln; Treasurer, Charles E. Bardwell, Lincoln; Historian, J. Reid Green, Lincoln.

Chapter Officers (1920 Report)

Lincoln Chapter.—President, John D. Bushnell; Secretary, Carl Carpenter.
Crete Chapter.—Secretary-Treasurer, J. M. Dunham.
Fremont Chapter.—President, Burnell Colson; Secretary, Frederick C. Laird.

NEVADA SOCIETY

Organized February 19, 1910

(No report. Society inactive.)

---

* Deceased September 25, 1922.

NEW HAMPSHIRE SOCIETY

185 Members

Organized April 24, 1889; Annual Meeting, April 19

Officers Elected 1922

President, Ashley K. Hardy, Hanover; Vice-Presidents, Elbert Wheeler, Nashua; Walter S. Baker, Concord, and Sewall W. Abbott, Wolfboro; Secretary-Treasurer, Rufus H. Baker, Concord; Registrar, Charles C. Jones, Concord; Historian, Henry H. Metcalf, Concord; Chaplain, Rev. J. W. Presby, Grasmere.

Chapter Officers

Keene Chapter.—President, Fred E. Howe; Secretary, Charles G. Shedd.

NEW JERSEY SOCIETY

1,852 Members

Organized March 7, 1889; Annual Meeting, April 22

Officers Elected 1922

President, Hon. Adrian Lyon, Perth Amboy; Vice-Presidents, Harry Frank Brewer, Elizabeth, and Elvord G. Chamberlain, Montclair; Secretary, David Lawrence Pierson, 33 Lombardy St., Newark; Treasurer, Frank E. Quinby, East Orange; Registrar, William Johnson Conkling, Newark; Assistant Registrar, Lieut.-Col. Charles A. Andrews, Newark; Historian, Rev. Masheim Steck Waters, Newark; Chaplain, Rev. Frank A. Smith, D. D., Elizabeth; Genealogist, Samuel Copp Worthen, East Orange; Chancellor, Raymond Townley Parrot, Elizabeth; Librarian, Russell B. Rankin, Newark.

Chapter Officers

Elizabethtown Chapter, No. 1.—President, Richard S. Earl; Vice-President, William C. Hope; Secretary, James J. Gerber; Treasurer, Walter C. Tenney; Chaplain, Rev. Dr. Charles A. Campbell; Registrar, Prof. William C. Armstrong; Historian, Fred. B. Bassett.

Orange Chapter, No. 2.—President. James L. Garabrant; Vice-President, I. Woodruff Faulks; Secretary, Elbert L. Sloat; Treasurer, Oscar Stanley Thompson, Jr.; Historian, Rev. Charles B. Bullard; Chaplain, Rev. George P. Eastman; Registrar, Rev. S. Ward Righter.

Montclair Chapter, No. 3.—President, J. Stewart Gibson; First Vice-President, Gilbert D. Maxwell; Second Vice-President, Arthur H. Churchill; Secretary, William H. Sutton, Jr.; Treasurer, Albert W. Ballentine; Historian, Charles B. Alling; Chaplain, Rev. Luke M. White.

Newark Chapter, No. 4.—President, Sylvester Halsey Moore Agens; Vice-President, Col. Charles A. Andrews; Secretary, George H. Renton, Jr.; Treasurer, Benjamin J. Coe; Historian, John Willis Weeks; Chaplain, Rev. Dr. Charles Lee Reynolds; Registrar, Russell B. Rankin.

Monmouth Chapter, No. 5, Asbury Park.—President, William C. Gallagher; Secretary, William A. Squire; Treasurer, Robert G. Poole.

Paramus Chapter, No. 6, Ridgewood.—President, Willet Weeks; Vice-President, Capt. Joseph C. Fitts; Secretary, Edmond Morey; Treasurer, Louis F. Halsted; Registrar, Richard T. Wilson; Historian, Everett L. Zabriskie; Chaplain, Rev. John A. Van Neste.

Morris County Chapter, No. 7.—President, Edward Q. Keasbey; Secretary and Treasurer, Henry C. Pitney, Jr.

Passaic Valley Chapter, No. 8, Summit.—President, Alfred W. Alesbury; Vice-President, Malcolm McDougal; Secretary, Edwin E. Beach; Treasurer, Edward G. Hotchkiss; Registrar, H. Donald Holmes; Historian, Schuyler M. Cady; Chaplain, John Hobart Egbert.

Washington Rock Chapter, No. 9, Plainfield.—President, Col. Charles R. Banks; Secretary, Harvey R. Linbarger.

Second River Chapter, No. 10, Belleville.—President, John N. Klein; Secretary, Henry L. Denison; Treasurer, Brewster H. Jones; Chaplain, Rev. J. Garland Hamner.

West Fields Chapter, No. 11, Westfield.—President, Harold B. Wright; Treasurer, John J. High; Secretary, Lawrence A. Clark; Registrar, Rutherford O. Pierson; Historian, Ray E. Mayham; Chaplain, Rev. William W. Coe.

Captain Abraham Godwin Chapter, No. 12, Paterson.—President, Albert Lincoln Wyman; Vice-President, Ide G. Sargeant; Recording Secretary, Major Augustus Van Gieson; Registrar, Dr. Frank R. Sandt; Historian, Louis E. Schermerhorn; Chaplain, Rev. Geo. W. Labaw; Treasurer, Fred. W. Wentworth; Corresponding Secretary, Dr. William H. Rauchfuss.

South Jersey Chapter, No. 13, Haddonfield, Organized May 6, 1922.—President, Rear-Admiral Reynold T. Hall; Vice-President, Edward C. Geehr; Secretary and Treasurer, J. Sterling Stockton; Historian and Registrar, Col. Winfield S. Price.

NEW MEXICO SOCIETY

64 MEMBERS

Organized December 26, 1908; Annual Meeting, February 22

Officers Elected 1922

President, C. C. Manning, Gallup; Vice-Presidents, Donald J. McClanahan, Albuquerque; Francis Cushman Wilson, Santa Fe; Keith M. Edwards, Ft. Sumner, and James F. Hinkle, Roswell; Secretary, Frank William Graham, Albuquerque; Treasurer, Orville Arthur Matson, Albuquerque; Registrar, Frank W. Clancy, Santa Fe; Historian, Arthur Henry Sisk, Albuquerque; Chaplain, Rev. Walter S. Trowbridge, Santa Fe.

NEW YORK (THE EMPIRE STATE SOCIETY)

1,770 MEMBERS

Organized February 11, 1890; Annual Meeting, April 19

Officers Elected 1922

President, George D. Bangs; Vice-Presidents, Maj. Walter B. Hopping and Col. Henry W. Sackett; Secretary, Maj. Charles A. Du Bois; Treasurer, James De La Montanye; Registrar, Teunis D. Huntting; Historian, Hon. James B. Laux; Chaplain, Rev. Joseph Fort Newton, D. D., all of New York City.

Chapter Officers

Buffalo Chapter.—President, Comm. Thomas W. Harris; Vice-Presidents, William W. Reilley and Maj. Henry A. Brown; Secretary, Frank B. Steele; Treasurer, Millard F. Dake; Registrar, William A. Galpin; Chaplain, Rev. Walter Smith, Dunkirk.

New York Chapter.—President, Brig. Gen. Oliver B. Bridgman; Vice-Presidents, Col. Henry W. Sackett, Hon. Job E. Hedges, and William C. Demorest; Secretary, George McK. Roberts, 220 Broadway; Treasurer, Ward Belknap; Registrar, Jesse H. Clute; Historian, Hon. James B. Laux; Chaplain, Rev. Joseph Fort Newton, D. D.

Ft. Johnston Chapter, Johnstown.—Secretary, Rev. Wolcott W. Ellsworth, D. D.

Huntington Chapter.—President, Isaac R. Swezey; Vice-President, James H. Conklin; Secretary, Everest Sammis; Treasurer, Edwin W. Sammis; Registrar, Daniel B. Young.

Mohawk Valley Chapter, Herkimer.—President, Hon. John W. Vrooman; Secretary, E. W. Christman; Treasurer, Ralph D. Earl.

Newburgh Chapter.—President, W. R. Perkins; Vice-Presidents, Charles F. Burnett and Rev. J. W. Babbitt; Secretary, Andrew E. Layman; Treasurer, Frank E. Forsyth; Registrar, Rev. Marinus S. Purdy; Historian, D. W. Jagger; Chaplain, Rev. Frank E. Whitney; Color Bearer, L. J. White.

Newton Battle Chapter, Elmira.—President, Jesse L. Churchill; Vice-Presidents, Hiram H. Bickford and Harrison S. Chapman; Secretary, George M. Diven, 615 Hoffman Street; Treasurer, Capt. Charles L. Hart; Registrar, H. Carlyle Millspaugh; Historian, Ichabod A. Olmstead; Chaplain, Joseph H. Pierce.

The Painted Post Chapter, Corning.—President, Hon. Alanson B. Houghton; Vice-President, E. Stuart Underhill; Secretary, John L. Chatfield; Treasurer, William J. Heermans; Historian, Uri Mulford.

Rochester Chapter.—President, Raymond G. Dann; Vice-President, William B. Boothby; Secretary, Charles A. Brady, 178 Culver Road; Treasurer, John B. Howe; Registrar, Edward R. Foreman; Historian, Fred L. Yates; Chaplain, Rev. James T. Dickinson, D. D.

Saratoga Chapter, Saratoga Springs.—Secretary, Dr. Earl H. King.

Syracuse Chapter.—President, Newell B. Woodworth; Vice-President, William W. Wiard; Secretary, Charles C. Cook, 202 Wieting Block; Treasurer, Willis E. Gaylord; Historian, Hon. D. Raymond Cobb; Registrar, J. Frank Durston; Chaplain, Rev. Walter R. Ferris.

Col. Cornelius Van Dyck Chapter, Schenectady.—69 members; chartered June 4, 1915. President, E. R. Whitney; Vice-Presidents, George E. Young and E. J. Hand; Secretary, Hanford Robison, 322 State Street; Treasurer, H. S. Stedman; Registrar, P. S. Miller; Historian, E. A. Shaw; Chaplain, Heber Williams.

Genesee Chapter, Batavia.—President, W. H. A. Spink; Vice-President, G. G. Dexter; Secretary, C. Randall Howe; Treasurer, G. A. Paddock; Historian, F. H. Dunham; Chaplain, Rev. Lafayette Congdon, D. D.

NORTH CAROLINA SOCIETY

Organized February 22, 1911; Annual Meeting, February 22

(Society now being reorganized under Maj. John F. Jones, Blacksburg, S. C.)

NORTH DAKOTA SOCIETY

83 MEMBERS

Organized February ?, 1911; Annual Meeting, February 22 (Postponed this year to April 19)

Officers Elected 1922

President, Howard E. Simpson, Grand Forks; Vice-President, John O. Hanchett, Valley City; Secretary-Registrar, Walter R. Reed, Fargo; Treasurer, Willis E. Fuller, Grand Forks; Historian, Frank Drew Hall, Fargo; Chaplain, William J. Clapp, Fargo.

Grand Forks Chapter.—Organized February 27, 1922; charter delivered April 19. President, Vernon P. Squires; Vice-President, John Adams Taylor; Secretary-Registrar, George F. Rich; Treasurer, F. F. Burchard; Historian, A. H. Yoder; Chaplain, Dr. S. Paige Johnson.

OHIO SOCIETY

853 MEMBERS

Organized April 11-22, 1889; Annual Meeting, April 19

Officers Elected 1922

President, Edwin L. Shuey, Dayton; Vice-President, Frederick H. Gates, Cleveland; Secretary-Registrar, William L. Curry, Columbus; Treasurer, S. G.

Harvey, Toledo; Historian, W. L. Mattoon, Columbus; Chaplain, Rev. Frederick B. Avery, Cleveland.

Chapter Officers

Alexander Hamilton Chapter, Coshocton.—President, Dr. William P. Reeves, Gambier; Secretary, Harry S. Lybarger.

Anthony Wayne Chapter, Toledo.—President, O. S. Brumbach; Secretary, Charles R. Barefoot.

Benjamin Franklin Chapter, Columbus.—President, John L. Hamilton, Jr.; Secretary, Hugh Huntington.

Cincinnati Chapter.—President, Dr. E. R. Booth; Secretary, Rev. E. P. Whallon, 422 Elm Street.

Ethan Allen Chapter, Warren.—President, Fred W. Adams; Secretary, Dr. James W. Tyler; Vice-President, James E. Bebee; Treasurer, Frederick K. Smith; Historian, Norman W. Adams.

Gen. Francis Marion Chapter, Marion.—President, Fred Hoch; Secretary, James A. Knapp.

John Stark Chapter, Massillon.—President, Dr. Henry Clinton Eyman; Secretary, Loren E. Souers, Canton.

Nathan Hale Chapter, Youngstown.—President, Hon. B. F. Wirt; Secretary, J. J. Brant.

Olentangy Valley Chapter, Delaware.—President, Robert B. Powers; Secretary, H. A. Spaulding.

Richard Montgomery Chapter, Dayton.—President, Edward F. Brown; Vice-President, Robert Patterson; Secretary, Miles S. Kuhns; Registrar, Ira H. Vogt; Chaplain, Rev. Allen K. Zartman.

Tarhe Chapter, Lancaster.—President, Henry K. Beck; Secretary, Curtis L. Berry.

Western Reserve Chapter, Cleveland.—President, Robert A. Bishop; Vice-Presidents, Francis W. Treadway, Edward M. Hall, O. W. Carpenter, and Theodore A. Cooper; Secretary-Treasurer, Robert P. Boggis, 3171 Coleridge Road; Assistant Secretary-Treasurer, George H. Barber; Registrar, Jesse A. Fenner; Historian, Fred S. Dunham; Chaplain, Rev. F. B. Avery, D. D.

OKLAHOMA SOCIETY

119 Members

Organized February 22, 1905; Charter Issued May 18, 1909; Annual Meeting, February 22

Officers Elected 1922

President, George L. Bowman, Kingfisher; Vice-Presidents, Barritt Galloway, Oklahoma City; George E. Bennett, Tulsa, and L. A. Morton, Duncan; Secretary-Treasurer, Edward F. McKay, Oklahoma City; Registrar, E. K. Jennings, Oklahoma City; Historian, J. B. Thoburn, Oklahoma City; Chaplain, Bowman F. Stockwell, Oklahoma City.

Tulsa Chapter.—Secretary, H. H. Hagan.

Oklahoma City Chapter.—President, Stewart Mitchell.

OREGON SOCIETY

260 Members

Organized June, 1891; Annual Meeting, February 22

Officers Elected 1922

President, B. B. Beekman; Vice-President, Winthrop Hammond; Secretary, B. A. Thaxter; Treasurer, A. A. Lindsley; Registrar, Alfred F. Parker, all of Portland.

PENNSYLVANIA SOCIETY

763 MEMBERS

Organized November 23, 1893; Annual Meeting, February 22

Officers Elected 1922

President, W. C. Lyne, Pittsburgh; Vice-Presidents, A. C. Shaw, Pittsburgh; H. W. Fernberger, Philadelphia, and Dr. H. C. Westervelt, Pittsburgh; Secretary, Francis Armstrong, Jr., Pittsburgh; Treasurer, A. W. Wall, Pittsburgh; Registrar, W. J. Askin, Jr., Pittsburgh; Historian-Chaplain, Rev. Grafton T. Reynolds, D. D., Pittsburgh.

Chapter Officers

Wayne Chapter, Erie.—Chartered 1899. (No report.)
New Castle Chapter.—55 members; annual meeting, January 8. President, F. G. Simonton; Vice-President, Harry W. McKee, Jr.; Secretary, William J. Caldwell; Treasurer, W. Fulton Jackson; Registrar, J. S. Du Shane.*
Philadelphia Chapter.—President, Herman W. Fernberger; Vice-President, Walter Gabell; Secretary-Treasurer, I. B. Blain; Registrar, Hiram L. Wynne; Historian, James K. Helms.
Ft. Bedford Chapter, Bedford.—(No report.)
Shenango Chapter, Sharon.—28 members. President, Andrew C. McLean; Vice-President, Guy Thorne; Secretary-Treasurer, George H. Allen; Registrar, Leroy S. Runser; Historian, William A. McCormick.
McKeesport Chapter—Organzied February 10, 1922. President, A. E. Leffler; Vice-President, A. B. Holmes; Secretary, John A. Kelso; Treasurer, Gilbert F. Myer; Historian, J. C. Miller; Registrar, Marion M. Ginn; Chaplain, Rev. George R. Phillips.
Middletown Chapter.—Organized May, 1922. President, R. P. Raymond; Vice-Presidents, Truman P. Ettele, Harrisburg, and Colin S. Few; Secretary, W. K. Lemon, Jr.; Assistant Secretary, H. B. Etter; Treasurer, Le Roy H. Markly; Registrar, R. F. Keiper; Chaplain-Historian, Joseph Montgomery, 2d, Harrisburg.

RHODE ISLAND SOCIETY

380 MEMBERS

Organized February 1, 1890; Annual Meeting, February 22

Officers Elected 1922

President, Herbert Ambrose Rice, Providence; Vice-President, Addison Pierce Munroe, Providence; Secretary, Theodore E. Dexter, 104 Clay Street, Central Falls; Treasurer, William Luther Sweet, Providence; Registrar, Edward Kimball Aldrich, Providence; Historian, Howard Millar Chapin, Providence; Chaplain, Rev. Frederick S. Penfold, Providence; Poet, William Mabley Muncy, Providence.

Chapter Officers

Bristol Chapter, No. 1.—Chartered January 1, 1898. President, Hezekiah C. Wardwell; Vice-President, Lewis B. Waldron; Secretary, Joseph Franklin Farrally; Treasurer, William L. Manchester; Historian, George U. Arnold; Poet, Orrin L. Bosworth.
Providence Chapter, No. 2.—Chartered April 17, 1901. President, Frederick Dickman Carr; Vice-President, Albert Lawton Calder, 2d; Secretary-Treasurer, Arthur Preston Sumner; Historian, Wilfred H. Munro; Poet, George F. Weston.

---

* Deceased.

Pawtucket Chapter, No. 3.—Chartered February 18, 1909. President, Henry Clinton Dexter; Vice-President, Charles Henry French; Secretary-Treasurer, Theodore E. Dexter.

Kent County Chapter, No. 4, East Greenwich.—Chartered February 18, 1909. President, Henry Greene Jackson, Riverpoint; Vice-President, Benjamin F. Tefft; Secretary, Elisha Waterman Bucklin; Treasurer, Frank Bailey Smith; Registrar, William Arnold Browning; Historian, Albert Rodman Nichols; Chaplain, Rev. Charles F. Roper.

SOUTH CAROLINA SOCIETY

Organized March 22, 1911

(No report.) (Society now being reorganized under Maj. John F. Jones, Blacksburg.)

SOUTH DAKOTA SOCIETY

78 MEMBERS

Organized March 27, 1911; Annual Meeting, April 19

Officers Elected 1922

President, A. B. Sessions, Sioux Falls; Secretary-Registrar, T. W. Dwight, Sioux Falls; Treasurer, B. H. Requa, Sioux Falls; Historian, Doane Robinson, Pierre.

TENNESSEE SOCIETY

159 MEMBERS

Organized December 2, 1889; Annual Meeting, October 7

Officers Elected 1922

President, Wm. K. Boardman, Nashville; Vice-President at Large, F. W. Millspaugh, Nashville; Vice-President East Tenn., C. K. Hill, Harriman; Vice-President Middle Tenn., Paul De Witt, Nashville; Vice-President West Tenn., John D. McDowell, Memphis; Secretary-Registrar, J. Tyree Fain, Nashville; Treasurer, Carey A. Folk, Nashville; Historian, John H. De Witt, Nashville; Surgeon, M. G. Buckner, M. D., Nashville; Chaplain, Jas. I. Vance, D. D., Nashville.

Chapter Officers

Memphis Chapter.—18 charter members; organized March 17, 1922. President, W. Lawson Wilhoite; Vice-Presidents, John Davis McDowell and Thomas W. Ham; Secretary-Treasurer, W. W. Swift; Registrar, E. E. Joyner; Historian, Dr. R. E. Bullington.

TEXAS SOCIETY

98 MEMBERS

Organized December 8, 1896; Annual Meeting, February 22

Officers Elected 1921 (No Annual Meeting 1922)

President, C. B. Dorchester, Sherman; Vice-Presidents, F. F. Downs, Temple, and John Charles Harris, Houston; Secretary-Treasurer, Walter S. Mayer, Galveston; Registrar-Historian, Edwin E. Rice, Galveston; Chaplain, J. T. Huffmaster, Galveston.

UTAH SOCIETY

212 MEMBERS

Organized January 29, 1895; Annual Meeting, February 22

Officers Elected 1922

President, Robert E. McConaughy; Vice-President, John Quale Cannon; Secretary, Gordon Lines Hutchins; Treasurer, Seth Warner Morrison; Registrar, Chauncey P. Overfield; Historian, Levi Edgar Young; Chaplain, Hoyt E. Henriques, all of Salt Lake City.

VERMONT SOCIETY

196 MEMBERS

Organized April 2, 1889; Annual Meeting in February

Officers Elected 1922

President, William H. Jeffrey, Montpelier; Vice-President, Charles A. Plumley, Northfield; Secretary, Walter H. Crockett, Burlington; Treasurer, Clarence L. Smith, Burlington; Registrar, Dorman B. E. Kent, Montpelier; Chaplain, Rev. I. C. Smart, Burlington.

VIRGINIA SOCIETY

263 MEMBERS

Organized July 7, 1890; Annual Meeting, February 22

Officers Elected 1922

President, Arthur B. Clarke, Richmond; Vice-Presidents, Hon. H. H. Pollard, Richmond; Frederick B. Emerson, Norfolk, and Dr. George Ross, Richmond; Secretary-Treasurer-Registrar, William E. Crawford, Richmond; Historian, James Branch Cabell, Dumbarton.

WASHINGTON SOCIETY

265 MEMBERS (1920)

Organized June 17, 1895; Annual Meeting, February 22

Officers Elected 1922

President, Walter Burgess Beals, Seattle; Vice-Presidents, Charles Barton Wood, Seattle; John W. Bell, Jr., Spokane, and Jesse Martin Hitt, Olympia; Secretary, Henry J. Gorin, Seattle; Treasurer, Kenneth P. Hussey, Seattle; Registrar, John N. Wilson, Seattle; Historian, Ovid A. Byers, Seattle; Chaplain, Sherman Landon Divine, Spokane.

Chapter Officers

Spokane Chapter.—President, John Chester Ralston; Vice-President, Luther N. Flagg; Secretary-Treasurer, John William Bell, Jr.; Registrar, John Wellman MacIntosh; Chaplain, Rev. J. Neilson Barry.

Seattle Chapter.—President, Percy Bradford Hunting; Vice-President, Charles Baron Whitney Raymond; Secretary-Treasurer-Historian, Will George Crosby; Chaplain, Rev. Frederick Levi Forbes; Senior Trustee, G. E. Tilton; Junior Trustee, John Charles Gregory.

Alexander Hamilton Chapter, Tacoma.—President, Leavenworth Kershaw; Vice-President, Walter B. Hotchkiss; Secretary-Registrar, George O. Swasey; Treasurer, A. E. Grafton.

Gov. Isaac Ingalls Stevens Chapter, Olympia.—President, John G. Gerwick; Vice-President, Elmer F. Walker; Secretary-Historian, J. M. Hitt; Treasurer, Fred. W. Stocking.

WISCONSIN SOCIETY

140 MEMBERS

Organized February 25, 1890; Annual Meeting in June

Officers Elected 1922

President, Henry S. Sloan; Vice-Presidents, C. B. Traver and Walter F. Meyer; Secretary, Emmett A. Donnelly; Treasurer, William Stark Smith; Registrar, William W. Wight; Historian, Ellis B. Usher; Chaplain, Rt. Rev. William Walter Webb, all of Milwaukee.

WYOMING SOCIETY

44 MEMBERS

Organized March 28, 1908; Annual Meeting, February 22

Officers Elected 1922

President, David A. Haggard; Vice-President, Thomas G. Gilson; Secretary, Maurice Groshon; Treasurer, James B. Guthrie; Registrar, Harold L. Vaughan; Historian, Ichabod S. Bartlett, all of Cheyenne.

ANNOUNCEMENTS

The President General was the speaker of the day at the meeting held on the steps of the Subtreasury on Wall Street, New York (where Washington took the oath of office as first President of the Republic), Saturday noon, September 16, under the auspices of the New York Chapter.

The subject of his address was "Defend the Constitution," and he was listened to by an audience of from eight to ten thousand interested people. After referring to the fact that similar meetings, to the number of more than fifty thousand, were being held under the auspices of the Sons of the American Revolution throughout the entire country, Major Adams went on to say:

"And it is eminently right and proper that we should do this, particularly at this time of national and world unrest, when the sinister forces which are unfriendly to our Constitution and to all constitutions are making their determined and organized efforts to overthrow it. If we would save our Constitution and the representative Republic which is founded upon it, we who revere and respect its authority, whether descendants of patriotic American Ancestry or foreign born (for all are true Americans who have the American spirit), must stand together now in its defense.

"The present revolutionary unrest which threatens the entire world, and which has manifested itself so disastrously in Russia, is not an outgrowth of the World War, as many have supposed, but has its root-causes much deeper than that. The same evil forces are at work here to overthrow our Government which have been successful in the Old World; and it devolves upon us who have faith in our Constitution and believe in our Republic as the best form of Government which the World has ever known, to resist every attack of its foes, whether from without or within.

"As our ancestors pledged their lives, property, and their sacred honor to establish our stately and stable Constitution, which has truly been pronounced the most wonderful document ever devised by man, so we, their descendants, the Sons of the American Revolution, must pledge ourselves, by all that we have and are, to maintain that same noble charter of our rights and liberties."

And he concluded a notable address by declaring that—

"The American Constitution stands for law and order, for equal rights and liberty under the law for all. The destiny of the Nation rests upon this Constitution, and its maintenance, with the blessings secured to us all under its wise and just provisions, is worthy of our greatest sacrifices."

The President General spoke again on the Constitution the following afternoon in Newark, N. J., where the New Jersey Society held a well-attended meeting before its Headquarters on Lombardy Street. State President Judge Adrian Lyon made the principal address on this occasion.

Several members of the Society have been remembered by the family of the late Dr. Moses Greeley Parker with a beautiful memorial volume of Dr. Parker's biography. This volume is beautifully bound in soft morocco and printed with fine taste and style. It is a worthy tribute to one of the noted members of our organization, President General in 1911-12, President of the Massachusetts Society in 1905, and prominent in many other organizations of a patriotic and civic nature and in humanitarian and professional endeavors.

The President General has accepted an invitation of Mr. Will H. Hays, chairman, to become a member of the General Committee of Social and Civic Agencies, as the Representative of the National Society, Sons of the American Revolution.

Treasurer General Roberts was one of the speakers at the Old Home Day celebration at Montgomery, Mass., on September 4, 1922. Mr. Roberts gave a short talk on "Montgomery in the Revolution and Early Settlers," and those in attendance were interested in knowing that the graves of several Revolutionary soldiers had been located in Montgomery cemeteries. Mr. Roberts also explained the organization and objects of the Sons of the American Revolution and told of its accomplishments and the various celebrations of important historical anniversaries. Montgomery is famous for being the site of the armory of Lt. Richard Falley, whose well-made guns helped materially to win the war. The ruins of the armory can still be seen, and near by is his old homestead, in an excellent state of preservation.

Hon. Eugene C. Bonniwell, Chancellor General of the National Society, was the guest of honor and principal speaker at the celebration of the anniversary of the birthday of General Lafayette, held at the Washington Club, Washington, D. C., on September 6, under the auspices of the Order of Lafayette. The meeting was preceded by a business session and election of officers, at which Judge Bonniwell was elected Vice-President of the order. Marshal Foch is Honorary President General of the organization.

The BULLETIN Editor takes pleasure in publishing the following copy of a letter received from the American Legion through National Director Alvin M. Owsley, Indianapolis, Ind.:

SEPTEMBER 16, 1922.

President, Sons of the American Revolution.

MY DEAR SIR: The American Legion, the National Education Association, and the United States Bureau of Education have joined together to hold the second annual American Education Week throughout the United States from December 3 to 9, inclusive. The underlying purpose of American Education Week is to arouse all the nation to a truer sense of our educational needs along broad, constructive, patriotic lines. By bringing our people to concentrate upon the training of the masses of uneducated, we shall go far toward eliminating illiteracy in our land and take a forward step in the solution of our national problems. An educated patriotic citizenship is the best investment to insure the safety and perpetuity of the Republic. Nothing can save us, if we are a nation of weaklings and illiterates.

The American Legion extends to the Sons of the American Revolution a cordial and urgent invitation to co-operate with it to make successful this undertaking. Your acceptance will be our pleasure and authority to use your name on the official program and in national publicity.

Faithfully yours,
(Signed)

ALVIN M. OWSLEY,
National Director.

THE FLAG

Flag Day, June 14; Constitution Day, September 17

Pledge of Allegiance: I pledge allegiance to my flag and to the Republic for which it stands—one nation, indivisible, with liberty and justice for all.

WHEN AND HOW TO DISPLAY THE FLAG OF THE UNITED STATES

Holidays, When the Flag Should be Displayed at Full Staff

Lincoln's Birthday_____February 12
Washington's Birthday_____February 22
Jefferson Day_____April 17
Battle of Lexington (Patriots Day)_____April 19
Memorial Day*_____May 30
Flag Day_____June 14
Battle of Bunker Hill_____June 17
Independence Day_____July 4
La Fayette Day_____September 6
"Star Spangled Banner" Day_____September 13
Paul Jones Day_____September 23
Columbus Day_____October 12
Battle of Saratoga_____October 17
Surrender of Yorktown_____October 19
Evacuation Day (New York)_____November 25

Stars and Stripes is the official name of the National Flag of the United States. In the Army our National Flag is called the Standard; also the Colors. When

*On Memorial Day, May 30, the flag should fly at half staff from sunrise to noon and full staff from noon to sunset.

borne with another flag, the regimental color, the two flags are called a "Stand of Colors." In the Navy our National Flag is known as the U. S. Ensign.

To show proper respect for the flag, the following should be observed:

Display

The flag should not be hoisted before sunrise nor allowed to remain up after sunset.

At "retreat" sunset, civilian spectators should stand at "attention" and uncover during the playing of the "Star Spangled Banner." Military spectators are required by regulation to stand at "attention" and give the military salute. During the playing of the National Hymn at "retreat" the flag should be lowered, but not then allowed to touch the ground.

When the flag is flown at half staff as a sign of mourning, it should be hoisted to the top of the staff and then lowered to position, dropping it from the top of the staff the distance of the width of the flag, and preliminary to lowering from half staff it should first be raised to the top.

On ship board the National Flag is the flag to be raised first and lowered last.

Where several flags are displayed on poles with the National Flag, the Stars and Stripes should be hoisted first and on the tallest and most conspicuous staff. Where two flags are displayed, one our National Flag, it should be placed on the right. (To ascertain the right of a building, face in the same direction as the building.) No flag should be flown from the same staff as the U. S. Flag, except in the Navy; then only during Divine service, when the Church Pennant may be displayed above the National Flag—God above country.

When, in parade, the National Flag is carried with any other flag, it should have the place of honor, at the right. If a number of flags are carried, the National Flag should either precede the others or be carried in the center, above the others, on a higher staff.

When flags are used in unveiling a monument, tablet or statue, they should not fall to the ground, but be carried aloft, forming a distinctive feature of the ceremony.

When the National Flag is used as a banner, the union should be at the right (as you face the flag). When used as an altar covering, the union is at the right (as you face the altar), and nothing should ever be placed upon the flag except the Holy Bible.

The flag should never be flown reversed except in case of distress at sea.

Portraying the Flag

To properly illustrate the flag, the staff should always be at the left of the picture, with the flag floating to the right. When two flags are crossed, the National Flag should be at the right. If the National Flag is pictured as a banner, the union is at the right.

Salute

When the National Colors are passing in parade or in review, the spectator should, if walking, halt, and if sitting, arise and stand at "attention" and uncover.

The national salute is one gun for every State.

The international salute is, under the laws of nations, 21 guns.

On shore the flag should not be dipped by way of salute or compliment.

THE TEMPLE OF THE CONSTITUTION

(An original ode, read by former Chaplain General Rev. Lyman Whitney Allen, at the
Constitution Day meeting, September 17, 1922, in Newark, N. J.)

The Temple of the Constitution, builded
Across the crimson trails of revolution,
After high Freedom's pattern in the Mount,
Whence incensed Law, and Love, and Justice rise,
    And God came down and wrote again
    His Word with fiery fingers.

The Temple of the Constitution, founded
Inviolate on the rock of truth eternal
By the great commoners of liberty—
America's forever-cherished fathers.
    And God was pleased and filled anew
    His house with power and glory.

The Temple of the Constitution 'stablished
To hold the people's governmental altars,
Whence incensed Law, and Love, and Justice rise.
The will of God, the hope of man exalting.
    And all the wide-flung gates of hell
    Shall not prevail against it.

LET'S GO!

Now that the summer and fall campaign for new members is over, don't stop even for breath, but let this be the greatest year in the history of our great organization!

Word has been received from the Registrar's office that the number of new members accepted and taken in during this past summer is the largest in the same period for any year. Of course, there is no doubt that to a great extent this was due to the fact that the initiation fee was waived until October 1. It was good business judgment to go out after new members to save them the extra fee, just as it is in business when prices are to rise. But you never hear of a business man laying down after the prices go up. He just speeds up his salesmen to do a little better, and if he has energy and enthusiasm, the very impetus that he has accumulated during his drive helps that much to carry on his future selling campaign. The Sons of the American Revolution all over the country can profit by this example, and now that we have made such a fine start, all we need do is to keep up the pace and the accomplishment of this year will be unrivaled.

As was so well said at the Congress in Springfield, this Society is one that appeals to the best in the land, and one that every man who can prove his eligibility should have an ardent desire to join and help in the work we are doing. No one who appreciates what this Society stands for, what it means to him to become a member, what it means to his country to have a body of sterling men throughout the country standing for the principles that the Sons of the American Revolution stands for, will hesitate an instant when asked to become a compatriot, and the matter of expense will not enter into the argument at all. In fact, it must be made so desirable to be associated with this Society that men will seek us rather than we find it necessary to go after them.

Compatriots, get to work and see what you can do! One member each from every member would not be hard, and if we do just one-quarter of that, or a member to each four, five thousand new members would be added. And this is not beyond the possibilities! Our great sister organization has over 130,000 members, and this alone should make us feel that the men are at least as patriotic and proud of their inheritance as the women. Keep it in mind every minute; work with your Chapters and your State Societies; volunteer your services. There never was a better time to carry on this work of our organization, and if you will do your part a splendid result will be achieved at the close of the year.

JUDGE McCAMANT'S REVIEW OF MUZZEY'S SCHOOL HISTORY

Past President General McCamant is vigorously carrying on the work of purging the public schools of the country of inaccurate, unfair, and prejudiced school histories.

In his clean-cut and logical way he goes after the recent edition of Muzzey's School History of the United States which, through the business enterprise of the publishers, has been introduced and maintained in many public schools throughout the country. Judge McCamant believes this work to be utterly unfit for school use and brands the author as one having "no abiding conviction in American fundamentals; no enthusiastic veneration for the great men who founded the Republic." Then our Past President General goes on to show the unfairness and inaccuracy of this book. Space forbids publishing in the BULLETIN the complete review, but, as this organization is particularly interested in this part of the work, a few of the unfair statements and omissions will be given here to show our members what is going on in this country.

Judge McCamant shows that in one place the people who engaged in the demonstrations against the Stamp Act are called "the mob"; that Hancock, Warren Otis, and the Adams's are spoken of contemptuously and called "patriots" with these quotation-marks attached to the word; that the author gives his views on taxation without representation, and there is no condemnation of the principle contended for by George III or his ministers; he characterizes the matter as a "debatable one," and in another place he contemptuously refers to the speeches of Patrick Henry and the Adams's as "their rhetorical warnings against being reduced to slavery." This author devotes one sentence to the Battle of Bunker Hill and makes no mention of the death of Joseph Warren. The Battle of Lexington is mentioned in one sentence, as follows: "In April occurred the Battle of Lexington." The taking of Ticonderoga is covered in the following way: "In May came the bold capture of Fort Ticonderoga." Then Judge McCamant goes on to make a most pertinent statement:

"Except for the sentences to each of the battles of Lexington, Ticonderoga, and Bunker Hill, he (Muzzey) undertakes to cover the Revolutionary War in seven pages. I am not contending that a school history should discuss in detail the tactics of battles and the strategy of campaigns, but I do say that students in our public schools should be taught that our free institutions were won by heroism and self-sacrifice. They should know the story in sufficient detail to insure that they will revere the men who founded the Republic, and that they will prize our institutions as a treasure bought with a great price. They should understand references in literature to Valley Forge and Bunker Hill. They should have some conception of the far-sighted wisdom of the great men of the Revolution, of the hardships endured in order to win the Revolution and the high type of manhood and character exemplified by the patriots of the Revolutionary period. . . . Some of the incidents of the Revolution are particularly adapted to captivate the imagination of the younger students. Any red-blooded American, whatever his age, will be impressed with the stories of Lexington and Concord, of Anthony Wayne and Stony Point, the sufferings of the army at Valley Forge and Morristown; the heroism displayed in crossing the Delaware and fighting the battles of Trenton and Princeton; the partisan warfare in South Carolina and the uprising of the people of New York and New England to encompass the surrender of Burgoyne."

Judge McCamant, with members of our organization in New York, protested against the use of certain books then in use in the schools and helped crystallize the sentiment in that city. This led to the appointment of a committee of twenty-one educators by the superintendent of schools in Greater New York. This committee, with commendable research and patience, has investigated the subject and made a report which should be in the hands of every board charged with the selection of school books on American History. The following is quoted by Judge McCamant from this report:

"The pupil should be inspired by the vivid and glowing pictures of the sacrifices made by the patriots, the things they did and the things they said. In the words of Abbe Reynal:

"'With what grandeur, with what enthusiasm, should I speak of those generous men who erected this grand edifice, by their patience, their courage—Hancock, Franklin, Adams! Posterity shall know them all. Their honored names shall be transmitted to it by a happier pen than mine. Brass and marble shall show them to the remotest ages. In beholding them shall the friend of freedom feel his heart palpitate with joy, feel his eyes float in delicious tears. Under the bust of one of them has been written, "He wrested thunder from heaven and the scepter from tyrants." Of the last words of this eulogy shall the whole of them partake.'"

Judge McCamant further shows that there are three lines devoted to the Battle of Oriskany and a mere reference to Valley Forge; that this author ascribes the French alliance to a desire on the part of France for revenge. This is inaccurate and unfair. The services rendered by France to this country in our Revolutionary period were knightly, and so generous that it is no small fault in a school history to ascribe them to a selfish and unworthy motive. There is no mention of Marion, Sumpter, Pickens, and Williams. The work contains no mention of Bennington, or John Starke, of Anthony Wayne or Stony Point, of Light Horse Harry Lee or Paulus Hook.

These are some of the glaring and unfair statements concerning the Revolutionary War. They are enough, but Judge McCamant shows in the balance of this review that this whole work is permeated with inaccuracies, unfairness, partisanship, and socialism.

When we stop to contemplate the effect of such a book upon the young minds of our country, it makes the blood boil, and we who, above any others in this country, are the descendants of those men who gave themselves to make this land of ours what it was and what it is, should in every community where there is a possibility of such propaganda being spread use our utmost influence to stamp it out.

Do not be passive about this really serious menace, but stamp on it while it is raising its head, and it will be another achievement to the credit of this great organization of ours. Past President General McCamant is leading the way; let us work with him and back him up to the limit.

A REPRINT FROM THE LIBERTY BELL, ISSUE OF OCTOBER, 1922

OFFICIAL ORGAN OF THE SONS OF THE REVOLUTION OF CALIFORNIA

[The following account is intended to record the circumstances attending the organization of the two National Revolutionary Societies. Some apparent inaccuracies are corrected in the appended letter by Compatriot Edward Hagaman Hall to a former President General, Col. Louis Annin Ames.

The article makes no mention, however, of the unsuccessful efforts to merge the two organizations into one large National Society which would be satisfactory to both. The account of these efforts to combine is too long for repetition at this time; it is contained in a pamphlet by Edward Hagaman Hall, which was reprinted from the register for 1899 of the Empire State Society, Sons of the American Revolution, to which we refer the interested reader.

This pamphlet reveals the fact that the efforts to combine into one Society all the descendants of Revolutionary Sires failed through no fault of the representatives of the Sons of the American Revolution.]

Chronological History of the Revolutionary War Societies

"CANTONMENT OF THE AMERICAN ARMY ON
HUDSON RIVER, 10th May, 1783."

"Proposals for establishing a Society, upon principles therein mentioned, whose Members shall be Officers of the American Army," . . . were considered at this time. It resulted in the formation of the Society of the Cincinnati, having among its purposes the following:

"To perpetuate, therefore, as well the Remembrance of this Vast Event, as the mutual Friendships which have been formed under the Pressure of common Danger and in many Instances Cemented by the Blood of the capital Parties, the Officers of the American Army do hereby in the Most Solemn Manner associate, constitute and combine themselves into one Society of Friends, to endure as long as they shall endure or any of their Eldest Male Posterity, and in failure thereof the Collateral Branches who may be judged worthy of becoming its Supporters and Members."

"An Incessant Attention to preserve inviolate those exalted Rights and Liberties of Human Nature for which they have fought and bled and without which the high rank of a Rational Being is a Curse Instead of a Blessing.

"An unalterable determination to promote and cherish between the respective States that Union and national Honour so essentially necessary to their happiness, and the future dignity of the American Empire." (Society of the Cincinnati, Pennsylvania, July 4, 1881, pages 5, 6, and 7.)

"In December of 1873 several efforts were made by Mr. John Austin Stevens, of New York, to induce the Society of the Cincinnati, through its President General, Honorable Hamilton Fish, to change the policy of that organization so as to provide for admission to membership upon more extended lines, so that the doors of the organization should be open to a larger number of Revolutionuary Descendants. These efforts did not meet with any response. As a result of this rebuff, the ideas and thoughts of Mr. Stevens were crystallized in a purpose to organize a new Society, to be carried upon broader lines of membership than the older organization." (Spirit of Patriotism, 1915, page 27.)

"Anticipating the Centennial Celebration, a few men met at the office of Dr. James L. Cogswell, 230 Kearney Street, San Francisco, on October 22, 1875, and formed a temporary organization only. Nothing more was done until some of them helped to organize the Sons of Revolutionary Sires." ("Addresses," California Society, S. A. R., 1917, page 69.)

"Mr. John Austin Stevens is truly the founder of the Society, Sons of the Revolution. He gathered about him a number of associates who adopted and supported his cause, and on the 18th day of December, 1875, in the rooms of the New York Historical Society, a meeting was held to determine the possibilities of the new organization. Mr. Stevens there proposed a definite organization, and the name 'Sons of the Revolution' was adopted at this preliminary meeting.

"Later a meeting was held at the same place on January 15, 1876, a constitution presented by Mr. Stevens was unanimously adopted and signed by all who were present. The new organization was launched with much hope and certain confidence in its future growth and prosperity."

A circular letter was then issued stating the purposes of the newly formed Society, inviting those eligible to join with them. To quote:

"A meeting will be held for the organization at the rooms of the New York Historical Society on the morning of Tuesday, the 22d of February next (1876), at 12 o'clock. All persons having a right and desire to become members may send their names and the names of those they represent to the undersigned (Box 88, Station D, New York post-office). (Signed) John Austin Stevens." (Spirit of Patriotism, 1915, pages 27, 28, and 29; Supplement to section 1 of "Heroes of the Revolution and their Descendants, 1899.")

"A call for the descendants of the Revolutionary fathers to meet at 212 Kearney Street, San Francisco, California, on the evening of June 29, 1876, was published in the *Alta Californian* of that date, at the request of James P. Dameron, for the purpose of celebrating the Centennial Anniversary. In response to the call several men met there and on July 4, 1876, they formed a permanent organization, called the 'Sons of the Revolutionary Sires.'" ("Addresses," California Society, S. A. R., 1917, page 69.)

"Elaborate preparations were made for a dinner at Faunce's Tavern (New York City), to be given on December 4, 1883, in commemoration of the close of Washington's military career," . . .

"Here, at the time indicated, in the identical 'Long Room,' assembled a company of representative New York citizens . . ." An opportunity at this time was offered those present to join the already established Society, Sons of the Revolution.

"The Constitution of the Society, Sons of the Revolution, was presented by Mr. Stevens and his associates, and it was received with enthusiastic acclaim. The original document was brought from the archives of the New York Historical Society, where it had been deposited, and it was signed by all present who were eligible by Revolutionary descent, more than forty gentlemen affixing their signatures (many of these gentlemen were members of the Society of the Cincinnati), and the New York Society (Sons of the Revolution) was organized by the election of John Austin Stevens President; John Cochrane, Vice-President; Austin Huntington, Secretary, and George H. Potts, Treasurer.

"On the 29th day of April, 1884, a certificate of incorporation was executed." . . . (Spirit of Patriotism, 1915, pages 28 and 29.)

In March, 1889, one of the members of the New York Society, Sons of the Revolution, then living in New Jersey, in conjunction with a second member of the same society and a third man, a Scotchman, not eligible to membership, met in Newark, N. J., and there formed what they called the New Jersey Society, "Sons of the Revolution." They started a campaign to organize other State societies based upon the constitution adopted by them at the time they organized. Their constitution differed somewhat from the purposes of the original Society, Sons of the Revolution in New York. Among the differences was this: some of these newly forming societies did not prevent the admission of women to membership. The three organizers of the New Jersey "Sons of the Revolution" also started a small newspaper to advance their work, but it did not last long.

"March 7th, 1889, there were in existence only the California Society of Sons of Revolutionary Sires and the New York, Pennsylvania, and New Jersey Societies Sons of the Revolution. . . . Printed slips were sent to all the leading newspapers in the United States, setting forth the desire for the formation of State Societies and requesting correspondence with the New Jersey Committee on the part of those interested." . . . (Year Book, National Society, Sons of the American Revolution, 1890.)

After the formation of a few societies in different States, the three original organizing members of the New Jersey Society, "Sons of the Revolution," petitioned the New York Society, Sons of the Revolution, to be admitted, together with their recently formed Societies, as part of their organization. However, the material differences adopted by some of the Societies in their constitutions made it impossible as they then stood. They were requested to change them to conform to that of the original purposes of the New York Society, Sons of the Revolution, when they would be accepted. But this was never carried out.

During the Centennial Celebration of the adoption of the Constitution of the United States, in New York City, on April 30, 1889, about twenty members of these hastily organized "Sons of the Revolution" Societies met at Faunce's Tavern for the purpose of forming a National Organization, "Sons of the Revolution." The oldest of these Societies, "Sons of the Revolution," were at that time less than two months old, while the remaining Societies were from a few weeks to a few hours old.

"Pursuant to call, the National Convention assembled at Faunce's Tavern, in the City of New York, at 9 a. m., April 30th, 1889. . . .

"A draft of the Constitution was made or dictated by Hon. Lucius P. Deming.

"*Name.*—Article I of the Constitution declares the name to be 'The Society of the Sons of the Revolution.' . . .

"*Eligibility for Membership.*—Article III states that Any person (did not exclude women) may be eligible for membership in a State Society who is above the age of twenty-one years and who is descended from an ancestor that assisted," . . . (Supplement to section 1 of the Heroes of the American Revolution and their Descendants, 1898, pages 5 and 6, and History National Society, S. A. R.)

However, before the convention came to a close, it was decided to change the name of their organization. This they did by inserting the name "American" before the word "Revolution." On this date the "Society, Sons of the American Revolution," first came into existence.

Those interested in the formation of this "National Society" at this time decided that one of their men in the east should represent a worthy organization in San

Francisco that had been in existence for some time, namely, the Society "Sons of the Revolutionary Sires." This latter organization, while organized to commemorate the Revolutionary period, differed considerably with the original "Sons of the Revolution" Society and its purposes. The Sons of the Revolutionary Sires admitted to membership in an auxiliary men between the ages of 20 and 40 years, who had no Revolutionary War ancestors; likewise women were admitted to an auxiliary, and minors also were admitted to membership.

At this same meeting in New York a Constitution was adopted for the newly formed "National Society, Sons of the American Revolution." This Constitution differed from that of the Society, Sons of the Revolutionary Sires. These two Societies up to as late as April 30, 1889, were two separate organizations, though many members of the earlier Society joined the newly formed San Francisco Society, Sons of the American Revolution. About this time the membership of these two Societies was about 175 members for the Sons of the Revolutionary Sires and about 73 members for the newer organization, the Society, Sons of the American Revolution.

"There is no relation of identity between the Sons of Revolutionary Sires and the Sons of the American Revolution. The California Society, Sons of Revolutionary Sires, was never merged into or identified with the S. A. R. or the S. of R. Societies, but the members thereof transferred themselves in a body to the Sons of the American Revolution." (Historical Bulletin, December 1, 1904.)

While the membership of the earlier Society went over to the recently organized Society, the former Society did not then officially go out of existence, so far as published records disclose.

April 9, 1890. the National Society, Sons of the American Revolution, was incorporated by Congress. (Historical Sketch, Sons of the Revolution, 1893) and (Genesis and Revelations of the Former California Society, Sons of the Revolutionary Sires, but now the California Society, Sons of the American Revolution, 1905.)

The year following the organization of the National Society, Sons of the American Revolution, that organization decided to do the very thing insisted upon by the New York Society, Sons of the Revolution, at the time they sought to be admitted with their hurriedly formed Societies as part of the original organization, Sons of the Revolution. We note:

"Only a sudden jar was needed to crystallize this thought into action. This needed impulse was supplied by the Society of the Sons of the American Revolution, in the spring of 1890, when they refused to admit women to the membership in an organization intended to promote patriotism." . . .

"Interest in this grew and there were several meetings and much correspondence. On October 11, 1890, a formal meeting was held at the Strathmore Arms, 810 12th Street (Washington, D. C.) . . . Eleven of them (those present) became members that evening. It was determined that the Society should be national, with headquarters in Washington, and that the head of the new organization should be a woman of national repute. A constitution was provisionally adopted and officers elected. Mrs. Caroline Scott Harrison, wife of the President of the United States, was elected President General." . . . (Report National Society, D. A. R., 1890, page 36.)

Up to 1895 there remained in the Constitution an article containing a clause reading: "from the mother of such a patriot"; also, from "a recognized patriot," which permitted membership in the Society from descent from collateral lines of those in the Revolution, such as from brothers or sisters of Revolutionary soldiers, or those whom the Society might at any time decide to qualify as "a recognized patriot."

On February 20, 1896, the National Society, Daughters of the American Revolution, was incorporated by Congress.

August 20th, 1891, the General Society of the Daughters of the Revolution was organized in New York City, upon the same general basis the other societies are now founded upon, not admitting to membership those descended from collateral lines of ancestry, "from the mother of such a patriot," or from "a recognized patriot." Today it has Societies and Chapters in many of the States throughout the Union.

SONS OF THE REVOLUTION,
By Pierson Worrall Banning and Edward Thomas Harden.
SONS OF THE AMERICAN REVOLUTION,
By W. I. Lincoln Adams and George Eltweed Pomeroy.

Compatriot Hall's letter follows:

154 NASSAU STREET, NEW YORK, *October* 11, 1922.
Col. LOUIS ANNIN AMES,
    99 *Fulton Street, City.*

DEAR COLONEL AMES:

I have received from Mr. de la Montanye the inclosed proof and correspondence for perusal and criticism.

I think the article in proof is unfair to the S. A. R., in that it calls the California organization of 1875 "a temporary organization only," while it does not show that the organization of John Austin Stevens of 1876 was even more temporary.

The order of events appears to have been as follows:

October 22, 1875, a meeting was held at the office of Dr. Cogswell, in San Francisco, as mentioned in the proof.

December 18, 1875, Mr. Stevens had his meeting in New York, as mentioned in the proof.

The sixth paragraph in the proof, beginning "In December, 1873," is in error by two years, and should read "In December, 1875," which makes all the difference in the world. In my brother Henry Hall's book, entitled "Year Book of the Societies Composed of Descendants of the Men of the Revolution," written in 1890, is a statement furnished by Mr. Stevens himself, in which he says:

"In the fall of 1875 John Austin Stevens . . . addressed a letter to Hamilton Fish, President of the Society of the Cincinnati, to ascertain what the intentions of the Cincinnati were with reference to the approaching Centennial celebration," etc.

Mr. Stevens' own statement goes on to say that after Mr. Fish's reply he "devised the plan of a society to which he then gave the name of Sons of the Revolution. . . . A circular was prepared, inviting a meeting at the rooms of the Historical Society, February 22, 1876, the special object of which was to arrange for representation at the Philadelphia Centennial. But the time was not ripe and the interest was not sufficiently awakened in Revolutionary matters. All this, however, came later, and the celebration in New York City in 1883 of Evacuation Day was taken advantage of, and the Society of Sons of the Revolution was organized," . . . etc.

If Mr. Stevens had projected the Sons of the Revolution in 1873 he would have claimed it in that statement. It was in 1875, after the California meeting, that Mr. Stevens' first meeting was held, although the two movements may have originated spontaneously, from the same historical suggestions of the year 1875 and the approaching Centennial.

Now, what ensued? The California Society, on July 4, 1876, resolved to continue as a Society of Sons of Revolutionary Sires, and on July 11 elected permanent officers. It remained in continuous existence and its literature spread to the East.

Mr. Stevens' organization, according to his own statement, was not effectual in 1876. Permanent organization was not effected till 1883, the Centennial of Evacuation of New York.

Prior to 1889 there appear to have been only three societies permanently organized: The Sons of Revolutionary Sires of California in 1876, the New York Society of Sons of the Revolution in 1883, and the Pennsylvania Society of Sons of the Revolution in 1888.

The claim that the New Jersey Society of Sons of the Revolution antedates the New Jersey Society of the Sons of the American Revolution appears to me disingenuous, if I understand the circumstances.

The New Jersey Society was organized March 7, 1889, as Sons of the Revolution in New Jersey and applied to the New York Society for a charter. The New York Society *refused* to recognize them and objected to their use of the name Sons of the Revolution. The Jerseymen therefore, on April 20, changed their name to the New Jersey Society of the Sons of Revolutionary Sires, and when the National Society of Sons of the American Revolution was formed they adopted the name of the Sons of the American Revolution.

In 1889 about nine new Societies of Sons of the American Revolution were formed and two new societies of Sons of the Revolution.

It seems to me that it will avoid heartburnings if invidious comparisons and characterizations are avoided, and it is conceded (a) that the idea originated naturally in both the East and the West in 1875, from the association of ideas connected with the centennial of Concord and Lexington and the approach of 1876; (b) that efforts to organize, which proved temporary, were made in 1875 in both California and New York; (c) that in 1876 the first permanent organization was made in the West and in 1883 the first permanent organization in the East; and (d) that the existing societies are the product of those two parental movements.

Yours sincerely,

E. H. HALL.

NEW JERSEY'S QUARTET

Credit is given the New Jersey Society for having within its organization the only vocal quartet in the Society. Features of colonial life and of the creative period of the country, during the War for Independence, have been dealt with in recent years almost wholly from the viewpoint of suffering, trial, and hardship. But now, under the leadership of four members of Newark Chapter, Sons of the American Revolution, an entirely different aspect has been raised. It is expected that during the coming season this group of men, who compose the Newark Chapter Quartet, will exploit the music of the era when the country was instituted.

Rehearsals have been regularly held by these singers since the idea was first launched, about three months ago, by Edmund D. Poole, one of the members. After long research he has concluded that "Yankee Doodle" was not the only American rallying tune during the War of the Revolution, but that "Chester," composed by William Billings, who was born in Boston on October 7, 1746, and who died in that city September 29, 1800, was the favorite. Billings was a self-taught musician. An apprentice to a tanner, he wrote his first attempts at harmony with chalk upon the sides of leather. His first publication was entitled "The New England Psalm Singer and American Chorister." It was issued in 1770 and contained 108 pages of 120 tunes.

Billings was a believer in the effects of florid counterpoint, Mr. Poole says, being entirely ignorant of its rules, however. He early began to introduce into his work "fuguetunes," which really were not fugues at all. In such pieces the different parts naturally presented more of contrast than was possible in choral-like harmony, and this diversity was the charm which moved Billings to his musical tasks.

Several other books were found by Mr. Poole to have been issued by Billings. The soldiers of the New England regiments introduced his melodies to the other colonies through which they marched. At the occupation of Morristown by Washington and his army, particularly in the winter of 1779-1780, Billings's tunes were sung almost entirely by the soldiers. "Chester," the best known of them all, was often played by the Continental fifers and sung around the camp-fires of the boys in buff, white, and blue.

The Newark Chapter Quartet is composed of Russell B. Rankin, first tenor; Jonathan H. Huntington, 3d, second tenor; Mr. Poole, baritone, and Edwin G. Gould, bass. Mr. Huntington arranged the score of "Chester" so that it could be sung by the men with freedom, and at a recent rehearsal the effect of this grand old hymn, for such it is, was striking. It probably exerted an impelling force in sustaining the drooping spirits of the soldiers in cantonments and other quarters where the necessaries of life were limited, as they were at Morristown and at Valley Forge.

IMMIGRATION AND NATURALIZATION

Within a few weeks after the National Congress met in Springfield the Secretary General received a most cordial letter from the Secretary of Labor, Hon. James J. Davis, acknowledging the receipt of the Lillian Russell and immigration resolutions passed by the National Society, Sons of the American Revolution Congress. Secretary Davis said that President Harding had referred the matter to him, and that he, Secretary Davis, was deeply interested and wished to thank the Society for its stand on these matters.

At the same time Secretary Davis sent to the Secretary General a copy of a letter written by him to Senator Shortridge, of California, giving his views on the matter of naturalization and citizenship legislation which was then pending in the Senate. This letter is very illuminating and shows Secretary Davis to be thoroughly and intimately acquainted with this subject that our Society is so deeply interested in. The Secretary tells how he came to this country as a boy of eight; how he worked with his father in the mills; and having lived most of his life among immigrants of many nationalities, he can speak sympathetically of the needs of the alien from his viewpoint, as well as with consideration relative to serving the best interests of our country.

Secretary Davis gives a summary of the bill, which provides:

1. A required standard of education for citizenship.

2. Ability to use and understand a common language, making it possible for every citizen to communicate with each other, understand his work and the regulations made for his protection in industry, increase his opportunities for entertainment, and add greatly to his ability to use and enjoy the full advantages of residence in America.

3. Facilities for the naturalization process, eliminating the necessity for furnishing witnesses who have known the alien five years. It is estimated that this will save the aliens becoming naturalized between $3,500,000 and $7,000,000 each year.

There is substituted for this a most simple process, and the machinery for carrying out the work is comprehensive and not difficult for the foreigner. All that is necessary for the alien is to enroll and pay a small fee, which goes into a fund to be used for his own education and betterment. Not one cent of the fees collected is to go into the coffers of the National Treasury as a tax upon aliens for the purposes of the government. It is merely a small charge for education and insurance. Upon enrolling, the alien is given a card, and periodically upon this card is entered his record, which will show the progress he has made in his studies and the status of his eligibility for citizenship. Another advantage of the card, which, it is understood, has his photograph attached, is that it is authentic identification, should the alien ever be in a strange place and find it necessary to prove his identity.

4. Protection against destitution for himself and family should he become permanently disabled, and for his family should be die and leave dependents unable to care for themselves.

5. Machinery to accomplish the purposes of the act, through enrollment and the payment of a small annual fee.

The contemplated new citizenship legislation is essentially a program of education, in which every alien enrolls for citizenship training. The desire is first to teach English, so that we will be a nation with a common language. It actually means dollars and cents to the workman to be able to understand orders given to him and not follow blindly what some one else is doing. Many accidents in industry are caused through inability to understand the regulations made for the protection of the workman.

Many sources of amusement are closed to those who do not understand the national language. Being unable to read our books, our periodicals, and our newspapers, the foreign-born gets a very limited knowledge of our history and our institutions. The greatest menace to American institutions is ignorance, led by selfish education—the man who has to get his information from any one who sees fit to give him only such as serve selfish interests. The alien should be made to think and argue for himself. He should not be allowed to take for gospel truth those statements made from a soap-box by some red leader in his campaign of anarchy. Good citizenship would mean the practical elimination of anarchy and the reduction of labor disturbances to a minimum. By knowing English and being able to read and reason for himself, the alien-born would soon learn the relationship existing between capital and labor.

The Secretary advocates the teaching of history, government, and economy; the visual education by the movies, by the drama and practical teaching; also by community singing and by amusements that will interest and instruct the alien.

It is also shown by a comprehensive table that even of the aliens most responsive in taking out their citizenship papers, from Wales, Germany, Sweden, Norway, Ireland, England, Scotland, and Canada—more than 25 per cent have failed to avail themselves of the privilege, and in the southern European countries it goes as low as 10 per cent.

One of the most important factors in deterring aliens from becoming citizens is their inability to produce qualified witnesses. The enrollment feature does away with all this requirement of witnesses. There is no getting away from the card record, which he carries with him and a copy of which is made a part of the permanent records of the Government. It gives mute testimony in vouching for his eligibility to become one of us who are running and operating this greatest of all governments.

Some objection has been raised on the ground that the enrollment provision would constitute a system of espionage similar to that which is practiced in Europe. If this was so, the measure would not be considered for a moment. This legislation is an honest effort on the part of the Government to co-operate with every private organization and individual in raising the standard of citizenship and making it easier to attain that standard and acquire the privilege. True, as an incident to the working of the law, those aliens of anarchistic blood and selfish motives for aggrandizement would be discouraged. The immigration law already provides that those aliens in America in violation of law and with motives to overthrow our government institutions shall be deported, and this registration provision will but assist materially in checking up these undesirable aliens.

The foregoing is but a brief outline of Secretary of Labor Davis' letter to Senator Shortridge, but it will give our compatriots sufficient information to comprehend what a far-reaching and important measure this is and it should appeal deeply to every one who has the best interests of our country at heart. We have as a nation been all too careless in the past in the manner in which we have handled the vast hordes of people who have come from all parts of the world to these welcoming shores. We opened our arms to them; we have taken them in and said, Here are our fields and storehouses, our mines and our factories. Come, work with us and be part of us, and there will be nothing of what we have that cannot be yours and your children's merely for the asking. They came, at first, timid and afraid and in small companies, and then, seeing and realizing what was here, they sent the news back to their fatherland, and others came after them, and then others—sturdy, honest, clean, and desirable. But then, in recent years, through the machinations of unscrupulous and selfish men, great masses of undesirable immigrants were dumped down upon us, and we suddenly awoke to the fact that if something was not done at once, this great land of ours would be in the grip of a discordant and anarchistic element that would shake the country to its very foundation. Perhaps it is too late even now to cure some of the terrible evils that have crept in, and it is necessary for us who feel that our traditions have been threatened to stand up and face this problem and do our best to overcome the danger.

Accordingly, every Society of the Sons of the American Revolution, every Chapter, and every compatriot should deem it a duty to look into this bill, which will no doubt be brought up at the next session of Congress, and use whatever influence that can be brought to bear upon the Representatives and Senators from all parts of the country, urging them to support this measure. We have a membership of nearly twenty thousand, composed of men who in their communities are influential and prominent. Letters or personal communications to your representatives will have great weight, and there is no doubt would help greatly in the ultimate passage of this or a similar measure, which goes to the very heart of one of our most serious problems.

ORAL REPORT OF VICE-PRESIDENT GENERAL, NEW ENGLAND DISTRICT, GEORGE HALE NUTTING

I have great pleasure in reporting that the members of the Massachusetts Society, Sons of the American Revolution, have held their meetings this year in a satisfactory and regular manner. Notwithstanding the predictions of some of the foreboders of ill in some sections that, owing to the raising of dues in Massachusetts, a large proportion of the members would fall out, we find that we have a larger number than ever before on our roster. The Massachusetts Society has given out this year Washington and Franklin medals for excellency in the study of history, at least something like one hundred and forty in all, among the leading high schools and academies of the State. This is deemed to be one of the most important lines of our work and brings us in close contact with the public, interesting both pupils and parents in the study of United States history and, as we believe, promoting better citizenship among our youth. The probability is that for the ensuing year there will be a demand for in the vicinity of 200 from high schools and academies in the Commonwealth.

It will be particularly interesting to you to know that as the result of efforts of this Society 42 unmarked graves of Revolutionary soldiers have been located in the old cemetery in the town of Grafton, on which markers have been placed with a suitable memorial, and this will be dedicated with appropriate exercises on June 17 next. It may interest you to hear the names of those Revolutionary heroes. I will read them: Andres Adams, Nathaniel Adams, Thomas Axtell, Perley Batchelor, Capt. Noah Brooks, Elijah Brooks, Joel Brooks, Simon Bruce, Ebenezer Cutler, Moses Cutler, Thomas Davidson, Col. Luke Drury, Thomas Drury, Benj. Goddard, John Goulding, Jonathan Hall, Ephraim Harrington, Moses Harrington, Moses Hayden, Moses Holbrook, Simeon Keith, Aaron Kimball, Noah Brooks Kimball, David W. Leland, Ebenezer Leland, Eleazer Leland, Phineas Leland, Samuel Leland, Joseph Meriam, Timothy Meriam, Zadock Putnam, Thaddeus Read, Zebedec Reading, John Roberts, Benj. Rockwood, Nahum Stone, Jonathan Stow, Shelomith Stow, Ebenezer Wadsworth, Joseph Warren, Samuel Warren, James Whipple, and John Whipple.

The interest in the welfare of the Massachusetts Society has not lagged and the growth in membership has been substantial, but I felt considerable pain this morning when I learned that the New Jersey Society had passed us. I feel humiliated to have to admit it, but they are a little ahead of the Massachusetts Society.

During the year the principal celebration which we had was the Benjamin Franklin celebration, in honor of the statue which was carried from Philadelphia to its final resting place in Connecticut. That was a two-day celebration and was very successful, as also were the other celebrations at Philadelphia and various points on the line. I think that is about all that I can give you of interest at this time.

REPORT OF VICE-PRESIDENT GENERAL FOR MIDDLE AND COAST DISTRICT

Mr. President General and Compatriots of the Thirty-third Annual Congress:

The several States assigned to the jurisdiction of the Middle and Coast District comprise practically one-third of the entire membership of our National Society. They are States of which a majority are under able and devoted management, having officers who from time to time, at great expenditure of time and energy, have contributed to the maintenance of the high and commanding positions of their organizations in the ranks of our Society. In that statement will be found the real and substantial reason for the success and rank of those Societies.

The events of the year show that the New York (Empire State) Society has continued its interest in our work, which has been especially notable in the case of the New York, Buffalo, Rochester, Syracuse, and other Chapters, these Chapters having held or taken part in numerous patriotic assemblies during the year. While the figures covering additions to and the annual net membership of the National Society by States are not available at this time, the records show that the Empire State Society on April 1, 1921, having a total membership of 1,701, has added new members during the twelve months ending March 1, 1922, amounting to 140.

The New Jersey State Society and its various Chapters have had a year of the most energetic and inspiring character, marked throughout by great enthusiasm and a determination to make the Society a strong factor in our work. It is, therefore, not surprising that I note this State, with a membership last year of 1,590, has produced in the past twelve months about 380 new members.

Of the many patriotic and interesting events occurring in this State during the year should be mentioned the dedication, in the burying ground of the old First Presbyterian Church at Elizabeth, of a granite boulder in memory of Rev. Dr. William Force Whitaker, Chaplain General of the National Society in 1913-1915, who will be well remembered by those having his friendship and acquaintance at our Congresses during his official term.

In several places the Society arranged for the ringing of church bells for three minutes at noon on Independence Day, the occasion being very generally observed by nearly all the Chapters throughout the State.

About three weeks ago, upon invitation of the New Jersey State Society, I attended the very interesting ceremonies connected with the unveiling of a marker presented by the Oregon State Society and erected upon the battlefield of Princeton. Appropriate addresses were delivered by President Hibben, of Princeton University, and also by the son of President General McCamant, a student at the University, who also unveiled the marker and made the presentation in the name of the Oregon Society.

Conspicuous among the events of interest in New Jersey during the year and worthy of special mention is the purchase of a State headquarters in Newark, a three-story stone building, the purchase price therefor, amounting to many thousands of dollars, being paid in less than two months through an issue of bonds. The Society is to be congratulated upon such a good business enterprise.

When we consider that, as I have stated, this State has brought in about 380 new members in the past year, and one Chapter (Newark) has doubled its membership in the same time, it would seem that there is no limit to the energies and accomplishments of such an organization.

The Pennsylvania Society reports the receipt of many new applications, one member alone having secured eleven, and I note a new membership secured in twelve months amounting to 107, a substantial percentage on its total enrollment, now amounting to 764. Two new Chapters have been established in the State and more expected. The Society was represented in Washington on Armistice

Day at the services for the Unknown Soldier by a special committee of seven, who joined the District of Columbia Society in the parade to Arlington and attended the burial service. The committee placed a large floral piece on the grave at the close of the services.

The Delaware Society, under efficient management, has during the past two years shown a commendable degree of interest in the work of the organization. With a membership two years ago of 46, last year reaching 99, it has during the past year reported a new enrollment of 27, a ratio of additions which if followed by our larger organizations would mean an immense increase of membership in the National Society. A recent visit to Delaware convinces me that the Society is in the hands of competent and active officials, who are striving to place the organization on a firm and satisfactory basis, both as to number and quality of membership.

The Maryland Society has maintained interest in the work and made a material gain in the addition of new members for the year. The Society during the past year has suffered a great loss through the sudden death, by an accident, of its President, Osborne I. Yellott, a faithful and devoted member of the organization. On invitation of the Maryland Society and at the special request of our President General, I attended the funeral services at Towson, Md., near Baltimore, as a representative of the National Society, and was impressed by the very large and representative gathering of fellow-citizens of the deceased assembled to do honor to his memory.

The District of Columbia Society has had a very active and prosperous year, numerous meetings have been held with good attendance. With 55 additions in membership during the year, the net roll now numbers well above 500. Notwithstanding the comparatively small population in the District, this Society has a membership exceeding in number 35 of the States. Out of debt, the Society has in hand, well invested, a reserve fund amounting to $11,000 and stands as a splendid example of financial foresight and management.

The Virginia Society, under the active care and direction of President Arthur B. Clarke, has been doing good work, making a substantial addition of new members during the year. The Society has participated in various patriotic and historical events. On a visit to Richmond a few months ago, I was unable to see President Clarke, who was at that time confined to a hospital on account of severe illness.

The remaining States in the Middle and Coast District, viz., North Carolina, South Carolina, Georgia, and Florida, comprise but a very small proportion of our membership. Georgia, with a membership of sixteen a year ago, appears to have secured about 25 new members, making the net membership much less than the one hundred expected during the past year. Florida, with 47 members last year, has added only three in twelve months.

I regret that I am unable to report progress in the matter of the restoration of the Societies in the States of North and South Carolina, where there is so much material which might be of value in our organization. Of the members representing these States assigned to my Committee on Organization, I found several months ago by correspondence that the representative from South Carolina had died, and no response could be secured from the North Carolina representative. On a visit to North Carolina during the past winter, I took with me a list of names and addresses of members who had several years ago enrolled from those States, in the hope that I would be able to get in touch with several who would aid in the work, but my efforts were unsuccessful. A few months ago, through the kindly assistance of Secretary Millspaugh, of the Tennessee Society, I came in touch with a member of that Society in Washington, on whose recommendation I took up the subject of reviving the North Carolina Society with a well-known gentleman in that State. I have had correspondence with him, and have supplied him with necessary literature, as well as advice, and am hoping for successful results.

During the year I have made visits to the States of New Jersey, Pennsylvania, Delaware, Maryland, Virginia, and North Carolina. I believe the district as a whole has shown a substantial growth and accomplished much, not only in the general work of the organization, but also in the broad field of patriotism.

A report being due from me at this time, I have sought to present a few outstanding facts and figures connected with this district. I feel that there is much encouragement in the work, and that we may look forward to even greater results in the year before us.

Respectfully submitted,

PHILIP F. LARNER,
Vice-President General for Middle and Coast District.

REPORT OF VICE-PRESIDENT GENERAL, EAST MISSISSIPPI VALLEY DISTRICT

Mr. President General and Compatriots:

Details of the work of the active Societies in the East Mississippi Valley District have been published in the OFFICIAL BULLETIN, and this report, therefore, will only touch upon those matters that seem to be worthy of comment.

There are three State Societies within the district which have not functioned for several years, viz., Alabama, Mississippi, and West Virginia. In entering upon my duties as Vice-President General last year, my hope and intention was to come to this Congress and report that a resurrection had taken place, and that the Societies of those States were once more actively functioning.

After writing about 150 letters, with the net result of two answers, both absolutely discouraging, the attempt to do anything by mail in these States was reluctantly abandoned. If interest is ever revived in those States, it seems to me it will have to be done by personal contact, and that it will be necessary for some one to undertake it who can afford either to give considerable time or else by a paid organizer.

The other States within my jurisdiction are Michigan, Wisconsin, Illinois, Indiana, Ohio, Kentucky, and Tennessee. In all of these the organizations have been active.

The Ohio Society reports a net gain of 60 members. The official figures will show a net gain of 88, but part of this is accounted for by an error in reporting last year's result. This Society has been particularly active along the lines of patriotic education, having distributed copies of the Constitution of the United States through the schools and also booklets giving important information to immigrants relating to naturalization. One chapter reports that it assisted one hundred foreigners who made application for citizenship during the year. Copies of a patriotic letter from President Warren G. Harding, a member of the Ohio Society, mailed to county school superintendents, coupled with the request that Constitution Day be observed in each school, met with favorable response. This plan, in line with a letter from the Vice-President General, seems to have been followed by all the active Societies of the district, with the result that in practically all the public schools Constitution Day was celebrated.

The Ohio Society has been active in its efforts for an appropriation by the State to improve the grounds surrounding Fort Laurens, the first fort erected in the territory of Ohio during the War of the Revolution, and also in favor of the movement to erect two monuments in memory of Mad Anthony Wayne— one on the battlefield of Fallen Timbers, near Toledo, and one near Greenville, an historic spot, where important treaties were signed by the Indians. The Society has also been active in the work of identifying and locating the graves of Revolutionary soldiers.

It was my very great pleasure to be the dinner guest of the Anthony Wayne Chapter at Toledo on April 17, but owing to the postponement of the annual meeting date, it was impossible for me to attend the State Convention. A new register containing information relating to the activities of the Ohio Society for the years of 1917-21, inclusive, is just off the press.

The net increase of the Indiana Society for the year is fifty. The report of the Committee on Patriotic Markers revealed considerable progress in the compiling of an historical record of revolutionary soldiers who spent their last days in Indiana, and many of their graves have been located. Graves that are unmarked are being marked with marble headstones similar to those of the United States War Department, while for those which already have suitable headstones special bronze markers are used. All markers erected are dedicated with an appropriate ceremony. Great credit is due Cornelius F. Posson, the newly elected President of the Indiana Society, for the work he has done in locating the graves of patriots. Mr. Posson estimates there are at least 1,500 soldiers of the Revolution buried in Indiana.

The net gain in membership of the Illinois Society for the year is 31, the membership now standing at 1,220. A notable celebration was held by the Society on Lincoln's Birthday, when 352 members attended a dinner at which President General McCamant and General John J. Pershing were guests of honor. Four additional patriotic celebrations were held by the Society, and the local chapters at Springfield and Peoria were very active. The Society is making, through its board of managers, a study of naturalization conditions in Chicago and has distributed 1,000 copies of the book of "The American's Creed" in the public schools.

The Tennessee Society began the year with 107 members and no chapter organization and ended the year with 159 members. A chapter at Memphis was formed March 17, 1922; petitions are pending for Chapters in Pulaski and Nashville and a movement is under way for the organization of a Chapter in Chattanooga. A recent survey indicates there are at least 1,500 men in Nashville eligible to membership.

The annual meeting of the Society was held October 7, the anniversary of the

Battle of King's Mountain, with Past President General Thruston and myself as guests of honor. During the year nineteen markers have been placed at the graves of Revolutionary heroes.

State-wide observance of Flag Day, Constitution Day, and Washington's Birthday was urged with much success. A letter from the President General on "George Washington, the Gentleman," was the feature article on the front page of the Nashville papers on February 22. History text-books have been censored in several counties and found to be 100 per cent American.

On February 25 the Tennessee Society, assisted by other patriotic organizations of Nashville, produced the play "America First" for the benefit of the 114th Machine-gun Battalion, which made such a heroic record in France.

The aim of the Tennessee Society has been civic achievement rather than social entertainment, and much credit is due to the officers of the Society for the able way in which its affairs have been conducted.

A net gain of 27 members is reported by the Michigan Society. This Society and its various chapters have been very active in patriotic matters. At a reception tendered to newly admitted citizens by the Board of Commerce of Detroit, the Detroit Chapter, Sons of the American Revolution, with appropriate ceremony, presented to each new citizen a silk United States Flag. On the 6th of last December this Chapter gave a dinner in honor of Rear-Admiral Snowden Sims, United States Navy, at which 400 guests were present.

Aside from the fact that the Wisconsin Society held its annual meeting and elected new officers, there is no report. However, information received indirectly is to the effect that the Society is functioning.

Kentucky reports a net gain in membership of twenty. The Society has this year purchased a bronze tablet, which will shortly be placed in the Library Building, upon which the following inscription appears:

> "The trees planted on these grounds in memory of the Sons and Daughters of Jefferson County, Kentucky, who made the supreme sacrifice in the World's War, were given by fifty-eight public-spirited organizations. 1920."

Thus the Society has completed the work which it sponsored and managed—that of planting fifty-eight trees as a living memorial.

The Society also appropriated and expended $190 in a patriotic essay contest. Five prizes were offered for the best essays, the competition being open to students of the senior classes of the high schools of the State. The first prize of $150 was a scholarship in either the University of Louisville or University of Kentucky. This contest attracted great interest and will probably be repeated next year.

At the request of the Mayor of Louisville, the Society undertook plans for putting on a large pageant, to be given three successive nights in Cherokee Park, beginning on Constitution Day. The subject proposed was the "Founding and History of Louisville," with a masque having for its background Kentucky history. Mr. Percy Mackaye was brought to Louisville and preliminary plans were made which involved a total expenditure of about $25,000. Mr. Mackaye agreed to undertake the task of writing the drama, and everything was going smoothly until the Cherokee Golf Club began opposition because of the fear that its links might be damaged. A hard fight resulted before the Park Board, which denied the request for the site, though permission to use it previously had been tacitly given. There being no other site with a lake of water available to carry out the idea originated by Mr. Mackaye, the project had to be abandoned. However, Constitution Day was appropriately celebrated, and the Kentucky Society hopes to publish a patriotic pageant, written by Miss Ethel Allen Murphy, entitled "The Heritage," which should in due course be available to other State Societies.

The various meetings held during the year were well attended. On February 25 the Society celebrated the anniversary of George Rogers Clark's second capture of Vincennes, with President General McCamant as the guest of honor. He delivered a splendid and inspiring address on George Rogers Clark.

The project for the purchase of Federal Hill, known as "My Old Kentucky Home," as a State shrine has now been completed. While this was not a Society matter, it was first sponsored by one of our members, and it was due to a resolution adopted by the Society which induced the writer of this report to head the committee which raised the funds. The Old Homestead has now been fully paid for and will shortly be deeded to the State, which has passed an act providing for its maintenance and appropriated, in addition to the $62,000 raised by private subscription, $20,000 for improvements. One of the historic spots of the State will, therefore, be permanently preserved to the public as a result of work sponsored and executed very largely by members of the Kentucky Society.

There is one thought, Mr. President General, that I wish to leave with the Congress. It is this: There are two forces contending in America today. On the one side are those who stand up for and defend American standards, American institutions, and American citizenship. They are concerned first and last with America and the protection of American life and progress. On the contrary side are those who would break down American ideals and institutions; those whose pocket-books are dominant over their patriotism, and those who are more devoted to the ties of alien race and culture rather than to America and her purposes. Let the activities of the Sons of the American Revolution along patriotic lines leave no doubt as to where they stand; that they may be faithful trustees; that they may keep the heritage.

Very respectfully,

MARVIN H. LEWIS,
Vice-President General, East Mississippi Valley District.

REPORT OF CHANCELLOR GENERAL FOR THE YEAR ENDING APRIL 1, 1922

The Chancellor General has the honor to report that shortly after the close of the last Convention the Treasurer General called upon him to furnish a legal opinion as to the validity of the amendment adopted at the Annual Congress held at Buffalo May 16 and 17, 1921, which provided that the annual dues of the National Society should be in the sum of one ($1) dollar per year instead of fifty ($0.50) cents per year. After an examination of the minutes of the meeting and a consideration of the law and decisions applicable to such cases, I reported to the proper officers the following opinion:

Opinion

"Following the Congress of the National Society of the Sons of the American Revolution, held at Buffalo May 16 and 17, 1921, Mr. John H. Burroughs, Treasurer General of the Society, formally required of the Chancellor General an opinion as to the legality and validity of the amendment adopted at said Convention, increasing the dues of the members of the Society.

"An examination of the minutes of the proceedings as of the date of May 17, 1921, discloses that the Committee on Resolutions reported an amendment to the Constitution providing for an initiation fee of five ($5) dollars upon each member duly elected. Due notice of this amendment under the Constitution and By-Laws of the Society had been given, as required by law. Upon a question upon the adoption or rejection of the amendment, the purposed amendment was amended by substituting for the initiation fee an annual dues. This amendment to the proposed amendment was duly adopted and thereafter declared carried by the chairman.

"Your Chancellor General is of the opinion that an amendment to a constitution must stand or fall upon the original motion. There is no question of parliamentary law herein contained. The constitution is the written charter of rights and privileges of an organization. It is provided that it may be altered or amended by giving due notice in writing of the proposed alteration or amendment. This notice in relation to the original amendment was duly given. The membership of the national organization were able to determine whether they approved or opposed. Those who approved could justly ignore any further activity in the matter, because they did approve, and those who did oppose had the opportunity to present their objections. But the amendment as amended, while it related to the subject of dues, was a complete antithesis of the original amendment; it substituted an annual dues for an initiation fee and affects the work of the State Societies in a very marked degree.

"Your Chancellor General is of the opinion that the amendment as proposed, and of which notice was duly given, was the only business properly before the meeting at that time, and that it should have been either accepted or rejected. A constitutional amendment could not be amended, in the judgment of your law officer. It might be further pointed out that all amendments to the Constitution require a two-thirds vote. It is true that the amendment to the amendment did receive a two-thirds vote, 60 to 30. There is naught that appears of record than that the amendment upon final passage received a majority vote. It does not appear that the necessary two-thirds vote was cast on final passage. This, in the opinion of the Chancellor General, is fatal to its validity, even if the other objection did not exist.

"Under all circumstances, I am of the opinion that the amendment as adopted is null and void."

The necessity of limiting for a period of even twelve months the activities of our Society by this legislative decision was one that was most distasteful to your Chancellor General, but it did not appear to me that there was any reasonable or sound legal ground upon which I could uphold this amendment, upon which no notice had been given the membership.

In November, 1921, the Chancellor General was requested by the Executive Committee to prepare an amendment to section 4 of our Charter, enlarging the number of Trustees, which section then read: "There shall not be more than sixty, nor less than forty Trustees," and it was desired to amend that section to read: "There shall not be more than one hundred, nor less than sixty Trustees." The request for the proposed amendment also showed that we have 48 State Societies, the District of Columbia Society, the Far East Society, and eleven General Trustees, which gives us more than sixty Trustees.

Your Chancellor General, being on a visit to Washington, conferred with the Honorable Stephen G. Porter, Chairman of the Foreign Relations Committee of Congress, who suggested as a bill for amendment a form which Mr. Porter himself had submitted as an amendment to the National Red Cross Society and which had been duly approved by the Congress of the United States. The Chancellor General therefore submitted to the Executive Committee the following bill:

A bill to amend section 4 of act entitled "An act to incorporate National Society of Sons of the American Revolution," Approved June 9, 1906.

Be it enacted by the Senate and House of Representatives of the United States of America in Congress assembled, That section 4 of the Act for the incorporation of the National Society of the Sons of the American Revolution, approved June the 9th, 1906, be, and the same hereby is, amended, so that the number of Trustees therein provided for shall be "not more than one hundred, nor less than sixty," instead of "not more than sixty, nor less than forty" Trustees.
SECTION 2. That this act shall take effect immediately.

and which he has been informed has been turned over to Senator Frelinghuysen, who has the matter in charge for the National Society.

There were no other matters of official note brought to the attention of your Chancellor General.

All of which is respectfully submitted.

EUGENE C. BONNIWELL,
Chancellor General.

ANNUAL REPORT OF THE HISTORIAN GENERAL

Mr. President General and Compatriots of the Thirty-third Annual Congress of the National Society of the Sons of the American Revolution, Greeting:

The earliest medium of exchange that we find in use between European colonists on these shores and the Indian natives was wampum, or strings of shells ground down to about the size of a grain of corn, which was early recognized in New England, and valuations were placed upon it from time to time by the General Court.

In 1637 the General Court of Massachusetts ordered "that wampum should pass at six a penny for any sum under twelve pence;" in 1640, the same court ordered that white wampum should pass for four a penny, blue for two a penny, etc., and not until 1661 was the law authorizing its use as a legal tender repealed.

In 1651 the colonial life had so advanced that metallic currency was demanded, and in 1652 the first silver coins made in America were coined in the Boston, (Mass.) mint. They were known as the New England pieces, and consisted of silver planchets, stamped incuse; the obverse bearing N. E. (New England); the reverse the values XII, VI, or III, respectively, of the same stardard and fineness as the corresponding English coin.

These being easily clipped and counterfeited, were soon objected to and were replaced by the Massachusetts Willow, Oak, and Pine Tree series, consisting of a shilling, six, three, and two pence. The design on the obverse of these coins has "MASATHVSETS . IN." between two beaded circles, and within the inner circle a tree; the reverse, "NEW ENGLAND : AN : DOM." between beaded circles and 1652 with denomination therein, as illustrated below.

John Hull was the mint master of the Boston (Mass.) mint and received a certain percentage for all the money he struck.

When Mr. Hull's daughter was married to Judge Samuel Sewall, the founder of the town of Newbury, Mass., the father said nothing about any portion for her; but the marriage went on, and while all the guests were congratulating the married couple in the way that Puritan fashions permitted, a large steel-yard was brought into the room and the blushing bride placed upon one of the platforms, while into a chest upon the other side of the scale were poured uncirculated Pine Tree shillings until the steel-yard balanced.

MASSACHUSETTS 1652 PINE TREE XII PENCE (SHILLING)

"There, son Sewall," cried the good mint master, "take these shillings as my daughter's portion, use her kindly, and thank Heaven for her, for it is not every wife that is worth her weight in silver."

THE JERSEY PRISON SHIP

What pen can fitly describe the experience of the prison ship "martyrs," which constitutes one of the most frightful chapters in American history; for during the Revolutionary War the British confined the American seamen taken prisoners in old hulks anchored in Wallabout Bay off what is now Wallabout Market, East River.

These hulks were mainly old vessels, unseaworthy, which had long passed their days of usefulness; and thousands of American seamen who refused to take an oath of allegiance to England were herded like cattle in their holds rather than disgrace themselves under the British flag.

Of the floating dungeons, the *Jersey* was the most prominent. She was originally a British ship of the line, rated and registered as a sixty-four-gun ship, but had usually mounted seventy-four guns.

At the commencement of the Revolution, being an old vessel, badly decayed, she was stripped of everything warlike and moored in East River at New York. In 1780 she was fitted out as a prison-ship and was used for that purpose during the remainder of the war.

Infected with contagion and reeking with filth of the crowded captives, dead and dying, the *Jersey* was removed and moored with chain and cable at the Wallabout, about three-quarters of a mile to the eastward of Brooklyn Ferry, near a tide-mill, a solitary and unfrequented place on the shore of Long Island.

Her rudder was now unhung and she was generally dismantled, her only spars being the bowsprit, a derrick for taking aboard supplies of water, bread, etc., and a flagstaff at the stern, all together presenting a most repulsive appearance, suggestive of the death and despair that reigned within.

In a ship constructed to accommodate only four hundred men, over eleven hundred prisoners were usually crushed. Two tiers of small holes were cut through her sides, fitted with iron bars, to enable the human misery confined in the hold of the vessel to have a little light by day and sufficient air to keep them alive.

Among the seamen from Rhode Island confined on the *Jersey* were Captain Daniel Aborn, of Pawtuxet, R. I., and his crew of the privateer *Chance*, a new vessel, owned by Clarke and Nightingale, of Providence.

The *Chance* sailed from Providence in the month of May, 1782. She mounted twelve six-pound cannon, had a complement of 65 men, and was officered as follows:

Daniel Aborn, Pawtuxet, R. I._____Commander.
John Tillinghast, Providence, R. I._____First lieutenant.
James Hawkins, Pawtuxet, R. I._____Second lieutenant.
Sylvester Rhodes, Pawtuxet, R. I. (great-great-great-uncle of
   your Historian General)_____Sailing master.
Thomas Dring, Providence, R. I._____Master's mate.
Joseph Bowen, Providence, R. I._____Surgeon.
Robert Carver, Providence, R. I._____Gunner.
Joseph Arnold, Providence, R. I._____Carpenter.
John W. Gladding, Providence, R. I._____Prize master.

The cruise of the *Chance*, however, was short, for in a few days she was captured by the *Belisarius*, Captain Graves, 26 guns, of the British Navy, to which all were conveyed prior to being confined on the floating prison *Jersey*.

The prison-ship was found to be filthy beyond description. The provisions served were not fit for any human being to make use of. Putrid beef, pork, and worm-eaten bread, condemned on board their ships of war, were furnished the prisoners; but eat it, worms and all, they must or starve.

Dreadful beyond description was the condition of these unfortunate prisoners of war. Rarely would they live six months and, as a rule, died within three, being borne ashore by their fellow-prisoners and buried in unmarked graves on the sandy shores near the Wallabout.

Messrs. Aborn, Bowen, Dring, and Rhodes were later exchanged, with thirty-one other members of the *Chance* crew, for English prisoners, all arriving in Providence early in October, 1782, with the exception of Sylvester Rhodes, who died of yellow fever en route and was buried at New Haven, Conn.

After the war the old *Jersey* was permitted to rot away in Wallabout, and for a number of years the remains of the old hulk could be plainly seen at low tide.

In 1792, at a Brooklyn town meeting, definite steps were first urged to properly bury the remains, yet bleaching on the shore of Long Island and daily exposed by the falling down of the high bank on which the prisoners were buried. Nothing was done, however, until 1808, when the Tammany Society secured funds for the temporary wooden tomb which was constructed on Hudson Street. To this the bodies, dug from the trenches along the Wallabout banks, where they had been hastily interred, were removed. With passing years the structure fell into decay, the bones again became exposed, children often playing with them, and in 1875 the city of Brooklyn removed all that could be collected to a tomb at Fort Green Park, under the stairs of the entrance.

In 1908 the present prison-ship "martyrs" monument was dedicated, the monument being an imposing Doric column of Maine granite 270 feet high, surmounted by a funeral urn and flagstaff, and is one of the largest and most beautiful of the kind in America, being the last design of the gifted Stanford White. Below the column is the opening to the crypt, in which are interred, in metallic coffins, the remains of twelve thousand patriots, of which your Historian has the names of over eight thousand of the martyrs, obtained from the Revolutionary Records of the War Office in England.

Respectfully submitted,

GEORGE CARPENTER ARNOLD,

MAY 15, 1922.   *Historian General.*

The United States Ambassador to Germany, Hon. Alanson B. Houghton, is a member of the Empire State Society, and President of the Painted Post Chapter of Corning, New York.

ORAL REPORT OF GENEALOGIST GENERAL, WALTER K. WATKINS

MR. PRESIDENT AND GENTLEMEN, COMPATRIOTS:

I have received about 150 letters from all parts of the United States, two from Manila, and one from China, asking for genealogical information, some of which I could give and some of which I could only suggest the means of obtaining. Some letters contained a 2-cent stamp and others did not contain anything; so that the postage came out of my salary.   (Laughter.)   I was very glad, however, to give the information, although it took two or three hours in some cases to get the material.

Last year I asked that the blank of the Society should be changed so that the localities will appear in the form filled out for the pedigree as well as the dates. The Trustees have recently decided that such a form may be used, and although compatriots in the western part of the United States may be at a loss to get information, I suppose I shall have to offer, being the author of the change, to furnish any information that I may be able in the future, to any one wishing to complete their forms on application.

REPORT OF THE COMMITTEE ON NAVAL AND MILITARY WAR RECORDS

MR. PRESIDENT GENERAL:

Your Committee on War Records has the honor to report progress. The records have not been moved from the Munitions Building, in this city, since our last report.

Your committee has, however, discovered a record in the State of New Jersey which, we think, claims our attention and, we think, might properly be referred to the Committee on Memorials. We refer to the shocking condition of the little marker at the grave of a Colonial Governor and Revolutionary soldier, David Brearley. It is in the graveyard connected with Saint Michaels Episcopal Church, at Trenton, N. J. The marker is badly broken, but, when assembled, the inscription reads:

Sacred
To the memory of the Honorable
DAVID BREARLEY
Who died August 16th, 1790,
In the 45th year of his age.

The expense of restoring or replacing the little memorial is not so great, and we could afford it. We should do so unless the New Jersey Society or his own descendants or his church claim the privilege. We are inclosing a picture of the memorial as it now exists.

Respectfully submitted,

GEORGE W. BAIRD,
Chairman.

MEMORIAL MENTIONED IN PRECEDING REPORT

EVENTS OF STATE SOCIETIES

The Arizona Society mourns the recent death, in Paris, in September, of its honored member and former President in 1910, Dr. F. E. Shine, a valued member of the Order, scion of an historic family, a gentleman, and an honored and respected professional man. He greatly strengthened and made permanent the Arizona Society and will be deeply missed.

The California Society.—The monthly luncheon custom of the California Society seems to have been successful and is being continued. The members meet monthly at one of the hotels or down-town clubs and hold short business and social sessions over the luncheon repast, for which a nominal price per plate is charged. It serves admirably to keep a live interest and a spirit of fellowship among members in the Society, and the occasion can be enlarged to something more important and pretentious at any time circumstances warrant. The California Society has issued a call for volunteers to form a quartet or glee club to assist in making this luncheon hour attractive. The Society sponsored and had the co-operation of other patriotic and fraternal bodies in promoting a special commemoratory ceremony on Constitution Day in the Scottish Rite Auditorium, at which Hon. Harry F. Atwood, of Chicago, was the speaker, with a fine musical program. On Independence Day the usual civic ceremonies incident to naturalization of new citizens took place in San Francisco, followed by a great patriotic demonstration, presenting pictorially in song and tableaux the nation's history for the benefit, instruction, and entertainment of some 2,000 of these new citizens. Members of our Society and the Daughters of the American Revolution were actively represented in all the activities. The Society celebrated the Surrender of Cornwallis at Yorktown at a dinner at the Hotel Oakland on Thursday, October 19. Members were privileged to invite guests. The address of the evening was given by Rev. Charles L. Kloss on "America's Right to Optimism," who was followed by Mr. Harry F. Atwood, of Chicago, on "Restoring Constitutional Government, Our Imperative Task."

The Colorado Society, among others of our State Societies, has suffered a recent bereavement in the passing of its highly beloved Secretary, Dr. James Polk Willard, of Denver. Dr. Willard has been ill for something over a year and spent the past few months in California in an effort to regain his health. He seemed for a time to be on the road to recovery. His loss is a great one, not only to the local Society, but to the community, and the sympathy of the National Society goes out to our compatriots. His duties have for several months been assumed by Charles B. Toppan, elected Assistant Secretary of the Colorado Society some months ago.

The Hawaiian Society.—At the annual business meeting of the Hawaiian Society, S. A. R., held at the office of the secretary of the Y. M. C. A., at noon, Saturday, June 17, 1922, the following officers were elected to serve for the ensuing year: Donald S. Bowman, President; Dr. C. B. Cooper, Vice-President; Elmer T. Winant, Treasurer; James T. Taylor, Secretary; Gerrit P. Wilder, Registrar. President Bowman made a short oral report of the activities of the Society, followed by the annual report of the Secretary, James T. Taylor. Resolutions of sympathy on the death of Compatriot P. C. Jones were adopted. A committee on celebration and entertainment was appointed to arrange for future activities. The Society took active part during the year in the observance of Armistice Day and the celebration of Lexington Day and adopted resolutions in support of house joint resolution No. 171, relative to labor conditions in Hawaii.

The Idaho Society.—Constitution Day, or rather week, was observed in Boise by sermons on Sunday in all of the Protestant churches, and by addresses before luncheon clubs, the Kiwanis, Rotary, and Exchange, and by especial assembly of the fifteen hundred high-school students. The Governor of Idaho issued a proclamation relative to the observance of this day, at the request of the General Chairman, Mr. Ames.

The Illinois Society promoted a fine patriotic service on Constitution Day, at the Fourth Presbyterian Church, Michigan Avenue and Delaware Place, Chicago. Dr. John Timothy Stone, formerly Chaplain General of the National Society, made the address and a large audience attended. Compatriots were requested to wear the Society rosette.

The Indiana Society held two fall meetings, one in the northern part of the State and one in the southern, of a very interesting nature. On Sunday, October 15, at 2.30 p. m., members met at the grave of Lieutenant William Ray, in a hillside pasture, near Riley, Vigo County, to unveil and dedicate a marker placed there by the Society. William Ray was a lieutenant under "Mad" Anthony Wayne, in the Revolutionary War. A most interesting patriotic program took place. On Sunday, October 29, meeting at the grave of William Tuffs, in the old Bonneyville Cemetery, just east of Bristol, Elkhart County, a boulder with bronze tablet was placed by the Society. William Tuffs was not only a soldier of the Revolutionary War, as well as of the War of 1812, but was also a participant in the famous "Boston Tea Party." The public was urged to attend these meetings. Several hundred people from the adjacent countryside, were present at both meetings, which were well worth while, and both ceremonies were a fine example of the good work this Society is doing in preserving historical spots.

The Iowa Society.—A witch bonfire was one of the many features of entertainment indulged in by members of Lexington Chapter, No. 4, Sons of the American Revolution, in their celebration of Bastille Day at the summer home of Compatriot Edward F. Carter, at Sandusky. Mr. Carter invited the Chapter to be his guests and entertained the members royally. Following supper President W. G. Blood called the Society together for a short business session. Three new members were received. President Blood told a few facts about the Bastille, or Castle of Paris, which was destroyed 133 years ago.

Rev. Fred W. Long, chairman of the Membership Committee, read a list of prospects, 72 in number, and each member volunteered to see these prospects about joining. Lexington Chapter has a slogan, "Each member get a member," for this year. Following this business, the Committee on the Suppression of Witchcraft made its report, and the Sons condemned to death a witch which had committed such heinous crimes as were set out in a bill of complaint. As the torch was applied to the pile of driftwood on the shores of Lemoliese Creek at Sandusky, there was a shout of approval, from all but two. A minister of the gospel and a descendant of Quakers voiced their protest against the burning. As the flames licked up the witch's broomstick legs, caught her flimsy clothing, and shriveled up her cardboard face, there was a hum of approval. She sputtered and exploded in firecracker fashion.

As the witch fire died down, Dr. Long expressed the appreciation of the Chapter for the hospitality extended by Mr. Carter, who was called on to make a speech. Mr. Carter, who is a student of local history and has made quite a study of the pioneer days of the county, said that the Chapter members were celebrating Bastille Day on one of the most historic spots in the West and without question on the most historic spot in Lee County. It was at this point on the river that Lemoliese, a French pioneer, built his cabin before Dr. Muir settled in Keokuk, in 1820. It was on this spot, too, that Father Marquette, on his trip down the river, landed and made his camp. Mr. Carter told of the finding of Indian skeletons and bones, indicating that there was an old Indian burial ground here. The burial ground was submerged when the water-power project was completed, but frequently bones are washed on the banks. He has several collections of these bones, which were exhibited. Past President General Elmer T. Wentworth was instrumental in sending out Constitution Day propaganda throughout the State, something over two thousand copies of a pertinent editorial on the subject being distributed.

The Louisiana Society, with its able and enthusiastic President, Col. C. Robert Churchill leading and encouraging, succeeded in bringing about a very wide observance of Constitution Day throughout the State. A personal letter from President Churchill to mayors, ministers, and school authorities brought about a general observance, and not alone in New Orleans and Louisiana towns, but in Greenwood, Miss., particularly, was there a notable effort to recognize the day. The efforts of Colonel Churchill and Compatriot Millspaugh, of the Tennessee Society, to revive and resuscitate the Mississippi Society seem to be meeting with success, and great hopes are entertained that this Society will be functioning again before the Nashville Congress.

"The Kellers of Hamilton Township, Pennsylvania," by Compatriot David H. Keller, of the Louisiana State Society, Sons of the American Revolution, will be published on December 1, 1922. It will contain complete histories of the Keller families also the allied families of Bossards, Drachs, Dills, Browns, and Butzs. Important historical chapters have been contributed by Mr. Charles R. Roberts and Mr. Horatio G. Shull, of Pennsylvania. The work is of more than usual interest, as practically all of the lines of descent are proven by wills, deeds and other papers, many of which are given in full. The book will be extensively illustrated, over 30 full-page illustrations amplifying the text. The war record of all the Revolutionary soldiers in the family is given in full. While the book was printed for private circulation only, a limited number have been reserved for historical societies and those interested in genealogical research.

Colonel Churchill, President of the Louisiana Society, is deeply interested in promoting a new chapter in London, England, to be known as the "London Society," from the nucleus of our members now residing there. There are not at this time a sufficient number of members to form a separate Society under the rules for formation of State Societies, but there are several applications pending, and it is hoped that before long this may be an accomplished fact.

The Maine Society secured general recognition of Constitution Day and was particularly fortunate in securing the co-operation of the superintendent of schools and the newspapers of Portland. The latter gave excellent space and the former sent out a general letter to the schools requesting recognition and special instruction relative to the day and the document. Many special exercises were held.

The Maryland Society.—From June 4 to June 8, inclusive, there was held on the Pro-Cathedral grounds, Baltimore, a "Fête of Lights and Flowers," and Tuesday, June 6, was designated as Patriotic Day. The service that afternoon consisted of a processional of the members of the various patriotic societies and the flags of each, and the service at the outdoor altar ended with the blessing of the flags by Right Reverend John Murray, Bishop of Maryland. This service was taken part in by twenty-two patriotic organizations, including the Sons of the American Revolution, and was the first time that any meeting has been held in this city in which the flags and official representatives of all the patriotic organizations were present. It was a very imposing ceremony.

On Wednesday June 14, the monument erected by Congress to the memory of Francis Scott Key was unveiled, and the official reception committee at the unveiling ceremony consisted of the members of the Maryland Society, Sons of the American Revolution, the Society of 1812, and the Colonial Wars, some of whom acted as personal escort to President Harding during the ceremony. Notably among our compatriots on the reception and escort committees were Past President General James Harry Preston, Registrar General Francis B. Culver, Secretary Robertson of the Maryland Society; Matthew Page Andrews, John H. K. Shannahan, Milton W. Gatch, and many others.

The Maryland Society held a dinner in honor of the President General on Thursday, October 19, preceding its annual meeting. President General Adams spoke informally at the banquet, and more formally at the meeting on "History and Patriotism." Historian Bacon, of the Maryland Society, spoke on the "Causes which Led to the Revolution," and Compatriot Matthew Page Andrews, author of the "American's Creed," recited the Creed most eloquently and presented to the Society some original letters in the handwriting of Washington, Cornwallis, and others, which are priceless and most interesting.

The Massachusetts Society.—This Society was well represented and most active in the events which took place in Boston in celebration of the Bicentenary of Samuel Adams' birth, September 27. The committee in behalf of the Sons of the American Revolution consisted of Rev. Lewis Wilder Hicks, T. Julien Silsby, van Cortlandt Lawrence, and George Hale Nutting, and the Massachusetts Society decorated both the birthplace of Samuel Adams, on Purchase Street, and his later home, on Winter Street, and members took active part in the street parade. The day's program included a procession from the Adams birthplace, 252 Purchase Street, to City Hall, the Old State House, the Old South Meeting House, the Adams grave in the Granary burying ground, and a "Town Meeting" in Faneuil Hall, where Louis A. Coolidge, president of the Sentinels of the Republic, officiated as "moderator." The celebration began with delegations meeting in front of the Adams birthplace on Purchase Street. There were representations from the Sons of the American Revolution, Society of Colonial Wars, G. A. R., American Legion, Spanish War Veterans, Ancients, Fusiliers, and other patriotic societies. A company of sailors from the local navy yard assisted in the trooping of the colors and two military bands, one from Fort Banks and the other from the National Guard Coast Defense, furnished music.

William H. Doyle, commander of the Massachusetts department of the American Legion, was marshal of the parade. More than 1,500 persons were in line. The parade was reviewed at City Hall by Mayor Curley and other city officials. At the Old State House, Senator Lodge spoke in the council chamber where Adams spoke during the Revolution. He said in part:

"Adams was pre-eminently a man of law and order. He intended that all the substantial progress which he and his companions were seeking should be achieved by law and order.. Moreover, I believe that he had something of the vision of the great country that was to come, the nation which was to lead the way in government among all the nations of his time."

Before the "town meeting" adjourned the following resolutions were adopted:

"*Resolved,* That the citizens of Boston, gathered in town meeting in Faneuil Hall on the 200th anniversary of the birth of Samuel Adams, with firm faith in the destiny of the United States and of the State of Masschusetts, declare the following to be their unalterable purposes:
"First. The fundamental principles of the American Constitution must be maintained.
"Second. The Federal encroachment upon the rights of the States and of the individual citizen must be opposed.
"Third. The insidious growth of socialism must be stopped.

GEORGE WASHINGTON CHAPTER AT CELEBRATION IN CONNECTION WITH OPENING OF NEW BRIDGE OVER CONNECTICUT RIVER AT SPRINGFIELD

"Fourth. Further power of concentration in Washington through the multitude of administrative bureaus, under a precarious interpretation of the general-welfare clause, must be prevented.
"Fifth. A free republican form of government in the United States must be preserved."

The entire celebration was a splendid series of tributes to the "Father of the Revolution" from morning till night.

GEORGE WASHINGTON CHAPTER, SPRINGFIELD.—At the celebration in connection with the opening of the new bridge over the Connecticut River at Springfield, Mass., on August 3, George Washington Chapter took a prominent part. In the historical parade they were placed near the head of the line and carried the Society's colors. Then followed five horsemen, representing General George Washington and party as they rode through Springfield on June 30, 1775, on the famous journey from Philadelphia to Cambridge, where Washington took command of the Continental Army.

Friday, August 18, President General Adams met the Board of Managers and other members of the Massachusetts Society at an informal luncheon at the Boston City Club. A very pleasant hour was spent, chiefly in conversation and discussion of features of the work of the Sons of the American Revolution in the coming year. Vice-President General for New England, Harry T. Lord, Esq., of New Hampshire, and National Trustee George Hale Nutting took part in the discussion following a short address by Major Adams, in which he referred with much appreciation to his Massachusetts ancestry and designated himself as a spiritual son of the Commonwealth. The luncheon was followed by the meeting of the Board of Managers of the Massachusetts Society, at which considerable business was transacted. Governor Cox, of Massachusetts, was invited to be present at the luncheon, but was unable to accept.

The Massachusetts Society now occupies its new headquarters in the building of the New England Historic and Genealogical Society. They are worthy of the Society and well worth seeing. The anniversary of the Surrender of Cornwallis October 19 was the occasion of a "house-warming" and ladies' night at the new headquarters for members, their families, and guests. Several members spoke briefly and informallly of the plans and hopes of the Society, some with lantern slide illustrations, after which a buffet luncheon was served. Members were urged to bring as a guest some friend who might become interested in the Society.

The Michigan Society.—The Detroit Chapter held its annual meeting on June 14, 1922, at the Detroit Athletic Club. Dinner was first served. The meeting was then called to order by President Carl F. Clarke, with an opening address. Secretary Raymond E. Van Syckle presented his annual report and read the annual report of Historian Albert H. Finn. Treasurer Frank G. Smith read his annual report. Compatriots John W. Starrett, of the Membership Committee; Harold H. Emmons, chairman of the Program Committee; George E. Bushnell, chairman of the Patriotic Legislation Committee; Dr. Earl C. Barkley, chairman of the National Defense Committee, and Edgar M. Bosley, chairman of the Publicity Committee, reported on the activities of their respective committees. Compatriot Allen G. Ludington, chairman of the Flag Committee, told of the distribution of flags by the Detroit Chapter to the newly admitted citizens at the Board of Commerce and of the presentation thereof by Compatriot Dr. Minot C. Morgan, chairman of the Patriotic Educational Committee. The President then called upon the delegates to the National Congress at Springfield, Mass., Almon B. Atwater and Dr. Frank Ward Holt, who responded with interesting accounts of the program and entertainment at the National Congress. The President then called upon Vice-President George E. Bushnell, who responded with an appropriate and inspiring address upon "Flag Day."

The following officers were elected for the ensuing year: President, Carl F. Clarke; Vice-President, George E. Bushnell; Second Vice-President, Julius E. Thatcher; Secretary, Raymond E. Van Syckle; Treasurer, Frank G. Smith; Historian, Allen G. Ludington; Chaplain, Rev. Jos. A. Vance, D. D.; Board of

Governors: Dr. Earl C. Barkley, Edgar M. Bosley, C. E. Frazer Clark, Harold H. Emmons, Hugh C. Chedester, Lloyd G. Grinnell, Fred C. Lawton, John W. Starrett, Palmer E. Winslow.

Compatriot Harold H. Emmons followed with a most interesting account of the experimental bombing from aëroplanes of the German war vessels off the Virginia coast, illustrated by moving films taken from the attacking planes.

The newly elected Board of Managers of Detroit Chapter were entertained at dinner at the home of President Carl F. Clarke, 92 Peterboro Street, on Monday evening, June 26, 1922. Plans for the coming year were formulated and chairmen of the committees announced. The second meeting of the Board of Governors was held on August 18, 1922, in the officers' dining-room of the First National Bank of Detroit, where the members were served lunch as guests of the bank and of Treasurer Frank G. Smith. The Board voted $500 as a contribution to the Army and Navy Club toward the furnishing of a room therein. It was decided to hold the Chapter meetings on the first Tuesday of each month.

Detroit Chapter observed Constitution Day, through the courtesy of the *Detroit News,* by broadcasting through WWJ, Detroit News Radio Station, an address by George E. Bushnell, Vice-President of Detroit Chapter. Compatriot Bushnell called to the attention of the people of Detroit and vicinity the significance of the day which was being observed throughout the nation as Constitution Day. He explained that the observance of the day was made in commemoration of the adoption of the Constitution of the United States. "The Constitution has been called the foundation stone of our present governmental structure, and one who thinks that our Constitution can preserve itself makes a serious mistake," Mr. Bushnell stated. "Its very life and existence depend upon wholesome, intelligent public opinion. Because of this fact, the observance of Constitution Day has become an annual occasion."

Detroit Chapter held its first meeting for the present season at the Army and Navy Club on Tuesday evening, October 3. Compatriot Clarence M. Burton, former President of Michigan Society, Sons of the American Revolution, gave an interesting account of Detroit during the period intervening between the end of the Revolution and the surrender of this territory to the United States by the British. Prior to the meeting, many of the members gathered for dinner at the club. Compatriot George E. Bushnell was the chairman in charge of the meeting.

THE SARA CASWELL ANGELL CHAPTER of the Daughters of the American Revolution and the WASHTENAW CHAPTER of the Sons of the American Revolution, Ann Arbor, recently co-operated in placing a monument to mark the place where the old territorial trail left Ann Arbor, the ladies furnishing the tablet and the men the boulder. The boulder is a splendid specimen, about 90 per cent granite and weighing, as near as can be estimated, five tons. It was brought in to Ann Arbor by a four-horse team from about seven miles west on the Jackson Road.

Regent Beal, of the university, gave a very instructive talk on old trails, and Dean W. B. Hinsdale told how the boulders were brought to this part of the State from north of the Great Lakes by the glaciers. He called them the "first immigrants to the United States."

Miss Sara Whedon, Regent of the Sara Caswell Angell Chapter of the Daughters of the American Revolution, presented the monument to the city, and Mayor George E. Lewis, on the part of the city, acceptd it, and in his remarks said that he wished there were more societies like the Sons of the American Revolution and the Daughters of the American Revolution to assist in beautifying the city and in placing monuments to mark the old historic places which abound in this region. The tablet was unveiled by Mrs. Herbert M. Slauson and Milton E. Osborn, the chairmen of the committees of their respective societies. Those passing through Ann Arbor will observe the monument, about a mile out West Huron Street, at the fork of the roads leading to Dexter and Jackson.

The Minnesota Society.—Minneapolis Chapter, No. 1, Sons of the American Revolution, since its organization late last year has been very active. First, as to membership, a list of State Society members in Minneapolis was furnished by the State Secretary, 83 in all, and these members have been roused to their privileges and obligations to the extent that nearly 70 have to date become affiliated with the new Chapter. The applications of new members to the number of 58 have been submitted, and five members of other State societies living in Minneapolis have completed their demit papers. When these papers are finally approved the charter membership roll will show at least 130, with a total membership of about 150. As to the character of the Chapter membership, some of the mmebers are: Mayor of Minneapolis, George E. Leach (Colonel of 151st F. A., Rainbow Division) ; Hon. Walter H. Newton, Congressman, 5th District (Minneapolis) ; Hon. E. J. Westlake, former State Senator; Hon. Wallace G. Nye, former mayor of Minneapolis; Hon. Levi Longfellow,˙National Patriotic Instructor, G. A. R.; Dr. Hugh S. Willson (formerly with Mayo Clinic), a lieutenant-colonel, in command of a base hospital in France; Hon. Arch Coleman, former State Senator and chairman Republican County Committee (now postmaster of Minneapolis) ; Judge Edward F. Waite, District Court, Hennepin County, and Hon. Earle Brown, Sheriff of Hennepin County. The above are only a few; there are at least a dozen Reserve officers and some National Guard officers in the membership; also two members, Charles J. Gotshall and William W. Gilbert, are grandsons of Revolutionary soldiers.

Activities: The Chapter has gone ahead while getting applications for membership and getting organized. A Washington's Birthday dinner was given at the Radisson Hotel, February 22, with 44 present. Dr. C. A. Prosser, Director of the William Hood Dunwoody Industrial Institute; District Judge E. F. Waite, and Charles G. Davis, Minneapolis Chief of the American Protective League during the war and a capitain in the Military Intelligence Reserve Corps, gave splendid talks dealing with the immigration problem. At that meeting a telegram was sent to President Harding asking him to veto the then pending legislation in Congress to extend the 3 per cent immigration for three years. A smoker was held at the West Hotel on the anniversary of the Battle of Lexington, April 19, with about 78 present, and a talk was given by Hon. George T. Simpson, former Attorney General of Minnesota, on the problem of immigration. Business was transacted and some music and buffet supper were furnished. A May meeting, with a lunch at the Minneapolis Elks Club at noon, was held. Dr. Lotus D. Coffman, President of the University of Minnesota, was the speaker, his talk dealing with the evolution of our educational system from the days of our Colonial ancestors through to the present time. The attendance was 40. Recognition of Flag Day was another noonday lunch, held on Wednesday, June 14, at the Elks Club, which was addressed by Dr. Marion D. Shutter, pastor of the Church of the Redeemer. This meeting was attended by 37 members and developed into a business meeting of the highest importance.

The Minneapolis Officers' Reserve Corps Mess invited as their guests, at their last dinner of the year, at the Radisson Hotel, Thursday, July 6, the Minneapolis Chapter of the Loyal Legion and Minneapolis Chapter, No. 1, Sons of the American Revolution, representatives of the G. A. R., and other patriotic bodies. Although a hot night, over two hundred guests were present, including several officers and students from the R. O. T. C. camp at Fort Snelling. Dr. A. C. Sweeney, of St. Paul, neurologist, gave a wonderful talk on the army intelligence tests given during the war. Judge Ell Torrance, Past National Commander of the G. A. R., responded for the Loyal Legion. (He is also a member of the Sons of the American Revolution.) Senator E. J. Westlake responded for Minneapolis Chapter, No. 1, Sons of the American Revolution, of which there were 29 members present. Action was taken at that meeting to form a committee of five members each from the Officers' Reserve Corps Mess, Loyal Legion, and Minneapolis Chapter, No. 1, Sons of the American Revolution, to form the nucleus of a Council of Associated Patriotic Orders, which shall include representatives from the American Legion, Spanish War Veterans, Veterans of Foreign Wars, Military Order of the World War, Sons of Veterans, Grand Army of the Republic, and their auxiliaries, Daughters of the American Revolution, Daughters of the Revolution, and similar organizations, so that duplication of patriotic work may possibly be avoided and the influence of all the organizations may be obtained to combat radical and un-American propaganda when the occasion arises.

There are three permanent standing committees: Arrangements and Publicity, having charge of arrangements for all meetings and the publicity for same; Membership, which is self-explanatory, and Activities, to canvass thoroughly all matters of patriotic and Americanization work in the city, in the schools, and among immigrants and new citizens, and to recommend and outline the course of activities and procedure of the Chapter. There is also a special committee, to have complete charge of four prize essay contests in the city schools. The Chapter is giving $200, divided among four contests during the coming school year, the contests to be on four different Revolutionary events, unless the committee decides that present-day Americanization subjects are better.

The Chapter invited Vice-President Coolidge to address it at a noon or evening meeting, to be arranged at his convenience, when in Minneapolis in September to speak at the Minnesota State Fair. The Chapter invited for this meeting the Minneapolis Officers' Reserve Corps Mess and the Loyal Legion to be guests.

The proper observance of Constitution Day was duly encouraged by the Chapter by circularizing the clergy, school authorities and others, and a special meeting held by the Chapter on Monday, September 18, at which the Secretary of the local Board of Education, Hon. C. E. Purdy, spoke on "America's Responsibility Today." The Chapter is sincere in a desire to co-operate with the National and State Society, particularly in an endeavor to encourage the formation of other local chapters throughout the State, and has already assisted in promoting the organization of one other, namely, in Duluth, an account of which will soon be given.

The Missouri Society.—On May 4 a get-together meeting was held in the evening at the Washington Hotel, in St. Louis. Linn Paine, President of the Missouri Society, called the meeting and made the announcement of the future activities of the Society, including Flag Day Celebration and the annual banquet, which is to be held on October 19 to commemorate the surrender of Cornwallis at Yorktown. Former President W. D. Vandiver, having recently returned from an extended trip abroad, was the principal speaker of the evening and delighted all present with narratives of his experiences in Egypt, the Holy Land, Italy, and other places of equal importance. Short speeches were made by Compatriot Breckenridge Jones, Vice-President Charles W. Bates, and Rev. Joseph H. Harvey, the recently elected Chaplain. A talented quartet of male singers was engaged for the evening and a program of patriotic songs was rendered. On June 14 a Flag Day celebration was held in the Jefferson Memorial Building. The program consisted of an invocation by Rev. Joseph H. Harvey; an address of welcome, delivered by Linn Paine, President of the Missouri Society; an address, "Our Flag," by Rev. Marvin T. Haw, and another, "Heroes of the Recent War," by Dr. L. H. Renfrow, Chairman of American Legion Committee on Memorial Celebrations. The officials of the local D. A. R. Chapters were invited as guests of honor. On June 17 a memorial tablet bearing the names of all St. Louis and St. Louis County men and women who died in the service of the United States during the World War was unveiled by Mayor Kiel, in the City Hall rotunda. The Sons of the American Revolution, Society of Colonial Wars, Spanish War Veterans, D. A. R. Chapters, Women's Auxiliary of the American Legion, and the Missouri Historical Society participated in the ceremonies. Music was furnished by the Jefferson Barracks Band. On June 25 the monument erected by members of the 12th United States Engineers to their comrades who made the supreme sacrifice on the fields of France was unveiled at the "Chain-of-Rocks." Hon. Charles M. Hay, Vice-President of the Sons of the American Revolution, delivered the dedicatory address. A ten-piece Scottish pipe band, obtained by permission of the British Embassy at Washington, D. C., and the Scottish Rite Choir participated in the ceremonies, as did many of the military and patriotic organizations of the city.

On September 17 Constitution Day was celebrated in the Fountain Park Congregational Church, Fountain and Aubert Avenues, St. Louis. This celebration was in accordance with the request of the National Society to formally celebrate the 135th Anniversary of the Adoption of the Constitution of the United States. Rev. Frank G. Beardsley, pastor, a newly elected member of the Missouri Society, delivered the principal address of the evening. His subject was "The Flag of Our Country." A beautiful silk flag, recently purchased for the Congregational Church, was dedicated during the services. A musical program consisting of patriotic songs was rendered. Reading (in unison) of The American Creed, lead by Linn Paine, President of the Missouri Society, Sons of the American Revolution, and the benediction by Rev. Joseph H. Harvey, Chaplain, concluded the exercises. Constitution Day was also generally observed in Missouri by exercises in schools and churches.

The Montana Society has suffered deep bereavement in the loss by death of its esteemed President, Paris B. Bartley, of Helena, who was called suddenly on September 25. Appropriate resolutions were adopted by the Montana Society, expressing their high esteem and deep and sincere sense of loss. The National Society joins in these expressions of deep regret.

The New Hampshire Society held its annual meeting and election of officers on the usual date, April 19, in the hall of the New Hampshire Historical Society

Building, at Concord, N. H. At the business meeting, in addition to routine business, tributes to the memory of several deceased members were presented and appropriate resolutions adopted. We would particularly mention as among the number the late Hon. Jeremiah Smith, the last surviving *real son* within the membership of this Society and the last, with a single exception, so far as is known, in the entire country. The public exercises included a brief address by the President, Prof. Ashley K. Hardy, of Dartmouth College; the invocation by Rev. George H. Reed, of Concord; several vocal selections by the Temple Male Quartet of Concord, and "a dignified, scholarly, and inspiring address of appreciation of John Langdon," by Compatriot Judge Charles R. Corning. In addition to the members present, these exercises were enjoyed by a considerable number of "Daughters" and friends.

Officers elected for the year were: President, Ashley K. Hardy, of Hanover; Vice-Presidents, Gen. Elbert Wheeler, Nashua; Walter S. Baker and Levin J. Chase, Concord; Secretary-Treasurer, Col. Charles L. Mason, Concord; Historian, Henry H. Metcalf, Concord; Registrar, Charles C. Jones, Concord; Board of Managers, Hon. Harry T. Lord, Manchester; Major Otis G. Hammond and Major Louis C. Merrill, Concord; Chaplain, Rev. J. W. Presby, Tilton. Hon. Harry T. Lord was chosen Trustee of the National Society.

Since the annual meeting the Society has suffered a grave loss in the sudden death of the Secretary-Treasurer, Col. Charles L. Mason, on the 26th day of June. He was a worthy Compatriot and an efficient and loyal officer of the Society. On July 25 the Board of Managers chose Rufus H. Baker, of Bow, to fill out his unexpired term.

The New Hampshire Society considers itself particularly fortunate in the fact that President General Adams is a long-time summer resident of our State. Accordingly, to give this concrete expression and to honor him personally, an informal reception and dinner were tendered him on September 8, at the Eagle Hotel, Concord, N. H., by such members as could be gathered on short notice, through the efforts of Vice-President General Lord and Compatriot Merrill, of the Board of Managers. Prior to the reception, at 4 o'clock, President Adams had an opportunity to visit the New Hampshire Historical Society Building to see the Revolutionary battle flags of the State and exhibits of that and other periods on view there. The dinner was served at 5 o'clock. Following this President Adams briefly set forth the three main lines of activity of the National Society, and, after a general discussion, resolutions were adopted thanking President Adams for his visit and pledging the hearty and loyal support of the New Hampshire Society to the aims and efforts of the National body. A goodly number were present from Concord and Manchester, including many officers of the State Society. President Hardy was unable to be present and Vice-President General Lord acted as master of ceremonies and presiding officer.

Although the New Hampshire Society arranged no program meetings of its own for "Constitution Week," it sought to have the week observed in various ways. Ministers made mention of Constitution Week, for which the Sons of the American Revolution this year has chosen the theme, "Respect for Law and Order." In the schools during the week there were special observances generally on Monday.

The New Jersey Society was never better organized than it is at the present time for intensive activities under the banners of the Stars and Stripes and Buff, White, and Blue. There is no diminution of the strength injected into the plans for increasing the usefulness of the Society and of encouraging those outside our portals to become identified with the fellowship which is rapidly nearing the 2,000th mark. This notable event in the history of the Society will be observed during the winter with a ceremony of induction worthy of the exalted character of our organization and of the proposed applicant. A custom established in the spring of 1921 was reinaugurated on Saturday, October 7, when a reception was given the new members at the headquarters, at 33 Lombardy Street, Newark. All who attended were made acquainted with the engagements of the Society and new workers were added to the list of enthusiastic supporters.

Notable indeed was the observance of Constitution Day, under the auspices of the New Jersey Society, a mass meeting being held in front of the headquarters at 3 o'clock in the afternoon of Sunday, September 17, and the guest of honor was our President General, Major Washington Irving Lincoln Adams, who is also a Past President of our New Jersey Society and of the Montclair Chapter. David L. Pierson, Secretary, who prepared the program and who first proposed the observance of Constitution Day in 1917, was in charge of the program by unanimous desire of the Board of Managers. The Salvation Army Band of Newark, consisting of twenty-five pieces, volunteered its services for the occasion, which was one of the most inspirational conducted by the Society. Secretary Pierson said that the theme of the hour was divided into three parts—love, law, and liberty—love for the Creator of the Universe, love for country, and love for the homes of the land; law—obedience thereto creates order and advances society in the arts of civilization. Liberty, as a result, follows in just the proportion as the former two principles are observed.

Mr. Pierson read a letter from President Harding, which said in part: "It would give me the greatest pleasure to accept your invitation to address your meeting, if it were possible. Unfortunately for me, public duties which are impossible for me to leave at this time necessitate my remaining in Washington. I most sincerely hope that your celebration will be entirely successful and worthy both of your Society's interest and of the inspiration which so notable an occasion must give."

President General Adams sounded the call for service in a brief address, in which he brought greetings from the National Society, and urged the members to stand fast in the forward movement patriotically. The Society in general is greatly needed in combatting the forces of evil, said the President General, and the need of observing Constitution Day is most apparent to every thinking man and woman.

Judge Adrian Lyon, President of the State Society, the orator of the day, electrified his audience with an admirable address, in which he declared the Constitution to be the most perfect instrument given to mankind in the Christian era, and quoted Gladstone, who also said that it was the greatest document ever struck off by mortal man. The Constitution safeguarded the Declaration of Independence, which declared the equality of man before the law and in opportunity. The speaker spoke of the horror perpetrated in Smyrna, and while deploring the awful loss of life and waste of property, offered the challenge to the world if it was not time for the Christian nations to check the outrages of Turkey. Under our Constitution, liberty and freedom are vouchsafed and for 135 years it has stood the tests placed upon it, and now there are a number of well-intentioned men who are criticizing it because of a certain amendment, which is only a part of the Constitution and not all of it. The blessings to mankind under the government are so numerous that the Constitution ought to have the loyal support of every thinking individual living under its protection.

Secretary Pierson alluded to the fact that the people of Essex County could not wait for the regularly called convention to ratify the Constitution, but that on October 12, 1787, twenty-five days after the Philadelphia Convention had completed its labors, the people assembled and unanimously ratified the instrument, the State following on December 18.

An original poem on the Constitution was read by Rev. Dr. Lyman Whitney Allen, former Chaplain General, and several selections were given by the band during the exercises.

A procession was formed and proceeded to the Washington Statue, where a wreath was placed by Secretary Pierson, in behalf of the Society, "in loving memory of the Father of the Country." "America" was then sung and the benediction pronounced by Rev. Dr. Frank A. Smith, of Elizabeth, Chaplain of the Society, and who also delivered the invocation at the opening of the ceremonies. Chester N. Jones, former President, gave the Pledge to the Flag most impressively.

THE NEWARK CHAPTER offered its tribute to the Constitution and its framers at a well attended meeting on Monday night, September 18, at the State headquarters. President Sylvester H. M. Agens, who presided, led in the Pledge to the Flag. An innovation suggested by President Agens was presented at this meeting, and which will be followed at every one held in the future—the reading of a chapter of American history. Following this thought, Rev. Warren Patten Coon, chaplain in the World War and member of the Chapter, read dramatically the story of the death-bed scene of Benedict Arnold. The Newark Chapter Quartet sang with much feeling Kipling's Recessional and other selections. John O. Bigelow, prosecutor of the Court of Common Pleas of Essex County, gave an exposition of the Constitution, during which he said that none of the commissioners of the Philadelphia Convention of 1787 had any idea that they had wrought a perfect instrument; yet time had demonstrated that fact.

Chaplain Warren P. Coon addressed the employees of Seabury & Johnson, East Orange, on Tuesday, September 19, on the general subject of the Constitution, and Secretary Pierson made two appointments, one on the 20th and the other on the 22d, at noonday factory meetings, at which the story of the Constitution was told.

ORANGE CHAPTER observed Independence Day with an open-air meeting in the morning of July 4 at the Military Common, Orange, the training ground during the War for American Independence. The tavern of Samuel Munn is still standing, as in days of yore. Chaplain Warren P. Coon was the speaker, David L. Pierson read the Declaration of Independence, and addresses were given by Mayor Charles H. Martens, of East Orange; Mayor Frank J. Murray, of Orange, and Walter D. Van Riper, who had recently retired as mayor of West Orange. This chapter met evening of October 20 at the Central Presbyterian Church, Orange, and the address was given by Rev. Dr. Samuel D. Chambers, on "Outdoor Sports of Canada," and Samuel C. Worthen, Genealogist of the State Society, gave a sketch of "Outdoor Sports in the Days of General George Washington."

CAPTAIN ABRAHAM GODWIN CHAPTER, of Paterson, also met on this evening and observed its first anniversary, at the United States Hotel, the speaker of the evening being Judge Adrian Lyon, State President. Under the direction of President Albert Lincoln Wyman, the Chapter is planning a drive through the winter season, the goal being to double its membership.

MONTCLAIR CHAPTER, co-operating with Eagle Rock Chapter, D. A. R., dedicated a boulder and tablet at the home of Dr. Maurice Cohen, Claremont Avenue and Valley Road, Montclair, on October 28, marking the site of the homestead of William Crane, where General Washington established his temporary headquarters on October 26, 1780, while Lafayette conducted an expedition against the British, then encamped upon Staten Island, and which proved unsuccessful because the train bringing boats overland from the Great Falls, now Paterson, was retarded on account of a storm.

MONTCLAIR CHAPTER also observed Independence Day, co-operating with the city officials and Eagle Rock Chapter, D. A. R. J. Stewart Gibson, President of Montclair Chapter, presided, and the address was given by Rev. Warren P. Coon.

Rev. M. S. Waters, Historian of the New Jersey Society and chairman of the State Society Committee on Study of History in the Public Schools, reported at the October meeting of the Board of Managers, on October 13, that the inspection of text-books used in New Jersey public schools would be undertaken with dispatch at an early day. His committee was preparing a plan of procedure which will be very thorough, co-operation being given by Judge Wallace McCamant, former President General and now chairman of the National Committee on the Text-book Investigation. The meeting of the Board was enlivened with a number of important reports, chief among them being that of the Finance Committee, which reported through its chairman, Compatriot Carl M. Vail, that a plan suggested by Compatriot Sylvester H. M. Agens, President of Newark Chapter, for increasing the revenue would be presented at a specially called meeting of the Society if the Board concurred. This was heartily given, and it is expected that the dues will be increased at the beginning of the next fiscal year, on April 1. Meanwhile a number of changes will be inaugurated in anticipation of securing the increased funds, in the re-arrangement of the work at the headquarters, which has increased so rapidly that the Secretary has found it necessary to have assistance. Registrar William J. Conking, who made his first appearance after an illness of over three months, reported that since the last Board meeting, on September 8, a total of 49 applications were received and sent to the Registrar General. The membership is now 1,958 and a large number of applications now being considered will bring the total up to 2,000 before the advent of the new calendar year.

PASSAIC VALLEY CHAPTER, headquarters of which are at Summit, entertained royally at a banquet given at the Canoe Brook Country Club on Thursday, October 12, in honor of Major W. I. Lincoln Adams, President General, and Judge Adrian Lyon, President of the New Jersey Society. Both delivered addresses of an inspirational character and encouraged the members and guests to continue the forward stride in securing new members for the Society and in acquainting the people with the high type of citizenship required by the Federal Constitution. Hon. Oliver B. Merrill, Mayor of Summit and member of the local Chapter, also delivered a very inspiring address. Alfred W. Alesbury, President of the Chapter, presided and acted the part of toastmaster very acceptably. This affair was one of the most delightful ever carried out in the circle of the New Jersey Society, the entire evening being one of complete satisfaction. H. Donald Holmes, former President of the Chapter, gave the Pledge to the Flag, and a feature was the singing of the Passaic Valley Chapter Quartet, which made its appearance for the first time on this occasion.

SOUTH JERSEY CHAPTER, the latest to be organized by the New Jersey Society, on May 6 last, conducted a very successful pilgrimage on September 23 to the Frank Horner Farm, near Woodston, in south Jersey, where a wreath and a flag of thirteen stars was placed on the grave of Major Christian Piercy, a soldier of the War for American Independence, by Rear-Admiral Reynold ·T. Hall, President of the Chapter. Part in the exercises was taken by Edward C. Geehr, Vice-President, and by Colonel Winfield S. Price, Historian. The party also visited Hancock Bridge, where an engagement took place during the Revolutionary War. The day ended with supper at the Indian King Inn, antedating the war, at Haddonfield, where the Chapter has established its headquarters.

NEWARK CHAPTER observed Yorktown Day on Friday, October 20, at the headquarters of the State Society, 33 Lombardy Street, Newark. The speaker was Dr. William R. Ward, and a chapter in the country's history was read.

PARAMUS CHAPTER, of Ridgewood, presented a flag to the Chestnut Ridge Rest Farm, of Ridgewood, June 17. The place, serving as a retreat for the disabled soldiers and sailors of the World War, ·overlooks the beautiful Saddle River Valley, and the day on which the presentation was made proved ideal in every way. Miss Grace Isabel Weeks, daughter of Compatriot Willett Weeks, President of the Chapter, raised the emblem to the top of the Liberty Pole, and the Sons of the American Revolution pledge to the Flag was given by Compatriot Ira W. Travell, superintendent of the Ridgewood public schools.

The annual pilgrimage of Paramus Chapter to historical places was to the Sterling Iron Mines, Orange County, N. Y., and about 25 miles southwest from West Point, on September 30. It was at this place that the links of the famous chain stretched across the Hudson River at West Point were forged in the early spring of 1778. The historical addresses were given by Judge Cornelius Doremus, former President of the Chapter, and Benjamis Moffatt, Jr., Treasurer of the Sterling Iron and Foundry Company. It was a delightful trip and greatly enjoyed by over one hundred members and guests.

SUMMIT CHAPTER gave a complimentary banquet to the President General and to Judge Adrian Lyon, State President, on the evening of Columbus Day at the Canoe Brook Country Club, in Summit. The affair was attended by about one hundred compatriots, and was a great success in every way. Both Judge Lyon and Mayor Adams spoke informally after the banquet.

New York (Empire State) Society, NEW YORK CHAPTER.—The ceremony of receiving, blessing, and pouring upon the grave of Etienne Nicolas Marie Béchet, Sieur De Rochefontaine, later known as Lieut.-Col. Stephen Rochefontaine, earth from his native city of Ay, France, and water from the neighboring river, Marne, was conducted under the auspices of the Sons of the American Revolution, - New York Chapter, in St. Paul's Chapel and churchyard of the parish of Trinity Church at Broadway, Fulton, and Vesey streets, New York City, on Lafayette-Marne Day, Wednesday, September 6, 1922. The committee of arrangements consisted of Brigadier-General Oliver B. Bridgman, President; Edward Hagaman Hall, L. H. D., chairman; Major Charles A. Du Bois, marshal; Col. William P. Alexander, Col. Louis Annin Ames, Mr. William C. Demorest, Prof. Norman P. Heffley, Hon. James B. Laux, Col. Henry W. Sackett. Honorary member, Monsieur Marcel Mailly, Mayor of Ay-Champagne, Councilor General of the Department of the Marne, Chevalier of the Legion of Honor, etc. The following fine program was held in the chapel at 12 o'clock noon, Rev. J. P. McComas, D. D., vicar of St. Paul's Chapel, officiating, and Rev. A. E. Ribourg, D. D., rector of St. Andrew's Church, assisting: Processional; national anthems of the United States and France, instrumentally; prayer for the Presidents of the United States and France and all in civil authority; prayer of thanksgiving for victory; hymn, "Come, Thou Almighty King"; address by the Very Rev. George B. Myers, D. D., dean of Trinity Cathedral, Havana, Cuba; hymn, "Praise, My Soul, the King of Heaven"; the presentation of the earth, by Hon. James B. Laux; the presentation of the water, by Ira B. Stewart, Esq.; the receiving and blessing of the earth and the water, by Rev. Joseph P. McComas, D. D.; benediction; recessional. At the grave, at 12:30 p. m., Brigadier-General Oliver B. Bridgman, President of the New York Chapter of the Sons of the American Revolution, presided. The program consisted of "The Star Spangled Banner"; welcome, by Brigadier-General Oliver B. Bridgman; address, by Edward Hagaman Hall, L. H. D.; "The Marseillaise," by Mlle. Madelaine Cardinal; sentences, by Rev. Joseph P. McComas, D. D.; the pouring of the earth, by Col. Henry W. Sackett; the pouring of the water, by Col. Louis Annin Ames; prayers for the repose of the soul of the deceased and the concord of nations, by the Rev. J. P. McComas, D. D.; tribute to France, by John H. Finley, L. H. D., LL. D.; response, by M. Gaston Liebert, Consul General of France; benediction.

COLONEL SACKETT DEPOSITING THE EARTH FROM THE CITY OF AY, FRANCE, AND PAST PRESIDENT GENERAL LOUIS ANNIN AMES WITH THE WATER READY TO POUR

COLONEL CORNELIUS VAN DYKE CHAPTER, SCHENECTADY.—The Society's prize of ten dollars for the best work done in the American History course for the year was awarded to Mary E. Clark, with an average of 96 per cent. This award is eagerly sought and prized by the students of the High School—H. H. Van Cott, Principal. The Chapter has been active in its work during the last few months.

SARATOGA CHAPTER.—Members of Saratoga Chapter, Daughters of the American Revolution, and of the Sons of the American Revolution, gathered for the observance of Constitution Day and heard an eloquent address on the Constitution by the Rev. A. H. Boutwell, whose topic was "A Scrap of Paper." Mr. Boutwell cited expressions from historians to the effect that the American Constitution is one of the world's greatest documents, and that without it the thirteen States, despite their Declaration of Independence, would have drifted into anarchy. He explained the need for such an instrument at the time, giving many illustrations of the bitterness between the individual colonies and the lack of unity manifested after the War for Independence. He spoke of the opposition of the Constitution after it had been drafted and of the difficulty with which ratification was secured. "Events since that time," he continued, "have justified the action of the Federalists, for under the Constitution the United States has grown to its present power, so pliable has this 'scrap of paper' proved. As the country has expanded and the habits and texture of people have changed, the Constitution," he said, "has met every changing condition."

He concluded with the declaration that the Constitution entails on every citizen the duty of maintaining it and observing its provisions. Unless this is done, anarchy will ensue.

The Ohio Society—ETHAN ALLEN CHAPTER.—On March 6, at a meeting held at the Masonic Club, Warren, Ohio, the Ethan Allen Chapter was organized. The following officers were elected: President, Fred W. Adams; Vice-President, James Beebe; Secretary-Registrar, James J. Tyler, M. D.; Historian, Norman W. Adams; Treasurer, Frederick K. Smith, M. D.; Executive Committee, Fred W. Adams, James J. Tyler, Lynn B. Dana, F. Dean Adams, and Jesse N. Baldwin. A letter received at this time from President General Wallace McCamant stated in part: "I note with much pleasure the organization of the Ethan Allen Chapter of the Ohio Society, Sons of the American Revolution. Located as you are, in the heart of the Western Reserve, you should find plenty of material from which to recruit your membership, and I bespeak for you a prosperous and useful career. There is much to be done by the patriotic societies in these days, and they should have the support of all eligible gentlemen. If we did nothing but perpetuate the memory of the good men and true to whom we owe our political institutions, the Society would still be very much worth while. As a matter of fact, the Society is doing a great many other things intimately related to present-day life. The nation-wide celebration of Constitution Day is the last big thing which the National Society has brought about. There is a great work to be done in the matter of Americanization, and patriotic education is a cause which should never be lost sight of."

Later the certificate of organization of the Chapter and a letter from J. G. Butler, Jr., President of The National McKinley Birthplace Memorial Association, together with Mr. Butler's badge, presented to him when Vice-President General of the National Society, Sons of the American Revolution, were framed and given a place in the Relic Room of the McKinley Memorial at Niles, Ohio.

A letter received from Secretary Wm. L. Curry at this time stated: "I recall very distinctly when Governor McKinley joined the Sons of the American Revolution. He requested me to look up the record of his ancestor and I found that he was a Minute Man and had enlisted, as I recall, eight different times during the War of the Revolution. When I took that record into Governor McKinley he was very much pleased and said very enthusiastically, 'Bring on your application blank,' and I had the pleasure of signing his application as one of the members of the Ohio Society." The Chapter has increased its membership and taken an active part in Flag Day and Constitution Day observance. On Sunday, September 17, the members of Mary Chesney Chapter, Daughters of the American Revolution, and Ethan Allen Chapter, Sons of the American Revolution, were special guests at a Constitution Day service at Christ Episcopal Church. The address was given by Rev. Rudolph E. Schulz.

The day was noted by the local Rotary and Kiwanis clubs, and a letter received from Mr. H. B. Turner, superintendent of the public schools, stated that the principals had been notified to bring it to the attention of the pupils.

RICHARD MONTGOMERY CHAPTER, DAYTON.—The activities of this Chapter were renewed for the winter season with a dinner, notice of which went out to the members in a bulletin issued by the President of the Chapter, Edward F. Brown, and the Secretary, Miles S. Kuhns, urging appropriate observance of Constitution Day and informing the members of the new amendment to the Constitution regarding initiation fee, and other details of the workings of the National Society. The new President of the Ohio Society, E. L. Shuey, is a member of the Richard Montgomery Chapter and a resident of Dayton. The Chapter numbers 54 members.

WESTERN RESERVE SOCIETY of Cleveland elected new officers early in the year, as follows: President, Robert A Bishop; Vice-Presidents, Francis W. Treadway, Edward M. Hall, O. W. Carpenter, and Theodore A. Cooper; Secretary-Treasurer, Robert P. Boggis; Assistant Secretary, George H. Barber; Registrar, Jesse A. Fenner; Assistant Registrar, John C. Pearson; Historian, Fred S. Dunham, and Chaplain, Rev. F. B. Avery. Active chairmen of committees were appointed on Membership, Life Membership, Entertainment, Resolutions, Americanization, Naturalization, American Flag, and Press. A fine address on "The Civil and Military Life of George Washington" was given by Brig.-Gen. John R. McQuigg, on the conclusion of which General McQuigg was unanimously elected as honorary member of the Society and presented with the bronze War Service Medal of the National Society.

The Oregon Society.—A very delightful smoker was held by the Oregon Society of the Sons of the American Revolution on the evening of Saturday, June 17, a feature of which was some very interesting remarks by Past President General McCamant relative to the National Congress held in Springfield, Mass.

An exceedingly instructive paper on "The Constitutional Convention of 1787" was read by George L. Koehn, Professor of American History and International Law at Reed College, Portland, Oregon. Professor Koehn, after outlining the development of the ideas and principles underlying the Constitution and vividly sketching the membership of the Convention, gave a clear and informative account of the discussions and compromises which paved the way to the finished work of that great deliberative and constructive body.

Another interesting feature of the gathering was the report of the ceremonies connected with the dedication of the Princeton Battlefield tablets erected by the Oregon Society. In connection with that report the addresses delivered on April 29 were read, Compatriot Winthrop Hammond reading the address of President Hibben, of Princeton University; Compatriot General Charles F. Beebe the address of Thomas McCamant, official representative of the Oregon Society, and Compatriot Alfred F. Parker the address of Prof. T. J. Wertenbaker, of Princeton University. These addresses were greatly enjoyed by those present, and, together with the general report presented, gave a very clear idea of the exercises connected with the dedication and unveiling of the tablets.

A committee consisting of Compatriots H. B. Augur, C. C. Chapman, and Frank L. Griffin was announced and will have in charge the matter of the prize-essay competition among the school children of Oregon during the ensuing scholastic year. A committee of nine was appointed to conduct the observance of Constitution Day, Sunday, September 17, 1922. As the anniversary of Constitution Day fell this year on Sunday, special attention was voted to its observance by churches. The observance by civic organizations was held during the week of September 18-23, at their various luncheons. The Daughters of the American Revolution, through their numerous chapters throughout the State, took special charge of many of the local observances in the numerous towns of Oregon. There was a very general observance of the day in Oregon last year, and it was felt that the celebration was still more general this year.

The Pennsylvania Society was called upon early in the summer to give tribute to one of its oldest and most revered members, Col. Robert W. Guthrie, who died on July 24 at the age of seventy-six years. Colonel Guthrie was Trustee of the National Society for Pennsylvania and a well-known figure at all of our National Congresses for many years. The Society has elected Past President James A. Wakefield, of Pittsburgh, as National Trustee to fill the vacancy.

Pittsburgh compatriots will hold an Armistice Day dinner on Saturday evening, November 11. The speakers will be General Tasker H. Bliss, Mrs. John Brown Heron, State Reginet of the Daughters of the American Revolution, and the toastmaster, Hon. Clyde Kelly. Ladies and other guests will be present.

MIDDLETOWN CHAPTER.—The first meeting of the newly organized. Middletown Chapter of the Sons of the American Revolution was held on Friday evening, June 9, 1922, in Krauss Hall, for the purpose of the installation of the local officers by the State officers. About 125 guests, together with the local members of the Society and the eight members of the State Board from Pittsburgh, were present. The meeting was called to order by W. J. Lynne, President of the State Society, and two verses of "America" were sung, followed by an invocation by Joseph Montgomery, 2nd, Chaplain of Middletown Chapter. The officers were installed by R. C. Schanck, chairman of the Membership Committee of the State Society, and each officer was obligated by the State President. The following constitute the officers of the Middletown Chapter: President, Robert P. Raymond; First Vice-President, Truman P. Ettele; Second Vice-President, Colin S. Few; Secretary, William K. Lemon, Jr.; Assistant Secretary, Harry B. Etter; Treasurer, Le Roy H. Markley; Registrar, Robert F. Keiper; Chaplain and Historian, Joseph Montgomery, 2nd, of Harrisburg, Pa.

President Lynne then delivered a remarkable address, bringing to mind the Huguenots who found succor in this country and whose descendents are among the nationally prominent citizens, such as Dewey, Pershing, etc.; also Martin Luther, who meant so much to a community and whose followers are counted among the highest of the Nation. He spoke of the memorial services on November 11, 1921, held in the Amphitheater at Arlington, Va., in memory of our Unknown Soldier and said that in the notable gathering were many who were descended from Revolutionary ancestors. He also stated that a law was passed by Congress that officers and enlisted men of the United States Army and Navy may be privileged to wear the insignia of the Sons of the American Revolution, the only decoration permitted, other than those authorized by Congress. Flag Day, June 14, is one of the days to be honored by the Sons of the American Revolution. He besought those who are eligible to join the Society and become charter members of this Chapter.

President Raymond, of Middletown Chapter, in a few well-chosen words, presented the Chapter with a beautiful silk American Flag, which was accepted for the Chapter by First Vice-President Truman P. Ettele. Mr. R. C. Schanck spoke and gave great credit to Mrs. R. P. Raymond, "the little mother of the Middletown Chapter," as he termed her, for her assistance in creating interest to organize this Chapter. He presented a button, the insignia of the Society, to each member.

President Raymond introduced the chief speaker of the evening, the Rev. Fuller Bergstresser, pastor of St. Peter's Lutheran Church, and a member of the Kansas State Society, who delivered an interesting, instructive, and powerful address. He requested the audience to rise and pledge allegiance to the American Creed. In closing he gave a poem by Henry Holcomb Bennett, entitled "The Flag Goes By." Other State officers and visitors were called upon for short talks, among them, Miss Cora Lee Snyder, Regent of the Harrisburg Chapter, Daughters of the American Revolution, who extended the good wishes of her Chapter and presented this Chapter with their Year Book. Mrs. Rachel Springer, Regent of the Swatara Pine Ford Chapter, D. A. R., of Middletown, expressed her pleasure in having a Chapter of the Sons of the American Revolution in this community, and hoped that this Chapter would grow as rapidly as the Daughters of the American Revolution, which, when they celebrated their second birthday, May 18, 1922, had a membership of 140. Music and refreshments concluded the evening.

The Middletown Chapter, true to its enthusiastic beginning, exerted itself to bring about a proper observance of Constitution Day, and was most successful in having it recognized generally in the schools and churches, and promoted a fine patriotic service on the afternoon of September 17 in the Old Lutheran Church, a historic meeting-house of the community.

The Tennessee Society.—Members of the Society in Nashville attended Christ Church on June 18 and listened to an inspiring address by the Rector, Dr. Maxon, commemorating the Battle of Bunker Hill. For several years it has been the custom of the compatriots in Nashville to observe the anniversary in this manner, and the annual meeting of the Society on October 7 voted to request members in all parts of the State to arrange for observance of the day annually. Constitution Day was observed generally throughout the State, in 79 cities and towns, the celebration in every instance being prompted by the Tennessee Society. The press in many of our cities commented flatteringly on this movement and urged that the Sons of the American Revolution be given cordial support by every true American. In Memphis, under the auspices of the new Chapter there, Vice-President McDowell broadcasted a Constitution Day speech by radio.

The unveiling of the marker at the grave of Andrew Kennedy, in Baker's Creek Cemetery, on Sunday, September 17, Constitution Day, was an interesting event. The services began at 2 p. m., with prayer by Rev. R. W. Post, returned missionary of the Presbyterian Church. Major Will A. McTeer, representing the Sons of Revolution, gave a fine résumé of the care with which the nations have remembered the graves of their dead, and said that especially ought we to care for those who fell in 1775-1783.

Mrs. Alice Gamble, representing the Mary Blount Chapter of the D. A. R., gave an address showing that, although young, the chapter of Blount County is not behind in hunting for the historical points, graves, and keeping alive "the spirit of 1776."

Mrs. Cora Kennedy-Whitlock spoke on "What Our Forefathers Stood For," as a member of the Tennessee Daughters of the American Revolution and a descendant of the patriot.

The presentation of the marker to the descendants and to the memory of "our fathers" was made by Will E. Parham, for the Sons of the American Revolution, who had provided the marker which was sent from the head office at Nashville, Tenn. Mr. Parham also presided as master of ceremonies. Dr. Edwin Wexler Kennedy, a grandson, replied and accepted the marker.

The annual meeting on October 7, the anniversary of the Battle of King's Mountain, in which so many Tennesseeans took part, was the largest in the history of the Society. The Secretary's report showed an increase of 52 per cent in membership in the past year and 81 per cent in two years. Several hours were devoted to serious consideration of work for the coming year, and a businesslike division of the work was made. Extension was assigned to the Vice-President at Large; patriotic anniversaries to the President; censorship of text-books was placed in charge of a special committee. The officers for the new year are: President, Wm. K. Boardman; Vice-President at Large, F. W. Millspaugh; Vice-President for East Tennessee, C. K. Hill; Vice-President for Middle Tennessee, Dr. Paul De Witt; Vice-President for West Tennessee, John Davis McDowell; Secretary-Registrar, J. Tyree Fain; Treasurer, Carey A. Folk; Historian, Judge John Hibbett De Witt; Surgeon, Dr. Matthew Gardner Buckner; Chaplain, Dr. James I. Vance; Executive Committee: Leland Hume, W. R. Manier, Jr., A. L. Hayes, and W. L. Wilhoite; Fraternal Delegate to State D. A. R., Leland Hume. Delegate Hume will address this meeting on November 3 on "What the Sons of the American Revolution is and what it accomplishes."

General W. H. Washington was elected chairman of committee to co-operate with and assist the Daughters of the American Revolution in an effort to have statues of John Sevier and Andrew Jackson placed in Hall of Fame.

Resolution was unanimously passed commending the University of the South at Sewanee, Tenn., for the action of its board of trustees making a year's study of the Constitution of the United States a requisite for all academic degrees, and committee was appointed to endeavor to have the other institutions of learning in the State adopt a similar rule. Report has been received that an objectionable text-book on U. S. History is being used in several schools of the State, and the work of eliminating this book has been started.

The Tennessee Society wishes officially to congratulate the Sons of the Revolution for their splendid work in July, when the body of Mrs. Kate Sherrill Sevier ("Bonny Kate"), wife of Tennessee's first Governor, Governor John Sevier, was brought from Russellville, Ala., and placed by the side of her hero husband in Knoxville, Tenn. Our Society felt honored by the privilege of sending flowers to the ceremony in Knoxville, which was most impressive and carried through by the Sons of the Revolution and Daughters of the American Revolution.

The Utah Society, led by Vice-President General George Albert Smith, was active in procuring almost a State-wide observance of Constitution Day, and the *Deseret News*, a leading newspaper of Salt Lake City, devoted much space to the encouragement of a recognition of the day. Among other efforts is noted an advertisement of an essay contest open to school children on "What the Constitution Means to Me," offering cash prizes ranging from $5 to $25. This was undoubtedly at the instigation of our National Officer for that district.

The Vermont Society promoted a general observance of Constitution Day throughout the State in schools and churches, with a special inspirational service of music and addresses at Burlington. The ceremonies were conducted at Battery Park and were presided over by Judge C. H. Darling. Hon. F. L. Fish was the orator, and made a memorable address on "The American Constitution, the Defense of Our Liberties." Both Judge Darling and Judge Fish are former Presidents of the Vermont Society. Community singing was a feature of the program.

The Wisconsin Society is showing renewed spirit of late, and in view of the new initiation fee in effect October 1, promoted a membership drive which has been productive of good results. An active committee on membership and ways and means of promoting interest and activity has been appointed and will present a plan of action for the coming winter.

ADDITIONS TO MEMBERSHIP

There have been enrolled in the office of the Registrar General, from May 30, 1922, to October 1, 1922, 504 new members, distributed as follows: Arkansas, 2; California, 16; Colorado, 2; Delaware, 2; District of Columbia, 11; Florida, 2; Georgia, 2; Hawaii, 1; Idaho, 2; Illinois, 25; Indiana, 10; Iowa, 14; Kansas, 7; Kentucky, 3; Louisiana, 6; Maine, 5; Maryland, 29; Massachusetts, 44; Minnesota, 39; Missouri, 14; Nebraska, 3; New Jersey, 75; New Mexico, 1; New York, 34; North Dakota, 1; Ohio, 33; Oregon, 13; Pennsylvania, 40; South Dakota, 1; Tennessee, 25; Texas, 8; Utah, 7; Virginia, 5; Washington State, 7; Wisconsin, 7.

The first application to be received and accepted since October 1st, when the new initiation fee went into effect, was from the Florida Society for Compatriot William Henry Gillette, admitted October 11, 1922. Compatriot Gillette's National number is 29924, Florida number 110. He is a descendant of Benjamin Bissell.

In Memoriam

GEORGE W. ALDRIDGE, Empire State Society, died June 13, 1922.
PARIS B. BARTLEY, President of the Montana Society, died September 25, 1922.
WILLIAM WELLS BERRY, Tennessee Society, died July 30, 1922.
WALDO E. BOARDMAN, Massachusetts Society, died August 14, 1922.
CHARLES J. BOWLBY, Nebraska Society, died April 23, 1922.
JOHN M. BRACEY, Arkansas Society, died July 17, 1922.
WILBUR FISKE BRAINERD, New Jersey Society, died September 27, 1922.
ANSEL H. BRIDGES, Maine Society, died February 19, 1922.
PRESCOTT CHAMBERLAIN, Massachusetts Society, died May 2, 1922.
URIAL W. CHASE, Massachusetts Society, died September —, 1922.
CLARENCE L. COLLINS, Empire State Society, died September 28, 1922.
ANDREW CONE, Empire State Society, died February 6, 1922.
HAMILTON S. CORWIN, Empire State Society, died July 16, 1922.
WILLIAM THOMAS EUBANK, Colorado Society, Real Son of a Revolutionary Soldier,
    died June 26, 1922.
JAMES M. FAY, Massachusetts Society, died July 26, 1921.
JOHN H. FLAGLER, Empire State Society, died September 8, 1922.
JOHN F. GOUCHER, Maryland Society, died July 19, 1922.
HENRY MARTIN GRANT, Oregon Society, died May 13, 1922.
SAMUEL B. GRISWOLD, Empire State Society, died December 20, 1921.
Colonel ROBERT W. GUTHRIE, Pennsylvania Society, Member Board of Trustees of
    National Society, died July 24, 1922.
WILMOT R. HASTINGS, Massachusetts Society, died —— —, 1922.
ROBERT HANDOLPH HENDERSON, Maryland Society, died December 20, 1921.
GEORGE EDMUND HERRICK, Massachusetts Society, died August 5, 1922.
DRAYTON MEADE HITE, Maryland Society, died May 9, 1922.
JOHN B. HUNDLEY, Kentucky Society, died June 14, 1922.
COLGATE HOYT, Empire State Society, died January 30, 1922.
FRANCIS DEMING HOYT, Empire State Society, died July 21, 1922.
HARLAN H. JOHNSON, Michigan Society, died September —, 1922.
JOHN LLEWELLYN JOHNSON, Maryland Society, died June 27, 1922.
CHARLES E. KANTER, Michigan Society, died July 16, 1922.
CHARLES D. LANNING, Massachusetts Society, died July 31, 1922.
MICHAEL W. LARENDON, Empire State Society, died August 20, 1922.
RICHARD W. LAVENDON, Empire State Society, died August 20, 1922.
GEORGE B. LOUD, Empire State Society, died July 31, 1922.
CHARLES MASON, New Hampshire Society, died June 26, 1922.
CHARLES B. MATTHEWS, Empire State Society, died June 16, 1922.
JOHN EDWARD MCCLELLAN, Massachusetts Society, died May 17, 1922.
EDWARD J. MILLSPAUGH, Empire State Society, died July —, 1922.
ISAAC WIMBERT MOHLER, JR., Maryland Society, died May 19, 1922.
WILLIAM P. MONTAGUE, Empire State Society, died January 26, 1922.
ADONIRAM J. MORSE, Wisconsin Society, died September 4, 1922.
CHARLES W. NOYES, Empire State Society, died December 20, 1921.
CHARLES ADAMS PATTERSON, Vice-President Delaware Society, died July 26, 1922.
JOHN L. PEARSON, Illinois Society, died June 14, 1922.
GEORGE PRATT, Massachusetts Society, died September 27, 1921.
WILLARD S. REED, Empire State Society, died October 23, 1921.
FRANCIS ELLES SHINE, Past President Arizona Society, died September 14, 1922.
EDWARD SMALL, Empire State Society, died August 17, 1922.
LOUIS C. SOUTHARD, Massachusetts Society, died September 29, 1922.
WELTON STANFORD, Empire State Society, died January 4, 1922.
CHAUNCEY C. STARKWEATHER, Empire State Society, died June 19, 1922.
FREDERICK P. TUTHILL, Empire State Society, died July 2, 1922.
PHILIP S. VINCENT, Massachusetts Society, died July 24, 1922.
DANIEL WHITE WELLS, Massachusetts Society, died May 14, 1922.
Brig.-Gen. EDWARD W. WHITAKER, District of Columbia Society, died July 31, 1922.
FRANK MERRILL WHITE, Massachusetts Society, died April 23, 1922.
JAMES POLK WILLARD, Secretary Colorado Society, died October 2, 1922.
GEORGE TWYMAN WOOD, Treasurer Kentucky Society, Member Board of Trustees of
    National Society, died July —, 1922.

RECORDS OF 504 NEW MEMBERS AND 78 SUPPLEMENTALS APPROVED AND ENROLLED BY THE REGISTRAR GENERAL FROM MAY 30, 1922, TO OCTOBER 1, 1922.

WILLARD GRANT ABORN, Brookline, Mass. (37391). Son of George W. and Mary Frances (Pennell) Aborn; grandson of John and Elizabeth (Gould) Aborn; great-grandson of Samuel and Mary (Flint) Aborn; great²-grandson of *Samuel Flint*, Captain, Essex County, Massachusetts Militia, killed at Stillwater.

FRANK DWIGHT ADAMS, Minneapolis, Minn. (37428). Son of Charles E. and Adeline Fidelia (Tower) Adams; grandson of Rodney and Fidelia (Robinson) Tower; great-grandson of Samuel and Anna (Tower) Robinson; great²-grandson of *Stephen Tower*, private, Hingham, Massachusetts Militia.

EARLE MARTIN ADNEY, Lebanon, Ind. (36445). Son of Isaac S. and Eva Lewis (Brown) Adney; grandson of James A. and Sarah Jane (Watkins) Brown; great-grandson of Jacob and Elizabeth (Lewis) Brown; great²-grandson of *Thomas Lewis*, Lieutenant, Eleventh Regt., Virginia Troops.

ROY WATKINS ADNEY, Lebanon, Ind. (36439). Same as Earle Martin Adney, Ind. (36445).

SYLVESTER TAYLOR AGENS, Newark, N. J. (37525). Son of Sylvester Halsey Moore and Elizabeth Walter (Taylor) Agens; grandson of Frederick Girard and Emma Louise (Moore) Agens; great-grandson of Thomas and Eliza Crane (Osborn) Agens; great²-grandson of *James Agens (Agin)*, private, Colonel Hall's and Colonel Willett's Regts., Cont'l Line.

CHARLES GERLOCK ALLEN, Keokuk, Iowa (36917). Son of James Madison and Katherine (Girlock) Allen; grandson of James Nehemiah and Phœbe Haskins (Burton) Allen; great-grandson of Robert Haskins and Lucinda (Wagley) Burton; great²-grandson of George and Mary (Miller) Wagley; great³-grandson of Joseph and Lillie (Allen) Miller; great⁴-grandson of *Joseph Miller*, private, Botetourt County, Virginia Militia, pensioned.

FREDERICK WILLIAM ALLEN, Reading, Mass. (37759). Son of Frederick and Elizabeth (Plummer) Allen; grandson of Luther and Janett Laing (Mann) Allen; great-grandson of *Nathaniel Allen*, private, Massachusetts Cont'l Line, pensioned.

JOHN ALFRED AMERMAN, Newark, N. J. (37519). Son of George Vroom and Alletta Jane (Quick) Amerman; grandson of William Dow and Garetta (Tunison) Amerman; great-grandson of John Covert and Margaret (Brown) Amerman; great²-grandson of Paul A. and Martha (Covert) Amerman; great³-grandson of *Albert Amerman*, private, Second Battalion, Somerset County, New Jersey Militia.

HARRY COMPTON ANDERSON, Springfield, N. J. (37511). Son of David M. and Etta (Compton) Anderson; grandson of Henry and Sarah (Tucker) Compton; great-grandson of John and Maria (Taylor) Tucker; great²-grandson of Elias and Nancy (Mills) Tucker; great³-grandson of *Joseph Tucker*, private and Ensign, Essex County, New Jersey Militia.

JAMES SUMTER ANDERSON, Pulski, Tenn. (37466). Son of Ed Frances and Beulah (Sumter) Anderson; grandson of James A. and Mary (Rhea) Sumter; great-grandson of Joseph C. and Catherine (Reynolds) Rhea; great²-grandson of William and Elizabeth (Breden) Rhea; great³-grandson of *Joseph C. Rhea*, Chaplain, First Regt., Virginia Cont'l Troops.

ELMER ELLSWORTH APPLETON, Freeport, Ill. (37205). Son of Samuel E. and Mary (Mikesell) Appleton; grandson of Joseph B. and Abbie Hale (Hunt) Appleton; great-grandson of Joseph B. and Hanna (Knowlton) Appleton; great²-grandson of Isaac and Sarah (Twitchell) Appleton; great³-grandson of *Isaac Appleton*, private, New Hampshire Militia, Member Provincial Congress and of Committees of Safety and Correspondence.

LUTHER ALBERT BAKER, Minneapolis, Minn. (37235). Son of Henry Chapman and Ellen Maria (Brewster) Baker; grandson of Luther Alexander and Mercy (Stanard) Baker; great-grandson of Ozi and Lucy (Hard) Baker; great²-grandson of *Remember Baker*, Captain, Vermont "Green Mountain Boys," killed in service.

WILLIAM PARCHER BANGS, Swampscott, Mass. (37397). Son of Charles Howard and Eva A. (Parcher) Bangs; grandson of William B. and Martha P. (Swett) Bangs; great-grandson of Sylvanus and Hannah E. (Bean) Bangs; great²-grandson of Ebenezer and Polly (Cobb) Bangs; great²-grandson of *Barnabas Bangs*, Matross, Cumberland County, Massachusetts Artillery.

ARTHUR UDELL BARCO, Edwardsville, Ill. (37217). Son of Harrison and Anna Maria (Mestre) Barco; grandson of Dempsy and Elizabeth Ann (Stallings) Barco; great-grandson of Henry and Rosannah (Emmert) Stallings; great²-grandson of *Abram Stallings*, private, Nansemond County, Virginia Militia.

MILTON EDWARD BARKER, Wilmette, Ill. (37206). Son of Milton Edward and Della (Dimock) Barker; grandson of John Harding and Mary E. (Dimock) Dimock; great-grandson of Davis and Betsey (Jenkins) Dimock; great²-grandson of *David Dimock*, Lieutenant, Connecticut Militia, pensioned.

NORMAN WICKFORD BARNS, East Hampton, N. Y. (37585). Son of Thomas Dixon and Adelaide T. (Huntting) Barns; grandson of James Madison and Mary (Van Conklin) Huntting; great-grandson of Abraham and Mary (Mulford) Huntting; great²-grandson of *Nathaniel Huntting*, East Hampton, New York Associator.

HERSCHEL BARTLETT, St. Joseph, Mo. (Mass., 37398). Son of David and Phobe (Elsworth) Bartlett; grandson of Josiah and Anna (Latham) Bartlett; great-grandson of *Samuel Latham*, private, Fourteenth Regt., Albany County, New York Militia.

IRA BENNETT BARTLEY, Chicago, Ill. (37216). Son of Samuel Moore and Virginia Catherine (Berry) Bartley; grandson of George and Elizabeth Grey (Moore) Bartley; great-grandson of *Joshua Bartley*, private and Corporal, Col. Benjamin Temple's Regt., Virginia Militia.

WILLIAM MARSHALL BARTON, St. Louis, Mo. (35571). Son of Jonathan Marshall and Katie May (Burgess) Barton; grandson of J. M. and Louisa (Hutson) Barton; great-grandson of William and Sarah (Dunning) Barton; great²-grandson of David and Hannah (Hill) Barton; great²-grandson of *Joshua Barton*, private, Col. John Sevier's Regt., North Carolina Troops at King's Mountain.

FREDERIC GEORGE BATES, Toledo, Ohio (37049). Son of George Chapman and Alice Emily (Moore) Bates; grandson of Apollas and Delina (Tuttle) Moore; great-grandson of Abel and Hannah (Gowdy) Tuttle, Jr.; great²-grandson of *Alexander Gowdy, Jr.*, private, Connecticut Militia, pensioned; great²-grandson of *Abel Tuttle*, grandson of Henry Miner and Nancy Farrar (Chapman) Bates; great-grandson of Jacob and Charity (Paddock) Bates; great²-grandson of *Thomas Paddock*, private Plymouth County, Massachusetts Militia; great-grandson of Daniel and Caroline (Shurtleff) Chapman; great²-grandson of *Benoni Shurtleff, Jr.*, private and Marine, Massachusetts Troops, pensioned.

ROBERT BAYLEY, Jamaica Plain, Mass. (37395). Son of Frank William and Mina (French) Bayley; grandson of William Henry and Lucy Ann (Chase) Bayley; great-grandson of Luther Rogers and Lucy Demond (Follansbee) Chase; great²-grandson of Nathan and Judith (Rogers) Chase; great²-grandson of *Edmund Chase*, Newbury, Mass., Minute Man at Lexington Alarm.

FRANK GRENVILLE BEARDSLEY, St. Louis, Mo. (37601). Son of Grenville S. and Mary Elizabeth (Clark) Beardsley; grandson of Leonard Everett and Nancy (Craumer) Beardsley; great-grandson of Everett and Olive (Peters) Beardsley; great²-grandson of *Whitmore Beardsley*, private, Connecticut Cont'l Troops, pensioned.

EDWIN BENJAMIN, Mt. Vernon, N. Y. (37189). Son of George W. and Mary Matilda (Bachtler) Benjamin; grandson of Martin Everett and Sarah Morrill (Shepard) Benjamin; great-grandson of Eleaser Benjamin; great²-grandson of John Benjamin; great³-grandson of *George Benjamin*, Captain, Col. G. S. Silliman's Regt., Connecticut State Troops.

RAYMOND BENJAMIN, San Francisco, Calif. (37250). Son of Erastus Moses and Ruth Slocum (Mahon) Benjamin; grandson of Michael and Susanne (Bailey) Benjamin; great-grandson of *Judah Benjamin*, private, Connecticut Militia.

NATHANIEL WALLIS BENNETT, Minneapolis, Minn. (37228). Son of Moses Sanders and Isabel (Wallis) Bennett; grandson of Nathaniel and Betsey (Edget) Wallis, Jr.; great-grandson of *Nathaniel Wallis*, private, Albany County, New York Militia, daughter pensioned.

JOHN OUTWATER BENSON, Paterson, N. J. (37776). Son of John and Jane Maria (Outwater) Benson; grandson of John and Sophia (Paulison) Outwater; great-grandson of Richard and Catherine (Kipp) Outwater; great²-grandson of *John Outwater (Jan Outwater)*, Captain, Bergen County, New Jersey Militia.

WEBSTER AUGUSTUS BENTON, Minneapolis, Minn. (37241). Son of Raphael Ward and Hannah W. (Leete) Benton; grandson of Raphael and Lois (Russell) Benton; great-grandson of Lot and Hannah (Chittenden) Benton; great²-grandson of *Timothy Benton*, private, Guilford, Connecticut Militia at Lexington Alarm.

GEORGE BERLET, Houston, Texas (37530). Son of Balthaser and Mary Emily (Montgomery) Berlet; grandson of James Nelson and Catharine (Batterson) Montgomery; great-grandson of Isaac and Amelia (Nash) Batterson; great²-grandson of *Stephen Batterson*, private, Col. Heman Swift's Regt., Connecticut Cont'l Troops, pensioned.

HENRY WILLIAM BISHOP, Eustis, Fla. (29922). Son of William and Mary Ann (Lapsley) Bishop; grandson of William and Sarah (Alcorn) Lapsley; great-grandson of *John Lapsley*, Lieutenant, Ninth Regt., Virginia Troops.

WALTER HUMBOLDT BISHOP, Eustis, Fla. (29923). Same as Henry W. Bishop, Fla. (29922).

HAROLD FERDINAND BLAKE, Georgetown, Mass. (37377). Son of Ferdinand Louis and Mary Nesbit (Chase) Blake; grandson of Josiah Tilton and Catherine (Fogg) Blake; great-grandson of *Jeremiah Fogg*, Paymaster and Captain, Second Regt., New Hampshire Cont'l Infantry.

MARVIN EDWARD BOISSEAU, St. Louis, Mo. (37603). Son of Daniel Thomas and Amanda Jane (——) Boisseau; grandson of Benjamin W. and Sybil (Duncan) Boisseau; great-grandson of Charles F. and Susan (Camden) Duncan; great²-grandson of *William Camden*, Sergeant, Lieutenant-Colonel John Pope's Regt., Virginia Volunteers.

LEON MAYNARD BOLTER, Minneapolis, Minn. (37230). Son of Edward G. and Harriet E. (Nutting) Bolter; grandson of Emerson and Harriet (Nash) Nutting; great-grandson of *John Nutting*, private, Hampshire County, Massachusetts Militia.

RICHARD WATSON BOND, Wilmington, Del. (35669). Son of William Vinton and Alice Saxton (Goodyear) Bond; grandson of John and Caroline (Flennard) Goodyear; great-grandson of John and Anna (Burkholder) Goodyear; great²-grandson of *Ludwick Goodyear*, private, Lancaster County, Pennsylvania Militia.

ROBERT MERMOD BOOTH, Cincinnati, Ohio (37632). Son of Emmons Rutledge and Mary (Mermod) Booth; grandson of Ebenezer and Margaret E. (Sering) Booth; great-grandson of Samuel and Elizabeth (Sharp) Sering, Jr.; great²-grandson of *John Sharp*, Corporal and Lieutenant, New Jersey Militia and Cont'l Troops; great²-grandson of Samuel and Sarah (Mann) Sering; great²-grandson of *Joseph Mann*, private, Westmoreland County, Pennsylvania Militia and Cont'l Line.

EDWARD L. BOUTON, Elizabeth, N. J. (37777). Son of Chauncey and Mary Meade (Lawrence) Bouton; grandson of John and Huldah G. (Keeler) Bouton; great²-grandson of *Jeremiah Keeler*, Corporal and Sergeant, Connecticut Militia.

EUGENE BOUTON, Bloomfield, N. J. (37516). Son of Ira and Emma (Foote) Bouton; grandson of William and Hannah (Carrington) Bouton; great-grandson of *William Bouton*, Corporal and Sergeant, Connecticut Militia and General Wooster's Cont'l Troops.

ROBERT OGDEN BOUTON, Elizabeth, N. J. (37778). Son of Adrian F. and Fanny (Ogden) Bouton; grandson of Chauncey and Mary Meade (Lawrence) Bouton; great-grandson of John and Huldah G. (Keeler) Bouton; great²-grandson of *Jeremiah Keeler*, Corporal and Sergeant, Connecticut Militia, pensioned.

HARRY WILSON BOVARD, Sharon, Pa. (37401). Son of James Chambers and Mary (Wilhelmina) (Orr) Bovard; grandson of Chambers and Hannah (Turney) Orr; great-grandson of *Robert Orr*, Captain, George Rogers Clark Expedition.

HAROLD KING BOWEN, Iowa (35608). Supplemental. Son of William Walker and Lydia May (King) Bowen; grandson of David and Lydia Ann (Hall) Wood; great-grandson of Phineas and Lydia (Huntley) Hall; great²-grandson of James and Lydia (Caulkins) Huntley, Jr.; great²-grandson of *Jonathan Caulkins*, Captain, Lieutenant-Colonel Storr's Regt., Connecticut Militia.

CHARLES FREDERICK BOWERS, Harmony Grove, Md. (37349). Son of Grayson Eichelberger and Chrisse Byrd Dell (Firestone) Bowers; grandson of Martin Luther and Katherine Virginia (Galle) Firestone; great-grandson of Joshua and Christiana (Stull) Firestone; great²-grandson of Jacob and Mary Magdaline (Hummel) Firestone; great³-grandson of *Matthias Firestone*, private, York County, Pennsylvania Militia.

RALPH FIRESTONE BOWERS, Harmony Grove, Md. (37350). Same as Charles Frederick Bowers, Md. (37349).

WALTER RAYMOND BOYD, Glen Ridge, N. J. (37373). Son of Frank Raymond and Julia Willis (Thorp) Boyd; grandson of Orange P. and Sarah A. (Sturtevant) Thorp; great-grandson of *Asa Sturtevant*, private and Fifer, Massachusetts Militia and Cont'l Troops.

JAMES MALCOLM BRECKENRIDGE, St. Louis, Mo. (35566). Son of George and Julia (Clark) Breckenridge; grandson of James and Elizabeth Ann (Bryan) Breckenridge; great-grandson of *George Breckenridge*, private, Virginia Militia at King's Mountain; great²-grandson of *Alexander Breckenridge*, private, Virginia Militia at King's Mountain; great-grandson of *James Bryan*, private, Col. Otho Williams' Regt., Virginia Cont'l Troops.

ARTHUR BRANTLY BRISTOW, Norfolk, Va. (36553). Son of Robert S. and Lelia Weston (Faulkner) Bristow; grandson of Larkin Stubblefield and Catharine (Seward) Bristow; great-grandson of Benjamin and Anne (Saunders) Bristow, Jr.; great²-grandson of *Benjamin Bristow*, private, Sixth Regt., Virginia Cont'l Troops.

WILLIS WARNER BROWN, San Diego, Calif. (37260). Son of Willis R. and Theresa Elizabeth (Warner) Brown; grandson of Peter R. and Lucina K. (Westcott) Warner; great-grandson of John and Elizabeth (Spraker) Warner; great²-grandson of *John Spraker*, private and Batteauman, Montgomery County, New York Militia, pensioned.

HENRY DAVID BROPHY, Fairfield, Maine (36593). Son of James and Harriet (Mullin) Brophy; grandson of David and Lydia (Green) Mullin; great-grandson of *Archibald McMullin*, private, Massachusetts Cont'l Troops, pensioned.

ALBERT WALKER BROWN, Chicago, Ill. (Ind. 36443). Son of James A. and Sarah Jane (Watkins) Brown; grandson of Jacob and Elizabeth (Lewis) Brown; great-grandson of *Thomas Lewis*, Lieutenant, Eleventh Regt., Virginia Militia.

CARL GROVER BROWN, San Francisco, Calif. (37253). Son of Albert Vincent and Sylvia H. (Grover) Brown; grandson of James Lyman and Hannah Folsom (Elsemore) Grover; great-grandson of William and Lucy G. (Folsom) Elsemore; great²-grandson of John Dearborn and Hannah (Gooch) Folsom; great³-grandson of *Benjamin Folsom*, Captain, New Hampshire Militia.

ROBERT LONGFELLOW BROWN, Boston, Mass. (37399). Son of William Henry and Elizabeth Mayhew (Longfellow) Brown; grandson of Jonathan Abel and Emmeline Love (Smith) Longfellow; great-grandson of Killiam Otis and Susan C. (Hoyt) Smith; great²-grandson of John and Love (St. Scott) Smith; great³-grandson of Stephen and Hannah (Hill) Smith; great⁴-grandson of *Stephen Smith*, Captain and Major, Massachusetts Militia for sea-coast defense, truckmaster and Commissary.

JOHN SANFORD BRUMBACK, Toledo, Ohio (37050). Son of David La'Doyt and Elizabeth (Pinkerton) Brumback; grandson of John Sanford and Ellen Perlena (Purmort) Brumback; great-grandson of Minor and Perlena (Nettleton) Purmort; great²-grandson of Joshua and Eunice (Walworth) Purmort; great³-grandson of *Charles Walworth*, Signer of Canaan, N. H. Association Test.

HUDSON FREELAND BRUNER, Kola, Nebr. (36991). Son of Uriah and Amelia (Brobst) Bruner; grandson of John Gangewere and Judith (Erdman) Bruner; great-grandson of *Andrew Brunner (Bruner)*, private, Northampton County, Pennsylvania Association.

MATTHEW GARDNER BUCKNER, Nashville, Tenn. (36798). Son of H. Bruce and Sadie McClung (Gardner) Buckner; grandson of Robert H. and Margaret (McClung) Gardner; great-grandson of Matthew B. and Eliza Jane (Morgan) McClung; great²-grandson of Charles and Margaret (White) McClung; great³-grandson of *James White*, Captain, Iredell County, North Carolina Militia.

NEWTON MORRIS BULLARD, Summit, N. J. (37512). Son of George Henry and Emily Jane (Van Keuren) Bullard; grandson of James A. and Harriet (Rundle) Bullard; great-grandson of *Nathan Bullard*, private, Corporal and Sergeant, Massachusetts Cont'l Troops and Militia.

GEORGE SAMUEL BURCH, Minneapolis, Minn. (37232). Son of George Benjamin and Ellen Harriet (Merrill) Burch; grandson of Samuel Day and Louisa (Heath) Merrill; great-grandson of Joseph and Susan (Day) Merrill; great²-grandson of *John Merrill*, Sergeant, Col. Samuel Herrick's Regt., Vermont Militia.

GUY HAMILTON BURRAGE, Contoocook, N. H. (Calif. 37254). Son of Hamilton and Mary (Davis) Burrage; grandson of John and Nancy (Dana) Burrage; great-grandson of John and Abigail (Pratt) Burrage; great²-grandson of *Thomas Burrage*, private, Massachusetts Militia.

PAUL J. BURRAGE, Savannah, Ga. (Mass. 37760). Son of George Dana and Clara G. (Johnson) Burrage; grandson of John and Nancy (Dana) Burrage; great-grandson of John and Abigail (Pratt) Burrage; great²-grandson of *Thomas Burrage*, private, Colonel McIntosh's Regt., Massachusetts Militia.

EGERTON VINSON BURRITT, East Orange, N. J. (37523). Son of Frank Hamilton and Eva (Burritt) Vinson; grandson of Harvey Hallock and Eliza Egerton (Wilson) Burritt; great-grandson of Benjamin and Diana (Plotts) Burritt; great²-grandson of *Stephen Burritt*, private, Col. Samuel Canfield's Regt., Connecticut Militia.

JOHN EDWARDS CALHOUN, Minneapolis, Minn. (37429). Son of John Franklin and Clara Zenora (Edwards) Calhoun; grandson of David and Caroline Matilda (Cunningham) Calhoun; great-grandson of Thomas and Jean (Gray) Calhoun; great²-grandson of *David Calhoun*, private, Col. Timothy Green's Battalion, Lancaster County, Pennsylvania Militia.

HERBERT GEORGE CANDEE, Milwaukee, Wis. (37280). Son of Henry and Hosanna (Stafford) Candee; grandson of Arnold and Ruby (Underwood) Stafford; great-grandson of Joseph and Susan (Hopkins) Stafford; great²-grandson of *Oliver Hopkins*, private, Rhode Island Militia, pensioned; great-grandson of Evander and Jerusha (Wood) Underwood; great²-grandson of *Nathan Wood*, private, Colonel Latimore's Regt., Connecticut Militia, pensioned.

EDWIN QUAYLE CANNON, Salt Lake City, Utah (32650). Son of George Quayle and Eliza Lamercia (Tenney) Cannon; grandson of William and Eliza (Webb) Tenney; great-grandson of William and Judith (Reed) Tenney; great²-grandson of *Benjamin Tenney*, private, New Hampshire Militia.

EDGAR MORTIMER CARNRICK, New York, N. Y. (37188). Son of John and Gertrude (Solmons) Carnrick; grandson of George and Mahala (Searles) Carnrick; great-grandson of George and Mary (Peck) Carnrick; great²-grandson of *Ichabod Peck*, private, Col. Joseph Read's Regt., Rhode Island Militia.

GEORGE ELY CARPENTER, Newark, N. J. (37779). Son of Adson M. and Ann Caroline (Watson) Carpenter, grandson of Benjamin Ely and Susan C. (Teed) Watson; great-grandson of John and Elizabeth (Ely) Watson; great²-grandson of *Moses Ely*, private and teamster, Essex County, New Jersey Militia.

JULIAN SHAKESPEARE CARR, Durham, N. C. (Va. 36556). Son of John Wesley and Eliza P. (Bullock) Carr; grandson of John Carr; great-grandson of *John Carr*, Ensign, First Regt., Virginia Cont'l Troops.

ALBERT CARROLL, Shawneetown, Ill. (37218). Son of Charles and Elizabeth (Clarey) Carroll; grandson of Charles and Elizabeth (Eddy) Carroll; great-grandson of Henry and Mary (Marshall) Eddy; great²-grandson of Nathan and Rebecca (Safford) Eddy, Jr.; great²-grandson of Nathan and Rebecca (Safford) Eddy; great³-grandson of *Nathan Eddy*, private, Col. Ebenezer Sprout's Regt., Massachusetts Cont'l Infantry.

ARTHUR JAY CARRUTH, Topeka, Kans. (36741). Son of Uri and Lucy Ann (Robinson) Carruth; grandson of Ira and Polly (Kibbee) Robinson; great-grandson of Zelotes and Alice (Mayo) Robinson; great²-grandson of *Elijah Robinson*, Captain, Connecticut Militia and State Troops.

ARTHUR JAY CARRUTH, Jr., Topeka, Kans. (36742). Son of Arthur Jay and Clara Belle (Wilkinson) Carruth; grandson of Uri and Lucy Ann (Robinson) Carruth; great-grandson of Ira and Polly (Kibbee) Robinson; great²-grandson of Zelotes and Alice (Mayo) Robinson; great²-grandson of *Elijah Robinson*, Captain, Connecticut Militia and State Troops.

EDGAR WILLIAM CARRUTH, Herrington, Kans. (36743). Same as Arthur Jay Carruth, Jr., Kans. (36742).

CLARENCE EDWARD CARY, Chicago, Ill. (37215). Son of William Miller and Caroline (George) Cary; grandson of James and Mercy (Weaver) Cary; great-grandson of *Jabez Weaver*, Sergeant, Vermont Militia.

EDWARD GEORGE CASEY, Toronto, Ohio (37047). Son of John Stanton and Hannah R. (Myers) Casey; grandson of Michael and Hannah K. (Bowles) Myers; great-grandson of George and Hannah (Robb) Myers; great²-grandson of *Michael Myers*, Indian Scout with rank of Captain.

LEVIN PATRICK CAUSEY, Springfield, Mass. (Md. 37327). Son of Franklin and Nancy D. (Miller) Causey; grandson of Patrick and Polly (Cropper) Causey; great-grandson of *Patrick Causey*, private, Wicomico County, Maryland Militia.

HERBERT GRISWOLD CHADWICK, Milwaukee, Wis. (37281). Son of Arthur Benjamin and Minnie Nixon (O'Donnell) Chadwick; grandson of James Eli and Martha Julia Clark) Chadwick; great-grandson of Joel Bushrod and Julia Ann (Griswold) Clark; great²-grandson of Abiel Buckland and Mary (Pinney) Griswold; great³-grandson of *Isaac Pinney*, Corporal and Sergeant, Connecticut Troops, pensioned.

CLARENCE BUFORD CHAMBERS, Gallup, N. Mex. (30100). Son of John G. and Mary (C. ——) Chambers; grandson of William and Catherine (Blaukenship) Chambers; great-grandson of *Alexander Chambers*, private, Seventh Regt., Virginia Militia and Cont'l Troops.

FREDERICK DORRANCE CHANDLER, Honolulu, Hawaii (38536). Son of William James Dawes and Matilda Evelyn (Burr) Chandler; grandson of Jarvis Platt and Lydia Evelyn (Carthwaite) Burr; great-grandson of *Wakeman Burr*, Lieutenant, Fifth Regt., Connecticut Militia.

SAMUEL MICHAEL ANDREW CHAPMAN, Huntington, Ind. (Mass. 37400). Son of William F. and Louise Augusta (Pollard) Chapman; grandson of Andrew and Elizabeth Newmarch (Cutts) Pollard; great-grandson of John Seward and Dorcas (Kennard) Cutts; great²-grandson of John and Dorothy (Seaward) Cutts; great³-grandson of *John Cutts*, Fifer, Col. Pierce Long's Regt., New Hampshire Militia.

TRUMAN B. CHAPMAN, Elizabeth, N. J. (37513). Son of Charles E. and Ella (Lillie) Chapman; grandson of William and Ann Betsy (Kimball) Lillie; great-grandson of William and Betsy Ann (Smith) Kimball; great²-grandson of *Joseph Kimball*, private, Massachusetts Cont'l Troops.

ATHOLBERT ELTON CHASE, Loup City, Neb. (36990). Son of Albert E. and Anna Lauretta (Sutton) Chase; grandson of Alonzo and Martha Ann (Dick) Sutton; great-grandson of Levi and Amytiah (Leeper) Dick; great²-grandson of Robert and Julia Frances (Summers) Leeper; great³-grandson of *Matthew Leeper*, North Carolina patriot who furnished provisions and money to Militia; great⁴-grandson of *Andrew Leeper*, patriot who furnished provisions and money to Militia of North and South Carolina and Virginia.

JOHN EDWIN MERRILL CHILDS, Roslindale, Mass. (37378). Son of James Root and Mary Ann (Shandrew) Childs; grandson of Levi and Eliza Hurd (Root) Childs; great-grandson of James and Elizabeth (Stocking) Root; great²-grandson of *Oliver Root*, Captain and Major, Massachusetts Militia.

ARTHUR LINCOLN CLARK, Nashville, Tenn. (37459). Son of William Adams and Mary E. (Bennett) Clark; grandson of Solomon Bradford and Emily S. (Hoisington) Clark; great-grandson of Daniel Randall and Lucy (Claflin) Clark; great²-grandson of *Timothy Clark*, private and Ensign, New Hampshire Militia.

CLARENCE BREEDLOVE CLARKE, West Park, Ohio (37626). Son of William Bradley and Alice Pheriba Breedlove (Winings) Clarke; grandson of Sumner and Maria Haddock (Wilcox) Clark; great-grandson of Enos and Susan (Allen) Clark; great²-grandson of *Solomon Allen*, Major Second Regt., Hampshire County, Massachusetts Militia.

JOHN PHILANDER CLOUGH, Oakland, Calif. (37255). Son of Oliver Kenney and Mercy Ann (Whaley) Clough; grandson of *Oliver Clough*, private, Colonel Scammell's Third Regt., New Hampshire Troops, pensioned.

FREDERICK BURFORD COBBETT, Morristown, N. J. (37355). Son of George and Mary Catherine (Potts) Cobbett; grandson of William and Maria (Voorhees) Potts; great-grandson of Coert A. and Margaret Ann (Bergen) Voorhees; great²-grandson of *Jacob G. Bergen*, Lieutenant, Somerset County, New Jersey Militia.

HARRIE CUTLER COBURN, San Francisco, Calif. (37261). Son of Jessie Milton and Abbie M. (Cutler) Coburn; grandson of Jessie Milton and Almira (Morse) Coburn; great-grandson of *Silas Coburn*, private, Col. Samuel Bullard's Regt., Massachusetts Militia.

SAMUEL POYNTZ COCHRAN, Dallas, Texas (37527). Son of John Carr and Samuella Tannehill (Dewees) Cochran; grandson of John and Mary (Wasson) Cochran; great-grandson of *Andrew* and Sarah (Baird) *Cochran*, private, Tryon County, New York Militia, and Captain Burhydt's Company of Bateaumen; great^2-grandson of *John Baird* (Beard), private, Col. Marinus Willett's Regt., Tyron County, New York Militia; great-grandson of *James Wasson*, private, Major Francis Chaudinette's Regt., New York Bateaumen; grandson of John Coburn and Maria (Bayless) Dewees; great-grandson of *Samuel* and Mary (Coburn) *Dewees*, private, Tenth Regt., Philadelphia County, Pennsylvania Militia; great^2-grandson of *John Coburn*, private, Chester County, Pennsylvania Militia; great-grandson of Benjamin and Elizabeth (Wood) Bayless; great^2-grandson of *George Wood*, Matross, Col. John Eyre's Regt., Pennsylvania Artillery Militia.

BENJAMIN EDMUND COLLISON, Providence, R. I. (36507). Son of John T. and Ellen May (French) Collison; grandson of Edmund Henry and Ellen Maria (Arnold) French; great-grandson of Ezra and Suky (Fuller) French; great^2-grandson of *Ezra French*, private, Massachusetts Militia.

GEORGE NEWELL COMFORT, Shaker Village, Ohio (37035). Son of John Collins and Elizabeth (Maltz) Comfort; grandson of Balkam Newell and Lucretia Goodwin (Collins) Comfort; great-grandson of Thomas and Abigail (David) Comfort; great^2-grandson of *Richard Comfort*, private, Dutchess County, New York Militia.

ARTHUR BURDETT CONNER, Brooklyn, N. Y. (37582). Son of James and Mary Elizabeth (Conner) Conner; grandson of John Dunbar and Paulina (Wardwell) Conner; great-grandson of William and Deborah (Littlefield) Wardwell; great^2-grandson of *Jeremiah Wardwell*, private, Colonel Frye's Regt., Massachusetts Militia.

MARSHALL HARVEY COOLIDGE, Minneapolis, Minn. (37430). Son of John Harvey and Mrs. Elizabeth (Coleman) (Davidson) Coolidge; grandson of John and Harriet (Towne) Coolidge; great-grandson of Archaelaus and Esther (Weston) Towne; great^2-grandson of *Archaeleus Towne*, Captain, Col. Moses Nichols' Regt., New Hampshire Militia.

CHARLES CYRUS COOMBS, Washington, D. C. (37152). Son of Charles William and Mary Catherine (——) Coombs; grandson of William and Barbara Ellen (——) Coombs; great-grandson of *John Coombs*, private, Colonel Alexander's Regt., Virginia Troops.

WILLIAM LESLIE COOMBS, Washington, D. C. (37153). Son of Charles Cyrus and Hattie Frances (Brooks) Coombs; grandson of Charles William and Mary Catherine (Belford) Coombs; great-grandson of William and Barbara Ellen (Macray) Coombs; great^2-grandson of *John Coombs*, private, Colonel Alexander's and Colonel Dabney's Regts., Virginia Troops; grandson of Albert Franklin and Abbie Frances (Bancroft) Brooks; great-grandson of Franklin and Rebecca A. (Batchelder) Brooks; great^2-grandson of *Joshua Brooks*, private and Corporal, Lincoln, Massachusetts Militia.

THOMAS ARMITAGE CORY, U. S. Navy, Little Rock, Ark. (31774). Son of Thomas Moses and Emma Josephine (Armitage) Cory; grandson of Azro Buck and Rhoda Scott (Hart) Cory; great-grandson of Thomas Robbins and Lytta (Howe) Cory; great^2-grandson of *Ebenezer Cory*, private, Massachusetts Cont'l Line, pensioned; great^2-grandson of *Asa Howe*, private, Connecticut Militia and Cont'l Troops; grandson of Joseph and Eleanora (Barnard) Armitage; great-grandson of Martin Moses and Emmeline (Benedict) Barnard; great^2-grandson of Thaddeus and Hannah (Goldsborough) Barnard; great^3-grandson of *Moses* and Hannah (Barnard) *Barnard*, private, Connecticut Militia, State and Cont'l Troops, widow pensioned; great^4-grandson of *Edward Barnard* (father of Hannah), Windsor, Connnecticut Selectman and Captain of Committee for providing for soldiers' families and for raising bounties; great^2-grandson of Stephen and Polly (Sherman) Benedict; great^3-grandson of *Jonathan Benedict*, Orderly-Sergeant, Danbury, Connecticut Militia, pensioned; great^4-grandson of *Nathaniel Benedict*, private, Captain Lockwood's Regt., Danbury, Connecticut Militia.

FRED GEORGE CORYELL, New York City, N. Y. (37182). Son of Charles Rollin and Dian (Armstrong) Coryell; grandson of George and Eliza (Sherwood) Coriell; great-grandson of Abraham and Annie (Covert) Coriell; great^2-grandson of *Abraham Coriell*, private, Middlesex County, New Jersey Militia.

HORACE R. COUDY, St. Louis, Mo. (37604). Son of Matthew and Mary C. (Seward) Coudy; grandson of Isreal and Margaret (Slaybeck) Seward; great-grandson of John and Mary (Butler) Seward; great²-grandson of *John Seward*, Colonel, Second Regt., Sussex County, New Jersey Militia.

GOLDSBOROUGH GREENFIELD COULBOURN, Suffolk, Va. (Md. 37331). Son of George and Mary (Fooks) Coulbourn; grandson of Uriah and Eliza Jane (Johnson) Fooks; great-grandson of Seth and Matty (——) Fooks; great²-grandson of *Jesse Fooks* (*Fooke*), private, Wicomico County, Maryland Militia.

JOHN IRVING COULBOURN, Overbrook, Pa. (Md. 37332). Same as Goldsborough G. Coulbourn, Md. (37331).

THOMAS BALL COUPER, Montclair, N. J. (37780). Son of William and Eliza Chickering (Ball) Couper; grandson of Thomas and Ellen Louisa (Wild) Ball; great-grandson of Thomas and Elizabeth Wyer (Hall) Ball; great²-grandson of *Jonathan Ball*, Sergeant, Colonel Whitney's Regt., Massachusetts Militia, pensioned; great-grandson of Daniel and Eliza B. (Plimpton) Wild; great²-grandson of *Jonathan Wild*, private, Massachusetts Militia, Surgeon on privateer "Speedwell" and sloop "Revenge," pensioned.

JOSEPH ERVING COWPERTHWAITE, Butte, Mont. (Utah 37551). Son of Allen Corson and Ida Estella (Erving) Cowperthwaite; grandson of Joel Fuller and Amelia Phœbe (Cadwell) Erving; great-grandson of John and Lydia Carlisle (Fuller) Erving; great²-grandson of *Joseph Fuller*, private, Massachusetts State Troops, pensioned.

CHANNING HARRIS COX, Boston, Mass. (37376). Son of Charles Edson and Eveline (Randall) Cox; grandson of Thomas Bartlett and Mary Gilman (Pickering) Randall; great-grandson of John and Martha (Pease) Pickering; great²-grandson of *James Pickering*, private, Capt. Joseph Parsons' Company, Portsmouth, New Hampshire Militia.

CHARLES HENRY CRANDON, Miami, Fla. (Mass. 37379). Son of Philip Howland and Emma Frances (Winslow) Crandon; grandson of Philip and Harriet Pierce (Sisson) Crandon; great-grandson of Philip and Rebecca (Hathaway) Crandon; great²-grandson of *Thomas Crandon*, Member Dartmouth, Mass. Committee of Safety and Supplies, Captain, Bristol County, Massachusetts Militia; great²-grandson of *Jacob Hathaway*, private, Second Regt., Bristol County, Massachusetts Militia; gradson of Jonathan and Laurana (Rogers) Winslow; great-grandson of Richard and Abigail (Small) Winslow; great²-grandson of *Richard Winslow*, private, Col. John Hathaway's Regt., Massachusetts Militia, at Rhode Island Alarm; great-grandson of Jeptha and Mercy (Pool) Rogers; great²-grandson of *Gideon Rogers*, Sergeant, Col. John Hathaway's Regt., Massachusetts Militia, at Rhode Island Alarm.

DE WITT CRANE, Newport News, Va. (36554). Son of Job Symmes and Helen Baxter (Watkins) Crane; grandson of Job and Mary B. (Woodruff) Crane; great-grandson of *Nathaniel Crane*, private, Essex County, New Jersey Militia.

HARRY H. CUNNINGHAM, Trenton, Ohio (37036). Son of Andrew and Sarah Jane (Weaver) Cunningham; grandson of John and Esther (Clark) Weaver; great-grandson of Philip and Catharine (Hursh) Weaver; great²-grandson of *Michael Weaver*, Captain, Fourth and Third Battalions, Northumberland County, Pennsylvania Militia.

JOHN McFERRIN CURLEE, St. Louis, Mo. (35569). Son of John Rufus and Luna (Rogers) Curlee; grandson of John McFerrin and Sally Ann (Norfleet) Curlee; great-grandson of Cullen and Eleanor Duncan (McFerrin) Curlee; great²-grandson of *John Curlee*, private, North Carolina Troops; great²-grandson of John and Mary (Barber) Curlee; great³-grandson of *John Barber*, Member Tryon County, North Carolina Committee of Safety and Delegate to North Carolina Provincial Congress.

JOHN RUFUS CURLEE, Kirkwood, Mo. (35568). Son of John McFerrin and Sarah Ann (Norfleet) Curlee; grandson of Cullen and Eleanor Duncan (McFerrin) Curlee; great-grandson of *John* and Mary (Barber) *Curlee*, private, North Carolina Troops; great²-grandson of *John Barber*, Member Tryon County, North Carolina Committee of Safety and Delegate to North Carolina Provincial Congress.

LOUIS DE V. DAY, Summit, N. J. (37524). Son of Stephen S. and Hattie (A. ——) Day; grandson of Samuel Thomas and Elizabeth (Crane) Day; great-grandson of Stephen and Betsey Coe (Wood) Day; great²-grandson of *Daniel Smith Wood*, Captain, First Regt., Essex County, New Jersey Militia and State Troops.

JAMES DE LA MONTANYE, London, Eng. (N. Y. 37581). Son of John and Lillie Jane (Hoffman) de la Montanye; grandson of Franklin and Blandina (Ten Eyck) de la Montanye; great-grandson of Isaac and Mary (Longyear) de la Montanye; great²-grandson of *Peter Montanye*, private and Sergeant, New York Levies.

FRED STEPHENS DOAK, Chicago, Ill. (Pa. 37422). Son of William and Margaret (Lockhart) Doak; grandson of Moses and Rachel (Stephens) Doak; great-grandson of *Robert Doak*, private, Fourth and Third Battalions, Northampton County, Pennsylvania Troops.

CHARLES DOBBS, Louisville, Ky. (36534). Son of C. E. W. and Mary (Barrett) Dobbs; grandson of William Drewry and Martha (Leslie) Dobbs; great-grandson of Willoughby Dobbs; great²-grandson of *Kedar Dobbs*, private, Col. Daniel Morgan's Regt., Virginia Troops.

HENRY DE WITT DOBBS, New Rochelle, N. Y. (37579). Son of William Henry and Esther (Carlough) Dobbs; grandson of Howell and Sarah (Wilson) Dobbs; great-grandson of *Jarvis Dobbs*, private, Colonel Lasher's Regt., New York Militia.

WILLIAM HENRY DOBBS, New Rochelle, N. Y. (37181). Son of Henry De Witt and Hattie (Hamlin) Dobbs; grandson of William Henry and Esther (Carlough) Dobbs; great-grandson of Howel and Sara (Wilson) (Willison) Dobbs; great²-grandson of *Jarvis Dobbs*, private, Colonel Lasher's Regt., New York Militia.

WALTER BURDEN DODGE, East Providence Center, R. I. (36508). Son of William Anthony and Sarah Mariah (Burdon) Dodge; grandson of Aaron and Mary (Walker) Burdon; great-grandson of *Jonathan Burdon*, private, Worcester County, Massachusetts Militia; great-grandson of *Asa* and Hannah (Dudley) *Walker*, private, Col. Ebenezer Learned's Regt., Massachusetts Militia; great²-grandson of *Jonathan Dudley*, Sergeant, Worcester County, Massachusetts Militia.

ALBERT RUSSELL DODSON, Humboldt, Tenn. (37456). Son of Watkins Hopkins and Jerusha Ann (Blakemore) Dodson; grandson of William Thornton and Leslie (Young) Dodson; great-grandson of *Caleb Dodson*, private, Halifax County, Virginia Militia.

HARRY CULBERSON DORER, East Orange, N. J. (37369). Son of George Andrew and Phœbe Louisa (Culberson) Dorer; grandson of Henry W. and Ellen Augusta (Jewel) Culberson; great-grandson of Aaron C. and Louisa (Baldwin) Jewel; great²-grandson of John and Martha (Ferris) Jewel, Jr.; great³-grandson of *John Jewel, Sr.*, private Westchester County, New York Militia.

JAMES HOOPER DORSEY, Baltimore, Md. (37681). Son of John Richardson and Lillian (Hooper) Dorsey; grandson of James Levin and Sarah A. W. (Richardson) Dorsey; great-grandson of John and Martha (Chisolm) Dorsey; great²-grandson of *Levin Dorsey*, Dorchester County, Maryland Volunteer, killed.

JESSE WRIGHT DOWNEY, JR., Baltimore, Md. (37333). Son of Jesse Wright and Mary (Hammond) Downey; grandson of William and Margaret (Wright) Downey; great-grandson of William and Cordelia (Dorsey) Downey; great²-grandson of *John Downey*, Lieutenant, Eighth Battalion, Cumberland County, Pa.

GEORGE W. DOWNS, Portland, Ore. (35075). Son of Samuel H. and Ann Swan (Freen) Downs; grandson of George and Polly (Crossman) Downs; great-grandson of *John Crossman*, private, Second Regt., Fairfield County, Connecticut Line.

CHARLES WAYLAND DREW, JR., Minneapolis, Minn. (37435). Son of Charles Wayland and Annah Reed (Kellogg) Drew; grandson of Homer Cassius and Lorinda (Roby) Drew; great-grandson of Ebenezer and Mehitable (Taplin) Roby; great²-grandson of Elisha and Martha (Newton) Taplin; great³-grandson of *Seth Newton*, Captain, Worcester County, Massachusetts Militia.

JAMES RICHMOND DRIGGS, Darlington, S. C. (N. Y. 37190). Son of Spencer Bartholomew and Anna (Adrain) Driggs; grandson of Spencer and Sarah (Turner) Driggs; great-grandson of *Seth Turner*, private, Col. Jedidiah Huntington's Regt., Connecticut Cont'l Troops, pensioned.

WILLIAM F. DUFFY, JR., Providence, R. I. (36509). Son of William J. and Ann Maria (Cole) Duffy; grandson of Nehemiah Knight and Sarah Ann (Goff) Cole; great-grandson of Nehemiah Pierce and Sarah (Gladding) Cole; great²-grandson of *Nehemiah Cole*, private, Colonel Whitney's and Carpenter's Regts., Massachusetts Militia.

CHARLES CLARKE DUKE, Baltimore, Md. (37334). Son of James O'Connor and Emily Jane (Benson) Duke; grandson of Perry and Susan Ellen (Kemp) Benson; great-grandson of James and Mary Anne (Hopkins) Benson; great²-grandson of *Perry Benson*, Captain, Talbot County, Maryland Militia.

HARRY LLEWELLYN DUNLAP, New Castle, Pa. (37727). Son of Hamilton Rowan and Annie (Bonham) Dunlap; grandson of Llewellyn and Matilda (Fry) Bonham; great-grandson of Jacob and Mary (Moore) Fry; great²-grandson of *James Moore*, Colonel, Pennsylvania Militia.

ROBERT ELLIS DUNLAP, Calif. (36422). Supplemental. Son of George Thomas and Emma May (Ellis) Dunlap; grandson of James Henry and Harriet (Zuck) Ellis; great-grandson of David and Maria Louise (Linton) Zuck; great²-grandson of Jeremiah and Mary (Gross) Linton; great³-grandson of Jonathan and Susanna (Gillam) Linton; great⁴-grandson of *Joseph Linton*, private, Sixth Battalion, Pennsylvania Troops.

CLYDE P. DYER, St. Louis, Mo. (37605). Son of John Barry and Mary Elizabeth (Still) Dyer; grandson of Abner Withers and Cynthia Elizabeth (Wilson) Dyer; great-grandson of Zacharias Steel and Jane (Collins) Wilson; great²-grandson of *Richard Collins*, private, Col. John Thomas' Regt., South Carolina Militia.

SAMUEL ALLETHORN DYKE, Melrose, Mass. (37380). Son of Thomas Jefferson and Jane (Allethorn) Dike; grandson of Samuel and Dorothy (Flanders) Dike; great-grandson of Benjamin and Dorothy (Stearns) Dike; great²-grandson of *Benjamin Dike*, private, Massachusetts Militia and Cont'l Troops.

CHARLES FINNEY EAGAN, Niles, Ohio (37633). Son of John J. and Melvia (Finney) Eagan; grandson of Theron C. and Fidelia (Andrews) Finney; great-grandson of Josiah and Clarissa (Bushnell) Finney; great²-grandson of *Josiah Finney*, private, Litchfield County, Connecticut Militia, pensioned.

FRANKLIN HUBERT EDMESTER, Ridgewood, N. J. (37356). Son of Elijah Briggs and Susan (Stimpson) Edmester; grandson of George and Sarah (Hiers) Stimpson; great-grandson of *Andrew Stimpson*, private, Charlestown, Massachusetts Militia.

H. GERARD EFFINGER, Portland, Ore. (37484). Son of John Robert and Lucretia (Knowles) Effinger; grandson of John Strother and Mary (Currie) Effinger; great-grandson of *John Ignatius von Effinger*, Corporal, Captain von Herr's Regt., Pennsylvania Light Dragoons.

HENRY CLIFFORD EGERTON, Passaic, N. J. (37362). Son of James Oliver and Frances Virginia (Walsh) Egerton; grandson of Oliver and Hannah (Converse) Egerton; great-grandson of Israel and Anna (Smith) Converse; great²-grandson of *Israel Converse*, Captain and Colonel, Connecticut Militia and Cont'l Troops.

CARLETON ELLIS, Montclair, N. J. (37371). Son of Marcus and Kate (C——) Ellis; grandson of Enoch and Marcia (Spalding) Ellis; great-grandson of Moses and Kate (Boyden) Ellis; great²-grandson of *Joseph Ellis*, private, Walpole, Massachusetts militia.

FRED LEON ELLSWORTH, Minneapolis, Minn. (37233). Son of Enoch B. and Julia (Knapp) Ellsworth; grandson of Elijah and Celia (Pullen) Knapp; great-grandson of Joseph and Eunice (Carver) Knapp, Jr.; great²-grandson of *Joseph Knapp*, private, Col. Thomas Marshall's Regt., Massachusetts Militia.

NELSON LEWIS ELMER, Springfield, Mass. (37121). Son of Willard N. and Clara (Holton) Elmer; grandson of Nelson Lee and Betsey (Parsons) Elmer; great-grandson of *Andrew Parsons*, private, Massachusetts Militia, pensioned.

JAMES WILLIAM ELMS, Parlin, N. J. (37781). Son of George and Harriett (Berce) Elms; grandson of Charles D. and Abbie S. (Luce) Berce; great-grandson of Isaac and Roxanda (Spalding) Berce; great²-grandson of John and Betsey (——) Spalding; great³-grandson of *Eleazer Spalding*, Lieutenant, Col. William Prescott's Massachusetts Militia.

DWIGHT CARYL ELY, New York City, N. Y. (37580). Son of Theodore Julius and Nettie (Willis) Ely, grandson of Benjamin Cornwall and Elizabeth Crippen (Caryl) Ely; great-grandson of Sumner and Hannah Knapp (Gilbert) Ely; great²-grandson of *Adriel Ely*, Second Lieutenant, Col. Erastus Wolcott's Regt., Connecticut Militia.

RICHARD HARRINGTON ELY, Jerseyville, Ill. (37704). Son of Archibald Forman and Mary Terese (Harrington) Ely; grandson of Richard R. and Mary Ann (Fitzgerald) Ely; great-grandson of Richard I. and Amy (Forman) Ely; great²-grandson of Isaac and Sarah (Johnson) Ely; great³-grandson of *John Ely*, New Jersey Assistant, Department of Quartermaster General.

FREDERICK EARLE EMMONS, Elizabeth, N. J. (37782). Son of Lucius Edward and Cornelia (Hull) Emmons; grandson of Eben and Mary (Tryon) Hull; great-grandson of *Zephaniah Hull*, private, Second Regt., Connecticut Cont'l Dragoons.

JOSEPH RIDDICK ESTES, JR., Birmingham, Ala. (D. C. 37154). Son of Joseph Riddick and Willie Franc (Redd) Estés; grandson of J. Francis and J. Willie (Edwards) Redd; great-grandson of J. W. B. and Margaret (Culbertson) Edwards; great²-grandson of Sterling and Susan Q. (Hicks) Edwards; great²-grandson of *John Edwards*, private, Brunswick County, Virginia Troops, pensioned.

DAVID AUGUSTUS EVANS, Ellwood City, Pa. (37407). Son of John R. and Mary (Shoemaker) Evans; grandson of Jonathan and Christiana (Ralston) Evans; great-grandson of John and Isabella (Hays) Ralston; great²-grandson of *John Hays*, Captain, Northampton County, Pennsylvania Militia; great-grandson of Eli and Elizabeth (McElhany) Evans; great²-grandson of George and Sophia (North) McElhany; great²-grandson of *Roger North*, Pennsylvania Patriot.

EARLE REMINGTON EVANS, New York City, N. Y. (Ill. 37219). Son of Jackson Murray and Elethea (Remington) Evans; grandson of Thomas and Catherine (Noggle) Evans; great-grandson of Miles and Ara (Whitehead) Evans; great²-grandson of *Amos Evans*; private, Fifth Battalion, Lancaster County, Pennsylvania Militia.

JACKSON MURRAY EVANS, Chicago, Ill. (37220). Son of Thomas and Catherine (Noggle) Evans; grandson of Miles and Ara (Whitehead) Evans; great-grandson of *Amos Evans*, private, Fifth Battalion, Lancaster County, Pennsylvania Militia.

JAMES MILES EVANS, Chicago, Ill. (37221). Same as Earle Remington Evans, Ill. (37219).

ALBERT GALLATIN EWING, JR., Nashville, Tenn. (37460). Son of Albert G. and Henrietta (Cockrill) Ewing; grandson of Mark Robertson and Susan (Collinsworth) Cockrill; great-grandson of *John R. Cockrill*, private, Tenth Regt., Virginia Troops.

CARLETON WILLIAM FINNEY, Niles, Ohio (37634). Son of Drayton Josiah and Luella M. (Ball) Finney; grandson of Theron L. and Fidelia (Andrews) Finney; great-grandson of Josiah and Clarissa (Bushnell) Finney; great²-grandson of *Josiah Finney*, private, Litchfield County, Connecticut Militia, pensioned.

DRAYTON JOSIAH FINNEY, Niles, Ohio (37635). Son of Theron L. and Fidelia (Andrews) Finney; grandson of Josiah and Clarissa (Bushnell) Finney; great-grandson of *Josiah Finney*, private, Litchfield County, Connecticut Militia, pensioned.

LEYBURN GREAR FISBACH, Pittsburgh, Pa. (37094). Son of David and Elizabeth Rebecca (Horner) Fisbach; grandson of Eaton Grear and Sarah J. (Gardner) Horner; great-grandson of William and Elizabeth (Wilson) Horner; great²-grandson of David and Mary (Love) Horner; great³-grandson of *Alexander Love*, Member South Carolina Provincial Congress.

CLARENCE A. FISHER, Canton, Ohio (37041). Son of Benjamin Hart and Elizabeth (Rittenhouse) Fisher; grandson of John and Jane (Hart) Fisher; great-grandson of *John Fisher*, private, Second Regt., Virginia Militia.

THOMAS JEROME FITZGERALD, Salt Lake City, Utah (32647). Son of Hart J. and Mary (Reynolds) Fitzgerald; grandson of Jerome B. and Isabel (Sweet) Fitzgerald; great-grandson of Kneeland and Julia (Kennedy) Sweet; great²-grandson of *Timothy Sweet*, Corporal, Colonel Graham's Regt., New York Militia.

COKE FLANNAGAN, Montclair, N. J. (37150). Son of Dallas and Elise (Coke) Flannagan; grandson of John Archer and Emma (Overbey) Coke; great-grandson of John and Eliza (Hankins) Coke; great²-grandson of Archer and Alice (Browne) Hankins; great³-grandson of *John Browne*, Commissary General, Virginia Troops.

NORMAN HARVEY FOLSOM, Montclair, N. J. (37147). Son of John Fulford and Sophia Ellen (Harvey) Folsom; grandson of Benjamin and Martha (Culver) Folsom; great-grandson of John and Hannah (Swasey) Folsom; great²-grandson of Edward and Elizabeth (Fulford) Swasey; great³-grandson of *John Fulford*, Captain and Major, Maryland Artillery.

HAROLD WILLIS FORD, Belleville, N. J. (37364). Son of Willis Pierson and Minnie M. (Seeley) Ford; grandson of Leander Bishop and Laura E. (Tuttle) Ford; great-grandson of Alfred and Mary (Bishop) Ford; great²-grandson of Charles and Rachel (Burroughs) Ford; great³-grandson of *Jonathan Ford*, private, Morris County, New Jersey Militia.

ROBERT ANDERSON FORNEY, Harrisburg, Pa. (37409). Son of Peter and Mary Ann (Witmeyer) Forney; grandson of John and Mary (Martin) Forney; great-grandson of *Peter Forney*, private, Second Battalion, Lancaster County, Pennsylvania Militia.

AUSTIN POWERS FOSTER, Nashville, Tenn. (37463). Son of Samuel and Abigail Phillips (Porter) Foster; grandson of Nathaniel and Phœbe (Phillips) Porter; great-grandson of Mark and Celia (Chamberlain) Phillips; great²-grandson of *Mark Phillips*, private and Corporal, Massachusetts Militia.

EDGAR MARTIN FOSTER, Nashville, Tenn. (37452). Son of Robert C. and Martha E. (Bradford) Foster; grandson of Ephraim Hubbard and Jean Mebane (Lytle) Foster; great-grandson of Robert Coleman and Ann Slaughter (Hubbard) Foster; great²-grandson of *Antony Foster, Jr.*, private, Col. William Christian's First Regt., Virginia Troops, pensioned; great-grandson of *William* and Anna Day (Taylor) *Lytle*, Captain, Sixth and First Regts., North Carolina Troops; great²-grandson of *John Taylor*, Ensign, First Regt., and Paymaster, Eighth Regt., North Carolina Troops.

GEORGE ORA FRANK, Mearnesburg, Ohio (37637). Son of John C. and Rebecca Ann (Slifer) Frank; grandson of Matthew and Barbara Ann (Loy) Frank; great-grandson of *Lawrence Frank*, private, Col. Van Renselear's New York Troops.

RUPERT LANNARD FRANK, Mearnesburg, Ohio (37638). Son of George Ora and Amelia Henrietta (Devine) Frank; grandson of John C. and Rebecca Ann (Stifer) Frank; great-grandson of Matthew and Barbara Ann (Loy) Frank; great²-grandson of *Lawrence Frank*, private, Colonel Van Renselear's Regt., New York Troop.

J. ANDERSON FRASER, Elizabeth, N. J. (37783). Son of James Harrison and Alice Van Arsdale (Clayton) Frazer; grandson of Joshua Anderson and Margaret (Skillman) Clayton; great-grandson of *Jonathan Ives Clayton*, Ensign, New Jersey Militia.

EDWARD WALLER FRENCH, St. Louis, Mo. (37606). Son of William Pierce and Fannie (Shivel) French; grandson of Jacob Weaver and Mary Elizabeth (Goodrich) French; great-grandson of Martin and Cynthia Ann (McGee) Goodrich; great²-grandson of Gideon and Elizabeth (Carter) Goodrich; great³-grandson of *Edward Goodrich*, Corporal, Col. Thomas Elliott's Regt., Virginia Troops.

WILLIAM PIERCE FRENCH, St. Louis, Mo. (35572). Son of Jacob Weaver and Mary Elizabeth (Goodrich) French; grandson of Martin P. and Cynthia Ann (McGee) Goodrich; great-grandson of Gideon C. and Elizabeth (Carter) Goodrich; great²-grandson of *Edward Goodrich*, private and Corporal, Fourth Virginia Regt., Cont'l Troops.

FREDERIC WHIP FRIDAY, Millville, N. J. (Md. 37335). Son of John Milton and Sarah Ellen (Whip) Friday; grandson of George Tobias and Lydia (Rouzahn) Whip; great-grandson of George and Mary (Cost) Whip; great²-grandson of George and Mary Elizabeth (Williard) Cost; great³-grandson of *Francis Cost*, Member Frederick County, Maryland Associators.

SAMUEL BERNARD FRISCHKORN, Richmond, Va. (36557). Son of Louis N. and Julia (Meredith) Frischkorn; grandson of Samuel and Eliabeth Holmes (Stewart) Meredith; great-grandson of Samuel and Nancy (Terry) Meredith; great²-grandson of *Samuel Meredith*, Colonel, Virginia Cont'l Service; great³-grandson of John and Nancy (Quarles) Terry; great⁴-grandson of *James Quarles*, Captain and Major, Virginia State Troops and Militia.

ALEN GARTON, Portland, Ore. (37476). Son of Albert H. and Nancy (Smith) Garton; grandson of George O. and Harriett (Wyckoff) Smith; great-grandson of John and Mary (McKenzie) Wyckoff; great²-grandson of *John Wyckoff*, private, Col. Abraham Brinkerhoff's Regt., New York Militia.

HORATIO HAMILTON GATES, Ridgewood, N. J. (37357). Son of William and Harriet Louise (Carter) Gates; grandson of *Lemuel Gates*, Bombardier and Sergeant, Colonel Prescott's and Colonel Crane's Regts., Massachusetts Cont'l Troops, pensioned.

PAUL CRANKSHAW GAUCHAT, Warren, Ohio. Son of William F. and Sarah Bradford (Crankshaw) Gauchat; grandson of David M. and Deliah (Randall) Crankshaw; great-grandson of Tritian and Emily (Engle) Randall; great²-grandson of Robert and Margaret (Shepherd) Engle; great³-grandson of *John Shepherd*, private, Philadelphia County, Pennsylvania Militia.

STANLEIGH KEYES GAVENEY, Arcadia, Wis. (37282). Son of John Comstock and
Isadore Delia (Rasey) Gaveney; grandson of Francis H. and Eliza Melissa (Schryver)
Rasey; great-grandson of Henry and Elizabeth (Lyke) Schryver; great²-grandson of
Cornelius and Lucretia (Bull) Schryver; great²-grandson of *Stephen Schryver*, private,
Ulster County, New York Militia.

JAMES MASON GAYLORD, Denver, Colo. (36347). Son of John Davis and Sarah Elizabeth (Kendall) Gaylord; grandson of Horace and Mary A. (Davis) Gaylord; great-
grandson of *John Davis*, Captain and Major, Rhode Island Militia, pensioned.

ARTHUR McCORNACK GEARY, Portland, Ore. (37485). Son of Edward P. and Agnes
(McCornack) Geary; grandson of Edward R. and Nancy M. (Woodridge) Geary; great-
grandson of Ebenezer and Electa (Hollister) Woodbridge; great²-grandson of *Hoel
(Howell) Woodbridge*, Colonel, Connecticut Militia.

DOUGLAS CLARK GIBSON, Ogden, Utah (32646). Son of Abner Clark and Edith
Alberta (Peterson) Gibson; grandson of Thomas Farnham and Mary Leona (Clark)
Gibson; great-grandson of Thomas and Lucretia (Farnham) Gibson; great²-grandson of
Thomas Farnham, private and Sergeant, Connecticut Militia, prisoner, pensioned.

RICHARD LAW GILBERT, Dallas, Texas (Ind. 36440). Son of Henry C. and Zelia
(Law) Gilbert; grandson of Curtis and Mary C. (King) Gilbert; great-grandson of *Benjamin Gilbert*, private, Colonel Shurburne's Regt., Connecticut Line, pensioned.

WILLIAM WERT GILBERT, Minneapolis, Minn. (37242). Son of Henry S. and Gertrude
(Nottingham) Gilbert; grandson of *Job* and Zebiah (Sweeting) *Gilbert*; Lieutenant, Col.
Josiah Whitney's Regt., Massachusetts Militia; great-grandson of *Louis Sweeting*, private,
Bristol County, Massachusetts Militia at Lexington Alarm.

ANDREW BOYD GILFILLAN, Buffalo, N. Y. (37185). Son of Andrew B. and Margaret
(Gordon) Gilfillan; grandson of Andrew B. and Anne (Caldwell) Gilfillan; great-grandson
of *Alexander Gilfillan*, private, Washington County, Pennsylvania Militia.

BRUCE L. GILFILLAN, Keokuk, Iowa (36918). Son of George and Susan Dora (Lock)
Gilfillan; grandson of John Frederick Oberlin and Sarah (Redd) Gilfillan; great-grandson
of Edward and Mary (McKinley) Gilfillan; great²-grandson of *James Gilfillan*, private,
Fourth and Seventh Battalions, Cumberland County, Pennsylvania Militia.

RICHARD SHERMAN GILFILLAN, Minneapolis, Minn. (37436). Son of Sherman Lewis
and Mathilde (Amundson) Gilfillan; grandson of William and Helen Selena (Tower)
Gilfillan; great-grandson of Rodney and Fidelia (Robinson) Tower; great²-grandson of
Samuel Robinson, private, Hingham, Massachusetts Militia.

SHERMAN LEWIS GILFILLAN, Minneapolis, Minn. (37243). Son of William and Helen
Selana (Tower) Gilfillan; grandson of Rodney and Fidelia (Robinson) Tower; great-
grandson of Samuel and Anna (Tower) Robinson; great²-grandson of *Stephen Tower*,
private, Hingham, Massachusetts Militia.

KENNETH WARDEN GILKERSON, Minneapolis, Minn. (37236). Son of Curtis Harvey
and Julia (Sultzbaugh) Gilkerson; grandson of Thomas and Janet (Strobridge) Gilkerson;
great-grandson of Ebenezer Hinds and Elizabeth (Harvey) Strobridge; great²-grandson of
William Strobridge, private, Middleborough, Massachusetts Militia.

ORRIN JUDSON GILKERSON, Minneapolis, Minn. (37431). Son of Thomas and Janet
(Strobridge) Gilkerson; grandson of Ebenezer Hinds and Elizabeth (Harvey) Strobridge;
great-grandson of *William Strobridge*, private, Plymouth County, Massachusetts Militia.

EDWIN STANTON GILL, Seattle, Wash. (36654). Son of Joshua Selmon and Eliza Ann
Caroline (Haynes) Gill; grandson of Selmon and Margaret (Dorrett) Gill; great-grandson
of *Jonathan Gill*, Matross, Col. Charles Harrison's Regt., Maryland Artillery.

HERBERT CLARK GILSON, Summitt, N. J. (37374). Son of Thomas Q. and Elizabeth
L. (Clark) Gilson; grandson of James M. and Emily V. (Shaddle) Clark; great-grandson
of John and Charlotte (King) Shaddle; great²-grandson of Henry and Susannah (Paulding) King; great²-grandson of *Joseph Paulding, Jr.*, private, Westchester County, New
York Militia.

WALTER SCOTT GINN, McKeesport, Pa. (37728). Son of Charles James nad Mary
Lucinda (Mason) Ginn; grandson of Lewis Marion and Emily Devol (Sprague) Mason;
great-grandson of Anthony Wayne and Lucinda (Devol) Sprague; great²-grandson of
Jonathan and Sabra (Seaans) Sprague; great²-grandson of *Joshua Sprague*, Major,
Colonel Stafford's Independent Massachusetts Volunteers and private, Colonel Chapin's
Regt., Massachusetts Cont'l Infantry.

ARTHUR EZRA GLEASON, North Adams, Mass. (37122). Son of Newton F. and Caroline I. (——) Gleason; grandson of Joseph D. and Mary (S—) Gleason; great-grandson of Newton and Antis (Mixer) Gleason; great²-grandson of Ezra and Polly (Newton) Gleason; great²-grandson of *Joseph Newton*, private, Marlborough, Massachusetts Militia.

CHARLES THOMAS GLINES, Providence, R. I. (36510). Son of Charles Edward and Mary Elizabeth (Carter) Glines; grandson of Simeon Dana and Eliza B. (Woods) Glines; great-grandson of Joseph and Nancy (Ditson) Woods; great²-grandson of *Joseph Woods*, private, Col. William Prescott's Regt., Massachusetts Militia.

WARREN FREDERICK GOFF, Fort Madison, Iowa (36915). Son of Newell Hale and Mary (Schenck) Goff; grandson of Peter and Eliza (Dagett) Schenck; great-grandson of Jacob and Mary (Lott) Schenck; great²-grandson of *John Schenck*, Captain, Second Regt., Middlesex County, New Jersey Militia.

PHILLIPS LEE GOLDSBOROUGH, Baltimore, Md. (37336). Son of Martin Worthington and Henrietta Maria (Jones) Goldsborough; grandson of Brice John and Leah (Goldsborough) Goldsborough; great-grandson of Richard and Achsah (Worthington) Goldsborough; great²-grandson of *Robert Goldsborough*, Delegate to Continental Congress, 1774-'75, Member Maryland Provincial Convention and Committee of Safety.

CHARLES NEWELL GOODNOW, Chicago, Ill. (37222). Son of Henry C. and Margaret T. (Newell) Goodnow; grandson of Thaddeus and Elizabeth (Woodruff) Goodnow; great-grandson of *Eliab Goodnow*, private, Massachusetts Militia.

CLINTON BURR GOODRICH, East Orange, N. J. (Mass. 37381). Son of John Calvin and Jennie L. (Paul) Goodrich; grandson of Truman and Sarah (Theyer) Paul; great-grandson of James and Zemah (Short) Paul; great²-grandson of *John Paul*, private and Sargeant, Col. Josiah Whitney's Regt., Massachusetts Militia.

PAUL MYRON GOODRICH, North Adams, Mass. (37382). Same as Clinton Burr Goodrich, East Orange, N. J. (Mass. 37381).

FIELDING GLASS GORDON, Nashville, Tenn. (37467). Son of Edward Andrew and Corinne (Glass) Gordon; grandson of Andrew and Rebecca Catherine (Dickerson) Gordon; great-grandson of Thomas Martin and Sallie (McLaurine) Gordon; great²-grandson of Thomas Kennedy and Elizabeth (Lane) Gordon; great²-grandson of *Martin Lane*, private, North Carolina Militia.

MORRIS ELTING GORE, Orange, N. J. (37504). Son of Adolph K. and Alice S. (Bennett) Gore; grandson of Obadiah and Matilda (Shaw) Gore; great-grandson of Avery and Sucy (Gore) Gore; great²-grandson of *Obadiah Gore, Jr.*, Lieutenant, Third Regt., Connecticut Troops.

CHARLES JACOB GOTSHALL, Minneapolis, Minn. (37244). Son of Daniel and Rebecca (Martin) Gotshall; grandson of *Michael Gotshall*, private, Lancaster County, Pennsylvania Associators.

WILLIAM HENRY GRAHAM, Washington, D. C. (37159). Son of Thomas Turbett and Margaret Alice (Rhinesmith) Graham; grandson of William James and Nancy (Hackett) Graham; great-grandson of John and Mary (Turbett) Graham; great²-grandson of *William Graham*, Ensign, Seventh Battalion, Pennsylvania Cont'l Line, Captain, Cumberland County Militia.

JOHN AVERY GRANNIS, Nashville, Tenn. (37453). Son of Herbert William and Mary M. (Grannis) Grannis; grandson of William J. and Lucy (Gates) Grannis; great-grandson of John Cotes and Marian (Dunlap) Grannis; great²-grandson of John and Nancy (Cotes) Grannis; great³-grandson of *Edward Grannis*, private and Captain, Stark's Brigade, New Hampshire Militia; grandson of Joseph Wells (father of Mary M.) and Mary Haven (Usher) Grannis; great-grandson of William and Mahala (Haven) Usher; great²-grandson of Nathaniel and Mary (Coolidge) Haven; great²-grandson of *Isaac Coolidge*, private, Colonel Patterson's Regt., Massachusetts Militia at Lexington Alarm; great²-grandson of *David Haven*, private, Col. Sam Bullard's Regt., Massachusetts Militia; great-grandson of Eliphas and Lucy (Lamb) Gates; great²-grandson of *David Lamb*, private, Connecticut and Vermont Militia, and Marine on U. S. S. "Providence."

JAMES G. GRANT, Akron, Ohio (37046). Son of Theron and Jane (Harrison) Grant; grandson of David and Jemima (Bancroft) Grant; great-grandson of Ephraim and Jemima (Loomis) Bancroft; great²-grandson of *Ephriam Bancroft*, Lieutenant, Seventeenth Regt., Connecticut Troops.

ALFRED SHIRLEY GRAY, West Roxbury, Mass. (37392). Son of George W. and Florence (Knapp) Gray; grandson of Alfred and Adeline J. (Field) Knapp; great-grandson of Paul and Mercy (Stearns) Field; great²-grandson of *Joshua Field*, private, New Hampshire Militia, pensioned.

LE ROY EDWARD GRAY, Chicago, Ill. (37223). Son of Frederick William and Sylva May (Hoyt) Gray; grandson of Hiram Currier and Sylva (Watkins) Hoyt; great-grandson of James and Mary (Horseford) Watkins; great²-grandson of Gilbert and Sara (Watkins) Watkins; great²-grandson of *Nathan Watkins*, Captain, Massachusetts Militia and Cont'l Infantry, prisoner.

SAMUEL BROWN GRAY, Scottdale, Pa. (37423). Son of Joseph and Sarah (Molleston) Gray; grandson of John F. and Jane (Whaley) Gray; great-grandson of James and Jane Vance (Moreland) Whaley; great²-grandson of *Benjamin Whaley*, Sergeant and Captain, Berkley County, Virginia Militia, and Cont'l Troops.

CHARLES JOSEPH GREGORY, Marianna, Ark. (31775). Son of Joseph Henry and Rebecca (——) Gregory; grandson of Thomas L. B. and Frances Whittaker (Pitman) Gregory; great-grandson of Thomas and Mary (Bradford) Gregory; great²-grandson of *John Bradford*, Member Halifax, North Carolina, Provincial Congress, State Senator and Colonel of Militia.

EDWARD McDONALD GRIGG, Dorchester, Mass. (37383). Son of Edwin and Elizabeth (Kitfield) Grigg; grandson of Jacob and Sarah (Littlefield) Kitfield; great-grandson of Jacob and Ann (Kellahan) Kitfield; great²-grandson of *Edward Kitfield*, Corporal and Sergeant, Massachusetts Militia.

CHARLES BRYANT GROVE, Washington, D. C. (37155). Son of Harry Colfax and Jessie Elizabeth (Bryant) Grove; grandson of Charles Morton and Amanda M. (Camp) Bryant; great-grandson of Philip Durkee and Sarah Paulina (Searl) Bryant; great²-grandson of Philip and Sophia (Shepard) Bryant; great³-grandson of *John Bryant*, private, Connnecticut Militia.

ROBERT RUSSELL GUNN, Crawfordville, Ga. (36829). Son of Uly S. and Olive Belle (Alford) Gunn; grandson of William Hathan and Fannie (Nunn) Gunn; great-grandson of John R. and Sarah (Chapman) Gunn; great²-gradson of William and Pleasance (Stephens) Gunn; great³-grandson of *Richard Gunn, Sr.*, private, Virginia Militia.

GEORGE EDWIN HAGENBUCH, Cleveland, Ohio (37640). Son of Edwin and Nellie (Howard) Hagenbuch; grandson of George Pearl and Celestine (Chapman) Howard; great-grandson of Anson and Olive (Pearl) Howard; great²-grandson of *William Howard*, private and Sergeant, Connecticut Militia.

CHARLES A HALL, San Francisco, Calif. (37262). Son of William Harmon and Alice B. (Anderson) Hall; grandson of James P. and Myra (Bradley) Hall; great-grandson of Harmon and Harriet (Bishop) Bradley; great²-grandson of *Abraham Bradley*, private, Captain Farrington's Company, Freyburg, Massachusetts Militia.

LUKE HALL, Sharon, Mass. (37751). Son of Luke and Mary H. (Smith) Hall; grandson of Sylvanus and Judith W. (McGlanthlin) Smith; great-grandson of Jonathan and Zilpah (Drew) Smith; great²-grandson of *Sylvanus Drew*, Captain, Massachusetts boat service.

WILLARD I. HAMILTON, Newark, N. J. (37784). Son of Edward Livingston and Sarah C. (Lum) Hamilton; grandson of Caleb W. and Mary (Vail) Hamilton; great-grandson of William and Phebe (——) Hamilton; great²-grandson of *William Hamilton*, private, New Jersey Troops; grandson of Stephen and Catherine A. (Conklin) Lum; great-grandson of Moses and Nancy (Morehouse) Lum; great²-grandson of *Stephen Lum* private, Essex County, New Jersey Militia; great²-grandson of *Simeon Morehouse*, private, Essex County, New Jersey Militia, State Troops and Third Battalion, Second Establishment, Cont'l Line.

ROBERT CLARENCE HANNA, Minneapolis, Minn. (37237). Son of Jason R. and Margaret Ashley (Lewis) Hanna; grandson of Joshua and Susan (McFarlane) Hanna; great-grandson of Benjamin and Rachel (Dixon) Hanna; great²-grandson of *Robert Hanna*, Member Philadelphia Provincial Committee.

MARSHALL CHESTER HANNAH, Keokuk, Iowa (36923). Son of Jesse Fremont and Jennie (Huntoon) Hannah; grandson of Chester H. and Emma (Dunan) Huntoon; great-grandson of Benesley and Florinda (Nye) Huntoon; great²-grandson of *Josiah Huntoon*, private, Colonel Reed's and Colonel Bellon's Regts., New Hampshire Militia.

CHARLES PARKER HANNUM, Everett, Mass. (37752). Son of Daniel Lapham and Mary Rebecca (Pease) Hannum; grandson of Alpheus and Lucy (Foster) Pease; great-grandson of Jonathan and Hannah (Cutter) Foster; great²-grandson of *Benjamin Cutter*, Ensign, New Ipswich, New Hampshire Militia.

SAMUEL WALKER HARDY, Casper, Wyo. (D. C. 37156). Son of William Baldwin and Lucretia (Walker) Hardy; grandson of Samuel Hamilton and Sallie Lucretia (Brody) Walker; great-grandson of Jonathan Thomas and Jane Amelia (Benson) Walker; great²-grandson of Nathan and Elizabeth (Thomas) Walker; great³-grandson of *Isaac Walker*, Lieutenant, Prince George County, Maryland Militia.

GEORGE WENTZ HARRIS, New Jersey (37006). Supplemental. Son of William J. and Phœbe L. (Baldwin) Harris; grandson of William H. and Phœbe H. (Baldwin) Harris; great-grandson of Robert and Mary (Gould) Baldwin; great²-grandson of *Zadoc Baldwin*, private, New Jersey Militia.

JOSEPH LE ROY HARRISON, Northampton, Mass. (37384). Son of John Le Roy and Ellen Maria (Hawks) Harrison; grandson of Elihu Smead and Sophia Elizabeth (Abby) Hawks; great-grandson of *Samuel Hawks*, private, Hampshire County, Massachusetts Militia; grandson of John and Irene (Van Dyke) Harrison; great-grandson of John and Esther (Garner) Van Dyke; great²-grandson of *Jacob Van Dyke*, private, Albany County, New York Militia.

SCHUYLER GOULD HARRISON, East Orange, N. J. (37521). Son of Thomas Gould and Winefred (Jones) Harrison; grandson of Caleb Gould and Charlotte (Washburn) Harrison; great-grandson of Caleb and Jane (Gould) Harrison; great²-grandson of *Isaac Harrison*, private, Essex County, New Jersey Militia, State and Cont'l Troops, pensioned.

JAMES TRUE HAZARD, Minneapolis, Minn. (37245). Son of William Silliman and Mary Will (True) Hazard; grandson of Silas Holmes and Delia Hoagland (Beach) Hazard; great-grandson of Samuel Serren and Jane (Hoff) Beach; great²-grandson of Charles and Hannah F. (Tuttle) Hoff, Jr.; great³-grandson of Moses and Jane (Ford) Tuttle; great⁴-grandson of *Jacob Ford*, Member New Jersey Provincial Congress and Chairman Committee of Correspondence.

HENRY W. B. HEWEN, Southbend, Wash. (36655). Son of Loring and Seddie S. (Truesdell) Hewen; grandson of Jesse and Dorothy (Talcott) Truesdell; great-grandson of Elizur and Dorothy (Lord) Talcott, Jr.; great²-grandson of *Elizur Talcott*, Colonel, Sixth Regt., Connecticut Militia.

JAMES EDWIN HEWSON, Irvington, N. J. (37514). Son of James Starr and Mary Gertrude (Kerns) Hewson; grandson of Theodore Crowell and Elizabeth Woodruff (Dunnington) Hewson; great-grandson of James and Desire (Crowell) Hewson; great²-grandson of James and Martha (——) Hewson; great³-grandson of *John Hewson*, Captain, Philadelphia County, Pennsylvania Militia.

HENRY C. HIBBS, Nashville, Tenn. (37455). Son of Jonathan Kirkbride and Anna W. (Kirkpatrick) Hibbs; grandson of Jonathan and Mary A. (Twining) Hibbs; great-grandson of Stephen and Sarah (Warner) Twining; great²-grandson of Jacob and Margery (Croasdale) Twining; great³-grandson of Stephen and Mary (Wilkinson) Twining; great⁴-grandson of *John Wilkinson*, Lieutenant-Colonel, Bucks County, Pennsylvania Militia, Member of Pennsylvania Assembly, and Judge of Common Pleas.

LOUIS EMMONS HILL, Lakewood, Ohio (37628). Son of Hosea Emmons and Mary Ellen (Pilsbury) Hill; grandson of Samuel and Sally (Garvin) Pilsbury; great²-grandson of *Stephen Pilsbury*, private, Col. Loammi Baldwin's Regt., Massachusetts Militia.

ROGER HILSMAN, Captain, U. S. Army, Texas (37529). Son of Lee James and Jennie (Powell) Hilsman; grandson of Jeremiah and Martha Ann (Janes) Hilsman; great-grandson of Edward and Jane Sheppard (Beall) Janes; great²-grandson of *Reasin Beall*, Brigadier-General, Maryland Flying Camp.

DAVID CLARK HILTON, Nebraska (33894). Supplemental. Son of John B. W. and Mary Elizabeth (Redgate) Hilton; grandson of Edmund and Lydia Ann (Miller) Redgate; great-grandson of Stephen and Elizabeth (Weeks) Miller; great²-grandson of *Increase Miller*, private, Westchester County, New York Militia.

EARLE ROY HIMES, New Bethlehem, Pa. (37424). Son of Joseph C. and Margaret (Rutherford) Himes; grandson of John and Sylvina (Space) Himes; great-grandson of Zephaniah and Katie (Armstrong) Space; great²-grandson of *John Space*, private, First Battalion, Second and First Regts., New Jersey Cont'l Line.

JOHN BENJAMIN HIRSCH, Dormont Boro, Pa. (37419). Son of William Lincoln and Harriet (Roberts) Hirsch; grandson of Joseph G. and Mary (Wentworth) Hirsch; great-grandson of George A. and Betsy (McCoy) Wentworth; great²-grandson of *Henry Wentworth*, private and Fife Major, Colonel Badger's Regt., New Hampshire Militia.

JOSEPH HENRY HIRSCH, Dormont Boro, Pa. (37420). Same as John Benjamin Hirsch, Pennsylvania (37419).

FRANCIS E. HITCHCOCK, Coraopolis, Pa. (37406). Son of Milton Stebbins and Jane (Hazlett) Hitchcock; grandson of Tidal and Mary (Polly) (Cowdry) Hitchcock; great-grandson of *Daniel Hitchcock*, private, Captain Clift's Company, Connecticut Line.

JOHN D. HITCHCOCK, Cleveland, Ohio (37639). Son of Alvin C. and Mary J. (Drennen) Hitchcock; grandson of Tidal and Mary (Cowdrey) Hitchcock; great-grandson of *Ambrose Cowdrey*, private, Second Regt., Connecticut Troops, pensioned.

THORNTON HODGE, Keokuk, Iowa (36920). Son of Hugh Cambell and Nettie (Crane) Hodge; grandson of Frank C. and Ellena M. (Burnett) Crane; great-grandson of Uzziel and Helen (Shaw) Burnett; great²-grandson of Lucas and Mehitabel (Ellis) Shaw; great³-grandson of *Sylvanus Shaw*, private, Massachusetts Cont'l Line, pensioned.

JAMES SHANOR HOFFMAN, Wilkinsburg, Pa. (37425). Son of John L. and Ellen (Shanor) Hoffman; grandson of Mathias and Mary (Hains) Shanor; great-grandson of David and Ruth (Peirsol) Shanor; great²-grandson of *Sampson Peirsol*, (*Pearsall*), private, Col. William Crawford's Regt., Pennsylvania Militia, pensioned.

FRANKLIN HOLLAND, Baltimore, Md. (37679). Son of Joseph and Margaret Ann (Mountain) Holland; grandson of *Joseph Holland*, private, Col. Jonathan Holman's Regt., Massachusetts Militia.

FRANKLIN ERNEST HOLLAND, Montreal, Que. (Md. 37677). Son of Franklin and Margaret Jane (Stark) Holland; grandson of Joseph and Margaret Ann (Mountain) Holland; great-grandson of *Joseph Holland*, private, Col. Jonathan Holman's Regt., Massachusetts Militia.

HERBERT STANLEY HOLLAND, Baltimore, Md. (37680). Same as Franklin Ernest Holland (Md. 37677).

HOWARD ERWIN HOLLAND, Baltimore, Md. (37678). Same as Franklin Ernest Holland (Md. 37677).

WARREN J. REEVE HOOSE, Cleveland, Ohio (37629). Son of Leon Beckwith and Lillian (Reeve) Hoose; grandson of Warren L. and Sarah (Hanson) Hoose; great-grandson of Cornelius and Jane (Hanson) Hoose; great²-grandson of Jacob and Sabrina (Burhite) Hoose; great³-grandson of —— and Olive (Messenger) Burhite; great⁴-grandson of *Isaac Messenger*, private, Col. Roger Enos' Regt., Connecticut Cont'l Troops.

SELDEN RICH HOPKINS, Montclair, N. J. (37785). Son of Oney Rice and Artemissa (Sawyer) Hopkins; grandson of Prescott and Zernia (Lamb) Sawyer; great-grandson of *Cornelius Sawyer*, private, Connecticut and Vermont Militia; great²-grandson of *Jonas Sawyer*, private, Pomfret, Connecticut Militia, at Lexington Alarm.

CHARLES AUGUSTUS HORTON, Providence R. I. (36511). Son of Charles Albert and Elizabeth Bruce (Winship) Horton; grandson of Danforth Gardiner and Mary (Simmons) Horton; great-grandson of Silvanus and Hannah (Slade) Horton; great²-grandson of *Daniel Horton*, private and Sergeant, Col. Thomas Carpenter's Regt., Massachusetts Militia.

CARRINGTON HOWARD, Caldwell, N. J. (37786). Son of John Raymond and Susan R. (Merriam) Howard; grandson of John Tasker and Susan Taylor (Raymond) Howard; great-grandson of Joseph and Austiss (Smith) Howard; great²-grandson of *John Howard*, Corporal and Drill-Sergeant, Col. John Glover's Regt., Massachusetts Militia, Sail-maker on armed schooner "Hancock."

FRANK AZRO HOWE, Minneapolis, Minn. (37231). Son of Charles Morgan and Mary Jane (Bickford) Howe; grandson of Benjamin Clough and Sabra (Washburn) Howe; great-grandson of *Samuel Howe*, private, Col. Jonathan Chase's Regt., New Hampshire Militia.

GEORGE C. LA B. HUCHET DE KERNION, New Orleans, La. (36964). Son of Anatole La B. and Fanny Evelina Heloise (Campbell) Huchet de Kernion; grandson of Charles La B. and Euphemie Aimee (Lambert) Hucket de Kernion; great-grandson of *Jean Rene Huchet de Kernion*, Spanish officer, under Galvez, in campaigns against English; grandson of James and Francoise Zoe (Lambert) Campbell; great-grandson of Francois Martin and

Julie Heloise (Trepagnier) Lambert; great²-grandson of *Pedro (Pierre) Trepagnier,* Lieutenant, of Cabahanou Company, under Galvez; great-grandson of Pierre Joseph and Marie Constance (Wiltz) Lambert; great²-grandson of Jean Baptiste and Suzanne (Langliche) Wiltz; great²-grandson of *Don Lorenso Wilts,* Lieutenant of Artillery, under Galvez.

HOWARD DAVENPORT HUDSON, Shreveport, La. (36963). Son of W. R. and Sue (Davenport) Hudson; grandson of Charles C. and Sarah J. (Lyon) Davenport; great-grandson of Thomas Gilliam and Lucinda (Jones) Davenport; great²-grandson of Charles and Sarah (Gary) Davenport; great³-grandson of James Madison and Eliabeth (Gilliam) ·Davenport; great⁴-grandson of *Robert Gilliam (Gillam),* Major, South Carolina Militia.

STANLEY E. HUNTING, Rochester, N. Y. (37583). Son of Mars Breed and Ann Jane (Converse) Hunting; grandson of Hiram and Fanny (Converse) Converse; great-grandson of Therou and Nancy (Case) Converse; great²-grandson of *Thomas Converse,* Adjutant and Captain, Third and Second Regts., Connecticut Cont'l Line, Brigade Inspector in 1781.

DANIEL WITMER HUNTZBERGER, Middletown, Pa. (37415). Son of David and Catharine (Witmer) Huntzberger; grandson of David and Sarah (Missimer) Witmer; great-grandson of Jacob S. and Elizabeth (Hohman) Missimer; great²-grandson of *Henry Brandt Missimer, (Masoner),* private, Fifth Battalion, Lancaster County, Pennsylvania Militia.

LAURENCE KAYE HYDE, Minneapolis, Minn. (37238). Son of Ora L. and Esther (Kerr) Hyde; grandson of George W. and Jane (Lane) Hyde; great-grandson of William W. and Louisa (Ferry) Hyde; great²-grandson of Eleazer and Mary (Brown) Hyde; great³-grandson of *Asa Brown,* private, Connecticut Militia.

RALPH WALDO IMMEL, Denver, Col. (36346). Son of Cassius M. and Minerva (Prickett) Immel; grandson of Isaiah and Rosannah (Jones) Immel; great-grandson of Jacob and Catherine (Byerly) Immel; great²-grandson of Jacob and Maria Elizabeth (Parthemore) Byerly; great³-grandson of *John Pattimore (Parthemore),* private, Fourth and Tenth Battalions, Lancaster County, Pennsylvania Militia.

JOHN RANKIN IRWIN, Keokuk, Iowa (36919). Son of John Nichol and Mary (Love) Rankin; grandson of John Walker and Sara Dupuy (Thomasson) Rankin; great-grandson of William Poindexter and Charlotte (Leonard) Thomasson; great²-grandson of David A. and Mary (Peirce) Leonard; great³-grandson of *David Leonard,* Second Lieutenant, Bridgewater, Massachusetts Minute Men, at Lexington Alarm.

ROBERT JAMES IZANT, Sr., East Cleveland, Ohio (37042). Son of Silas and Sarah L. (Heard) Izant; grandson of Stephen and Betsy Ruggles (Holman) Heard; great-grandson of *Thomas Holman,* private, Middletown, Connecticut Militia.

FRANK WATTERSON JACKSON, Montclair, N. J. (37507). Son of Enos Sturgis and Clara (Bayley) Jackson; grandson of James W. and Elizabeth (Sturgis) Jackson; great-grandson of Enos and Diana (Jones) Sturgis; great²-grandson of Phineas and Elizabeth (West) Sturgis; great³-grandson of *John Sturgis,* private, Pennsylvania Militia.

GEORGE JACKSON, Battle Ground, Ind. (36446). Son of Hugh Alexander and Mary (Forrest) Jackson; grandson of George and Fannie (Alexander) Jackson; great-grandson of Joseph and Margaret (Wilson) Jackson; great²-grandson of *George Jackson,* Second Lieutenant, Third Battalion, Bedford County Pennsylvania Militia.

THOMAS WELDON JACKSON, Jr., Orange, N. J. (37505). Son of Thomas Weldon and Mary L. (Egbert) Jackson; grandson of Abraham and Emmeline (Sutton) Egbert; great-grandson of *Abraham Egbert,* private, Third Regt., Middlesex County, New Jersey Militia.

CHARLES JABEZ JOHNSON, Minneapolis, Minn. (37246). Son of Simon Lowell and Leonora Augusta (Day) Johnson; grandson of Daniel Averill and Lydia (Palmer) Day; great-grandson of William and Sarah (Averill) Day; great²-grandson of Daniel and Abigail (Hanscom) Averill; great³-grandson of *Joseph Averill,* Sergeant, Lincoln County, Massachusetts Militia.

LOUIS RAUB JOHNSON, San Diego, Calif. (37263). Son of Louis D. and Emma James (Smith) Johnson; grandson of James R. and Angelina (James) Smith; great-grandson of Charles Whitehead and Vamelias (Meeker) James; great²-grandson of Thomas and Deborah (Derrick) James; great³-grandson of *Thomas James,* private, Second Regt., Middlesex County, New Jersey Militia and Cont'l Troops.

ABRAM TILLMAN JONES, Nashville, Tenn. (36799). Son of Ira Philander and Martha Elizabeth (Paul) Jones; grandson of Isaac and Susan Massy (Nance) Paul; great-grand-son of William Howe and Elizabeth Venable (Morton) Nance; great²-grandson of *Joseph Morton*, Sergeant, Pittsylvania County, Virginia Troops.

HARRIS STAFFORD JONES, Minneapolis, Minn. Son of William Herbert and Edith Harris (Stafford) Jones; grandson of John Francis and Mary Frances (Harris) Stafford; great-grandson of Herman Brimmer and Louisa Maria (McClary) Harris; great²-grandson of Andrew and Mehitable H. (Duncan) McClary; great²-grandson of *Michael McClary*, Captain, Colonel Scammel's Regt., New Hampshire Troops.

IRA PHILANDER JONES, Jr., Nashville, Tenn. (36800). Same as Abram Tillman Jones, Tenn. (36799).

JUDSON WALDO JONES, Port Jefferson, N. Y. (37191). Son of Adoniram Judson and Mary Elizabeth (Bryant) Jones; grandson of Lewis Hutchinson and Jemima (Roberts) Bryant; great-grandson of Jonathan Owsley and Martha (Kissinger) Bryant; great²-grandson of *John Bryant*, Sergeant, Powhatan County, Virginia Militia.

VERNER MOORE JONES, Nashville, Tenn. (37454). Son of Edgar and Susan (Cheatham) Jones; grandson of Edward and Ellen Jean (Foster) Cheatham; great-grandson of Ephraim Hubbard and Jean Mebane (Lytle) Foster; great²-grandson of *William Lytle*, Captain, First and Fourth Regts., North Carolina Troops.

CLYDE ROYAL JOY, Keokuk, Iowa (36914). Son of Royal Noah and Rodelia Elizabeth (Epps) Joy; grandson of Noah and Mary (Ford) Joy; great-grandson of *Nehemiah Joy*, Corporal, Weymouth, Massachusetts Militia and Artillery.

TULLY ALFRED JOYNES, Baltimore, Md. (37328). Son of George Goodwin and Sally Wright (Northam) Joynes; grandson of Tully Armistead and Sabra Polk (Fitchett) Joynes; great-grandson of Joshua and Martha (Polk) Fitchett; great²-grandson of *William Polk*, Captain, Accomack County, Virginia Militia.

JOSEPH SCOTT JUNKIN, Chicago, Ill. (37207). Son of Samuel James and Ida (Lanham) Junkin; grandson of Joseph Buchanan and Mary (Baker) Junkin; great-grandson of Benjamin and Anna Maria (Agnew) Junkin; great²-grandson of *Joseph Junkin*, Lieutenant, Third Battalion, Cumberland County, Pennsylvania Militia.

DAVID HENRY KELLER, Louisiana (35998), Supplemental. Son of James E. M. and Laura A. (Whitesell) Keller; grandson of David and Ellen (Brown) Keller; great-grandson of John and Sarah (Trach) Keller; great²-grandson of John George and Rachael (Diehls) (Dils) Keller; great²-grandson of *Christopher Keller*, Captain, Northampton County, Pennsylvania Militia; grandson of Henry and Elizabeth (George) Whitesell; great-grandson of Abraham and Christina (Myers) George; great²-grandson of Henry and Elizabeth (Reiswick) George; great²-grandson of *John Conrad George*, private, Northampton County, Pennsylvania Militia.

ANDREW PARK KELLY, Baltimore, Md. (37337). Son of Andrew J. and Mary Park (Redgrave) Kelly; grandson of William Sands and Catherine Louisa (Park) Redgrave; great-grandson of Samuel Hance and Sarah Lambdin (Richardson) Redgrave; great²-grandson of *Thomas Richardson*, sailor on Maryland barge "Fearnought."

JAMES EDWARD KELSEY, Asbury Park, N. J. (37370). Son of James Seely and Jennie (Loveland) Kelsey; grandson of James and Jurusha Seely (Matthews) Kelsey; great-grandson of Joseph and Adaline (Seely) Matthews; great²-grandson of *John Seely*, private, New Jersey Militia, State and Cont'l Troops.

CALVIN IRA KEPHART, California (29964), Supplemental. Son of George Elwood and Anna C. (Weisel) Kephart; grandson of Henry Harman and Amy T. (Hyde) Kephart; great-grandson of Jacob and Mary Magdalene (Ruth) Kephart; great²-grandson of *Abraham Ruth*, private, Col. William Robert's Battalion, Bucks County, Pennsylvania Militia; great²-grandson of *Andrew Ruth*, private in same company.

JOHN WHITE KEY, Higbee, Mo. (35573) Son of Philip and Euphrates F. (Martin) Key; grandson of John Hall and Juliet M. (Reeder) Key; great-grandson of *Philip Key*, Member St. Mary's County, Maryland Committee of Correspondence and Member of Maryland Assembly.

ARTHUR SPENCER KIMBALL, East Orange, N. J. (37375). Son of Charles H. and Anna Frances (Crane) Kimball; grandson of Nathaniel J. and Elizabeth J. (Ward) Crane; great-grandson of Eleazar D. and Elizabeth W. (Dodd) Ward; great²-grandson of Isaac and Mary (James) Dodd; great³-grandson of *Amos Dodd*, Captain, Second Regt., Essex County, New Jersey Militia.

GEORGE ILGENFRITZ KING, Middletown, Pa. (37096). Son of Arthur and Lydia Ann (Ilgenfritz) King; grandson of George W. and Isabella (Emmitt) Ilgenfritz; great-grandson of Daniel and Elizabeth (Deitch) Ilgenfritz; great²-grandson of *Hartman Deitch*, Captain, Second Company, York County, Pennsylvania Militia.

JUSTUS J. KLEINE, Highland Park, N. J. (37354). Son of Justus J. and Caroline (Willett) Kleine; grandson of Samuel and Maria (Sherwood) Willett; great-grandson of *Hartshorne Willett*, private, Middlesex County, New Jersey Militia.

JOSEPH PERCY KNIGHT, Jr., New York City, N. Y. (37192). Son of Joseph P. and Clara (Salter) Knight; grandson of George Ferry and Annie M. (Stivers) Salter; great-grandson of John Walgrove and Sarah A. (Ferry) Salter; great²-grandson of Noah Taylor and Drusilla (Barnum) Ferry; great³-grandson of *Eliphalet Ferry*, Sergeant, Sixteenth Regt., Connecticut Troops.

CHARLES RICHARDSON KNOX, San Francisco, Calif. (37264). Son of Charles Silas and Harriett (Richardson) Knox; grandson of Samuel and Mindwell (Hine) Richardson; great-grandson of Israel and Juliette O. (Boardman) Hine; great²-grandson of Benjamin and Sabra (Brown) Boardman; great³-grandson of *Joseph Boardman*, Captain, Eighth Regt., Connecticut Militia.

FRANK HOWARD KURTZ, Minneapolis, Minn. (37234). Son of Edward and Alice (Alerams) Kurtz; grandson of John Nicholas and Ann (Murphy) Kurtz; great-grandson of Benjamin and Elizabeth (Gardiner) Kurtz; great²-grandson of *John Nicholas Kurtz*, Minister at York, Pa., who collected supplies for Valley Forge Camp.

FRANCIS WARD LANGSTROTH, Jr., New York City, N. Y. (37180). Son of Francis Ward and Charlotte Louise (Barnes) Langstroth; grandson of William E. and Lavinia Maria (Townsend) Barnes; great-grandson of Horace and Rebecca Brush (Cornell) Townsend; great²-grandson of *William Cornell*, Ensign, Tryon County, New York Militia.

FRANK HERBERT LANGWORTHY, Lynn, Mass. (37761). Son of John Erwin and Esther Parthenia (Macomber) Langworthy; grandson of Stephen and Sarah B. (Francis) Macomber; great-grandson of Elijah and Eliza (Swett) Macomber; great²-grandson of *Joseph Macomber*, Lieutenant, Thirteenth Regt., Massachusetts Cont'l Infantry.

WILLIAM BARNY LEAVENS, Jr., Maplewood, N. J. (37522). Son of William Barry and Annie (M.—) Leavens; grandson of Philo French and Helen Josephine (Barry) Leavens; great-grandson of Paschal Paoli and Ann Eliza (Bowen) Leavens; great²-grandson of Pennel and Sally (Cross) Leavens; great³-grandson of *Charles Leavens*, Lieutenant, Third Regt., Vermont Militia.

DANIEL TALCOTT SMITH LELAND, Boston, Mass. (37385). Son of Daniel and Julia Ann (Bigelow) Leland; grandson of Daniel and Betsey (Hurd) Leland; great-grandson of *Moses Leland*, private, Massachusetts Militia.

EDWARD IRVING LELAND, Concord, Mass. (37393). Son of Daniel and Julia Ann (Bigelow) Leland; grandson of Daniel and Elizabeth (Heard) Leland; great²-grandson of *Moses Leland*, private, Massachusetts Militia.

JAMES HENRY LEMON, Middletown, Pa. (37404). Son of William Kemp and Catherine (Heckert) Lemon; grandson of Simon and Jane (Sweigert) Lemon; great-grandson of *George Leamon (Lemon)*, private, Lancaster County, Pennsylvania Militia.

STANLEY GRANT LEMON, Wilmington, Del. (37416). Son of James Henry and Emma Minerva (Shaffer) Lemon; grandson of William Kemp and Catherine (Heckert) Lemon; great-grandson of Simon and Jane (Sivergert) Lemon; great²-grandson of *George Leamon (Lemon)*, private, Lancaster County, Pennsylvania Militia.

WALTER MAGRUDER LEONARD, Sr., Cleveland, Ohio (37033). Son of William and Elizabeth Cooke (Magruder) Leonard; grandson of Julian and Margaret Ann (Johnson) Magruder; great-grandson of W. P. C. and Ann Elisa (Washington) Johnson; great²-grandson of Bushrod and Henrietta (Spottswood) Washington; great³-grandson of *William Augustine Washington*, Lieutenant-Colonel, Third Virginia Dragoons.

EDWARD VAN KIRK LESLIE, Pittsburgh, Pa. (37729). Son of Homer Ellsworth and Mabel Blanche (Leslie) Leslie; grandson of John Wilson and Rachel Alice Clendenning (Humphreys) Scott; great-grandson of Joseph and Ruth (Van Kirk) Scott; great²-grandson of *James Scott*, Lieutenant, Westmoreland County, Pennsylvania Militia; great²-grandson of *Samuel Van Kirk*, private, Middlesex County Militia and Cont'l Troops.

DONALD MACY LIDDELL, Elizabeth, N. J. (37365). Son of Oliver Brown and Josephine (Major) Liddell; grandson of Daniel Symmes and Catherine Eliza (Guard) Major; great-grandson of David and Beulah Miller (Millar) Guard; great²-grandson of *Alexander Guard*, private, Morris County, New Jersey Militia; great-grandson of William and Mary (Patterson) Major; great²-grandson of *James Major*, private, Chester County, Pennsylvania Militia; great-grandson of David nad Beulah Miller (or Millar) Guard; great²-grandson of Thomas and Pricilla (Hayes) Millar; great²-grandson of *Joseph Hayes II*, Captain, Col. Otho William's Regt., Pennsylvania Cavalry.

ALBERT WILLIAM LILIENTHAL, Jr., New York City, N. Y. (37193). Son of Albert William and Florence Cornelia Brooks (Ellwanger) Lilienthal; grandson of George Herman and Harriette Lawson (Stillson) Ellwanger; great-grandson of George and Cornelia (Brooks) Ellwanger; great²-grandson of Micah and Mary (Hall) Brooks; great²-grandson of *David Brooks*, Delegate to Connecticut Constitutional Convention, Chaplain and Quartermaster, Connecticut Militia.

GEORGE HENRY LINCOLN, Providence, R. I. (36512). Son of Thomas and Lucy Coolidge (Stone) Lincoln; grandson of Asa and Mary (Coolidge) Stone; great-grandson of *Samuel Coolidge*, private, Suffolk County, Massachusetts Cont'l Troops.

THOMAS GREEN LINNELL, Minneapolis, Minn. (37247). Son of Lewis M. and Elizabeth (Green) Linnell; grandson of Lewis T. and Isabella A. (Longley) Linnell; great-grandson of Wm. Ferguson and Lydia Sears (Bassett) Longley; great²-grandson of Edmund and Olive (Field) Longley, Jr.; great²-grandson of *Edmund Longley*, Captain, Colonel Cogswell's Regt., Massachusetts Militia.

JOHN HOWARD LITTLE, Pittsburgh, Pa. (37421). Son of John Wilder nad Elizabeth (Watterson) Little; grandson of John Wilder and Mary (Loomis) Little; great-grandson of Jonathan Colton and Electa (Stockbridge) Loomis; great²-grandson of *Abner Loomis*, private, Massachusetts Militia.

JOHN ARTHUR LOGAN, Chicago, Ill. (37224). Son of Earl C. and Elizabeth (Spaulding) Logan; grandson of William Abiel and Mary (Hoisington) Spaulding; great-grandson of Jonathan and Milanda (Parr) Spaulding; great²-grandson of Abiel and Susannah (Marshall) Spaulding; great²-grandson of *Jonathan Spaulding*, private, Col. Israel's Chapin's Regt., Massachusetts Militia.

HAROLD J. LONG, ——, Ohio (37039). Son of Berton J. and Nellie E. (Musser) Long; grandson of David and Mary (Armstrong) Musser; great-grandson of James and Ellen (Pinkerton) Armstrong; great²-grandson of James and Martha (Fairfield) Armstrong; great³-grandson of *John Armstrong*, Major and Aide-de-Camp, Pennsylvania Militia.

CHARLES E. LONGENECKER, Middletown, Pa. (37092). Son of Isaac Kinportz and Anna Dora (Sheaffer) Longenecker; grandson of Christian and Mary (Kinportz) Longenecker; great-grandson of Daniel and Anna (Oberholtzer) Longenecker; great²-grandson of *Abraham Longenecker*, private, Sixth Battalion, Lancaster County, Pennsylvania Militia

LEVI LONGFELLOW, Minneapolis, Minn. (37239). Son of Jacob and Martha Jane (Getchell) Longfellow; grandson of Enoch and Anna (——) Longfellow; great-grandson of *Nathan Longfellow*, Lieutenant, Lincoln County, Massachusetts Militia.

ELISHA RISLEY LOOMIS, West Union, Iowa (36925). Son of Austin R. and Ellen M. (Nestle) Loomis; grandson of Russell and Sally (Risley) Loomis; great-grandson of *Israel Loomis*, private, Connecticut Cont'l Troops, pensioned.

JOHN JAY LOUIS, Minneapolis, Minn. (37440). Son of John Henry and Traunie B. (Fetter) Louis; grandson of Jacob Lobingier and Charlotte R. (Palmer) Fetter; great-grandson of Christian and Sarah (Lobingier) Fetter; great²-grandson of John and Sophia (Moyer) Lobingier; great³-grandson of *Christopher Lobingier*, Member Committee of Correspondence and Delegate to first Pennsylvania Constitutional Convention.

WILLIAM ALEXANDER LOVE, Columbus, Miss. (La. 36660). Son of Drennan and Elizabeth Lovelace (Cook) Love; grandson of James and Jane (Lockhart) Love; great-grandson of *James Love*, South Carolina Volunteer at battle of Fishing Creek.

EDWIN HALFORD LYBARGER, Cleveland, Ohio (37043). Son of Elijah Crum and Julydia Workman (Winterringer) Lybarger; grandson of James Thompson and Amelia Eagle (Crum) Lybarger; great-grandson of Andrew and Naomi (Thompson) Lybarger; great²-grandson of *Ludwick Lybarger*, private, Bedford County, Pennsylvania Militia.

JESSE JAMES LYBARGER, Cleveland, Ohio (37044). Same as Edwin Halford Lybarger, Ohio (37043).

JOHN WALKER STAUNFORD McCALL, Fort Worth, Texas (Mo. 35570). Son of John Peter and Frances Elizabeth (Hancock) McCall; grandson of Abram Booth and Martha Elizabeth (Walker) Hancock; great-grandson of Benjamin and Elizabeth (Booth) Hancock; great²-grandson of Lewis and Celia (Duncan) Oglesby Hancock; great³-grandson of *George Duncan*, Captain, Fluvanna County, Virginia Militia; great-grandson of Moses and Frances Elizabeth (Glass) Walker; great²-grandson of Elisha and Judith (Kirby) Walker; great³-grandson of *John Kirby*, private, Pittsylvania County, Virginia Militia.

THOMAS CALVIN McCARRELL, Middletown, Pa. (37410). Son of Alexander and Martha (McClean) McCarrell; grandson of Samuel and Elizabeth (McConnell) McCarrell; great-grandson of *Thomas McCarrell*, private, York County, Pennsylvania Militia.

HUGH KING McCLENAHAN, Sharon, Pa. (37730). Son of Henry Irvine and Margaret (Kennedy) McClenahan; grandson of Samuel Pew and Betsy (Adams) Kennedy; great-grandson of Jay and Sarah Gates (Simmons) Adams; great²-grandson of *Asahel Adams*, private, Seventh Regt., Connecticut Cont'l Line.

DONALD McCURDY, Warren, Ohio (37048). Son of Samuel Henry and Helen (Tayler) McCurdy; grandson of Matthew Bannon and Adaline Adams (Hapgood) Tayler; great-grandson of George and Adaline (Adams) Hapgood; great²-grandson of *Asael Adams*, private, Col. Heaman Swift's Seventh Regt., Connecticut Line; great³-grandson of *Phineas Adams*, private, Colonel Moseley's Regt., Connecticut Militia.

CICERO DECATUR McCUTCHEON, II, Dalton, Ga. (36830). Son of Cicero Decatur and Frances Cornelia (Kelly) McCutcheon; grandson of Thomas Davis and Phœbe Caroline (Bryan) Kelly; great-grandson of Andrew and Delphia Garnett (Jones) Bryan; great²-grandson of *Andrew Bryan* (*O'Brian*), private, Chester County, Pennsylvania Militia.

ARCHIBALD HOWARD McELRATH, Mercer, Pa. (37402). Son of John and Jane (Brandon) McElrath; grandson of James and Nancy (McDowell) Brandon; great-grandson of *William Brandon*, Ensign, First Battalion, York County, Pennsylvania Militia.

CLARENCE BRANDON McELRATH, Mercer, Pa. (37731). Son of Archibald Howard and Mary (McJunkin) McElrath; grandson of John and Jane (Brandon) McElrath; great-grandson of James and Nancy (McDowell) Brandon; great²-grandson of *William Brandon*, Ensign, First Battalion, York County, Pennsylvania Militia.

JOHN BERRY McFERRIN, Collierville, Tenn. (37462). Son of John H. and Tommie Jessie (Matthews) McFerrin; grandson of William M. and Louise (Lapsley) McFerrin; great-grandson of James and Jane Campbell (Berry) McFerrin; great²-grandson of *William McFerrin*, private, Virginia Militia.

FREDERICK WILLIAM McKEE, Ware Neck, Va. (36555). Son of Joseph Allen and Susan (Church) McKee; grandson of Francis and Joanna (Allen) McKee; great-grandson of *John McKee*, private, Pennsylvania Militia, pensioned.

FREDERICK VALLETTE McNAIR, Annapolis, Md. (N. Y. 37194). Son of Frederick V. and Clara (Warren) McNair; grandson of John and Mary (Yerkes) McNair; great-grandson of Stephen and Alice (Watson) Yerkes; great²-grandson of *Harmon Yerkes*, private in Warminster Company, Pennsylvania Associators.

KEAN CORNELIUS McNALLY, Washington, D. C. (37157). Son of James Clifford and Agnes (Keane) McNally; grandson of Henry Thomas and Jane (Bishop) Keane; great-grandson of Michael and Ruth (Vanderhof) O'Keane; great²-grandson of *Cornelius Vanderhof*, Matross, Col. John Lamb's Regt., New York Cont'l Artillery.

FRANKLIN MADDOX, Baltimore, Md. (37338). Son of Edward and Mary (Causey) Maddox; grandson of Franklin and Nancy D. (Miller) Causey; great-grandson of Patrick and Polly (Cropper) Causey, Jr.; great²-grandson of *Patrick Causey*, private, Wicomico Company, Somerset County, Maryland Militia.

RUSSELL WILLIAM MAGNA, Holyoke, Mass. (37386). Son of Albert and Harriet S. (Goss) Magna; grandson of William and Mary (Hallett) Goss; great-grandson of William and Eunice (Wood) Goss; great²-grandson of *Zebulon Goss*, private, Col. Nathan Tyler's Regt., Massachusetts Militia.

THOMAS MILLER MANIER, Nashville, Tenn. (37468). Son of Will Rucker and Mary (Owsley) Manier; grandson of John Samuel and Susan Malinda (Miller) Owsley; great-grandson of Thomas W. and Mary Jane (Hocker) Miller; great²-grandson of Daniel and Susannah (Woods) Miller; great³-grandson of *Robert Miller, Jr.*, Captain, Orange County, Virginia Militia.

WILLIAM ARTHUR MARKELL, Baltimore, Md. (37676). Son of Francis and Caroline Matilda Map (Caine) Markell; grandson of John Leelap and Sophia (Charlton) Caine; great-grandson of *John Usker Charlton*, Member Frederick County, Md., Committee of Safety and Captain of Militia.

JOHN HASSLER MARKLEY, Peoria, Ill. (37703). Son of Christian and Sarah (Swenk) Markley; grandson of Levi and Eliza (Atherholt) Markley; great-grandson of *George Markley*, private, Lancaster County, Pennsylvania Militia.

CHARLES ABSALOM MARSHALL, Nashville, Tenn. (37461). Son of Jonathan R. and Martha (Wiggins) Marshall; grandson of Allen and Catherine (Fudge) Wiggins; great-grandson of *William Wiggins, Jr.*, private, Georgia Militia.

CHARLES REMBERT MARSHALL, Nashville, Tenn. (36796). Son of Charles A. and Ella (Holton) Marshall; grandson of William David and Priscilla Smith (Williams) Holton; great-grandson of Samuel Z. and Elizabeth (Smith) Williams; great²-grandson of Robert and Priscilla (Parker) Smith; great²-grandson of William and Kitty (Matthews) Parker; great⁴-grandson of *John Parker*, private, Col. John Haslet's Regt., Delaware Militia.

WALTER SANDS MARVIN, Montclair, N. J. (37501). Son of Charles A. and Mabel Starbuck (Metcalf) Marvin; grandson of Aaron Burr and Sarah Stilwell (Sands) Marvin; great-grandson of Ephraim and Mercy (Sears) Marvin; great²-grandson of *Ephraim Marvin*, Lieutenant, Suffolk County, New York Militia.

HUGH MacVEIGH MATHEWS, Arlington, N. J. (37502). Son of Joseph William and Rosannah Cecelia (MacVeigh) Mathews; grandson of Hiram and Mary Elizabeth (White) MacVeigh; great-grandson of John and Nancy (McIlhany) White; great²-grandson of *James McIlhany*, Captain, Fifth Regt., Virginia Troops.

STANLEY ROBERT MAXEINER, South Minneapolis, Minn. (37248). Son of John R. and Clara Maria (——) Maxeiner; grandson of Frederick G. and Julia Ann (Nethaway) Stanley; great-grandson of Whiting Day and Maria (Castle) Stanley; great²-grandson of Daniel and Rachel (Jones) Castle; great²-grandson of *Lemuel Castle*, private, Dutchess County, New York Militia.

HARRY VICTOR MAYO, East Providence, R. I. (36513). Son of Charles Henry Victor and Sarah Bowers (Munro) Mayo; grandson of John Black and Elizabeth Wardwell (Fales) Mayo; great-grandson of Jesse and Dorcas (Brewer) Mayo; great²-grandson of *Thomas Mayo*, Captain, First Suffolk County, Massachusetts Militia.

SUMNER ADELBERT MEAD, Chicago, Ill. (37208). Son of Adelbert Francis and Theodosia Bertha (Wright) Mead; grandson of Varnum Balfour and Direxa (Stearns) Mead; great-grandson of Nathaniel and Lucy (Taylor) Mead; great²-grandson of *Oliver Mead*, private, Col. John Whitcomb's Regt., Massachusetts Minute Men.

JAMES HENRY MEREDITH, Lometa, Texas (36334). Son of William Wesley and Nancy Jane (Robbins) Meredith; grandson of William and Susan (Christman) Meredith; great-grandson of *Samuel Meredith*, Dragoon, Col. Henry Lee's Regt., Virginia Troops, widow pensioned.

CHARLES WINCHESTER MERRILL, Boston, Mass. (37123). Son of Franklin C. and —— (Winchester) Merrill; grandson of Amos and Abigail Allen (Upton) Merrill; great-grandson of Eben Sprague and Sally (Richardson) Upton; great²-grandson of *Charles Richardson*, private, Col. Cyprian Howe's Regt., Massachusetts Militia.

SMITHER MERRILL, Galveston, Texas (36335). Son of Frank E. and Annie (Butler) Merrill; grandson of E. D. and Mary (Anderson) Butler; great-grandson of Mark and Lavinia (Heady) Anderson; great²-grandson of *James Heady*, private, Captain Gaddis' Company, Virginia Militia.

SAMUEL FREDERICK MESSER, Warren, Ohio (37636). Son of Marcellus O. and Fanny (Dickey) Messer; grandson of Lauren Sanborn and Chestina Waterbury (Cook) Messer; great-grandson of Ebenezer and Lydia (Streeter) Messer, Jr.; great²-grandson of *Ebenezer Messer*, private, Suffolk County, Massachusetts Militia.

HOWARD FARR METCALF, Holyoke, Mass. (37387). Son of Joseph and Clara Wheeler (Farr) Metcalf; grandson of Marshall H. and Diana (Randall) Farr; great-grandson of Eleasar and Clara (Wheeler) Randall; great²-grandson of *Benjamin Wheeler*, private, Col. James Reid's Regt. Massachusetts Militia.

THOMAS DRAKE METCALF, Portland, Ore. (37481). Son of George Peabody and Emily Strong (Dwight) Metcalf; grandson of William Cecil and Laura (Talbot) Dwight; great-grandson of Theodore Foster and Elizabeth Cox (Truxtun) Talbot; great²-grandson of *Silas Talbot*, Rhode Island, Lieutenant-Colonel, Cont'l Army, and Captain, U. S. Navy, prisoner; great²-grandson of *Thomas Truxton*, Lieutenant, Cont'l Navy.

WILLIAM DRUMMOND MIDDLETON, Captain, U. S. Army, New York (37586). Son of William Drummond and Susan Yandall (Modemann) Middleton; grandson of George and Mary Van Sindern (Webb) Modemann; great-grandson of Henry Wilson and Eliza Milligan (Smith) Webb; great²-grandson of Samuel and Mary (Wilson) Webb; great²-grandson of *Charles Webb*, Member Connecticut General Assembly and Colonel, Connecticut Militia and Cont'l Troops.

MAYNARD BOYDEN MILES, Clarion, Iowa (36922). Son of John and Harriet Eliza (Boyden) Miles; grandson of Sanford and Cyntha (Hotchkiss) Boyden; great-grandson of Joseph and Abigail (Gilmore) Boyden; great²-grandson of *Jonathan Boyden*, private, Walpole, Massachusetts Militia.

GEORGE HENRY MIX, Ridgewood, N. J. (37503). Son of John Goodwin and Clarissa Champion (Isham) Mix; grandson of John and Elizabeth (Gilbert) Isham, Jr.; great-grandson of *John Isham, Jr.*, Captain of Colonel Chester's Connecticut State Regt.

ALVIN MOORE, Summit, N. J. (37352). Son of Eliphalet and Christianna (Martin) Moore; grandson of Crowell and Sarah (Burwell) Martin; great-grandson of *David Martin*, private and Corporal, Connecticut and New Jersey Militia, Cont'l and State Troops.

HAROLD MOORE, Summit, N. J. (37353). Son of Alvin and Juliet (Horning) Moore; grandson of Eliphalet and Christiana (Martin) Moore; great-grandson of Crowell and Sarah (Burwell) Martin; great²-grandson of *David Martin*, private and Corporal, Connecticut and New Jersey Militia, Cont'l and State Troops.

HARRY BEAUMONT MOORE, Portland, Ore. (37477). Son of Arthur W. and Nettie (Morgan) Moore; grandson of Heard L. and Bathsheba (Higgins) Moore; great-grandson of Josiah and Mary (Cousins) Higgins; great²-grandson of *Levi Higgins*, Lieutenant, Lincoln County, Massachusetts Militia.

MORRIS EDWIN MOORE, Minneapolis, Minn. (37437). Son of Morris Ellsworth and Carrie (Taylor) Moore; grandson of Azro Benton and Jane Eliza (Woodruff) Taylor; great-grandson of Jared Morcy and Mary (Benton) Taylor; great²-grandson of *Felix Benton*, private, Berkshire County, Massachusetts Militia, pensioned.

WILLIAM MANNING MORGAN, Galveston, Texas (37526). Son of George Dickinson and Jean Coventree (Scrimgeour) Morgan; grandson of William and Sarah A. (Thomas) Morgan; great-grandson of Seabury and Hannah Avery (Haley) Thomas; great²-grandson of *Daniel Thomas*, private, Connecticut Militia and Cont'l Troops.

WILLIAM MARSHALL MORRILL, Boston, Mass. (37753). Son of James Edward and Hannah Jane (Marshall) Morrill; grandson of Samuel and Hannah (Brown) Marshall; great-grandson of *Nathaniel Brown*, Signer New Hampshire Association Test.

PERCY MULFORD MORSE, Eugene, Ore. (37478). Son of Amos Addison and Ellen G. (Keeney) Morse; grandson of Amos Marsh and Louisa (Mulford) Morse; great-grandson of Amos and Letty (Halsey) Morse; great²-grandson of *Amos Morse*, Captain, Col. Moses Jaques' Battalion, New Jersey State Troops.

WALLACE WYNNE MORSE, Tacoma, Wash. (Ore. 37479). Same as Percy Mulford Morse, Ore. (37478).

EDWARD MOSHER, Westfield, N. J. (37787). Son of John M. and Flora (Whitford) Mosher; grandson of Horatio and Malvina (Satterlee) Whitford; great-grandson of Joshua and Avis (Satterlee) Whitford; great²-grandson of John and Margaret (Coon) Whitford; great²-grandson of *Joshua Whitford*, private, Connecticut Militia, pensioned.

FRANCIS CLARK MURGOTTEN, Reno, Nev. (Calif. 37268). Son of Alexander P. and Mattie (Munroe) Murgotten; grandson of Henry Clay and Susan (Shaffer) Murgotten; great-grandson of Adam Shaffer; great²-grandson of *George Shaffer*, Sergeant, Eighth Battalion, Lancaster County, Pennsylvania Militia.

HENRY MURGOTTEN, San Francisco, Calif (37269). Same as Francis Clark Murgotten, Calif. (37268).

WALTER EMMONS NASON, Dallas, Texas (Mass. 37394). Son of Walter Leroy and Evangeline Sappho (Patterson) Nason; grandson of William Emmons and (——) Nason; great-grandson of George Warren and Peacry B. (Cook) Nason; great²-grandson of Jesse and Hannah (Clark) Nason; great³-grandson of *Willoughby Nason*, private, Massachusetts Militia.

JOSHUA THOMAS NEEL, Donora, Pa. (37095). Son of Aliff Shepard and Maria Louisa (Thomas) Neel (O'Neal); grandson of Barnett and Martha (Hughes) O'Neal, Jr.; great-grandson of *Barnett (Bryan) O'Neal*, private, Washington County, Pennsylvania Militia.

MORTIMER E. NEWCOMB, Westfield, N. J. (37788). Son of Frederick J. and Julia A. (Miller) Newcomb; grandson of William Frederick and Louisa Jane (Gleason) Newcomb; great-grandson of Charles and Fanny (Hitchcock) Newcomb; great²-grandson of *William Newcomb*, private, Bristol County, Massachusetts Militia.

CHARLES MAHLON NIEZER, Fort Wayne, Ind. (36447). Son of John Bernard and Sarah Theresa (Eyanson) Niezer; grandson of Thomas Eyanson; great-grandson of *John Eyanson (Ireson)*, private, Third Battalion, New Jersey Cont'l Troops and Lancaster County, Pennsylvania Militia.

BEN W. NORTHCOTT, Kansas City, Mo. (37602). Son of Robert S. and Mary (Bollenbacher) Northcott; grandson of Benjamin H. and Janet (Stevenson) Northcott; great-grandson of William and Fanny Lewis (Goddard) Northcott; great²-grandson of *Joseph Goddard*, private and Corporal, Farquier County, Virginia Militia, pensioned.

HENRY W. NULL, West Newton, Pa. (37411). Son of Andrew Jackson and Lucinda Perry (Robinson) Null; grandson of Henry and Elizabeth (Pool) Null; great-grandson of *Philip Null*, private, Lancaster County, Pennsylvania Militia, and Captain, General Gates' Regt., North Carolina Militia; grandson of Thomas and Achsah Loma (Bailey) Robinson; great-grandson of Daniel and Lucinda (Perry) Bailey; great²-grandson of *James Perry*, Captain, Massachusetts Militia and Sixteenth Regt., Cont'l Infantry.

EDWARD FRANCIS O'BRIEN, Havana, Cuba (Mass. 37390). Son of William and Louise Stark (Hodeker) O'Brien; grandson of Rufus and Elvira (Bartlett) Stark; great-grandson of John and Annie (Rogers) Stark; great²-grandson of *John Stark*, Sergeant, New Hampshire Militia, pensioned.

ARTHUR OLIVER, New York City, N. Y. (N. J. 37366). Son of James and Emily Augusta (Jayne) Oliver; grandson of Addison A. and Eleanor Wiatt (Fordyce) Jayne; great-grandson of John and Zipporah (Wiatt) Fordyce; great²-grandson of *Henry Fordyce*, private, Essex County, New Jersey Militia, pensioned.

JOSEPH RAOUL OLIVIER, St. Martinville, La. (36965). Son of Felix and Theodora (Ledoux) Olivier; grandson of Charles St. Maurice and Aminthe (Berard) Olivier; great-grandson of Pierre and Marie Josephe (Latiolais) Olivier Duclozel; great²-grandson of *Hugues Charles Honore Olivier De Vezin*, soldier in Galvez Expedition.

MILTON EPHRAIM OSBORN, Michigan (28141), Supplemental. Son of David and Eliza Maria (Faxon) Osborn; grandson of Ephraim and Lois (Wakeman) Osborn; great-grandson of Ephraim and Mary (Merwin) Osborn; great²-grandson of *Peter Osborn*, Sergeant, Lieut.-Col. Jonathan Dimon's Fourth Regt., Connecticut Militia; grandson of Samuel Ervin and Azuba (Gray) Faxon; great-grandson of Samuel and Martha (Spooner) Faxon; great²-grandson of *Shearjashub Spooner*, private, Col. Nathan Sparhawk's Regt., Massachusetts Militia.

WILLIAM CARLISLE OSBORN, Sioux City, Iowa (37651). Son of Walter W. and Arabella (Carlisle) Osborn; grandson of Daniel and Hannah Lewis (Glover) Carlisle; great-grandson of David and Tammerson (Hall) Glover; great²-grandson of *Henry Glover*, private, Massachusetts Militia.

AUBREY PHILIP OTTARSON, Nashville, Tenn. (36795). Son of Aubrey Dean and Pauline (Nelson) Ottarson; grandson of Franklin J. and Marietta (Dean) Ottarson; great-grandson of Joseph and Anna (Taylor) Ottarson; great²-grandson of *David Taylor*, Quartermaster, Colonels Can Ness' and Alden's Regts., New York Militia, pensioned.

CARLTON BYNNER OVERTON, Montclair, N. J. (37359). Son of Frank Carlton and Ruth (Bynner) Overton; grandson of Robert Henry and Agnes (Conine) Overton; great-grandson of Richard Carlton and Arietta (Elting) Overton; great²-grandson of Maltiah and Lucretia (Davis) Overton; great³-grandson of *Nathaniel Overton*, Minute Man, Suffolk County, New York Militia.

FRANK CARLTON OVERTON, Montclair, N. J. (37358). Son of Robert Henry nad Agnes (Conine) Overton; grandson of Richard Carlton and Arietta (Elting) Overton; great-grandson of Maltiah and Lucretia (Davis) Overton; great²-grandson of *Nathaniel Overton*, Minute Man, Suffolk County, New York Militia.

IRA JUNE OWEN, Grand Rapids, Mich. (Ill. 37225). Son of William Russell and Mary Frances (June) Owen; grandson of Frank Thomas and Jennie Agnes (Sturtevant) June; great-grandson of Isaac Doty and Susan (Summers) Sturtevant; great²-grandson of Perez and Dorothy (Kimball) Sturtevant; great³-grandson of *Church Sturtevant*, private, Col. Thomas Lothrop's Regt., Massachusetts Militia.

PHILIP CLARKSON PACK, Chicago, Ill. (37209). Son of Ambrose Clarkson and Roba (Pulcipher) Pack; grandson of Milo and Isabelle (Drake) Pulcipher; great-grandson of Zera and Caroline Louise (Doty) Pulcipher (Pulsipher); great²-grandson of *Samuel Doty*, Sergeant, Col. Samuel Elmore's Regt., Connecticut Cont'l Troops.

LOUIS HOOKER PALMER, Baltimore, Md. (37339). Son of John William and Flora Elizabeth (Hooker) Palmer; grandson of James Louis and Harriet Frances (Luff) Hooker; great-grandson of Samuel Filer and Mary Smith (Brewster) Hooker; great²-grandson of Jacob W. and Esther (Douglass) Brewster; great³-grandson of *Hezikiah Douglass*, Ensign, Third Battalion, Connecticut Troops.

SAMUEL CLARK PARCELLS, New Providence, N. J. (37518). Son of James Miller and Sarah (Baldwin) Parcells; grandson of Samuel and Mary (Coddington) Baldwin; great-grandson of John nad Sally (Parsons) Coddington; great²-grandson of *Samuel Parsons*, Sergeant, Essex County, New Jersey Light Horse and private, Spencer's Regt., Cont'l Army.

CHARLES MARCO PARKER, Minneapolis, Minn. (37229). Son of Marco Luther and Mary Jane (Eads) Parker; grandson of Charles Durham and Angeline (Southworth) Parker; great-grandson of Luther and Alletta (French) Parker; great²-grandson of Joshua and Polly (Taylor) Parker; great³-grandson of Asa and Hepzibah (Nichols) Parker; great⁴-grandson of *Benjamin Parker*, private, Colonel Green's Regt. at Lexington Alarm.

LYMAN TRUMBALL PARKER, Minneapolis, Minn. (37249). Son of Charles and Almira (Lyman) Parker; grandson of Azel and Mary (Bates) Lyman; great-grandson of *Abel Lyman*, Lieutenant, Col. Jonathan Chase's Regt., New Hampshire Militia.

ARTHUR JACOB PEAVEY, Idaho (35114). Supplemental. Son of Jacob Cummings and Angeline Abbie (Harris) Peavey; grandson of Jacob S. and Susan (Campbell) Peavey; great-grandson of *Peter Peavey*, private, Massachusetts Militia and Colonel Tupper's Cont'l Troops, pensioned; great-grandson of Peter and Lucy (Cummings) Peavey; great²-grandson of *Ebenezer Cummings*, private, Fifth Regt., Hollis, New Hampshire Militia, died in service.

FRANK WASSON PENDEXTER, Chicago, Ill. (37210). Son of Albion Winslow and Roxanna Eunice (Stevens) Pendexter; grandson of Henry and Nancy (Libby) Pendexter; great-grandson of *Paul Pendexter*, private, Tenth and Sixth Regts., Massachusetts Militia; grandson of Philander and Eunice Wing (Brown) Stevens; great-grandson of Jeremiah and Jerusha (Buell) Stevens; great²-grandson of *Asa Buell*, private, Colonel Swift's Seventh Regt., Connecticut Cont'l Troops, pensioned.

CHARLES HUNTINGTON PENNOYER, Attleboro, Mass. (37754). Son of Henry Jesse and Mary Emma (Huntington) Pennoyer; grandson of Jesse and Pamelia (Blossom) Pennoyer; great-grandson of *Jesse Pennoyer*, Drummer, Col. James Holmes' Regt., New York Cont'l Troops.

WARREN A. PERDEW, Keokuk, Iowa (36916). Son of Warren Areleyton and Anna Elizabeth (Beeteasteen) Perdew; grandson of Eugene J. and Lizzie (V.—) Perdew; great-grandson of John and Maria (Vrooman) Perdew; great²-grandson of Samuel A. and Sallie (Dillenback) Vrooman; great³-grandson of Adam and Elizabeth (Ziele) Vrooman; great⁴-grandson of *Samuel Vrooman*, private, Fifteenth Regt., Albany County, New York Militia.

WILLIAM HENRY PERKINS, Baltimore, Md. (37340). Son of William Henry and Mary (McCoy) Perkins; grandson of William Henry and Laura Ann (Pachon) Perkins; great-grandson of John and Harriet (Gorsuch) Perkins; great²-grandson of Robert and Sarah (Donovan) Gorsuch; great³-grandson of *Richard Donovan*, Lieutenant, Sixth Regt., Maryland Troops, killed.

CHARLES NEWTON PHILLIPS, Marion, Ohio (37040). Son of Samuel and Mary Ann (Ellis) Phillips; grandson of Richard and Mary P. (Selover) Ellis; great-grandson of John and Abilena (Phillips) Ellis, Jr.; great²-grandson of *John Ellis*, Second Lieutenant, Hampshire County, Massachusetts Militia.

JAMES EDWARD PHILLIPS, Newark, N. J. (37368). Son of Jesse Collum and Sarah Henrietta (Shoemaker) Phillips; grandson of James Dalrymple and Maria (Collum) Phillips; great-grandson of John and Elizabeth (Dalrymple) Phillips; great²-grandson of *David Phillips*, private and Wagon-master, Sussex County, New Jersey Militia.

LLOYD PEIXOTTO PHILLIPS, New York City, N. Y. (37584). Son of Sydney A. and Ethel (Levin) Phillips; grandson of Jonas Naptali and Esther (Peixotto) Phillips; great-grandson of Naphtali and Rachel Mendez (Seixas) Phillips; great²-grandson of *Jonas Phillips*, private, Col. William Bradford's Btaalion, Philadelphia Militia.

FRED ALONZO PIERCE, Cleveland, Ohio (37630). Son of Charles Alonzo and Abbie Arabella (Flagg) Pierce; grandson of Charles and Margery Thompson (Allen) Pierce; great-grandson of Samuel and Elizabeth (Hovey) Pierce; great²-grandson of *Isaac Pierce*, private, Middlesex County, Massachusetts Militia.

LYALL JULIAN PINKERTON, Neenat, Wis. (37283). Son of Samuel and Harriet Louise (Perkins) Pinkerton; grandson of Lewis and Lucy (Phelps) Perkins; great-grandson of Milo and Welthea (Kellogg) Phelps; great²-grandson of Frederick and Mary (Phelps) Kellogg; great³-grandson of *Asa Kellogg*, Sergeant, Col. John Brown's Regt., Massachusetts Militia.

SCOTT HOWELL PLUMMER, Minneapolis, Minn. (37432). Son of George Albert and Mary Thornton (Taylor) Plummer; grandson of William Henry Harrison and Anna Tuttle (Harrison) Taylor; great-grandson of William Henry and Anna (Symmes) Harrison; great²-grandson of *Benjamin Harrison*, Signer of Declaration of Independence.

LAURENCE NORTON POLK, Nashville, Tenn. (37457). Son of James Knox and Mary F. (Hibbler) Polk; grandson of Marshall Tate and Evalina McNeal (Bills) Polk; great-grandson of John Houston and Prudence (McNeal) Bills; great²-grandson of Thomas and Clarissa (Polk) McNeal; great³-grandson of *Ezekiel Polk*, Captain, South Carolina Rangers.

MATTHIAS JUDD PRICE, Newark, N. J. (37367). Son of Matthias and Emily Catherine (Judd) Price; grandson of George B. and Abby Ward (Sòverel) Judd; great-grandson of Elizur and Temperance (Scott) Judd; great²-grandson of *Herman Judd*, private, Col. Erastus Wolcott's Regt., Connecticut Militia.

HENRY DARLINGTON PUGH, Scottdale, Pa. (37726). Son of Marshall Rodger and Helen (Darlington) Pugh; grandson of John Blackwell and Elizabeth Sergeant (Fox) Pugh; great-grandson of *John Pugh*, Ensign, Third Battalion, Pennsylvania Militia; great-grandson of John and Margery (Rodman) Fox; great²-grandson of *Gilbert Rodman*, Major, Col. Joseph Hart's Battalion, Bucks County, Pennsylvania Militia.

HAROLD STEWART PURSELL, New Castle, Pa. (37405). Son of W. Wallace and Catherine (Bachman) Pursell; grandson of Amos Franklin and Laura (Frisbie) Bachman; great-grandson of Levi and Chole (Chubbuck) Frisbie; great²-grandson of Levi and Phebe (Gaylord) Frisbie; great³-grandson of *Aaron Gaylord*, private, Twenty-fourth Regt., Connecticut Militia, killed at Wyoming Valley.

HARRY HARVIE QUINBY, Chicago, Ill. (37701). Son of Henry Harvie and Molly L. (Watson) Quinby; grandson of Austin Rayner and Theresa (Gray) Quinby; great-grandson of Nathaniel Etheride and Margaret (Raynerd) Quinby; great²-grandson of Enoch and Sarah (Libby) Quinby; great³-grandson of *Aaron Quinby*, Captain, Colonel Kelly's Regt., New Hampshire Militia.

WILLIAM O'GORMAN QUINBY, East Orange, N. J. (37372). Son of James Milnor and Mary V. (Casey) Quinby; grandson of James Moses and Phœbe A. (Sweazy) Quinby; great-grandson of Jotham and Lillias (Smith) Quinby; great²-grandson of Moses and Mary (Baldwin) Quinby; great³-grandson of *Josiah Quinby*, Second Lieutenant, Col. Elias Dayton's Regt., New Jersey Cont'l Line.

JAMES ALEXANDER RACKERBY, St. Louis, Mo. (37607). Son of Joseph H. and Mary Ann (Gilkison) Rackerby; grandson of John H. and George Ann (Dudley) Rackerby; great-grandson of Robert and —— (Parish) Dudley; great²-grandson of *Ambrose Dudley*, Captain, Virginia Militia.

WILLIAM LUTHER RAMEY, Escondido, Calif. (37256). Son of William and Frances (Neff) Ramey; grandson of Daniel and Melvina (Huffman) Neff; great-grandson of *Jacob Neff*, private, Lancaster County, Pennsylvania Militia.

FREDERICK LUCIEN RAY, Anderson, Ind. (36448). Son of Martin and Rhoda E. (Prendergast) Ray; grandson of James and Nancy (McCosky) Ray; great-grandson of John and Barbara (Lutz) Ray; great²-grandson of *William Ray*, Lieutenant in Col. Anthony Wayne's Regt., Pennsylvania Troops.

EDWIN AUGUSTUS RAYNER, New Jersey (6095). Supplemental. Son of Warren G. and Catherine (Babbidge) Rayner; grandson of John Laurens and Nancy (Kimball) Babbidge; great-grandson of *William Kimball*, private, Col. Abijah Stern's Regt., Massachusetts Militia; great-grandson of *John Babbidge*, sailor on Massachusets sloop "Race Horse"; grandson of Thomas and Mary (Parker) Rayner; great-grandson of *David Parker*, private, Col. Ebenezer Bridges's Regt., Massachusetts Minute Men.

JESSE MOTT READ, Salt Lake City, Utah (37552). Son of Edward F. and Edna M. (Aldrich) Read; grandson of William Earl and Salina Almeda (Spooner) Aldrich; great-grandson of Alton and Mary (Earl) Aldrich; great²-grandson of Ralph and Betsy (Davis) Earl; great³-grandson of *William Davis*, Second Lieutenant, First Regt., Rhode Island Troops.

JOSEPH HENRY READING, Chicago, Ill. (37211). Son of Joseph and Sarah (Fox) Reading; grandson of William and Eizabeth (Sergeant) Reading; great-grandson of William and Ann (Emley) Reading; great²-grandson of *Joseph Reading*, Justice for Hunterdon County, New Jersey, 1778-'80.

GEORGE NELSON REED, Reedville, Va. (D. C. 37160). Son of Elijah W. and Rebecca Sargent (Herrick) Reed; grandson of George and Hannah (Allen) Reed; great-grandson of Isaac and Sarah (Freeman) Reed; great²-grandson of *William Reed*, Captain, Lincoln County, Massachusetts Militia.

STANLEY BELL REID, Nashville, Tenn. (36797). Son of Francis Thorpe and Josephine (Wood) Reid; grandson of Robert Fulton and Marina Turner (Cheatham) Woods; great-grandson of George W. and Marina Bryan (Turner) Cheatham; great²-grandson of Jack Edwards and Marina Brickel (Bryan) Turner; great³-grandson of *Jacob Turner*, Captain, Third Regt., North Carolina Cont'l Line.

ALAN RICE, Brooklyn, N. Y. (37183). Son of George Trowbridge and Lillian Alice (Oaks) Rice; grandson of George and Emma Elizabeth (Flower) Rice; great-grandson of Reuben and Elinor Paris (Root) Rice; great-²-grandson of Joel and Elinor (Strong) Root; great³-grandson of *John Strong*, Captain, Torington, Connecticut Militia; great³-grandson of *Elisha Root*, Colonel, Torington, Connecticut Militia, died in service.

ARTHUR HAYS RICHARDSON, Montclair, N. J. (37149). Son of Andrew Jackson and Euphemia (Hays) Richardson; grandson of Joseph and Lucina (Allen) Richardson; great-grandson of Bradbury Moulton and Sarah (Lee) Richardson; great²-grandson of *Bradbury Richardson*, Major, Col. Thomas Stickney's Regt., New Hampshire Militia.

BRENT NEVILLE RICKARD, Salt Lake City, Utah (32649). Son of Stephen and Constance Maude (Neville) Rickard; grandson of Thomas J. and Amelia Elizabeth (Ransom) Neville; great-grandson of Leander and Anna Matilda (Johnstone) Ransom; great²-grandson of Bliss and Wealthy (Adams) Ransom, Jr.; great³-grandson of *Bliss Ransom*, Sergeant, Colchester, Connecticut Militia.

PHILIP LIGHTFOOT ROBB, Baltimore, Md. (37341). Son of Philip Lightfoot and Helen Struan (Bernard) Robb; grandson of Robert Gilchrist and Fannie Bernard (Lightfoot) Robb; great-grandson of Philip and Sarah Savin (Bernard) Lightfoot; great²-grandson of *Philip Lightfoot*, Lieutenant, First Regt., Virginia Cont'l Artillery.

JOHN CUTTER ROBERTS, Providence, R. I. (36514). Son of John Nichols and Ann Batchelder (Cutter) Roberts; grandson of Caleb and Susan Ann (Norris) Cutter; great-grandson of John and Mary (Batchelder) Cutter; great²-grandson of *Joseph Cutter*, Sergeant and Lieutenant, Jaffrey County, New Hampshire Militia, pensioned.

LEONARD FIELD ROBLEE, Lockport, Ill. (37702). Son of Henry Scott and Alice L. (Partridge) Roblee; grandson of Frederick H. and Mary E. (Root) Partridge; great-grandson of Stephen Eastman and Hannah (Moxley) Root; great²-grandson of *John Root*, private, Connecticut Militia, pensioned.

JOHN ORES ROGERS, Chicago, Ill. (37212). Son of George Baumgarner and Eva (Coates) Rogers; grandson of John and Nancy (Rinard) Rogers; great-grandson of Thornton and Sarah (Massey) Rogers; great²-grandson of Aaron Grigsby and Elizabeth (Baumgarner) Rogers; great³-grandson of *Joseph Rogers*, private, Massachusetts and Virginia Militia.

DICK R. ROSS, Salem, Ore. (35074). Son of Enoch W. and Charlotte (Porter) Ross; grandson of John R. and Emily Ann (Baker) Ross; great-grandson of Daniel and Ann (McClintock) Ross; great²-grandson of *John Ross*, private, Fourteenth and Tenth Regts., Virginia Cont'l Line.

GEORGE HARMON ROSS, Morristown, N. J. (37361). Son of George Harmon and Anne Madeleine (Rafferty) Ross; grandson of George Washington and Juliette (Turner) Ross; great-grandson of Jesse and Betsey (Hancock) Ross; great²-grandson of *Perrin Ross*, Lieutenant, Connecticut Cont'l Troops, killed at Wyoming Massacre.

WARREN PAUL ROSS, Lincoln, Nebr. (36989). Son of James M. and Elizabeth A. (Sanders) Ross; grandson of Robert and Elizabeth (Hornerton) Ross; great-grandson of *Reuben Ross*, private, Maryland and Virginia Troops, pensioned.

JOHN TULLER ROYSE, Terre Haute, Ind. (36444). Son of James S. and Mabel (Tuller) Royse; grandson of John and Lavinia (Mann) Royse; great-grandson of Samuel and Martha (Nichol) Royse; great²-grandson of *Solomon Royse*, private and spy, Colonel Barret's Regt., Maryland Line, pensioned.

HORACE CHARLES RUBERT, Topeka, Kans. (36739). Son of David and Eunice R. (Moll) Rubert; grandson of Eli and Elizabeth (Schock) Moll; great-grandson of George and Margaret (Seibert) Schock; great²-grandson of *Matthias (Michael) Schock*, private, Northumberland County, Pennsylvania Militia.

HORACE CHARLES RUBERT, JR., Topeka, Kans. (36740). Son of Horace Charles and Blanche M. (Campbell) Rubert; grandson of David and Eunice R. (Moll) Rubert; great-grandson of Eli and Elizabeth (Schock) Moll; great²-grandson of George and Margaret (Seibert) Schock; great³-grandson of *Matthias (Michael) Schock*, private, Northumberland County, Pennsylvania Militia.

HORACE EDSALL RUDE, Paterson, N. J. (37520). Son of John Wesley and Anne (Hopper) Rude; grandson of Caleb and Elizabeth (Stockman) Rude; great-grandson of James and Mary (Edsall) Rude; great²-grandson of Caleb and Elizabeth (Simpson) Rude; great³-grandson of *Caleb Rude*, private, Colonel Seeley's Battalion, Morris County, New Jersey Militia.

J. L'VERNE RUSSELL, Adel, Iowa (36921). Son of Willard and Flora (Frush) Russell; grandson of Adoniram and Sarah (North) Russell; great-grandson of Joseph and Sarah (Russell) North; great²-grandson of *Thomas North*, Orderly and Quartermaster-Sergeant, Charlotte County, Virginia Militia.

WILLIAM DEAN SANFORD, Westfield, N. J. (37789). Son of Edward Hoyle and Mary Elizabeth (McNabb) Sanford; grandson of John Lowry and Mary Hoyle (Knight) Sanford; great-grandson of Nathaniel and Elizabeth (Hoyle) Knight; great²-grandson of *Nathaniel Knight*, Corporal, Essex County, Massachusetts Militia, for seacoast defense.

SHERMAN COFFIN SAWTELLE, Medina, Wash. (36659). Son of Charles W. and Annie Emery (Smith) Sawtelle; grandson of Charles F. and Lois B. (Emery) Smith; great-grandson of Charles A. and Eliza A. (Jennerson) Smith; great²-grandson of Jonas L. and Abigail (Kemp) Jennerson; great³-grandson of *Moses Jennerson*, private, Colonel Whitcomb's and Colonel Dike's Regts., Massachusetts Militia.

CARL HOWELL SAWYER, Waukesha, Wis. (37284). Son of Walter Putnam and Eleanor (Williams) Sawyer; grandson of Silas Stearns and Julia (Sargeant) Sawyer; great-grandson of Joseph and Dorcas (Edgell) Sawyer; great²-grandson of *Abraham Sawyer*, private, Massachusetts Militia and Cont'l Troops; great²-grandson of *John Edgell*, Corporal, Major Bridge's Regt., Massachusetts Militia; great-grandson of Ezra and Betsy (Putman) Sargeant; great²-grandson of *John Putman*, private, Col. Asa Whitcomb's Regt., Massachusetts Militia; great²-grandson of *Ezra Sargeant (Sargent)*, private, Massachusetts Militia, at Lexington Alarm.

HUGH SWENEY SCAMMON, Minneapolis, Minn. (37250). Son of Frank and Mary
(——) Scammon; grandson of William and Hannah (Smith) Scammon; great-grandson
of Nicholas and Margaret (Cort) Scammon; great²-grandson of *Samuel Scammon*, Second
Lieutenant, Col. Lemuel Robinson's Regt., Massachusetts Militia.

CHARLES PEARSALL SCHOUTEN, Minnesota (19940). Supplemental. Son of John
William and Mary Louise (Pearsall) Schouten; grandson of Lewis and Harriet (Hustis)
Pearsall; great-grandson of James Haight and Sarah Elizabeth (Stevens) Hustis; great²-
grandson of *Robert Hustis*, private, Seventh Regt., Dutchess County, New York Militia;
great³-grandson of *Joseph Hustis*, private, Seventh Regt., Dutchess County, New York
Militia; grandson of Jerome and Isabella (Stotesbury) Schouten; great-grandson of
Stephen and Elizabeth (Van Voorhis) Schouten; great²-grandson of *Jerome Van Voorhis*,
private, Second and Sixth Regts., Dutchess County, New York Militia.

JOHN WILLIAM SCHOUTEN, Minneapolis, Minn. (37434). Son of Jeromus and Isabella
(Stotesbury) Schouten; grandson of Stephen and Elizabeth (Van Voorhis) Schouten;
great-grandson of *Jerome Van Voorhis*, private, Dutchess County, New York Militia.

PAUL REVERE SCHRIVER, Totowa Borough, N. J. (37790). Son of Andrew and Martha
Alida (Wiltse) Schriver; grandson of Hiram and Charlotte Ann (Schoonmaker) Wiltse;
great-grandson of Ambrose and Magdalene (Miller) Wiltse; great²-grandson of *William
Wiltse*, private, Sixth and Second Regts., Dutchess County, New York Militia.

DE ELTON V. SEEBER, Cape Vincent, N. Y. (37195). Son of Walter and Celestia
(Reynolds) Seeber; grandson of Henry W. and Susan (Overacker) Seeber; great-grandson
of William H. and Hannah (or Annatie) (Kitts); great²-grandson of *Henry Seeber*,
private, First Regt., Tryon County, New York Militia; great³-grandson of *William Seeber*,
Member Committee of Safety, Lieutenant-Colonel, Tryon County, New York Militia, killed
in service.

MYRON JAMES SEELY, Montclair, N. J. (37506). Son of James P. and Ida (Dealing)
Seely; grandson of Uriah and Nancy (Hopping) Seely; great-grandson of James and
Amanda (Mason) Seely; great²-grandson of *John Seely*, private, Monmouth County,
New Jersey Militia, and Cont'l Troops.

URIAH SEELY, Jr., East Orange, N. J. (37508). Son of Uriah and Nancy (Hopping)
Seely; grandson of James and Amanda (Mason) Seely; great-grandson of *John Seely*,
private, Monmouth County, New Jersey Militia, and Cont'l Troops.

HENRY CLAY SESSIONS, Jr., Sioux Falls, S. D. (30672). Son of Henry Clay and
Margaret Matilda (Sessions) Sessions; grandson of Alonzo (father of Margaret) and
Celia (Dexter) Sessions; great-grandson of Samuel and Anna (Fargo) Dexter; great²-
grandson of *Samuel Dexter*, private, Colonel Lippett's Regt., Rhode Island Troops.

ARTHUR P. SHANKLIN, Jr., Baltimore, Md. (37342). Son of Arthur P. and Jane G.
(Staub) Shanklin; grandson of Richard P. H. and Adelia A. (Goshorn) Staub; great-
grandson of William Scott and Priscilla Jane (——) Goshorn; great²-grandson of John
and Mary (Farrier) Goshorn; great³-grandson of William and Isabella (Scott) Farrier;
great⁴-grandson of *Joseph Scott*, private, Seventh Battalion, Cumberland County, Pennsylvania Militia.

RICHARD GOSHORN SHANKLIN, Baltimore, Md. (37343). Same as Arthur P. Shanklin,
Jr., Md. (37342).

WILLIAM B. SHANNAHAN, Easton, Md. (37682). Son of William Elston Shannahan;
grandson of John Henry Kelley Shannahan; great-grandson of Jesse and Rachel
(Cheezum) Shannahan; great²-grandson of *John Shannahan*, Lieutenant, "Hearts of Oak"
Company, Maryland Militia.

RALPH HAKE SHEAFFER, Interville, Pa. (37099). Son of William Eckert and Ann
Catharine (Schreiner) Sheaffer; grandson of Henry and Christianna (Bomberger)
Schreiner; great-grandson of John and Rachel (Blattenberger) Bomberger; great²-grandson
of *John Bomberger*, private, Lancaster County, Pennsylvania Militia.

ADELBERT BRYANT SHEHAN, Biddeford, Me. (36594). Son of James R. and Lizzie E.
(Walden) Shehan; grandson of Benjamin and Pauline (Bryant) Shehan; great-grandson
of *Stephen Bryant*, Corporal, Colonel Storer's Regt., York County, Massachusetts
Militia.

DANIEL LEROY SHIRLEY, Newark, N. J. (37515). Son of George David and Cornelia
Deyo (Terwilliger) Shirley; grandson of Daniel C. and Emilie A. (Sprague) Terwilliger;

great-grandson of Jonathan B. and Ellen J. (King) Sprague; great²-grandson of Evans and Lavinia (Mullenix) Sprague; great³-grandson of *Amasa Sprague*, private, Fourth Regt., Ulster County, New Jersey Militia.

JOHN EDWARD SHOEMAKER, Washington, D. C. (37158). Son of Joseph Lucas and Elizabeth (Moxley) Shoemaker; grandson of Loyd and Elizabeth (Kraft) Moxley; great-grandson of *William Kraft*, private, Colonel Weltner's Regt., Maryland Militia, pensioned.

WILLIAM MORRIS SHOTWELL, Salina, Kans. (36744). Son of John Warder and Julia (E.——) Shotwell; grandson of Jabez and Elizabeth (Warder) Shotwell; great-grandson of *John Shotwell*, private, Morris County, New Jersey Militia.

WILLIAM E. SIMONS, Bluffton, Ind. (36441). Son of William and Anna (M.——) Simons; grandson of Adriel and Patty (Merrit) Simons; great-grandson of *Adriel Simons*, private, Connecticut Militia.

WILLIAM ELLIS SIMONTON, Portland, Ore. (37483). Son of Jas. and Melinda (Koser) Simonton; grandson of William and Katharine (Carlon) Simonton; great-grandson of Robert and Margaret (Richards) Simonton; great²-grandson of *William Richards*, private, First Regt., Pennsylvania Cont'l Line, pensioned.

PAUL L. SLOAN, Nashville, Tenn. (37465). Son of Vaniah S. and Letitia A. (Lowe) Sloan; grandson of George L. and Caroline (Townsend) Sloan; great-grandson of Thomas and Hannah (——) Sloan; great²-grandson of *Thomas Sloan*, munition maker and private, Connecticut guard service.

HARRY SPEER SMITH, McKeesport, Pa. (37408). Son of Wilson Speer and Elvira (McCune) Smith; grandson of Robert McFarland and Caroline (Black) Smith; great-grandson of *Phillip Smith*, private, Pennsylvania Militia.

JULIUS FRED SMITH, Herkimer, N. Y. (37587). Son of Isaac Eugene and Elizabeth (Kingsbury) Smith; grandson of Samuel Faron and Maria (Cox) Smith; great-grandson of Ebenezer and Maria (Keller) Cox; great²-grandson of *Ebenezer Cox*, Lieutenant Colonel, New York Militia, killed.

RALSTON FOX SMITH, Cleveland, Ohio (37631). Son of Robert Ralston and Minnie (Simmons) Smith; grandson of John Cottin and Ellen Content (Fox) Smith; great-grandson of Asa and Mary Brainard (Beckwith) Smith; great²-grandson of *Matthew Smith*, private, Connecticut Militia at Lexington Alarm.

STERLING EDWARD SMITH, North Adams, Mass. (37124). Son of Edward N. and Eva S. (Rich) Smith; grandson of Charles and Sarah A. (Lewis) Rich; great-grandson of Nelson and Naomi (Amy) (Goodell) Rich; great²-grandson of *Lemuel Rich*, private, Connecticut Cont'l Line and State Troops.

WILLIAM GIDEON SPENCER, Westfield, N. J. (37148). Son of William Gideon and Nannie E. (Smith) Spencer; grandson of Thomas Flournoy and Sarah A. (Bouldin) Spencer; great-grandson of *Gideon Spencer*, Lieutenant, Virginia State Troops, Captain, Charlotte, Virginia Militia.

IRA ROBERT SPRINGER, Middletown, Pa. (37098). Son of George W. and Anne K. (Whitney) Springer; grandson of Simon Carver and Elizabeth (Critson) Springer; great-grandson of George and Christina (Heppich) Critson; great²-grandson of Christian and Elizabeth Catherine (Ettele) Heppich; great³-grandson of *Gottlieb David Ettelin (Ettele)*, Patriot who furnished supplies to army, Signer of Oath of Allegiance.

HENRY ETTER STARR, Philadelphia, Pa. (37093). Son of John William and Christ-Anne (Etter) Starr; grandson of Henry Augustus and Mary Elizabeth (Schreiner) Etter; great-grandson of Henry and Christianna (Bomberger) Schreiner; great²-grandson of John and Rachel (Blattenberger) Bomberger; great³-grandson of *John Bomberger*, private, Ninth and Third Battalions, Lancaster County, Pennsylvania Militia.

HERBERT FOSTER STATESIR, Washington, D. C. (37161). Son of Benjamin T. and Emilie Augusta (Foster) Statesir; grandson of John and Mary Morris (Tilton) Statesir; great-grandson of *John Statesir*, private, Monmouth County, New Jersey Militia, prisoner, pensioned.

WILLIAM HENRY STAUB, Baltimore, Md. (37344). Son of Richard P. H. and Adelia A. (Goshorn) Staub; grandson of William Scott and Priscila Jane (Zinn) Goshorn; great-grandson of John and Mary (Farrier) Goshorn; great²-grandson of William nad Isabella (Scott) Farrier; great³-grandson of *Joseph Scott*, private, Seventh Battalion, Cumberland County, Pennsylvania Militia.

MARSHALL W. STEADMAN, Tyringham, Mass. (37389). Son of Martin V. B. and Maria (Baker) Steadman; grandson of William S. and Lucinda (Heath) Steadman; great-grandson of Thomas and Lydia (Sweet) Steadman; great²-grandson of *William Steadman*, Ensign, Rhode Island Militia, pensioned.

ELIJAH HUBERT STEELE, Oakland, Calif. (37270). Son of Elijah and Louisa C. (Lanze) Steele; grandson of Orlo and Fanny (Abby) Steele; great-grandson of Peter and Hannah (Alden) Abbey; great²-grandson of *Thomas Abbey (Abbe)*, Captain, Connecticut State and Cont'l Troops.

VARIAN STEELE, Buffalo, N. Y. (37187). Son of Frank Bartlett and Helen (Varian) Steele; grandson of Charles G. and Harriet V. (Snyder) Steele; great-grandson of Oliver G. and Sarah (Hull) Steele; great²-grandson of William and Rhoda (Barker) Steele; great³-grandson of *Zenas Barker*, private, Col. Marinus Willett's Regt., New York Troops; grandson of William and Ann E. (Litchfield) Varian; great-grandson of Alexander and Elizabeth Amelia (Atlee) Varian; great-grandson of Ichabod and Elizabeth (Patchen) Varian; great³-grandson of *James Varian*, Captain, Westchester County, New York Minute Men; great²-grandson of William Pitt and Sarah (Light) Atlee; great³-grandson of *William Augustus Atlee*, Chairman, Lancaster County, Pennsylvania Committee of Safety and Superintendent of Arsenals and Barracks; great-grandson of Eleazer and Marina Lavinia (Hovey) Litchfield; great²-grandson of Jacob and Olive (Grow) Hovey; great³-grandson of *Nathaniel Hovey*, private, Eighth Regt., Connecticut Militia at Lexington Alarm.

HENRY CHAMBLISS STERLING, Port Arthur, Texas (37528). Son of Thomas Sill and Eleanor (Walker) Sterling; grandson of William J. and Amanda (Burton) Sterling; great-grandson of Thomas Sill and Mary P. (Falconer) Sterling; great²-grandson of William and Jerusha (Ely) Sterling; great³-grandson of *William Sterling*, Captain, Sixth Company, Third Regt., Connecticut State Troops, and purchaser of army supplies; great²-grandson of *Robert Ely*, private, Connecticut Militia.

ALBION MORSE STEVENS, Atlantic, Mass. (37755). Son of Isaac Gilkey and Meriam (Fernald) Stevens; grandson of Frederick and Betty (Gilkey) Stevens; great-grandson of *Nathaniel Stevens*, Corporal, Col. Edmund Phinney's Regt., Massachusetts Militia.

ALBERT FLETCHER STEVENSON, Ridgewood, N. J. (37517). Son of Joseph Henry and Helen Louisa (Fletcher) Stevenson; grandson of Joseph and Hannah (Bickford) Stevenson; great-grandson of Thomas and Sarah (Johnson) Stevenson; great²-grandson of *Phineas Johnson*, private, Col. James Frye's Regt., Massachusetts Militia; great²-grandson of *Samuel Johnson*, Colonel, Essex County, Massachusetts Militia, and Member Committee of Inspection; grandson of Elbridge Erastus and Miriam Bird (Fowle) Fletcher; great-grandson of Michael and Sally (Fowle) Fletcher; great²-grandson of *Samuel Fowle*, private, Colonel Baldwin's Regt., Massachusetts Militia; great-grandson of Samuel and Miriam Channel (Bird) Fowle; great²-grandson of James and Hannah (Channel) Bird; great³-grandson of *Louis Channel*, private and Corporal, Massachusetts Militia, and guard service; great²-grandson of Samuel and Rachel (Lawrence) Fowle; great²-grandson of *Jonathan Lawrence*, Treasurer for Woburn, Massachusetts, 1777-'78

RALPH DE MERRITT STILES, Minneapolis, Minn. (37426). Son of Cyrus Dwight and Flora (De Merritt) Stiles; grandson of Joseph and Mary (Eustis) De Merritt; great-grandson of Samuel and Maria (Knapp) De Merritt; great²-grandson of Davis and Abigail (Emerson) De Merritt; great³-grandson of John and Lois (Davis) De Merritt, 3d; great⁴-grandson of *John De Merritt, Jr.*, Major, Second Regt., New Hampshire Militia.

WILLIAM PAUL STILLMAN, Red Bank, N. J. (37791). Son of William Howard and Elizabeth B. (Dingwell) Stillman; grandson of Louis Mortimer and Sarah C. (Moores) Stillman; great-grandson of Ebenezer and Rhoda (Francis) Stillman; great²-grandson of *Joseph Stillman*, Connecticut Minute Man at Lexington Alarm.

PAUL STINCHFIELD, San Francisco, Calif. (37257). Son of Edwin Hovey and Pauline Lucinda (Kennedy) Stinchfield; grandson of Jeremiah and Harriet Ansenath (Foster) Stinchfield; great-grandson of Jeremiah and Desire (Butterfield) Stinchfied; great²-grandson of *William Stinchfield*, private, Cumberland County, Massachusetts Militia.

ALVIN GLENN STITH, Louisville, Ky. (36535). Son of Richard Luther and Eugenia (Carrico) Stith; grandson of Milton and Martha (Stith) Stith; great-grandson of John and Lucy (Hardaway) Stith; great²-grandson of *Joseph Stith*, Ensign, Bedford County, Virginia Militia; great³-grandson of *Richard Stith*, Member Bedford County, Va., Committee of Correspondence.

WALTER LINCOLN STOCKWELL, Fargo, N. D. (36942). Son of Silvanus and Charlotte (Bowdish) Stockwell; grandson of Peter and Huldah (Putnam) Stockwell; great-grandson of *Solomon Stockwell*, private, Colonel Tyler's Regt., Massachusetts Militia.

HENRY HOYT STONE, Oberlin, Ohio (37034). Son of Demmon C. and Eveline (Hustid) Stone; grandson of Daniel and Mary A. (Wildman) Stone; great-grandson of Ezra and Anne (Hoyt) Wildman; great²-grandson of Comfort and Eunice (Mallory) Hoyt, Jr.; great³-grandson of *Comfort Hoyt*, Captain, Sixteenth Regt., Connecticut Militia for Cont'l service.

JOHN DANA STONE, Minneapolis, Minn. (37240). Son of John West and Kate Gleason (Dana) Stone; grandson of John Denniston and Martha (Allen) Stone; great-grandson of Gardner and Sally Ann (Denniston) Stone; great²-grandson of *Windsor Stone*, private, Massachusetts Militia and Cont'l Troops, pensioned.

ROBERT LEE STRICKLER, Indiana (36427). Supplemental. Son of William Lewis and Mary Margaret (Swink) Strickler; grandson of Daniel and Mary Jane (Brown) Strickler; great-grandson of Jacob and Elizabeth (Lewis) Brown; great²-grandson of Thomas and Elizabeth (Payne) Lewis; great³-grandson of *Edward Payne*, Member Fairfax County, Va., Committee of Safety; great³-grandson of *William Lewis*, Major, Tenth Virginia Regt., Cont'l Troops.

CARLTON STRONG, Pittsburgh, Pa. (37097). Son of Howard Marshall and Julia Stillwell (Bowne) Strong; grandson of Alfred and Annis (Spicer) Strong; great-grandson of Timothy and Clarissa (Stoddard) Tyrrell Strong; great²-grandson of *Nathan Stoddard*, Captain, Connecticut Militia, prisoner and killed at Fort Mifflin.

HAROLD JOSEPH SWEZEY, Wilmington, Del. (35670). Son of Joseph Benjamin and Ida W. (Jagger) Swezey; grandson of Nathaniel Tuttle and Phebe (Robinson) Swezey; great-grandson of Phineas and Beulah (Tuthill) Robinson; great²-grandson of *James Tuthill, Jr.*, private, Col. Thomas Terry's Third Regt., New York Minute Men.

GEORGE REED TABOR, Oklahoma (36245). Son of John W. and Martha Jane (Anderson) Tabor; grandson of Elijah and Margaret (Ellison) Anderson; great-grandson of Lewis and Margaret (Powers) Ellison; great²-grandson of *Robert Ellison*, Captain, Third Regt., South Carolina Troops, prisoner; great-grandson of Henry and Jane (Coffee) Anderson, Jr.; great²-grandson of *Henry Anderson*, Captain, Col. Levi Casey's Regt., South Carolina Troops, killed.

CHARLES CORNWELL TALCOTT, Montclair, N. J. (37509). Son of Augustus Lyman and Caroline (Cornwell) Talcott; grandson of Samuel Lyman and Elizabeth B. (Collins) Talcott; great-grandson of Lyman and Harriet (Hatch) Talcott; great²-grandson of *Joseph Talcott*, Second Lieutenant, Colonel Johnson's Regt., Connecticut Militia, and private, Colonel Chester's Regt., Connecticut State Troops.

GEORGE ABERT TAYLOR, Massachusetts (37118). Supplemental. Son of James Truman and Helen Frances (Peters) Taylor; grandson of John Rogers and Abby (Covil) Peters; great-grandson of *Silas Covil*, Corporal, Pomfret, Connecticut Militia, and Cont'l Line; great-grandson of Silas and Rebecca (Thurber) Covil; great²-grandson of *Samuel Thurber*, Third Steward, Province, R. I., Hospital; great-grandson of Absalom and Mary (Rogers) Peters; great²-grandson of *Nathaniel Rogers*, Deputy to New Hampshire Convention of '75; great²-grandson of *John Peters*, Hebrun, Connecticut Moderator and Selectman, 1777'-79.

GEORGE EDWIN TAYLOR, Pittsburgh, Pa. (37732). Son of Samuel W. and Margaret E. (Barrickman) Taylor; grandson of George E. and Mary V. E. M. (Larkin) Taylor; great-grandson of Michael (Micah) and Julian (Burgess) Larkin; great²-grandson of John and Elenor (Griffith) Burgess; great³-grandson of *John Burgess*, Captain and Colonel, Anne Arundel County, Maryland Militia, Member Committee of Observation and other war commissions.

SPENCER HANNUM TAYLOR, Acton, Mass. (37756). Son of Arthur Orison and Lucy Mitty (Hannum) Taylor; grandson of Daniel Lapham and Mary Rebecca (Pease) Hannum; great-grandson of Alpheus and Lucy (Foster) Pease; great²-grandson of Jonathan and Hannah (Cutter) Foster; great³-grandson of *Benjamin Cutter*, Ensign, New Ipswich, New Hampshire Militia.

WALTER PIERCE TEEGARDIN, Seattle, Wash. (36656). Son of Levi and Mary (R.—) Teegardin; grandson of Aaron and Sarah (Hoyt) Teegardin; great-grandson of George and Christiana (Brobst) Teegardin; great²-grandson of Aaron and Margaret (Dieble) Teegardin; great³-grandson of *Abraham Teegardin, Jr. (Tiegarten)*, Pennsylvania Frontier Ranger.

MENTER BRADLEY TERRILL, Dallas, Texas (36333). Son of James William and Elizabeth (Bradley) Terrill; grandson of Benjamin and Delilah (Chrisler) Terrill; great-grandson of Robert and Mary (Polly) (Lacey) Terrill; great²-grandson of *Edmund Terrill*, Sergeant, Culpepper County, Virginia Militia.

RUSSELL PAUL THIERBACH, Milwaukee, Wis. (37285). Son of Edwin and Alice (Martin) Thierbach; grandson of John and Mary (Johnson) Martin; great-grandson of Allan and Mary (Chalfont) Johnson; great²-grandson of Aaron nad Elizabeth (Barrick) Chalfont; great³-grandson of Russell and Mary (Timberlake) Barrick; great⁴-grandson of *John Timberlake*, private, Virginia Cont'l Line.

GEORGE CURTIS TINGLEY, Jamaica Plain, Mass. (37396). Son of Ernest De Witt and Alice Ruphelle (Churchill) Tingley; grandson of George Curtis and Georgiana Harriet Matilda (Sage) Tingley; great-grandson of Hartford and Freelove (Backus) Tingley; great²-grandson of *Nathan Tingley*, private, Massachusetts Militia.

ALEXANDER DIX TITTLE, Johnstown, Pa. (37412). Son of James Whitesides and Mary (Ringler) Tittle; grandson of John and Mary (Snodgrass) Tittle; great-grandson of James and Ann (Fraeme) Tittle; great²-grandson of *Peter Tittle, Jr.*, private, Westmoreland County, Pennsylvania Rangers.

JOHN WARREN TITTLE, Johnstown, Pa. (37418). Son of James and Mary Ringler (Orr) Tittle; grandson of John and Mary (Snodgrass) Tittle; great-grandson of James and Ann (Fraeme) Tittle; great²-grandson of *Peter Tittle, Jr.*, private, Westmoreland County, Pennsylvania Rangers.

HOWARD GOODELL THOMPSON, Walla Walla, Wash. (36657). Son of Archibald Brewer and Mary E. (Eddy) Thompson; grandson of James and Nancy M. (Baird) Thompson; great-grandson of Sylvanus and Betsey (Brewer) Thompson; great²-grandson of *Jonathan Thompson (Thomson)*, Lieutenant, Brimfield, Massachusetts Militia.

FRED A. TOLMAN, Boise, Idaho (35115). Son of Sidney E. and Addie L. (Kinsman) Tolman; grandson of Elisha H. and Rusina (Beard) Tolman; great-grandson of Henry and Mary (Harris) Tolman; great²-grandson of *Benjamin Tolman*, private, New Hampshire and Massachusetts Militia; great²-grandson of *Micah Chaplin*, Corporal and Sergeant, New Hampshire Militia and Cont'l service, pensioned.

BURTON AUGUSTUS TOWNE, Lodi, Calif. (37265). Son of Horace Alonzo and Emma M. (Scoville) Towne; grandson of Nelson Parker and Julia A. (Dresser) Towne; great-grandson of Moses and Susannah (Towne) Dresser, Jr.; great²-grandson of Josiah and Elizabeth (Ware) Towne, Jr.; great³-grandson of *Josiah Towne*, private, Worcester County, Massachusetts Militia; great²-grandson of Moses and Abigail (Blood) Dresser; great³-grandson of *Richard Dresser, Jr.*, private, Massachusetts Militia; grandson of Augustus J. and Elizabeth Moore (Wilde) Scoville; great-grandson of James A. and Mary (Phelps) Scoville; great²-grandson of Horace and Mary (Rice) Phelps; great³-grandson of *Ebenezer Phelps*, Fifer and Lieutenant, Connecticut Troops, pensioned.

GEORGE CLEVELAND TRIPP, Chicago, Ill. (37213). Son of George Monroe and Catherine Adelaide (Hall) Tripp; grandson of William and Margaret (Ward) Tripp; great-grandson of William and Rary (Rathburn) Tripp; great²-grandson of *Acus Tripp*, Corporal and private, Barnstable County, Massachusetts Militia.

CARROLL VIETS TUCKER, Warren, Ohio (37037). Son of Frank Eugene and Nira Estelle (Whitney) Tucker; grandson of John Viets and Mrs. Mary (Lansing) Graves Whitney; great-grandson of Samuel Platt and Lois (Buttles) Whitney; great²-grandson of *Jonathan Buttles, 3d, (Buttolph)*, Captian, Eighteenth Regt., Connecticut Militia.

GLENN GRANVILLE TUCKER, Warren, Ohio (37038). Same as Carroll Viets Tucker, Ohio (37037).

NATHANIEL TUTTLE, Croton-on-Hudson, N. Y. (37186). Son of Nathaniel and Ellanora Jordan (Clark) Tuttle; grandson of James Horton and Phœbe A. (Tucker) Tuttle; great-grandson of Reuben and Rachel (Boice) Tucker; great²-grandson of *Nathaniel Tucker*, Lieutenant, Westchester County, New York Militia.

FRANK WARNER TYLER, Buffalo, N. Y. (37196). Son of Charles Parker and Ella Katherine (Chamberlain) Tyler; grandson of Asahel Ruben and Minerva Catherine

(Barnard) Chamberlain; great-grandson of Othniel Fitzhenry and Susan Adelia (Ransom) Barnard; great²-grandson of Selah and Dorothy (Taylor) Barnard; great²-grandson of *Othniel Taylor*, Captain and Adjutant, Tenth Regt., Massachusetts Cont'l Line.

ROBERT STANNARD UNDERWOOD, Summit, N. J. (37792). Son of Bert Elias and Susan (Stannard) Underwood; grandson of Elias and Livina (Elmer) Underwood; great-grandson of Abishai Sabine and Mary (Alvord) Underwood; great²-grandson of *Daniel Alvord*, private, Hampshire County, Massachusetts Militia.

JOHN ROLLINS UPTON, Chicago, Ill. (37214). Son of Charles and Jennie (Kemmer) Wesley; grandson of Daniel and Amanda M. (Rollins) Upton; great-grandson of Daniel and Rebecca (Teel) Upton; great²-grandson of *Jacob Upton*, private, Reading, Massachusetts Militia.

EDWIN CORTLANDT VAN CISE, Summit, N. J. (37360). Son of Joel Garrettson and Laura Helen (Marsh) Van Cise; grandson of William S. and Abigail S. (Knowles) Marsh; great-grandson of Amasa and Mercey (Simpson) Knowles; great²-grandson of Freeman and Esther (Myrick) Knowles; great²-grandson of *Seth Knowles*, private, Col. William Shepherd's Regt., Massachusetts Cont'l Troops.

GEORGE G. VAN HORN, Monroeville, Ohio (37045). Son of William H. and Edna (Hicks) Van Horn; grandson of William D. and Lydia (Griswold) Van Horn; great-grandson of —— and Elizabeth (Strope) Van Horn; great²-grandson of *Sebastian Strope*, private, at Wyoming, Pa., Massacre.

CECIL WOODS VEST, Baltimore, Md. (37245). Son of William Edward and Alice Gertrude (Woods) Vest; grandson of Porter and Ellen (Watson) Woods; great-grandson of Samuel and Mary (Richardson) Watson; great²-grandson of *John Richardson*, Ensign, Middle District, Frederick County, Maryland Flying Camp.

ARTHUR MILLER VINJE, Madison, Wis. (37286). Son of Aad John and Alice Idell (Miller) Vinje; grandson of John Cody and Adelia Maria (Wait) Miller; great-grandson of John and Statira (Booth) Miller; great²-grandson of James Harrington and Lucy (Pratt) Miller; great³-grandson of *Phine(h)as Pratt*, private, Col. Nathan Sparhawk's Regt., Massachusetts Militia.

HARRY VINSONHALER, St. Louis, Mo. (35574). Son of George and Sarah (Rea) Vinsonhaler; grandson of Jacob and Nancy (MacDonald) Vinsonhaler; great-grandson of Hugh and Jane (Montgomery) MacDonald; great²-grandson of *William MacDonald*, private, Col. William Crawford's Regt., Pennsylvania Troops.

CECIL ROY WADE, Bandon, Ore. (37480). Son of Elza Thomas and Manta (Hall) Wade; grandson of James A. and Sarah (Christie) Wade; great-grandson of Israel and Elizabeth (Cook) Christie; great²-grandson of *James Christie*, private, Pittsylvania County, Virginia, pensioned.

WALTER EDWIN WAITE, Washington, D. C. (37162). Son of George Ervin and Mary Alice (Ingalls) Waite; grandson of Edwin Putnam and Charlotte (Stickney) Ingalls; great-grandson of Theophilus and Electa (Cook) Stickney; great²-grandson of Moses and Mary (Hastings) Stickney; great³-grandson of *Moses Stickney*, private, Col. Josiah Whitney's Regt., Massachusetts Militia, pensioned.

FREDERICK WILLIAM WALKER, Roselle, N. J. (37363). Son of John Henry Hobart and Lilian Montgomery (Johnstone) Walker; grandson of Frederick William and Alida Ritzma (Bogert) Walker; great-grandson of John C. and Ann (Roberts) Walker; great²-grandson of *Samuel Walker*, Captain, Vermont Militia.

BURROUGHS BENJAMIN WALLING, Summit, N. J. (37510). Son of James Snyder and Emma (Aumack) Walling; grandson of Benjamin Bennett and Eliza Ann (——) Welling; great-grandson of Joseph and Eliza (——) Walling; great²-grandson of *Joseph Walling*, Lieutenant, Monmouth County, New Jersey Militia, pensioned.

HENRY CARR WARD, Newark, N. J. (37351). Son of Joseph Grover and Julia Smith (Cochran) Ward; grandson of Aaron Condit and Mary Oliver (Munn) Ward; great-grandson of Jacob and Abigail (Dodd) Ward, Jr.; great²-grandson of *Jacob Ward*, private, Essex County, New Jersey Militia.

EUGENE WARDEN, Mt. Pleasant, Pa. (37403). Son of James S. and Sarah Jane (Cunningham) Warden; grandson of Joseph and Jane (Gault) Cunnnigham; great-grandson of William and Mary (Huston) Cunningham; great²-grandson of *Joseph Huston*, private and Captain, Crawford's Expedition, and Westmoreland County, Pennsylvania Rangers.

FRANK OSMAN WARNER, New York City, N. Y. (37197). Son of James M. and Roselle (Brewer) Warner; grandson of Osman and Deluana (Spencer) Brewer; great-grandson of Martin and Polly (Holmes) Spencer; great²-grandson of Thomas and Rachel (Arnold) Spencer, Jr.; great³-grandson of *Thomas Spencer*, Corporal and Sergeant, Fourth Battalion, Connecticut Troops.

ROBERT NEWTON WASHABAUGH, Pittsburgh, Pa. (37733). Son of George W. and Mariah E. Arnold Washabaugh; grandson of David and Sarah (Huey) Wahabaugh; great-grandson of John and Catharine (McKnight) Washabaugh; great²-grandson of *Henry Washabaugh*, private, Bedford County, Pennsylvania Militia.

FRANCIS WHITING WASHINGTON, Nashville, Tenn. (36794). Son of Allen Hall and Sallie (Garner) Washington; grandson of Francis Whiting and Eliza Mason (Hall) Washington; great-grandson of Warner and Mary (Whiting) Washington; great²-grandson of *Francis Whiting*, Lieutenant, Virginia Cont'l Dragoons, Colonel, Gloucester County, Virginia Militia.

O'BRYAN WASHINGTON, Nashville, Tenn. (37451). Son of Allen Hall and Sallie (Garner) Washington; grandson of Francis Whiting and Eliza Mason (Hall) Washington; great-grandson of Warner and Mary (Whiting) Washington; great²-grandson of *Francis Whiting*, Lieutenant in Thurston's and Baylor's Regts., Virginia Cont'l Dragoons.

LEIGH WEBBER, Hallowell, Me. (36595). Son of Horatio Nelson and Helen Paine (Leigh) Webber; grandson of Charles E. and Catherine (Grant) Webber; great-grandson of Horatio Nelson and Dorothy (Harlow) Webber; great-grandson of Jeremiah and Balsora (Horne) Webber; great³-grandson of *Charles Webber*, Second Lieutenant, Lincoln County, Massachusetts Militia.

JOHN L. WELLINGTON, Rochester, N. Y. (37588). Son of Erasmus and Helen (——) Wellington; grandson of John L. and Julia (——) Wellington; great-grandson of Ebenezer and Rebecca (——) Wellington; great²-grandson of *John Wellington*, private, Massachusetts Militia.

ALTON LYNN WELLS, Croton, N. Y. (37184). Son of Allen Baker and Etta Clara (Frary) Wells; grandson of Calvin and Hannah M. (Waterbury) Wells, Jr.; great-grandson of Calvin and Thankful (Crafts) Wells; great²-grandson of *John Crafts*, private and Sergeant, Whately, Massachusetts Militia.

LEWIS EMMOR WELLS, McKeesport, Pa. (37100). Son of James Truman and Ann Appleton (Rhoades) Wells; grandson of Joseph and Sophia (Boyd) Wells; great-grandson of William and Martha (Langhead) Wells; great²-grandson of Joseph and Sarah (Farquhar) Wells; great³-grandson of *Thomas Wells*, Captain, Third Battalion, Washington County, Pennsylvania Militia.

WILLIAM NORRIS WENTWORTH, Madison, Wis. (Iowa 36924). Son of Elmer Marston and Elizabeth Tilton (Towne) Wentworth; grandson of John Norris and Nancy (Titcomb) Wentworth; great-grandson of Benjamin and Hannah (Ames) Wentworth; great²-grandson of Ephraim and Anne (Nancy) (Titcomb) Wentworth; great³-grandson of *Benjamin Titcomb*, Lieutenant-Colonel of Enoch Poor's Regt., New Hampshire Troops.

FRANK WEYMOUTH, Bar Mills, Me. (36596). Son of Edmund and Hannah (Roberts) Weymouth; grandson of John and Charlotte (Clark) Weymouth; great-grandson of *Stephen Weymouth*, private, Massachusetts Cont'l Troops; grandson of Gristram and Betsy (Page) Roberts; great-grandson of Joshua and Abigail (Hubbard) Roberts; great²-grandson of *Joseph Hubbard, Jr.*, Corporal, Massachusetts Cont'l Troops.

ORRIN PLUMMER WEYMOUTH, Portland, Me. (36597). Same as Frank Weymouth, Maine (36596).

GEORGE WILLIAM PRESTON WHIP, Baltimore, Md. (37346). Son of George Tobias and Lettie M. (Culler) Whip, Jr.; grandson of George Tobias and Barbara (Maught) Whip; great-grandson of George and Mary (Cost) Whip; great²-grandson of George and Mary Elizabeth (Williard) Cost; great³-grandson of *Francis Cost*, Member Maryland Associators.

PAUL CULLER WHIPP, New York City, N. Y. (Md. 37347). Same as George William Preston Whip, Maryland (37346).

CARTER PARRY WHITCOMB, Cotuit, Mass. (37762). Son of Franklin Luther and Mary Piatt (Parry) Whitcomb; grandson of Rees H. and Mary Frances (Piatt) Parry; great-grandson of Abram Sedam and Mary Pope (McCoy) Piatt; great²-grandson of *Jacob Piatt*, Captain, First Regt., New Jersey Troops.

FRANKLIN LUTHER WHITCOMB, Jr., Cotuit, Mass. (37763). Same as Carter Parry Whitcomb, Cotuit, Mass. (37762).

PEMBERTON WHITCOMB, Cotuit, Mass. (37764). Same as Carter Parry Whitcomb, Cotuit, Mass. (37762).

DAVID WALKER WHITE, Nashville, Tenn. (37464). Son of James Park and Harriet (Baker) White; grandson of George McNutt and Sophia (Park) White; great-grandson of Moses and Sophia (Moody) White; great²-grandson of *James White*, Captain, North Carolina Militia.

GEORGE McNUTT WHITE, Nashville, Tenn. (37458). Same as David Walker White, Tenn. (37464).

HERBERT E. WHITE, Sacramento, Calif. (37271). Son of Clinton L. and Olive (McKinney) White; grandson of Joshua Vose and Emeline (Garwood) McKinney; great-grandson of William and Jane (Shirley) McKinney; great²-grandson of James and Mary (Moor) Shirley; great³-grandson of *Daniel Moor*, Colonel, Ninth Regt., New Hampshire Militia.

JOHN WHITE, Terre Haute, Ind. (36442). Son of Joseph and Ann (Viers) White; grandson of Benjamin and Rachel (Chiswell) White; great-grandson of Nathan Smith and Margaret Presbury (Chiswell) White; great²-grandson of *William White*, Lieutenant, Prince Georges County, Maryland Militia.

ALLAN HIRAM WHITMAN, Malden, Mass. (37125). Son of James H. and Minerva B. (Rogerson) Whitman; grandson of Hiram and Hannah E. (Gove) Whitman; great-grandson of Samuel and Sarah (Smith) Gove; great²-grandson of *Winthrop Gove*, Mustermaster, Seabrook, New Hampshire Militia.

ARTHUR DARE WHITESIDE, Westport, Conn. (N. Y. 37198). Son of Newton Elkhanah and Elizabeth (Hankins) Whiteside; grandson of William Philips and Mary Clothida (Dare) Whiteside; great-grandson of Abraham and Isabella (Ross) Whiteside; great²-grandson of *Thomas Whiteside*, Captain, Col. Thomas Porter's Battalion, Lancaster County, Pennsylvania Militia.

NORMAN NEWTON WHITESIDE, New York City, N. Y. (37199). Same as Arthur Dare Whiteside, N. Y. (37198).

RAY BELMONT WHITMAN, Bridgeport, Conn. (N. Y. 37200). Son of William W. and Mattie A. (Dearborn) Whitman; grandson of Edwin J. and Susan N. (Georgia) Dearborn; great-grandson of Mark and Electa (Bull) Dearborn; great²-grandson of *Nathaniel Dearborn*, private, General Stark's Brigade, New Hampshire Militia.

HENRY CLAUSEN WHITNEY, Brooklyn, N. Y. (37576). Son of Scudder and Elizabeth (Titus) Whitney; grandson of Daniel and Nancy (Valentine) Whitney; great-grandson of *Darling Whitney*, private, Col. Phillip Bradley's Regt., Connecticut Militia.

MERRILL HENRY WHITNEY, North Adams, Mass. (37757). Son of Charles R. and Diantha (Davis) Whitney; grandson of Eliphalet and Sally (Ryan) Whitney; great-grandson of *Eliphalet Whitney*, private, Windham County, Vermont Militia.

THOMAS HAYES WHITNEY, Atlantic, Iowa (37652). Son of Franklin Huntington and Elinor (Graham) Whitney; grandson of John and Nancy (Huntington) Whitney; great-grandson of *Cornelius Whitney*, private, Seventh Regt., Connecticut Troops.

HARRY RUSSELL WILBERN, Minneapolis, Minn. (37433). Son of Cyrus D. and Mary Ann (Bushnell) Wilbern; grandson of Calvin and Mary Ann (Stokes) Bushnell; great-grandson of Richard and Mary Ann (Kirtland) Stokes; great²-grandson of *Richard Stokes*, private, Col. Zebulon Butler's Regt., Connecticut Cont'l Troops, pensioned.

RAYMOND ABRAM WILDRICK, Paterson, N. J. (37794). Son of Edward A. and Jennie Helen (Burtt) Wildrick; grandson of Robert J. and Cynthia Goodyear (Bateman) Burtt; great-grandson of Stephen and Maria (Benham) Bateman; great²-grandson of Elihu and Esther (Griffin) Benham, Jr.; great³-grandson of *Elihu Benham*, private, Connecticut Militia, pensioned.

GEORGE BARTLETT WILLARD, Waltham, Mass. (37758). Son of George Henry and Helen May (Hall) Willard; grandson of Emery and Irene (Felton) Benjamin Willard; great-grandson of John and Deborah (Wilder) Willard; great²-grandson of *John Willard*, Corporal and Ensign, Lancaster, Massachusetts Militia.

CHARLES SEYBURN WILLIAMS, New Orleans, La. (36961). Son of Francis Bennett and Emily Williamson (Seyburn) Williams; grandson of I. D. and Mary Anne (Rogers) Seyburn; great-grandson of John Michael and Elizabeth (Reynolds) Rogers; great²-grandson of Bernard and Monica (McKeon) Reynolds, Jr.; great²-grandson of *Bernard Reynolds,* private, Virginia Cont'l Troops.

HOWARD ALFRED WILLIAMS, Newark, N. J. (37795). Son of George P. and Annie (Mason) Williams; grandson of George Washington and Amy O. (Wright) Williams; great-grandson of Frederick W. and Mariah (Romer) Williams; great²-grandson of Jacob and Hannah (Van Tassell) Romer; great³-grandson of *John Van Tassell,* private, Westchester County, New York Militia, and Fourth Regt. Cont'l Line, pensioned.

LAURENCE MOORE WILLIAMS, New Orleans, La. (36962). Same as Charles Seyburn Williams, Louisiana (36961).

SAMUEL TANKERSLEY WILLIAMS, Captain U. S. Army, Washington (36660). Son of Darwin Herbert and Ida (Cessna) Williams; grandson of Charles and Mary Ann (Dibert) Cessna; great-grandson of James and Elizabeth (Lysinger) Cessna; great²-grandson of *John Cessna,* Major, Bedford County, Pennsylvania Militia.

HUGH SPALDING WILLSON, Minneapolis, Minn. (37438). Son of Frank Arthur and Henrietta (Spalding) Willson; grandson of George and Emeline Augusta (Larcorn) Spalding; great-grandson of Simeon and Rhoda Bradley (Hovey) Spalding; great²-grandson of Micah and Mary (Chamberlain) Spalding; great³-grandson of *Simeon Spalding,* Lieutenant-Colonel, Second Regt., Middlesex County, Massachusetts Militia, Member Massachusetts Constitutional Convention.

CLAUDE ORONBY WINANS, Saratoga, Calif. (37272). Son of Jonas Wood and Alice Emily (Jones) Winans; grandson of Jonas Wood and Sarah (Stiles) Winans; great-grandson of John and Phebe (Crane) Stiles; great²-grandson of *Jacob Crane,* Captain, Morris County, New Jersey Militia, Member Committee of Safety and Delegate to Philadelphia Convention of '74.

CHESTER MERRILL WITHINGTON, Weston, Conn. (N. Y. 37577). Son of Albert Merrill and Alice Josephine (Nelson) Withington; grandson of Warren and Waitstill (Young) Withington; great-grandson of Otis and Sarah (——) Withington; great²-grandson of *John Withington,* private, Stoughton, Massachusetts Militia at Lexington Alarm; great²-grandson of *Edward Withington,* private, Stoughton, Massachusetts Militia.

WILLIAM FLETCHER WOODFORD, Logan, Utah (Kans. 36738). Son of William D. and Mary (Fetcher) Woodford; grandson of John R. and Armenia E. (Fortner) Woodford; great-grandson of Ira and Parthenra (Hulbert) Woodford; great-grandson of *Bissell Woodford,* private, Connecticut Militia, pensioned.

JAMES LLOYD WOODRUFF, Salt Lake City, Utah (32648). Son of James Jackson and Fanny (Lloyd) Woodruff; grandson of Elias and Lucy (Brown) Smith; great-grandson of Asael and Mary (Duty) Smith; great³-grandson of *Samuel Smith,* Member Massachusetts Committee of Safety, Delegate to General Court and Provincial Congress.

TROWBRIDGE BLANCHARD WOODRUFF, Sparrows Point, Md. (37348). Son of Jerome Joseph and Myra Blanchard (Wheat) Woodruff; grandson of Orrin and Eliza Ann (Woodruff) Woodruff; great-grandson of *Gurdon Woodruff,* private, Col. Erastus Wolcott's Regt., Connecticut Troops.

EVAN MORRISON WOODWARD, Jr., Wenonah, N. J. (37796). Son of Evan Morrison and Ella Louisa (Ritter) Woodward; grandson of James Darrah and Marie Louisa (Stokley) Ritter; great-grandson of Jacob and Susannah (Bradford) Ritter, Jr.; great²-grandson of Thomas and Mary (Fisher) Bradford; great³-grandson of *William Bradford, 3d,* Colonel, Philadelphia Associators, Chairman Pennsylvania Navy Board.

GEORGE HENRY WOOLLEY, Newton Highlands, Mass. (37388). Son of James and Hannah Elizabeth (Hildreth) Woolley; grandson of Charles and Catherine Elizabeth (Colburn) Woolley; great-grandson of Charles and Susannah (Bentley) Woolley; great²-grandson of *Joshua Bentley,* Volunteer boatman to Paul Revere April 18, '75, and Captain, Massachusetts Commissary Service; great-grandson of Calvin and Catherine Sybil (Lakin) Colburn; great²-grandson of *Nathan Colburn,* private and Corporal, Massachusetts Militia; grandson of Levi and Adeline Matilda (Conant) Hildreth; great-grandson of *Zachariah Hildreth,* Second Lieutenant, Sixth Regt., Middlesex County, Massachusetts Militia; great-grandson of *Nathan* and Mrs. Hannah (Petts) Potter *Conant,* Corporal,

Massachusetts Militia at Lexington Alarm; great²-grandson of *Lemuel Petts*, Lieutenant, Colonel Webb's Regt., Massachusetts Troops, Member Committee of Safety and Correspondence.

JAMES TERRELL WOOSLEY, Lake Charles, La. (Ky. 36533). Son of James W. and Sallie (Edwards) Woosley; grandson of Terrell and Nancy Jane (Oller) Woosley; great-grandson of George Washington and Julia (Siler) Woosley; great²-grandson of Samuel and Phœbe (——) Woosley; great³-grandson of *Moses Woosley*, private, Eleventh and Fifteenth Regts., Virginia Cont'l Troops.

JAMES STEWART WROTH, New York City, N. Y. (37578). Son of James Henry and Ella (Forrest) Wroth; grandson of Frederic D. and Abby Ursula (Stewart) Forrest; great-grandson of John Church and Abby Jones (Ridgway) Stewart; great²-grandson of Henry and Sophia (Church) Stewart; great³-grandson of *John Church*, Drummer, private, and Corporal Massachusetts Militia, pensioned; great³-grandson of *Hugh Stewart*, private, Capt. Benjamin Smith's Company, for seacoast defense, widow pensioned; great²-grandson of James and Relipha (Roach) Ridgway; great²-grandson of *James Ridgway*, Massachusets Militia, three years' service, widow pensioned; great³-grandson of *John Roach*, private, Col. Michael Jackson's Regt., Massachusetts Militia, pensioned.

GENTRY WEST YATES, Portland, Ore. (37482). Son of Weldon D. and Margaret L. (Williams) Yates; grandson of John N. and Selina J. (Harwood) Yates; great-grandson of John and Elizabeth (Blue) Yates; great²-grandson of John I. and Penscelia (Reeves) Blue; great²-grandson of *John Blue*, private, Hampshire County, Virginia Militia.

JAMES REED YOCOM, Tacoma, Wash. (36658). Son of Thomas Smith and Caroline Matilda (Reed) Yocom; grandson of Abel and Elizabeth Ann (Smith) Reed; great-grandson of Abel and Ruth (Lane) Reed; great²-grandson of *Moses Reed*, private, Capt. Edmund Munroe's Massachusetts Company at Lexington Alarm.

WILLIAM ARTHUR YODER, Minneapolis, Minn. (37427). Son of William Henry and Cathrine (Addie) Yoder; grandson of Henry and Ruth Ann (Rader) Yoder; great-grandson of Jacob and Cathrine (Dellinger) Yoder; great²-grandson of *John Dellinger*, Captain, North Carolina Militia, Member Tryon County Committee of Safety, and Signer of Bill of Rights, pensioned.

SIMON CAMERON YOUNG, Middletown, Pa. (37417). Son of James and Elizabeth Ann (Redsecker) Young; grandson of Peter and Catharine Sophia (Ettele) Young, Jr.; great-grandson of *Peter Young*, Lieutenant, Sixth Battalion, Berks County, Pennsylvania Militia.

Index of Ancestors to be Found in Bulletins June and October, 1922

Breckenridge, Alexander, Oct., 78
Breckenridge, George, Oct., 78
Breedlove, William, June, 97
Brewer, Gaius, June, 109
Brewster, Samuel, June, 88
Brigden, Michael, June, 85
Briggs, Samuel, June, 121
Brinsmode, Abraham, June, 88
Bristol, Bazaliel (Bizaleel), June, 87
Bristow, Benjamin, Oct., 78
Brodhead, Daniel, June, 99
Brogan, John, June, 120
Brokaw, George, June, 115
Bronson, James, June, 119
Brooks, David, Oct., 95
Brooks, James, June, 96
Brooks, Joshua, Oct., 81
Brown, Abraham, June, 88
Brown, Asa, Oct., 92
Brown, John, Oct., 85
Brown, Joshua, June, 85
Brown, Josiah, June, 88
Brown, Nathaniel, Oct., 98
Brunner, Andrew, Oct., 78
Bryan, Andrew, Oct., —
Bryan, James, Oct., 78
Bryant, ohn, Oct., 89, 93, 96
Bryant, Stephen, Oct., 104
Buell, Asa., Oct., 100
Bullard, Nathan, Oct., 78
Burdon, Jonathan, Oct., 83
Burgess, John, Oct., 107
Burks, Samuel, June, 88
Burpee, Moses, June, 119
Burr, Wakeman, Oct., 80
Burrage, Thomas, Oct., 79
Burritt, Stephen, Oct., 79
Buttles (Buttolph), Jonathan, Oct., 108
Byerly, Jacob, June, 91

Cabell, Nicholas, June, 86
Cady, David, Jr., June, 93
Calhoun, David, Oct., 79
Camden, William, Oct., 77
Cameron, Alexander, June, 120
Cameron, John, June, 120
Capron, Seth, June, 105
Carlton, John, June, 118
Carpenter, Ashabel, June, 121
Carr, John, Oct., 79
Carrigan, Gilbert, June, 119
Cary, Ebenezer, June, 94
Casler, Jacob, June, 89
Casterer (Castor), John, June, 114
Castle, Lemuel, Oct., 97
Castner, Samuel, June, 106
Cattell, Jonas, June, 111
Caulkins, Jonathan, Oct., 77
Causey, Patrick, Oct., 80, 96
Cessna, John, Oct., 112
Chambers, David, June, 101

Chapin, Ephraim, June, 100
Chase, Edmund, June, 85
Cessna, John, Oct., —
Chambers, Alexander, Oct., 80
Channel, Louis, Oct., 106
Chaplin, Micah, Oct., 108
Charlton, John Usher, Oct., 97
Chase, Edmund, Oct., 76
Chatfield, Oliver, June, 93
Christie, James, Oct., 109
Church, John, Oct., 113
Cilley, Joseph, June, 115
Clark, Abraham, June, 114
Clark, Greenleaf, June, 115
Clark, Isaac, June, 89
Clark, James, June, 109
Clark, Jesse, June, 89
Clark, John, June, 89
Clark, Timothy, Oct., 80
Clark, William, June, 103
Clayton, Jonathan Ives, Oct., 86
Clendenin, James, June, 120
Cleveland, Benjamin, June, 97
Cline, Conrad, June, 102
Clough, Oliver, Oct., 80
Coburn, John, Oct., —
Coburn, Silas, Oct., 81
Cochran, Andrew, Oct., 81
Cockrill, John R., Oct., 85
Codwise, George, June, 92
Colburn, Nathan, Oct., 112
Cole, Nehemiah, Oct., 83
Cole, Simeon, June, 90
Collins, Richard, Oct., 84
Comfort, Richard, Oct., 81
Conant, Nathan, Oct., 112
Condit, Abner, June, 119
Conkling, Joshua, June, 90
Converse, Israel, Oct., 84
Converse, Thomas, Oct., 92
Cook (Cooke), Daniel, June, 90
Cook, Lemuel, June, 90
Coolidge, Isaac, Oct., 88
Coolidge, Samuel, June, 109; Oct., 95
Coombs, John, Oct., 81
Coriell, Abraham, Oct., 81
Cornell, William, Oct., 94
Corwin, Joseph, June, 98
Cory, Ebenezer, Oct., 81
Cost, Francis, Oct., 86, 110
Covil, Silas, Oct., 107
Cowdrey, Ambrose, Oct., 91
Cox, Ebenezer, Oct., 105
Crafts, John, Oct., 110
Craig, Elizabeth Sanders, June, 111
Craig, John, June, 91
Craig, Lewis, June, 111
Craig, Polly Hawkins, June, 111
Crandon, Thomas, Oct., 82
Crane, Jacob, Oct., 112
Crane, Josiah, June, 91

Crane, Nathaniel, Oct., 82
Crary, Nathan, June, 91
Cribbs, John, June, 91
Crosby, Josiah, June, 92
Cross, Ralph, June, 93
Crossman, John, Oct., 83
Culbertson, Alexander, June, 92
Cummings, Abraham, June, 92
Cummings, Ebenezer, Oct., 100
Cunningham, Barnet (Barnett), June, 99
Curlee, John, Oct., 82
Cutler, Elisha, June, 90
Cutter, Benjamin, Oct., 90, 107
Cutter, Joseph, Oct., 102
Cutts, John, Oct., 80

Dake, William Gould, June, 92
Davis, Aaron, June, 110
Davis, John, Oct., 87
Davis, Joseph, June, 90
Davis, William, Oct., 102
Day, Jonathan, June, 93
Day, Nehemiah, June, 93
Dayton, Michael, June, 117
Dearborn, Nathaniel, Oct., 111
Deitch, Hartman, Oct., 93
de Kernion, Jean Rene Huchet, Oct., 91
Dellinger, John, June, 121; Oct., 113
De Maranville, Louis, June, 104
De Meritt, John, Oct., 106
Denman, Christopher, June, 91
Dennis, John, June, 107
De Saussure, John Daniel Hector, June, 94
De Vezin, Hugues Charles Honore Olivier,
    Oct., 99
Dewees, Samuel, Oct, 81
Dexter, Samuel, Oct., 104
Dey, John, June, 93
Dike, Benjamin, Oct., 76, 84
Dimock, David, Oct., —
Dismukes, Paul, June, 88
Doak, Robert, Oct., 83
Dobbs, Kedar, Oct., 83
Dobbs, William, June, 88
Dodd, Amos, Oct., 94
Dodd, Bishop, June, 105
Dodson, Caleb, Oct., 83
Donovan, Richard, Oct., 101
Doremus, Thomas, June, 94
Dorsey, Levin, Oct., 83
Doty, John, June, 113
Doty, Samuel, Oct., 100
Douglass, Hezekiah, Oct., 100
Downey, John, Oct., 83
Dresser, Richard, Jr., Oct., 108
Drew, Sylvanus, Oct., 89
Dudley, Ambrose, Oct., 102
Dudley, Jonathan, Oct., 83
Dunbar, Hamilton, 115
Duncan, George, Oct., 96
Dunham, Jonathan, June, 112

Dunn, Jeremiah, June, 95
Dutton, Thomas, June, 95

Eastman, Enoch, June, 117
Eddy, Nathan, June, 118; Oct., 79
Edgell, John, Oct., 103
Edmonstone, Thomas, June, 93
Edwards, John, Oct., 85
Eels, Jeremiah Beard, June, 91
Egbert, Abraham, Oct., 92
Egerton, Ariel, June, 114
Elliott, John, June, 84
Ellis, John, Oct., 101
Ellis, Joseph, Oct., 84
Ellison, Robert, Oct., 107
Ely, Adriel, Oct., 84
Ely, John, Oct., 84
Ely, Moses, Oct., 79
Ely, Robert, Oct., 106
Emerson, Jonathan, June, 96
Emerson, Nathaniel, June, 95
Ettelin, David Gottlieb, Oct., 105
Eustis, Thomas, June, 96
Evans, Amos, Oct., 85
Evans, Peter, June, 112
Everitt, Abner, June, 117
Ewell, John, June, 96
Eyanson, John, Oct., 99

Farnham, Thomas, Oct., 87
Farnsworth, Gershom, June, 115
Feeter, William, June, 84
Ferry, Eliphalet, Oct., 94
Field, Joshua, Oct., 89
Finney, Josiah, Oct., 84, 85
Finney, Lazarus, June, 103
Firestone, Matthias, Oct., 78
Fisher, John, Oct., 85
Fisk, Stephen, June, 96
Fiske, William, June, 93
Fitch, Elisha, June, 103
Fletcher, Daniel, June, 108
Flint, Samuel, Oct., 75
Fogg, Jeremiah, Oct., 77
Folsom, Benjamin, Oct., 78
Fooks, Jesse, Oct., 82
Forbush, David, June, 112
Ford, Jacob, Oct., 90
Ford, Jonathan, Oct., 85
Fordyce, Henry, Oct., 99
Forney, Peter, Oct., 86
Foster, Antony, Jr., Oct., 86
Foster, Henry, June, 92
Foster, Jedidiah, June, 96
Fowle, Samuel, Oct., 106
Fowler, Samuel, June, 97
Frank, Lawrence, Oct., 86
Freeman, Samuel, June, 104
French, Ezra, Oct., 81
Friend, Tobias, June, 114
Fulford, John, Oct., 85

Fuller, Amos, June, 100
Fuller, Joseph, Oct., 82

Gabbert, Michael, June, 121
Gage, Nathaniel, June, 110
Galbreath (Gilbreath), Robert, June, 97
Gallup, Nathan, June, 117
Gannett, Henry, June, 97
Gantt, Edward, June, 97
Gardner, Aaron, June, 110
Garnsey (Guernsey), Joel, June, 87
Gaston, James, June, 95
Gaston, John, June, 95
Gaston, Stephen, June, 95
Gates, Lemuel, Oct., 86
Gates, Luther, June, 88
Gaylord, Aaron, Oct., 101
Gaylord, David, June, 96
George, John Conrad, Oct., 93
Gerrish, Henry, June, 121
Gibbs, Julius, June, 98
Gibson, Abraham, June, 84
Gilbert, Benjamin, Oct., 87
Gile, Ezekill (Ezekiel), June, 89
Giles, Samuel, June, 118
Gilfiillan, Alexander, Oct., 87
Gilfillan, James, Oct., 87
Gill, Jonathan, Oct., 87
Gilliam, Robert, Oct., 92
Giben, David, June, 108
Glover, Henry, Oct., 99
Goddard, Joseph, Oct., 99
Goff, Ezra, June, 97
Goldsborough, Robert, Oct., 88
Goodenow, Eliab, Oct., 88
Goodrich, Edward, Oct., 86
Goodridge, Allen, June, 92
Goodwin, William, June, 92
Goodyear, Ludwick, Oct., 77
Gore, Obadiah, June, 84; Oct., 88
Gore, Obadiah, Jr., June, 93
Gorton, Samuel, June, 85
Gould, Jacob, June, 101
Goss, Zebulon, Oct., 96
Gotshall, Michael, Oct., 88
Gould, William, June, 98
Gove, Winthrop, Oct., 111
Gowdy, Alexander, Oct., 76
Graff, Andrew, June, 110
Graff, George, June, 97
Graham, William, Oct., 88
Grannis, Edward, Oct., 88
Gregory, Ebenezer, June, 86
Gregory, Joseph, June, 86
Gregory, Nathan, June, 98
Griggs, Ichabod, June, 121
Grout, Elijah, June, 102
Guard, Alexander, Oct., 95
Guild, Jesse, June, 98
Gunn, Richard, Oct., 89

Hadden, Thomas, June, 113
Hadden, Thomas, Jr., June, 113
Hall, Richard, June, 85
Hallock, Richard, June, 122
Hall, Zephaniah, Oct., 85
Halsey, John, June, 116
Hamilton, William, Oct., 89
Hammer, Samuel, June, 91
Handy, Ebenezer, June, 116
Hanna, Robert, Oct., 89
Hansell, Anthony, June, 113
Harman, George, June, 98
Harrington, Thaddeus, June, 98
Harris, Benjamin, June, 103
Harris, George, June, 85
Harris, Robert, June, 86
Harris, Squire, June, 84
Harrison, Benjamin, Oct., 101
Harrison, Isaac, Oct., 90
Harrison, Silas, June, 94
Hart, James, June, 109
Hart, Joseph, June, 103
Harvey, Nathan, June, 89
Haskins, Joshua, June, 109
Hathaway, Jacob, Oct., 82
Haven, David, Oct., 88
Hawley, Amos, June, 111
Hawks, Samuel, Oct., 90
Hayes, Joseph, II, Oct., 95
Hays, John, Oct., 85
Heady, James, Oct., 97
Heald, Daniel, June, 98
Healy, Jabez, June, 98
Heath, Daniel, June, 120
Hendee, Caleb, Jr., June, 99
Hendricks, Isaac, June, 91
Herrick, Israel, June, 95
Hershey, Christian, June, 99
Hess, Han Jost, June, 106
Heuston, William, June, 100
Hewson, John, Oct., 90
Higgins, Eleazer, June, 85
Higgins, Levi, June, 98
Hildreth, Zachariah, Oct., 112
Hill, Ebenezer, June, 119
Hill, George, June, 99
Hill, Green, June, 99
Hitchcock, Benjamin, June, 111
Hitchcock, Daniel, Oct., 91
Hogeboom, Lawrence, June, 98
Holcomb, Asahel, June, 106
Holden, John, June, 100
Holland, Joseph, Oct., 91
Holland, Richard, June, 98
Holman, Thomas, Oct., 92
Holt, William, June, 100
Hopkins, Oliver, Oct., 79
Horton, Daniel, Oct., 91
Horton, Lemuel, June, 85
Hough, Justus, June, 109
Hovey, Nathaniel, Oct., 106

Howard, John, Oct., 91
Howard, William, Oct., 89
Howe, Asa, Oct., 81
Howe, Samuel, Oct., 91
Howell, Richard, June, 89
Hoyt, Comfort, Oct, 107
Hubbard, Joseph, Jr., Oct., 110
Huber, John, June, 94
Hueston, William, June, 100
Huff, Jacob, June, 104
Hughes, Chas. Honore Olivier de Vezin, Oct., —
Humrickhouse, Peter, June, 104
Huntoon, Josiah, Oct., 89
Huntting, Nathaniel, Oct., 76
Hurd, Samuel, June, 100
Hustis, Joseph, Oct., 104
Hustis, Robert, Oct., 104
Huston, Joseph, June, 105; Oct., 109
Huston, William, June, 103
Hutchin, William, June, 100
Hutchison, Cornelius, June, 100
Hutson, Thomas, June, 94

Ingraham, Jeremiah, June, 100
Irish, Benjamin, June, 100
Irwin (Irvin), Samuel, June, 84
Isham, John, Jr., Oct., 98

Jackson, George, Oct., 92
Jacobs, Simeon, June, 95
James, Thomas, Oct., 92
Jennerson, Moses, Oct., 103
Jewel, John, Oct., 83
Johnson, Daniel, June, 115
Johnson, John Boswell, June, 101
Johnson, Phineas, Oct., 106
Johnson, Samuel, Oct., 106
Judd, Herman, Oct., 101
Judd, Noah, June, 117
Junkin, Joseph, Oct., 93
Joy, Nehemiah, Oct., 93

Keffer, Martin, June, 107
Keller, Christopher, Oct., 93
Keller, Jeremiah, Oct., 77
Kellogg, Asa, Oct., 101
Kellogg, Levi, June, 122
Kellogg, Phineas, June, 98
Kelsey, Thomas, June, 101
Kendrick, William, June, 101
Kennedy, Daniel, June, 102
Key, Philip, Oct., 93
Kimball, Aaron, June, 102
Kimball, Daniel, Jr., June, 110
Kimball, Joseph, Oct., 80
Kimball, William, Oct., 102
Kingsbury, Daniel, June, 102
Kip, Cornelius, June, 102
Kirby, John, Oct., 96
Kitfield, Edward, Oct., 89

Kithcart, Joseph, June, 99
Knapp, Joseph, Oct., 84
Knight, Nathaniel, Oct., 103
Knowles, Seth, Oct., 109
Kraft, William, Oct., 105
Kurtz, John Nicholas, Oct., 94

Lamb, David, Oct., 88
Lamb, Joseph, June, 111
Lane, Ephraim, June, 105
Lane, Martin, June, 94; Oct., 88
Lansing, Jacob Jacoke, June, 98
Lapsley, John, June, 103; Oct., 77
Latham, Samuel, Oct., 76
Lawrence, Jonathan, Oct., 106
Leake, Elisha, June, 91
Leaman, George, Oct., 94
Leavens, Charles, Oct., 94
Le Baron, James, June, 107
Leeper, Andrew, Oct., 80
Leeper, Matthew, Oct., 80
Leland, Moses, Oct., 94
Leonard, Asa, June, 103
Leonard, David, Oct., 92
Lewis, Thomas, June, 88; Oct., 75, 78
Lewis, William, Oct., 107
Lightfoot, Philip, Oct., 102
Lillie, David, June, 111
Linton, Joseph, Oct., 84
Little, Benjamin, June, 103
Little, Moses, June, 96
Livingston, William, June, 96
Livingston, William, Jr., June, 96
Lobingier, Christopher, Oct., 95
Long, Nicholas, June, 99
Longenecker, Abraham, Oct., 95
Longfellow, Nathan, Oct., 95
Longley, Edmund, Oct., 95
Loomis, Abner, June, 103; Oct., 95
Loomis, Israel, Oct., 95
Losee, Simeon, June, 86
Lott, John, June, 120
Love, Alexander, Oct., 85
Love, James, Oct., 95
Lum, Stephen, Oct., 89
Lybarger, Ludwick, Oct., 95
Lyford, Francis, June, 116
Lyman, Abel, Oct., 100
Lynn, Felix, June, 107
Lytle, William, June, 89; Oct., 86, 93

MacDonald, William, Oct., 109
McAllister, William, June, 104
McCarrell, Thomas, Oct., 96
McClanahan, Thomas, June, 115
McClary, Michael, June, 115; Oct., 93
McCrory, Thomas, June, 119
McFerrin, William, Oct., 96
McIlhany, James, Oct., 97
McIlhenny, Robert, June, 102
McKee, John, June, 105; Oct., 96

McKee, Joseph, June, 117
McMullin, Archibald, Oct., 78
McWilliams, William, June, 106
Macdonough, Thomas, June, 109
Mackey, John, 103, 105
Macomber, Joseph, Oct., 94
Magaw, William, June, 105
Magill, Charles, June, 90
Major, James, Oct., 95
Mann, Andrew, June, 104
Mann, Joseph, Oct., 77
Markley, George, Oct., 97
Marsh, Daniel, June, 117
Marsh, Simeon, June, 92
Marshall, Thomas, June, 84
Martin, David, Oct., 98
Martin, James, June, 104
Marvin, Ephraim, Oct., 97
Massie, Nathaniel, June, 94
Massie, Thomas, June, 106
Matlack, Timothy, June, 94
Matthews, Thomas, June, 118
Maxson, Zacheus, June, 106
Mayberry, Richard, June, 116
Mayberry, William, June, 116
Maynard, Malachi, June, 106
Mayo, Thomas, Oct., 97
Mead, Ethan, June, 106
Mead, Oliver, Oct., 97
Meeks, Joseph, June, 90
Meredith, David, June, 108
Meredith, Samuel, Oct., 86, 97
Merrill, John, Oct., 79
Mertz, George Henry, June, 116
Messer, Ebenezer, Oct., 97
Messinger, Isaac, Oct., 91
Meullion, Ennemond, June, 101
Miller, Increase, Oct., 90
Miller, Joseph, Oct., 75
Miller, Robert, Jr., June, 105; Oct., 97
Missimer (Masoner), Henry, Oct., 92
Mitchell, John, June, 106
Mitchell, William, June, 107
Montanye, Peter, Oct., 83
Moor, Daniel, Oct., 111
Moore, James, Oct., 84
Moore, Josiah, June, 110
Morehouse, Simeon, Oct., 89
Morgan, William, June, 117
Morrill, Joseph, June, 101
Morse, Amos, June, 114; Oct., 98
Morton, Joseph, Oct., 93
Moseley, Joseph, June, 106
Moulthrop, John, June, 107
Moulton, Freeborn, June, 107
Moulton, Joseph, June, 107
Moulton, Jotham, June, 107
Mount, Adam Dobbs, June, 112
Mumford, David, June, 120
Munday, Samuel, June, 88
Munroe, Nathan, June, 107

Munson, Walter, June, 100
Murray, Leckey, June, 87
Myers, Michael, Oct., 80

Nason, Willoughby, Oct., 99
Neff, Jacob, Oct., 102
Nelson, Robert, June, 103
Newberry, Amasa, June, 108
Newcomb, William, Oct., 99
Newkirk, John, June, 113
Newton, Joseph, Oct., 88
Newton, Seth, Oct., 83
Nicholls, William, June, 112
North, Roger, Oct., 85
North, Thomas, Oct., 103
Norton, Jonathan, June, 109
Null, Philip, Oct., 99
Nutt, William, June, 108
Nutting, John, Oct., 77

Olds, Benjamin, June, 114
Oliver, John, June, 116
Olmstead, Jared, June, 87
Olmstead, Samuel, June, 87
O'Neal, Barnett (Bryan), Oct., 99
Oram, Darby, June, 99
Orr, Robert, Oct., 77
Osborn, Peter, Oct., 99
Outwater, John, Oct., 77
Overbagh, John Jurry, June, 108
Overbagh, John Jurry, Jr., June, 108
Overton, Nathaniel, Oct., 100
Owens, Thomas, June, 108

Packer, Job E., June, 105
Paddock, Thomas, Oct., 76
Paine, David, June, 115
Parke, Joseph, June, 101
Parker, Benjamin, Oct., 100
Parker, David, Oct., 102
Parker, John, Oct., 97
Parkhurst, Jonathan, June, 108
Parson, Andrew, Oct., 84
Parsons, Samuel, Oct., 100
Patrick, William, June, 107
Pattimore, John, Oct., 92
Patton, John, June, 107
Paulding, Joseph, Jr., Oct., 87
Paul, John, Oct., 88
Payne, Edward, Oct., 107
Peach, William, June, 109
Peavey, Peter, Oct., 100
Peck, Darius, June, 109
Peck, Ichabod, Jr., Oct., 79
Peck, Nathan, June, 92
Peden, Thomas, June, 97
Peirsol (Pearsall), Sampson, Oct., 91
Pendexter, Paul, Oct., 100
Penneyer, Jesse, Oct., 100
Perkins, Ithial, June, 116
Perin, Lemuel, June, 91

Perrin, David, June, 109
Perrin (Perin), Jesse, June, 91
Perrine, James, June, 93
Perry, James, Oct., 99
Perry, Micah, June, 110
Pershing, Frederick, June, 110
Peters, Absalom, June, 117
Peters, John, Oct., 107
Petrie (Petry), William, 121
Petts, Lemuel, Oct., 113
Phelps, Ebenezer, Oct., 108
Philips, Jonas, June, 103, 110
Phillips, David, Oct., 101
Phillips, Jonas, Oct., 101
Phillips, Mark, Oct., 86
Phillips, Samuel, Jr., June, 110
Piatt, Jacob, Oct., 110
Pickering, James, Oct., 82
Pierce, Isaac, Oct., 101
Pierson, David, June, 110
Pike, Benjamin, June, 106
Pilsbury, Stephen, Oct., 90
Pinney, Eleazer, June, 95
Pinney, Isaac, Oct., 80
Plummer, Beard, June, 110
Plummer, Bitfield, June, 103
Polk, Ezekiel, Oct., 101
Polk, William, Oct., 93
Pollard, Joseph, June, 110
Pond, Elijah, June, 88
Pool, Samuel, June, 105
Pope, Seth, June, 111
Powers, Josiah, June, 97
Pratt, Phineas, Oct., 109
Prudden, Newton, June, 111
Pugh, John, Oct., 101
Putman, John, Oct., 103
Putnam, David, June, 112
Putnam, Israel, June, 111

Quarles, James, Oct., 86
Quick, Jacobus, June, 89
Quimby, Aaron, Oct., 101
Quimby, Josiah, Oct., 101

Ransom, Bliss, Oct., 102
Rathbun, Samuel, Jr., June, 112
Ray, William, Oct., 102
Read, Jonathan, June, 92
Read, Martin, June, 92
Read, Nathan, June, 92
Reading, Joseph, Oct., 102
Reading, Thomas, 91
Reed, Benjamin, June, 111
Reed, Moses, Oct., 113
Reed, William, Oct., 102
Reese, David, June, 108
Reese, Thomas, June, 108
Reid, George, June, 104
Revere, Paul, June, 102
Reynolds, Bernard, Oct., 112

Rhea, Joseph Campbell, Oct., 75
Rhoades, Samuel, June, 111
Rice, William, June, 101
Rich, Lemuel, Oct., 105
Richards, John, June, 118
Richards, William, Oct., 105
Richardson, Bradbury, Oct., 102
Richardson, Charles, Oct., 97
Richardson, John, Oct., 109
Richardson, Thomas, Oct., 93
Richardson, Tilley, June, 87
Ridgway, James, Oct., 113
Ritter, Casper, June, 112
Roach, John, Oct, 113
Robbins, Luther, June, 112
Robins, Brintinel, June, 111
Robinson, Elijah, Oct., 79
Robinson, Randall, June, 112
Robinson, Samuel, Oct., 87
Rodman, Gilbert, Oct., 101
Rogers, Gideon, Oct., 82
Rogers, Joseph, Oct., 103
Rogers, Nathaniel, Oct., 107
Rosekrans, Jacobus, June, 107
Ross, John, Oct., 103
Ross, Perrin, Oct., 103
Ross, Reuben, Oct., 103
Root, Elisha, Oct., 102
Root, John, Oct., 103
Root, Oliver, Oct., 80
Royse, Solomon, Oct., 103
Rude, Caleb, Oct., 103
Russell, Aquila, June, 118
Ruth, Abraham, Oct., 93
Ruth, Andrew, Oct., 93

Sanborn, Josiah, June, 116
Sanders, John, June, 120
Sands, John, June, 112
Sargent, Ezra, Oct., 103
Sawyer, Abraham, Oct., 103
Sawyer, Cornelius, Oct., 91
Sawyer, Jonas, Oct., 91
Scammon, Samuel, Oct., 104
Schenck, Garret, June, 91
Schenck, John, Oct., 88
Schock, Matthias (Michael), Oct., 103
Schryver, Stephen, Oct., 87
Scott, Hugh, June, 112
Scott, Hugh, Jr., June, 112
Scott, James, Oct., 94
Scott, Joseph, Oct., 104, 105
Scoville, Edward, June, 119
Scudder, Richard, June, 102
Scurlock, Mial, June, 104
Seeber, Henry, Oct., 104
Seeber, William, Oct., 104
Seeley, John, June, 113
Seely, John, Oct., 93, 104
Selleck, Nathan (Nathaniel), June, 92
Sellew, Philip, June, 102, 113

Sevier, John, June, 97
Seward, John, Oct., 82
Shaffer, Frederick, June, 113
Shaffer, George, Oct., 98
Shannahan, John, Oct., 104
Sharp, John, Oct., 77
Shaw, Sylvanus, Oct., 91
Shedd, Oliver, June, 113
Shepherd, John, Oct., 86
Sherman, George, June, 113
Sherman, Thomas, June, 98
Shotwell, Isaiah, June, 113
Shotwell, John, June, 113; Oct., 105
Shurtleff, Benoni, Jr., Oct., 76
Simons, Adriel, Oct., 105
Simpson, Peter, Jr., June, 104
Skilton, Henry, June, 114
Sloan, Thomas, Oct., 105
Smith, Caleb, June, 90
Smith, Isaac, June, 114
Smith, John, June, 114
Smith, Matthew, Oct., 105
Smith, Michael, June, 114
Smith, Moses, June, 98
Smith, Phillip, Oct., 105
Smith, Samuel, Oct., 112
Smith, Stephen, Oct., 78
Smith, Theophilus Miles, June, 91
Smock, Hendrick, June, 91
Smock, John, June, 91
Snow, Benjamin, June, 102
Snow, Silas, June, 113
Space, John, June, 99; Oct., 90
Southard, Thomas, June, 110
Spalding, Eleazer, Oct., 84
Spalding, Jacob, June, 104
Spalding, Simeon, Oct., 112
Spaulding, Jonathan, Oct., 95
Spencer, Gideon, Oct., 105
Spencer, Thomas, Oct., 110
Spinning, Benjamin, June, 114
Spooner, Charles, June, 108
Spooner, Shearjashub, Oct., 99
Sprague, Amasa, Oct., 105
Sprague, James, June, 121
Sprague, Joshua, Oct., 87
Spraker, John, Oct., 78
Sproat, Ebenezer, June, 106
Stallings, Abram, Oct., 76
Stanhope, Joseph, June, 110
Stark, John, Oct., 99
Starr, Daniel, June, 92
Starr, Ezra, June, 92
Statesir, John, Oct., 105
Steadman, William, Oct., 106
Stebbins, Nehemiah, June, 115
Sterling, William, Oct., 106
Stetson (Stutson), Stephen, June, 109
Stevens, Nathaniel, Oct., 106
Stevens, Stephen A., June, 115
Stewart, Alexander, June, 115, 116

Stewart, Hugh, Oct., 113
Stickney, Moses, Oct., 109
Stillman, Joseph, Oct., 106
Stimpson, Andrew, Oct., 84
Stinchfield, William, Oct., 106
Stith, Joseph, Oct., 106
Stith, Richard, Oct., 106
Stockwell, Solomon, Oct., 107
Stoddard, Nathan, Oct., 107
Stokes, Richard, Oct., 111
Stone, Windsor, Oct., 107
Stow, Jonathan, June, 116
Stoy, Daniel, June, 114
Straight, Jacob, June, 88
Strayer, John, June, 113
Strayhorn, John, June, 109
Strowbridge, William, Oct., 87
Strope, Sebastian, Oct., 109
Sturtevant, Asa, Oct., 78
Sturtevant, Church, Oct., 100
Strong, John, Oct., 102
Sturgis, John, Oct., 92
Sumney, Jacob, June, 116
Sweet, Timothy, Oct., 85
Sweeting, Louis, Oct., 87
Sylvester, Peter, June, 117

Talbot, Matthew, Jr., 96
Talbot, Silas, Oct., 98
Talcott, Elizur, Oct., 90
Talcott, Joseph, Oct., 107
Taylor, David, Oct., 99
Taylor, James, 101
Taylor, John, Oct., 86
Taylor, Othniel, Oct., 109
Teegardin, Abraham, Oct., 108
Tempest, Robert, June, 97
Tenny, Benjamin, Oct., 79
Tenney, John, June, 110
Terrill, Amos, June, 87
Terrill, Edmund, Oct., 108
Tewksbury, James, June, 86
Thomas, Daniel, Oct., 98
Thomson, William, June, 97
Thompson, Jonathan, Oct., 108
Thralls, Richard, June, 117
Thurber, Samuel, Oct., 107
Tillman, John, June, 106
Timberlake, John, Oct., 108
Tingley, Nathan, Oct., 108
Titcomb, Benjamin, Oct., 110
Tittle, Peter, Jr., Oct., 108
Titus, Joseph, June, 117
Tiegarten, Abraham, Oct., 108
Todd, Jehiel, June, 117
Todd, Levi, June, 121
Tolman, Benjamin, Oct., 108
Torrey, Lemuel, June, 86
Tower, Stephen, Oct., 75, 87
Towne, Archaelaus, Oct., 81
Towne, Josiah, Oct., 108

Tracy, Thomas, June, 86
Treadwell, Moses, June, 121
Tremper, Michael, June, 86
Trepagnier, Pedro (Pierre), Oct., 92
Tripp, Acus, Oct., 108
Trousdale, James, June, 84
Trowbridge, Luther S., June., 106
Truxton, Thomas, Oct., 98
Tucker, Joseph, Oct., 75
Tucker, Nathaniel, Oct., 108
Turner, Jacob, Oct., 102
Turner, Seth, Oct, 83
Turrill, James, June, 120
Tuthill, James, Jr., Oct., 107
Tuttle, Abel, Oct., 76
Tyler, Asa, June, 115
Tyler, James, June, 119

Upton, Jacob, Oct., 109

Van Buskirk, Isaac, June, 121
Vance, William, June, 118
Vanderhof, Cornelius, Oct., 96
Van Dorn, Jacob, June, 91
Van Dorn, Peter, June, 91
Van Dyke, Jacob, Oct., 90
Van Horn, Henry, June, 118
Van Horn, Isaiah, June, 118
Van Kirk, Samuel, Oct., 94
Van Reipen, Daniel, June, 87
Van Tassell, John, Oct., 112
Vantreese, Joseph, June, 106
Van Voorhis, Jerome, Oct., 104
Van Vorst (Voast), Johannes Jacobus, June, 118
Van Woert, Jacob R., June, 118
Van Woert, Johannes (John), June, 98
Varian, James, Oct., 106
Vegthe (Vetter), Garrit, June, 94
Von Effinger, John Ignatius, Oct., 84
Vrooman, Samuel, Oct., 100

Wadsworth, Joseph, June, 88
Waggoner, John, June, 111
Wainwright, Thomas, June, 118
Waldo, Daniel, June, 118
Waldo, Edward, June, 96
Wales, Oliver, June, 118
Walker, Asa, Oct., 83
Walker, Isaac, Oct., 90
Walker, James, June, 119
Walker, Samuel, Oct., 109
Walling, Joseph, Oct., 109
Wallis, Nathaniel, Oct., 76
Walworth, Charles, Oct., 78
Ward, Andrew, June, 89
Ward, Jacob, Oct., 109
Wardwell, Jeremiah, Oct., 81
Washabaugh, Henry, Oct., 110
Washburn, Jonah, Jr., June, 119
Washburn, Jonah M., June, 119

Washington, Wm. Augustine, Oct., 94
Wasson, James, Oct., 81
Watkins, Nathan, Oct., 89
Watson, Thomas, June, 119
Weare, Mescheh, June, 85
Weaver, Jabez, June, 89; Oct., 80
Weaver, Michael, Oct., 82
Webb, Charles, Oct., 98
Webb, Ezekial, June, 95
Webb, Francis, June, 115
Webber, Charles, Oct., 110
Webster, Constant, June, 98, 119
Webster, David, June, 117
Weeks, Andrew, June, 119
Welcocks, William, June, 101
Weld, David, June, 109
Wellington, John, Oct., 110
Wells, James, June, 120
Wells, Thomas, Oct., 110
Welsh, John, June, 99
Wentworth, Daniel, June, 98
Wentworth, Henry, Oct., 91
Wentworth, William, June, 120
Westervelt, Casparus, June, 91
West, William, June, 120
Weymouth, Stephen, Oct., 110
Whaley, Benjamin, Oct., 89
Wheeler, Benjamin, Oct., 98
Wheeler, Elisha, June, 95
Whicker, William, June, 120
Whipple, Abraham, June, 106
Whipple, Jonathan, June, 116
Whitcomb, John, June, 119
White, James, Oct., 78, 111
Whiteside (Whitesides), Thomas, June, 120
Whiteside, Thomas, Oct., 111
White, William, Oct., 111
Whitford, Joshua, Oct., 98
Whiting, Francis, Oct., 110
Whitlock, John, June, 90
Whitmarsh, Jacob, June, 105
Whitney, Cornelius, Oct., 111
Whitney, Darling, Oct., 111
Whitney, Eliphalet, Oct., 111
Whitney, Jonathan, June, 109
Wiggins, William, Jr., Oct., 97
Wigton, John, June, 92
Wilcox, Josiah, June, 120
Wild, Jonathan, Oct., 82
Wilkins, Aquila, June, 93
Wilkinson, John, Oct., 90
Willard, John, Oct., 111
Willett, Hartshorne, Oct., 94
Willey, Edward, June, 108
Willoughby, Edlyne, June, 121
Wiltse, William, Oct., 104
Wiltz, Don Lorenzo, Oct., 92
Winchester, William, June, 85
Winslow, Richard, Oct., 82
Witherspoon, John, June, 121
Withington, Edward, Oct., 112

THE PRESIDENT GENERAL .

OFFICIAL BULLETIN

OF THE

National Society
of the Sons of the American Revolution

Organized April 30, 1889

Incorporated by
Act of Congress, June 9, 1906

President General
W. I. LINCOLN ADAMS
Montclair, New Jersey

Published at Washington, D. C., in June, October, December, and March.
Entered as second-class matter, May 7, 1906, at the post-office at Washington, D. C., under the act of July 16, 1894.

Volume XVII	DECEMBER, 1922	Number 3

The OFFICIAL BULLETIN records action by the General Officers, the Board of Trustees, the Executive and other National Committees, lists of members deceased and of new members, and important doings of State Societies. In order that the OFFICIAL BULLETIN may be up to date, and to insure the preservation in the National Society archives of a complete history of the doings of the entire organization, State Societies and local Chapters are requested to communicate promptly to the Secretary General written or printed accounts of all meetings or celebrations, to forward copies of all notices, circulars, and other printed matter issued by them, and to notify him at once of dates of death of members.

PURPOSES AND OBJECTS OF THE S. A. R.

(EXTRACTS FROM CONSTITUTION)

The purposes and objects of this Society are declared to be patriotic, historical, and educational, and shall include those intended or designed to perpetuate the memory of the men who, by their services or sacrifices during the war of the American Revolution, achieved the independence of the American people; to unite and promote fellowship among their descendants; to inspire them and the community at large with a more profound reverence for the principles of the government founded by our forefathers; to encourage historical research in relation to the American Revolution; to acquire and preserve the records of the individual services of the patriots of the war, as well as documents, relics, and landmarks; to mark the scenes of the Revolution by appropriate memorials; to celebrate the anniversaries of the prominent events of the war and of the Revolutionary period; to foster true patriotism; to maintain and extend the institutions of American freedom, and to carry out the purposes expressed in the preamble of the Constitution of our country and the injunctions of Washington in his farewell address to the American people.

Qualifications for Membership

Any man shall be eligible to membership in the Society who, being of the age of twenty-one years or over and a citizen of good repute in the community, is the lineal descendant of an ancestor who was at all times unfailing in his loyalty to, and rendered active service in, the cause of American Independence, either as an officer, soldier, seaman, marine, militiaman or minute man, in the armed forces of the Continental Congress, or of any one of the several Colonies or States, or as a Signer of the Declaration of Independence, or as a member of a Committee of Safety or Correspondence, or as a member of any Continental, Provincial, or Colonial Congress or Legislature, or as a recognized patriot who performed actual service by overt acts of resistance to the authority of Great Britain.

Provided, however, that any male person, above the age of 18 years and under the age of 21 years, whose qualifications in regard to ancestry and personal character are as above prescribed, shall be eligible to a qualified membership to be known and designated as junior membership. . . .

Application for membership is made on standard blanks furnished by the State Societies. These blanks call for the place and date of birth and of death of the Revolutionary ancestor and the year of birth, of marriage, and of death of ancestors in intervening generations. Membership is based on one original claim; additional claims are filed on supplemental papers. The applications and supplementals are made in duplicate.

GENERAL OFFICERS ELECTED AT THE SPRINGFIELD CONGRESS, MAY 16, 1922

President General:

W. I. LINCOLN ADAMS, Montclair, New Jersey.

Vice-Presidents General:

HARRY T. LORD, Manchester, New Hampshire.
> New England (Maine, New Hampshire, Vermont, Massachusetts, Rhode Island, and Connecticut).

PHILIP F. LARNER, 918 F Street N. W., Washington, District of Columbia.
> Middle and Coast District (New York, New Jersey, Pennsylvania, Delaware, Maryland, District of Columbia, Virginia, North Carolina, South Carolina, Georgia, and Florida).

LOUIS A. BOWMAN, 30 North La Salle Street, Chicago, Illinois.
> Mississippi Valley, East District (Michigan, Wisconsin, Illinois, Indiana, Ohio, West Virginia, Kentucky, Tennessee, Alabama, and Mississippi).

HENRY B. HAWLEY, Des Moines, Iowa.
> Mississippi Valley, West District (Minnesota, North Dakota, South Dakota, Nebraska, Iowa, Kansas, Missouri, Oklahoma, Arkansas, Louisiana, and Texas).

GEORGE ALBERT SMITH, Utah Savings & Trust Building, Salt Lake City, Utah.
> Mountain and Pacific Coast District (Montana, Idaho, Wyoming, Nevada, Utah, Colorado, Arizona, New Mexico, Oregon, Washington, California, Hawaii, and Philippines).

Secretary General:

FRANK BARTLETT STEELE, 183 St. James Place, Buffalo, New York.

Registrar General:

FRANCIS BARNUM CULVER, 2203 North Charles Street, Baltimore, Maryland; 918 F Street N. W., Washington, District of Columbia.

Treasurer General:

GEORGE McK. ROBERTS, Room 2126, 120 Broadway, New York City.

Historian General:

JOSEPH B. DOYLE, Steubenville, Ohio.

Chancellor General:

EUGENE C. BONNIWELL, City Court Building, Philadelphia, Pennsylvania.

Genealogist General:

WALTER K. WATKINS, 9 Ashburton Place, Boston, Massachusetts.

Chaplain General:

Rev. FREDERICK W. PERKINS, D. D., 27 Deer Cove, Lynn, Massachusetts.

BOARD OF TRUSTEES

The General Officers, together with one member from each State Society, constitute the Board of Trustees of the National Society. The following Trustees for the several States were elected at the Springfield Congress, May 16, 1922, to serve until their successors are elected at the Congress to be held at Nashville, Tenn., in May, 1923:

Alabama, (vacant) ; Arizona, W. B. Twitchell, Phœnix ; Arkansas, George W. Clark, Little Rock; California, Seabury C. Mastick, New York City; Colorado, Victor E. Keyes, Denver; Connecticut, Herbert H. White, Hartford; Delaware, Hon. Horace Wilson, Wilmington; District of Columbia, Albert D. Spangler, Washington; Far Eastern Society, H. Lawrence Noble, Manila; Florida, Dr. F. G. Renshaw, Pensacola; Society in France, (vacant); Hawaiian Society, Donald S. Bowman, Honolulu; Georgia, Allan Waters, Atlanta; Idaho, M. A. Wood, Boise; Illinois, Dorr E. Felt, Chicago; Indiana, Charles C. Jewett, Terre Haute; Iowa, Elmer E. Wentworth, State Center; Kansas, John M. Meade, Topeka; Kentucky, Marvin Lewis, Louisville, Louisiana, Col. C. Robert Churchill, New Orleans; Maine, William B. Berry, Gardiner; Maryland, Hon. Henry Stockbridge, Baltimore; Massachusetts, George Hale Nutting, Boston; Michigan, Albert M. Henry, Detroit; Minnesota, Charles E. Rittenhouse, Minneapolis; Mississippi, Hon. Gordon G. Lyell, Jackson; Missouri, George R. Merrill, St. Louis; Montana, Marcus Whritenour, Helena; Nebraska, Benjamin F. Bailey, Lincoln; Nevada, (vacant); New Hampshire, Hon. Harry T. ' Lord, Manchester; New Jersey, Charles Symmes Kiggins, Elizabeth; New Mexico, George G. Klock, Albuquerque; New York, Louis Annin Ames, New York; North Carolina, (vacant); North Dakota, Howard E. Simpson, Grand Forks; Ohio, Hon. Warren G. Harding, Washington, D. C.; Oklahoma, W. A. Jennings, Oklahoma City; Oregon, Wallace McCamant, Portland; Pennsylvania, James A. Wakefield, Pittsburgh; Rhode Island, Hon. Arthur P. Sumner, Providence; South Carolina, (vacant); South Dakota, F. M. Mills, Sioux Falls; Tennessee, Leland Hume, Nashville; Texas, C. B. Dorchester, Sherman; Utah, Daniel S. Spencer, Salt Lake City; Vermont, William Jeffrey, Montpelier; Virginia, Arthur B. Clarke, Richmond; Washington, Ernest B. Hussey, Seattle; Wisconsin, Walter H. Wright, Milwaukee; Wyoming, Warren Richardson, Cheyenne.

PRESIDENTS AND SECRETARIES OF STATE SOCIETIES

ARIZONA—President, Lloyd B. Christie, 116 N. 1 Avenue, Phœnix.
  Secretary, Clarence P. Woodbury, 1509 Grand Avenue, Phœnix.
  Treasurer, Kenneth Freeland, Phœnix.

ARKANSAS—President, John M. Bracey,* Little Rock.
  Vice-President, Frank D. Leaming.
  Secretary, Fay Hempstead, Little Rock.
  Treasurer, Thomas M. Cory, Little Rock.

CALIFORNIA—President, Charles E. Hale, 51 Main Street, San Francisco.
  Secretary-Registrar, Thomas A. Perkins, Mills Building, San Francisco.
  Treasurer, John C. Currier, 713 Merchants' Exchange Building, San Francisco.

COLORADO—President, Hon. George H. Bradfield, Greeley.
  Secretary, R. Harvey Boltwood, 511 15th St., Denver.
  Treasurer, Walter D. Wynkoop, Mt. States T. & T. Co., Denver.

CONNECTICUT—President, Hon. Rollin S. Woodruff, 210 Edwards Street, New Haven.
  Secretary, Frederick A. Doolittle, 117 Middle Street, Bridgeport.
  Treasurer, Charles G. Stone, P. O. Box 847, Hartford.

DELAWARE—President, Robert H. Richards, 1415 Delaware Avenue, Wilmington.
  Secretary-Treasurer-Registrar, Charles A. Rudolph, 900 Vanburen Street, Wilmington.

DISTRICT OF COLUMBIA—President, Selden M. Ely, Gales School Building, Washington.
  Secretary, Kenneth S. Wales, 110 Florence Court, E., Washington.
  Treasurer, Hilleary F. Offcutt, Jr., 1501 Crittenden Street N. W., Washington.

FAR EASTERN SOCIETY—President-Secretary, H. Lawrence Noble, P. O. Box 940, Manila, Philippine Islands.
  Treasurer, Herman Roy Hare.

FLORIDA—President, Dr. F. G. Renshaw, Pensacola.
  Secretary, John Hobart Cross, Pensacola.
  Treasurer-Registrar, F. F. Bingham, Pensacola.

SOCIETY IN FRANCE—Administered by Empire State Society.

GEORGIA—President, Allen Waters, P. O. Box 361, Atlanta.
  Secretary-Registrar, Arthur W. Falkinburg, 1301 Atlanta Trust Co. Building, Atlanta.
  Treasurer, William Alden, Box 172, Decatur.

HAWAII—President, Donald S. Bowman, Honolulu.
  Secretary, James T. Taylor, 207 Kauikeolani Building, Honolulu.
  Treasurer, Elmer T. Winant, Honolulu.

IDAHO—President, Albert H. Conner, Boise.
  Secretary and Treasurer, Frank G. Ensign, Boise.

ILLINOIS—President, James Edgar Brown, 30 North La Salle Street, Chicago.
  Secretary, Louis A. Bowman, 30 North La Salle Street, Chicago.
  Treasurer, Henry R. Kent, 30 North La Salle Street, Chicago.

INDIANA—President, Cornelius F. Posson, 538 East Drive, Woodruff Place, Indianapolis.
  Secretary and Treasurer, Edmund L. Parker, 511 East Walnut Street, Kokomo.

IOWA—President, Frank D. Harsh, Des Moines.
  Secretary, Captain Elbridge D. Hadley, 409 Franklin Avenue, Des Moines.
  Treasurer, William E. Barrett, 4815 Grand Avenue, Des Moines.

KANSAS—President, John M. Meade, Topeka.
  Secretary, Arthur H. Bennett, 434 Woodlawn Avenue, Topeka.
  Treasurer-Registrar, Walter E. Wilson, Topeka.

KENTUCKY—President, J. Swigert Taylor, Frankfort.
  Secretary, Ben F. Ewing, II, 903 Realty Building, Louisville.
  Treasurer, Alexander W. Tippett, U. S. Trust Co. Building, Louisville.

---

*Deceased.

LOUISIANA—President, C. Robert Churchill, 408 Canal Street, New Orleans.
    Secretary, Herbert P. Benton, 403 Carondelet Building, New Orleans.
    Treasurer, S. O. Landry, 616 Maison Blanche Building, New Orleans.

MAINE—President, William B. Berry, 42 Pleasant Street, Gardiner.
    Secretary, Francis L. Littlefield, 246 Spring Street, Portland.
    Treasurer, Enoch O. Greenleaf, Portland.

MARYLAND—President, Herbert Baker Flowers, 3008 N. Calvert Street, Baltimore.
    Secretary, George Sadtler Robertson, 1628 Linden Avenue, Baltimore.
    Treasurer, Benson Blake, Jr., 2320 N. Calvert St., Baltimore.

MASSACHUSETTS—President, Dr. Charles H. Bangs, Swampscott.
    Secretary, Walter K. Watkins, 9 Ashburton Place, Boston.
    Treasurer, Lieut.-Col. Charles M. Green, 78 Marlboro Street, Boston.

MICHIGAN—President, William P. Holliday, Detroit.
    Secretary, Raymond E. Van Syckle, 1729 Ford Building, Detroit.
    Treasurer, Frank G. Smith, 1183 W. Boston Boulevard, Detroit.

MINNESOTA—President, Kenneth G. Brill, 43 South Hamline Avenue, St. Paul.
    Secretary, Charles H. Bronson, 48 East Fourth Street, St. Paul.
    Treasurer, Charles W. Eddy, 302 Pittsburg Building, St. Paul.

MISSISSIPPI—President, Judge Gordon Garland Lyell, Jackson.
    Secretary and Treasurer, William H. Pullen, Mechanics' Bank Building, Jackson.

MISSOURI—President, Linn Paine, 904 Locust Street, St. Louis.
    Secretary, J. Alonzo Matthews, 901 Pontiac Building, St. Louis.
    Treasurer, I. Shreve Carter, 308 Merchant La Clede Building, St. Louis.

MONTANA—President, Paris B. Bartley,* Helena.
    Secretary and Treasurer, Leslie Sulgrove, Helena.

NEBRASKA—President, Benjamin F. Bailey, 506 1st National Bank Building, Lincoln.
    Secretary, Addison E. Sheldon, 1319 South 23d Street, Lincoln.
    Treasurer, C. E. Bardwell, 522 Terminal Building, Lincoln.

NEVADA—President, Rt. Rev. George C. Huntting, 505 Ridge Street, Reno.

NEW HAMPSHIRE—President, Prof. Ashley K. Hardy, Hanover.
    Secretary and Treasurer, Rufus H. Baker, 12 Liberty Street, Concord.

NEW JERSEY—President, Hon. Adrian Lyon, Perth Amboy.
    Secretary, David L. Pierson, 33 Lombardy Street, Newark.
    Treasurer, Frank E. Quinby, 33 Lombardy Street, Newark.

NEW MEXICO—President, C. C. Manning, Gallup.
    Secretary, Frank W. Graham, Albuquerque.
    Treasurer, Orvil A. Matson, Albuquerque.

NEW YORK—President, George D. Bangs, Tribune Building, New York City.
    Secretary, Major Charles A. Du Bois, 220 Broadway, New York City.
    Treasurer, James de la Montanye, 220 Broadway, New York City.

NORTH CAROLINA—Special Organizer for North and South Carolina, Maj. John F. Jones,
    Internal Revenue Office, Columbia, S. C.

NORTH DAKOTA—President, Howard E. Simpson, University of North Dakota, Grand Forks.
    Secretary-Registrar, Walter R. Reed, 407 7th Avenue, So., Fargo.
    Treasurer, Willis E. Fuller, Northern National Bank, Grand Forks.

OHIO—President, Edward L. Shuey, Dayton.
    Secretary-Registrar, W. L. Curry, Box 645, Columbus.
    Treasurer, S. G. Harvey, 650 Oakwood Avenue, Toledo.

OKLAHOMA—President, George L. Bowman, Kingfisher.
    Secretary-Treasurer, Edward F. McKay, 536 West 31st Street, Oklahoma City.

OREGON—President, B. B. Beekman, 601 Platt Building, Portland.
    Secretary, B. A. Thaxter, Post Office Box 832, Portland.
    Treasurer, A. A. Lindsley, Henry Building, Portland.

---

*Deceased.

PENNSYLVANIA—President, W. C. Lyne, Farmers' Bank Building, Pittsburgh.
    Secretary, Francis Armstrong, Jr., 515 Wood Street, Pittsburgh.
    Treasurer, A. W. Wall, Farmers' Bank Building, Pittsburgh.

RHODE ISLAND—President, Herbert A. Rice, 809 Hospital Trust Building, Providence.
    Secretary, Theodore E. Dexter, 104 Clay Street, Central Falls.
    Treasurer, William L. Sweet, Box 1515, Providence.

SOUTH CAROLINA—Special Organizer for North and South Carolina, Maj. John F. Jones,
    Internal Revenue Office, Columbia, S. C.

SOUTH DAKOTA—President, Col. A. B. Sessions, Sioux Falls.
    Secretary-Registrar, T. W. Dwight, Sioux Falls.
    Treasurer, B. H. Requa, Sioux Falls.

TENNESSEE—President, William K. Boardman, Nashville.
    Vice-President-at-Large, Frederick W. Millspaugh, Nashville.
    Secretary-Registrar, J. Tyree Fain, 315 North 2d Avenue, Nashville.
    Treasurer, Carey Folk, 411 Union Street, Nashville.

TEXAS—President, C. B. Dorchester, Sherman.
    Secretary-Treasurer, Walter S. Mayer, 1404 39th Street, Galveston.

UTAH—President, Robert E. McConaughy, 1079 E. 2d South Street, Salt Lake City.
    Secretary, Gordon Lines Hutchins, Dooly Building, Salt Lake City.
    Treasurer, Seth Warner Morrison, Jr., 32 S. 7th East Street, Salt Lake City.

VERMONT—President, William H. Jeffrey, Montpelier.
    Secretary, Walter H. Crockett, Burlington.
    Treasurer, Clarence L. Smith, Burlington.

VIRGINIA—President, Arthur B. Clarke, 616 American National Bank Building, Richmond.
    Secretary and Treasurer, William E. Crawford, 700 Travelers' Building, Richmond.

WASHINGTON—President, Walter Burges Beals, Haller Building, Seattle.
    Secretary, Henry J. Gorin, 322 Central Building, Seattle.
    Treasurer, Kenneth P. Hussey, 903 Boylston Avenue, Seattle.

WISCONSIN—President, Henry S. Sloan, 216 W. Water Street, Milwaukee.
    Secretary, Emmett A. Donnelly, 1030 Wells Building, Milwaukee.
    Treasurer, William Stark Smith, 373 Lake Drive, Milwaukee.

WYOMING—President, David A. Haggard, Cheyenne.
    Secretary, Maurice Groshon, Cheyenne.
    Treasurer, James B. Guthrie, Cheyenne.

Minutes of the Meeting of the Executive Committee of the National Society, Sons of the American Revolution, Held at the Union League Club, New York, N. Y., October 31, 1922.

Present: The President General, W. I. Lincoln Adams, of New Jersey; Directors General Louis Annin Ames, of New York; George E. Pomeroy, of Ohio; Arthur P. Sumner, of Rhode Island; Marvin Lewis, of Kentucky, and Director General and Vice-President General Harry T. Lord, of New Hampshire.

The meeting was called to order by the chairman, President General Adams, who presided.

The Secretary General recorded.

The report of the Secretary General was read and ordered filed.

The report of the Treasurer General was read and ordered filed.

On motion of Director General Ames, the courtesies of the floor were granted to President George D. Bangs, of the Empire State Society, and George McK. Roberts, Treasurer General, who were present by invitation.

Upon the report of the Treasurer General that he had reduced the outstanding indebtedness of the Society to an almost nominal sum, it was moved by Director

General Sumner that certain uncollectable claims against certain societies should be charged off the books. Carried.

The following resolution was presented by Director General Lewis, of Kentucky:

Resolved, That the proper officers of this Society of the Sons of the American Revolution be authorized to borrow a sum, not to exceed seven thousand dollars ($7,000), upon the securities of the Society, if necessary, and that said sum be borrowed from the Corn Exchange National Bank.

The resolution was unanimously adopted.

The matter of the cost of printing the BULLETIN and other necessary documents, blanks, etc., was fully and thoroughly discussed.

It was moved by Director General Pomeroy that the matter of printing in all its aspects, as to cost, location, and printing firm, be left to the President General and the Secretary General, with full power to act. Carried.

The matter of accepting advertising for the BULLETIN was fully and freely discussed, and it was moved by Director General Pomeroy that a committee upon publication be appointed from the Executive Committee, with authority to accept a limited amount of advertising of a character appropriate to our publication. Carried.

The chairman called for nominations for this committee, and President General Adams, Director General Ames, and Secretary General Steele were appointed such committee, with power to accept such advertising and publish it in the next and following issues of the BULLETIN.

The matter of issuing blanks for North and South Carolina for Major Jones and the same for Alabama and Mississippi for Colonel Churchill was discussed, and it was moved by Director General Lord that no charge be made for these blanks, and that Major Jones be reimbursed for any expense he has incurred for printing and postage. Carried.

It was moved by Director General Lewis that the dues of the members of the Texas Society who were in the service of the United States during the World War be remitted during their period of service. Carried.

The matter of the formation of a Society in London, England, was discussed, and it was the sense of the committee that any new members who join from London or England be allowed to join any State Society desired by them, and when enough members have joined to form a new Society under the National Constitution that these members be authorized to form such Society.

On motion of Director General Pomeroy, the matter of a standard membership card was referred to the Committee on Publication.

It was moved by Director General Ames that the Secretary General have the power to issue a short folder of information as to the objects, purposes, and qualifications for membership.

The matter of an extension of time to file applications without initiation fee from the Indiana Society was discussed, and the committee decided that it had no power to extend such time. The Secretary General was directed to write to the Indiana Society that all applications dated and received by said Society on or before October 1 will be accepted.

The matter of publishing the American's Creed was left to President General Adams to take up with Mr. Matthew Page Andrews.

The matter of the restriction of the use of historical names was referred to Director General Sumner for consideration.

It was moved by Director General Pomeroy that the matter of the pledge to the flag and a ritual to be used at the meetings and gatherings of the State Societies and Chapters of the Society be referred to the Committee on Colors and Ceremonies, and it is suggested that they prepare a ritual for use at such meetings and gatherings, with a uniform pledge. Carried.

The Secretary General was directed to send expressions of the deepest sympathy to former Director General Albert M. Henry, of Detroit, on account of his serious illness.

The Secretary General was directed to answer the letter of Past President General Wallace McCamant and extend the greetings of the Executive Committee to him.

Meeting adjourned.

Frank B. Steele

Secretary General.

ANNOUNCEMENTS

At the time of the meeting of the Executive Committee held recently in New York there was a strong sentiment that when the Congress was held in Nashville next May a special train or at least special cars should be run. It is known that the plans that are developing by the enthusiastic compatriots of that hospitable southern city are not only unique, but will show the visiting delegates from all over the country that no mistake was made in holding the Congress of 1923 in Nashville. This Congress should be one of the largest in the history of the organization and every man who is elected a delegate should not only decide to attend, but also plan to take his wife and family with him. Word has been received from the committee in charge that the women who are assisting the Nashville compatriots are making a special feature of entertaining the ladies accompanying delegates and many delightful functions will be held.

As the delegates from the northern and eastern States will attend in large numbers, there will be little trouble in securing a special train at no greater expense than the regular fare and possibly at less expense. Accordingly this appeal is made to delegates who when elected contemplate attending to get in touch with the Secretary General or with their respective State officers at as early a date as possible in order that plans for such special train or cars can be made and that if possible announcement of details may be made in the March OFFICIAL BULLETIN.

The Secretary General respectfully requests all State Secretaries and others sending in material for publication in the BULLETIN, to kindly get all copy to the office of the Secretary General on or before the 15th of the month of publication, namely, October, December, March, and June.

Year Books of the National Society for the following years may be obtained by applying to the office of the Registrar General, 918 F Street N. W., Washington, D. C., and enclosing 14 cents postage for each copy: 1903, 1905, 1910, 1911, 1913, 1915, 1920.

IN MEMORIAM

The Sons of the American Revolution mourn the loss of that sterling patriot, Albert McKee Henry, who was called to his reward on November 3, 1922.

Compatriot Henry was born at Grand Rapids, Mich., September 20, 1845, graduated from the University of Michigan 1867, and resided in Detroit since 1875. He became a member of the Michigan Society, S. A. R., October 25, 1895, serving as its Vice-President in 1909, President 1913-14 and 1915, and as a delegate to the National Congress since 1906.

In the National Society Compatriot Henry served with distinction on many important committees and was always active in the deliberations of the Congress. The value of his work during the twelve years of his membership on the Board of Trustees, five years on the National Executive Committee, and a year as Vice-President General cannot be overestimated.

In civil affairs his talents and judgment were early recognized, both city and State calling him to their service from time to time.

His stalwart manhood, high character, genial personality, and true Americanism, exemplifying the best of American inheritance, endeared him to all.

(Signed)   ELMER M. WENTWORTH, *Chairman.*
LOUIS ANNIN AMES.
MORRIS B. BEARDSLEY.

MRS. MARY SMITH LOCKWOOD

Mrs. Mary Smith Lockwood, one of the founders of the Daughters of the American Revolution, died November 10, at the Jordan Hospital, Plymouth, Mass., where she had beeen a patient since September. She was 91 years old.

Mrs Lockwood, "Little Mother to the Daughters of the American Revolution," was the last survivor of the little group of 18 women patriots who organized that body more than 30 years ago; and despite her nearly full century of years, she was one of the most active members of the organization almost up to the time of her last illness.

ROBERT W. HEMPHILL, JR.

Following is a resolution drafted by Washtenaw Chapter, No. 3, S. A. R., in commemoration of Robert W. Hemphill, Jr., whose death occurred December 8, 1922, in Ypsilanti:

"In the death of Robert W. Hemphill, Jr., Washtenaw Chapter, No. 3, Sons of the American Revolution, loses the third member of the original Chapter. Compatriot Hemphill always manifested a helpful interest in all things pertaining to the Society's welfare and served as President of the Chapter in the year 1917. He was admitted to Michigan Society in 1898.

"True to his inheritance as a member of the S. A. R., Compatriot Hemphill volunteered his services to his country during the World War, filling several important positions with great credit.

"His memory will always be cherished by his many friends both because of his sterling worth as a man and of his appreciation of his fellows.

"It is, therefore, with a feeling of a very distinct loss that the members of this Society extend to the bereaved family and relatives their heartfelt sympathy.

"The Secretary of the Chapter is directed to convey a copy of these resolutions to the family and to have them publish in *The Times-News* and in the OFFICIAL BULLETIN of the National Society.
"Washtenaw Chapter, No. 3, S. A. R.

W. B. HINSDALE,
President.
W. HACKLEY BUTLER,
Secretary.

Request endorsed by *Raymond E. Van Syckle*, Secretary Michigan Society.

ACTIVITIES OF THE PRESIDENT GENERAL

As will be seen from the following reports of our various State Societies, the President General has not only maintained his earlier services to our organization, but during the past quarter has actually increased his official activities.

He continues his practice to accept invitations from all State Societies which do not conflict, and he is in demand, of course, for other patriotic organizations and occasions as well.

When distance, or a conflict of dates, prevents him from being present at some function of importance, he often sends a letter or telegram of official greeting. Thus he telegraphed the California compatriots, through T. A. Perkins, on the occasion of their celebration of the Surrender at Yorktown, his official and personal greetings.

To Compatriot Linn Paine, President of the Missouri Society and formerly Vice-President General of the National Society, he likewise sent a letter-message on the occasion of their annual banquet in St. Louis the same night. He personally attended the banquet and meeting of the Maryland Society in Baltimore that evening and made the principal address.

To Compatriot A. W. Wall, Treasurer of the Pennsylvania Society, he sent the following message, which was read at the meeting of the Pennsylvania compatriots on the evening of Armistice Day, together with similar messages from Compatriot Warren G. Harding, President of the United States; Compatriot Charles E. Hughes, Secretary of State, and General John J. Pershing. The President General's message was as follows:

"I desire to convey to my Pennsylvania compatriots, through you, sir, my most cordial official and personal greetings on this historic anniversary.

"And may I remind them of the significant and encouraging fact that in the Great World War, as in all of our other wars, the descendants of Revolutionary stock were true to the ideals of their heroic forefathers.

"They promptly and proudly volunteered their services, many enlisting in the armies of our Allies even before our country entered the great struggle, and they bore themselves throughout the war like men worthy of their illustrious sires.

"Many sleep tonight beneath the poppies of Flanders Fields, and I hope you will remember them with gratitude and pride as you celebrate the victorious Armistice which they so gallantly fought and died to achieve."

Major Adams addressed the assembled high-school students of his home city of Montclair, N. J., on the morning of Armistice Day. Later, the same day, he reviewed the parade at Westfield, N. J., and he was the orator of the day at the open-air mass meeting which followed the official review. In the evening he held an official reception to his New Jersey compatriots in their headquarters at Newark, which was very largely attended and was an enthusiastic success.

The President General was host at the luncheon to the Executive Committee at the Union League Club, October 31, and presided at the executive meeting which followed. The same night he was the guest of honor of the New York compatriots in the Army and Navy Club of that city, and made an address on "The Proper Teaching of History." The following message was sent by Major Adams to the Tennessee compatriots:

"In response to the invitation of Vice-President Millspaugh, of your State Society, I gladly avail myself of the opportunity to extend to you all my most cordial personal and official greetings, and in doing so I wish to remind you in a word for what our patriotic organization stands, and something of its obligations, its responsibilities, and its opportunities.

"We stand for the Constitution, the Americanization of our foreign-born, and for patriotic education. We must always protect and uphold the dignity of our Flag, suitably celebrate the outstanding anniversaries in our history, and cultivate in ourselves and in others an active, enlightened, and public-spirited interest in our duties as American citizens at all times.

"We acquire no personal merit, of course, through our descent from patriotic ancestors; but we do inherit from them a solemn obligation to acquit ourselves like men worthy of these heroic forefathers; and we recall the deeds and the characters of our illustrious sires, not for personal glory, but that we may establish them as the standards which we and all others, should emulate in these present difficult times of unrest and readjustment following the upheavals of the Great World War."

The President General spoke at the dedication of the Washington Memorial in Montclair on October 28, as reported elsewhere, and has participated officially in various other functions of patriotic import, before and since that event, in New Jersey and New York.

With the advent of the new year he begins his official transcontinental trip, which will be reported later. He makes his principal stops at Chicago, Salt Lake, Portland, Oregon, Seattle, San Francisco, Los Angeles, New Orleans, St. Louis, Louisville, Washington, Philadelphia, and will be back East in time to fill engagements for the February anniversaries in New York, New Jersey, Connecticut, and Massachusetts.

RESPONSIBILITY OF THE WELL-BORN

History shows us that no civilization in the past has long endured except through the superior characters of its leaders. When they have failed in this respect, that civilization has invariably collapsed.

This was true of the ancient Oriental civilizations—the Egyptians, the Greeks, the Romans—and it will be true of our modern western civilization, which is now imperiled, unless our leaders maintain a superiority in character which will enable them to successfully dominate and control the trend of events.

The present revolutionary unrest which threatens the entire world, and which has manifested itself so disastrously in Russia, is not an outgrowth of the World War, as many have supposed, but its root-causes are much deeper than that. The same sinister forces are at work now to overthrow our civilization (right here in the United States of America) which have succeeded in the past to destroy whenever decadence in the character of a people have invited that disaster.

History also shows that a comparatively small number of high-spirited and patriotic people can preserve a nation and a civilization if they have sufficient courage and wisdom. There were not more than fifty thousand Athenians who successfully controlled the destiny of the Greeks, and they reached in many respects the highest civilization which history has recorded; and those in our own time and country, descendants of patriotic ancestry, and others who hold with them, are sufficiently strong in numbers, if they prove strong enough in character, to successfully preserve our modern Republic, and our own enlightened civilization, from the attacks of all their threatening foes, whether from without or within.

Scientists are now almost unanimous in asserting that the dominant qualities of superior character, such as courage and patriotism, are inherited by descent rather than acquired from favorable environment; and those who are descended from brave and strong ancestry have inherited therefrom a solemn responsibility which they are in duty bound to assume and fulfill.

The destinies of our nation and our civilization rest largely with them, and those like them, who accept this patriotic obligation; and the future of our Republic is secure only so long as its patriotic leaders prove worthy of this sacred trust which devolves upon them. If they are brave and true and strong and good, as were their illustrious ancestors, then this representative Republic of ours will endure and this Christian Civilization will survive.

Washington I. L. Adams

TWO UNUSUAL APPLICATIONS

The following official letter from the President General to the Registrar General is self-explanatory:

MR. FRANCIS B. CULVER, *Registrar General,*
  2203 *North Charles Street, Baltimore, Md.*

MY DEAR COMPATRIOT CULVER:

Replying to your letter of November 22, which encloses Compatriot Parker's communication referring to the application of George A. Gordon, the patriotic centenarian who attended the Indiana Constitutional Convention of 1850 and who participated in two of our wars, I hasten to assure you that I am sure our National Executive Committee will approve of the action of the Indiana Society in electing Compatriot Gordon an honorary member, and will gladly waive his initiation fee.

I have recommended that this action be taken in connection with a Real Son of the American Revolution who was elected to honorary membership by the Maine Society, and I shall gladly do so also in the case of Compatriot Gordon. I have no doubt that the Executive Committee will waive the initial fee in both of these notable cases with much pleasure, and may refer the matter for final approval to the Nashville Congress that our delegates there assembled may have the gratification of acting favorably upon two such unusual, and highly interesting, applications.

Faithfully yours,

Washington I. L. Adams

President General.

We reprint also, in this connection, a copy of the letter which the President General wrote the centenarian Compatriot, George A. Gordon, of the Indiana Society:

GEORGE A. GORDON, ESQ.,
 Eureka, Kansas.

MY DEAR COMPATRIOT GORDON:

I have learned with much pleasure, and great interest, of your recent election as an honorary member of the Indiana Society of the Sons of the American Revolution. I wish to send you my most cordial official, and personal, congratulations and good wishes.

It must be very gratifying to you to recall, at this advanced age, the long life of patriotic service that you have rendered our country; having attended, as a member, the Indiana Constitutional Convention of 1850, and having participated in two of our wars.

The Indiana Society honored itself, and us, in honoring you, and I trust you will yet live many years in good health to continue your public-spirited services as a member of our great patriotic organization.

Faithfully yours,

Washington J. L. Adams

President General.

A PROTEST AND REPLY

SOUTH DAKOTA STATE COLLEGE OF AGRICULTURE AND MECHANIC ARTS
Office of Librarian—Wm. H. Powers

BROOKINGS, SOUTH DAKOTA, *November 21, 1922.*

Secretary, Sons of the American Revolution, Washington, D. C.

SIR: I enclose a few notes on McCamant's criticism of Muzzey's History. Such criticism seems to many members of the S. A. R. harmful and I hope you can give space to the protest.

Yours truly,

WM. H. POWERS.

Upon the article in the October number of the OFFICIAL BULLETIN of the S. A. R., entitled "Judge McCamant's Review of Muzzey's School History," I wish to make a few remarks. It seems to me liable to hinder the cause it seems designed to promote and to belittle the society.

How successful the publishers have been in promoting the sale of Muzzey's book I do not know. They would not seem to be under any necessity of resorting to improper means, since the book is approved by a preface from the pen of that most eminent American scholar, James H. Robinson. A study of that preface would render futile some of the criticisms offered. The book is not designed for the youngest readers. It can, therefore, presuppose some familiarity with the heroic stories of our early days. It aims to trace the development of federal power, our westward expansion, and the influence of economic factors on political history; especially does it deal with the history of our country since the Civil War. "Dr. Muzzey has undertaken the arduous task of giving the great problems and preoccupations of today their indispensable historic setting." To accomplish this and to keep within the limits set in a school history, great condensation in dealing with the Colonial and Revolutionary periods is necessary. It would not be fair, then, to bring as an accusation the limitation of the history of the Revolution to seven pages. However, this statement is not true.

Part II of the history is entitled "Separation of the Colonies from England," and occupies forty-five pages. The subsection, "The Revolutionary War," occupies eleven pages; besides several earlier pages are given to the Boston Massacre and other warlike events which preceded the actual declaration, including, not as one would think from Judge McCamant's article, a single sentence on the Battle of Lexington, but a paragraph of two-thirds of a page. Moreover, as contributing more effectively than words to pride in the event, Muzzey gives on the opposite page four pictures, no one of which can be looked at without a thrill.

Of course, writers will differ as to the relative importance of details, but we cannot justly blame a man, who is clearly condensing in these earlier chapters in order to have more room for later matters, because he omits certain heroic names like Warren, Marion, and Starke. Anthony Wayne, by the way, is noted for his Indian victory at Fallen Timbers.

The historian's first responsibility is to tell the truth. Aside from the generalization, "The whole work is permeated with inaccuracies," which, of course, falls of its own weight, there is nothing in the article as printed to show that Muzzey is in fault. Sometimes the truth will cause a blush of shame. How proud we should be that telling the truth about the Revolution is not incompatible with the glow and pride of patriotism. One reader must declare such to be the effect of reading Muzzy's account, all the more effective, perhaps, for the air of impartiality and restraint. Who can read without a thrill the paragraph summarizing the events of 1775? Who will not be moved by more respect for the law after reading the clear-cut distinction between Tory and traitor set forth on page 129? Who would not be moved to larger views by the account of England's dealings with the Loyalists after the peace?

One must surmise that Judge McCamant came to the book determined to be displeased. Was not the Stamp Act demonstration in Boston the work of a mob? They destroyed property and hanged an officer in effigy. If any contempt is meant in the reference to Otis and Adams as "patriots," it is not apparent. So far as relates to George III, the author's condemnation of him and his ministers could hardly be more severe.

To say, moreover, that there is no condemnation of the king's views on taxation merely proves that the critic either has read too hastily or with too little understanding of what he reads. Muzzey writes: "The British Parliament had struck at the most precious right of the colonies, that of voting their own taxes." . . . For them a "representative meant a man of their own town, county, or hundred, elected by their own votes. As well tell a Virginian that he was 'represented' in the Assembly of New York as that he was represented in the British Parliament!" Even the exclamation point is Muzzey's, although in general he avoids mere exclamation, thinking, I suppose, that patriotism, to endure, must be more substantial than Fourth of July oratory.

The youth of today see clearly that men, because they live outside the bounds of the United States, are not therefore "villains all." The best service that

teachers can do them, then, is to show that in the earlier crises of our history likewise a cultivated judgment is required, able equally to see what must be granted
to opponents and yet to approve the action taken. Muzzey is clearly writing for
rational beings, who know that men's motives are mixed, who must themselves in
today's affairs choose for the greater good.

It is cause for profound regret to have such notions as Judge McCamant's
sponsored by the Sons of the American Revolution.

Judge McCamant's Reply to the Above

The portion of Muzzey's History entitled "The Revolutionary War" begins on
page 116, and what the author has to say about the surrender at Yorktown is
found on page 123. It is true, as is pointed out in my pamphlet, the author before
reaching page 116 has published the following account of the Battle of Bunker
Hill: "In June Gage's army stormed the American breastworks on Bunker Hill in
three desperate and bloody assaults, and burned the adjacent town of Charlestown."
In similar brief and unsympathetic fashion he has treated several other military
events.

It is contended that this passing over of important events in our Revolutionary
War is proper because the aim of the author is to emphasize economic factors in
our history. I object to the presence in our schools of a text-book on history
written from this point of view. If the instruction given the rising generation
emphasizes our achievements in acquiring wealth and minimizes our sacrifices in
winning freedom, we must expect a generation of Americans with great affection
for the dollar and slight veneration for the flag.

Passing Muzzey's omissions for the present, let us consider his treatment of the
men of the American Revolution. On page 102, in speaking of Hancock, Warren,
Otis, and the Adamses, he refers to them as patriots with quotation-marks about
the word. There is no rule of punctuation which calls for these quotation-marks.
The use of these marks can only mean that these Revolutionary leaders are so-called
patriots, whose patriotism the author is unwilling to concede.

On page 108 Muzzey refers to the speeches of Patrick Henry and the Adamses
as "their rhetorical warnings against being reduced to slavery." He puts quotation-
marks about the words "reduced to slavery." Here is a clear intimation given to
students using this book that the author has no sympathy with the views expressed
by Henry and the Adamses in their great speeches, which exerted so powerful
an influence in arousing public opinion.

On page 162 Muzzey quotes Alexander Hamilton as saying, "Your people, sir,
is a great beast." What purpose is subserved in publishing this in a school history?
Can there be any difference of opinion as to its effect on school children? Is there
any justification for publishing that which tends to awaken antagonism for this
great man, whom we should venerate both for his military and his civic service?

I have reread section 120, in which Muzzey sets up the colonists' view of taxation
without representation, and section 121, in which he states the British view of the
same subject. There is nothing in the text to indicate with which side of the
controversy Muzzey sympathizes. He says in section 131 that it was a debatable
question. I want our school children taught that our forefathers were right and
the British were wrong on this subject.

Contrary to the views above expressed, I maintain that a work such as Muzzey's will not "thrill" the student. An author cannot inspire patriotism unless he is himself a patriot. The matters referred to in my pamphlet and the tone and temper of the first edition of Muzzey's work justify the impression that his loyalty is to class rather than to country.

I might answer the concluding sentence of the communication by calling attention to the fact that the Muzzey History is condemned by the National Association for Constitutional Government, in a well-considered article found in the July issue of its magazine; that the Daughters of the Confederacy blacklisted the book at their convention held at Birmingham, Alabama, in November, 1922; that the Oregon Department of the Grand Army of the Republic, at its 1917 encampment, demanded its exclusion from the schools.

I prefer to say that the duty of vindicating the men of the American Revolution and the cause for which they fought devolves peculiarly on their descendants. In no work can the membership of this Society be better employed than in insisting that school text-books shall properly stress the value of our political heritage and the debt due to the founders of the Republic.

THE PROPER TEACHING OF HISTORY

By W. I. Lincoln Adams

(Reprinted from Current History, July, 1922)

The Sons of the American Revolution and other hereditary and patriotic organizations are very greatly interested in the proper teaching of American history in our schools and colleges. They are also interested in the much-needed censorship of the text-books employed in those institutions. We have a National Committee, under the chairmanship of Judge Wallace McCamant, of Portland, Ore., former President General of the National Society, Sons of the American Revolution, on Patriotic Education, which expects to be very active in this important work during the present year.

The two chief requisites for the advantageous study of American history in our schools and colleges are, first, teachers who are properly equipped to instruct, by temperament, character, and knowledge of the real facts and their true significance, and, second, well written and truthful text-books, which present the historical facts in their proper relation to each other and in their true proportions.

It is astonishing to find how many of those who are attempting to teach American history are not in sympathy with their subject. Some are frankly "international" in their ideas, as they rather grandiloquently characterize what they consider a finer and broader point of view; they deprecate patriotism as "provincial," "selfish," "ignorant," and "prejudiced," and they minimize and misrepresent the acts and motives of our heroes and the great leaders of our past.

Some are admittedly socialistic, and even communistic, in their convictions, while others are agnostic or worse in their religious faith, or lack of it. And yet these misguided teachers are permitted to continue their false instructions to our young people at a time when the latter are forming their opinions and characters for the country's future weal or woe.

Surely, rigid censorship is sorely needed for those who teach, as well as for what is taught. Personally, I wish that every teacher of history in this country might be required to declare, with Daniel Webster: "I shall know but one country! The ends I aim at shall be my country's, my God's, and truth's. I was born an American; I lived an American; I shall die an American, and I intend to perform the duties incumbent upon me in that character to the end of my career."

However, it is the defective character of many of our text-books of history which has most concerned us; our patriotic societies and, indeed, all good citizens, must recognize as a very promising sign the censorship of school histories which has been undertaken in New York. We hope that this worthy example may be followed throughout the entire Republic. I strongly believe that our school histories should be written from an American standpoint, and that the facts contained in them should be truthfully set forth, regardless of whom they may offend.

Our text-books need not be anti-British to be truly American. They should always record that the action of our Revolutionary forefathers in breaking away from the mother country was commended by a large body of enlightened Englishmen at that time, as it is approved by the judgment of most Englishmen of the present time. It should not be omitted that many Englishmen of the Revolutionary period were in active sympathy with our patriotic ancestors and felt that, in a certain sense, they were fighting to preserve English civil liberty in America for the benefit of the whole world. These significant facts are properly emphasized in Sir George Trevelyan's excellent four-volume history of the American Revolution.

Our quarrel was not with the English people, but with a king who was not truly English, either by birth or in spirit. Our forefathers were distinctly not out of sympathy with the true English traditions which they brought to this country and which were and are our common inheritance. In fact, it was largely just because they were descended from the English barons, who exacted the Magna Charta from King John, that they resisted, even to the point of an armed conflict, the encroachments of King George III on their hard-won political rights and privileges in America.

It should be remembered that King George III employed German mercenaries to suppress the efforts of our heroic ancestors to preserve their precious liberties, and that our allies in that glorious struggle, as in the great World War, were the gallant French. While we should never allow these important facts to be omitted or minimized, it should also be recorded that in the World War the English and the French and the Americans fought side by side in the common cause for liberty.

In treating of the Revolutionary period—for it is that phase of our history which I have now principally in mind—I think our text-books should point out most clearly the fact that King George and his ministers, acting contrary to the best English sentiment, were clearly in the wrong in their encroachments on the liberties of our American ancestors, and that our forefathers were right in defending these liberties. They should tell the dramatic story of that Revolutionary struggle, from Lexington to Yorktown, with sufficient charm of style to impress the principal events indelibly on the youthful mind. John Fiske's admirable history of the Revolutionary period is a good example of fidelity to fact and literary charm.

Our school histories should certainly not malign the characters of our military leaders and statesmen of any period, as some do, but, on the contrary, should present them, sympathetically, in their true light and with proper relation to each other and to the times in which they lived. No period in the history of any people was richer in great and good men, according to so distinguished and unprejudiced an authority as the late Lord Bryce, than that of our own Revolution.

Hero worship is good for the young, for it stimulates manly aspirations and gives to a people the highest standards of manhood. As Charles Grant Miller has truly said: "The better instincts of the human race have, through all the ages, exalted and consecrated its heroes into something like objects and tenets of religious worship, and a people's greatness may be measured by the characters and traditions it cherishes in love and emulation, as it can be known by its gods." Good biographies and autobiographies of our outstanding historical characters, in war and peace, could, with great profit, be added as text-books in our schools. This is a feature of historical teaching which is largely, if not entirely, neglected at present. Such works as Irving's "Life of Washington," Franklin's autobiography, Lodge's "Hamilton," and Hay's condensed "Life of Lincoln" could profitably be added to our school curricula.

REPORT OF COMMITTEE ON THE OBSERVANCE OF CONSTITUTION DAY, SEPTEMBER 17, 1922

DECEMBER 1, 1922.

MR. PRESIDENT GENERAL AND MEMBERS OF THE NATIONAL EXECUTIVE COMMITTEE:

Again credit is due the Sons of the American Revolution for a nation-wide observance of Constitution Day. Space will permit of only a summary of the thousands of gatherings of patriotic citizens who voiced their loyalty to the Constitution of the United States of America. We have had the co-operation of not alone all the compatriots of the Sons of American Revolution, but our distinguished compatriots, the President and the Vice-President of the United States, took a deep interest in these celebrations.

Proclamations calling for the observance of the day were issued by the Governors of the following States: Arizona, Florida, Idaho, Kansas, Maryland, Nevada, South Carolina, South Dakota, Utah, Vermont, and Wisconsin.

With the Sons of the American Revolution co-operated State and local chambers of commerce, boards of trade, bar associations, Masonic bodies, Order of Elks, Rotary, Kiwanis, Lions, American Legion, Boy Scouts, Y. M. C. A., and other commercial organizations. The theatrical profession, community centers, churches, boards of education, and the newspapers were generous in not only recording these celebrations, but editorial articles were published covering over 360,000 newspaper columns.

Arizona.—Agreeable to the request of Governor Thomas E. Campbell, of Arizona, Constitution Day was generally observed throughout the State. The Governor especially requested that the day be observed by all of the churches, and that from each pulpit there should be stressed the privileges and safeguards embodied in the Constitution of the United States. The American Flag was displayed on all of the State buildings, and throughout the week following a period of time was devoted by all schools, public and private, to the study and explanation of the Constitution. This is the second year the State has observed Constitution Day and much credit is due to the State Society, Sons of the American Revolution.

California.—The California Society was extremely active in the observance of Constitution Day. Not being contented with merely holding a banquet at the Commercial Club on the evening of September 14 and having an address, "The Constitution of the United States Our Safeguard," delivered by Harry F. Atwood, they held a public meeting at the Scottish Rite Auditorium at San Francisco and had present representatives of the following patriotic, civic, and fraternal organizations: California Society, Sons of the American Revolution; California Society, Daughters of the American Revolution; Accountants' Association, American Legion, Business League, Grand Army of the Republic, Ladies of the Grand Army of the Republic, Masonic Committee on Education, Military Order of the Loyal Legion, National Progress Club, One Hundred Per Cent Club, Public Spirit Club, Purchasing Agents' Association of Northern California, San Francisco Advertising Club, S. F. Lodge B. P. O. Elks, No. 3; Society of California Pioneers, The Soroptimist Club, To Kalon Club, United Spanish War Veterans, U. S. Veteran Navy, and Young Men's and Young Women's Hebrew Association.

It was one of the largest gatherings ever held in the city of San Francisco. The meeting was largely advertised. Posters 30 x 15 inches, advertising the meeting, were displayed throughout the city. The speaker was Hon. Harry F. Atwood. A fine musical program was rendered throughout the State and the day was generally observed by press and pulpit. The following week the various commercial organizations at their meetings held exercises in commemoration of the anniversary of the adoption of the United States Constitution. Special exercises were held in all of the higher grade schools of the State.

Connecticut.—The Connecticut Society, Sons of the American Revolution, and the Daughters of the American Revolution held a large public meeting on Sunday afternoon, September 17, in the First Congregational Church of Bridgeport, in observance of the anniversary of the adoption of the Constitution of the United States.

In New Haven the Sons of the American Revolution held an outdoor meeting in Center Church. Rev. Dr. Oscar E. Maurer spoke from the porch of the church. There was an attendance of 300. The speaker remarked that the Constitution is the fundamental law, all other laws and later constitutions according with it.

All throughout the State Constitution Day was observed the following week by special exercises in the higher grade schools and at the dinners of Rotary, Kiwanis, and Lions Clubs.

The Connecticut Society, Sons of the American Revolution, were more active this year than any previous year in the observance of the day.

District of Columbia.—The Secretary of the District of Columbia Society, Sons of the American Revolution, has suggested that the great Convention Hall, which is erected at our Nation's Capital, should be called Constitution Hall; and it is further suggested that Constitution Hall should house a National Library of American History; likewise a national school for the study of representative government, with a lecture course on the Constitution.

Florida.—At the request of Governor Cary A. Hardee, celebrations were held in the various cities, towns, and communities throughout the State of Florida. Regret we have no details to report on these celebrations.

Idaho.—Idaho observed Constitution Week. In answer to the proclamation of Governor Davis, flags were displayed throughout the State. Exercises were held in the public schools; sermons were preached in the churches. Boards of trade, chambers of commerce, Lions, Kiwanis, Rotary, and civic clubs all joined in paying honor to the Constitution of the United States. Hayden I. Sawyer declared, in his address before the Idaho Society, Sons of the American Revolution, that no group or class of men would ever rule this nation as long as we stood by the Constitution of our forefathers. Dr. H. W. Hoover urged the Sons to be true to the ideals of the Nation and the Constitution.. The meeting was held at the Y. M. C. A. and was preceded by a banquet of the Lexington Chapter, Sons of the American Revolution.

Illinois.—The Illinois Society held a great patriotic service on Sunday afternoon, September 17, in the Fourth Presbyterian Church. The address was delivered by Dr. John Timothy Stone, former Chaplain General of the National Society, Sons of the American Revolution.

Exercises commemorating the adoption of the Constitution of the United States were held in the schools throughout the State. Not only were addresses delivered from most of the pulpits of the State, but there were addresses made by the judges at the opening of the courts on Monday, September 18. Civic organizations remembered the adoption of the Constitution of the United States at their meetings held the following week. The day was observed in nearly every town and hamlet of the State.

Iowa.—The Iowa Society, Sons of the American Revolution, and other patriotic societies in the State observed Constitution Day generally. Past President General Elmer M. Wentworth wrote an editorial on "Constitution Day" which was published throughout the State. Over 2,000 copies of this editorial appeared in the various daily and weekly papers of the State.

Kansas.—Many celebrations were held throughout Kansas in the courts, public schools, and churches and a proclamation was issued by the Governor.

Kentucky.—Under the inspiration of the Sons of the American Revolution, Constitution Day was generally observed throughout Kentucky. Luncheon clubs observed Constitution Day Week by setting aside their meeting day as a special day commemorating the signing of the Constitution and to discuss the subject "Respect for Law and Order." The speakers were furnished from the Sons of the American Revolution. The Society of the Sons of the American Revolution addressed a letter to all the leading high schools in the State, and Prof. Zenos E. Scott, Superintendent of Public schools, requested that some particular notice be taken of Constitution Day, either immediately before or after September 17, in all of the schools. The ministers of the State were also requested to observe the day by appropriate reference to the same during their sermons.

Maine.—The Maine Society secured a State-wide recognition of Constitution Day, and was particularly fortunate in securing the co-operation of the Superintendent of Schools and the newspapers of the State. Many special exercises were held. The day, coming on Sunday, was the subject of patriotic addresses in most of the churches.

Maryland.—The Maryland Society observed the day fittingly, beginning with Saturday evening, September 16. The motion-picture houses used pictures telling the story of the Constitution. The churches recognized the day. A mass meeting was held in Baltimore under the auspices of the Maryland Society, Sons of the American Revolution, in which all the patriotic and civic organizations co-operated.

Massachusetts.—Not only did the Sons of the American Revolution organize celebrations, but they supplied a corps of speakers and furnished slides for use at various clubs, schools, and other assemblages, and their efforts met with such hearty response that the Massachusetts Society has decided to continue the work during the next three months, sending speakers to various organizations, and to make use of slides telling the story of the adoption of the Constitution of the United States, so as to fix facts pertaining to the Constitution of the United States on the minds of many people that it is especially desirable to reach. The Massachusetts Society, Sons of the American Revolution, are strong for patriotic education.

Michigan.—Unique was the work of the Michigan Society in regard to the observance of Constitution Day. On Saturday evening, September 16, arrangements were made for a radio program to be broadcasted by W W J, *Detroit News* Radio Station. An address was made by George E. Bushnell, District Attorney, Vice-President of the Detroit Chapter, Sons of the American Revolution, who called the attention of the people of Detroit and the State of Michigan to the significance of Constitution Day. The day was fittingly observed throughout the State by special exercises in the schools and by addresses from many of the pulpits. Commercial organizations set aside part of their meetings during Constitution Day week for patriotic addresses.

Minnesota.—To the Minnesota Society, Sons of the American Revolution, is due credit for the proper observance of Constitution Day, not only in Minneapolis, but throughout the State. A special meeting of the Minneapolis Chapter was held on the evening of Monday, September 18, at which the Secretary of the local board of education, Hon. C. E. Purdy, spoke on "America's Responsibility Today."

The importance of the day was called to the attention of the clergy, schools, and patriotic societies by sending out a circular prepared for the purpose, which carried with it a call to civic duty, reverence for the Constitution, and a love of country. The response was most generous from 25 patriotic organizations; from the Ministerial Federation, the Superintendent of the Board of Education, and notable was the hearty co-operation of the American Legion, Veterans of Foreign Wars, Minneapolis Business Men's Association, Knights of Columbus, and Superintendent of the Board of Education. The Lincoln Club held a meeting, at which Vice-President Coolidge was the orator, and invited the Sons of the American Revolution as its special guests.

New Jersey.—The activities of the Sons of the American Revolution in observance of Constitution Day reached all parts of the State. Compatriot Edward Q. Keasbey made arrangements for the clergymen to impress upon their congregations the importance of the Constitution as the charter of our Government and the importance of maintaining the principles of the Constitution and a respect for law and order. He also arranged with the officers of Rotary and Lions Clubs and chambers of commerce for addresses or resolutions on one or the other of the days of the week. Notable was the interest the American Legion took in arranging for the observance to be carried on in the individual churches. He also had the co-operation of the Y. M. C. A. and the superintendent of schools.

A notable observance of Constitution Day under the auspices of the New Jersey Society, Sons of the American Revolution, was the holding of a mass meeting in front of the Sons of the American Revolution headquarters at 3 o'clock on the afternoon of Sunday, September 17. The guest of honor was our President General, Major Washington Irving Lincoln Adams. The chairman was David L. Pierson, who first proposed the observance of Constitution Day in 1917. Compatriot Pierson read a letter from President Harding. President General Adams delivered a brief address and was followed by Judge Adrian Lyon, President of the New Jersey Society, who delivered the oration of the day. An original poem on the Constitution was read by Rev. Lyman Whitney Allen, D. D., former Chaplain General. At the close of the exercises the Sons of the American Revolution marched to Washington Square, where a wreath was laid by Compatriot Pierson at the foot of Washington's statue "in loving memory of the Father of our Country." "America" was sung, after which the benediction was pronounced by Rev. Dr. Frank A. Smith, Chaplain of the Society. Former President Chester N. Jones gave the pledge to the flag.

The Newark Chapter, Sons of the American Revolution, held a "Constitution Day" night on Monday, September 18, at the State headquarters. Addresses were made by President Sylvester H. M. Agens and Compatriot Rev. Warren Patten Coon. Music was furnished by the S. A. R. quartet. Hon. John O. Bigelow, of the Court of Common Pleas of Essex County, delivered an address on the Constitution.

On Tuesday, September 19, in East Orange, at the plant of Seabury & Johnson, Compatriot Rev. Warren P. Coon delivered an address on the general subject of the Constitution. Compatriot Pierson made similar addresses on the 20th and 23d at noonday factory meetings held in other parts of Orange, at which the story of the Constitution was told. All through New Jersey arrangements were perfected for bringing the story of the Constitution to the workers in most of the factories.

Empire State Society (New York City Chapter).—In the presence of 2,000 persons, exercises to commemorate the 135th anniversary of the adoption of the Constitution of the United States were held on the steps of the Sub-Treasury, Wall and Nassau streets, by the New York Chapter of the Sons of the American Revolution. Members of the Chapter met at St. Paul's Chapel, Broadway and Fulton Street, and marched in procession down Broadway. General Oliver B. Bridgman, President of the Chapter, presided at the exercises. The principal speech was made by Major Washington I. L. Adams, President General of the National Society, Sons of the American Revolution, who said in part:

"The present revolutionary unrest which threatens the entire world, and which has manifested itself so disastrously in Russia, is not an outgrowth of the World War, as many have supposed, but has its root-causes much deeper than that. The same evil forces are at work here to overthrow our Government which have been successful in the Old World, and it devolves upon us who have faith in our Constitution and believe in our Republic, as the best form of government which the world has ever known, to resist every attack of its foes, whether from without or within.

"As our ancestors pledged their lives, property, and their sacred honor to establish our stately and stable Constitution, which has truly been pronounced the most wonderful document ever devised by man, so we, their descendants, the Sons of the American Revolution, and all true Americans, must pledge ourselves, by all that we have and are, to maintain that same noble charter of our rights and liberties."

Announcement that "Constitution Day" exercises would be held on Monday in many New York City schools was made by Lloyd Taylor, Secretary of the National Security League. "The Constitution Day celebration is part of the plan to teach future American citizens the 'rules of the game.'" Mr. Taylor said, "To know your rights as an American citizen and to know the rights of others under the Constitution is one of the most important factors in Americanization today. We believe the place to teach the Constitution is in the schools, and we are seeking to have the Legislature of every State pass laws making this mandatory."

The Fifth Avenue Association observed Constitution Day by having all of its members decorate their shops with the National Colors.

The Huntington Chapter, Sons of the American Revolution, displayed slides telling the story of the Constitution in the local theaters on Saturday afternoon and evening and on Sunday evening in the Central Presbyterian Church, and on Monday in the schools of Huntington and at Huntington Station, a most cosmopolitan section of Long Island.

The Saratoga Chapter, Sons of the American Revolution, in conjunction with the Daughters of the American Revolution, gathered for the observance of Constitution Day and listened to an elegant address on the Constitution by Rev. A. H. Boutwell. (A more detailed description will be found on page 68 of the October, 1922, BULLETIN.)

All of the daily and weekly papers of the State had editorials on Constitution Day, as well as fine reports of meetings held, not alone by the patriotic societies, but of the exercises in schools, addresses in the churches, meetings of Boy Scouts, American Legion, Rotary, Kiwanis, Lions, and other commercial bodies. The Bar Association took an active part in the observance of the day.

Nevada.—In response to a proclamation issued by Governor Emmet D. Boyd September 17, celebrations in honor of Constitution Day were held throughout the State.

Ohio.—The Ohio Society, Sons of the American Revolution, through its Chapters, generally observed Constitution Day, September 17 and 18, with patriotic services. A letter prepared by the Secretary of the State Society was distributed to all Chapter officers, requesting they take the advance in arousing public interest. Not only members of the Sons of the American Revolution, but various other organizations joined in active co-operation. Rotary and all civic clubs, schools of all grades, chambers of commerce, churches and church organizations observed the day, emphasizing practical loyal citizenship, and that "respect for law and order" should be the general theme.

Mention must be made of the valuable assistance by the Daughters of the American Revolution. Reports received showed that this important anniversary was more generally observed than in any former year.

Oregon.—The observance of Constitution Day, September 17, 1922, in Oregon was quite general and very successful. Churches, courts, high schools, grammar schools, and patriotic and civic organizations observed the anniversary on September 17 or immediately before or after that date. The press of the State published many editorials and articles relating to the Constitution and its adoption.

Early in August arrangements were perfected by the State organizations of the Daughters of the American Revolution and the Sons of the American Revolution for joint effort and co-operation in securing observance of the anniversary throughout the State. The nineteen Chapters of the Oregon Daughters of the American Revolution rendered invaluable assistance and arranged for Chapter or public meetings in the various towns in which the Chapters are located. In this work they were in numerous instances aided by resident compatriots of the Oregon Society, Sons of the American Revolution, there being no Chapters of the Sons of the American Revolution in Oregon, owing to insufficiency of members in any town, with the exception of Portland, to insure an efficient Chapter organization.

The following-named members of the Oregon Society, Sons of the American Revolution, constituted the general committee for securing observance of the day in Oregon, in conjunction with President B. B. Beekman, *ex-officio* Director for the State: Judge Robert Tucker, chairman; H. H. Ward and Walter E. Bliss, for schools; C. D. Tillson and A. A. Lindsley, for churches; Winthrop Hammond and H. C. Ewing, for civic and patriotic organizations in Portland; P. P. Dabney and H. M. Tomlinson, for courts and bar associations; Rollin K. Page and C. E Ingalls, for civic and patriotic organizations in State at large.

Patriotic sermons and references to the day were very general in the many churches of the city of Portland. The Sons of the American Revolution and Daughters of the American Revolution provided speakers for the eight high schools, and short talks were given by the teachers in the sixth, seventh, and eighth grades of the grammar schools during the week, September 18-22. The committee in charge, Compatriots H. H. Ward and Walter E. Bliss and Mrs. H. H. Ward, Mrs. Pearson, and Mrs. Crowe, representing the Multnomah and Willamette Chapters, Daughters of the American Revolution, received enthusiastic reports as to the character and excellence of the addresses delivered at the various high-school assemblies. Past President General Wallace McCamant addressed three of the high schools, and in the case of the Jefferson High School addressed the students in two assemblies. It need hardly be said that his addresses were able and patriotic in the highest degree and were enthusiastically received by the high-school teachers and students.

The high-school program for the week, September 15-22, was as follows: September 15—Girls' Polytechnic High School, Past President General Wallace McCamant. September 18—Franklin High School, Jacob Weinstein, senior student at Reed College. September 19—Commerce High School, Jacob Weinstein, senior student at Reed College; Lincoln High School, Cassius R. Peck, of the Multnomah County bar. September 20—Benson Polytechnic High School, Past President General Wallace McCamant. September 21—Jefferson High School, Past President General Wallace McCamant; James John High School, Jacob Weinstein, senior student at Reed College. September 22—Washington High School, Jerry Bronaugh, of the Multnomah County bar.

Other Portland observances were as follows: September 16—Circuit Court of Multnomah County, public meeting, addressed by Ex-Judge John P. Kavanaugh, of Portland. September 18—Multnomah Chapter, Daughters of the American Revolution tea; addresses by Bishop Charles H. Brent, of New York, and Bishop Arthur W. Moulton, of Utah. September 18—Public meeting under the auspices of the Catholic Civic Rights Association, addressed by Bishop Irving P. Johnson, of Denver, Colorado. September 19—Kiwanis Club luncheon; addresses by Bishop Joseph M. Francis, of Indianapolis, and Colonel James J. Crossley, Commander of Portland Post of the American Legion. September 21—East Side Business Men's Club, address by Ex-Judge John P. Kavanaugh. September 21—Progressive Business Men's Club, address by Canon Henry Russell Talbot, of Washington, D. C. September 22—Realty Board, address by Ex-Judge John P. Kavanaugh. September 22—City Club, address by Compatriot Henry M. Tomlinson.

The Dalles, September 21—Public meeting presided over by Compatriot Fred W. Wilson, Judge of Circuit Court of Wasco County; addresses by various members of the bar.

Brownsville, September 17—Public observance in Methodist Episcopal Church; addresses by Rev. C. G. Morris and A. A. Tussing.

Eugene, September 17—St. Mary's Catholic Church; patriotic service and address by Frank J. Lonergan, attorney, of Portland. September 17—Congregational Church, public meeting, Daughters of the American Revolution and Sons of the American Revolution members attending, with patriotic sermon by the pastor, Rev. Marshall. September 16—Kiwanis Club luncheon. An interesting feature of this luncheon gathering was a folder place-card prepared by Compatriot Frederick S. Dunn. This folder was also distributed to all the teachers of the city and read by them to their classes. (Eugene Kiwanis Club luncheon place-card:) "A Babylonian despot once graved his code on columns of stone; the Cæsars once bound their edicts to their legions' spears; knout and mailed fist had made the world long since aged and heavily aweáried with the travail of its past, when, as in the days of Genesis, a cry rang out over the chaos. It was the voice of Democracy from her refuge on the shores of the new continent, proclaiming, in the words of that immortal preamble, the birth of America. A new nation, far remote from the world's acknowledged centers, had flung out a challenge and erected a trophy toward which all peoples turned in wonderment. Like the Cross itself, which drew the world to its foot, was the Constitution of the United States of America, for its adoption, one hundred and thirty-five years ago today, proved the greatest achievement yet attained in political history and still wants but little of marking as great a cleavage as the Christian Era between all times previous and subsequent. We Americans have become almost idolatrous of our dear old cracked Liberty Bell and we have made of Independence Day a tumult of riot and revelry; but far above both totem and the Fourth of July should be reverenced that event which created of us a real people and gave America a high seat at the world's Round Table. Marathon, the Metaurus, the First Christmas, Magna Charta, the Reformation, the Renaissance, the defeat of Prussianism—to such a family of epochal names belongs our own September 17th, 1787." (This folder constituted a new feature in Constitution Day programs in Oregon.)

Medford, September 15—Daughters of the American Revolution Chapter meeting; instructive paper on "History of the Constitution," by Mrs. Stella Owens Adams. September 20—Chamber of Commerce luncheon; address by Porter J. Neff, of the Jackson County bar. September 18-21—Address to Medford High School students by Porter J. Neff, and also addresses by local attorneys to 6th, 7th, and 8th grade classes of the grammar schools.

Springfield, September 17—General meeting; address by Col. W. G. D. Mercer, Patriotic Instructor, Grand Army of the Republic, Department of Oregon.

Junction City, September 17—Public meeting, address by Col. W. G. D. Mercer.

Salem, September 16—Daughters of the American Revolution Chapter meeting; address by Hon. John R. McCourt, of the Oregon Supreme Court.

Ashland—Daughters of the American Revolution Chapter meeting. Paper on "Constitution Day" (writer's name not reported) read and published in full in Ashland daily paper. (No copy mailed to Daughters of the American Revolution or Sons of the American Revolution State organization.)

Astoria—Patriotic sermons on Sunday, September 17, in Presbuterian and Episcopal churches; special articles published in the local papers, *The Astorian* and *The Budget;* appropriaite addresses at Astoria High School assembly (no details reported).

Dallas, September 17—Patriotic service and sermon in Presbyterian Church.

Baker—The observance in Baker was under the charge and direction of Compatriot Irving Rand and Mrs John L. Soule, Regent of Matthew Starbuck Chapter, Daughters of the American Revolution. September 18 (morning)—Baker High School. Program of patriotic vocal and instrumental music and address on "The History of the Constitution and Its Leading Principles," by Hon. Fred Packwood. September 18 (evening)—Baker Bar Association. Public meeting, held in High School Auditorium. Program as follows: Address, "Political History of the Constitution," Hon. C. T. Godwin; address, "Capital and Labor under the Constitution," Hon. A. A. Smith; address, "The Relation of the State to the Federal Government," Hon. James T. Donald; address, "All Men Equal before the Law," Judge Gustav Anderson. The program included selections of patriotic songs by Miss Alma Payton, with Miss Florence French accompanist. The meeting was attended by the Daughters of the American Revolution Chapter in a body, by Civil Government classes of the high school, and by the public generally. September 19—Kiwanis Club luncheon; address by Frank C. Wynne, of Portland, and general discussion of various phases of the Constitution.

Roseburg, September 18—Roseburg High School; address by Compatriot O. P. Coshow, who came to the rescue when the scheduled speaker was unavoidably called from town just prior to the meeting.

Burns, September 20—Harney County Bar. Public meeting, with Captain A. W. Gowan, presiding. The following program was given: Invocation, Rev. C. A. Waterhouse; assembly singing, "Battle Hymn of the Republic"; address, "Constitution and Constitution Changing," Hon. Wells W. Wood, of Ontario; vocal solo, Prof. E. E. Hurley; address, "Duty of Upholding the Constitution and the Laws thereunder," Judge Dalton Biggs; assembly singing, "America"; benediction.

Other towns, institutions, and organizations not enumerated held similar meetings, marked by like exercises and addresses. Observance of Constitution Day has met with popular favor and approval in this State and may be made a permanent annual custom if the various patriotic and civic organizations will make proper provision for attractive exercises and furnish competent speakers.

Pennsylvania.—Never before was Constitution Day so generally observed throughout the State as this year.

Pittsburgh.—The Pennsylvania State Society attended in a body, on Sunday, September 17, at 11 a. m., the patriotic meeting at the First Baptist Church of Pittsburgh, where a patriotic address was delivered by the Rev. Carl Wallace Petty, D. D.

Middletown.—Under the auspices of the local Sons of the American Revolution, a wonderful meeting was held at the Old Lutheran Church Sunday afternoon at 3 o'clock. The services were in charge of Compatriot Rev. Fuller G. Bergstresser, D. D. After the address a quartet composed of members of the Swatara Pineford Chapter, Daughters of the American Revolution, rendered that great patriotic song, "Beloved America," after which all pledged allegiance to our country's flag and sang "The Star-Spangled Banner." This ended one of the most enjoyable and impressive services ever held in Middletown was the opinion of all present. The Sons of Veterans, P. O. S. of A., I. O. of Americans, and other organizations, Boy Scout troops from the United Brethren, Presbyterian, and Methodist churches attended in a body. The Middletown Chapter, Sons of the American Revolution, acted as ushers. They wish to thank the trustees of St. Peter's Lutheran Church for kindly allowing the use of the historic old church, which is kept in excellent condition for services, being built in 1767; also to thank all those who took part and helped make this Constitution Day one long to be remembered.

Steubenville.—The day was observed by addresses delivered from all of the pulpits and the day was observed in the following week by all fraternal orders and civic organizations. Throughout the State there was a general observance of the day and the newspapers devoted considerable space to editorials on Constitution Day.

Additional reports will be made for Pennsylvania.

Tennessee.—The Tennessee Society is to be congratulated upon its part in observing Constitution Day. Its efficient Secretary, F. W. Millspaugh, was not satisfied to arrange for celebrations in 79 cities and towns, but also five celebrations in Mississippi and five in Alabama. He also made arrangements with the Superintendent of Schools, and with churches and civic organizations throughout the State, for a fitting observance of the day.

Two compatriots, Gov. A. A. Taylor and Hon. Austin Teay, were rival candidates and each gubernatorial candidate devoted considerable attention to Constitution Day. The old Volunteer State was a willing volunteer in the spirit of co-operation for a respect for law and order.

The *Commercial-Appeal,* one of Memphis' leading papers, contained an article on "The Constitution," written by John Davis McDowell, Vice-President of the Tennessee Society and a member of the Memphis Chapter. The Sons of the American Revolution were directly responsible for 501 observances of Constitution Day, with an estimated attendance at these meetings of over 60,000.

No report would be complete without mention of the splendid work done by Compatriots T. D. Lee, of Union City; W. E. Parkham, of Maryville, and Dr. W. T. Wilkins, of Olive Branch, Mississippi.

Vice-President John Davis McDowell was not satisfied by having an article on Constitution Day appear in the daily press, but broadcasted by radio a call for the observance of the anniversary of Constitution Day that was listened to by thousands. Colored slides depicting the Constitution as a document of the people were used in the schools and theaters of Nashville. In all of the editorials and reports of the observance of the day the press gave full credit to the Sons of the American Revolution.

This report would not be complete if due credit were not given to Compatriot Thomas W. Ham, who sent out more than 1,000 letters to the various newspapers, asking their aid in making a state-wide observance of Constitution Day. Unlimited space was given by the newspapers of Nashville, Chattanooga, Memphis, and Knoxville. In Nashville during the week prior to Constitution Day, each of the daily papers had about four columns, possibly more, in addition to the editorials, in each paper on the observance of Constitution Day. At the Rotary Constitution Day meeting the Sons of the American Revolution distributed 200 copies of the Constitution. At every meeting of the Boy Scout troops during Constitution Day Week a talk was delivered to the boys regarding the Constitution and its makers, and especially "Respect for Law and Order."

If any one meeting was of more importance than another, it was the one held under the auspices of the Sons of the American Revolution, at the First Presbyterian Church, Nashville, Sunday, September 17, at which was delivered an address on "The Constitution," by John H. De Witt, Historian of the Sons of the American Revolution. The Daughters of the American Revolution Chapters of the city were in attendance.

This entire issue of the BULLETIN would not contain space enough to give a detailed account of the observance of Constitution Day this year in the State of Tennessee.

South Carolina.—Governor Wilson G. Harvey, in an official proclamation, designated September 17 as Constitution Day in the State of South Carolina. Governor Harvey is now President of the California Society, Sons of the Revolution, and he interested the Society of Colonial Dames in Charleston, and the State Society of the Daughters of the American Revolution in the observance of Constitution Day. The Sons of the American Revolution were responsible for many exercises being held in the churches of the State commemorative of the day, and on the following Monday in the schools of the State.

South Dakota.—The South Dakota Society held an appropriate observance of Constitution Day in the Colosseum, Sioux Falls. The President of the Society, Mr. Amos E. Ayres, presided. The orator of the day was Rev. L. Wendell Fifield, and the subject of his address was "The Constitution Then and Now." President

Ayers is also President of the Board of Education of Sioux Falls and arranged with the Superintendent of Schools to have fitting observances held in all the schools of the city on Friday, September 15. A state-wide committee was appointed by President Ayres, which was successful in having suitable ceremonies held in all of the larger cities and towns of the State. South Dakota was among those States whose governors issued a proclamation calling for appropriate recognition of the day.

Utah.—At the request of Hon. George Albert Smith, Vice-President General of the Sons of the American Revolution, the following call was issued in the *Deseret News* of Saturday, September 16:

CONSTITUTION DAY

Next Sunday, September 17, being Constitution Day, designated and set apart for commemoration of the great document which is the organic law and foundation of our glorious Republic, we earnestly desire that bishops and presidents of States arrange to have the speakers in their respective services on that day address themselves to the Constitution, its history, meaning, and importance.

HEBER J. GRANT,
CHARLES W. PENROSE,
ANTHONY W. IVINS,
First Presidency.

In addition thereto there appeared a column editorial on the Constitution, and the *Deseret News* conducted an essay contest on "What the Constitution Means to Me." The contest was open to all pupils enrolled in the grade high schools and accredited private schools, and published daily a chapter from the work recently compiled by Judge Martin J. Wade, eminent jurist, former member of Congress, and Dean Wm. F. Russell, of the University of Iowa. This book is known as "The Short Constitution." The *Tribune* of Salt Lake City also carried a column editorial in its Sunday issue of September 17, entitled "Constitution Day."

No greater observance of the anniversary of the adoption of the Constitution was held in any other State. Scarcely a church, school, civic or commercial organization failed to hold special services in honor of the day, all under the inspiration of the Utah Society, Sons of the American Revolution. Hon. George Albert Smith, our Vice-President General, was chairman of the committee for the State of Utah.

Vermont.—On the afternoon of Sunday, September, 17, hundreds of compatriots and members of other patriotic societies assembled at Battery Park, Burlington, Vermont, for the celebration of Constitution Day. An eloquent address was delivered by Judge Frank L. Fish on "The American Constitution, the Defense of Our Liberties." Judge C. H. Darling presided. Both Judge Darling and Judge Fish were former Presidents of the Vermont State Society, Sons of the American Revolution. The day was generally observed throughout the State.

Wisconsin.—Governor John J. Blaine was instrumental in having Constitution Day observed throughout the State of Wisconsin.

Your committee, although active in collecting records of the observance of Constitution Day by means of newspaper clippings, accounts sent in by departments of education, chambers of commerce, civic organizations, and fraternal orders, can make only a partial report. Many State Societies, Sons of the American Revolution, have to date failed to send in records of their celebrations.

The total number of celebrations throughout the United States were in excess of 60,000.

Respectfully submitted,

LOUIS ANNIN AMES,
Chairman.

REPORT OF VICE-PRESIDENT GENERAL FOR MISSISSIPPI VALLEY, WEST DISTRICT

The Mississippi Valley, West District, had a healthy and prosperous year. The activities of the various Societies have been covered in the report of the Secretary General and the Registrar General, to which we refer for the details.

The numerical growth has not been as large as we had hoped for, but the interest has been maintained and the patriotic activities carried forward with commendable zeal.

The unrest following the war brought new problems of great importance to our citizenship, and the obligations of our membership to hold a sane and steady course, in harmony with American ideals as charted in the Constitution, has been accepted with good results, especially where local Chapters exist.

We feel that, if for no other reason than this, a strong effort should be made by each State Society to establish local Chapters as rapidly as possible, and to encourage the work along the lines of better citizenship and a closer observance of the duties and obligations devolving upon said citizenship. As a nucleus around which this work should be centered, we can conceive no group that would have a greater influence and we would heartily urge co-operation by the members of the Sons of the American Revolution with the various activities carried on by the Rotary, Kiwanis, Lions Clubs, and kindred organizations.

It is generally conceded that there has been a marked growth of laxness in the observance of our duties as citizens and in the respect for the laws of the land. As an organization and as individuals, it is the duty of each Son of the American Revolution to use every effort to restore sane thinking and a decent respect for the rights of others.

The work of the North Dakota Society is especially commendable along these lines. We feel that it is the most forceful unit in that State and desire to publicly recognize and commend its work. During the coming year we trust that the other State Societies and Chapters will give special thought to their local conditions with the view of leadership along the constitutional lines upon which the nation was founded.

The Iowa Chapters, though few in number, have done most excellent work. This is especially true as to Lexington Chapter of Keokuk and Ben Franklin Chapter of Des Moines. Ben Franklin Chapter has over 115 members and holds monthly meetings, at which topics of historic interest and profitable studies in good citizenship are subjects discussed by prominent speakers. Strong efforts are being made to strengthen the State Societies through Chapter organizations throughout the district.

Past President Wentworth, whose home is in Des Moines, is a source of great inspiration to all compatriots, not only in his home city and State, but throughout the entire Mississippi Valley, and his visit to North Dakota Society last winter, in the time of her need, has been a potent factor in bringing that State back to more sane Americanism.

With such good work going on throughout our field, I am pleased to make this encouraging report.

H. B. HAWLEY,
Vice-President General, Mississippi Valley, West District.

AN EXPLANATION

In the October OFFICIAL BULLETIN it was announced that the selection called "Chester" was first discovered by Compatriot Edmund D. Poole, of Newark, in the narrative dealing with the organization and progress of the Newark Chapter Quartet, of the New Jersey Society. It is true that he conducted the independent research and, to his own knowledge, was the first one of modern days to bring it to light and into use. It appears, however, that Compatriot R. C. Ballard Thruston, former President General, during his very successful administration discovered the composition in the possession of Mr. Ernest Newton Bragg, of Springfield, aid it so impressed him that on December 11, 1914, he sent out a number of copies, at his own expense, to the various State Societies. For some unaccountable reason the musicians of the Society failed to realize the importance of the hymn in its application to the work of the Society; so, while the honor belongs to Compatriot Thruston for first presenting and thus preserving in the Society this famous music and words, it remained for Compatriot Poole to have it sung before audiences of compatriots. It is a very inspiring selection and should be sung by the Society in general.

DAVID L. PIERSON,
Secretary, New Jersey Society.

REPORT OF MEMORIAL COMMITTEE AT SPRINGFIELD, MASS.

MAY 11, 1922.

MR. PRESIDENT GENERAL AND COMPATRIOTS:

The work of your Memorial Committee and that of the Joint Committee with the Descendants of the Signers is one and the same, and therefore the one report will convey to you the information as to what the two committees have accomplished.

The Joint Committee had a meeting in New York City in June last, which was attended by Judge Albert McC. Matthewson, Mr. John Calvert, substituting for Mr. Russell Duane, their President, and Mr. Charles T. Adams, on behalf of the Descendants of the Signers, and by Mr. Matthew Page Andrews, Col. George A. Elliott, and your chairman of the Memorial Committee as our representatives. The meeting was an enthusiastic one. The Descendants of the Signers were anxious to increase the membership of this committee from six to eight, and, that being entirely agreeable to all parties, they added Mr. John Calvert, their Secretary. As yet I have not made a recommendation to our President General as to who should be the fourth member of our committee, the desire being that all representatives shall be active workers.

In my last report I gave the list of twelve of the Signers whose wills had not been located or the administration upon whose estates had not been found.

Immediately after our last Congress, Compatriot Granville H. Norcross, of Boston, located the administration upon the estate of Elbridge Gerry in East Cambridge and kindly sent us an abstract of the proceedings.

President Arthur B. Clarke, of the Virginia Society, obtained for us the will of Thomas Nelson, Jr., which has been carefully edited by one of his descendants, Compatriot Roswell Page, of Virginia.

Compatriot Harry Orville Hall, of our District of Columbia Society, a collateral descendant of Lyman Hall, after reading the report of your committee in the October BULLETIN, kindly wrote to our President General and sent a copy of what purported to be the will of Lyman Hall, but what really is a power of attorney for disposing of his estate, which amounted to virtually the same thing. Through him and his daughter, a D. A. R. Regent, we have been able to obtain information regarding this Signer and his family.

Therefore, instead of twelve, I can now report that we are lacking the copies of the wills or the administration upon the estate of the following nine Signers:

James Wilson, of Pennsylvania; George Clymer, of Pennsylvania; Samuel Chase, of Maryland; George Wythe, of Virginia; Carter Braxton, of Virginia; William Hooper, of North Carolina; Thomas Heyward, Jr., of South Carolina; Thomas Lynch, Jr., of South Carolina, and George Walton, of Georgia.

Now, as to the location of the graves of the Signers, in my last I reported that there were ten whose graves had been located within a close degree of approximation, such as the churchyard or burial-ground. George Wythe was among these. Since then a certain group of organizations in Richmond, Va., of which our Virginia Society is one, has determined the location of the grave of George Wythe and erected at the head of that grave a handsome granite monument. His name, therefore, should be transferred to those the location of whose graves is definitely known.

In my previous report I gave the names of three the location of whose graves was unknown or merely surmised. My information is, after a most careful study of the question, the late Mr. Caperton Braxton, a descendant of Carter Braxton, the Signer, was firmly convinced that Carter Braxton was buried at "Chericoke" in an unmarked grave. I think we will have to accept his conclusions as correct.

Compatriot John Scott Harrison, descendant of Benjamin Harrison, the Signer, of our Montana Society, upon reading the October BULLETIN, wrote, giving me the name of Benjamin Harrison Wilkins, Tullahoma, Tenn, whom he thought would be able to give me definite information regarding the burial-place of his Signer ancestor. Mr. Wilkins wrote me that he was reared on the adjoining plantation to Berkeley, had often been to the burial-ground there, and, although he had not been there for many years, he was certain the Signer was buried within the family burial-ground not far from the gate in the iron railing surrounding it, and that the grave was covered with a marble slab. In reply to my suggestion that he might have been buried at Westover, he replied, "You can dismiss from your mind any probability of his having been buried at Westover; the bones of a Harrison could never have remained quiet in the burial-ground of the old 'Tory' Byrd family, that owned Westover at that time." I accordingly arranged with a man in Richmond, Va., who had previously taken me there, to visit the burial-ground, take with him a sharp stick, and make search for either slab or fallen headstone which might be within that burial-ground hidden from sight by the mass of myrtle and undergrowth. He wrote me that within that railing there was no space even a foot square that he had not searched in this way, but was not able to locate either, but from Mr. Jamison, the present owner of the place, he has learned that Benjamin Harrison was buried within that burial-ground and the location of his grave is known, and the next time I go to Richmond, Va., he will arrange for me to be shown the spot. I feel, therefore, that regarding the burial-place of the 56 Signers our present information is there were:

Lost at sea.. 1
Exact spot of the original burial-place known, with none of their remains
    disturbed 33
Those whose remains have been removed and reinterred.................... 10
Location of whose graves are known with close degree of approximation... 11
    Francis Lewis, New York.
    Francis Hopkinson, New Jersey.
    Rich'd Stockton, New Jersey.
    Geo. Ross, Pennsylvania.
    Cæsar Rodney, Delaware.
    Richard Henry Lee, Virginia.
    Carter Braxton, Virginia.
    Benjamin Harrison, Virginia.
    Joseph Hewes, North Carolina.
    Arthur Middleton, South Carolina.
    Thos. Heyward, South Carolina.
Location of whose graves are unknown or merely surmised................ 1
    Button Gwinnett, Georgia.
                                                    ——
                                                   56

Regarding the grave of Richard Henry Lee, I am informed that Mr. Lawrence R. Lee, Washington, D. C., is actually engaged in having the graveyard inclosure at Old Burnt House, in Westmoreland County, Virginia, restored, and he hopes to determine the exact location of the grave of Richard Henry Lee and place a monument to him there.

It was my idea to take the field this year, as I did last, to personally visit the homes, graves, and families of the Signers in the Southern States, thus obtaining that information which can be acquired only through the personal touch, but unfortunately circumstances over which I had no control have prevented my doing so. I hope that conditions during the coming year may be more propitious for carrying on the class of work I hope to accomplish.

    Respectfully submitted,   R. C. BALLARD THRUSTON,
                                    Chairman Memorial Committee.

The following letter is of interest in connection with the foregoing report:

                                    NEW ORLEANS, LA., 6, 9, '22.

Mr. E. M. WENTWORTH,
    National Society, Sons of the
        American Revolution, Des Moines, Iowa.

MY DEAR MR. WENTWORTH:

    Through the kindness of our member, Compatriot J. St. Clair, Favrot, of Baton Rouge, I ran across something that will probably be of interest to you relative to your work in the matter of burial-places of the Signers of the Declaration of Independence.

In one of the old graveyards in Baton Rouge there is a very old headstone to Robert Cain Morris, and it reads approximately as follows:

ROBERT CAIN MORRIS,
Son of Thomas and Sarah Morris,
of the City of New York,
and
Grandson of Robert Morris, Signer of
the Declaration of Independence and
first Treasurer of the United States.

The headstone goes on to relate that he was en route from Pittsburgh to New Orleans and was taken with the cholera at Vicksburg and died just before he arrived at Baton Rouge. He was buried in Baton Rouge.

The above for your information. I don't know how valuable it is, but it may lead on to something else.

Yours very truly,

C. ROBT. CHURCHILL,
President Louisiana Society, S. A. R.

REPORT OF COMMITTEE ON NATIONAL ARCHIVES BUILDING

For the past eight years the Special Committee on a National Archives Building has been interested in the project of erecting at the National Capital a building suitable for safeguarding the valuable records of the Federal Government. The pressing need of such a building is recognized by every one and the necessity steadily grows more imperative. It is now nearly half a century since the idea of protecting our immensely valuable historical records was first urged upon Congress. Twenty years ago a suitable site was purchased by authority of Congress, but the land was diverted to other uses. Two years ago options were taken on another site, but Congress took no action and the options expired.

Plans for the building have been prepared in the office of the Supervising Architect of the Treasury. The Fine Arts Commission and the Public Buildings Commission are committed to the project. The Secretary of the Treasury has authority under present legislation to contract for a site. He has in mind a centrally located square of land, part of which is already owned by the Government.

No further progress can, however, be made until Congress acts, and Congress is slow to act. The Congress is a greatly overworked body with sufficient routine business work on hand to occupy its time. The state of the national finances requires the strictest economy. There is no impelling public sentiment demanding an appropriation for an Archives Building. The necessity for such a building is fully recognized, but there is no public demand for it, as there is for good roads, soldiers' bonus, public buildings, river and harbor improvements, etc. Until pressure is brought to bear upon Senators and Congressmen by their constituents the project will be deferred to a more favorable time and many years of delay will follow. Until the necessary legislation is enacted this Congress and the State Societies should be insistent and unceasing in exerting all influence possible to accomplish that desired end. Every year of delay means greater danger of the destruction of documents and records of inestimable value.

Very respectfully submitted,

FRED'K C. BRYAN,
Chairman.

REPORT OF COMMITTEE ON AMERICANIZATION AND ALIENS

SPRINGFIELD, MASS., *May* 16, 1922.

Your Committee upon Americanization and Aliens present the following report:

As in former years, the members of the committee have submitted to the chairman an account of the activities in their various localities. Dr. Samuel Judd Holmes reports for the Washington Society that at the present time the American Legion is interested in the proper education of the alien and furthering the teaching, in the city of Seattle and vicinity of the State, principles of government, reverence for our national institutions, and appreciation of the privileges enjoyed in this country. An interesting pamphlet was prepared and circulated by the Department at Washington of the American Legion on "The Reason Why," written by Dr. William C. Hicks, director of Americanization work in that State. This pamphlet is worthy of general circulation and contains a fine pledge to America.

The Legion is seeking to secure legislative enactment requiring the teaching throughout the State of higher ideals of citizenship, the history of the founders of our institutions, etc.

The Y. M. C. A. and Knights of Columbus have also been active in this good work.

Dr. Holmes states, from his own experience, that he is confident that personal contact in teaching carries the lesson home more effectually and is more impressive, coupled, as it should be, with true interest and sympathy. In the work in the legislative, judicial, and executive departments, as taught in their schools, specialists were called in from each department, they being successful in securing a Governor, a Congressman, members of the Legislature, a member of the President's Cabinet, and heads of the city and county departments. These carried such an interest to the classes that the true value was clearly shown, and proved a wonderful stimulus to the members of the class.

Past President General Jenks, of the Illinois Society, reports that, under the direction of Secretary Bowman, of that Society, there has been a large circulation of the American's Creed, particularly in the public schools. There has been much personal work by individual members of the Illinois Society. Many addresses have been delivered in the schools by speakers upon topics tending to promote patriotism and patriotic endeavor and the enlightenment of the foreign-born as to the ideals held by all true Americans. There has also been co-operation with the judiciary in the various courts at the naturalization sessions.

Harry T. Lord, of New Hampshire, reports that they have in that State very satisfactory laws tending to aid in Americanization work:

"No child is allowed to work until he is sixteen or a graduate of grammar school (eight grades). From sixteen to twenty-one no one may work who does not attend evening school sixty nights per year. These two sections give a good hold on all foreign people.

"We have classes in home management of various types for mothers, as well as typical English courses. The men, and some women, also are provided with classes for the study of history and government for direct preparation for citizenship papers. We have examination arrangements with the U. S. Government whereby our graduates are not questioned in court, being accepted by diploma. One independent French organization has been conducting similar classes, but is to merge with us this fall because of this privilege. In this city of less than 80,000 people there are over 2,000 in regular attendance at evening schools—a proportion not generally found, I think.

"Meetings and lectures are provided at intervals, as are patriotic entertainments. Personal service by the teachers and officials of the school department has more than any other work brought the foreign or 'New American' group to a realization of the spirit of equality and mutual helpfulness so necessary to the preservation of our form of government and society. This last is by no means confined to the night school pupils.

"As to needs, the greatest need in Manchester is real trained workers who can go to the homes of mothers who are unable to get to the schools. I would suggest that your Society go on record and use its influence to see that funds are provided by the city or other agency for this purpose.

"During the last few years, as immigration has been slowed up, first by the war, and then by the unemployment situation, it has seemed that we have gained in the fight. However, it is very certain that when conditions become normal again we can never keep up if the previous unrestricted flow of undesirables is permitted. Congress is now, in its slow, laborious manner, considering some means of checking this flow. I hope your Society will use its strength to see that Congress makes some provision to check the undesirables (in large numbers), and that at their homes, rather than after they have made the trip to America."—*Extract from letter of Assistant Superintendent of Schools, Manchester, New Hampshire.*

Dr. Charles Bangs, of the Massachusetts Society, reports that the Department of Education of Massachusetts, the cities and towns and by-organizations, have accomplished much in the interest of Americanism. The study of American history or civics is compulsory in the high schools of Massachusetts. The State Society has for the past three years given the Washington and Franklin medal to the pupil of the graduating class of any school making seasonable application who has obtained the highest rank in that study. In 1921 one hundred and forty-two high schools applied for the medal and all reported that it had greatly stimulated interest in the study of history. This year the number will approximate two hundred.

He reported that the problem of the alien has been one that confronted us for the past three hundred years, and that its solution necessarily varies from time to time. He states that the Pilgrims set the example of assimilation or deportation, and they also set forth the ideals of Americanism more clearly than any other unit of the various elements of colonization. Dr. Bangs inclosed a number of clippings showing the widespread interest in this subject.

Mr. McMathewson, of Connecticut, writes that under the will of Compatriot L. Wheeler Beecher, of New Haven, one-fifth of the residue of his estate was given to the General Davis Humphrey Branch of the Connecticut Society, S. A. R., to be used in its discretion for promoting the patriotic purposes of the Society. This fund gives this Society a generous yearly income, which is used for prizes in high schools and grammar schools and is co-operating with the American Legion in assisting it in its complicated work, and these specific lines of work are producing substantial results. He urges that the most important work is with the school children and with the veterans of the late war. He writes that they are now drifting and skeptical; that during the war they were idealistic; that politicians will exploit them, but we can reach them and help them.

Thomas W. Williams, of the New Jersey Society, reports that much has been done in the New Jersey Chapters in the line of addresses, lectures in classes, and the distribution of literature among the aliens; that the Y. M. C. A. and Salvation

Army are accomplishing much, and that the incoming President of the New Jersey State Society, Judge Lyon, has devoted much time to this work within the past year. Mr. Williams suggests the factories as a fruitful field for Americanization work.

In New York very much is being done to assist the alien. The chambers of commerce of a number of cities are now making appropriations for this work. In the Rochester Chamber of Commerce the Council for Better Citizenship is composed of the leading citizens. Many members of our organization are members of that council. During the past year it had a series of six lectures and entertainments in six different centers of the city, the meetings being held in the larger schools, public and parochial. Members of the faculty of the University of Rochester tendered their services for lectures upon American history. Talks were given upon the importance of conserving the public health and moving pictures were put on, with addresses by prominent citizens. This series of thirty-six meetings was largely attended and very popular.

The Council for Better Citizenship is very active. One of its aims is to impress upon the new citizens their privileges and responsibilities and to interest the native-born in his new brother.

The council consists of five committees, namely: New Citizens' Committee, Service Bureau Committee, Education Committee, Legislation Committee, and Racial Advisory Committee. The members of the New Citizens' Committee appear in court on naturalization days and greet the newly made citizens. During the year five large dinners were given at the Chamber of Commerce, at which the new citizens are invited. Here the members of the chamber mingle with the new citizens in the proportion of about two to six or seven, exercises are held, and the final certificates of citizenship delivered. In 1921, 1,370 citizens were greeted, and of this number about 1,000 attended dinners.

The Service Bureau in 1921 maintained a central office at the chamber for the help and information of the foreign-born. During the year there were over 5,000 callers and the new citizens and foreign-born were rendered every conceivable service.

The Education Committee recently conducted a "Learn English Drive," with 250 teams consisting of one Chamber of Commerce member and an interpreter, or Team Head. These teams canvassed foreign-born homes, receiving pledges from those upon whom they called to the effect that they would join a class in English or citizenship. Reports show that approximately 2,000 pledged themselves, and within a few weeks about 50 per cent of those registered became members of such classes. There is no end to the avenues of such work for that committee. I would advise any one who desires to know more specifically about this work to correspond with the most efficient secretary of this council, Miss Melissa Bingeman, of the Rochester Chamber of Commerce.

President Harding has suggested that July 4th might properly and with profit be turned to the promotion of Americanism work among America's great foreign-born population. This situation is all the more timely, in that as the result of the restriction of immigration by the 3 per cent law and of the continued departure of aliens, the increase of population by the influx of aliens has been halted.

There is proposed legislation before the present session of Congress tending to correct some of the absurdities of our naturalization law. At present in the United States 10,000 petitions for citizenship are not granted and of these 9,000 are refused upon technicalities. For instance, in many jurisdictions a petitioner cannot be admitted unless two witnesses swear they have known him for five consecutive years immediately preceding his petition, and that these two witnesses must accompany him when he has his court hearing before the Supreme Court Justice. A man might move from New York to Buffalo after living in one city for two or three years, and thus be deprived of securing his citizenship until he had lived five years in his new home. It is desired that this injustice be corrected by permitting depositions to be present~d from witnesses who have known the applicant in his former home.

In addition to about 100,000 who are annually admitted to citizenship, 80,000 come into citizenship incidentally by reason of the domestic relations. It is highly desirable that the naturalization law be modified and the State laws affecting the status and voting qualifications of citizens conform with the Federal statutes.

The new citizen in many cases is as plastic as the little child. He appreciates attention and I think in the great majority of cases appreciates the efforts which are being made for his advancement and uplift. Our great organization can do no better work than to co-operate with all agencies which are working to this end. The welfare of our country is fast passing into the hands of those whose ancestors migrated to this country long after the Revolution, and we need to be most alert to preserve these ideals.

Respectfully submitted,

HARVEY F. REMINGTON,
Chairman.

REPORT OF COMMITTEE ON PATRIOTIC EDUCATION, SPRINGFIELD, MASS., MAY 15, 1922

To the Thirty-third Annual Congress of the National Society of the Sons of the American Revolution.

MR. PRESIDENT GENERAL AND COMPATRIOTS:

Your Committee on Patriotic Education begs to report that the usefulness of our organization in the cause of good citizenship has been advanced by the attention of our compatriots to several enterprises assigned to their care.

As foremost in importance mention should be made of the beginning of a survey of school histories and text-books in use throughout the United States of America. Through the efforts of the President General the Society has obtained for examination a collection of these publications, numbering over sixty volumes, recently written or revised by various authors.

All reports of the survey are not yet complete, and it now appears advisable to continue the examinations through the summer months. The committee gratefully acknowledges the assistance and example of President General McCamant for the able criticisms herewith submitted on Muzzey's School History; A History of the United States, by John P. O'Hara; History of the United States, by McLaughlin and Van Tyne.

The latter two publications, together with the 'School Histories of Hart, Ward, Guitteau, and Everett Barnes, have received unfavorable criticism in the pamphlet of Charles Grant Miller, entitled "Treason to American Tradition."

It was hoped that at this Congress announcement could be made to the conclusion of this entire survey; but the work undertaken has required much more time than was expected and was delayed in some measure owing to the distance separating the compatriots who have the examination in charge.

The following plan of survey has been furnished by our President General:

"What is of value is a detailed criticism, noting an error on one page, an objectionable statement on another, and a characterization of such an event as the Boston Tea Party or the Surrender of Yorktown or the French Alliance. I think it is important to ascertain whether or not histories in use adequately emphasize the American Revolution and record the hero tales incident thereto.

"They should be correct in their statement of facts; they should tell the story in a dramatic manner and in such a way as to grip the imagination of the students.

"They should strongly stress the value of our form of government and the sacrifices necessary to secure it.

"They should be free from partisan bias in the discussion of the events of the last twenty-five years. They should be particularly free from anything which can minister to class hatred or which can stir up hatred by the poor for the rich. This valuable plan of action is proving a great aid to members of the Society who are engaged in the text-book examinations."

The Sons of the American Revolution during the past year have surpassed all former achievements by assisting high schools and other educational institutions in their celebrations of a patriotic character on anniversaries of Constitution Day, Washington's Birthday, and other special occasions.

The idea of awarding medals for patriotic essays in the schools has proved very effective. Valuable suggestions regarding such prizes have been made by compatriot J. W. Brooman.

The advisability of using motion pictures to promote patriotic education has been considered by members of this committee. Recommendations have been made to introduce some themes and striking incidents which we feel should be emphasized before the youth of our country, and also by bringing influence to bear in favor of such high-class productions when they are finally produced. We could also be of service in criticising and preventing the production of false or incorrect history.

Much has been said—and yet not enough—in praise of the American's Creed. This keynote of true Americanism has been very helpful to those interested in patriotic education.

Your committee recommends a larger distribution in its several forms. The popularity of the American's Creed is largely due to the untiring efforts of Compatriot Matthew Page Andrews.

The National Association for Constitutional Government makes a very strong appeal to the Sons of the American Revolution and to all loyal citizens for support in its endeavor to maintain throughout the country a profound appreciation of the Constitution of the United States and a better understanding of its benefits. This association, by frequent publication of bulletins and pamphlets, has given valuable information to your committee regarding the attitude of instructors in universities and colleges appertaining to their loyalty to the Constitution and their ability and willingness to teach the great truths of our nation's history.

Without attempting to offer a detailed account of all matters that have received attention, the committee gratefully acknowledges the assistance and suggestions so kindly rendered by compatriots and friends of this Society.

The opportunities for service in the line of patriotic education have been unlimited. It must be admitted that our efforts are but a beginning of works that are yet to be accomplished. Our service has a national character. The greatest requisite for useful citizenship is a high-minded desire to maintain and perpetuate the American institutions of good government.

LINN PAINE,
Chairman.

REPORT OF THE FLAG COMMITTEE, 1922

COMPATRIOTS:

The Flag Committee of the National Society, Sons of the American Revolution, reports once more that the Congress of the United States has failed up to this time to enact a law to protect the Flag of the United States from abuse, misuse, and commercial degradation. The bill introduced by Hon. W. E. Andrews, a hundred per cent American from Nebraska, which was approved by this Society, remains in the Committee on the Judiciary, and will likely stay there unless unearthed and rescued by the united efforts of those who believe in a clean Flag. If protective legislation is ever secured, as stated in former reports, it will be necessary to have united effort. Today it is said that Congress is so jammed with bills and resolutions to settle problems of the World's War that it will be impossible at this session to secure even a hearing on the protection of the Flag.

The fact that congressional action has not been had in the past and that our country has not severely suffered by absence of legislation is used as an argument that Flag legislation is unnecessary; that without a law the Flag will be forcibly protected by forceful Americans, should flagrant acts be committed against the symbol of our Government, the Flag.

Your committee does not agree to arguments akin to lynch law. It insists that the Government should be in a position to promptly proceed in a lawful, orderly, and systematic way against those who would debase or deface the Flag representing the Government and our institutions. It is unfair for Congress to neglect taking action, and by so doing force lovers of the Flag perhaps to do unlawful things when aroused by overt acts of those who do not love country, Flag, and the institutions established by our fathers and defended by their sons. Come what may, the Flag unsullied must remain waving aloft unfurled.

Twelve years have passed since your chairman took up the work of the committee laid down by General Vincent, and it still, as in the beginning, urges Congress to enact the Andrews bill or one equally as good, and by doing so protect the Flag that Congress created. It will not do, without a law, to rely on patriotic sentiment to protect the symbol of Government, and it is not fair to force the States of the Union to enact measures to protect the Flag, not the creation of a State, but the creation of the Congress of the United States.

All States honor the Flag. Many of them, becoming tired of waiting for a Federal law, have, in its absence, enacted laws, although limited in jurisdiction and differing in their provisions, these laws have filled a useful purpose by arousing patriotic sentiment, teaching the meaning and proper use of the Flag, and enforcing the law by punishing those who willfully misuse it.

It is interesting to recall that since the introduction in Congress, by S. S. Cox, of the first Flag bill, forty-four years ago, Americanization has been advocated and practiced by the Sons of the American Revolution with good results and without expense to Government or individual not a member of the organization.

When the United States entered the World War, the Sons of the American Revolution were relieved "officially" of this patriotic work.

It is thought by the enlargement of patriotic instruction the protection of the Flag will follow, for Congressmen are not likely to remain negligent of responsibilities when urged by large numbers of thoughtful patriots to support a law that will prevent the desecration of the Flag. The committee is encouraged by the fact that there never was a time when the Flag was more respected, used, and intelligently displayed than today. This noticeable change is attributed to the examples set by our soldiers from overseas, patriotic instructions of patriotic instructors, observance of Flag Day in the schools and elsewhere, and the teaching of Flag etiquette. This change was especially noticeable in Washington during the Conference of the Limitation of Armaments (1921). The regulations promulgated by the Secretary of War were strictly followed by delegates and the citizens.

The regulations stated that—

"Foreign flags should not be displayed until November 11 except on days when delegates arrive in town.

"On November 11 all United States flags should be at half-staff from sunrise to sunset. Foreign flags cannot be placed at half-staff, but should be held to the staff at the bottom, so as not to fly free.

"Flags should be flown every day for the first week of the conference. After November 19 foreign flags should be flown only on public holidays and during the last two weeks of the conference.

"Flags should be arranged in the following order from left to right looking from the building toward the street: Portugal, China, Japan, France, United States (center), Great Britain, Italy, Belgium, Netherlands."

During the Arms Conference an effort was made by the Interparliamentary Union to have Congress adopt a "Peace Flag" by attaching a white border to the Flag of the United States. Senator Smoot, a man of vision, deserves the thanks of the country for his successful efforts in preventing the adoption of the resolution. Thinking of similar misuses of the Flag, Senator Smoot said, "Our Flag is good enough as it is and needs no decoration when displayed at any peace or other conference or at any place in all the world. The Stars and Stripes represent American ideals of Government and all that is good in society and in government," and the Senate agreed to his statement.

Many books, papers, addresses, reports, congressional hearings, etc., have been written with the Flag as a text. These publications have proven instructive, interesting, and helpful and the writers deserve great praise for their part in educating and making better and more patriotic citizens.

The committee urges that the forty years' wandering in the wilderness seeking a law to protect the Flag (the Ark of the Covenant) be continued. It recommends that the Americanizing of the alien within the gate and the native be continued until there shall be one America, one language, and one Flag— the Red, White, and Blue.

W. V. Cox.

May 10, 1922.

THE AMERICAN FLAG ASSOCIATION

This patriotic organization, which numbers among its founders many prominent compatriots of our own National Society, after twenty-five years of constructive patriotic work for the flag, in which it has aided the adoption of flag laws in thirty-eight States of our Union, has now incorporated and received its charter from the State of New York.

On Thursday, December 4, a meeting of the new directors was held in the Governor's Room, New York City Hall, at 2 o'clock p. m., at which the following officers were elected: President, Cornelius A. Pugsley; Secretary, Edward Hagaman Hall; Treasurer, W. I. Lincoln Adams; Registrar, Clarence E. Leonard, and 100 charter members were named on the executive committee. It is expected that thousands of citizens will join the Association throughout the United States. It is non-political and non-sectarian, and for the fee of $5 for life membership a certificate is furnished free. This certificate is lithographed from an engraved plate and bears the American flag in colors.

Among the charter members are Louis Annin Ames, who is a Vice-President; Wallace McCamant, George Albert Smith, Lewis B. Curtis, Chancellor Jenks, Thomas W. Williams, Carl M. Vail, Stuyvesant Fish, John A. Stewart, Admiral Harrington, General Oliver Bridgeman, Eugene C. Bonniwell, Mrs. George Minor, President General of the National Society, Daughters of the American Revolution; Mrs. Bleakley, Mrs. Ten Eyck and other representative men and women in our patriotic organizations.

Those of our Society who desire to join this newly incorporated Association may do so by sending their names and addresses, accompanied by a check for five dollars (which pays their life membership), to the Treasurer, Major W. I. Lincoln Adams, at his New York office, 135 West 14th Street.

THE FLAG

Flag Day, June 14; Constitution Day, September 17

Pledge of Allegiance: I pledge allegiance to my flag and to the Republic for which it stands—one nation, indivisible, with liberty and justice for all.

When and How to Display the Flag of the United States

Holidays, When the Flag Should be Displayed at Full Staff

Lincoln's Birthday	February 12
Washington's Birthday	February 22
Jefferson Day	April 17
Battle of Lexington (Patriots Day)	April 19
Memorial Day*	May 30
Flag Day	June 14
Battle of Bunker Hill	June 17
Independence Day	July 4
La Fayette Day	September 6

---

*On Memorial Day, May 30, the flag should fly at half staff from sunrise to noon and full staff from noon to sunset.

"Star Spangled Banner" Day--September 13
Paul Jones Day---September 23
Columbus Day--October 12
Battle of Saratoga--October 17
Surrender of Yorktown--October 19
Evacuation Day (New York)-------------------------------------November 25

Stars and Stripes is the official name of the National Flag of the United States. In the Army our National Flag is called the Standard; also the Colors. When borne with another flag, the regimental color, the two flags are called a "Stand of Colors." In the Navy our National Flag is known as the U. S. Ensign.

To show proper respect for the flag, the following should be observed:

Display

The flag should not be hoisted before sunrise nor allowed to remain up after sunset.

At "retreat" sunset, civilian spectators should stand at "attention" and uncover during the playing of the "Star Spangled Banner." Military spectators are required by regulation to stand at "attention" and give the military salute. During the playing of the National Hymn at "retreat" the flag should be lowered, but not then allowed to touch the ground.

When the flag is flown at half staff as a sign of mourning, it should be hoisted to the top of the staff and then lowered to position, dropping it from the top of the staff the distance of the width of the flag, and preliminary to lowering from half staff it should first be raised to the top.

On ship board the National Flag is the flag to be raised first and lowered last.

Where several flags are displayed on poles with the National Flag, the Stars and Stripes should be hoisted first and on the tallest and most conspicuous staff. Where two flags are displayed, one our National Flag, it should be placed on the right. (To ascertain the right of a building, face in the same direction as the building.) No flag should be flown from the same staff as the U. S. Flag, except in the Navy; then only during Divine services, when the Church Penant may be displayed above the National Flag—God above country.

When, in parade, the National Flag is carried with any other flag, it should have the place of honor, at the right. If a number of flags are carried, the National Flag should either precede the others or be carried in the center, above the others, on a higher staff.

When flags are used in unveiling a monument, tablet or statue, they should not fall to the ground, but be carried aloft, forming a distinctive feature of the ceremony.

When the National Flag is used as a banner, the union should be at the right (as you face the flag). When used as an altar covering, the union is at the right (as you face the altar), and nothing should ever be placed upon the flag except the Holy Bible.

The flag should never be flown reversed except in case of distress at sea.

Portraying the Flag

To properly illustrate the flag, the staff should always be at the left of the picture, with the flag floating to the right. When two flags are crossed, the National

Flag should be at the right. If the National Flag is pictured as a banner, the union is at the right.

Salute

When the National Colors are passing in parade or in review, the spectator should, if walking, halt, and if sitting, arise and stand at "attention" and uncover.

The national salute is one gun for every State.

The international salute is, under the laws of nations, 21 guns.

On shore the flag should not be dipped by way of salute or compliment.

EVENTS OF STATE SOCIETIES

The District of Columbia Society.—The District of Columbia Society of the Sons of the American Revolution held a "Field Day" meeting in Rock Creek Cemetery on Tuesday, October 24, 1922, for the purpose of commemorating the setting of four Revolutionary gravestone markers at the graves of Chaplain Abraham Baldwin, Lieut. Thomas Boyd, Ensign Peter Faulkner, and William Deakins, Jr.

The program consisted of an inspection of the markers, followed by addresses on Abraham Baldwin and Peter Faulkner by Compatriot Josiah A. Van Orsdel, Justice of the Court of Appeals of the District of Columbia, and on Thomas Boyd and William Deakins, Jr., by Compatriot Allen C. Clark, President of the Columbia Historical Society. Compatriot John Clagett Proctor contributed an original poem appropriate to the time and place. Mrs. Harriet Harding Guthrie was the soloist of the occasion, and with the assistance of the cornetist, Mr. T. W. Harvey led the singing of patriotic songs. The inspection of the markers afforded a splendid opportunity for the compatriots and their guests to view also the famous St. Gaudens' Statue in memory of Mrs. Henry Adams.

After the exercises in the cemetery the Society proceeded to Rock Creek Parish Hall, where an outing supper was served. After the supper greetings were extended on behalf of the Vestry and Men's Club of the Parish by Compatriot Walter B. Patterson, who related some of the interesting early history of the cemetery and the parish. Compatriot William L. Boyden, librarian, made an after-supper talk on Quaint Epitaphs and Compatriot William A. Miller gave an address on A Few Famous Epitaphs. Several compatriots gave humorous or specially appropriate epitaphs.

The Society participated officially in the unveiling ceremonies in connection with the presentation to the city of Washington of the monument to Edmund Burke by the Sulgrave Institution of England through the Sulgrave Institution of the United States. President Ely, of the District of Columbia Society, presented a beautiful wreath on behalf of the Society. On October 27 the Society participated in the program for Navy Day. Exercises at the grave of the unknown soldier in Arlington in the morning and a program at the monument of John Paul Jones during the afternoon constituted the ceremonies. The District of Columbia Society feels that its increasing membership shows a healthy interest and activity in the work of our organization.

The Society held a November meeting on Wednesday evening, November 15, at the Lafayette Hotel.

There was an election of two members of the Board of Management, one to succeed Compatriot Eugene E. Stevens, recently deceased, and the other to succeed Compatriot Alfred B. Dent, who has recently moved to New York City and resigned from the Board of Management, but not from the Society.

The formal address of the evening was delivered by Dr. J. W. Crabtree, Secretary of the National Education Association, on the subject "Education, the Foundation of Democracy," and was an unanswerable argument for the equalization upward of educational opportunities in the United States. The address was intended as an introduction to "Educational Week," December 3 to 9. Compatriot George W. Young, recently returned from a diplomatic post in Asia Minor, made a brief report on "American *versus* Foreign Conditions." Music of a high order completed the program. The formal program was followed with a social hour, during which a buffet luncheon and smoker was enjoyed.

The Idaho Society.—The Idaho Society was honored by a visit, on December 4, from Vice-President General George Albert Smith, and a delightful dinner was held by the Society in his honor at the Owyhee Hotel, Boise. Compatriot C. P. Overfield, Registrar of the Utah Society, accompanied Vice-President General Smith. It is hoped that this visit will greatly stimulate the interest in the Society in Idaho, where we have a creditable membership, but so scattered over the State that it is difficult to promote general activities. There is a large field, however, for increase, and we have reason to hope for this to soon make itself felt.

The Illinois Society.—The annual meeting of the Society was held on December 4, at the Hamilton Club. No formal program was presented, but the announcement of the meeting requested members to think over and discuss various aspects of the organization, especially with regard to proposed increase in initiation fees and dues, with helpful suggestions for increase of membership attendance at meetings and other modifications and improvements. An interesting feature of the meeting was a roll call of 97 new members elected during the past year, with responses in seven words, either in person or by postal card, to the question, "Why I joined the Society?" The prevailing note of the replies gave as a reason "Perpetuating early American ideals," while one compatriot attracted considerable attention and comment by saying, "To help Americanize America." An election of officers followed the social hour with the following result: James Edgar Brown, President; William G. Adkins, First Vice-President; William P. Reed, Second Vice-President; Louis A. Bowman, Secretary; Henry R. Kent, Treasurer; George A. Brennan, Historian; John D. Vandercook, Registrar; William W. Johnstone, D. D., Chaplain, and Cecil R. Boman, Sergeant-at-Arms. Members of Board of Managers elected were: Henry W. Austin, Arthur R. Camp, Dorr E. Felt, Chancellor L. Jenks, Carroll H. Sudler, and David V. Webster.

The retiring President, Brigadier-General James M. Eddy, was presented with the official insignia and the President's emblem on his retirement from the Presidency. A special dinner is being arranged for Saturday evening, January 6, when the Society is to entertain the President General, Maj. W. I. Lincoln Adams, as he starts on his western tour, visiting several State Societies en route, an outline of this trip being printed elsewhere in this issue of the BULLETIN.

At the November meeting of the Springfield Chapter a subject of vital importance to the rising generation was presented, viz., the teaching of American history in the public schools, by one who has spent much time as a public-school teacher and knows the subject—Compatriot W. E. Archibald.

At this meeting the question of purchasing a State and city flag was proposed, but action was postponed until the December meeting. At the close of the meeting nearly half of the necessary amount was voluntarily promised by seven members.

At the St. Nicholas Hotel, Friday December 15, the Chapter met for dinner and an address by Mr. A. L. Bowen on "Some Facts About Ancestry."

The annual meeting and election of officers will be held Friday, January 5, 1923, at which time the Program Committee hopes to have two compatriots whose ancestors spent the winter with Washington at Valley Forge give some of the important results from the terrible suffering the Continental Army endured during that trying ordeal. These events have not been presented so far at any of the meetings and will bear thoughtful consideration.

The Indiana Society of the Sons of the American Revolution has been quite active during the past year along several different lines. An active membership campaign has resulted quite satisfactorily and the number of new members secured during the year is around forty, which number by the end of the Society's fiscal year, which is February 25, will probably be increased to fifty. This number of accessions exceeds the new membership for any year for the last decade with the single exception of 1921, when the number of new members secured was also around the fifty mark. In this matter of membership much credit is due our Secretary, Mr. Edmund L. Parker, of Kokomo, who has been most diligent and active in bringing up delinquents and in looking out for new members at all times. During the past three years the membership of the Indiana Society has been doubled, a record of which Mr. Parker, Secretary; Mr. Austin H. Brown, Past President and present chairman of the Membership Committee, may well feel proud, as they have had much to do with the increased membership.

In this connection we cannot pass without referring to the very sad bereavement which came to Secretary Parker in October in the loss of his wife, and we feel sure that the entire membership throughout the State sympathizes keenly with him.

Cornelius F. Posson, President of the State Society, changed his place of residence from Brazil, Indiana, to 538 East Drive, Woodruff Place, Indianapolis, in July. Mr. Posson is auditor for the Knox Consolidated Coal Company of Indianapolis, one of the largest coal operating companies in the country.

The leading activity for the year has been the compiling of a list of Revolutionary soldiers who are known to have spent their last days and to have died in Indiana. This list is being daily added to by data coming in on the subject all the time, and many unmarked graves of Revolutionary soldiers will be marked during the year 1923. Several bronze markers with the Society's insignia and several marble headstones have already been ordered and arrangements will be made for the marking of these graves.

Two most interesting and impressive fall ceremonies were held, one at the grave of Lieutenant William Ray in Vigo County, Indiana, and the other at the grave of William Tuffs in Elkhart County, Indiana. These ceremonies occurred on October 15 and 29 respectively, both of which days were delightful autumn days suitable for outdoor exercises. Mention has already been made in these columns concerning the finding of the grave of Lieutenant William Ray. At the grave of William Tuffs a boulder with bronze tablet was erected and dedicated with a most appropriate and impressive ceremony. Cut of the boulder with bronze tablet is here shown.

The tablet reads as follows:

Beneath this stone reposes the dust
of a patriot
WILLIAM TUFFS
of Massachusetts
Participant in the Boston Tea Party
Soldier of the Revolution
Soldier of the War of 1812.

This tablet erected by the Indiana Society of the Sons of the American Revolution.

President Posson has been called upon to speak on different occasions at meetings of a patriotic nature. On the Memorial Day in Brazil, Indiana, he delivered a patriotic address in connection with the Memorial Day service. On Lafayette Day, September 6, a ten-minute patriotic address was broadcasted by radio from the Star-Hatfield Radio Station in Indianapolis. In connection with the observance of Armistice Day by the "Men of Meridian Club" of Indianapolis, Mr. Posson was called upon for an address, which was well received. On Flag Day the John Morton Chapter, S. A. R., of Terre Haute, in connection with the Fort Harrison Chapter, D. A. R., of Terre Haute, observed the day with appropriate exercises. At Rushville on June 22 the inactive General Pleasant A. Hackleman Chapter, S. A. R., was reorganized, some fourteen members assembling at the home of Compatriot Earl H. Payne, who entertained the members with a most elaborate dinner, entertaining on this occasion also President Posson.

The Indiana Society now begins to look forward to the big event of the year, their annual meeting, which is always on February 25, the anniversary of the only Revolutionary event occurring on Indiana soil, the capture of Fort Sackville, Vincennes, by General George Rogers Clark. The Society is anticipating a larger attendance on the occasion of the annual meeting this year than it has enjoyed for many years and the Board of Managers will get together early in January to outline the program, and it is the intention to make this program more interesting than any that has been enjoyed in many years. An attempt will be made to get together at this meeting a collection of relics of the Revolutionary War, of which there are quite a few, pricelessly treasured by their owners, in different parts of the State. It is the Society's intention to have as guests at their annual meeting the owners of these historic relics, asking them to bring with them these interesting and valuable treasures. There is a Continental uniform actually worn in the Revolutionary War still in existence. There is a canteen which was used by a Revolutionary soldier. There is General Anthony Wayne's battle flag, and other things.

Professor Herbert Briggs, of the Terre Haute public schools, has continued throughout the year his active and energetic efforts in behalf of a better recognition in the text-books on history (and for a better teaching in the schools of the State of Indiana history and local history). He has worked most diligently, having sent letters to all of the more than two hundred public libraries in the State, the county superintendents, and others of influence in connection with school matters and has been financed to the full extent of his asking by the Society. This effort has met with some opposition on the part of some who for selfish and mercenary purposes would prefer to have text-books of their own choosing, and only for Compatriot Briggs' determination and great faith in the justice of his cause, we would not now be at the goal of success. Other State societies, inspired by this effort on our part, are taking up similar activity in their respective States.

The Iowa Society.—Lexington Chapter of Keokuk held an Armistice Day meeting and celebrated this anniversary jointly with a recognition of Constitution Day, which had been necessarily postponed. An address by President William G. Blood on the Evacuation of New York and General Washington's entry was supplemented by readings from John Marshall's Life of Washington. Other addresses were made by Mr. Hazen L. Sawyer and Dr. H. D. Hoover, of Carthage. A brief business meeting followed, at which reports were given of progress in Americanization work and plans for the memorial Victory Park, and new members elected. An exhibit of an old powder-horn, with traditions connected with it, by one of the chapter members, Mr. J. A. Dunlap, created much interest.

The Maine Society.—At the February 22d, 1920, annual meeting and banquet of the Maine Society of the Sons of the American Revolution, President William K. Sanderson appointed Hon. A. M. Spear, of Augusta; Hon. O. B. Clason, of Gardiner, and Converse E. Leach, Esq., of Portland, to appear before the Maine Legislature and solicit an appropriation of six hundred dollars ($600) to build a bronze tablet to place upon the granite marker at Valley Forge, and it was granted. The Board of Managers of the Maine Society appointed a committee comprising W. B. Berry, Esq., of Gardiner, chairman; Hon. A. M. Spear, of Augusta; Chas.

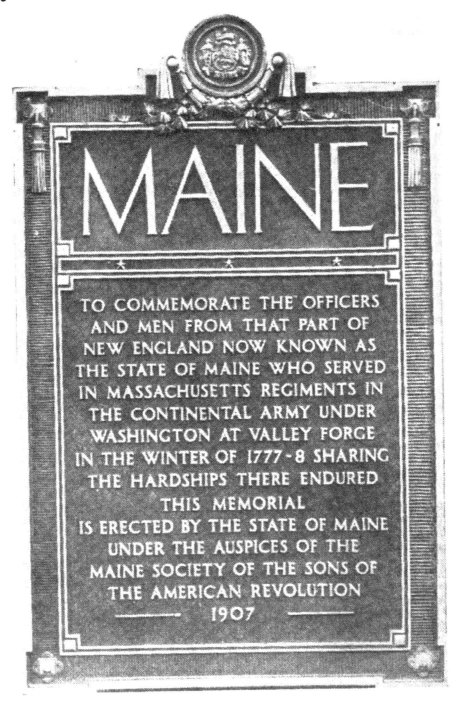

FINE BRONZE TABLET NOW AT VALLEY FORGE IN HONOR OF MAINE MEN THERE IN 1777-8

Erected by the State of Maine through efforts of the Sons of the Revolution and under direction of a committee composed of W. P. Berry, A. M. Spear, Wm. H. Sanderson, and Charles L. Hutchinson.

Lyman Hutchinson, Esq., and William K. Sanderson, Esq., of Portland, Me., to look after all the details of the building of the tablet. Mr. Leander Higgins, of Portland, was chosen as the architect and the sketch was drawn by him.

The tablet is made of statuary bronze and is 32 inches wide and 52 inches high. The seal of the State of Maine is on the top and in the center, with pine cones and ornamental trimmings. The inscription was written by Governor William T. Cobb. The letters were made large so they could be easily read by occupants of vehicles without getting out of the vehicle and pedestrians passing by. The tablet is placed upon the granite marker at Valley Forge.

The lowest bid and architect's fee exceeded the appropriation by sixty-five dollars ($65), but arrangements were made. to keep within the appropriation and still have the same design, material, and workmanship. The committee have devoted considerable of their time, thought, and money to complete the work and are perfectly satisfied with the results and sincerely trust the citizens of Maine and the Valley Forge Memorial Committee and all interested will be pleased and equally satisfied.

The Massachusetts Society.—The Massachusetts Society, Sons of the American Revolution, held its housewarming on the evening of Thursday, the 19th of October, at its rooms, 9 Ashburton Place, at eight o'clock. The meeting was presided over by the President, Charles H. Bangs, M. D., whose address of welcome related the activities of the Society during the present year. Vice-President J. Morton Davis gave account of the awards of the Washington and Franklin Medal to the best pupils in American history in the various schools of the Commonwealth. The Secretary, W. K. Watkins, presented to the Society a sword carried by Isaac Collier, a Marblehead soldier, during the Revolution. The Chaplain General, Rev. Frederic Williams Perkins, D. D., of Lynn, spoke on Americanization, and presented the War Service Medal of the Society to one of its members, Major Frederic Gilbert Bauer, still in the Advocate General's Department of the United States Army. Mr. Van Courtlandt Lawrence, chairman of the Committee of Entertainment, showed the lantern slides which were used in various moving-picture houses last month as illustrating the history of the Constitution of the United States. Other slides were also shown illustrating the Battle of Yorktown, which occurred on the 19th of October, 1781. There was exhibited an original plan of the battle, which is owned by the New England Historic Genealogical Society. After an inspection of the rooms of the Society, those present partook of a buffet lunch served in the small hall of the Society's building.

Isaac Lewis Chapter, Walpole.—Among the recent activities of this chapter have been the restoration and preservation of two old family burial-grounds containing the graves of Revolutionary patriots, which had become so completely obscured that no one knew of them. One had been sold several times as a part of the surrounding wood-lot. These graves, with 140 others, were decorated with Betsy Ross Flags by the President of the Chapter, Mr. Isaac Newton Lewis, thus relieving the solitude and neglect of former years. The Chapter has also given assistance to needy descendants of patriots living in the South and West and who know but little about their ancestry in the East. All State and National patriotic days have been appropriately observed, including ovations to Foch and Clemenceau as coming from Lafayette's land. A medal was presented to a high-school student for excellence in United States history.

THE SETH POMEROY CHAPTER, Northampton, held an open meeting Tuesday evening, December 12, in the First Church parlors in celebration of the 149th anniversary of the Boston Tea Party. The speaker of this occasion was Prof. John C. Hildt, of Smith College, who delivered an extremely instructive as well as entertaining address on "The Medieval University." Professor Hildt pointed out that the twelfth century, in which the chief of the European universities came into being, was one of the energetic awakenings and something approaching universal peace. This resulted in a revival of learning such as Europe had scarcely known since the days of Roman supremacy. A general desire to learn took hold of the classes, and students flocked eagerly around such teachers as Abelarde and William of Champeaux, forming the "studium" or the "studium generale." The latter gave instruction in more than one branch of learning, and was, therefore, more apt to attract foreign as well as native students. From the "studium generale" we derive our modern university. Professor Hildt closed his address with a reading from letters, drinking songs, and poems of a more or less humorous nature written by medieval students. The meeting was well attended, and the subject of the address, as arranged by Professor Hildt, proved strikingly appropriate to the occasion.

George H. Sergeant was elected Vice-President to fill the vacancy caused by the death of Arthur L. Kingsbury.

Seth Pomeroy Chapter entertained the ladies of Betty Allen Chapter, Daughters of the American Revolution, at this meeting.

Following the lecture tea and sandwiches were served, the meeting being held in celebration of the Boston Tea Party, which occurred December 16, 1773.

The Michigan Society.—Detroit Chapter met on November 7 at the University Club, Detroit. Dr. Earl C. Barkley, in charge of the program, had secured Prof. J. A. Frayer, of the University of Michigan, who spoke on "The Near East Today." Prior to the meeting many members gathered together for dinner in honor of the speaker.

WASHTENAW CHAPTER met on November 17 at the residence of its President, Dr. W. B. Hinsdale, 716 Forest Avenue, Ann Arbor. Prof. A. S. Aiton gave an address upon "American History in Spanish Archives." Reports from committees were received, and the matter of co-operating with the D. A. R. in the forthcoming centennial was considered. It was announced that the University of Michigan has established in its museum a department of Michigan archeology, and Dr. W. B. Hinsdale has been appointed to assist in the organization of the department and to act as custodian of the collections. It is desired to assemble there every possible item of information concerning the Michigan Indians—their history, remains, and relics. A permanent collection of specimens and data is contemplated. Co-operation and correspondence is invited.

At the unveiling of a statue to Theodore Roosevelt, at St. Joseph, Mich., on Armistice Day, a large American Flag was presented by Leonard J. Merchant, a member of the Connecticut State Society and veteran and founder of the Benton Harbor Palladium.

OAKLAND CHAPTER held a dinner on Thursday, December 7, 1922, at the Board of Commerce, Pontiac, attended by fourteen members, at which Charles I. Shattuck, President of Oakland Chapter, presided. The toastmaster was Roy V. Barnes. The guests of honor and speakers were Compatriot Julius E. Thatcher, Vice-

President of Detroit Chapter, who told of the activities of Detroit Chapter, and Compatriot John P. Antisdel, Detroit, member of Board of Managers of Michigan Society, who outlined the purposes, activities, and accomplishments of the Sons of the American Revolution and offered pertinent suggestions for local activities. Other speakers were Alfred L. Smith, Secretary of Oakland Chapter; Compatriot Thadeus D. Seeley, Mayor of Pontiac, and Compatriots Taylor, George H. Kimball, Dr. Le Baron, Franklin A. Slater, and Dr. Phillips. It was voted to offer the services of the Chapter to the Pontiac Board of Commerce for civic aid along patriotic lines.

LENAWEE CHAPTER held a dinner on Thursday evening, November 23, at Adrian, at which its own ladies were invited and also members of the D. A. R. Rev. Jos. A. Vance, D. D., Chaplain of the Detroit Chapter, was the guest of honor and speaker.

KENT CHAPTER held its first regular meeting for the season on Tuesday, November 14, at 8 p. m., at the Peninsular Club, Grand Rapids. The hosts for the evening were Compatriots Wm. R. Shelby and A. S. Goodman. Hon. Willis P. Perkins, Circuit Judge, was the speaker, his subject being "The Injunction."

Kent Chapter held its second meeting for the season on Tuesday, December 12, at the Peninsular Club. The hosts for the evening were Compatriots Frederick K. Tinkham and Frank E. Spraker. The speaker was Hon. George Clapperton, on the subject "Some Phases of Modern Taxation."

The officers mentioned on page 14 of the October number of the BULLETIN for Kent Chapter are superseded by the following: President, Albert M. Davis; Vice-President, Wm. R. Shelby; Secretary, Daniel W. Tower; Treasurer, L. S. Hillman; Registrar, Charles N. Remington.

Tuesday evening, December 5, the meeting of Detroit Chapter was held at the University Club. There were 50 present.

Wilbert B. Hinsdale, A. M., M. D., President of Washtenaw Chapter, Sons of the American Revolution, was guest and speaker. Dr. Hinsdale, who has been a professor and dean of the Homœopathic Medical College and director of the hospital of the University of Michigan since 1895, has been lately designated to organize a department of Michigan archeology in the University Museum, of which he has been appointed curator. It is the intention of the university to collect and preserve historical material, relics, and remains of the Indians of Michigan and gather data for publication concerning the life of primitive man in this State. Interest in the same has been obvious, as has been manifested in the many private collections of Indian remains gathered by Michigan families and by the many traditions and stories handed down to us from the Michigan pioneers. Much of this material has been lost or dispersed, but before it is forever too late the university has determined to make an effort to preserve the same, and to seek from the citizens of Michigan their legends, traditions, and stories of Indian life, as well as such specimens as can be gathered together. To those who have lived long in Michigan the Indian was a familiar character and his customs were known, but the great majority of the present inhabitants of Michigan have little knowledge thereof. Dr. Hinsdale gave a most interesting talk on "Primitive Man in Michigan," describing his customs, mounds, burial grounds, camp sites, trails, mines, earthworks, etc., illustrated with stereopticon views. President Carl F. Clark presided. A dinner in honor of the speaker was held prior to the meeting, which was attended by twenty members.

The Minnesota Society.—Under the guidance of President Kenneth G. Brill, of St. Paul, this Society has taken on renewed life, and with the assistance of the splendid chapter of 75 members in Minneapolis the State Society will make a substantial growth in 1923. On December 5 a new Chapter was formed in St. Paul, with a charter list of 35 members.

Duluth, under the direction of C. F. Graff, is about to institute a new Chapter, and Fergus Falls expects to organize a Chapter in January. The Society has made splendid progress during the year.

THE MINNEAPOLIS CHAPTER has had a very successful year and has taken in approximately 60 new members locally during the first year of the Chapter's existence, and for the coming year a strong Membership Committee has been appointed and many additions are expected. On December 4 the Chapter had its first annual meeting and elected the following officers: President, Charles P. Schouten; Vice-Presidents, Walter H. Wheeler and Benjamin A. Ege; Secretary, Louis P. Chute; Treasurer, Frank H. Coyle; Historian, Levi Longfellow, with Luther A. Baker, Ward H. Benton, and Robert J. Jordan as Directors.

The Missouri Society.—The annual banquet of the State organization was held in the new Hotel Chase, St. Louis, October 17, celebrating the 141st anniversary of the Yorktown victory in the War for American Independence. Following an invocation by the Rev. Joseph Harris Harvey, Linn Paine, President of the Missouri organization, welcomed the assembly, reviewed the activities of the State Society, and read letters of felicitation and regret from President Warren G. Harding, who is a member of the Sons of the American Revolution, President General Washington I. L. Adams, Governor Hyde, and Mayor Kiel. The principal speaker of the evening was Frederic A. Hill, chancellor of the Washington University, who delivered a very instructive address on patriotic education and highly commended the spirit of the soldiers of the World War, many of whom were present as members and guests of the Society.

Mrs. John Trigg Moss, Vice-President General of the Daughters of the American Revolution, brought the greetings of our sister society and urged that the two great organizations should continue working for the betterment and advance of America for Americans. A program of orchestral concert music was rendered under the direction of P. G. Anton and patriotic songs, arranged for the occasion, were sung by the Temple Male Quartette of St. Louis. A reception committee of fifty members was in charge of Compatriot David R. Francis, former Ambassador to Russia and President of the Missouri Historical Society. Compatriots I. Shreve Carter, J. Alonzo Matthews, and Cabell Gray were in charge of arrangements and provided all present with beautifully engraved souvenir programs. The banquet was the largest and probably the most notable event in the history of the Missouri Society.

The New Jersey Society.—One of the most notable events in the annals of the New Jersey Society was the reception tendered by President General Major Washington I. L. Adams to the entire membership on the evening of Armistice Day, November 11, at the headquarters, 33 Lombardy Street, Newark. Chester N Jones, Past President of the New Jersey Society, was master of ceremonies, and during the early evening hours the rooms, all decorated with palms and flags, were the scene of animated groups of compatriots discussing various forms of forward movements of the Society. Besides President General Adams, those in the receiving line were Past Presidents Carl M. Vail and Rev. Dr. Lyman Whitney Allen and President Adrian Lyon. At the conclusion of the receiving hours the party adjourned to the third floor for refreshments, after which the President General was prevailed upon to deliver an address, during which he said:

"It is a time for serious thinking and of realization of the sacrifices made for civilization. I was at Westfield today, where I met the mother of Mark Wallberg, born of foreign parents, who was the first man to carry the American flag over the top. The young man, under age, had volunteered his services in the Federal Army, but before he left for overseas duty his mother gave him a small American Flag, which he carried with him till the zero hour arrived; then he fastened the flag to his bayonet, and as he started to go through No Man's Land he fell, pierced by an enemy bullet. The flag was secured, however, by another soldier and is preserved today here, in the United States. I told the mother that although she had made a sacrifice for the flag she was the proud possessor of something more precious than could be computed by human standards, and that even if she were called upon to make many more sacrifices, how fortunate it would be for her that this could be done. We owe more than we can ever repay to the young men who went overseas under the Flag of Stars and Stripes, and Armistice Day will give us all an opportunity to express our gratitude to those who served so nobly in the World War. There were many of our own Society enrolled, some of whom never returned, but their deeds are in our safe keeping and we shall not forget them."

Several losses have occurred in the New Jersey Society during recent weeks, among them being Frederick B. Bassett, who had served for several years as a member of the Board of Managers and was also at one time President of the Elizabethtown Chapter, No. 1. His death occurred on November 11. Major James Soulard Tomkins, first President of Monmouth County Chapter, also died on this day, and De Forrest P. Lozier died on October 28. These three compatriots were members of the Grand Army of the Republic. Herbert Royal Crane, who died on November 8, was also a member of the Board of Managers for several years and was President of Newark Chapter in 1919 and 1920.

A most enjoyable pilgrimage was enjoyed by members of the New Jersey Society and members of their families to the Washington Headquarters, at Morristown, on October 21. The affair was in charge of Secretary David L. Pierson, and it proved delightful and instructive in every way. The party met at Springfield and, proceeding in automobiles to the historical mansion, there enjoyed luncheon, with an address by Judge Adrian Lyon, President, and by the Secretary. The remainder of the afternoon was spent in visiting the rooms in the headquarters used by Washington and his generals in the winter of 1779-1780.

Under the direction of Rev. M. S. Waters, chairman, vigorous and consistent action is being taken in the inspection of school histories. It is the plan of the committee to proceed with every possible care and recommend to the proper authorities that all irrelevant matter be expunged from the text-books used in the public schools.

Resolutions adopted by the Board of Managers on December 2 were forwarded to the Congress of the United States, urging its co-operation in the building of a memorial bridge over the Delaware River, connecting with a park on the New Jersey side and one on the Pennsylvania side of the river. These will all mark the historical night of December 25 and the morning of December 26, 1776, when Washington crossed the now famous stream and fought the Battle of Trenton. Resolutions have also been passed requesting the passage by Congress of a bill, now before it, providing for the erection of an archives building in Washington for the storage of documents. This has long been agitated by the National Society.

A reception, the second of a series, was tendered newly-elected members at the headquarters on the afternoon of December 2, when Compatriot Selden R. Hopkins, who was in the Union Army during the Civil War, read an intensely interesting paper on "How a Boy Telegrapher Saved an Army Brigade." He told the story of an operator receiving dispatches before Nashville, in the late autumn of 1864; that the line was suddenly broken, and when he discovered the cause to be the presence of the Confederate Army, the commanding officer of the brigade was notified, who changed his line of march; otherwise he and his men would have fallen into the hands of the enemy. Secretary Pierson, at the conclusion, announced that the hero of the story was Compatriot Hopkins. The third in the series will be given on January 6, when Rev. M. S. Waters will read a paper on "French and English Struggle for Supremacy in America and Braddock's Defeat." This will be open to all members of the Society.

Librarian Russell B. Rankin is arranging the library so that the reference books will be much more available to those seeking information for membership. The immediate future is full of promise of large accretions to the membership and a brilliant winter and spring campaign is assured for the New Jersey Society.

Judge Adrian Lyon, President, was the speaker at the annual meeting of the New Jersey Historical Society, on October 25.

Unanimity prevailed at the special meeting of the New Jersey Society on December 9, when the only business brought before it was soon dispatched—the amending of the by-laws to provide for the increase in annual dues, beginning on April 1, 1923, from $3 to $5 per annum.

Elizabethtown Chapter, No. 1, resolved, at a meeting held on October 24, to offer three money prizes to students of the Battin High School and Pingry School of Elizabeth, in the annual competition for essays on subjects pertaining to the War for American Independence. This has been named in honor of Judge Edward S. Atwater, former President of the New Jersey Society. Charles B. Newton, headmaster of the Pingry School, gave an address on the Near East situation.

Orange Chapter, at its meeting on November 17, listened to a very able address by Rev. George A. Edmison, pastor of Trinity Presbyterian Church, South Orange, on the welding of the bond of friendship between the English-speaking peoples. Rev. George P. Eastman, Chaplain, is chairman of a committee which is arranging to place a tablet, if permission can be secured, on the outer wall of the Federal building in Orange next Constitution Day, September 17, and in commemoration of that event.

At the December meeting of the Chapter, on the evening of December 15, New Jersey Day, which occurs on December 18 and marks the ratification by the State of the Federal Constitution, in 1787 was observed. The speakers were Rev. S. Ward Righter, Elroy Headley, A. P. Bachman, Philemon Woodruff, O. Stanley Thompson, and David L. Pierson.

Newark Chapter observed Evacuation Day on the eve of November 24, when Compatriot Carl E. Sutphen, M. D., opened his home on Roseville Avenue, Newark, for the occasion. An instructive and illuminating paper dealing with the general subject, beginning with the granting of the Magna Charta by King John in 1215, was given by Rev. Robert Scott Ingliss. Chaplain Warren P. Coon read the report submitted by Lord Cornwallis to King George upon the evacuation of Yorktown, and the Chapter Quartet gave a number of excellent selections. At the October meeting, held on the 19th, anniversary of Yorktown Day, the speaker was Dr. William R. Ward, his theme being "Newark, Its Progress Through the Years." The Chapter is preparing to observe the anniversary of the Battle of Trenton on December 26, when a Christmas party will also be given, both taking place at the State headquarters.

MONTCLAIR CHAPTER.—On Saturday afternoon, October 28, a Memorial Tablet in honor of General George Washington was dedicated and unveiled by the Eagle Rock Chapter, Daughters of the American Revolution, and the Montclair Chapter, Sons of the American Revolution, upon the sight of the Old Crane Homestead, Montclair, N. J. This Homestead was occupied as Washington's

THE OLD CRANE HOMESTEAD
Occupied as Washington's Headquarters, October 26 and 27, 1780

headquarters in the month of October, 1780. The members of the Montclair Chapter assembled at their headquarters and, with their guests, among whom were President General W. I. Lincoln Adams, Past President Louis Annin Ames, Secretary General Frank B. Steele, and Judge Adrian Lyon, President of the New Jersey Society, marched in a body to the site of the tablet. There they were met by the Eagle Rock Chapter of the Daughters of the American Revolution, and the exercises were held in front of the house which now stands upon the old site. The chairman of the day was Mr. J. Stewart Gibson, President of the Montclair Chapter, Sons of the American Revolution, and the vice-chairman was Mrs. Edward V. Cary, Regent of Eagle Rock Chapter, Daughters of the American Revolution. The invocation was given by Rev. Luke White,

Chaplain, Sons of the Revolution. Then came the presentation of colors and the pledge to the flag. After the singing of the "Star-Spangled Banner," Mr. J. Stewart Gibson made a few appropriate introductory remarks, and the tablet was unveiled by Mrs. Theodore Greene Sullivan, founder of the Eagle Rock Chapter, Daughters of the American Revolution. The deed of the site of the tablet and boulder was presented by Mrs. Edward V. Cary, Regent of Eagle Rock Chapter, and accepted on behalf of the town by Hon. Howard F. McConnell, Mayor of the city of Montclair. After the singing of "America the Beautiful," President General Adams, of the National Society, Sons of the American Revolution, and a lifelong resident of Montclair, told of some interesting local history of this attractive and always loyal town. The oration of the day was delivered by Judge Adrian Lyon, of Perth Amboy, who spoke most eloquently on the patriotic lessons to be learned from occasions of this kind and work that can be accomplished by our organizations. The program ended with the singing of "America."

Montclair Chapter is taking up an intensive form of Americanization originated by Compatriot Gilbert D. Maxwell, whose son, Charles Edward Maxwell, was given as his birthday present, on attaining his majority, his membership papers in the New Jersey Society.

PARAMUS CHAPTER held its annual meeting on December 8 and elected Ira W. Travell President; B. H. H. Noble, Vice-President; Edmond Morey, Secretary; Louis E. Halsted, Treasurer; Hiram Calkins, Registrar; Everett L. Zabriskie, Historian; Rev. John A. Van Neste, Chaplain. The Chapter is located in Ridgewood and has a membership of eighty-six.

WEST FIELDS CHAPTER held a meeting on December 8, when Carolus T. Clark read a paper on the historical points around Elizabeth, and dealing with the march of the British and Hessians on Springfield, via the Galloping Hill road, on June 23, 1780.

ROSELLE CHAPTER is the name of the newest organization within the New Jersey Society, which was organized by State President Adrian Lyon on December 14, at the home of Compatriot John L. Warner, of Roselle. The officers are: William C. Hope, President; John L. Warner, Vice-President; Edgar M. Gibby, Secretary; Oliver P. Schneeweiss, Treasurer; Charles A. Smith, Registrar; Stephen B. Ransom, Historian, Rev. Herbert K. England, Chaplain; additional members of the Board of Trustees, Frederick Provost, Edmund A. Merrill, and Horace G. Benedict; Delegate to the State Board of Managers, President Hope.

The Empire State Society—NEW YORK CHAPTER.—The regular meeting of the Chapter was held on Tuesday, October 31, at 8 p. m., the anniversary of the organization of the Sons of Liberty, at the Army and Navy Club of America, New York City.

The guests of honor were President General W. I. Lincoln Adams and the Executive Committee of the National Society. Preceding the meeting the usual "get together" dinner was served at 6.30 p. m. Many compatriots attended, including the national officers. About 200 members and guests attended the dinner and meeting. The meeting was presided over by General Oliver B. Bridgman, President. Interesting and instructive addresses were made by the President General and other speakers. Colonel Louis Annin Ames in his remarks drew the members' attention to the fact that the President General's name not only included the names of three Presidents of the United States, but that President General Washington Irving Lincoln Adams was a descendant from each of these great men.

ROCHESTER CHAPTER.—The annual election of officers and a literary program marked the October meeting of Rochester Chapter, at the Daughters of the American Revolution Chapter House in Livingston Park. The meeting was the opening of the 1922-23 season and marked the anniversary of the Battle of Saratoga, a momentous day in the country's history. The Rt. Rev. David Lincoln Ferris, suffragan bishop of the Episcopal Diocese of Western New York, delivered an address on "The Battle of Saratoga" and the story of the surrender of General Burgoyne. Preceding the literary program, officers presented their annual reports. President Raymond G. Dann delivered the annual address.

SYRACUSE CHAPTER.—The annual meeting and election of officers of the Chapter was held in November, at the University Club. About 40 members attended and officers were elected for the ensuing year as follows: Newell B. Woodworth, President; William W. Wiard, Vice-President; Edward Kies Ives, Secretary; Willis E. Gaylord, Treasurer; J. Frank Durston, Registrar; Prof. Frederick F. Moon, Historian; Rev. Dr. Albert C. Fulton, Chaplain.

BUFFALO CHAPTER.—The Buffalo Chapter opened its season with a most delightful meeting at the New Saturn Club on Tuesday evening, November 28, with a dinner at which more than seventy were present. The speaker of the evening was Lieut. Commander Ewart G. Haas, who for more than two years commanded the U. S. S. *Sturtevant* in European waters. Commander Haas gave a most interesting and illuminating talk on the conditions in Russia and Turkey. The dinner was presided over by the new President of the Chapter, Commander Thomas W. Harris. Commander Harris, with a few pleasant words, welcomed into the Chapter seven new members who have been admitted since the last meeting.

On Tuesday, December 5, the Chapter gave a luncheon in honor of William Lawrence Sullivan, D. D., of New York, who was conducting a mission in Buffalo. Doctor Sullivan gave a most inspiring address on the Constitution and some of the dangers that confront the American people at this time. The luncheon was held at the Buffalo Club and was well attended. The Chapter has plans for active work for this year and a definite campaign is being carried out for a larger and more active membership.

The Ohio Society was represented at an enjoyable occasion of the Daughters of the American Revolution by Historian General Joseph B. Doyle, who spoke before the Chapter at Steubenville at the Hotel Fort Steuben on November 11. The Regent, Mrs. Sinclair, presided and introduced our Historian General, who spoke on the ideals of the S. A. R., which were honoring the memory of the patriots who founded the United States, prompting patriotism in the citizenship of the country and instilling Americanism into the lives of the immigrants, whose influence will mold the future of America. Mr. Doyle gave an interesting review of "The Iron Puddler," a book lately written by Secretary of Labor James J. Davis, which is the story of his life. The description of his progress through thrift, hard work and determination to make good reads like a romance. The Golden Rule and Ten Commandments were his guiding stars and obedience was a decided influence in his life. Mr. Doyle closed with the expressed hope that

America might sift her ever-increasing number of immigrants retaining the type described in the Iron Puddler and keeping out the vicious and law-defying.

The Oregon Society.—The annual fall smoker of the Oregon Society of the Sons of the American Revolution was held on the evening of Saturday, November 18, and proved a most enjoyable occasion. Lieutenant-Colonel Charles Wellington Furlong, of the Massachusetts Society, was the guest of the evening and delivered a very forceful address upon "Our Heritage," in which he discussed numerous problems confronting America, and particularly in our international relations. At the request of the Massachusetts Society, the Oregon Society presented to Lieutenant-Colonel Furlong the Sons of the American Revolution Service medal in attestation of his World War service. Compatriot H. B. Augur contributed materially to the success of the evening's program by reading an informative and scholarly paper on "The Peace Negotiations of 1782-1783." There was a goodly attendance and the evening was one of general enjoyment.

The Oregon Society has sustained a heavy loss in the death of General Charles F. Beebe, whose passing occurred on November 20. General Beebe was for many years a loyal and enthusiastic member of our Society, frequently participating in its activities, and at the time of his death was Vice-President of the Society. By his many admirable personal qualities and intense patriotism he had endeared himself to our members and will be greatly missed by them.

Our Society is looking forward with pleasant anticipation to the visit of President General W. I. Lincoln Adams during the middle of January. Vice-President General George Albert Smith will probably accompany President General Adams, and the Oregon Society will likely have the pleasure of entertaining two officers of the National Society.

The Pennsylvania Society.—Major Gen. Tasker H. Bliss, former Chief of the Staff of the American Army during the World War, gave an account of the origin of the armistice before one of the largest gatherings of Pennsylvania State Sons of the American Revolution that has ever been drawn together by that body, at the Armistice Day dinner, in McCreery's banquet hall, in Pittsburgh, Saturday evening, November 11. Prior to his address Mrs. John Brown Heron, State Regent of the Pennsylvania Chapter, Daughters of the American Revolution, presented a beautiful gold flag to the Sons, bearing their insignia. The colors were yellow, white, and blue.

Clyde Kelly was toastmaster, and the invocation was read by Rev. Dr. Grafton T. Reynolds, Chaplain.

Armistice Day telegrams were received from both President Harding and Gen. John J. Pershing.

After explaining in detail the exchange of notes between the Allied Powers and Germany, as well as conferences between representatives of both which led up to the signing of the armistice, General Bliss said in part:

"As to the propriety of having an armistice, there was at the time no difference of opinion among responsible men, nor has there been since. I fully agreed with the expressed view of Marshal Foch that, if we secured an armistice that made it impossible for Germany to resume the war, to be followed by terms of peace that would still further guarantee this impossibility and secure all our just war aims, it would be nothing short of wanton murder of Allied troops to refuse. It might have cost another million lives and billions of money, to be followed by the same terms with lessened ability on the part of the enemy to meet them. Nor, in the long history of war, do I know of any civilized nation, even in a war with the most barbarous people, refusing an armistice for the purpose of making peace."

General Bliss then related in detail the difficulties which confronted the peace conference as a result of the failure to make the armistice definite, and also told of the renewals of 30 days each three times of the armistice. "All of this was due," he said, "not to the fact of the armistice, but to the form of it." Concluding, he said:

"The armistice was made because all the Allied world wanted it, and for no other reason. But its defective form, for which America was in no way whatever responsible, invited and permitted in a considerable degree the delays which proved the bane of the peace conference and which had much to do in preventing the re-establishment of the peace of the world."

Distinguished guests at the banquet included: Gen. A. J. Logan, Brig.-Gen. and Mrs. Lloyd M. Brett, Mrs. John Brown Heron, W. C. Lyne, President of the Pennsylvania Society; General Bliss, former President James A. Wakefield, National Trustee for Pennsylvania.

At a recent meeting of the Board of Managers of the Pennsylvania Society Mr. James A. Wakefield was elected to fill the unexpired term of Col. Robert W. Guthrie as National Trustee, and Mr. G. L. Neel as a member of the Board, in place of J. S. Du Shane.

The Tennessee Society.—One of our Tennessee compatriots, "a plain country doctor," has in his yard ivy grown from a slip taken from Washington's tomb. Each fall he gives ivy cuttings to the school children and tells them the story of the Father of their Country.

This "plain country doctor in West Tennessee" has a ten-year-old boy, and the little fellow has a scrap-book in which is pasted the story of Bunker Hill, of Nathan Hale, of many other heroic incidents of the war that are not given in Muzzey's text-book. In the scrap-book is also the story of the boy's own ancestor, who died of cold and starvation during the winter at Valley Forge.

The Tennessee Society claims that this "plain country doctor in West Tennessee" is an example for us all, and that his boy's scrap-book is a better text for red-blooded Americans than are the insipid books of the revisionist school.

Muzzey's School History has been withdrawn by request from Middle Tennessee State Normal, Columbia Military Academy, St. Cecelia Academy, Central High School, Nashville, and the Tennessee Society secured "black-listing" of the book by the National Convention of the United Daughters of the Confederacy on November 16.

THE HERMITAGE

Preserved as a sacred memorial to a great American who, having caught in boyhood the spirit of the American Revolution, led the citizen army which at New Orleans gave substantial victory to the American arms in the War of 1812, "The Hermitage," home and burial-place of Andrew Jackson, soldier, statesman, and President, is chief among the historic attractions of Nashville, where the National Congress will meet in May, 1923. On the grounds, owned by the State of Tennessee and managed by a patriotic association of women, there stand the

THE HERMITAGE

mansion house, built in 1819, in the best tradition of the time and a gem of spacious Colonial architecture, and rebuilt after a fire in 1835, near the close of General Jackson's second term as President; the tomb where lie the General and his beloved wife, whose death occurred just after he was elected President, in 1828, and part of the original cabin home, built in 1804, which was the residence of the stern old warrior when he came back from the Battle of New Orleans, in 1815, the hero of the nation. House, outbuildings, garden, and grounds are preserved as nearly as may be as they were in the old General's time. The house is a veritable museum of the history of the period of Jackson.

NASHVILLE!

Nashville, the capital of Tennessee, is in the heart of the famous blue-grass section, in the central part of the State. It lies in the beautiful rolling valley of the Cumberland River, one of the great waterways of the South. It was successively known as French Salt Lick, the Bluffs, then Nashborough in memory of Gen. Francis Nash, a brave patriot of the Revolution, and finally, in 1806, as Nashville. From that time the development of Nashville was rapid, being in the center of an enormously productive region. Nashville's fame was materially advanced by the achievements and growing prominence of Andrew Jackson, whose home was at "The Hermitage," near Nashville. Under his influence and that of other men of his vigorous type, Nashville became a center of national politics.

From Nashville marched the troops that forever broke the power of the southern Indians. Here, too, were marshaled the forces that won that great American victory—the Battle of New Orleans. This beautiful height was the scene of much interest during the war between the States, when 55,000 Federal and 23,000 Confederate troops occupied the hills in and around the city, while both armies were ice-bound for a week prior to the great battle of December 14 and 15, 1864, General Grant making his headquarters here when made Lieutenant General of the Federal Army.

The Cumberland River cuts its way through the high bluffs upon which the city is built. The State Capitol, of Grecian architecture, commands the most elevated position, and Capitol Hill is adorned with terraces, upon which are statues of Andrew Jackson, the tomb of President and Mrs. Polk, and the statue of Sam Davis, a Confederate scout, who died a martyr's death on the gallows.

Nashville is a city of beautiful residences, churches, and schools. It has a number of beautiful parks. In one of them, the Centennial Park, stands an exact reproduction of the Parthenon of Athens, the only one extant. The city has long been recognized as the "Athens of the South," being the educational and cultural center of the Southern States.

ERRATA

In the BULLETIN of October, 1922, page 97, the pedigree of William Arthur Markell should read as follows: Son of Francis and Caroline Matilda (Delaplaine) Markell; grandson of John and Sophia (Charlton) Delaplaine; great-grandson of *John Usher Charlton*, etc.

INCREASE IN MEMBERSHIP

The Registrar-General has to report the largest increase in membership in the history of the Society for the summer months. The State Societies have admitted from June 1 to October 1, 692 new members and likewise approved 130 Supplemental papers. The greatest number, 79, were admitted to the New Jersey Society, while New York, Illinois, and Massachusetts admitted 60, 52, and 48 respectively, while increased activity was noted in many other States. It is hoped that the interest in securing additional members will continue during the winter months, in spite of the amendment to Article VI of the Constitution, providing for an Initiation Fee of five dollars to the National Society, passed at the last Congress, and which went into effect on the first of October.

ADDITIONS TO MEMBERSHIP

There have been enrolled in the office of the Registrar General, from September 30, 1922, to December 1, 1922, 249 new members, distributed as follows: Arkansas, 1; California, 19; Connecticut, 14; District of Columbia, 16; Florida, 2; Idaho, 2; Illinois, 27; Indiana, 17; Iowa, 3; Kentucky, 5; Louisiana, 10; Maine, 4; Maryland, 3; Massachusetts, 10; Michigan, 20; Minnesota, 5; Missouri, 3; Nebraska, 4; New Jersey, 16; New Mexico, 1; New York (Empire State), 27; Ohio, 10; Oregon, 1; Pennsylvania, 2; Tennessee, 16; Texas, 2; Vermont, 3; Washington State, 2; Wisconsin, 1.

The Maine Society has admitted a real son of the Revolution—Mr. Peter Brackett of Biddeford, own son of William Brackett, who was born at Falmouth, Mass., in 1752, and served as a Sergeant in the Mass. Militia and Continental Troops. Mr. Brackett was born March 4, 1838, and saw service in the Civil War.

In Memoriam

CHARLES HENRY ALLEN, Rhode Island Society, died October 13, 1922.
NORMAND F. ALLEN, Connecticut Society, died May 30, 1922.
JOHN MACDOUGALL ARMSTRONG, New Jersey Society, died November 1, 1922.
LUCIUS ALBERT BARBOUR, Connecticut Society, died November 6, 1922.
FREDERICK B. BASSETT, New Jersey Society, died November 11, 1922.
CHARLES F. BEEBE, Oregon Society, died November 20, 1922.
CHARLES UPHAM BELL, Massachusetts Society, died November 11, 1922.
SAMUEL HAVENS BERRY, Connecticut Society, died June 10, 1922.
WILBUR FISKE BRAINERD, New Jersey Society, died September 27, 1922.
HIRAM H. BREWER, District of Columbia Society, died October 26, 1922.
CHARLES ORSON BRITTON, Connecticut Society, died September 19, 1922.
HON. MORGAN GARDNER BULKELEY, Past-President Connecticut Society, Ex-United
    States Senator, etc., died November 6, 1922.
ARCHIE HAMILTON BURRAGE, Massachusetts Society, died November 10, 1922.
CHARLES H. COOLIDGE, Michigan Society, died November 14, 1922.
HENRY S. COLWELL, New Jersey Society, died February 14, 1922.
WILLIAM L. CONDIT, New Jersey Society, died October 8, 1922.
HERBERT ROYAL CRANE, New Jersey Society, died November 8, 1922.
EDMUND L. FRENCH, Empire State Society, died August 31, 1922.
ROBERT C. GEMMELL, Utah Society, died October 25, 1922.
GEORGE BARNETT GUILD, Massachusetts Society, died October 14, 1922.
WENDELL PHILLIPS HALE, Rhode Island Society, died December 15, 1922.
WILMOT REED HASTINGS, Massachusetts Society, died April 7, 1922.
ALBERT M. HENRY, Past President Michigan Society, Member Board of Trustees of
    National Society, died November 3, 1922.
JOHN ALFRED HULL, Connecticut Society, died July 5, 1922.
EDWARD BRYANT HUTCHINSON, Massachusetts Society, died November 9, 1922.
GEORGE STEPHEN JELLERSON, New Jersey Society, died October 10, 1922.
DE FOREST PARSONS LOZIER, New Jersey Society, died October 28, 1922.
WILLIAM G. MARKHAM, Empire State Society, died May 16, 1922.
EDWARD CARRINGTON MAYO, Virginia Society, died September 5, 1922.
SEYMOUR MORRIS, Illinois Society, died September 27, 1921.
CHARLES E. POINDEXTER, Connecticut Society, died August 6, 1922.
CHARLES HOOKER RISLEY, Connecticut Society, died October 14, 1922.
JOSEPH HEWES SHEPHERD, Massachusetts Society, died March, 2, 1922.
WILLIAM SMITH SIMMONS, Connecticut Society, died August 2, 1922.
SAMUEL WHEELER SMITH, Connecticut Society, died April 16, 1922.
HERBERT W. SNOW, Connecticut Society, died July 16, 1922.
LOUIS CARVER SOUTHARD, Massachusetts Society, died September 29, 1922.
WILLIAM E. SPANDOW, Empire State Society, died November 17, 1922.
ALEXANDER RAMSEY SPEEL, District of Columbia Society, died October 21, 1922.
EUGENE ENSIGN STEVENS, Member Board of Management District of Columbia So-
    ciety, died September 26, 1922.
JOHN C. STROTHER, Kentucky Society, died August 16, 1922.
JOHN A. THOMPSON, Empire State Society, died July 13, 1922.
JAMES SOULARD TOMKINS, New Jersey Society, died November 11, 1922.
ROGER ALLEN TOWNSEND, Connecticut Society, died July 27, 1922.
HARRY VAUGHAN, New Jersey Society, died June 21, 1921.
WILLIAM HOWARD WALKER, Rhode Island Society, died October 19, 1922.
CHARLES HEMPSTED WELLS, Ohio Society, died February —, 1919.
RUSSELL T. WHITING, Connecticut Society, died July 11, 1922.
CHARLES J. WHITTEN, Connecticut Society, died April 22, 1922.
JOHN R. WILLIAMS, New Jersey Society, died November —, 1921.
THOMAS HOOD YEAGER, District of Columbia Society, died September 12, 1922.

RECORDS OF 249 NEW MEMBERS AND 55 SUPPLEMENTALS APPROVED AND ENROLLED BY THE REGISTRAR GENERAL FROM SEPTEMBER 30, 1922, TO DECEMBER 1, 1922.

NOBLE WAYNE ABRAHAMS, Washington, D. C. (37173). Son of Edward Ward and Maud Virginia (Carson) Abrahams; grandson of Edward Ward and Susan (Ayres) Abrahams; great-grandson of James Armistead and Sarah Truly (Ward) Abrahams; great²-grandson of Jacob Levy and Theodotia (Armistead) Abrahams; great²-grandson of *Mordecai Abrahams*, Captain, King William County, Virginia Militia.

THOMAS YOUNG ABY, New Orleans, La. (36970). Son of Thomas Young and Emily (Turney) Aby; grandson of Samuel Hulett and Sarah Ann (Brown) Aby; great-grandson of Jonas and Barbara (Hulett) Aby; great²-grandson of *Charles Hulett*, private, New Jersey Militia and Cont'l Troops, prisoner, pensioned.

FRANK DWIGHT ADAMS, Minn. (37428). Supplemental. Son of Charles Edward and Adeline Fidelia (Tower) Adams; grandson of Hector Dwight and Lucy (Jones) Adams; great-grandson of Origin and Anna (Wilcox) Adams; great²-grandson of *Ebenezer Adams, Jr.*; Corporal, Col. Benjamin Simond's Regt., Massachusetts Cont'l Troops.

JOSEPH ALEXANDER, Haddonfield, N. J. (37798). Son of Henry Clay and Sarah M. (Gibbs) Alexander; grandson of Thomas A. and Elizabeth (Stevenson) Alexander; great-grandson of Thomas and Rebecca (Thorne) Stevenson; great²-grandson of *Joseph Thorne*, Captain, Gloucester County, New Jersey Militia.

WILLIAM HENRY SNOWDEN ALEXANDER, Haddonfield, N. J. (37799). Son of Joseph and Emma (Snowden) Alexander; grandson of Henry Clay and Sarah (Gibbs) Alexander; great-grandson of Thomas A. and Elizabeth (Stevenson) Alexander; great²-grandson of Thomas and Rebecca (Thorne) Stevenson; great²-grandson of *Joseph Thorne*, Captain, Gloucester County, New Jersey Militia.

FORREST FRANCIS ALLEN, Nashville, Tenn. (38052). Son of James Walter and Flora (Hamel) Allen; grandson of John and Sarah Louisa (Harwood) Allen; great-grandson of John and Nancy Caroline (Morton) Allen; great²-grandson of Vincent and Mary (Bowdon) Allen; great²-grandson of *Charles Allen*, Captain, Second and Fifth Regts., North Carolina Militia.

ABRAM PHILLIPS ANCKER, Evansville, Ind. (37810). Son of Jacob and Julia (Phillips) Ancker; grandson of Gustave and Ester Ella Virginia (Pettigrew) Ancker; great-grandson of Jacob and Rachel (Pettigrew) Phillips; great²-grandson of *James Pettigrew*, Lieutenant, Second, Fifteenth and Eleventh Regts., Pennsylvania Cont'l Line.

DE WITT CLINTON JAMES ANCKER, Lieut. U. S. Army (Texas 37532). Son of Abram Phillips and Eliza Frances (James) Ancker; grandson of Jacob and Julia (Phillips) Ancker; great-grandson of Adolph and Hetty (Pettigrew) Ancker; great²-grandson of *James Pettigrew*, Lieutenant, Eleventh Regt., Pennsylvania Cont'l Line.

JAMES GILBERT ANTHONY, Washington, D. C. (36449). Son of Cassius M. and Florence L. (Coy) Anthony; grandson of John and Caroline Virginia (Martin) Coy; great-grandson of John and Nancy (Perkins) Martin; great²-grandson of *John Martin*, Captain, North Carolina Troops, prisoner, pensioned.

ROBERT PRESTON APPLETON, Cincinnati, Ohio (Ill. 37706). Son of Elmer Ellsworth and Mary A. (Kibler) Appleton; grandson of Samuel E. and Mary (Mikesell) Appleton; great-grandson of Joseph B. and Abbie Hale (Hunt) Appleton; great²-grandson of Joseph B. and Hanna (Knowlton) Appleton; great²-grandson of *Isaac Appleton*, private, Col. Enoch Hale's Regt., New Hampshire Militia, Member Provincial Congress and of Committee of Correspondence and Safety.

GEORGE WASHINGTON ARMSTRONG, Adrian, Mich. (37952). Son of Henry H. and Mary A. (Robinson) Armstrong; grandson of Ephraim and Anna (Fitch) Robinson, Jr.; great-grandson of *Ephraim Robinson*, Corporal, Eighth Regt., Connecticut Militia.

HENRY CLAIBOURNE ARMSTRONG, Louisville, Ky. (36536). Son of Henry Claibourne and Josephine (McGee) Armstrong; grandson of James Watson and Josephine (Wheeler) McGee; great-grandson of Samuel and Aarah (Yocum) McGee; great²-grandson of *Robert McGee*, Lieutenant, Philadelphia Rifle Battalion, wounded, pensioned.

STERLING ARMSTRONG, New Orleans, La. (36971). Son of Henry Sweppe and Geraldine (Duval) Armstrong; grandson of Francis and Susan H. (Sweppe) Armstrong; great-grandson of John and Deborah (Hart) Armstrong; great²-grandson of Jesse and Martha (Mattison) Hart; great²-grandson of *John Hart*, New Jersey Signer of the Declaration of Independence.

ARTHUR ELMER BALDWIN, Omaha, Nebr. (36994). Son of Jacob and Abigail (Briggs) Baldwin; grandson of Elisha and Jemima (Ryder) Baldwin, Jr.; great-grandson of *Elisha* and Elizabeth (Cornwell) *Baldwin*, private, Dutchess County, New York Militia; great²-grandson of *Daniel Cornwell*, private, Col. Ludington's Regt., Dutchess County, New York Militia; great-grandson of Joshua and Fanny (Pugsley) Ryder; great²-grandson of *William Pugsley*, private, Sixth Regt., Dutchess County, New York Militia.

ALBERT MAHARD BARKER, Sparta, Ill. (37707). Son of Daniel Perry and Anna Jane (Rosbrough) Barker; grandson of Daniel M. and Rachel (Jarrard) Barker; great-grandson of *Zebediah Barker*, Corporal and Sergeant, Massachusetts Militia, widow pensioned.

MAITLAND DEFOREST BARSTOW, Cœur d'Alene, Idaho (35117). Son of Elam Spencer and Hannah (Walker) Barstow; grandson of James and Jane (Paget) (Padget) Walker, Jr.; great-grandson of *James Walker*, private, New Hampshire Militia, pensioned.

J. GARDNER BARTLETT, Cambridge, Mass. (37771). Son of Joseph E. and Antoinette F. (Carpenter) Bartlett; grandson of Daniels and Abigail (Payson) Carpenter; great-grandson of Ezra and Mary (Daniels) Carpenter; great²-grandson of *Nehemiah Carpenter*, Captain, Third Regt., Suffolk County, Massachusetts Militia.

DONALD DURANT BATTELLE, Dayton, Ohio (37644). Son of Louis G. and Annie Ella (Sellars) Battelle; grandson of Andrew Brimmer and Mary Elizabeth (Barker) Battelle; great-grandson of Ebenezer and Mary (Greene) Battelle; great²-grandson of *Ebenezer Battelle*, Captain, guarding Massachusetts Cont'l stores, private, Colonel Pierce's Regt., Massachusetts Militia.

GORDON SELLERS BATTELLE, DAYTON, Ohio (37645). Same as Donald Durant Battelle, Ohio (37644).

LOUIS G. BATTELLE, Dayton, Ohio (37646). Son of Andrew Brimmer and Mary Elizabeth Barker) Battelle; grandson of Ebenezer and Mary (Greene) Battelle; great-grandson of *Ebenezer Battelle*, Captain, guarding Massachusetts Cont'l stores, private, Col. Pierce's Regt., Massachusetts Militia.

ELMER HOPPER BEACH, East Orange, N. J. (37988). Son of William Wallace and Sarah Caroline (Syms) Beach; grandson of William and Sally (Remington) Beach; great-grandson of Asa Alexander and Mary (Hunter) Beach; great²-grandson of *Joseph Beach*, Captain, Eastern Battalion, Morris County, New Jersey Militia.

LEONARD STANDRING BEARD, San Francisco, Calif. (37866). Son of Lewis William and Nellie Protherer (Standring) Beard; grandson of William and Sarah Maria (Hammond) Beard; great-grandson of Mathew Brown and Susan (McCormick) Hammond; great²-grandson of *James Hammond*, private, Northumberland County, Pennsylvania Militia; great-grandson of *Mathew Brown*, member Pennsylvania Flying Camp.

FLOYD LAFAYETTE BIDWELL, Stratford, Conn. (37303). Son of George Melville and Mary (Ammerman) Bidwell; grandson of Ashabel and Polly (Griffing) Bidwell; great-grandson of Ephraim and Dorcas (Andrews) Bidwell; great²-grandson of *Daniel Andrews*, private, Second Regt., Connecticut Line.

EDWIN LAWRENCE BIGELOW, Middlebury, Vt. (38026). Son of Edwin R. and Celeste (E—) Bigelow; grandson of Jonathan Brooks and Relief (Newhall) Bigelow; great-grandson of Phineas and Wealthy Willis (Newcomb) Newhall; great²-grandson of *Ebenezer Newhall*, private and Sergeant, Bristol County, Massachusetts Militia.

WILLIAM CHARLES BILLMAN, Trenton, N. J. (37982). Son of Washington Daniel and Joanna (Ritter) Billman; grandson of Joseph and Sarah (Tobias) Ritter; great-grandson of Isaac and Anna (Deter) Ritter; great²-grandson of *Ferdinand Ritter*, Captain, Berk's County, Pennsylvania Militia.

CLARENCE EUGENE BISSELL, Manchester, Conn. (37304). Son of Robert Palmer and Henrietta (Brough) Bissell; grandson of Lewis and Cornelia (Palmer) Bissell; great-grandson of Lewis Glover Bissell; great²-grandson of Ozias Bissell; great²-grandson of *Ozias Bissell*, Captain, Col. Eno's Regt., Connecticut Militia, pensioned.

CHARLES LESTER BLANCHARD, Dover, N. J. (37797). Son of John Edward and Jennie Baker (Davenport) Blanchard; grandson of Charles and Apphia J. (Spencer) Davenport; great-grandson of Enos and Frances (Keeper) Davenport; great²-grandson of *Frances Keeper*, private, Eastern Battalion, Morris County, New Jersey Militia.

HENRY BOND, Chattanooga, Tenn. (38056). Son of Henry and Mary Lippett (Bradley) Bond; grandson of Alfred Owen and Eliza (Lippett) Bradley; great-grandson of William H. and Mary H. (Bernard) Lippett; great²-grandson of *Moses Lippett*, Ensign, Cranston, Rhode Island Militia, Captain of privateer "Columbia," prisoner.

ALFRED CLARK BOUGHTON, Chicago, Ill. (Mo. 37610). Son of Chauncey K. and Emily Josephine (James) Boughton; grandson of Jehiel and Eunice (Waterbury) Boughton (Bouton); great-grandson of *John* and Elizabeth (Roberts) *Bouton*, private, Col. Crane's Regt., Westchester County, New York Militia; great²-grandson of *Jehiel Bouton*, Sergeant, Westchester County, New York Levies and Militia.

EDWARD EVERETT BOWEN, Idaho (21356). Supplementals. Son of Caleb Tillinghast and Lydia Waterman (Knight) Bowen; grandson of Joseph and Abagail (Tillinghast) Bates Bowen; great-grandson of *Ichabod Bowen*, private, Kent County, Rhode Island Militia; grandson of Andrew Waterman and Lydia Sheldon (Fiske) Knight; great-grandson of Peleg and Orpha (Knight) Fiske, Jr.; great²-grandson of *Peleg Fiske*, Captain, First Company, Scituate, Rhode Island Militia; great-grandson of Earl and Betsey (Waterman) Knight; great²-grandson of *Andrew Knight*, private, Col. Benjamin Slack's Regt., Rhode Island Militia; great²-grandson of Peleg and Lydia (Sheldon) Fiske; great²-grandson of *Philip Sheldon*, private, Fourth Company, Providence, Rhode Island Train Band.

WILL M. BOWLBY, Sharpsville, Ind. (36450). Son of William and Phebe (Sippy) Bowlby; grandson of Joseph and Mary (Bonnell) Bowlby; great-grandson of Clement and Rachel (Woolverton) Bonnell; great²-grandson of *Abraham Bonnell*, Lieutenant-Colonel, Third Regt., Hunterdon County, New Jersey Militia.

PETER BRACKETT, Biddeford, Maine (36601). Son of *William* and Judith (——) *Brackett*, Sergeant, Col. Phinney's Regt., Massachusetts Cont'l Infantry and of Cumberland County, Massachusetts Militia.

FREDERICK LANE BROWN, New Brunswick, N. J. (37800). Son of James and Gertrude Potter (Lane) Brown; grandson of Frederick Howell and Mary Ann (Craig) Lane; great-grandson of Matthew P. and Anna (Howell) Lane; great²-grandson of Peter and Elizabeth (Smock) Lane; great²-grandson of *John Smock*, Lieutenant-Colonel, New Jersey Militia, prisoner.

LEE LOTHROP BROWN, Ill. (24777). Supplemental. Son of Walter Lee and Ina Belle (Brown) Brown; grandson of George Hansberger and Mary Virginia (Burt) Brown; great-grandson of Morris and Mary (Sullard) Burt; great²-grandson of *Benjamin Sullard*, private, Middlesex County, New Jersey Militia, pensioned.

HENRY LINDSAY BROWNING, Jr., Indianapolis, Ind. (37801). Son of Henry Lindsay and Maria (Frazee) Browning; grandson of Woodville and Mary (Brown) Browning; great-grandson of William John and Susan (Tomkins) Brown; great²-grandson of *George Brown*, Sergeant, Col. George Gibson's Regt., First Virginia State Troops.

FREDERICK CONGER BRYAN, Washington, D. C. (37163). Son of Frederick Carlos and Blanche (Conger) Bryan; grandson of Constant and Susan Louise (Barnum) Bryan; great-grandson of *Elijah Bryan*, private, Connecticut Cont'l Line, six years service, pensioned.

THOMAS DOBYNS BUFORD, Chattanooga, Tenn. (38057). Son of William Robertson and Sallie Bristow (Dobyns) Buford; grandson of William McDowell and Margaret Eliza (Robertson) Buford; great-grandson of *Abraham Buford*, Colonel, Eleventh and Third Regts., Virginia Cont'l Line.

MARION DIXON CALDER, Seattle, Wash. (36662). Son of Joseph Edward and Nina L. (French) Calder; grandson of George W. and Charlotte E. (Olney) French; great-grandson of William and Charlotte (Tanner) Olney; great²-grandson of *Stephen Olney*, Captain, Gloucester, Rhode Island Militia.

EUGENE WILLARD CALVIT, Dallas, Texas (La. 36972). Son of Montfort Wells and Louise Elizabeth (Albert) Calvit; grandson of Tacitus Garllard and Jeannette Dent (Wells) Calvit; great-grandson of Montfort and Jeannette (Dent) Wells; great²-grandson of Hatch and Jeannette (Merrillion) Dent; great²-grandson of *Hezekiah Dent*, Captain, Twelfth Battalion, Charles County, Maryland Militia.

MONTFORT CALVIT, Pensacola, Fla. (La. 36973). Same as Eugene Willard Calvit (La. 36972).

BIRUM GOULD CAMPBELL, Pontiac, Mich. (37063). Son of Edwin William and Ella Mary (Gould) Campbell; grandson of William and Addie E. (Lyman) Campbell; great-grandson of Alfred and Maltida (McCrory) Lyman; great²-grandson of Nathan and Mary (Bissell) Lyman; great²-grandson of *David Bissell*, Lieutenant, Fourth Regt., Connecticut Troops.

GEORGE WASHINGTON CARR, Grand Island, Nebr. (36995). Son of William and Jane (Stanford) Carr; grandson of *Peter Carr*, private, New Jersey Militia, State Troops and Cont'l Line.

CHARLES ROBINSON CARRUTH, New York, N. Y. (37590). Son of Uri and Lucy Ann (Robinson) Carruth; grandson of Ira and Polly (Kibbe) Robinson; great-grandson of Zelotes and Alice (Mayo) Robinson; great²-grandson of *Elijah Robinson*, Captain, Connecticut Militia and State Troops.

CLARENCE URI CARRUTH, New York, N. Y. (37591). Same as Charles Robinson Carruth, New York (37590).

CLARENCE URI CARRUTH, Jr., New York, N. Y. (37592). Son of Clarence Uri and Elizabeth Judith (Hutt) Carruth; grandson of Uri and Lucy Ann (Robinson) Carruth; great-grandson of Ira and Polly (Kibbe) Robinson; great²-grandson of Zelotes and Alice (Mayo) Robinson; great²-grandson of *Elijah Robinson*, Captain, Connecticut Militia and State Troops.

FREDERIC COUDERT CARRUTH, New York, N. Y. (37593). Son of Charles Robinson and Mary Louise (Palmer) Carruth; grandson of Uri and Lucy Ann (Robinson) Carruth; great-grandson of Ira and Polly (Kibbe) Robinson; great²-grandson of Zelotes and Alice (Mayo) Robinson; great²-grandson of *Elijah Robinson*, Captain, Connecticut Militia and State Troops.

HOWARD WILLISTON CARTER, Norfolk, Conn. (37305). Son of Frederick William and Sarah Maria (Tuller) Carter; grandson of Thomas and Ann (Joslyn) Carter; great-grandson of *Benoni Carter*, Sergeant, Thirteenth Regt., Connecticut Militias.

RALPH WHITNEY CASE, Maynard, Mass. (37765). Son of William Bradford and Lucy J. (Whitney) Case; grandson of Artemus and Lucy (Pease) Whitney; great-grandson of Alpheus and Lucy (Forster) Pease; great²-grandson of Jonathan and Hannah (Cutter) Forster; great²-grandson of *Benjamin Cutter*, Ensign, New Hampshire Militia.

FRANK BRITTAIN CHAMBERLIN, Ohio (29157). Supplementals. Son of William Clark and Lydia (Brittain) Chamberlin; grandson of Robert and Rebecca (Taggart) Chamberlin; great-grandson of John and Rebecca (Clark) Taggart; great²-grandson of James and Nancy (Reed) Clark; great²-grandson of *John Reed*, Captain, First Pennsylvania Battalion of the Flying Camp; great²-grandson of *James Clark*, Captain, Fifth Company, Fourth Battalion, Pennsylvania Troops.

FRED POPE CLARK, Stockton, Calif. (37273). Son of Asa and Mary E. (Mountjoy) Clark; grandson of Curtis and Electra (Meacham) Clark; great-grandson of *Abraham Meacham*, private, Williamstown, Massachusetts Militia.

LESTER L. CLARK, Stockton, Calif. (37274). Son of Fred Pope and Edith H. (Cross) Clark; grandson of Asa and Mary E. (Mountjoy) Clark; great-grandson of Curtis and Electra (Meacham) Clark; great²-grandson of *Abraham Meacham*, private, Williamstown, Massachusetts Militia.

JAMES DANA COIT, Norwich, Conn. (37306). Son of George Douglass and Frances H. (Dana) Coit; grandson of Charles and Sarah Perkins (Grosvenor) Coit; great-grandson of Lemuel and Sarah (Perkins) Grosvenor; great²-grandson of *Elisha Perkins*, Surgeon, Col. John Douglas' Regt., Connecticut Troops and Member Committee of Correspondence.

JAMES EDGAR COLE, Minn. (35692). Supplemental. Son of Edgar H. and Eva (Sharpley) Cole; grandson of George Horatio and Clementine Erphelia (Rorman) Cole; great-grandson of Richard and Emily (Morgan) Cole; great²-grandson of Benjamin and Phœbe (Williams) Morgan; great²-grandson of *William Williams*, Colonel, Vermont Militia.

PHILIP PEARSON COLE, Captain, A. E. F., Nashville, Tenn. (38053). Son of Herbert Elmore and Mary Cass (Fogg) Cole; grandson of Albert and Addie Pearson (Cass) Fogg; great-grandson of Daniel and Hannah (Whitney) Fogg, Jr.; great²-grandson of Daniel and Eunice (March) Fogg; great³-grandson of *Reuben Fogg*, Colonel, Cumberland County, Massachusetts Militia; great²-grandson of Samuel and Hannah (Snow) Whitney; great²-grandson of Asa and Patience (Weston) Whitney; great⁴-grandson of *Nathan Whitney*, Member, Gorham, Maine, Committee of Safety.

ARCHIBALD COLEMAN, Minneapolis, Minn. (37441). Son of Silas Bunker and Rebecca Fitzhugh (Backus) Coleman; grandson of Frederick William and Emily Louise (Montgomery) Backus; great-grandson of Harvey and Eleanor (Rochester) Montgomery; great²-grandson of *Nathaniel Rochester*, Paymaster and Colonel, North Carolina Militia, and Commissary General.

ALFRED FILLMORE COMPTON, Moundsville, W. Va. (D. C. 37164). Son of Millard and Mary N. (Tomlinson) Compton; grandson of Henry and Ruth (Hardman) Compton; great-grandson of *Robert Compton*, Guide and Messenger to General Washington, New Jersey Campaign.

HARRY CRAWFORD COMPTON, Grafton, W. Va. (D. C. 37165). Same as Alfred Fillmore Compton, (D. C. 37164).

HARRY CUSTIS COMPTON, Grafton, W. Va. (D. C. 37166). Son of Henry and Ruth (Hardman) Compton; grandson of *Robert Compton*, Guide and Messenger to General Washington, New Jersey Campaign.

HENRY TOMLINSON COMPTON, Moundsville, W. Va. (D. C. 37167). Same as Alfred Fillmore Compton, (D. C. 37164).

JAY GOULD CONDERMAN, Chicago, Ill. (37881). Son of Caleb and Sally Ann (Mulholland) Conderman; grandson of Adam J. and Elizabeth (Bruner) Conderman; great-grandson of *John A. Contreman (Conderman)*, private, Tryon County, New York Militia.

HAROLD LESLIE CONKLIN, King's Park, L. I., N. Y. (37599). Son of Charles A. and Sarah A. (Blydenburgh) Conklin; grandson of John Washington and Ann Eliza (Newton) Blydenburgh; great-grandson of Jonas Beecher and Cecelia A. (Darling) Blydenburgh; great²-grandson of John and Elizabeth (Payne) Blydenburgh; great³-grandson of *Joseph Blydenburgh*, Signer, New York Association Test.

JOHN HOLMES CONVERSE, Washington, D. C. (37168). Son of John H. and Jane Baker (Jones) Converse; grandson of Freeman and Emily (Miller) Converse; great-grandson of Solvin and Sarah (Holmes) Converse; great²-grandson of *Asa Converse*, private, Col. Benjamin Simond's Regt., Connecticut Militia.

W. LORRAIN COOK, Washington, D. C. (37169). Son of Henry Trevor and Eliza (Hempstead) Cook; grandson of Charles Wilt and Elizabeth (Cooper) Hempstead; great-grandson of Charles Smith and Rachel (Wilt) Hempstead; great²-grandson of *Stephen Hempstead, 2d*, Sergeant, Col. Webb's Regt., Connecticut Rangers.

EARNEST ERASMUS CORRELL, Nebr. (24822). Supplemental. Son of Erasmus Michael and Lucy L. (Wilder) Correll; grandson of Landis Jacob and Mary Jane (Van der Cook) Correll; great-grandson of Michael M. and Mathilda (Brown) Van der Cook; great²-grandson of Michael S. and Mahitable (Haskins) Van der Cook; great³-grandson of *Simon Van der Cook*, Ensign, Albany County, New York Militia; great⁴-grandson of *Michael Van der Cook*, patriot who furnished pay to Albany County, New York Militia; great²-grandson of Simon and Fevina (Van der Hoff) (Hoof) Van der Cook; great²-grandson of *Hendrick Van der Hoof*, Captain, Col. Yates' Regt., Albany County, New York Militia.

THOMAS MOSES CORY, Ark. (18870). Supplemental. Son of Azro Buck and Rhoda Scott (Hart) Cory; grandson of Thomas Robbins and Lytta (Howe) Cory; great-grandson of Ebenezer and Joanna (Fletcher) Cory; great²-grandson of *Ebenezer Fletcher*, private, Col. Prescott's Regt., Massachusetts Minute-Men.

BAIRD FAVILLE COX, Osgood, Ind. (37802). Son of Lafayette Thomas and Ezraetta (Callicotte) Cox; grandson of Francis M. and Amney (Hughs) Cox; great-grandson of Vardamon and Frances (Wells) Hughs; great²-grandson of *John Hughs*, private, Capt. Fox's Company, Sixth Regt., Virginia Cont'l Troops.

WATKINS CROCKETT, Nashville, Tenn. (37471), Son of Robert Payne and Mary Eliza (Watkins) Crockett; grandson of Overton and Evalina (Smith) Crockett; great-grandson of *Anthony Crockett*, Lieutenant, Virginia Militia, pensioned.

LOUIS WILKINS CULBREATH, Stanton, Tenn. (38058). Son of William Jackson and Missouri Ann (Pinson) Culbreath; grandson of William E. and Elizabeth (Hughes) Culbreath; great-grandson of William Linnen and Tempe (Wiles) Culbreath (Colbreath); great²-grandson of *Thomas Culbreath (Colbreath)*, private, Col. Henry Luddington's Regt., Dutchess County, New York Militia.

HERBERT JOHN CUTLER, Buffalo, N. Y. (37913). Son of Francis Eli and Emma (Baines) Cutler; grandson of Samuel J. and Hulda Rebecca (Josselyn) Cutler; great-grandson of Samuel and Rebecca (Teachout) Josselyn; great²-grandson of Amasa and Mary (Hooker) Josselyn; great²-grandson of *Simeon Hooker*, Sergeant, Massachusetts Militia, pensioned.

FRANCIS CUTTING, Stockton, Calif. (37275). Son of Lewis Morrison and Catharine Sophia (Howland) Cutting; grandson of Lewis and Susan Julia (Morrison) Cutting; great-grandson of John and Jennette (Paul) Morrison; great²-grandson of *John Morrison, 3rd*, private, Col. John Stark's Regt., New Hampshire Troops.

LEWIS MILTON CUTTING, Stockton, Calif. (37851). Son of Francis and Helena L. (Henderson) Cutting; grandson of Lewis M. and Catherine Sophia (Howland) Cutting; great²-grandson of John and Jennette (Paul) Morrison; great²-grandson of *John Morrison, 3d*, private, Col. Stark's Regt., New Hampshire Troops.

CHARLES ALBERT DAVIS, San Francisco, Calif. (37861). Son of Joseph W. and Ellen Lucina (Robinson) Davis; grandson of Harmon and Cynthia (Fair) Robinson; great-grandson of Otis and Hannah (Reed) Robinson; great²-grandson of *Enoch Robinson*, Captain, Massachusetts Militia.

FRANK PATTERSON DAVIS, Chicago, Ill. (37708). Son of James May and Susannah Trotter (Patterson) Davis; grandson of Nathaniel Green and Catherine (Simpson) Patterson; great-grandson of Benjamin Franklin and Eliza Odom (Farver) Simpson; great²-grandson of Richard Duke and Henrietta (Williams) Simpson; great²-grandson of *John Williams*, Lieutenant, Second Regt., North Carolina Troops, Delegate to Provincial Congress.

GUY WILFRED DAVIS, Portland, Maine (36598). Son of Horace F. and Grace (A——) Davis; grandson of Joseph C. and Ann M. (Coffren) Whitman; great-grandson of *Robert Coffren*, private, Third and First Regts., New Hampshire Cont'l Troops.

HERBERT ROWAN DAVIS, Buffalo, N. Y. (37600). Son of Edward Smith and Hannah (Gregory) Davis; grandson of Caleb Smith and Hannah Smith (Dodd) Davis; great-grandson of *Joseph Davis*, private and Wagonmaster, Essex County, New Jersey Militia.

PAUL H. DAY, Paterson, N. J. (37976). Son of Waters B. and Mame (C——) Day; grandson of Samuel Thomas and Elizabeth (Crane) Day; great-grandson of Stephen and Elizabeth (Wood) Day; great²-grandson of *Daniel Smith Wood*, Captain, First Regt., Essex County, New Jersey Militia.

MARTIN HENRY DEFFENBAUGH, Nebr. (36992). Son of Sylvester and Virginia Martin (Young) Deffenbaugh; grandson of Isaac K. and Fannie (McCormick) Kelly Young; great-grandson of George and Fannie Malone (Armstrong) McCormick; great²-grandson of *George McCormick*, Captain, Thirteenth Regt., Virginia Cont'l Line.

LOUIS DENNISTON, West Hartford, Conn. (37307). Son of Marvin R. and Eliza A. (Greene) Denniston; grandson of Eli and Matilda (Crofoot) Denniston; great-grandson of *John Denniston*, private, Second Regt., Ulster County, New York Militia.

ROBERT CLARENCE DERIVAUX, Nashville, Tenn. (38054). Son of Armand and Georgine (Schepp) Derivaux; grandson of Jean Baptiste and Theodorine (Scheibel-Girardey) Derivaux; great-grandson of *Mathieu Derivaux*, Regimental Surgeon with Rochambeau.

JAMES DINKINS, La. (26300). Supplemental. Son of Alexander Hamilton and Cynthia (Springs) Dinkin; grandson of William Polk and Margaret Polk (Springs) Springs; great-grandson of *Richard Springs*, (father of Margaret), Captain, Merklinburg County, North Carolina Troops; great-grandson of *John Springs* (father of William), Captain, Merklinburg County, North Carolina Troops; great-grandson of John and Sarah (Alexander) Springs; great²-grandson of Adam and Mary (Shelby) Alexander; great²-grandson of *Evan Dhu Shelby*, Brig.-General, Virginia Militia.

FRANCIS ASBURY DONY, Washington, D. C. (37174). Son of James H. and Charlotte (Clark) Dony; grandson of Jesse W. and Emma (Titchenor) Clark; great-grandson of Pardee and Polly (Woodward) Clark; great²-grandson of *Daniel Clark*, private, Fifth Regt., Connecticut Cont'l Line and Corporal Connecticut Militia, pensioned.

WILLIAM ALVA DORAN, San Marcos, Calif. (37853). Son of David Chapman and Harriet Alice (Lancaster) Doran; grandson of William Henry and Alice (Looker) Lancaster; great-grandson of Samuel and Hannah (Irwin) Looker; great²-grandson of *Othneil Looker*, private, New Jersey Militia, pensioned.

FREDERICK WILLIAM DORR, Alameda, Calif. (37854). Son of Charles Wesley and Laura Bell (McKnight) Dorr; grandson of James Edmond and Susan Belle (Potter) Dorr; great-grandson of Matthew and Ann (Mudge) Dorr; great²-grandson of Matthew and Dinah (Mudge) Dorr; great²-grandson of *Matthew Dorr*, Captain in Colonel Jonathan Latimer's Regt., Connecticut Militia.

ROBERT HAROLD DOWNELL, San Diego, Calif. (37852). Son of Alvin Herbert and Dorcas L. (Kilby) Donnell; grandson of Robert Page and Rachel (Litchfield) Donnell; great-grandson of Joseph and Lucy (Fitts) Donnell; great²-grandson of *John Donnell*, Massachusetts sailor on privateer "Black Prince."

ROGER ARNOLD DREW, Tampa, Fla. (29925). Son of Joseph Nickerson and Lucille Winchester (Cochran) Drew; grandson of William Bradbury and Mary Rogers (Johnson) Drew; great-grandson of Holton and Margaret Brewer (Witt) Johnson; great²-grandson of John Legree and Sarah (Rogers) Johnson; great²-grandson of *Benjamin Johnson*, Lieutenant, Lynn Company, Massachusetts Militia at Lexington Alarm, Member Committee of Safety and Correspondence.

DANIEL HERBERT DUVALL, Baltimore, Md. (37684). Son of Daniel and Elizabeth (Waters) Duvall; grandson of Daniel and Isabella (Cruse) Duvall; great-grandson of Tobias and —— (Willett) Duvall; great²-grandson of *Samuel Duvall*, private, Second Regt., Maryland Militia for Cont'l service.

JOHN EARLY, Nashville, Tenn. (37470). Son of John F. and Eliza (Bostick) Early; grandson of Hardin Perkins and Margaret Rebecca (Litton) Bostick; great-grandson of *John Bostick*, Sergeant, Hazen's Regt., North Carolina Cont'l Troops.

EARNEST EAST, Peoria, Ill. (37709). Son of Thomas Wheatly and Sarah Catherine (Barber) East; grandson of Stillman and Mary (Clark) Barber; great-grandson of Moses and Elizabeth (Belcher) Barber; great²-grandson of *James Barber*, private, Rhode Island Militia, mother pensioned.

FRANK HENRY EASTEY, San Jose, Calif. (37862). Son of Henry and Adeline (Moses) Estey; grandson of Anson George and Mary Ann (Bowen) Moses; great-grandson of Ruben and Lucinda (Stevens) Moses; great²-grandson of *Zebulon Moses*, private, Col. Allen's Regt., Vermont Militia.

MURRAY FRENCH EDWARDS, Kirkwood, Mo. (37608). Son of Nelson Green and Emma Nelson (Carter) Edwards; grandson of Henry Shreve and Mary (Palmer) Carter; great-grandson of Walker Randolph and Rebecca Ann (Shreve) Carter; great²-grandson of Henry Miller and Mary (Blair) Shreve; great²-grandson of *Israel Shreve*, Colonel, Second Regt., New Jersey Troops; grandson of Nelson Green and Harriet Josephine (Cooper) Edwards; great-grandson of Cyrus and Nancy Harriet (Reed) Edwards; great²-grandson of *Benjamin Edwards*, Lieutenant, Maryland Cont'l Line, member Maryland Legislature.

CHARLES THORBURN, St. Louis, Mo. (37609). Son of Charles Reid and May (Tappen) Thorburn; grandson of Charles Edmondson and Rebecca (Reid) Thorburn; great-grandson of James Donaldson and Ann Moore (Howison) Thorburn; great²-grandson of James and Ann Roy (Buckner) Thorburn; great²-grandson of *William Buckner*, Captain, Caroline County, Virginia Militia.

THOMAS RICHMOND EDWARDS, Brooklyn, N. Y. (37594). Son of William Henry and Elizabeth (Cranston) Edwards; grandson of Richmond and Chloe Hyde (Collier) Cranston; great-grandson of James and Anne (Hempstead) Cranston; great²-grandson of *Robert Hempstead*, Sergeant, Eighth Regt., Connecticut Militia.

FREDERICK ARTHUR EGERTON, Westfield, N. J. (37927). Son of James Oliver and Frances Virginia (Walsh) Egerton; grandson of Oliver and Hannah (Converse) Egerton; great-grandson of Israel and Anna (Smith) Converse; great²-grandson of *Israel Converse*, Captain, Col. Levi Wells' Regt., Connecticut Militia.

OTTO RAYMOND ELLARS, Fitzgerald, Ga. (37803). Son of Otto and Martha (Lovejoy) Ellars; grandson of James Sullivan and Phebe Ann (Cox) Lovejoy; great-grandson of David J. and Rozina (Bake) Cox; great²-grandson of *James* and Anne Borden (Potts) *Cox;* Brig.-General, Monmouth Brigade, New Jersey Militia; great²-grandson of *William Potts*, private, New Jersey Militia and member Committee of Observation; great²-grandson of *Peter Bake*, private, Third Regt., Hunterdon County, New Jersey Militia; great-grandson of *Samuel Lovejoy*, private, Massachusetts Militia; great²-grandson of *Isaac Lovejoy*, private, Col. John Nixon's Regt., Massachusetts Militia of 1775; great-grandson of Samuel and Esther (Morse) Lovejoy; great²-grandson of *William Morse*, private, Massachusetts Militia at Cambridge.

LEE ELLIS, Sullivan, Ind. (37811). Son of William and Nellie (H——) Ellis; grandson of *Robert Ellis*, private, Second and Tenth Regts., North Carolina Cont'l Line.

WILLIAM SCOTT FAULKNER, Alameda, Calif. (37867). Son of Thomas Peatry and Elizabeth Jane (Scott) Faulkner; grandson of Jeremiah Robinson and Elizabeth (Smith) Scott; great-grandson of Samuel and Jane (Robinson) Scott; great²-grandson of *Jeremiah Robinson*, private, Chester and Cumberland Counties, Pennsylvania Militia.

DOUGLASS HEWITT FERRY, Murray, Idaho (35116). Son of John Howard and Clara (Smith) Ferry; grandson of Sumner Ives and Mary (Hayes) Smith; great-grandson of Joel and Ann (Mills) Hayes; great²-grandson of Joel and Mary (Bliss) Hayes; great²-grandson of *Joel Hayes*, Lieutenant, Connecticut Militia at Lexington and Bennington Alarms.

CLAUDE CARLTON FINNEY, Warren, Ohio (37641). Son of Theron L. and Fidelia (Andrews) Finney; grandson of Josiah and Clarissa (Bushnell) Finney; great-grandson of *Josiah Finney*, private, Connecticut Militia, pensioned.

FULTON BROOKS FLICK, New Kensington, Pa. (Iowa 37655). Son of Albert Edward and Berthania E. (Weatherby) Flick; grandson of Charles Murray and Charlotte Edsall (de Lorimier) Weatherby; great-grandson of Henry Chester and Elizabeth (Brooks) Weatherby; great²-grandson of Ephraim and Susanna (Estabrook) Brooks, Jr.; great²-grandson of *Ephraim Brooks*, private, Concord, Massachusetts Militia, and Corporal, Col. Jackson's Regt., Massachusetts Cont'l Line.

CHAUNCEY C. FOSTER, Nashville, Tenn. (37469). Son of William and Caroline Matilda (Bertine) Foster, Jr.; grandson of William and Eliza Ann (Hall) Foster; great-grandson of Rawsley and Sally (Mansfield) Hall; great²-grandson of *Ebenezer Mansfield*, private, Connecticut State Troops and Militia, pensioned.

CHARLES KIRKLEY FROST, Washington, D. C. (37175). Son of Henry Hunter and Mary Walker (Creswell) Schley; grandson of George Hanson and Zemula Walker (Douglass) Schley; great-grandson of William and Charlotte (Kirkley) Schley; great²-grandson of John Jacob and Anna Maria (Shellman) Schley; great²-grandson of *John Thomas Shley*, member Maryland Council of Safety and of Committees of Correspondence, Observation and Vigilance.

JOSEPH WEBSTER GARRISON, Chicago, Ill. (37710). Son of James Manly and Sarah Jane (Mulligan) Garrison; grandson of James and Sarah Norton (Webster) Coffinger Mulligan; great-grandson of Calvin Price and Betsey (Parks) Webster; great²-grandson of Robert and Polly (Smith) Parks; great²-grandson of Robert and Elizabeth (Hall) Parks; great²-grandson of *Joseph Parks,* private, Connecticut Infantry.

CLAUDE GIGNOUX, Berkeley, Calif. (37864). Son of John Francis and Elizabeth (Hughes) Gignoux; grandson of Miles and Elizabeth (Galloway) Hughes; great-grandson of George and Mary (Coffey) Galloway; great²-grandson of *Alexander Galloway*, Second Lieutenant, Col. Jesse Woodhull's Regt., New York Militia.

RAYMOND CLARK GILES, Nashville, Tenn. (38059). Son of George E. and Anna (Haslett) Giles; grandson of Clark and Sally Ann (Thomas) Giles; great-grandson of James and Eliza N. (Olmstead) Giles, Jr.; great²-grandson of *James Giles*, Second Lieutenant and Adjutant, Second Regt., New York Cont'l Artillery.

JOSEPH ROGERS GILLARD, Grand Rapids, Mich. (37070). Son of James and Sylvia Ruth (Brown) Gillard; grandson of Solomon and Ziltha (Campbell) (Camel) Brown; great-grandson of Joseph Rogers and Ruth (Smith) Brown; great²-grandson of *Daniel Brown*, private, Third Regt., New York Troops.

WILLIAM HENRY GILLETTE, Jacksonville, Fla. (29924). Son of Otis E. and Cornelia L. (Bissell) Gillette; grandson of William and Amanda (J——) Bissell; great-grandson of Hiram and Beatta (Wetmore) Bissell; great²-grandson of *Benjamin Bissell*, Sergeant, Col. Andrew Ward's Regt., Connecticut State Troops.

RICHARD PARSONS GILLUM, Terre Haute, Ind. (37812). Son of Robert G. and Helen (Gilbert) Gillum; grandson of Joseph and Sarah (Morgan) Gilbert; great-grandson of Curtis and Mary A. (King) Gilbert; great²-grandson of *Benjamin Gilbert*, private, Connecticut Cont'l, State Troops and Militia, pensioned.

HAROLD ALBEN GILMORE, Chicago, Ill. (37711). Son of Harry Alben and Grace (Hutson) Gilmore; grandson of William Milton and Elizabeth (Merryman) Gilmore; great-grandson of William and Angelia (Bartholomew) Merryman; great²-grandson of *Joseph Bartholomew*, Sergeant, Chester County, Pennsylvania Militia.

GEORGE ANDREW GORDON, Eureka, Kans. (Ind. 37815). [Aged 101 years, 11 months.] Son of John and Ann (Armstrong) Gordon; grandson of *George Gordon*, private and Corporal, Col. William Irwin's Regt., Pennsylvania Troops.

ALEXANDER HARBERT GRAY, Brownsville, Tenn. (37472). Son of John Turner and Mary Ora (Battle) Gray; grandson of William Bennett and Sarah A. (Rice) Battle; great-grandson of William and Chloe Crudup (Boddie) Battle; great²-grandson of *William Battle*, Captain, North Carolina Militia.

JOHN TURNER GRAY, Jr., Brownsville, Tenn. (38055). Same as Alexander Harbert Gray, Tenn. (37472).

FRANKLIN THEODORE GREEN, San Francisco, Calif. (37855). Son of Theodore and Phœbe Marie (Le Vere) Green; grandson of William and Maria (Prindle) Le Vere; great-grandson of Joel and Phœbe (Cogswell) Prindle; great²-grandson of *Zalmon Prindle*, private, Eighth, Fifth and Second Regts., Connecticut Line, widow pensioned; great²-grandson of Zalmon and Mary (Williams) Prindle; great²-grandson of *Abraham Williams*, private, Westchester County, New York Militia, died in prison.

RALPH ROBINSON GREENE, Boston, Mass. (37772). Son of Marlon E. and Mary Ella (Jaques) Greene; grandson of Addison Brown and Emily Rebecca (Farnsworth) Jaques; great-grandson of Eliphalet and Elizabeth (Davis) Jaques; great²-grandson of *Parker Jaques*, Corporal from Newbury, Massachusetts, at Lexington Alarm, private, Essex County, Massachusetts sea-coast defense.

WILLIAM MARTIN GREER, Chicago, Ill. (37712). Son of William Henry and Mary Bonner (Byrkit) Greer; grandson of Martin Bonner and Hannah (Waggoner) Byrkit; great-grandson of John and Mary (Bonner) Byrkit; great²-grandson of *Joseph Burkett*, private, First Regt., South Carolina Militia.

CHARLES CLIFTON GRIGGS, Washington, D. C. (38000). Son of Lewis Theodore and Carrie E. (Gale) Griggs; grandson of Lucien David and Mary Townsend (Kirk) Griggs; great-grandson of John and Huldah (Carpenter) Griggs; great²-grandson of *Joseph Griggs*, Corporal, Col. Joseph Spencer's Regt., Connecticut Militia of 1775.

EGBERT CHARLES HADLEY, Fairfield, Conn. (37308). Son of Harry Clifton and Carrie Augusta (Starr) Hadley; grandson of Enoch and Mary Ann (Gove) Hadley; great-grandson of Enoch and Abigail (George) Hadley; great²-grandson of *George Hadley*, Captain, Col. Daniel Moore's Regt., New Hampshire Militia, member New Hampshire Legislature of 1777.

STANDISH HALL, Chicago, Ill. (37713). Son of Harry Newberry and Anne (Russell) Hall; grandson of Henry Clinton and Emma Theresa (Dunbar) Hall; great-grandson of James and Evaline (Allen) Hall; great²-grandson of Daniel and Ruth (Josselyn) Hall; great²-grandson of *Joshua Hall*, Captain, Plymouth County, Massachusetts Militia.

BENJAMIN SAWTELLE HANCHETT, Grand Rapids, Mich. (37074). Son of Benjamin Sawtelle and Betsey (Jenison) Hanchett; grandson of Lemuel and Sally (Sanderson) Jenison; great-grandson of *Abijah Jenison*, private, Col. John Rand's Regt., Massachusetts Militia.

GERALD JENISON HANCHETT, Grand Rapids, Mich. (37075). Son of Benjamin Sawtelle and Elizabeth Anne (Husband) Hanchett, Jr.; grandson of Benjamin Sawtelle and Betsey (Jenison) Hanchett; great-grandson of Lemuel and Sally (Sanderson) Jenison; great²-grandson of *Abijah Jenison*, private, Col. John Rand's Regt., Massachusetts Militia.

ALFRED ALLEN HANKS, Montpelier, Vt. (38027). Son of Edwin Page and Susan Augusta (Allen) Hanks; grandson of Frederick Freeman and Abigail (Page) Hanks; great-grandson of Rodney and Olive (Freeman) Hanks; great²-grandson of *Frederick Freeman*, private, Capt. Jonathan Nichols' Company, Connecticut Militia at Lexington Alarm.

HARRIS ALLEN HARDISON, Nashville, Tenn. (37473). Son of Humphrey A. and Annie Laura (Bowen) Hardison; grandson of Humphrey and Harriet (Woolard) Hardison; great-grandson of *James Hardison*, private, Martin County, North Carolina Militia.

HORACE FREDERIC HARDY, Chicago, Ill. (37714). Son of Tucker and Helen (Stave) Hardy; grandson of Horace F. and Laura S. (Tucker) Hardy; great-grandson of Pierce A. and Ophelia (Breedlove) Hardy; great²-grandson of James W. and Maria (Winchester) Breedlove; great³-grandson of *James Winchester*, Captain, Third Regt., Maryland Troops.

FREDERICK KING HARRIS, Detroit, Mich. (37065). Son of George Henry and Juliza (Turner) Harris; grandson of John and Elizabeth (Allcott) Harris; great-grandson of Simeon Plumb and Jane Ann (Whitmore) Allcott; great²-grandson of *Asa Allcott*, private, Connecticut State Troops and Col. Baldwin's Regt., Artillery Artificers.

RALPH CLYMER HAWKINS, N. Y. (34560). Supplemental. Son of Eunest Clymer and Ada Sanford (Hallock) Hawkins; grandson of Henry Webb and Alice Estelle (Miller) Hallock; great-grandson of Daniel Roe and Mary Halsey (Rogers) Hallock; great²-grandson of Zophar and Hannah (Roe) Hallock; great³-grandson of *Daniel Hallock*, Signer of Suffolk County, New York, Association Test.

HENRY W. B. HEWEN, Wash. (36655). Supplemental. Son of Loring and Seddie (Truesdell) Hewen; grandson of Jesse and Dorothy (Talcott) Truesdell; great-grandson of *Jabish Truesdell*, private, Fourth Regt., West Chester County, New York Militia.

JOHNSON HEYWOOD, Yonkers, N. Y. (37915). Son of John Wicks and Flora Mills (Johnson) Heywood; grandson of Daniel Wicks and Sarah (Hood) Heywood; great-grandson of Russell Hubbard and Sarah (Wicks) Heywood; great²-grandson of Daniel and Sally (Hubbard) Heywood; great³-grandson of *Jonas Hubbard*, Captain, Col. Ward's Regt., Massachusetts Militia, prisoner, died in service.

WILLIAM MORTIMER HIGLEY, Minneapolis, Minn. (37444). Son of Wellington W. and James E. (Farnum) Higley; grandson of Mowry and Avelina Johnson (Gibson) Farnum; great-grandson of Solomon and Sarah (Willard) Gibson; great²-grandson of *Isaac Gibson*, private, Col. Asa Whitcomb's Regt., Massachusetts Militia.

HENRY CLARKE HILL, Galesburg, Ill. (37715). Son of Thomas A. and Ellen White (Lynde) Hill; grandson of Henry and Ann Clarke (Shaw) Lynde; great-grandson of Nathaniel and Sarah (Hitchcock) Lynde; great²-grandson of *Samuel Lynde*, private, Second Regt., Connecticut Cont'l Line.

ROSS A. HINDMAN, Fort Wayne, Ind. (37804). Son of Thomas J. and Laura O. (Unger) Hindman; grandson of Crooks and Matilda R. (Brown) Hindman; great-grandson of James and Ruth (Crunkhilton) Hindman; great²-grandson of *James Hindman*, private, Cumberland County, Pennsylvania Militia.

THOMAS J. HINDMAN, Fort Wayne, Ind. (37808). Son of Crooks and Matilda R. (Brown) Hindman; grandson of James and Ruth (Crunkhilton) Hindman; great-grandson of *James Hindman*, private, Cumberland County, Pennsylvania Militia.

WILLIAM HENRY HOGG, Mountain Lakes, N. J. (N. Y. 37901). Son of William and Maria Eliza (Patterson) Hogg; grandson of Robert and Sarah (Van Metre) Patterson; great-grandson of *John Van Metre*, Captain, Westmoreland County, Pennsylvania Militia and Cont'l Line.

FREDERIC CLARK HOOD, Brookline, Mass. (37773). Son of George Henry and Frances Henrietta (Janvrin) Hood; grandson of Jacob and Sophia (Needham) Hood; great-grandson of *John Hood*, private, Massachusetts Cont'l Troops and Sergeant, Essex County, Massachusetts Militia.

HAROLD LYNDE HOPKINS, Forest Grove, Oregon (37486). Son of Joseph Bower and Emily (Lynde) Hopkins; grandson of Joseph and Parnelia (Pickett) Hopkins; great-grandson of *Joseph Hopkins*, private, Lieut.-Col. Baldwin's Tenth Regt., Connecticut Cont'l Infantry.

MYRON HARRIS HOPKINS, Grand Rapids, Mich. (37071). Son of Mordicai Low and Sarah (Rathbone) Hopkins; grandson of Benjamin and Catherine (Low) Hopkins; great-grandson of *Cornelius Low (Lowe)*, private, New York Militia.

ALLEN ASA HORTON, Highland Park, Mich. (37951). Son of Henry Wilber and Cora Eliza (Bailey) Horton; grandson of Henry Witter and Mary (Allen) Horton; great-grandson of Pliney and Sarah (Porter) Allen; great²-grandson of *Noah Allen*, Captain and Major, Berkshire County, Massachusetts Troops, pensioned; grandson of Asa Harts-horn and Harriet Maria (Fusselman) Bailey; great-grandson of James and Betsey (Brewster) Bailey; great-grandson of *Frederick Brewster*, private and Coast Guard, Connecticut Militia.

GEORGE BURT HOYER, Buffalo, N. Y. (37912). Son of Burt Prindle and Harriett (Lambart) Hoyer; grandson of George A. and Dorothea (Prindle) Hoyer; great-grandson of Frederick and Eva (Kaynor) Hoyer; great²-grandson of *Peter Hoyer*, private, Fourth Regt., Tyron County, New York Militia.

JAMES ALFRED HOYT, Detroit, Mich. (37062). Son of James Alfred and Rebecca Caroline (Webb) Hoyt; grandson of Elijah and Elizabeth Rebecca (Gaillard) Webb; great-grandson of *Charles Gaillard*, private, South Carolina Militia; grandson of Jonathan Perkins and Jane (Johnson) Hoyt; great-grandson of *Nathan Hoyt*, private, Col. Joseph Badger's Regt., New Hampshire Militia.

LEVERETT MARSDEN HUBBARD, Hartford, Conn. (37309). Son of Leverett M. and —— (——) Hubbard; grandson of Eli and Georgiana (Leach) Hubbard; great-grandson of Leverett W. and Deborah (Scranton) Leach; great²-grandson of *Timothy Scranton*, private, Fourth Regt., Connecticut Line, pensioned.

GEORGE ANDREW GORDON HUTCHISON, Oakland, Calif. (37856). Son of Andrew and Edelia Jane (Gordon) Hutchison; grandson of John and Anna (Armstrong) Gordon; great-grandson of *George Gordon*, private and Corporal, Colonel William Irvin's Regt., Pennsylvania Troops.

LUTHER TAYLOR JACKMAN, Huntington, N. Y. (37902). Son of Lewis and Syrena A. (Buzzell) Jackman; grandson of Royal and Lucretia (Ladd) Jackman; great-grandson of *Samuel Jackman*, private, Fifth Regt., New Hampshire Cont'l Infantry.

LESLIE E. JACOBY, Lieut. U. S. Army, Ohio (37642). Son of Charles Wesley and Mary (Zeig) Jacoby; grandson of Michael and Catharine (Emery) Jacoby, Jr.; great-grandson of Michael and Elizabeth (Worline) Jacoby; great²-grandson of Henry and Catharine (Cline) Worline; great²-grandson of *Conrad Cline*, private, Second Regt., Pennsylvania Cont'l Line.

LAWRENCE GAMALIEL JACQUA, Humboldt, Iowa (37654). Son of John Franklin and Alice Loretta (McCaffrey) Jaqua; grandson of Gamaliel and Christina (Thomas) Jaqua; great-grandson of Darius and Freelove (Gaistin) Jaqua; great²-grandson of *Gamaliel Jaqua*, private, Major Elijah Humphrey's Regt., Connecticut Troops, widow pensioned.

McCLURE KELLY, San Francisco, Calif. (Ky. 36537). Son of Walter and Martha Agnes (McClure) Kelly; grandson of John D. and Agnes Haley (Todd) McClure; great-grandson of George and Mary Ellis (Montague) Todd; great²-grandson of *William Todd*, private, Fifth and Eleventh Regts., Virginia Militia.

WALLACE KELLY, Plainfield, N. J. (Ky. 36538). Same as McClure Kelly, Ky. (36537).

AUSTIN KILBOURN, Hartford, Conn. (37310). Son of Joseph Austin and Sarah Alacoque (Dooley) Kilbourn; grandson of Horace and Mary (Young) Kilbourn; great-grandson of Joseph and Hannah (Sellew) Kilbourn; great²-grandson of *Philip Sellew*, member Connecticut Committee for Purchasing Clothing for Cont'l Army, member Connecticut General Assembly of 1783.

WILLIAM RANKIN KING, Washington, D. C. (38001). Son of Joseph Cicero and Emma (Rankin) King; grandson of William Rufus and Mary (Arnott) King; great-grandson of Edward Sanders and Polly (Ashley) King; great²-grandson of *Edward King*, private, Tenth Regt., North Carolina Troops, pensioned.

ROBERT CASWELL KINGSLEY, Detroit, Mich. (37068). Son of Frederick Alonzo and Jane (Caswell) Kingsley; grandson of Edwin and Bethiah (Wells) Caswell; great-grandson of Lemuel and Jennet (Nevins) Caswell; great-grandson of *Lemuel Caswell*, private and Sergeant, Plymouth County, Massachusetts Militia and Cont'l Troops, pensioned.

HARRY FREDERICK KLEIST, Detroit, Mich. (37955). Son of Henry G. and Aleda (Groves) Kleist; grandson of John and Melissa (Spear) Groves; great-grandson of Robert H. and Eliza Dyckman (Springsteen) Spear; great-grandson of Harmon and Welliampe (Onderdunk) Springsteen; great-grandson of *Thomas Onderdunk*, private, Orange County, New York Militia, widow pensioned.

CHARLES ELLSWORTH KNAPP, Springfield, Ill. (37716). Son of George and Mahalath Berry (Shank) Knapp; grandson of John Smith and Susan (Hoke) Shank; great-grandson of *Christian Shank*, private and Corporal, New Jersey and Maryland Militia, pensioned.

HAL GREENWOOD KNIGHT, Akron, Ohio (38076). Son of Charles M. and Seraph May (Acomb) Knight; grandson of James L. and Seraph (Oliver) Acomb; great-grandson of Charles and Pheba (Willson) Oliver; great-grandson of Moses and Lois W. (Humphrey) Oliver; great-grandson of *John Oliver*, Captain, Col. Nathan Sparhawk's Regt., Massachusetts Militia.

FREDERICK KRAISSL, Jr., River Edge, N. J. (37978). Son of Frederick and Anna M. (Van Sann) Kraissl; grandson of John A. and Sophia A. (Post) Van Sann; great-grandson of Albert J. and Margaret (Weaver) Van Sann; great-grandson of Jacob and Jane (Van Keuren) Weaver; great-grandson of Abraham and Nellie (Wilsey) Van Keuren; great-grandson of *Abraham Van Keuren*, Lieutenant, Fourth Regt., Dutchess County, New York Militia.

GEORGE PASPILD KREIDER, Springfield, Ill. (37717). Son of George Noble and Emma (Pasfield) Kreider; grandson of Edmund Cicero and Mary (Gates) Kreider; great-grandson of Michael Zimmerman and Sidney Ann (Rees) Kreider; great-grandson of Daniel and Salome (Carpenter) Kreider; great-grandson of *Michael Kreider (Cryder)*, private, Lancaster County, Pennsylvania Militia, Commissary and Frontierman, Cont'l Army.

PAUL GATES KREIDER, Springfield, Ill. (37718). Same as George Pasfield Kreider, Ill. (37717).

DOC LYTLE LEDBETTER, Murfreesboro, Tenn. (38060). Son of William and Mary Catherine (Lytle) Ledbetter; grandson of William F. and Mary (Henderson) Lytle; great-grandson of *William Lytle*, Captain, Fourth Regt., North Carolina Cont'l Line.

SAMUEL BOUTON WHITMAN LEYENBERGER, Newark, N. J. (37979). Son of John and Emeline (Whitman) Leyenberger; grandson of Samuel B. and Elizabeth (Symons) Whitman; great-grandson of Jacob and Emeline (Hayward) Whitman; great-grandson of *Isaac Whitman*, private, Suffolk County, New York Militia.

PHILIP JAMES LINE, Chicago, Ill. (37719). Son of Charles and Olive Hawkes (Dunton) Line; grandson of James and Esther Marion (Hawkes) Dunton; great-grandson of Asa and Lois (Hawkes) Dunton; great-grandson of *Thomas Dunton*, private, Vermont and Connecticut Militia.

WILTON LLOYD-SMITH, New York, N. Y. (37908). Son of Walter and Jessie E. (Gonzales) Lloyd-Smith; grandson of Horace Boardman and Ellen (Hays) Smith; great-grandson of Nathaniel and Francis (Boardman) Smith; great-grandson of *Hezekiah Smith*, Major, Hampshire County, Massachusetts Militia, member Provincial Congress and Constitutional Convention.

FREDERICK E. McCAIN, Detroit, Mich. (37067). Son of Edmund Seely and Ann Judson (Ferguson) McCain; grandson of William McCain; great-grandson of *William McCain*, private, Fourth Regt., Orange County, New York Militia.

MILTON HIRAM McCREERY, East St. Louis, Ill. (37720). Son of Joel Marshall and Isabella Laura (Slawson) McCreery, grandson of John Warren and Mary E. (Pace) McCreery; great-grandson of Alexander and Ann (Harrell) McCreery; great-grandson of Thomas and Nancy (Lewis) Harrell; great-grandson of *Thomas Lewis*, Lieutenant, Virginia Troops.

HUNTER McDONALD, Jr., Nashville, Tenn. (37474). Son of Hunter and Mary Eloise (Gordon) McDonald; grandson of Angus William and Cornelia (Peake) McDonald;

great-grandson of Angus and Mary (McGuire) McDonald; great²-grandson of *Angus McDonald*, member Virginia Committee of Safety of 1776, member Virginia Cont'l Line.

MALCOLM FIZER McFARLAND, Fort Madison, Iowa (37653). Son of Corey Fuller and Mamie Dunn (Fizer) McFarland; grandson of Jacob Corey and ·May (Woodcock) McFarland; great-grandson of David and Polly (Stevens) McFarland; great²-grandson of Elijah and Sarah (Marshall) MacFarlin, Jr.; great³-grandson of *Elijah MacFarlin (MacFarling)*, private, Col. Bradford's Regt., Massachusetts Cont'l Troops, died in service.

EDWARD WALTER McNEAL, Kokoma, Ind. (37813). Son of J. Hugh and Malinda (Lytle) McNeal; grandson of Richard Finley and Elizabeth (Welsh) Lytle; great-grandson of *William Welsh*, private, Col. William Heth's Third Regt., Virginia Troops.

GEORGE McNEIR, New York City, N. Y. (37595). Son of Thomas Shepherd and Emily Ridgly (Schwarar) McNeir; grandson of George and Elizabeth (Thompson) McNeir; great-grandson of Thomas and Elizabeth (Cobreth) McNeir; great²-grandson of Thomas and Nancy (Burgess) McNeir; great³-grandson of *Edward Burgess*, Captain, First Battalion, Maryland Flying Camp, member House of Delegates, Committee of Observation and Justice of Montgomery County Court.

DAVID CLINTON MACKEY, Plainfield, N. J. (37980). Son of Robert and Lydia White (Yerkes) Mackey; grandson of Andrew Long and Susan Austin (Jarrett) Yerkes; great-grandson of William and Letitia Esther (Long) Yerkes; great²-grandson of *Andrew Long*, Captain, First Battalion, Miles', Pennsylvania Rifle Regt.

MALCOLM ELWOOD MACKEY, Muncie, Ind. (37805). Son of Henry Clay and Sarah (Baker) Mackey; grandson of Absalom and Margaret Ann (Rowe) Mackey; great-grandson of Jacob and Sarah (Conlin) Rowe; great²-grandson of *George Rowe (Row)*, Lieutenant, North Hampton County, Pennsylvania Militia.

EDWIN HENRY MARBLE, Worcester, Mass. (37768). Son of Edwin T. and Harriet H. (Chase) Marble; grandson of Royal Tyler and Ann B. (Clement) Marble; great-grandson of Andrew and Sarah (Harback) Marble; great²-grandson of *Malachi Marble*, Massachusetts Powder-maker, Constable and Collector of Taxes 1778.

WILL HAMMOND MARSHALL, Little Rock, Ark., (37926). Son of William Henry and Mary Jane (McCorkle) Marshall; grandson of Hammond and Mary (Maddox) Marshall; great-grandson of Peletiah and Martha (Skillings) Marshall; great²-grandson of *Simeon Skillings*, private, Col. Jonathan Mitchell's Regt., Massachusetts Militia.

PAUL BERNARD MEDBERY, Chicago, Ill. (37721). Son of Hiram and Lucy (Royce) Medbery; grandson of Hiram and Nancy (Chambers) Medbery; great-grandson of Nathan and Rhoda (Harris) Medbury; great²-grandson of *Benjamin Medberry*, private and Corporal, Rhode Island and Massachusetts Militia and Cont'l Troops.

DAYTON BALL MEEKER, New York, N. Y. (37903). Son of Joseph Frank and Harriet Georgette (Fisher) Meeker; grandson of Robert William and Sarah Elizabeth (Clawson) Fisher; great-grandson of Robert and Mary Elizabeth (Auspake) Fisher; great²-grandson of Frederick and Catharine (Bogardus) Auspake; great³-grandson of *John Bogardus*, private, Dutchess County, New York Militia.

FRANK BOGARDUS MEEKER, Yonkers, N. Y. (37904). Son of Joseph Frank and Harriet Georgett (Fisher) Meeker; grandson of Robert William and Sarah Elizabeth (Clawson) Fisher; great-grandson of Robert and Mary Elizabeth (Anspake) Fisher; great³-grandson of Frederick and Catharine (Bogardus) Anspack; great²-grandson of *John Bogardus*, private, Second Regt., Dutchess County, New York Militia.

GEORGE FISHER MEEKER, New York, N. Y. (37905). Same as Frank Bogardus Meeker, N. Y. (37904).

EDGAR NELSON MENDENHALL, Fort Wayne, Ind. (37809). Son of Noah M. and Anna (Wroe) Mendenhall; grandson of Noah Madison and Mary Jane (Quick) Mendenhall; great-grandson of James and Elizabeth (McClure) Quick; great²-grandson of John and Mary (Eads) Quick; great³-grandson of *Henry Eads*, private, Kent County, Maryland Militia, pensioned.

CHARLES PLATT MERCHANT, Irvington, N. J. (37983). Son of Frank M. and Leonora E. (Bryant) Merchant; grandson of Daniel P. and Ann Eliza (Cary) Merchant; great-grandson of *Lewis Cary*, Matross, Ebenezer Stewart's Corp, Massachusetts Cont'l Artillery.

EDWIN AUSTIN MERRITT, Portland, Maine (36599). Son of James Henry and Sarah J. (Lowell) Merritt; grandson of Henry and Betsey (Rice) Lowell; great-grandson of John and Mary (Hanscom) Rice; great²-grandson of *Moses Hanscom*, private, Col. Jonathan Mitchell's Regt., Massachusetts Militia.

LINDSLEY ROSS MIDDLEBROOKE, Malden, Mass. (37766). Son of Frank H. and Katherine (Ross) Middlebrook; grandson of James H. and Margaret (Lindsley) Middlebrook; great-grandson of Hiram and Louise (Garrett) Middlebrook; great²-grandson of Hezekiah and Rebecca (Fitch) Middlebrook, Jr.; great³-grandson of *Hezekiah Middlebrook*, Chairman, Ballston, New York, Committee of Safety.

CLINTON RALPH MILLER, Omaha, Nebr. (36993). Son of Franklin Delos and Mary (Enright) Miller; grandson of Hiram Barlow and Maria (Deming) Miller; great-grandson of Lyman and Celia B. (Wheeler) Miller; great²-grandson of *Benjamin Wheeler*, private and Sergeant, Massachusetts Militia, pensioned.

FREDERICK W. MILLSPAUGH, Tenn. (27912). Supplemental. Son of Charles Edward and Elizabeth Susan (Tozer) Millspaugh; grandson of Homer and Sarah Elosia (Groesbeck) Millspaugh; great-grandson of John Quakenbos and Hannah (Arnold) Groesbeck; great²-grandson of Jonathan and Mary (Hoogoboom) Arnold; great³-grandson of *David Arnold*, private, New York Levies and Fourth Regt., Albany County, New York Militia.

GEORGE B. MILLER, Milwaukee, Wis. (37287). Son of Andrew Galbraith and Martha Elizabeth (Goodwin) Miller; grandson of Andrew Galbraith and Cornelia Augusta (McVicker) Miller; great-grandson of Andrew Galbraith and Caroline Elizabeth (Kurtz) Miller; great²-grandson of Matthew and Jean (Galbraith) Miller; great³-grandson of *Andrew Galbraith*, Major, Col. Watt's Battalion, Pennsylvania Flying Camp.

ROBERT E. MILLING, JR., New Orleans, La. (36966). Son of Robert E. and —— (——) Milling; grandson of Thomas David and Mary A. (Teddlie) Milling; great-grandson of David T. and Maria (Latham) Milling; great²-grandson of *Hugh Milling*, Captain, Sixth Regt., South Carolina Cont'l Line, prisoner.

OSCAR MITCHELL, Duluth, Minn. (37442). Son of Jackson Gates and Sarah Elizabeth (Hubbell) Mitchell; grandson of Anderson and Elzira (Whitlock) Mitchell; great-grandson of Charles and Patsy (Wilson) Whitlock; great²-grandson of *Moses Wilson*, private, Capt. John Holder's Company, Virginia Troops.

FREDERICK ISAIAH MODDELL, Bridgeport, Conn. (37311). Son of Frederick Willis and Mary Jeanett (Rogers) Moddell; grandson of Isaiah and Mary Huntington (Colby) Rogers; great-grandson of John and Ruth (Titus) Rogers, Jr.; great²-grandson of *Jonathan Titus*, Captain, Fourth Regt., New York Line.

ALBERT C. MURPHY, Detroit, Mich. (37060). Son of Albert L. and Sarah (McDonald) Murphy; grandson of John and Margaret (Morrow) Murphy; great-grandson of John and Elizabeth (Boyle) Murphy; great²-grandson of *Owen Murphy*, private, Eighth Regt., Virginia Cont'l Line.

EARL STIMSON NIBLACK, Terre Haute, Ind. (37814). Son of Sanford Lee and Susan (Brooks) Niblack; grandson of Thomas Jefferson and Susanna (Poore) Brooks; great-grandson of John and Hannah (Chute) Poore; great²-grandson of *James Chute*, private, Yarmouth, Massachusetts Militia.

JAMES K. NICHOLS, Highland Park, Mich. (37066). Son of George E. and Harriet (Kennedy) Nichols; grandson of James and Eliza (Moseman) Kennedy; great-grandson of Elias D. and Harriet (N——) Moseman; great²-grandson of Eben and Zilpha (Weeks) Moseman; great³-grandson of *Marcus Moseman, Jr.*, Captain, New York Militia, prisoner.

FREDERICK MANTHANO NOYES, Gardiner, Maine (36600). Son of Manthano and Lydia (Stuart) Noyes; grandson of *Thomas Noyes*, private, Cumberland County, Massachusetts Militia.

WILLIAM ALEXANDER ORR, Morristown, Tenn. (37475). Son of David Murphey and Rebecca (Wynne) Orr; grandson of Robert Whitley and Mary (Crabtree) Wynne; great-grandson of *William Wynne*, private, Virginia Militia at Chesterfield Court House.

CHARLES DUSTIN PARKER, Chicago, Ill. (37722). Son of Charles Aubrey and Emma Elizabeth (Kuchs) Parker; grandson of Dustin Merrill and Celestia (Melvin) Parker; great-grandson of Daniel and Harriett (Gregg) Melvin; great²-grandson of *Reuben Gregg*, private, New Hampshire Militia, pensioned.

THOMAS WELLER PARKHILL, Burlington, Vt. (38028). Son of Edward W. and Mary (W——) Parkhill; grandson of Ezra and Elizabeth Rebecca (Hill) Parkhill; great-grandson of Thomas Chittenden and —— (——) Hill; great-grandson of James and Betsey (Chittenden) Hill; great-grandson of *Thomas Chittenden*, President, Vermont Council of Safety and Governor 1778-1783.

OLIVER PARIS PARTHEMORE, Roslyn, Va. (D. C. 37170). Son of Daniel and Nancy (Ebersole) Parthemore; grandson of George and Eve (Winagle) Parthemore; great-grandson of *John Philip Parthemore*, private, Fourth Battalion, Lancaster County, Pennsylvania Militia.

CLARENCE E. PEARSALL, Eureka, Calif. (37857). Son of George Alfred and Eliza Catharine (Larime) Pearsall; grandson of John and Deborah Ann (Brill) Pearsall; great-grandson of Peter and Mary Phebe (Burtis) Pearsall; great-grandson of *George Pearsall*, private, Fourth Regt., Dutchess County, New York Militia.

EBEN HOMER PENNELL, Bedford, Pa. (37735). Son of Edward McPherson and Amand (Homer) Pennell; grandson of Eben and Mary Anna Barbara (Over) Pennell; great-grandson of John and Catharine (Zollinger) Over; great-grandson of David and Barbara (Zollinger) Over; great-grandson of *Nicholas Zollinger*, Second Lieutenant, First Battalion, Lancaster County, Pennsylvania Militia.

CHARLES WILLIAM PEYTON, Temple, Texas (37531). Son of Charles Lewis and Agnes (Stuart) Peyton; grandson of Craven and Jane Jefferson (Lewis) Peyton; great-grandson of *Valentine Peyton*, Captain, Third Company, Third Regt., Virginia Troops.

ALEXANDER ROY PHILLIPS, Montclair, N. J. (37985). Son of George Pierce and Florence (Minney) Phillips; grandson of Edwin and Mary (Walton) Phillips; great-grandson of *George Phillips*, private, Sixth Regt., Virginia Cont'l Troops.

DAN GRIGSBY POLAND, Ardmore, Okla. (36967). Son of Robert P. and Enver Mildred (Grigsby) Poland; grandson of Daniel Jefferson and Lily (Cox) Grigsby; great-grandson of Silas and Emer Jane (Keene) Gex; great-grandson of John Anthony and Lyrena (Price) Gex; great-grandson of John M. and Sallie (Craig) Price; great-grandson of Benjamin and Mary (Hawkins) Craig; great-grandson of *Toliver (Talliferro) Craig*, Captain, Orange County, Virginia Militia.

ALEXANDER TAYLOR RANKIN, Buffalo, N. Y. (37906). Son of William and Mary L. (Wilson) Rankin; grandson of Alexander Taylor and Mary M. (Lowry) Rankin; great-grandson of Richard and Jane (Steel) Rankin; great-grandson of *Thomas Rankin*, private, Washington County, Pennsylvania Cont'l Line.

WILLIAM ARTHUR RANKIN, Buffalo, N. Y. (37907). Same as Alexander Taylor Rankin, N. Y. (37906).

EUGENE HOWARD RAY, Ky. (34711). Supplementals. Son of Samuel and Ellen Thomas (Howard) Ray, Jr.; grandson of Jesse and Lucy (Mayfield) Howard; great-grandson of *John Mayfield*, private, Virginia Militia; grandson of Samuel and Mary (Chism) Ray; great-grandson of James T. and Phebe (Breed) Chism; great-grandson of *James Chism*, private, Second and Tenth Regts., Virginia Cont'l Line.

WILLIAM HARRY RAY, Monroe, Mich. (37072). Son of Hiram Wentworth and Isabella Houston-Wynkoop; grandson of John and Lucy (Wentworth) Ray; great-grandson of Elegah and Lucy (Walker) Wentworth; great-grandson of *Elegah Wentworth*, private and Sergeant, Asabel Smith's Company, Massachusetts Militia.

ALBERTUS DELAFIELD RAYNOR, Montclair, N. J. (37981). Son of Clark H. and Harriet Cloves (Carter) Raynor; grandson of George Cobeat and Mary Catherine (Roe) Raynor; great-grandson of James and Cornelia (Roe) Roe; great-grandson of Benjamin Strong and Sarah (Hudson) Roe (father of Cornelia); great-grandson of *Phillips Roe*, Adjutant, First Regt., Suffolk County, New York Militia.

HERBERT ELLSWORTH RECTOR, Brooklyn, N. Y. (37589). Son of Lincoln Ellsworth and Mary Elizabeth (Blair) Rector; grandson of Lewis R. and Katharine (Harrison) Blair; great-grandson of Daniel and Sarah Ann (Blair) Blair; great-grandson of *Robert Blair*, private, Second Regt., New Jersey Troops, six years service, pensioned.

GEORGE ELBERT REED, Freemont, Ind. (37806). Son of Ira and Harriet C. (Fisher) Reed; grandson of James and —— (Dexter) Fisher; great-grandson of —— and ——

(Tuffs) Dexter; great²-grandson of *William Tuffs*, private, Massachusetts Militia, pensioned.

STANLEY FORMAN REED, Ky. (34715). Supplemental. Son of John and Frances (Forman) Reed; grandson of Samuel and Anna Frinces (Soward) Forman; great-grandson of Joseph and Mary (Dye) Forman; great²-grandson of *Thomas Forman*, member Monmouth County, New Jersey, Drafting Committee, private, New Jersey Cont'l Troops.

HENRY KAUFFMAN REIGHARD, Bedford, Pa. (37734). Son of Absalom and Margaretta (Kauffman) Reighard; grandson of Henry and Rachel (Dibert) Kauffman; great-grandson of Henry and Rachel (Dibert) Kauffman; great²-grandson of *George Kauffman*, Second Lieutenant, Third Battalion, Berks County, Pennsylvania Militia.

JOHN ERWIN REYNOLDS, Minneapolis, Minn. (37443). Son of Frederick A. and Lucy A. (Evans) Reynolds; grandson of Ira P. and Elizabeth (Perkins) Evans; great-grandson of Luke and Betsey (Otis) Perkins; great²-grandson of *Obadiah Perkins*, Lieutenant, Col. Ledyard's Regt., Connecticut Militia.

CHARLES FRANCIS RICE, Somerville, Mass. (37769). Son of Charles Albion and Miranda (Rawson) Rice; grandson of Artemus and Dorcas B. (Rice) Rawson; great-grandson of *Artemus Rawson*, private, Third Regt., Worcester County, Massachusetts Militia.

LEWIS A. RICE, Frederick, Md. (37685). Son of Albert Thomas and Ann Sibana (Mantz) Rice; grandson of Gideon and Eliza (Sides) Mantz; great-grandson of *Peter Mantz*, Major, Maryland Flying Camp.

WILLIAM ALFRED ROBBINS, Brooklyn, N. Y. (37597). Son of Thomas Herrick and Adelia Stevens (Jordan) Robbins; grandson of Noah and Sarah (Stevens) Jordan; great-grandson of Benjamin and Sarah (Sawyer) Stevens; great²-grandson of *Jonathan Sawyer*, Captain, Col. Phinney's Regt., Massachusetts Militia.

THEODORE E. A. ROSE, Grand Rapids, Mich. (37069). Son of Henry Arnold and Zada Arminda (Martin) Rose; grandson of Samuel and Melinda (Crofut) Martin; great-grandson of Samuel and Phebe (Sanford) Martin; great²-grandson of *Daniel Sanford*, private, Connecticut State and Cont'l Troops, prisoner, pensioned.

ERBERT EMERSON RUSSELL, Chicago, Ill. (37705). Son of Benjamin Franklin and Elizabeth Gilman (Colby) Russell; grandson of Jason and Elizabeth (Thorp) Russell; great-grandson of Noah and Eunice (Bemis) Russell; great²-grandson of *Jason Russell*, killed at battle of Lexington.

AARON GRIGSBY ROGERS, Parker, Ind. (Ill. 37723). Son of Thornton and Eliza (Lluellen) Rogers; grandson of Aaron Grigsby and Elizabeth (Baumgarner) Rogers; great-grandson of *Joseph Rogers*, private, Col. Wigglesworth's Regt., Massachusetts Militia.

GEORGE ALFRED SAWIN, Washington, D. C. (Mass. 37774). Son of Alfred and Jane (Oakes) Sawin; grandson of Zadoc and Abigail (Allen) Oakes; great-grandson of *Samuel Oakes*, private, Col. John Greaton's Regt., Massachusetts Troops, carpenter on brigantine "Tyrannicide."

GEORGE HARRISON SCHAEFFER, Germantown, Ohio (37643). Son of John C. and Laura (Banker) Schaeffer; grandson of William Henry Harrison and Catherine (Negley) Schaeffer; great-grandson of John C. and Mary (Shuey) Negley; great²-grandson of *Philip Neagley (Negley)*, private, Major Lewis Farmer's Regt., Pennsylvania State Troops.

JOHN SEWARD, Chevy Chase, Md. (D. C. 37171). Son of John Leddel and Eliza (Kimber) Seward; grandson of George Washington and Tempe Wicke (Leddel) Seward; great-grandson of Samuel Swayze and Mary (Jennings) Seward; great²-grandson of *John Seward*, Colonel, New Jersey Militia.

WILLIAM McKINLEY SHEPHERD, Adrian, Mich. (37953). Son of William F. and Emma A. (Bovee) Shepherd; grandson of James H. and Roxanna (McMath) Shepherd; great-grandson of Paul and Asenath (Mack) Shepherd; great²-grandson of Alexander and Martha (McConnell) Shepherd; great³-grandson of *Paul Shepherd*, Captain of Home Guard, Northumberland County, Pennsylvania Militia.

TIMOTHY WALLACE SHERWOOD, Ind. (35512). Supplemental. Son of Thomas Russell and Anna Maria (Wallace) Sherwood; grandson of Timothy and Olive (Sherman)

Wallace; great-grandson of Ebenezer and Annie (Snow) Wallace; great²-grandson of *Benoni Wallace*, private, Massachusetts Militia, at Lexington Alarm.

EDWIN GLENDINNING SHOUP, Santa Clara, Calif. (37859). Son of William and Samantha C. (Whipple) Shoup; grandson of Russell G. and Mary (Allen) Whipple; great-grandson of Persons and Chloe (Tuttle) Allen; great²-grandson of *Phineas Allen*, private, First Regt., Connecticut Militia, pensioned.

DONALD BAIRD SKINNER, Chicago, Ill. (37724). Son of James Graden and Ida (Baird) Skinner; grandson of William Franklin and Caroline (Mills) Skinner; great-grandson of James H. and Catherine (Reid) Skinner; great²-grandson of Peter and Sarah (Roberts) Skinner; great³-grandson of *Richard Skinner*, private, Fourth, Eighth and Twelfth Regts., Virginia Troops.

HENRY RICHMOND SLACK, Jr., Baltimore, Md. (La. 36974). Son of Henry Richmond and Ruth (Bradfield) Slack; grandson of Henry Richmond and Louisiana Tennessee (Worlfolk) Slack; great-grandson of Eliphalet and Abigail (Cutter) Slack; great²-grandson of *John Slack*, private, Col. William McIntosh's Regt., Massachusetts Militia.

PAUL LOWE SLOAN, Tenn. (37465). Supplemental. Son of Vaniah S. and Latitia (Lowe) Sloan; grandson of George L. and Caroline (Townsend) Sloan; great-grandson of Thomas and Hannah (Barnard) Sloan; great²-grandson of *John Barnard*, Captain, Third Regt., Connecticut Cont'l Line.

BENJAMIN FRANKLIN SLOAT, Jr., N. J. (26934). Supplemental. Son of Benjamin Franklin and Mary Evelyn (Gwynne) Sloat; grandson of Henry Corquet and Laura (Parmlee) Sloat; great-grandson of Johannes C. and Martha (Corquet) Slott (Sloat); great²-grandson of Cornelius and Charity (Cumings) Slott (Sloat); great³-grandson of Cornelius and Ellen (McKinney) Slot (Sloat); great⁴-grandson of *Arthur McKinney*, private, Second Regt., Ulster County, New York Militia.

JOHN VANDERBILT SMALE, San Diego, Calif. (37858). Son of John Apsley and Sarah (Felt) Smale; grandson of Orson and Sarah (How) Felt; great-grandson of Jehiel and Mehitabel (Davis) Felt; great²-grandson of *Samuel Felt*, Captain, Connecticut Militia.

FREDERICK A. SMART, Jr., Detroit, Mich. (37073). Son of Frederick A. and Hattie A. (Lee) Smart; grandson of James Shirley and Elmira (Carter) Smart; great-grandson of David and Mary Louisa (Davis) Carter; great²-grandson of Samuel and Sarah (Newcomb) Carter; great³-grandson of *Samuel Carter*, private and Lieutenant, Connecticut Militia and Cont'l Line.

WILLIAM McPHERSON SMITH, Howell, Mich. (37061). Son of Frederick A and Ella McPherson) Smith; grandson of Henry Francis and Lydia (Smith) Smith; great-grandson of Albert G. W. and Caroline (Carver) Smith; great²-grandson of Benjamin and Clarinda (Lee) Carver; great³-grandson of *Noah Lee*, Captain, Connecticut Militia, Colonel, Vermont Militia in 1781.

WILLIAM MEREDITH SMITH, Frederick, Md. (37683). Son of Francis Fenwick and Maria (Lee) Smith; grandson of Leonard and Eliza (Jamison) Smith; great-grandson of *John Smith*, (Frederick County), Captain, Third Regt., Maryland Troops, prisoner.

DANIEL T. SMITHWICK, Louisburg, N. C. (Tenn. 38051). Son of James Robert and Frances (Allen) Smithwick; grandson of Turner and Elizabeth Willis (Watson) Allen; great-grandson of Vinson (Vincent) and Mary (Bowden) Allen; great²-grandson of *Charles Allen*, Captain, Second and Fifth Regts., North Carolina Troops.

JOSEPH CLYDE SNELL, Toledo, Ohio (37647). Son of Frank Clyde and Marie (Gilroy) Snell; grandson of Oscar Clyde and Jennie (Moore) Snell; great-grandson of Levi and Jane (Clyde) Snell; great²-grandson of Matthew and Jane (Clark) Clyde; great³-grandson of *Samuel Clyde*, Lieutenant-Colonel, New York Militia.

FRANKLIN MAYNARD SPEAR, Minneapolis, Minn. (37446). Son of Frederick Augustus and Laura Ann (Stiles) Spear; grandson of Zebadiah and Jane Gallison (Dennis) Spear; great-grandson of Zebadiah and Mary (Bucknam) Spear; great²-grandson of Zebadiah and Elizabeth (Farron) Spear; great³-grandson of *William Spear, Jr.*, private, Braintree, Massachusetts Militia.

CHARLES LUTHER SPENCER, Jr., Hartford, Conn. (37312). Son of Charles Luther and —— (——) Spencer; grandson of Israel Luther and Julia (Pease) Spencer; great-grandson of Hezekiah and Cecelia (Spencer) Spencer; great²-grandson of Hezekiah and Jerusha (Nelson) Spencer; great²-grandson of *Hezekiah Spencer*, private, Connecticut Militia, at Lexington Alarm.

HENRY FRANCIS SPENCER, West Haven, Conn. (37313). Son of Henry Green and Sarah Elizabeth (Wood) Spencer; grandson of George Addison and Eliza Hayward (Robbins) Wood; great-grandson of Jonathan Coolidge and Phœbe (Guild) Wood; great²-grandson of *Holland Wood*, private and Sergeant, Massachusetts Militia and Cont'l Artillery.

HENRY JOSEPH STEVENSON, East Boston, Mass. (37767). Son of Joseph Henry and Helen Louisa (Fletcher) Stevenson; grandson of Joseph and Hannah (Bickford) Stevenson; great-grandson of Thomas and Sarah (Johnson) Stevenson; great²-grandson of *Phineas* and Hannah (Poor) *Johnson*, private, Col. James Frye's Regt., Massachusetts Militia; great²-grandson of *Samuel Johnson*, Colonel, Fourth Regt., Essex County, Massachusetts Militia; grandson of Elbridge Erastus and Miriam Bird (Fowle) Fletcher; great-grandson of Samuel and Miriam Channel (Bird) Fowle; great²-grandson of Samuel and Rachel (Lawrence) Fowle; great²-grandson of *Jonathan Lawrence*, Treasurer, town of Woburn, Massachusetts, 1777-78; great²-grandson of James and Hannah (Channel) Bird; great²-grandson of *Louis Channel*, private, Corporal and Guard, Massachusetts Militia; great²-grandson of *Samuel Fowle*, private and Guard, Lieut.-Colonel Baldwin's Regt., Massachusetts Militia.

ELMER STEWART, Washington, D. C. (38002). Son of Joseph and Jessie Stewart (Bailey) Stewart; grandson of Benjamin Franklin and Ellen Jane (Stewart) Bailey; great-grandson of Jonathan and Catherine (Stewart) Bailey, Jr.; great²-grandson of *Jonathan Bailey*, private, Fifth Regt., Col. Lewis Duboy's Regt., New York Cont'l Line.

CHARLES HENRY STINAFF, Ohio (37027). Supplemental. Son of Charles Henry and Vernie E. (Smith) Stinaff; grandson of Henry William and Lydia (Button) Stinaff; great-grandson of Charles and Susan (T——) Button; great²-grandson of Charles F. and Hannah (Kinne) Button; great²-grandson of *Charles Button*, private, Vermont Militia; great²-grandson of *Asa Kinne*, Captain, Connecticut State Troops.

HERBERT RICHMOND STODDARD, New York City, N. Y. (37911). Son of Frank Wyman and Helen A. (Nay) Stoddard; grandson of Ephraim Samuel and Deucie L. (Crafts) Stoddard; great-grandson of Levi and Ermina (Wyman) Stoddard; great²-grandson of Samuel Stoddard; great²-grandson of *David Stoddard*, Sergeant, Col. James Reed's Regt., New Hampshire Troops, died in service.

JAMES CLIFTON STONE, Lexington, Ky. (36539). Son of Samuel Hanson and Pattie (Duncan) Stone; grandson of John D. and Nancy Jane (White) Harris; great-grandson of William and Malinda (Duncan) Harris; great²-grandson of John and Margaret (Maupin) Harris; great²-grandson of *Christopher Harris*, private and Frontiersman, Virginia Militia; great²-grandson of John and Frances (Dabney) Maupin; great⁴-grandson of *Daniel Maupin*, private, Albamarle County, Virginia Militia.

SAMUEL HANSON STONE, Jr., Louisville, Ky. (36540). Same as James Clifton Stone, Ky. (36539).

WILLIAM LEON STONE, Allston, Mass. (37770). Son of Leon Ashton and Marcia Ann (Simmons) Stone; grandson of William Henry and Rhoda Jane (Lull) Stone; great-grandson of Moses and Rhoda (Gove) Lull; great²-grandson of *David Lull*, private, Massachusetts Militia, widow pensioned.

CLAYTON FRANK BLOOMFIELD STOWELL, Chicago, Ill. (37725). Son of Frank Bloomfield and Frances (Hobson) Stowell; grandson of Abijah Delos and Mary Ann (Burdick) Stowell; great-grandson of Jacob and Mary (Jackson) Stowell; great²-grandson of Abijah and Lydia (Richards) Stowell; great²-grandson of *Abijah Stowell*, private, Col. McIntosh's Regt., Massachusetts Militia.

LEONARD WESTCOTT SMITH STRYKER, Youngstown, Ohio (37650). Son of Peter Wilson and Margaret (Tibbits) Stryker; grandson of James and Hannah Maria (Halsey) Stryker; great-grandson of *Luther Halsey*, Lieutenant and Adjutant, Second Regt., New Jersey Troops, seven years' service.

LOUIS KOSSUTH SUNDERLIN, Washington, D. C. (37172). Son of Arthur Vaughn and Eliza Jennings (Coffin) Sunderlin; grandson of John Davis and Margaret (Harrah)

Wood; great²-grandson of *Jeremiah Wood*, private, First Regt., Suffolk County, New York Militia; great-grandson of Daniel and Ann Jane (Lowery) Slote; great²-grandson of *Daniel Slote*, private, Col. Baldwin's Regt., New York Artificers; grandson of William Lawrence and Lydia A. (Mundy) Hartshorn; great-grandson of David Hunt and Sarah (Lawrence) Hartshorn; great²-grandson of *Beriah Hartshorn*, private, Capt. Mott's Connecticut Company, at defense of New London; great²-grandson of *David Lawrence*, private, Second Regt., Orange County, New York Militia; great²-grandson of *Jonathan Lawrence*, Captain, Sappers and Miner's New York Regt.; great²-grandson of David and Elizabeth (Poppino) Lawrence; great²-grandson of *John Poppino*, Major, Orange County, New York Militia; great-grandson of Edward Nelson and Margaret (Fran) (Sisco) Mundy; great²-grandson of *Jacob (Fran) Sisco*, private, Morris County, New Jersey Militia.

NORMAN ASA WOOD, Ann Arbor, Mich. (37954). Son of Jesup Scott and Lydia P. (Ingraham) Wood; grandson of Ira and Maria (Scott) Wood; great-grandson of Daniel and Wealthy (Munrow) Wood, Jr.; great²-grandson of *Daniel Wood*, private, Connecticut Militia at New Haven Alarm, member Connecticut War Committees.

WILL CHRISTOPHER WOOD, Sacramento, Calif. (37863). Son of Emerson and Martha Jane (Turner) Wood; grandson of Joel and Hannah (Rockwell) Wood; great-grandson of *Samuel Wood*, private, Worcester County, Massachusetts Militia.

REYNIER JACOB WORTENDYKE, Jr., Jersey City, N. J. (37987). Son of Reynier Jacob and Carolyn (Cooley) Wortendyke; grandson of Jacob Reynier and Susan Jane (Doremus) Wortendyke; great-grandson of Nicholas Jones and Elizabeth (Haring) Doremus; great²-grandson of Peter Thomas and Susan (Jacobus) Doremus; great²-grandson of *Thomas Doremus*, private, Essex County, New Jersey Militia.

JACK DOUGLAS WRIGHT, Chicago, Ill. (37880). Son of Louie Douglas and Gertrude Maude (Allensworth) Wright; grandson of Jack Douglas and Isabelle (Hodges) Wright; great-grandson of Asa Douglas and Lucy (Cabanis) Wright; great²-grandson of Orson and Elizabeth (Judd) Wright; great²-grandson of Isaac and Sarah (Douglas) Wright; great⁴-grandson of Asa and Sarah (Robbins) Douglas; great⁵-grandson of *Asa Douglas*, Captain, Connecticut "Silver Grays."

PAST PRESIDENT GENERAL MORRIS B. BEARDSLEY
Died March 2, 1923

OFFICIAL BULLETIN

OF THE

National Society
of the Sons of the American Revolution

Organized April 30, 1889

Incorporated by
Act of Congress, June 9, 1906

President General
W. I. LINCOLN ADAMS
Montclair, New Jersey

Published at Washington, D. C., in June, October, December, and March.
Entered as second-class matter, May 7, 1906, at the post-office at Washington, D. C., under the act of July 16, 1894.

| Volume XVII | MARCH, 1923 | Number 4 |

The OFFICIAL BULLETIN records action by the General Officers, the Board of Trustees, the Executive and other National Committees, lists of members deceased and of new members, and important doings of State Societies. In order that the OFFICIAL BULLETIN may be up to date, and to insure the preservation in the National Society archives of a complete history of the doings of the entire organization, State Societies and local Chapters are requested to communicate promptly to the Secretary General written or printed accounts of all meetings or celebrations, to forward copies of all notices, circulars, and other printed matter issued by them, and to notify him at once of dates of death of members.

PURPOSES AND OBJECTS OF THE S. A. R.

(Extracts from Constitution)

The purposes and objects of this Society are declared to be patriotic, historical, and educational, and shall include those intended or designed to perpetuate the memory of the men who, by their services or sacrifices during the war of the American Revolution, achieved the independence of the American people; to unite and promote fellowship among their descendants; to inspire them and the community at large with a more profound reverence for the principles of the government founded by our forefathers; to encourage historical research in relation to the American Revolution; to acquire and preserve the records of the individual services of the patriots of the war, as well as documents, relics, and landmarks; to mark the scenes of the Revolution by appropriate memorials; to celebrate the anniversaries of the prominent events of the war and of the Revolutionary period; to foster true patriotism; to maintain and extend the institutions of American freedom, and to carry out the purposes expressed in the preamble of the Constitution of our country and the injunctions of Washington in his farewell address to the American people.

Qualifications for Membership

Any man shall be eligible to membership in the Society who, being of the age of twenty-one years or over and a citizen of good repute in the community, is the lineal descendant of an ancestor who was at all times unfailing in his loyalty to, and rendered active service in, the cause of American Independence, either as an officer, soldier, seaman, marine, militiaman or minute man, in the armed forces of the Continental Congress or of any one of the several Colonies or States, or as a Signer of the Declaration of Independence, or as a member of a Committee of Safety or Correspondence, or as a member of any Continental, Provincial, or Colonial Congress or Legislature, or as a recognized patriot who performed actual service by overt acts of resistance to the authority of Great Britain.

Provided, however, that any male person, above the age of 18 years and under the age of 21 years, whose qualifications in regard to ancestry and personal character are as above prescribed, shall be eligible to a qualified membership to be known and designated as junior membership. . . .

Application for membership is made on standard blanks furnished by the State Societies. These blanks call for the place and date of birth and of death of the Revolutionary ancestor and the year of birth, of marriage, and of death of ancestors in intervening generations. Membership is based on one original claim; additional claims are filed on supplemental papers. The applications and supplementals are made in duplicate.

GENERAL OFFICERS ELECTED AT THE SPRINGFIELD CONGRESS, MAY 16, 1922

President General:

W. I. LINCOLN ADAMS, Montclair, New Jersey.

Vice-Presidents General:

HARRY T. LORD, Manchester, New Hampshire.
New England (Maine, New Hampshire, Vermont, Massachusetts, Rhode Island, and Connecticut).

PHILIP F. LARNER, 918 F Street N. W., Washington, District of Columbia.
Middle and Coast District (New York, New Jersey, Pennsylvania, Delaware, Maryland, District of Columbia, Virginia, North Carolina, South Carolina, Georgia, and Florida).

LOUIS A. BOWMAN, 30 North La Salle Street, Chicago, Illinois.
Mississippi Valley, East District (Michigan, Wisconsin, Illinois, Indiana, Ohio, West Virginia, Kentucky, Tennessee, Alabama, and Mississippi).

HENRY B. HAWLEY, Des Moines, Iowa.
Mississippi Valley, West District (Minnesota, North Dakota, South Dakota, Nebraska, Iowa, Kansas, Missouri, Oklahoma, Arkansas, Louisiana, and Texas).

GEORGE ALBERT SMITH, Utah Savings & Trust Building, Salt Lake City, Utah.
Mountain and Pacific Coast District (Montana, Idaho, Wyoming, Nevada, Utah, Colorado, Arizona, New Mexico, Oregon, Washington, California, Hawaii, and Philippines).

Secretary General:

FRANK BARTLETT STEELE, 183 St. James Place, Buffalo, New York.

Registrar General:

FRANCIS BARNUM CULVER, 2203 North Charles Street, Baltimore, Maryland; 918 F Street N. W., Washington, District of Columbia.

Treasurer General:

GEORGE McK. ROBERTS, Room 2126, 120 Broadway, New York City.

Historian General:

JOSEPH B. DOYLE, Steubenville, Ohio.

Chancellor General:

EUGENE C. BONNIWELL, City Court Building, Philadelphia, Pennsylvania.

Genealogist General:

WALTER K. WATKINS, 9 Ashburton Place, Boston, Massachusetts.

Chaplain General:

REV. FREDERICK W. PERKINS, D. D., 27 Deer Cove, Lynn, Massachusetts.

BOARD OF TRUSTEES

The General Officers, together with one member from each State Society, constitute the Board of Trustees of the National Society. The following Trustees for the several States were elected at the Springfield Congress, May 16, 1922, to serve until their successors are elected at the Congress to be held at Nashville, Tenn., in May, 1923:

Alabama, (vacant); Arizona, W. B. Twitchell, Phœnix; Arkansas, George W. Clark, Little Rock; California, Seabury C. Mastick, New York City; Colorado, Victor E. Keyes, Denver; Connecticut, Herbert H. White, Hartford; Delaware, Hon. Horace Wilson, Wilmington; District of Columbia, Albert D. Spangler, Washington; Far Eastern Society, H. Lawrence Noble, Manila; Florida, Dr. F. G. Renshaw, Pensacola; Society in France, (vacant); Hawaiian Society, Donald S. Bowman, Honolulu; Georgia, Allan Waters, Atlanta; Idaho, M. A. Wood, Boise; Illinois, Dorr E. Felt, Chicago; Indiana, Charles C. Jewett, Terre Haute; Iowa, Elmer E. Wentworth, State Center; Kansas, John M. Meade, Topeka; Kentucky, Marvin Lewis, Louisville; Louisiana, Col. C. Robert Churchill, New Orleans; Maine, William B. Berry, Gardiner; Maryland, Hon. Henry Stockbridge, Baltimore; Massachusetts, George Hale Nutting, Boston; Michigan, Albert M. Henry,* Detroit; Minnesota, Charles E. Rittenhouse, Minneapolis; Mississippi, Hon. Gordon G. Lyell, Jackson; Missouri, George R. Merrill, St. Louis; Montana, Marcus Whritenour, Helena; Nebraska, Benjamin F. Bailey, Lincoln; Nevada, (vacant); New Hampshire, Hon. Harry T. Lord, Manchester; New Jersey, Charles Symmes Kiggins, Elizabeth; New Mexico, George S. Klock, Albuquerque; New York, Louis Annin Ames, New York; North Carolina, (vacant); North Dakota, Howard E. Simpson, Grand Forks; Ohio, Hon. Warren G. Harding, Washington, D. C.; Oklahoma, W. A. Jennings, Oklahoma City; Oregon, Wallace McCamant, Portland; Pennsylvania, James A. Wakefield, Pittsburgh; Rhode Island, Hon. Arthur P. Sumner, Providence; South Carolina, (vacant); South Dakota, F. M. Mills, Sioux Falls; Tennessee, Leland Hume, Nashville; Texas, C. B. Dorchester, Sherman; Utah, Daniel S. Spencer, Salt Lake City; Vermont, William Jeffrey, Montpelier; Virginia, Arthur B. Clarke,* Richmond; Washington, Ernest B. Hussey, Seattle; Wisconsin, Walter H. Wright, Milwaukee; Wyoming, Warren Richardson, Cheyenne.

*Deceased.

PRESIDENTS AND SECRETARIES OF STATE SOCIETIES

ARIZONA—President, Harold Baxter, Phœnix.
    Secretary, E. L. Freeland, Phœnix.
    Treasurer, Kenneth Freeland, Phœnix.

ARKANSAS—President, Frank D. Leaming, Little Rock.
    Secretary, Fay Hempstead, Little Rock.
    Treasurer, Thomas M. Cory, Little Rock.

CALIFORNIA—President, Charles E. Hale, 51 Main Street, San Francisco.
    Secretary-Registrar, Thomas A. Perkins, Mills Building, San Francisco.
    Treasurer, John C. Currier, 713 Merchants' Exchange Building, San Francisco.

COLORADO—President, Hon. George H. Bradfield, Greeley.
    Secretary, R. Harvey Boltwood, Central Business College, Denver.
    Treasurer, Walter D. Wynkoop, Mt. States T. & T. Co., Denver.

CONNECTICUT—President, Hon. Rollin S. Woodruff, 210 Edwards Street, New Haven.
    Secretary, Frederick A. Doolittle, 117 Middle Street, Bridgeport.
    Treasurer, Charles G. Stone, P. O. Box 847, Hartford.

DELAWARE—President, Robert H. Richards, 1415 Delaware Avenue, Wilmington.
    Secretary-Treasurer-Registrar, Charles A. Rudolph, 900 Vanburen Street, Wilmington.

DISTRICT OF COLUMBIA—President, Samuel Herrick, Westory Building, Washington.
    Secretary-Treasurer, Kenneth S. Wales, 110 Florence Court, E., Washington.

FAR EASTERN SOCIETY—President, Austin Craig, University of the Philippines, Manila, Philippine Islands.
    Secretary-Registrar, Harry J. Cushing, P. O. Box 119, Manila.

FLORIDA—President, Dr. F. G. Renshaw, Pensacola.
    Secretary, John Hobart Cross, Pensacola.
    Treasurer-Registrar, F. F. Bingham, Pensacola.

SOCIETY IN FRANCE—Administered by Empire State Society.

GEORGIA—President, Allen Waters, P. O. Box 361, Atlanta.
    Secretary-Registrar, Arthur W. Falkinburg, 1301 Atlanta Trust Co. Building, Atlanta.
    Treasurer, William Alden, Box 172, Decatur.

HAWAII—President, Donald S. Bowman, Honolulu.
    Secretary, James T. Taylor, 207 Kauikeolani Building, Honolulu.
    Treasurer, Elmer T. Winant, Honolulu.

IDAHO—President, Albert H. Conner, Boise.
    Secretary and Treasurer, Frank G. Ensign, Boise.

ILLINOIS—President, James Edgar Brown, 30 North La Salle Street, Chicago.
    Secretary, Louis A. Bowman, 30 North La Salle Street, Chicago.
    Treasurer, Henry R. Kent, 30 North La Salle Street, Chicago.

INDIANA—President, Cornelius F. Posson, 538 East Drive, Woodruff Place, Indianapolis.
    Secretary and Treasurer, Edmund L. Parker, 511 East Walnut Street, Kokomo.

IOWA—President, Frank D. Harsh, Des Moines.
    Secretary, Captain Elbridge D. Hadley, 409 Franklin Avenue, Des Moines.
    Treasurer, William E. Barrett, 4815 Grand Avenue, Des Moines.

KANSAS—President, John M. Meade, Topeka.
    Secretary, Arthur H. Bennett, 1708 Laurel Avenue, Topeka.
    Treasurer-Registrar, Walter E. Wilson, Topeka.

KENTUCKY—President, J. Swigert Taylor, Frankfort.
    Secretary, Ben F. Ewing, II, 903 Realty Building, Louisville.
    Treasurer, Alexander W. Tippett, U. S. Trust Co. Building, Louisville.

LOUISIANA—President, C. Robert Churchill, 408 Canal Street, New Orleans.
    Secretary, Herbert P. Benton, 403 Carondelet Building, New Orleans.
    Treasurer, S. O. Landry, 616 Maison Blanche Building, New Orleans.

MAINE—President, Charles L. Hutchinson, 135 Spring St., Portland.
    Secretary, Francis L. Littlefield, 246 Spring Street, Portland.
    Treasurer, Enoch O. Greenleaf, Portland.

MARYLAND—President, Herbert Baker Flowers, 3008 N. Calvert Street, Baltimore.
    Secretary, George Sadtler Robertson, 1628 Linden Avenue, Baltimore.
    Treasurer, Benson Blake, Jr., 2320 N. Calvert St., Baltimore.

MASSACHUSETTS—President, Dr. Charles H. Bangs, Swampscott.
    Secretary, Walter K. Watkins, 9 Ashburton Place, Boston.
    Treasurer, Lieut.-Col. Charles M. Green, 78 Marlboro Street, Boston.

MICHIGAN—President, William P. Holliday, 1500 Seminole Ave., Detroit.
    Secretary, Raymond E. Van Syckle, 1729 Ford Building, Detroit.
    Treasurer, Frank G. Smith, 1183 W. Boston Boulevard, Detroit.

MINNESOTA—President, Dr. Douglas F. Wood, 4121 Linden Hills Blvd., Minneapolis.
    Secretary, Charles H. Bronson, 48 East Fourth Street, St. Paul.
    Treasurer, Charles W. Eddy, 302 Pittsburg Building, St. Paul.

MISSISSIPPI—President, Judge Gordon Garland Lyell, Jackson.
    Secretary and Treasurer, William H. Pullen, Mechanics' Bank Building, Jackson.

MISSOURI—President, Linn Paine, 904 Locust Street, St. Louis.
    Secretary, J. Alonzo Matthews, 901 Pontiac Building, St. Louis.
    Treasurer, I. Shreve Carter, 308 Merchant La Clede Building, St. Louis.

MONTANA—President, Hon. Lyman H. Bennett, Virginia City.
    Secretary and Treasurer, Leslie Sulgrove, Helena.

NEBRASKA—President, Benjamin F. Bailey, 506 1st National Bank Building, Lincoln.
    Secretary, Addison E. Sheldon, 1319 South 23d Street, Lincoln.
    Treasurer, C. E. Bardwell, 522 Terminal Building, Lincoln.

NEVADA—President, Rt. Rev. George C. Huntting, 505 Ridge Street, Reno.

NEW HAMPSHIRE—President, Prof. Ashley K. Hardy, Hanover.
    Secretary and Treasurer, Rufus H. Baker, 12 Liberty Street, Concord.

NEW JERSEY—President, Hon. Adrian Lyon, Perth Amboy.
    Secretary, David L. Pierson, 33 Lombardy Street, Newark.
    Treasurer, Frank E. Quinby, 33 Lombardy Street, Newark.

NEW MEXICO—President, C. C. Manning, Gallup.
    Secretary, Frank W. Graham, Albuquerque.
    Treasurer, Orvil A. Matson, Albuquerque.

NEW YORK—President, George D. Bangs, Tribune Building, New York City.
    Secretary, Major Charles A. Du Bois, 220 Broadway, New York City.
    Treasurer, James de la Montanye, 220 Broadway, New York City.

NORTH CAROLINA—Special Organizer for North and South Carolina, Maj. John F. Jones,
    Internal Revenue Office, Columbia, S. C.

NORTH DAKOTA—President, Howard E. Simpson, University of North Dakota, Grand Forks.
    Secretary-Registrar, Walter R. Reed, 407 7th Avenue, So., Fargo.
    Treasurer, Willis E. Fuller, Northern National Bank, Grand Forks.

OHIO—President, Edward L. Shuey, Dayton.
    Secretary-Registrar, W. L. Curry, Box 645, Columbus.
    Treasurer, S. G. Harvey, 650 Oakwood Avenue, Toledo.

OKLAHOMA—President, Ben W. Riley, 1501 West 31st Street, Oklahoma City.
    Secretary-Treasurer, Edward F. McKay, 536 West 31st Street, Oklahoma City.

OREGON—President, B. B. Beekman, 601 Platt Building, Portland.
    Secretary, B. A. Thaxter, Post Office Box 832, Portland.
    Treasurer, H. C. Ewing, 207 Northwestern Bank Building, Portland.

PENNSYLVANIA—President, R. C. Schanck, 609 Chamber of Commerce, Pittsburgh.
    Secretary, Robert E. Grove, Keenan Bldg., Pittsburgh.
    Treasurer, A. W. Wall, Farmers' Bank Building, Pittsburgh.

RHODE ISLAND—President, Hon. Addison Pierce Munroe, 66 Paterson Street, Providence.
    Secretary, Theodore E. Dexter, 104 Clay Street, Central Falls.
    Treasurer, William L. Sweet, Box 1515, Providence.

SOUTH CAROLINA—Special Organizer for North and South Carolina, Maj. John F. Jones,
    Internal Revenue Office, Columbia, S. C.

SOUTH DAKOTA—President, Col. A. B. Sessions, Sioux Falls.
  Secretary-Registrar, T. W. Dwight, Sioux Falls.
  Treasurer, B. H. Requa, Sioux Falls.
TENNESSEE—President, William K. Boardman, Nashville.
  Vice-President-at-Large, Frederick W. Millspaugh, Nashville.
  Secretary-Registrar, J. Tyree Fain, 315 North 22d Avenue, Nashville.
  Treasurer, Carey Folk, 411 Union Street, Nashville.
TEXAS—President, C. B. Dorchester, Sherman.
  Secretary-Treasurer, Walter S. Mayer, 1404 39th Street, Galveston.
UTAH—President, John Q. Cannon, *Deseret News*, Salt Lake City.
  Secretary, Gordon Lines Hutchins, Dooly Building, Salt Lake City.
  Treasurer, Elias Smith Woodruff, 2315 Winsor Street, Salt Lake City.
VERMONT—President, Wiilliam H. Jeffrey, Montpelier.
  Secretary, Walter H. Crockett, Burlington.
  Treasurer, Clarence L. Smith, Burlington.
VIRGINIA—President, Col. Eugene C. Massie, Mutual Building, Richmond.
  Secretary and Treasurer, William E. Crawford, 700 Travelers' Building, Richmond.
WASHINGTON—President, William D. Totten, New York Block, Seattle.
  Secretary, Kenneth P. Hussey, Leary Building, Seattle.
WISCONSIN—President, Henry S. Sloan, 216 W. Water Street, Milwaukee.
  Secretary, Emmett A. Donnelly, 1030 Wells Building, Milwaukee.
  Treasurer, William Stark Smith, 373 Lake Drive, Milwaukee.
WYOMING—President, David A. Haggard, Cheyenne.
  Secretary, Maurice Groshon, Cheyenne.
  Treasurer, James B. Guthrie, Cheyenne.

ON TO NASHVILLE

There is no doubt that the most important matter that is before the members of this Society at this time is the next Congress of the National Society, Sons of the American Revolution, to be held from Sunday, May 20, 1923, through Tuesday, May 22.

That this Congress will be not only one of the most interesting from the standpoint of the work to be accomplished by the Congress itself, but the fact that it is the first that has been held so far in the southland and in the attractive city of Nashville, should make it wonderfully attractive to our members, not only from the South itself, but from the East, West, North, and Middle West especially.

Then again the mere outline of the program that is printed in this issue of the BULLETIN is but a slight evidence of what those hospitable compatriots from the Tennessee Society, and Nashville especially, are planning to do to entertain the delegates. It is not necessary to have to read between the lines of the enthusiastic letters from Compatriot Millspaugh, who is the moving spirit of this Society, to understand that the welcome and entertainment to be given to the visiting compatriots will be probably as enthusiastic as ever given to a National Congress. It is impossible to tell here of the numerous plans and preparations that the committees have awaiting the delegates, but the members from the other States are urged now to plan to go to this Congress and see for themselves what is in store for them.

Application is now pending for a special rate of a fare and one-half to Nashville, and if granted notice will be given to the State secretaries. However, this special fare is predicated upon the attendance of not less than two hundred and fifty persons from outside places, and it is up to the members to make this good. If you are a delegate and will attend the Congress, get in touch with your State Secretary and he will give you the details of this special fare proposition if it is granted.

A further project is on foot to have a special train or special cars from the East and North. This would take in delegates from all of the New England States, New York, New Jersey, possibly part of Pennsylvania, Maryland, and Delaware. If this plan is found to be possible and enough members signify their intention of going on this train or cars, due notice will be given to the several State officials and announcement made to the delegates in that manner. It would greatly assist the National officers if the delegates will notify either their State secretaries or the Secretary General at an early date if they will be able to attend the Congress in Nashville.

Let us make this a great event in the history of the Society. Nashville deserves it, for this Society has had a wonderful year. It has gone ahead by leaps and bounds. The compatriots in that city have shown what can be done by real push, energy, and true patriotism, and they deserve the support of their sister societies in every part of the country.

The program of the Congress follows, and compatriots who desire further information will get enthusiastic answers from compatriot Fred W. Millspaugh, Nashville, Tenn. No other address is needed; for if he is not the best-known man in Nashville now, he will be after this Congress meets there.

ARRANGEMENTS FOR NASHVILLE CONGRESS

Headquarters.—Hotel Hermitage, corner Sixth Avenue and Union Street. The Hermitage Club, next door to the hotel, was Federal headquarters during the war.

Registration.—Begins 2.30 p. m. Sunday, May 20, in loggia of the Hotel Hermitage.

Church Service.—Delegates will assemble at Hotel Hermitage and leave for First Presbyterian Church, two blocks distant, at 7.45 p. m.

Sessions.—Monday, May 21, at 10 a. m. and 2 p. m. Monday noon, luncheon by Tennessee Society.

Reception.—Monday night, given by the Daughters of the American Revolution, the Colonial Dames in the State of Tennessee, the United States Daughters of 1812, and the Centennial Club.

Tuesday.—Business session, 9 a. m. 12.30 p. m., luncheon, followed by automobile drive to the historic Hermitage, home of President Andrew Jackson. 7 p. m., banquet by Tennessee Society.

Ladies' Entertainment.—Mrs. Edward West Foster, assisted by her committee, composed of the Regents of the Daughters of the American Revolution Chapters, the Colonial Dames, Daughters of 1812, and Centennial Club, will meet the ladies at the Hotel Hermitage at 12.30, Monday noon, and will entertain them at formal luncheon, which will be followed by an automobile drive during the afternoon, with stops at several homes where teas will be given in honor of the visitors. Visiting ladies will be entertained with the delegates at luncheon Tuesday, with automobile drive to the Hermitage, and late in the afternoon a tea at the beau-

THE SECRETARY GENERAL

tiful country home of Mrs. E. W. Cole. Ladies will join the delegates at the formal banquet Tuesday night.

Hotels and Rates.—Hermitage, single rooms, $2.50 to $5.00; double rooms, $4.50 to $7.00 (125 rooms reserved). Tulane, single rooms, $3.00; double rooms, $5.00 (50 rooms reserved). Maxwell, single rooms, $3.00; double rooms, $5.00.

For information, address W. K. Boardman, President Tennessee Society, Nashville; F. W. Millspaugh, chairman National Committee on Arrangements, Nashville.

National Committee on Arrangements.—F. W. Millspaugh, chairman; Hon. John Hibbett De Witt, Leland Hume, Edward West Foster, William Kellogg Boardman, Edwin Warner, Director General Marvin H. Lewis, Past President General R. C. Ballard Thruston, Colonel C. Robert Churchill, Augustus F. Meehan, Chattanooga; Garnett Andrews, Chattanooga; John Davis McDowell, Memphis.

Credentials.—Teunis D. Huntting, chairman, New York; William J. Conkling, vice-chairman, New Jersey; Lieutenant Commander A. G. Dibrell, U. S. N.; Stanley Bell Reid, J. Avery Grannis, Captain Robert Selph Henry.

Ceremonies and Colors.—Colonel George V. Lauman, chairman, Illinois; Captain R. W. Brown, Pennsylvania, acting chairman; Joseph Atwood Lynn, Massachusetts; Joseph M. Shields, Washington; Joseph Hammond, Oregon; Major Philip Pearson Cole, Captain Will Rucker Manier, Captain Douglas Henry, Lieutenant Hunter McDonald, Jr., Lieutenant Laurence Norton Polk, all of Tennessee.

Ladies' Entertainment Committee.—Mrs. Edward West Foster, chairman; Mrs. Alex. G. Hunter, secretary; Mrs. John Hill Eakin, President Centennial Club; Mrs. Frederick W. Millspaugh, Regent, Daughters of 1812; Mrs. Frank W. Ring, Regent, Colonial Dames; Mrs. R. E. Donnell, Regent, Cumberland Chapter, Daughters of the American Revolution; Mrs. Charles A. Marshall, Regent, Campbell Chapter, Daughters of the American Revolution; Mrs. T. Graham Hall, Regent, Colonel Thomas McCrory Chapter, Daughters of the American Revolution.

ANNOUNCEMENTS

President General Adams has appointed Mr. Carl M. Vail, of the New Jersey Society, as chairman of the Special Committee to Arrange for the Celebration of the 150th Anniversary of Historical Events of the American Revolution. This committee was appointed in fulfillment of a resolution adopted at the Springfield Congress. Other appointments on this committee are Judge Adrian Lyon, of New Jersey; Albert L. Wyman, of New Jersey; David L. Pierson, of New Jersey; Edward Hagaman Hall, of New York; Dr. Charles H. Bangs, of Massachusetts; Walter K. Watkins, Historian of the Massachusetts Society, and the Historians of the State societies in those States where Revolutionary events occurred. Additions to this committee will be made from time to time.

For the information of State Society officers, the new certificate issued by the National Society to each new member and which has been in effect since October first, is sent directly from the office of the Secretary General to the new compatriot. This is a small certificate, 11 x 9 inches, and bears the signature of the

President General and the Secretary General, the National number, and the seal of the Society. This does not preclude the purchase by the compatriot of the former certificate, which will be issued as usual upon application to the Registrar General.

The Secretary General respectfully requests all State Secretaries and others sending in material for publication in the BULLETIN to kindly get all copy to the office of the Secretary General on or before the 15th of the month of publication, namely, October, December, March, and June.

ANNOUNCEMENT OF PROPOSED AMENDMENT TO CONSTITUTION

Compatriots are advised that at the 33d Annual Congress of the National Society, Sons of the American Revolution, held in the city of Springfield, Mass., May 15, 1922, the following amendment to the Constitution of the National Society was proposed and will be presented as an amendment for consideration to the annual Congress to be held in the city of Nashville, Tenn., on May 21, 1923.

That Article VI of the Constitution of the National Society be amended to read as follows:

"Each State Society shall pay annually to the Treasurer General to defray the expense of the National Society *one dollar* for each member thereof, unless intermitted by the National Congress.

"Such dues shall be paid on or before the first day of April for the ensuing year in order to secure representation in the Congress of the National Society."

(Italics indicate amendments added or changed.)

This notice has been sent to officers and State Societies in accordance with the requirements of our Constitution.

ADVERTISING—A NEW VENTURE FOR THE BULLETIN

The compatriots will notice that in this issue of the BULLETIN there appear a few advertisements that should appeal to our members. At the meeting of the Executive Committee held in New York in October, a committee, consisting of the President General, the Secretary General, and Past President General Ames, was appointed with power to solicit and publish in a future BULLETIN a few desirable advertisements, It was felt that some of the space of the BULLETIN could be used to advantage in this way, and thus help to very materially reduce the cost of its publication. The few that are published in this issue, it is hoped, are but a start in this direction, and it is thought that with the assistance of our compatriots in all parts of the country this venture will substantially reduce the cost of publication, if not pay for it in full, in due time. The circulation of our BULLETIN, as is well known, is of the highest order, and though approximately but 20,000 now, will no doubt grow to much higher figures in the near future.

With the help of the members, this venture in desirable advertising can be made a great success and get the results desired. If the compatriots throughout the many States and Chapters will do a little missionary work among National advertisers in the community in which they live by not only telling of this chance to get to high-class readers, but, if possible, secure a page or part of a page of good advertising, this plan will be a great success. There is no desire to make money out of this idea, but merely to reduce the cost of our publication. Kindly communicate with the Editor of the BULLETIN if you wish further information.

"A CLARION CALL"

Compatriot Louis Wilkins Culbreath, of Stanton, Tenn., writing to Vice-President F. W. Millspaugh, of the Tennessee Society, has this to say of the President General's article in the December BULLETIN, on "The Responsibility of the Well Born":

"I cannot close without referring to the article in the BULLETIN by our President General, on 'The Responsibility of the Well Born.' In these trying times of unrest, of 'isms and 'cisms, of propaganda for this and that, a spasm of uncertainty and the wild rush of madmen and peoples for place and power, such preachments as his fall upon our troubled souls as the dew of Hermon that ran down upon Aaron's beard, even to the hem of his garment. His is a clarion call to patriotic duty, clean cut, clear, and unmistakable. He said more in thirty lines than I have gleaned from volumes. I wish I could place this one article in the hands of every boy and girl, man and woman, under the American Flag today."

"Though a member of less than three months' standing," writes Mr. Millspaugh, "Dr. Culbreath has already recruited four members in his little town and is going to enlist others soon. There is no man in his county who stands higher or is more beloved than this country doctor."

WASHINGTON, THE STATESMAN

The President General sent the following letter to the Secretaries of all of our State Societies, to be read by them to the members of their respective organizations at some meeting during the month of February:

OFFICE OF PRESIDENT GENERAL,
MONTCLAIR, N. J., *February 2, 1923.*

COMPATRIOTS:

Last year, at this patriotic season, we considered George Washington as the gentleman, in accordance with the request of our honored President General at that time.

This year may I suggest that compatriots will think of him principally as the far-seeing and constructive statesman; for it is in the contemplation of that important side of this many-sided man that we may find, perhaps, the greatest aid in solving the perplexing problems which confront us at this time.

Let us read and reread the state papers and public addresses of President Washington, particularly the immortal Farewell Address, the prophetic wisdom and sound political judgment of which was never more needed than now.

Commending to all compatriots, then, the thoughtful consideration of Washington, the statesman, at this time, I am, with every good wish for one and all,

Faithfully and fraternally yours,

WASHINGTON I. L. ADAMS,
President General.

EXTRACT OF LETTER FROM PRESIDENT HARDING TO PRESIDENT GENERAL ADAMS

"I have been particularly proud of my membership in this Society, and of the fact that I am eligible to such membership. I look upon it as one of the worthy and uniformly well-directed enginleries of patriotism that have sought to crystallize into national sentiments and public policies the best thought and purpose of the American Nation; therefore I have pleasure in wishing the success of the forthcoming Congress and the continuance of the Society's splendid service.

"Most sincerely yours,

(Signed)　　　　　　　　　　　　　WARREN G. HARDING.

The White House, Washington, D. C., February 1, 1923."

LETTER FROM ONE OF OUR REAL SONS

Major WASHINGTON I. L. ADAMS,
　　　President General of National Society, S. A. R., Montclair, New Jersey:

DEAR MR. ADAMS:

I wish to express my most sincere thanks to the National Society of the Sons of the American Revolution for the distinguished honor they bestowed upon me in electing me a member of the National Society. I accept with deepest gratitude, as my 102d birthday present, the beautifully engraved certificate of membership.

　　　Sincerely yours,

　　　　　　　　　　　　　　　　　GEORGE A. GORDON.

EUREKA, KANSAS, *January 29, 1923.*

Illustration is here given of the new Membership Card, which can be supplied to State Societies by application to the Secretary General, at current printing rates. The card is in two colors, with imprint of the Insignia and space for signature of State Treasurer and President.

OFFICIAL INSIGNIA AND WAR SERVICE BARS

Illustration is again given of our Official Insignia, and the War Service Bars to be worn upon its ribbon. The former is obtained by application for permit to purchase from the officers of the State Societies or the Registrar General. The latter should be applied for directly to the Secretary General. In applying for the latter, copies of discharge papers or commissions should accompany applications.

PRESIDENT GENERAL HONORED BY D. A. R.

The President General has accepted the invitation of the President General of the National Society, Daughters of the American Revolution, to make the opening address at their annual Congress, in Continental Hall, on the 16th of April.

THE PRESIDENT GENERAL'S OFFICIAL TRIP

The President General left New York on his official transcontinental trip on the afternoon of January 5, and made his first stop in Chicago, where he was entertained by the Illinois Society.

He attended a luncheon of the officers and members of the Board of Managers at the Union League Club, in that city, on the afternoon of January 6. State President James Edgar Brown presided, and Vice-President General Louis A. Bowman, who is also Secretary of the Illinois Society, recorded. About twenty representative members of the Society were present, and to them the President General spoke informally in regard to the various activities of the National Organization.

In the evening the regular meeting of the entire Society was held at the Great Western Hotel, about 100 being present. The President General made the principal address of the occasion, taking for his subject "History and Patriotism" and speaking principally about the value of the proper study of history as a means of cultivating true patriotism.

His next stop was at Salt Lake City, where he was met at the station, on the afternoon of January 9, by a large delegation of the Utah Society, including Vice-President General George Albert Smith; State President John Q. Cannon, Compatriots D. S. Spencer, Samuel P. Dobbs, and other representative members of the Utah Society. That evening an informal dinner was given for the President General at the Hotel Utah by the officers of the Utah Society and an informal conference followed.

A luncheon was held in the Alta Club the next day, at which the officers and the members of the Board of Managers were present, about 20 in number. Compatriot Russell L. Tracey was host. Governor Mabey, of Utah, who is a compatriot, spoke informally, as did also the President General. He visited the United States Army Post at Fort Douglas, Salt Lake City, and addressed the assembled officers there, in an informal manner, as one brother officer to others.

Later in the afternoon he was invited to address the Utah Legislature, which had met in joint session, and his remarks there met with cordial approval. Many Senators and representatives of the Utah Legislature are members of our organization.

In the evening the banquet of the Utah Society was held at the beautiful Hotel Utah, which was largely attended by both ladies and compatriots. The meeting was addressed by Governor Mabey and the Mayor of Salt Lake City, as well as by the President General, who made the principal address.

Referring to the visit of the President General in Utah, *The Deseret News,* which is the oldest paper of the State, has this to say of the President General, at the conclusion of an editorial in its issue of January 10, entitled

"A DISTINGUISHED VISITOR"

"Utah is pleased and proud to welcome Major Adams and to extend to him the hand of friendship and hospitality. He will find among his compatriots here a burning patriotism akin to his own, and in the hearts of the people in general he will discern a love of country, a pride in its accomplishments, and an abiding faith in its high destiny."

From Salt Lake City the President General was accompanied by George Albert Smith, Vice-President General for the Mountain Region and the Pacific Coast.

Their first stop was in Portland, Oregon, which they reached Friday morning, January 12. They were entertained the same day at luncheon at the Arlington Club by former President General Wallace McCamant, at which a number of the officers and members of the Board of Managers were present. The general officers attended a dinner in the same club that night, at which there was a fine group of Portland's leading citizens and members of our organization.

The luncheon on the following day was given by the Board of Managers of the Oregon Society and the officers of that State organization. Both the President General and Vice-President General Smith made informal addresses at this luncheon in regard to the active work of the Society.

A dinner and reception at the University Club, under the auspices of the Oregon Society, was held the same evening, with about one hundred present. The President of the State Society, B. B. Beekman, presided. Director General Wallace McCamant introduced the President General, and he was followed by Vice-President General Smith. Justice McBride, Chief Justice of the State of Oregon, and representatives of the G. A. R., the American Legion, as well as officers of the United States Army and Navy, were in attendance.

The President General spoke of the importance of censoring the teaching and teachers of American history, as well as the text-books, and he concluded his address with the Pledge to the Flag of the New Jersey State Society, as follows:

> "Flag of our great Republic, hallowed by noblest deeds and loving sacrifice, guardian of our homes, an inspiration in every battle for the right, whose stars and stripes stand for Beauty, Purity, Truth, Patriotism, and the Union,
>
> ### WE SALUTE THEE,
>
> and for thy defense, the protection of our country, and the conservation of the liberty of the American people, we pledge our hearts, our lives, and our sacred honor."

Major Adams was greatly impressed while in Portland, Oregon, with the patriotic attitude of the Portland Chapter in appointing Compatriot Pratt, formerly of Meriden, Conn., as lecturer on American history and American ideals. Mr. Pratt goes about among the schools each day and, taking some historical personage or incident in American history, speaks on patriotism before the children.

Their next stop was at San Francisco, where the general officers were entertained by the California Society. A dinner and reception were held, under the auspices of the Sons and Daughters of the American Revolution, at the Commercial Club of that city on the evening of January 16. On Thursday, the eighteenth, the officers and members of the Board of Managers entertained the general officers informally at luncheon in the Commercial Club, and a profitable conference in regard to the interests of the organization was held at that time.

The general officers were then conducted to "Telegraph Hill," where they both spoke over the radio. The President General's address was entitled "A Message of Patriotism," and he has heard approvingly of it from all over the country. Among other things, he said:

> "I consider every man a true American who has the American spirit, whether he was born in this country or in a foreign land. . . .
>
> "It is true our race is becoming less, both proportionately and in numbers, which is certainly a grave condition; but we must make up for our losses in numbers by the strength and force of our character; what we lose in quantity we must gain in the quality of our citizenship. . . .

"We who were born in favored circumstances, and who have advantages that are denied to many, should set an example to all in patriotic service and public-spirited, unselfish devotion to the country."

At Los Angeles the general officers were entertained at luncheon on Friday, January 19, by officers and representatives of the Sons of the Revolution and members of the Society of Colonial Wars. President General Adams, who is also Governor of the New Jersey Society of Colonial Wars, brought the greetings of that Society to the California organization. He found in this city that a very cordial feeling existed between the Sons of the Revolution and Sons of the American Revolution, a sentiment which he did everything in his power to strengthen. The next day the President General made the address at the Saturday noonday meeting of the City Club, on "Practical Patriotism," which was well received and was followed by an interesting and animated discussion, during which questions were freely asked and frankly answered.

Later, the same day, he visited the Harvard Military School and the Page Military School, for younger boys, near Hollywood. At the latter school Major Page held battalion drill and review in honor of Major Adams.

Vice-President Smith returned to Utah from Los Angeles, while the President General proceeded to New Orleans. He arrived in the Crescent City on the evening of Tuesday, January 23, and was met there by Colonel C. Robert Churchill, President of the Louisiana State Society, and a delegation of the members and officers of that active organization.

The next day he was entertained at luncheon by the officers of the Louisiana Society in one of the historic old French restaurants in that interesting city. The dinner and annual meeting of the Louisiana State Society was held the same evening, in the Sazerac restaurant, and was an enthusiastic success from every point of view. There were about 75 present. Addresses were made by Compatriot Edwin T. Merrick, a former President of the Louisiana Society; Compatriot J. Edward Kirby, former President of the Iowa Society; Hon. Thomas W. Robertson, Speaker of the House of Representatives of Louisiana, and by the President General, who made the principal address of the evening.

An interesting feature of this meeting was the automatic roll-call of the members. Each member in turn arose, gave his name, profession or business, and address, and then stated his ancestor or ancestors, through whom he qualified for membership. The following day a group of the officers of the Louisiana Society took the President General for a trip on the river, which was greatly enjoyed by all who participated.

The President General was joined on his trip from New Orleans to Louisville by Compatriot F. W. Millspaugh, Vice-President of the Tennessee Society, who attended the banquet and meeting of the Kentucky Society in Louisville, Friday, January 26, at the Pendennis Club, and spoke for the Tennessee Society in soliciting the co-operation of the Kentucky Society in making the forthcoming Congress at Nashville the success it should be. Mr. Helm Bruce, of Louisville, spoke on the subject "Why We Are" in a most eloquent manner.

The President General made an address in which he described the vast patriotic activities of our organization, and was followed by the Governor of Kentucky, Edwin P. Morrow, who is a member of the Kentucky Society. Dr. Curran Pope, Vice-President of the Society, was toastmaster in the place of President J. Swigert Taylor, who had recently met with a bereavement in his family. Colors were presented in due form and saluted and the installation of new members followed in the following form:

INSTALLATION OF NEW MEMBERS

PRESIDENT: "The following gentlemen have been elected members since the last installation." (Reads their names.) "They will now come forward."

The president then said: "Gentlemen, the interests, objects, and principles of this Society are consecrated to our united care. We are pledged to protect the institutions of our sovereign nation; to guard the flag; to foster true 100 per cent Americanism; to resist to the utmost of our strength every act or sentiment unfriendly to our country. Does each one of you so pledge yourself?"

In unison, each says: "I do. As my ancestors offered their lives and fortunes that this sovereign nation of United States might be born and prosper, I, in their names, pledge myself to defend it against enemies; to protect its flag from danger and calumny; to stand at all times watchful of its safety; to be quick to attack every sentiment or alien propaganda that threatens it; to foster love of country and true 100 per cent Americanism. I serve but one God, one flag, one country."

PRESIDENT (to older members): "Your properly constituted authorities have, after due care, recommended and elected these gentlemen, and they are now formally accepted as members of this Society."

OLDER MEMBERS: "Compatriots, we give you hearty welcome."

The custodian of the colors then returned with the flag. After he had done this, the older members sang the first verse of "America," during which the newly installed compatriots returned to their seats.

The menu contained the following references to the name of the President General:

WASHINGTON

"The very idea of the power and right of the people to establish government presupposes the duty of every individual to obey the established government."—*George Washington.*

IRVING

"The flag which he had contributed to ennoble, and had died to defend is a picture that will remain treasured up in the dearest recollection of every American."—*Irving's Sketch of Lawrence.*

LINCOLN

"Continue to execute all the express provisions of the National Constitution and the Union will endure forever."—*Lincoln.*

ADAMS

"Think of your forefathers! Think of your posterity!"—*John Quincy Adams.*

The next day Major Adams was entertained at luncheon by former President General R. C. Ballard Thruston and Director General Marvin H. Lewis, at the Pendennis Club. He delivered his "Message of Patriotism" over the *Louisville Courier Journal* radio (WHAS) at 8 o'clock the same evening, and later spoke from the stage of Macauley's Theater at the conclusion of the premier performance of the "Man Without a Country," which was given in that historic theater by the American Legion. In this address, which of necessity was a brief one, Major

Adams explained to the large audience, which packed the theater from orchestra to gallery, that "the Sons of the American Revolution are not ancestor worshippers or idealers of the past; they do not think for one moment that they acquire any personal merit by virtue of descent from a long line of patriotic American ancestry; but they do believe that they inherit from their heroic forefathers a solemn obligation, in these present critical times, to acquit themselves like the men of 'seventy-six'." He concluded his impressive address by saying: "How different would have been the sad ending of Philip Nolan, hero of the moving picture of 'The Man Without a Country,' if, instead of cursing his country as he did in his youth, he had said, with Daniel Webster:

"'I shall know but one country. The ends I seek shall be my country's, my God's, and Truth. I was born an American, I have lived an American, I shall die an American; and the duties incumbent upon me in that capacity I shall continue to discharge to the end of my career.'"

The next day the President General proceeded to Washington, D. C., where he was entertained by the District of Columbia Society. A reception was held under the auspices of this Society in his honor, to which the Daughters were also invited. After the reception, at which Mrs. Adams assisted the President General in receiving the members and guests, a meeting was held in a connecting hall, attended by several hundred people.

Selden Marvin Ely, President of the Society, introduced Major Adams as a man, "patriotic as the Constitution, as American as the Flag." The President General then spoke on "The Responsibility of the Well Born," and was followed by Mrs. George Maynard Minor, President General of the Daughters of the American Revolution, and others. A substantial supper was then served, followed by dancing.

While in Washington the President General called upon Mrs. Minor, by appointment, at her executive offices in Continental Memorial Hall. He was also at the offices of our National Headquarters every day during his stay at Washington, signing certificates and transacting other official business with Registrar General Culver and Mrs. Clark.

Mr. Samuel Herrick, a former President of the District of Columbia Society, entertained the President General with the officers and Board of Managers, at a luncheon Wednesday, January 31. He was also entertained by Vice-President General Larner and his daughter and son-in-law, Mrs. and Captain Gore.

The President General was unable to see the President in person while in Washington, on account of the President's illness at the time; so Major Adams wrote him the following letter, to which he received the appended reply:

WASHINGTON, D. C., *January 30, 1923.*

HON. WARREN G. HARDING,
President of the United States, Washington, D. C.

MY DEAR MR. PRESIDENT AND COMPATRIOT:

I am sincerely sorry to learn from your secretary that your recent illness is the reason which prevents me from paying my respects to you in person while I am in Washington.

I am completing an official trip of the country, and had the honor of writing you the other day from New Orleans about the effect of an address of mine before the City Club in Los Angeles, which was a most hearty endorsement of your bonus veto.

In behalf of the National Society of the Sons of the American Revolution, of which you are our most honored member, may I, its President General, now extend to you in this way what I desired to do in person, a most cordial invitation to attend our next National Congress, which will be held in Nashville, Tennessee, from May twentieth to the twenty-third.

If it were possible for you to be present, for only one day, during our Congress, I can promise you a delightful and most interesting time amongst fellow-Americans, who are almost kinsfolk of yours.

And would not an old-fashioned American speech from you, our honored President and compatriot, on such an occasion as this, appeal to the imagination and the patriotism of our fellow-Americans, and indeed to all the world, at this crisis in the history of the world, which would be most timely and impressive.

I earnestly pray you keep the date in mind and, if possible, accept our most sincere and fraternal invitation.

With all respect and solicitude for the early and complete return of your health and strength,

    I am, faithfully yours,

       (Signed)   WASHINGTON I. L. ADAMS,
                                      President General.

          THE WHITE HOUSE, WASHINGTON, *February* 1, 1923.

MY DEAR MR. ADAMS:

Please be assured of my sincere regrets that it was impossible for me to receive you in person when you were in Washington, owing to my indisposition. I have now received, through your very kind letter, the invitation which you had intended to present in person, asking me to attend the National Congress of the Society at Nashville in the late days of May. I want you, and the members of the Society, to know how much I appreciate the invitation and how greatly I regret that, owing to other arrangements which entirely dispose of my time at that period, acceptance is impossible. I have been particularly proud of my membership in this Society and of the fact that I am eligible to such membership. I look upon it as one of the worthy and uniformly well directed engineries of patriotism that have sought to crystallize into national sentiments and public policies the best thought and purpose of the American Nation; therefore I have pleasure in wishing the success of the forthcoming Congress and the continuance of the Society's splendid service.

    Most sincerely yours,

       (Signed)   WARREN G. HARDING.

The President General was everywhere received with the utmost courtesy and (as he writes) "with distinguished attention far beyond any personal merit." The public press was uniformly friendly and very generous in the amount of space which they accorded to the reports of the meetings which Major Adams addressed and to the reports of his speeches.

The principal themes of his addresses, as reported in the press, were the necessity for all true Americans to stand together in these critical times in defense of the fundamental principles of our Republic, and by example, by education and patriotic propaganda, endeavor to offset the evil influences of those who are antagonistic to our ideals and standards of government. He repeatedly pointed out that "all are true Americans who have the American spirit, whether descendants from a long line of American ancestry or foreign born, and he called upon all "to defend our country from its foes, whether from without or within."

This notable official journey of our President General, which occupied just a month in duration, and during which he covered nearly 10,000 miles, visited 26 States, and made 25 formal addresses, besides the informal talks which he gave at luncheons and at conferences, may be recorded as a successful trip in every way. He not only advanced the highest interests of our National Organization, as well as the various local Societies which he visited, but, what is of far greater importance, he extended and promoted the great cause of American patriotism.

OTHER OFFICIAL VISITS OF THE PRESIDENT GENERAL

Since his return from the official transcontinental trip which the President General completed in February, he has made a number of official visits in the East.

Thursday evening, February 20, he was the guest of honor of the New Jersey Society in Newark, where he delivered an address on the outstanding features of his coast-to-coast official trip.

The following night he spoke in similar vein before the New York Chapter at the Army and Navy Club in New York City. On this occasion former Ambassador Wilson to Mexico made the address on Washington, and Col. C. Robert Churchill, of the Louisiana Society, brought the greetings of that active organization.

On the 22d the President General spoke in two States: First, after the luncheon of the Connecticut Society in the Hotel Taft, New Haven, and the same evening before the George Washington Chapter, in Springfield, Mass. State President Dr. Charles H. Bangs spoke on "The Enduring Washington" on this occasion.

All of these meetings were well attended with enthusiastic compatriots, who gave our President General a most cordial welcome home after his long official trip.

The New Jersey compatriots gave a reception on the evening of March 16 at the home of former Vice-President General T. W. Williams, in Orange.

DECEASED COMPATRIOTS

It would not seem proper if something was not said at this time about the three beloved and honored compatriots who have passed away within the last few months. Many others have died during this year, but it seems fitting that some special mention should be made of these three men, who a few years ago were the leaders in the achievements, ideals, and progress of the Society. Albert M. Henry, of Detroit, Mich.; Commander John H. Moore, of Washington, D. C., and Hon. Morris B. Beardsley, of Bridgeport, Conn., were compatriots who were typical of the best that this organization stands for and who left their impress on its pages of history so that it can never be erased. All of these gentlemen were singularly alike—genial, kindly, progressive, and able. They at all times had the best interests of the Society at heart and gave of their time and abilities without stint and with a patriotic fervor and enthusiasm that accomplished results that will never be forgotten.

Judge Beardsley was elected President General in 1909 and served for one year. He had been Vice-President General before that and was on many committees of importance, including the Executive Committee. His interest never flagged, and it is known that he attended every Congress up to and including the one at Springfield, in 1922. He was always accompanied by his devoted wife, and the older members who have enjoyed their friendship and looked for their presence will miss them with a sorrow that cannot be expressed in words.

Commander John H. Moore, although he would never accept the office of President General, had been at one time one of our most influential and devoted members. As he expressed it on several occasions when urged to take the highest office of this organization, "I would rather help run it than have to run it." He was Vice-President General in 1911, elected at Louisville, Ky. But his great work was as the chairman of the Committee on Alien Education. It was through his persistent and untiring efforts that the three pamphlets were issued for distribution to the foreigner on our shores. The pamphlet so clearly written by Judge Stockbridge, of Maryland, was published in more than a dozen languages. The little booklet on naturalization and the handy copy of the United States Constitution were published in English. All three of these were at one time printed and distributed at the expense of the Government, under the direction of our Society and through the personal efforts of Commander Moore. Thousands of these were sent to schools, patriotic societies, and welfare workers throughout the country, and that a deep impression was made wherever received was shown by the constant demand for additional copies. Truly it may be said that Commander Moore was one of the pioneers in the so-called Americanization work in this country.

Albert M. Henry, of Detroit, had long been deeply interested in the work of the Sons of the American Revolution. His genial and kindly spirit endeared him to many of the compatriots who worked with him for many years for the good of the Society. Whenever it was possible he was in attendance at the yearly meetings of the Congress and it was only when failing health prevented that he was absent. He, too, will be missed from the ranks of the splendid men who have helped make the National Society what it is today.

CONCLUSION OF THE ARBUCKLE INCIDENT

Too late for the last number of the OFFICIAL BULLETIN came word of the conclusion of the Arbuckle incident.

It was announced from Mr. Will H. Hays' office on January 31 that the films in which Roscoe Arbuckle appeared would not be released, nor would he act again.

The President General represents the Sons of the American Revolution on Mr. Hays' Committee on Public Relations, which was active in bringing this situation to its satisfactory conclusion.

We are glad to know of the interest which the Sons of the American Revolution are taking in motion pictures. Such a wide and important influence is exercised by motion pictures in the nation that it becomes one of our civic duties to help them into their greatest usefulness.

The Executive Secretary of the Committee on Public Relations has had hundreds of fine letters from our members containing sympathetic and constructive suggestions. These are all passed on to the industry and are having their beneficial influence on new productions.

While we do not waiver our right and duty to criticise severely any evil practice we may notice, let us encourage the fine examples of better pictures and better practices, to the end that this potent force may become a powerful instrument for constructive entertainment, instruction, and patriotism.

PAST PRESIDENT GENERAL MORRIS B. BEARDSLEY

On Friday, March 2, 1923, in the city of Bridgeport, Conn., there fell asleep the beloved compatriot of the Sons of the American Revolution, Past President General Morris B. Beardsley.

Morris Beach Beardsley, son of Samuel G. and Mary (Beach) Beardsley, was born August 13, 1849, at Trumbull, Conn.; was prepared for college at Stratford, Conn., and graduated from Yale in the class of 1870. He studied law at the Columbia Law School, New York, and in the office of William K. Seeley. On June 25, 1872, he was admitted to practice and formed a partnership with Mr. Seeley, under the name of Seeley & Beardsley. The partnership was dissolved January 1, 1874, when he was elected city clerk of Bridgeport, which office he held until he was elected judge of probate, January 1, 1877. He was continuously re-elected judge of probate until 1893, when he declined a renomination and was elected Representative in the General Assembly of Connecticut.

Politically, Judge Beardsley had been a Democrat of the old school. In 1894 he was a candidate of his party for Lieutenant Governor and in 1916 he headed the Democratic ticket as Governor. Judge Beardsley was a Mason, a member of Lafayette Consistory and a 32d degree Mason.

From 1893 to 1923 he practiced law in Bridgeport. He married Lucy J. Fayerweather June 5, 1873. He became a member of the Connecticut Society, Sons of the American Revolution, in 1896 and was its Vice-President in 1903-04. He was elected Vice-President General at the Congress in Independence Hall, Philadelphia, May 3, 1905, and during that year was chairman of the Educational Committee. On May 2, 1905, Judge Beardsley was made chairman of a special committee to secure a charter from the United States Congress—a work to which he devoted careful attention, resulting in the incorporation of the National Society of the Sons of the American Revolution, approved by President Roosevelt June 9, 1906. In 1906 he was chairman of a Committee on Revision of the Constitution and By-Laws, and at the Denver Congress, in June, 1907, submitted a new Constitution and By-Laws, in accordance with the terms of the National Charter, which were adopted. In 1907 and 1908 he served on the National Executive Committee. In 1909 he was elected President General.

He was a member and Past Governor of the Society of Colonial Wars, in the State of Connecticut. He was a member of the New England Society of New York City, of the Brooklawn, University and Contemporary Clubs, and a member of the Board of Park Commissioners of the Park City. At the time of his death he was the president of the People's Savings Bank of Bridgeport. He had been connected with the management of this institution for the past thirty-three years, as trustee, corporator, chairman of the Finance Committee, first vice-president, and then as president. He was for many years a member of the Bridgeport Library Board and for twenty years he was on the Board of Governors of the Burroughs Home.

Judge Beardsley was a descendant of one of the oldest families of Fairfield County. On the paternal side he was a descendant of William Beardsley, who settled in Stratford in 1639. Another direct ancestor was Samuel Gregory, and he and Samuel Beardsley were two of the original members of the First Church of Christ, now the United Congregational Church of Bridgeport, in which church his funeral services were held. The National Society, Sons of the American Revolution, was represented by President General W. I. Lincoln Adams and Past President General Louis Annin Ames, who acted as honorary pall-bearers.

Judge Beardsley is survived by his widow, Lucy J. Fayerweather Beardsley; one son, Major Samuel F. Beardsley, his law partner and member of the Connecticut Society, Sons of the American Revolution; two daughters, Mrs. Emile C. Canning and Miss Amelia L. Beardsley, all residents of Bridgeport.

Throughout his long and useful life Judge Beardsley gave evidence that he was a worthy scion of old New England stock of the Colonial and Revolutionary periods, which has made America great and contributed so much to the high ideals that a democracy must possess if it is to endure the test of time.

The National Society, Sons of the American Revolution, has appointed a committee, consisting of Past Presidents General Louis Annin Ames, Wm. A. Marble, and Cornelius A. Pugsley, to draft a memorial in memory of Judge Beardsley and present same to the National Congress of the Sons of the American Revolution, to be held in the city of Nashville, Tenn., May 21, 1923.

COMMANDER JOHN H. MOORE

Commander John H. Moore, U. S. Navy, retired, and a former Vice-President General of the National Society, Sons of the American Revolution, died in Washington, D. C., on Saturday, February 3, at the Naval Hospital.

Commander Moore was born in Buffalo, N. Y., February 18, 1849, the son of George A. Moore, one of the early settlers of that city. He was graduated from the Naval Academy, at Annapolis, in 1869 and was president of his class. He twice circulated the globe and assisted in laying the first cable to Honolulu. He retired from active service in 1889 and during the last thirty years he devoted himself to active business and patriotic work in Washington. However, he was detailed in Washington many times in active service, being assistant superintendent of the Naval Gun Factory at the outbreak of the Spanish-American War; he volunteered in 1917 for active service in the World War, and was placed on the active list in the Bureau of Ordnance, remaining until November, 1919.

Commander Moore was one of the founders of the Army and Navy Club and its president in 1903. He was also a member of the Naval Institute, Vice-President of West End National Bank, and later of the National Metropolitan Bank, and in 1904 was president of the Bankers' Association of Washington, D. C.

Compatriots of the Society will best remember him when he was active in its work, a few years ago. He was President of the District of Columbia Society of Washington and served on many of the National Society committees, the most important being the chairman and vice-chairman of the Committee on Aliens and Americanization. It was during the time that he was vice-chairman of this committee that he had full charge of the distribution of pamphlets that were prepared under the direction of former Secretary General Clark and which were translated into eleven different languages. It is known that more than one hundred thousand of these pamphlets were distributed while he had charge of this work. It was largely through his and Mr. Clark's influence that these pamphlets were printed and distributed gratis by the Government.

Commander Moore served on the National Executive Committee and was also Vice-President General in 1911. He attended many of the Congresses of the

National Society and his deep interest in its welfare, his devotion to its principles and objects, and his good counsel and advice, given when needed most, made him one of the outstanding figures in its growth and development for many years.

THE SCHOOL HISTORIES

This Society is interested in no subject more important than that of the one that relates to school histories that are being used in public schools. The fact that the State of Oregon has passed a bill which will no doubt prevent the use in public schools of histories which are not in accord with our best traditions; that a bill, which is even more explicit in its terms, has been introduced in the New York State Legislature and it is hoped will pass, and that a similar bill has been introduced in the State of Washington, at the request of the Seattle Chapter of the Sons of the American Revolution; the fact that many letters have been received from compatriots from all over the country commending the stand taken by Judge McCamant and his committee on patriotic education— all of these facts go to show the deep interest in this subject, and that it is one of the vital questions that is being met and solved by our Society. The bill that was passed in Oregon is as follows and it is to the credit of that State that as the pioneers of the early days led the way to the settlement of the great Northwest, so this State now leads the way for the preservation of our historic ideals:

A BILL for an act to define the principles to govern those who are charged with the selection of textbooks for use in the public schools.

Be it enacted by the people of the State of Oregon:
SECTION I. It shall be the duty of every board, commission, committee, or officer charged with the selection of textbooks for use in the public schools to select and install textbooks on American history and civil government which adequately stress the services rendered by the men who achieved our national independence, who established our form of constitutional government, and who preserved our Federal Union. No textbook shall be used in our schools which speaks slightingly of the founders of the Republic, or of the men who preserved the Union, or which beittes or undervalues their work.

The Seattle Chapter's committee, which made an exhaustive study of Muzzey's History in comparison with Gordy's, rendered a most illuminating report. It concludes that Muzzey's History should be discarded for the following reasons:

I. It is almost wholly lacking in incidents calculated to inspire patriotism in the children studying it.

2. It is not sufficiently accurate, nor so written as to give the student a proper understanding of the Revolutionary War, and the causes leading to it, and we believe the book as a whole is unsuitable.

The committee then gives a careful analysis of Muzzey's History and says, among other things:

"What is the object of teaching history in our schools? Is it to fill the mind of the pupil with dry-as-dust facts, soon to be forgotten, to substitute for national feeling a vapid internationalism leading to Bolshevism, or is it to teach our youth red-blooded patriotism, and should the time ever come when they should be called upon to make the great sacrifice, that they may say with Nathan Hale, 'I regret that I have only one life to give to my country'?

Hero-worship is good for the young, for it stimulates the aspirations and gives to the people the highest standards of manhood. Therefore the character sketches of such men as Prescott, Stark, Putnam, Nathan Hale, Mad Anthony Wayne, Sumpter, Light Horse Harry Lee, Commander Barry, Molly Pitcher, and many others should be taught with all the glamour, color, eloquence, and dramatic effect upon the minds of our children at the age when they are most susceptible to such impressions."

A letter from Mr. Moulton Houk, former Vice-President General of Ohio, takes a similar view and is so excellent in its analysis that if we had space it would be printed in full; but there is one point that surely must appeal to our compatriots. In speaking of the statement made by the publishers of one of these objectionable stories that we do not want hero-worship, but we do want facts, Mr. Houk does not hesitate to take issue with this idea. He says: "To the contrary, we do want hero-worship and we do not want *all* the facts. Is it not better to remember Grant's heroism than that he had failings in other directions? And should the latter go into history?" Mr. Houk cites one or two other instances in the lives of our great heroes, and then goes on to say: "We do not want facts unless they are creditable; unless they will add to our glory in our Americanism, but we do want credit, and all credit only, given to our heroes. We easily pass over such works (these histories), but such works will form our children's ideas of our past and make either for patriot or internationalist; it must be one or the other."

A letter written by Captain A. H. Connor has been issued by Judge McCamant with comments. Captain Connor is President of the Idaho Society, Sons of the American Revolution, and Attorney General of that State. The letter is written to the editor of the *Idaho Statesman* and is a sharp criticism of the History of the American People by William Mason West. Captain Connor says:

"The author of this text-book quite evidently lacks the national viewpoint, is strongly inclined toward socialism, and has no pride in the achievements of the founders of the Republic. The whole Revolutionary period is sketchily treated. The Tories are stated to have represented respectability and refinement, leaving the inference that the fathers who fought for the liberties we now enjoy were neither respectable nor refined. The book refers to those who took part in the resistance to the Stamp Act and the Boston Tea Party as 'mobs.' No reference is made to Bunker Hill, and this author enlarges upon Washington's temper and his ability to swear. The great battles and achievements of the Revolutionary War are dismissed in a few lines."

This history, which is full of socialism and bias partisanship, is in use in the Boise high schools. Captain Connor says that "discussion of controversal subjects has no place in a history; it should not be found in a single school in the United States of America."

These few quotations from some of our red-blooded compatriots show, it seems, the general feeling that pervades our organization, though there comes a note of disapproval of this stand from one or two of our pedagogic members, who, though not altogether agreeing with what is said in these so-called histories, yet raise the question that these books should not be censured, as they are teaching the older student, who is capable of thinking for himself. Compatriot William H. Powers, of the South Dakota State College, takes this view, and makes as a constructive suggestion, this statement:

THE TREASURER GENERAL

"Should we not get further in our schools, for example, if our school boards choose teachers of history for their intelligence, their learning, and their character; then hold them responsible for results? Is it not better to fix trust where you expect results than to dilute it by passing it through a chain of peering investigators? If our association is committed to the business of censorship, do we not owe it to ourselves at least to see that our charges are not based on trivial instances and are not expressed in a manner inviting contempt?"

It would seem that Compatriot Powers misses the point completely. In the first place, the high-school students of today, ranging from fourteen to eighteen, are still at a most impressionable age, and at no time does a boy get his ideals of men and events stronger than at that time in his life. It would seem that to be compelled to study a history that practically eliminates all of the great characters and events of our great struggle for liberty, and is filled later with biased partisanship and socialistic teachings, is not the sort to make for high ideals and patriotism; and no teacher, however good his learning, intelligence, and character, could counteract the impressions that would emanate from such a book. It can hardly be said that what these books teach in many of their pages, as Judge McCamant and Colonel Connor have pointed out, can be called "trivial instances." They go to the very heart of our national life, to the foundation of our Republic, based on its splendid traditions and the character of its great founders and builders; and when they teach partisanship and socialism and hatred toward class, they strike at the very roots of our Constitution.

REPORT OF COMMITTEE TO EXAMINE AND HARMONIZE CHARTER, CONSTITUTION, AND BY-LAWS

To the Compatriots of the National Society of the Sons of the American Revolution:

At the 33d Annual Congress of the National Society, held on May 15-16, 1922, at Springfield, Mass., it was moved and carried—

"That the incoming President General and the incoming Chancellor General be a committee charged with the duty to examine the Charter, Constitution, and By-Laws and make such recommendations as shall harmonize the three documents one with the other, they to report to the Society through the BULLETIN at the earliest possible date."

Your committee begs to report:

A careful and detailed scrutiny of the Charter, Constitution, and By-Laws has been made, not only by the two members of this committee, but the year books and proceedings have been examined for a period of ten years prior to this date in order to ascertain the questions and discussions which have arisen in connection with doubtful points in relation to either the Constitution or By-Laws. In order to bring the said Constitution and By-Laws the one with the other, the following changes are necessary and are hereby recommended to the National Society for action at the forthcoming convention:

CONSTITUTION

In place of Article VI as it exists in the printed Constitution, there shall be substituted the new amendment adopted May 16, 1922, at Springfield, Mass., as follows:

"ARTICLE VI—*Initiation Fees and Dues*

"SECTION 1. In addition to the initiation fee, if any, charged by a State Society, there shall be paid an initiation fee of five dollars for membership in the National Society, Sons of the American Revolution. Said fee shall be forwarded to the Registrar General with each application for membership and shall entitle the newly elected compatriot to receive an engraved certificate of membership.

"SEC. 2. Each State shall pay annually to the Treasurer General to defray the expense of the National Society fifty cents for each member thereof, unless intermitted by the National Congress.

"SEC. 3. Such dues shall be paid on or before the first day of April in each year for the ensuing year in order to secure representation in the Congress of the National Society."

You are further notified that under a resolution adopted by the Congress (see page 41 of the OFFICIAL BULLETIN, June, 1922) all initiation fees were waived on applications received prior to October 1, 1922.

BY-LAWS

Amend and correct By-Laws:

ARTICLE XII—*State Societies*

Strike out section 2 as printed in present By-Laws and substitute therefor:

"Transmit to the Registrar General duplicate applications of all accepted members, together with the initiation fee of five dollars for membership in the National Society, and promptly notify him of the resignation or death of all members thereof, the names of those dropped from the roll for non-payment of dues."

ARTICLE XIII—*Board of Trustees*

Strike out the word "five" in section 4, line 3, and insert the word "seven" to conform with section 3, Article V, of Constitution.

ARTICLE XV—*Seal*

Add to present section the following words:

"The seal of the Society shall be used upon all documents and large certificates, but a seal 2 inches in diameter may be used on the smaller certificates presented by the National Society."

ARTICLE XVII—*Insignia*

Clarify Article XVII, section 1, by striking out all of the remainder of section 1 following the words "on ceremonial occasions only" and substitute the following:

"and shall be carried on the left breast or at the collar by active or Past Officers General of the National Society (the President General shall wear the distinctive badge of his office) or the President, active or past, of a State Society and the active President of a local Chapter.

"The insignia of a National officer and a State President, active or past, may be jeweled by the insertion of the diamond in the space between the talons of the eagle and the upper arm of the chevalier's cross.

"The President General, during his term of office and while acting in that capacity on official and ceremonial occasions, shall wear the distinctive badge of his office. It may be carried at the left breast or suspended from the neck ribbon.

In full dress he shall wear a sash of the Society colors, three and one-half inches in width, extending from the right shoulder to the left hip. Past Presidents General and Vice-Presidents General, while in office, in full dress may wear a sash of the Society colors, three and one-half inches wide, extending from the right shoulder to the left hip."

ARTICLE XVIII—*Official Standard*

This flag consists of three equal vertical bars, blue, white, and buff, the blue bar at the hoist. Upon the center or white bar is the insignia of the Society and the name "The Society of the Sons of the American Revolution."

Article XVIII changed to Article XIX.
Article XIX changed to Article XX.

ARTICLE XXI—*Amendments*

"These By-Laws may be altered or amended by a vote of three-fourths of the members present at any meeting of the Board of Trustees, notice thereof having been given at a previous meeting."

A PROPOSED PLAN FOR THE DISTRIBUTION OF MEDALS TO PUPILS IN PUBLIC SCHOOLS

For many years, in different parts of the country, the State Societies and local Chapters of the Sons of the American Revolution have awarded medals for the best essays on subjects dealing with Revolutionary History. These medals have usually been awarded to high-school students, and the results have been most satisfactory, so far as this idea was carried out. However, it has seemed that the work of the Society could be extended and made more far-reaching and the plan which follows is one that is being worked out by the Secretary General with the advice and suggestions of Superintendent Ernest Hartwell, of the Buffalo public schools.

The underlying idea of this proposed plan is that it will reach the pupil at an age when character and citizenship is in the making, and that every boy that wins one of these medals will, it is hoped, become a loyal and patriotic citizen, following along the lines of his endeavor to achieve this honor.

There are two other most vital reasons why this method of distribution should appeal to our State Societies and local Chapters: First, it will mean a wider distribution of the medals, for grammar schools are far more numerous than high schools; and, second, it will reach more of the people who need this standard of citizenship. Where the high schools reach many of our foreign-born or children of foreign-born citizens, the grammar schools reach the mass of these citizens. It can easily be understood what the effect of winning these medals by the children of either native or foreign-born will have, not only upon the immediate family, but also the relatives and friends.

It is with this idea in mind that the plan which is here proposed will be carried out, and it is felt that if the Societies throughout the country will work along these lines, far-reaching results will be obtained in the work we are striving for in our organization.

It is hoped and expected that the cost of these medals will be insignificant compared with the results achieved. By ordering in large quantities, the National

Society expects to be able to supply them to the State Societies and Chapters in bronze for approximately $1.50 each. This price has not been definitely fixed as yet, but will depend upon how large a response there is to this plan. The Buffalo Chapter has already given its order for enough to supply every grammar school in Buffalo something over sixty each year. Chapters in New Jersey have signified their intention to take a quantity of these medals for distribution, and it is known that many other societies throughout the country stand ready to carry out this idea.

It is proposed to have the plan or announcement which follows printed in blue, with our insignia at the top, and one or more of these hung in the school where the medal is to be awarded. There may possibly be some minor changes in the wording and construction of this announcement, but this follows the general plan.

The above dignified and attractive design for the medal is under consideration by the committee.

PLAN OF AWARD

The Sons of the American Revolution have as one of their chief purposes the stimulation of a vigorous patriotism. They believe that such a purpose is to be secured only as the youth of our schools become imbued with high ideals of character and citizenship. The Sons of the American Revolution have, therefore, decided annually to award a medal to the boy in the eighth grade graduating class of each elementary school who shall have best exemplified the principles of good citizenship.

The qualities to be considered in making this award shall be:

I. Dependability, as evidenced by the record of the boy in punctuality, truthfulness, honesty, loyalty, trustworthiness, and self-control.

II. Co-operation, as evidenced by the record of the boy in respect for authority, respect for property, respect for the rights of others, and courtesy.

III. Leadership, as evidenced by what the boy has done to make his school a better school.

No boy shall receive the Sons of the American Revolution Medal who is not clean in speech and in personal habits.

He must also be a non-user of tobacco, inasmuch as no eighth-grade boy in New York State can use tobacco without violating the law of the Commonwealth.

The method of determining what boy shall receive the medal shall be as follows:

Some time within the ten days preceding the eighth-grade commencement exercises, each division of the senior eighth grades in each school shall meet and by vote of the class nominate not more than five boys whom the class considers to be eligible to receive the medal. From this five the final selection shall be made by the principal of the school and a majority vote of all of the teachers who have had the nominees in class during the eighth-grade year.

Further information may be had from the Secretary General.

NEW JERSEY'S THIRTY-FOURTH ANNIVERSARY

Broadcasting the message of the Society of the Sons of the American Revolution was an innovation delightfully experienced by a group of members of the New Jersey Society, which met in the studio of the Westinghouse Company, at the Waldorf-Astoria, New York, on the evening of March 7, the thirty-fourth anniversary of the organization. Arrangements had been made for the patriotic program by the Newark Chapter quartet. After several selections were rendered, the address on the New Jersey Society was given by David L. Pierson, Secretary, who spoke as follows:

"Organized on March 7, 1889, the New Jersey Society, Sons of the American Revolution, has today attained its thirty-fourth birthday. It is composed of descendants of ancestors who assisted in creating the independence of the United States, is non-sectarian, non-political, and, while it has many lines of patriotic activity, the dominant thought and action are in the maintenance of the principles and traditions of the founders of the Republic.

"The Society came into being clothed with the pure spirit of patriotism on the mighty wave of aroused public sentiment incident to the preparation and carrying out of the plans for the celebration of the centenary of General George Washington's inauguration as the first President of the United States, on April 30, 1889. On this day, in accordance with the request of the New Jersey Society, delegates from many of the States met in the Fraunces Tavern, New York, and effected the National organization. There are now fifty separate societies.

"Constructive work of the Society includes the institution of Flag Day, on June 14, and Constitution Day, September 17, now so well remembered by the people; the enacting of flag laws, preventing the use of the flag of Stars and Stripes for commercial and other wrongful purposes; helping the aliens to become citizens; the restoring of innumerable genealogical lines of the older American families; awarding of prizes to students for their essays on American history; marking of scenes connected with the War for Independence, and of the lives of eminent Americans connected therewith; correcting defects in text-books relating to historical narrative of our country and encouraging the study of history by all the people.

"Let us not forget the injunction of the immortal Washington, whose birthday anniversary was so recently and widely celebrated. In his Farewell Address, declining a third term as President of the United States, he there declared a sound principle for the American people, that 'in time of peace prepare for war,' not to prepare for the destruction of life and property, but to so order our daily routine that we might give a full measure of individual service for the stability and uplift of the government of the people, by the people, and for the people; and not wait till war clouds hover over the horizon before demonstrating our fealty to the institutions of our country.

"New Jersey, the Belgium of the Revolutionary War, has many patriotic shrines connected with the great awakening of a liberty-loving people. Old Nassau, the famous seat of learning at Princeton, is the identical building around which waged the battle of Princeton, on January 3, 1777; the Ford Mansion, at Morristown, where Washington made his headquarters in the rigorous winter of 1779-1780, is preserved forever as a repository of notable possessions of the chieftain and of the people of his time; the Wallace House, at Somerville, headquarters of the commander in the winter of 1778-1779; Rocky Hill, the headquarters, near Princeton, where the farewell address to the soldiers of the army was written on November 2, 1783; the Springfield battlefield, where was fought the decisive engagement of the war, on June 23, 1780; the battle of Trenton, December 26, 1776; the battle of Monmouth, June 28, 1778, are all among the many other prized possessions of the Jersey folk.

"We have come into our great heritage over a long and tedious route, often beset with danger. Sentinels of freedom have always and will forever guard and guide the way for the Ship of State to pass along. Eternal vigilance is the price of Liberty!

"At the beginning of the War for American Independence the music sung in the colonies was entirely of foreign origin till William Billings, a native of Massachusetts, wrote the hymns in the era immediately preceding the opening of hostilities with the mother country, and which have made his name immortal as the Father of American Music.

"Among the compositions emanating from the pen of this gifted son of New England was the call to heroic service of the soldiers enrolled in Washington's Army, and which he named "Chester." This was sung on the march, around the camp fires at the bivouac, and in the cantonments. The spirited music to which the ennobling words were set was provocative of incomparable results, cheering the weary soldiers as they trudged over the frozen roadways, in the quiet of the evening hour at the end of the long day's march, or as they sat huddled together in their huts at Valley Forge and at Morristown, waiting for the advent of the season of life and warmth to begin anew the struggle for supremacy of right over wrong."

This hymn was then sung by the Newark Chapter quartet.

Compatriot Rev. Warren P. Coon gave an address on "One Hundred Per Cent Patriotism," during which he declared for the perpetuity and sanctity of the American home, and in defining the sentiment of simplicity spoke of three things necessary for the proper equipment of every domicil—the Bible, the flag, and the red tablecloth. This latter was found in nearly every home, the speaker declared, a third of a century ago, particularly in the New England home.

The Board of Managers of the New Jersey Society enjoyed a dinner at the Essex Club, Newark, on Friday night, March 9, in remembrance of the thirty-fourth anniversary of the organization. Judge Adrian Lyon, President, presided, and the address was delivered by Rev. Dr. Lyman Whitney Allen, past Chaplain General of the National Society and past President of the New Jersey Society. He also read an original poem on the Constitution.

Adjournment was then made to the headquarters at 33 Lombardy Street, where the regular monthly meeting was held. A letter was read from Compatriot Louis A. Bowman, Secretary of the Illinois Society, expressing the felicitations of that Society upon the attainment of the birthday anniversary. A letter was also read from Compatriot F. W. Millspaugh, Vice-President of the Tennessee Society, also extending felicitations and expressing the hope that a large delegation would be sent to the Congress which will meet in Nashville in May.

A tribute was offered in memory of Dr. Carlyle E. Sutphen, of Newark, who died on March 7, and who was one of the well-known members,

THE ROOSEVELT MEMORIAL

The following letter from the Woman's Roosevelt Memorial Association to the New York Chapter of the Empire State Society was referred to the National Society with the request that it be published in the Bulletin:

NEW YORK CHAPTER, SONS OF THE AMERICAN REVOLUTION,
GENERAL OLIVER B. BRIDGMAN, PRESIDENT, 220 BROADWAY, NEW YORK CITY.

MY DEAR GENERAL BRIDGMAN:

The building of Roosevelt House has gone forward only as money has been received, and we have now enough to complete the building up to the auditorium. To do this we need $12,000, and we see a sure way of raising it if the men's patriotic societies throughout the United States will come to our assistance.

The auditorium should be finished at once, in order that the real work of Roosevelt House, which is educational, may begin without delay. In the auditorium we expect to have lectures given on the life and ideals of Roosevelt; there also we expect to show moving pictures which will bring the living Roosevelt vividly before the eyes of the children of New York. That work is greatly worth doing. New York needs it, and it needs it *now*. When Roosevelt House is opened that work should promptly begin.

Since we started our work, four years ago, we have faithfully kept our purpose before us, and now that we are in sight of its fulfillment we ask your aid in this our final effort. If you feel that we have done well, will you help us raise a part of the $12,000 we need to complete Roosevelt House?

Make checks payable to the Woman's Roosevelt Memorial Association and kindly mention your society.

Very sincerely yours,

EMILY V. HAMMOND,
(MRS. JOHN HENRY HAMMOND),
President.

January 30, 1923.

KENMORE

In Fredericksburg, Va., stands a beautiful old Colonial mansion, "Kenmore," once the home of Betty Washington, George Washington's only and well-beloved sister. She was just sixteen months younger, and always there existed between them the tenderest devotion. When seventeen years old, George Washington gave her in marriage to Colonel Fielding Lewis, whose generous nature, fine family, and fortune made him a worthy mate.

In 1752 Colonel Lewis bought the land, upon which he at once began to build this stately home. It is a solid brick structure, walls two feet thick, with large, handsome rooms and its interior wood-work finished with the most exquisite refinement of detail. George Washington took the greatest pride and interest in his sister's·home. He helped to plan the home and grounds and he suggested and designed the ornate walls and ceilings, which are a distinctive feature of the mansion. It is an attested fact that the mantel in the reception-room, illustrating the fable of "The Fox, the Crow, and the Piece of Cheese," he chose, to teach his nephews to beware of flatterers. It is said that at one time General Washington lived with his sister; certainly he was a frequent guest.

Kenmore stands now unchanged, on a large lawn surrounded by many of the same old trees. For years it has had the loving care of appreciative owners, but last spring it was thrown on the market, the grounds subdivided into building lots, the house to be turned into an apartment-house. Then it was that the patriotic women of Fredericksburg, with little means or backing, formed themselves into the Kenmore Association, and stormed the nation with their appeals. They secured the $10,000 necessary to hold the property. The price is $30,000. Since then they have collected $5,000 more. They have taken possession and the property is rented for enough to meet the interest on the deferred payments. They are appealing now to the patriotic societies, Daughters of the American Revolution and Colonial Dames. Both have lent their aid.

But there is an especial appeal to the Sons of the American Revolution, because Colonel Fielding Lewis, owner and builder of Kenmore, made the first guns for the Continental Army. The "Manufactory of Small Arms" was established in Fredericksburg July, 1775. Colonel Lewis was chief commissioner, and he sacrificed his entire fortune in this vital enterprise. At one time he was so embarrassed he could not raise the money to meet his taxes (Calendar of State Papers, Vol. I, page 503).

To the descendants of the men whom Washington led comes this appeal. Memorials of General Washington, costing thousands of dollars, are being erected everywhere, and here stands this place, dearer to him than any other, except Mount Vernon, and alive with intimate associations with him and his friends, threatened with destruction. Will not every son feel it his duty to respond to this urgent need? Will it not be a privilege to save for future generations this memorial of our glorious past?

Perpetual beneficent guardian	$1,000.00
Hereditary guardian	500.00
Life guardian	100.00
Hereditary life member	50.00
Honorary life member	25.00
Ten-year member	10.00
Active member	5.00
Associate member	1.00 annually

Kindly make checks payable to Planters National Bank of Fredericksburg, Va., treasurer for Kenmore Association, Inc.

MRS. V. M. FLEMING,
President Kenmore Association, Inc.

FREDERICKSBURG, VA.

EVENTS OF STATE SOCIETIES

The Arizona Society.—The twenty-seventh annual business meeting of the Arizona Society was held on February 22 at the office of the President. The following officers were unanimously elected: President, Harold Baxter; Vice-President, H. H. Wilson; Secretary, E. L. Freeland; Treasurer, W. B. Twitchell; Registrar, B. L. Purvines; Historian, Rt. Rev. J. W. Atwood; Chaplain, Rev. J. Rockwood Jenkins; additional members of the Board of Managers, J. C. Greenway, M. B. Hazeltine, Willard S. Wright; Delegate to National Congress, W. B. Twitchell; National Trustee, E. E. Ellinwood.

At the twenty-seventh annual dinner of the Society, held the same evening, at the Woman's Club, Phœnix, Compatriots E. E. Ellinwood and Dwight B. Heard responded to the toasts of the evening, taking as their respective subjects "Beaumarchais" and "Our Forefathers."

The Society voted to take an active part in the reception of newly made citizens upon the occasion of naturalization of candidates for citizenship in the District Court of the United States at Phœnix.

The annual oratorical contest was held, and the first prize of $20 was awarded to Floyd Davidson, student of the Chandler High School, whose oration was upon the topic "The Father of Our Country." The second prize of $10 was awarded to John L. Mixon, student of the Phœnix Union High School, whose oration was upon the topic of "The Soul of Washington."

The newly elected officers were introduced and a social hour concluded the entertainment.

The Arkansas Society, Sons of the American Revolution, held its annual business meeting at the Hotel Marion February 23, 1923, and elected the following officers for the ensuing year: Frank D. Leaming, President; J. O. Blakeney, First Vice-President; S. S. Wassell, Second Vice-President; Fay Hempstead, Secretary; E. C. Newton, Registrar; T. M. Cory, Treasurer; Alyn Smith, Historian; T. M. Cory, Representative to the National Meeting; B. W. Green, G. W. Clark, Randall Peck, and E. R. Wiles, members of the Board of Governors.

Memorials were presented and adopted concerning the late P. K. Roots and John M. Bracey. A. R. Snodgrass was recommended for National Trustee. It was agreed that the Society hold suitable celebrations of "Flag Day" and "Constitution Day." It was announced that the National Meeting will be held in Nashville, Tenn., in May.

After the business session, the Society and guests attended a banquet in one of the hotel private dining-rooms. Music was furnished by the Misses Claudia and Virginia Askew. Addresses were made by S. S. Wassell on "Francis Marion," Governor McRae on "Character of Washington," Fay Hempstead on "Count Pulaski"; Admiral A. O. Wright, of Jacksonville, Fla., explained the origin of the cherry-tree story. Greetings on behalf of the State Society, Daughters of the American Revolution, were given by Mrs. A. M. Barrow, State Regent, in verse. Greetings on behalf of the Colonial Dames were presented by Mrs. Fred'k Hanger.

The California Society.—Major Washington I. L. Adams, President General, addressed the members of the California Society of the Sons and Daughters of the American Revolution at a dinner at the Commercial Club on the evening of January 5.

The dinner was given in honor of Major Adams, who is a descendant of John Quincy Adams.

With Major Adams at the reception as a guest of honor was George Albert Smith, Vice-President General of the Sons of the American Revolution, who came out from Salt Lake City.

San Francisco, with the rest of the Nation, paid tribute to the memory of George Washington on the 191st anniversary of his birth, February 22.

Special commemorative exercises were held by the Sons and Daughters of the American Revolution at the General's statue at the Marina at 2 p. m. David Starr Jordan, chancellor of Stanford University, was the orator of the occasion.

Many patriotic organizations and societies were represented at the ceremonies, a feature of which was the placing of wreaths on the statue of the man who was "first in war, first in peace, and first in the hearts of his countrymen." Among those taking part in the tribute were veterans' organizations, including the Sons and Daughters of the American Revolution, Grand Army of the Republic, Spanish-American War Veterans, and a host of others.

The District of Columbia Society, Sons of the American Revolution, Daughters of the American Revolution, and Sons of the Revolution of the District of Columbia united in their ninth annual joint celebration on February 22, in Memorial Continental Hall. Mr. Selden Marvin Ely, Mrs. William B. Hardy, and Brigadier General George Richards, the respective heads of the three organizations, presided jointly. An elaborate and impressive program was participated in by a large audience. The invocation was made by Rev. Robert Johnston, D. D., of St. John's Episcopal Church. The presentation of the Colors was accompanied by a group representing the Spirit of '76, the Marine Band, and followed by the Pledge to the Flag, the American's Creed, and the singing of the Star-Spangled Banner. Addresses by Mrs. William B. Hardy, the Hon. Samuel M. Shortridge, of California, and the presentation of medals for prize essays by the participating societies completed the program, which was interspersed by musical selections by the Marine Band.

The annual election of officers of the District of Columbia Society took place on this date and resulted as follows: President, Mr. Samuel Herrick; Vice-Presidents, Henry L. Bryan, Admiral Hugh Rodman, and Hon. Josiah A. Van Orsdel; Secretary and Treasurer, Mr. Kenneth S. Wales; Registrar, Major Overton C. Luxford; Assistant Registrar, Charles M. Bryant; Historian, Henry White Draper; Librarian, William L. Boyden, and Chaplain, William Curtis White.

The Far Eastern Society has taken on a new lease of life under the inspiration of its new President, Prof. Austin Craig, of the University of the Philippines, and progress and increased membership in this far station of our Society may be looked for. Other officers are Hon. T. A. Street, Vice-President; Harry J. Cushing, Secretary-Treasurer, and Hayward and Samuel A. Dewing, Managers. The Society desires to establish chapters in Japan, Korea, North China, South China, Siam, Malaysia, and India and appeals to present members in these localities or compatriots in the States who have friends in the Far East to co-operate in promulgating this ambition.

The Idaho Society.—The fifteenth annual meeting of the Idaho Society was held in the Owyhee Hotel, Boise, on February 22.

The President, Compatriot A. H. Conner, reported that this Society has so successfully opposed the use of such un-American American histories as Muzzy's and West's in our public schools that they are now used only in three schools in the State.

Compatriot Addison T. Smith having called attention to the fact that forty-four States have exercised their right to place a tablet in the Washington Monument at Washington, D. C., and that Idaho is one of the four States which has not done so, a discussion ensued in connection with this matter, and it is hoped during the year to have Idaho properly represented.

The Utah Society having invited the National Congress to Salt Lake City in 1924, this selection was endorsed by the Idaho Society.

The new officers elected are: President, Charles L. Longley; Vice-Presidents, Dean Driscoll, Boise; S. E. Anderson, Pocatello; M. H. Brownell, Hailey; Bowen Curley, Idaho Falls; Stanly A. Easton, Kellogg; William H. Eldridge, Twin Falls; J. M. Elder, Cœur d'Alene; Asher A. Getchell, Boise; W. H. Gibson, Mountain Home; Rev. W. S. Hawkes, Caldwell; Miles S. Johnson, Lewiston; George N. Osborne, Wallace; Samuel H. Hays, Boise; Secretary-Treasurer-Registrar, Frank G. Ensign; Chaplain, Rev. R. B. Wright, D. D.; Historian, M. W. Wood, Lieutenant-Colonel, U. S. A. (retired).

The ladies of the Daughters of the American Revolution joined the annual Washington dinner. Compatriot Miles S. Johnson delivered a forceful address on Washington as a statesman.

The Illinois Society.—The annual celebration of Washington's Birthday, under the joint auspices of the Sons and Daughters of the American Revolution, was held Thursday evening, February 22, with a banquet, in the First Christian Church. The arrangements were in the hands of the Daughters of the American Revolution.

Reminiscences of Valley Forge as told to Oliver McDaniel, of Buffalo, by his grandfather, who was a soldier with Washington, were the basis of an interesting talk on "Valley Forge of Revolutionary Times," by Mr. McDaniel. As Compatriot McDaniel celebrated his 85th birthday a short time ago, he remembers his grandfather telling his experiences of those trying times, as he lived to be quite an old man. Very few present-day members are "grandson's" and probably fewer still can remember their grandfathers telling of events of the Revolutionary War. Compatriot McDaniel was in the Civil War for three years, and attends more regularly than many younger members. Attorney J. B. Searcy also gave an address on Valley Forge gathered from historical accounts of the memorable winter camp of Washington during the Revolution.

Grover C. Rockwood was elected President of the Association; James B. Searcy, Vice-Preseident; Isaac R. Diller, Secretary-Treasurer; Dr. E. P. Bartlett, Historian; J. Ralph Tobin, Registrar, and Nelson L. Allyn, Chaplain.

PEORIA CHAPTER.—Resolutions urging that the Government purchase the Kahokia Mounds, near East St. Louis, and convert the ground into a park were adopted at a meeting of the Peoria Chapter, Sons of the American Revolution, in the Creve Cœur Club Saturday.

The meeting was called by the new President of the organization, Mark D. Batchelder, for the purpose of becoming acquainted with all the members. Following dinner in the club dining-room, the body went into business session, where the resolution concerning the historic mounds was discussed. Other business included appointment of Philip Gregg as chairman of the Membership Committee, Louis A. Howes as chairman of the Publicity Committee, and A. H. Hiatt as chairman of the Entertainment Committee. There are a large number of Peorians eligible for membership and steps will be taken to bring them into the fold.

The Kentucky Society.—In an atmosphere reminiscent of America's glorious traditions, members of the Kentucky Society, Sons of the American Revolution, were fervently urged at their annual dinner, January 26, at the Pendennis Club, to keep aloft the American light of liberty by sacred regard for the Constitution and respect for laws of the land. Governor Morrow, Helm Bruce, and Major W. I. Adams made speeches.

Allegiance to the flag was repledged, and the speaker, Major Washington Irving Lincoln Adams, of Montclair, N. J., President General of the National Society, appealed for added stimulus and application of that spirit in law enforcement and the spread of 100 per cent Americanism.

Attention was called at the meeting to the "open violation" of the Eighteenth Amendment; thoughts were turned to the Nation's heroic dead and the heritage of American citizens; steps were advocated to combat insidious un-American propaganda, and the need was emphasized for improvement of text-books dealing with American history.

Dr. Curran Pope, Vice-President of the Society, presided at the dinner, with Dean Richard L. McCready pronouncing the invocation. F. W. Millspaugh, Vice-President of the Tennessee Society, urged members of the Kentucky Society to attend the National Congress of that body to be held at Nashville in May.

New members taken into the Society, with special installation ceremonies, were William B. Pirtle, Normal Milner Cooty, Ellerbee W. Carter, Henry Clayborn Armstrong, Ranson Haselip Bassett, Murray Brawner, J. Carter Stewart, John B. Lewman, all of Louisville; George M. Covington, Russellville; Hansford Lee Threlkeld, Morganfield; James Clinton Stone, Lexington; Samuel Hanson Stone, Lexington; Dr. John G. South, resident of Panama, but a native of Frankfurt.

Talented entertainers gave a program over W H A S, the radiophone of *The Courier-Journal* and *The Louisville Times*. Major Adams also made an address over W H A S. He was introduced by Mayor Huston Quin. R. C. Ballard Thruston and Marvin H. Lewis gave a reception at the Pendennis Club at 1:30 o'clock in the afternoon in honor of Major Adams.

The Louisiana Society held its annual meeting on Wednesday, January 24. The entertainment of Major W. I. Lincoln Adams, President General, took place at the Sazerac Restaurant. The occasion was a purely informal one. The business features of the affair were conducted briefly, and following the election of officers the meeting was given over to the guest of honor and the speakers of the evening, the whole constituting the regular annual meeting of the Louisiana Society deferred from the first Saturday in December, 1922.

The program included an invocation and automatic roll-call, in which each member in turn rose, stated his name, his business, city of residence, and his Revolutionary ancestor or ancestors; reports of the Treasurer, Financial Secretary, and President. The toastmaster, Henry W. Robinson, introduced the speakers, and addresses were made by Mr. Edwin T. Merrick, Past President of the Louisiana Society, on "England and America"; Mr. J. Edward Kirby, late President of the Iowa Society, national speaker, Near East Relief, on "America and Russia"; Hon. Thomas W. Robertson, late Vice-President of the Louisiana Society, on "Uncensored School Books," and Major W. I. Lincoln Adams, President General of the National Society.

The Louisiana Society has again issued a splendid Year Book, with roster of its members, which it has widely distributed.

The Maine Society.—Charles L. Hutchinson, of Portland, was elected President of the Maine Society, Sons of the American Revolution, at their annual meeting, February 22, at the Congress Square Hotel. Other officers elected were: Vice-Presidents, Oliver L. Hall, of Bangor; Willis Blake Hall, of Cape Elizabeth; Albert M. Spear, of Augusta; Treasurer, Enoch O. Greenleaf of Portland; Secretary, Francis L. Littlefield, of Portland; Registrar, James C. Woolley, of Portland; Historian, John Francis Sprague, of Dover-Foxcroft; Chaplain, the Very Rev. Edmund Randolph Laine, Jr., of Portland; Librarian, William T. Cousens, of Portland; Associate Managers, Frederic L. Tower, of Portland; Dr. J. Fred Hill, of Waterville; Converse E. Leach, of Portland; Mark A. Barwise, of Bangor; Edwin J. Haskell, of Westbrook.

It was voted to endorse the efforts of Lucy Knox Chapter, Daughters of the American Revolution, to obtain funds sufficient to enable them to build a Henry Knox Memorial at Thomaston.

The new President, Charles L. Hutchinson, was elected a Trustee of the National Society.

The principal after-dinner speaker was Rev. Dr. Henry Stiles Bradley, pastor of the State Street Church, who spoke of George Washington. Dr. Bradley exhibited some curious documents which once belonged to Washington and read extracts from them. He also read a long description of Washington, which traced his lineage back to nearly all of the great men and women of the old world.

The Massachusetts Society of the Sons of the American Revolution and its junior organization, the Washington Guard, observed the 191st anniversary of Washington's Birthday, February 22, 1923, at the headquarters of the Society, 9 Ashburton Place, Boston. This meeting was in the nature of a father-and-son gathering, and each member of the Sons of the American Revolution in attendance was requested to bring as his guest a son or a member of the Washington Guard.

The program for the day included an assembly at the headquarters, 9 Ashburton Place, in the morning, followed by attendance at the Governor's reception at the State House in a body, the Sons of the American Revolution escorting the Washington Guard. An informal reception was held by the officers and guests of the Society at headquarters and dinner was served in Wilder Hall; reception of the Colors; an address, "George Washington," by Frederick Jackson Turner, Professor of History, Harvard University; an address to the Washington Guard, Rev. Frederic W. Perkins, D. D., Chaplain General, National Society; presentation of service medals, and roll-call of chapters. Each chapter was requested to respond with a three-minute table talk.

Each Chapter of the Massachusetts Society, Sons of the American Revolution, was requested to send a delegation to the meeting of February 22, to arrive in season to attend the reception to be given in the Hall of Flags at the State House by Governor Channing H. Cox, who is one of our compatriots. There was also a good representation from the Washington Guard upon that occasion. Headquarters at 9 Ashburton Place is within two minutes' walk of the State House and within one minute of the Boston City Club, Ford Hall, and the Court House. It is open daily, except Sunday, from 9 to 5, and is at the service of the members as a place of meeting. Several of the Greater Boston Chapters are finding it very convenient to hold their meetings there.

THE GEORGE WASHINGTON CHAPTER, Sons of the American Revolution, of Springfield, held its annual meeting and banquet at the Nayasset Club, at Springfield, on the evening of February 22. The chief officers of the National and State societies, namely, President General Washington Irving Lincoln Adams, of Montclair, N. J.; Vice-President General Harry T. Lord, of Manchester, N. H., and Dr. Charles H. Bangs, President of the Massachusetts Society, were guests of the local chapter. Officers or members of the National or State societies were cordially invited to attend this meeting.

Dr. Bangs spoke on "The Enduring Washington," in an inspiring address, in which he declared that from the perspective of nearly a century and a quarter we now behold that figure of history that stands out as the enduring Washington.

After dinner came the business session, President Charles F. Warner presiding. In his annual report President Warner told of the six meetings in addition to the annual meeting held during the year, referred particularly to the bridge celebration and the Chapter's part in it, to the National Congress held here last year, and closed by urging the campaign for introduction of new blood into the Chapter, which as it is has a record membership of 243 active members, 12 having been voted in during the year.

The Nominating Committee brought in the following nominations for new officers, who were unanimously elected: President, Frank P. Forbes; Vice-President, Henry C. Haile; Secretary, Henry A. Booth; Treasurer, Frederick M. Jones; Historian, Moses Lyman; Registrar, Seth H. Clark; Auditor, Harry M. Seabury.

Just previous to the meeting the municipal chime vesper program, rung between 6 and 6:45 o'clock in recognition of Washington's Birthday, included the group of tunes used in the larger cities whenever the President General and other officers of the National Society, Sons of the American Revolution, are present. The airs in regulation order were: "America," "Doxology," "America the Beautiful," "Hail, Columbia," "Old Haddam," "Chester" (first American battle song), "Onward, Christian Soldiers," and "Taps."

Reference was made prior to the address of the President General that this is his birthday, which he had been celebrating in two States, Connecticut and Massachusetts. Major Adams, who was here at the National Congress, as was Dr. Bangs, brought a message of the success of Sons of the American Revolution chapters everywhere throughout the country, as he has recently observed their activities in his tour through 26 States.

OLD ESSEX CHAPTER.—Rev. Frederic W. Perkins, Chaplain General of the National Society, Sons of the American Revolution, invited the compatriots of Old Essex Chapter, with their wives and friends, to attend a special service in commemoration of Washington's Birthday on Sunday afternoon, February 18, at 5 o'clock, in the First Universalist Church, Lynn.

Appropriate music by an enlarged choir and an address by Dr. Perkins were given. An organ recital at 4:25 preceded the service. Representatives of the official board of the State Society were present.

OLD MIDDLESEX CHAPTER, Sons of the American Revolution, of Lowell, held its twenty-seventh annual meeting and dinner on Friday evening, February 9, at the Richardson Hotel. The officers of the Massachusetts Society, Sons of the American Revolution, were invited to attend in a body. Burton N. Wiggin, the First Vice-President of the Massachusetts Society, was one of the charter members of Old Middlesex Chapter when it was organized, on January 17, 1896. It was the home Chapter of Moses Greeley Parker, who served the Society long and faithfully and filled the offices of President of the Massachusetts Society and President General of the National Society. The late Brigadier-General Philip Reade, U. S. A. (retired), also was a member of Old Middlesex.

OLD SALEM CHAPTER.—The annual meeting of Old Salem Chapter, Sons of the American Revolution, was held at the Salem Club, in Salem, on February 26. Dr. Frank A. Gardner gave a talk on the Black Watch Regiment and the origin and use of the Scotch plaids and tartans.

The following officers were elected for 1923-24: President, Isaac H. Sawyer; Vice-Presidents, William W. Woodman, William D. Chapple; Treasurer, Samuel D. Lord; Secretary, Osborne Leach; Executive Committee, Walter P. Richardson, Lawrence W. Jenkins, Warren R. Bowen, Jesse H. Wade.

SETH POMEROY CHAPTER, Sons of the American Revolution, of Northampton and Holyoke, met for luncheon at Boyden's in observance of Lincoln's Birthday. President of the Chapter, Rev. Dr. Henry G. Smith, presided and opened the meeting by a reading of the Governor's proclamation. President Smith then called upon L. L. Campbell to read the "Gettysburg Address." All present stood during this reading.

In his introduction of the speakers who were to give personal reminiscenses of Lincoln, President Smith said that in his thinking upon the subject he knew of only three now alive in Northampton who were old enough to vote at the time of Lincoln's first election. To be able to claim such an honor one must be 83 years of age or over.

After the formalities of speaking had been finished, John E. Morse, of Hadley, who had a selected portion of his Lincolniana arranged for the members' inspection, explained to those interested the significance of the numerous medals and other memorabilia in the collection.

The recent sudden death in Boston of Thomas Munroe Shepherd, one of the most prominent citizens and a descendant of one of the oldest families, has been a great loss to this Chapter and community.

Secretary William L. Root, of this city, represented Pittsfield at the annual Washington's Birthday dinner of Berkshire Chapter, Sons of the American Revolution, at the Richmond Hotel, at North Adams. Twenty-five members of the Chapter and guests were present. The Chapter extended hearty congratulations to Dr. Crosby A. Perry, of Pittsfield, a *real son* of the American Revolution now living, who will be 85 on March 1. Dr. Perry is a life member of the Chapter. An interesting address on "Washington, the American," was delivered by Mortimer W. Thomas, vice-principal of North Adams High School.

NEW BEDFORD CHAPTER, Sons of the American Revolution, was organized January 26 with about thirty members and the pledge to make the number one hun-

DR. CROSBY A. PERRY, REAL SON OF MASSACHUSETTS

dred within the year. Its members include leading business and professional men of the city, and there is much enthusiasm displayed. The meeting of the organization was held at the New Bedford House. Compatriot Clarence R. O'Brion has taken the lead in organizing the Chapter. A full board of officers was elected, of whom Herbert E. Cushman was elected President; Arthur W. Forbes, Secretary, and Clarence R. O'Brion, Treasurer. A delegation of officers in the Massachusetts Society attended the meeting and were very much pleased by the enthusiasm manifested. Lieutenant-Colonel John S. Barrows (retired) is chairman of the Publicity Committee.

The Michigan Society.—This year the Detroit Chapter observed Washington's Birthday with a dinner, to which the ladies were invited, given in the ladies' dining-room of the Detroit Athletic Club, Thursday evening, February 22. There was an attendance of about 100.

Addresses were made by Professor Thomas Harrison Reed, of the University of Michigan, upon "Washington and Present Affairs," and Compatriot Col. Frederick M. Alger, of Detroit, upon "Preparedness." Rev. James A. Vance, D. D., Chaplain of the Chapter, pronounced the invocation. President Carl F. Clarke presided. Others at the speakers' table were William P. Holliday, President of the Michigan Society; Raymond E. Van Syckle, Secretary, and General Charles A. Coolidge, ex-President. Captain Donald McMillan, the Arctic explorer, was also a guest.

KENT CHAPTER.—A dinner meeting of Kent Chapter, Sons of the American Revolution, was held at the Peninsular Club, Tuesday, January 16, to which ladies and guests were invited. Dr. Mary L. Hinsdale, of Junior College, spoke on the subject, "Shall the United States Mix in World Politics? or, Echoes from Williams Institute." Miss Hinsdale, a forceful speaker, based her address on impressions received at the Conference on International Relations held last summer at Williams College, Massachusetts. This conference has been addressed by diplomats, bankers, and others, of world-wide fame, who are qualified to discuss international relations, particularly as they affect the United States. Miss Hinsdale also touched upon our "Debt to France" and the tender friendship which existed between Washington and Lafayette.

WASHTENAW CHAPTER.—Professor George W. Patterson and Mrs. Patterson entertained the Sons of the American Revolution and their wives at their home, on Hill street, Thursday evening, in celebration of Washington's Birthday. This was the occasion of the annual meeting and election of officers, and at a brief business session preceding the evening's program the following were chosen for the ensuing year: President, Dr. W. B. Hinsdale; Vice-President, J. J. Goodyear; Secretary, W. Hackley Butler; Treasurer, Milton E. Osborn; Chaplain, Junius E. Beal; Historian, George W. Patterson.

Arthur L. Cross, professor of European History, standing before a large draped American flag at one end of the living-room, read a most interesting and valuable paper, entitled "Importance of Country History."

The Minnesota Society of the Sons of the American Revolution went on record at their annual dinner meeting at the Minneapolis Club as opposed to the activities of the Ku Klux Klan and all violators of the Eighteenth amendment to the Constitution.

A resolution expressing condemnation of the present movement of spreading activities of the Ku Klux organization was introduced by Judge E. F. Waite, of the Hennepin County District Bench, and adopted unanimously. Dr. Douglas F. Wood, President of the Minneapolis Chapter, No. 1, during 1922, was elected President of the State Society at the meeting. Other officers elected were: Judge Grier M. Orr, St. Paul, First Vice-President; Walter Wheeler, Minneapolis, Second Vice-President; Charles H. Bronson, St. Paul, Secretary; Charles W. Eddy, St. Paul, Treasurer; H. C. Varney, St. Paul, Registrar; the Rev. M. D. Edwards, St. Paul, Historian; the Rev. S. W. Dickinson, St. Paul, Chaplain. Kenneth G. Brill, of St. Paul, retiring President, presided at the dinner.

Following the dinner a roster of members who have died since the last annual meeting was read, with short sketches of their lives, and Color Sergeants Patton and Wellinger, of the Third Infantry, at Fort Snelling, attired in their Colonial uniforms, marched in with Buglers Pintar and Camadula, of the same regiment, who sounded "taps." A program of entertainment was furnished by members.

MINNEAPOLIS CHAPTER No. 1 held a Washington's Birthday meeting at which the members of the Officers' Reserve Corps Mess, 7th Corps Area, were guests. There was an attendance of 80, about equally divided between the Chapter members and the officers. The principal address was given by the Rev. Phillips E. Osgood, Rector of St. Mark's Episcopal Church, who spoke on Washington's personal traits. At this meeting a joint resolution was adopted commending Congressman Walter H. Newton, of Minneapolis, for his successful efforts in detecting and greatly assisting in warding off a blow at the Amended National Defense Act of June 4, 1920, and the effort to strike at the heart of the act by the omission from the Army Appropriation Bill of the item providing for the maintenance of the various divisional and regimental headquarters of the organized reserve divisions. His determined stand in Congress saved the citizen army and the plans of the Government under the National Defense Act and provided $60,000 for rental of headquarters throughout the country. This retains in Minneapolis the divisional and regimental headquarters of the 88th Reserve Division and keeps the reserve division intact. In case of an emergency, mobilization of troops in Minnesota, Iowa, and North Dakota would be directly from the divisional headquarters in Minneapolis, where quicker action could be had than in case they were located at Fort Snelling, where an attempt was made to locate them, in an effort to partly cripple the service.

Since then the Chapter has listened to overtures from the Children of the American Revolution with a view to encouraging the Society and leading gradually to the further upbuilding of the Sons of the American Revolution. There was a conference likewise with the Loyal League committee of Daughters of the American Revolution in reference to the promotion of patriotic work among the children of the schools.

Matters of a substantial nature are now in consideration and announcement will be made later. We expect to make preparation for an interesting meeting on Lexington Day.

Minneapolis Chapter has lately received the application of Earle Brown, the sheriff of the county in which Minneapolis is situated, descendant of Captain David Brown, who fired the first shot in the Revolutionary War. Information in the application reads as follows:

"Captain David Brown lived at Concord, Massachusetts, and commanded the Concord Minute Men on April 19, 1775, when at the North Bridge the regulars poured their first volley across the river into the ranks of the farmer boys and instantly killed Captain Davis, of the Acton Company. Captain Brown, raising his own gun to ready, gave the command, 'Fire!' at the same time firing his own gun and bringing down the first Britisher in the War of the Revolution."

The Missouri Society held its annual meeting at the Hotel Statler, March 3, and elected the following officers: President, Linn Paine; Vice-Presidents, Charles W. Bates, Samuel McKnight Green, Charles M. Hay, and J. W. Fristoe; Honorary Vice-Presidents, George M. Shields, William B. Homer, James M. Withrow, L. D. Kingsland, Harmon J. Bliss; National Trustee, George R. Merrell; Secretary, J. Alonzo Matthews; Treasurer, I. Shreve Carter; Registrar, Homer Hall; Historian and Genealogist, W. H. H. Tainter; Chaplain, Rev. Joseph Harris Harvey; Board of Managers, Ashley Cabell, Charles M. Hay, Casper S. Yost,

G. S. Johns, L. D. Kingsland, E. R. Kinsey, Samuel McK. Green, C. Walter Hughes, Isaac H. Orr, Norman E. Tevis, Paul V. Bunn, and Cabell Gray.

President Linn Paine addressed the Society, outlining the purposes and objects of the organization, and announced a program of activities that had been approved for the advancement of the highest ideals in American citizenship. The program includes an observance of the anniversary of the battles of Lexington and Concord on the 19th of April, a celebration on Flag Day, June 14, and the annual banquet of the Society, October 19. It was further proposed to arrange a general celebration of the 136th anniversary of the adoption of our Federal Constitution, which will occur September 17.

President Paine included in his address a tribute to the memory of Amedee B. Cole, former State President and former Vice-President General of the Sons of the American Revolution, and Robert E. Adreon, who had also served our Society as State President.

The Montana Society.—The 29th annual convention of the compatriots of the Montana State Society of the Sons of the American Revolution was held Thursday evening and the 191st anniversary of the birth of George Washington was celebrated by the united Sons and Daughters of the American Revolution at a reception held at the Sulgrove home.

The business meeting was presided over by Judge Lyman H. Bennett, who wielded the historic cherrywood hatchet-gavel, made from a tree on the Westmoreland home of Washington.

Officers elected for 1923 are: Lyman H. Bennett, Virginia City, President; John N. Wolfe, Roundup, Vice-President; Leslie Sulgrove, Helena, Secretary-Treasurer; Robert H. Howey, Helena, Registrar; Alfred G. Badger, Butte, Historian; W. R. Burroughs, Helena, Chaplain; Scott Harrison, Helena, Librarian.

Appropriate resolutions were passed relating to the decease during the past year of the President, Paris B. Bartley; the Registrar, Willis J. Egleston, and of Dr. L. H. Thurston, of Roundup, who died February 19, 1923.

The Nebraska Society.—The annual meeting of the Nebraska Society, held February 22, was preceded by a joint luncheon of the Sons of the American Revolution and Daughters of the American Revolution at the Lincoln Hotel in celebration of Washington's Birthday; 135 sat down to luncheon. The program was in charge of President B. F. Bailey, and included music, brief responses by Mrs. A. R. Congdon, Regent of Deborah Avery Chapter, and by Mrs. E. L. Troyer, Regent of St. Leger Cowley Chapter. Brief addresses were given by Dr. Joshi, Hindu lecturer from Baroda College, India, and by Colonel John N. Banister, of Omaha, a member of the Nebraska Society. President Bailey presented Rev. Harmon Bross, Adjutant General of the Nebraska Grand Army of the Republic, and Judge J. B. Strode, past President of the Nebraska Sons of the American Revolution, as the two oldest and best loved members of our order. They were greeted with cheers.

The annual business meeting of the Nebraska Society was well attended. The Secretary's report showed 252 members of the State Society at the beginning of the year, an addition of 28 new members and the loss of two, one of them ex-Congressman W. L. Stark, of Aurora, by death.

The principal accomplishments of the Society during the past year include:

A compilation of a printed year book; presentation of a steel engraving, "Washington Crossing the Delaware," to the Masonic Home at Plattsmouth, October 28, 1922; participation in patriotic meetings and plans; Sons of the American Revolution dinners, with addresses, under auspices of Lincoln Chapter; Nebraska historical sites; co-operation with the other organizations in patriotic instruction and civic welfare.

A resolution by Compatriot Bobbitt favoring English in schools was adopted.

The present officers were re-elected. A new board of managers was chosen as follows: Ralph Moseley, Lincoln; E. D. Crites, Chadron; H. E. Newton, Aurora; M. H. Deffenbaugh, Fairmont; George Rogers, Omaha; T. N. Bobbitt, Lincoln.

The presentation of the steel engraving to the Masonic Home at Plattsmouth last October was a noteworthy occasion. The presentation speech was made by President Bailey and responded to by Judge Begley, of Plattsmouth.

A delegate convention was held in Lincoln, at the Chamber of Commerce Building, February 14, to celebrate the Birthday of Abraham Lincoln and to plan an original permânent celebration of the day throughout the years. Sixteen delegates from each of the patriotic societies of Lincoln were in attendance. Dr. B. F. Bailey, President of the Nebraska Society, Sons of the American Revolution, was chairman. A fife and drum corps, composed entirely of members of the Grand Army of the Republic, rendered stirring patriotic music. It was a splendid revival of patriotic sentiment. Lincoln, as the only capital city of the United States named in honor of President Abraham Lincoln, recognizes its great privilege in making each Lincoln Birthday a great patriotic celebration.

The New Jersey Society.—Under the happiest auspices the New Jersey Society observed the birthday anniversary of General George Washington with a banquet at the Washington Restaurant, Newark, on the evening of Tuesday, February 20. This date was selected because of the many celebrations planned for the day itself, and nearly 200 compatriots answered the call of the Committee of Arrangements, of which Compatriot John W. Halsey was chairman. Features of the celebration, aside from the excellent addresses delivered, were the turning on of a spotlight on the statue of Washington, in Washington Park, near the dining hall, by the city authorities, in compliance with the request of the committee; the appearance of the Newark Chapter quartet, dressed in the uniform of Continental soldiers and imitating the Spirit of '76 as the members marched into the banquet hall to the music of the fife and drum; the wearing by all the members of the three-cornered Continental hat, and the wonderful spirit of harmony patriotically and fraternally prevailing throughout the evening.

Judge Adrian Lyon, President, was the toastmaster, and the ceremony of the presentation of the Colors, the pledge to the Flag, singing of the "Star-Spangled Banner," and the special singing of the hymn "Chester," used by the troops of Washington, were features.

Fulfillment of the hope that the Sons of the American Revolution and the Sons of the Revolution will be merged in one organization is among the possibilities of the not distant future, Major Washington Irving Lincoln Adams, President General of the Sons of the American Revolution, stated in his address. Major Adams urged the Society to stand by the Constitution and to encourage citizens generally to do likewise. He read a letter from President Harding, who has been invited to deliver an address at the Nashville Congress of the Sons of the American Revolution next May.

"General George Washington" was the theme of Rev. Dr. Frank A. Smith, Chaplain.

Exercises were held at the headquarters of the Society, 33 Lombardy Street, Newark, on the morning of Washington's Birthday anniversary, in charge of the Newark Chapter. Compatriot Sylvester H. M. Agens, President, presided. The invocation was offered by Rev. M. S. Waters, Historian of the State Society, and David L. Pierson, Secretary, gave an address on "The Stalwart Character of Washington." Afterward a procession was formed, and proceeding to the Washington statue, in Washington Park, a block away, a wreath was there placed as a tribute to the Father of His Country, in behalf of the Society.

NEWARK CHAPTER attended services at the Centenary M. E. Church, that city, on Sunday evening, February 18, when the pastor, Rev. James Brett McKenna, preached a patriotic sermon in remembrance of Washington.

A reception was tendered Major Washington I. L. Adams at the home of Compatriot Thomas W. Williams, former Vice-President General, at 78 North Arlington Avenue, East Orange, on Friday evening, March 16. The affair was arranged by Orange Chapter, and during the evening there were addresses by the guest of honor, Judge Adrian Lyon, President of the State Society, and by the host.

The annual meeting of the New Jersey Society will be held on Saturday, April 21, and the annual church service, in remembrance of Lexington and Concord, will be held in the Trinity Church Cathedral, Newark, on Sunday, April 22.

On Lincoln's Birthday anniversary, February 12, the State Secretary conducted, as he has done for the past twelve years, exercises at the East Orange City Hall, in memory of the martyred President, after which a procession was formed, and proceeding to the statue of Lincoln on the Parkway, a wreath was there placed as a tribute of the people of the city. Rev. Dr. George M. Gordon, a member of the Orange Chapter, offered the invocation.

Secretary David L. Pierson spoke at the meeting of the Rotary Club, Morristown, at noon and at the Hillside Grammar School in the afternoon of February 21. Members of the State organization attended the annual exercises at the Washington Headquarters, in Morristown, at noon on February 22. It was reported that the day was more generally observed than it had been at any other time in recent years in New Jersey, and that it was a hopeful sign of a return to the old-time patriotic standards in the era of peace.

A conference of the clergy of the State Society, Chapter Presidents, and members of the Board of Managers was held at the headquarters, 33 Lombardy Street, on January 31. Secretary David L. Pierson, who arranged the program, opened the meeting by announcing Rev. M. S. Waters, Historian, as the presiding officer, and from 11 a. m. till late in the afternoon there was a constant flow of ideas for increasing the usefulness of the Sons of the American Revolution, and particularly as to its relationship with the church, which was the theme of the morning session. Addresses were delivered by Judge Adrian Lyon, President; Bishop Wilson R. Stearly, Rev. Dr. Frank A. Smith, Rev. Joseph F. Folsom, Rev. George P. Eastman, Gilbert D. Maxwell, Vice-President Elvord G. Chamberlin, Rev. George P. Liggitt, Superintendent Frederick E. Emmons of the Elizabeth public schools, and a number of others. Bishop Stearly advocated the establishment of a Bureau of Speakers for the purpose of supplying speakers to organizations desiring patriotic addresses. This is now being considered by the Executive Committee, with these suggestions offered by Secretary Pierson:

That the clergymen recommend to presbyteries, classes, diocesan and other organizations of clergymen that either sermons be preached on the Sundays nearest the patriotic anniversaries or that some mention be made from the pulpit.

That the Flag of Stars and Stripes be presented at the altar of churches following the offertory or some other point in the service, and that "America" be sung.

That the men's clubs be requested to have a patriotic or a Sons of the American Revolution meeting once each year at least.

That the church women have one patriotic festival each year for children, with historical tableaux, flag drills, etc.

That the clergy induce their fellow-clergy to become members of the Sons of the American Revolution if eligible.

That the singing of patriotic selections be encouraged at meetings of the various church societies.

That the clergy enjoin upon congregations the display of the Flag of Stars and Stripes on the patriotic anniversaries, announcing them on the Sunday nearest the date.

That special effort be made to observe Constitution Day, September 17, and, where possible, have the church bell ring at the noon hour on the anniversary, calling the attention of the people to its advent.

That Sons of the American Revolution members pledge themselves in every possible way to assist the aliens to understand the living in harmony with the Constitution and the institutions of the country.

That all clubs, societies, and organizations of men be invited to co-operate in the forward movement patriotically.

That a Bureau of Speakers be established and all Sons of the American Revolution members gifted with public speaking enroll therein.

Illness prevented Major W. I. L. Adams, President General of the National Society of the Sons of the American Revolution, from being present Saturday afternoon, February 10, at a reception given in his honor at the headquarters of the State Society, 33 Lombardy Street. A framed picture of Major Adams, showing him in the regalia of his office, was presented to the Society by J. Stewart Gibson, President of the Montclair Chapter.

Mr. Gibson praised the work of Major Adams, who was both a charter member and past President of the Montclair Chapter, as National Executive, referring to the recent transcontinental trip, in which he visited many State Societies.

The picture was formally received by Judge Adrian Lyon, President of the New Jersey Society, in which he expressed appreciation to the Montclair members.

Memorials for Frederick B. Bassett and Augustus S. Crane, both long and active members of the Society, were read.

The reports of Secretary Pierson, Treasurer Frank E. Quinby, Registrar William J. Conkling, and Librarian Russell B. Rankin all showed the Society to be in a flourishing condition.

The Secretary was directed to write the Governor, the Senate, and the House of Assembly, favoring the bill now before the Legislature, which grants an appropriation for assistance with the Congress at Washington in building the memorial bridge across the Delaware River in commemoration of the crossing of the river by Washington and his troops.

Secretary Pierson reported he had attended a conference on Friday at the Y. W.

C. A., at which plans were discussed for a concentration of all Americanization work in the city under one management.

A series of patriotic luncheons, arranged for the second and fourth Wednesdays of each month, at the Essex Club, Newark, for members of the New Jersey Society, and inaugurated on February 14, have been proving a success in developing the spirit of good fellowship and general interest in the Society's welfare. They are given at noon, and after the menu has been served a speaker dwells on a popular subject for twenty minutes, bringing the entire assembly within the hour usually allowed for the lunch period. The speaker at the first one was President General Major Washington I. L. Adams. Judge Adrian Lyon addressed the compatriots on February 28 on the "Constitution of the United States and Its Relation to the Sons of the American Revolution."

The State Secretary gave an address at the annual Historian's Day of Orange Mountain Chapter, Daughters of the American Revolution, held in East Orange on February 26. On January 7 he addressed the Rotary Club of Newark at the Robert Treat Hotel, and at the meeting of the New England Society of Orange, on February 24, told the members of the wonderful awakening all over the country in the celebration of Washington's Birthday. Compatriot Thomas W. Williams, a former Vice-President General of the National Society, is President of this influential organization.

At a reception held at the headquarters on January 8 for newly elected members Rev. M. S. Waters, Historian, gave a very instructive address on "The Struggle of the English and the French for Supremacy on the North American Continent." He also exhibited a number of relics—bullets, buckles, etc.—taken from the battle-field at Fort Duquesne, at the time of Braddock's defeat, July 9, 1755.

The New Jersey Society has suffered a severe loss in the death of Augustus S. Crane, publisher of the *Elizabeth Daily Journal*, whose State and National number were 162. Compatriot Crane died at Summit, N. J., January 9.

ELIZABETHTOWN CHAPTER has been engaged in Americanization work through its committee, of which Compatriot Harry F. Brewer is chairman, by instructing aliens desiring to become citizens. The certificates of the Department of Labor have been given to a large number who have been passed by the superintendent of schools, thus saving the tedious waiting in the court of naturalization.

ORANGE CHAPTER held a very enjoyable meeting on January 19, the subject being "How to Make a National Anthem Poetically and Musically." During the program a number of slides containing musical scores were thrown upon a screen and concluded with the music of a new hymn, "America."

The Chapter also met on the evening of February 16, when Rev. Charles Thomas Walkley gave an address on "Some Side Lights of Colonial Literature," dealing principally with the conditions in England about the period of the Puritan disturbance. A. P. Bachman gave a paper on "The Witch of Whiskey Lane."

MONTCLAIR CHAPTER rose to very great heights on Sunday, February 25, when, under its auspices, the annual service at the beautiful First Congregational Church, in remembrance of the immortal Washington and his 191st birthday, attracted a congregation of over 1,500 persons.

J. Stewart Gibson, President of the Chapter, was in charge of the ceremonies, and the Pledge to the Flag was given by Major Washington I. L. Adams, President General, who is a member of the Board of Trustees of the church. Judge

NATIONAL SOCIETY, S. A. R.

Adrian Lyon, President of the State Society, brought the greetings of that organization, and the address was delivered by Rev. Dr. Howard Duffield, pastor of the First Presbyterian Church of New York City. He said that while Washington inveighed against entangling alliances he said nothing about "ennobling alliances."

NEWARK CHAPTER, at its meeting held at the home of Compatriot Edward S. Rankin on January 24, listened to three addresses—by Compatriot Rankin, on "Newark's Wonderful Heritage"; Rev. M. S. Waters, on "The Struggle of the English and the French for Supremacy in America," and Secretary David L. Pierson, on "The Suffering of the Troops of Washington at Morristown in the Winter of 1779-1780." The Newark Chapter quartet gave a number of excellent vocal selections.

Under the auspices of Montclair Chapter and the American Legion, a meeting will be held in the Wellmont Hall, Bloomfield Avenue, Montclair, on Thursday, April 26, for the reception of newly made citizens. Compatriot Gilbert D. Maxwell, chairman of the Chapter committee, is deeply interested in making the affair a great success, which it promises to be.

The President General has presented to the Montclair High School, through his home Chapter, a solid gold Sons of the American Revolution medal for the best essay by a senior of that school on an historical subject connected with our national history.

THE PASSAIC VALLEY CHAPTER, Sons of the American Revolution, and the Beacon Fire Chapter, Daughters of the American Revolution, both of Summit, N. J., held a joint reception in the Y. M. C. A. auditorium on the evening of February 22, 1923, in celebration of Washington's Birthday.

American flags were used artistically in a decorative effect. Instead of the guests and speakers being on the platform, they sat on the main floor, in a semicircle, with a background of palms and ferns. The effect was very homelike and cozy. The flags were fastened to the walls and suspended from the chandeliers. On the stage was draped a large flag, below which was a picture of the immortal Washington. In the center of the room was a long serving table, presided over by Mrs. Corby and Mrs. Meyer, dressed in colonial costumes, who supplied each guest with a small American flag.

The guests of honor were Mrs. Henry Dusenbury Fitts, New Jersey State Regent of the Daughters of the American Revolution, and John Lenord Merrill, of East Orange, past State President of New Jersey, Sons of the American Revolution, who made the principal address. After the addresses a social hour was enjoyed, during which refreshments were served by high-school boys and girls in colonial costume, in which they had previously danced a minuet.

The Beacon Fire Chapter, Daughters of the American Revolution, was organized only last December. It is a very wide-awake organization and will do much toward increased activity in Passaic Valley Chapter, Sons of the American Revolution.

PASSAIC VALLEY CHAPTER, at its meeting on January 13, discussed pro and con Muzzy's History and other text-books. An address on "The Patriotism of Abraham Lincoln" was given by Rev. Oscar R. Hawes.

CAPTAIN ABRAHAM GODWIN CHAPTER, of Paterson, at its meeting on January 29, received a report of its Committee on Pageant, of which Compatriot Ide Gill Sargeant is chairman. A most ambitious presentation is to be made in one of the parks of the city in the early summer, dealing in episodes relating to the history of Passaic County and of the city. It was here that Alexander Hamilton, in 1792, installed "The Society for Useful Manufactures," being the beginning of the industrial life of the country. Dr. Frank R. Sandt, who is actively engaged in furthering the observance of events leading to and through the War for American Independence, said that he hoped to have a general exhibition in the moving-picture theaters in the country of these scenes, beginning with the anniversary of the Boston Tea Party next December.

WEST FIELDS CHAPTER on February 15 enjoyed an evening devoted to the life of Washington, and on Sunday, February 18, attended service at the First Congregational Church, Westfield, at 4 p. m., when Rev. George P. Eastman, Chaplain of Orange Chapter, gave an address on Washington.

The New York (Empire State) Society.—Compatriot Col. Henry W. Sackett has presented to the Society a silk "Bunker Hill" flag, and Compatriot William L. Allen a silk "Bourbon" flag, a replica of the one used by Lafayette in the Revolution. Compatriot George Royce Brown has presented the Color Guard with a set of 36 brassards. The annual meeting of the Society will be held on April 19, at the Army and Navy Club, 112 West 59th Street, New York City, at which time the election of officers and delegates to the National Society Congress will take place.

Compatriot Louis Annin Ames, Past President General of the National Society, represented the Society at the funeral of the late Hon. Morris B. Beardsley, Past President General, at Bridgeport, on March 7, and was one of the pall-bearers.

NEW YORK CHAPTER.—The regular meeting of the Chapter was held on Wednesday evening, February 21, at 8 p. m. As usual, the dinner was held at 6.30 p. m., at which over 150 members were in attendance. The guests were President General W. I. Lincoln Adams, Director General Marvin H. Lewis, of the National Society; Col. C. Robert Churchill, President of the Louisiana Society, and Hon. Henry Lane Wilson, member of the Indiana Society and former Ambassador from the United States to Mexico, who as speaker of the evening made a most interesting address on "George Washington," which was received with much appreciation by the compatriots present. This address will be published in the April Bulletin of the Empire State Society and sent to each member. The next meeting of the Chapter will be held on April 19, 1923.

The annual church service was held on February 18, at the Church of the Divine Paternity. The sermon was by Rev. Joseph Fort Newton, D. D., Chaplain of the Chapter, and a reception was held in the parish house after the service.

BUFFALO CHAPTER.—The Buffalo Chapter celebrated Washington's Birthday with a dinner at the Lafayette Hotel on February 22. The Chapter was fortunate in having some very distinguished guests at this banquet, and the occasion was one of the most delightful ever held by this Society. The guest of honor and principal speaker was Rev. Josiah Sibley, D. D., of the Second Presbyterian Church of Chicago. Doctor Sibley came to the Buffalo Chapter on the recommendation of Vice-President General Louis A. Bowman. The high praise bestowed upon Doctor Sibley by Compatriot Bowman was more than borne out when that eloquent and scholarly gentleman addressed the Chapter. Doctor Sibley is a speaker of rare charm and great force. He carries his hearers with him from the moment of beginning to the final eloquent closing, and there is never an instant that his audience is not stirred with his remarkable power of expression and his original

NATIONAL SOCIETY, S. A. R. 53

and stirring thoughts. His subject was the "Soul of America," and his masterful treatment of that great idea was such that the Chapter will remember this event for many years to come. The Chapter was more than fortunate to have with it on this occasion not only the splendid Regent of the Buffalo Chapter, Daughters of the American Revolution, Mrs. John Millor Horton, who spoke in her usually delightful and charming manner, but also, on account of our sister Chapter having had a Washington's Birthday celebration on the same afternoon, the dinner was graced by the presence of Mrs. Anthony Wayne Cook, of Cooksville, Pa., who it is understood is a candidate for President General of the Daughters of the American Revolution, and also by the presence of Mrs. Charles Nash, the State Regent of New York State Daughters of the American Revolution. Both of these charming ladies gave delightful greetings from their respective National and State Organizations. The dinner was presided over by the President, Commander Thomas W. Harris, and about seventy-five ladies and gentlemen attended.

THE NEWBURGH CHAPTER.—At the meeting of this Chapter on February 27th, a "Flag Etiquette" was adopted, and it will be printed for distribution among the various patriotic organizations. The business meeting was preceded by a dinner. The Rev. S. F. White addressed the members on the "Greatness of a Country." The Chapter is to place a Sons of the American Revolution marker on the grave of Jeremiah Webb, a Revolutionary soldier, at Andes, Delaware County, New York at an early date.

THE ROCHESTER CHAPTER.—At the annual meeting of the Chapter the following officers were elected to act for the coming year: Raymond G. Dann, President; Wm. B. Boothby, Vice-President; Edward J. Seeber, Secretary; John B. Howe, Treasurer; Edward R. Foreman, Registrar; A. Emerson Babcock, Historian; Rev. James T. Dickinson, D. D., Chaplain.

SYRACUSE CHAPTER.—The Syracuse Chapter held a very pleasant and profitable meeting on the evening of February 22, in commemoration of Washington's Birthday, at the home of Compatriot and Mrs. H. Winfield Chapin, in James Street. The meeting was addressed by Mr. Franklin H. Chase, Associate Editor of the Syracuse *Journal*, giving some interesting data of his recent trip of two years in the Orient and Europe.

NEWBURGH CHAPTER.—At the banquet of the Sons of the American Revolution given in the banquet hall of Crook's restaurant, Newburgh, the Rev. Dr. S. F. White, the speaker of the evening, spoke on the greatness of the United States and the qualities in a man necessary to make him a fit American citizen. After the address regular business of the organization was transacted.

During the regular business, the Chapter approved of the appointment of Samuel L. Stewart and the Rev. J. Woodman Babbitt as delegates to the National Congress, which will be held in Nashville, Tenn., in May, and James W. Barnes as member of the board of managers of the Empire State Society. The Rev. Mr. Babbitt, for the Committee of Flag Etiquette, told of the modification by headquarters of the displaying of flags. He was authorized to procure 250 copies of these modified regulations. They are on cardboard 7½ inches by 13 inches and will be distributed among the schools and organizations in Newburgh for their guidance and use of flags on patriotic occasions.

Communications were received from the Empire State Society and a relative in LaPorte, Indiana, asked that the Newburgh Chapter mark the grave of Jeremiah Webb, a Revolutionary soldier, who died at Stamford, Conn., on

October 22, 1830, and who was buried at Andes, Delaware County, New York. As soon as the weather permits, the Newburgh Chapter will set a bronze marker over the grave. Webb served in two companies of the Connecticut militia. President Perkins approved of a membership committee of the board of managers of the Empire State Society. A number of requests have been received from citizens of Newburgh to become members of the organization.

It was voted that hereafter the regular monthly meeting will be held on the fourth Tuesday of the month. The entertainment committee will endeavor to procure interesting speakers for these meetings. There was also some talk about the annual banquet, to be held in the Palatine Hotel on April 19, the anniversary of the Battle of Lexington. The committee will try to obtain the services of the Rev. S. Parkes Cadman, of Brooklyn, as speaker.

The Ohio Society.—The Chapters in the larger cities have been quite active along Americanization lines—assisting foreigners in preparing their applications for naturalization; distributing copies of the Constitution of the United States and of our booklet, "Information for Immigrants," and holding public ceremonies before judges of the United States courts, to which the families of the applicants are invited. These meetings, with short patriotic addresses by members and inspiring patriotic songs, have been interesting and greatly enjoyed by the families, who take pride in their new citizenship. The State officers have distributed hundreds of copies of the Constitution of the United States and our booklet, "How to display the Flag," to the public schools in the State, and a number of appreciative letters have been received from superintendents of these schools, and many of the schools observed the birthday anniversaries of both Washington and Lincoln.

One Chapter has been organized—Lafayette Chapter, at Akron. A petition was filed December 28, 1922, by members of the Society residing in Summit County, Ohio, requesting authority to organize a Chapter with jurisdiction in the County of Summit. January 4, 1923, a warrant was issued by the State officers authorizing the organization of a Chapter. The members of this Chapter have a good field for recruiting. They are enthusiastic and give promise of active service along patriotic lines.

RICHARD MONTGOMERY CHAPTER, at Dayton, seems to have the lead in the number of interesting meetings held during the year, which is reported for the encouragement of other Chapters. This Chapter reports nine special meetings during the year, celebrating patriotic anniversaries with members of the D. A. R., and are assisting them in building up a reference library.

ETHAN ALLEN CHAPTER, organized just one year ago, has doubled its membership. An interesting meeting was held at Steubenville February 22. The members joined the Daughters of the American Revolution in observance of the day with a banquet and a number of fine addresses, interspersed with patriotic songs. Hon. Joseph B. Doyle, Historian General of the National Society, was one of the speakers, who made a patriotic talk on Washington and his high character, and he said there were two great traits of his character which in the passing years we did not hear much about—his truthfulness and his religion. He was a sincere Christian and had faith in God and called upon Him in the crisis of our Government. In evidence of this great trait of character Mr. Doyle read Washington's prayer, sent out to the Governors of the States on June 8, 1783, which is as apropos today as it was in the founding of the American Government.

The alphabetical list of battles of the Revolution, published in the Year Book for 1922, is commended very highly by librarians in the State, as they have so many inquiries with reference to them. Sixty members have been admitted to the State Society since the last annual meeting, April last, and it has been a busy and prosperous year in patriotic service.

LAFAYETTE CHAPTER of Akron is the newest organization of the Ohio Society and held its initial organization meeting on January 31. Cordial letters of greeting and encouragement were received on this occasion from Mrs. J. M. Allen, Regent of the Cuyahoga Portage Chapter of the Daughters of the American Revolution, and Mrs. E. E. Crites, President of the Anna Hudson Chapter of the Children of the American Revolution, both of whom expressed great satisfaction at the realization of the efforts of those who had interested themselves in the new organization, and assuring personal co-operation in interesting new members to join. Officers of Lafayette Chapter were elected as follows: President, Edward L. Howe; Vice-President, James G. Grant; Registrar, Charles Henry Stinaff; Secretary-Treasurer, Mason Jay Snow. A second meeting was held shortly after, at which Hon. D. C. Rybolt, Mayor of Akron, addressed the members on patriotism. A later meeting is scheduled for April 19, when, if weather permits, the grounds of the beautiful home of President Howe will be opened for a patriotic meeting befitting the occasion.

The Oklahoma Society.—A most enjoyable meeting was held on February 22, with a splendid address on George Washington by Compatriot H. H. Hagan, of Tulsa.

Compatriot Hagan drew a picture of Washington's life and character that was not only inspiring and brilliant, but also gave his auditors an insight into the daily life of this great man that was most clear and enlightening. Among other things he said: "Unfortunately, Washington has become a tradition, a vague demigod enveloped in a cloud of dignity, and our age scoffs at tradition and has forgotten dignity. The strong, incorruptible, unselfish, clear, and far-sighted Washington has become a dim personality, whose example is rarely followed and whose only precept generally remembered is his warning against entangling alliances. . . . Yet there is no one from whom the present generation could with greater profit catch inspiration. Washington loved freedom. . . . Unless a halt is made, we are rapidly approaching the day when the conduct of the individual will be so circumscribed by oppressive, petty, and obnoxious regulation that individual liberty in this country will be completely destroyed. . . . Washington rose superior to the fetters of partisanship and the clamors of factions. He recognized only one guide, one mentor, the good of the whole commonwealth, the welfare of the entire citizenship. When he thought the best interests of the Government dictated otherwise, he was unswerving and uncompromising in his determination, and no amount of public outcry could change his decision or influence his course of action." After a most comprehensive summing up of Washington's life and character, Mr. Hagan ended his masterly address with these impressive words: "Let us resolve that the priceless heritage of Washington, he of whom it has been fittingly said that God left him childless in order that he might be the father of his country—let us resolve that his heritage, the heritage of a nation united, of a nation proud and inviolate, of a nation whose people are free, just, contented, and God-fearing, of a nation whose institutions are unoppressive, whose motives are pure, whose traditions are glorious, whose ideals are unsullied—let us resolve that that heritage shall not be lost or surrendered or little by little frittered away, but that we will hand it down to our children as it was bequeathed to us by our fathers, intact and reverenced, so that to them and to all mankind America may continue to be a land of liberty, of justice, of tolerance—the hope and inspiration of the world."

The election of officers resulted as follows: Ben W. Riley, Oklahoma City, President; L. A. Norton, Duncan, H. H. Hagan, Tulsa, and W. S. Kerfoot, Hinton, Vice-Presidents; E. F. McKay, Secretary-Treasurer (re-elected); J. B. Thoburn, Historian (re-elected); George R. Tabor, Oklahoma City, Registrar; George L. Bowman, Kingfisher, Trustee; L. C. Murray, Tulsa, Chaplain; A. N. Leecraft, H. T. Deupree, and L. H. Buxton, Managers.

A committee, headed by Compatriot R. L. Williams, judge of the United States District Court for the Eastern District of Oklahoma, was appointed to arrange a marker or tablet at the grave of Montfort Stokes, the only veteran of the Revolutionary War known to have been buried in the soil of what is now the State of Oklahoma. Because the exact location of the grave is not known, the memorial will be built in a small inclosure on a little knoll near Fort Gibson, where the veteran rests with others of his fellows.

The Oregon Society was favored by a visit of President General W. I. Lincoln Adams and Vice-President General George Albert Smith on January 12-13. A most cordial welcome was extended to the distinguished guests by officials and members of the State Society. They were entertained at luncheon and dinner on January 12 by Past President General Wallace McCamant. On January 13 the Board of Managers of the Oregon Society gave a luncheon to the President General, the Vice-President General, and Past President General McCamant. On the evening of January 13 a most enjoyable reception was held, more than one hundred compatriots and numerous guests, representing the Grand Army of the Republic, the American Legion, and other patriotic societies, being present. Dr. Stuart McGuire, a favorite Portland singer, added to the enjoyment of the evening with several finely rendered vocal selections. The visit of the National Society officials was a season of refreshment and inspiration to the Oregon Society, and will undoubtedly result in more general interest and activity among the members.

The annual meeting of the Oregon Society was held on February 22, and officers for the ensuing year were elected as follows: President, B. B. Beekman; Vice-President, Winthrop Hammond; Secretary, B. A. Thaxter; Treasurer, H. C. Ewing; Registrar, Alfred Parker; members of the Board of Managers, B. S. Sanford, P. P. Dabney, J. S. Cooper, Jr., and H. L. Bates. Compatriot H. C. Ewing was elected as successor to Compatriot A. A. Lindsley, who has served as Treasurer for seventeen consecutive years, but whom ill-health compelled to resign on February 8. In recognition of Compatriot Lindsay's long and devoted service to the Society, he was elected a life member and awarded the insignia of the Sons of the American Revolution as a token of appreciation. Compatriot Bates was elected a member of the Board of Managers to fill the vacancy caused by the death of Compatriot Charles F. Beebe. All the other named officers were re-elected. The election of Delegates to the Annual Congress to be held at Nashville in May and nomination of Trustee of the National Society for Oregon were delegated to the Board of Managers.

The Society at the annual meeting authorized the offering of the customary prizes of $25.00, $15.00, and $10.00 for the best three essays on subjects relating to the American Revolution, submitted by school children of the State during the scholastic year of 1923-24.

The Society also voted an appropriation of $100.00 to the Oregon State Library for traveling libraries made up of volumes dealing with the Revolutionary War period. The State Library already has sixteen such traveling libraries, provided from funds donated by the Oregon Society. The report of the State Librarian shows that these libraries have been in constant use and have been forwarded to all sections of the State. These traveling libraries have been very helpful in connection with the annual essay competitions, but their use has not been confined to school children.

The annual banquet of the Oregon Society was held on the evening of February 22, at the University Club, in Portland. There was a good attendance and a most enjoyable program of addresses and music. The addresses were as follows: "Washington—the Sleepless Sentinel of Our Free Institutions," by Dr. William Wallace Youngson; "Then and Now," by Compatriot Captain James S. Gay, Jr., Past State Commander, Veterans of Foreign Wars; "An Associate of Washington," by Compatriot Judge Robert Tucker. Mr. A. E. Davidson was soloist of the evening, with Compatriot Ralph W. Hoyt as accompanist.

On the evening of February 22 a reception was tendered at the Portland Public Auditorium to seven hundred citizens naturalized during the past year. The meeting was held under the auspices of the Portland Americanization Council, a beneficiary of the Portland Community Chest, and sponsored and conducted by representatives of numerous civic and patriotic organizations. Both the Daughters and the Sons of the American Revolution are affiliated withh this Council. The Auditorium was thronged and splendid addresses of welcome and encouragement were delivered. Each of the new citizens was presented with a silk American flag.

The Rhode Island Society.—The annual meeting of the Rhode Island Society was held on Thursday, February 22, at 12 o'clock, noon, at the rooms of the Rhode Island Historical Society, on Waterman Street, in Providence, for the election of officers and transaction of other business.

Luncheon was served at the rooms of the Historical Society after the meeting. The annual dinner was held at 6:30 o'clock that evening, at the Turks Head Club. The banquet exercises included addresses by Telfair Minton, Esq., of Boston, whose subject was "History and Evolution of the Flag of the United States of America"; Hon. Marvin H. Lewis, of Louisville, Ky., Director General of the National Society, who was the guest of honor, and Hon. Chester W. Barrows, of Providence, Justice of the Superior Court of Rhode Island.

Resolutions "viewing as un-American," any proposal to substitute another language for English as the vehicle of instruction in Rhode Island schools were unanimously adopted. Copies of the resolutions, which urge the General Assembly to "keep intact the educational legislation of 1922," were ordered forwarded to the Senate, the House of Representatives, and the Governor.

Addison Pierce Munroe, Vice-President of the Society, was elected President to succeed Herbert A. Rice, and Dr. George Thurston Spicer was elected Vice-President. Other officers elected at the business meeting were: Secretary, Theodore Everett Dexter; Treasurer, William Luther Sweet; Registrar, Edward Kimball Aldrich; Historian, Charles Dean Kimball; Chaplain, Rev. Alfred H. Wheeler; Poet, William Mabley Muncy.

The Tennessee Society.—The annual February 22 dinner of the Tennessee Society, held at the Chamber of Commerce, in Nashville, brought out the largest gathering of the compatriots in the history of the Society. President Boardman briefly touched upon the plans made for the entertainment of the Thirty-fourth Annual Congress in May, and the short business session was followed by an able and eloquent address by Dr. Charles Turck, of Vanderbilt University Law School. The flag ceremony was in charge of Captain Douglas Henry, Commander of Davidson County Post, No. 6, of the American Legion. Twenty-eight gentlemen were admitted to membership at the meeting. Some years ago, while visiting Mount Vernon, Compatriot L. W. Culbreath, of Stanton, Tenn., was presented with a root of the ivy growing on Washington's tomb. He brought it home and planted it. Dr. Culbreath sent to us for the dinner a generous box of the ivy, which formed the table decorations.

The Texas Society.—Owing to the fact that it was impossible to secure a quorum for an annual meeting on Washington's birthday, February 22, this meeting was postponed until April 21, 1923, San Jacinto Day, commemorating the battle of San Jacinto, when Texas gained her freedom from Mexico, at Hotel Galvez, at 10 o'clock a. m. San Jacinto Day is a Texas holiday.

It is the desire of the officers and Board of Managers to have as large a meeting as possible, as it has been several years since this Society has had a meeting, and there are many matters of importance to be brought up and voted on.

At the National Convention to be held this year in Nashville, Tenn., on May 21 and 22, it is the desire that as large a representation from the Southern states as possible attend this meeting. Delegates will be appointed from the Texas Society to attend this Congress at the meeting to be held April 21.

The Utah Society.—At the annual meeting of this Society, held on December 26, 1922, the following officers were chosen for the ensuing year: President, John Quayle Cannon; Vice-President, Abbot Rodney Heywood; Secretary, Gordon Lines Hutchins; Treasurer, Elias Smith Woodruff; Registrar, Chauncey P. Overfield; Historian, Levi Edgar Young; Chaplain, Rev. Hoyt E. Henriques; National Trustee, Daniel Samuel Spencer.

At the same meeting of the Society it was unanimously decided to invite the National Society of the Sons of the American Revolution to hold the Thirty-fifth Annual Congress in Salt Lake City during the summer of 1924. The Utah Society is composed of two hundred and twenty members and is both numerically and financially able to properly entertain the National Congress and will esteem it an honor and a privilege to have an opportunity of extending a very cordial western welcome.

The official reception and entertainment of President General W. I. Lincoln Adams took place on January 10. The President General was met at Ogden by Vice-President General Hon. George Albert Smith and a committee of compatriots as escort to Salt Lake City, where he was escorted to the Utah Hotel, afterward being taken on a tour of the city by the Vice-President General and the President of the Society. In the evening he was entertained at a dinner at the Hotel Utah, attended by President General John Q. Cannon, former Presidents Judge M. L. Ritchie, G. L. Hutchins, D. R. Gray, Vice-President General George Albert Smith, Professor Levi Edgar Young, Dr. E. S. Wright, George J. Gibson, and Joseph Kimball. A most delightful evening was enjoyed.

He was entertained at a special organ recital at the Tabernacle, after which he was tendered a luncheon at the Alta Club, the guests including many present and past officers of the Society. After the luncheon the President General was escorted to Ft. Douglas, where a reception was tendered in his honor by the officers at the Post.

The President General then proceeded to the Utah State Capitol and addressed a joint session of the Utah State Legislature.

In the evening a banquet was given at the Hotel Utah in his honor, which was attended by ninety-seven compatriots, guests, and their ladies. This was one of the most delightful occasions in the history of the Society in Utah.

With deep regret the Utah Society announces the death of Hon. Abbot Rodney Heywood, Vice-President of the Utah Society of the Sons of the American Revolution, which occurred at Ogden, Utah, January 9, 1923. We do not have to dwell upon the unusual and magnificent qualities of Major Heywood, and his passing leaves a niche that it will be difficult to fill.

The Washington Society.—SEATTLE CHAPTER, at its meeting on November 4, 1922, adopted the following resolution with regard to school text-books:

WHEREAS, The free public school, originating and developing in America, giving American youth the education and training so necessary to a life of usefulness and good citizenship, is one of the most valuable of all American institutions and one of the principal bulwarks of liberty and independence; and

WHEREAS, National safety and national unity demand the maintenance of our public-school system free from the influences, whether foreign or domestic, which tend to degrade American ideals and to corrupt our national traditions; and

WHEREAS, Among America's richest treasures are its Revolutionary history, the Boston tea party, Paul Revere's ride, Putnam leaving his plow in the field, Lexington, Bunker Hill, Patrick Henry's speech, Valley Forge, Saratoga, Yorktown, great landmarks of a heroic race, as daring in conception, as thrilling in execution, as momentous in result as anything in ancient romance, the divine birthright of every American child, in which he absorbs and lives and breathes the very spirit that made this United States; and

WHEREAS, Indisputable evidence proves an insidious and treacherous propaganda in operation to place in our public schools American history text-books designed to destroy faith in the forefathers and respect for American history and institutions;

Now, therefore, be it Resolved, That Seattle Chapter, Sons of the American Revolution, realizing that eternal vigilance is the price of peace, freedom, and security, regards with grave concern this condition in our schools, and urges upon our educational authorities (school boards, superintendents, supervisors, principals, and teachers) the vital need for a careful review of American history text-books, that steps may be taken to bar obnoxious books from our schools, and that only such text-books be permitted therein as teach the simple heroic truth of American history, and written not by aliens, but by American historians.

House Bill No. 170, referring to the proper selection of school history text-books, was introduced in the Washington State Legislature at the session just closed. This bill was drawn by a member of Seattle Chapter, Compatriot Harry Denton Moore, and was introduced into the House by another member of Seattle Chapter, Compatriot William Phelps Totten. It passed the House by a vote of 70 to 4. It was placed on the Senate calendar too late, and the Senate adjourned before it was reached. There seems little doubt that it would have been passed if the Senate had been given a chance to vote on it.

Since March 8, 1922, there were held by this Chapter 35 luncheons (meetings of the Chapter) to December 31, 1922, and during 1923, to date, 10 luncheon meetings—a total of 45 meetings since the last election of officers. The Chapter marched in the Independence Day parade, July 4, 1922, and again with the Americanization parade, directed by the Veterans of Foreign Wars, August 19, 1922, with our Bunker Hill Phalanx in Revolutionary uniform.

Gold, silver, and bronze medals were presented to the winners of the annual high school oratorical contest, held Wednesday evening, February 21, in the Broadway High, the presentation being made at the annual banquet following the annual meeting of the Washington State Society, February 22, 1923.

ADDITIONS TO MEMBERSHIP

There have been enrolled by the Registrar-General from November 30, 1922, to March 1, 1923, 245 new members as follows: California, 15; District of Columbia, 7; Illinois, 9; Indiana, 13; Iowa, 5; Kansas, 3; Kentucky, 7; Louisiana, 15; Maine, 8; Maryland, 7; Massachusetts, 16; Michigan, 2; Minnesota, 10; Missouri, 2; Nebraska, 3; New Jersey, 15; New Mexico, 2; New York (Empire State), 24; North Dakota, 1; Ohio, 3; Oklahoma, 2; Oregon, 8; Pennsylvania, 19; Rhode Island, 17; South Dakota, 3; Tennessee, 17; Texas, 1; Utah, 2; Virginia, 4; Washington, 3; Wyoming, 2.

In Memoriam

EDWARD M. ADAMS, California Society, died April 13, 1922.

GILMER SPEED ADAMS, Kentucky Society, died November 26, 1922.

J. DEXTER ADAMS, Rear-Admiral, U. S. Navy, Massachusetts Society, died February —, 1922.

ROBERT E. ADRION, Missouri Society, died January 6, 1923.

HENRY CLAY ALDRICH, Minnesota Society, died September 28, 1922.

DWIGHT B. BAKER, Empire State Society, died December 12, 1922.

MORRIS BEACH BEARDSLEY, Past President-General, National Society, Past Vice-President General, Past President Connecticut Society, died March 2, 1923.

CHARLES F. BEEBE, Oregon Society, died November 20, 1922.

ORRIN LUTHER BOSWORTH, Rhode Island Society, died December 25, 1922.

GEORGE SAMUEL BURCH, Minnesota Society, died May 4, 1922.

WILLIAM S. CARR, Empire State Society, died July 16, 1922.

CHARLES E. CLARK, Rear-Admiral, U. S. Navy, Vermont Society, died October 1, 1922.

EDWIN CLARK, Minnesota Society, died — —, 1922.

ARTHUR B. CLARKE, President, Virginia Society, Member National Board of Trustees, died December 24, 1922.

RENSSELAER JAY COE, Wisconsin Society, died February —, 1923.

AMEDEE B. COLE, Missouri Society, died November 2, 1922.

CHARLES CUMMINGS COLLINS, Missouri Society, died September 21, 1922.

HENRY F. CONDICT, California Society, died March 19, 1922.

CLEMENT H. CONE, Vermont Society, died January 13, 1922.

PEREZ DICKINSON COWAN, New Jersey Society, died February 10, 1923.

AUGUSTUS S. CRANE, New Jersey Society, died January 9, 1923.

OLIVER CROSBY, Minnesota Society, died December 8, 1922.

HENRY T. CUSHMAN, Vermont Society, died May 14, 1922.

WALTER ALONZO DAVIS, Massachusetts Society, died October 17, 1921.

WILLIAM BEAKE DEAN, Minnesota Society, died December 5, 1922.

CHARLES L. DENISON, New Jersey Society, died December 16, 1922.

JOHN W. DINSMORE, California Society, died April 3, 1922.

JAMES BARTLETT EDGERLY, New Hampshire Society, died November 1, 1922.

GEORGE BRAYTON EVANS, Minnesota Society, died June 7, 1922.

IRA H. EVANS, California Society, died April 19, 1922.

SHERMAN EVARTS, Vermont Society, died — —, 1922.

CHARLES WESLEY FAITOUT, New Jersey Society, died December 4, 1922.

JOHN R. FISHER, New Jersey Society, died February 26, 1923.

WALTER K. FLETCHER, California Society, died July 24, 1922.

ELKANAH M. GIBSON, California Society, died May 10, 1922.

HENRY A. GOODRICH, Massachusetts Society, died April 20, 1922.

EDGAR FLETCHER GOULD, Minnesota Society, died February 18, 1923.

ELIJAH ATWOOD GOVE, Minnesota Society, died September 5, 1922.

ALBERT BALLARD HAMMOND, Massachusetts Society, died October 22, 1922.

EDWARD J. HAND, Empire State Society, died December 6, 1922.

SAMUEL HASKINS, California Society, died October 24, 1922.

JOHN W. HATCH, California Society, died October 24, 1922.

CHARLES D. HAVEN, California Society, died October 10, 1922.

ROBERT W. HEMPHILL, JR., Michigan Society, died December 8, 1922.

In Memoriam

CHARLES OSCAR HENNION, New Jersey Society, died December 21, 1922.

GEORGE E. HERRICK, Massachusetts Society, died August 5, 1922.

FRED A. HODGE, Minnesota Society, died June 19, 1922.

ANSEL A. HOWARD, Michigan Society, died February 23, 1923.

GEORGE T. JESTER, Texas Society, died July 19, 1922.

EDWARD EVERETT KEITH, Massachusetts Society, died June 10, 1921.

FRANK W. KENT, New Jersey Society, died February 27, 1923.

ARTHUR LITTLE KINGSBURY, Massachusetts Society, died November 20, 1922.

GEORGE KITCHELL, New Jersey Society, died February 9, 1923.

ALBERT E. LAYMAN, Empire State Society, died November 28, 1922.

HOMER LEE, Empire State Society, died January 25, 1923.

HARVEY D. LOVELAND, California Society, died June 11, 1922.

BRIANT HALSEY MARSH, New Jersey Society, died January 1, 1923.

ALBERT M. MARSHALL, Michigan Society, died February 4, 1923.

FREEMONT RUSSELL McMANIGAL, Minnesota Society, died March 9, 1923.

CAPTAIN JOHN H. MOORE, U. S. Navy (retired), Past Vice-President General National Society and Past President, District of Columbia Society, died February 3, 1923.

CHARLES B. MORRISON, Virginia Society, died —— ——, 1919.

CHARLES MYERS, Indiana Society, died February 12, 1920.

ICHABOD A. OLMSTEAD, Empire State Society, died October 27, 1922.

EDGAR PAINTER, California Society, died June 11, 1922.

BOWDOIN STRONG PARKER, Massachusetts Society, died December 19, 1922.

ALLEN MILLARD PECK, Rhode Island Society, died November 9, 1922.

JAMES K. PENFIELD, Empire State Society, died February 8, 1923.

BENJAMIN FRANKLIN QUACKENBUSH, New Jersey Society, died December 21, 1922.

RUXTON MOORE RIDGLY, Maryland Society, died December 7, 1922.

CHARLES E. RITTENHOUSE, Past President Minnesota Society, died January 13, 1923.

EDWIN W. SAMMIS, Empire State Society, died January 16, 1923.

THOMAS MUNROE SHEPHERD, Massachusetts Society, died February 4, 1923.

FRANK E. SMITH, Vermont Society, died July 19, 1922.

FRANKLIN T. SMITH, Wisconsin Society, died February ——, 1923.

FREDERICK B. SPELMAN, Minnesota Society, died February 1, 1923.

CHARLES B. SWARTWOOD, Empire State Society, died February 8, 1923.

LLEWELLYN H. THURSTON, Montana Society, died February 19, 1923.

DANIEL W. TOWER, Michigan Society, died February ——, 1923.

FRANK B. TURPIN, California Society, died September 30, 1922.

WALLACE VAN NESS, New Jersey Society, died January 18, 1923.

EDWARD H. WALES, Empire State Society, died October 31, 1922.

PAUL T. M. WATE, California Society, died December 13, 1922.

J. FRANK WATSON, Oregon Society, died December 23, 1922.

LEWIS ANTHONY WATERMAN, Rhode Island Society, died January 12, 1923.

FLOYD WELLMAN, Kansas Society, died November 29, 1922.

A. G. WHITTEMORE, Vermont Society, died January 11, 1922.

AUSTIN WILKINS, Vermont Society, died March 19, 1922.

HENRY C. WORTH, California Society, died June 1, 1922.

JOHN M. WRIGHT, California Society, died November 2, 1922.

RECORDS OF 245 NEW MEMBERS AND 60 SUPPLEMENTALS APPROVED AND ENROLLED BY THE REGISTRAR-GENERAL FROM DECEMBER 1, 1922, TO APRIL 1, 1923.

GEORGE ARETAS AGNEW, Central City, Nebr. (36997). Son of George Crawford and Nannie Bell (Richards) Agnew; grandson of Isaiah S. and Jane (Secrest) Richards; great-grandson of John and Margaret (Spaid) Richards; great²-grandson of John and Hannah (Anderson) Spaid; great³-grandson of George Nicholas and Elizabeth (Cale) Spaid; great⁴-grandson of *John Cale*, private, Eighth Regt., Virginia Militia.

WILLIAM VINCENT ALLABEN, Iowa City, Iowa (37657). Son of W. N. and Vinnie M. (Redmond) Allaben, Jr.; grandson of W. N. and Martha (Todd) Allaben; great-grandson of Samuel and Abigail (Abels) Todd, Jr., great²-grandson of *Samuel Todd, Sr.*, private, Fifth Regt., Connecticut Cont'l Line, pensioned.

ABRAM PIATT ANDREW, La Porte, Ind. (37820). Son of Abraham Piatt and Viola Jane (Armstrong) Andrew; grandson of James and Catherine (Piatt) Andrew; great-grandson of *John Andrew (Andrews)*, Surgeon, New Jersey Militia; great-grandson of *Abraham Piatt*, Major, Somerset County, New Jersey Militia and Captain, Northumberland County, Pennsylvania Troops; grandson of *John* and Tabitha (Goforth) *Armstrong*, Lieutenant and Captain, Third Regt., Pennsylvania Cont'l Troops; great-grandson of *William Goforth*, Major, Second Battalion, Col. Philip Van Cortlandt's Regt., New York Troops.

F. DUVAL ARMSTRONG, New Orleans, La. (38105). Son of Henry Sweppe and Geraldine (Duval) Armstrong; grandson of Francis and Susan H. (Sweppe) Armstrong; great-grandson of John and Deborah (Hart) Armstrong; great²-grandson of Jesse and Martha (Matteson) Hart; great³-grandson of *John Hart*, Signer of the Declaration of Independence, Captain, New Jersey Blues.

HARRY SAXE ARMSTRONG, New Orleans, La. (38106). Same as F. Duval Armstrong, Louisiana (38105).

EDWARD CROSBY BADEAU, Staten Island, N. Y. (37925). Son of Charles Benson and Kate (Rose) Badeau; grandson of Edward Crosby and Cynthia (Dean) Badeau; great-grandson of Samuel and Cynthia (Chichester) Dean; great²-grandson of *Samuel Dean*, private, Connecticut Militia and Cont'l Troops.

DONALD BAKER, Terre Haute, Ind. (37816). Son of Harry J. and Elizabeth (Hamill) Baker; grandson of Samuel Ripley and Martha (Wood) Hamill; great-grandson of George and Mary (Ripley) Hamill; great²-grandson of *Samuel Ripley*, private, Col. Samuel Lyon's Regt., Pennsylvania Militia.

HAMILL WOOD BAKER, Terre Haute, Ind. (38278). Same as Donald Baker, Indiana (37816).

HENRY FENIMORE BAKER, Md. (21741). Supplemental. Son of Milton and Henrietta (Boozer) Baker; grandson of William and Susanna Pettinger (Maxwell) Boozer; great-grandson of Joseph and Rachel (Fenimore) Boozer; great²-grandson of *Jonathan Fenimore (Fenemore)*, Matross, Fourth Regt., Pennsylvania Cont'l Artillery.

HENRY SILL BALDWIN, Swampscott, Mass. (38134). Son of James Garrison and Hannah Arnold (Sill) Baldwin; grandson of Henry Ward and Sophia Matilda (Arnold) Sill; great-grandson of Thomas and Clarissa (Treadway) Sill; great²-grandson of *Micah Sill*, private, Capt. Jewett's Co., Connecticut Militia at Lexington Alarm.

EDWIN PERRY BANTA, West New York, N. J. (37916.) Son of Edwin Perry and Sarah Ann (Gibson) Banta; grandson of George Weart and Martha Melissa (Hovell) Banta; great-grandson of Petrus and Catherine (Bruce) Banta; great²-grandson of *Jan (John) Banta*, private, Bergen County, New Jersey Militia.

FLOYD NELSON BARBER, Crafton, Pa. (37736). Son of Brewster Oliver and Ann Elizabeth (Henry) Barber; grandson of Harmon and Locena L. (Daniels) Barber; great-grandson of Reuben and Polly (Larkom) Daniels; great²-grandson of *Paul Larkcom*, private, Berkshire County, Massachusetts Militia.

ROBERT STEVENS BARTLETT, New York City, N. Y. (37917). Son of John Stevens and Maria (Maxwell) Bartlett; grandson of Silas and Hester Ann (Maxwell) Haight;

great-grandson of Moses and Phoebe (Mosher) Haight; great²-grandson of *Silas Haight,* private, Sixth Regt., Dutchess County, New York Militia.

MARK ALTON BARWISE, Bangor, Me. (38178). Son of Frank Herbert and Nellie Emma (Mills) Barwise; grandson of Mark Leighton and Mary Lord (Copp) Mills; great-grandson of Roger and Abigail (Blaisdell) Copp; great²-grandson of *Samuel Copp,* Lieutenant, New Hampshire Militia, Lebanon Selectman and Member Committee of Safety.

WILLIAM DORRANCE BEACH, San Diego, Calif. (37868). Son of Joshua Munson and Sarah E. (Ford) Beach; grandson of James and Charity (Kitchel) Ford; great-grandson of *James Kitchel,* private, New Jersey Militia and Cont'l Line.

CHARLES STUART BEATTIE, Stuart, Iowa (37658). Son of John James and Elizabeth Cameron (Stuart) Beattie; grandson of James Milligan and Margaret Sophia (Nelson) Beattie; great-grandson of John and Mary (Finlay) Nelson; great²-grandson of Hugh and Jane (Cochran) Finley; great³-grandson of *Joseph Finlay,* Captain, Londonderry, New Hampshire Volunteers.

HENRY LYMAN PARSONS BECKWITH, Providence, R. I. (36524). Son of Truman and Harriet (Parsons) Beckwith; grandson of Amos N. and Clara C. (Lippitt) Beckwith; great-grandson of Warren and Eliza (Seamans) Lippitt; great²-grandson of *Charles Lippitt,* Assistant Commissary of Issues.

WILLIAM TECUMSEH SHERMAN BEEKS, Seattle, Wash. (36665). Son of Matthew Lambdin Barnes and Mary Elizabeth (Fleming) Beeks;; grandson of Samuel and Elizabeth Beal (Lambdin) Beeks; great-grandson of *Christopher Beeks,* private, First Regt., Virginia Cont'l Troops.

LUTHER MELANCHTON BERNHISEL, Chicago, Ill. (37882). Son of Luther Melanchton and Sarah Bell (Clark) Bernhisel; grandson of Solomon and Hannah (Dunkleberger) Bernheisel; great-grandson of *John* and Cathern (Loy) *Bernheisel,* private, Berks County, Pennsylvania Militia; great²-grandson of *Michael Loy,* private, Lancaster County, Pennsylvania Musketry; great-grandson of John and Catherine (Sunday) Dunkelberger; great²-grandson of *Clemeses Dunkelberger,* private, Berks County, Pennsylvania Militia.

RICARDO LANE BERTOLACCI, Berkeley, Calif. (37869). Son of George Thomas and Anna Augusta (Lane) Bertolacci; grandson of Moses A. and Ann (Sargent) Lane; great-grandson of Moses and Olive (Fellows) Lane; great²-grandson of *Nathan Fellows,* private, Essex County, Massachusetts Militia and Massachusetts Cont'l Troops.

ROBERT McPHERRAN BETTS, Cornicopia, Ore. (37489). Son of Chauncey Grove and Leah (McPherran) Betts; grandson of Charles H. and Amelia (Mather) Betts; great-grandson of Chauncey and Maria (Mather) Betts; great²-grandson of *Nathan Betts,* private, Second Co., Westchester County, New York Militia; grandson of Andrew and Maria (Brubaker) McPherran; great-grandson of John and Elizabeth (Stewart) McPherran; great²-grandson of *Andrew McPherran (McPharen),* private, First Regt., Pennsylvania Troops and Fifth Regt., Cont'l Line, 5 years' service.

WILLIAM CLAYTON BOARDMAN, Aberdeen, So. Dak. (30675). Son of Grant Clinton and Agnes (Brady) Boardman; grandson of Alonzo Clinton and Margaret (Spence) Boardman; great-grandson of Stephen Charles and Bethania (Coit) Boardman; great²-grandson of *Nathaniel* and Philomelia (Huntington) *Boardman, Jr.,* private, Col. Peter Olcott's Regt., Vermont Militia; great³-grandson of *Nathaniel Boardman,* private, Col. Olcott's Regt., Vermont Militia.

JAMES CALDERWOOD BOLTON, Alexandria, La. (38101). Son of James Wade and Mary Esther Calderwood; grandson of George Washington and Tennessee (Wade) Bolton; great-grandson of Absalom and Melinda Kennedy (Porter) Wade; great²-grandson of William and Hannah (Kennedy) Porter; great³-grandson of *William Porter,* Captain, Second Battalion, Chester County, Pennsylvania Militia.

GEORGE HOOD BONELLI, Brookline, Mass. (38126). Son of Louis Henry and Ada (Hood) Bonelli; grandson of George and Hermione (Breed) Hood; great-grandson of *Aaron Breed,* private, Essex County, Massachusetts Militia.

EUGENE CAHILL BONNIWELL, JR., W. Philadelphia, Pa. (37748). Son of Eugene Cleophas and Madeline (Cahill) Bonniwell; grandson of Evander Berry and Elizabeth Ann (O'Doherty) Bonniwell; great-grandson of James and Phebe Brooks Bonniwell; great²-grandson of William and Sally (Brooks) Capes; great³-grandson, of Henry and

Phebe (Youngs) Brooks; great⁴-grandson of John and Elizabeth (Youngs) Brooks; great⁵-grandson of *Samuel Youngs*, Captain, Connecticut Train Band and Member of Committees.

HAROLD KING BOWEN, Iowa (35608). Supplemental. Son of William Walker and Lydia May (King) Bowen; grandson of David and Lydia Ann (Hall) Wood; great-grandson of Phineas and Lydia (Huntley) Hall; great²-grandson of Stephen Russell and Hannah (Wilson) Hall; great³-grandson of Ephraim and Lydia (Russell) Hall; great⁴-grandson of *Stephen Russell*, Captain, Massachusetts Militia, Member Committee of Correspondence, Inspection and Safety.

FREDERICK McCAUSLAND BRADDOCK, Stockton, Calif. (37870). Son of Joshua C. and Rosalie Bailey (Meady) Braddock; grandson of David and Katherine (Headington) Braddock; great-grandson of Nicholas and Ruth (Phillips) Headington; great²-grandson of *James Phillips* (Baltimore County, Md.), Commander of Sloop "General Lee."

GEORGE PRESTON BRECKENRIDGE, Pelham Manor, N. Y. (37918). Son of George and Julia (Clark) Breckenridge; grandson of James and Elizabeth Ann (Bryan) Breckenridge; great-grandson of *George Breckenridge*, private, Virginia Militia at King's Mountain; great²-grandson of *Alexander Breckenridge*, private, Washington County, Virginia Militia; great-grandson of *James Bryan*, private, Col. Otho Williams' Regt., Virginia Line.

ROBERT LAWRENCE BROWN, Richmond, Va. (36561). Son of William Cabell and Ida Mason (Dorsey) Brown; grandson of Robert Lawrence and Margaret Baldwin (Cabell) Brown; great-grandson of Mayo and Mary Cornelia Brisco (Daniel) Cabell; great²-grandson of *William Cabell*, Member Virginia Convention and of Committee of Safety.

WILLIAM CABELL BROWN, Richmond, Va. (36559). Son of Robert Lawrence and Margaret Baldwin (Cabell) Brown; grandson of Mayo and Mary Cornelia Briscoe (Daniel) Cabell; great-grandson of *William Cabell*, Member Committee of Safety and Virginia Convention of 1775.

JAY FISK BROWNE, New York City, N. Y. (38214). Son of Charles Nichols and Lucy Ann (Moses) Browne; grandson of William and Louisa (Haines) Moses; great-grandson of Dudley and Elizabeth (Carr) Haines; great²-grandson of *Simson Haines*, private, Col. Long's and Col. Poor's Regts., New Hampshire Militia.

GAIUS MARCUS BRUMBAUGH, Washington, D. C. (38005). Son of Andrew Boelus and Maria B. (Frank) Brumbaugh; grandson of Jacob and Rachel (Boyer) Brumbaugh; great-grandson of Henry and Catherine (Roberts) Boyer; great²-grandson of *Abraham Boyer*, private, Philadelphia County, Pennsylvania Militia.

HORACE GREELEY BYERS, Montclair, N. J. (37993). Son of Ambrose and Mary (McCracken) Byers; grandson of William and Elizabeth (Bissell) Byers; great-grandson of *John Partridge Bissell*, private, Col. Latimer's Regt., Connecticut Militia.

EDWARD POTTER CARPENTER, Caterham Valley, Surrey, Eng. (La. 38113). Son of Edwin Burnham and Tabitha (Potter) Carpenter; grandson of Cyrus and Betsey (Putnam) Carpenter; great-grandson of *Benjamin Carpenter*, Colonel, Vermont Militia, Lieutenant-Governor and Member of Council, 1779.

ELLERBE WINN CARTER, Louisville, Ky. (36543). Son of William Douglass and Julia Reese (Winn) Carter; grandson of Henry Jasper and Eliza Evans (Ellerbe) Winn; great-grandson of William Alexander and Catherine E. (Pegues) Ellerbe; great²-grandson of Christopher Butler and Eliza Hodges (Evans) Pegues; great³-grandson of *Claudius Pegues, Jr.*, Captain, Marion's Brigade, South Carolina Militia; great⁴-grandson of *Claudius Pegues*, Delegate to Cont'l Congress, Member Provincial Congress, Council of Safety and General Assembly.

CHARLES L. CHAMBERLIN, Colfax, Wash. (36667). Son of Orson N. and Ellen G. (Maxwell) Chamberlin; grandson of Orson and Philena (Kellogg) Chamberlin; great-grandson of *Martin Kellogg*, private, Western, Massachusetts Militia and Cont'l Troops.

LE ROY WILDER CHANDLER, Stamford, Conn. (38127). Son of Roscoe Lincoln and Katy Adaline (Wilder) Chandler; grandson of Ephraim Hartwell and Mary Keyes (Swallow) Chandler; great-grandson of Ephraim and Mary (Powers) Chandler; great²-grandson of *John Chandler*, private, Col. Josiah Whitney's Regt., Massachusetts Militia.

FRANK HOMER CHURCHWELL, Brooklyn, N. Y. (37923). Son of Herbert R. and Nellie (Brush) Churchwell; grandson of Cornelius and Elizabeth (Knapp) Churchwell; great-grandson of William and Cornelia (Van Nostrand) Churchwell; great²-grandson of *John Churchwell (Churchill)*, private, Second Regt., Dutchess County, New York Militia.

HARMAN BENSON COEN, Columbus, Ohio (38079). Son of Jacob S. and Lydda C. (Craft) Coen; grandson of David S. and Betsie (Beard) Craft; great-grandson of *John Beard*, private and Ensign, Cumberland County, Pennsylvania Militia.

LOUIS LOREN COLLINS, Minneapolis, Minn. (38301). Son of Loren W. and Ella Margaret (Stewart) Collins; grandson of Charles Pierce and Abigail (Libby) Collins; great-grandson of Shuball and Abigail (Hoyt) Collins; great²-grandson of *Benjamin Collins*, private, Col. Bedell's and Col. Cilley's Regts., New Hampshire Troops, died in service.

ALBERT GEORGE COOK, Jr., Ens. U. S. N., Monroe, La. (38102). Son of Albert George and Ella (Frierson) Cook; grandson of William Gardiner and Fannie (Eagan) Frierson; great-grandson of Gardiner and Lavinia Tipton (Williams) Frierson; great²-grandson of Samuel and Ruth (Davidson) Williams; great³-grandson of *William Davidson*, Lieutenant, Captain James Houston's Co., North Carolina Rangers.

ROBERT FRIERSON COOK, Monroe, La. (38103). Son of Albert George and Ella (Frierson) Cook; grandson of William Gardiner and Fannie (Eagan) Frierson;; great-grandson of Gardiner and Lavinia Tipton (Williams) Frierson; great²-grandson of Samuel and Ruth (Davidson) Williams; great³-grandson of *William Davidson*, Lieutenant, Captain James Houston's Co., North Carolina Rangers.

HARRY WEBSTER COOKE, Baltimore, Md. (37688). Son of Theodore and Sophia (Webster) Cooke; grandson of Israel and Areetta (Clark) Cooke; great-grandson of John and Sarah (Root) Cooke; great²-grandson of Daniel and Elizabeth (Crowell) Root; great³-grandson of *Henry Crowell*, Signer, Frederick County, Maryland Association Agreement.

NORMAN MILNER COUTY, Louisville, Ky. (36541). Son of Charles Edward and Jane E. (Witt) Couty; grandson of David Richard and Nancy (Wade) Witt; great-grandson of *Elisha Witt*, private, Amherst County, Virginia Militia, pensioned; great-grandson of William and Sarah (Allen) Wade; great²-grandson of *Richard Wade*, private, Virginia Militia, twice prisoner, pensioned.

GEORGE MILBURN COVINGTON, Jr., Russellville, Ky. (36542). Son of George M. and Lucy (—) Covington; grandson of F. Marion and Delia (Clark) Covington; great-grandson of Coleman and Mary Jane (Robinson) Covington; great²-grandson of Francis and Lucy (Hughes) Covington, Jr.; great³-grandson of *Francis Covington*, Captain, Culpeper County, Virginia Militia.

MANFORD ALLAN COX, Oklahoma City, Okla. (35246). Son of Spruce McCoy and Susan Ida (—) Cox; grandson of Louis Allan and Caroline (Baird) Cox; great-grandson of Andrew and Elizabeth (Smith) Baird; great²-grandson of *Frederick Smith*, private and Captain, Virginia Line, pensioned.

ALMERON CRANDALL, Portland, Ore. (37493). Son of Smith Elliott and Mary (Walker) Crandall; grandson of Silas and Zada (Elliott) Crandall; great-grandson of *Edward Crandall*, private, First Regt., Connecticut Line, pensioned.

CLAUDE GRANVILLE CRANE, Brooklyn, N. Y. (38215). Son of Harrison N. and Mary Elizabeth (Moorehouse) Crane; grandson of William Henry and Mary Jane (Gillen) Crane; great-grandson of Josiah and Keziah Saxton (Sturgis) Crane; great²-grandson of Benjamin and Phebe (Allien) Crane; great³-grandson of *Josiah Crane*, Lieutenant, Eastern Battalion, Morris County, New Jersey Militia.

JOHN ALLEN CREAMER, Louisville, Ky. (36545). Son of George Morgan and Lida (Stephens) Creamer; grandson of John Q. A. and Eliza Price (Bowles) Stephens; great-grandson of Lyddall Bacon and Sally Waller (Price) Bowles; great²-grandson of *Thomas Philip Bowles*, Lieutenant, Col. Shepherd's Virginia Riflemen.

WILLIAM BROADDUS CRIDLIN, Richmond, Va. (36558). Son of Ransdall White and Emma Haseltine (Snelling) Cridlin; grandson of Creed Thomas and Mary Susan (Chiles) Snelling; great-grandson of Elliot Francis and Eliza S. (Broaddus) Chiles; great²-grandson of *William Chiles*, private, Caroline County, Virginia Militia.

LEWIS ABBOTT CROSSETT, Mass. (27950). Supplementals. Son of Robert and Ruth Ellen (Lewis) Crossett; grandson of Robert and Mary (Abbott) Crossett; great-grandson of Samuel and Abigail (Cady) Crossett; great²-grandson of *Samuel Cady*, private, Col. David Leonard's Regt., Massachusetts Militia; great-grandson of *Joel Abbott*, private, Brookfield, Massachusetts Militia; great²-grandson of *Peter Abbott*, private, Brookfield, Massachusetts Militia; grandson of Jason and Ruth (Wilkinson) Lewis; great-grandson of *David Lewis*, private, Col. Joseph Webb's Regt., Massachusetts Militia; great²-grandson of *John Lewis*, private, Capt. Seth Bullard's Mass. Co., Lexington; great-grandson of David and Priscilla (Guild) Lewis; great²-grandson of *Aaron Guild*, Member Com. of Correspondence and Safety, and Captain, Col. Lemuel Robinson's Regt., Massachusetts Militia; great-grandson of *David Wilkinson, Jr.*, private, Col. John Crane's Regt., Massachusetts Cont'l Troops; great²-grandson of *David Wilkinson*, private, Col. Samuel Robinson's Regt., Massachusetts Militia; great-grandson of David and Ruth (Allen) Wilkinson, Jr.; great²-grandson of *Joshua Allen*, private, Walpole, Massachusetts Militia; great²-grandson of Joshua and Patience (Ide) Allen; great²-grandson of *Jacob Ide*, Captain, Col. Daggett's Regt., Massachusetts Militia and Member Massachusetts Committee of Safety.

ALBERT WILLARD DAMON, Kingston, R. I. (36515). Son of Samuel Chester and Elizabeth (Taylor) Damon; grandson of Samuel Reed and Sarah (Bond) Damon; great-grandson of Samuel and Patty (Reed) Damon; great²-grandson of *Benjamin Damon*, private, Reading, Massachusetts Militia, pensioned.

FRANK FENNER DAVIS, Chepacket, R. I. (36516). Son of Gilbert Henry and Abigail Alverson (Briggs) Davis; grandson of Dexter and Rebecca (Cook) Davis; great-grandson of *John Wanton Cook*, private, Col. Archibald Crary's Regt., Rhode Island Militia; also in Continental Line, pensioned.

HARRY ALEXANDER DAVIS, Washington, D. C. (38004). Son af David Roger Williams and Mary (Deering) Davis; grandson of Alexander Warren and Helen Margaret (Grant) Deering; great-grandson of Noah and Elizabeth (Cummings) Deering; great²-grandson of *Joseph Deering*, private and Fifer, Col. Edmund Phinney's Regt., Massachusetts Militia, also sea-coast defense; great²-grandson of *Nathaniel Cummings*, private, Col. Gill's Regt., Massachusetts Militia; great²-grandson of Nathaniel and Sarah (Junkin) Cummings; great²-grandson of *Paul Junkins*, Member York County, Massachusetts Committee of Safety; great²-grandson of Joseph and Hannah (Jameson) Deering; great²-grandson of *William Jameson*, seaman on brig "Charming Sally"; grandson of David Roger Williams and Mary White (Norris) Davis; great-grandson of John Bradford and Harriet C. (Billingsley) Norris; great²-grandson of *Thomas Norris*, private, First Co., Maryland Troops.

FAYETTE FRANK DEAN, San José, Calif. (38152). Son of George Wesley and Louisa Ellen (Barnhill) Dean; grandson of Moses and Priscilla (Suddeth) Dean; great-grandson of Frank and Sarah (Weaver) Suddeth; great²-grandson of *William Suddeth*, Corporal, Col. Daniel Morgan's and Col. Butler's Regts., Virginia Troops.

CHARLES CAMILLE DE GRAVELLES, Morgan City, La. (38110). Son of St. Clair and Eva (Haifleigh) de Gravelles; grandson of William Frederick and Azelie C. (Charpantier) Haifleigh; great-grandson of Jacob and Celeste (Carlin) Haifleigh; great²-grandson of Celestin and Theresa (Provast) Carlin; great²-grandson of *Joseph Carlin*, private and Sergeant, Atakapas, Louisiana Militia.

LYNN HAMILTON DINKINS, La. (30812). Supplementals. Son of James and Sue (Hart) Dinkins; grandson of Alexander Hamilton and Cynthia (Springs) Dinkins; great-grandson of William Polk and Margaret Polk (Springs) Springs; great²-grandson of *John Springs* (father of William Polk Springs), Captain, Mecklinburg County, North Carolina Troops; great²-grandson of *Richard Springs* (father of Margaret Polk Springs), Captain, Mecklinburg County, North Carolina Troops.

OSCAR DINWIDDIE, Ind. (13671). Supplemental. Son of John Wilson and Mary Janette (Perkins) Dinwiddie; grandson of Thomas and Mary Ann (Wilson) Dinwiddie; great-grandson of David and Susannah (Patterson) Dinwiddie; great²-grandson of *David Dinwiddie*, Member Pennsylvania General Assembly during Revolution.

ARTHUR CHAMBERLIN DODDS, New York City, N. Y. (38201). Son of William Black and Jenny (Chamberlin) Dodds; grandson of James Roswell and Jane (Bellows) Chamberlin; great-grandson of Ortin and Calista (—) Chamberlin; great²-grandson of *Amasa Chamberlin*, private, Capt. John Alger's Co., Vermont Militia.

ALBION NOYES DOE, Kingston, R. I. (36525). Son of Charles P. and Mary Linnie (Russ) Doe; grandson of Charles Albion and Hannah (Noyes) Doe; great-grandson of Harrison and Lydia Ann (Harriman) Doe; great²-grandson of Charles and Rachael (Varnum) Doe; great²-grandson of *Nathaniel Doe, Jr.*, private, Col. Samuel McCobb's Regt., Massachusetts Militia.

LYTTON WARWICK DOOLITTLE, Providence, R. I. (38326). Son of William Shearman and Esther Amelia (Warwick) Doolittle; grandson of Charles Hutchins and Julia Tyler (Shearman) Doolittle; great-grandson of Harvey W. and Hannah (Hutchins) Doolittle; great²-grandson of *Joel Doolittle*, private, First, Fifth, and Third Regts., Connecticut Cont'l Troops, six years' service.

GEORGE RAYMOND DU BOIS, Brooklyn, N. Y. (37919). Son of James Madison and Mary Etta Osborne (Andrews) Du Bois; grandson of Andre Lefevre and Marie (Ville-fidele, or Winfield) Du Bois; great-grandson of Wessel and Catherine (LeFevre) Du Bois; great²-grandson of *Louis Jonathan Du Bois*, Captain, Third Regt., Ulster County, New York Militia.

DONALD FERRIC DU SHANE, New Castle, Pa. (38352). Son of Jonathan and Adela (McMiller) Du Shane; grandson of Joseph Townsend and Jane (Smith) Du Shane; great-grandson of *Jonathan Smith*, Lieutenant, Fifth Regt., Virginia Troops, pensioned.

THOMAS WILLIAM EDWARDS, Colombia, So. A. Tenn. (38067). Son of Will Ware and Kittie Lowry (Meredith) Edwards; grandson of Thomas and Sarah Francis (Ware) Edwards; great-grandson of Thomas and Leah (Ford) Edwards; great²-granson of *Thomas Edwards*, private, Fourth Regt., South Carolina Artillery, pensioned.

GEORGE HAMLIN ELDREDGE, Adrian, Mich. (37958). Son of Nathaniel Buel and Jannette (Patten) Eldredge; grandson of Daniel E. and Mehitable (Bristol) Eldredge; great-grandson of *Daniel Eldredge (Eldridge)*, Lieutenant, Ashford, Connecticut Militia and Second Regt., Connecticut Cont'l Troops.

SAMUEL EWART EMMONS, Baltimore, Md. (37687). Son of Charles De Moss and Edith Bertha (Ewart) Emmons; grandson of Samuel and Mary (Brackenridge) Ewart; great-grandson of Alexander M. and Mary (Porter) Brackenridge; great²-grandson of *Hugh Henry Brackenridge*, Chaplain, Pennsylvania Troops.

JOHN REDDEN EVERETT, Minneapolis, Minn. (38302). Son of Charles F. and Mary Elizabeth (Van Winkle) Everett; grandson of Redden H. and Mary Ann (Flowers) Everett; great-grandson of Charles M. and Margaret Hooper (Rhodes) Flowers; great²-grandson of *James Flowers*, private, First Battalion, Buck's County, Pennsylvania Associators.

GLENN BLACKMER EWELL, New York (36882). Supplementals. Son of Jirah Blackmer and Mary Florine (Mallory) Ewell; grandson of Henry Bancroft and Fanny (Blackmer) Ewell; great-grandson of Jirah and Sally (Joslin) Blackmer; great²-grandson of Joseph and Thankful (Spear) Blackmer; great²-grandson of *Joseph Blackmer*, private, Berkshire County, Massachusetts Militia; great-grandson of Henry and Betsy (Bancroft) Ewell; great²-grandson of *James Ewell*, private, Col. Woodbridge's Regt., Massachusetts Militia.

CHARLES KELLER FINCKEL, Washington D. C. (38006). Son of George Keller and Sophie Louise (—) Finckel; grandson of Samuel De Vin and Harriet (Keller) Finckel; great-grandson of John Christian and Sabina (De Vin) Finckel; great²-grandson of *Philip Finckel*, Surgeon, Sixth Battalion, Berk's County, Pennsylvania Militia.

CHARLES WHITMORE FLOYD, Washington, D. C. (38007). Son of Daniel Pattee and Charlotte (Parker) Floyd; grandson of Leonard and Lucia (Brown) Parker; great-grandson of Abel and Priscilla (Hodgkins) Brown; great²-grandson of *Elisha Brown*, private and Corporal, Col. Doolittle's Regt., and Winchendon, Massachusetts Militia.

DAVID NATHANIEL FOSTER, Fort Wayne, Ind. (37817). Son of John Lyman and Harriet (Scott) Foster; grandson of David and Sarah (Werd) Foster; great-grandson of *Jesse Foster* private and Quartermaster Sergeant, Connecticut Militia, and Artificer Col. Baldwin's Regt., Connecticut Artillery, pensioned.

REYNOLDS CRAIG FRAMPTON, St. Louis, Mo. (37611). Son of David Thomas and Annie M. (Stuart) Frampton; grandson of Samuel and Evaline (Reynolds) Frampton; great-grandson of David and Hannah (Lobaugh) Frampton; great²-grandson of *William*

Frampton, private, Cumberland County, Pennsylvania Militia; grandson of Charles and Nancy (Craig) Stuart; great-grandson of Samuel and Maria (Hill) Craig; great²-grandson of Joseph and Nancy (Morehead) Craig; great³-grandson of *Samuel Craig,* Lieutenant First Battalion, Westmoreland County, Pennsylvania Provincials, killed.

CHARLES JEFFERSON FRYE, Saqua La Grande, Cuba (Me. 38179). Son of Charles Jefferson and Harriet Whipple (Cook) Frye; grandson of George Henry and Selina Atwood (Aiken) Cook; great-grandson of Charles and Elizabeth (Burbeck) Cook; great²-grandson of Edward and Jane (Milk) Burbeck; great³-grandson of *William Burbeck,* Lieutenant-Colonel, Gridley's Massachusetts Cont'l Artillery, Comptroller and Superintendent of Laboratory.

HARVEY ELBERT GARRETT, Louisville, Ky. (36546). Son of Harvey Elbert and Mary Eliza (Hawkins) Garrett; grandson of James Russell and Mary Frances (Davis) Hawkins, Jr.; great-grandson of James Russell and Sarah Adaline (Bowles) Hawkins; great²-grandson of Lyddal Bacon and Elizabeth (Smith) Bowles; great³-grandson of *Thomas Philip Bowles,* Lieutenant, Col. Shepherd's Virginia Artillery.

ROBERT ARTHUR GIBSON, Butler, Pa. (37749). Son of Wilmot Byron and Helen (Stewart) Gibson; grandson of James B. and Charlotte (Vail) Gibson; great-grandson of James and Priscilla (Evans) Gibson; great²-grandson of *Robert Gibson,* Captain, Buck's County, Pennsylvania Associators.

ERROL CLARENCE GILKEY, Oakland, Calif. (38153). Son of Herbert Louville and Mary Olive (Kerr) Gilkey; grandson of William and Nancy Gustavia (Smart) Gilkey; great-grandson of Samuel and Betsey (Whitney) Gilkey; great²-grandson of Joseph and Betty (Phinney) Whitney; great³-grandson of *Edmund Phinney,* Colonel, Eighteenth Regt., Massachusetts Cont'l Infantry; grandson of James Anderson and Abigail Boutwell (Walker) Karr (Kerr); great-grandson of Elkanah and Mary (Richardson) Karr; great²-grandson of Joseph and Charlotte (Thompson) Richardson; great³-grandson of Isaac Snow and Charlotte (Hay) Thompson; great⁴-grandson of *Daniel Thompson,* Massachusetts Minute Man, killed at Concord.

DARWIN CRAYON GIVENS, Charlottesville, Va. (36560). Son of Darwin Branch and Annie E. (Morris) Givens; grandson of James E. and Rebecca (—) Morris; great-grandson of James and Mary (—) Morris; great²-grandson of Jermiah and Elizabeth (—) Morris; great³-grandson of *Thomas A. Morris,* Corporal and Sergeant, Col. Wm. Thompson's Third Regt., South Carolina Rangers.

CHARLES BERTIE GLEASON, San José, Calif. (37871). Son of Charles Willard and Jane Grey (Story) Gleason; grandson of Joseph and Abigail (Read) Gleason; great-grandson of *Winser Gleason,* private, Col. Hobart's Regt., New Hampshire Militia.

ROBERT E. GOLDEN, Walla Walla, Wash. (Ore. 37487). Son of Frank A. and Jeanette Smith Ray Golden; grandson of George S. and Elizabeth (Hayes) Ray; great-grandson of Thomas Patrick and Jeanette (Smith) Ray; great²-grandson of Alexander and Volender (Suter) Smith; great³-grandson of *John Suter,* Second Lieutenant, Middle Battalion, Montgomery County, Maryland Militia.

TAYLOR BANKER GRANT, Brooklyn, N. Y. (37924). Son of Robert Silliman and Mary Lucas (Taylor) Grant; grandson of Adolph Banker and Rhoda (Silliman) Grant; great-grandson of Peter and Hannah (Banker) Grant; great²-grandson of *Adolph Banker,* private and Corporal, Westchester County, New York Militia.

ALBERT HENRY STARR HAFFENDER, Portland Ore. (37491). Son of Albert and Hadassah (Starr) Haffender; grandson of William Henry and Mary (Foster) Starr; great-grandson of Seth and Lucy (Bacon) Starr; great²-grandson of Jonah and Phebe (Middlebrook) Starr; great³-grandson of *Joseph Starr,* private, Col. Nathan Gallup's Regt., Connecticut Militia.

GEORGE DENNY HALLOCK, Newark, N. J. (37998). Son of Herbert Andrew and Annie Bell (Denny) Hallock; grandson of John William and Mary Baxter (Milne) Denny; great-grandson of William Henry and Rebecca (Bell) Denny; great²-grandson of William and Sarah (Bailey) Denny; great³-grandson of *Henry Denny,* Sergeant, Bergen County, New Jersey Militia.

RONALD EDWARD HALLOCK, Newark, N. J. (37999). Same as George Denny Hallock, New Jersey (37998),

WILLARD I. HAMILTON, N. J. (37784). Supplementals. Son of Edward Livingston and Sarah Celia (Lum) Hamilton; grandson of Stephen and Catherine A. (Conkling) Lum; great-grandson of Moses and Nancy (Morehouse) Lum; great²-grandson of Simeon and Rebecca (Meeker) Morehouse; great²-grandson of *James Meeker*, private, Essex County, New Jersey Militia; grandson of Caleb Whitfield and Mary (Vail) Hamilton; great-grandson of Henry and Lucinda (Dodd) Vail; great²-grandson of *Usal Dodd*, private, Essex County, New Jersey Militia.

WHITTIER LORENZ HANSOM, Boston, Mass. (38135). Son of Samuel Conrad and Nancy Elizabeth (Edmondson) Hansom; grandson of John and Alcinda (Cox) Hansom; great-grandson of Conrad and Catharine (Shultz) Hansom; great²-grandson of *John Hansom*, private, Twelfth Regt., Virginia Troops.

GALEN CAMPBELL HARTMAN, Pittsburgh, Pa. (37737). Son of (Johan Herman) Robert and Rebecca J. (Perrine) Hartman; grandson of Isaac and Margaret (Irwin) Perrine; great-grandson of *Peter Perrine*, private, Somerset County, New Jersey Militia, pensioned.

GEORGE JUAN HATFIELD, San Francisco, Calif. (37872). Son of William M. and Harriet Juanita (Bingham) Hatfield; grandson of Isaac and Katharine Melick (Perrine) Hatfield; great-grandson of John and Hannah (Billings) Perrine; great²-grandson of *Peter Perrine*, Captain, Third Battalion, Somerset County, New Jersey Militia.

WILLIAM STARKS HAWES, Oak Park, Ill. (37883). Son of Lucius A. and Harriet Martha (Starks) Hawes; grandson of Elijah and Eliza (Hoar) Hawes; great-grandson of David and Angellette (Peirce) Hoar; great²-grandson of Jonathan and Sarah (Heard) Hoar; great³-grandson of *Josiah Hoar*, Sergeant and Lieutenant, Middlesex County, Massachusetts Militia; great³-grandson of *Richard Heard*, private, Sudbury, Massachusetts Militia; great²-grandson of *Nathaniel Peirce*, private, Stoughton, Massachusetts Militia; great³-grandson of *Seth Peirce*, Captain, Colonel Samuel Williams Regt., Hampshire County, Massachusetts Militia.

HOWARD DOUGLAS HENDERSON, Murfreesboro, Tenn. (38068). Son of Albert G. and Mattie (Holt) Henderson; grandson of Berry D. and Lucretia (Hart) Holt; great-grandson of Henry and Betty (McGuire) Holt; great²-grandson of *William McGuire*, Lieutenant, Third Regt., Virginia Cont'l Troops; grandson of Albert G. and Elizabeth (Love) Henderson; great-grandson of James and Fanny (Henderson) Henderson; great².grandson of *Samuel Herderson*, private, Second Regt., South Carolina Troops.

EDWIN HENSHAW, Des Moines, Iowa (37660). Son of John Brace and Cynthia (—) Henshaw; grandson of William and Jerusha (Brace) Henshaw, Jr.; great-grandson of *William Henshaw*, Lieutenant and Paymaster, Connecticut Cont'l Line.

CHARLES WILLIAM HESS, Goshen, Ind. (37818). Son of Joseph and Filenia Isora (Harden) Hess; grandson of Balser and Sarah Ann (Immel) Hess; great-grandson of Balser and Sarah B. (Immel) Hess; great²-grandson of *Baltzer (Balser) Hess*, private, Bedford County, Pennsylvania Militia.

FRANK E. HESS, Goshen, Ind. (37819). Son of Henry B. and Sarah Ann (Rensbarger) Hess; grandson of John and Hannah (Rowand) Hess; great-grandson of Balser and Sarah B. (Immell) Hess; great²-grandson of *Baltzer (Balser) Hess*, private, Bedford County, Pennsylvania Militia.

OSBORN FORT HEVENER, Newark, N. J. (38226). Son of Archibald Osborn and Margaret (Fort) Hevener; grandson of Jacob Platt and Margaret (Force) Fort; great-grandson of Andrew and Nancy (Platt) Fort; great²-grandson of *John Fort*, private, Burlington County, New Jersey Militia.

GEORGE TAYLOR HICKOK, New York City, N. Y. (38211). Son of William and Mary E. (Hall) Hickok, Jr.; grandson of Edward D. and Mary J. (Westervelt) Hall; great-grandson of Daniel and Mary (Hall) Westervelt; great²-grandson of Peter and Catlyntje (—) Westervelt; great³-grandson of *Daniel Westervelt*, Lieutenant and Ensign, Bergen County, New Jersey Militia, died in prison.

ROBERT SHERRARD HILL, Steubenville, Ohio (36494). Supplementals. Son of Joseph Welsh and Mary Ann (Sherrard) Hill; grandson of Robert Andrew and Mary (Kithcart) Sherrard; great-grandson of *John Shearer (Sherrard)*, Commissary-General, Matross and Captain, Pennsylvania Troops; great-grandson of *Joseph Kithcart (Cathcart) (Hithcart)*, private, Second Regt., Monmouth County, New Jersey Militia.

BURTON ABRAM HOFFMAN, Buffalo, N. Y. (38202). Son of Abram and Lillian (Bartels) Hoffman; grandson of Abram and Carrie (King) Hoffman; great-grandson of Cornelius and Elizabeth (Lounsbury) Hoffman; great²-grandson of *Adam Hoffman*, private, Third Regt., Ulster County, New York Militia.

DONALD HOLBROOK, Newton, Mass. (38128). Son of Walter Hills and Katherine T. (Hatch) Holbrook; grandson of Charles Soper and Abbie P. (Hills) Holbrook; great-grandson of Hessey Jesse and Fannie (Seabury) Holbrook; great²-grandson of David and Mehitable (Soper) Holbrook; great³-grandson of *Edmund Soper*, Major, Fifth Regt., Suffolk County, Massachusetts Militia.

WILLIAM LE ROY HOLTZ, Emporia, Kans. (36746). Son of D. F. and Hannah (Sheppard) Holtz; grandson of Jacob and Eleanor (Douglass) Holtz; great-grandson of *Jacob Holtz*, private, Second Battalion, Lancaster County, Pennsylvania Militia.

DONALD TUCKER HOOD, Brookline, Mass. (38129). Son of Frederick Clark and Myra (Tucker) Hood; grandson of George Henry and Frances Henrietta (Janvrin) Hood; great-grandson of Jacob and Sophia (Needham) Hood; great²-grandson of *John Hood*, private and Sergeant, Essex County, Massachusetts Militia and Cont'l Troops.

JOSEPH WILLETT HORN, Horn Springs, Tenn. (38069). Son of James Adams and Abill (Herd) Horn; grandson of Joseph Walling and Nancy (Green) Herd; great-grandson of Thomas and Sarah (Friar) Green; great²-grandson of John and Rachel (Mackey) Green; great³-grandson of *Jarvis Greene* (*Green*), private, Tryon County, North Carolina Militia.

DAVID J. HOWELL, Cheyenne, Wyo. (38251). Son of David James and Elizabeth Elvina (Stewart) Howell; grandson of David and Susan (Martin) Howell; great-grandson of *Nathan Martin*, private, Albany County, New York Militia.

MARION GROSS HOY, Evanston, Ill. (37884). Son of Jeremiah W. and Susan B. (Gross) Hoy; grandson of Phillip and Elizabeth (Schoch) Gross; great-grandson of Jacob and Elizabeth (Hendrick) Schoch; great²-grandson of *Michael Schoch*, private, Northumberland County, Pennsylvania Militia.

EARLE REGINALD HOYT, Chicago, Ill. (37885). Son of Benjamin Joseph and Helen (Earle) Hoyt; grandson of Avery Atkins and Caroline (Hoyt) Hoyt; great-grandson of Benjamin and Susan (Hayes) Hoyt; great²-grandson of *Joseph Hoyt*, private, Gen. Stark's Regt., New Hampshire Militia.

CHARLES CALVIN HUESTIS, Greencastle, Ind. (37822). Son of Calvin Walker and Margaret (Phelps) Huestis; grandson of Elihu and Margaret (Cruikshank) Phelps; great-grandson of *John Phelps*, Lieutenant and Captain, Connecticut Cavalry.

MILAN HULBERT HULBERT, Chicago, Ill. (37886). Son of William Augustus and Helen (Moore) Hulbert; grandson of Samuel Augustus and Mary Robinson (Plunkett) Hulbert; great-grandson of *Amos Hurlbut* (*Hulbert*), private, Wadsworth's Brigade, Connecticut Militia, pensioned.

HAROLD EVERETT HUNT, Portland, Ore. (37494). Son of James E. and Addie M. (Chapman) Hunt; grandson of James J. and Nancy (Converse) Hunt; great-grandson of Nelson and Sally (Jewel) Hunt; great²-grandson of *Daniel Hunt*, private, Col. Bedell's Regt., New Hampshire Troops; grandson of Samuel J. and Eveline (Greene) Chapman; great-grandson of Caleb and Mary (Oaks) Greene; great²-grandson of Thomas and Dorcas (—) Greene; great³-grandson of *Caleb Greene*, Lieutenant, Providence and Kent Counties, Rhode Island Militia.

JAMES EVERETT HUNT, Portland, Ore. (37490). Son of James Everett and Nancy (Converse) Hunt; grandson of Nelson and Sally (Jewell) Hunt; great-grandson of *Daniel Hunt*, private, Col. Timothy Bedel's Regt., New Hampshire Troops.

WALTER KING HUNT, Utica, N. Y. (N. J. 28228). Son of William Walter and Thankful Gaines (King) Hunt; grandson of Walter and Susanna (Deming) Hunt; great-grandson of *Ziba* (*Zeba*) *Hunt*, private, 17th Regt., Albany County, New York Militia.

RICHARD HUDSON IMHOFF, Hopewell, N. J. (38227). Son of Charles Hudson and Grace Rae (Douglas) Imhoff; grandson of Joseph T. and Mary Ellen (Rector) Imhoff; great-grandson of Joseph and Catherine (Heffley) Imhoff; great²-grandson of Peter and Sarah (Johnson) Heffley; great³-grandson of *George Johnson*, Fifer, Col. Buford's Regt., Virginia Cont'l Line, pensioned.

DONALD JACKSON, Barrington, R. I. (36517). Son of Benjamin Aborn and Lucy Anna (Greene) Jackson; grandson of Henry Lehré and Marcy Gooding (Wilbur) Greene; great-grandson of Simon Henry and Caroline Cornelia (Aborn) Greene; great²-grandson of Job and Abigail (Rhodes) Greene; great²-grandson of *Christopher Greene*, Colonel, First Regt., Rhode Island Continental Troops, killed in action.

JOHN FRANKLIN JAQUA, Humboldt, Iowa (37656). Son of Gamaliel and Christena (Thomas) Jaqua; grandson of Darius and Frelove (Gustin) Jaqua; great-grandson of *Gamaliel Jaqua*, private, Sixth Regt., Connecticut Cont'l Troops, widow pensioned.

MAURICE VARNEY JENNESS, Minneapolis, Minn. (38303). Son of Benjamin Franklin and Lucia Amand (Fancher) Jenness; grandson of Elisha and Sarah Amanda (Kingsley) Fancher; great-grandson of John and Pleiades (Brewster) Kingsley; great²-grandson of *Oliver Brewster*, Surgeon, Col. John Brown's Regt., Massachusetts Militia.

HOWARD HIRAM JOHNSON, San Francisco, Calif. (37873). Son of Louis D. and Emma (James) Johnson; grandson of James R. and Angelina (James) Smith; great-grandson of Charles Whitehead and Vanelia (Meaker) James; great²-grandson of Thomas and Deborah (Derrick) James; great³-grandson of *Thomas James*, private, Middlesex County, New Jersey Militia, State Troops and Cont'l Line.

JOHN WILLIAM JOHNSON, Jr., Ky. (34702). Supplemental. Son of John William and Sallie (Abbott) Johnson; grandson of William Henry and Judith Ann Martin (Shockley) Abbott; great-grandson of Thomas and Ann (Stephens) Shockley; great²-grandson of *John Stephens*, private, Virginia Militia, pensioned.

STANLEY CLARK JOHNSON, Providence, R. I (38327). Son of Gilbert and Susan Montgomery (Higgins) Johnson; grandson of Silas and Susan Montgomery (Turner) Higgins; great-grandson of Edward and Cynthia (Sexton) Turner; great²-grandson of *Jonathan Sexton*, private, Connecticut Militia at Lexington and Boston.

THOMAS ALEXANDER JOHNSON, Buffalo, N. Y. (38205). Son of Alexander and Mary (Rawlins) Johnson; grandson of Alexander and Sarah (Perkins) Johnson; great-grandson of Benjamin and Sarah (Kershaw) Perkins; great²-grandson of *Joseph Kershaw*, Colonel, South Carolina Militia, Member Provincial Congress.

WILLIAM CARTER JOHNSON, Providence, R. I. (36518). Son of William Reed and Mary E. (Atwood) Johnson; grandson of Charles Walton and Caroline (Reynold) Atwood; great-grandson of John Walton and Catherine (Budlong) Atwood; great²-grandson of *Caleb Atwood*, private, Col. Peck's Regt., Rhode Island Militia; also a Minute Man.

WILLIAM KNAPP JONES, Cheyenne, Wyo. (38252). Son of William R. and Emma (Knapp) Jones; grandson of Henry Wright and Emily C. (Kendall) Knapp; great-grandson of Asa and Mary (Wright) Knapp; great²-grandson of *Isaac Knapp*, Sergeant, Col. Van Alstyn's Regt., New York Militia.

WILLIAM PAIGE KARNER, Pittsburgh, Pa. (37750). Son of Courtland S. and Margaret (Love) Karner; grandson of George and Angeline (Bentley) Carner; great-grandson of *Philip Carner*, Albany County, New York Militia.

EDSON WILFORD KEELER, Portland, Ore. (37495). Son of Harry Spear and Minnie Aletha (Jacobs) Keeler; grandson of Jeremiah W. and Augusta (Brinkerhoff) Keeler; great-grandson of Thaddeus H. and Laura Ann (Avery) Keeler; great²-grandson of *Jeremiah Keeler*, Corporal and Sergeant, Ninth Regt., Connecticut Militia and private Connecticut Line, pensioned.

NEWTON HOMER KEISTER, Cumberland, Ind. (37823). Son of Elijah Newton and Elizabeth Catherine (Walp) Keister; grandson of Daniel and Jane (Aber) Keister; great-grandson of *George Philip Keister*, private and Corporal, Westmoreland County, Pennsylvania Rangers.

ARTHUR LESLIE KEITH, Vermilion, S. Dak. (30673). Son of John Lawson and Mary Ann (Robertson) Keith; grandson of Henry and Ssan Hardridge Lawson; great-grandson of Jonathan and Elizabeth (Irwin) Keith; great²-grandson of *Alexander Keith*, private, Lieut. David Enoch's Co., Virginia Militia.

DAVID HENRY KELLER, La. (35988). Supplementals. Son of James E. M. and Laura A. (Whitesell) Keller; grandson of Henry and Elizabeth (George) Whitesell; great-grandson of Abraham and Christiana (Meyers) George; great²-grandson of Henry and Elizabeth (Reiswick) George; great³-grandson of *John Reiswick*, private, Northampton County, Pennsylvania Militia; grandson of David and Ellen (Brown) Keller; great-grandson of John and Sarah (Trach) Keller; great²-grandson of Rudolph and Maria Magdelene (Winner) Trach; great²-grandson of *Adam Trough* (*Trach—Drah—Drach*), private, Buck's County, Pennsylvania Associators.

WALTER YOUNG KEMPER, Jr., Franklin, La. (38107). Son of Walter Young and Leonora (Barton) Kemper; grandson of William Peter and Monica Reynolds (Rogers) Kemper; great-grandson of William Peter and Eliza (Hulick) Kemper; great²-grandson of Nathan and Mary (Whitaker) Kemper; great²-grandson of *Peter Kemper*, Ensign, Virginia Militia.

WILLIAM PETER KEMPER, Franklin, La. (38108). Same as Walter Young Kemper, Louisiana (38107).

ARTHUR STERLING KERFOOT, Lemon Grove, Calif. (37874). Son of George Thomas and Alice Rebecca (Allemong) Kerfoot; grandson of George Alexander and Lucinda (Fretwell) Kerfoot; great-grandson of William G. and Eliza (—) Kerfoot; great²-grandson of George and Sarah Elizabeth (—) Kerfoot; great²-grandson of *William Kerfoot* (*Kerfwoot*), Sergeant, Fourth Regt., Virginia Troops.

WILLIAM FRANKLIN KERFOOT, Oklahoma City, Okla. (35245). Same as Arthur Sterling Kerfoot, California (37874).

GEORGE EDWIN KNAPP, Oshkosh, Wis. (Ill. 37887). Son of George and Mahalath Berry (Shank) Knapp; grandson of John Smith and Susan (Hoke) Shank; great-grandson of *Christian Shank* (*Schenck*), private and Corporal, New Jersey and Maryland Militia, pensioned.

LEWIS HARDENBERGH KNAPP, Freeport, N. Y. (38203). Son of George Conover and Margaret (Hardenberg) Knapp; grandson of Richard and Maria (Crispell) Hardenberg; great-grandson of Lewis and Catherine (Daily) Hardenberg; great²-grandson of *Johannis Hardenberg*, Colonel, Ulster County, New York Militia, Member First Provincial Congress.

CHARLES WISNER KNIGHT, Minneapolis, Minn. (37447). Son of James Merrit and Lydia (Thorne) Knight; grandson of George Washington and Ruth (Albertson) Knight; great-grandson of *Thomas Knight*, private, Orderly Sergeant, and Quartermaster, Orange and Ulster Counties, New York Militia.

RALPH THOMAS KNIGHT, Minneapolis, Minn. (37448). Son of Charles Wisner and Alma Phebe (Roberts) Knight; grandson of James Merrit and Lydia (Thorne) Knight; great-grandson of George Washington and Ruth (Albertson) Knight; great²-grandson of *Thomas Knight*, private, Orderly Sergeant, and Quartermaster, Orange and Ulster Counties, New York Militia.

RAY ROBERTS KNIGHT, Minneapolis, Minn. (37449). Same as Ralph Thomas Knight, Minn. (37448).

AUGUST KOHN, Jr., Columbia, S. C. (Mass. 38136). Son of August and Irene (Goldsmith) Kohn;; grandson of Abram Alexander and Rose (Hilziem) Goldsmith; great-grandson of Moses and Ellen (Alexander) Goldsmith; great²-grandson of Abram and Hannah (Aarons) Alexander, Jr.; great²-grandson of *Abram Alexander*, Second Lieutenant, Sumter's Brigade, South Carolina Troops, pensioned.

EARL McLEAN KYLE, New Castle, Pa. (37738). Son of John Barnett and Celia (McLean) Kyle; grandson of James Ross and Elizabeth (Keck) McLean; great-grandson of William and Elizabeth (Ross) McLean;; great²-grandson of *Andrew McLean*, private, Col. James Dunlap's Battalion, Cumberland County, Pennsylvania Militia.

WALTER JOHN LANGENDORFER, Philadelphia, Pa. (31739). Son of William H. and Sallie R. (Hiskey) Langendorfer; grandson of Thomas and Mary (Follweiler) Hiskey; great-grandson of David and Catharine (Wanamacher) Follweiler; great²-grandson of Daniel and Barbara (Lieser) Follweiler; great²-grandson of *Frederick Lieser* (*Liesser*), private, Seventh Class, Sixth Battalion, Northampton County, Pennsylvania Militia.

LUKE LEA, Nashville, Tenn. (38071). Son of Overton and Ella (Cooke) Lea; grandson of John M. and Elizabeth (Overton) Lea; great-grandson of John and Mary McConnell (White) Overton; great²-grandson of *James White*, Captain, Iredel County, North Carolina Militia.

LESTER LEE, Madison, Tenn. (38070). Son of James Elsy and Margaret Ann (Stephenson) Lee; grandson of Sidney and Anna Eliza (Alexander) Lee; great-grandson of Elsy Culpepper and Sarah Ann (Murphy) Lee; great²-grandson of *Peter Perrine Lee*, private, New Jersey Militia.

JOSEPH MASTELLA LE GRAND, Baltimore, Md. (37691). Son of Richard Virginius and Cora Anne (Clarke) Le Grand; grandson of Charles Washington and Virginia (Pye) Le Grand; great-grandson of Claudius Francois and Anna Maria (Croxall) Le Grand; great²-grandson of *Charles Moale Croxall*, Lieutenant, Tenth Regt., Pennsylvania Troops, prisoner, pensioned.

CLAUD FREDERICK LESTER, N. Y. (28935). Supplemental. Son of Fred Volney and Eva Melinda (Conklin) Lester; grandson of Volney and Mary Jane (Smith) Lester; great-grandson of Martin and Esther (Bronson) Smith; great²-grandson of Sylvanus and Esther (Remington) Bronson; great³-grandson of David and Jerusha (Cooley) Bronson; great⁴-grandson of *Abner Cooley*, private, Col. Danielson's Regt., Massachusetts Militia.

JOHN BUREL LEWMAN, Ky. (36528). Supplemental. Son of Moses T. and N. L. (Conover) Lewman; grandson of John and Mary (Grisemer) Lewman; great-grandson of Jacob and Mary (Treichler) Grisemer; great-grandson of *Jacob Grisemer*, Second Lieutenant, First Battalion, Berks County, Pennsylvania Militia.

CHARLES CURTIS LOMMASSON, Topeka, Kans. (36747). Son of Samuel and Nettie (Curtis) Lommasson; grandson of Lawrence and Mary Ann (Winters) Lommasson; great-grandson of Andrew and Christian (Smith) Lommasson; great²-grandson of *Lawrence Lommasson*, Second Lieutenant Sussex County, New Jersey Militia.

DANIEL WEBSTER LONGFELLOW, Minneapolis, Minn. (38307). Son of Jacob and Jane (Getchell) Longfellow; grandson of Enoch and Anna (Longfellow) Longfellow; great-grandson of *Nathan Longfellow* (father of Enoch), Lieutenant, Lincoln County, Massachusetts Militia.

HORACE M. LUKENS, Evansville, Ind. (38277). Son of Horace and Anna M. (Strauss) Lukins; grandson of Richard M. and Caroline (Thomas) Lukens; great-grandson of Perry and Mary (Moore) Lukens; great²-grandson of *Henry Moore*, private, Seventh Battalion, Cumberland County, Pennsylvania Militia.

EUGENE PENFIELD LYNCH, Providence, R. I. (36519). Son of William Penfield and Elizabeth (Penfield) Lynch; grandson of Orrin S. and Margaret (Kedzie) Penfield; great-grandson of David and Voadicia (Scovill) Penfield; great²-grandson of *Peter Penfield*, Lieutenant, Col. Silliman's Connecticut State Regt., and Captain Connecticut Militia, pensioned.

HENRY WILLIAMSON MANN, St. Paul, Minn. (38304). Son of Edward H. and Catherine L. (Lewis) Mann; grandson of William E. and Adaline (Donaldson) Lewis; great-grandson of Isaac and Catherine (Evertson) Lewis; great²-grandson of *Isaac Lewis* Chaplain, Col. Philip Bradley's Battalion, Connecticut State Troops.

MORRIS MARCUS, San Francisco, Calif. (38154). Son of José Arnaldo and Emma Clara (Willcocks) Marquez (Marcus); grandson of Lewis and Margaret Ellinor (Morris) Willcocks; great-grandson of *William Willcocks (Willcox)*, Captain, Lasher's Regt., New York Militia and Aid-de-Camp to Gen. Alexander, pensioned.

LOUIS HUDSON MARTENSEN, Boston, Mass. (38137). Son of Charles and Jennie Irene (Adams) Martensen; grandson of Abel Parlin and Eliza (Hudson) Adams; great-grandson of Abial A. and Irene (Gray) Adams; great²-grandson of *Martin Adams*, Drummer, Col. Fletcher's Regt., Vermont Militia and Capt. Hutchin's Independent Company.

MILTON LUCIEN MASSON, New York City, N. Y. (38212). Son of Milton Increase and Elizabeth Rogers (Guild) Masson; grandson of Henry James and Fanny Jane (Slawson) Masson; great-grandson of Milton and Prudence (Wood) Slawson; great²-grandson of Elihu and Esther (Case) Slawson; great³-grandson of *Joseph Case*, Second Lieutenant, Orange County, New York Militia; grandson of Josiah Fiske and Lucy Walker (Bradshaw) Guild; great-grandson of Chester and Harriet (Fiske) Guild; great²-grandson of Nathaniel and Rebecca (Hart) Guild; great³-grandson of *Nathaniel Guild*, private, Col. Ephraim Wheelock's Regt., Massachusetts Militia.

CHARLES EDWARD MAXWELL, Montclair, N. J. (37989). Son of Gilbert Dudley and Priscilla (Kennaday) Maxwell; grandson of Charles Edward and Alice Gilbert (Perry) Maxwell; great-grandson of Henry C. and Abigail Farrington (Crandell) Perry; great²-grandson of Lemuel and Sarah (Makepeace) Perry; great³-grandson of *Ichabod Perry*, private, Norton, Massachusetts Militia.

BARNABY McAUSLAN, Providence, R. I. (38328). Son of William A. and Grace Ellen (Barnaby) McAuslan; grandson of Abner J. and Betsey J. (Wallace) Barnaby; great-grandson of Stephen and Lucy (Hathaway) Barnaby; great²-grandson of *Ambrose Barnaby*, private, Freetown, Massachusetts Militia and in Cont'l Troops.

MORTON LEWIS McBRIDE, Dickinson, N. Dak. (36943). Son of James Albert and Caroline Amanda (MacKune) McBride; grandson of Lewis and Laura Etta (Corse) MacKune; great-grandson of Joshua and Esther (Lewis) MacKune; great²-grandson of Nathaniel and Sarah Heart (Cole) Lewis, Jr.; great²-grandson of *Nathaniel Cole*, private, Connecticut and Vermont Militia.

THOMAS McCAMANT, Portland, Ore. (37488). Son of Wallace and Katherine S. (Davis) McCamant; grandson of Thomas and Delia (Rollins) McCamant; great-grandson of Graham and Mary (Meadville) McCamant; great²-grandson of *James McCamant*, Major, Col. Abraham Smith's Regt., Pennsylvania Militia; great-grandson of Joseph and Mary (Howard) Rollins; great²-grandson of *Eliphalit Rollins*, private, Col. Sherburne's Third Regt., Lincoln County, Massachusetts Militia.

ROBERT EDWIN McCONAUGHY, Jr., Salt Lake City, Utah (37554). Son of Robert E. and Nora (Losee) McConaughy; grandson of John McCurdy and Mary (Neal) McConaughy; great-grandson of John and Margaret (McCurdy) McConaughy; great²-grandson of *James McCurdy*, Frontier Guard, Western Pennsylvania Militia.

ROBERT WILSON McKNIGHT, Sewickley, Pa. (37740). Son of Charles and Eliza Cochran (Wilson) McKnight; grandson of Charles and Jeanie (Baird) McKnight; great-grandson of Thomas Harlan and Nancy (McCulough) Baird; great²-grandson of *Absalom Baird*, Surgeon, Col. Baldwin's Pennsylvania Regt., Artillery Artificers.

WILLIAM SCOTT McMAHEN, Stanton, Tenn. (38072). Son of W. V. and Cathrine (Hill) McMahen; grandson of William and Nancy (Peebles) Hill; great-grandson of Green and Mary (—) Hill; great²-grandson of *Green Hill*, Second Major, Bute County, North Carolina Militia and Member Provincial Congress.

MERRITT C. MECHEM, Santa Fe, N. Mex. (37827). Son of Homer Clark and Martha S. (Davenport) Mechem; grandson of John Adrian and Ellen (Davenport) Davenport; great-grandson of John and Martha (Coulson) Davenport; great²-grandson of *John Davenport*, Corporal, Seventh Regt., Virginia Cont'l Troops.

RAYMOND FOGG MERRIAM, Minneapolis, Minn. (38305). Son of Leander O. and Georgiana E. (Humphreys) Merriam; grandson of Artemas and Angelina Jenks (Fogg) Merriam; great-grandson of Josiah and Sally (Hill) Merriam; great²-grandson of Ezra and Susanna (Elliott) Merriam; great²-grandson of *Abraham Merriam*, private, Mason, New Hampshire Militia for Cont'l Service.

EUGENE LAWRENCE MESSLER, Pittsburgh, Pa. (37741). Son of Thomas D. and Marie Remsen (Varrick) Messler; grandson of Abraham and Elmer (Doremus) Messler; great-grandson of *Cornelius Messelaer* (*Messler*), private, New Jersey Militia.

CLYDE WEBSTER METCALF, Augusta, Me. (38180). Son of Charles Cutts and Sadie (Webster) Metcalf; grandson of William Lovett and Maria Colburn (Cutts) Colburn; great-grandson of James and Olive (Colburn) Cutts; great²-grandson of *Reuben Colburn*, private, Massachusetts Cont'l Troops.

EDWARD DUNCAN MIDDLETON, P. A. Surgeon, U. S. Army, Chelsea, Mass. (38138). Son of William Drummond and Susan Yandall (Modemann) Middleton; grandson of George and Mary Van Zindren (Webb) Modemann; great-grandson of Henry Wilson and Eliza Mulligan (Smith) Webb; great²-grandson of Samuel and Mary (Wilson) Webb; great²-grandson of *Charles Webb*, Member Connecticut General Assembly, Colonel, Nineteenth and Second Regts., Connecticut Cont'l Infantry.

CHARLES ALONZO MILLER, Toledo, Ohio (38077). Son of Cyrus A. and Kathryn (Kelley) Miller; grandson of Tunis and Marinda (Black) Miller; great-grandson of Joseph and Pamelea (Harris) Miller; great²-grandson of *George Harris*, Sergeant, Second Regt., New Jersey Militia, State and Cont'l Troops.

JOHN DOUGLAS MITCHELL, Providence, R. I. (38329). Son of John Baker and Jessie Richmond (Manton) Mitchell; grandson of Joseph P. and Mary Richmond (Spooner) Manton; great-grandson of Salma and Austis P. (Dyer) Manton; great²-grandson of Jeremiah and Mary Austis (Borden) Manton; great²-grandson of *Daniel Manton*, Lieutenant and Captain, Rhode Island Light Horse.

ROBERT LEVIS MITCHELL, Baltimore, Md. (37689). Son of Arthur Whiteley and Mary (Levis) Mitchell; grandson of George Edward and Mary (Hooper) Mitchell; great-grandson of *Abraham Mitchell*, Maryland Volunteer Surgeon who gave his home for a hospital.

ALFRED REUBEN MOORE, Garrett, Ind. (37825). Son of Samuel B. and Mary A. (Young) Moore; grandson of John and Hannah (Lindesmith) Young; great-grandson of Jacob and Susanna (Crissinger) Lindesmith; great²-grandson of *Joseph Lindesmith*, Bugler and Fifer, Pennsylvania Militia.

PAUL ALBERT MOORE, Huntington, Ind. (38276). Son of Albert B. and Claudia (Miller) Moore; grandson of Franklin and Mary (Baum) Miller; great-grandson of Giddian and Elizabeth (Smith) Baum; great²-grandson of Charles and Susan (Mayer) Baum; great³-grandson of *Charles Baum*, private, Second Battalion, Cumberland County, Pennsylvania Militia.

JOHN WILLIAMS MORGAN, Harrisburg, Pa. (38351). Son of Edward Robbins and Mary Catharine (Winter) Morgan; grandson of Stephen and Rowena Abigail (Broadbent) Morgan; great-grandson of Guy and Nancy Clark (Griswold) Morgan; great²-grandson of *Stephen Morgan*, private, Col. Oliver Smith's Regt., Connecticut Volunteers.

HORACE CHESTER MOSES, Montclair, N. J. (37994). Son of Linus A. and Mary (Bowen) Moses; grandson of Pliny and Rachel L. (Holcomb) Moses; great-grandson of Linus and Emily (Grimes) Moses; great²-grandson of Zebina and Theodosia (Curtis) Moses; great³-grandson of *Daniel Moses*, private, Col. Jedediah Huntington's Regt., Connecticut Cont'l Infantry.

LAWSON HILL MYERS, Fayetteville, Tenn. (38073). Son of John C. and Sue (Hill) Myers; grandson of H. L. W. and Virginia (Dearing) Hill; great-grandson of William Lynch S. and Mary Terry (Harrison) Dearing; great²-grandson of *James Deering (Dearing)*, private, Second Regt., Virginia Troops.

THOMAS S. MYERS, Chattanooga, Tenn. (38062). Son of John C. and Sue (Hill) Myers; grandson of H. L. W. and Virginia (Dearing) Hill; great-grandson of William Lynch S. and Mary Terry (Harrison) Dearing; great²-grandson of *James Deering (Dearing)*, private and Ensign, Second Regt., Virginia Cont'l Troops.

EDWARD CURTIS NEAL, Fresno, Calif. (38155). Son of John and Mary Jane (Day) Neal; grandson of William Allen and Ruth (Leaps) Neal; great-grandson of *Charles Neal*, Sergeant-Major, Virginia Cont'l Troops; grandson of *John Leap*, private, Twelfth Regt., Virginia Troops.

JOHN NEAL, Fresno, Calif. (37875). Same as Edward Curtis Neal, California (38155).

GEORGE WALDEMAR NELSON, Goodman, Miss. (38063). Son of William J. and Carrie (Croft) Nelson; grandson of George N. and Charlotte Elmore (Cherry) Croft; great-grandson of Robert M. and Caroline (Crenshaw) Cherry; great²-grandson of Samuel and Susan Polk (Reese) Cherry; great³-grandson of Thomas and Jane (Harris) Reese; great⁴-grandson of *David Reese*, Signer of Mecklenburg Declaration of Independence; great⁴-grandson of *Thomas Polk*, Brigadier-General, North Carolina Troops.

HIRAM WINNETT ORR, Lincoln, Nebr. (36996). Son of Andrew Wilson and Frances J. (Winnett) Orr; grandson of William and Julia Ann (Bowen) Orr; great-grandson of *John Orr*, private, Westmoreland County, Pennsylvania Militia.

ARTHUR HEATH ONTHANK, San Francisco, Calif. (38151). Son of Arthur Nahum Ball and Annabel Genevieve (McDermott) Onthank; grandson of Nahum Ball and Caroline Heath (Clancey) Onthank; great-grandson of William Newton and Susan Forbes (Ball) Onthank; great²-grandson of *William* and Mittie (Newton) *Onthank, Jr.*, private, Worcester County, Massachusetts Militia and Cont'l Service; great³-grandson of *William Onthank*, Lieutenant, Massachusetts Militia.

DONELSON CAFFERY PALFREY, Franklin, La. (38114). Son of Henry Sterling and Willie Winans (Wall) Palfrey; grandson of William T. and Susan Cornelia (Gates) Palfrey; great-grandson of John Palfrey; great²-grandson of *William Palfrey*, Aide-de-Camp to Gens. Washington and Lee, and Paymaster-General.

WENDELL PALFREY, New Orleans, La. (38112). Son of Herbert and Jessie (Campbell) Palfrey; grandson of George and Gertrude Elizabeth (Wendell) Palfrey; great-grandson of Henry William and Mary Bloomfield (Inskeep) Palfrey; great²-grandson of *William Palfrey*, Aide-de-Camp to Gen. Washington, Paymaster-General and appointed Consul-General to France.

CLARENCE EUGENE PEARSALL, Calif. (37857). Supplementals. Son of George Alfred and Eliza Catherine (Larimer) Pearsall; grandson of John and Deborah Ann (Brill) Pearsall; great-grandson of *David I. Brill*, private, Dutchess County, New York Militia; great-grandson of *Peter Pearsall*, private, Col. Malcolm's Fourth Regt., New York Cont'l Troops.

CELSUS PRICE PERRIE, New York City, N. Y. (38216). Son of Charles Thomas and Mary Nancy (Reid) Perrie; grandson of Edward Swann and Harriet (Forman) Perrie; great-grandson of Francis Richard and Letitia (Swann) Perrie; great²-grandson of *John Perrie (Perry)*, Captain, Prince George County, Maryland Militia and Member of a War Committee.

ALBERT HOVEY PEYTON, U. S. Army, Ga. (35222). Supplemental. Son of Thomas West and Mary Thornburg (Hovey) Peyton; grandson of Thomas West and Sarah (O'Dowd) Peyton, Jr.; great-grandson of Thomas West and Sophia Matilda (Dundas) Peyton, Sr.; great²-grandson of *John Dundas*, Ensign, Second Battalion, Philadelphia, Pennsylvania Militia.

GORDON CUTLER POOLE, Hackensack, N. J. (38210). Son of Francis Alden and Marion Kaler (Rounds) Poole; grandson of Edmund Alden and Laura Anna (Mackintosh) Poole; great-grandson of Fitch and Mary Ann (Poor) Poole; great²-grandson of Fitch and Elizabeth (Cutler) Poole; great³-grandson of *Manasseh Cutler*, Chaplain, Eleventh Regt., Massachusetts Militia.

FRED H. POORE, Kansas (22373). Supplemental. Son of John A. and Julia A. (Jordan) Poore; grandson of John and Mary Osgood (Bradley) Poore (Poor); great-grandson of John and Chloe (Lovejoy) Poor; great²-grandson of *Joshua Lovejoy*, Lieutenant, Col. Whitney's Regt., Massachusetts Militia.

HIRAM WILBUR POTTER, Gardiner, Me. (38176). Son of William C. and Lucinda (Preble) Potter; grandson of Amos and Hannah (Clark) Potter; great-grandson of *William Potter*, private, Col. Joseph Pierce's Regt., Massachusetts Militia.

JOHN RANDALL POWELSON, New York City, N. Y. (38217). Son of John H. and Anna B. (Randall) Powelson; grandson of Lyman Wolcott and Joanna Wiker (Loomis) Randall; great-grandson of Amos and Dolly Sharp (Fuller) Loomis; great²-grandson of Avander and Joanna (Wiker) Fuller; great³-grandson of *Ebenezer Fuller*, private, Connecticut Militia, pensioned.

ARTHUR BERGE PRATT, Burlingame, Kans. (36745). Son of Berge Elijah and Lottie Jane (Hoover) Pratt; grandson of David and Mary McHenry (Jamison) Hoover; great-grandson of Archibald and Mary (Lydick) Jamison; great²-grandson of Patrick and Mary (McHenry) Lydick; great³-grandson of *John Lydick*, private, Capt. Thomas Fletcher's Company, Pennsylvania Frontier Rangers. ·

WILLIAM GLADDING PRICE, New York City, N. Y. (R. I. 36520). Son of Raymond H. and Caroline F. (Atwood) Price; grandson of Charles Walton and Caroline F. (Reynolds) Atwood; great-grandson of John Walton and Catherine (Budlong) Atwood; great²-grandson of *Caleb Atwood*, private, Col. Peck's Regt., Rhode Island Militia, also a Minute Man.

OSCAR BLOUNT RALLS, Washington, D. C. (38008). Son of Oscar Black and Lucy Clara (Slade) Ralls; grandson of Thomas Blount and Catherine Irby (Comegys) Slade; great-grandson of Marmaduke Johnson and Ann Gray (Blount) Slade; great²-grandson of Thomas and Martha (Emanuel) Blount; great³-grandson of *David Emanuel (Emmanuel)*, Lieutenant, Gen. John Twigg's Regt., Georgia Militia.

HENRY SMITH RAMEY, Louisville, Ky. (36547). Son of Henry and Mary Waller (Bowles) Ramey; grandson of Lyddall Bacon and Sally Waller (Price) Bowles; great-grandson of *Thomas Philip Bowles*, Lieutenant, Col. Shepherd's Virginia Artillery.

ALBERT BORLAND RANDALL, Whitestone, L. I., N. Y. (38204). Son of William F. and Sarah E. (Smith) Randall; grandson of Jacob and Eliza (Davis) Smith; great-grandson of John and Sarah (Corwin) Smith; great²-grandson of *Jacob Corwin*, private, Ninth Company, First Regt., Suffolk County, New York Militia.

JAMES EMILE REYNOLDS, Wickford, R. I. (38330). Son of Charles Boyer and Emile C. (J. —) Reynolds; grandson of Stephen Boyer and Harriet Cottrell (Gardiner) Reynolds; great-grandson of Beriah and Elizabeth (Hammond) Gardiner; great²-grandson of *Nicholas* and Deborah (Vincent) *Gardiner, Jr.*, Delegate to Rhode Island General

Assembly of 1782; great²-grandson of *Nicholas Gardiner (Gardner)*, Lieutenant-Colonel, King's County, Rhode Island Militia; great-grandson of William Job and Mary (Davis) Reinolds; great²-grandson of *William Reynolds*, private, North Kingston, Rhode Island Militia, pensioned.

JAMES FRANCIS ROOKER, Oak Park, Ill. (37888). Son of Clement H. and Hattie (Davis) Rooker; grandson of Francis Evans and Harriet (Flanders) Davis; great-grandson of Levi and Sarah (Brown) Flanders; great²-grandson of Levi and Vashti (Hall) Flanders; great²-grandson of *John Hall*, private and Surgeon's Mate, Col. Ebenezer Bridge's Regt., Massachusetts Militia, pensioned.

ARTHUR RUSSELL ROSENBERGER, Harrisonburg, Va. (37742). Son of George W. and Barbra Ann (Kagey) Rosenberger; grandson of George Rosenberger; great-grandson of *George Rosenberger*, private, Third Battalion, Cumberland County, Pennsylvania Militia.

WOLCOTT LORD RUSSELL, Tucumcari, N. Mex. (37828). Son of Joseph Somers and Henrietta Wolcott (Lord) Russell; grandson of Benjamin Meade and Phebe (Tillinghast) Lord; great-grandson of John and Susan Caroline (Avery) Tillinghast; great²-grandson of Pardon and Mary (Sweet) Tillinghast; great³-grandson of *Charles Tillinghast*, Rhode Island Recruiting Officer, died in prison; great²-grandson of *Elisha Avery*, private and Corporal, Col. Jedediah Huntington's Regt., Connecticut Militia and Cont'l Line.

SAMUEL WAGNER RUSSELL, Sioux Falls, S. Dak. (30674). Son of Benjamin Stillman and Mary (Gaskill) Russell; grandson of Hamlin and Sarah (Norcross) Russell; great-grandson of *Nathaniel Russell*, Minuteman and Corporal, Connecticut Militia and State Troops.

WALTER MARTIN SANBORN Augusta, Me. (38181). Son of Bigelow T. and Emma F. (Martin) Sanborn; grandson of Warren and Jane (Warren) Sanborn; great-grandson of *John Sanborn*, private, Col. Vose's Regt., Massachusetts Cont'l Infantry, pensioned.

JOHN WHEATON SARGENT, Chicago, Ill. (37889). Son of John Robert Wheaton and Maud L. (Timmerman) Sargent; grandson of Homer Earle and Rebecca Eddy (Wheaton) Sargent; great-grandson of Asa and Charlotte (Earle) Sargent; great²-grandson of *John Sargent*, private, Leicester, Massachusetts Militia.

LEWIS PERKINS SAWIN, Everett, Mass. (38130). Son of George Alfred and Harriet Emeline (Perkins) Sawin; grandson of Alfred and Jane (Oakes) Sawin; great-grandson of Zadock and Abigail (Allen) Oakes; great²-grandson of *Samuel Oakes*, private, Col. Greaton's Regt., Massachusetts Militia and Carpenter on Brigantine "Tyrannicide."

CHASE HOUGHTON SAYRE, Fresno, Calif. (38156). Son of James Henry and Aggie J. (Payne) Sayre; grandson of Charles L. and Abby Jane (Jennings) Payne; great-grandson of James and Louisa (Richmond) Jennings; great²-grandson of *Jona Perry Jennings*, private, Connecticut Militia, Light Dragoons and Fifth Regt., Connecticut Cont'l Line.

FRED GOTLEIB SCHAAL, Terre Haute, Ind. (37824). Son of George A. and Mary E. (Sibley) Schaal; grandson of Wallace and Harriet Esther (Vickery) Sibley; great-grandson of John and Mary Elizabeth (May) Sibley; great²-grandson of *Elisha Sibley*, private, Massachusetts Militia.

HAROLD DACKINS SCHERER, Mankato, Minn. (37450). Son of Archibald H. and Genevieve (Dackins) Scherer; grandson of Luther and Catharine (Correll) Scherer; great-grandson of John and Margaret (Reitzel) Scherer; grand²-grandson of *Frederick Shurer (Scherer)*, private, Tenth Regt., North Carolina Cont'l Line.

CHARLES PEARSALL SCHOUTEN, Minn. (19940). Supplemental. Son of John William and Mary Louise (Pearsall) Schouten; grandson of Lewis and Harriet (Hustis) Pearsall; great-grandson of George and Charity (Parmaley) Pearsall; great²-grandson of George and Hepsebeth (Ammerman) Pearsall; great³-grandson of Derrick and Margaret (Ranons) Ammerman; great⁴-grandson of *Cornelius Ammerman*, private and Corporal, Fourth and Second Regts., New York Line.

JOSEPH TILFORD SCOTT, New Orleans, La. (38109). Son of Joseph Thompson and Dora Churchill (Dean) Scott; grandson of Joseph and Lucy Caroline (Webb) Scott; great-grandson of *Matthew Scott*, Captain, Thirteenth Pennsylvania State Regt., prisoner on prison-ship "Jersey."

WALLACE SPILMAN SCOTT, New Salem, Ind. (38078). Son of Seneca Logan and Annie Gertrude (Spillman) Scott; grandson of Smith and Sophronia Snow (Le Rue) Scott; great-grandson of Berrian Heath and Mary Ann (Nye) La Rue; great²-grandson of

Joshua and Anna (Snow) Nye; great²-grandson of *Lemuel Snow,* private, Col. Marshall's and Col. Freeman's Regts., Massachusetts Militia.

ALEC HERBERT SEYMOUR, New York City, N. Y. (37920). Son of George Robbins and Jennie (Parsons) Seymour; grandson of Charles A. and Sarah Merrill (Brainard) Seymour; great-grandson of Ira and Ruth (Paterson) Seymour; great²-grandson of *John Paterson,* Colonel, Massachusetts Cont'l Infantry, Brigadier-General, and Major-General, Continental Army.

JOHN NEWTON SHANNAHAN, Hampton, Va. (Md. 37686). Son of William and Abigail Jane (Dean) Shannahan; grandson of Ezra B. and Harriet (Newton) Dean; great-grand-son of *Paul Newton,* private, Col. Jonathan Ward's Regt., Massachusetts Militia, pensioned.

GEORGE MASON SHEARER, Buffalo, N. Y. (38209). Son of Matthew L. and Rosamond (Mason) Shearer; grandson of Luther M. and Emily (Gould) Mason, Jr.; great-grandson of Luther M. and Clarissa Ann (Haskins) Mason; great²-grandson of Ira and Clara (Baldwin) Haskins; great³-grandson of *Anthony Haskins (Hoskins),* Sergeant, Col. Charles Burrall's Regt., Connecticut State Troops.

CHESTER MERTON SHEPPARD, Washington, D. C. (38009). Son of David W. and Annie E. (Davis) Sheppard; grandson of Joab and Mary A. (Whitaker) Sheppard; great-grandson of Jonadab and Sarah (B. —) Sheppard; great²-grandson of *Jonadab Shepherd (Sheppard),* Captain, First Battalion, Cumberland County, New Jersey Militia.

TIMOTHY WALLACE SHERWOOD, Ind. (35512). Supplemental. Son of Thomas Russell and Anna Maria (Wallace) Sherwood; grandson of Timothy and Olive (Sherman) Wallace; great-grandson of Nathan and Mary (Carpenter) Sherman; great²-grandson of *Jabez Carpenter,* private, Col. Thomas Carpenter's Regt., Massachusetts Militia.

BERRY DON SHRIVER, Nashville, Tenn. (38074). Son of Thomas Abraham and Elizabeth (Holt) Shriver; grandson of Berry D. and Lucretia (Hart) Holt; great-grandson of Henry and Bettie (McGuire) Holt; great²-grandson of *William McGuire,* Lieutenant, Third Regt., Virginia Troops.

THOMAS ABRAHAM SHRIVER, Jr., Nashville, Tenn. (38075). Same as Berry Don Shriver, Tennessee (38074).

DILWORTH M. SILVER, Buffalo, N. Y. (38206). Son of Solomon and Hannah (George) Silver; grandson of David and Alletta (Sheppard) George; great-grandson of Elisha and Alletta (Smock) Sheppard; great²-grandson of *John Smock,* Captain, Major, and Colonel, Monmouth County, New Jersey Militia and State Troops, prisoner.

EATON KITTREDGE SIMS, Donaldsville, La. (38111). Son of Robert Nicholls and Emma (Kittredge) Sims; grandson of Ebenezer Eaton and Elizabeth (Eaton) Kittredge; great²-grandson of *Francis Kittredge, II,* Surgeon, Massachusetts Militia.

WILLIAM ERNEST ANDREW SLAGHT, Mt. Vernon, Iowa (37659). Son of Philander and Catherine (Malcolm) Slaght; grandson of Job and Sarah (Corlis) Slaght; great-grandson of Uriah and Mehitable (Lynch) Corlis (Curlis); great²-grandson of *James Curlis,* private, Essex County, New Jersey Militia.

GEORGE ARTHUR SLOAN, New York City, N. Y. (Tenn. 38064). Son of Paul Lowe and Anne (Joy) Sloan; grandson of Vaniah S. and Letitia (Lowe) Sloan; great-grandson of George L. and Caroline (Townsend) Sloan; great²-grandson of Thomas and Hannah (Barnard) Sloan; great³-grandson of *John Barnard,* Lieutenant, Connecticut Militia and State Troops, Captain, Third Regt., Connecticut Line.

HUGH WEIR SMEATON, Jr., Rochester Mills, Pa. (37743). Son of Hugh Weir and Jeanetta W. (Gorman) Smeaton; grandson of James and Sarah (Lydick) Gorman; great-grandson of James and Sarah (Chapman) Lydick; great²-grandson of Patrick and Mary (McHenry) Lydick; great³-grandson of *John Lydick,* private, Westmoreland County, Pennsylvania Rangers.

RICHMOND SMITH, Ill. (34617). Supplemental. Son of Alfred Hall and Margaret (Galloway) Smith; grandson of Charles Hinsdale and Elizabeth (Norman) Galloway; great-grandson of Henderson H. and Mary Elizabeth (Caffey) Norman; great²-grandson of Thomas and Mary B. (Patrick) Caffey; great³-grandson of *John Caffey,* private, Dorchester County, Maryland and in North Carolina Militia.

SYDNEY SCOTT SMITH, Washington, D. C. (38010). Son of Archibald E. and Emily (Scott) Smith; grandson of James Spaulding and Susan Amanda (Perry) Smith; great-grandson of James and Lucy Candace (Jones) Smith; great²-grandson of *Samuel Smith*, private, Newberry, Massachusetts Militia, pensioned.

WILLIAM GORIN SMITH, Ill. (24618). Supplemental. Same as Richmond Smith, Illinois (34617). Supplemental.

NOAH Q. SPEER, Berkeley Springs, W. Va. (Pa. 37745). Son of Louis Marchand and Jane (Finley) Speer; grandson of William and Margaret M. (Wilson) Finley; great-grandson of *James Finley*, Justice of the Peace and a recognized patriot.

GEORGE DAYTON SPINNING, Newark, N. J. (37995). Son of Charles Frederick and Eleanor (Brown) Spinning;; grandson of Dayton Martin and Eliza Jane (Douglas) Spinning; great-grandson of Henry B. and Sarah (Comstock) Douglas; great²-grandson of *Caleb Comstock*, private and guard, Fairfield County, Connecticut Militia.

WILLIAM FRANKLIN LESLIE, Spokane, Wash. (36666). Son of Samuel Chase and Mary Ann (Dolbier) Leslie; grandson of Nathan and Polly (Dyer) Dolbier; great-grand-son of *Benjamin Dolbier*, private, Needham, Massachusetts Militia and Cont'l Troops.

CHARLES RICHARD STEEDMAN, Providence, R. I. (38331). Son of Charles John and Mary Balch (Lippitt) Steedman; grandson of Henry and Mary Ann (Balch) Lippitt; great-grandson of Warren and Eliza (Scamans) Lippitt; great²-grandson of *Charles Lippitt*, Warwick, Rhode Island Assistant Commissary of Issues.

HOWARD WARREN STEERE, Providence, R. I. (36521). Son of Warren Hunt and Adelaide Sophia (Phillips) Steere; grandson of Mowry and Sally (Sargent) Phillips; great-grandson of Edwin Darling and Sophia (Kilburn)' Sargent; great²-grandson of Simeon and Lucy (Aldrich) Kilburn; great³-grandson of Rufus and Lucy (Lovett) Aldrich; great⁴-grandson of *Levi Aldrich*, Lieutenant, Col. Joseph Read's Regt., and Captain, Col. Whitney's Regt., Massachusetts Militia.

KENYON STEVENSON, Lancaster, Pa. (38353). Son of Charles Astor and Viola Jane (Lane) Stevenson; grandson of George and Jane (Gregory) Stevenson; great-grandson of Peter and Phoebe (Carroll) Gregory; great²-grandson of *William Carroll*, private, New Jersey Cont'l Line, and Cumberland County, Pennsylvania Militia.

WILLIAM ARTHUR STOCKMAN, Portland, Me. (38182). Son of David and Amelia Rogers (Dole) Stockman, Jr.; grandson of *Amos Dole, Jr.*, private and Orderly-Sergeant Massachusetts Militia and Cont'l Troops, pensioned.

THOMAS FOSTER STRONG, Preston, Idaho (Utah 37553). Son of Edward N. and Edna Linda (Foster) Strong; grandson of Thomas Williams and Martha Amanda (Niccolls) Foster; great-grandson of Jesse Franklin and Huldah E. (Rhame) England Foster; great²-grandson of John and Ann (Vanoy) Foster; great³-grandson of *Thomas Foster*, private, Orange County, Virginia Cont'l Line; great²-grandson of *Nathaniel Vanoy*, private, Col. Benjamin Cleveland's Regt., North Carolina Militia.

GEORGE WALTER SUMMERSBY, Waltham, Mass. (38142). Son of Walter Henry and Etta Frances (Weymouth) Summersby; grandson of Calvin Hiram and Sarah (Dorr) Weymouth; great-grandson of Solomon and Betsey (Whitcomb) Weymouth; great²-grand-son of *Benjamin Weymouth*, private, Massachusetts Militia, and Col. John Bailey's Regt., Cont'l Infantry.

WILLIAM CALVIN SUMMERSBY, Waltham, Mass. (38143). Same as George Walter Summersby, Massachusetts (38142).

FREDERICK JAQUES SWAN, Dorchester, Mass. (38139). Son of Robert Hinckley and Jessie (Jaques) Swan; grandson of Frederick Phillips and Abbie (Severns) Jaques; great-grandson of Nathan Eames and Pamelia (Pinkham) Jaques; great²-grandson of *John Jaques*, private, Massachusetts Militia at Siege of Boston.

WILLIAM B. SWIFT, Chicago, Ill. (37890). Son of Robert Z. and Amarilla T. (Chamberlin) Swift; grandson of Cyrus and Adeline (Gillette) Chamberlin; great-grandson of Eliphas and Amarilla (Sanford) Gillette; great²-grandson of *Benoni Gillette*, private, Connecticut Militia, pensioned.

WEBSTER TALLMADGE, Montclair, N. J. (38229). Son of Daniel Webster and Mary Woodruff (Spencer) Tallmadge; grandson of John and Mary (Avery) Tallmadge; great-grandson of *Ezra* and Anna (Polley) *Tallmadge*, private, Col. Van Rensselaer's Regt., New York Militia; grandson of Henry Savage and Martha Bigelow (Benton) Spencer; great-grandson of James and Eunice (Stanley) Benton; great²-grandson of

Samuel Benton, private, Second Regt., Connecticut Troops, and Member of Governor's Guard.

EUGENE THORPE, New Orleans, La. (38115). Son of Thomas J. Horace and Mary Louise (Fisher) Thorpe (Tharp); grandson of Thomas H. James and Sarah Anna (Roane) Tharp; great-grandson of Fayette and Elizabeth (Hunt) Roane; great²-grandson of Spencer and Anne (Henry) Roane; great²-grandson of *Patrick Henry,* Delegate to Cont'l Congress, and Commander in Chief, Virginia Troops.

HANSFORD LEE THRELKELD, Colonel, U. S. Army (retired), Morgansfield, Ky. (36544). Son of Uriel Hansford and Mary Catherine (Taylor) Threlkeld; grandson of James and Mary Sims (Peters) Threlkeld; great-grandson of John and Elizabeth Crosby (Floyd) Peters; great²-grandson of *Henry Helm Floyd,* private, Col. Churill's and Col. Edmund's Regts., Virginia Militia, pensioned.

WALTER LIVINGSTON TITUS, New York City, N. Y. (37921). Son of James Livingston and Harriet Louisa (Pratt) Titus; grandson of David Lee and Phobe Ann (Van Cleve) Titus; great-grandson of Benjamin and Anna (Lee) Titus; great²-grandson of *Samuel Titus,* private, First Regt., Hunterdon County, New Jersey Militia.

CHARLES ROSS VAN HOUTEN, Springfield, N. J. (38231). Son of Abraham and Susan Frances (Whaley) Van Houten; grandson of Horace and Mary (Hand) Van Houten; great-grandson of Ira and Rhoda (Crowel) Hand; great²-grandson of *David Hand,* private, Essex County, New Jersey Militia, and Express Rider, New Jersey Troops.

HARRY TOWSEND VIALL, Jr., Providence, R. I. (36522). Son of Harry Towsend and Fannie Earle (Simmons) Viall; grandson of Edward Henry and Hannah E. (Freeman) Viall; great-grandson of Benjamin and Hannah (Kinnient) Viall; great²-grandson of *John Viall,* private and Sergeant, Bristol County, Massachusetts Militia.

ALLEYNE VON SCHRADER, Long Beach, Calif. (38157). Son of Frederick and Arabella (Alleyne) von Schrader; grandson of Frederick and Olivia Gill (Morrison) von Schrader; great-grandson of William and Eliza S. (Bissell) Morrison; great²-grandson of Daniel and Deborah (Seba) Bissell; great³-grandson of *Ozias Bissell,* Captain, Connecticut Militia and Seventeenth Regt., Connecticut Cont'l Troops, prisoner.

ALEXIS VOORHIES, New Iberia, La. (38116). Son of Martin and Marguerite Alice (Leroy) Voorhies; grandson of Cornelius and Cidalise (Mouton) Voorhies, Jr.; great-grandson of Cornelius and Aimee (Gradenigo) Voorhies; great²-grandson of *Daniel Voorhees (Voorhies),* Lieutenant, Third Regt., Middlesex County, New Jersey Militia.

STEPHEN EARLE VOSBURGH, West Pownal, Me. (38183). Son of Stephen and Ella Augusta (Carter) Vosburgh; grandson of Everet and Polly (Pultz) Vosburgh; great-grandson of Richard Evert and Catherine (Tobias) Vosburgh; great²-grandson of *Evert Vosburgh,* Lieutenant, Seventh Regt., Albany County, New York Militia.

FOSTER WATT WALKER, McKeesport, Pa. (37744). Son of William E. and Letitia (Watt) Walker; grandson of Nathaniel Foster and Mary Ann (Van Gelder) Walker; great-grandson of Michael and Hannah (Young) Van Gelder (Van Gilder); great²-grandson of *Peter Van Gelder (Van Gilder),* Jr., private, New Jersey Light-Horse.

FRANK DENHAM WALKER, Houston, Texas (37533). Son of Roy T. and Cora (Denham) Walker; grandson of Frank James and Rosa Gage (Wright) Denham; great-grandson of George Skirvin and Susan Mary (West) Wright; great²-grandson of Lewis and Sally (Mahoney) West; great³-grandson of Lynn and Susana (Jackson) West; great⁴-grandson of *James West,* private, Col. Cabell's Regt., Virginia Troops; great⁴-grandson of *Charles Jackson,* private, Virgina Militia.

FRANK GEORGE WALTON, N. J. (37986). Supplemental. Son of John and Jane Eliza (Westney) Walton; grandson of John and Sarah Goodwin (Allen) Walton; great-grandson of John and Mary (Bullard) Walton; great²-grandson of John and Keziah (Viles) Walton; great³-grandson of *John Walton,* Captain, Col. David Green's Massachusetts Regt., at Lexington Alarm and of Reading, Massachusetts Train-band.

GEORGE WESTNEY WALTON, Rutherford, N. J. (37991). Son of Frank G. and Marie Louise (Jennings) Walton; grandson of John and Jane Eliza (Westney) Walton; great-grandson of John and Sarah Goodwin (Allen) Walton; great²-grandson of John and Mary (Bullard) Walton; great³-grandson of *John Walton,* Captain, Middlesex County, Massachusetts Militia and Guards.

ROBERT WOODS WASHINGTON, Cedar Hill, Tenn. (38376). Son of George Augustine Washington and M. G. (Queenie) Woods; grandson of Robert and Marina Turner

(Cheatam) Woods; great-grandson of George W. and Marina Brickel (Turner) Cheatham; great²-grandson of Jack Edwards and Mariana Brickel (Bryan) Turner; great³-grandson of *Jacob Turner*, Captain, Third Regt., North Carolina Cont'l Line.

FREDERICK NOBLE WATERMAN, Mass. (34414). Supplemental. Son of James F. and Caroline J. (Simmons) Waterman; grandson of John and Melinda (Randall) Waterman; great-grandson of James and Polly (Payson) Waterman; great²-grandson of *Anthony Waterman*, Lieutenant, Plymouth County, Massachusetts Militia and of Col. Job Cushings' Troops.

FRANCIS HUTCHINS WATERS, Fort Riley, Kans. (37692). Son of Francis and Sophia (Cooke) Waters; grandson of Theodore and Sophia (Webster) Cooke; great-grandson of Israel and Arietta (Clark) Cooke; great²-grandson of John and Sarah (Root) Cooke; great³-grandson of Daniel and Elizabeth (Crowell) Root; great⁴-grandson of *Henry Crowell*, Signer, Frederick County, Maryland Association Agreement.

LEWIS DUDLEY WATERS, New York, N. Y. (Mich. 37956). Son of Oliver S. and Louise Spalding (Worden) Waters; grandson of John and Louise (Eves) Spalding; great-grandson of Jonathan and Susannah (Potter) Spalding; great²-grandson of *Elijah Spalding*, private and Sergeant, Fourteenth Regt., Albany County, New York Militia.

THEODORE COOKE WATERS, Baltimore, Md. (37690). Son of Francis H. and Sophia (Cooke) Waters; grandson of Theodore and Sophia (Webster) Cooke; great-grandson of Israel and Arietta (Clark) Cooke; great²-grandson of John and Sarah (Root) Cooke; great³-grandson of Daniel and Elizabeth (Crowell) Root; great⁴-grandson of *Henry Crowell*, signer, Frederick County, Maryland Association Agreement.

RODERICK JOSEPH WATTERSTON, Long Island, N. Y. (38207). Son of Charles and Mary Kate (Hutchison) Watterston; grandson of George Wedderburn and Rebecca (Bookter) Watterston; great-grandson of George and Maria A. (Shanley) Watterston; great²-grandson of Bernard and Sarah (Magruder) Shanley; great³-grandson of *Nathaniel Magruder*, Lieutenant, Md. Militia and Judge of Elections.

RAYMER BALCH WEEDEN, Providence, R. I. (36523). Son of William Babcock and Hannah Raymer (Balch) Weeden; grandson of Joseph and Mary Ann (Bailey) Balch; great-grandson of Joseph and Hannah (Pope) Balch;; great²-grandson of *Joseph Balch*, Captain, Col. Craft's Regt., Massachusetts Troops.

MARSHALL McMAHEN WELCH, Mason, Tenn. (38065). Son of T. J. and Martha (McMahen) Welch; grandson of W. V. and Cathrine (Hill) McMahen; great-grandson of William and Nancy (Peebles) Hill; great²-grandson of Green and Mary (—) Hill; great³-grandson of *Green Hill*, Member North Carolina Provincial Congress, Second Major, Bute County Regt., North Carolina Militia.

PAUL WILEY WELCH, Braden, Tenn. (38377). Same as Marshall McMahen Welch, Tennessee (38065).

TERELIUS JONATHAN WELCH, Stanton, Tenn. (38066). Same as Marshall McMahan Welch, Tennessee (38065).

GEORGE ALFRED WESSNER, Ridgewood, N. J. (38230). Son of Alfred S. and Emma (Kistler) Wessner; grandson of Henry D. and Caroline (Swoyer) Kistler; great-grandson of John J. and Elizabeth (Detrich) Kistler; great²-grandson of Jacob S. and Anna Barbara (Bausch) Kistler; great³-grandson of *Samuel Kistler*, private and Ensign, Northampton County, Pennsylvania Militia.

CALVIN ROBERTS WEYMOUTH, Hollis, Me. (38177). Son of Edmund and Hannah (Roberts) Weymouth; grandson of John and Charlotte (Clark) Weymouth; great-grandson of *Stephen Weymouth*, private, Massachusetts Cont'l Troops; grandson of Tristram and Betsy (Page) Roberts; great-grandson of Joshua and Abigail (Hubbard) Roberts; great²-grandson of *Joseph Hubbard, Jr.*, Corporal, Col. James Scammon's Thirtieth Regt., Massachusetts Cont'l Troops.

ALFRED HENRY WHITE, St. Louis, Mo. (37612). Son of Alfred and Emily (Cady) White; grandson of Hezekiah and Nancy (Hale) Cady; great-grandson of *Jonathan Hale*, Second Lieutenant, Springfield, Massachusetts Militia at Lexington Alarm.

GEORGE BRADFORD WHITE, Braintree, Mass. (38132). Son of Loring Quincy and Mary (Bradford) White; grandson of George Washington and Betsey (Burrell) White; great-grandson of Jonathan and Polly (Loud) White; great²-grandson of *Benjamin White*, private and Drummer, Massachusetts Militia.

RALPH WHITTEMORE WHITE, Bridgewater, Mass. (38133). Son of Loring Quincy and Edith Morton (Whittemore) White; grandson of Loring Quincy and Mary (Bradford) White; great-grandson of George Washington and Betsey (Burrell) White; great²-grandson of Jonathan and Polly (Loud) White; great³-grandson of *Benjamin White*, private and Drummer, Massachusetts Militia.

ELMER E. WIBLE, Pittsburgh, Pa. (37746). Son of William E. and Elizabeth (Truxal) Wible; grandson of Henry and Susanna (Thomas) Wible; great-grandson of Barnett and Mary Magdalina (Mechlin) Thomas; great²-grandson of *Dewalt Mechlin*, Ensign, Eighth Regt., Westmoreland County, Pennsylvania Troops.

HARRY PALMERSTON WILLIAMS, La. (36968). Supplemental. Son of Frank Bennet and Emily W. (Seyburn) Williams; grandson of Charles and Emily Caroline (Moore) Williams; great-grandson of Lawrence and Lettice (Foster) Williams; great²-grandson of *Obediah Williams*, Surgeon, First Regt., New Hampshire Troops and Hospital Department.

LOUIS KEMPER WILLIAMS, La. (36969). Supplemental. Same as Harry Palmerston Williams, Louisiana (36968). Supplemental.

THOMAS J. WILSON, Corydon, Ind. (37821). Son of Joshua T. and Mary C. (Jordan) Wilson; grandson of Benjamin and Nancy (Hunter) Jordan; great-grandson of *Patrick Hunter*, Ensign, Westmoreland County, Pennsylvania Militia, pensioned.

FRANK HENRY WITMEYER, Annville, Pa. (37747). Son of Adam and Priscilla (Yeakley) (Yeagley) Witmeyer; grandson of John and Elizabeth (Tittle) Yeagley; great-grandson of *Henry Yeakley (Yeagley)*, private, Eighth Regt., Lancaster County, Pennsylvania Militia.

THOMAS WOLFE, JR., David City, Neb. (36998). Son of Thomas and Minnie Madessa (Guist) Wolfe; grandson of John C. and Mary (Myers) Guist; great-grandson of Peter and Mary (Grove) Myers; great²-grandson of *Peter Grove (Groff)*, Lieutenant, Cumberland County, Pennsylvania Frontier Rangers.

THOMAS VICTOR WOOTEN, Allston, Mass. (38131). Son of Sylvanus Bagby and Harriet N. (Hodgen) Wooten; grandson of Isaac and Phoebe (Trabue) Hodgen; great-grandson of William and Elizabeth (Haskins) Trabue; great²-grandson of *John James Trabue*, Ensign, Fifth Regt., Virginia Troops.

REYNIER JACOB WORTENDYKE, JR., N. J. (37987.) Supplemental. Son of Reynier Jacob and Carolyn (Cooley) Wortendyke; grandson of Albert and Jane Maria (Blakesley) Cooley; great-grandson of James Manning and Jane Maria (Colt) Blakesley; great²-grandson of Eliada and Lucina (Wedge) Blakesley; great³-grandson of *Asahel Wedge*, Corporal, Thirteenth Regt., Connecticut Militia.

JOHN LINDSAY YOUNG, Reno, Nev. (Pa. 38354). Son of John G. and Anna M. (Lindsay) Young; grandson of Samuel D. and Margaret Ann (Buhoup) Lindsay; great-grandson of John L. and Mary Ann (Bartelow) Buhoup; great²-grandson of William and Christina (Fry) Bartelow; great³-grandson of *Michael Fry*, private, Eighth Battalion, Cumberland County, Pennsylvania Militia.

CHARLES JACOB YOST, JR., Wenonah, N. J. (37996). Son of Charles J. and Mary Hart (Brittain) Yost; grandson of David and Eliza H. (Anderson) Brittain; great-grandson of John Hoppock and Mary (Hart) Anderson; great²-grandson of Joshua and Elizabeth (Hoppock) Anderson; great³-grandson of *John Anderson*, Captain, Fourth Regt., New Jersey Cont'l Line and Hunterdon County, New Jersey Militia.

ALLEN KING ZARTMAN, Ohio (31570). Supplementals. Son of Isaac and Rebecca (King) Zartman; grandson of Alexander and Salome (Kobel) Zartman; great-grandson of *Henry* and Elizabeth (Hauser) *Zartman*, Member Northumberland County, Pennsylvania Committee of Safety; great²-grandson of *Jacob Zartman*, private, Northumberland County, Pennsylvania Militia; grandson of Peter and Mary Magdalene (Whitmer) King; great-grandson of *Peter Whitmer*, private, Northumberland County, Pennsylvania Militia.

PARLEY E. ZARTMAN, Ind. (29656). Supplementals. Son of Solomon King and Malinda (Vegt) Zartman; grandson of Isaac and Rebecca (King) Zartman; great-grandson of Alexander and Salome (Kobel) Zartman; great²-grandson of *Henry* and Elizabeth (Hauser) *Zartman*, Member Northumberland County, Pennsylvania Committee of Safety; great³-grandson of *Jacob Zartman*, private, Northumberland County, Pennsylvania Militia; great-grandson of Peter and Mary Magdalene (Whitmer) King; great²-grandson of *Peter Whitmer*, private, Northumberland County, Pennsylvania Militia.

Index of Ancestors of New Members Published in Bulletins of December, 1922, and March, 1923

Clyde, Samuel, Dec., 82
Coffin, Tristam, Dec., 84
Coffren, Robert, Dec., 71
Colburn, Reuben, Mar., 75
Cole, Nathaniel, Mar., 75
Collins, Benjamin, Mar., 66
Compton, Robert, Dec., 70
Comstock, Caleb, Mar., 80
Connor, Benjamin, Dec., 85
Contreman (Conderman), John A., Dec., 70
Converse, Asa, Dec., 70
Converse, Israel, Dec., 73
Cook, John Wanton, Mar., 67
Cooley, Abner, Mar., 74
Copp, Samuel, Mar., 64
Cornwell, Daniel, Dec., 67
Corwin, Jacob, Mar., 77
Cox, James, 73
Covington, Francis, Sr., Mar., 66
Craig, Samuel, Mar., 69
Craig, Toliver (Talliferro), Dec., 80
Crandell, Edward, Mar., 66
Crane, Josiah, Mar., 66
Crockett, Anthony, Dec., 71
Crowell, Henry, Mar., 66, 82
Croxall, Charles Moal, Mar., 74
Culbreath (Colbreath), Thomas, Dec., 71
Cummings, Nathaniel, Mar., 67
Curlis, James, Mar., 79
Cutler, Manassah, Mar., 77
Cutter, Benjamin, Dec., 69

Damon, Benjamin, Mar., 67
Davenport, John, Mar., 75
Davidson, William, Mar., 66
Davis, Joseph, Dec., 71
Day, Moses, Dec., 85
Dean, Samuel, Mar., 63
Deering (Dearing), Mar., 76
Deering, Joseph, Mar., 67
Denniston, John, Dec., 71
Denny, Henry, Mar., 69
Dent, Hezekiah, Dec., 69
Derivaux, Mathieu, Dec., 71
De Witt, John L., Dec., 84
Dinwiddie, David, Mar., 67
Dodd, Uzal, Mar., 70
Doe, Nathaniel, Jr., Mar., 68
Dolbier, Benjamin, Mar., 80
Dole, Amos, Jr., Mar., 80
Donnell, John, Dec., 72
Doolittle, Joel, Mar., 68
Doremus, Thomas, Dec., 86
Douglas, Asa, Dec., 86
Dow, Matthew, Dec., 72
Du Bois, Louis, Jr., Mar., 68
Dundas, John, Mar., 77
Dunkelberger, Clemens, Mar., 64
Dunton, Thomas, Dec., 77
Duvall, Samuel, Dec., 72

Eads, Henry, Dec., 78
Edwards, Benjamin, Dec., 72
Edwards, Thomas, Mar., 68
Eldridge, Daniel, Mar., 68
Ellis, Robert, Dec., 73
Ellison, Robert, Dec., 84
Emanuel, David, Mar., 77
Ewell, James, Mar., 68

Fellows, Nathan, Mar., 64
Felt, Samuel, Dec., 82
Fenimore, Jonathan, Mar., 63
Finckel, Philip, Mar., 68
Finlay, Joseph, Mar., 64
Finley, James, Mar., 80
Finney, Josiah, Dec., 73
Fiske, Peleg, Dec., 83
Fletcher, Ebenezer, Dec., 70
Flowers, James, Mar., 68
Floyd, Henry Helm, Mar., 81
Fogg, Reuben, Dec., 70
Forman, Thomas, Dec., 81
Fort, John, Mar., 70
Foster, Jesse, Mar., 68
Foster, Thomas, Mar., 80
Fowle, Samuel, Dec., 83
Frampton, William, Mar., 69
Freeman, Frederick, Dec., 75
Fry, Michael, Mar., 83
Fuller, Amasa, Dec., 84
Fuller, Ebenezer, Mar., 77

Gaillard, Charles, Dec., 76
Galbraith, Andrew, Dec., 79
Galloway, Alexander, Dec., 73
Gardiner, Nicholas, Mar., 77, 78
Gibson, Isaac, Dec., 75
Gibson, Robert, Mar., 69
Gilbert, Benjamin, Dec., 74
Giles, James, Dec., 73
Gillette, Benoni, Mar., 80
Gleason, Winsor, Mar., 69
Goforth, William, Mar., 63
Gordon, George, Dec., 76, 74
Greene, Caleb, Mar., 71
Greene, Christopher, Mar., 72
Greene, Jarvis, Mar., 71
Gregg, Reuben, Dec., 79
Griggs, Joseph, Dec., 74
Grisemer, Jacob, Mar., 74
Grove, Peter, Mar., 83
Guild, Aaron, Mar., 67
Guild, Nathaniel Mar., 74

Hadley, George, Dec., 79
Haight, Silas, Mar., 64
Haines, Simson, Mar., 65
Hale, Johnathan, Mar., 82
Hall, John, Mar., 78
Hall, Joshua, Dec., 74
Hallock, Daniel, Dec., 75
Halsey, Luther, Dec., 83

Hammond, James, Dec., 67
Hand, David, Mar., 81
Hanscom, Moses, Dec., 79
Hanson, John, Mar., 70
Hardenberg, Johannis, Mar., 7-
Hardison, James, Dec., 75
Harris, Christopher, Dec., 83
Harris, George, Mar., 75
Hart, John, Dec., 67, Mar., 63
Hartshorn, Beriah, Dec., 86
Haskins (Hoskins), Anthony, Mar., 79
Hayes, Joel, Dec., 73
Heard, Richard, Mar., 70
Heiser, John, Dec., 85
Hempstead, Robert, Dec., 72
Hempstead, Stephen, Dec., 70
Henderson, Samuel, Mar., 70
Henry, Patrick, Mar., 81
Henshaw, William, Mar., 70
Hess, Baltzer, Mar., 70
Hill, Green, Mar., 75, 82
Hindman, James, Dec., 75
Hoar, Josiah, Mar., 70
Hoar, Jonathan, Mar., 70
Hoffman, Adam, Mar., 71
Holtz, Jacob, Mar., 71
Hood, John, Dec., 75, Mar., 71
Hooker, Simeon, Dec., 71
Hopkins, Joseph, Dec., 76
Hoyer, Peter, Dec., 76
Hoyt, Joseph, Mar., 71
Hoyt, Nathan, Dec., 76
Hubbard, Jonas, Dec., 75
Hubbard, Joseph, Jr., Mar., 82
Hughes, John, Dec., 70
Hulbert, Amos, Mar., 71
Hulett, Charles, Dec., 66
Hunt, Daniel, Mar., 71
Hunt, Zeba, Mar., 71
Hunter, Patrick, Mar., 71

Ide, Jacob, Mar., 67

Jackman, Samuel, Dec., 76
Jackson, Charles, Mar., 81
James, Thomas, Mar., 72
Jameson, William, Mar., 67
Jaqua, Gamaliel, Dec., 76, Mar., 72
Jaques, John, Mar., 80
Jaques, Parker, Dec., 74
Jenison, Abijah, Dec., 74, 75
Jennings, Jona Perry, Mar., 78
Johnson, Benjamin, Dec., 72
Johnson, George, Mar., 71
Johnson, Phineas, Dec., 83
Johnson, Samuel, Dec., 83
Jenkins, Paul, Mar., 67

Kauffman, George, Dec., 81
Keeler, Jeremiah, Mar., 72
Keeper, Frances, Dec., 68

Keister (Kiester), George Philip, Mar., 72
Keith, Alexander, Mar., 72
Kellogg, Martin, Mar., 65
Kelsey, George, Dec., 85
Kemper, Peter, Mar., 73
Kendall, Joshua, Dec., 85
Kerfoot (Kerfwoot), William, Mar., 73
Kershaw, Joseph, Mar., 72
King, Edward, Dec., 76
Kinne, Asa, Dec., 83
Kistler, Samuel, Mar., 82
Kitchel, James, Mar., 64
Kithcart, Joseph, Mar., 70
Kittridge, Francis, Mar., 79
Knapp, Isaac, Mar., 72
Knight, Andrew, Dec., 68
Knight, Thomas, Mar., 73
Kreider (Cryder), Michael, Dec., 77

Larkcom, Paul, Mar., 63
Lawrence, David, Dec., 86
Lawrence, Jonathan, Dec., 83
Lawrence, Jonathan, Dec., 86
Lay, Michael, Mar., 64
Leap, John, Mar., 76
Lee, Noah, Dec., 82
Lee, Peter Perrine, Mar., 73
Lewis, David, Mar., 67
Lewis, Isaac, Mar., 74
Lewis, John, Mar., 67
Lewis, Thomas, Dec., 77
Lieser, Frederick, Mar., 73
Lighthall, John, Dec., 84
Lindesmith, Joseph, Mar., 76
Lippett, Moses, Dec., 68
Lippitt, Charles, Mar., 64, 80
Lommasson, Lawrence, Mar., 74
Long, Andrew, Dec., 78
Longfellow, Nathan, 74
Looker, Othneil, Dec. 72
Lovejoy, Isaac, Dec., 73
Lovejoy, Joshua, Mar., 77
Lovejoy, Samuel, Dec., 73
Low (Lowe), Cornelius, Dec., 76
Loy, Michael, Mar., 64
Luff, David, Dec., 83
Lydick, John, Mar., 77, 79
Lynde, Samuel, Dec., 75
Lytle, William, Dec., 77

McCain, William, Dec., 77
McCamant, James, Mar., 75
McCormick, George, Dec., 71
McCurdy, James, Mar., 75
McDonald, Angus, Dec., 78
McFarlin (McFarling), Elijah, Dec., 78
McGee, Robert, Dec., 66
McGuire, William, Mar., 70, 79
McKinney, Arthur, Dec., 82
McLean, Andrew, Mar., 73
McPheran, Andrew, Mar., 64

Magruder, Nathaniel, Mar., 82
Mansfield, Ebenezer, Dec., 73
Manton, Daniel, Mar., 75
Mantz, Peter, Dec., 81
Marble, Malachi, Dec., 78
Martin, John, Dec., 66
Martin, Nathan, Mar., 71
Maupin, Daniel, Dec., 83
Mayfield, John, Dec., 80
Meacham, Abraham, Dec., 69
Mead, Jeremiah, Dec., 84
Mechlin, Dewalt, Mar., 83
Medbury, Benjamin, Dec., 78
Meeker, James, Mar., 70
Merriam, Abraham, Mar., 75
Messelaer, Cornelius, Mar., 75
Middlebrook, Hezekiah, Dec., 79
Mitchell, Abraham, Mar., 76
Milling, Hugh, Dec., 79
Moore, Henry, Mar., 74
Morgan, Stephen, Mar., 76
Morrison, John, 3d, Dec., 71
Morris, Thomas A., Mar., 69
Morse, William, Dec., 73
Moseman, Marcus, Jr., Dec., 79
Moses, Daniel, Mar., 76
Moses, Zebulon, Dec., 72
Murphy, Owen, Dec., 79

Neagley (Negley), Philip, Dec., 81
Neal, Charles, Mar., 76
Newhall, Ebenezer, Dec., 67
Newton, Paul, Mar., 79
Norris, Thomas, Mar., 67
Norton, Jonathan, Dec., 85
Noyes, Thomas, Dec., 79

Oakes, Samuel, Dec., 81, Mar., 78
Oliver, John, Dec., 77
Olney, Stephen, Dec., 68
Onderdunk, Thomas, Dec., 77
Onthank, William, Mar., 76
Orr, John, Mar., 76
Outwater, John, Dec., 84

Palfrey, William, Mar., 76
Parks, Joseph, Dec., 73
Parthemore, John Philip, Dec., 80
Paterson, John, Mar., 79
Pearsall, George, Dec., 80
Pearsall, Peter, Mar., 77
Pegues, Cladius, Mar., 65
Peirce, Nathaniel, Mar., 70
Peirce, Seth, Mar., 70
Penfield, Peter, Mar., 74
Perkins, Elisha, Dec., 69
Perkins, Obadiah, Dec., 81
Perkins, Stephen, Dec., 85
Perrie, John, Mar., 77
Perrine, Peter, Mar., 70
Perry, Ichabod, Mar., 74

Pettigrew, James, Dec., 66
Peyton, Valentine, Dec., 80
Phelps, John, Mar., 71
Phillips, George, Dec., 80
Piatt, Abraham, Mar., 63
Phillips, James, Mar., 64
Phinney, Edmund, Mar., 69
Polk, Thomas, Mar., 76
Poppino, John, Dec., 86
Porter, William, Mar., 64
Potter, William, Mar., 77
Potts, William, Dec., 73
Prindle, Zalmon, Dec., 74
Pugsley, William, Dec., 67

Rankin, Thomas, Dec., 80
Rawson, Artemus, Dec., 81
Reed, John, Dec., 69
Reese, David, Mar., 76
Reiswick, John, Mar., 72
Reynolds, Bernard, Dec., 85
Reynolds, William, Mar., 78
Ripley, Samuel, Mar., 63
Ritter, Ferdinand, Dec., 87
Robinson, Elijah, Dec., 69
Robinson, Enoch, Dec., 71
Robinson, Ephraim, Dec. 66
Robinson, Jeremiah, Dec., 73
Rochester, Nathaniel, Dec., 70
Roe, Phillips, Dec., 80
Rogers, Joseph, Dec. 81
Rollins, Eliphalit, Mar., 75
Rosenberger, George, Mar. 78
Rowe (Row), George, Dec., 78
Russell, Jason, Dec., 81
Russell, Nathaniel, Mar., 78
Russell, Stephen, Mar., 65

Sanborn, John, Mar., 78
Sanford, Daniel, Dec., 81
Sargent, John, Mar., 78
Sawyer, Jonathan, Dec., 81
Schock, Mathias Michael, Mar., 71
Scott, Matthew, Mar., 78
Smith, Frederick, Mar., 66
Scranton, Timothy, Dec., 76
Sellow, Philip, Dec., 76
Seward, John, Dec., 81
Sexton, Jonathan, Mar., 72
Shank, Christian, Dec., 77, Mar., 73
Shearer, John, Mar., 70
Shelby, Evan Dhu, Dec., 72
Sheldon, Philip, Dec., 68
Shepherd, Jonadab, Mar., 79
Shepherd, Paul, Dec., 81
Shreve, Israel, Dec., 72
Shurer, Frederick, Mar., 78
Sibley, Elisha, Mar., 78
Sill, Micah, Mar., 63
Sisco, Jacob (Fran), Dec., 86
Skillings, Simeon, Dec., 78

ec., 85

Thomas, Dec., 73

ec., 82

6

., 66

77

68

9

___, 08, Mar., 79

___w, Lemuel, Mar., 79
Soper, Edmund, Mar., 71
Spalding, Elijah, Mar., 82
Spear, William, Jr., Dec., 82
Spencer, Hezekiah, Dec., 83
Springs, John, Mar., 67
Springs, Richard, Dec., 71, Mar., 67
Starr, Joseph, Mar., 69
Stephens, John, Mar., 72
Stoddard, David, Dec., 83
Stowell, Abijah, Dec., 83
Suddeth, William, Mar., 67
Sullard, Benjamin, Dec., 68
Suter, John, Mar., 69

Tallmadge, Ezra, Mar., 80
Taylor, Robert, Dec., 84
Terry, Elnathan, Dec., 84
Thompson, Daniel, Mar., 69
Thompson, James, Dec., 84
Thompson, Sylvanus, Dec., 84
Thorne, Joseph, Dec., 66
Tillinghast, Charles, Mar., 78
Titus, Jonathan, Dec., 79
Titus, Samuel, Mar., 81
Todd, Samuel, Sr., Mar., 63
Todd, William, Dec., 76
Trabue, John James, Mar., 83
Trabue, William, Mar., 83
Trough, Adam, Mar., 73
Truesdall, Jabish, Dec., 75
Tuffs, William, Dec., 81
Turner, Jacob, Mar., 82

Upson, Stephen, Jr., Dec., 85

Van der Cook, Michael, Dec., 70
Van der Cook, Simon, Dec., 70
Van der Hoof, Hendrik, Dec., 70
Van Gelder (Gilder), Peter, Jr., Mar., 81

Van Keuren, John, Dec., 77
Van Metre, John, Dec., 75
Vanoy, Nathaniel, Mar., 80
Viall, John, Mar., 81
Voorhees, Daniel, Mar., 81
Vosburgh, Evert, Mar., 81

Wade, Richard, Mar., 66
Walker, James, Dec., 67
Wallace, Benoni, Dec., 82
Walton, John, Dec., 84, Mar., 81
Waterman, Anthony, Mar., 82
Webb, Charles, Mar., 75
Wedge, Asahel, Mar., 83
Welsh, William, Dec., 78
Wentworth, Elegah, Dec., 80
Westervelt, Daniel, Mar., 70
West, James, Mar., 81
Weston, Joseph, Dec., 85
Weymouth, Benjamin, Mar., 80
Weymouth (Waymouth), Stephen, Mar., 82
Wheeler, Benjamin, Dec., 79
White, Benjamin, Mar., 82, 83
White, James, Mar., 73
Whitman, Isaac, Dec., 77
Whitmer, Peter, Mar., 83
Whitney, Nathan, Dec., 70
Wilkinson, David, Sr. and Jr., Mar., 67
Willcocks, William, Mar., 74
William, Obediah, Mar., 84
Williams, Abraham, Mar., 74
Williams, John, Dec., 71
Williams, William, Dec., 69
Winchester, James, Dec., 75
Wilson, Moses, Dec., 79
Witt, Elisha, Mar., 66
Wood, Daniel, Dec., 86
Wood, Daniel Smith, Dec., 71
Wood, Holland, Dec., 83
Wood, Jeremiah, Dec., 86
Wood, Samuel, Dec., 86
Wyman, Abujah, Dec., 85
Wynne, William, Dec., 79

Yeakley (Yeagley), Henry, Mar., 83
Youngs, Samuel, Mar., 65

Zartman, Henry, Mar., 83
Zartman, Jacob, Mar., 83
Zollinger, Nicholas, Dec., 80

OFFICIAL BULLETIN

OF THE

National Society

of the

Sons of the American Revolution

Volume XVII   MARCH, 1923   Number 4

EDITED AND COMPILED BY

FRANK B. STEELE

SECRETARY GENERAL

CPSIA information can be obtained
at www.ICGtesting.com
Printed in the USA
BVHW02s1303220118
505976BV00008B/108/P